Anderson's MANUAL FOR NOTARIES PUBLIC

Anderson's
MANUAL FOR NOTARIES PUBLIC

A Complete Guide for Notaries Public and
Commissioners of Deeds, with Glossary,
Charts and Index

FOR USE IN ALL STATES AND U.S. TERRITORIES

QUALIFICATIONS, APPOINTMENT, JURISDICTION,
TERM, POWERS, DUTIES, FEES, RECORDS, SEAL,
LIABILITIES, PENALTIES, REMOVAL

Sixth Edition

BY

The Publisher's Staff

CINCINNATI
ANDERSON PUBLISHING CO.

ANDERSON'S MANUAL FOR NOTARIES PUBLIC

© 1940, 1956, 1962, 1966 by The W.H. Anderson Company
© 1976, 1991 by Anderson Publishing Co.

Library of Congress Cataloging-in-Publication Data

Anderson's manual for notaries public: a complete guide for notaries
    public and commissioners of deeds, with glossary, charts, and index:
    qualifications, appointment, jurisdiction, term, powers, duties,
    fees, records, seal, liabilities, penalties, removal / by the
    publisher's staff. — 6th ed.
        p.   cm.
    Rev. ed. of: Anderson's manual for notaries public / Wesley
Gilmer, Jr. 5th ed. c1976.
    "For use in all states."
    Includes index.
    ISBN 0-87084-040-1
    1. Notaries—United States—Handbooks, manuals, etc. I. Gilmer,
Wesley. Anderson's manual for notaries public. II. Anderson
Publishing Co. (Cincinnati, Ohio)
KF8797.G54   1991
347.73′16—dc20
[347.30716]   91-35126
                                                          CIP

CONTENTS

Part II
STATUTES

PREFACE

A very large number of persons hold commissions as notaries public under the laws of the 50 states of the United States, the District of Columbia, Puerto Rico, and the Virgin Islands. While the laws of each of the jurisdictions under which the notaries are appointed are different, there are also large areas of common ideas and rules which appear in the law of each of those jurisdictions. In the main, notaries have the same duties and authority, and labor under the same constraints, regardless of the state or other jurisdiction by which they are appointed.

Most notaries are not full-time "professional" notaries. Instead, they hold their commissions as incidents to other occupations, such as accountant, attorney, automobile dealer, banker, bookkeeper, court reporter, insurance agent, legal assistant, loan officer, police officer, real estate broker, secretary, and the like. Despite the fact that they are not full-time "professional" notaries, their every act as a notary must be accomplished in a professional manner, however, because they are held to high accountability and are relied upon by the public because of the high degree of responsibility which they exercise. For this reason, among others, each notary public needs a reliable manual at hand to which he or she may turn for prompt answers to the questions, problems, and dilemmas which from time to time present themselves. With such a need in mind, it was the publisher's goal to prepare, as best the various statutes permitted, a manual of concrete statutes and text which would be responsive to a large number of such needs.

The text covers various topics with which a notary public is likely to be concerned, such as appointment, authority and duties, fees chargeable, oaths, affidavits, acknowledgments, depositions, seals, commercial paper, and the like. Following the general text material appear the statutes of each state, the District of Columbia, Puerto Rico, and the Virgin Islands relative to notaries.

One way to consult this book is through the index in the back. It provides an alphabetical analysis of the book's contents. The table of contents in the front is useful, however, for the purpose of scanning the sequence of the contents of the book and generally locating topics and specific state or other jurisdictions' statutes concerning the topics therein. The reader is encouraged to utilize both avenues of access.

Attention is called to the charts which are provided in the book; they have been prepared for the purpose of providing graphic comparisons of the variations among the jurisdictions. The glossary of definitions should also be remembered; its purpose is to aid the reader to grasp the meanings of the legal terms which a notary public is obligated to understand.

The publisher would be grateful if readers who have suggestions to offer concerning the future improvement of *Anderson's Manual for Notaries Public* would communicate those suggestions.

PART I
TEXT

	APPOINTMENT					FEE	BOND
	Governor	Governor, with consent of Senate	Governor, with advice of council	Secretary of State	Court		
Alabama					x	$1.00	$10,000
Alaska	[2]					20.00	1,000
Arizona				x			1,000
Arkansas				x		20.00	4,000
California				x		50.00[5]	10,000
Colorado				x			5,000
Connecticut				x		40.00	
Delaware	x						
District of Columbia	[7]					30.00	2,000
Florida	x					25.00	1,000
Georgia					[8]	8.00	
Hawaii	[9]					35.00[10]	1,000
Idaho				x		30.00	10,000
Illinois				x		10.00	5,000
Indiana	x					10.00	5,000
Iowa				x		30.00	
Kansas				x		10.00	7,500
Kentucky				x		10.00	[11]
Louisiana		x					5,000
Maine			x			25.00	
Maryland		x				11.00	
Massachusetts			x			[12]	
Michigan	x					3.00	10,000
Minnesota		x				10.00	
Mississippi	x						5,000

[1] The probate judges may appoint a competent number for each county.
[2] Now Lieutenant Governor.
[3] Postmasters are automatically notaries public and need not post bond.
[4] As to acknowledgments.
[5] Fee not to exceed $50.00 per commission.
[6] *See* DEL. CODE ANN. tit. 29, §§ 4301 to 4305.
[7] Appointed by Mayor of District of Columbia.

TERM (years)	JURISDICTION		STATUTORY REFERENCES
	State	County	
4		x[1]	ALA. CODE §§ 36-20-1 to 36-20-32
4	x[3]		ALASKA STAT. §§ 44.50.010 to 44.50.180
4	x[4]	x	ARIZ. REV. STAT. ANN. §§ 41-311 to 41-317
10	x		ARK. STAT. ANN. §§ 21-14-101 to 21-14-111
4	x		CAL. GOV'T CODE §§ 8200 to 8230
4	x		COLO. REV. STAT. ANN. §§ 12-55-101 to 12-55-123
5	x		CONN. GEN. STAT. ANN. §§ 3-91 to 3-95
6	x		DEL. CODE ANN. tit. 29, §§ 4301 to 4313
5			D.C. CODE ANN. §§ 1-801 to 1-817
4	x		FLA. STAT. ANN. §§ 117.01 to 117.10
4		x	GA. CODE ANN. §§ 45-17-1 to 45-17-32
4	x		HAW. REV. STAT. §§ 456-1 to 456-18
6	x		IDAHO CODE §§ 51-101 to 51-123
4	x		ILL. ANN. STAT. ch. 102, ¶201-101 to 208-104
4	x		IND. CODE ANN. §§ 33-16-1-1 to 33-16-8-5
3	x		IOWA CODE ANN. §§ 77A.1 to 77A.11
4	x		KAN. STAT. ANN. §§ 53-101 to 53-118
4	x		KY. REV. STAT. ANN. §§ 423.010 to 423.990
Indefinite[13]		x[14]	LA. REV. STAT. ANN. 35:1 to 35:555
	x		ME. REV. STAT. ANN. tit. 4, §§ 951 to 958
4	x		MD. ANN. CODE art. 68, §§ 1 to 13
7	x		MASS. ANN. LAWS ch. 222, §§ 1 to 11
4	x		MICH. COMP. LAWS ANN. §§ 55.103 to 55.251
6	x		MINN. STAT. ANN. §§ 359.01 to 359.12
4	x		MISS. CODE ANN. §§ 25-33-1 to 25-33-23

[8] Appointed by clerk of superior court of county in which commission applies.
[9] Appointed by attorney general.
[10] $15.00 for renewal.
[11] Amount not stated. *See* KY. REV. STAT. ANN. § 423.010.
[12] Fee determined annually by commissioner of administration.
[13] During good behavior.
[14] Parish.

	APPOINTMENT					FEE	BOND
	Governor	Governor, with consent of Senate	Governor, with advice of council	Secretary of State	Court		
Missouri				x		$15.00	$10,000
Montana	x					2.00	5,000
Nebraska	x					20.00	4,000
Nevada				x		35.00	10,000
New Hampshire			x			30.00	
New Jersey				x		25.00	
New Mexico	x					10.00	500
New York				x		20.00	
North Carolina				x		15.00	
North Dakota				x		20.00	7,500
Ohio	x						
Oklahoma				x		25.00	1,000
Oregon				x		20.00	
Pennsylvania				x		25.00	[15]
Rhode Island	x					40.00	
South Carolina	x					25.00	
South Dakota				x		5.00	500
Tennessee	x[16]					3.00	5,000[17]
Texas				x		10.00	2,500
Utah[19]							5,000
Vermont					x		
Virginia	x					25.00	
Washington[22]						[23]	10,000
West Virginia	x					50.00	
Wisconsin	x					15.00	500
Wyoming				x		30.00	500

[15] Fixed by secretary of commonwealth.
[16] Elected by members of county legislative body; commissioned by governor.
[17] $10,000 in counties with population of more than 600,000.
[18] Special provisions for qualifying in additional counties.
[19] Commissioned by director of Division of Corporations and Commercial Code.

TERM (years)	JURISDICTION		STATUTORY REFERENCES
	State	County	
4	x		Mo. Ann. Stat. §§ 486.200 to 486.405
3	x		Mont. Code Ann. §§ 1-5-401 to 1-5-420
4	x		Neb. Rev. Stat. §§ 64-101 to 64-116
4	x		Nev. Rev. Stat. §§ 240.010 to 240.230
5	x		N.H. Rev. Stat. Ann. §§ 455:1 to 455:11
5	x		N.J. Stat. Ann. §§ 52:7-10 to 52:7-21
4	x		N. M. Stat. Ann. §§ 14-12-1 to 14-12-20
2	x		N.Y. Exec. Law §§ 130 to 138
5	x		N.C. Gen. Stat. §§ 10-1 to 10-17
6	x		N.D. Cent. Code §§ 44-06-01 to 44-06-14
5	x		Ohio Rev. Code Ann. §§ 147.01 to 147.14
4	x		Okla. Stat. Ann. tit. 49, §§ 1 to 10
4	x		Or. Rev. Stat. §§ 194.005 to 194.990
4	x		Pa. Stat. Ann. tit. 57, §§ 148 to 169
5	x		R.I. Gen. Laws Ann. §§ 42-30-3 to 42-30-14
10	x		S.C. Code Ann. §§ 26-1-10 to 26-1-120
8	x		S.D. Codified Laws Ann. §§ 18-1-1 to 18-1-14
4		x[18]	Tenn. Code Ann. §§ 8-16-101 to 8-16-309
4	x		Tex. Gov't Code Ann. §§ 406.001 to 406.024 (Vernon 1986)
4	x		Utah Code Ann. §§ 46-1-1 to 46-1-17
[20]	x		Vt. Stat. Ann. tit. 24, §§ 441 to 446
4	[21]		Va. Code Ann. §§ 47.1-1 to 47.1-30
4	x		Wash. Rev. Code Ann. §§ 42.44.010 to 42.44.903
10	x		W. Va. Code Ann. §§ 29C-1-101 to 29C-9-101
4[24]	x		Wis. Stat. Ann. § 137.01
4		x	Wyo. Stat. Ann. §§ 32-1-101 to 32-1-113

[20] Term corresponds to term of office of appointing judges.
[21] Certain powers outside of commonwealth as well.
[22] Appointed by director of Licensing.
[23] Fee established by director by rule.
[24] Attorneys entitled to permanent commission.

Chapter 1.
INTRODUCTION

§ 1.1 Generally.

A notary public (sometimes called a notary) is a public official appointed under authority of law with power, among other things, to administer oaths, certify affidavits, take acknowledgments, take depositions, perpetuate testimony, and protest negotiable instruments. Notaries are not appointed under federal law; they are appointed under the authority of the various states, districts, territories as in the case of the Virgin Islands, and the commonwealth in the case of Puerto Rico. The statutes which define the powers and duties of a notary public frequently grant the notary authority to do all acts justified by commercial usage and the law merchant.

The law merchant, or custom of merchants as it is occasionally called, is the general body of commercial usages which have become an established part of the law of the United States and England and which relate chiefly to the transactions of merchants, mariners, and those engaged in trade. Unless displaced by particular provisions of the Uniform Commercial Code, the law merchant supplements its provisions.

For other definitions see the *Glossary* and concerning the Uniform Commercial Code see *Commercial Paper under the Uniform Commercial Code*, § 2.22.

§ 1.2 Origin and early history of office.

In the early days of the Roman Republic there were persons who made it a business to draw important documents, and do other writing for whoever might employ them. Their number and importance increased with the growth of the wealth and power of the Roman Empire, under various titles such as *scriba, cursor, tabularius, tabellio, exceptor, actuarius,* and *notarius,* according to the time in which they lived and the duties which they performed. In the latter days of the Empire, they had become more or less subject to regulation by law. Some of their acts had been accorded such a degree of authenticity as to be specially designated as public instruments themselves, and were required to be deposited in public archives.

These quasi officials, and the regulations by law concerning them, spread to a greater or lesser degree into the various provinces of Rome, including, among others, the present nations of France, Spain, and England.

They were well known functionaries in the territories of Charlemagne, who invested their acts with public authority and provided for their appointment by his deputies in every locality. He provided that each bishop, abbot, and count should have a notary. That they acted as conveyancers, in some instances at least, in England, even before the Norman conquest, is shown by the fact that a grant of lands and manors was made by King Edward the Confessor, to the Abbot of Westminster by a charter written and attested by a notary.

In England, notaries have always considered themselves authorized to administer oaths, and this power is now expressly conferred on them by statute. They protest foreign bills of exchange, and their certificate of the presentment, demand, and dishonor of such bills, and of their protest thereof on account of such dishonor, is itself proof of these matters. The law in the United States is similar, and is often so declared by the statutes of the various states and other jurisdictions.

§ 1.3   What a notary should know.

Before entering upon his duties, a notary public should know and understand:

The qualifications necessary for his appointment;

How to prepare an application for a commission;

Who appoints notaries public in his state, district, or other jurisdiction;

The amount of the bond which he must furnish, if one is required;

The fee which he must pay for his commission;

Where his commission must be recorded;

The number of years he holds office;

The extent of his territorial jurisdiction;

The scope of his powers and duties;

Circumstances which will disqualify him from acting;

The manner of signing his official certificate;

The requisites of his official seal, or stamp, if one is required;

What records he must keep;

The fees which he may charge for performing particular services;

His, and his surety's liability for negligent and fraudulent acts;

The fines and penalties to which he may be subject;

The grounds for his removal from office;

The manner of administering oaths;

The forms and purpose of affidavits;

His duties in connection with taking acknowledgments, depositions, the perpetuation of testimony, and safe deposit boxes;

His duties in presenting and protesting commercial paper, sometimes called
 negotiable instruments; and

What constitutes the unauthorized practice of law.

§ 1.4 What a notary may not do.

A notary public, who is not also a licensed attorney at law in the particular
state, district or other jurisdiction, has no authority to perform any act or service
which constitutes practicing law, as that term has been defined by the courts of the
various states, districts and other jurisdictions. Like any other individual, he is free
to prepare legal documents under directors from a competent person, but it is
contrary to law for him to draft legal papers, such as deeds, mortgages, wills, trust
agreements, and the like, at his own discretion and charge a fee for the service
rendered. Such constitutes the practice of law, even though the individual so engaged makes no attempt to appear in court or to give the impression that he is
entitled to do so.

A notary public may be enjoined from preparing instruments for compensation,
and from giving legal advice to those for whom he prepares them. A person who
gives legal advice to those for whom he draws instruments, or holds himself out as
competent to do so, does work of a legal nature, when the instruments he prepares
either define, set forth, limit, terminate, specify, claim, grant, or otherwise affect
legal rights. Instruments coming within the scope of this limitation are deeds,
mortgages, leases, agreements, contracts, bills of sale, security agreements, wills,
promissory notes, options, powers of attorney, liens, bonds, mortgage assignments,
releases, or satisfactions, and any other documents requiring the use of knowledge
of law in their preparation.

§ 1.5 Authority and duties.

In the main, the authority and duties of notaries public are strictly controlled by
the various state, district, territorial and other statutes. At common law, notaries
had limited powers and functions, which were mainly commercial in nature. They
related to dealings between merchants, were controlled by the law merchant, and
were respected by the law of nations.

There are major differences between the notary public statutes of the various
states, the District of Columbia, Puerto Rico, and the Virgin Islands. The statutes
of each of these various jurisdictions concerning authority and duties of notaries
are quoted below. In general, the statutes usually grant to a notary public power
to administer oaths, certify affidavits, present and protest commercial paper
(sometimes called negotiable instruments), take depositions, and take acknowledgments of instruments relating to the transfer or encumbrance of real property, and
instruments relating to commerce and navigation. In addition, many jurisdictions

by express statutory provision authorize a notary public to do all other acts justified by commercial usage and the law merchant.

The authority of a notary frequently corresponds with the authority of a justice of the peace. The right to issue subpoenas and compel the attendance of witnesses is occasionally granted.

§ 1.6   Removal.

In a large number of states and other jurisdictions the statutes expressly specify grounds for the removal of a notary public, and designate the authority or officer who has the power to remove. Frequently those matters are stated in the same section that provides for the appointment of the notary. Concerning removal of notaries in specific states and other jurisdictions, see the specific state statutes.

Chapter 2.
THE OFFICE OF NOTARY PUBLIC

§ 2.1   Qualifications of applicant.

Ordinarily, an applicant must be of legal age, which for most purposes today is 18 years old, a citizen of the state, district, or other jurisdiction, and a person of good moral character. In many instances he must be a resident of the county or judicial district within which he is to act. Several of the states require filing some evidence of qualifications. As an example, an applicant might be required to file a certificate from a judge or other local official that he is of good moral character, of legal age, a citizen of the county in which he resides, and is possessed of sufficient qualifications and ability to discharge the duties of the office. In some states a similar certificate must be signed by a certain number of ordinary citizens. Other states require the applicant to pass an examination satisfying the appointing authority that the applicant possesses the knowledge to fulfill the duties of the office.

§ 2.2   Application.

An applicant usually obtains the necessary forms from the governor, secretary of state, or other appointing authority. As a matter of convenience, surety companies occasionally furnish forms.

In recent years there has developed a practice of submitting questionnaires to each applicant, preliminary to the approval of the application. Questions such as the following must be answered: how long the applicant has lived in the county; place and date of his birth; his business or employment; education; whether his commission has ever been revoked; whether he has ever been convicted of any offense; and the name and address of surety company or individual who will execute indemnity bond.

§ 2.3   Appointment.

In most of the states, notaries public are appointed by the governor of the state. In some states the appointments are made by the governor by and with the advice and consent of the senate, or with the advice of his council. In other states the secretary of state has authority to make the appointment. Notaries are appointed by courts in a few of the states.

§ 2.4   Bond.

In most states, and other jurisdictions, a notary is required to file a bond with approved sureties. The public officer with whom the bond must be filed is designated by the statutes of the various states and other jurisdictions.

The amount of bond required varies among the several states and other jurisdictions, from none up to $10,000. The purpose of the bond is often stated in the specific statute applicable, but may be generally described as being to assure the faithful performance of duties, and to compensate any person who may suffer a loss as a result of the notary's misconduct.

§ 2.5 Oath of office.

An oath of office is required in every state. Occasionally the oath is endorsed on the notary's commission or on his bond. Both the oath and bond are ordinarily filed with the secretary of state or other designated public officer.

§ 2.6 Commission.

Upon the payment of a fee, usually to the secretary of state, a commission will be issued to a qualified applicant. The amount of this fee varies among the states and other jurisdictions from $1.00 up to $100.00. In a few jurisdictions, there is apparently no fee. For concrete information in this regard, see the specific statute.

The commission, signed by the appointing power, is evidence of the notary's official authority. In many states the notary, before entering upon his duties, must leave the commission with some officer designated by law, generally the clerk of court, to be recorded. A small additional fee is charged by the clerk, to cover the cost of recording the commission.

§ 2.7 Term of office.

The statutes of most states and other jurisdictions prescribe a certain number of years as the term of office of a notary public. These terms range from two to ten years, and in some jurisdictions the term of office is indefinite. In some instances a particular statute provides that a notary holds office during good behavior, during the pleasure of the governor, or during the term of the appointing judge.

The death of a notary will terminate his office, although he was appointed for a definite term. It will not create a vacancy for the unexpired part of his term.

§ 2.8 Territorial jurisdiction.

In some jurisdictions a notary public can act only within the county or judicial district for which he has been appointed, or within the locality named in his commission. The statutes of many states, however, permit a notary to act anywhere throughout the state. He has no jurisdiction outside the state of his appointment.

Some states allow the notary to act in any other county, or in a county adjoining the county of his residence, if he files a certified copy of his appointment with the clerk of such other county. Where the city in which a notary resides is located in two or more counties, he may often perform his duties in either county.

These matters are strictly controlled by the concrete provisions of the specific state, district or other jurisdiction statutes, however.

§ 2.9 Disqualifications.

In a number of states, there is a statute which declares that no banker, broker, cashier, director, teller, clerk, or other person holding an official relationship to a bank, banker or broker, shall be competent to act as a notary public in any matter in which the bank, banker, or broker is interested.

Contrary to the situation in those states, most states have adopted a more liberal attitude. They allow any notary public who is a stockholder, director, officer or employee of a bank or other corporation to take the acknowledgment of any party to any written instrument to or by such corporation, or to administer an oath to any other stockholder, director, officer, employee or agent of such corporation, or to protest for nonacceptance or nonpayment bills of exchange, drafts, checks, notes, or other negotiable instruments which may be owned or held for collection by such corporation. Such notary is disqualified from acting, however, if he is a party to the instrument, either individually or as a representative of the corporation, or has a financial interest in the subject thereof.

Readers interested in the statutory provisions in this regard, relative to any specific jurisdiction, should consult the specific state statute.

§ 2.10   Signature.

A notary public must sign his name to each official certificate. Some states require the notary's name to be engraved on his official seal or stamp, or printed, stamped or typewritten on the document.

§ 2.11   Expiration of commission.

Perhaps for the purpose of preventing a notary public from performing a notarial act after his term of office expires, a large number of states and other jurisdictions require him to add to his jurat, or other certificate, the date of expiration of his commission. The usual form for such state is:

My commission expires — [date].

Some jurisdictions have statutes which provide that any act done by a notary after the expiration of his term is valid, but in addition impose a fine or other penalty for performing the act after his commission has expired. Some states also impose a fine or other penalty for the failure to state the date when the commission expires.

Regardless of the formal requirements in the local state or other jurisdiction, it is good practice to always state the date of the expiration of the commission when the document is intended to be used in another state.

§ 2.12   Seal.

Under the law merchant and the law of nations, notaries must attest their official certificates and other writings with their seal of office. This is also a requirement imposed by statute in most of the states and other jurisdictions. The statutes in a few jurisdictions provide that a seal is not necessary, or are silent concerning a seal. It is universal good practice, however, to affix an official seal to every certificate or affidavit.

The requisites of a notary seal must be determined according to the statutes of the state or other jurisdiction from which the notary derives his authority. In states which prescribe the words and devices which the seal must contain, the statutory provisions in this regard must be strictly complied with.

§ 2.13   Records.

In many of the states and other jurisdictions, the statutes require a notary public to keep a record or register of his official acts. This is particularly so concerning protests of commercial paper. Some states require a record of all instruments acknowledged, and of all depositions taken. Ordinarily, a notary must furnish a certified copy of any notarial record in his office to any person who applies therefor and pays the notary the necessary fee.

Statutes often provide that at the expiration of the notary's term of office, or upon his resignation, disqualification, death, removal from the county, or removal from office, his records must be deposited in some designated public office. A penalty is frequently imposed upon anyone who fails to so deposit the records.

Penalties are also often provided for destroying or defacing the records of a notary public.

§ 2.14   Fees.

The compensation of a notary public for his services is received in the form of fees, the amount of which is usually fixed by statute in each state. The statutes ordinarily prescribe precisely what a notary may charge for protesting commercial paper, administering an oath, taking a deposition or acknowledgment, or performing some other act.

Several states have enacted laws prohibiting a notary from making a charge for any service to honorably discharged soldiers, sailors, airmen, or marines, in connection with applications for pensions.

§ 2.15   Civil liability.

A notary public must perform his duties honestly, skillfully, and with reasonable diligence. He owes these duties to anyone who officially employs him, and who relies on his certificates. Nominally the state, the governor, or some official is the obligee of the notary's bond, but the real beneficiaries of the bond are the persons who may incur a loss as a proximate result of a notary's misconduct.

Both the notary and the sureties on his official bond are liable for any loss which is the proximate result of the failure of the notary to perform his duties. Liability will arise from a notary's negligence in taking an acknowledgment or for making a false certificate of acknowledgment. If a notary certifies to an acknowledgment of an instrument without personal knowledge concerning the identity of the party acknowledging, and without a careful investigation, he is guilty of negligence and liable for all damage resulting therefrom. The public is entitled to rely upon the truth of a notary's certificate. The notary can therefore be held liable for falsely certifying that particular persons, such as grantors or mortgagors, personally appeared before him and acknowledged the execution of a deed or mortgage.

§ 2.16   Offenses and penalties.

Notaries public of course, are not above the law. When they perform their functions, they must observe the same laws as other persons. In addition to the ordinary statutory prohibitions which all persons, including notaries public, must observe, there are various statutes in many of the states and other jurisdictions which prohibit and punish specified wrongful acts by notaries and other public officials. Some states and other jurisdictions also have statutes which relate to persons who commit offenses against notaries or their records.

§ 2.17   Safe deposit boxes.

In an increasing number of states and other jurisdictions, notaries public are being assigned duties concerning safe deposit boxes on which the rent has not been paid. Typically, the various statutes provide that when the rent due on a safe deposit box has remained unpaid for a specified number of months, the bank or other institution owning the box may give notice to the lessee of the box that the rent is unpaid and the contents will be removed if the rent is not paid within a certain specified period of time. If the rent is not paid within that period, the bank or other institution owning the box may open it in the presence of an officer of the bank and a notary public who is not in the general employment of the bank. The notary is authorized to remove the contents of the box, list them, and seal the contents in a package marked with a legend identifying the lessee of the box from which the contents were removed. A certificate by the notary public, listing the contents is mailed to the lessee of the box. The statutes usually provide additional details concerning how the contents of the package shall be stored and eventually liquidated by sale by the bank or other institution which owns the safe deposit box.

§ 2.18   Oaths.

(A) General.

An oath is an outward pledge, given by the person taking it, that his attestation or promise is made under an immediate sense of his responsibility to God for the truth of what is stated or the faithful performance of what is undertaken.

An affirmation is a solemn declaration without oath. Generally, the term "oath" includes an affirmation, and whenever an oath is required or authorized by law, an affirmation may be taken in lieu of an oath by any person having conscientious scruples against taking an oath. The statutes in most states and other jurisdictions provide that an affirmation has the same force and effect as an oath.

See also the definitions in the *Glossary*.

(B) Manner of administering.

The form of administering an oath may be varied to conform to the religious belief of the individual, so as to make it binding on his conscience. One form consists of the person taking the oath or affirmation holding up his right hand while the officer repeats to him the words of the oath, which begins, "You do solemnly swear that * * *" and ends "so help you God" or "this you do as you shall answer unto God."

In the case of an affirmation, the officer's statement begins, "You do solemnly, sincerely and truly affirm and declare that * * *" and ends "this you do under the pains and penalties of perjury." The person being sworn or affirmed then gives an affirmative answer.

In the case of a public official taking an oath of office, a Christian may place his right hand on the Holy Bible, instead of raising his hand while the words are repeated by the officer administering the oath. A Jewish person should be sworn on the Old Testament; a Mohammedan on the Koran.

Occasionally these matters are specified in the state and other jurisdiction statutes.

(C) Forms of oath.

In addition to, and between, the introductory and closing clauses, the oath may contain a statement such as: "That the various matters and things set forth in this paper which you have here signed before me are true"; or "that the statements contained in the pleading you have just heard read are true"; or "that you will faithfully and diligently perform your duties as director of the _____ Company."

The form of oath which is ordinarily administered to a witness whose deposition is to be taken is as follows: "You do solemnly swear that you will testify the truth, the whole truth, and nothing but the truth in the deposition you are about to give in the case now pending in the _____ Court, wherein A B is plaintiff and C D is defendant, and this you do as you shall answer to God."

A common form of oath administered to a witness during a trial is: "You do solemnly swear that the evidence you are about to give in the cause now here pending shall be the truth, the whole truth, and nothing but the truth, so help you God."

The ordinary form of oath of office is as follows: "You do solemnly swear that you will support the Constitution of the United States, the constitution of the state of _____, and that you will faithfully discharge the duties of the office of _____, during the term for which you have been elected (or, appointed), so help you God."

(D) Who may administer.

In nearly every state and other jurisdiction the statutes authorize a notary public to administer an oath. In cases in which, under the laws of the United States, oaths are authorized or required to be administered, they may be administered by, among others, notaries public duly appointed in any state, district, territory, or possession of the United States. (*See* 5 U.S.C. § 2903.)

§ 2.19 Affidavits.

(A) General.

An affidavit is a declaration reduced to writing, signed by the affiant, and sworn to before an officer authorized by law to administer oaths. An affidavit is generally given or taken without notice to an adverse party, and without cross-examination, differing in this and other respects from a deposition.

An affiant, occasionally called a deponent, is the person who swears or affirms that the matters contained in the affidavit are true.

(B) Component parts.

An affidavit consists of: (1) the caption, which may include the title and venue; (2) the body of the affidavit, which includes the introductory statement and the allegations; and (3) the conclusion, being the signatures, seal and jurat.

(C) The caption.

In an affidavit which is not to be used in any proceeding in court, no title need be given. If, however, an affidavit is to be used in court, the title must show the court in which it is to be used, the names of the parties to the suit, the file number of the suit, and it must generally conform to the captions on pleadings, motions, and orders.

The venue, or name of the state and county where the affidavit is taken, must never be omitted. It precedes the body of the affidavit and fixes the place where the affidavit is made, to show that it is within the jurisdiction of the officer. The letters "ss," or "sct," frequently added to the venue, have no legal significance and are not essential.

(D) Introductory statement.

The body of the affidavit usually begins with a formal statement, such as "Before me, G H, a notary public in and for said county, personally came E F, who, being duly sworn according to law, deposes and says that * * *." If desired, the phrase "authorized by law to administer oaths" may be inserted after the word "County." The affidavit may begin with a more simple introductory statement, such as, "E F, being duly sworn, says that * * *." Another form is, "E F, being first duly sworn, makes this his affidavit and states: * * *."

Where an agent or attorney makes an affidavit, it must expressly state that the affiant is such agent or attorney. One correct way is to say, "E F, being duly sworn, says that he is the agent of A B"; it is incorrect to begin the affidavit, "E F, agent of A B, being duly sworn, says that." Similarly, an affidavit for a partnership in proof of a claim due the partnership must be sworn by one of the partners as agent for the firm. Such an affidavit could begin: "E F, being duly sworn, says that he is a member of the firm of _____ Company."

Where it is necessary to show the residence of the affiant, the place of his residence should not be added as a matter of description to his name; instead the locality should be expressly stated and verified.

(E) Allegations.

The affiant's allegations may be classified as positive and not positive. Positive allegations are those that state facts and not opinions, and are not modified by any such phrase as "to the best of affiant's knowledge and belief," or "as he verily believes."

Allegations which are not positive may be described as: (1) allegations made upon knowledge and belief; (2) upon information and belief; or (3) upon belief.

It is common practice for the affiant to add, at the close of his statements the words, "to the best of his knowledge and belief," even when the matters stated are not merely matters of opinion but are clearly within his own knowledge, and could be positively averred, lest he might unwittingly make oath to an untruth by reason of the infirmity of his memory.

It is customary in some jurisdictions to close the allegations with the words "and further saith not," or "and further affiant saith not."

(F) Signatures.

Even in the absence of an express statutory requirement, the affiant should sign his name to the affidavit at the close of the allegations made by him.

To complete an affidavit taken before a notary public, it is essential that the notary sign his name thereto and comply with the various formalities specified by the appropriate statutes. *See also* § 2.10 above.

(G) Jurat.

The jurat is that part of an affidavit in which the notary states that it was sworn to before him. The omission of words such as "before me," in the jurat may void the affidavit. A common form for the jurat is: "Sworn to before me and subscribed in my presence this _____ day of _____, 19__." Shorter forms, such as: "Subscribed and sworn to before me this [date]," are acceptable.

(H) Seal.

In most states requiring the notary public to have an official seal, he must further attest the affidavit by affixing his seal. *See also* § 2.12 above.

(I) General forms of affidavits.

State of _____,
County of _____, Sct.

E F, after being first duly sworn, makes this his affidavit and states: [allegations].

This [date]

[Signature of affiant]

The foregoing was subscribed and sworn to before me by E F this [date].

(SEAL)

G H, Notary Public
My commission expires [date].

Alternate Form

State of _____,
County of _____, ss.

E F, being first duly sworn, says that _____ [allegations.]

Sworn to before me and subscribed in my presence by E F this _____ day of _____ , 19__.

(SEAL)

G H, Notary Public
My commission expires [date].

(J) Specimen form of affidavit in legal proceeding.

In the _____ Court of _____
Case No. _____

A B, Plaintiff
　　　v.
C D, Defendant

Affidavit of E F

State of _____,
County of _____, Sct.

E F, being first duly sworn, makes this his affidavit and states: [allegations]. And further affiant saith not.

[Signature of affiant.]

The foregoing was subscribed and sworn to before me by E F this _____ day of _____, 19__.

(SEAL)

G H, Notary Public
My commission expires [date].

(K) Before whom affidavits made.

When an affidavit is made in the state or other jurisdiction where it is to be used, it may be made before a notary public within the limits of his jurisdiction. Usually, the statutes also authorize the following officers to take affidavits in the jurisdiction where they are to be used: justice of the peace, mayor, clerk of court, judge of any court of record, and court commissioner.

When an affidavit is made within the United States, but out of the jurisdiction where it is to be used, it may be made before a notary public in a majority of the states and other jurisdictions. The statutes also permit such affidavit to be taken by a commissioner of the state where it is to be used, or by anyone authorized to administer oaths or take depositions.

When the affidavit is made out of the United States, it may usually be made before a notary public. The statutes of many states and other jurisdictions also authorize the following officers to take such affidavits: ambassador of the United States, consul, and consular agent.

§ 2.20 Acknowledgments.

(A) General.

Acknowledgment is a formal declaration before a public officer, by the person who has signed an instrument, that it is his or her voluntary act and deed. The term also includes the written certificate of the officer, as to the act of acknowledgment, upon the same sheet as the instrument or attached thereto. Acknowledgment must be distinguished from attestation, which is merely the act of witnessing the execution of a paper and subscribing one's name thereto as a witness.

The purpose of acknowledgment is to entitle the instrument to record, and to provide official evidence of its execution.

(B) Instruments requiring acknowledgment.

An instrument need not be acknowledged unless required by statute, because acknowledgment was unknown to the common law. The statutory provisions of each state or other jurisdiction must be consulted to determine what particular instruments require acknowledgment. Some idea of the scope of such statutes will be gained from the following list of instruments which, under the laws of various states, must be acknowledged: deeds, mortgages, land contracts and leases of any interest in real property; powers of attorney to convey, mortgage or lease the same; satisfactions and releases of mortgages, when not made on the original mortgage or on the margin of the record thereof; plats of towns, additions and subdivisions; deeds of sheriffs, master commissioners, and other officers selling real property in pursuance of an order of court; written agreements of owners of adjoining lands fixing the corners or boundary lines; certificates of limited partnership; trademarks of timber dealers.

Some statutes provide that certain instruments need not be acknowledged; for example, leases for a short term, releases of mortgages when made on the original mortgage, security agreements, and financing statements.

(C) Officers authorized to take.

Acknowledgments can be taken only by those officers specifically authorized by statute. Three different situations are recognized in the statutory provisions of most states and other jurisdictions, designating in separate lists what officers may take acknowledgments (1) within the state, (2) elsewhere in the United States, and (3) outside the United States. A notary public, among others, has authority under the laws of virtually every state and other jurisdiction to take acknowledgments in the three situations. Other officers frequently authorized by the various statutes are: justices of the peace, magistrates, mayors, judges of courts of record, clerks of courts, commissioners of deeds, and consuls.

(D) Disqualification of officer.

The fact that the notary public is related to one of the parties signing the instrument does not usually disqualify him from taking the signer's acknowledgment. If, however, the notary is interested as grantor or grantee, or has some financial interest in the transaction, he is disqualified. *See also* § 2.9 above.

Several states have enacted laws permitting a notary public who is a stockholder, director, officer, or employee of a bank, savings and loan association, or other corporation to take acknowledgment of any party to any written instrument to or by such corporation, provided such notary is not a party to the instrument, either individually or as a representative of the corporation.

(E) Manner of taking acknowledgment.

Before taking the acknowledgment of the person who is signing a deed or other instrument, a notary public should read to himself the certificate of acknowledgment. By doing this, he will be reminded of his responsibility to act only within the locality for which he has been appointed, and he also will be aware of the necessity of knowing the signer and having the signer personally appear before him. In addition, the wording of the certificate of acknowledgment will enable the notary to know what to say to the signer.

After asking the signer to raise his right hand and be sworn, the notary ordinarily says: "Do you acknowledge the signing of this instrument to be your voluntary act and deed?" The signer should respond "I do" before the notary completes the certificate of acknowledgment by inserting the date, signing his name at the end of the certificate, affixing his notarial seal, and stating the date when his commission expires where that is required by law.

Some notaries have been tempted to accommodate various persons by taking acknowledgments over the telephone. Such a practice is hazardous, and should be scrupulously avoided. A majority of states and other jurisdictions hold that acknowledgments via telephone are invalid. The pertinent statutes usually require the personal presence of the party "before" the officer taking the acknowledgment, and an acknowledgment given by a person via telephone when he or she is not in fact "before" or in the presence of the officer, is therefore void. A notary's official acts as directed by legislation are not insignificant formalities "which may be smiled out of the law." Court cases have held that a signing, which is not in fact acknowledged before the notary, is not properly executed, is not entitled to be recorded, and the recording in fact does not constitute constructive notice to a subsequent mortgagee. A notary public who affixes his name and seal to an acknowledgment or affidavit which states that the parties appeared before him when in effect they did not do so is himself making an untrue statement which may be followed by both civil and criminal liability.

(F) Corporate acknowledgment.

Corporate officers should swear that they are officers of the corporation; that the seal affixed to the instrument they have just signed is the seal of the corporation; that they have signed and sealed the instrument on behalf of the corporation and by authority of its board of directors; and that the signing of the instrument is their free act and deed individually and as such officers, and the free and corporate act of the corporation.

(G) Certificate of acknowledgment.

The certificate should be written on the same sheet with the instrument acknowledged. This requirement is mandatory under the laws of a number of states, although a few states allow it to be on a separate paper, attached to the instrument. In both printed forms and typewritten documents the certificate follows immediately after the signatures to be acknowledged.

1. Component parts.

The officer's certificate of acknowledgment may be analyzed as consisting of the following parts:

    (1) Venue, or statement of locality;
    (2) Body of certificate, which states:
        (a) Introductory clause
        (b) Date when acknowledged
        (c) Name and identity of officer
        (d) Presence of grantor
        (e) Name of grantor
        (f) Officer's knowledge of grantor's identity
        (g) Voluntary nature of acknowledgment
    (3) Testimonium clause
    (4) Officer's signature
    (5) Seal of officer
    (6) Date of expiration of officer's commission

2. General form.

With the exception of those states which have adopted the Uniform Acknowledgment Act, few states prescribe a form of certificate. The figures and letters in parentheses in the following general form have been inserted only for the purpose of identifying the component parts as outlined in the preceding section.

(*1*) State of _____,
      County of _____, ss.

(*2*) (*a*) Be it remembered that (*b*) on the _____ day of _____, 19__, (*c*) before me, G H, a notary public in and for said county, (*d*) personally came and appeared (*e*) A B, C D and E D, the grantors in the foregoing deed (*f*) to me known to be the same persons described in and who executed the foregoing instrument, (*g*) and acknowledged the signing thereof to be their voluntary act and deed, for the uses and purposes therein mentioned.

(*3*) In testimony whereof, I have hereunto subscribed my name and affixed my notarial seal, on the day and year last above mentioned.

(*4*)   G H, Notary Public

(*5*) (SEAL)

(*6*) My commission expires _____ (date).

3. Venue.

The state and county where the acknowledgment is made should appear at the beginning of each certificate. It is then presumed that the officer acted within that locality. This statement is important by reason of the fact that an acknowledgment can be taken by an officer only within the locality for which he has been appointed.

4. Introductory clause.

The phrase, "Be it remembered that," is of no legal significance and can be omitted if desired.

5. Date.

The date when the acknowledgment is taken should always be given in the certificate. It generally is the same as the date of signing the instrument. The date of acknowledgment cannot be earlier than the day of execution of the instrument.

There is not reason why an instrument may not be acknowledged years after its execution, or at different times and places by various grantors. If several persons acknowledge before the same officer, but on different days, he can state the facts as follows:

"Before me, G H, a notary public in and for said county, on the first day of June, 19__, personally came A B and C D, two of the grantors in the foregoing deed, and on the third day of June, 19__, personally came E D, another of said grantors."

(H) Name and identity of officer.

The certificate should contain the name and title of the officer before whom the acknowledgment is taken, together with a reference to the locality within which he is authorized to act. The words "in and for said county," or "within and for said county," are sufficient if the state and county are named in the venue at the beginning of the certificate.

1. Presence of grantor.

It is essential that the grantor personally appear before the notary public at the time of acknowledging the instrument. Acknowledgments should not be taken over a telephone. An officer who falsely certifies that a person has appeared before him, when in fact he has not, is guilty of misconduct and becomes liable on his bond. Concerning acknowledgments over the telephone, see § 2.20(E), above.

2. Name of grantor.

Usually, all the acknowledging grantors should be named in the certificate of acknowledgment. The name of the wife of each grantor should likewise be included, even if she joins in the execution of the deed for the sole purpose of relinquishing her right of dower. Care should be exercised that the name of the grantor as it appears in the certificate is the same as that in the instrument being acknowledged. Furthermore, the certificate should identify the party by showing that it was the grantor or other signer of the instrument who acknowledged it. A phrase such as "the grantors in the foregoing deed," or "the parties to the within lease," may be used immediately after the names of the parties in order to accomplish this purpose.

3. Knowledge of identity.

The certificate uniformly must state that the signer is known to the officer, or has been proved to him to be the person who signed. The phrase "known to me" or "proved to me on the oath of _____" precedes the general statement, "to be the same person whose name is subscribed to the foregoing instrument." It is not enough for the officer to say that he is "satisfied" as to the identity.

4. Voluntary nature of acknowledgment.

The fact that the person who has signed the instrument also acknowledges it must be stated in the certificate. The usual phrases are "acknowledged that he executed the same as his free act and deed," or "acknowledged the signing thereof to be his voluntary act and deed." Failure to include such statement will render the acknowledgment invalid.

In some states it is necessary to add the words "for the uses and purposes therein mentioned.

5. Married woman.

Formerly, when a married woman was a party to a deed, the laws of some states required that the officer examine her separate and apart from her husband. When this examination was required, the certificate had to show that, upon being examined separate and apart from her husband, and the contents of the instrument being explained to her, she declared that she signed and acknowledged the same voluntarily, and was still satisfied therewith.

Today, in virtually every state, however, a wife need not be examined separately.

6. Testimonium clause.

The certificate of acknowledgment frequently contains a statement by the officer that the signature and seal to his certificate are his signature and seal. Instead of the long sentence, "In testimony whereof, I have hereunto subscribed my name and affixed my notarial seal, on the day and year last above mentioned," one of the following brief statements is often used: "Witness my hand and seal of office;" "Given under my hand and seal this _____ day of _____, 19__;" "Before me."

The forms of acknowledgments in a number of states omit the testimonium clause as being unnecessary.

7. Officer's signature.

The notary public must sign his name at the end of the certificate of acknowledgment. His mere personal signature is not sufficient, the words "Notary Public" should be added to his name. If the description of the officer in the body of the certificate has not already stated his locality, it is proper to sign, "G H, Notary Public, in and for _____ County, State of _____." The omission of the officer's signature renders the certificate of acknowledgment void. *See also* § 2.10 above.

8. Seal of officer.

Custom generally, and the statutes or decisions in many of the states, require that the certificate of acknowledgment should be authenticated by the officer's seal, if he be required by law to have a seal. In view of the well-known principle of law that a notary's seal proves itself, he should affix his seal to every acknowledgment taken by him. *See also* § 2.12 above.

9. Date of expiration of commission.

In those states which by statute require a notary public to add to his certificate the date of the expiration of his commission, a certificate of acknowledgment must conclude with the statement: "My commission expires _____ (date)." *See also* § 2.11 above.

(I) Authentication of officer's authority.

Unless required by a particular statute, no certificate of authentication need accompany an acknowledgment made before a notary public of another state, attested by his official seal.

When a justice of the peace, mayor, or similar officer takes the acknowledgment of a deed to land outside of his own state, there often must be affixed to his certificate of acknowledgment a certificate of the clerk of the court of his county, under the seal of the court, as to the official capacity of such justice or mayor, that he is authorized by law to take acknowledgments, that the clerk is acquainted with the handwriting of such justice, and that the signature to the certificate of acknowledgment is that of such justice.

(J) Proving deeds.

It is lawful and customary in some states and other jurisdictions to prove deeds as an alternative to acknowledging them. One or more of the subscribing witnesses goes before an officer authorized to administer oaths, and makes an affidavit that the grantor executed and acknowledged the instrument in the presence of the affiant and the other witness. The officer then prepares a certificate of this oath on the deed in the same manner as a certificate of acknowledgment is made. In some states this procedure is called probating the deed. *See also* § 2.24 below.

§ 2.21 Depositions.

(A) General.

A deposition is the testimony of a witness which is reduced to writing by a notary public or other public officer for various purposes incident to a lawsuit. It is made under oath and upon notice to the adverse party, who may attend and cross-examine the witness.

(B) Right to take depositions.

The use of depositions was not permitted in the early common law courts, except by consent of the parties. Courts of equity, however, had power to obtain testimony by deposition, having created three different forms of relief: (1) A bill to take testimony de bene esse; (2) a bill to perpetuate testimony; and (3) a bill of discovery. To correct these limitations, most states and other jurisdictions have enacted statutes, and most courts have adopted rules of procedure, which now permit the use of depositions and prescribe the manner in which they are to be taken. Strict compliance with these statutory provisions and rules of procedure is necessary. The Federal Rules of Civil Procedure (Fed. R. Civ. P.) incorporate and broaden the former provisions of the United States statutes concerning depositions, and have served as a model for various state rules of civil procedure which has been closely followed by a large number of state courts.

(C) Classification.

Depositions are frequently mentioned under different names and phrases in the various statutory provisions, with references chiefly to the manner, authorization, purpose, and time of their taking. They may be classified accordingly.

 1. Depositions taken in reply to (a) oral interrogatories or questions, and (b) written interrogatories or questions.

 2. Depositions taken (a) on notice; (b) under commission, or dedimus potestatem; (c) under notice and commission; (d) by stipulation or agreement; (e) under letters rogatory.

3. Depositions taken (a) de bene esse (conditionally); (b) to perpetuate testimony.

(D) Who may take depositions.

Statutes or rules of procedure, or both, usually identify the officers before whom depositions may be taken. Not only notaries public, but frequently the clerk of a court, a judge of a court, a justice of the peace, and various commissioners are authorized to take depositions. Some statutes and rules of procedure confer such power generally upon any officer authorized to administer an oath.

If the witness whose deposition is to be taken resides out of the state, a commission may be issued by the clerk of the court in which the suit is pending, to any person agreed upon by the parties to the suit, or to a notary public selected by the officer issuing the commission, or to a commissioner appointed by the governor to take depositions in other states.

The statutes of many states, and the rules of procedure of many courts, expressly provide that the officer before whom the deposition is taken must not be related to, or the attorney or agent of, either of the parties, or interested in the result of the law suit.

(E) Notice of intention to take.

The written notice of intention to take a deposition, given to the adverse party, usually contains the following information: (1) Names of the parties to the lawsuit; (2) court in which the deposition is to be used; (3) date, time, and place where it will be taken; (4) name of the witness or witnesses; (5) name or identity of officer who will take; (6) purpose of the deposition; (7) whether the examination is to be adjourned from day to day; (8) occasionally, the matters upon which the witness is to be examined; and (9) signature of the attorney of the party giving notice.

The manner and time of serving such notice are regulated by the statutes of the various states and other jurisdictions, and the rules of procedure of the various courts.

Depositions taken on notice are generally taken in answer to oral questions propounded by the attorneys of the parties, the notice being the only writing which comes to the notary public as evidence of the right to take the deposition. He must, therefore, be an officer expressly authorized by statute to take depositions.

(F) Manner of taking depositions—in general.

Depositions in reply to oral questions are ordinarily taken pursuant to notice or agreement, before a duly authorized officer, with whom the parties have arranged to be present and to have the witnesses present, at the time and place mentioned in the notice or agreement. Either or both parties have the right to be present at such taking, by attorney or in person, or both. The officer, after having written out the proper caption and preamble, records the names of the attorneys, parties, and witnesses present. This is often listed under the title, "Appearances." The officer proceeds to write, or to have written, the questions submitted orally to the witnesses by the attorneys, and the answers of each witness.

Depositions in reply to written interrogatories are taken under a commission, at which taking neither party to the lawsuit has a right to be present or to be represented by attorney or agent, the interrogatories being put to the witness by the officer, and the answers thereto written by him or some authorized person. In addition to the interrogatories prepared by the attorney of the party desiring the deposition, cross-interrogatories may be submitted by the opposing attorney. Both the interrogatories and cross-interrogatories are attached to the commission. The law of the state or other jurisdiction whence the commission issues governs such depositions and the manner of their taking.

(G) Taken under agreement or stipulation.

The parties to a lawsuit may agree or stipulate that the deposition of a witness or witnesses may be taken before a certain officer, at a designated date, time and place, and waive some of the strict formalities as to adjournments or other particulars. Such agreement or stipulation is usually reduced to writing, and takes the place of a commission or similar authority. As to matters not provided for in the agreement, the statutes and rules of procedure in the state or other jurisdiction where the deposition is to be used should be carefully observed.

(H) Swearing the witness.

The witness must be sworn before he gives his testimony. The usual form of oath to the witness is as follows:

"You do solemnly swear that you will testify the truth, the whole truth, and nothing but the truth in answer to the several questions (or interrogatories and cross-interrogatories) about to be put to you in the case now pending in the _____ Court, wherein A B is plaintiff and C D is defendant, and this you do as you shall answer unto God?"

(I) Writing of depositions.

Under the statutes and rules of procedure of most states and other jurisdictions, only the officer, or the witness who is deposing, or some disinterested third person, is allowed to write the answers to the questions put to the witness. They often provide that the officer before whom the deposition is taken shall personally, or by someone acting under his direction and in his presence, record the testimony of the witness. Usually, depositions may be taken stenographically and transcribed. When the testimony is fully transcribed, the deposition is submitted to the witness for examination and will be read to or by him for his correction or approval. Any changes in form or substance which the witness desires to make should be noted upon the deposition by the notary public with a statement of the reasons given by the witness for making them.

(J) Signing the deposition.

Unless the requirement is waived by the witness and by the parties, the deposition must be signed by the witness at the end thereof. Such waivers are often given. Some states and other jurisdictions require the witness to sign the deposition not only at the end, but also upon each piece of paper upon which any portion of his testimony is written. If, from ignorance, disability, or illness, the witness is unable to write his signature at the end of the deposition, the notary public may write the witness' name for him as follows: "William Brown, by George Houston;" or: "William (his x mark) Brown," the mark x being made by the witness, or by the notary public while the witness is touching the pen.

In some states, the officer must certify, after the signature of each witness, as follows: "Sworn to and subscribed before me, by the said E F, this _____ day of _____, 19__, at the place and within the hours above mentioned. G H, Notary Public."

(K) Caption, preamble, and appearances.

The introductory portion of the deposition should show: (1) Name and title of officer before whom taken; (2) date and time when, and (3) place where taken; (4) by what authority taken; (5) in what court to be used; (6) names of the parties to suit; (7) names and residences of witnesses; (8) in whose behalf taken; (9) who was present in behalf of each party; and (10) that the witness was duly sworn.

(L) Form of deposition.

The statutes and rules of procedure of a few states and other jurisdictions prescribe the form of a deposition. In the absence of specific contrary directions in the appropriate statutes and rules of procedure, the following general form may be used:

Deposition of E F taken before me, G H, a notary public in and for _____ County, State of _____, pursuant to the annexed notice (*or*, commission; *or* agreement) at the time and place therein specified, to be read in evidence on behalf of the plaintiff (*or*, defendant), in an action pending in the _____ Court of _____ County, State of _____, in which A B is plaintiff, and C D is defendant. L M appeared as attorney for the plaintiff and R S appeared as attorney for the defendant.

E F, of lawful age, being first duly sworn, deposes and says as follows:

Question.*

Answer.

Q.

A.

[And so continue until the direct examination is finished. If the deposition is taken under written interrogatories, the officer or stenographer writes, not the interrogatory, but only: "To the first interrogatory he says:" and "To the second interrogatory he says:" etc.]

Cross-examination of E F, by _____, in behalf of _____:

Q.

A. (and so proceed to the close of the cross-examination).

Re-direct examination of E F by _____:

Q.

Q. (and so to the end of his testimony)

(Signature) E F
Witness

* Note: The questions and answers are often identified by the abbreviations "Q." and "A." respectively.

(M) Officer's certificate.

After the testimony of all the witnesses has been taken, the officer usually must add to the deposition a certificate stating: (1) That the witness was first sworn to testify the truth, the whole truth, and nothing but the truth; (2) by whom the deposition was written, and if written by deponent or some disinterested person, that it was written in the presence and under the direction of the officer; (3) the date, time and place of taking the deposition; (4) that the witness signed it, or that the signing by the witness was waived; (5) that the officer is not counsel, attorney or relative of either party, or otherwise interested in the result of the lawsuit; (6) that the deposition is a true record of the evidence and testimony given by deponent. The officer must sign the certificate and affix his seal.

(N) Interpreters.

Even in the absence of express statutory authority, the right to take testimony would imply the power to employ an interpreter when the witness does not understand English, or cannot intelligently testify in that language. If the officer taking the deposition understands the witness' language, he may interpret the testimony.

An oath, in substantially the following form, should be administered to the interpreter: "You do solemnly swear that you know the English and the _____ languages, and can interpret from either of them into the other; and that you will truly and impartially interpret from the English language into to the _____ language to E F, the witness, the oath that shall be administered to him, and the questions that shall be put to him as a witness, and that you will truly and impartially interpret from the _____ language into the English language the answers that said witness shall give; and this you do as you shall answer unto God."

An interpreter also must sign the deposition with the witness whose testimony he interprets. The following statement should be inserted in the deposition, just preceding the testimony: "It appearing that the witness, E F, could not understand the English language (or, could not intelligently testify in the English language), and did understand the _____ language, one L M, who also well understands said _____ language, was employed as interpreter and sworn to impartially interpret the oath, questions and answers."

(O) Adjournments.

Ordinarily, when the deposition has not been finished and the closing hour of the day has come, or for other good reason an adjournment is necessary, the further taking of the deposition should be adjourned to the next day unless it be Sunday or a legal holiday. A notice to take depositions usually provides for adjournment from day to day.

The adjournment should be to the same place, unless the parties agree to some other place. The taking of a deposition under commission, at which the parties cannot be present, may be adjourned to such times and places as will suit the convenience of the officer and the witnesses.

There being more testimony than can be taken conveniently in one day, or a witness in attendance becoming sick and unable to attend longer on that day, or a witness duly subpoenaed failing to attend, are good reasons for an adjournment to the next day.

The adjournment may be noted by the officer as follows: "The taking of said deposition not being finished at _____ o'clock of said _____ day of _____, 19__, the further taking thereof was adjourned to _____ o'clock of the _____ day of _____, 19__ [the next business day, omitting Sundays and legal holidays]."

The resumption of taking testimony, after adjournment, may be noted: "The taking of said E F's deposition commenced on the _____ day of _____, 19__, was resumed on _____ _____, 19__, at _____ o'clock __.M."

(P) Objections.

The adverse party or his attorney may object to questions, and occasionally answers, for various reasons. The objections should be recorded by the officer. At the appropriate place in the record of the examination, the officer writes, "The plaintiff (*or*, defendant) objects to this question (*or*, answer) as [state the reason given]," and then, nevertheless, writes the answer. The court before which the lawsuit is pending will rule on the objections when the deposition is filed in court.

(Q) Exhibits.

If a letter, telegram, or other paper is introduced in evidence during the taking of a deposition, it should be marked for identification as required by the statutes or custom of the state or other jurisdiction in which the deposition is to be used. In many jurisdictions, such papers are described carefully in the deposition, the witness then adding such words as "which letter is hereto attached, marked Exhibit A." The next one is called "Exhibit B," the next one "Exhibit C," and they are all fastened to the deposition.

In other jurisdictions, such exhibits must be annexed to the deposition, subscribed by the witness, and endorsed by the officer as follows:

"At the execution of a commission for the examination of witnesses in a suit

between A B, plaintiff, and C D, defendant, the paper writing was produced and
shown to E F and by him deposed unto at the time of the examination before.

G H

Commissioner"

(R) Filing of deposition.

After the deposition has been completed, it must be fastened together with the
notice, commission, or agreement, written interrogatories, if any, and exhibits into
one package. All of these papers, including each page of the deposition, may be
held firmly together by means of a fastener run through holes placed near the top
of all the sheets or along one side of the sheets. To prevent any one from tampering
with the package, a seal may be placed over the ends of the fastener and an
impression of the officer's seal made on it.

The deposition must be enclosed in some suitable cover such as a large envelope,
and sealed. The package, so sealed, ordinarily must be addressed to the clerk of
the court in which the lawsuit is pending, as follows:

A B, Plaintiff   No. _____

v.   Pending in

C D, Defendant   _____ Court

Deposition of E F, taken in behalf of
the plaintiff (*or*, defendant), before G H,
Notary Public

To the Clerk of the _____ Court

(name of postoffice),

_____ County,

(State)

Across the back of the envelope, or sealed place of the cover, the officer should
write:

Deposition taken
before me, and
sealed, addressed
and transmitted
by me.

G H,

Notary Public in
and for _____
County, State of

_____.

The object of this is to identify the deposition without opening it, and prevent its being opened by the wrong parties. The endorsements should, therefore, not be omitted even where not required by statute.

(S) Compelling attendance of witness.

In many states and other jurisdictions, the various officers authorized to take depositions are empowered to subpoena witnesses to attend and to testify, and to compel them to do so in case of their neglect or refusal to do either. In several jurisdictions, however, compulsory measures to secure attendance, answers, and signatures of witnesses at the taking of depositions must be secured through the court. In some jurisdictions, both provisions exist, and the persons taking the depositions may choose either alternative. Often, the proof of service of a notice to take a deposition constitutes a sufficient authorization for the issuance by the clerk of the court of subpoenas for the persons named or described therein. A subpoena commanding the production of documentary evidence on the taking of a deposition ordinarily cannot be used without an order of the court.

(T) Punishment for contempt.

Disobedience of a subpoena, a refusal to be sworn, a refusal to answer as a witness, or to subscribe a deposition, may be punished as a contempt of the court or officer by whom the attendance or testimony of the witness is required. The statutes of several states and other jurisdictions authorize the officer to impose a fine or commit the witness to jail.

If a party or other deponent refuses to answer a question propounded upon oral examination, or an interrogatory, the examination should be completed on other matters or adjourned, as the proponent of the question may prefer. Thereafter, on reasonable notice to all persons affected thereby, the proponent of the question may apply to the court for an order compelling an answer. The failure to comply with such an order would be considered a contempt of court.

§ 2.22 Commercial paper under the Uniform Commercial Code.

(A) General.

A large number of state and other jurisdiction statutes place large importance on the functions of notaries public in relation to commercial paper, sometimes called negotiable instruments. These functions are to some extent affected by the provisions of Articles 3 and 4 of the Uniform Commercial Code, which was recommended to the various state and other legislatures for adoption by the American Law Institute and the National Conference of Commissioners on Uniform State Laws. First adopted and made effective in Pennsylvania in 1954, Massachusetts in 1958, and Kentucky in 1960, the other states and jurisdictions followed by adopting it, as modified to a relatively small degree by the legislatures of the adopting states and other jurisdictions. The Uniform Commercial Code is now at least in part, the law in 50 states, the District of Columbia and the Virgin islands.

Article 3 concerns commercial paper and Article 4 concerns bank deposits and collections. The text that follows is a general discussion of the Official Text of the Uniform Commercial Code or UCC as it is commonly called. Few states have adopted it without modification. Therefore the reader is cautioned to consult the specific statute for particular requirements.

(B) Presentment of bills for acceptance.

Presentment is a demand for acceptance or payment made upon the maker, acceptor, drawee or other payor by or on behalf of the holder.[1] The holder of a bill or his agent, generally a notary public, must call upon the drawee, exhibit the bill to him and ask whether the drawee will pay it at its maturity.

Presentment for acceptance is necessary to charge the drawer and indorsers of a draft where the draft so provides, or is payable elsewhere than at the residence or place of business of the drawee, or its date of payment depends upon such presentment. The holder may at his option present for acceptance any other draft payable at a stated date.[2]

Presentment may be made: (1) by mail, in which event the time of presentment is determined by the time of receipt of the mail; (2) through a clearing house; or (3) at the place of acceptance specified in the instrument or if there be none at the place of business or residence of the party to accept. If neither the party to accept nor anyone authorized to act for him is present or accessible at such place, presentment is excused.[3]

Presentment may be made to: (1) any one of two or more makers, acceptors, drawees or other payors; or (2) any person who has authority to make or refuse the acceptance. A draft accepted or a note made payable at a bank in the United States must be presented at such bank.[4]

1. Time.

Unless a different time is expressed in the instrument the time for presentment is determined as follows: (1) where an instrument is payable at or a fixed period after a stated date any presentment for acceptance must be made on or before the date it is payable; (2) where an instrument is payable after sight it must either be presented for acceptance or negotiated within a reasonable time after date or issue whichever is later; (3) with respect to the liability of any secondary party presentment for acceptance of any other instrument is due within a reasonable time after such party becomes liable thereon.[5]

A reasonable time for presentment is determined by the nature of the instrument, any usage of banking or trade and the facts of the particular case. Where any presentment is due on a day which is not a full business day for either the

---

[1] Uniform Commercial Code (hereinafter U.C.C.) § 3-504(1).

[2] U.C.C. § 3-501(1)(a).

[3] U.C.C. § 3-504(2).

[4] U.C.C. § 3-504(3), (4).

[5] U.C.C. § 3-503(1).

person making presentment or the party to accept, presentment is due on the next following day which is a full business day for both parties. Presentment to be sufficient must be made at a reasonable hour, and if at a bank during its banking day.[6]

2. Excused.

Delay in presentment is excused when the party is without notice that it is due or when the delay is caused by circumstances beyond his control and he exercises reasonable diligence after the cause of delay ceases to operate.[7]

Presentment is entirely excused when either: (1) the party to be charged has waived it expressly or by implication either before or after it is due; (2) such party has himself dishonored the instrument or has countermanded payment or otherwise has no reason to expect or right to require that the instrument be accepted; (3) by reasonable diligence the presentment cannot be made; (4) the maker, acceptor or drawee of any instrument except a documentary draft is dead or in insolvency proceedings instituted after the issue of the instrument; or (5) acceptance is refused but not for want of proper presentment.[8]

A waiver of protest is also a waiver of presentment. Where a waiver of presentment is embodied in the instrument itself it is binding upon all parties; but where it is written above the signature of an indorser it binds him only.[9]

(C) Dishonor by nonacceptance.

An instrument is dishonored when: (1) a necessary or optional presentment is made and due acceptance is refused or cannot be obtained within the prescribed time or in case of bank collections the instrument is seasonably returned by the midnight deadline; or (2) presentment is excused and the instrument is not duly accepted.[10]

Return of an instrument for lack of proper indorsement is not dishonor. A term in a draft or an indorsement thereof allowing a stated time for re-presentment in the event of any dishonor of the draft by nonacceptance if a time draft or by nonpayment if a sight draft gives the holder as against any secondary party bound by the term an option to waive the dishonor without affecting the liability of the secondary party. He may present again up to the end of the stated time.[11]

Where a draft has been dishonored by nonacceptance a later presentment for payment and any notice of dishonor and protest for nonpayment are excused unless in the meantime the instrument has been accepted.[12]

(D) Presentment for payment.

Unless excused (Section 3-511; see § 2.22(B) 2. above), presentment for payment

---

[6] U.C.C. § 3-503(2)–(4). See § 2.22(M), *Legal Holidays*, below.

[7] U.C.C. § 3-511(1).

[8] U.C.C. § 3-511(2), (3).

[9] U.C.C. § 3-511(5), (6).

[10] U.C.C. § 3-507(1).

[11] U.C.C. § 3-507(3), (4).

[12] U.C.C. § 3-511(4).

is necessary to charge any indorser. In the case of any drawer, the acceptor of a draft payable at a bank or the maker of a note payable at a bank, presentment for payment is necessary, but failure to make presentment discharges the drawer, acceptor or maker only as stated in Section 3-502(1)(b).[13]

Where the maker or acceptor of an instrument payable otherwise than on demand is able and ready to pay at every place of payment specified in the instrument when it is due, it is equivalent to tender. Any party making tender of full payment to a holder when or after it is due is discharged to the extent of all subsequent liability for interest, costs and attorney's fees.[14]

1. Time.

Unless a different time is expressed in the instrument the time for presentment is determined as follows: (1) where an instrument shows the date on which it is payable presentment for payment is due on that date; (2) where an instrument is accelerated presentment for payment is due within a reasonable time after the acceleration; (3) with respect to the liability of any secondary party presentment for payment of any other instrument is due within a reasonable time after such party becomes liable thereon.[15]

A reasonable time for presentment is determined by the nature of the instrument, any usage of banking or trade and the facts of the particular case. In the case of an uncertified check which is drawn and payable within the United States and which is not a draft drawn by a bank the following are presumed to be reasonable periods within which to present for payment or to initiate bank collection: (1) with respect to the liability of the drawer, thirty days after date or issue whichever is later; and (2) with respect to the liability of an indorser, seven days after his indorsement.[16]

Where any presentment is due on a day which is not a full business day for either the person making presentment or the party to pay or accept, presentment is due on the next following day which is a full business day for both parties. Presentment to be sufficient must be made at a reasonable hour, and if at a bank during its banking day.[17]

2. Sufficiency.

Presentment is a demand for payment made upon the maker, acceptor, drawee or other payor by or on behalf of the holder. Presentment may be made by mail, in which event the time of presentment is determined by the time of receipt of the

---

[13] U.C.C. § 3-501(1)(b)(c). U.C.C. § 3-502(1)(b) provides that where without excuse any necessary presentment or notice of dishonor is delayed beyond the time when it is due, any drawer or the acceptor of a draft payable at a bank or the maker of a note payable at a bank who because the drawee or payor bank becomes insolvent during the delay is deprived of funds maintained with the drawee or payor bank to cover the instrument may discharge his liability by written as-

signment to the holder of his rights against the drawee or payor bank in respect of such funds, but such drawer, acceptor or maker is not otherwise discharged.

[14] U.C.C. § 3-604.

[15] U.C.C. § 3-503(1).

[16] U.C.C. § 3-503(2).

[17] U.C.C. § 3-503(3), (4). See § 2.22(M), *Legal Holidays*, below.

mail, or through a clearing house.[18] Presentment to be sufficient must be made at a reasonable hour, and if at a bank during its banking day.[19]

3. Place.

Presentment for payment may be made at the place of payment specified in the instrument or if there be none at the place of business or residence of the party to pay. If neither the party to pay nor anyone authorized to act for him is present or accessible at such place presentment is excused.[20]

(E) To whom made.

Presentment for payment may be made to any one of two or more makers, acceptors, drawees or other payors, or to any person who has authority to make or refuse the payment.[21]

The party to whom presentment is made may without dishonor require any or all of the following: (1) exhibition of the instrument; (2) reasonable identification of the person making presentment and evidence of his authority to make it if made for another; (3) that the instrument be produced for acceptance or payment at a place specified in it, or if there be none at any place reasonable in the circumstances; and (4) a signed receipt on the instrument for any partial or full payment and its surrender upon full payment. Failure to comply with any such requirement invalidates the presentment but the person presenting has a reasonable time in which to comply and the time for payment runs from the time of compliance.[22]

1. Delay excused.

Delay in presentment is excused when the party is without notice that it is due or when the delay is caused by circumstances beyond his control and he exercises reasonable diligence after the cause of the delay ceases to operate.[23]

2. Dispensed with.

Presentment is entirely excused when: (1) the party to be charged has waived it expressly or by implication either before or after it is due; (2) such party has himself dishonored the instrument or has countermanded payment or otherwise has no reason to expect or right to require that the instrument be accepted or paid; (3) by reasonable diligence the presentment cannot be made; (4) the maker, acceptor or drawee of any instrument except a documentary draft is dead or in insolvency proceedings instituted after the issue of the instrument; or (5) payment is refused but not for want of proper presentment.[24]

Where a draft has been dishonored by nonacceptance a later presentment for payment is excused unless in the meantime the instrument has been accepted. A

---

[18] U.C.C. § 3-504(1), (2).
[19] U.C.C. § 3-503(4).
[20] U.C.C. § 3-504(2).
[21] U.C.C. § 3-504(3).

[22] U.C.C. § 3-505.
[23] U.C.C. § 3-511(1).
[24] U.C.C. § 3-511(2), (3).

waiver of protest is also a waiver of presentment. Where a waiver of presentment is embodied in the instrument itself it is binding upon all parties; but where it is written above the signature of an indorser it binds him only.[25]

(F) Dishonor by nonpayment.

An instrument is dishonored when: (1) a necessary or optional presentment is duly made and due payment is refused or cannot be obtained within the prescribed time or in case of bank collections the instrument is seasonably returned by the midnight deadline; or (2) presentment is excused and the instrument is not duly paid.[26]

(G) Protest.

A protest is a declaration in writing made by, among others, a notary public, on behalf of the holder of a bill or note, that acceptance or payment has been refused. This written declaration itself is also called a certificate of dishonor or the certificate of protest, which is only the evidence of the fact of protest. Although in a technical sense the term "protest" means only the formal declaration drawn up and signed by the notary, in commercial usage it includes all the steps necessary to charge the indorser.[27]

Unless excused (Section 3-511; see § 2.22(G) 5. below), protest of any dishonor is necessary to charge the drawer and indorsers of any draft which on its face appears to be drawn or payable outside of the states, territories, dependencies and possessions of the United States, the District of Columbia, and the Commonwealth of Puerto Rico. The holder may at his option make protest of any dishonor of any other instrument and in the case of a foreign draft may on insolvency of the acceptor before maturity make protest for better security. Protest is not necessary to charge an indorser who has indorsed an instrument after maturity.[28]

1. Time for making.

With one exception, any necessary protest is due by the time that notice of dishonor is due.[29] Any necessary notice of dishonor must be given by a bank before its midnight deadline and by any other person before midnight of the third business day after dishonor or receipt of notice of dishonor.[30] The exception is that if, before protest is due, an instrument has been noted for protest by the officer to make protest, the protest may be made at any time thereafter as of the date of the noting.[31]

2. Place.

Under the Code, protest need not be made at the place where dishonor occurs.[32]

---

[25] U.C.C. § 3-511(4)–(6).

[26] U.C.C. § 3-507(1).

[27] See also the definition in the *Glossary* below.

[28] U.C.C. § 3-501(3), (4).

[29] U.C.C. § 3-509(4), (5).

[30] U.C.C. § 3-508(2).

[31] U.C.C. § 3-509(4), (5).

[32] U.C.C. § 3-509, Official Comment 3.

3. Contents of certificate.

The protest must identify the instrument and certify either that due present-ment has been made or the reason why it is excused and that the instrument has been dishonored by nonacceptance or nonpayment. The protest may also certify that notice of dishonor has been given to all parties or to specified parties.[33]

A complete certificate of protest should ordinarily include the following items: (1) the notary's venire or locality within which he is authorized to act; (2) his name and title; (3) for whom he acted, or the holder's name; (4) a copy of the instrument presented; (5) the fact and manner of presentment and demand; (6) the time; (7) the place; (8) to whom presented, and of whom demand was made; (9) the fact of dishonor; (10) the fact of protest; (11) the reason assigned for refusal to honor; (12) who was notified; (13) the manner of notification; and (14) the notary's official seal and signature.[34]

4. Form of protest.

[This certificate follows a copy of the bill or note protested]

United States of America, State of _____,

_____ County, ss.

Be it known by this instrument of Protest, that at the close of banking hours on _____ the _____ day of _____, 19__, I, G H, notary public within and for said county of _____, did, at the request of _____, holder of the original _____, dated _____, a copy of which appears above, present the same to _____ at _____ in the city of _____, _____, and demanded payment (*or*, acceptance) thereof, which was refused. Said dishonor of said _____ occurred for the following assigned reason: _____.

Whereupon I protested the same for nonpayment (*or*, nonacceptance) and noti-fied the following named drawer and indorsers thereof of said presentment and protest, by a separate notice to each, enclosed in (the same, or separate) enve-lope— and addressed as follows: _____; and deposited the same in the post office of _____ in said county, the same day, postage paid; and the following named drawer and indorsers thereof, by delivering to each of them such notices personally on the same or the next day _____.

Whereupon, I, the said notary, upon the authority aforesaid, have protested and do hereby solemnly protest as well against the drawer and indorsers of the said _____ as against all others whom it doth or may concern, for exchange, re-exchange, and all costs, charges, damages and interest, suffered or to be suffered, for the want of payment (*or*, acceptance) thereof, and I certify that I have no interest in the above-protested instrument.

---

[33] U.C.C. § 3-509(2), (3).

[34] U.C.C. § 3-509(2) says that the protest must iden-tify the instrument and certify either that due present-ment has been made or the reason why it is excused and that the instrument has been dishonored by nonac-ceptance or nonpayment. U.C.C. § 3-509(3) says that the protest may also certify that notice of dishonor has been given to all parties or to specified parties.

Witness my hand and notarial seal this _____ day of _____, 19__.

Protest fees, $_____.

(SEAL)   G H, Notary Public.

My commission expires _____.

5. Dispensed with.

Protest is entirely excused when either: (1) the party to be charged has waived it expressly or by implication either before or after it is due; (2) such party has himself dishonored the instrument or has countermanded payment or otherwise has no reason to expect or right to require that the instrument be accepted or paid; (3) by reasonable diligence the protest cannot be made; or (4) a draft has been dishonored by nonacceptance, unless the instrument has been accepted in the meantime. Where a waiver of protest is embodied where it is written above the signature of an indorser it binds him only.[35]

6. Record.

Statutes in many states and other jurisdictions require, and well established custom in other states and jurisdictions permits, a notary to make a minute on the dishonored instrument, or in this register, of the presentment, refusal to accept or pay, the month, day and year, and his charges of protest.[36] This is called noting, and must be done, if not at the very time, at least not later than the day of the dishonor. The protest may be written out in full at any convenient time afterward.[37]

Because the notary may be called upon to testify in relation to his acts as notary by deposition or orally, it is important that he should keep a register or record containing detailed information with regard to the protesting of commercial paper.

7. National bank notes.

Whenever any national banking association fails to redeem in the lawful money of the United States any of its circulating notes, upon demand of payment duly made during the usual hours of business, at the office of such association, or at its designated place of redemption, the holder may cause the same to be protested, in one package, by a notary public, unless the president or cashier of the association whose notes are presented for payment, or the president or cashier of the association at the place at which they are redeemable, offers to waive demand and notice of the protest, and, in pursuance of such offer, makes, signs, and delivers to the party making such demand an admission in writing, stating the time of the demand, the amount demanded, and the fact of the nonpayment thereof. The no-

---

[35] U.C.C. § 3-511(2), (6). See also § 2.22(G), above, wherein it is pointed out that there is no requirement of protest except dishonor of a draft which on its face appears to be either drawn or payable outside of the states, territories, dependencies, and possessions of the United States, the District of Columbia and the Commonwealth of Puerto Rico.

[36] See § 2.13.

[37] See § 1.5.

tary public, on making such protest, or upon receiving such admission, shall forthwith forward such admission or notice of protest to the Comptroller of the Currency, retaining a copy thereof. If, however, satisfactory proof is produced to the notary public that the payment of the notes demanded is restrained by order of any court of competent jurisdiction, he shall not protest the same. When the holder of any notes causes more than one note or package to be protested on the same day, he shall not receive pay for more than one protest.[38]

(H) Acceptance supra protest.

Acceptance is the drawee's signed engagement to honor the draft as presented. It must be written on the draft, and may consist of his signature alone. It becomes operative when completed by delivery or notification. A draft may be accepted although it has not been signed by the drawer or is otherwise incomplete or is overdue or has been dishonored.[39]

(I) Payment for honor.

Payment or satisfaction may be made with the consent of the holder by any person including a stranger to the instrument. Surrender of the instrument to such a person gives him the rights of a transferee.[40]

(J) Notice of dishonor.

Unless excused,[41] notice of any dishonor is necessary to charge any indorser. In the case of any drawer, the acceptor of a draft payable at a bank or the maker of a note payable at a bank, notice of any dishonor is necessary, but failure to give such notice discharges such drawer, acceptor or maker only as stated in Section 3-502(1)(b);[42] however, notice of dishonor is not necessary to charge an indorser who has indorsed an instrument after maturity.[43] Notice operates for the benefit of all parties who have rights on the instrument against the party notified.[44]

1. Given by agent.

An agent or bank in whose hands the instrument is dishonored may give notice to his principal or customer or to another agent or bank from which the instrument was received.[45]

2. Essentials.

Notice may be given in any reasonable manner. It may be oral or written and in

---

[38] 12 U.S.C. § 131.

[39] U.C.C. § 3-410(1), (2).

[40] U.C.C. § 3-603(2).

[41] U.C.C. § 3-511 provides that delay in notice of dishonor is excused when the party is without notice that it is due or when the delay is caused by circumstances beyond his control and he exercises reasonable diligence after the cause of the delay ceased to operate. When a draft has been dishonored by nonacceptance a later presentment for payment and any notice of dis-

honor is excused unless in the meantime the instrument has been accepted. A waiver of protest is also a waiver of notice of dishonor even though protest is not required.

[42] Concerning U.C.C. § 3-502(1)(b), see § 2.22(D) above at n.13.

[43] U.C.C. § 3-501(2), (4).

[44] U.C.C. § 3-508(8).

[45] U.C.C. § 3-508(1).

any terms which identify the instrument and state that it has been dishonored. A misdescription which does not mislead the party notified does not vitiate the notice. Sending the instrument bearing a stamp, ticket or writing stating that acceptance or payment has been refused or sending a notice of debit with respect to the instrument is sufficient.[46]

3. Form of notice of dishonor.

_____ (Place)

_____ (Date)

Take notice, that a bill of exchange (or, promissory note) for _____ Dollars dated _____, drawn by _____, in favor of _____, on _____ Bank (accepted by _____), indorsed by _____, payable _____, was this day presented for acceptance (or, payment), which was refused, and therefore was this day protested by the undersigned notary public for non-acceptance (or, nonpayment).

The holder therefore looks to you for payment thereof, together with interest, damages, costs, you being indorser (or, drawer) thereof.

To: _____

G H, Notary Public
My commission expires _____.

4. To whom given.

Notice of dishonor may be given to any person who may be liable on the instrument by or on behalf of the holder or any party who has himself received notice, or any other party who can be compelled to pay the instrument. In addition an agent or bank in whose hands the instrument is dishonored may give notice to his principal or customer or another agent or bank from which the instrument was received.[47]

Notice to one partner is notice to each although the firm has been dissolved. When any party is in insolvency proceedings instituted after the issue of the instrument, notice may be given either to the party or to the representative of his estate.[48]

5. Time of giving.

Any necessary notice must be given by a bank before its midnight deadline and by any other person before midnight of the third business day after dishonor or receipt of notice of dishonor. Written notice is given when sent although it is not received.[49]

6. Place.

When any party is dead or incompetent notice may be sent to his last known address or given to his personal representative.[50]

---

[46] U.C.C. § 3-508(3).
[47] U.C.C. § 3-508(1).
[48] U.C.C. § 3-508(5), (6).

[49] U.C.C. § 3-508(2), (4).
[50] U.C.C. § 3-508(7).

7. Waiver.

Where a waiver of notice of dishonor is embodied in the instrument itself it is binding upon all parties; but where it is written above the signature of an indorser it binds him only. A waiver of protest is also a waiver of presentment and of notice of dishonor even though protest is not required.[51]

8. Dispensed with.

Notice of dishonor is entirely excused when: (1) the party to be charged has waived it expressly or by implication either before or after it is due; (2) by reasonable diligence the notice cannot be given. Where a draft has been dishonored by nonacceptance a later presentment for payment and any notice of dishonor are excused unless in the meantime the instrument has been accepted.[52]

9. Delay excused.

Delay in notice of dishonor is excused when the party is without notice that it is due or when the delay is caused by circumstances beyond his control and he exercises reasonable diligence after the cause of the delay ceases to operate.[53]

(K) Promissory note.

A promissory note is an unconditional promise in writing made by one person to another, signed by the maker engaging to pay on demand, or at a definite time, a sum certain in money to the order of such other or to bearer. The person who signs such unconditional written promise is called the maker and the person to whom the order is payable, the payee. If the payee transfers it to a third person by indorsement, the payee is the endorser and the third person, the indorsee. The following is an ordinary form of a promissory note:

FORM

_____ (City) _____ (State)
_____ (Date)

$ _____

On _____ (date) (or, _____ days, or, months, or, years, after date; or, on demand), for value received, I promise to pay to the order of C D (or, bearer) the sum of _____ Dollars, with interest thereon after date, at the rate of _____ % per year, payable quarterly (or, semi-annually, or, annually) at the _____ Bank, of _____.

A B

(L) Bill of exchange.

A bill of exchange, or draft, is an unconditional, written and signed, order to

---

[51] U.C.C. § 3-511(5), (6).

[52] U.C.C. § 3-511(2), (4).

[53] U.C.C. § 3-511(1).

pay a sum certain in money to someone, drawn by a person on a third party. The person who signs such order is called the drawer; the person who is directed to pay, the drawee; and after accepting the order, the drawee is also the acceptor. The following is an ordinary form of a bill of exchange.

FORM

_____ (City) _____ (State)
_____ (Date)

_____ days after date (or, on demand; or, at sight) pay to the order of E F, _____ Dollars, for value received, and charge to account of

A B

To: C D, _____ (City) _____ (State)

(M) Legal holidays.

Information concerning various state and other holidays is important to the notary public in connection with his duties under the Uniform Commercial Code. In the context of commercial paper, there is superimposed on the various state, federal, and other statutes, the provisions concerning legal holidays in U.C.C. § 3-503(3), which is uniformly in effect in each of the states, the District of Columbia, and the Virgin Islands. Under § 3-503(3), where any presentment is due on a day which is not a full business day for either the person making the presentment or the party to pay or accept, e.g., a holiday, presentment is due on the next following day which is a full business day for both parties. This provision in the U.C.C. replaces the former analogous Uniform Negotiable Instruments Law §§ 85 and 146. Section 3-503(3) is intended to make allowance for the increasing practice of closing banks or businesses on Saturday or other days of the week. It is not intended to mean that any drawee or obligor can avoid dishonor of instruments by extended closing.

§ 2.23 Commissioners of Deeds.

(A) Appointments.

A commissioner of deeds is an officer authorized by the laws of one state to perform certain duties in another state or country where he resides. As an example, a resident of Ohio may be appointed by the governor of Illinois to take acknowledgments, administer oaths, or perform other duties in Ohio, for use in Illinois. The statutes of most of the states expressly provide for such officers. They are appointed by the governor of the state for which they are to act, though in a few of the states the appointment of such commissioners must be by and with the advice and consent of the senate or the governor's council. The number to be appointed is ordinarily left to the discretion of the governor.

Commissioners are ordinarily appointed for a term of years, varying from two to seven; and in a few states, during the pleasure of the governor. Sometimes a bond is required.

(B) Oath and seal.

Many of the states require commissioners of deeds to take an oath of office for the faithful performance of their duties. Some states also require them to procure an official seal. The form of such seal, as prescribed by statutes, frequently consists of the following: the words "Commissioner of Deeds for the State of _____" (the state appointing him), the name of the commissioner, and the name of the state in which he has authority to act. Before entering upon the duties of his office, the commissioner must usually send to the secretary of state for which he is appointed his executed oath of office, an impression of his seal, and his signature.

(C) Powers.

Commissioners are commonly authorized to administer oaths, take depositions and affidavits, and take acknowledgments or proof of the execution of deeds, leases, mortgages, or other written instruments, to be used in evidence or recorded in the state from which the commission has been issued. If appointed for a foreign country, a commissioner may often certify to the existence of a patent, record, or other document recorded in a public office or under official custody in such country, and to the correctness of a copy thereof.

Frequently there are statutory provisions regulating the fees which commissioners may charge for their services in connection with administering oaths or taking depositions or acknowledgments.

All acts of a commissioner in the state for which he is appointed must be authenticated by his official seal and signature. Although not required by all states, it is advisable for the commissioner to add the date of the expiration of his commission. *See also* § 2.20 (J) above.

§ 2.24 Legal holidays.

Legal holidays are creatures of statute. As such, they have precisely the meaning given them by the statute, no more and no less. At common law, in the absence of a specific statute, holidays have no legal significance. Some statutes, make specific provision for the delegation of authority to the Governor to declare other holidays, in addition to those expressly created by the statute. It is therefore important that a person interested in whether a particular day is a holiday and if so, what its significance is, should examine not only the chart of legal holidays which is provided at page 649, but must read the precise words of the various applicable state, federal, and other statutes which create the holidays and which are included in this book. In addition to legal holidays, a large number of states, the federal government, and other jurisdictions, have days of special observance or commemoration which are not legal holidays, but which have more or less special significance within the jurisdiction. In some instances, a particular day will be a legal holiday in one state and only a day of special observance or commemoration in another state.

PART II
STATUTES

ALABAMA

NOTARIES PUBLIC

[ALA. CODE]

§ **36-20-1.** Appointment and commissioning; term of office; fee of probate judge for issuance of notary commissions; report to secretary of state by probate judge as to notaries appointed and commissioned.

A competent number of notaries public for each county shall be appointed and commissioned by the probate judges of the several counties of the state and shall hold office for four years from the date of their commissions. The probate judges shall collect a fee of $1.00 for each such notary commission issued. The probate judges shall also report to the secretary of state the name, county, date of issuance and date of expiration of the commission of each notary public appointed and commissioned under this section.

§ **36-20-2.** Vacation of office by removal from county.

Notaries public shall vacate their office by removal from the county.

§ **36-20-3.** Bond.

Notaries public must give bond with sureties, to be approved by the judge of probate of the county for which they are appointed, in the sum of $10,000.00, payable to the state of Alabama and conditioned to faithfully discharge the duties of such office so long as they may continue therein or discharge any of the duties thereof. Such bond must be executed, approved, filed and recorded in the office of the judge of probate before they enter on the duties of such office.

§ **36-20-4.** Seal.

For the authentication of his official acts, each notary must provide a seal of office, which must present, by its impression, his name, office, state and the county for which he was appointed.

§ **36-20-5.** Powers.

Notaries public shall have authority to:
(1) Administer oaths in all matters incident to the exercise of their office;
(2) Take the acknowledgment or proof of instruments of writing relating to commerce or navigation and certify the same and all other of their official acts under their seal of office;
(3) Demand acceptance and payment of bills of exchange, promissory notes and all other writings which are governed by the commercial law as to days of grace, demand and notice of nonpayment and protest the same for nonacceptance or nonpayment and to give notice thereof as required by law; and
(4) Exercise such other powers as, according to commercial usage or the laws of this state, may belong to notaries public.

§ 36-20-6. Fees.

Notaries public are entitled to the following fees: the sum of $1.50 and necessary postage for all services rendered in connection with the protest of any bill of exchange for acceptance, or of any bill of exchange, promissory note, check or other writing for payment and shall not charge any other fees therefor; for any oath, certificate and seal taken under subdivision (1) of section 36-20-5, $.50; for giving copies from register, $.20 for each 100 words; for each certificate and seal to such copy, $.25; and for giving any other certificate and affixing seal of office, $.50.

§ 36-20-7. Notary public to maintain register of official acts; provision of certified copies from register generally.

Each notary public must keep a fair register of all his official acts and give a certified copy therefrom, when required, on payment of his legal fees.

§ 36-20-8. Register to be delivered to probate judge upon death, resignation, etc., of notary; liability of person failing to deliver notary's register to probate judge on demand generally.

In case of the death, resignation, removal or expiration of his term of office, the registers of any notary must, within 30 days thereafter, be delivered to the judge of probate of the county, and any person having the same in possession and refusing to deliver them on demand to such judge is liable to an action for the recovery thereof in the name of such judge.

§ 36-20-9. Penalty for failure to deliver notary's register to probate judge on demand.

Any person who, after the death, resignation, removal or expiration of the term of office of any notary public, having in possession the register kept by such notary public, refuses, on demand, to deliver the same to the judge of probate of the county, shall, on conviction, be fined not less than $100.00.

§ 36-20-10. Probate judge may deliver register to another notary; provision of certified copies from register.

The registers referred to in section 36-20-8 may, by such judge, be delivered to any other notary of his county, who must give certified copies from the same to any person making application therefor on payment of the legal fees. While the registers are in the possession of the judge of probate, he must give certified copies from the same on application and the payment of the fees therefor in the same manner as notaries public.

§ 36-20-11. Performance or assumption of authority to perform notarial act without commission.

Any person who, having been a notary or a notary public for the state at large, willfully performs or assumes the authority to perform a notarial act after his commission expires or any person who without a notary's commission assumes the authority and performs a notarial act shall be guilty of a misdemeanor and, upon conviction, shall be punished by imprisonment for not more than one year.

Notaries Public for State at Large

§ 36-20-30. Appointment and commissioning; term of office; powers, duties and territorial jurisdiction; fee of probate judge for issuance of notary commissions; report to secretary of state by probate judge as to notaries appointed and commissioned.

A competent number of notaries public for the state at large shall be appointed and commissioned by the probate judges of the several counties of the state and shall hold office for four years from the date of their commission. Such notaries public for the state at large shall perform all the acts and exercise all authority now performed and exercised by notaries public under the general laws of the state of Alabama. The jurisdiction of such notaries public shall not be limited to the counties of their residence but shall extend to any county of the state. The probate judges shall collect a fee of $1.00 for each such notary commission issued. The probate judges shall also report to the secretary of state the name, county of residence, date of issuance and date of expiration of the commission of each notary public appointed and commissioned under this section and the fact that said notary was appointed and commissioned for the state at large.

§ 36-20-31. Bond.

Notaries public appointed under this article must give bond with sureties to be approved by the judge of probate of the county of their residence in the sum of $10,000.00, payable to the state of Alabama and conditioned to faithfully discharge the duties of such office so long as they may continue therein or discharge any of the duties thereof. Such bond must be executed, approved, filed and recorded in the office of the judge of probate of the county of their residence before they enter on the duties of such office. Such notaries public for the state at large, in the event of any breach of the conditions of their official bonds, may be sued in the county of their residence or in the county in which the breach was committed or in the county where the party or parties who suffered damages from the breach reside.

§ 36-20-32. Seal.

For the authentication of his official acts, each such notary must provide a seal of office which must present, by its impression, his name, office and the state for which he was appointed.

ACKNOWLEDGMENTS

§ 35-4-24. Officers authorized to take acknowledgments, etc., in this state.

Acknowledgments and proofs of conveyances may be taken by the following officers within this state: Judges of the supreme court, the court of civil appeals, the court of criminal appeals, circuit courts and district courts, and the clerks of such courts; registers of the circuit court, judges of the court of probate, and notaries public.

§ 35-4-29. Form of acknowledgment of conveyance.

The following are substantially the forms of acknowledgment to be used in this state, on conveyances and instruments of every description admitted to record:

ACKNOWLEDGMENT FOR INDIVIDUAL

The State of _____}
_____ County   }

I (name and style of officer) hereby certify that _____ whose name is signed to the foregoing conveyance, and who is known to me, acknowledged before me on this day that, being informed of the contents of the conveyance, he executed the same voluntarily on the day the same bears date. Given under my hand this _____ day of _____, A. D. 19___.

A. B. Judge, etc. (or as the case may be)

ACKNOWLEDGMENT FOR CORPORATION

The State of _____}
_____ County   }

I, _____, a _____ in and for said County in said State, hereby certify that _____, whose name as _____ of the _____, a corporation, is signed to the foregoing conveyance and who is known to me, acknowledged before me on this day that, being informed of the contents of the conveyance, he, as such officer and with full authority, executed the same voluntarily for and as the act of said corporation.

Given under my hand this the _____ day of _____, 19___.

_____
(Style of Officer)

ACKNOWLEDGMENT FOR AN OFFICIAL OR OTHER PERSON IN REPRESENTATIVE CAPACITY

The State of _____}
_____ County   }

I, _____, a _____, in and for said County in said State, hereby certify that _____, whose name as _____ (here state representative capacity) is signed to the foregoing conveyance and who is known to me, acknowledged before me on this day that, being informed of the contents of the conveyance, he, in his capacity as such _____, executed the same voluntarily on the day the same bears date.

Given under my hand this the _____ day of _____, 19___.

_____
(Style of Officer)

ACKNOWLEDGMENT FOR CORPORATION, IN REPRESENTATIVE CAPACITY

The State of _____}
_____ County   }

I, _____, a _____ in and for said County, in said State, hereby certify that _____ whose name as _____ of _____, a corporation as _____ of the estate of _____ (or as the case may be) is signed in the foregoing _____, and who is known to me, acknowledged before me on this day, that being informed of the contents of said _____, he, as such officer, and with full authority, executed the same voluntarily for and as the act of said corporation, acting in its capacity as _____ as aforesaid.

Given under my hand this the _____ day of _____, 19___.

_____
(Style of Officer)

DEPOSITIONS

[ALA. R. CIV. P.]

RULE 28. Persons before whom depositions may be taken.

(a) **Depositions taken within the United States to be used in this state.** Within the United States or within a territory or insular possession subject to the jurisdiction of the United States, depositions to be used in this state shall be taken before an officer authorized to administer oaths by the laws of the United States, or of the state of Alabama, or of the place where the examination is held, or before a person appointed by the court in which the action is pending. A person so appointed has power to administer oaths and take testimony.

(b) **Depositions taken in foreign countries to be used in this state.** In a foreign country, depositions to be used in this state may be taken (1) on notice before a person authorized to administer oaths in the place in which the examination is held, either by the law thereof or by the law of the United States, or (2) before a person commissioned by the court, and a person so commissioned shall have the power, by virtue of his commission, to administer any necessary oath and take testimony, or (3) pursuant to a letter rogatory or a letter of request, or (4) pursuant to any applicable treaty or convention. A commission or a letter rogatory or a letter of request shall be issued on application and notice and on terms that are just and appropriate. It is not requisite to the issuance of a commission or a letter rogatory or a letter of request that the taking of the deposition in any other manner be impracticable or inconvenient; and both a commission and a letter rogatory or a letter of request may be issued in proper cases. A notice or commission may designate the person before whom the deposition is to be taken either by name or by descriptive title. A letter rogatory or request may be addressed "To the appropriate authority in [here name the country]." When a letter of request or any other device is used pursuant to any applicable treaty or convention, it shall be styled in the form prescribed by that treaty or convention. Evidence obtained in response to a letter rogatory or a letter of request need not be excluded merely for the reason that it is not a verbatim transcript or that the testimony was not taken under oath or for any similar departure from the requirements for depositions taken within the United States under these rules.

(c) **Depositions taken within this state to be used outside this state.** A person desiring to take depositions in this state to be used in proceedings pending in the courts of any other state or country may produce to a judge of the circuit where the witness resides a commission authorizing the taking of such depositions or proof of notice duly served, whereupon it shall be the duty of the judge to issue, pursuant to Rule 45, the necessary subpoenas. Orders of the character provided for in Rules 30(d), 37(a)(1), 37(b)(1), and 45(b) may be made upon proper application therefor by the person to whom such a subpoena is directed. Failure by any person without adequate excuse to obey a subpoena served upon him pursuant to this rule may be deemed a contempt of the court from which the subpoena issued.

(d) **Disqualification for interest.** No deposition shall be taken before a person who is a relative, employee, attorney or counsel of any of the parties, or who is a relative or employee of such attorney or counsel, or who is financially interested in the action.

(dc) **District court rule.** Rule 28(a), Rule 28(b), and Rule 28(d) apply in the district courts in those instances when depositions on written questions or depositions on oral examination are permitted by Rule 26(dc). Rule 28(c) does not apply in the district courts.

COMMISSIONERS

[ALA. CODE]

§ 36-1-1. Appointment of commissioners in other states.

The governor may appoint commissioners in other states and territories of the United States to take and certify depositions, to receive the acknowledgment and take the proof of conveyances of property within this state and the proof of wills, executed by persons without the state, devising or bequeathing property within this state. Commissioners appointed under this section shall hold office for four years.

LEGAL HOLIDAYS

§ 1-3-8. Holidays enumerated; observance of Veterans' day by closing of schools, banks and government offices; bank closings on certain other holidays.

(a) Sunday, Christmas day, New Year's day, Martin Luther King, Jr.'s birthday, Robert E. Lee's birthday, George Washington's birthday, Thomas Jefferson's birthday, Mardi Gras, Confederate Memorial day, Jefferson Davis' birthday, the Fourth day of July, Labor day, Columbus day and Fraternal day, Veterans' day and the day designated by the governor for public thanksgiving shall each be deemed a holiday. If any holiday falls on Sunday, the following day is the holiday. If any holiday falls on Saturday, the preceding day shall be the holiday. Veterans' day shall be observed by the closing of all state, county and municipal offices, all banks located within this state and the public schools on such day. The superintendent of banks, with the concurrence of not less than two members of the state banking board, may authorize any state bank to close on National Memorial day, the last Monday in May, and on such other days as may be declared by the governor to be state holidays in honor of a special event. In the event any authorized state holiday falls on Friday, the superintendent of banks may authorize the Saturday following that Friday to be a holiday. The superintendent may also authorize the closing of banks at 12:00 noon on the day prior to Christmas day, and the day prior to New Year's day, if such days fall on business days.

(b) Of the above enumerated legal public holidays, the following shall be observed on the dates herein prescribed:

(1) Robert E. Lee's birthday — the third Monday in January.

(2) George Washington's birthday — the third Monday in February.

(3) Confederate Memorial day — the fourth Monday in April.

(4) Jefferson Davis' birthday — the first Monday in June.

(5) Columbus day and Fraternal day — the second Monday in October.

(6) Veterans' day — the eleventh day of November.

(7) Martin Luther King, Jr.'s birthday — the third Monday in January.

(c) All state holidays shall be observed by the closing of all state offices. Any state office may remain open on a state holiday upon written notice by the appointing authority to the state personnel board at least 60 days in advance of the holiday. Provided, that any state office may be opened in the event of an emergency and the state personnel board may grant a blanket approval for the openings of state offices needing to be open on holidays on a regular basis for essential services. Any state employee working on a state holiday shall receive a day of compensatory leave or paid compensation in lieu of the holiday as provided herein.

(d) Each employee shall attempt to schedule any compensatory leave day provided in lieu of a regularly scheduled holiday, subject to the approval of the supervisor, during the quarter that the regularly scheduled holiday occurred. In the event that any compensatory leave day cannot be scheduled during the designated quarter, then the compensatory leave day may be accumulated at the request of the employee for up to one year. Supervisors failing to schedule compensatory leave days for employees within the quarter, unless the day is carried forward at the request of the employee, must justify that action in writing to the director of state personnel and the employee shall receive pay at a rate not less than the employee's usual and customary rate of pay for any compensatory leave day to which he may be entitled and which has not been taken.

ALASKA

NOTARIES PUBLIC

[Alaska Stat.]

§ 44.50.010. Appointment and commission.

The lieutenant governor may appoint and commission notaries public for the state.

§ 44.50.020. Qualifications.

A person appointed a notary public shall be, at the time of submitting an application, a resident of this state and at least 19 years of age. In this section, "resident" means a person who maintains his permanent place of abode in the state and is in fact living in the state.

§ 44.50.030. Term of office.

The term of office of a notary public is four years from the date of commission. SLA 1961, ch. 99, § 3.

§ 44.50.040. Fees.

A fee of $20 shall be paid to the lieutenant governor for each commission issued other than to a state employee. SLA 1961, ch 99, § 4.

§ 44.50.060. Duties.

A notary public shall

(1) when requested, demand acceptance and payment of foreign and inland bills of exchange, or promissory notes, protest them for nonacceptance and nonpayment, and exercise the other powers and duties which by the law of nations and according to commercial usages, or by the laws of any other state, government, or country, may be performed by notaries;

(2) take the acknowledgment or proof of powers of attorney, mortgages, deeds, grants, transfers, and other instruments of writing, and give a certificate of the proof or acknowledgment endorsed on or attached to the instrument; the certificate shall be signed by the notary in the notary's own handwriting;

(3) take depositions and affidavits, and administer oaths and affirmations, in all matters incident to the duties of the office, or to be used before a court, judge, officer, or board in the state; a deposition, affidavit, oath, or affirmation shall be signed by the notary in the notary's own handwriting, and the notary shall endorse after the signature the date of expiration of the notary's commission.

§ 44.50.070. Presence and identification required.

A notary public shall require oaths and affirmations to be given in the notary's presence and require persons appearing before the notary to produce identification. SLA 1961, ch. 99, §§ 5, 6.

§ 44.50.080. Seal.

(a) A notary public shall provide and keep an official seal, upon which shall appear the words, "State of Alaska" and "Notary Public," together with the name of the notary. The notary shall authenticate all official acts with the seal.

(b) The seal of every notary public whose commission is issued on or after July 1, 1972 may be affixed by a seal press or stamp that will print or emboss a seal which legibly reproduces under photographic methods the words "State of Alaska" and "Notary Public" and the name of the notary. The seal may be circular not over two inches in diameter, or may be a rectangular form not more than an inch in width by two and one-half inches in length, and must contain the information required by this section.

§ 44.50.090. Protest of bill or note.

The protest of a notary public, under the notary's hand and official seal, of a bill of exchange or promissory note for nonacceptance or nonpayment is prima facie evidence of the facts recited in it, if the protest recites (1) the time and place of presentment; (2) the fact that presentment was made and the manner of presentment; (3) the cause or reason for protesting the bill; (4) the demand made and the answer given, or the fact that the drawee or acceptor could not be found.

§ 44.50.100. Return of papers to lieutenant governor.

If a notary public dies, resigns, is disqualified, removed from office, or removes from the state, all the notary's public papers shall be delivered to the lieutenant governor.

§ 44.50.110. Application of Administrative Procedure Act to revocation of notary commission.

The procedures set out in the Administrative Procedure Act (AS 44.62) shall be followed in the revocation of the commission of a notary public.

§ 44.50.120. Bond.

Every person appointed a notary public after July 1, 1961, shall execute an official bond of $1,000, approved by the clerk of the superior court.

§ 44.50.130. Filing oath and bond.

(a) An application for a notary public commission shall include a statement under oath that the applicant is a resident, as defined in AS 44.50.020.

(b) A person appointed a notary public shall file a bond and the oath set out in AS 39.05.045 with the lieutenant governor. The oath must be notarized and signed by the appointee.

§ 44.50.140. Disposition of bond.

The lieutenant governor shall keep the bond for one year after the end of the term of the commission for which the bond is issued. Disposition of the bond after the end of the commission does not affect the time for starting an action on the bond.

§ 44.50.150. Copy of bond as evidence.

A certified copy of the record of the official bond with all affidavits, acknowledgments, endorsements, and attachments may be read in evidence with the same effect as the original, without further proof.

§ 44.50.160. Misconduct or neglect.

A notary and the sureties on the official bond are liable to persons injured for the damages sustained on account of misconduct or neglect of the notary.

§ 44.50.170. State employees as notaries.

(a) The lieutenant governor may appoint and commission state employees as notaries public of the state to act for and in behalf of a department of the state government as the lieutenant governor considers proper. If a state employee is appointed and commissioned, the head of the department shall execute a certificate that the appointment is made for the purposes of the department. When the certificate is filed with the lieutenant governor, the notary may not charge fees for filing or issuing a document in connection with the appointment.

(b) A department for which a notary public is appointed and commissioned under this section may pay from funds available for its support the premiums on the bond and the cost of stamps, seals, or other supplies required in connection with the appointment, commission, or performance of the duties of the notary public.

(c) Fees collected or obtained by a notary public whose documents have been filed without charge and for whom bond premiums have been paid by a state agency shall be remitted by the notary to the state department by which the notary is employed and paid into the general fund of the state. Notwithstanding AS 44.50.030, the termination of employment revokes the commission of a notary whose documents have been filed without charge and for whom bond premiums have been paid by a state agency.

§ 44.50.180. Postmasters as notaries.

(a) Each postmaster in the state may perform the functions of a notary public in the state.

(b) Each official act of a postmaster as a notary public shall be signed by the postmaster, with a designation of the person's title as postmaster, shall have the cancellation stamp of the post office affixed, and shall state the name of the post office and the date on which the act was done.

(c) The postmaster may charge and receive the same fees as a notary for similar services.

(d) Nothing in this chapter requires a postmaster to post a bond or to have a commission.

ADDITIONAL AUTHORITY

§ 10.25.450. Directors, officers or members as notaries.

No person authorized to take acknowledgments under the laws of this state is disqualified from taking acknowledgments of instruments to which a cooperative is a party because the person is an officer, director or member of the cooperative.

ACKNOWLEDGMENTS

§ 09.63.010. Oath, affirmation, and acknowledgment.

The following persons may take an oath, affirmation, or acknowledgment in the state:

(1) a justice, judge, or magistrate of a court of the State of Alaska or of the United States;

(2) a clerk or deputy clerk of a court of the State of Alaska or of the United States;

(3) a notary public;

(4) a United States postmaster;

(5) a commissioned officer under AS 09.63. 050(4); or

(6) a municipal clerk carrying out the clerk's duties under AS 29.20.380.

§ 09.63.030. Notarization.

(a) When a document is required by law to be notarized, the person who executes the document shall sign and swear to or affirm it before an officer authorized by law to take the person's oath or affirmation and the officer shall certify on the document that it was signed and sworn to or affirmed before the officer.

(b) The certificate required by this section may be in substantially the following form:

Subscribed and sworn to or affirmed before me at _____ on _____.

(date)

_____
Signature of Officer

_____
Title of Officer

(c) If the document is sworn to or affirmed before a notary public of the state, the notary public shall

(1) endorse after the signature of the notary public the date of expiration of the notary's commission;

(2) print or emboss the notary's seal on the document;

(3) comply with AS 44.50.060 — 44.50.080 or other applicable law.

§ 09.63.040. Verification.

(a) When a document is required by law to be verified, the person required to verify it shall certify under oath or affirmation that the person has read the document and believes its content to be true.

(b) The person who makes the verification shall sign it before a person authorized by law to take the person's oath or affirmation.

(c) A verification made under this section may be in substantially the following form:

I _____ say on oath or affirm that I have read the foregoing (or attached) document and believe all statements made in the document are true.

_____
Signature

Subscribed and sworn to or affirmed before me at _____ on _____.

(date)

_____
Signature of Officer

_____
Title of Officer

(d) If the verification is sworn to or affirmed before a notary public of the state, the notary public shall

(1) endorse after the signature of the notary public the date of expiration of the notary's commission;

(2) print or emboss the notary's seal on the document;

(3) comply with AS 44.50.060 — 44.50.080 or other applicable law.

Uniform Recognition of Acknowledgments Act

§ 09.63.050. Recognition of notarial acts performed outside the state.

Notarial acts may be performed outside the state for use in the state with the same effect as if performed by a notary public of the state by

(1) a notary public authorized to perform notarial acts in the place in which the act is performed;

(2) a justice, judge, magistrate, clerk, or deputy clerk of a court of record in the place in which the notarial act is performed;

(3) an officer of the foreign service of the United States, a consular agent, or a person authorized by regulation of the United States Department of State to perform notarial acts in the place in which the act is performed;

(4) a commissioned officer in active service with the armed forces of the United States or a person authorized by regulation of the armed forces to perform notarial acts if the notarial act is performed for a merchant seaman of the United States, a member of the armed forces of the United States, a person serving with or accompanying the armed forces of the United States, or their dependents; or

(5) a person authorized to perform notarial acts in the place in which the act is performed.

§ 09.63.060. Authentication of authority of officer.

(a) If the notarial act is performed by a person described in AS 09.63.050(1) — (4) other than a person authorized to perform notarial acts by the laws or regulations of a foreign country, the signature, rank or title and, if appropriate, the serial number of the person are sufficient proof of the authority of a person to perform the act.

(b) If the notarial act is performed by a person authorized by the laws or regulations of a foreign country to perform the act, there is sufficient proof of the authority of that person to act if

(1) either a foreign service officer of the United States resident in the country in which the act is performed or a diplomatic or consular officer of the foreign country resident in the United States certifies that a person holding that office is authorized to perform the act;

(2) the official seal of the person performing the notarial act is affixed to the document; or

(3) the title and indication of authority to perform notarial acts of the person appear either in a digest of foreign law or in a list customarily used as a source of that information.

(c) If the notarial act is performed by a person other than a person described in this section, there is sufficient proof of the authority of the person to act if the clerk of a court of record in the place in which the notarial act is performed certifies to the official character of the person and to the person's authority to perform the notarial act.

(d) The signature and title of the person performing the act are prima facie evidence that the person has the designated title and that the signature is genuine.

§ 09.63.070. Certificate of person taking acknowledgment.

The person taking an acknowledgment shall certify that

(1) the person acknowledging appeared before the person taking the acknowledgment and acknowledged that the person executed the instrument; and

(2) the person acknowledging was known to the person taking the acknowledgment or the person taking the acknowledgment had satisfactory evidence that the person acknowledging was the person described in and who executed the instrument.

§ 09.63.080. Recognition of certificate of acknowledgment.

The form of a certificate of acknowledgment used by a person whose authority is recognized under AS 09.63.010 or 09.63.050 shall be accepted in the state if

(1) the certificate is in a form prescribed by the laws or regulations of the state;

(2) the certificate is in a form prescribed by the laws or regulations applicable in the place in which the acknowledgment is taken; or

(3) the certificate contains the words "acknowledged before me" or their substantial equivalent.

§ 09.63.090. Certificate of acknowledgment.

The words "acknowledged before me" mean that

(1) the person acknowledging

(A) appeared before the person taking the acknowledgment;

(B) acknowledged that the person executed the instrument;

(C) in the case of

(i) a natural person, acknowledged that the person executed the instrument for the purposes stated in it;

(ii) an officer or agent of a corporation, acknowledged that the person held the position or title set out in the instrument and certificate, signed the instrument on behalf of the corporation by proper authority, and the instrument was the act of the corporation for the purposes stated in it;

(iii) a partner or agent of a partnership, acknowledged that the person signed the instrument on behalf of the partnership by proper authority and executed the instrument as the act of the partnership for the purposes stated in it;

(iv) a person acknowledging as a principal by an

attorney in fact, acknowledged that the person executed the instrument by proper authority as the act of the principal for the purposes stated in it;

(v) a person acknowledging as a public officer, trustee, administrator, guardian, or other representative, acknowledged that the person signed the instrument in the capacity and for the purposes stated in it; and

(2) the person taking the acknowledgment either knew or had satisfactory evidence that the person acknowledging is the person named in the instrument or certificate.

§ **09.63.100.** Forms of acknowledgment.

(a) The forms of acknowledgment set out in this subsection may be used and are sufficient for their respective purposes under a law of the state. The authorization of the forms in this section does not preclude the use of other forms.

(1) For an individual acting in the individual's own right:

State of _____ Judicial District (or County of _____)

The foregoing instrument was acknowledged before me this (date) by (name of person who acknowledged).

_____
Signature of Person Taking
Acknowledgment

_____
Title or Rank

_____
Serial Number, if any

(2) For a corporation:

State of _____ Judicial District for County of _____)

The foregoing instrument was acknowledged before me this (date) by (name of officer or agent, title of officer or agent) of (name of corporation acknowledging) a (state or place of incorporation) corporation, on behalf of the corporation.

_____
Signature of Person Taking
Acknowledgment

_____
Title or Rank

_____
Serial Number, if any

(3) For a partnership:

State of _____ Judicial District (or County of _____)

The foregoing instrument was acknowledged before me this (date) by (name of acknowledging partner or agent), partner (or agent) on behalf of (name of partnership), a partnership.

_____
Signature of Person Taking
Acknowledgment

_____
Title or Rank

_____
Serial Number, if any

(4) For an individual acting as principal by an attorney in fact:

State of _____ Judicial District (or county of _____)

The foregoing instrument was acknowledged before me this (date) by (name of attorney in fact) as attorney in fact on behalf of (name of principal).

_____
Signature of Person Taking
Acknowledgment

_____
Title or Rank

_____
Serial Number, if any

(5) By a public officer, trustee, or personal representative:

State of _____ Judicial District (or County of _____)

The foregoing instrument was acknowledged before me this (date) by (name and title of position).

_____
Signature of Person Taking
Acknowledgment

_____
Title or Rank

_____
Serial Number, if any

(b) If a document is acknowledged before a notary public of the state, the notary public shall

(1) endorse after the notary's signature the date of expiration of the notary's commission;

(2) print or emboss the notary's seal on the document;

(3) comply with AS 44.50.060 — 44.50.080 or other law.

§ **09.63.110.** Uniformity of interpretation.

AS 09.63.050 — 09.63.110 shall be interpreted as to make uniform the laws of those states which enact them.

§ **09.63.120.** Definition.

In AS 09.63.010 — 09.63.130, "notarial acts" means acts that the laws and regulations of the state authorize notaries public of the state to perform, including the administering of oaths and affirmations, taking proof of execution and acknowledgment of instruments, and attesting documents.

§ 09.63.130. Title.

AS 09.63.050 — 09.63.100 may be cited as the Uniform Recognition of Acknowledgments Act.

§ 34.15.150. Execution of conveyances.

(a) A conveyance executed in the state of land or an interest in land in the state shall be acknowledged before a person authorized to take acknowledgments in AS 09.63.010 or proved in accordance with AS 34.15.210 or 34.15.220. The officer taking an acknowledgment shall endorse on it a certificate of the acknowledgment of the conveyance and the date of making the acknowledgment.

(b) A conveyance executed before March 12, 1953, in due form but without two witnesses is validated, shall be received in evidence in all courts of the state, and is evidence of the title to the land or interest in land against the grantor, his heirs and assigns of the grantor.

DEPOSITIONS

[ALASKA R. CIV. P.]

RULE 28. Persons before whom depositions may be taken.

(a) **Within the State.** Within the state, depositions shall be taken before an officer authorized by the laws of this state to administer oaths, or before a person appointed by the court in which the action is pending. A person appointed has power to administer oaths and take testimony.

(b) **Without the State but within the United States.** Without the state but within the United States, or within a territory or insular possession subject to the dominion of the United States, depositions shall be taken before an officer authorized to administer oaths by the laws of the United States or of the place where the examination is held.

(c) **In foreign counties.** In a foreign country, depositions may be taken (1) on notice before a person authorized to administer oaths in the place in which the examination is held, either by the law thereof or by the law of the United States, or (2) before a person commissioned by the court, and a person so commissioned shall have the power by virtue of his commission to administer any necessary oath and take testimony, or (3) pursuant to a letter rogatory. A commission or letter rogatory shall be issued on application and notice and on terms that are just and appropriate. It is not requisite to the issuance of a commission or a letter rogatory that the taking of the deposition in any other manner is impracticable or inconvenient; and both a commission and a letter rogatory may be issued in proper cases. A notice or commission may designate the person before whom the deposition is to be taken either by name or descriptive title. A letter rogatory may be addressed "To the Appropriate Authority in [here name the country]." Evidence obtained in response to a letter rogatory need not be excluded merely for the reason that it is not a verbatim transcript or that the testimony was not taken under oath or for any similar departure from the requirements for depositions taken within the United States under these rules.

(d) **Disqualification for interest.** No deposition shall be taken before a person who is a relative or employee or attorney or counsel of any of the parties, or is a relative or employee of such attorney or counsel, or is financially interested in the action, except that in the case of an audio or audio-visual deposition, an attorney involved in the case may also operate or direct the operation of the recording machinery.

LEGAL HOLIDAYS

[ALASKA STAT.]

§ 44.12.010. Legal holidays.

(a) The following days are legal holidays:

(1) the first of January, known as New Year's Day;

(2) the third Monday of January, known as Martin Luther King, Jr.'s Birthday as provided in (b) of this section;

(3) the third Monday in February, known as Presidents' Day;

(4) the last Monday of March, known as Seward's Day;

(5) the last Monday in May, known as Memorial Day;

(6) the fourth of July, known as Independence Day;

(7) the first Monday in September, known as Labor Day;

(8) the 18th of October, known as Alaska Day;

(9) the 11th of November, known as Veterans' Day;

(10) the fourth Thursday in November, known as Thanksgiving Day;

(11) the 25th of December, known as Christmas Day;

(12) every Sunday;

(13) every day designated by public proclamation by the President of the United States or the governor of the state as a legal holiday.

(b) For employment purposes, Martin Luther King, Jr.'s Birthday is a legal holiday for state employees who

(1) are not covered by a collective bargaining agreement; or

(2) are covered by a collective bargaining agreement whose terms

(A) include by name Martin Luther King, Jr.'s Birthday; or

(B) have been amended to substitute a holiday on the third Monday of January for Martin Luther King, Jr.'s Birthday in place of another paid holiday.

§ 44.12.020. Holiday falling on Sunday.

If a holiday listed in AS 44.12.010, except AS 44.12.010(2), falls on a Sunday, Sunday and the following Monday are both legal holidays.

§ 44.12.025. Holiday falling on Saturday.

If a holiday listed in AS 44.12.010 falls on a Saturday, the Saturday and the preceding Friday are both legal holidays for officers and employees of the state.

ARIZONA

NOTARIES PUBLIC

[Ariz. Rev. Stat. Ann.]

§ 41-311. Appointment; term; oath and bond.

A. The secretary of state may appoint notaries public in each county to hold office for four years who shall have jurisdiction in the county in which they reside and in which they are appointed. Acknowledgments of instruments may be taken and executed and oaths may be administered by a notary public in any county of the state although the commission is issued to the notary public in and for another county.

B. The secretary of state shall transmit the commission of the person appointed as notary public to the clerk of the superior court in the county for which the notary was appointed. The clerk shall give notice thereof to the person appointed, who shall, within twenty days after receiving such notice, take the oath prescribed by law, and give a bond to the state, with sureties approved by the chairman of the board of supervisors, in the amount of one thousand dollars, and file it with the clerk. Upon filing the official oath and bond the clerk shall deliver the commission to such person, and give notice to the secretary of state of the time and filing of the oath and bond.

§ 41-312. Duties.

Notaries public shall, when requested:

1. Demand acceptance and payment of foreign, domestic and inland bills of exchange or promissory notes, and protest them for nonacceptance and nonpayment, and exercise with respect thereto such other powers and duties as by the laws of other jurisdictions and according to commercial usages may be performed by notaries.

2. Take acknowledgments and give a certificate of them endorsed on or attached to the instrument.

3. Take depositions and administer oaths and affirmations.

4. Keep a record of all their official acts, and a record of the parties to, date and character of every instrument acknowledged or proved before them, date of acknowledgment and description of the property affected by the instrument, and furnish, when requested, a certified copy of any record in their office.

5. Provide and keep official seals upon which shall be engraved the words "Notary Public," the name of the county for which they are commissioned, and the name of the notary.

6. Authenticate with their official seals all official acts, and affix the date of the expiration of their commissions as such notaries on every certificate or acknowledgment signed and sealed by them.

§ 41-313. Protest or certificate of notary as evidence.

A. The protest of the notary, under his hand and official seal, of a bill of exchange or promissory note for nonacceptance or nonpayment, stating the facts required by law to be stated in the protest, is prima facie evidence of the facts contained therein.

B. The certificate of a notary public under his hand and seal of office of official acts done by him as a notary shall be received in court as prima facie evidence of the facts therein contained.

§ 41-314. Fees.

Notaries public may receive the following fees:

1. Protesting a bill or note for nonacceptance or nonpayment, registering and affixing a seal, two dollars.

2. Each notice of protest, fifty cents.

3. Protest in all other cases, for each one hundred words, twenty cents.

4. Certificate and sale to such protest, seventy-five cents.

5. Taking the acknowledgment or proof of any deed or other instrument of writing for registration, including certificate and sale, seventy-five cents.

6. Taking the acknowledgment of a bill of sale of livestock, including certificate and seal, twenty-five cents.

7. Administering an oath or affirmation with the certificate and seal, seventy-five cents.

8. All certificates under seal not otherwise provided for, seventy-five cents.

9. Copies of all records and papers in their office, including certificate and seal, if less than two hundred words, seventy-five cents, or if more than two hundred words, for each one hundred words in excess of two hundred, in addition to the fee, twenty cents.

10. All notarial acts not otherwise provided for, fifty cents.

11. Taking the deposition of a witness, for each one hundred words, forty cents.

12. Swearing a witness to depositions, making certificate thereof with seal, and all other business connected with taking depositions, seventy-five cents.

§ 41-315. Depositing notarial records upon vacancy in office; failure to comply; storing of records; certified copies.

A. When the office of a notary public becomes vacant, his records and official papers shall be deposited in the office of the county recorder, and a notary who neglects for three months thereafter to deposit such records and papers, or the personal representative of a deceased notary who neglects for three months after his appointment to deposit such records and papers, shall forfeit to the state not less than fifty nor more than five hundred dollars.

B. The recorder shall keep all records and papers of notaries public deposited in his office and give certified copies thereof when required, and for the copies he shall receive the same fees as are by law allowed to notaries public. Such copies shall be as valid and effectual as if given by a notary public.

§ 41-316. Wilful destruction of records; penalty.

Any person who knowingly destroys, defaces or conceals any records or papers belonging to the office of a notary public, shall forfeit to the state an amount not exceeding five hundred dollars, and shall be liable for damages to any party injured thereby.

§ 41-317. Competency of bank and corporation notaries.

A. It is lawful for a notary public who is a stockholder, director, officer or employee of a corporation to take the acknowledgment or oath of any party to any written instrument executed to or by the corporation, or to administer an oath to any other stockholder, director, officer, employee or agent of the corporation, or to protest for nonacceptance or nonpayment of bills of exchange, drafts, checks, notes and other negotiable instruments which may be owned or held for collection by the corporation.

B. It is unlawful for any notary public to take the acknowledgment of an instrument executed by or to a corporation of which he is a stockholder, director, officer or employee, where the notary is a party to the instrument, either individually or as a representative of the corporation, or to protest any negotiable instrument owned or held for collection by the corporation where the notary is individually a party to the instrument.

FEES

§ 38-412. Posting schedule of fees.

[Among other officers] notaries public shall keep posted at all times in a conspicuous place in their respective offices a complete list of the fees they are allowed to charge.

§ 41-126. Fees; expedited services.

A. The secretary of state shall receive the following fees:

* * *

2. filing and recording each official bond and transmitting a commission for a notary public, twelve dollars fifty cents.

* * *

OFFENSES

§ 38-413. Charging excessive fees; penalty.

A. If an officer demands and receives a higher fee than prescribed by law, or any fee not so allowed, such officer shall be liable to the party aggrieved in an amount four times the fee unlawfully demanded and received by him.

B. an officer who violates this section is guilty of a class 5 felony.

ACKNOWLEDGMENTS

Uniform Recognition of Acknowledgments Act

§ 33-501. Recognition of notarial acts performed outside this state.

For the purposes of this article, "notarial acts" means acts which the laws and regulations of this state authorize notaries public of this state to perform, including the administering of oaths and affirmations, taking proof of execution and acknowledgments of instruments, and attesting documents. Notarial acts may be performed outside this state for use in this state with the same effect as if performed by a notary public of this state by the following persons authorized pursuant to the laws and regulations of other governments in addition to any other person authorized by the laws and regulations of this state:

1. A notary public authorized to perform notarial acts in the place in which the act is performed.

2. A judge, clerk, or deputy clerk of any court of record in the place in which the notarial act is performed.

3. An officer of the foreign service of the United States, a consular agent, or any other person authorized by regulation of the United States Department of State to perform notarial acts in the place in which the act is performed.

4. A commissioned officer in active service with the armed forces of the United States and any other person authorized by regulation of the armed forces to perform notarial acts if the notarial act is performed for one of the following or his dependents: a merchant seaman of the United States, a member of the armed forces of the United States, or any other person serving with or accompanying the armed forces of the United States.

5. Any other person authorized to perform notarial acts in the place in which the act is performed.

§ 33-502. Authentication of authority of officer.

A. If the notarial act is performed by any of the persons described in § 33-501, paragraphs 1 to 4, inclusive, other than a person authorized to perform notarial acts by the laws or regulations of a foreign country, the signature, rank, or title and serial number, if any, of the person are sufficient proof of the authority of a holder of that rank or title to perform the act. Further proof of his authority is not required.

B. If the notarial act is performed by a person authorized by the laws or regulations of a foreign county† to perform the act, there is sufficient proof of the authority of that person to act if:

1. Either a foreign service officer of the United States resident in the country in which the act is performed or a diplomatic or consular officer of the foreign country resident in the United States certifies that a person holding that office is authorized to perform the act, or

2. The official seal of the person performing the notarial act is affixed to the document, or

3. The title and indication of authority to perform notarial acts of the person appears either in a digest of foreign law or in a list customarily used as a source of such information.

C. If the notarial act is performed by a person other than one described in subsection A and B, there is sufficient proof of the authority of that person to act if the clerk of a court of record in the place in which the notarial act is performed certifies to the official character of that person and to his authority to perform the notarial act.

D. The signature and title of the person performing the act are prima facie evidence that he is a person with the designated title and that the signature is genuine.

† So in original. Probably should read "country."

§ 33-503. Certificate of person taking acknowledgment.

The person taking an acknowledgment shall certify that:

1. The person acknowledging appeared before him and acknowledged he executed the instrument, and

2. The person acknowledging was known to the person taking the acknowledgment or that the person taking the acknowledgment had satisfactory evidence that the person acknowledging was the person described in and who executed the instrument.

§ 33-504. Recognition of certificate of acknowledgment.

The form of a certificate of acknowledgment used by a person whose authority is recognized under § 33-501 shall be accepted in this state if:

1. The certificate is in a form prescribed by the laws or regulations of this state; or

2. The certificate is in a form prescribed by the laws or regulations applicable in the place in which the acknowledgment is taken, or

3. The certificate contains the words "acknowledged before me," or their substantial equivalent.

§ 33-505. Certificate of acknowledgment.

The words "acknowledged before me" mean that:

1. The person acknowledging appeared before the person taking the acknowledgment.

2. He acknowledged he had executed the instrument.

3. In the case of:

(a) A natural person, he executed the instrument for the purposes therein stated.

(b) A corporation, the officer or agent acknowledged he held the position or title set forth in the instrument and certificate, he signed the instrument on behalf of the corporation by proper authority, and the instrument was the act of the corporation for the purpose therein stated.

(c) A partnership, the partner or agent acknowledged he signed the instrument on behalf of the partnership by proper authority and he executed the instrument as the act of the partnership for the purposes therein stated.

(d) A person acknowledging as principal by an attorney in fact, he executed the instrument by proper authority as the act of the principal for the purposes therein stated.

(e) A person acknowledging as a public officer, trustee, personal representative, administrator, guardian, conservator or other representative, he signed the instrument by proper authority and he executed the instrument in the capacity and for the purposes therein stated.

4. The person taking the acknowledgment either knew or had satisfactory evidence that the person acknowledging was the person named in the instrument or certificate.

§ 33-506. Short forms of acknowledgment.

The forms of acknowledgment set forth in this section may be used and are sufficient for their respective purposes under any law of this state. The forms shall be known as "Statutory Short Forms of Acknowledgment" and may be referred to by that name. The authorization of the following forms does not preclude the use of other forms:

1. For an individual acting in his own right:

State of _____
County of _____

The foregoing instrument was acknowledged before me this (Date) by (Name of person acknowledged.)

    (Signature of person taking acknowledgment)
    (Title or rank)
    (Serial number, if any)

2. For a corporation:

State of _____
County of _____

The foregoing instrument was acknowledged before me this (Date) by (Name of officer or agent, title or officer or agent) of (Name of corporation acknowledging) a (State or place of incorporation) corporation, on behalf of the corporation.

    (Signature of person taking acknowledgment)
    (Title or rank)
    (Serial number, if any)

3. For a partnership:

State of _____
County of _____

The foregoing instrument was acknowledged before me this (Date) by (Name of acknowledging partner or agent), partner (or agent) on behalf of (Name of partnership), a partnership.

    (Signature of person taking acknowledgment)
    (Title or rank)
    (Serial number, if any)

4. For an individual acting as principal by an attorney in fact:

State of _____
County of _____

The foregoing instrument was acknowledged before me this (Date) by (Name of attorney in fact) as attorney in fact on behalf of (Name of principal).

    (Signature of person taking acknowledgment)
    (Title or rank)
    (Serial number, if any)

5. By any public officer, trustee, or personal representative.

State of _____
County of _____

The foregoing instrument was acknowledged before me this (Date) by (Name and title of position).

    (Signature of person taking acknowledgment)
    (Title or rank)
    (Serial number, if any)

§ 33-507. Acknowledgments not affected by this article.

A notarial act performed prior to the effective date of this article is not affected by this article. This article provides an additional method of proving notarial acts. Nothing in this article diminishes or invalidates the recognition accorded to notarial acts by other laws or regulations of this state.

§ 33-508. Uniformity of interpretation.

This article shall be so interpreted as to make uniform the laws of those states which enact it.

Uniform Acknowledgment Act

§ 33-511. Acknowledgment within the state.

The acknowledgment of any instrument may be made in this state before:
1. A judge of a court of record.
2. A clerk or deputy clerk of a court having a seal.
3. A recorder of deeds.
4. A notary public.
5. A justice of the peace.
6. A county recorder.

§ 33-512. Acknowledgment by a married woman.

An acknowledgment of a married woman may be made in the same form as though she were unmarried.

§ 33-513. Action to correct certificate of acknowledgment.

When an acknowledgment is properly made, but defectively certified, any party interested may bring an action in the superior court to obtain a judgment correcting the certificate.

DEPOSITIONS

[ARIZ. R. CIV. P.]

RULE 28. Persons before whom depositions may be taken.

28(a) Within the United States; commission or letters rogatory.

Within the United States or within a territory or insular possession subject to the jurisdiction of the United States, depositions shall be taken before an officer authorized to administer oaths by the laws of the United States, the State of Arizona, or of the place where the examination is held, or before a person appointed by the court in which the action is pending. A person so appointed has power to administer oaths and take testimony. Depositions may be taken in this state or anywhere upon notice provided by these Rules without a commission, letters rogatory or other writ. The term officer as used in Rules 30, 31 and 32 includes a person appointed by the court or designated by the parties under Rule 29.

Upon proof that the notice to take a deposition outside this state has been given as provided by these Rules, the party seeking such deposition may, but is not required, after one full day's notice to the other parties, have issued by the clerk, in the form given in such notice, a commission or letters rogatory or other like writ either in lieu of the notice to take the deposition or supplementary thereto. Failure to file written objections to such form before or at the time of its issuance shall be a waiver of any objection thereto. Any objection shall be heard and determined forthwith by the court or judge thereof.

28(b) In foreign countries. In a foreign country, depositions may be taken (1) on notice before a person authorized to administer oaths in the place in which the examination is held, either by the law thereof or by the law of the United States, or (2) before a person commissioned by the court, and a person so commissioned shall have the power by virtue of the commission to administer any necessary oath and take testimony, or (3) pursuant to a letter rogatory. A commission or a letter rogatory shall be issued on application and notice and on terms that are just and appropriate. It is not requisite to the issuance of a commission or a letter rogatory that the taking of the deposition in any other manner is impracticable or inconvenient; and both a commission and a letter rogatory may be issued in proper cases. A notice or commission may designate the person before whom the deposition is to be taken either by the name or descriptive title. A letter rogatory may be addressed "To the Appropriate Authority in (here name the country)." Evidence obtained in response to a letter rogatory need not be excluded merely for the reason that it is not a verbatim transcript or that the testimony was not taken under oath or for any similar departure from the requirements for depositions taken within the United States under these rules.

28(c) Disqualification for interest. No deposition shall be taken before a person who is a relative or employee or attorney or counsel of any of the parties, or is a relative or employee of such attorney or counsel, or is financially interested in the action.

LEGAL HOLIDAYS

[ARIZ. REV. STAT. ANN.]

§ **1-301.** Holidays enumerated.

A. The following days shall be holidays:
1. Sunday of each week.
2. January 1, "New Year's Day."
3. Third Monday in January, "Martin Luther King, Jr./Civil Rights Day."
4. Second Monday in February, "Lincoln Day".
5. Third Monday in February, "Washington Day."
6. Second Sunday in May, "Mothers' Day."
7. Last Monday in May, "Memorial Day."
8. Third Sunday in June, "Fathers' Day."
9. July 4, "Independence Day."
10. First Sunday in August, "American Family Day."
11. First Monday in September, "Labor Day."
12. September 17, "Constitution Day."
13. Second Monday in October, "Columbus Day."
14. November 11, "Veterans' Day."
15. Fourth Thursday in November, "Thanksgiving Day."
16. December 25, "Christmas Day."

B. When any of the holidays enumerated in subsection A falls on a Sunday, the following Monday shall be observed as a holiday, with the exception of the holidays enumerated in subsection A, paragraph 1, 6, 8, 10 and 12.

C. When any of the holidays enumerated in subsection A, paragraphs 2, 9, 14 and 16 falls on a Saturday, the preceding Friday shall be observed as a holiday.

D. When the holiday enumerated in subsection A, paragraph 12 falls on a day other than Sunday, the Sunday preceding September 17 shall be observed as such holiday.

§ **1-302.** Closing of offices and courts; transaction of certain judicial business.

A. Public officers shall not be open, and no court of justice shall be open or any judicial business transacted on a legal holiday, except for the following purposes:
1. To give upon its request, instructions to a jury deliberating on its verdict.
2. To receive a verdict or discharge a jury.
3. For the exercise of the powers of a magistrate in a criminal action or in a proceeding of a criminal nature.

B. Injunctions, attachments, process for claim and delivery and writs of prohibition may be issued and served on any day.

ARKANSAS

NOTARIES PUBLIC

[Ark. Stat. Ann.]

§ 21-14-101. Appointment and commission.

(a)(1) The Secretary of State may appoint and commission individual persons as notaries public in this state.

(2) Notaries public may perform notarial acts in any part of the state for a term of ten (10) years.

(b) Every applicant for appointment and commission as a notary public shall complete an application to be filed with the Secretary of State stating:

(1) That he is a bona fide citizen of the United States;

(2) That he is eighteen (18) years of age or older;

(3) That he is a legal resident of the State of Arkansas or a legal resident of an adjoining state and employed in the State of Arkansas;

(4) That he is able to read and write English;

(5) The address of his business or residence in this state;

(6) That during the past ten (10) years, his commission as a notary public has not been revoked.

(c) The application shall be sent to the Secretary of State with a twenty dollar ($20.00) fee for the notary public commission.

(d) Notaries public shall file in the office of the recorder of deeds for the county in which the notary public resides, or, in the case of a resident of an adjoining state, in the county in Arkansas in which employed, either:

(1) A surety bond executed by a surety insurer authorized to do business in Arkansas to the state for the faithful discharge of their duties, in the sum of four thousand dollars ($4,000), to be approved by the clerk of the circuit court of the county; or

(2) A surety contract guaranteeing the notaries' faithful discharge of their duties executed to the state of Arkansas for not more than an aggregate four thousand dollars ($4,000) issued by a general business corporation, validly organized and formed under the laws of this state pertaining to domestic corporations, and which:

(A) Has previously registered with the Insurance Commissioner on forms prescribed by him evidencing its purpose to issue only surety contracts for notaries public pursuant to the provisions of this section; and

(B) Has previously deposited and thereafter maintains with the Insurance Commissioner securities in the sum of not less than ten thousand dollars ($10,000) executed to the state of Arkansas which are issued by a nonaffiliated corporate entity and are approved by the Insurance Commissioner; and

(C) Is not otherwise transacting any insurance business in this state which requires compliance with the provisions of the Arkansas Insurance Code, § 23-60-101 et seq.

§ 21-14-102. Change of residence.

(a) In instances where a person appointed and commissioned a notary public under § 21-14-101 changes residence, or in case of a resident of an adjoining state changes his place of employment, to a county within this state other than the county wherein the notary resided or was employed on the date of commission, upon receiving notification of the change of residency, the Secretary of State shall transfer the notary's appointment and commission to the new county of residence or employment.

(b) The original bond shall also be filed in the new county of residence or county of employment.

§ 21-14-103. Death, resignation, or removal.

If any notary public dies, resigns, removes from the county, or is removed from office, his record book and all his public papers shall be delivered to the clerk of the county court, to be delivered to his successor.

§ 21-14-104. Power and authority generally.

The powers and authority of notaries public shall be coextensive with the state for:

(1) The purpose of swearing witnesses;

(2) Taking affidavits and depositions; and

(3) Taking acknowledgments of deeds and other instruments in writing and authorized by law to be acknowledged.

§ 21-14-105. Administration of oaths.

Each notary public shall have power to administer oaths in all matters incident to or belonging to the exercise of his notarial office.

§ 21-14-106. Acknowledgments and authentications.

A notary public may:

(1) Take the proof or the acknowledgment of all instruments of writing relating to commerce and navigation;

(2) Receive and authenticate acknowledgments of deeds, letters of attorney, and other instruments of writing;

(3) Make declarations and protests; and

(4) Certify under his official seal the truth of all matters and things done by virtue of his office.

§ 21-14-107. Signature—Seal.

(a) At the time of notarization, the notary public shall sign his official signature on every notary certificate.

(b)(1) Under or near his official signature on every notary certificate, a notary public shall provide a seal of his office, which shall be either a rubber stamp seal or a seal embosser. The seal shall be clear and legible, capable of photographic reproduction.

(2) The seal should include:

(A) His name exactly as he writes his official signature;

(B) The name of the county where his bond is filed;

(C) The words "notary public" and "Arkansas."

§ 21-14-108. Expiration date of commission.

(a)(1) All notaries public shall attach to any certificate of acknowledgment or jurat to an affidavit that he may make a statement of the date on which his commission will expire.

(2) No acknowledgment or other act of a notary shall be held invalid on account of the failure to comply with this section.

(b) If any notary public shall fail to attach the statement to any certificate of acknowledgment or other official act, he shall be guilty of a misdemeanor and be punished by a fine not to exceed five dollars ($5.00).

§ 21-14-109. Performance of duties for corporation.

(a) It shall be lawful for any notary public who is a stockholder, director, officer, or employee of a bank or other corporation to take the acknowledgment of any party to any written instrument executed to or by the corporation, or to administer an oath to any other stockholder, director, officer, employee, or agent of the corporation, or to protest for nonacceptance or nonpayment bills of exchange, drafts, checks, notes, and other negotiable instruments which may be owned or held for collection by the corporation.

(b) It shall be unlawful for any notary public to take the acknowledgment of an instrument executed by or to a bank or other corporation of which he is a stockholder, director, officer, or employee where the notary is a party to the instrument, either individually or as a representative of the corporation, or to protest any negotiable instrument owned or held for collection by the corporation, where the notary is individually a party to the instrument.

§ 21-14-110. Admissibility of acknowledged instruments.

All declarations and protests made, and acknowledgments taken by notaries public, and certified copies of their records and official papers shall be received as evidence of the facts therein stated in all the courts of this state.

§ 21-14-111. Unlawful act—Penalty.

(a) It is unlawful for any notary public to witness any signature on any instrument unless the notary either:

(1) Witnesses the signing of the instrument and personally knows the signer or is presented proof of the identity of the signer; or

(2) Recognizes the signature of the signer by virtue of familiarity with the signature.

(b) Any notary public violating this section shall be guilty of a Class A misdemeanor. In addition, the commission of any notary public convicted of a violation of this section shall be revoked and the person shall be ineligible to be recommissioned as a notary public.

ADDITIONAL AUTHORITY

§ 1-4-108. Official seals.

(a) It shall be the duty of the Governor to procure a seal for the State of Arkansas, which shall present the following impressions, devices, and emblems, to wit: An eagle at the bottom, holding a scroll in its beak, inscribed "Regnat Populus," a bundle of arrows in one claw and olive branch in the other; a shield covering the breast of the eagle, engraved with a steamboat at top, a beehive and plow in the middle, and sheaf of wheat at the bottom; the Goddess of Liberty at the top, holding a wreath in her right hand, a pole in the left hand,

surmounted by a liberty cap, and surrounded by a circle of stars outside of which is a circle of rays; the figure of an angel on the left, inscribed "Mercy," and a sword on the right hand, inscribed "Justice," surrounded with the words "Seal of the State of Arkansas."

(b) The Secretary of State, Auditor of State, and Treasurer of State shall each have a seal of office presenting the impressions, devices, and emblems presented by the Seal of State except that the surrounding words on the Secretary of State's seal shall be "Seal of the Secretary of State, Arkansas," on the Auditor of State's seal shall be "Seal of the Auditor of State, Arkansas," and on the Treasurer of State's seal shall be "Seal of the Treasurer of State, Arkansas."

(c) All official seals used in the state shall present the same impressions, emblems, and devices presented by the Seal of State, except that the surrounding words shall be such as to indicate the office to which each seal belongs.

§ 16-45-102. Officials before whom affidavits may be made.

(a) An affidavit may be made in this state before a judge of the court, justice of the peace, notary public, clerk of a court, or mayor of a city or incorporated town.

(b) An affidavit may be made out of this state before a commissioner appointed by the Governor of this state to take depositions, or before a judge of a court, mayor of a city, notary public, or justice of the peace, whose certificate shall be proof of the time and manner of its being made.

FEES

§ 21-6-309. Notaries public.

Each notary public in this state shall charge and collect the following fees:

(1) For protest and record of same .... $ 5.00
(2) For each notice of protest 5.00
(3) For each certificate and seal 5.00

(b) Any notary public who shall knowingly charge, demand, or receive any fees not provided by law, or who shall charge, demand, or receive any greater fees than are provided in this section shall be deemed guilty of a misdemeanor. Upon conviction he shall be fined in any sum not less than one hundred dollars ($100) for each and every offense.

ACKNOWLEDGMENTS

§ 16-47-103. Officers authorized to take proof or acknowledgment of real estate conveyances.

(a) The proof or acknowledgment of every deed or instrument of writing for the conveyance of any real estate shall be taken by one of the following courts or officers:

(1) When acknowledged or proven within this state before the Supreme Court, the circuit court, the chancery court, or any judges thereof, the clerk of any court of record, any county or probate judge, or before any justice of the peace or notary public;

(2) When acknowledged or proven outside this state, and within the United States or its territories, or in any of the colonies or possessions or dependencies of the United States, before any court of the United States, or any state or territory, or colony or possession or dependency of the United States, having a seal, or a clerk of any such court, or before any notary public, or before the mayor of any incorporated city or town, or the chief officer of any city or town having a seal, or before a commissioner appointed by the Governor of this state;

(3) When acknowledged or proven outside the United States, before any court of any state, kingdom, or empire having a seal; any mayor or chief officer of any city or town having an official seal; or before any officer of any foreign country who by the laws of that country is authorized to take probate of the conveyance of real estate of his own country if the officer has, by law, an official seal.

(b) The acknowledgment of any deed or mortgage, when taken outside the United States, may be taken and certified by a United States consul.

Uniform Acknowledgment Act

§ 16-47-201. Acknowledgment of instruments.

Any instrument may be acknowledged in the manner and form provided by the laws of this state, or as provided by this act.

§ 16-47-202. Officials authorized to take within the state.

The acknowledgment of any instrument may be made in this state before:

(1) A judge of a court of record or before any former judge of a court of record who served at least four (4) or more years;

(2) A clerk of any court of record;

(3) A commissioner or registrar or recorder of deeds;

(4) A notary public;

(5) A justice of the peace; or

(6) A master in chancery or registrar in chancery.

§ 16-47-203. Officials authorized to take within the United States.

The acknowledgment of any instrument may be without the state but within the United States or a territory or insular possession of the United States and within the jurisdiction of the officer, before:

(1) A clerk or deputy clerk of any federal court;

(2) A clerk or deputy clerk of any court of record of any state or other jurisdiction;

(3) A notary public;

(4) A commissioner of deeds;

(5) Any person authorized by the laws of such other jurisdiction to take acknowledgments.

§ 16-47-204. Officials authorized to take without the United States.

The acknowledgment of any instrument may be made without the United States before:

(1) An ambassador, minister, charge d'affaires, counselor to or secretary of a legation, consul general, consul, vice-consul, commercial attache, or consular agent of the United States accredited to the country where the acknowledgment is made.

(2) A notary public of the country where the acknowledgment is made.

(3) A judge or clerk of a court of record of the country where the acknowledgment is made.

§ 16-47-205. Proof of identity of person making.

The officer taking the acknowledgment shall know or have satisfactory evidence that the person making the acknowledgment is the person described in and who executed the instrument.

§ 16-47-206. Acknowledgment by a married woman.

An acknowledgment by a married woman may be made in the same form as though she were unmarried.

§ 16-47-207. Forms of certificates.

An officer taking the acknowledgment shall endorse thereon or attach thereto a certificate substantially in one (1) of the following forms:

(1) By Individuals:

"State of ....

County of . . . .

On this the . . . . . day of . . . ., 19. . .,
before me, ..., the undersigned officer,
personally appeared . . . ., known to me
(or satisfactorily proven) to be the person whose
name . . . . . . subscribed to the within instrument
and acknowledged that . . . . . . he . . . . . . executed the same for the purposes therein contained.

In witness whereof I hereunto set my hand and
official seal.

. . . .
. . . .
Title of Officer."

(2) By a Corporation:

"State of . . . .
County of . . . .

On this the . . . . . day of . . . ., 19. . .,
before me, ..., the undersigned officer,
personally appeared . . . ., who acknowledged himself to be the . . . . of . . . .
., a corporation, and that he, as such . . . .,
being authorized so to do, executed the foregoing
instrument for the purposes therein contained, by
signing the name of the corporation by himself as
. . . .

In witness whereof I hereunto set my hand and
official seal.

. . . .
. . . .
Title of Officer."

(3) By an Attorney in Fact:

"State of . . . .
County of . . . .

On this the . . . . . day of . . . ., 19. . .,
before me, ..., the undersigned officer,
personally appeared . . . ., known to me
(or satisfactorily proven) to be the person whose
name is subscribed as attorney in fact for . . . .
. . ., and acknowledged that he executed the same
as the act of his principal for the purposes therein
contained.

In witness whereof I hereunto set my hand and
official seal.

. . . .
. . . .
Title of Officer."

(4) By Any Public Officer or Deputy Thereof, or
by Any Trustee, Administrator, Guardian, or Executor:

"State of . . . .
County of . . . .

On this the . . . . . day of . . . ., 19. . .,
before me, ..., the undersigned officer,
personally appeared . . . ., of the State
(County or City as the case may be) of . . . .,
known to me (or satisfactorily proven) to be the

person described in the foregoing instrument, and
acknowledged that he executed the same in the capacity therein stated and for the purposes therein
contained.

In witness whereof I hereunto set my hand and
official seal.

. . . .
. . . .
Title of Officer."

§ 16-47-208. Execution of certificate by officer.

The certificate of the acknowledging officer shall
be completed by his signature, his official seal if he
has one, the title of his office, and if he is a notary
public, the date his commission expires.

§ 16-47-209. Authentication of acknowl-edgments.

(a) If the acknowledgment is taken within this
state or is made without this state but in the United
States by one (1) of the officers designated in § 16-
47-203, or without the United States by an officer
of the United States, no authentication shall be necessary.

(b) If the acknowledgment is made without the
United States and by a notary public or a judge or
clerk of a court of record of the country where the
acknowledgment is made, the certificate shall be
authenticated by a certificate under the great seal
of state of the country, affixed by the custodian of
such seal, or by a certificate of a diplomatic, consular, or commercial officer of the United States
accredited to that country, certifying as to the official character of such officer.

§ 16-47-210. Acknowledgments under laws of other states.

Notwithstanding any provision in this act contained the acknowledgment of any instrument
without this state in compliance with the manner
and form prescribed by the laws of the place of its
execution, if in a state, a territory or insular possession of the United States, or in the District of Columbia, or in the Phillipine Islands, verified by the
official seal of the officer before whom it is acknowledged, shall have the same effect as an acknowledgment in the manner and form prescribed
by the laws of this state for instruments executed
within the state.

§ 16-47-211. Validation of unauthenti-cated writings affecting title to property.

All deeds, conveyances, deeds of trust, mortgages, mineral leases, marriage contracts, and other instruments in writing, affecting or purporting to affect title to any real estate or personal property situated in this state, which have been recorded or executed prior to July 19, 1971, and which may be defective or ineffectual because of the failure to have the authentication formerly required by Acts 1943, No. 169, §§ 9 and 10, prior to these amendments, shall be binding and effectual as though such instruments contained the required authentication.

§ 16-47-212. Act cumulative.

This act shall be cumulative to other acts of the General Assembly relating to acknowledgments.

§ 16-47-213. Acknowledgments by persons serving in or with the armed forces of the United States within or without the United States.

In addition to the acknowledgment of instruments in the manner and form and as otherwise authorized by this act, persons serving in or with the armed forces of the United States or their dependents may acknowledge the same wherever located before any commissioned officer in active service of the armed forces of the United States with rank of second lieutenant or higher in the Army, Air Force or Marine Corps, or ensign or higher in the Navy or United States Coast Guard. The instrument shall not be rendered invalid by the failure to state therein the place of execution or acknowledgment. No authentication of the officer's certificate of acknowledgment shall be required but the officer taking the acknowledgment shall endorse thereon or attach thereto a certificate substantially in the following form:

"On this . . . . . . day of . . . ., 19. . ., before me, ..., the undersigned officer, personally appeared . . . . (Serial No. . . . .), known to me or satifactorily proven to be (serving in or with the armed forces of the United States) (a dependent of . . . ., (Serial No. . . . .) a person serving in or with the armed forces of the United States) and to be the person whose name is subscribed to the within instrument and acknowledged that . . . . he . . . . executed the same for the purposes therein contained. And the undersigned does further certify that he is at the date of this certificate a commissioned officer of the rank stated below and is in the active service of the armed forces of the United States.

. . . .
Signature of the Officer

. . . .
Rank and Serial No. of Officer and Command to which attached."

§ 16-47-214. Acknowledgments previously taken unaffected.

No acknowledgment heretofore taken shall be affected by anything contained in this act.

§ 16-47-215. Uniformity of interpretation.

This act shall be so interpreted as to make uniform the laws of those states which enact it.

§ 16-47-216. Title of act.

This act may be cited as the "Uniform Acknowledgment Act."

§ 16-47-217. Validation of prior acknowledgments—Construction of uniform act.

It is the intent and purpose of this section that all acknowledgments taken subsequent to Acts 1957, No. 411 either in accordance with the Uniform Acknowledgment Act or in accordance with the laws of this state in effect at the time of adoption of the Uniform Acknowledgment Act be cured and validated for all purposes; and that neither Acts 1957, No. 411 nor the Uniform Acknowledgment Act to which it is amendatory shall be construed to repeal or modify any laws relative to the taking of acknowledgments and the authentication thereof which were in effect in this state at the time of adoption of the Uniform Acknowledgment Act, but that the Uniform Acknowledgment Act shall be deemed to provide an alternative system for taking and authenticating acknowledgments.

§ 16-47-218. Validation of acknowledgments—Construction of acts.

All acknowledgments taken subsequent to Acts 1959, No. 127 either in accordance with the Uniform Acknowledgment Act or in accordance with the laws of this state in effect at the time of adoption of the Uniform Acknowledgment Act are cured and validated for all purposes; and that neither Acts 1959, No. 127 nor the Uniform Acknowledgment Act shall be construed to repeal or modify any laws relative to the taking of acknowledgments and the authentication thereof which were in effect in this state at the time of adoption of the Uniform Acknowledgment Act, but that the Uniform Acknowledgment Act shall be deemed to provide an alternative system for taking and authenticating acknowledgments.

DEPOSITIONS

[Ark. R. Civ. P.]

RULE 28. Persons before whom depositions may be taken.

(a) **Within this State and Elsewhere in the United States.** Within this state and elsewhere in the United States or within a territory or insular possession subject to the dominion of the United States, depositions shall be taken before an officer authorized to administer oaths by the laws of this State or of the place where the examination is held, or before a person appointed by the court in which the action is pending. A person so appointed has power to administer oaths and take testimony.

(b) **In Foreign States or Countries.** In a foreign state or country, depositions may be taken (1) on notice before a person authorized to administer oaths in the place in which the examination is held, either by the law thereof or by the law of the United States, or (2) before a person commissioned by the court, and a person so commissioned shall have the power by virtue of his commission to administer any necessary oath and take testimony, or (3) pursuant to a letter rogatory. A commission or a letter rogatory shall be issued on application and notice and on terms that are just and appropriate. It is not requisite to the issuance of a commission or a letter rogatory that the taking of the deposition in any other manner is impractical or inconvenient; and both a commission and a letter rogatory may be issued in proper cases. A notice or commission may designate the person before whom the deposition is to be taken either by name or descriptive title. A letter rogatory may be addressed "To The Appropriate Authority in (here insert the country)." Evidence obtained in response to a letter rogatory need not be excluded merely for the reason that it is not a verbatim transcript or that the testimony was not taken under oath or for any similar departure from the requirements for depositions taken within the United States under these rules.

(c) **For Use in Foreign Countries.** A party desiring to take a deposition or have a document or other thing produced for examination in this state, for use in a judicial proceeding in a foreign country, may produce to a judge of the circuit, chancery or probate court in the county where the witness or person in possession of the document or thing to be examined resides or may be found, letter rogatory, appropriately authenticated, authorizing the taking of such deposition or production of such document or thing on notice duly served; whereupon it shall be the duty of the court to issue a subpoena requiring the witness to attend at a specified time and place for examination. In case of failure of the witness to attend or refusal to be sworn or to testify or to produce the document or thing requested, the court may find the witness in contempt.

(d) **Disqualification for Interest.** No deposition shall be taken before a person who is a relative or employee or attorney or counsel of any of the parties, or is a relative or employee of such attorney or counsel, or is financially interested in the action.

[ARK. STAT. ANN.]

§ 21-6-501. Officers taking depositions.

(a) The fees allowed an officer for taking depositions shall be two dollars ($2.00) for each deposition and five cents (5¢) per mile for each mile that an officer has to travel in going to and returning from the place of the taking.

(b) The distance to be traveled shall be estimated from his office but if a number of depositions are taken in one (1) day for the same party in any action, the fees shall not exceed five dollars ($5.00).

(c) If the officer shall be engaged more than one (1) day in taking a deposition, he shall receive two dollars ($2.00) per day for each day he may be engaged in taking one (1) deposition.

COMMISSIONERS

§ 25-16-204. Appointment of commissioners in other states.

(a) The Governor may nominate, appoint, and commission, under the Great Seal of Arkansas, or may continue in office one (1) or more commissioners within any other state or territory of the United States. The commissioners shall serve at the pleasure of the Governor then in office and shall have power to administer oaths and affirmations and to take depositions, affidavits, and the proof and acknowledgment of deeds or other instruments of writing, under seal, to be used or recorded in this state.

(b) All oaths administered by the commissioners, all affidavits and depositions taken by them, and all acknowledgments, etc., certified by them shall be as effectual in law, to all intents and purposes, as if done and certified by any justice of the peace or other authorized officer within this state.

(c) Before any commissioner shall proceed to discharge any of the duties of his appointment, he shall take and subscribe an oath before some justice of the peace, or other officer authorized to administer oaths in the state for which the commissioner is appointed, that he will well and faithfully discharge all the duties of his appointment. The oath, together with the signature and an impression of the seal of the commissioner, shall be filed in the office of the Secretary of State within six (6) months after its taking.

LEGAL HOLIDAYS

§ 1-5-101. Official holidays.

(a) The following days are declared to be the sole official holidays applicable to state government in Arkansas:

(1) New Year's Day — January 1;

(2) Dr. Martin Luther King' Jr.'s Birthday and Robert E. Lee's Birthday — the third Monday in January;

(3) George Washington's Birthday — the third Monday in February;

(4) Memorial Day — the last Monday in May;

(5) Independence Day — July 4;

(6) Labor Day — the first Monday in September;

(7) Veteran's Day — November 11;

(8) Thanksgiving Day — the fourth Thursday in November;

(9) Christmas Eve — December 24;

(10) Christmas Day — December 25;

(11) The employee's birthday — employee is granted one (1) holiday to observe his or her birthday.

(b) Holidays falling on a Saturday will be observed on the preceding Friday. Holidays falling on a Sunday will be observed on the succeeding Monday.

(c) It is the specific intent of the General Assembly that all state employees shall be entitled to eleven (11) paid holidays per year. The Office of Personnel Management of the Department of Finance and Administration shall promulgate rules and regulations to assure this legislative intent.

§ 1-5-102. State offices to be closed on holidays — Exceptions.

(a) All state offices shall be closed on all days declared to be legal holidays under the laws of this state, and all persons employed thereby shall not be required to work on legal holidays. However, this section shall not apply to those state government offices wherever located and to those employees that are essential to the preservation and protection of the public peace, health, and safety, nor to the offices of the various constitutional officers who may use their own discretion in the matter of closing their offices on legal holidays.

(b) It is the specific intent of this section that all state offices be closed on all legal holidays even though one (1) or more legal holidays shall fall during a general or special session of the General Assembly, provided that, with respect to state offices located in Pulaski County, those offices shall not be closed for any legal holiday during any general or special session of the General Assembly unless they are permitted to close by resolution of the General Assembly, but those offices shall maintain only a minimum number of employees necessary to carry on the business of the offices.

(c) Any state employee who is required to work on a legal holiday, for any reason, shall be entitled to equivalent time off at a later date.

(d) Nothwithstanding the provisions of subsection (a) of this section, state-supported instititutions of higher learning in this state may require the employees of the institutions to work on any of the holidays established in § 1-5-101, but if the employees are required to work on any day declared as a legal holiday, the employees shall be entitled to equivalent time off on another date.

§ 1-5-103. State office closings by proclamation.

Nothing in this chapter shall be construed as prohibiting the Governor from establishing by executive proclamation additional days when state offices shall be closed in observance of special events, or for other reasons at his discretion.

§ 1-5-104. Entitlement to paid holiday or equivalent time.

(a) To be eligible for holiday pay, the employee must be on pay status his last scheduled work day before the holiday and his first scheduled work day after the holiday.

(b) When a holiday falls while an employee is on annual or sick leave, that day is charged as a holiday and that day will not be charged against his annual or sick leave.

(c) When a holiday falls on an employee's regular scheduled day off, he will be given equivalent time off.

(d) The following provisions apply to employees who cannot take holidays as scheduled:

(1) Employees must work on holidays when the needs of the agency require it. Department or agency directors will determine the need;

(2) Days off for holidays worked may be taken at a time approved by the employee's supervisor. They are to be taken as soon as it is practical;

(3) Supervisors are responsible for scheduling days off in lieu of holidays for their employees. Department heads and supervisors are responsible for informing their employees of the schedule and the observance of all provisions.

§ 1-5-105. Commercial paper payable day after holiday.

All bills of exchange, drafts, or promissory notes which shall become payable on a legal holiday shall be payable on the day next succeeding the holiday.

CALIFORNIA

NOTARIES PUBLIC

[Cal. Gov't. Code]

§ 8200. Appointment and commission; number; jurisdiction; fees.

The Secretary of State may appoint and commission notaries public in such number as the Secretary of State deems necessary for the public convenience. Notaries public may act as such notaries in any part of this state.

§ 8201. Qualifications.

Every person appointed as notary public shall:

(a) Be at the time of appointment a legal resident of this state, except as otherwise provided in Section 8203.1.

(b) Be not less than 18 years of age.

(c) Have satisfactorily completed a written examination prescribed by the Secretary of State to determine the fitness of the person to exercise the functions of the office of notary public. All questions shall be based on the law of this state as set forth in the booklet of laws of California relating to notaries public distributed by the Secretary of State.

§ 8201.1. Additional qualifications; determination; identification; fingerprints.

Prior to granting an appointment as a notary public, the Secretary of State shall determine that the applicant possesses the required honesty, credibility, truthfulness, and integrity to fulfill the responsibilities of the position. To assist in determining the identity of the applicant and whether the applicant has been convicted of a disqualifying crime specified in subdivision (b) of Section 8214.1, the Secretary of State shall require that applicants be fingerprinted.

§ 8201.5. Application form; confidential nature; use of information.

The Secretary of State shall require an applicant for appointment and commission as a notary public to complete an application form prescribed by the Secretary of State. Information on this form filed by an applicant with the Secretary of State, except for his name and address, is confidential and no individual record shall be divulged by an official or employee having access to it to any person other than the applicant, his authorized representative, or an employee or officer of the federal government, the state government, or a local agency, as defined in subdivision (b) of Section 6252 of the Government Code, acting in his official capacity. Such information shall be used by the Secretary of State for the sole purpose of carrying out the duties of this chapter.

§ 8202.5. State, county and school district employees; certificate; expenses.

The Secretary of State may appoint and commission such number of state, county, and public school district employees as notaries public to act for and on behalf of the governmental entity for which appointed as the Secretary of State deems proper. Whenever such a notary is appointed and commissioned, a duly authorized representative of the employing governmental entity shall execute a certificate that the appointment is made for the purposes of the employing governmental entity, and whenever such certificate is filed with any state or county officer, no fees shall be charged by the officer for the filing or issuance of any document in connection with such appointment.

The state or any county or school district for which the notary public is appointed and commissioned pursuant to this section may pay from any funds available for its support the premiums on any bond and the cost of any stamps, seals or other supplies required in connection with the appointment, commission or performance of the duties of such notary public.

Any fees collected or obtained by any notary public whose documents have been filed without charge and for whom bond premiums have been paid by the employer of the notary public shall be remitted by such notary public to the employing agency which shall deposit such funds to the credit of the fund from which the salary of the notary public is paid.

§ 8202.7. Private employers; agreement to pay premium on bonds and costs of supplies; remission of fees to employer.

A private employer, pursuant to an agreement with an employee who is a notary public, may pay the premiums on any bond and the cost of any stamps, seals, or other supplies required in connection with the appointment, commission, or performance of the duties of such notary public. Such agreement may also provide for the remission of fees collected by such notary public to the employer, in which case any fees collected or obtained by such notary public while such agreement is in effect shall be remitted by such notary public to the employer which shall deposit such funds to the credit of the fund from which the compensation of the notary public is paid.

§ 8202.8. Private employers; limitation on provision of notarial services.

Notwithstanding any other provision of law, a private employer of a notary public who has entered into an agreement with his or her employee pursuant to Section 8202.7 may limit, during the employee's ordinary course of employment, the providing of notarial services by the employee solely to transactions directly associated with the business purposes of the employer.

§ 8203.1. Military and naval reservations; appointment and commission of notaries; qualifications.

The Secretary of State may appoint and commission notaries public for the military and naval reservations of the Army, Navy, Coast Guard, Air Force, and Marine Corps of the United States, wherever located in the state; provided, however, that such appointee shall be a citizen of the United States, not less than 18 years of age, and must meet the requirements set forth in subdivision (c) of Section 8201.

§ 8203.5. Military and naval reservations, jurat.

In addition to the name of the State, the jurat shall also contain the name of the reservation in which the instrument is executed.

§ 8204. Term of office.

The term of office of a notary public is for four years commencing with the date specified in the commission.

§ 8205. Duties.

(a) It is the duty of a notary public, when requested:

(1) To demand acceptance and payment of foreign and inland bills of exchange, or promissory notes, to protest them for nonacceptance and nonpayment, and to exercise such other powers and duties as by the law of nations and according to commercial usages, or by the laws of any other state, government, or country, may be performed by notaries.

(2) To take the acknowledgment or proof of powers of attorney, mortgages, deeds, grants, transfers, and other instruments of writing executed by any person, and to give a certificate of such proof or acknowledgment, endorsed on or attached to the instrument. Such certificate shall be signed by the notary public in the notary public's own handwriting.

(3) To take depositions and affidavits, and administer oaths and affirmations, in all matters incident to the duties of the office, or to be used before any court, judge, officer, or board. Any deposition, affidavit, oath or affirmation shall be signed by the notary public in the notary public's own handwriting.

(b) It shall further be the duty of a notary public, upon written request:

(1) To furnish to the Secretary of State certified copies of the notary's journal.

(2) To respond within 30 days of receiving written requests sent by certified mail from the Secretary of State's office for information relating to official acts performed by the notary.

§ 8206. Sequential journal; contents; copies of pages.

A notary public shall keep a sequential journal of all official acts performed as a notary public. The journal shall be in addition to and apart from any copies of notarized documents which may be in the possession of the notary public and shall include:

(a) Date, time and type of each official act.

(b) Character of every instrument acknowledged or proved before the notary.

(c) The signature of each person whose signature is being notarized.

(d) A statement as to whether the identity of a person making an acknowledgment was based on personal knowledge or satisfactory evidence. If identity was established by satisfactory evidence pursuant to Section 1185 of the Civil Code, then the journal shall contain the signature of the credible witness swearing or affirming to the identity of the individual or the type of identifying document, the governmental agency issuing the document, the serial or identifying number of the document, and the date of issue or expiration of the document.

(e) If the identity of the person making the acknowledgment was established by the oaths or affirmations of two credible witnesses whose identities are proven upon the presentation of satisfactory evidence, the type of identifying documents, the identifying numbers of the documents and the dates of issuance or expiration of the documents presented by the witnesses to establish their identity.

(f) The fee charged for the notarial service.

Upon written request of any member of the public, which request shall include the name of the parties, the type of document, and the month and year in which notarized, the notary shall supply a photostatic copy of the line item representing the requested transaction at a cost of not more than thirty cents ($0.30) per page.

§ 8207. Seal.

A notary public shall provide and keep an official seal, which shall clearly show, when embossed, stamped, impressed or affixed to a document, the name of the notary, the State Seal, the words "Notary Public" and the name of the county wherein the bond and oath of office are filed, and the date the notary public's commission expires. The seal of every notary public commissioned after January 1, 1992, shall contain the sequential identification number assigned to the manufacturer or vendor. The notary public shall authenticate with the official seal all official acts.

A notary public shall not use the official notarial seal except for the purpose of carrying out the duties and responsibilities as set forth in this chapter. A notary public shall not use the title "notary public" except for the purpose of rendering notarial service.

The seal of every notary public shall be affixed by a seal press or stamp that will print or emboss a seal which legibly reproduces under photographic methods the required elements of the seal. The seal may be circular not over two inches in diameter, or may be a rectangular form of not more than an inch in width by two inches and one-half in length, with a serrated or milled edged border, and shall contain the information required by this section.

§ 8208. Protest of bill or note for nonacceptance or nonpayment.

The protest of a notary public, under his or her hand and official seal, of a bill of exchange or promissory note for nonacceptance or nonpayment, specifying any of the following prima facie evidence of the facts recited therein:

(a) The time and place of presentment.

(b) The fact that presentment was made and the manner thereof.

(c) The cause or reason for protesting the bill.

(d) The demand made and the answer given, if any, or the fact that the drawee or acceptor could not be found * * *

§ 8209. Resignation, disqualification or removal of notary; records delivered to clerk; misdemeanor; death; destruction of records.

(a) If any notary public resigns, is disqualified, removed from office, or allows his or her appointment to expire without obtaining reappointment within 30 days, all notarial records and papers shall be delivered within 30 days to the clerk of the county in which the notary public's current official oath of office * * * is on file. If the notary public willfully fails or refuses to deliver all notarial records and papers to the county clerk within 30 days, the person is guilty of a misdemeanor and shall be personally liable for damages to any person injured by that action or inaction.

(b) In the case of the death of a notary public, the personal representative of the deceased shall promptly notify the Secretary of State of the death of the notary public and shall deliver all notarial records and papers of the deceased to the clerk of the county in which the notary public's official oath of office * * * is on file.

(c) After 10 years from the date of deposit with the county clerk, if no request for, or reference to such records has been made, they may be destroyed upon order of court.

§ 8211. Fees.

Fees charged by a notary public for the following services shall not exceed the fees prescribed by this section.

(a) For taking an acknowledgment or proof of a deed, or other instrument, to include the seal and the writing of the certificate, the sum of five dollars ($5) for each signature.

(b) For administering an oath or affirmation to one person and executing the jurat, including the seal, the sum of five dollars ($5).

(c) For all services rendered in connection with the taking of any deposition, the sum of ten dollars ($10), and in addition thereto, the sum of two dollars ($2) for administering the oath to the witness and the sum of two dollars ($2) for the certificate to such deposition.

(d) For every protest for the nonpayment of a promissory note or for the nonpayment or nonacceptance of a bill of exchange, draft, or check, the sum of four dollars ($4).

(e) For serving every notice of nonpayment of a promissory note or of nonpayment or nonacceptance of a bill of exchange, order, draft, or check, the sum of two dollars ($2).

(f) For recording every protest, the sum of two dollars ($2).

§ 8212. Bond; amount; form.

Every person appointed a notary public shall execute an official bond in the sum of ten thousand dollars ($10,000). The bond shall be in the form of a bond executed by an admitted surety insurer and not a deposit in lieu of bond.

§ 8213. Bonds and oaths; filing; certificate; copy of oath as evidence; transfer to new county; fees.

(a) No later than 30 days after the beginning of the term prescribed in the commission, every person appointed a notary public shall file an official bond, and take, subscribe, and file an oath of office in the office of the county clerk of the county within which the person maintains a principal place of business as shown in the application submitted to the Secretary of State, and the commission shall not take effect unless this is done within the 30-day period. Upon filing the oath and bond, the county clerk shall forthwith transmit to the Secretary of State a certificate setting forth the fact of such filing and containing a copy of the official oath, personally signed by the notary public in the form set forth in the commission and shall forthwith deliver the bond to the county recorder for recording. The county clerk shall retain the oath of office for one year following the expiration of the term of the commission for which the oath was taken, after which the oath may be destroyed or otherwise disposed of. The copy of the oath, personally signed by the notary public, on file with the Secretary of State may at any time be read in evidence with like effect as the original oath, without further proof.

(b) If a notary public transfers the principal place of business from one county to another, the notary public may file a new oath of office and bond, or a duplicate of the original bond with the county clerk to which the principal place of business was transferred. If the notary public elects to make a new filing, the notary public shall, within 30 days of the filing, obtain an official seal which shall include the name of the county to which the notary public has transferred. In such a case, the same filing and recording fees are applicable as in the case of the original filing and recording of the bond.

(c) The recording fees specified in Section 27361 of the Government Code shall be paid by the person appointed a notary public. The fee may be paid to the county clerk who shall transmit it to the county recorder.

(d) The county recorder shall record the bond and shall thereafter mail, unless specified to the contrary, it to the person named in the instrument and, if no person is named, to the party leaving it for recording.

§ 8213.5. Change in location or address; notice.

A notary public shall notify the Secretary of State by certified mail within 30 days as to any change in the location or address of the principal place of business.

§ 8214. Misconduct or neglect.

For the official misconduct or neglect of a notary public, the notary public and the sureties on the notary public's official bond are liable in a civil action to the persons injured thereby for all the damages sustained.

§ 8214.1. Grounds for refusal, revocation or suspension of commission.

The Secretary of State may refuse to appoint any person as notary public or may revoke or suspend the commission of any notary public upon any of the following grounds.

(a) Substantial and material misstatement or omission in the application submitted to the Secretary of State.

(b) Conviction of a felony or of a lesser offense involving moral turpitude or of a nature incompatible with the duties of a notary public. A conviction after a plea of nolo contendere is deemed to be a conviction within the meaning of this subdivision.

(c) Revocation, suspension, restriction, or denial of a professional license, if such revocation, suspen-

sion, restriction, or denial was for misconduct, dishonesty, or any cause substantially relating to the duties or responsibilities of a notary public.

(d) Failure to fully and faithfully discharge any of the duties or responsibilities required of a notary public.

(e) When adjudged liable for damages in any suit grounded in fraud, misrepresentation or violation of the state regulatory laws or in any suit based upon a failure to discharge fully and faithfully the duties as a notary public.

(f) The use of false or misleading advertising wherein the notary public has represented that the notary public has duties, rights or privileges that he or she does not possess by law.

(g) The practice of law in violation of Section 6125 of the Business and Professions Code.

(h) Charging more than the fees prescribed by this chapter.

(i) Commission of any act involving dishonesty, fraud, or deceit with the intent to substantially benefit the notary public or another, or substantially injure another.

(j) Failure to complete the acknowledgment at the time the notary's signature and seal are affixed to the document.

(k) Failure to administer the oath or affirmation as required by paragraph (3) of subdivision (a) of Section 8205.

(l) Execution of any certificate as a notary public containing a statement known to the notary public to be false.

(m) Violation of Section 8223.

§ 8214.2. Fraud relating to deed of trust; single-family residence; felony.

A notary public who knowingly and willfully with intent to defraud performs any notarial act in relation to a deed of trust on real property consisting of a single-family residence containing not more than four dwelling units, with knowledge that the deed of trust contains any false statements or is forged in whole or in part, is guilty of a felony.

§ 8214.3. Hearing prior to revocation, suspension or denial of commission; law governing; exceptions.

Prior to a revocation or suspension pursuant to this chapter or after a denial of a commission, the person affected shall have a right to a hearing on the matter and the proceeding shall be conducted in accordance with Chapter 5 (commencing with Section 11500) of Part 1 of Division 3 * * * , except that a person shall not have a right to a hearing after a denial of an application for a notary public commission in either of the following cases:

(a) The Secretary of State has, within one year

previous to the application, and after proceedings conducted in accordance with * * * Chapter 5 (commencing with Section 11500) of Part 1 of Division 3 * * * , denied or revoked the applicant's application or commission.

(b) The Secretary of State has entered an order pursuant to Section 8214.4 finding that the applicant has committed or omitted acts constituting grounds for suspension or revocation of a notary public's commission.

§ **8214.4.** Resignation or expiration of commission not a bar to investigation or disciplinary proceedings.

Notwithstanding * * * this chapter or Chapter 5 (commencing with Section 11500) of Part 1 of Division 3 * * * , if the Secretary of State determines, after proceedings conducted in accordance with * * * Chapter 5 (commencing with Section 11500) of Part 1 of Division 3 * * * , that any notary public has committed or omitted acts constituting grounds for suspension or revocation of a notary public's commission, the resignation or expiration of the notary public's commission shall not bar the Secretary of State from instituting or continuing an investigation or instituting disciplinary proceedings. Upon completion of the disciplinary proceedings, the Secretary of State shall enter an order finding the facts and stating the conclusion that the facts would or would not have constituted grounds for suspension or revocation of the commission if the commission had still been in effect.

§ **8214.5.** Revocation of commission; filing copy with county clerk.

Whenever the Secretary of State revokes the commission of any notary public, the Secretary of State shall file with the county clerk of the county in which the notary public's principal place of business is located a copy of the revocation. The county clerk shall note such revocation and its date upon the original record of such certificate.

§ **8216.** Release of surety.

When a surety of a notary desires to be released from responsibility on account of future acts, * * * the release shall be pursuant to Article 11 (commencing with Section 996.110), and not by cancellation or withdrawal pursuant to Article 13 (commencing with Section 996.310), of Chapter 2 of Title 14 of Part 2 of the Code of Civil Procedure. For this purpose the surety shall make application to the superior court of the county in which the notary public's principal place of business is located and the copy of the application and notice of hearing shall be served on the Secretary of State as the beneficiary.

§ **8219.5.** Advertising in language other than English; posting of notice relating to legal advice and fees; translation of notary public into Spanish; suspension.

(a) Every notary public who is not an attorney who advertises the services of a notary public in a language other than English by signs or other means of written communication, with the exception of a single desk plaque, shall post with such advertisement a notice in English and in the other language which sets forth the following:

(1) This statement: I am not an attorney and, therefore, cannot give legal advice.

(2) The fees set by statute which a notary public may charge.

(b) The notice required by subdivision (a) shall be printed and posted as prescribed by the Secretary of State.

(c) Literal translation of the phrase "notary public" into Spanish is prohibited. For purposes of this subdivision, "literal translation" of a word or phrase from one language to another means the translation of a word or phrase without regard to the true meaning of the word or phrase in the language which is being translated.

(d) The Secretary of State shall suspend for a period of not less than one year or revoke the commission of any notary public who fails to comply with subdivision (a), provided, however, that on the third offense the license of such notary public shall be revoked permanently.

§ **8220.** Rules and regulations.

The Secretary of State may adopt rules and regulations to carry out the provisions of this chapter.

The regulations shall be adopted in accordance with the Administrative Procedure Act, Chapter 4.5 (commencing with Section 11371) of Part 1 of Division 3 of this title.

§ **8221.** Destruction, defacement or concealment of records or papers; misdemeanor; liability for damages.

If any person shall knowingly destroy, deface, or conceal any records or papers belonging to the office of a notary public, such person shall be guilty of a misdemeanor and be liable in a civil action for damages to any person injured as a result of such destruction, defacing, or concealment.

§ 8222. Injunction; reimbursement for expenses.

(a) Whenever it * * * appears to the Secretary of State that any person has engaged or is about to engage in any acts or practices which constitute or will constitute a violation of any provision of this chapter or any rule or regulation prescribed under the authority thereof, the Secretary of State may apply for an injunction, and upon a proper showing, any court of competent jurisdiction * * * has power to issue a permanent or temporary injunction or restraining order * * * to enforce the provisions of this chapter, and any party to * * * the action * * * has the right to prosecute an appeal from the order or judgment of the court.

(b) The court may order a person subject to an injunction or restraining order provided for in this section to reimburse the Secretary of State for expenses incurred in the investigation related to the petition. The Secretary of State shall refund any amount received as reimbursement should the injunction or restraining order be dissolved by an appellate court.

§ 8223. Notary public with expertise in immigration matters; prohibition against advertising status as notary public; change in immigration status; fee.

No notary public who holds himself or herself out as being an immigration specialist, immigration consultant or any other title or description reflecting an expertise in immigration matters shall advertise in any manner whatsoever that he or she is a notary public.

The fee of a notary public, exclusive of signature verification, shall not exceed ten dollars ($10) per individual for each set of forms relating to a change of that individual's immigration status. This fee limitation shall apply whether the notary is acting in his or her capacity as a notary or not but shall not apply to an attorney, who is also a notary public, who is rendering professional services regarding immigration matters.

§ 8224. Conflict of interest; financial or beneficial interest in transaction; exceptions.

A notary public who has a direct financial or beneficial interest in a transaction shall not perform any notarial act in connection with such transaction.

For purposes of this section, a notary public has a direct financial or beneficial interest in a transaction if the notary public:

(a) With respect to a financial transaction, is named, individually, as a principal to the transaction.

(b) With respect to real property, is named, individually, as a grantor, grantee, mortgagor, mortgagee, trustor, trustee, beneficiary, vendor, vendee, lessor, or lessee, to the transaction.

For purposes of this section, a notary public has no direct financial or beneficial interest in a transaction where the notary public acts in the capacity of an agent, employee, insurer, attorney, escrow, or lender for a person having a direct financial or beneficial interest in the transaction.

§ 8224.1. Writings, depositions or affidavits of notary public; prohibitions against proof or taking by that notary public.

A notary public shall not take the acknowledgment or proof of instruments of writing executed by the notary public nor shall depositions or affidavits of the notary public be taken by the notary public.

§ 8225. Improper notarial acts, solicitation, coercion or influence of performance; misdemeanor.

Any person who solicits, coerces, or in any manner influences a notary public to perform an improper notarial act knowing such act to be an improper notarial act shall be guilty of a misdemeanor.

§ 8227.1. Unlawful acts by one not a notary public; misdemeanor.

It shall be a misdemeanor for any person who is not a duly commissioned, qualified, and acting notary public for the State of California to do any of the following:

(a) Represent or hold himself or herself out to the public or to any person as being entitled to act as a notary public.

(b) Assume, use or advertise the title of notary public in such a manner as to convey the impression that the person is a notary public.

(c) Purports to act as a notary public.

§ 8227.3. Unlawful acts by one not a notary public; deeds of trust on a single-family residence; felony.

Any person who is not a duly commissioned, qualified, and acting notary public who does any of the acts prohibited by Section 8227.1 in relation to any document or instrument affecting title to, placing an encumbrance on, or placing an interest secured by a mortgage or deed or trust on, real property consisting of a single-family residence containing not more than four dwelling units, is guilty of a felony.

§ 8228. Enforcement of chapter; examination of notarial books, records, etc.

The Secretary of State may enforce the provisions of this chapter through the examination of a notary public's books, records, letters, contracts, and other pertinent documents relating to the official acts of the notary public.

§ 8230. Identification of affiant; verification.

If a notary public executes a jurat and the statement sworn or subscribed to is contained in a document purporting to identify the affiant, and includes the birthdate or age of the person and a purported photograph or finger or thumbprint of the person so swearing or subscribing, the notary public shall require, as a condition to executing the jurat, that the person verify the birthdate or age contained in the statement by showing either:

(a) A certified copy of the person's birth certificate, or

(b) An identification card or driver's license issued by the Department of Motor Vehicles.

For the purposes of preparing for submission of forms required by the United States Immigration and Naturalization Service, and only for such purposes, a notary public may also accept for identification any documents or declarations acceptable to the United States Immigration and Naturalization Service.

FEES

§ 12197.1. Application and fee; use of funds.

The Secretary of State shall establish by regulation an application, examination, and commission fee which shall be sufficient to cover the costs of commissioning notaries public and the enforcement of laws governing notaries public. The fee shall not exceed fifty dollars ($50) per commission. It is the intention of the Legislature that these funds, which are to be deposited in the General Fund, shall be used to support the notary public program to the extent that appropriations are made in the Budget Act from year to year.

[DEPOSITIONS]

[CAL. CODE OF CIVIL PROCEDURE]

§ 2025. Oral depositions; protective orders; sanctions; audio or video tapes; stenographic transcripts; use of depositions at trial or hearing.

* * *

(k) Except as provided in paragraph (3) of subdivision (d) of Section 2020, the deposition shall be conducted under the supervision of an officer who is authorized to administer an oath. This officer shall not be financially interested in the action and shall not be a relative or employee of any attorney of any of the parties. Any objection to the qualifications of the deposition officer is waived unless made before the deposition begins or as soon thereafter as the ground for that objection becomes known or could be discovered by reasonable diligence.

* * *

§ 2026. Oral depositions in another state or territory of the United States.

* * *

(c) A deposition taken under this section shall be conducted (1) under the supervision of a person who is authorized to administer oaths by the laws of the United States or those of the place where the examination is to be held, and who is not otherwise disqualified under subdivision (k) of Section 2025, or (2) before a person appointed by the court. This appointment is effective to authorize that person to administer oaths and to take testimony. When necessary or convenient, the court shall issue a commission on such terms and with such directions as are just and appropriate.

§ 2027. Oral deposition in a foreign nation.

* * *

(c) A deposition taken under this section shall be conducted (1) under the supervision of a person who is authorized to administer oaths or their equivalent by the laws of the United States or of the foreign nation, and who is not otherwise disqualified under subdivision (k) of Section 2025, or (2) a person or officer appointed by commission or under letters rogatory; or (3) any person agreed to by all the parties.

§ 2093. Officers authorized to administer oaths or affirmations.

(a) Every court, every judge, or clerk of any court, every justice, and every notary public, and every officer or person authorized to take testimony in any action or proceeding, or to decide upon evidence, has the power to administer oaths or affirmations.

* * *

§ **2094.** Oath to witness; form.

An oath, or affirmation, in an action or proceeding, may be administered as follows, the person who swears, or affirms, expressing his assent when addressed in the following form: "You do solemnly swear (or affirm, as the case may be), that the evidence you shall give in this issue (or matter), pending between _____ and _____, shall be the truth, the whole truth, and nothing but the truth, so help you God."

§ **2095.** Oath to witness; variation to suit belief of witness.

FORM MAY BE VARIED TO SUIT WITNESS' BELIEF. Whenever the court before which a person is offered as a witness is satisfied that he has a peculiar mode of swearing, connected with or in addition to the usual form of administration, which, in his opinion, is more solemn or obligatory, the court may, in its discretion, adopt that mode.

§ **2096.** Oath to witness; admininstration according to ceremonies of his religion. SAME.

When a person is sworn who believes in any other than the Christian religion, he may be sworn according to the peculiar ceremonies of his religion, if there be any such.

§ **2097.** Oath to witness; option to declare or affirm.

ANY PERSON WHO PREFERS IT MAY DECLARE OR AFFIRM. Any person who desires it may, at his option, instead of taking an oath make his solemn affirmation or declaration, by assenting, when addressed, in the following form: "You do solemnly affirm (or declare) that," etc., as in Section 2094.

LEGAL HOLIDAYS

[CAL. GOV'T CODE]

§ **6700.** State holidays; memorandum of understanding; altered holiday.

The holidays in this state are:
(a) Every Sunday.
(b) January 1st.
(c) The third Monday in January, known as "Dr. Martin Luther King, Jr. Day."
(d) February 12th, known as "Lincoln Day."
(e) The third Monday in February.
(f) The last Monday in May.
(g) July 4th.

(h) The first Monday in September.
(i) September 9th, known as "Admission Day."
(j) The second Monday in October, known as "Columbus Day."
(k) November 11th, known as "Veterans Day."
(l) December 25th.
(m) Good Friday from 12 noon until 3 p.m.
(n) Every day appointed by the President or Governor for a public fast, thanksgiving, or holiday.

Except for the Thursday in November appointed as Thanksgiving Day, this subdivision and subdivision (c) shall not apply to a city, county, or district unless made applicable by charter, or by ordinance or resolution of the governing body thereof.

If the provisions of this section are in conflict with the provisions of a memorandum of understanding reached pursuant to Chapter 12 (commencing with Section 3560) of Division 4 of Title 1, the memorandum of understanding shall be controlling without further legislative action, except that if those provisions of a memorandum of understanding require the expenditure of funds, the provisions shall not become effective unless approved by the Legislature in the annual Budget Act.

§ **6701.** Holidays falling on Saturdays and Sundays.

If January 1st, February 12th, July 4th, September 9th, November 11th, or December 25th falls upon a Sunday, the Monday following is a holiday. If November 11th falls upon a Saturday, the preceding Friday is a holiday.

If any holiday designated in Section 6700 falls on a Saturday, the board of supervisors of any county may by ordinance or resolution provide that an alternate day shall be a holiday for the employees of the county, except those employees of the county working as court attaches or as clerks of the superior, municipal, or justice courts * * *

§ **6702.** Saturday half-holiday; closing city offices on holidays.

Every Saturday from noon to midnight is a holiday as regards the transaction of business in the public offices of the state and political divisions where laws, ordinances, or charters provide that public offices shall be closed on holidays. This section shall not be construed to prevent or invalidate the issuance, filing, service, execution, or recording of any legal process or written instrument during such period. Public offices of a city shall be closed on those holidays enumerated in Section 6700 unless otherwise provided by charter, ordinance or resolution.

COLORADO

NOTARIES PUBLIC

[COLO. REV. STAT. ANN.]

§ 12-55-101. Short title.

This part 1 shall be known and may be cited as the "Notaries Public Act".

§ 12-55-102. Definitions.

As used in this part 1, unless the context otherwise requires:

(1) "Notarial acts" means those acts which the laws and regulations of this state authorize notaries public to perform including, but not limited to, administering oaths and affirmations, taking proof of execution and acknowledgments of instruments, and attesting documents.

(2) "Notarization" means the performance of a notarial act.

(3) "Notary" or "notary public" means any individual appointed and commissioned to perform notarial acts.

§ 12-55-103. Appointment — terms.

Upon application pursuant to this part 1, the secretary of state may appoint and commission individuals as notaries public for a term of four years, unless said commission is revoked as provided in section 12-55-107. An applicant who has been denied appointment and commission may appeal such decision pursuant to article 4 of title 24, C.R.S. The secretary of state shall promptly notify the applicant in writing of such denial.

§ 12-55-104. Application.

(1) Every applicant for appointment and commission as a notary public shall complete an application form furnished by the secretary of state to be

filed with the secretary of state, stating:

(a) If he is a citizen of the United States, that he is a qualified elector of this state at the time of his appointment;

(b) That he is able to read and write the English language;

(c) The addresses and telephone numbers of his business and residence in this state;

(d) That his commission as a notary public has never been revoked;

(e) That he has not been convicted of a felony.

(2) The application shall include a handwritten sample of the applicant's official signature, which contains his surname and at least the initial of his first name, and the affirmation as provided in section 12-55-105.

§ 12-55-105. Applicant's affirmation.

Every applicant for appointment and commission as a notary public shall take the following affirmation in the presence of a person qualified to administer an affirmation in this state:

"I, ____(name of applicant)____ solemnly affirm, under the penalty of perjury in the second degree, as defined in section 18-8-503, Colorado Revised Statutes, that I have carefully read the notary law of this state, and, if appointed and commissioned as a notary public, I will faithfully perform, to the best of my ability, all notarial acts in conformance with the law.

_____
                 (signature of applicant)

Subscribed and affirmed before me this _____ day of _____, 19__.

_____
    (official signature and seal of person qualified to administer affirmation)   ."

§ 12-55-106. Bond.

Every applicant for appointment and commission as a notary public shall submit to the secretary of state, together with his application, an executed bond covering his term of commission in the sum of five thousand dollars, with, as surety thereon, a company qualified to write surety bonds in this state. The bond shall be conditioned upon the faithful performance of all notarial acts in accordance with this article.

§ 12-55-107. Revocation of commission.

(1) The secretary of state may deny the application of any person for appointment or reappointment, or revoke the commission of any notary public during his term of appointment if the notary public:

(a) Submits an application for commission and

appointment which contains substantial and material misstatement or omission of fact;

(b) Is convicted of official misconduct under the provisions of this part 1 or any felony;

(c) Fails to exercise the powers or perform the duties of a notary public in accordance with this part 1;

(d) Knowingly uses false or misleading advertising in which he represents that he has powers, duties, rights, or privileges that he does not possess by law;

(e) Is found by a court of this state to have engaged in the unauthorized practice of law;

(f) Ceases to fulfill the requirements applicable to his most recent appointment.

(2) A notary's commission may be revoked under the provisions of this part 1 only if action is taken pursuant to article 4 of title 24, C.R.S.

(3) After a notary public receives notice from the secretary of state that his commission has been revoked, and unless such revocation has been enjoined, such notary shall immediately send by certified mail or have delivered to the secretary of state his journal of notarial acts, all other papers and copies relating to his notarial acts, and his official seal.

§ 12-55-108. Reappointment — failure to be reappointed.

Every notary public, before or at the expiration of his commission, may submit an application for reappointment by submitting the same information, documents, and executed bond as required by sections 12-55-104 to 12-55-106 for the initial application. The secretary of state shall then determine whether the person shall be reappointed as notary public. If the secretary of state determines he shall not be reappointed, the applicant may appeal such determination pursuant to article 4 of title 24, C.R.S.

§ 12-55-109. Certificate of appointment — recording.

(1) The secretary of state is authorized to issue a certificate of authority qualifying said person as a notary public. The certificate shall also state the date of expiration of the commission and any other fact concerning such notary public which is required by the laws of this state.

(2) A notary public may record his certificate of authority in any county of this state and, after such recording, the county clerk and recorder of such county may issue a certificate that such person is a notary public, the date of expiration of his commission, and any other fact concerning such notary public which is required by the laws of this state.

(3) A notary public may exhibit to the judge or clerk of any court of record his certificate of authority, and the said judge or clerk may thereupon issue a certificate that such person is a notary public, the date of expiration of his commission, and any other fact concerning such notary which is required by the laws of this state.

§ 12-55-110. Powers and limitations.

(1) Every notary public is empowered to:

(a) Take acknowledgments;

(b) Administer oaths and affirmations;

(c) Certify that a copy of a document is a true copy of another document;

(d) Take depositions; and

(e) Perform any other act permitted by law.

(2) A notary public who has a disqualifying interest in a transaction may not legally perform any notarial act in connection with such transaction. For the purposes of this section, a notary public has a disqualifying interest in a transaction in connection with which notarial services are requested if he:

(a) May receive directly, and as a proximate result of the notarization, any advantage, right, title, interest, cash, or property exceeding in value the sum of any fee properly received in accordance with this part 1; or

(b) Is named, individually, as a party to the transaction.

§ 12-55-111. Journal.

Every notary public shall keep a journal of every acknowledgment taken by him to an instrument affecting the title to real property and, if required, give a certified copy of or a certificate as to any such journal or any of his acts, upon payment of his fee therefor.

§ 12-55-112. Official signature — rubber stamp seal — seal embosser.

(1) At the time of notarization, a notary public shall sign his official signature on every notary acknowledgment.

(2) Under or near his official signature on every notary acknowledgment, a notary public shall rubber stamp or emboss clearly and legibly his official seal. The official notary seal shall contain only the outline of the seal, the name of the notary, exactly as he writes his official signature, the words "STATE OF COLORADO," and the words "NOTARY PUBLIC."

(3) Under of near his official signature on every notary acknowledgment, a notary public shall write or stamp "my commission expires (commission expiration date)".

(4) Every notary public may provide, keep, and use a seal embosser engraved to show his name and the words "NOTARY PUBLIC" and "STATE OF COLORADO." The indentations made by the seal embosser shall not be applied on the notary acknowledgment or document to be notarized in a manner that will render illegible or incapable of photographic reproduction any of the printed marks or writing.

(5) The illegibility of any of the information required by this section does not affect the validity of a transaction.

§ 12-55-113. Lost journal or official seal.

Every notary public shall send by certified mail or have delivered notice to the secretary of state within thirty days after he loses or misplaces his journal of notarial acts or official seal. The fee payable to the secretary of state for recording notice of a lost journal or seal shall be determined and collected pursuant to section 24-21-104(3), C.R.S.

§ 12-55-114. Change of name or address.

(1) Every notary public shall send by certified mail or have delivered notice to the secretary of state within thirty days after he changes the address of his business or residence in this state. The fee payable to the secretary of state for recording notice of change of address shall be determined and collected pursuant to section 24-21-104(3), C.R.S.

(2) Every notary public shall send by certified mail or have delivered notice to the secretary of state within thirty days after he changes his name, including with the notification a sample of his handwritten official signature which contains his surname and at least the initial of his first name. The fee payable to the secretary of state for recording notice of change of notary's name shall be determined and collected pursuant to section 24-21-104(3), C.R.S.

§ 12-55-115. Death — resignation — removal from state.

(1) If a notary public dies during the term of his appointment, his heirs or personal representative, as soon as reasonably possible after the notary's death, shall send by certified mail or have delivered to the secretary of state the deceased notary's journal of notarial acts and his seal, if available.

(2) If a notary public no longer desires to be a notary public or has ceased to have a business or residence address in this state, he shall send by certified mail or have delivered to the secretary of state a letter of resignation, his journal of notarial acts, and all other papers and copies relating to his no-

tarial acts, including his seal. His commission shall thereafter cease to be in effect.

§ 12-55-116. Official misconduct by a notary public — liability of notary or surety.

(1) A notary public who knowingly and willfully violates the duties imposed by this part 1 commits official misconduct and is guilty of a class 2 misdemeanor.

(2) A notary public and the surety or sureties on his bond are liable to the persons involved for all damages proximately caused by the notary's official misconduct.

§ 12-55-117. Willful impersonation.

Any person who acts as, or otherwise willfully impersonates, a notary public while not lawfully appointed and commissioned to perform notarial acts is guilty of a class 2 misdemeanor.

§ 12-55-118. Wrongful possession of journal or seal.

Any person who unlawfully possesses and uses a notary's journal, an official seal, or any papers or copies relating to notarial acts is guilty of a class 3 misdemeanor.

§ 12-55-119. Affirmation procedures — form.

If an affirmation is to be administered by the notary public in writing, the person taking the affirmation shall sign his name thereto, and the notary public shall write or print under the text of the affirmation the fact that the document has been subscribed and affirmed, or sworn to before me in the county of _____, state of Colorado, this _____ day of _____, 19___.

_____(official signature, seal, and commission expiration date of notary)_____ .

§ 12-55-120. Certified facsimiles of documents — procedure and form.

(1) A notary public may certify a facsimile of a document if the original of the document is exhibited to him, together with a signed written request stating that:

(a) A certified copy or facsimile of the document cannot be obtained from the office of any clerk and recorder of public documents or custodian of documents in this state; and

(b) The production of a facsimile, preparation of a copy, or certification of a copy of the document does not violate any state or federal law.

(2) The certification of a facsimile shall be substantially in the following form:

"State of _____, County (or City) of _____, I, _____(name of notary)_____, a Notary Public in and for said state, do certify that on _____(date)_____, I carefully compared with the original the attached facsimile of _____(type of document)_____ and the facsimile I now hold in my possession. They are complete, full, true, and exact facsimiles of the document they purport to reproduce.

_____(official signature, official seal, and commission expiration date of notary)_____."

§ 12-55-121. Fees.

The fees of notaries public may be, but shall not exceed, two dollars for each acknowledgment, except as otherwise provided by law. Notaries public shall administer the absent voter's oath, as described in section 1-8-115, C.R.S., for any voter requesting to make said affidavit, and no notary shall make any charge whatsoever for administering such oath.

§ 12-55-122. Applicability.

This part 1 shall apply to all applications, both new and for reappointment, submitted to the office of secretary of state on or after July 1, 1981. Nothing in this part 1 shall be construed to revoke any notary public commission existing on July 1, 1981.

§ 12-55-123. Termination of functions.

The appointment function of the secretary of state as set forth in this article it terminated on July 1, 1992. Prior to such termination, the appointment function shall be reviewed as provided for in section 24-34-104, C.R.S.

ADDITIONAL AUTHORITY

§ 24-12-103. Oaths administered by whom.

All courts in this state and each judge, justice, clerk, and any deputy clerk thereof, members and referees of the division of labor, members of the public utilities commission, and all notaries public shall have power to administer oaths and affirmations to witnesses and others concerning any matter, thing, process, or proceeding pending, commenced, or to be commenced before them respectively. Such courts, judges, clerks, and deputy clerks within their respective districts or counties, and notaries public within any county of this state, shall have the power to administer all oaths of office and other oaths required to be taken by any person upon any lawful occasion and to take affidavits and depositions concerning any matter or thing, process, or proceeding pending, commenced, or to be commenced in any court or on any occasion wherein such affidavit or deposition is authorized or by law required to be taken.

§ 24-12-104. Officers in armed forces empowered to perform notarial acts.

(1) In addition to the acknowledgment of instruments and the performance of other notarial acts in the manner and form and as otherwise authorized by law, instruments may be acknowledged, documents attested, oaths and affirmations administered, depositions and affidavits executed, and other notarial acts performed before or by any commissioned officer in active service of the armed forces of the United States with the rank of second lieutenant or higher in the army or marine corps, or with the rank of ensign or higher in the navy or coast guard, or with equivalent rank in any other component part of the armed forces of the United States, by or for any person who is a member of the armed forces of the United States, or is serving as a merchant seaman outside the limits of the United States included within the fifty states and the District of Columbia, or is outside said limits by permission, assignment, or direction of any department or official of the United States government, in connection with any activity pertaining to the prosecution of any war in which the United States is then engaged.

(2) Such acknowledgment of instruments, attestation of documents, administration of oaths and affirmations, execution of depositions and affidavits, and performance of other notarial acts, whenever made or taken, are hereby declared legal, valid, and binding, and instruments and documents so acknowledged, authenticated, or sworn to shall be admissible in evidence and eligible to record in this state under the same circumstances and with the same force and effect as if such acknowledgment, attestation, oath, affirmation, deposition, affidavit, or other notarial act had been made or taken within this state before or by a duly qualified officer or official as otherwise provided by law.

(3) In the taking of acknowledgments and the performing of other notarial acts requiring certification, a certificate indorsed upon or attached to the instrument or document which shows the date of the notarial act and which states, in substance, that the person appearing before the officer acknowledged the instrument as his act or made or signed the instrument or document under oath, shall be sufficient for all intents and purposes. The instrument or document shall not be rendered invalid by the failure to state the place of execution or acknowledgment.

(4) If the signature, rank, and branch of service or subdivision thereof, of any such commissioned officer appears upon such instrument or document or certificate, no further proof of the authority of such officer

so to act shall be required and such action by such commissioned officer shall be prima facie evidence that the person making such oath or acknowledgment is within the purview of this section.

(5) If any instrument is acknowledged substantially as provided in this section, whether such acknowledgment has been taken before or after February 27, 1943, such acknowledgment shall be prima facie evidence of proper execution of such instrument and shall carry with it the presumptions provided for by section 38-35-101, C.R.S. 1973.

ACKNOWLEDGMENTS

§ 38-30-126. Acknowledgments, before whom taken.

(1) Deeds, bonds, and agreements in writing conveying lands or any interest therein, or affecting title thereto, may be acknowledged or proved before the following officers when executed within this state:

(a) Any judge of any court of record, the clerk of any such court of record, or the deputy of any such clerk, such judge, clerk, or deputy clerk certifying such acknowledgment under the seal of such court;

(b) The clerk and recorder of any county, or his deputy, such clerk or deputy clerk certifying the same under the seal of such county;

(c) Any notary public, certifying the same under his notarial seal; or

(d) Prior to the second Tuesday in January, 1965, any justice of the peace within his county, except that if such deed, bond, or agreement is for the conveyance of lands situated beyond the county of such justice of the peace, there shall be affixed to his certificate of such acknowledgment a certificate of the county clerk and recorder of the proper county, under his hand and the seal of such county, as to the official capacity of such justice of the peace, and that the signature to such certificate of acknowledgment is the true signature of such justice.

(2) When executed out of this state, and within the United States or any territory thereof, before:

(a) The secretary of any such state or territory, certifying such acknowledgment under the seal of such state or territory;

(b) The clerk of any court of record of such state or territory, or of the United States within such state or territory, having a seal, such clerk certifying the acknowledgement under the seal of such court;

(c) Any notary public of such state or territory, certifying the same under his notarial seal;

(d) Any commissioner of deeds for any such foreign state or territory appointed under the laws of this state, certifying such acknowledgment under his hand and official seal;

(e) Any other officer authorized by the laws of any such state or territory to take and certify such acknowledgment if there is affixed to the certificate of such officer, other than those above enumerated, a certificate by the clerk of some court of record of the county, city, or district, wherein such officer resides, under the seal of such court, that the person certifying such acknowledgment is the officer he assumes to be, that he has the authority by the laws of such state or territory to take and certify such acknowledgment, and that the signature of such officer to the certificate of acknowledgment is the true signature of such officer.

(3) When executed or acknowledged out of the United States, before:

(a) Any judge, or clerk, or deputy clerk of any court of record of any foreign kingdom, empire, republic, state, principality, province, colony, island possession, or bailiwick, such judge, clerk, or deputy clerk certifying such acknowledgment under the seal of such court;

(b) The chief magistrate or other chief executive officer of any province, colony, island possession, or bailiwick or the mayor or the chief executive officer of any city, town, borough, county, or municipal corporation having a seal, of such foreign kingdom, empire, republic, state, principality, province, colony, island possession, or bailiwick, such chief magistrate or other chief executive officer or such mayor certifying such acknowledgment under such seal; or

(c) Any ambassador, minister, consul, vice-consul, consular agent, vice-consular agent, charge d'affaires, vice-charge d'affaires, commercial agent, vice-commercial agent, or diplomatic, consular, or commercial agent or representative or duly constituted deputy of any thereof of the United States or of any other government or country appointed to reside in the foreign country or place where the proof of acknowledgment is made, he certifying the same under the seal of his office.

(4) When executed or acknowledged out of the state and within any colony, island possession, or bailiwick belonging to or under the control of the United States, before:

(a) Any judge or clerk or deputy clerk of any court of record of such colony, island possession, or bailiwick, such judge, clerk, or deputy clerk certifying such acknowledgment under the seal of such court;

(b) The chief magistrate or other chief executive officer of any such colony, island possession, or bailiwick, he certifying the same under his official seal, or before the mayor or the chief executive officer of any city, town, borough, county, or municipal corporation having a seal, of such colony, island possession, or bailiwick, such mayor or other chief officer certifying such acknowledgment under his official seal; or

(c) Any notary public within such colony, island possession, or bailiwick, such notary public certifying such acknowledgment under his seal.

§ 38-30-127. Acknowledgments by persons in armed forces.

In addition to the acknowledgment of instruments as provided by articles 30 to 44 of this title, instruments may be acknowledged by members of the armed forces of the United States and certain other persons, as provided by section 24-12-104.

§ 38-30-129. Clerk of U. S. courts may take acknowledgments.

Deeds, bonds, and agreements in writing, conveying lands or any interest therein, or affecting title thereto, may be acknowledged or proved before any clerk of the circuit or district court of the United States, for the district of Colorado, or any deputy of such clerk; such clerk certifying such acknowledgment under the seal of such court respectively.

§ 38-30-135. Officer shall subscribe certificate.

Every certificate of the acknowledgment or proof of any deed, bond, agreement, power of attorney, or other writing for the conveyance of real estate, or any interest therein or affecting title thereto, shall be subscribed by the officer certifying the same with his proper hand and shall be endorsed upon or attached to such deed or other writing.

§ 38-30-136. Subsequent proof of execution — proof or acknowledgment of copy.

(1) When any deed or instrument of writing has been executed and not acknowledged according to law at the time of the execution thereof, such deed or instrument of writing may at any subsequent time be acknowledged by the makers thereof in the manner provided in this article, or proof may be made of the execution thereof before any officer authorized to take acknowledgments of deeds in the manner provided in this section. Such officer, when the fact is not within his own knowledge, shall ascertain from the testimony of at least one competent, credible witness, to be sworn and examined by him, that the person offering to prove the execution of such deed or writing is a subscribing witness thereto. Thereupon such officer shall examine such subscribing witness upon oath or affirmation, and shall reduce his testimony to writing and require the witness to subscribe the same, endorsed upon or attached to such deed or other writing, and shall thereupon grant a certificate that such witness was personally known or was proved to him by the testimony of at least one witness (who shall be named in such certificate) to be a subscribing witness to the deed or instrument of writing to be proved,

that such subscribing witness was lawfully sworn and examined by him, and that the testimony of the said officer was reduced to writing and by said subscribing witness subscribed in his presence.

(2) If by the testimony it appears that such witness saw the person, whose name is subscribed to such instrument of writing, sign, seal, and deliver the same or that such person afterwards acknowledged the same to the said witness to be his free and voluntary act or deed and that such witness subscribed the said deed or instrument of writing in attestation thereof, in the presence and with the consent of the person so executing the same, such proof if attested and the authority of the officer to take the same duly proved in the same manner as required in the case of acknowledgment, shall have the same force and effect as an acknowledgment of said deed or instrument of writing by the person executing the same, and duly certified.

(3) When any such deed or instrument of writing has been executed and recorded without due proof, attestation or acknowledgment as required by law, a certified copy from such record may be proved or acknowledged in the same manner and with like effect as the original thereof. No person shall be permitted to use such certified copy so proved as evidence except upon satisfactory proof that the original thereof has been lost or destroyed or is beyond his power to produce.

§ 38-35-103. Acknowledgment before notary.

In addition to the officers now empowered by law to take acknowledgments within or without the United States, deeds and other instruments in writing may be acknowledged before any notary public having a notarial seal.

Uniform Recognition of Acknowledgments Act

§ 12-55-201. Short title.

This part 2 shall be known and may be cited as "Uniform Recognition of Acknowledgments Act".

§ 12-55-202. Definition.

As used in this part 2, unless the context otherwise requires:

(1) "Notarial acts" means acts which the laws and regulations of this state authorize notaries public of this state to perform, including, but not limited to, the administering of oaths and affirmations, taking proof of execution and acknowledgments of instruments, and attesting documents.

§ 12-55-203. Recognition of notarial acts performed outside this state.

(1) Notarial acts may be performed outside this state for use in this state with the same effect as if performed by a notary public of this state by the following persons authorized pursuant to the laws and regulations of other governments, in addition to any other person authorized by the laws and regulations of this state:

(a) A notary public authorized to perform notarial acts in the place in which the act is performed;

(b) A judge, clerk, or deputy clerk of any court of record in the place in which the notarial act is performed;

(c) An officer of the foreign service of the United States, a consular agent, or any other person authorized by regulation of the United States department of state to perform notarial acts in the place in which the act is performed;

(d) A commissioned officer in active service with the armed forces of the United States and any other person authorized by regulation of the armed forces to perform notarial acts if the notarial act is performed for one of the following or his dependents: A merchant seaman of the United States, a member of the armed forces of the United States, or any other person serving with or accompanying the armed forces of the United States; or

(e) Any other person authorized to perform notarial acts in the place in which the act is performed.

§ 12-55-204. Authentication of authority of officer.

(1) If the notarial act is performed by any of the persons described in section 12-55-203 (1)(a) to (1)(d), other than a person authorized to perform notarial acts by the laws or regulations of a foreign country, the signature, rank, or title and serial number, if any, of the person are sufficient proof of the authority of a holder of that rank or title to perform the act. Further proof of his authority is not required.

(2) If the notarial act is performed by a person authorized by the laws or regulations of a foreign country to perform the act, there is sufficient proof of the authority of that person to act if:

(a) Either a foreign service officer of the United States resident in the country in which the act is performed or a diplomatic or consular officer of the foreign country resident in the United States certifies that a person holding that office is authorized to perform the act;

(b) The official seal of the person performing the notarial act is affixed to the document; or

(c) The title and indication of authority to perform notarial acts of the person appears either in a digest of foreign law or in a list customarily used as a source of such information.

(3) If the notarial act is performed by a person other than one described in subsections (1) and (2) of this section, there is sufficient proof of the authority of that person to act if the clerk of a court of record in the place in which the notarial act is performed certifies to the official character of that person and to his authority to perform the notarial act.

(4) The signature and title of the person performing the act are prima facie evidence that he is a person with the designated title and that the signature is genuine.

§ 12-55-205. Certificate of person taking acknowledgment.

(1) The person taking an acknowledgment shall certify that:

(a) The person acknowledging appeared before him and acknowledged he executed the instrument; and

(b) The person acknowledging was known to the person taking the acknowledgment or that the person taking the acknowledgment had satisfactory evidence that the person acknowledging was the person described in and who executed the instrument.

§ 12-55-206. Recognition of certificate of acknowledgment.

(1) The form of a certificate of acknowledgment used by a person whose authority is recognized under section 12-55-203 shall be accepted in this state if:

(a) The certificate is in a form prescribed by the laws or regulations of this state; or

(b) The certificate is in a form prescribed by the laws or regulations applicable in the place in which the acknowledgment is taken; or

(c) The certificate contains the words "acknowledged before me," or their substantial equivalent.

§ 12-55-207. Certificate of acknowledgment.

(1) "Acknowledged before me" means:

(a) That the person acknowledging appeared before the person taking the acknowledgment; and

(b) That he acknowledged he executed the instrument; and

(c) That, in the case of:

(I) A natural person, he executed the instrument for the purposes therein stated;

(II) A corporation, the officer or agent acknowledged he held the position or title set forth in the instrument and certificate, he signed the instrument on behalf of the corporation by proper authority, and the instrument was the act of the corporation for the purpose therein stated;

(III) A partnership, the partner or agent acknowl-

edged he signed the instrument on behalf of the partnership by proper authority and he executed the instrument as the act of the partnership for the purposes therein stated;

(IV) A person acknowledging as principal by an attorney in fact, he executed the instrument by proper authority as the act of the principal for the purposes therein stated;

(V) A person acknowledging as a public officer, trustee, administrator, guardian, or other representative, he signed the instrument by proper authority and he executed the instrument in the capacity and for the purposes therein stated; and

(d) That the person taking the acknowledgment either knew or had satisfactory evidence that the person acknowledging was the person named in the instrument or certificate.

§ 12-55-208. Short forms of acknowledgment.

(1) The forms of acknowledgment set forth in this section may be used and are sufficient for their respective purposes under any law of this state. The forms shall be known as "Statutory Short Forms of Acknowledgment" and may be referred to by that name. The authorization of the following forms does not preclude the use of other forms:

(a) For an individual acting in his own right:

"State of . . . .
County of . . . .
The foregoing instrument was acknowledged before me this (date) by (name of person acknowledged).

       (signature of person taking acknowledgment)
       (title or rank)
       (serial number, if any)";

(b) For a corporation:

"State of . . . .
County of . . . .
The foregoing instrument was acknowledged before me this (date) by (name of officer or agent, title of officer or agent) of (name of corporation acknowledging) a (state or place of incorporation) corporation, on behalf of the corporation.

       (signature of person taking acknowledgment)
       (title or rank)
       (serial number, if any)";

(c) For a partnership:

"State of . . . .
County of . . . .
The foregoing instrument was acknowledged before me this (date) by (name of acknowledging partner or agent), partner (or agent) on behalf of (name of partnership), a partnership.

(signature of person taking acknowledgment)

(title or rank)

(serial number, if any)";

(d) For an individual acting as principal by an attorney in fact:

"State of . . . .

County of . . . .

The foregoing instrument was acknowledged before me this (date) by (name of attorney-in-fact) as attorney in fact on behalf of (name of principal).

(signature of person taking acknowledgment)

(title or rank)

(serial number, if any)";

(e) By any public officer, trustee, or personal representative:

"State of . . . .

County of . . . .

The foregoing instrument was acknowledged before me this (date) by (name and title of position).

(signature or person taking acknowledgment)

(title or rank)

(serial number, if any)".

§ 12-55-209. Acknowledgments not affected by this part 2.

A notarial act performed prior to July 1, 1969, is not affected by this part 2. This part 2 provides an additional method of proving notarial acts. Nothing in this part 2 diminishes or invalidates the recognition accorded to notarial acts by other laws or regulations of this state.

§ 12-55-210. Uniformity of interpretation.

This part 2 shall be so interpreted as to make uniform the laws of those states which enact it.

DEPOSITIONS

[Colo. R. Civ. P.]

RULE 28. Person before whom depositions may be taken

(a) **Outside the State of Colorado.** Depositions outside the State of Colorado shall be taken only upon proof that notice to take deposition has been given as provided in these rules. The deposition shall be taken before an officer authorized to administer oaths by the laws of this state, the United States or the place where the examination is to be held, or before a person appointed by the court in which the action is pending. A person so appointed has the power to administer oaths and take testimony.

(b) **Disqualification for Interest.** No deposition shall be taken before a person who is a relative or employee of attorney or counsel of any of the parties, or is financially interested in the action.

(c) **Commission or Letter Rogatory.** A commission or letters rogatory shall be issued when necessary, on application and notice, and on terms that are just and appropriate. It is not a requisite to the issuance of a commission or letter rogatory that the taking of the deposition in any other manner is impracticable or inconvenient. Both a commission and letters rogatory may be issued in proper cases. Officers may be designated in the commission either by nam e or descriptive title. Letters rogatory may be add essed "to the appropriate authority in (here name the appropriate place)." The clerk shall issue a commission or letters rogatory in the form prescribed by the jurisdiction where the deposition is to be taken, such form to be prepared by the party seeking the deposition. The commission or letters rogatory shall inform the officer that the original sealed deposition shall be filed according to subsection (d) of this rule. Any error in the form or in the commission or letters rogatory is waived unless an objection is filed and served before the time fixed in the notice.

(d) **Filing of the Deposition.** The officer transcribing the deposition shall file the original sealed deposition pursuant to C.R.C.P. 30(f)(1).

COMMISSIONERS

[Colo. Rev. Stat. Ann.]

§ 38-30-130. Governor may appoint commissioners of deeds.

The governor may appoint and commission, in any other state, in the District of Columbia, in each of the territories of the United States, and in any foreign country one or more commissioners, who shall keep a seal of office and continue in office during the pleasure of the governor and shall have authority to take the acknowledgment or proof of the execution of any deed or other conveyance or lease of any lands lying in this state or of any contract, letters of attorney, or any other writing under seal, or note to be used and recorded in this state, and such commissioners appointed for any foreign country shall also have authority to certify to the official character, signature, or seal of any officer within their district who is authorized to take acknowledgments or declarations under oath.

§ 38-30-131. Oath of commissioner of deeds.

Every such commissioner, before performing any duty or exercising any power by virtue of his appointment, shall take and subscribe an oath or affirmation before a judge or clerk of one of the courts of record of the district, territory, state or country in which such commissioner shall reside, or before any ambassador, minister, consul or vice-consul, consular agent, vice-consular agent, charge d'affaires or any diplomatic, consular or commercial agent or representative of the United States appointed for the foreign state or country in which such commissioner resides, well and faithfully to execute and perform all the duties of such commissioner under and by virtue of the laws of the state of Colorado, which oath, and an impression of the seal of office, together with his signature thereto, shall be filed in the office of the secretary of state of this state within six months after the date of appointment.

§ 38-30-132. Effect of commissioner's acknowledgment.

Such acknowledgment or proof so taken according to the laws of this state, and certified by any such commissioner under his seal of office, annexed to or endorsed on such instrument, shall have the same force and effect as if the same has been made before a judge or any other officer authorized to perform such act in this state.

§ 38-30-133. Commissioner shall have power to administer oath.

Every commissioner shall have power to administer any oath, which may be lawfully required in this state, to any person willing to take it, and to take and certify all depositions to be used in any of the courts of this state, in conformity with the laws thereof, either on interrogations proposed under commission from a court of this state or by consent of parties, and all such acts shall be as valid as if done and certified according to law by a magistrate of this state.

§ 38-30-134. Fees of commissioners.

Commissioners for like services, shall be allowed the same fees as are allowed by law to notaries public of this state.

LEGAL HOLIDAYS

§ 24-11-101. Legal holidays — effect.

(1) The following days, viz: The first day of January, commonly called New Year's day; the third Monday in January, which shall be observed as the birthday of Dr. Martin Luther King, Jr.; the third Monday in February, commonly called Washington-Lincoln day; the last Monday in May, commonly called Memorial day; the fourth day of July, commonly called

Independence day; the first Monday in September, commonly called Labor day; the second Monday in October, commonly called, Columbus day; the eleventh day of November, commonly called Veterans' day; the fourth Thursday in November, commonly called Thanksgiving day; the twenty-fifth day of December, commonly called Christmas day; and any day appointed or recommended by the governor of this state or the president of the United States as a day of fasting or prayer or thanksgiving, are hereby declared to be legal holidays and shall, for all purposes whatsoever, as regards the presenting for payment or acceptance and the protesting and giving notice of the dishonor of bills of exchange, drafts, bank checks, promissory notes, or other negotiable instruments and also for the holding of courts, be treated and considered as is the first day of the week commonly called Sunday.

(2) In case any of said holidays or any other legal holiday so designated falls upon a Sunday, then the Monday following shall be considered as the holiday, and all notes, bills, drafts, checks, or other negotiable instruments falling due or maturing on either of said days shall be deemed to be payable on the next succeeding business day. In case the return or adjourned day in any suit, matter, or hearing before any court comes on any day referred to in this section, such suit, matter, or proceeding, commenced or adjourned as aforesaid, shall not, by reason of coming on any such day, abate, but the same shall stand continued to the next succeeding day at the same time and place, unless the next day is Sunday, when in such case the same shall stand continued to the next succeeding secular or business day at the same time and place. Nothing in this section shall prevent the issuing or serving of process on any of the days mentioned in this section or on Sunday.

(3) The provisions of this section shall not operate to prohibit agencies in the executive branch of state government from doing business on any of the legal holidays named in this article. Employees under the jurisdiction of the state personnel system who are required to work on any of the legal holidays named in this article shall be granted an alternate day off in the same fiscal year or be paid in accordance with the state personnel system or state fiscal rules in effect on April 30, 1979.

§ 24-11-103. Saturday half holiday — effect.

In every city of this state having a population of twenty-five thousand or over, every Saturday during the months of June, July, and August from 12 noon until 12 midnight is hereby designated a public holiday, and the same shall be recognized, classed, and treated as other holidays under the laws of this state. In the case of a half holiday, bills of exchange, bank checks, and promissory notes shall be presentable for acceptance or payment at or before 12 noon of that day; and, for the purpose of protesting or otherwise holding liable any party to any bill of exchange, check, or promissory note which has not been paid before 12 noon on any Saturday during said months, a demand of acceptance or payment thereof may be made and notice of protest or dishonor thereof may be given on the next succeeding secular or business day. When any person receives for collection any check, bill of exchange, or promissory note due and presentable for acceptance or payment on any Saturday during said months, such person shall not be deemed guilty of any neglect or omission of duty nor incur any liability in not presenting for payment or acceptance or collecting such check, bill of exchange, or promissory note on that day. In construing this section, every Saturday during said months, unless a whole holiday, until 12 noon, shall be deemed a secular or business day.

§ 24-11-110. Effect of closing public offices.

If, on a holiday designated in section 24-11-103, or on any day when the public office concerned is closed, or on a Saturday, any document is required to be filed with any public office of the state of Colorado, its departments, agencies, or institutions, or with any public office of any political subdivision of the state, or any appearance or return is required to be made at any such public office, or any official or employee of such public office is required to perform any act or any duty of his office, then any such filing, appearance, return, act, or duty so required or scheduled shall neither be abated nor defaulted, but the same shall stand continued to the next succeeding full business day at such public office at the same time and place.

CONNECTICUT

NOTARIES PUBLIC

[CONN. GEN. STAT. ANN.]

§ 3-91. Notaries public. Appointment, term and qualifications. Waiver of fees.

The secretary may, upon application as hereinafter provided, accompanied by a fee of forty dollars, appoint a convenient number of notaries public, each for the term of five years from April first in the year of appointment, and may revoke any such appointment for cause. Appointees shall be at least eighteen years of age and shall have resided in the state at least one year immediately preceding their appointment. The secretary shall cause a certificate, bearing a facsimile of his signature and countersigned by his executive assistant or an employee designated by the secretary, to be issued to each such appointee. A notary public may exercise the functions of his office at any place in the state. Each application for appointment to such office, except an application for the renewal of a certificate made prior to, or not more than one year after, its expiration, shall be in the handwriting of the applicant and shall bear the recommendation of the town clerk of the town where such applicant resides, made after investigation, and shall be upon a form furnished by the secretary of the state. The fee of sixty dollars shall be waived for all state police majors, captains, lieutenants and sergeants making application for appointment as notary public, except that such police officers may exercise their authority as notaries public only in the administration of oaths and affirmations and the taking of acknowledgments pertaining to official police matters, and in such case, the seal of the state police shall be the notarial seal. The secretary of the state shall notify each appointee, by mail, of the expiration date of his certificate. The notice shall be mailed not later than thirty days prior to such expiration date.

§ 3-92. Record of certificate and oath of notary.

The certificate of each notary public, and his

oath of office taken and subscribed to by him before proper authority, shall be recorded by the town clerk of the town in which such notary resides; and any notary having his principal place of business in a town other than that in which he resides may also have his certificate and oath recorded in the town in which he has such place of business; and such clerks or assistants may certify to the authority and [sic] official acts of any notary whose certificate and oath have been recorded in the books in their charge.

§ 3-93. Notice of revocation of appointment.

Notice of the revocation of the appointment and certificate of any notary public shall be given in such manner as the secretary directs, and the executive assistant or the employee designated by the secretary shall, within five days after such revocation, give notice thereof to the town clerk of the town in the records of which such certificate is required to be recorded under the provisions of section 3-92. Such clerk shall note such revocation and its date upon the original record of such certificate.

§ 3-94. Change of name of notary.

Whenever any notary public has his name changed by reason of marriage or by reason of a change of name legally adjudicated, the secretary shall change the name of such person on his records upon receipt of such proof of such change of name as said secretary deems sufficient and upon the payment of a fee of twenty-five dollars. Any clerk who is required to make record of the certificate and oath of a notary under section 3-92 shall record the change of name of such notary upon payment by such notary to such clerk of a fee of one dollar for such record.

§ 3-95. Fees of notary.

The fee for any act performed by a notary public in accordance with the provisions of the general statutes shall not exceed one dollar plus an additional fifteen cents for each mile of travel.

ADDITIONAL AUTHORITY

§ 7-33a. Issuance of certificates of authority of justices of peace, notaries and superior court commissioners.

The town clerk of a town wherein a justice of the peace, notary public or commissioner of the superior court resides or is employed is authorized to issue certificates of the authority of such person.

FEES

§ 52-259. Court fees.

* * * [Clerks shall receive] for recording the commission and oath of a notary public or certifying under seal to the official character of any magistrate, two dollars; * * *.

§ 52-262. Fees for signing process, administering oaths, acknowledgments.

Any person legally authorized, except when otherwise provided and except for judges, prosecutors and clerks of court, shall be paid the following fees: (1) For signing an attachment, summons, warrant or subpoena, taking a bond or recognizance or an affidavit, or administering an oath out of court, ten cents; (2) for taking the acknowledgment of any instrument, or signing and issuing a subpoena or capias, twenty-five cents; and (3) for causing notices of the seizure of intoxicating liquors to be posted, or issuing an order for their destruction, fifty cents.

OATH

§ 1-25. Forms of oaths.

The forms of oaths shall be as follows, to wit:

FOR NOTARIES PUBLIC

You do solemnly swear (or affirm, as the case may be) that you will support the constitution of the United States, and the constitution of the state of Connecticut; and that you will faithfully discharge, according to law, the duties of the office of notary public to the best of your abilities; so help you God.

ACKNOWLEDGMENTS

§ 47-7. Conveyances and releases executed outside this state.

(a) Notwithstanding the provisions of section 1-36, any conveyance of real estate situated in this state, any mortgage or release of mortgage or lien upon any real estate situated in this state, and any power of attorney authorizing another to convey any interest in real estate situated in this state, executed and acknowledged in any other state or territory in conformity with the laws of that state or territory relating to the conveyance of real estate therein situated or of any interest therein or with the laws of this state, is valid.

(b) No county clerk's certificate or other authenticating certificate is required for such conveyance, mortgage, release, lien or power of attorney to be valid, provided the officer taking the acknowledgment indicated thereon the date, if any, on which his current commission expires.

Uniform Acknowledgment Act

§ 1-28. Permissible forms of acknowledgment.

Any instrument may be acknowledged in the manner and form now provided by other laws of this state, or as provided by this chapter.

§ 1-29. Acknowledgments within state.

The acknowledgment of any instrument may be made in this state before: (1) A judge of a court of record or a family support magistrate; (2) a clerk or deputy clerk of a court having a seal; (3) a commissioner of deeds or town clerk; (4) a notary public; (5) a justice of the peace; or (6) an attorney admitted to the bar of this state.

§ 1-30. Acknowledgments in other states, territories or possessions.

The acknowledgment of any instrument may be made without the state but within the United States or a territory or insular possession of the United States and within the jurisdiction of the officer, before: (1) A clerk or deputy clerk of any federal court; (2) a clerk or deputy clerk of any court of record of any state or other jurisdiction; (3) a notary public; (4) a commissioner of deeds; (5) any person authorized by the laws of such other jurisdiction to take acknowledgments.

§ 1-31. Acknowledgments without United States.

The acknowledgment of any instrument may be made without the United States before: (1) An ambassador, minister, charge d'affaires, counselor to or secretary of a legation, consul general, consul, vice-consul, commercial attache, or consular agent of the United States accredited to the country where the acknowledgment is made; (2) a notary public of the country where the acknowledgment is made; (3) a judge or clerk of a court of record of the country where the acknowledgment is made.

§ 1-32. Identification of person making acknowledgment.

The officer taking the acknowledgment shall know or have satisfactory evidence that the person making the acknowledgment is the person described in and who executed the instrument.

§ 1-33. Married women.

An acknowledgment of a married woman may be made in the same form as though she were unmarried.

§ 1-34. Certificate of officer.

An officer taking the acknowledgment shall endorse thereon or attach thereto a certificate substantially in one of the following forms:

(1) By individuals:

State of . . .

County of . . .

On this the . . . day of . . ., 19. ., before me, . . ., the undersigned officer, personally appeared . . ., known to me (or satisfactorily proven) to be the person whose name . . . subscribed to the within instrument and acknowledged that . . . he . . . executed the same for the purposes therein contained.

In witness whereof I hereunto set my hand.

....

....

Title of Officer.

(2) By a corporation:

State of . . .

County of . . .

On this the . . . day of . . ., 19. ., before me, . . ., the undersigned officer, personally appeared . . . who acknowledged himself to be the . . . of . . ., a corporation, and that he, as such . . ., being authorized so to do, executed the foregoing instrument for the purposes therein contained, by signing the name of the corporation by himself as . . . . .

In witness whereof I hereunto set my hand.

....

....

Title of Officer.

(3) By an attorney in fact:

State of . . .

County of . . .

On this the . . . day of . . ., 19. ., before me, . . ., the undersigned officer, personally appeared . . ., known to me (or satisfactorily proven) to be the person whose name is subscribed as attorney in fact for . . ., and acknowledged that he executed the same as the act of his principal for the purposes therein contained.

In witness whereof I hereunto set my hand.

....

....

Title of Officer.

(4) By any public officer or deputy thereof, or by any trustee, administrator, guardian, or executor:

State of . . .

County of . . .

On this the . . . day of . . ., 19. ., before me, . . ., the undersigned officer, personally appeared . . ., of the State (County or City as the case may be) of . . ., known to me (or satisfactorily proven) to be the person described in the foregoing instrument, and acknowledged that he executed the same in the capacity therein stated and for the purposes therein contained.

In witness whereof I hereunto set my hand.

....

....

Title of Officer.

§ 1-35. Identification of acknowledging officer.

The certificate of the acknowledging officer shall be completed by his signature, his official seal if he has one, the title of his office and, if he is a notary public, the date his commission expires.

§ 1-36. Authentication.

(1) If the acknowledgment is taken within this state or is made without the United States by an officer of the United States no authentication shall be necessary.

(2) If the acknowledgment is taken without this state, but in the United States, or a territory or insular possession of the United States, the certificate shall be authenticated by a certificate as to the official character of such officer, executed, if the acknowledgment is taken by a clerk or deputy clerk of a court, by the presiding judge of the court or, if the acknowledgment is taken by a notary public, or any other person authorized to take acknowledgments, by a clerk of a court of record of the county, parish or district, or the clerk of the town, in which the acknowledgment is taken. The signature to such authenticating certificate may be a facsimile printed, stamped, photographed or engraved thereon when the certificate bears the seal of the authenticating officer. A judge or clerk authenticating an acknowledgment shall endorse thereon or attach thereto a certificate in substantially the following form:

State of . . .

County of . . .

I . . . (judge or clerk) of the . . . in and for said county, which court is a court of record, having a seal, (or I, clerk of the town of . . . in said county,)

do hereby certify that . . . . . . by and before whom the foregoing (or annexed) acknowledgment was taken, was at the time of taking the same a notary public (or other officer) residing (or authorized to act) in said county, and was authorized by the laws of said state to take and certify acknowledgments in said state, and, further, that I am acquainted with his handwriting and that I believe that the signature to the certificate of acknowledgment is genuine.

In this testimony whereof I have hereunto set my hand and affixed the seal of the court this . . . day of . . ., 19. . .

(3) If the acknowledgment is taken without the United States and by a notary public or a judge or clerk of a court of record of the country or the clerk of the town where the acknowledgment is taken, the certificate shall be authenticated by a certificate under the great seal of the state of the country, affixed by the custodian of such seal, or by a certificate of a diplomatic, consular or commercial officer of the United States accredited to that country, certifying as to the official character of such officer. The officer authenticating an acknowledgment shall endorse thereon or attach thereto a certificate in substantially the form prescribed in subsection (2) of this section.

§ 1-37. Acknowledgment in compliance with law of other jurisdiction.

Notwithstanding any provision in this chapter, the acknowledgment of any instrument without this state in compliance with the manner and form prescribed by the laws of the place of its execution, if in a state, a territory or insular possession of the United States, or in the District of Columbia, verified by the official seal of the officer before whom it is acknowledged, and authenticated in the manner provided by subsection (2) of section 1-36, shall have the same effect as an acknowledgment in the manner and form prescribed by the laws of this state for instruments executed within the state.

§ 1-38. Acknowledgment of person in armed forces.

In addition to the acknowledgment of instruments in the manner and form and as otherwise authorized by this chapter, persons serving in or with the armed forces of the United States or their dependents, wherever located, may acknowledge the same before any commissioned officer in active service of the armed forces of the United States with the rank of second lieutenant or higher in the army, air force or marine corps, or ensign or higher in the navy or coast guard. The instrument shall not be rendered invalid by the failure to state therein the place of execution or acknowledgment. No authentication of the officer's certificate of acknowledgment shall be required but the officer taking the acknowledgment shall endorse thereon or attach thereto a certificate substantially in the following form:

On this the . . . . day of . . . ., 19. . ., before me, ..., the undersigned officer, personally appeared . . . . (Serial No.) (if any) . . . ., known to me (or satisfactorily proven) to be (serving in or with the armed forces of the United States) (a dependent of . . . ., (Serial No.) (if any) . . . ., a person serving in or with the armed forces of the United States) and to be the person whose name is subscribed to the within instrument and acknowledged that . . . . . . he . . . . . . executed the same for the purposes therein contained. And the undersigned does further certify that he is at the date of this certificate a commissioned officer of the rank stated below and is in the active service of the armed forces of the United States.

. . . .
Signature of the Officer

. . . .
Rank and Serial No. of Officer and Command to which attached.

§ 1-39. Prior acknowledgments unaffected.

No acknowledgment taken prior to October 1, 1961, shall be affected by anything contained in this chapter.

§ 1-40. Interpretation of chapter.

This chapter shall be so interpreted as to make uniform the laws of those states which enact it.

§ 1-41. Citation of chapter.

This chapter may be cited as the Uniform Acknowledgment Act.

Uniform Recognition of Acknowledgments Act

§ 1-57. Definitions. Authorized officers.

For the purposes of this chapter, "notarial acts" means acts which the laws and regulations of this state authorize notaries public of this state to perform, including the administering of oaths and affirmations, taking proof of execution and acknowledgments of instruments, and attesting documents. Notarial acts may be performed outside this state for use in this state with the same effect as if performed by a notary public of this state by the following persons authorized pursuant to the laws and regulations of other governments in addition to any other person authorized by the laws and regulations of this state: (1) A notary public authorized to perform notarial acts in the place in which the act is performed; (2) a judge, clerk, or deputy clerk of any court of record in the place in which the notarial act is performed; (3) an officer of the foreign service of the United States, a consular agent, or any other person authorized by regulation of the United States Department of State to perform notarial acts in the place in which the act is performed; (4) a commissioned officer in active service with the armed forces of the United States and any other person authorized by regulation of the armed forces to perform notarial acts if the notarial act is performed for one of the following or his dependents: A merchant seaman of the United States, a member of the armed forces of the United States, or any other person serving with or accompanying the armed forces of the United States; or (5) any other person authorized to perform notarial acts in the place in which the act is performed.

§ 1-58. Proof of authority to perform notarial act.

(a) If the notarial act is performed by any of the persons described in subdivisions (1) to (4), inclusive, of section 1-57, other than a person authorized to perform notarial acts by the laws or regulations of a foreign country, the signature, rank or title and serial number, if any, of the person are sufficient proof of the authority of a holder of that rank or title to perform the act. Further proof of his authority is not required.

(b) If the notarial act is performed by a person authorized by the laws or regulations of a foreign country to perform the act, there is sufficient proof of the authority of that person to act if: (1) A foreign service officer of the United States resident in the country in which the act is performed or a diplomatic or consular officer of the foreign country resident in the United States certifies that a person holding that office is authorized to perform the act; or (2) the official seal of the person performing the notarial act is affixed to the document; or (3) the title and indication of authority to perform notarial acts of the person appears either in a digest of foreign law or in a list customarily used as a source of such information.

(c) If the notarial act is performed by a person other than one described in subsections (a) and (b), there is sufficient proof of the authority of that person to act if the clerk of a court of record in the place in which the notarial act is performed certifies to the official character of that person and to his authority to perform the notarial act.

(d) The signature and title of the person performing the act are prima facie evidence that he is a person with the designated title and that the signature is genuine.

§ 1-59. Certification by person taking acknowledgment.

The person taking an acknowledgment shall certify that: (1) The person acknowledging appeared before him and acknowledged he executed the instrument; and (2) the person acknowledging was known to the person taking the acknowledgment or that the person taking the acknowledgment had satisfactory evidence that the person acknowledging was the person described in and who executed the instrument.

§ 1-60. Form of certificate.

The form of a certificate of acknowledgment used by a person whose authority is recognized under section 1-57 shall be accepted in this state if: (1) The certificate is in a form prescribed by the laws or regulations of this state; (2) the certificate is in a form prescribed by the laws or regulations applicable in the place in which the acknowledgment is taken; or (3) the certificate contains the words "acknowledged before me," or their substantial equivalent.

§ 1-61. "Acknowledged before me" defined.

The words "acknowledged before me" mean: (1) That the person acknowledging appeared before the person taking the acknowledgment; (2) that he acknowledged he executed the instrument; (3) that, in the case of: (i) A natural person, he executed the instrument for the purposes therein stated, (ii) a corporation, the officer or agent acknowledged he held the position or title set forth in the instrument and certificate, he signed the instrument on behalf of the corporation by proper authority, and the instrument was the act of the corporation for the purpose therein stated, (iii) a partnership, the partner or agent acknowledged he signed the instrument on behalf of the partnership by proper authority and he executed the instrument as the act of the partnership for the purposes therein stated, (iv) a person acknowledging as principal by an attorney in fact, he executed the instrument by proper authority as the act of the principal for the purposes therein stated and (v) a person acknowledging as a public officer, trustee, administrator, guardian, or other representative, he signed the instrument by proper authority and he executed the instrument in the capacity and for the purposes therein stated; and (4) that the person taking the acknowledgment either knew or had satisfactory evidence that the person acknowledging was the person named in the instrument or certificate.

§ 1-62. Statutory short forms of acknowledgment.

The forms of acknowledgment set forth in this section may be used and are sufficient for their respective purposes under any law of this state. The forms shall be known as "Statutory Short Forms of Acknowledgment" and may be referred to by that name. The authorization of the forms in this section does not preclude the use of other forms.

(1) For an individual acting in his own right:

State of . . .
County of . . .

The foregoing instrument was acknowledged before me this (date) by (name of person acknowledged.)

(Signature of person taking acknowledgment)
(Title or rank)
(Serial number, if any)

(2) For a corporation:

State of . . .
County of . . .

The foregoing instrument was acknowledged before me this (date) by (name of officer or agent, title of officer or agent) of (name of corporation acknowledging) a (state or place of incorporation) corporation, on behalf of the corporation.

(Signature of person taking acknowledgment)
(Title or rank)
(Serial number, if any)

(3) For a partnership:

State of . . .
County of . . .

The foregoing instrument was acknowledged before me this (date) by (name of acknowledging partner or agent), partner (or agent) on behalf of (name of partnership), a partnership.

(Signature of person taking acknowledgment)
(Title or rank)
(Serial number, if any)

(4) For an individual acting as principal by an attorney in fact:

State of . . .
County of . . .

The foregoing instrument was acknowledged before me this (date) by (name of attorney in fact) as attorney in fact on behalf of (name of principal).

(Signature of person taking acknowledgment)
(Title or rank)
(Serial number, if any)

(5) By any public officer, trustee or personal representative:

State of . . .

County of . . .

The foregoing instrument was acknowledged before me this (date) by (name and title of position).

(Signature of person taking acknowledgment)

(Title or rank)

(Serial number, if any)

§ 1-63. Prior acts unaffected. Method additional.

A notarial act performed prior to October 1, 1969, is not affected by this chapter. This chapter provides an additional method of proving notarial acts. Nothing in this chapter diminishes or invalidates the recognition accorded to notarial acts by other laws or regulations of this state.

§ 1-64. Uniform interpretation.

This chapter shall be so interpreted as to make uniform the laws of those states which enact it.

§ 1-65. Short title.

This chapter may be cited as the Uniform Recognition of Acknowledgments Act.

DEPOSITIONS

§ 1-23. When affirmation may be used.

When any person, required to take an oath, from scruples of conscience declines to take it in the usual form or when the court is satisfied that any person called as a witness does not believe in the existence of a Supreme Being, a solemn affirmation may be administered to him in the form of the oath prescribed, except that instead of the word "swear" the words "solemnly and sincerely affirm and declare" shall be used and instead of the words "so help you God" the words "upon the pains and penalties of perjury or false statement" shall be used.

§ 1-24. Who may administer oaths.

The following officers may administer oaths: * * * [Among others] (2) * * * judges and clerks of any court, family support magistrates, justices of the peace, commissioners of the superior court, notaries public, commissioners appointed by the governor to take acknowledgment of deeds, town clerks and assistant town clerks, in all cases where an oath may be administered, except in a case

where the law otherwise requires; * * * (5) commissioners appointed by the governors of other states to take the acknowledgment of deeds, in the discharge of their official duty; * * *

§ 1-25. Forms of oaths.

The forms of oaths shall be as follows, to-wit:

* * *

For Witnesses

You solemnly swear that the evidence you shall give, concerning the case now in question, shall be the truth, the whole truth and nothing by the truth; so help you God.

§ 52-148c. Before whom depositions may be taken.

(a) Within this state, depositions shall be taken before a judge or clerk of any court, justice of the peace, notary public or commissioner of the superior court.

(b) In any state or country, depositions for use in a civil action or probate proceeding within this state shall be taken before a notary public, a commissioner appointed by the governor of this state, any magistrate having power to administer oaths or a person commissioned by the court before which such action or proceeding is pending, or when such court is not in session, by any judge thereof. Any person so commissioned shall have the power by virtue of his commission to administer any necessary oath and to take testimony. Additionally, if a deposition is to be taken out of the United States, it may be taken before any foreign minister, secretary of a legation, consul or vice-consul, having authority under the laws of the country where the deposition is to be taken; and the official character of any such person may be proved by a certificate from the Secretary of State of the United States.

§ 52-148d. Requirements for taking of depositions. Party subject to taking of deposition.

(a) All witnesses or parties giving depositions shall be cautioned to speak the whole truth and be carefully examined, and shall subscribe their depositions, and make oath before the authority taking the depositions.

(b) The authority taking a deposition shall: (1) Attest the subscribing of the deposition and oath of the person deposed, (2) certify whether each adverse party or his agent was present and notified, (3) certify the reason for taking the deposition, and (4) seal the deposition and direct it to the court where it is to be used and deliver it, if requested, to the party at whose request it was taken.

(c) The party on whose behalf the deposition of an adverse party is taken shall be subject to having his deposition taken on behalf of such adverse party. The party on whose behalf a deposition is taken shall at his expense provide a copy of the deposition to each adverse party.

§ 52-148e. Issuance of subpoena for taking of depositions. Deposition to be used outside the state.

(a) Each judge or clerk of any court, justice of the peace, notary public or commissioner of the superior court, in this state, may issue a subpoena, upon request, for the appearance of any witness before him to give his deposition in a civil action or probate proceeding, if the party seeking to take such person's deposition has complied with the provisions of sections 52-148a and 52-148b and may take his deposition, each adverse party or his agent being present or notified.

(b) The subpoena may command the person to whom it is directed to produce and permit inspection and copying of designated books, papers, documents or tangible things which are material to the cause of action or the defense of the party at whose request the subpoena was issued and within the possession or control of the person to be examined. However, no subpoena may compel the production of matters which are privileged or otherwise protected by law from discovery.

(c) Any person to whom a subpoena commanding production of books, papers, documents or tangible things has been directed may, within fifteen days after the service thereof or on or before the time specified in the subpoena for compliance if such time is less than fifteen days after service, serve upon the issuing authority designated in the subpoena written objection to inspection or copying of any or all of the designated materials. If objection is made, the party at whose request the subpoena was issued shall not be entitled to inspect and copy the disputed materials except pursuant to an order of the court in which the cause is pending. The party who requested the subpoena may, if objection has been made, move upon notice to the deponent for an order at any time before or during the taking of the deposition.

(d) The court in which the cause is pending may, upon motion made promptly and in any event at or before the time for compliance specified in a subpoena authorized by subsection (b) of this section, (1) quash or modify the subpoena if it is unreasonable and oppressive or if it seeks the production of materials not subject to production under the provisions of subsection (b) of this section, or (2) condition denial of the motion upon the advancement by the party who requested the subpoena of the rea-

sonable cost of producing the materials which he is seeking.

(e) If any person to whom a lawful subpoena is issued under any provision of this section fails without just excuse to comply with any of its terms, the court before which the cause is pending, or any judge thereof, may issue a capias and cause him to be brought before such court or judge, as the case may be, and, if the person subpoenaed refuses to comply with said subpoena, such court or judge may commit him to jail until he signifies his willingness to comply with it.

(f) Deposition of witnesses living in this state may be taken in like manner to be used as evidence in a civil action or probate proceeding pending in any court of the United States or of any other state of the United States or of any foreign country, on application of any party to such civil action or probate proceeding.

COMMISSIONERS

§ 4-21. Commissioners for Connecticut.

The governor may appoint and commission a convenient number of commissioners in each of the other states of the United States, in any territory thereof and in the District of Columbia, for the term of five years, commencing with the date of their respective commissions, unless the appointments and commissions are sooner revoked. Each commissioner so appointed and commissioned shall have power to take the acknowledgment of deeds and of any instruments required by the laws of this state to be acknowledged, to administer oaths or affirmations, examine witnesses and take depositions relating to any cause pending, or to be brought, in any of the courts of this state; but no commissioner shall act as such until he has filed with the secretary an affidavit, signed and sworn to by him before proper authority, that he will faithfully perform his duties as such commissioner.

LEGAL HOLIDAYS

§ 1-4. Days designated as legal holidays.

In each year the first day of January (known as New Year's Day), the fifteenth day of January of each year prior to 1986, and commencing on the twentieth day of January in 1986, the first Monday occurring on or after January fifteenth (known as Martin Luther King Day), the twelfth day of February (known as Lincoln Day), the third Monday in February (known as Washington's Birthday), the last Monday in May (known as Memorial Day or

Decoration Day), the fourth day of July (known as Independence Day); the first Monday in September (known as Labor Day), the second Monday in October (known as Columbus Day), the eleventh day of November (known as Veterans' Day) and the twenty-fifth day of December (known as Christmas) and any day appointed or recommended by the governor of this state or the president of the United States as a day of thanksgiving, fasting or religious observance, shall each be a legal holiday, except that whenever any of such days which are not designated to occur on Monday, occurs upon a Sunday, the Monday next following such day shall be a legal holiday and whenever any of such days occurs upon a Saturday, the Friday immediately preceding such day shall be a legal holiday. When any such holiday occurs on a school day, there shall be no session of the public schools on such day.

DELAWARE

NOTARIES PUBLIC

[DEL. CODE. ANN.]

Tit. 29, § 4301. Appointment of notaries in general; number from each county; qualifications; revocation.

(a) In addition to the notaries public authorized to be appointed under sections 4302-4304 of this title, the Governor may appoint as many notaries public as he may decide is necessary and proper in each county of the State.

(b) Any citizen who desires to become a notary shall be at least 18 years of age and shall provide such evidence as the governor may require to show:

(1) Good character and reputation;

(2) A reasonable need for a notary commission; and

(3) Legal residence of at least 1 year within the State.

(c) The Governor may revoke any notary commission for cause.

§ 4302. Appointment of certain officers as notaries; term.

(a) The Governor shall appoint every person who is appointed by him to the office of the justice of the peace and as Secretary of Finance revenue also as a notary public.

The Secretary of Finance revenue shall only act as a notary public in connnection with work performed in carrying out the duties of his office.

The term of office of any person appointed a notary public under the provisions of this section: (1) whose appointment as a justice of the peace or collector of State revenue is not confirmed by the Senate; or (2) who fails to qualify, resigns or is removed from the office of the justice of the peace or collector of state revenue shall terminate at the same time his term of office as justice of the peace or collector of state revenue terminates.

(b) The Governor shall appoint as a notary public the Register in Chancery in Kent County, and his successors, from time to time, in the office.

The term of office of the Register in Chancery in Kent County as a notary public shall expire at the same time as his term of office as such Register in Chancery.

§ 4303. Appointment of notary for each bank or branch.

The Governor shall appoint 1 notary public for each trust company, bank, banking association or branch or branches thereof in this State, whether state or national, chartered or organized under the laws of this State, or of the United States.

§ 4304. Appointment of court reporters as notaries public.

The Governor may, upon the request of the Chief Justice of the Supreme Court, appoint any of the official court reporters as a notary public. Such court reporter need not be a legal resident of this State for 1 year at the time of his appointment, if he is a resident of this State at the time of his appointment as a notary public.

§ 4305. Appointment of notaries for certain service organizations; limitations.

(a) The Governor may, upon request of the department commander of the Spanish-American War Veterans, of the Veterans of Foreign Wars of the United States, of the Disabled American Veterans, of the Jewish War Veterans, of the American Legion, of the Paralyzed Veterans of America, and of the Vietnam Veterans of America, appoint 1 notary public for each requesting organization for a term of 4 years, without charge to any appointee, commander or organization.

(b) Any such notary, so appointed, shall have no authority to perform any duties with respect to such office or to take affidavits or acknowledgments, except on documents and papers in connection with and for the benefit of any veteran, their families or dependents. The notaries public, so appointed, shall make no charge for any service rendered.

§ 4308. Seal and powers.

The notary shall have a seal and shall exercise the powers and perform the duties belonging to that office. He shall also have power to take the acknowledgment of deeds and other instruments. The notary public must ensure, by requiring identification through use of a driver's license, personal identification by someone known to the notary or other appropriate means, that the individual whose presence and signature is being certified is in fact the person he or she claims to be.

§ 4309. Engraving of seal; effect of use of nonconforming seal.

The seals required by § 4308 of this title shall be used in the transaction of official business and shall have engraved thereon the name of the officer, either in full or using the initials of his Christian name; official title, the date of his appointment and anything additional which he may see fit to have engraved thereon.

If the official seal of any notary public is not engraved in conformity with the provisions of this section, it shall not invalidate his official act, but such act shall be as valid as though the seal had been engraved in conformity with the requirements of this section.

Any notary public failing to comply with the requirements of this section may be removed by the Governor for his neglect.

§ 4310. Fees for services.

(a) The fees of a notary public, for the services specified, shall be as follows—

Taking and certifying an affidavit . . . . $ .25

For protest of a promissory note, bill of exchange, draft or cheque, and registering the same 80

Giving notice of a protest, personal or otherwise, and registering the notice and manner thereof, for each notice 20

For exemplification, under hand and notarial seal, of such protest 25

Protest of a foreign bill of exchange (to wit, a bill of exchange drawn beyond sea), and registering the same 1.00

Giving notice of such protest, personal or otherwise, and registering the notice and manner thereof, for each notice. 37

Exemplification under hand and notarial seal of such protest 75

Registering a bill of exchange, promissory note, bank note, or cheque, where no fee for probate is charged 20

Registering a common sea protest 75

Registering a foreign sea protest. 1.00

Registering a protest against merchant, or other person, for detaining vessel beyond proper time, with answers and persistence to the protest 4.00

Exemplification under hand and notarial seal of either of said three last mentioned protests 1.00

And additionally 2 cents a line of 10 words.

Registering an obligation, letter of attorney, bill of sale, or other writing of similar length 1.00

Taking and certifying under hand and notarial seal, the acknowledgment of a deed, letter of attorney, or other instrument 50

Administering and certifying oaths to applicants for registration and titling of motor vehicles and operator's licenses not to exceed 50 cents for first certificate and 25 cents for each additional.

Drawing affidavit, or deposition, 2 cents a line of 10 words.

Taking depositions under order of court, a sum to be taxed by the court.

Certificate under hand and notarial seal, when no other service for which a fee is allowed is performed 35

Taking depositions, a reasonable sum, to be taxed by the court from which the commission issued.

(b) The fees prescribed in this section shall be the minimum fees to be charged by any notary public, and upon violation of this provision the Governor may revoke the commission of such notary and such notary shall not be reappointed within a period of 2 years.

(c) Every notary public, who keeps a public office, shall always keep hung up, in some convenient and conspicuous place therein, a printed or written list of the fees prescribed in this section.

(d) The provisions of this section shall be construed strictly and no fee shall be allowed for any service, except where otherwise expressly provided, until it has been actually performed.

(e) Notary fees for affidavits in connection with the indigent sick of Kent and Sussex Counties shall not be in excess of 10 cents for each such affidavit.

§ 4311. Duties and fees of notaries public with respect to conveyances of land in Sussex County.

Notaries public in this State, before whom any deed conveying land situated in Sussex County is acknowledged, shall make a certificate on blanks to be furnished by the Board of Assessment of Sussex County, showing the transfer, and return the same to the Board of Assessment in the same month in which the transfer was made.

For every deed reported under the provisions of this section the notary public shall be entitled to a fee of 25 cents to be paid by the Levy Court of Sussex County.

§ 4312. Special fee provisions for certain services to members of the armed forces and to veterans; penalties; jurisdiction of justices of peace.

(a) No notary public or other person who is authorized by law to take the acknowledgment of instruments or to administer oaths or affirmations shall charge any person serving in the armed forces of the United States, or a veteran of any war, or the widow or children of a soldier or soldier's parents or widower or other relative of any person in the armed services the fee provided by law, when an acknowledgment, oath or affirmation is taken in connection with any paper or papers required to be executed by the Veterans Administration or in support of any claim or other papers connected with or referring to the service of any male or female now serving or who hereafter may serve or who, in the past, has served in the armed forces of the United States.

(b) Whoever violates subsection (a) of this section shall be fined not less than $10 nor more than $25 and, in default of the payment of such fine, shall be imprisoned for not more than 5 days.

(c) Justices of the peace shall have jurisdiction of offenses under this section.

§ 4313. Commission; signature of Governor; seal.

(a) The commission appointing a notary public shall be in such form as the Secretary of State shall designate, shall be executed with the signature of

the Governor or with a facsimile signature of the Governor, which may be engraved, printed or stamped thereon, and shall be signed by the Secretary of State.

(b) The commission shall have placed thereon the impression of the Great Seal of the State, or a facsimile of the Great Seal shall be engraved or printed thereon.

FEES

Tit. 29, § 2315 Fees.

The fees to be charged by the Secretary of State for the use of the State are as follows:

* * *

For commission to Attorney General, coroners, and notaries public, each..........$15.00

ACKNOWLEDGMENTS

Tit. 25, § 110. Certificates of notaries public; validity.

No official certificate of any notary public shall be invalid or defective because the impression of the official seal of such officer upon the certificate does not strictly comport with the requirements of section 4309 of Title 29. All such certificates shall be valid in all respects; and in all cases where such certificates are annexed to papers proper to be recorded, the several recorders shall admit such papers to record. The record of the same, or a duly certified copy thereof, shall be competent evidence, and every such paper shall be as good and effectual in law as though the seal used by the officer certifying the acknowledgment of the same had been engraved in exact conformity with the provisions of the law.

§ 123. Certification of acknowledgment or proof.

Acknowledgment or proof shall be certified under the hand and seal of office of the clerk, or Prothonotary, of the court in which, or under the hand of the judge, notary public or justices of the peace before whom, the acknowledgment or proof is taken, in a certificate indorsed upon or annexed to the deed.

§ 128. Certification of acknowledgments by Mayor of Wilmington; fee.

The Mayor of Wilmington may take and certify under his hand and seal of office the acknowledgment of deeds and letters of attorney in like manner as a judge or notary public may. For such service he shall receive a fee of 75 cents, and no more, whether there are 1 or more parties to the deed.

§ 129. Acknowledgment or proof outside state.

(a) A deed, concerning lands, tenements or hereditaments within this State may be acknowledged or proved, or may be taken out of the State before any consul general, consul, vice-consul, consular agent, or commercial agent of the United States, duly appointed in any foreign country, at the places of their respective official residence, the judge of any United States District Court or United States Court of Appeals, or any judge of a court of record of any state, territory or country, or the mayor or chief officer of any city or borough, and certified under the hands of such judge, mayor or officer, and the seal of his office, court, city, or borough, by certificate indorsed upon or annexed to the deed; or such acknowledgment or proof may be taken in such court and certified under the hand of the clerk, or other officer of the court, and the seal of the court in like manner. If certified by a judge, the seal of his court may be affixed to his certificate or to a certificate of attestation of the clerk, or keeper of the seal.

(b) Acknowledgment and proof of a deed may also be taken out of this State by any commissioner of deeds, appointed by the governor in any of the states, or territories of the United States, or in the District of Columbia, or in the possessions of the United States, or in foreign countries, the deed to be certified, in like manner, under the hand and seal of the commissioner.

(c) Any deed concerning lands, tenements or hereditaments within this State, any other instrument of writing whatsoever, or any affidavit or other statement requiring acknowledgment or proof may be so acknowledged and proved out of this State before a notary public of any state or territory or of the District of Columbia. The provisions of this paragraph shall extend to affidavits of demand and defense as provided for in § 3901 of Title 10.

DEPOSITIONS

[DEL. R. CIV. P.]

RULE 28. Persons before whom deposition may be taken

(a) **Within the United States.** Within the United States or within a territory or insular possession subject to the dominion of the United States, depositions shall be taken (1) before an officer authorized to administer oaths by the laws of the place where the examination is held, or (2) before such person or officer as may be appointed by commission or under letters rogatory.

(b) **In Foreign Countries.** In a foreign country, depositions may be taken (1) on notice before a person authorized to administer oaths in the place in which the examination is held, either by the law thereof or by the law of the United States, or (2) before a person commissioned by the court, and a person so commissioned shall have the power by virtue of his commission to administer any necessary oath and take testimony, or (3) pursuant to a letters rogatory. A commission or a letters rogatory shall be issued on application and notice and on terms that are just and appropriate. It is not requisite to the issuance of a commission or a letter rogatory that the taking of the deposition in any other manner is impracticable or inconvenient; and both a commission and a letter rogatory may be issued in proper cases. A notice or commission may designate the person before whom the deposition is to be taken either by name or descriptive title. A letter rogatory may be addressed "To the Appropriate Authority in [here name the country]." Evidence obtained in response to a letter rogatory need not be excluded merely for the reason that it is not a verbatim transcript or that the testimony was not taken under oath or for any similar departure from the requirements for depositions taken within the United States under these rules.

(c) **Disqualification for Interest.** No deposition shall be taken before a person who is a relative or employee or attorney or counsel of any of the parties, or is a relative or employee of such attorney or counsel, or is financially interested in the action.

(d) **Designation of Officers.** The officers referred to in paragraphs (a) and (b) hereof may be designated in notices or commissions either by name or descriptive title and letters rogatory may be addressed "To the Appropriate Judicial Authority in (here name the State or Country)."

LEGAL HOLIDAYS

[DEL. CODE ANN.]

Tit. 1, § 501. Designation.

(a) The following days shall be legal holidays in this State: The 1st of January, known as New Year's Day; the third Monday in January, known as Martin Luther King, Jr. Day; the third Monday in February, known as Presidents' Day; Good Friday; the 4th of July, known as Independence Day; the first Monday in September, known as Labor Day; the second Monday in October, known as Columbus Day; the eleventh day of November, known as Veterans' Day; the fouth Thursday in November, known as Thanksgiving Day; the Friday following

Thanksgiving Day; the 25th of December, known as Christmas; Saturdays; the day of the General Election as it biennially occurs; and in Sussex County, Return Day, the second day after the General Election, after 12:00 Noon.

If any of the legal holidays fall on Sunday, the Monday following shall be a legal holiday. If any of the legal holidays other than Saturday fall on Saturday, the Friday preceding shall be a legal holiday.

(b) The last Monday in May shall be the legal holiday, known as Memorial Day, in the State.

§ 502. Validity of acts, transactions, legal procedures, etc.

(a) No contract made, instrument executed, or act done on any of the legal holidays designated in § 501 of this title shall be thereby rendered invalid, and nothing in that section shall be construed to prevent or invalidate the entry, issuance, service or execution of any writ, summons, confession, judgment, order or decree, or other legal process whatever, or the proceedings of any court or judge or board of canvass on any of such holidays.

DISTRICT OF COLUMBIA

NOTARIES PUBLIC

[D.C. CODE ANN.]

§ 1-801. Appointment; representation of clients before government departments; license fee; rules.

(a) The Mayor of the District of Columbia shall have power to appoint such number of notaries public, residents of said District, or whose sole place of business or employment is located within said District, as, in his discretion, the business of the District may require: Provided, that the appointment of any person as such notary public, or the acceptance of his commission as such, or the performance of the duties thereunder, shall not disqualify or prevent such person from representing clients before any of the departments of the United States government in the Distict of Columbia or elsewhere: Provided further, that such person so appointed as a notary public who appears to practice or represent clients before any such departments is not otherwise engaged in government employ, and shall be admitted by the heads of such departments to practice therein in accordance with the rules and regulations prescribed for other persons or attorneys who are admitted to practice therein: And provided further, that no notary public shall be authorized to take acknowledgments, administer oaths, certify papers, or perform any official acts in connection with matters in which he is employed as counsel, attorney, or agent, or in which he may be in any way interested before any of the deparments aforesaid.

(b) Each notary public before obtaining his commission, and for each renewal thereof, shall pay to the Director of the Department of Finance and Revenue of the District of Columbia a license fee of $30: Provided, that no license fee shall be collected from any notary public in the service of the United States government or the District of Columbia government whose notarial duties are confined solely to government official business: And provided further, that no notary fee shall be collected at any time by a notary public who is authorized to refund, in the manner prescribed by law for the refunding of erroneously paid taxes, the amount of any fee erroneously paid or collected under this section.

(c) The Council of the District of Columbia shall issue rules necessary to carry out the provisions of §§ 1-801 to 1-815: Except, that the Mayor of the District of Columbia shall amend by rule from time to time the amount of any fee established pursuant to §§ 1-801 to 1-815.

§ 1-802. Term of office.

Said notaries public shall hold their offices for the period of 5 years, removable at discretion.

§ 1-803. Oath; bond.

Each notary public, before entering upon the

duties of his office, shall take the oath prescribed for civil officers in the District of Columbia, and shall give bond to the District of Columbia in the sum of $2,000, with security, to be approved by the Mayor of the District of Columbia or his designated agent, for the faithful discharge of the duties of his office. Where any such notary public is an officer or employee of the government of the District of Columbia whose notarial duties are confined solely to government official business, any bond covering such officer or employee for the faithful performance of such notarial duties obtained by the Mayor of the District of Columbia pursuant to the authority conferred on him by law shall be in lieu of the bond required by the 1st sentence of this section.

§ 1-804. Seal.

Each notary public shall provide a notarial seal with which he shall authenticate all his official acts.

§ 1-805. Filing of signature; depositing impression of seal; certification as to authenticity.

Each notary public shall file his signature and deposit an impression of his official seal with the Mayor of the District of Columbia or his designated agent, and the Mayor or his designated agent may certify to the authenticity of the signature and official seal of the notary public.

§ 1-806. Exemption from execution.

A notary's official seal and his official documents shall be exempt from execution.

§ 1-807. Foreign bills of exchange.

Notaries public shall have authority to demand acceptance and payment of foreign bills of exchange and to protest the same for nonacceptance and nonpayment, and to exercise such other powers and duties as by the law of nations and according to commercial usages notaries public may do.

§ 1-808. Inland bills of exchange; promissory notes and checks.

Notaries public may also demand acceptance of inland bills of exchange and payment thereof, and of promissory notes and checks, and may protest the same for nonacceptance or nonpayment, as the case may require. And on the original protest thereof he shall state the presentment by him of the same for acceptance or payment, as the case may be, and the nonacceptance or nonpayment thereof, and the service of notice thereof on any of the par-

ties to the same, and the mode of giving such notice, and the reputed place of business or residence of the party to whom the same was given; and such protest shall be prima facie evidence of the facts therein stated. And any notary public failing to comply herewith shall pay a fine of $10 to the District of Columbia, to be collected in the Superior Court of the District of Columbia as are other fines and penalties.

§ 1-809. Other acts for use and effect beyond District.

Notaries public may also perform such other acts, for use and effect beyond the jurisdiction of the District, as according to the law of any state or territory of the United States or any foreign government in amity with the United States may be performed by notaries public.

§ 1-810. Certification of certain instruments; depositions; administration of oaths and affirmations; affidavits.

Each notary public shall have power to take and to certify the acknowledgment or proof of powers of attorney, mortgages, deeds, and other instruments of writing, to take depositions and to administer oaths and affirmations and also to take affidavits to be used before any court, judge, or officer within the District.

§ 1-811. Record of official acts; certified copies.

Each notary public shall keep a fair record of all his official acts, except such as are mentioned in § 1-810. and when required, shall give a certified copy of any record in his office to any person upon payment of the fees therefor.

§ 1-812. Copy of record as evidence.

The certificate of a notary public, under his hand and seal of office, drawn from his record, stating the protest and the facts therein recorded, shall be evidence of the facts in like manner as the original protest.

§ 1-813. Fees.

(a) The Mayor of the District of Columbia shall adjust from time to time the schedule of fees to be charged by notaries public. The Mayor shall adjust the schedule by rule to provide fees in amounts which, in the Mayor's judgment, will defray the notary public's necessary expenses in connection with performinng his services.

(b) Until the schedule of fees is adjusted by the Mayor in accordance with subsection (a) of this section, the schedule of fees in subsection (c) of this section will be in effect.

(c) The fees of notaries public shall be:

(1) For taking an acknowledgment of proof of a deed or other instrument including the seal and writing of the certificate, $2 for each signature;

(2) For administering an oath or for taking an affidavit, including the jurat and seal, $2;

(3) For any other notarial act, $2.

§ 1-814. Penalties for taking higher fees.

Any notary public who shall take a higher fee than is prescribed by § 1-813 shall pay a fine of $100 and be removed from office by the Superior Court of the District of Columbia.

§ 1-815. Custody of records and official papers upon death, resignation, and removal from office.

Upon the death, resignation, or removal from office of any notary public, his records, together with all his official papers, shall be deposited in the Office of the Mayor of the District of Columbia or his designated agent.

§ 1-816. Certificates issued by Mayor.

Certificates issued by the Mayor of the District of Columbia may be signed by the Executive Secretary.

§ 1-817. Authorization for appropriation; inclusion of expenses in Mayor's annual estimates.

Appropriation is hereby authorized to be made to carry out the provisions of this section and §§ 1-803 and 1-806, and the Mayor of the District of Columbia is authorized to include in his annual estimates provision for all expenses incident to such purposes, including the purchase of equipment and supplies and the payment of salaries to personnel.

ADDITIONAL AUTHORITY

§ 26-110. Authority of notaries public associated with corporations.

It shall be lawful for any notary public who is a stockholder, director, officer, or employee of a bank, trust company, or other corporation to take the acknowledgment of any party to any written instrument executed to or by such corporation, or to administer an oath to any other stockholder, director, officer, employee, or agent of such corporation, or to protest for nonacceptance or nonpayment drafts, checks, notes, acceptances, or other negotiable instruments which may be owned or held for collection by such corporation: Provided, that it shall be unlawful for any notary public to take the acknowledgment of an instrument executed by or to a bank or corporation of which he is a stockholder, director, officer, or employee, where such notary is a party to such instrument, either individually or as a representative of such corporation, or to protest any negotiable instrument owned or held for collection by such corporation, where such notary is individually a party to such instrument: Provided further, that it shall be unlawful for any notary public to take the oath of an officer or director of any bank or trust company of which he is an officer, or to take an oath of any person verifying a report of such bank or trust company to the Comptroller of the Currency.

ACKNOWLEDGMENTS

§ 45-601. No acknowledgment of deed by attorney.

No deeds of conveyance of either real or personal estate by individuals shall be executed or acknowledged by attorney.

§ 45-602. Manner of acknowledgment; form of certificate.

Acknowledgment of deeds may be made in the District of Columbia before any judge of any of the courts of said District, the Clerk of the United States District Court for the District of Columbia, or any notary public, or the Recorder of Deeds of said District, and the certificate of the officer taking the acknowledgment shall be to the following effect:

I, AB, a notary public (or other officer authorized) in and for the District of Columbia, do hereby certify that CD, party to a certain deed bearing date on the . . . . . . day of . . . . ., and hereto annexed, personally appeared before me in said District, the said CD being personally well-known to me as (or proved by the oath of credible witnesses to be) the person who executed the said deed, and acknowledged the same to be his act and deed.

Given under my hand and seal this . . . . . . day of . . . . . .

§ 45-603. Acknowledgment out of District.

When any deed or contract under seal is to be

acknowledged out of the District of Columbia, but within the United States, the acknowledgment may be made before any judge of a court of record and of law, or any chancellor of a state, any judge or justice of the Supreme, district, or territorial courts of the United States, any justice of the peace or notary public: Provided, that the certificate of acknowledgment aforesaid, made by any officer of the state or territory not having a seal, shall be accompanied by the certificate of the register, clerk, or other public officer that the officer taking said acknowledgment was in fact the officer he professed to be.

§ 45-604. Acknowledgment in foreign country.

Deeds made in a foreign country may be acknowledged before any judge or notary public, or before any secretary of legation or consular officer, or acting consular officer of the United States, as such consular officer is described in former § 51 of Title 22, United States Code; and when the acknowledgment is made before any other officer than a secretary of legation or consular officer or acting consular officer of the United States, the official character of the person taking the acknowledgment shall be certified in the manner prescribed in § 45-603.

§ 45-605. Acknowledgments in Guam, Samoa, and Canal Zone.

Deeds and other instruments affecting land situate in the District of Columbia may be acknowledged in the islands of Guam and Samoa or in the Canal Zone before any notary public or judge, appointed therein by proper authority, or by any officer therein who has ex officio the powers of a notary public: Provided, that the certificate by such notary in Guam, Samoa, or the Canal Zone, as the case may be, shall be accompanied by the certificate of the governor or acting governor of such place to the effect that the notary taking said acknowledgment was in fact the officer he purported to be; and any deeds or other instruments affecting lands so situate, so acknowledged since the 1st day of January, 1905, and accompanied by such certificate shall have the same effect as such deeds or other instruments hereafter so acknowledged and certified.

§ 45-606. Acknowledgments in Phillipine Islands and Puerto Rico.

Deeds and other instruments affecting land situate in the District of Columbia may be acknowledged in the Phillipine Islands and Puerto Rico be-fore any notary public appointed therein by proper authority, or any officer therein who has ex officio the powers of a notary public: Provided, that the certificate by such notary in the Phillipine Islands or in Puerto Rico, as the case may be, shall be accompanied by the certificate of the Executive Secretary of Puerto Rico, or the Governor or Attorney General of the Phillipine Islands to the effect that the notary taking said acknowledgment was in fact the officer he purported to be.

DEPOSITIONS

[D.C. Super. Ct. R. Civ. P.]

RULE 28. Persons before whom depositions may be taken

(a) **Within the United States.** Within the United States or within a territory or insular possession subject to the dominion of the United States, depositions shall be taken before an officer authorized to administer oaths by the laws of the United States or of the place where the examination is held, or before a person appointed by the court. A person so appointed has power to administer oaths and take testimony.

(b) **In Foreign Countries.** In a foreign country, depositions may be taken (1) on notice before a person authorized to administer oaths in the place in which the examination is held, either by the law thereof or by the law of the United States, or (2) before a person commissioned by the court, and a person so commissioned shall have the power by virtue of his commission to administer any necessary oath and take testimony, or (3) pursuant to a letter rogatory. A commission or a letter rogatory shall be issued on application and notice and on terms that are just and appropriate. It is not requisite to the issuance of a commission and a letter rogatory that the taking of the deposition in any other manner is impracticable or inconvenient; and both a commission and a letter rogatory may be issued in proper cases. A notice or commission may designate the person before whom the deposition is to be taken either by name or descriptive title. A letter rogatory may be addressed "To the Appropriate Authority in [here name the country]." Evidence obtained in response to a letter rogatory need not be excluded merely for the reason that it is not a verbatim transcript or that the testimony was not taken under oath or for any similar departure from the requirements for depositions taken within the United States under these rules.

(c) **Disqualification for Interest.** No deposition shall be taken before a person who is a relative or employee or attorney or counsel of any of the parties, or is a relative or employee of such attorney or counsel, or is financially interested in the action.

RULE 28-I. Person commissioned to take depositions

(a) **By This Court.** Any party to a civil action pending in this court may file with the court a motion for appointment of an examiner to take the testimony of a witness who resides outside the District of Columbia. The motion shall state the name and address of each witness sought to be deposed and the reasons why the testimony of such witness is required in the action. The motion shall be served on all other parties to the action who may within five days file opposition to the motion as prescribed in Rule 12. If the motion is granted, the court shall appoint an examiner to take the testimony of such witnesses as are designated in the order of appointment and shall issue a commission to the examiner who shall take the testimony in the manner prescribed in these rules.

(b) **By Another Court.** Any person appointed by a court of a state, territory, commonwealth, possession, or place under the jurisdiction of the United States to take the testimony of a witness found within the District of Columbia for use in an action pending in such court may cause to be filed with this court a copy of his commission or other evidence of authority together with a motion for leave of court to take the designated testimony. If the motion and evidence of authority so filed are in order, the court shall grant the motion and may, upon application, issue a subpoena compelling the designated witness to present himself for deposition at a specified time and place. Testimony taken under this section shall be taken in the manner prescribed in these rules and the court may entertain any motion, including motions for quashing service of a subpoena and for issuance of protective orders, in the same manner as if the action were pending in this court.

LEGAL HOLIDAYS

[D.C. CODE ANN.]

§ 28-2701. Holidays designated — Time for performing acts extended.

The following days in each year, namely, New Year's Day, January 1; Dr. Martin Luther King Jr.'s Birthday, the third Monday in January; Washington's Birthday, the third Monday in February; Memorial Day, the last Monday in May; Independence Day, July 4; Labor Day, the first Monday in September; Columbus Day, the second Monday in October; Veteran's Day, November 11; Thanksgiving Day, the fourth Thursday in November; Christmas Day, December 25; every Saturday, after twelve o'clock noon; any day appointed by the President of the United States as a day of public feasting or thanksgiving; and the day of the inauguration of the President, in every fourth year, are holidays in the District for all purposes. When a day set apart as a legal holiday, other than the day of the inauguration of the President, falls on a Saturday, the next preceding day is a holiday. When a day set apart as a legal holiday falls on a Sunday, the next succeeding day is a holiday. In such cases, when a Sunday and a holiday or holidays fall on successive days, all commercial papers falling due on any of those days shall, for all purposes of presenting for payment or acceptance, be deemed to mature and be presentable for payment or acceptance on the next secular business day succeeding. Every Saturday is a holiday in the District for (1) every bank or banking institution having an office or banking house located within the District, (2) every Federal savings and loan association whose main office is in the District, and (3) every building association, building and loan association, or savings and loan association, incorporated or unincorporated, organized and operating under the laws of and having an office located within the District. An act which would otherwise be required, authorized, or permitted to be performed on Saturday in the District at the office or banking house of, or by, any such bank or bank institution, Federal savings and loan association, building association, building and loan association, or savings and loan association, if Saturday were not a holiday, shall or may be so performed on the next succeeding business day, and liability or loss of rights of any kind may not result from such delay.

FLORIDA

NOTARIES PUBLIC

[FLA. STAT. ANN]

§ 117.01. Appointment, application, fee, term of office, powers, bond, and oath.

(1) The Governor may appoint as many notaries public as he shall deem necessary, each of whom shall be at least 18 years of age and a permanent resident of the state.

(2)(a) Application for appointment shall be signed by the applicant, shall be accompanied by a fee of $25 and the oath and bond required by subsection (4), and shall be in a form prescribed by the Department of State which shall require, but not be limited to, the following information: full name and residence or business address, home and business telephone numbers, date of birth, citizenship, status, affidavit of good character from someone unrelated to the applicant, declaration of permanent residence, and a statement of all felony convictions. Each applicant must certify that the application is true and correct to the best of his knowledge.

(b) The fee required by paragraph (a) shall be deemed to include the fee required by § 113.01 for issuance of a commission.

(3) Said notaries public shall hold their respective offices for 4 years and shall use and exercise such office of notary public for such places and within the boundaries of the state, to whose protestations, attestations, and other instruments of publication due credence shall be given. The Governor may remove any notary public for cause.

(4) Every notary public shall, prior to his executing the duties of said office, give bond to the Governor for the time being, in the penalty of $1,000, conditioned for the due discharge of his said office and also take an oath that he will honestly, diligently, and faithfully discharge the duties of a notary public. The bond shall be approved and filed with the Department of State. Such bond shall be executed by a surety company for hire, duly authorized to transact business in Florida. The bond must be approved by the Department of Banking and Finance before issuance of the commission.

(5) No person shall obtain or use a notary public commission in other than his legal name, and it shall be deemed unlawful for a notary public to notarize his own signature. Any person applying for a notary public commission may be required to submit proof of his identity to the Department of State if so requested. Any person violating the provisions of this subsection shall be guilty of a felony of the third degree, punishable as provided in § 775.082, § 775.083, or § 775.084.

§ 117.02. Women eligible.

Any woman who is commissioned as a notary public and subsequently changes her name by marriage or any other method may continue to hold her commission under the name in which it was issued until the commission shall have expired. Upon expiration, she shall then apply for a new commission using her new legal name.

§ 117.03. Administration of oaths; penalties for false oaths.

(1) In all cases in which it may be necessary to the due and legal execution of any writing or document whatever to be attested, protested, or published under the seal of his office, any notary public may administer an oath and make certificate thereof. The notary shall not take an acknowledgment of execution, as provided in § 117.07, in lieu of an oath when an oath is required.

(2) Any person making a false oath before a notary public shall be guilty of perjury and be subject to the penalties, forfeitures, and disabilities that are prescribed by law in cases of perjury under chapter 837.

§ 117.04. May solemnize marriages and take acknowledgments; fees.

Notaries public are authorized to solemnize the rites of matrimony and to take renunciation and relinquishment of dower and the acknowledgments of deeds and other instruments of writing for record, as fully as other officers of this state are; and, for so doing, they shall be allowed fees not to exceed those allowed by law to clerks of the circuit court for like services.

§ 117.05. Fees.

The fees of the notaries public may be prescribed by the Department of State but shall not exceed those provided by law to clerks of the circuit court for like services.

§ 117.06. Validity of acts prior to April 1, 1903.

Any and all notarial acts that were done by any notary public in the state prior to April 1, 1903, which would have been valid had not the term of office of the notary public expired, are declared to be valid.

§ 117.07. Statement of time of expiration of commission; seal.

(1) Unless the date of expiration of his commis-sion is included on the notary seal, a notary public in the state shall add to his official signature to any certificate of acknowledgment made before him a statement of the time of the expiration of his commission as notary public in words and figures as follows: "My commission expires ___(Herein insert the date when the commission expires.).*"

(2) A notary seal shall be affixed to all documents notarized, which may be of the rubber stamp or impression type and shall include the words "Notary Public—State of Florida." The seal shall also include the name of the notary public and may include the date of expiration of the commission of the notary public.

§ 117.08. Notary public acting after expiration of commission.

Every notary public in this state who shall take any acknowledgment of any instrument as a notary public, or who makes any certificate as such, after the expiration of his commission, shall be guilty of a misdemeanor of the second degree, punishable as provided in § 775.082 or § 775.083.

§ 117.09. Penalties.

(1) Every notary public in the state shall require reasonable proof of the identity of the person whose signature is being notarized and such person must be in the presence of the notary public at the time the signature is notarized. Any notary public violating the above provision shall be guilty of a misdemeanor of the second degree, punishable as provided in § 775.082 or § 775.083. It shall be no defense under this section that the notary public acted without intent to defraud.

(2) Any notary public in this state who shall falsely or fraudulently take any acknowledgment of any instrument as a notary public or who falsely or fraudulently makes any certificate as a notary public or who falsely takes or receives and acknowledgment of the signature on any written instrument shall be guilty of a felony of the third degree, punishable as provided in § 775.082, § 775.083, or § 775.084.

§ 117.10. Law enforcement officers and correctional officers.

Law enforcement officers and correctional officers, as defined in § 943.10, are notaries public for the purpose of notarizing, certifying, or attesting to documents in connection with the performance of official dutie§ Sections 117.01, 117.04, 117.05, 117.07, and 117.08 do not apply to the provisions of this section. An officer may not notarize his own signature.

ADDITIONAL AUTHORITY

§ 741.07. Persons authorized to solemnize matrimony.

(1) All regularly ordained ministers of the gospel or elders in communion with some church, or other ordained clergy, and all judicial officers, clerks of the circuit courts, and notaries public of this state may solemnize the rights of matrimonial contract, under the regulations prescribed by law. Nothing in this section shall make invalid a marriage which was solemnized by any member of the clergy, or as otherwise provided by law prior to July 1, 1978.

* * *

§ 741.08. Marriage not to be solemnized without a license.

Before any of the persons named in § 741.07 shall solemnize any marriage, he shall require of the parties a marriage license issued according to the requirements of § 741.01, and within 10 days after solemnizing the marriage he shall make a certificate thereof on the license, and shall transmit the same to the office of the county court judge from which it issued.

FEES

§ 113.01. Fee for commissions issued by Governor.

A fee of $10 is prescribed for the issuance of each commission issued by the Governor of the state and attested by the Secretary of State for an elected officer or a notary public. However, no fee shall be required for the issuance of a commission as a notary public to a veteran who served during a period of wartime service as defined in § 1.01(15)[(14)] and who has been rated by the United States Government or the Veterans Administration to have a disability rating of 50 percent or more; such disability is subject to verification by the Secretary of State, who has authority to adopt reasonable procedures to implement this act.

§ 320.04 Registration service charge.

* * *

(2) * * * No tax collector, deputy tax collector, or employee of the state or any county shall charge, collect, or receive any fee or compensation for services performed as notary public in connection with or incidental to the issuance of license plates or titles. The provisions of this subsection and of § 116.38(2) prohibiting the charging, collecting, or receiving of notary public fees do not apply to any privately owned license plate agency appointed by the county manager of a charter county which has an appointed tax collector.

PENALTIES

§ 775.082. Penalties.

(1) A person who has been convicted of a capital felony shall be punished by life imprisonment and shall be required to serve no less than 25 years before becoming eligible for parole unless the proceeding held to determine sentence according to the procedure set forth in § 921.141 results in findings by the court that such person shall be punished by death, and in the latter event such person shall be punished by death.

(2) In the event the death penalty in a capital felony is held to be unconstitutional by the Florida Supreme Court or the United States Supreme Court, the court having jurisdiction over a person previously sentenced to death for a capital felony shall cause such person to be brought before the court, and the court shall sentence such person to life imprisonment as provided in subsection (1).

(3) A person who has been convicted of any other designated felony may be punished as follows:

(a) For a life felony committed prior to October 1, 1983, by a term of imprisonment for life or for a term of years not less than 30 and, for a life felony committed on or after October 1, 1983, by a term of imprisonment for life or by a term of imprisonment not exceeding 40 years;

(b) For a felony of the first degree, by a term of imprisonment not exceeding 30 years or, when specifically provided by statute, by imprisonment for a term of years not exceeding life imprisonment;

(c) For a felony of the second degree, by a term of imprisonment not exceeding 15 years;

(d) For a felony of the third degree, by a term of imprisonment not exceeding 5 years.

(4) A person who has been convicted of a designated misdemeanor may be sentenced as follows:

(a) For a misdemeanor of the first degree, by a definite term of imprisonment not exceeding 1 year;

(b) For a misdemeanor of the second degree, by a definite term of imprisonment not exceeding 60 days.

(5) Any person who has been convicted of a noncriminal violation may not be sentenced to a term of imprisonment nor to any other punishment more severe than a fine, forfeiture, or other civil penalty, except as provided in chapter 316 or by ordinance of any city or county.

(6) Nothing in this section shall be construed to alter the operation of any statute of this state au-

thorizing a trial court, in its discretion, to impose a sentence of imprisonment for an indeterminate period within minimum and maximum limits as provided by law, except as provided in subsection (1).

(7) This section does not deprive the court of any authority conferred by law to decree a forfeiture of property, suspend or cancel a license, remove a person from office, or impose any other civil penalty. Such a judgment or order may be included in the sentence.

§ 775.083. Fines.

(1) A person who has been convicted of an offense other than a capital felony may be sentenced to pay a fine in addition to any punishment described in § 775.082; when specifically authorized by statute, he may be sentenced to pay a fine in lieu of any punishment described in § 775.082. A person who has been convicted of a noncriminal violation may be sentenced to pay a fine. Fines for designated crimes and for noncriminal violations shall not exceed:

(a) $15,000, when the conviction is of a life felony.

(b) $10,000, when the conviction is of a felony of the first or second degree.

(c) $5,000, when the conviction is of a felony of the third degree.

(d) $1,000, when the conviction is of a misdemeanor of the first degree.

(e) $500, when the conviction is of a misdemeanor of the second degree or a noncriminal violation.

(f) Any higher amount equal to double the pecuniary gain derived from the offense by the offender or double the pecuniary loss suffered by the victim.

(g) Any higher amount specifically authorized by statute.

(2) If a defendant is unable to pay a fine, the court may defer payment of the fine to a date certain.

§ 775.084. Habitual felony offenders and habitual violent felony offenders; extended terms; definitions; procedure; penalties.

(1) As used in this act:

(a) "Habitual felony offender" means a defendant for whom the court may impose an extended term of imprisonment, as provided in this section, if it finds that:

1. The defendant has previously been convicted of any combination of two or more felonies in this state or other qualified offenses;

2. The felony for which the defendant is to be sentenced was committed within 5 years of the date of the conviction of the last prior felony or other qualified offense of which he was convicted, or

within 5 years of the defendant's release, on parole or otherwise, from a prison sentence or other commitment imposed as a result of a prior conviction for a felony or other qualified offense, whichever is later;

3. The defendant has not received a pardon for any felony or other qualified offense that is necessary for the operation of this section; and

4. A conviction of a felony or other qualified offense necessary to the operation of this section has not been set aside in any post-conviction proceeding.

(b) "Habitual violent felony offender" means a defendant for whom the court may impose an extended term of imprisonment, as provided in this section, if it finds that:

1. The defendant has previously been convicted of a felony or an attempt or conspiracy to commit a felony and one or more of such convictions was for:

   a. Arson,

   b. Sexual battery,

   c. Robbery,

   d. Kidnapping,

   e. Aggravated child abuse,

   f. Aggravated assault,

   g. Murder,

   h. Manslaughter,

   i. Unlawful throwing, placing, or discharging of a destructive device or bomb,

   j. Armed burglary, or

   k. Aggravated battery;

2. The felony for which the defendant is to be sentenced was committed within 5 years of the date of the conviction of the last prior enumerated felony or within 5 years of the defendant's release, on parole or otherwise, from a prison sentence or other commitment imposed as a result of a prior conviction for an enumerated felony, whichever is later;

3. The defendant has not received a pardon on the ground of innocence for any crime that is necessary for the operation of this section; and

4. A conviction of a crime necessary to the operation of this section has not been set aside in any post-conviction proceeding.

(c) "Qualified offense" means any offense, substantially similar in elements and penalties to an offense in this state, which is in violation of a law of any other jurisdiction, whether that of another state, the District of Columbia, the United States or any possession or territory thereof, or any foreign jurisdiction, that was punishable under the law of such jurisdiction at the time of its commission by the defendant by death or imprisonment exceeding 1 year.

(2) For the purposes of this section, the placing of a person on probation without an adjudication of guilt shall be treated as a prior conviction if the subsequent offense for which he is to be sentenced was committed during such probationary period.

(3) In a separate proceeding, the court shall determine if the defendant is a habitual felony offender or a habitual violent felony offender. The procedure shall be as follows:

(a) The court shall obtain and consider a presentence investigation prior to the imposition of a sentence as a habitual felony offender or a habitual violent felony offender.

(b) Written notice shall be served on the defendant and his attorney a sufficient time prior to the entry of a plea or prior to the imposition of sentence so as to allow the preparation of a submission on behalf of the defendant.

(c) Except as provided in paragraph (a), all evidence presented shall be presented in open court with full rights of confrontation, cross-examination, and representation by counsel.

(d) Each of the findings required as the basis for such sentence shall be found to exist by a preponderance of the evidence and shall be appealable to the extent normally applicable to similar findings.

(e) For the purpose of identification of a habitual felony offender or a habitual violent felony offender, the court shall fingerprint the defendant pursuant to § 921.241.

(4)(a) The court, in conformity with the procedure established in subsection (3), shall sentence the habitual felony offender as follows:

1. In the case of a felony of the first degree, for life.

2. In the case of a felony of the second degree, for a term of years not exceeding 30.

3. In the case of a felony of the third degree, for a term of years not exceeding 10.

(b) The court, in conformity with the procedure established in subsection (3), may sentence the habitual violent felony offender as follows:

1. In the case of a felony of the first degree, for life, and such offender shall not be eligible for release for 15 years.

2. In the case of a felony of the second degree, for a term of years not exceeding 30, and such offender shall not be eligible for release for 10 years.

3. In the case of a felony of the third degree, for a term of years not exceeding 10, and such offender shall not be eligible for release for 5 years.

(c) If the court decides that imposition of sentence under this section is not necessary for the protection of the public, sentence shall be imposed without regard to this section. At any time when it appears to the court that the defendant is a habitual felony offender or a habitual violent felony offender, the court shall make that determination as provided in subsection (3).

(d) A sentence imposed under this section shall not be increased after such imposition.

(e) A sentence imposed under this section shall not be subject to the provisions of § 921.001. The provisions of chapter 947 shall not be applied to

such person. A defendant sentenced under this section shall not be eligible for gain-time granted by the Department of Corrections except that the department may grant up to 20 days of incentive gain-time each month as provided for in § 944.275(4)(b).

ACKNOWLEDGMENTS

§ 695.03. Acknowledgment and proof; validation of certain acknowledgments; legalization or authentication before foreign officials.

To entitle any instrument concerning real property to be recorded, the execution must be acknowledged by the party executing it, proved by a subscribing witness to it, or legalized or authenticated by a civil-law notary or notary public who affixes his official seal, before the officers and in the form and manner following:

(1) **Within this state.**— An acknowledgment or proof made within this state may be made before a judge, clerk, or deputy clerk of any court; a United States commissioner or magistrate; or a notary public, and the certificate of acknowledgment or proof must be under the seal of the court or officer, as the case may be. All affidavits and acknowledgments heretofore made or taken in this manner are hereby validated.

(2) **Without this state but within the United States.**—An acknowledgment or proof made out of this state but within the United States may be made before a commissioner of deeds appointed by the Governor of this state; a judge or clerk of any court of the United States or of any state, territory, or district, a United States commissioner or magistrate; or a notary public, justice of the peace, master in chancery, or registrar or recorder of deeds of any state, territory, or district having a seal, and the certificate of acknowledgment or proof must be under the seal of the court or officer, as the case may be. If the acknowledgment or proof is made before a notary public who does not affix a seal, it is sufficient for the notary public to type, print, or write by hand on the instrument, "I am a Notary Public of the State of . . .(state). . ., and my commission expires on . . .(date). . . ."

(3) **Within foreign countries.**—If the acknowledgment, legalization, authentication, or proof is made in a foreign country, it may be made before a commissioner of deeds appointed by the Governor of this state to act in such country; before a civil-law notary or notary public of such foreign country who has an official seal; before an ambassador, envoy extraordinary, minister plenipotentiary, minister, commissioner, charge d'affaires, consul general, consul, vice consul, consular agent, or other diplomatic or consular officer of the United States ap-

pointed to reside in such country; or before a military or naval officer authorized by the Laws or Articles of War of the United States to perform the duties of notary public, and the certificate of acknowledgment, legalization, authentication, or proof must be under the seal of the officer. A certificate legalizing or authenticating the signature of a person executing an instrument concerning real property and to which a civil-law notary or notary public of that country has affixed his official seal is sufficient as an acknowledgment. For the purposes of this section, "civil-law notary" means an official of a foreign country who has an official seal and who is authorized to make legal or lawful the execution of any document in that jurisdiction, in which jurisdiction the affixing of his official seal is deemed proof of the execution of the document or deed in full compliance with the laws of that jurisdiction.

All affidavits, legalizations, authentications, and acknowledgments heretofore made or taken in the manner set forth above are hereby validated.

§ 695.05. Certain defects cured as to acknowledgments and witnesses.

All deeds, conveyances, bills of sale, mortgages or other transfers of real or personal property within the limits of this state, heretofore or hereafter made and received bona fide and upon good consideration by any corporation, and acknowledged for record before some officer, stockholder or other person interested in the corporation, grantee, or mortgagee as a notary public or other officer authorized to take acknowledgments of instruments for record within this state, shall be held, deemed and taken as valid as if acknowledged by the proper notary public or other officer authorized to take acknowledgments of instruments for record in this state not so interested in said corporation, grantee or mortgagee; and said instrument whenever recorded shall be deemed notice to all persons; provided, however, that this section shall not apply to any instrument heretofore made, the validity of which shall be contested by suit commenced within one year of the effective date of this law.

§ 695.09. Identity of grantor.

No acknowledgement or proof shall be taken, except as set forth in § 695.03(3), by any officer within or without the United States unless he knows, or has satisfactory proof, that the person making the acknowledgment is the individual described in, and who executed, such instrument or that the person offering to make proof is one of the subscribing witnesses to such instrument.

DEPOSITIONS

[FLA. R. CIV. P.]

RULE 1.300. Persons before whom depositions may be taken

(a) **Persons Authorized.** Depositions may be taken before any notary public or judicial officer or before any officer authorized by the statutes of Florida to take acknowledgments or proof of executions of deeds or by any person appointed by the court in which the action is pending.

(b) **In Foreign Countries.** In a foreign country depositions may be taken (1) on notice before a person authorized to administer oaths in the place in which the examination is held, either by the law thereof or by the law of Florida or of the United States or (2) before a person commissioned by the court, and a person so commissioned shall have the power by virtue of his commission to administer any necessary oath and take testimony or (3) pursuant to a letter rogatory. A commission or a letter rogatory shall be issued on application and notice and on terms that are just and appropriate. It is not requisite to the issuance of a commission or a letter rogatory that the taking of the deposition in any other manner is impracticable or inconvenient and both a commission and a letter rogatory may be issued in proper cases. A notice or commission may designate the person before whom the deposition is to be taken either by name or descriptive title. A letter rogatory may be addressed "To the Appropriate Authority in (herein name the country)." Evidence obtained in response to a letter rogatory need not be excluded merely for the reason that it is not a verbatim transcript or that the testimony was not taken under oath or any similar departure from the requirements for depositions taken within Florida under these rules.

(c) **Selection by Stipulation.** If the parties so stipulate in writing, depositions may be taken before any person at any time or place upon any notice and in any manner and when so taken may be used like other depositions.

(d) **Persons Disqualified.** Unless so stipulated by the parties no deposition shall be taken before a person who is a relative or employee or attorney or counsel of any of the parties or is a relative or employee of such attorney or counsel or is financially interested in the action.

COMMISSIONERS

[FLA. STAT. ANN.]

§ 118.01. Appointment [of commissioners] and power to take acknowledgments.

The governor may name, appoint and commission one or more commissioners in each of such of the states and territories of the United States, the District of Columbia, and in any foreign country, as he may deem expedient; and such commissioner shall continue in office for 4 years, and shall have authority to take the acknowledgment and proof of the execution of any deed, mortgage or other conveyance of any lands, tenements or hereditaments lying or being in this state, and any contract, letter of attorney, or any other writing under seal to be used or recorded in this state, and such acknowledgment or proof taken or made in the manner directed by the laws of this state and certified by any one of the said commissioners before whom the same shall be taken or made under his seal, which certificate shall be endorsed on or annexed to said deed or instrument aforesaid, shall have the same force and effect, and be as good and available in law for all purposes, as if the same had been made or taken before the proper officer of this state.

§ 118.02.   May administer oaths.

Every commissioner appointed by virtue of this chapter may administer an oath to any person who shall be willing and desirous to make such oath before him, and such affidavit made before such commissioner shall be as good and effectual to all intents and purposes as if taken by any magistrate resident in this state and competent to take the same.

§ 118.03.   Oath of office.

Every commissioner appointed as aforesaid before he shall proceed to perform any duty under and by virtue of this law shall take and subscribe an oath before a notary public in the city or county in which such commissioner shall reside, well and faithfully to execute and perform all the duties of such commissioner under and by virtue of the laws of this state, which oath shall be filed in the office of the Department of State.

LEGAL HOLIDAYS

§ 683.01.   Legal holidays.

(1) The legal holidays, which are also public holidays, are the following:

(a) Sunday, the first day of each week.

(b) New Year's Day, January 1.

(c) Birthday of Martin Luther King, Jr., January 15.

(d) Birthday of Robert E. Lee, January 19.

(e) Lincoln's Birthday, February 12.

(f) Susan B. Anthony's Birthday, February 15.

(g) Washington's Birthday, the third Monday in February.

(h) Good Friday.

(i) Pascua Florida Day, April 2.

(j) Confederate Memorial Day, April 26.

(k) Memorial Day, the last Monday in May.

(l) Birthday of Jefferson Davis, June 3.

(m) Independence Day, July 4.

(n) Labor Day, the first Monday in September.

(o) Columbus Day and Farmer's Day, the second Monday in October.

(p) Veteran's Day, November 11.

(q) General Election Day.

(r) Thanksgiving Day, the fourth Thursday in November.

(s) Christmas Day, December 25.

(t) Shrove Tuesday sometimes known as "Mardi Gras," in counties where carnival associations are organized for the purpose of celebrating the same.

(2) Whenever any legal holiday shall fall upon a Sunday, the Monday next following shall be deemed a public holiday for all and any of the purposes aforesaid.

§ 638.02.   Meaning of term "legal holidays" as used in contracts.

Whenever, in contracts to be performed in the state, reference is made to "legal holidays," the term shall be understood to include those holidays designated in § 683.01 and such others as may be designated by law.

GEORGIA

NOTARIES PUBLIC

[GA. CODE ANN.]

§ 45-17-1. Definitions.

As used in this article, the term:

(1) "Attesting" and "attestation" are synonymous and mean the notarial act of witnessing or attesting a signature or execution of a deed or other written instrument, where such notarial act does not involve the taking of an acknowledgment, the administering of an oath or affirmation, the taking of a verification, or the certification of a copy.

(2) "Notarial act" means any act that a notary public is authorized by law to perform and includes, without limitation, attestation, the taking of an acknowledgment, the administration of an oath or affirmation, the taking of a verification upon an oath or affirmation, and the certification of a copy.

(3) "Notarial certificate" means the notary's documentation of a notarial act.

§ 45-17-1-1. Power to appoint notaries public.

The power to appoint notaries public is vested in

the clerks of the superior courts and may be exercised by them at any time.

§ 45-17-2. Qualifications of notaries.

(a) Any individual applying for appointment to be a notary public must be:

(1) At least 18 years old;

(2) A resident of this state;

(3) A resident of the county from which such individual is appointed; and

(4) Able to read and write the English language.

(b) The qualifications of paragraphs (2) and (3) of subsection (a) of this Code section shall not apply to any individual applying for appointment as a notary public under the provisions of Code Section 45-17-7.

§ 45-17-2-1. Application to be a notary; endorsements and declarations.

(a) Any individual desiring to be a notary public shall submit application to the clerk of superior court of the county in which the individual resides or, when applying under the provisions of Code Section 45-17-7, to the clerk of superior court of the county in which the individual works or has a business. The applicant shall sign and swear or affirm as outlined in paragraph (2) of subsection (b) of this Code section to the truthfulness of the application which shall state:

(1) That the applicant resides or works or has a business in the county of application and the address of the residence or business;

(2) That the applicant is at least 18 years old;

(3) That the applicant can read and write the English language;

(4) All denials, revocations, suspensions, restrictions, or resignations of a notary commission held by the applicant; and

(5) All criminal convictions of the applicant, including any plea of nolo contendere, except minor traffic violations.

(b) In addition to the application required in subsection (a) of this Code section, every applicant for appointment as notary public shall also submit to the clerk of superior court of the county in which the individual makes application:

(1) Endorsements from two persons who are not relatives of the applicant, who are at least 18 years old, and who reside in the county in which the individual makes application. The endorsement shall be in the following form:

I, _____, being 18 years of age
   (name of endorser)

or older and a resident of _____,
                            (name of county)

believe the applicant for a notary public commission, _____, who is not re-
              (name of applicant)

lated to myself, to be a person of integrity, good moral character, and capable of performing notarial acts.

_____   _____
(signature of endorser)   (date)

_____
(address of endorser)

(2) A declaration of applicant which shall have been signed in the presence of a commissioned notary public of this state. The declaration of applicant shall be in the following form:

I, _____, do solemnly swear or
   (name of applicant)

affirm under penalty of perjury that the personal information I have written in this application is true, complete, and correct.

_____
(signature of applicant)

State of _____
County of _____

On this _____ day of _____, 19___, before me appeared, _____, the person who singed the preceding declaration of applicant in my presence and who swore or affirmed that _____ under-
                                              (he/she)

stood the document and freely declared it to be truthful.

_____
(official signature of the notary)
(official seal of the notary)

§ 45-17-2-2. Application information to be matter of public record.

The information in the application for appointment and commissioning as a notary public shall be a matter of public record.

§ 45-17-2-3. Grant or denial of commission.

(a) After an applicant submits to the clerk of superior court of the county the application, endorsements, and declaration of applicant as required in Code Section 45-17-2-1, the clerk of the superior court shall either grant or deny a commission as a notary public within ten days following the applicant's submission of the necessary documents.

(b) The clerk of superior court may in his discretion deny a commission to an applicant based on any of the following grounds:

(1) The applicant's criminal history;

(2) Revocation, suspension, or restriction of any notary commission or professional license issued to the applicant by this or any other state; or

(3) The commission in this or any state of any act enumerated in subsection (a) of Code Section 45-

17-15. whether or not criminal penalties or commission suspension or revocation resulted.

(c) Any applicant who is denied a notarial commission by the clerk of superior court shall upon demand be allowed a hearing and adjudication before the superior court clerk with the right of de novo appeal to the superior court, such appeal to be determined by the court without the intervention of a jury.

§ 45-17-3. Oath of office.

Before entering on the duties of his office, each notary public shall take and subscribe before the clerk of the superior court the following oath, which shall be entered on his minutes.

"I, _____, do solemnly swear or affirm that I will well and truly perform the duties of a notary public to the best of my ability; and I further swear or affirm that I am not the holder of any public money belonging to the state and unaccounted for, so help me God."

§ 45-17-4. Payment of fees to court clerk and Secretary of State; Secretary of State to keep record of notaries appointed; reappointment.

Before a certificate shall be issued to a notary public, he shall pay to the clerk of the superior court the sum prescribed by Code Section 15-6-77. relating to fees of clerks of the superior courts, from which amount the clerk shall be entitled to cover his services in issuing the certificate of appointment as notary public, administering the oath, and recording the same. The amount by which the sum prescribed by Code Section 15-6-77. exceeds the amount which the clerk is required by this Code section to forward to the Secretary of State is what the clerk shall use to cover his services. The clerk shall immediately send a copy of the certificate of appointment, under his seal of office, and $2.00 to the Secretary of State who shall keep a record in his office showing the names of the notaries public appointed with their addresses, signatures, ages, sex, and the terms for which their commissions run; and such amount shall cover the cost of the Secretary of State in keeping such records. On reappointment as notaries public, the sum prescribed by Code Section 15-6-77 shall be paid to the clerk of the superior court and disbursed in the same manner as the fee for the original appointment is disbursed under this Code section.

§ 45-17-5. Term of office; revocation; renewal of commission; issuance of certificates of appointment; maintenance of record of appointments; duplicate original of certificate of appointment as prerequisite to obtaining notary

public seal; holding self out as or exercising powers of notary without commission as misdemeanor.

(a) Each notary public shall hold office for four years, subject to revocation at any time by the clerk of the superior court, at the end of which time, on petition, his commission may be renewed by order of the clerk for a like term. Renewal of a notary public commission may be done in person or by mail at the discretion of the clerk of superior court. The clerk of the superior court shall issue to each notary public a certificate of his appointment and qualifications, which certificate shall contain the name, address, age, and sex of the appointee, the date the certificate was issued, and the term for which the appointment runs. The clerk shall also keep a record of the names, addresses, signatures, ages, sex, and the terms of all notaries public whom he appoints.

(b) At the time the clerk of the superior court issues a certificate of appointment as provided in subsection (a) of this Code section, said officer shall also issue to the appointee a duplicate original of such certificate. The presentation of such duplicate original, either by mail or in person, to the supplier of a notary public seal shall be necessary to authorize such supplier to make up a notary public seal and deliver it to the appointee.

(c) It shall be unlawful for any person to hold himself or herself out as a notary public or to exercise the powers of a notary public unless such person has an unexpired commission as a notary public.

§ 45-17-6. Seal of office.

(a)(1) For the authentication of his notarial acts each notary public must provide a seal of office, which seal shall have for its impression his name, the words "Notary Public," the name of the state, and the county of his residence; or it shall have for its impression his name and the words "Notary Public, Georgia, State at Large." Notaries commissioned or renewing their commission after July 1, 1985, shall provide a seal of office which shall have for its impression the notary's name, the words "Notary Public," the name of the state, and the county of his appointment. The embossment of notarial certificates by the notary's seal shall be authorized but not necessary, and the use of a rubber or other type stamp shall be sufficient for imprinting the notary's seal. A scrawl shall not be a sufficient notary seal. An official notarial act must be documented by the notary's seal.

(2) No document executed prior to July 1, 1986, which would otherwise be eligible for recording in the real property records maintained by any clerk of superior court or constitute record notice or actual notice of any matter to any person shall be ineligible for recording or fail to constitute such no-

tice because of noncompliance with the requirement that the document contain a notary seal.

(b) It shall be unlawful for any person, firm, or corporation to supply a notary public seal to any person unless the person has presented the duplicate original of the certificate commissioning the person as a notary public. It shall be unlawful for any person to order or obtain a notary public seal unless such person is commissioned as a notary public.

§ 45-17-7. Commissioning of nonresidents as notaries; powers and duties.

(a) Any person who is a resident of a state bordering on the State of Georgia and who carries on a business or profession in the State of Georgia or who is regularly employed in the State of Georgia may be commissioned as a notary public by the clerk of the superior court of the county in which the person carries on said profession, business, or employment.

(b) Such person wishing to be commissioned as a notary public must meet all the requirements of Code Section 45-17-2, as it applies to this Code section.

(c) Such person shall submit the application, endorsements, and declaration of application as required by Code Section 45-17-2-1 to the clerk of superior court in the county in which such person carries on such profession, business, or employment. The clerk of the superior court shall approve or deny such application based on the provisions of Code Section 45-17-2-3. Upon approval and payment of the usual fees to the clerk, the applicant shall be issued a certificate as a notary public of this state and shall be authorized to perform all of the duties and exercise all of the powers and authorities relating to notaries public who are residents of this state.

§ 45-17-8. Powers and duties generally.

(a) Notaries public shall have authority to:

(1) Witness or attest signature or execution of deeds and other written instruments;

(2) Take acknowledgments;

(3) Administer oaths and affirmations in all matters incidental to their duties as commercial officers and all other oaths and affirmations which are not by law required to be administered by a particular officer;

(4) Witness affidavits upon oath or affirmation;

(5) Take verifications upon oath or affirmation;

(6) Make certified copies, provided that the document presented for copying is an original document and is neither a public record nor a publicly recorded document certified copies of which are available from an official source other than a notary and provided that the document was photocopied under supervision of the notary; and

(7) Perform such other acts as they are authorized to perform by other laws of this state.

(b) No notary shall be obligated to perform a notarial act if he feels such act is:

(1) For a transaction which the notary knows or suspects is illegal, false, or deceptive;

(2) For a person who is being coerced;

(3) For a person whose demeanor causes compelling doubts about whether the person knows the consequences of the transaction requiring the notarial act; or

(4) In situations which impugn and compromise the notary's impartiality, as specified in subsection (c) of this Code section.

(c) A notary shall be disqualified from performing a notarial act in the following situations which impugn and compromise the notary's impartiality:

(1) When the notary is a signer of the document which is to be notarized; or

(2) When the notary is a party to the document or transaction for which the notarial act is required.

(d) A notary public shall not execute a notarial certificate containing a statement known by the notary to be false nor perform any action with an intent to deceive or defraud.

(e) In performing any notarial act, a notary public shall confirm the identity of the document signer, oath taker, or affirmant based on personal knowledge or on satisfactory evidence.

(f) The signature of a notary public documenting a notarial act shall not be evidence to show that such notary public had knowledge of the contents of the document so signed, other than those specific contents which constitute the signature, execution, acknowledgment, oath, affirmation, affidavit, verification, or other act which the signature of that notary public documents, nor is a certification by a notary public that a document is a certified or true copy of an original document evidence to show that such notary public had knowledge of the contents of the document so certified.

§ 45-17-8-1. Signature and date of notarial act.

(a) Except as otherwise provided in this Code section, in documenting a notarial act, a notary public shall sign on the notarial certification, by hand in ink, only and exactly the name indicated on the notary's commission and shall record on the notarial certification the exact date of the notarial act.

(b) The requirement of subsection (a) of this Code section for recording of the date of the notarial act shall not apply to an attestation of deeds or any other instruments pertaining to real property.

(c) No document executed prior to July 1, 1986, which would otherwise be eligible for recording in the real property records maintained by any clerk of superior court or constitute record notice of actual notice of any matter to any person shall be ineligible for recording or fail to constitute such notice because of noncompliance with the present or any prior requirements of this Code section.

§ 45-17-8-2. Misrepresentation prohibited.

A notary shall not make claims to have or imply he has powers, qualifications, rights, or privileges that the office of notary does not authorize, including the powers to counsel on immigration matters and to give legal advice.

§ 45-17-9. Where notarial acts may be exercised.

Notarial acts may be exercised in any county in the state.

§ 45-17-10. Notaries not to issue attachments or garnishments or approve bonds for the purpose of issuing same; not to issue summons in dispossessory case; may attest affidavit in attachment, garnishment, or dispossessory action.

It shall not be lawful for notaries public to issue attachments or garnishments, to approve bonds for the purpose of issuing attachments or garnishments, or to issue a summons in a dispossessory case; but a notary may attest an affidavit in an attachment, garnishment, or dispossessory action; provided, however, no writ or summons in said matter shall issue without first having judicial approval as provided by law.

§ 45-17-11. Fees of notaries.

(a) The fees of notaries public shall be as follows:

(1) Administering an oath in any case
.... $ 2.00
(2) Each attendance on any person to make proof as a notary public and certifying to same 2.00
(3) Every other certificate 2.00

(b) It shall not be lawful for any notary public to charge a greater sum than $4.00 for each service performed. Said sum shall include a fee of $2.00 for performing the notarial act and a fee of $2.00 for an attendance to make proof as a notary public and certifying to same if such certification, which shall be issued by the clerk of superior court of the county in which the notary public was appointed

or the Secretary of State, is required. Registering shall be paid for by the party who has the service performed. The fee for all official acts which the notary may perform shall be the same as those prescribed for other officers who are likewise permitted to perform them.

(c) A notary public need not charge fees for notarial acts.

(d) A notary public shall inform the person requesting any notarial act, prior to performing the act, the fees permitted for each act.

§ 45-17-12. Authority of notaries who are officers, employees, etc., of banks, corporations, etc., to witness execution of written instruments, etc.

(a) As used in this Code section, the term:

(1) "Bank" or "other corporation" means a bank or other corporation organized under the laws of this or any other state or the United States.

(2) "Written instrument," without limiting the generality of meaning of such words, means deeds, mortgages, bills of sale to secure debt, deeds to secure debt, deeds of trust, contracts, legal pleadings, affidavits, certificates, or any other like instruments.

(b) It shall be lawful for any notary public who is a stockholder, director, officer, or employee of a bank or other corporation to take the acknowledgment of any party to any written instrument executed to or by such corporation. Any such notary public may act and sign as official witness to the execution by any party of any written instrument executed to or by such bank or other corporation. Any such notary public may administer an oath to any other stockholder, director, officer, employee, or agent of such bank or other corporation or may protest for nonacceptance or nonpayment bills of exchange, drafts, checks, notes, and other negotiable instruments which may be owned or held for collection by such bank or other corporation, provided that it shall be unlawful for any notary public to act and sign as official witness to or take the acknowledgment of an instrument executed by or to a bank or other corporation of which he is a stockholder, director, officer, or employee where such notary would be witnessing or acknowledging his own signature as it appears on the instrument either in his capacity as an individual or in his representative capacity with the bank or other corporation or to protest any negotiable instrument owned or held for collection by such bank or other corporation where such notary is individually a party to such instrument.

§ 45-17-13. Change of residence, address, or name.

(a) Every notary public shall notify in writing

the appointing clerk of superior court, with a copy to the Secretary of State, of any change in the notary's residence or business address, whichever was used for the purpose of appointment. The notice shall contain both the old and new addresses and must be received by the clerk of superior court within 30 days of the change.

(b)(1) Every notary public shall notify in writing the appointing clerk of superior court, with a copy to the Secretary of State, of any change in the notary's name. The notice shall contain both the old and new names, the new signature, and any new address and must be received by the clerk of superior court within 30 days of the change.

(2) A notary with a new name may begin to officially sign the new name on notarial certificates when the following steps have been completed:

(A) The notice described in paragraph (1) of this subsection has been received by the appointing clerk of superior court;

(B) A confirmation of the notary's name change has been received from the appointing clerk of superior court; and

(C) A new seal bearing the new name exactly as indicated in the confirmation has been obtained.

§ 45-17-14. Notice of loss or theft of notarial seal.

Within ten days of the loss or theft of an official notarial seal, the notary public shall send to the appointing clerk of superior court, with a copy to the Secretary of State, a written notice of the loss or theft.

§ 45-17-15. Revocation of commission; denial of reappointment.

(a) The appointing clerk of superior court may by letter, with a copy to the Secretary of State, revoke the commission or deny the reappointment of any notary public who:

(1) Violates any provision of this chapter;

(2) Performs any notarial act in violation of Code Section 45-17-8;

(3) Is found to have submitted an application or endorsement for a notarial commission containing substantial and significant misstatement or omission of fact;

(4) Ceases to reside or work or have a business in this state; or

(5) Becomes incapable of reading and writing the English language.

(b) Any notary public whose commission has been revoked shall upon demand be allowed a hearing and adjudication before the superior court clerk with a right of de novo appeal to superior court, such appeal to be determined by the court without the intervention of a jury.

§ 45-17-16. Revocation of commission; return of papers; destruction of seal.

Within ten days after receiving notice from the appointing clerk of superior court that a notarial commission has been revoked, an individual shall send or deliver to the appointing clerk of superior court all papers of appointment. Such individual shall also destroy the official notarial seal.

§ 45-17-17. Resignation of commission; return of papers; destruction of seal.

A person who wishes to resign a notarial commission shall send a signed letter of resignation to the appointing clerk of superior court, with a copy to the Secretary of State, and all papers of appointment. The resigning notary public shall destroy the official notarial seal.

§ 45-17-18. Destruction of seal upon expiration or denial of renewal of commission.

A notary public whose commission expires and who does not apply for renewal of such commission or whose application for renewal of a commission is denied shall destroy the official notarial seal.

§ 45-17-19. Authenticity of official signature and term of office; fees; apostille.

(a) The authenticity of the official signature and term of office of a notary public may be evidenced by:

(1) A certificate of authority from the appointing clerk of superior court or the Secretary of State; or

(2) An apostille in the exact form prescribed by the Hague Convention from the Secretary of State.

(b) The fee for a certificate of authority shall be $2.00. The fee for an apostille shall be $3.00.

(c) An apostille as specified by the Hague Convention Abolishing the Requirement of Legalization for Foreign Public Documents shall be attached to any document requiring authentication that is bound for a nation that has signed and ratified the Hague Convention.

§ 45-17-20. Penalty; prosecution of violations of article.

(a) Any person who violates subsection (d) of Code Section 45-17 shall be guilty of a misdemeanor.

(b) Each clerk of superior court is authorized to recommend to the appropriate prosecuting officers that criminal proceedings be instituted for violations of this article.

§ 45-17-30. Commissioned officers of armed services constituted as ex officio notaries; authority generally; effect of acts generally; no seal required.

All commissioned officers of all branches of the armed services of the United States of America are constituted ex officio notaries public of this state and as such are authorized, within and outside this state and within and outside the United States of America, to administer oaths, take acknowledgments, and attest instruments conveying or affecting property in Georgia. Acts performed by such officers as authorized in this Code section shall have the same effect as if performed within this state by notaries public of this state. A statement of his rank following the signature of any such officer shall be evidence of the fact of his rank and no seal shall be necessary.

§ 45-17-31. Persons authorized to have notarial acts performed by commissioned officers.

Any person who (1) is a member of the armed forces of the United States, (2) is serving as a merchant seaman outside the limits of the United States, or (3) is outside the limits of the United States by permission, assignment, or direction of any department or official of the United States government in connection with any activity pertaining to the prosecution of any war in which the United States is then engaged and the spouse, dependent child, or other dependent of such person may have instruments acknowleged, documents attested, oaths and affirmations administered, depositions and affidavits executed, and other notarial acts performed by any commissioned officer in active service of the armed forces of the United States.

§ 45-17-32. Validity and effect of notarial acts.

The notarial acts authorized by Code Section 45-17-31 are declared legal, valid, and binding; and instruments, documents, oaths, affirmations, depositions, and affidavits acknowledged, authenticated, or sworn to shall be admissible in evidence and eligible to record in this state under the same circumstances and with the same force and effect as if they had been made or taken within this state before a duly qualified officer or official.

ADDITIONAL AUTHORITY

§ 1-2-7. Rights of female citizens generally.

Female citizens are entitled to the privilege of the elective franchise and have the right to hold any civil office or perform any civil function as fully and completely as do male citizens.

§ 7-1-788. Notaries and other officers not disqualified by interest in association; validation of prior instruments.

No notary public or other public officer shall be disqualified from taking the acknowledgment of or witnessing any instruments, in writing, in which a building and loan association or a savings and loan association is interested, by reason of his holding an office in or being a member of or being pecuniarily interested in or employed by such association so interested; and any such acknowledgments or attestations taken prior to April 1, 1975, are validated.

§ 15-19-5. Authority of attorney to bind clients; taking of client's affidavit authorized.

* * *

Attorneys who are otherwise authorized by law to take affidavits and administer oaths shall not be disqualified to take affidavits required of their clients in any matter or proceeding of any nature whatsoever.

§ 24-7-23. Notarial acts; proof by certificate.

All notarial acts of notaries public in relation to bills of exchange, drafts, and promissory notes, required to be done by law, may be proved by the certificate of such notary under his hand and seal, provided that such certificate is filed in the trial court at its first term and permitted to remain there until the trial.

FEES

§ 15-6-77. Fees; construction of other fee provisions.

(a) The clerks of the superior courts of this state shall be entitled to charge and collect the fees enumerated in subsection (b) through (f) of this Code section for official duties performed by them, provided that, in all counties in this state where the clerk of the superior court is on a salary basis, the fees provided for in this Code section shall be paid into the county treasury.

* * *

(d) Miscellaneous fees:

* * *

(5) Issuing certificates of appointment and reappointment to notaries

public, as provided by Code Section 45-17-4. .... 8.00

* * *

ACKNOWLEDGMENTS

§ 44-2-15. Officers authorized to attest registrable instruments.

Any of the instruments enumerated in Code Section 44-2-14 may be attested by a judge of a court of record, including a judge of a municipal court, or by a magistrate, a notary public, or a clerk or deputy clerk of a superior court or of a city court created by special Act of the General Assembly. With the exception of notaries public and judges of courts of record, such officers may attest such instruments only in the county in which they respectively hold their offices.

§ 44-2-16. Effect of acknowledgment subsequent to execution.

If subsequent to its execution a recordable instrument is acknowledged in the presence of any of the officers referred to in section 44-2-15, that fact, certified on the deed by such officer, shall entitle it to be recorded.

§ 44-2-21. Execution of instrument out of state; attestation and acknowledgment; validity of attestation by a state or county officer who appears to have no jurisdiction to attest the instrument, based on its caption and place of execution.

(a) To authorize the recording of a deed to realty or personalty executed outside this state, the deed must be attested by or acknowledged before:

(1) A counsul or vice-counsul of the United States, whose certificate under his official seal shall be evidence of the fact;

(2) A judge of a court of record in the state or county where executed, with a certificate of the clerk under the seal of such court of the genuineness of the signature of such judge;

(3) A clerk of a court of record under the seal of the court; or

(4) A notary public or justice of the peace of the county or city of the state or the state and the county, city, or country where executed, with his seal of office attached; if such notary public or justice of the peace has no seal, then his official character shall be certified by a clerk of any court of record in the county, city, or country of the residence of such notary or justice of the peace.

(b) A deed to realty must be attested by two witnesses, one of whom may be one of the officials named in subsection (a) of this Code section.

(c) Wherever any deed to realty or personalty executed outside this state appears by its caption to have been executed in one state and county and the official attesting witness appears to be an official of another state or county, which official would not have jurisdiction to witness such deed in the state and county named in the caption, the deed, notwithstanding the caption, shall be conclusively considered and construed to have been attested by the officer in the state and county in which he had authority to act.

DEPOSITIONS

§ 9-10-113. When verification sufficient.

All affidavits, petitions, answers, defenses, or other proceedings required to be verified or sworn to under oath shall be held to be sufficient when the same are sworn to before any notary public, magistrate, judge of any court, or any other officer of the state or county where the oath is made who is authorized by the laws thereof to administer oaths. The oath if made outside this state shall have the same force and effect as if it had been made before an officer of this state authorized to administer the same. The official attestation of the officer before whom the oath or affidavit is made shall be prima-facie evidence of the official character of the officer and that he was authorized by law to administer oaths. However, this Code section shall not apply to such affidavits as may be expressly required by statute to be made before some particular officer within the state.

§ 9-11-28. Persons before whom depositions may be taken.

(a) **Within the United States and its possessions.** Depositions shall be taken before an officer authorized to administer oaths by the laws of the United States or of the place where the examination is held or before a person appointed by the court in which action is pending. A person so appointed has power to administer oaths and take testimony.

(b) **In foreign countries.** In a foreign State or Country depositions shall be taken on notice before a secretary of embassy or legation, consul general, consul, vice-counsul, or consular agent of the United States, or before such person or officer as may be appointed by commission or under letters rogatory. A commission or letters rogatory shall be issued only when necessary or convenient, on application and notice, and on such terms and with such directions as are just and appropriate. Officers may be designated in notices or commissions either by name or descriptive title and letters rogatory may be addressed "To the Appropriate Judicial Authority in (here name the country)."

(c) **Disqualification for interest.** No deposition shall be taken before a person who is a relative, employee, attorney, or counsel of any of the parties, or who is a relative or employee of such attorney or counsel, or who is financially interested in the action, unless such disqualification is waived in writing by all parties to the action.

LEGAL HOLIDAYS

§ **1-4-1.** Public and legal holidays; leave for observance of religious holidays not specifically provided for.

(a) The State of Georgia shall recognize and observe as public and legal holidays:

(1) All days which have been designated as of January 1, 1984, as public and legal holidays by the federal government; and

(2) All other days designated and proclaimed by the Governor as public and legal holidays or as days of fasting and prayer or other religious observance. In such designation the Governor shall include at least one of the following dates: January 19, April 26, or June 3, or a suitable date in lieu thereof to commemorate the event or events now observed by such dates.

(b) The Governor shall close all state offices and facilities a minimum of 12 days throughout the year and not more than 12 days in observance of the public and legal holidays and other days set forth in subsection (a) of this Code section and shall specify the days state offices and facilities shall be closed for such observances.

(c) Employees of any state department or agency or of any other department or agency covered by the state merit system shall, upon request to their appointing authority or his designee at least seven days in advance, be given priority consideration for time away from work for observance of religious holy days not otherwise provided for in this Code section. Any paid leave time for such religious holy day observance shall be charged to accrued compensatory leave or accrued annual leave credits available to the employee at the time of the holy day observance. No employee may claim priority consideration for more than three work days each calendar year. A request by an employee for time away from work to observe a religious holy day shall not be denied unless the employee has inadequate accrued compensatory or annual leave credits to cover such period of absence or the duties performed by the employee are urgently required and the employee is the only person available who can perform the duties as determined by the appointing authority or his designee. The State Personnel Board shall provide by rule and regulation a procedure to be followed by agencies and departments in the granting of such holy days for employees in the classified service of the state merit system. The employing department or agency shall provide the procedures to be followed for all other employees.

§ **1-4-2.** Religious holidays.

The only days to be declared, treated, and considered as religious holidays shall be the first day of each week, called Sunday.

HAWAII

NOTARIES PUBLIC

[HAW. REV. STAT.]

§ 456-1. Appointment; tenure.

The attorney general may, in the attorney general's discretion, appoint and commission such number of notaries public for the State as the attorney general deems necessary for the public good and convenience. The term of office of a notary public shall be four years from the date of the notary's commission, unless sooner removed by the attorney general for cause after due hearing; provided that after due hearing the commission of a notary public may be revoked by the attorney general in any case where any change occurs in the notary's office, occupation, residence, or employment which in the attorney general's judgment renders the holding of such commission by the notary no longer necessary for the public good and convenience. Each notary shall, upon any change in the notary's office, occupation, residence, or employment, forthwith report the same to the attorney general.

§ 456-2. Qualifications; oath.

Every person appointed a notary public shall, at the time of the person's appointment, be a resident of the State, possess the other qualifications required of public officers and be at least eighteen years of age. Every person appointed to that office shall, before entering thereon, take and subscribe an oath for the faithful discharge of the person's duties, which oath shall be filed in the department of the attorney general.

§ 456-3. Seal.

Every notary public shall constantly keep an engraved seal of office or a rubber stamp facsimile seal which shall clearly show, when embossed, stamped or impressed upon a document, the notary's name, and the words, "notary public" and "State of Hawaii." The notary public shall authenticate all the notary's official acts, attestations, certificates, and instruments therewith, and shall always add to an official signature a statement showing the date that the notary's commission expires. Upon resignation, death, expiration of term of office without reappointment, or removal from or abandonment of office the notary public shall immediately deliver the notary's seal to the attorney general who shall deface or destroy the same. If any notary fails to comply with this section within ninety days of the date of the notary's resignation, expiration of term of office without reappointment, or removal from or abandonment of office or if the notary's personal representative fails to comply with this section within ninety days of the notary's death, then the notary public or the notary's personal representative shall forfeit to the State not more than $200, in the discretion of the court, to be recovered in an action to be brought by the attorney general on behalf of the State.

§ 456-4. Filing copy of commission; authentication of acts.

Each person appointed and commissioned a notary public under this chapter shall forthwith file a literal or photostatic copy of the person's commission, an impression of the person's seal, and a specimen of the person's official signature with the clerk of the circuit court of the circuit in which the notary public resides. Each person appointed and commissioned a notary public under this chapter may also, at the person's option, file the above-named documents with the clerk of any other circuit court. Thereafter any clerk, when thereunto requested, shall certify to the official character and acts of any such notary public whose commission, impression of seal, and specimen of official signature is so filed in the clerk's office.

§ 456-5. Official bond.

Each notary public forthwith and before entering upon the duties of the notary's office shall execute, at the notary's own expense, an official surety bond which shall be in the sum of $1,000. Each bond shall be approved by a judge of the circuit court.

The obligee of each bond shall be the State and the condition contained therein shall be that the notary public will well, truly, and faithfully perform all the duties of the notary's office which are then or may thereafter be required, prescribed, or defined by law or by any rule or resignation made under the express or implied authority of any statute, and all duties and acts undertaken, assumed, or performed by the notary public by virtue or color of the notary's office. The surety on any such bond shall be a surety company authorized to do business in the State. After approval the bond shall be deposited and kept on file in the office of the clerk of the circuit court of the judicial circuit in which the notary public resides. The clerk shall keep a book to be called the "bond record", in which the clerk shall record such data in respect to each of the bonds deposited and filed in the clerk's office as the attorney general may direct.

§ 456-6. Liabilities on official bond.

For the official misconduct or neglect of a notary

public or breach of any of the conditions of the notary's official bond, the notary and the surety on the notary's official bond shall be liable to the party injured thereby for all the damages sustained. The party shall have a right of action in the party's own name upon the bond and may prosecute the action to final judgment and execution.

§ 456-8. Rules.

The attorney general, subject to chapter 91, may prescribe such rules and regulations as the attorney general deems advisable concerning the administration of this chapter, the appointment and duties of notaries public and the duties of other officers thereunder. The rules or regulations shall have the force and effect of law.

§ 456-9. Fees.

The attorney general shall charge and collect the following fees:

For issuing the original commission, $35;

For renewal of commission, $15.

The clerk of each circuit court shall charge and receive the following fees

For filing a copy of a commission, $3;

For each certificate of authentication, $1.

The foregoing fees collected by the attorney general shall be deposited with the director of finance to the credit of the general fund.

§ 456-10. Duties, by mercantile usage.

It shall be a notary public's duty when requested, to enter on record all losses or damages sustained or apprehended, by sea or land, and also all averages, and such other matters as, by mercantile usage, appertain to the notary's office, and cause protest thereof to be made, duly and formally.

§ 456-11. Protests; negotiable paper.

All facts, extracts from documents, and circumstances, so noted, shall be signed and sworn to by all the persons appearing to protest. The notary public shall note, extend, and record the protest so made; and shall grant authenticated copies thereof, under the notary's signature and notarial seal, to those who request and pay for the same. The notary shall also, in behalf of any person interested, present any bill of exchange, or other negotiable paper, for acceptance or payment to any party on whom the same is drawn or who may be liable therefor; and notify all indorsers or other parties to such bill or paper. The notary may, in general, do all the acts to be done by notaries public by the usages of merchants, or which are authorized by the laws of the State.

§ 456-12. Protest, evidence of what.

The protest of any foreign or inland bill of exchange, or promissory note or order, duly certified by any notary public, under the notary's hand and official seal, shall be legal evidence of the facts stated in the protest, as to the same, and also as to the notice given to the drawer or indorser in any court of law.

§ 456-13. May administer oath.

Every notary public may administer oaths in all cases in which oaths are by law authorized or required to be taken or administered, or in which the administering of an oath may be proper. All oaths administered before June 23, 1888, by notaries public are declared valid and binding.

§ 456-14. Notary connected with a corporation or trust company; authority to act.

It shall be lawful for any notary public, although an officer, employee, shareholder, or director of a corporation or trust company to take the acknowledgment of any party to any written instrument executed to or by the corporation or trust company, or to administer an oath to any shareholder, director, officer, employee, or agent of the corporation of trust company, or to protest for nonacceptance or nonpayment of bills of exchange, drafts, checks, notes, and other negotiable instruments which may be owned or held for collection by the corporation or trust company; provided it shall be unlawful for any notary public to take the acknowledgment of any party to an instrument, or to protest any negotiable instrument, where the notary is individually a party to the instrument.

§ 456-15. Record; copies as evidence.

Every notary public shall record at length in a book of records all acts, protests, depositions, and other things, by the notary noted or done in the notary's official capacity. All copies or certificates granted by the notary shall be under the notary's hand and notarial seal, and shall be received as evidence of such transactions.

§ 456-16. Disposition of records, penalty.

The records of each notary public shall be deposited with the clerk of the circuit court of the judicial circuit in which the notary public resides upon the resignation, death, expiration of each term of office, or removal from or abandonment of office.

If any notary fails to comply with this section within ninety days of the date of the resignation, expiration of any term of office, or removal from or abandonment of office or if the notary's personal representative fails to comply with this section within ninety days of the notary's death, then the notary or the notary's personal representative shall forfeit to the State not less than $50 nor more than $500, in the discretion of the court, in an action brought by the attorney general on behalf of the State.

§ 456-17. Fees.

Subject to section 456-18, every notary public is entitled to demand and receive the following fees:

For noting the protest of mercantile paper, $5;

For each notice and certified copy of protest, $5;

For noting any other protest, $5;

For every notice thereof, and certified copy of protest, $5;

For every deposition, or official certificate, $5;

For the administration of oath, including the certificate of the oath, $4; for affixing the certificate of the oath to every duplicate original instrument beyond four, $2.50;

For taking any acknowledgment, $4 for each party signing; for affixing to every duplicate original beyond one of any instrument acknowledged before the notary, the notary's certificate of the acknowledgment, $2.50 for each person making the acknowledgment.

§ 456-18. Notaries in government service.

Except as otherwise provided for by law, the head of every department (which term as used in this chapter includes any department, board, commission, bureau, or establishment of the United States, or of the State, or any political subdivision thereof) may designate one or more of the head of every department's subordinates to be a notary public who, upon duly qualifying and receiving a commission as a notary public in government service, shall perform, without charge, the services of a notary public in all matters of business pertaining to the State, any political subdivision thereof, or the United States.

Any provision of this chapter to the contrary notwithstanding, a subordinate so designated and thus qualified and commissioned as a notary public in government service shall:

(1) Be authorized to perform the duties of a notary public in one or more of the judicial circuits of the State as the attorney general shall designate;

(2) Not be required (A) to pay any fee to the clerk of any circuit court for filing a copy of the notary's commission; (B) to pay any fee to the attorney general for the issuance of the notary's com-

mission or the renewal thereof; (C) to furnish and file an official bond unless such bond is required by the head of the department in which the notary is a subordinate, in which event, the expense of furnishing any such bond shall be borne by the department concerned;

(3) Not demand or receive any fee for the notary's service as a notary public; provided that where the occasion, in the judgment of the head of the department, is deemed one of urgent necessity and convenience, the notary may, but shall not be compelled to, administer oaths or take acknowledgments in nongovernmental matters, for which services the prescribed fees shall be demanded and received as governmental realizations and covered into the general fund of the State; provided further that with the prior written approval of the attorney general, the notary public, upon paying the fees prescribed by law and upon executing, depositing, and filing at the notary's own expense, the required official bond, may demand or receive the fees prescribed by law for services rendered by the notary in matters not pertaining to such public business.

ADDITIONAL AUTHORITY

§ 46-29. Certain notarial powers conferred upon county officers.

Wherever by law any affidavit under oath or any statement or other document to be acknowledged is required to be filed with the chief of police, treasurer, director of finance, clerk, or council of any county as a condition to the granting of any license or the performance of any act by any person, or by any county officer, the chief of police, treasurer, director of finance, or clerk, their deputy or deputies, of the county, shall take the oath or acknowledgment, free of charge, keeping records thereof as required by law of notaries public; provided that nothing herein shall prevent any person desiring so to do from making the oath or acknowledgment before any duly authorized notary public, subject to the notary's legal fees therefor.

§ 403-51. Notary connected with bank; authority to act.

It shall be lawful for any notary public, although an officer, employee, shareholder, or director of a bank, to take the acknowledgment of any party to any written instrument executed to or by the bank, or to administer an oath to any shareholder, director, officer, employee, or agent of the bank, or to protest for nonacceptance or nonpayment of bills of exchange, drafts, checks, notes, and other negotiable instruments which may be owned or held for collection by the bank, provided, it shall be unlawful for any notary public to take the acknowledgment of any party to an instrument, or to protest any negotiable instrument, where the notary is individually a party to the instrument.

§ 407-36. Notary public connected with association; authority to act.

It shall be lawful for any notary public, although an officer or employee of a building and loan association or a shareholder, member, or director thereof, to take the acknowledgment of any party to any written instrument executed to or by the association, or to administer an oath to any shareholder, member, director, officer, employee, or agent of the association, or to protest for nonacceptance or nonpayment of bills of exchange, drafts, checks, notes, and other negotiable instruments which may be owned or held for collection by the association; and in general, to do and perform any act pertaining to the powers and duties of a notary public; provided that it shall be unlawful for the notary public to take the oath or acknowledgment of any party to an instrument, or to protest any negotiable instrument, where the notary is individually a party to the instrument.

ACKNOWLEDGMENTS

§ 502-41. Certificate of acknowledgment; natural persons, corporations.

Except as otherwise provided by section 502-50 to 502-52, to entitle any conveyance or other instrument to be recorded there shall be endorsed, subjoined, or attached thereto an acknowledgment in the form provided or authorized in any of sections 502-42, 502-43, or 502-45, or in substantially the following form:

(Begin in all cases by a caption specifying the state or territory and the place where the acknowledgment is taken.)

1. In the case of natural persons acting in their own right:

On this _____ day of _____, 19___, before me personally appeared A. B. (A. B. or C. D.), to me known to be the person (or persons) described in and who executed the foregoing instrument, and acknowledged that he (or they) executed the same as his (or their) free act and deed.

2. In the case of natural persons acting by attorney:

On this _____ day of _____, 19___, before me personally appeared A. B., to me known to be the person who executed the foregoing instrument in behalf of C. D. and acknowledged that he executed the same as the free act and deed of said C. D.

3. In the case of corporations or joint stock associations:

On this _____ day of _____, 19__, before me appeared A. B., to me personally known, who, being by me duly sworn (or affirmed), did say that he is the president (or other officer or agent of the corporation or association) of (describing the corporation or association) and that the seal affixed to the instrument is the corporate seal of the corporation (or association), and that the instrument was signed and sealed in behalf of the corporation (or association) by authority of its board of directors (or trustees), and A. B. acknowledged the instrument to be the free act and deed of the corporation (or association).

In case the corporation or association has no corporate seal, omit "the seal affixed to the instrument is the corporate seal of the corporation (or association), and that" and add, at the end of the affidavit clause, "and that the corporation (or association) has no corporate seal."

4. In the case of a corporation or joint stock company acknowledging by an individual as its attorney, where the enabling power of attorney has previously been recorded, the acknowledgment of the instrument executed under the power of attorney shall be substantially in the following form:

On this _____ day of _____, 19__, before me personally appeared A. B., to me personally known, who being by me duly sworn (or affirmed) did say that he is the attorney in fact of C. D. (here name the corporation) duly appointed under power of attorney dated the _____ day of _____, 19__, recorded in book _____, at page _____; and that the foregoing instrument was executed in the name and behalf of said C. D. by A. B. as its attorney in fact; and A. B. acknowledged the instrument to be the free act and deed of C. D.

In case the enabling power of attorney has not previously been recorded, omit the reference to its place of record and insert in lieu thereof the words "which power of attorney is now in full force and effect."

5. In the case of a corporation or joint stock company acknowledging by another corporation or joint stock company as its attorney, where the enabling power of attorney has previously been recorded, the acknowledgment of the instrument executed under the power of attorney shall be substantially in the following form:

On this _____ day of _____, 19__, before me personally appeared A. B., to me personally known, who, being by me duly sworn (or affirmed) did say that he is the president (or other officer or agent of the corporation or joint stock company

acting as attorney) of C. D. (here name the corporation or joint stock company acting as attorney) and that C. D. is the attorney in fact of E. F. (here name the corporation or joint stock company in whose behalf the attorney is acting) duly appointed under power of attorney dated the _____ day of _____, 19__, recorded in book _____, at page _____; that the foregoing instrument was executed in the name and behalf of E. F. by C. D. as its attorney-in-fact; that the seal affixed to the foregoing instrument is the corporate seal of C. D., and the instrument was so executed by C. D. by authority of its board of directors; and A. B. acknowledged the instrument to be the free act and deed of E. F.

In case the corporation acting as attorney has no corporate seal, or no seal within the State, omit the words "the seal affixed to the foregoing instrument is the corporate seal of C. D." and insert in lieu thereof, "C. D. has no corporate seal," or "C. D. has no corporate seal within the State of Hawaii." In case the enabling power of attorney has not previously been recorded, omit the reference to its place of record and insert in lieu thereof the words "which power of attorney is now in full force and effect."

In all cases add signature and title of the officer taking the acknowledgment.

§ 502-42. Certificate, contents.

The certificate of acknowledgment shall state in substance that the person who executed the instrument appeared before the officer granting the certificate and acknowledged or stated that the person executed the same, and that such person was personally known to the officer granting such certificate to be the person whose name is subscribed to the instrument as a party thereto, or was proved to be such by the oath or affirmation of a credible witness known to the officer whose name shall be inserted in the certificate. It shall not be ground for the rejection of any such certificate, or for refusing to accept such instrument for record or in evidence, that the certificate fails to state that the person making the acknowledgment stated or acknowledged that the instrument was executed freely or voluntarily by the person or as the person's free act and deed.

§ 502-43. Form when person unknown.

When the person offering the acknowledgment is unknown to the officer taking the acknowledgment, the certificate may be substantially in the following form, to-wit:

State of Hawaii,

County of _____ ss.

On this _____ day of _____, 19__, personally appeared before me A. B., satisfactorily proved to me to be the person described in and who executed the within instrument, by the oath of C. D., a credible witness for that purpose, to me known and by me duly sworn, and he, A. B., acknowledged that he executed the same freely and voluntarily for the uses and purposes therein set forth.

§ 502-44. Married women.

The acknowledgment of a married woman when required by law may be taken in the same form as if she were sole and without any examination separate and apart from her husband.

§ 502-45. Acknowledgments without the State.

The proof or acknowledgment of any deed or other written instrument required to be proved or acknowledged in order to enable the same to be recorded or read in evidence, when made by any person without the State and within any other state, territory, district, or dependency of the United States, may be made before any officer of the state, territory, district, or dependency authorized by the laws thereof to take proof and acknowledgment of deeds and when so taken, and when the certificate of acknowledgment is in a form sufficient to entitle deeds of real property to be recorded in the appropriate office for recording in such state, territory, district, or dependency or in the form provided or permitted by any of sections 502-41 to 502-43, shall be entitled to be recorded and may be read in evidence in the State. The signature of such officer constitutes prima facie evidence that the acknowledgment is taken in accordance with the laws of the place where made and of the authority of the officer to take the acknowledgment. If the record of any such instrument, or a transcript thereof, is used in evidence in any proceeding the burden shall be on the party relying on such record to prove that the instrument was duly executed, in any proceeding where such fact is asserted by such party and is in dispute. The burden may be met by proof made in the manner provided in section 502-46.

§ 502-46. Same; certificate of authority of officer.

The burden of proving due execution of any conveyance or written instrument, acknowledged or proved under section 502-45, may be met by any admissible evidence sufficient for that purpose and shall also be met if at the time of recording or

thereafter there is indorsed, subjoined, or attached to the certificate of proof or acknowledgment, signed by such officer, a certificate of the secretary of state of the state or territory in which such officer resides, under the seal of the state or territory, or a certificate of clerk of a court of record of the state, territory, or district in the county in which the officer resides or in which the officer took such proof or acknowledgment, under the seal of the court, or a certificate of the executive officer or clerk of a court of record of such dependency, authorized to make such certificate, stating that the officer was, at the time of taking the proof or acknowledgment, duly authorized to take acknowledgments and proofs of deeds of lands in the state, territory, district, or dependency, and that the secretary of state, or other authorized executive officer, or clerk of court, is well acquainted with the handwriting of the officer taking the acknowledgment or proof, and that the secretary of state, executive officer, or clerk verily believes that the signature affixed to the certificate of proof or acknowledgment is genuine.

The authentication of the proof of acknowledgment of a deed or other written instrument when taken without the State and within any other state, territory, or district of the United States, shall be in substantially the following form:

(Begin with a caption specifying the state, territory, or district, and county or place, where the authentication is made.)

I, _____, clerk of the _____ in and for said county which court is a court of record, having a seal (or I, _____, the secretary of state of said state or territory) do hereby certify that _____ by and before whom the foregoing acknowledgment (or proof) was taken, was at the time of taking the same, a notary public (or other officer) residing (or authorized to act) in the county, and was duly authorized by the laws of the state (territory or district) to take and certify acknowledgment or proofs of deeds of land in the state (territory or district), and further that I am well acquainted with the handwriting of _____, and that I verily believe that the signature to the certificate of acknowledgment (or proof) is genuine. In testimony whereof, I have hereunto set my hand and affixed the seal of the court (or state) this _____ day of _____, 19__.

§ 502-47. Acknowledgment without the United States; by members of the armed forces; recordation where no official authorized to take proof.

(a) The proof or acknowledgment of any deed or other instrument required to be proved or acknowledged in order to entitle the same to be recorded or read in evidence, when made by any person without the United States may be made by:

(1) Any officer now authorized thereto by the laws of the State;

(2) Any officer of the United States diplomatic or consular service, resident in any foreign country or port, when certified by him under his seal of office; and

(3) Any person authorized by the law of any foreign country to take such acknowledgment or proof, when such acknowledgment or proof is accompanied by a certificate to the effect that the person taking the same is duly authorized thereto and that such acknowledgment or proof is in the manner prescribed by the laws of the foreign country. The certificate may be made by a diplomatic or consular officer of the United States under the seal of his office, or by a diplomatic or consular officer of the foreign country, resident in the State, under the seal of his office.

For the purposes of this section diplomatic or consular officer includes any minister, consul, vice-consul, charge d'affaires, consular, or commercial agent, or vice-consular or vice-commercial agent.

(b) Proof or acknowledgment may be made by any person in the armed forces of the United States, or by any person without the United States, before any officer of the armed forces authorized by Congress to exercise the powers of a notary public. The signature without seal of any officer acting as such notary public is prima facie evidence of his authority.

(c) Where it is established to the satisfaction of any judge of a circuit court of the state that any instrument required to be acknowledged or proved has been executed by a person then permanently or temporarily resident at some place where acknowledgment or proof cannot be made as hereinabove provided, such instrument shall be declared acceptable for recordation by order of the judge issued upon such testimony and evidence as are sufficient in the judgment of the judge to establish the genuineness and authenticity thereof, and a certified copy of the order shall be recorded together with and attached to any instrument so ordered acceptable for recordation.

(d) Any instrument so proved, acknowledged, or ordered acceptable for recordation is entitled to be recorded in the State, and may be read in evidence in any court of the State in the same manner and with like effect as if therein duly recorded or acknowledged.

§ 502-48. Identification of person making.

No acknowledgment of any conveyance or other instrument, except as provided by this chapter, whereby any real estate is conveyed or may be affected, shall be taken, unless the person offering to make the acknowledgment is personally known to the officer taking the same to be the person whose name is subscribed to the conveyance or instrument as a party thereto, or is proved to be such by the oath or affirmation of a credible witness known to the officer.

§ 502-49. Certificate of officer, or judge, necessary.

Every officer who takes the acknowledgment of any instrument shall indorse, subjoin, or attach a certificate thereof, signed by oneself, on the instrument.

Every judge who takes the proof of any instrument shall indorse, subjoin, or attach a certificate thereof, signed by oneself, on the instrument, giving the names of the witnesses examined before the judge, their places of residence, and the substance of the evidence by them given.

§ 502-50. How made; proof if not made.

(a) Except as otherwise provided, to entitle any conveyance or other instrument to be recorded, it shall be acknowledged by the person or persons executing the same, before the registrar of conveyances, or the registrar's deputy or before a judge of a court of record or a notary public of the State. If any person having executed an instrument within the State, dies, or departs from the State, without having acknowledged the instrument, or refuses to acknowledge it, or if the person has acknowledged it but such acknowledgment has not been duly certified by the officer before whom made and for any reason neither proper certification nor a new acknowledgment can be secured, the instrument may be entered as of record on proof of its execution by a subscribing witness thereto before the judge of the land court or a judge of a circuit court of the State. If all the subscribing witnesses to the conveyance or other instrument are dead or out of the State, the same may be proved before any court in the State by proving the handwriting of the person executing the same and any subscribing witness. For the purposes of this section a notary public or person who wrongfully undertakes to act as such, may be deemed a subscribing witness.

(b) If there is any interlineation, erasure, or other change in an instrument, not initialed as required by section 502-61, and for any reason compliance with section 502-61 cannot be secured, the instrument may be proved as provided in subsection (c), or, without the bringing of the proceeding therein provided for, the judge of the land court or a judge of a circuit court may certify that the instrument is entitled to be recorded, if it is established to the judge's satisfaction that such change was made before execution of the instrument, and the instrument thereupon shall be received for record notwithstanding section 502-63. If the record of any such instrument, received for record by reason of such certificate, or a transcript thereof, is used in evidence in any proceeding, the burden shall be on the party relying on such record to prove that such change was made before execution of the instrument, in any proceeding where such fact is asserted by the party and is in dispute.

(c) Any person interested under an instrument which if properly proved or acknowledged would be entitled to record, may institute a proceeding against the proper parties to obtain a judgment proving such instrument. The proceeding shall be brought in a circuit court or the land court. If the instrument affects the title to real property the proceeding shall be brought in the judicial circuit where the property is located. If judgment is obtained a certified copy thereof shall be appended to the instrument.

§ 502-53. No certificate of acknowledgment contrary hereto valid in court or entitled to be recorded; exception.

No certificate of acknowledgment contrary to this chapter is valid in any court of the State, nor is it entitled to be recorded in the bureau of conveyances, but no certificate of acknowledgment executed before July 29, 1872, shall in consequence of anything in this chapter contained be deemed invalid.

§ 502-54. Penalty for false certificate.

Any officer authorized to take acknowledgments to instruments who knowingly incorporates in the certificate of acknowledgment any false or misleading statement as to the facts therein contained, shall be fined not more than $1,000 or imprisoned not more than one year, or both. Nothing in this section shall be construed to do away with the liability for civil damages for such act.

§ 502-61. Changes noted in instrument.

Every notary public or officer authorized to take acknowledgments to instruments, before taking acknowledgment, shall first carefully inspect any instrument proposed to be acknowledged before the notary public or officer, and ascertain whether there are any interlineations, erasures, or changes in the instrument. If there are any interlineations, erasures, or changes, the notary public or officer shall call the attention thereto of the person offering to acknowledge the instrument. If they are approved, the acknowledging officer shall place the officer's initials in the margin of the instrument opposite each interlineation, erasure, or change. The initialing by the officer taking the acknowledgment

is prima facie evidence of the extent of the interlineations, erasures, or changes and of the fact that the same were made prior to acknowledgment of the instrument, but does not preclude proof to the contrary.

§ 502-62. Penalty for not noting changes.

Every notary public or other person authorized to take acknowledgments to instruments who takes the acknowledgment of any person to any instrument in which there are interlineations, erasures, or changes, and who fails to observe or perform the requirements, or any of them, of section 502-61, shall be fined not more than $200.

§ 502-63. Not recorded unless initialed.

No instrument in which there are interlineations, erasures, or changes shall be recorded by the registrar, unless the same are duly initialed by the officer or officers taking the acknowledgment or acknowledgments to the same.

§ 502-64. Noted in record.

Each and every interlineation, erasure, or change made in any record in the bureau of conveyances shall be indicated and initialed in the margin by the registrar or the registrar's deputy.

DEPOSITIONS

[HAW. R. CIV. P.]

RULE 28. Persons before whom depositions may be taken.

(a) **Within the United States.** Within the United States or within a territory or insular possession subject to the dominion of the United States, depositions shall be taken before an officer authorized to administer oaths by the laws of this State or of the United States or of the place where the examination is held, or before a person appointed by the court in which the action is pending. A person so appointed has power to administer oaths and take testimony.

(b) **In foreign countries.** In a foreign country, depositions may be taken (1) on notice before a person authorized to administer oaths in the place in which the examination is held, either by the law thereof or by the law of the United States, or (2) before a person commissioned by the court, and a person so commissioned shall have the power by virtue of his commission to administer any necessary oath and take testimony, or (3) pursuant to a letter rogatory. A commission or a letter rogatory shall be issued on application and notice and on terms that are just and appropriate. It is not requisite to the issuance of a commission or a letter rogatory that the taking of the deposition in any other manner is impracticable or inconvenient; and both a commission and a letter rogatory may be issued in proper cases. A notice or commission may designate the person before whom the deposition is to be taken either by name or descriptive title. A letter rogatory may be addressed "To the Appropriate Authority in [here name the country]." Evidence obtained in response to a letter rogatory need not be excluded merely for the reason that it is not a verbatim transcript or that the testimony was not taken under oath or for any similar departure from the requirements for depositions taken within the United States under these rules.

(c) **Disqualification for interest.** No deposition shall be taken before a person who is a relative or employee or attorney or counsel of any of the parties, or is a relative or employee of such attorney or counsel, or is financially interested in the action.

LEGAL HOLIDAYS

[Haw. Rev. Stat.]

§ 8-1. Holidays designated.

The following days of each year are set apart and established as state holidays:

The first day of January, New Year's Day;

The third Monday in February, Presidents' Day;

The twenty-sixth day of March, Prince Jonah Kuhio Kalanianaole Day;

The Friday preceding Easter Sunday, Good Friday;

The last Monday in May, Memorial Day;

The eleventh day of June, King Kamehameha I Day;

The fourth day of July, Independence Day;

The third Friday in August, Admission Day;

The first Monday in September, Labor Day;

The second Monday in October, Discoverers' Day;

The eleventh day in November, Veterans' Day;

The fourth Thursday in November, Thanksgiving Day;

The twenty-fifth day of December, Christmas Day;

All election days, except primary and special election days, in the county wherein the election is held;

Any day designated by proclamation by the President of the United States or by the governor as a holiday.

§ 8-2. Observance of holidays falling on Sundays and Saturdays.

If any of the State's legal holidays fall on Sunday, the following Monday shall be observed as a holiday. If the day falls on Saturday, the preceding Friday shall be observed as a holiday.

§ 8-3. Banking holidays.

Whenever in the opinion of the governor, a public emergency exists, and it seems to the governor to be in the public interest, the governor may by proclamation designate and proclaim as legal banking holidays in the State such number of consecutive days as in the governor's judgment the emergency may require. The governor may extend the same as the governor may deem advisable. The proclamation of bank holidays shall not relate to any business other than that of banking and kindred operations, nor as prohibiting, perforce, any voluntary conduct of banking business, in whole or in part, except to the extent declared in the proclamation or in any further proclamation in enlargement or modification thereof.

§ 1-32. Acts to be done on holidays.

Whenever any act of a secular nature other than a work of necessity or mercy is appointed by law or contract to be performed upon a particular day, which day falls upon a Sunday or holiday, the act may be performed upon the next business day with the same effect as if it had been performed upon the appointed day. When so provided by the rules of court, the act also may be performed upon the next business day with the same effect as if it had been performed upon the appointed day if the appointed day falls on a Saturday.

§ 502-32. Instrument recorded as of time of delivery; office hours.

Every instrument entitled by law to be recorded, shall be recorded in the order and as of the time when the same is delivered to the registrar for that purpose, and shall be considered as recorded from the time of such delivery; provided that it shall not be lawful for the registrar to accept or enter for record and record any instrument or other paper on any Sunday or legal holiday, or on any Saturday that the registrar's office remains closed pursuant to law, or on any other day except between the hours of 8:00 a.m. and 3:30 p.m.

IDAHO

NOTARIES PUBLIC

[IDAHO CODE]

§ 51-101. Short title.

This chapter may be cited as the "Idaho Notary Public Act."

§ 51-102. Definitions.

As used in this chapter:

(1) The masculine gender includes the feminine.

(2) "Notarial act" means any official act performed by a notary public under provisions of section 51-107, Idaho Code.

(3) "Resident" means a natural person who has fixed his habitation in the state of Idaho and who, whenever absent, intends to return to that place of habitation in Idaho.

(4) "Serious crime" includes any felony and any lesser crime, a necessary element of which, as determined by the statutory or common law definition of such crime, involves interference with the administration of justice, false swearing, misrepresentation, fraud, the unauthorized practice of law, deceit, bribery, extortion, misappropriation, theft, or an attempt, a conspiracy or the solicitation of another to commit a serious crime.

(5) "Affidavit" means a declaration in writing, under oath, and sworn to or affirmed by the declarant before a person authorized to administer oaths.

(6) "Verification" means an affidavit of the truth of the facts stated in the instrument to which it relates.

§ 51-103. Power of appointment—Term—Reappointment.

(1) The secretary of state shall appoint in and for the state of Idaho as many notaries public as he shall deem necessary.

(2) Each notary public so appointed shall serve for a term of six (6) years except as otherwise provided in this chapter.

(3) A notary public may be reappointed upon submission of a new application not earlier than ninety (90) days prior to the expiration of his term.

§ 51-104. Qualification for appointment.

Each person appointed and commissioned as a notary public:

(1) Shall be at least eighteen (18) years of age;

(2) Shall be a citizen of the United States;

(3) Shall be a resident of the state of Idaho;

(4) Must be able to read and write the English language; and

(5) Must not have been removed from the office of notary public for official misconduct nor have been convicted of a serious crime as defined in section 51-102, Idaho Code, within the ten (10) year period immediately preceding his appointment nor be serving a sentence for conviction of a serious crime, without regard to when convicted.

§ 51-105. Appointment procedure—Oath.

(1) Each person to be appointed a notary public shall submit an application to the secretary of state on a form prescribed by the secretary of state. The application shall include such information as the secretary of state shall deem proper and shall include that the applicant:

(a) Is at least eighteen (18) years of age;

(b) Is a citizen of the United States;

(c) Is a resident of the state of Idaho;

(d) Is able to read and write the English language; and

(e) Has not been convicted of a serious crime nor removed from office for official misconduct during the immediately preceding ten (10) year period.

The applicant shall also take the following oath, which shall appear on the application form:

"I, _____, solemnly swear (or affirm) that the answers to all questions in this application are true, complete and correct; that I have carefully read the notary laws of this State and I am familiar with their provisions; that I will uphold the Constitution of the United States and the Constitution and laws of the State of Idaho; and that I will faithfully perform, to the best of my ability, the duties of the office of notary public."

The oath shall be signed and sworn to (or affirmed) by the applicant in the presence of a notary public or other person authorized to administer oaths in this state.

(2) Each person to be appointed a notary public shall execute and append to the application a bond to the state of Idaho in the amount of ten thousand dollars ($10,000). The surety which provides the bond shall be a bonding or surety company authorized to do business in this state.

§ 51-106. Seal.

(1) Each notary public shall provide and keep an official seal which shall conform to one of the following configurations:

(a) A seal embosser engraved with the words "Notary Public", the notary public's name, and the words: "State of Idaho."

(b) A rubber stamp with a serrated or milled edge border in rectangular or circular form, which contains the same information required for the seal embosser.

(2) The seal shall be impressed below or near the notary public's official signature on each notary certificate which he administers.

§ 51-107. Powers and jurisdiction.

(1) Each notary public is empowered to:

(a) Take acknowledgments;

(b) Administer oaths and affirmations;

(c) Certify that a copy of an original document is a true copy thereof, only if a certified copy of such original cannot be obtained from an official custodian of such document;

(d) Certify affidavits (to include verifications) or depositions of witnesses; and

(e) Perform such other acts as may be specifically permitted by law.

(2) The powers of a notary public commissioned pursuant to the provisions of this chapter may be exercised anywhere within the state of Idaho and may be exercised outside the state only in connection with a deed or other writing to be admitted to record in the state of Idaho.

§ 51-108. Disqualifying interests.

(1) As used in this section, the term "transaction" shall not include judicial proceedings.

(2) A notary public who has a disqualifying interest, as hereinafter defined, in a transaction may not legally perform any notarial act in connection with the transaction.

(3) For the purposes of this chapter, a notary public has a disqualifying interest in a transaction in connection with which notarial services are requested if he is named as a party to the transaction or shares the same beneficial interest as a party to the transaction.

(4) Neither the notary public nor any party sharing the same beneficial interest as the notary public in the transaction may raise the issue of disqualifying interest in an attempt to invalidate the transaction. The issue of disqualifying interest may not be raised between parties neither of whom shares the same beneficial interest as the notary public.

§ 51-109. Forms for notarial acts.

(1) Certificates of acknowledgment shall substantially conform to the forms set forth in sections 55-710 through 55-715, Idaho Code.

(2) An oath or affirmation, which is in writing, shall be signed by the person who takes it, and the notary public shall enter thereunder substantially the following:

"State of Idaho   }
                     } ss
County of _____ }
Subscribed and sworn (or affirmed) before me this _____ day of _____, 19___."

_____(official signature and seal)

(3) An oath or affirmation administered verbally by a notary public shall be in substantially the following form:

"You do solemnly swear (or affirm) that the testimony you shall give in the matter in issue shall be the truth, the whole truth, and nothing but the truth." The person who takes the oath or affirmation must respond affirmatively.

(4) A certificate of verification of an instrument shall follow the maker's signature and shall identify the notary public and certify that the maker personally appeared, was sworn, stated his authority for making the instrument, and averred the truth of the statements therein. For example, the verification of a corporate document by an officer of the corporation should be in substantially the following form:

"State of Idaho   }
                     } ss
County of _____ }
I, _____, a notary public, do hereby certify that on this _____ day of _____, 19___, personally appeared before me _____, who, being by me first duly sworn, declared that he is the _____ of _____, that he signed the foregoing document as _____ of the corporation, and that the statements therein contained are true."

_____(official signature and seal)

(5) If a certified copy of a document cannot be obtained from any recorder or custodian of public documents, and if certification of a copy of the document by a notary public is otherwise permissible, a notary public may certify a copy of the docu-

ment in substantially the following form:

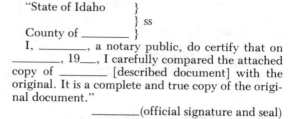

"State of Idaho   }
                     } ss
County of _____ }
I, _____, a notary public, do certify that on _____, 19___, I carefully compared the attached copy of _____ [described document] with the original. It is a complete and true copy of the original document."

_____(official signature and seal)

(6) On each notary certificate, the notary public shall immediately following his signature state the date of the expiration of his commission in substantially the following form:

"My commission expires on _____, 19___."

§ 51-110. Notary fee.

(1) A notary public may, for any notarial act, charge a fee not to exceed two dollars ($2.00).

(2) In addition to the fee, a notary public may be compensated for actual and reasonable expense of travel to a place where a notarial act is to be performed.

(3) An employer shall not require a notary public in his employment to surrender to him a fee, if charged, or any part thereof. An employer may, however, preclude such notary public from charging a fee for a notarial act performed in the scope of his employment.

§ 51-111. Duties.

(1) Each notary public shall exercise reasonable care in the performance of his duties generally, and shall exercise a high degree of care in ascertaining the identity of any person whose identity is the subject of a notarial act.

(2) Any notary public whose name or residence changes during his term of office shall within sixty (60) days after such change submit written notice thereof to the secretary of state.

§ 51-112. Official misconduct.

Official misconduct is the wrongful exercise of a power or the wrongful performance of a duty. In this context, wrongful shall mean unauthorized, unlawful, abusive, negligent, or reckless. Official misconduct by a notary public shall include, but not be limited to:

(a) Engaging in any fraudulent or deceptive conduct which is related in any way to his capacity as a notary public;

(b) Failure to exercise the required degree of care in identifying a person whose identity is an essential element of a notarial act;

(c) Representing or implying by the use of his title that he has qualifications, powers, duties, rights, or privileges that by the law he does not possess;

(d) Engaging in the unauthorized practice of law; or

(e) Charging a fee for a notarial act which is in excess of that provided by section 51-110, Idaho Code.

§ 51-113. Grounds for removal.

A notary public may be removed from the office upon any of the following grounds:

(a) Conviction of a serious crime within the immediately preceding ten (10) year period;

(b) Any action which constitutes official misconduct;

(c) Any material misstatement of fact in his application for appointment as a notary public;

(d) Failure of a conservator or guardian to submit a timely resignation after a notary public becomes incompetent;

(e) Failure of a notary public to submit a timely resignation when he becomes disqualified by virtue of no longer: (1) being a citizen of the United States; or (2) being a resident of Idaho; or

(f) Cancellation of the notary bond by the bonding or surety company.

§ 51-114. Removal procedure.

(1) If a notary public is convicted of a serious crime in any court of this state, the clerk of the court, if he knows that the convict is a notary public or upon the request of any person, shall forward to the secretary of state a certified copy of the judgment of conviction. If a notary public is convicted of a serious crime in a federal court or a court of another state, any person may obtain a certified copy of the judgment of conviction and forward it to the secretary of state. Upon receipt of a certified copy of a judgment of conviction of a serious crime in the preceding ten (10) year period, the secretary of state shall forthwith cancel the commission of the notary public.

(2) If in any civil or criminal case the court finds that a notary public has committed any act which constitutes official misconduct under section 51-112, Idaho Code, the clerk of the court, upon the request of any person, shall forward a certified copy of the findings of fact, or relevant extract therefrom, to the secretary of state. Upon receipt of the certified copy of the findings of fact or extract therefrom the secretary of state shall, if he finds that the act of the notary public as found by the court constitutes official misconduct, forthwith cancel the commission of the notary public.

(3) Upon receipt of proof on the public record of a material misstatement of fact in the application

of a notary public, certified by the custodian of such record, the secretary of state shall forthwith cancel the commission of the notary public.

(4) If the conservator or guardian of a notary public who has been adjudged incompetent fails to submit a timely resignation as required by subsection (3) of section 51-115, Idaho Code, the clerk of the court which found the notary public to be incompetent shall, upon the request of any person, forward to the secretary of state a certified copy of the order adjudging the notary to be incompetent. Upon receipt of such order, the secretary of state shall forthwith cancel the commission of the notary public.

(5) If the secretary of state receives credible information that a notary public is no longer a citizen of the United States or is no longer a resident of Idaho, the secretary of state shall send to the notary public at his last known address by certified return receipt mail a statement setting forth such information and a notice of opportunity to rebut. If the statement and notice cannot be delivered or if no rebuttal is received within forty-five (45) days after mailing the notice, the secretary of state shall cancel the commission of the notary public. If the statement is rebutted by statements which indicate that the notary public is not disqualified on citizenship or residency grounds, the secretary of state shall take no further action.

(6) A bonding or surety company shall file prompt written notice of cancellation of a notary's bond with the secretary of state who shall forthwith cancel the commission of the notary pubic. The cancellation of the bond shall be effective only upon receipt by the secretary of state of notice of cancellation.

§ 51-115. Resignation or death.

(1) A notary public may voluntarily resign by mailing or delivering to the secretary of state a letter of resignation.

(2) Any notary public who becomes ineligible to hold such office for any reason shall within thirty (30) days thereafter resign by mailing or delivering to the secretary of state a letter of resignation.

(3) If a notary public becomes incompetent, his conservator or guardian shall within thirty (30) days after the finding of incompetency mail or deliver to the secretary of state a letter of resignation on behalf of the notary public.

(4) If a notary public dies in office, his personal representative shall within thirty (30) days thereafter mail or deliver to the secretary of state notice thereof.

(5) Upon receipt of a letter of resignation or notice of death, the secretary of state shall forthwith cancel the commission of the notary public.

§ 51-116. Cancellation procedure.

Whenever the secretary of state is required by the provisions of sections 51-114 and 51-115, Idaho Code, to cancel the commission of a notary public, he shall:

(a) Mark the notary public's record "cancelled" and append thereto the supporting document; and

(b) Mail written notice to the resigned or removed notary public or to the conservator, guardian, or personal representative, as appropriate, instructing him to destroy the notary public commission and seal.

§ 51-117. Conditions impairing validity of notarial act.

Without excluding other conditions which may impair the validity of a notarial act, the following conditions invalidate the notarial act:

(a) Failure of the notary public to require a person whose acknowledgment is taken to personally appear before him;

(b) Failure of the notary public to administer an oath or affirmation when the notary certificate indicates that he has administered it;

(c) As to only the notary public who performs the notarial act and any party who shares the same beneficial interest in the transaction, the existence of a disqualifying interest.

§ 51-118. Civil liability of notary public and employer.

(1) A notary public shall be liable for all damages proximately caused by his official misconduct.

(2) The employer of a notary public shall be jointly and severally liable with such notary public for all damages proximately caused by the official misconduct of such notary public if:

(a) The notary public was acting within the scope of his employment; and

(b) The employer had actual knowledge of, or reasonably should have known of, the notary public's official misconduct.

§ 51-119. Criminal penalties.

(1) Any notary public who knowingly and willfully commits an act of official misconduct under the provisions of section 51-112, Idaho Code, shall be guilty of a misdemeanor.

(2) Any employer of a notary public who willfully induces such notary public to commit an act of official misconduct under the provisions of section 51-112, Idaho Code, shall be guilty of a misdemeanor.

(3) Any person who shall willfully act as or otherwise impersonate a notary public while not lawfully commissioned as such nor otherwise officially authorized to perform notarial acts shall be guilty of a misdemeanor.

(4) Any person who shall steal or wrongfully possess a notary public's seal with the intent to use it in the commission of any crime shall be guilty of a felony.

(5) The penalties prescribed in this section shall not be exclusive.

§ 51-120. Notary handbook.

The secretary of state shall prepare a handbook for notaries public which shall contain the provisions of this chapter and such other information as the secretary of state shall deem proper. A copy of the handbook shall be given to each applicant for appointment as a notary public.

§ 51-121. Filing fees.

(1) The fee for filing an application for appointment as a notary public shall be thirty dollars ($30.00).

(2) There shall be no fee charged for filing a letter of resignation, a certified copy of a judgment of conviction, a certified copy of findings of fact or extract therefrom, public record of proof of material misstatement of fact in an application, certified copy of order adjudging incompetency, or notice of death.

(3) The fee for filing notice of change of name or address shall be five dollars ($5.00).

(4) The fee for filing notice of cancellation of a notary bond shall be five dollars ($5.00).

§ 51-122. Severability.

If a court of competent jurisdiction shall adjudge to be invalid or unconstitutional any clause, sentence, paragraph, section or part of this act, such judgment or decree shall not affect, impair, invalidate or nullify the remainder of this act, but the effect thereof shall be confined to the clause, sentence, paragraph, section or part of this act so adjudged to be invalid or unconstitutional.

§ 51-123. Transition.

(1) Each notary commission which was granted under the prior law shall be terminated upon the expiration of the notary bond which was in effect on December 31, 1984.

(2) Except for sections 51-103, 51-104, and 51-105, Idaho Code, the provisions of this chapter shall apply to notaries public who were commissioned under the prior law.

(3) This section shall be in full force and effect from January 1, 1985, to January 1, 1989.

FEES

§ 65-301. Performance without fee—Services enumerated.

Any state, county, city or public officer, or board, or body, acting in his or her or its official capacity on behalf of the state, county, or city, including notaries public, shall not collect, demand or receive any fee or compensation for recording or indexing the discharge papers of any male or female veteran who had active service in any war or conflict officially engaged in by the government of the United States; or for issuing certified copies thereof, or for any service whatever rendered by any such officer or officers, in the matter of a pension claim, application, affidavit, voucher, or in the matter of any claim to be presented to the United States veterans bureau or United States bureau of pensions for the purposes of securing any benefits under the World War Veterans Act of June 7, 1924 and other acts of congress providing pension benefits for honorably discharged veterans of any war, and all acts or parts of acts amendatory thereto, or for furnishing a certified copy of the public record of a marriage, death, birth, divorce, deed of trust, mortgage, or property assessment, or making a reasonable search for the same, wherein the same is to be used in a claim for pension, or a claim for allotment, allowance, compensation, insurance, automatic insurance, or otherwise provided for by the provisions of the World War Veterans Act and amendments thereto or any and all legislation by congress providing pension benefits for honorably discharged veterans of any war.

ACKNOWLEDGMENTS

§ 55-701. By whom [acknowledgments] taken—Any place within state.

The proof or acknowledgment of an instrument may be made at any place within the state, before a justice or clerk of the Supreme Court, or a notary public, or the secretary of state, or United States commissioner.

§ 55-702. By whom taken—Within limited territory.

The proof of acknowledgment of an instrument may be made in this state within the city, county or district for which the officer was elected or appointed, before either:

1. A judge or a clerk of a court of record; or
2. A county recorder; or,
3. A justice of the peace.

§ 55-703. By whom taken—Outside of state.

The proof or acknowledgment of an instrument may be made without this state, but within the United States, and within the jurisdiction of the officer, before either:

1. A justice, judge or clerk of any court of record of the United States; or,
2. A justice, judge or clerk of any court of record of any state or territory; or,
3. A commissioner appointed by the governor of this state for that purpose; or,
4. A notary public; or,
5. Any other officer of the state or territory where the acknowledgment is made, authorized by its laws to take such proof or acknowledgment.

§ 55-704. By whom taken—Outside United States.

The proof of acknowledgment of an instrument may be made without the United States, before either:

1. A minister, commissioner or charge d'affaires of the United States, resident and accredited in the country where the proof or acknowledgment is made; or,
2. A consul or vice-consul of the United States resident in the country where the proof or acknowledgment is made; or,
3. A judge of a court of record of the country where the proof or acknowledgment is made; or,
4. Commissioners appointed for such purposes by the governor of the state pursuant to statute; or,
5. A notary public.

§ 55-705. By whom taken—Members of the armed forces.

Any officer of any component of any branch of the armed forces of the United States as may be designated to take a deposition, shall have the general powers of a notary public in the administration of oaths, the execution and acknowledgment of legal instruments, the attestation of documents and all other forms of notarial acts to be executed by persons in any of the armed forces of the United States or subject to military or naval law and/or their wives and/or dependents.

Such an acknowledgment or oath, whether heretofore or hereafter so taken within or without the state of Idaho or the United States and whether with or without seal or stamp, shall have the same force and effect as an acknowledgment or oath before a notary public duly commissioned by and residing in the state of Idaho. Recital in the certificate of such officer that he holds the office stated in the certificate and that the affiant is a member of the armed forces or subject to military or naval law, or wife or dependent of such member, shall be prima facie evidence of such facts.

§ 55-706. Acknowledgment before deputies.

When any of the officers mentioned in the four (4) preceding sections are authorized by law to appoint a deputy, the acknowledgment or proof may be taken by such deputy, in the name of his principal.

§ 55-707. Requisites of acknowledgment.

The acknowledgment of an instrument must not be taken, unless the officer taking it knows, or has satisfactory evidence, on the oath or affirmation of a credible witness, that the person making such acknowledgment is the individual who is described in, and who executed, the instrument; or, if executed by a corporation, that the person making such acknowledgment is the president or vice-president or secretary or assistant secretary of such corporation; or other person who executed on its behalf; or if executed in the name of the state of Idaho or that of any county, political subdivision, municipal or quasi-municipal or public corporation, that the person making such acknowledgment is one of its officers executing the same; or if executed in a partnership name, that the person making the acknowledgment is the partner or one of the partners subscribing the partnership name to such instrument.

§ 55-708. Acknowledgment by married woman.

The acknowledgment of a married woman to any instrument in writing shall be taken and certified to in the same manner and form as that of a single person, and must be substantially in the form prescribed by section 55-710.

§ 55-709. Certificate of acknowledgment.

An officer taking the acknowledgment of an instrument must indorse thereon a certificate substantially in the forms hereinafter prescribed.

§ 55-710. Form of certificate.

The certificate of acknowledgment, unless it is otherwise in this chapter provided, must be substantially in the following form:

State of Idaho, county of _____, ss.

On this _____ day of _____, in the year of _____, before me (here insert the name and quality of the officer), personally appeared _____, known to me (or proved to me on the oath of _____), to be the person whose name is subscribed to the within instrument, and acknowledged to me that he (or they) executed the same.

§ 55-711. Form of certificate—Acknowledgment by corporation.

The certificate of acknowledgment of an instrument executed by a corporation must be substantially in the following form:

State of Idaho, county of _____, ss.

On this _____ day of _____, in the year _____, before me (here insert the name and quality of the officer), personally appeared _____ known to me (or proved to me on the oath of _____) to be the president, or vice-president, or secretary or assistant secretary, of the corporation that executed the instrument or the person who executed the instrument on behalf of said corporation, and acknowledged to me that such corporation executed the same.

§ 55-712. Form of certificate—Acknowledgment by attorney.

The certificate of acknowledgment by an attorney in fact must be substantially in the following form:

State of Idaho, county of _____, ss.

On this _____ day of _____, in the year _____, before me (here insert the name and quality of the officer), personally appeared _____, known to me (or proved to me on the oath of _____) to be the person whose name is subscribed to the within instrument as the attorney in fact _____, and acknowledged to me that he subscribed the name of _____ thereto as principal, and his own name as attorney in fact.

§ 55-713. Form of certificate—Acknowledgment by official or fiduciary.

The certificate of acknowledgment of an instrument which is executed by a person in his own name as trustee or as executor, administrator, guardian, sheriff, receiver or other official or representative capacity, shall be substantially in the following form:

State of Idaho, county of _____, ss.

On this _____ day of _____, in the year _____, before me (here insert the name and quality of the officer) personally appeared _____, known to me (or proved to me on the oath of _____), to be the person whose name is subscribed to the within instrument as (here insert the official or representative capacity in which the instrument is executed) and acknowledged to me that he (or they) executed the same as such (here insert again the official or representative capacity in which the instrument is executed).

§ 55-714. Form of certificate—Acknowledgment by partnership.

The certificate of acknowledgment of an instrument executed in a partnership name must be substantially in the following form:

State of Idaho, county of _____, ss.

On this _____ day of _____, in the year _____, before me (here insert the name and quality of the officer), personally appeared _____, known to me (or proved to me on the oath of _____), to be one of the partners in the partnership of (here insert partnership name signed to instrument), and the partner or one of the partners who subscribed said partnership name to the foregoing instrument, and acknowledged to me that he executed the same in said partnership name.

§ 55-715. Form of certificate—Acknowledgment by state or political subdivision.

The certificate of acknowledgment of an instrument executed in the name of the state of Idaho or any county, political subdivision, municipal, quasi-municipal or public corporation, must be substantially in the following form:

State of Idaho, county of _____, ss.

On this _____ day of _____, in the year of _____, before me (here insert the name and quality of the officer), personally appeared _____, known to me (or proved to me on the oath of _____), to be the (here insert the official capacity of the officer making the acknowledgment) of the (here insert the name of state, county, subdivision or corporation executing the instrument) that executed the said instrument, and acknowledged to me that such (here insert name of state, county, political subdivision, municipal or public corporation executing the instrument) executed the same.

§ 55-716. Authentication of certificate.

Officers taking and certifying acknowledgments or proof of instruments for record must authenticate their certificates by affixing thereto their signatures, followed by the names of their offices; also their seals of office, if by the laws of the territory, state or country where the acknowledgment or proof is taken, or by authority of which they are acting, they are required to have official seals.

§ 55-717. Certificate of justice—Authentication.

The certificate of proof or acknowledgment, if made before a justice of the peace, when used in any county other than that in which he resides, must be accompanied by a certificate under the hand and seal of the recorder of the county in which the justice resides, setting forth that such justice, at the time of taking such proof or acknowledgment, was authorized to take the same, and that the recorder is acquainted with his handwriting, and believes that the signature to the original certificate is genuine.

§ 55-718. Proof of execution.

Proof of the execution of an instrument, when not acknowledged, may be made either:

1. By the parties executing it, or either of them; or,

2. By subscribing witness; or,

3. By other witnesses in the cases hereinafter mentioned.

§ 55-719. Identity of witness must be known or proved.

If by a subscribing witness such witness must be personally known to the officer taking the proof, to be the person whose name is subscribed to the instrument, as a witness, or must be proved to be such by the oath of a credible witness.

§ 55-720. Proof of identity of grantor.

The subscribing witness must prove that the person whose name is subscribed to the instrument as a party is the person described in it, and that such person executed it, and that the witness subscribed his name thereto as a witness.

§ 55-805. Acknowledgment necessary to authorize recording.

Before an instrument may be recorded, unless it is otherwise expressly provided, its execution must be acknowledged by the person executing it, or if executed by a corporation, by its president or vice-president or secretary or assistant secretary, or other person executing the same on behalf of the corporation, or if executed in name of the state of Idaho or any county, political subdivision, municipal, quasi-municipal, or public corporation, by one or more of the officers of such state, county, political subdivision, municipal, quasi-municipal, or public corporation executing the same, or if executed in a partnership name, by one or more of the partners who subscribed the partnership name thereto, or the execution must be proved and the acknowledgment or proof, certified in the manner prescribed by chapter 7 of this title; provided, that if such instrument shall have been executed and acknowledged in any other state or territory of the United States, or in any foreign country, according to the laws of the state, territory or country wherein such acknowledgment was taken, the same shall be entitled to record, and a certificate of acknowledgment indorsed upon or attached to any such instrument purporting to have been made in any such state, territory or foreign country, shall be prima facie sufficient to entitle the same to such record.

DEPOSITIONS

[IDAHO R. CIV. P.]

RULE 28. Persons before whom depositions may be taken.

(a). Persons before whom depositions may be taken—within the United States. Within the state of Idaho, depositions shall be taken before a person authorized by the laws of this state to administer oaths; without the state, but within the United States, or within a territory or insular possession subject to the dominion of the United States, depositions shall be taken before a person authorized to administer oaths by the laws of this state, by the United States, or of the place where the examination is held; within or without the state of Idaho, depositions may also be taken before a person appointed by the court in which the action is pending, which person so appointed shall have the power to administer oaths and take testimony.

(b). Taking in foreign countries. — In a foreign state or country depositions shall be taken (1) before a secretary of embassy or legation, consul, vice consul, or consular agent of the United States, or any officer authorized to administer oaths under the laws of this state, or of the United States or (2) before a person appointed by the court. The officer or person is empowered to administer oaths to take testimony. A commission shall be issued only when necessary or convenient, on application and notice, and on such terms and with such directions as are just and appropriate. Officers may be designated in notices or commissions either by name or descriptive title.

(c). Members of the armed forces. — The deposition of a person in any of the armed forces of the United States or of the state of Idaho or of their spouses and children or any other person subject to military or naval law or their spouses and dependents, may be taken before any officer of any component of any branch of such armed forces of the United States or the state of Idaho. Recital in the certificate of such officer that he holds the office stated in the certificate and that affiant is a member of such armed forces or subject to military or naval law or is a spouse or child of such member, shall be prima facie evidence of such facts. [Amended December 19, 1975, effective January 1, 1976.]

(d). Disqualification for interest. — No deposition shall be taken before a person who is a relative, employee or attorney or counsel of any party, or is a relative or employee of such attorney or counsel, or is financially interested in this action; provided that such disqualification shall not apply to an attorney acting as a notary public for the acknowledgment of a document, or the verification of an affidavit or pleading in an action.

Oaths and Affirmations

[IDAHO CODE]

§ 9-1401. Who may administer oaths.

Every court, every judge or clerk of any court, every justice and every notary public, the secretary of state, and every officer or person authorized to take testimony in any action or proceeding, or to decide upon evidence, has power to administer oaths or affirmations.

§ 9-1402. Form of oath.

An oath or affirmation in an action or proceeding, may be administered as follows, the person who swears or affirms, expressing his assent when addressed, in the following form:

You do solemnly swear (or affirm, as the case may be), that the evidence you shall give in the issue (or matter), pending between _____ and _____, shall be the truth, the whole truth, and nothing but the truth, so help you God.

§ 9-1403. Peculiar forms of oaths.

Whenever the court before which a person is offered as a witness is satisfied that he has a peculiar mode of swearing, connected with, or in addition to, the usual form of administration, which, in his opinion, is more solemn or obligatory, the court may, in its discretion, adopt that mode.

§ 9-1404. Peculiar forms of oath—Religions other than Christian.

When a person is sworn who believes in any other than the Christian religion, he may be sworn according to the peculiar ceremonies of his religion, if there be any such.

§ 9-1405. Affirmation in place of oath.

Any person who desires it, may, at his option, instead of taking an oath, make his solemn affirmation or declaration, by assenting when addressed, in the following form: "You do solemnly affirm (or declare) that," etc., as above provided.

Commissions to Examine Witnesses

§ 19-3201. Examination of nonresident witness.

When an issue of fact is joined upon an indictment the defendant may have any material witness, residing out of the state, examined in his behalf, as prescribed in this chapter and not otherwise.

§ 19-3202. Application for order.

When a material witness for the defendant resides out of the state the defendant may apply for an order that the witness be examined on a commission.

§ 19-3203. Commission defined.

A commission is a process issued under the seal of the court and the signature of the clerk, directed to some person designated as commissioner, authorizing him to examine the witness upon oath or interrogatories annexed thereto, to take and certify the deposition of the witness, and to return it according to the directions given with the commission.

§ 19-3209. Execution of commission.

The commissioner, unless otherwise specially directed, may execute the commission as follows:

1. He must publicly administer an oath to the witness, that his answers given to the interrogatories shall be the truth, the whole truth and nothing but the truth.

2. He must cause the examination of the witness to be reduced to writing, and subscribed by him.

3. He must write the answers of the witness as near as possible in the language in which he gives them, and read to him each answer as it is taken down, and correct or add to it until it conforms to what he declares is the truth.

4. If the witness declined answering a question, that fact, with the reason assigned by him for declining, must be stated.

5. If any papers or documents are produced before him and proved by the witness, they, or copies of them, must be annexed to the deposition subscribed by the witness and certified by the commissioner.

6. The commissioner must subscribe his name to each sheet of the deposition, and annex the deposition, with the papers and documents, proved by the witness, to the commission, and must close it up under seal, and address it as directed by the indorsement thereon.

7. If there is a direction on the commission to return it by mail, the commissioner must immediately deposit it in the nearest post office. If any other direction is made by the written consent of the parties, or by the court or judge, on the commission, as to its return, he must comply with the direction. A copy of this section must be annexed to the commission.

LEGAL HOLIDAYS

§ 73-108. Holidays enumerated.

Holidays, within the meaning of these compiled laws, are:

Every Sunday;

January 1 (New Year's Day);

Third Monday in January (Martin Luther King, Jr.-Idaho Human Rights Day);

Third Monday in February (Washington's Birthday);

Last Monday in May (Decoration Day);

July 4 (Independence Day);

First Monday in September (Labor Day);

Second Monday in October (Columbus Day);

November 11 (Veterans Day);

Fourth Thursday in November (Thanksgiving Day);

December 25 (Christmas);

Every day appointed by the President of the United States, or by the governor of this state, for a public fast, thanksgiving, or holiday.

Any legal holiday that falls on Saturday, the preceding Friday shall be a holiday and any legal holiday enumerated herein other than Sunday that falls on Sunday, the following Monday shall be a holiday.

ILLINOIS

NOTARIES PUBLIC

[ILL. ANN. STAT.]

Article I. General Provisions

Ch. 102, ¶ 201-101. Short title.

This Act shall be known and may be cited as "The Illinois Notary Public Act".

Ch. 102, ¶ 201-102. Purposes and rules of construction.

(a) This Act shall be construed and applied to promote its underlying purposes and policies.

(b) The underlying purposes and policies of this Act are:

(1) to simplify, clarify, and modernize the law governing notaries public; and protect the public interest.

(2) to promote, serve, and protect the public interest.

Ch. 102, ¶ 201-103. Prospective effect of Act.

This Act applies prospectively. Nothing in this Act shall be construed to revoke any notary public commission existing on the effective date of this Act. All reappointments of notarial commissions shall be obtained in accordance with this Act.

Ch. 102, ¶ 201-104. Notary public and notarization defined.

(a) The terms "notary public" and "notary" are used interchangeably to mean any individual appointed and commissioned to perform notarial acts.

(b) "Notarization" means the performance of a notarial act.

Article II. Appointment Provisions

Ch. 102, ¶ 202-101. Appointment.

The Secretary of State may appoint and commission as notaries public for a four year term as many persons resident in a county in this State as he deems necessary.

Ch. 102, ¶ 202-102. Application.

Every applicant for appointment and commission as a notary shall complete an application form furnished by the Secretary of State to be filed with the Secretary of State, stating:

(a) the applicant's official name, which contains his or her last name and at least the initial of the first name;

(b) the county in which the applicant resides;

(c) the applicant's residence address and business address, if any or any address at which an applicant will use a notary public commission to receive fees;

(d) that the applicant has resided in the State of Illinois for 30 days preceding the application;

(e) that the applicant is a citizen of the United States or an alien lawfully admitted for permanent residence in the United States;

(f) that the applicant is at least 18 years of age;

(g) that the applicant is able to read and write the English language;

(h) that during the past 10 years the applicant's commission as notary (if any) has not been revoked;

(i) that the applicant has not been convicted of a felony; and

(j) any other information the Secretary of State deems necessary.

Ch. 102, ¶ 202-103. Appointment fee.

Every applicant for appointment and commission as a notary public shall pay to the Secretary of State a fee of $10.

Ch. 102, ¶ 202-104. Oath.

Every applicant for appointment and commission as a notary public shall take the following oath in the presence of a person qualified to administer an oath in this State:

"I, _____ (name of applicant), solemnly affirm, under the penalty of perjury, that the answers to all questions in this application are true, complete, and correct; that I have carefully read the notary law of this State; and that, if appointed and commissioned as a notary public, I will perform faithfully, to the best of my ability, all notarial acts in accordance with the law.

_____ (Signature of applicant)

Subscribed and affirmed before me this _____ day of _____, 19___.

_____ (Official signature and official seal of notary)".

Ch. 102, ¶ 202-105. Bond.

Every application for appointment and commission as a notary public shall be accompanied by an executed bond commencing on the date of the appointment with a term of 4 years, in the sum of $5,000, with, as surety thereon, a company qualified to write surety bonds in this State. The bond shall be conditioned upon the faithful performance of all notarial acts in accordance with this Act. The Secretary of State may prescribe an official bond form.

Ch. 102, ¶ 202-106. Appointment recorded by county clerk.

The appointment of the applicant as a notary public is complete when the commission is recorded with the county clerk.

The Secretary of State shall forward the applicant's commission to the county clerk of the county in which the applicant resides. Upon receipt thereof, the county clerk shall notify the applicant of the action taken by the Secretary of State, and the applicant shall either appear at the county clerk's office to record the same and receive the commission or request by mail to have the commission sent to the applicant with a specimen signature of the applicant attached to the request. The applicant shall have a record of the appointment, and the time when the commission will expire, entered in the records of the office of the county clerk. When the applicant appears before the county clerk, the applicant shall pay a fee of $5, at which time the county clerk shall then deliver the commission to the applicant.

If the appointment is completed by mail, the applicant shall pay the county clerk a fee of $10.00, which shall be submitted with the request to the county clerk. The county clerk shall then record the appointment and send the commission by mail to the applicant.

If an applicant does not respond to the notification by the county clerk within 30 days, the county clerk shall again notify the applicant that the county clerk has received the applicant's notary public commission issued by the Secretary of State. The second notice shall be in substantially the following form:

"The records of this office indicate that you have not picked up your notary public commission from the Office of the County Clerk.

The Illinois Notary Public Law requires you to appear in person in the clerk's office, record your commission, and pay a fee of $5.00 to the county clerk or request that your commission be mailed to you. This request must be accompanied by a specimen of your signature and a $10.00 fee payable to the county clerk.

Your appointment as a notary is not complete until the commission is recorded with the county clerk. Furthermore, if you do not make arrangements with the clerk for recording and delivery of your commission within 30 days from the date of this letter, the county clerk will return your commission to the Secretary of State. Your commission will be cancelled and your name will be removed from the list of notaries in the State of Illinois.

I should also like to remind you that any person who attests to any document as a notary and is not a notary in good standing with the Office of the Secretary of State is guilty of official misconduct and may be subject to a fine or imprisonment."

The Secretary of State shall cancel the appointment of all notaries whose commissions are returned to his office by the county clerks. No application fee will be refunded and no bonding company is required to issue a refund when an appointment is cancelled.

Article III. Duties—Fees—Authority

Ch. 102, ¶ 203.101. Official seal.

Each notary public shall, upon receiving the commission from the county clerk, obtain an official rubber stamp seal with which the notary shall authenticate his official acts. The rubber stamp seal shall contain the following information:

(a) the words "Official Seal";

(b) the notary's official name;

(c) the words "Notary Public", "State of Illinois", and "My commission expires _____ (commission expiration date)"; and

(d) a serrated or milled edge border in a rectangular form not more than one inch in height by two and one-half inches in length surrounding the information.

Ch. 102, ¶ 203-102. Official signature.

At the time of notarization, a notary public shall officially sign every notary certificate and affix the rubber stamp seal clearly and legibly using black ink, so that it is capable of photographic reproduction. The illegibility of any of the information required by this Section does not affect the validity of a transaction.

Ch. 102, ¶ 203-103. Notice.

(a) Every notary public who is not an attorney who advertises the services of a notary public in a language other than English, whether by radio, television, signs, pamphlets, newspapers, or other written communication, with the exception of a single desk plaque, shall post or otherwise include with such advertisement a notice in English and the language in which the advertisement appears. This notice shall be of a conspicuous size, if in writing and shall state: "I AM NOT AN ATTORNEY LICENSED TO PRACTICE LAW IN ILLINOIS AND MAY NOT GIVE LEGAL ADVICE OR ACCEPT FEES FOR LEGAL ADVICE". If such advertisement is by radio or television, the statement may be modified but must include substantially the same message.

Literal translation of the phrase "Notary Public" into a language other than English is prohibited. For the purposes of this subsection, "literal translation" of a word or phrase from one language to another means the translation of a word or phrase without regard to the true meaning of the word or phrase in the language which is being translated.

(b) All notaries public required to comply with the provisions of subsection (a) shall prominently post at their place of business as recorded with the Secretary of State pursuant to Section 2-102 of this

Act a schedule of fees established by law which a notary public may charge. The fee schedule shall be written in English and in the non-English language in which notary services were solicited and shall contain the disavowal of legal representation required above in subsection (a), unless such notice of disavowal is already prominently posted.

(c) No notary public, agency or any other person who is not an attorney shall represent, hold themselves out or advertise that they are experts on immigration matters unless they are a designated entity as defined pursuant to Section 245a.1 of Part 245a of the Code of Federal Regulations (8 CFR 245a.1) or an entity accredited by the Board of Immigration Appeals.

(d) Any person who aids, abets or otherwise induces another person to give false information concerning immigration status shall be guilty of a Class A misdemeanor for a first offense and a Class 3 felony for a second or subsequent offense committed within 5 years of a previous conviction for the same offense.

Any notary public who violates the provisions of this Section shall be guilty of official misconduct and subject to fine or imprisonment.

Nothing in this Section shall preclude any consumer of notary public services from pursuing other civil remedies available under the law.

Ch. 102, ¶ 203-104. Maximum fee.

Maximum Fee. (a) Except as provided in subsection (b) of this Section, the maximum fee in this State is $1.00 for any notarial act performed.

(b) Fees for a notary public, agency, or any other person who is not an attorney filling out legalization forms or applications related to the Immigration Reform and Control Act of 1986 shall be as follows:

(1) $75 per person;

(2) $75 per person up to 4 persons per immediate family, with no additional charge for a fifth of subsequent person where all persons are legally related;

(3) $10 per page for the translation of a non-English language into English where such translation is required for legalization forms;

(4) $1 for notarizing; and

(5) $3 to execute any procedures necessary to obtain a document required to complete legalization forms.

Fees authorized under this subsection shall not include application fees required to be submitted with a legalization applicant in conformity with the Immigration and Control Act of 1986.

Any person who violates the provisions of this subsection shall be guilty of a Class A misdemeanor for a first offense and a Class 3 felony for a second or subsequent offense committed within 5 years of

a previous conviction for the same offense.

(c) Upon his own information or upon complaint of any person, the Attorney General or any State's Attorney, or their designee, may maintain an action for injunctive relief in the court against any notary public or any other person who violates the provisions of subsection (b) of this Section. These remedies are in addition to, and not in substitution for, other available remedies.

If the Attorney General or any State's Attorney fails to bring an action as provided pursuant to this subsection any person may file a civil action to enforce the provisions of this subsection and maintain an action for injunctive relief.

Ch. 102, ¶ 203-105. Authority.

A notary public shall have authority to perform notarial acts throughout the State so long as the notary resides in the same county in which the notary was commissioned.

Ch. 102, ¶ 203-106. Certificate of authority.

Upon the receipt of a written request, the notarized document, and a fee of $2 payable to the Secretary of State or County Clerk, the Office of the Secretary of State or County Clerk shall provide a certificate of authority in substantially the following form:

I _____ (Secretary of State or _____ County Clerk) of the State of Illinois, which office is an office of record having a seal, certify that _____ (notary's name), by whom the foregoing or annexed document was notarized, was, on the _____ day of _____, 19__, appointed and commissioned a notary public in and for the State of Illinois and that as such, full faith and credit is and ought to be given to this notary's official attestations. In testimony whereof, I have affixed my signature and the seal of this office this _____ day of _____, 19__. _____ (Secretary of State or _____ County Clerk).

Article IV. Change of Name or Move from County

Ch. 102, ¶ 204-101. Change of name or move from county.

When any notary public legally changes his or her name or moves from the county in which he or she was commissioned, the commission ceases to be in effect and should be returned to the Secretary of State. These individuals who desire to again become a notary public must file a new application, bond, and oath with the Secretary of State.

Article V. Reappointment as a Notary Public

Ch. 102, ¶ 205-101. Reappointment.

No person is automatically reappointed as a notary public. At least 60 days prior to the expiration of a commission the Secretary of State shall mail notice of the expiration date to the holder of a commission. Every notary public who is an applicant for reappointment shall comply with the provisions of Article II of this Act.

Ch. 102, ¶ 205-102. Solicitation to purchase bond.

No person shall solicit any notary public and offer to provide a surety bond more than 60 days in advance of the expiration date of the notary public's commission.

Nor shall any person solicit any applicant for a commission or reappointment thereof and offer to provide a surety bond for the notary commission unless any such solicitation specifically sets forth in bold face type not less than ¼ inch in height the following: "WE ARE NOT ASSOCIATED WITH ANY STATE OR LOCAL GOVERNMENTAL AGENCY".

Whenever it shall appear to the Secretary of State that any person is engaged or is about to engage in any acts or practices which constitute or will constitute a violation of the provisions of this Section, the Secretary of State may, in his discretion, through the Attorney General, apply for an injunction, and, upon a proper showing, any circuit court shall have power to issue a permanent or temporary injunction or restraining order without bond to enforce the provisions of this Act, and either party to such suit shall have the right to prosecute an appeal from the order or judgment of the court.

Any person, association, corporation, or others who violate the provisions of this Section shall be guilty of a business offense and punishable by a fine of not less than $500 for each offense.

Article VI. Notarial Acts and Forms

Ch. 102, ¶ 206-101. Definitions.

(a) "Notarial act" means any act that a notary public of this State is authorized to perform and includes taking an acknowledgment, administering an oath or affirmation, taking a verification upon oath or affirmation, and witnessing or attesting a signature.

(b) "Acknowledgment" means a declaration by a person that the person has executed an instrument for the purposes stated therein and, if the instrument is executed in a representative capacity, that the person signed the instrument with proper authority and executed it as the act of the person or entity represented and identified therein.

(c) "Verification upon oath or affirmation" means a declaration that a statement is true made by a person upon oath or affirmation.

(d) "In a representative capacity" means:

(1) for and on behalf of a corporation, partnership, trust, or other entity, as an authorized officer, agent, partner, trustee, or other representative;

(2) as a public officer, personal representative, guardian, or other representative, in the capacity recited in the instrument;

(3) as an attorney in fact for a principal; or

(4) in any other capacity as an authorized representative of another.

Ch. 102, ¶ 206-102. Notarial acts.

(a) In taking an acknowledgment, the notary public must determine, either from personal knowledge or from satisfactory evidence, that the person appearing before the notary and making the acknowledgment is the person whose true signature is on the instrument.

(b) In taking a verification upon oath or affirmation, the notary public must determine, either from personal knowledge or from satisfactory evidence, that the person appearing before the notary and making the verification is the person whose true signature is on the statement verified.

(c) In witnessing or attesting a signature, the notary public must determine, either from personal knowledge or from satisfactory evidence, that the signature is that of the person appearing before the notary and named therein.

(d) A notary public has satisfactory evidence that a person is the person whose true signature is on a document if that person:

(1) is personally known to the notary;

(2) is identified upon the oath or affirmation of a credible witness personally known to the notary; or

(3) is identified on the basis of identification documents.

Ch. 102, ¶ 206-103. Certificate of notarial acts.

(a) A notarial act must be evidenced by a certificate signed and dated by the notary public. The certificate must include identification of the jurisdiction in which the notarial act is performed and the official seal of office.

(b) A certificate of a notarial act is sufficient if it meets the requirements of subsection (a) and it:

(1) is in the short form set forth in Section 6-105;

(2) is in a form otherwise prescribed by the law of this State; or

(3) sets forth the actions of the notary public and those are sufficient to meet the requirements of the designated notarial act.

Ch. 102, ¶ 206-104. Acts prohibited.

(a) A notary public shall not use any name or initial in signing certificates other than that by which the notary was commissioned.

(b) A notary public shall not acknowledge any instrument in which the notary's name appears as a party to the transaction.

(c) A notary public shall not affix his signature to a blank form of affidavit or certificate of acknowledgment and deliver that form to another person with intent that it be used as an affidavit or acknowledgment.

(d) A notary public shall not take the acknowledgment of or administer an oath to any person whom the notary actually knows to have been adjudged mentally ill by a court of competent jurisdiction and who has not been restored to mental health as a matter of record.

(e) A notary public shall not take the acknowledgment of any person who is blind until the notary has read the instrument to such person.

(f) A notary public shall not take the acknowledgment of any person who does not speak or understand the English language, unless the nature and effect of the instrument to be notarized is translated into a language which the person does understand.

(g) A notary public shall not change anything in a written instrument after it has been signed by anyone.

(h) No notary public shall be authorized to prepare any legal instrument, or fill in the blanks of an instrument, other than a notary certificate; however, this prohibition shall not prohibit an attorney, who is also a notary public, from performing notarial acts for any document prepared by that attorney.

(i) If a notary public accepts or receives any money from any one to whom an oath has been administered or on behalf of whom an acknowledgment has been taken for the purpose of transmitting or forwarding such money to another and willfully fails to transmit or forward such money promptly, the notary is personally liable for any loss sustained because of such failure. The person or persons damaged by such failure may bring an action to recover damages, together with interest and reasonable attorney fees, against such notary public or his bondsmen.

Ch. 102, ¶ 206-105. Short forms.

The following short form certificates of notarial acts are sufficient for the purposes indicated.

(a) For an acknowledgment in an individual capacity:

State of _____

County of _____

This instrument was acknowledged before me on _____ (date) by _____ (name/s of person/s).

_____
(Signature of Notary Public)

(Seal)

(b) For an acknowledgment in a representative capacity:

State of _____

County of _____

This instrument was acknowledged before me on _____ (date) by _____ (name/s of person/s) as _____ (type of authority, e.g., officer, trustee, etc.) of _____ (name of party on behalf of whom instrument was executed).

_____
(Signature of Notary Public)

(Seal)

(c) For a verification upon oath or affirmation:

State of _____

County of _____

Signed and sworn (or affirmed) to before me on _____ (date) by _____ (name/s of person/s making statement).

_____
(Signature of Notary Public)

(Seal)

(d) For witnessing or attesting a signature:

State of _____

County of _____

Signed or attested before me on _____ (date) by _____ (name/s of person/s).

_____
(Signature of Notary Public)

(Seal)

Article VII. Liability and Revocation

Ch. 102, ¶ 207-101. Liability of notary and surety.

A notary public and the surety on the notary's bond are liable to the persons involved for all damages caused by the notary's official misconduct.

Ch. 102, ¶ 207-102. Liability of employer of notary.

The employer of a notary public is also liable to

the persons involved for all damages caused by the notary's official misconduct, if:

(a) the notary was acting within the scope of the notary's employment at the time the notary engaged in the official misconduct; and

(b) the employer consented to the notary public's official misconduct.

Ch. 102, ¶ 207-103. Cause of damages.

It is not essential to a recovery of damages that a notary's official misconduct be the only cause of the damages.

Ch. 102, ¶ 207-104. Official misconduct defined.

The term "official misconduct" generally means the wrongful exercise of a power or the wrongful performance of a duty and is fully defined in Section 33-3 of the Criminal Code of 1961. The term "wrongful" as used in the definition of official misconduct means unauthorized, unlawful, abusive, negligent, reckless, or injurious.

Ch. 102, ¶ 207-105. Official misconduct.

(a) A notary public who knowingly and willfully commits any official misconduct is guilty of a Class A misdemeanor.

(b) A notary public who recklessly or negligently commits any official misconduct is guilty of a Class B misdemeanor.

Ch. 102, ¶ 207-106. Willful impersonation.

Any person who acts as, or otherwise willfully impersonates, a notary public while not lawfully appointed and commissioned to perform notarial acts is guilty of a Class A misdemeanor.

Ch. 102, ¶ 207-107. Wrongful possession.

Any person who unlawfully possesses a notary's official seal is guilty of a misdemeanor and punishable upon conviction by a fine not exceeding $1,000.

Ch. 102, ¶ 207-108. Revocation of commission.

The Secretary of State may revoke the commission of any notary public who, during the current term of appointment:

(a) submits an application for commission and appointment as a notary public which contains substantial and material misstatement or omission of fact; or

(b) is convicted of any felony or official misconduct under this Act.

Ch. 102, ¶ 207-109. Action for injunction—Unauthorized practice of law.

Upon his own information or upon complaint of any person, the Attorney General or any State's Attorney, or their designee, may maintain an action for injunctive relief in the circuit court against any notary public who renders, offers to render, or holds himself or herself out as rendering any service constituting the unauthorized practice of the law. Any organized bar association in this State may intervene in the action, at any stage of the proceeding, for good cause shown. The action may also be maintained by an organized bar association in this State. These remedies are in addition to, and not in substitution for, other available remedies.

Article VIII. Repealer and Effective Date

Ch. 102, ¶ 208-101. Repealer.

Section 2 of "An Act to increase the fee for issuing commissions to notaries public", approved June 3, 1897, as amended, is repealed.

Ch. 102, ¶ 208-102. Repealer.

Section 28 of "An Act concerning fees and salaries, and to classify the several counties of this State with reference thereto", approved March 29, 1872, as amended, is repealed.

Ch. 102, ¶ 208-103. Repealer.

"An Act to provide for the appointment, qualification and duties or notaries public and certifying their official acts and to provide for fines and penalties for the violation thereof", approved April 5, 1872, as amended, is repealed.

Ch. 102, ¶ 208-104. Effective date.

This Act takes effect July 1, 1986.

OFFENSES

Ch. 38, ¶ 1005-9-1. Authorized fines.

(a) An offender may be sentenced to pay a fine

which shall not exceed for each offense:

(1) for a felony, $10,000 or the amount specified in the offense, whichever is greater, or where the offender is a corporation, $50,000 or the amount specified in the offense, whichever is greater;

(2) for a Class A misdemeanor, $1,000 or the amount specified in the offense, whichever is greater;

(3) for a Class B or Class C misdemeanor, $500;

(4) for a petty offense, $500 or the amount specified in the offense, whichever is less;

(5) for a business offense, the amount specified in the statute defining that offense.

(b) A fine may be imposed in addition to a sentence of conditional discharge, probation, periodic imprisonment, or imprisonment.

(c) There shall be added to every fine imposed in sentencing for a criminal or traffic offense, except an offense relating to parking or registration, or offense by a pedestrian, an additional penalty of $4 for each $40, or fraction thereof, of fine imposed. The additional penalty of $4 for each $40, or fraction thereof, of fine imposed, if not otherwise assessed, shall also be added to every fine imposed upon a plea of guilty, stipulation of facts or findings of guilty, resulting in a judgment of conviction, or order of supervision in criminal, traffic, local ordinance, county ordinance, and conservation cases (except parking, registration, or pedestrian violations), or upon a sentence of probation without entry of judgment under Section 10 of the Cannabis Control Act, as now or hereafter amended, or Section 410 of the Controlled Substances Act, as now or hereafter amended.

Such additional amounts shall be assessed by the court imposing the fine and shall be collected by the Circuit Clerk in addition to the fine and costs in the case. Each such additional penalty shall be remitted by the Circuit Clerk within one month after receipt to the State Treasurer for deposit into the Traffic and Criminal Conviction Surcharge Fund. Such additional penalty shall not be considered a part of the fine for purposes of any reduction in the fine for time served either before or after sentencing. Not later than March 1 of each year the Circuit Clerk shall submit a report of the amount of funds remitted to the State Treasurer under this subsection (c) during the preceding calendar year. Except as otherwise provided by Supreme Court Rules, if a court in imposing a fine against an offender levies a gross amount for fine, costs, fees and penalties, the amount of the additional penalty provided for herein shall be computed on the amount remaining after deducting from the gross amount levied all fees of the Circuit Clerk, the State's Attorney and the Sheriff. After deducting from the gross amount levied the fees and additional penalty provided for herein, less any other additional penalties provided by law, the clerk

shall remit the net balance remaining to the entity authorized by law to receive the fine imposed in the case. For purposes of this Section "fees of the Circuit Clerk" shall include, if applicable, the fee provided for under Section 27.3a of "An Act to revise the law in relation to clerks of courts", approved March 25, 1874, as amended, and the fee, if applicable, payable to the county in which the violation occurred pursuant to Section 25.45 of "An Act to revise the law in relation to counties", approved March 31, 1874, as amended.

The Circuit Clerk may accept payment of fines and costs by credit card from an offender who has been convicted of a traffic offense, petty offense or misdemeanor and may charge the service fee permitted where fines and costs are paid by credit card provided for in Section 27.3b of "An Act to revise the law in relation to clerks of courts", approved March 27, 1874, as now or hereafter amended.

(d) In determining the amount and method of payment of a fine, except for those fines established for violations of Chapter 15 of the Illinois Vehicle Code, the court shall consider:

(1) the financial resources and future ability of the offender to pay the fine; and

(2) whether the fine will prevent the offender from making court ordered restitution or reparation to the victim of the offense; and

(3) in a case where the accused is a dissolved corporation and the court has appointed counsel to represent the corporation, the costs incurred either by the county or the State for such representation.

(e) The court may order the fine to be paid forthwith or within a specified period of time or in installments.

ACKNOWLEDGMENTS

Ch. 17, ¶ 3305-14. Acknowledgments.

No acknowledgment of a deed, mortgage or other instrument shall be invalid because such acknowledgment was taken before an officer authorized by the laws of this State to acknowledge conveyances who is also a member, director, employee, or officer of an association which is a party to such deed, mortgage or other instrument.

Ch. 30, ¶ 18. Acknowledgment by married woman.

§ 19. The acknowledgment or proof of any deed, mortgage, conveyance, power of attorney, or other writing of or relating to the sale, conveyance, or other disposition of lands or real estate, or any interest therein, by a married woman, may be made and certified the same as if she were a feme sole, and shall have the same effect.

Ch. 30, ¶ 19. Acknowledgment or proof of deeds, mortgages, conveyances, releases, etc.— Courts or officers authorized to take—Attestation—Persons serving with armed forces—Validating provision.

§ 20. Deeds, mortgages, conveyances, releases, powers of attorney or other writings of or relating to the sale, conveyance or other disposition of real estate or any interest therein whereby the rights of any person may be affected, may be acknowledged or proven before some one of the following courts or officers, namely:

1. When acknowledged or proven within this State, before a notary public, United States commissioner, county clerk, or any court or any judge, clerk or deputy clerk of such court. When taken before a notary public or United States commissioner, the same shall be attested by his official seal; when taken before a court or the clerk thereof, or a deputy clerk thereof, the same shall be attested by the seal of such court.

2. When acknowledged or proved outside of this State and within the United States or any of its territories or dependencies or the District of Columbia, before a justice of the peace, notary public, master in chancery, United States commissioner, commissioner to take acknowledgments of deeds, mayor or city, clerk of a county, or before any judge, justice, clerk or deputy clerk of the supreme, circuit or district court of the United States, or before any judge, justice, clerk or deputy clerk, prothonotary, surrogate, or registrar of the supreme, circuit, superior, district, county, common pleas, probate, orphan's or surrogate's court of any of the states, territories or dependencies of the United States. In any dependency of the United States such acknowledgment or proof may also be taken or made before any commissioned officer in the military service of the United States. When such acknowledgment or proof is made before a notary public, United States commissioner or commissioner of deeds, it shall be certified under his seal of office. If taken before a mayor of a city it shall be certified under the seal of the city; if before a clerk, deputy clerk, prothonotary, registrar or surrogate, then under the seal of his court; if before a justice of the peace or a master in chancery there shall be added a certificate of the proper clerk under the seal of his office setting forth that the person before whom such proof or acknowledgment was made with a justice of the peace or master in chancery at the time of taking such acknowledgment of proof. As acknowledgment or proof of execution of any instrument above stated, may be made in conformity with the laws of the State, territory, dependency or district where it is made. If any clerk of any court of record within such state, territory, dependency or district shall, under his signature and the seal of such court, certify that such acknowledgment or proof was made in conformity with the laws of such state, territory, dependency or district, or it shall so appear by the laws of such state, territory, dependency or district such instrument or a duly proved or certified copy of the record of such deed, mortgage or other instrument relating to real estate heretofore or hereafter made and recorded in the proper county may be admitted in evidence as in other cases involving the admission of evidence of certified copies.

3. When acknowledged or proven outside of the United States before any court of any republic, dominion, state, kingdom, empire, colony, territory, or dependency having a seal, or before any judge, justice or clerk thereof or before any mayor or chief officer of any city or town having a seal, or before a notary public or commissioner of deeds, or any ambassador, minister or secretary of legation or consul of the United States or vice consul, deputy consul, commercial agent or consular agent of the United States in any foreign republic, dominion, state, kingdom, empire, colony, territory or dependency attested by his official seal or before any officer authorized by the laws of the place where such acknowledgment or proof is made to take acknowledgments of conveyances of real estate or to administer oaths in proof of the execution of conveyances of real estate. Such acknowledgments are to be attested by the official seal, if any, of such court or officer, and in case such acknowledgment or proof is taken or made before a court or officer having no official seal, a certificate shall be added by an ambassador, minister, secretary of legation, consul, vice consul, deputy consul, commercial agent or consular agent of the United States residing in such republic, dominion, state, kingdom, empire, colony, territory, or dependency under his official seal, showing that such court or officer was duly elected, appointed or created and acting at the time such acknowledgment or proof was made.

4. Any person serving in or with the armed forces of the United States, within or outside of the United States, and the spouse or former spouse of any such person, may acknowledge the instruments wherever located before any commissioned officer in active service of the armed forces of the United States with the rank of Second Lieutenant or higher in the Army, Air Force or Marine Corps, or Ensign or higher in the Navy or United States Coast Guard. The instrument shall not be rendered invalid by the failure to state therein the place of execution or acknowledgment. No authentication of the officer's certificate of acknowledgment shall be required and such certificate need not be at-

tested by any seal but the officer taking the acknowledgment shall indorse thereon or attach thereto a certificate substantially in the following form:

On _____, 19__, the undersigned officer, personally appeared before me, known to me (or satisfactorily proven) to be serving in or with the armed forces of the United States (and/or the spouse or former spouse of a person so serving) and to be the person whose name is subscribed to the instrument and acknowledged that _____ he _____ executed the same as _____ free and voluntary act for the purposes therein contained, and the undersigned further certifies that he is at the date of this certificate a commissioned officer of the rank stated below and is in the active service of the armed forces of the United States.

_____

Signature of Officer

_____

Rank of Officer and Command
to which attached.

5. All deeds or other instruments or copies of the record thereof duly certified or proven which have been acknowledged or proven prior to August 30, 1963, before either of the courts or officers mentioned in this Act and in the manner herein provided, shall be deemed to be good and effectual in law and the same may be introduced in evidence without further proof of their execution, with the same effect as if this amendatory Act of 1963 had been in force at the date of such acknowledgment or proof.

Ch. 30, ¶ 21. Foreign acknowledgment—Certificate of conformity.

Where any deed, conveyance or power of attorney has been or may be acknowledged or proved in any foreign state, kingdom, empire or country, the certificate of any consul or minister of the United States in said country, under his official seal, that the said deed, conveyance, or power of attorney is executed in conformity with such foreign law shall be deemed and taken as prima facie evidence thereof: Provided, that any other legal mode of proving that the same is executed in conformity with such foreign law may be resorted to in any court in which the question of such execution or acknowledgment may arise.

Ch. 30, ¶ 22. Foreign acknowledgment—Effect.

All deeds, conveyances and powers of attorney, for the conveyance of lands lying in this state, which have been or may be acknowledged or proved and authenticated as aforesaid or in conformity with the laws of any foreign state, kingdom, empire or country, shall be deemed as good and valid in law as though acknowledged or proved in conformity with the existing laws of this state.

Ch. 30, ¶ 23. Duty of officer taking acknowledgment.

No judge or other officer shall take the acknowledgment of any person to any deed or instrument of writing, as aforesaid, unless the person offering to make such acknowledgment shall be personally known to him to be the real person who and in whose name such acknowledgment is proposed to be made, or shall be proved to be such by a credible witness, and the judge or officer taking such acknowledgment shall, in his certificate thereof, state that such person was personally known to him to be the person whose name is subscribed to such deed or writing, as having executed the same, or that he was proved to be such by a credible witness (naming him), and on taking proof of any deed or instrument of writing, by the testimony of any subscribing witnesses, the judge or officer shall ascertain that the person who offers to prove the same is a subscribing witness, either from his own knowledge, or from the testimony of a credible witness; and if it shall appear from the testimony of such subscribing witness that the person whose name appears subscribed to such deed or writing is the real person who executed the same, and that the witness subscribed his name as such, in his presence and at his request, the judge or officer shall grant a certificate, stating that the person testifying as subscribing witness was personally known to him to be the person whose name appears subscribed to such deed, as a witness of the execution thereof, or that he was proved to be such by a credible witness (naming him), and stating the proof made by him; and where any grantor or person executing such deed or writing, and the subscribing witnesses, are deceased or cannot be had, the judge or officer, as aforesaid, may take proof of the handwriting of such deceased party and subscribing witness or witnesses (if any); and the examination of a competent and credible witness, who shall state on oath or affirmation that he personally knew the person whose handwriting he is called to prove, and well knew his signature (stating his means of knowledge), and that he believes the name of such person subscribed to such deed or writing, as party or witness (as the case may be), was thereto subscribed by such person; and when the handwriting of the grantor or person executing such deed or writing, and of one subscribing witness (if any there be), shall have been proved, as aforesaid, or by proof of signature of grantor where there is no subscribing witness, the judge or officer shall grant a certificate thereof stating the proof aforesaid.

Ch. 30, ¶ 25. Form of acknowledgment.

§ 26. A certificate of acknowledgment, substantially in the following form, shall be sufficient:

State of (name of state), }
} ss.
County of (name of county). }

I (here give name of officer and his official title) certify that (name of grantor, and if acknowledged by the spouse, his or her name, and add "his or her spouse") personally known to me to be the same person whose name is (or are) subscribed to the foregoing instrument, appeared before me this day in person, and acknowledged that—he—(she or they) signed and delivered the instrument as his (her or their) free and voluntary act, for the uses and purposes therein set forth.

Dated   19   . (Signature of officer.) (Seal.)

Ch. 30, ¶ 34c. Deeds and instruments of conveyances—Inclusion—Effect of absence or neglect.

§ 35c. Whenever any deed or instrument of conveyance or other instrument to be made a matter of record is executed there shall be typed or printed to the side or below all signatures the names of the parties signing such instruments including the witnesses thereto, if any, and the names of the parties or officers taking the acknowledgments. The absence or neglect to print or type the names of the parties under the signatures shall not invalidate the instrument.

* * *

Uniform Recognition of Acknowledgments Act

Ch. 30, ¶ 221. Short title.

§ 1. Short title. This Act may be cited as the Uniform Recognition of Acknowledgments Act.

Ch. 30, ¶ 222. Recognition of notarial acts performed outside this State.

§ 2. Recognition of notarial acts performed outside this State. For the purposes of this Act, "notarial acts" means acts which the laws and regulations of this State authorize notaries public of this State to perform, including the administering of oaths and affirmations, taking proof of execution and acknowledgments of instruments, and attesting documents. Notarial acts may be performed outside this

State for use in this State with the same effect as if performed by a notary public of this State by the following persons authorized pursuant to the laws and regulations of other governments in addition to any other person authorized by the laws and regulations of this State:

(1) a notary public authorized to perform notarial acts in the place in which the act is performed;

(2) a judge, clerk, or deputy clerk of any court of record in the place in which the notarial act is performed;

(3) an officer of the foreign service of the United States, a consular agent, or any other person authorized by regulation of the United States Department of State to perform notarial acts in the place in which the act is performed;

(4) a commissioned officer in active service with the Armed Forces of the United States and any other person authorized by regulation of the Armed Forces to perform notarial acts if the notarial act is performed for one of the following or his dependents: a merchant seaman of the United States, a member of the Armed Forces of the United States, or any other person serving with or accompanying the Armed Forces of the United States; or

(5) any other person authorized to perform notarial acts in the place in which the act is performed.

Ch. 30, ¶ 223. Authentication of authority of officer.

§ 3. Authentication of authority of officer. (a) If the notarial act is performed by any of the persons described in paragraphs 1 to 4, inclusive of Section 2, other than a person authorized to perform notarial acts by the laws or regulations of a foreign country, the signature, rank, or title and serial number, if any, of the person are sufficient proof of the authority of a holder of that rank or title to perform the act. Further proof of his authority is not required.

(b) If the notarial act is performed by a person authorized by the laws or regulations of a foreign country to perform the act, there is sufficient proof of the authority of that person to act if:

(1) either a foreign service officer of the United States resident in the country in which the act is performed or a diplomatic or consular officer of the foreign country resident in the United States certifies that a person holding that office is authorized to perform the act;

(2) the official seal of the person performing the notarial act is affixed to the document; or

(3) the title and indication of authority to perform notarial acts of the person appear either in a digest of foreign law or in a list customarily used as a source of such information.

(c) If the notarial act is performed by a person

other than one described in subsections (a) and (b), there is sufficient proof of the authority of that person to act if the clerk of a court of record in the place in which the notarial act is performed certifies to the official character of that person and to his authority to perform the notarial act.

(d) The signature and title of the person performing the act are prima facie evidence that he is a person with the designated title and that the signature is genuine.

Ch. 30, ¶ 224. Certificate of person taking acknowledgment.

§ 4. Certificate of person taking acknowledgment. The person taking an acknowledgment shall certify that:

(1) the person acknowledging appeared before him and acknowledged he executed the instrument; and

(2) the person acknowledging was known to the person taking the acknowledgment or that the person taking the acknowledgment had satisfactory evidence that the person acknowledging was the person described in and who executed the instrument.

Ch. 30, ¶ 225. Recognition of certificate of acknowledgment.

§ 5. Recognition of certificate of acknowledgment. The form of a certificate of acknowledgment used by a person whose authority is recognized under Section 2 shall be accepted in this State if:

(1) the certificate is in a form prescribed by the laws or regulations of this State;

(2) the certificate is in a form prescribed by the laws or regulations applicable in the place in which the acknowledgment is taken; or

(3) the certificate contains the words "acknowledged before me", or their substantial equivalent.

Ch. 30, ¶ 226. Certificate of acknowledgment.

§ 6. Certificate of acknowledgment. The words acknowledged before me mean:

(1) that the person acknowledging appeared before the person taking the acknowledgment;

(2) that he acknowledged he executed the instrument;

(3) that, in the case of:

(i) a natural person, he executed the instrument for the purposes therein stated;

(ii) a corporation, the officer or agent acknowledged he held the position or title set forth in the instrument and certificate, he signed the instrument on behalf of the corporation by proper au-

thority, and the instrument was the act of the corporation for the purpose therein stated;

(iii) a partnership, the partner or agent acknowledged he signed the instrument on behalf of the partnership by proper authority and he executed the instrument as the act of the partnership for the purposes therein stated;

(iv) a person acknowledging as principal by an attorney in fact, he executed the instrument by proper authority as the act of the principal for the purposes therein stated;

(v) a person acknowledging as a public officer, trustee, administrator, guardian, or other representative, he signed the instrument by proper authority and he executed the instrument in the capacity and for the purposes therein stated; and

(4) that the person taking the acknowledgment either knew or had satisfactory evidence that the person acknowledging was the person named in the instrument or certificate.

Ch. 30, ¶ 227. Short forms of acknowledgment.

§ 7. Short forms of acknowledgment. The forms of acknowledgment set forth in this Section may be used and are sufficient for their respective purposes under any law of this State, whether executed in this State or any other State. The forms shall be known as "Statutory Short Forms of Acknowledgment" and may be referred to by that name. The authorization of the forms in this Section does not preclude the use of other forms.

(1) For an individual acting in his own right:

State of . . . .

County of . . . .

The foregoing instrument was acknowledged before me this (date) by (name of person acknowledged).

(Signature of person taking acknowledgment)

(Title or rank)

(Serial number, if any)

(2) For a corporation:

State of . . . .

County of . . . .

The foregoing instrument was acknowledged before me this (date) by (name of officer or agent, title of officer or agent) of (name of corporation acknowledging) a (state or place of incorporation) corporation, on behalf of the corporation.

(Signature of person taking acknowledgment)

(Title or rank)

(Serial number, if any)

(3) For a partnership:

State of . . . .

County of . . . .

The foregoing instrument was acknowledged before me this (date) by (name of acknowledging partner or agent), partner (or agent) on behalf of (name of partnership), a partnership.

(Signature of person taking acknowledgment)
(Title or rank)
(Serial number, if any)
(4) For an individual acting as principal by an attorney in fact:

State of . . . .
County of . . . .

The foregoing instrument was acknowledged before me this (date) by (name of attorney in fact) as attorney in fact on behalf of (name of principal).

(Signature of person taking acknowledgment)
(Title or rank)
(Serial number, if any)
(5) By any public officer, trustee, or personal representative:

State of . . . .
County of . . . .

The foregoing instrument was acknowledged before me this (date) by (name and title of position).

(Signature of person taking acknowledgment)
(Title or rank)
(Serial number, if any)
(b) This amendatory Act of 1981 is to clarify that any uses of the short form of acknowledgment as herein provided within the State of Illinois prior to the effective date of this Amendatory Act have been valid.

Ch. 30, ¶ 228. Acknowledgments not affected by this Act.

§ 8. Acknowledgments not affected by this Act. A notarial act performed prior to the effective date of this Act is not affected by this Act. This Act provides an additional method of proving notarial acts. Nothing in this Act diminishes or invalidates the recognition accorded to notarial acts by other laws or regulations of this State.

Ch. 30, ¶ 229. Uniformity of interpretation.

§ 9. Uniformity of interpretation. This Act shall be so interpreted as to make uniform the laws of those states which enact it.

Ch. 30, ¶ 230. Time of taking effect.

§ 10. Time of taking effect. This Act shall take effect on January 1, 1970.

DEPOSITIONS

Ch. 101, ¶ 1. Administration of oaths to witnesses and others—Persons empowered.

All courts, and all judges and the clerk thereof, the county clerk, deputy county clerk, and notaries public, have power to administer oaths and affirmations to witnesses and others, concerning anything commenced or to be commenced, or pending before them respectively.

Ch. 101, ¶ 2. Administration of oath of office—Affidavits and depositions—Persons empowered.

All courts, and judges, and the clerks thereof, the county clerk, deputy county clerk, the Secretary of State and notaries public, may, in their respective districts, circuits, counties or jurisdictions, administer all oaths of office and all other oaths authorized or required of any officer or other person, and take affidavits and depositions concerning any matter or thing, process or proceeding commenced or to be commenced, or pending in any court or before them, or on any occasion wherein any affidavit or deposition is authorized or required by law to be taken.

The same functions may be performed by any commissioned officer in active service of the armed forces of the United States, within or without the United States. Oaths, affidavits or depositions taken by or affirmations made before such officers need not be authenticated nor attested by any seal nor shall any instruments executed or proceedings had before such officers be invalid because the place of the proceedings or of the execution is not state.

Ch. 101, ¶ 205. Persons before whom depositions may be taken.

(a) **Within the United States.** Within the United States or within a territory or insular possession subject to the dominion of the United States, depositions shall be taken (1) before an officer authorized to administer oaths by the laws of this state or of the United States or of the place where the examination is held, or (2) before a person appointed by the court. The officer or person is empowered to administer oaths and take testimony. Whenever the term "officer" is used in these rules, it includes a person appointed by the court unless the context indicates otherwise.

(b) **In foreign countries.** In a foreign state or country depositions shall be taken (1) before a secretary of embassy, consul general, consul, vice counsul, or consular agent of the United States, or any officer authorized to administer oaths under the laws of this state, or of the United States, or of the place where the examination is held, or (2) before a person appointed by the court. The officer or person is empowered to administer oaths and take testimony.

(c) **Issuance of commissions and letters rogatory.** A commission, dedimus potestatem, or letter rogatory is not required but if desired shall be issued by the clerk without notice. An officer may be designated in a commission either by name or descriptive title and a letter rogatory may be addressed "To the Appropriate Authority in (here name the country)."

(d) **Disqualification for interest.** No deposition shall be taken before a person who is a relative of or attorney for any of the parties, a relative of the attorney, or financially interested in the action.

LEGAL HOLIDAYS

Ch. 17, ¶ 2201. Legal holidays—Regular day to be closed—Closing on other than regular day to be closed—Days considered Sunday.

§ 17. (a) The following days shall be legal holidays in the State of Illinois upon which day a bank may, but is not required to, remain closed:

the first day of January (New Year's Day);

the third Monday in January (observance of Martin Luther King, Jr.'s birthday);

the twelfth day in February (Abraham Lincoln's birthday);

the third Monday in February (Presidents Day);

the first Monday in March (observance of Casimir Pulaski's birthday);

the Friday preceding Easter Sunday (Good Friday);

the thirtieth day of May (Memorial Day);

the fourth day of July (Independence Day);

the first Monday in September (Labor Day);

the second Monday in October (Columbus Day);

the eleventh day of November (Veterans' Day);

the fourth Thursday in November (Thanksgiving Day);

the twenty-fifth day in December (Christmas Day);

The days upon which the general elections for members of the House of Representatives are held, and any day proclaimed by the Governor of this State; as a legal holiday. From 12 o'clock noon to 12 o'clock midnight of each Saturday shall be considered a half-holiday. In addition to such holidays and half-holidays, a bank may select one day of the week to remain closed, as provided in subsection (b) of this Section.

(b) Any bank doing business within this State may select any one day of the week to remain closed on a regular basis upon adoption of a resolution by the board of directors of such bank designating the day selected and upon filing and publishing a copy of such resolution as hereinafter required. Any such resolution shall be deemed effective for the purpose of this Section only when a copy thereof, certified by an officer having charge of the records of such bank, is filed with the Recorder of the county in which such bank is located and published once each week for 3 successive weeks in a newspaper of general circulation in such county. Such publication shall be accomplished by, and at the expense of, the bank, and the bank shall submit to the Commissioner of Banks and Trust Companies such evidence of the publication as the Commissioner shall deem appropriate. Any such selection shall remain in full force and effect until a copy of the later resolution of the board of directors of such bank, certified in like manner, terminating or altering any such prior selection shall be filed and published in the same manner as such prior resolution.

(c) If an occasion arises when a state bank wishes to remain closed on a particular day, other than a day on which the bank has selected to remain closed on a regular basis as provided in this Section, such state bank may remain closed on such an occasion after first sending to the Commissioner a copy of a resolution adopted by the board of directors authorizing the bank to remain closed on such occasion and notice of the intent to remain closed on such occasion shall be conspicuously posted in the lobby of the main banking office and any branches of such bank for at least 3 weeks in advance of such occasion. Any day which any bank doing business within the State shall select to remain closed pursuant to this Section shall, with respect to such bank, be treated and considered as a Sunday.

(d) all legal holidays, the half holidays and any day selected by a bank doing business within the State to remain closed, shall, for all purposes whatsoever, as regards the presenting for payment or acceptance, the maturity and protesting and giving of notice of the dishonor of bills of exchange, bank checks and promissory notes and other negotiable or commercial paper or instrument, be treated and considered as a Sunday. When any such holidays fall on Sunday, the Monday next following shall be held and considered such holiday. All notes, bills, drafts, checks or other evidence of indebtedness, falling due or maturing on either of such days, shall be deemed as due or maturing upon the day following, and when 2 or more of these days come together, or immediately succeeding each other, then such instruments, paper or indebtedness shall be deemed as due or having matured on the day following the last of such days.

(e) Any act authorized, required or permitted to

be performed at or by or with respect to any bank doing business within the State on a day which it has selected to remain closed under this Section may be so performed on the next succeeding business day and no liability or loss of rights of any kind shall result from such delay.

(f) Nothing in this Act shall in any manner affect the validity of, or render void or voidable, the payment, certification, or acceptance of a check or other negotiable instrument, or any other transaction by a bank in this State, because done or performed on any Saturday, Sunday, holiday, or any day selected by a bank to remain closed, or during any time other than regular banking hours; but no bank in this State, which by law or custom is entitled to remain open or to close for the whole or any part of any day selected by it to remain open or to close, is compelled to close, or to remain open for the transaction of business or to perform any of the acts or transactions aforesaid except at its own option.

INDIANA

NOTARIES PUBLIC

[IND. CODE ANN.]

§ 33-16-1-1. Jurisdiction.

The jurisdiction of any notary public duly qualified in this state shall be co-extensive with the limits of the state, but no notary shall be compelled to act out of the limits of the county in which he resides.

§ 33-16-2-1. Qualifications; appointment; term; application; bond; fees.

Sec. 1. (a) Any applicant for a commission as a notary public must:

(1) be at least eighteen (18) years of age; and

(2) be a legal resident of Indiana.

(b) A notary public shall be appointed and commissioned by the governor. A notary public shall hold office for four (4) years. A notary public, when so qualified, shall be authorized to act throughout Indiana. A person may request an application to become a notary public from the secretary of state. The application form shall be prescribed by the secretary of state and shall include the applicant's county of residence, oath of office, and official bond. The application shall also contain any additional information necessary for the efficient administration of this chapter. The applicant shall personally appear with an application form before an officer, authorized by law to administer oaths, who shall administer an oath of office to the applicant.

(c) The applicant shall secure an official bond, with freehold or corporate security, to be approved by the secretary of state in the sum of five thousand dollars ($5,000). The official bond shall be conditioned upon the faithful performance and discharge of the duties of the office of notary public, in all things according to law, for the use of any person injured by a breach of the condition. The completed application shall be forwarded to the secretary of state. The secretary of state shall forward each commission issued by the governor to the applicant or the applicant's surety company.

(d) The secretary of state shall charge and collect the following fees:

(1) For each commission to notaries public, ten dollars ($10).

(2) For each duplicate commission to notaries public, five dollars ($5).

§ 33-16-2-2. Prohibited acts; investigation; violation; revocation of commission.

Sec. 2. (a) A notary public shall not do any of the following:

(1) Use any other name or initial in signing acknowledgments, other than that by which the notary has been commissioned.

(2) Acknowledge any instrument in which the notary's name appears as a party to the transaction.

(3) Take the acknowledgment of or administer an oath to any person whom the notary actually knows:

(A) has been adjudged mentally incompetent by a court of competent jurisdiction; and

(B) to be under a guardianship under IC-29-3 at the time the notary takes the acknowledgment or administers the oath.

(4) Take the acknowledgment of any person who is blind, without first reading the instrument to the blind person.

(5) Take the acknowledgment of any person who does not speak or understand the English language, unless the nature and effect of the instrument to be notarized is translated into a language which the person does speak or understand.

(6) Acknowledge the execution of:

(A) an affidavit, unless the affiant acknowledges the truth of the statements in the affidavit; or

(B) an instrument, unless the person who executed the instrument:

(i) signs the instrument before the notary; or

(ii) affirms to the notary that the signature on the instrument is the person's own.

(b) In the event any notary public violates any of the provisions of this article, the notary's appointment may be revoked by the judge of the circuit court in which the notary resides.

(c) The secretary of state may investigate any possible violation of this section by a notary public and may, under IC-4-21.5, revoke the commission of a notary public who violates any of the provisions of this section. Whenever the secretary of state revokes the commission of a notary public, the notary public is barred from reapplying for a new commission for five (5) years after the revocation.

§ 33-16-2-3. Appointment—Governor's discretion.

The governor may appoint notaries public in the several counties whenever, in his judgment, the public interest would be thereby promoted.

§ 33-16-2-4. Seal; attestation of notarial acts; requisite.

No notary shall be authorized to act until he shall have procured such a seal as will stamp upon paper a distinct impression, in words or letters, sufficiently indicating his official character, to which may be added such other device as he may choose and all notarial acts not attested by such seal shall be void.

§ 33-16-2-5. Powers.

Every notary has the power to:

(1) do all such acts which, by common law and the custom of merchants, they are authorized to do;

(2) take and certify all acknowledgments of deeds or other instruments of writing required or authorized by law to be acknowledged; and

(3) administer oaths generally, and to take and certify affidavits and depositions.

§ 33-16-2-6. Certificate attested by seal.

The official certificate of a notary public, attested by his seal, shall be presumptive evidence of the facts therein stated, in cases where, by law, he is authorized to certify such facts.

§ 33-16-2-7. Bank officer or public official acting as notary.

No person, being an officer in any bank, corporation, or association possessed of any banking powers, shall act as a notary public in the business of such bank, corporation or association. The aforesaid prohibition shall not apply to employees of any such bank, corporation or association, and a person who is a shareholder or member of a building and loan association or savings and loan association may act as a notary public in the business of such association. No person holding any lucrative office or appointment under the United States or under this state, and prohibited by the Constitution of this state from holing more than one (1) such lucrative office, shall serve as a notary public, and his acceptance of any such office shall vacate his appointment as such notary; but this provision shall not apply to any person holding any lucrative office or appointment under any civil or school city or town of this state. No person, being a public official, or a deputy or appointee acting for or serving under the same, shall make any charge for services as a notary public in connection with any official business of such office, or of any other office in the governmental unit in which such persons are serving, unless such charges are specifically authorized by some statute other than the statute fixing generally the fees and charges of notaries public.

§ 33-16-2-8. Lists; notice of change of county or name; revised commission.

Sec. 8. The secretary of state shall furnish to the clerk of the circuit court of a county, at his request, a list of all commissioned notaries public residing in that county. If any notary public shall change his name or county of residence during the term of his commission he shall notify the secretary of state in writing of the change. The secretary of state shall process a revised commission to reflect any change of name or county and such revised commission shall only be valid for the unexpired term of the original commission.

§ 33-16-2-9. Affixing printed name of notary on documents, etc.

Sec. 9. (a) Each notary, in addition to affixing his name, expiration date, and seal, shall print or type his name immediately beneath his signature on a certificate of acknowledgment, jurat, or other official document, unless his name appears:

(1) in printed form on the document; or

(2) as part of his stamp in such form as to be legible when the document is photographed;

and also shall indicate his county of residence on the document.

(b) Failure to comply with subsection (a) does not affect the validity of any document notarized before July 1, 1982.

§ 33-16-3-1. Certificate of acknowledgment, jurat or official document.

Sec. 1. It shall be the duty of every notary public holding a commission as such from the state of Indiana, at the time of signing any certificate of acknowledgment of a deed, mortgage or other instrument, or any jurat or other official document, to append to such certificate a true statement of the date of the expiration of his commission as such notary public.

§ 33-16-3-2. Omission of statement.

Sec. 2. A notary public who omits to make the statement required by section 1 of this chapter commits a Class C infraction.

§ 33-16-4-1. Public officials authorized to administer oaths and take acknowledgments.

Sec. 1. (a) Notaries public, judges of courts, in their respective jurisdictions, mayors, clerks, and clerk-treasurers of towns and cities, in their respective towns and cities, clerks of circuit courts, master commissioners, in their respective counties, judges of United States district courts of Indiana, in their respective jurisdictions, and United States commissioners appointed for any United States district court of Indiana, in their respective jurisdictions, are authorized to administer oaths and take acknowledgments generally, pertaining to all matters where an oath is required.

(b) County auditors, in their respective counties, shall be authorized to administer oaths to township trustees.

(c) Any member of the general assembly shall have full power and authority to subscribe and administer oaths and take acknowledgments of all documents whatsoever anywhere in Indiana.

§ 33-16-4-2. Fraudulent acts; felony.

Sec. 2. A person authorized to administer oaths or take acknowledgments who, with intent to defraud:

(1) affixes his signature to a blank form or affidavit or certificate of acknowledgment; and

(2) delivers that form to another person, with intent that it be used as an affidavit or acknowledgment;

commits a Class D felony.

§ 33-16-4-3. Fraudulent use of forms; felony.

Sec. 3. A person who knowingly uses a form that was delivered to him in violation of section 2 of this chapter commits a Class D felony.

§ 33-16-5-1. Manager, officers and employees becoming and acting as notary public.

Sec. 1. The manager, officers, and employees of any federal land bank association located within the state of Indiana may become and act as a notary public in the business of such association to take acknowledgments of deeds and real estate mortgages and to take and certify affidavits.

§ 33-16-6-1. Notary public also stockholder or association officer.

Sec. 1. Any notary public who may be a stockholder or officer of any cemetery association in which no officer or stockholder in such association can be a beneficiary from the sale of lots or otherwise, as provided by the constitution of such association, may and is hereby authorized to take acknowledgments of sales of such lots.

§ 33-16-7-1. Amount of fee.

Sec. 1. The maximum fee of a notary public is two dollars ($2) for each notarial act.

§ 33-16-8-1. Authorization; recording.

Sec. 1. A township trustee has the power to perform any act that a notary public may perform in Indiana. Acknowledgments to deeds or other instruments taken by a trustee shall be recorded as if they had been acknowledged before a notary public.

§ 33-16-8-2. Seal; requirement.

Sec. 2. Before a trustee may perform a notarial act, the trustee shall obtain a seal that can stamp upon paper a distinct impression that indicates the trustee's official character, along with any other information that the trustee chooses. A notarial act of a trustee that is not attested by a seal is void.

§ 33-16-8-3. Trustee's date of election; appendage.

Sec. 3. When signing any certificate of acknowledgment, jurat, or other official document, the trustee must append to it the trustee's date of election as a trustee.

§ 33-16-8-4. Fee barred.

Sec. 4. A trustee may not receive a fee for performing a notarial act.

§ 33-16-8-5. Prohibited acts.

Sec. 5. A trustee shall not perform any act that is prohibited to a notary public.

ADDITIONAL AUTHORITY

§ 2-3-4-1. Members or officers of general assembly.

Sec. 1. (a) Any member of the general assembly, the principal clerk of the house of representatives, or the secretary of the senate may:

(1) take acknowledgment to deeds or other instruments in writing;

(2) administer oaths, protest notes, and checks;

(3) take the deposition of a witness;

(4) take and certify affidavits and depositions; and

(5) perform any other duty conferred upon a notary public by the statutes of Indiana.

(b) Acknowledgments to deeds or other instruments taken by any such person shall entitle such deeds or other instruments to be recorded the same as though acknowledged before a notary public.

§ 2-3-4-2. General assembly—Members as notaries—Seal, impression, attestation.

No member of the general assembly shall be authorized to perform any of the duties mentioned in section one [§ 2-3-4-2] of this chapter until he shall have procured such seal as will stamp upon paper a distinct impression, in words or letters, sufficiently indicating his official character, to which may be added such other device as he may choose. All acts not attested by such seal shall be void.

§ 2-3-4-3. General assembly—Members as notaries—Date of election appended to jurat—Jurisdiction.

It shall be the duty of every member of the general assembly performing any of the acts as set forth in this act [§§ 2-3-4-1—2-3-4-4], at the time of signing any certificate of acknowledgment of a deed, mortgage or other instrument, or any jurat or other official document, to append to such certificate the date of his election to the general assembly. The jurisdiction of any such member to perform the duties herein mentioned shall be coextensive with the state of Indiana.

§ 2-3-4-4. Fees.

Any such member performing any of the acts or duties hereunder shall be entitled to the same fees as those charged by notaries public, and where any act by a notary public would be a violation of the law, it shall likewise be a violation of the law if committed by a member of said general assembly in the performance of any of the duties or acts authorized hereunder. All laws and parts of laws in conflict herewith are hereby repealed.

§ 33-15-24-1. Powers of notary public; taking examinations and depositions; bond; seal.

Sec. 1. (a) Every official circuit, superior, criminal, probate, juvenile, and county court reporter appointed under IC 33-15-23-1 or IC 33-10.5-8-2 is authorized and empowered to:

(1) take and certify all acknowledgments of

deeds, mortgages, or other instruments of writing required or authorized by law to be acknowledged;

(2) administer oaths generally;

(3) take and certify affidavits, examinations, and depositions; and

(4) perform any duty now conferred upon a notary public by the statutes of the state of Indiana.

(b) Any official reporter taking examinations and depositions shall have the right to:

(1) take them in shorthand;

(2) transcribe them into typewriting or long-hand; and

(3) have them signed by the deposing witness.

(c) Before performing any official duty as authorized, an official reporter shall:

(1) provide a bond as is required for notary publics; and

(2) procure a seal which will stamp a distinct impression indicating his official character, to which may be added to any other device as he may choose.

§ 36-2-11-16. Requirements for instruments to be received and recorded.

Sec. 16. (a) This section does not apply to:

(1) an instrument executed before November 4, 1943;

(2) a judgment, order, or writ of a court;

(3) a will or death certificate; or

(4) an instrument executed or acknowledged outside Indiana.

(b) Whenever this section prescribes that the name of a person be printed, typewritten, or stamped immediately beneath his signature, the signature must be written on the instrument, directly preceding the printed, typewritten, or stamped name, and may not be superimposed on that name so as to render either illegible. However, the instrument may be received for record if the name and signature are, in the discretion of the county recorder, placed on the instrument so as to render the connection between the two apparent.

(c) The recorder may receive for record an instrument only if:

(1) the name of each person who executed the instrument is legibly printed, typewritten, or stamped immediately beneath his signature or the signature itself is printed, typewritten, or stamped;

(2) the name of each witness to the instrument is legibly printed, typewritten, or stamped immediately beneath his signature or the signature itself is printed, typewritten, or stamped;

(3) the name of each notary public whose signature appears on the instrument is legibly printed, typewritten, or stamped immediately beneath his signature or the signature itself is printed, typewritten, or stamped; and

(4) the name of each person who executed the instrument appears identically in the body of the instrument, in the acknowledgment or jurat, in his signature, and beneath his signature;

or if subsection (d) is complied with.

(d) The recorder may receive for record an instrument that does not comply with subsection (c) if:

(1) a printed or typewritten affidavit of a person with personal knowledge of the facts is recorded with the instrument;

(2) the affidavit complies with this section;

(3) the affidavit states the correct name of a person, if any, whose signature cannot be identified or whose name is not printed, typewritten, or stamped on the instrument as prescribed by this section; and

(4) when the instrument does not comply with subsection (c)(4), the affidavit states the correct name of the person and states that each of the names used in the instrument refers to the person.

(e) The recorder may record a copy produced by a photographic process of any document presented for recording if:

(1) the document complies with other statutory recording requirements; and

(2) the copy is a clear, concise, and unobstructed copy.

All copies accepted for recording shall be marked as copies by the recorder.

(f) An instrument received and recorded by a county recorder is conclusively presumed to comply with this section.

FEES

§ 5-7-1-1. Fees authorized.

Sec. 1. The secretary of state, provided that no fees shall be charged against the United States, or this, or any other state, or any county of this state, nor against any officer of either of them, for any attestation, certificate or paper required by them for official use, shall be authorized to charge and collect on behalf of the state of Indiana, the following fees, to be paid by the parties requiring the service: for each attestation and seal, unless otherwise provided, fifty cents (50 cents); for each certified copy, six dollars ($6.00) plus the charge for copying; for all copying of records, papers and documents not otherwise provided for, ten cents (10 cents) per page; the fees and amounts so taxed and collected shall not belong to or be the property of the secretary of state, but shall belong to and be the property of the state.

ACKNOWLEDGMENTS

§ 32-1-2-18. Acknowledgment or proof.

To entitle any conveyance, mortgage, or instrument of writing to be recorded, it shall be acknowledged by the grantor, or proved before any judge, or clerk of a court of record, justice of the peace, auditor, recorder, notary public, or mayor of a city in this or any other state, or before any commissioner appointed in another state by the governor of this state, or before any minister, charge d'affaires, or consul of the United States in any foreign country.

§ 32-1-2-19. Certification of acknowledgment in another county.

When any conveyance, mortgage, or other instrument required to be recorded, is acknowledged in any county in this state, other than the one in which the same is required to be recorded, the acknowledgment shall be certified by the clerk of the circuit court of the county in which such officer resides, and attested by the seal of said court; but an acknowledgment before an officer, having an official seal, if attested by such official seal, shall be sufficient without such certificate.

§ 32-1-2-20. Foreign acknowledgment in another state; recording.

To entitle to record, in this state, conveyances acknowledged out of this state and within the United States, the same must be certified by the clerk of any court of record of the county in which the officer receiving the acknowledgment resides, and attested by the seal of said court; but an acknowledgment before an officer having an official seal, attested by his official seal, shall be sufficient without such certificate.

§ 32-1-2-21. Manner of proof. Proving deeds.

All deeds may be proved according to the rules of the common law, before any officer authorized to take acknowledgments, and being so proved, shall be entitled to record.

§ 32-1-2-23. Form; acknowledgment of deed or mortgage.

The following or any other form substantially the same, shall be a good or sufficient form of acknowledgment of any deed or mortgage:

"Before me, E. F. (a judge or justice, as the case may be) this _____ day of _____, _____,

A. B. acknowledged the execution of the annexed deed, (or mortgage, as the case may be)."

§ 32-1-2-24. Acknowledgment when grantor signs by mark. Explaining contents and purport of deed to grantor.

Whenever before any public officer duly authorized to receive acknowledgment of deeds, the grantor of any deed shall sign the same with his or her mark, and also in all other cases in which the said public officer shall have good cause to believe that the contents and purport of said deed are not fully known to the grantor thereof, it shall be the duty of the said public officer before signature, fully to explain to him or her, the contents and purport of the within deed. But the failure of such officer so to do shall not affect the validity of any deed.

§ 32-1-2-26. Certificate of acknowledgment; attaching to instrument; contents.

A certificate of the acknowledgment of the conveyance or other instrument in writing, required to be recorded, under the hand and seal of the officer taking the same, shall be written on or attached to such deed; and in all cases where, by law, the certificate of the clerk of the proper county is required to accompany the acknowledgment, the said certificate shall set forth that the officer before whom such acknowledgment was taken, was at the time, lawfully acting as such, and that his signature to the certificate of acknowledgment, is genuine.

§ 32-2-4-1. Acknowledgment in foreign country. Diplomatic or consular offices.

Conveyances, mortgages and other instruments in writing, of a character to admit them to record under the recording laws of this state, when executed in a foreign country, shall be acknowledged by the grantor or person executing the same, and proved before any diplomatic or consular officer of the United States, duly accredited, or before any officer of such country who, by the laws thereof, is authorized to take acknowledgments or proof of conveyances; and if such acknowledgment or proof is in the English language, and attested by the official seal of such officer, it shall be sufficient to admit such instrument to record; but if in some other language or not attested by such official seal, then such instrument must be accompanied by a certificate of an officer of the United States, as aforesaid, to the effect that it is duly executed according to the laws of such foreign country; that the officer certifying to the acknowledgment or proof had legal authority so to do, and the meaning of his certificate, if the same is made in a foreign language.

DEPOSITIONS

[IND. TRIAL RULE]

RULE 28. Persons before whom depositions may be taken; * * *

(A) Within the United States. Within the United States or within a territory or insular possession subject to the dominion of the United States, depositions shall be taken before an officer authorized to administer oaths by the laws of the United States, or of the state of Indiana, or of the place where the examination is held, or before a person appointed by the court in which the action is pending. A person so appointed has power to administer oaths and take testimony.

(B) In foreign countries. In a foreign country, depositions may be taken:

(1) on notice before a person authorized to administer oaths in the place in which the examination is held, either by the law thereof or by the law of the United States; or

(2) before a person commissioned by the court, and a person so commissioned shall have the power by virtue of his commission to administer any necessary oath and take testimony; or

(3) pursuant to a letter rogatory.

A commission or a letter rogatory shall be issued on application and notice and on terms that are just and appropriate. It is not requisite to the issuance of a commission or a letter rogatory that the taking of the deposition in any other manner is impracticable or inconvenient; and both a commission and a letter rogatory may be issued in proper cases. A notice or commission may designate the person before whom the deposition is to be taken either by name or descriptive title. A letter rogatory may be addressed "To the Appropriate Authority in (here name the country)." Evidence obtained in response to a letter rogatory need not be excluded merely for the reason that it is not a verbatim transcript or that the testimony was not taken under oath or for any similar departure from the requirements for depositions taken within the United States under these rules.

(C) Disqualification for interest. Unless otherwise permitted by these rules, no deposition shall be taken before a person who is a relative or employee or attorney or counsel of any of the parties, or is a relative or employee of such attorney or counsel, or is financially interested in the action.

* * *

LEGAL HOLIDAYS

[IND. CODE ANN.]

§ 1-1-9-1. List; observances.

Sec. 1. (a) The following are legal holidays within the state of Indiana for all purposes:

New Year's Day, January 1.

Martin Luther King, Jr.'s Birthday, the third Monday in January.

Abraham Lincoln's Birthday, February 12.

George Washington's Birthday, the third Monday in February.

Good Friday, a movable feast day.

Memorial Day, the last Monday in May.

Independence Day, July 4.

Labor Day, the first Monday in September.

Columbus Day, the second Monday in October.

Election Day, the day of any general, municipal, or primary election.

Veterans Day, November 11.

Thanksgiving Day, the fourth Thursday in November.

Christmas Day, December 25.

Sunday, the first day of the week.

(b) When any of these holidays, other than Sunday, comes on Sunday, the following Monday shall be the legal holiday. When any of these holidays comes on Saturday, the preceding Friday shall be the legal holiday.

(c) The provisions of this section shall not affect any action taken by the general assembly while in regular or special session, and any action taken by the general assembly on any such holiday shall be valid for all purposes.

IOWA

NOTARIAL ACTS

[Iowa Code Ann.]

§ 77A.1. Title.

This chapter shall be known as the "Iowa Law on Notarial Acts."

§ 77A.2. Definitions.

As used in this chapter, unless the context otherwise requires:

1. "Acknowledgment" means a declaration by a person that the person has executed an instrument for the purposes stated in the document and, if the instrument is executed in a representative capacity, that the person signed the instrument with proper authority and executed it as the act of the person or entity represented and identified in the document.

2. "Notarial act" means any act that a notary public of this state is authorized to perform, and includes, but is not limited to, taking an acknowledgment, administering an oath or affirmation, taking verification upon oath or affirmation, witnessing or attesting a signature, certifying or attesting a copy, and noting a protest of a negotiable instrument.

3. "Notarial officer" means a notary public or other officer authorized to perform notarial acts.

4. "Representative capacity" means any of the following:

a. A representative on behalf of a corporation, partnership, trust, or other entity, as an authorized officer, agent, partner, trustee, or other representative.

b. A public officer, personal representative, guardian, or other representative, in the capacity recited in the instrument.

c. An attorney in fact for a principal.

d. Any other capacity as an authorized representative of another.

5. "Verification upon oath or affirmation" means a declaration that a statement is true, made by a person upon oath or affirmation.

§ 77A.3. Appointment—revocation.

1. The secretary of state may appoint residents of this state as notaries public and may revoke an appointment for cause.

2. The secretary of state shall appoint members

of the general assembly as notaries public, upon request, and may revoke an appointment for cause.

3. The secretary of state may appoint as a notary public a resident of a state bordering Iowa if that person's place of work or business is within the state of Iowa. If a notary who is a resident of a state bordering Iowa ceases to work or maintain a place of business in Iowa, the notary commission expires.

§ 77A.4. Term of commission.

The term of a notary public who is an Iowa resident is three years. The term of a notary who is a resident of a state bordering Iowa and whose place of work or business is in Iowa, is one year. The term of a notary who is a member of the general assembly is the member's term of office.

§ 77A.5. Notice of expiration of term.

The secretary of state shall, two months preceding the expiration of a commission, notify the notary public of the expiration date and furnish a blank application for reappointment.

§ 77A.6. Application—fee—seal.

1. Before a commission is delivered to a person appointed as a notary public, the person shall:

a. Complete an application for appointment as a notary public on a form prescribed by the secretary of state.

b. Remit the sum of thirty dollars to the secretary of state. However, persons appointed as notaries public under section 77A.3, subsection 2, are not subject to the fee imposed by this subsection.

2. When the secretary of state determines that the requirements of this section are satisfied, the secretary shall execute and deliver a certificate of commission to the person appointed.

3. A notary public may procure a seal or stamp for use in performing notarial acts. A seal or stamp used by a notary public in the performance of notarial acts shall contain the words "Notarial Seal" and the word "Iowa". The stamp may include the name of the notary public. However, a notarial act is not invalid if a seal or stamp used in the performance of a notarial act fails to meet the requirements of this subsection. This subsection does not require the use of a seal or stamp in the performance of a notarial act.

§ 77A.7. Revocation—notice and hearing—rules.

If the commission of a person appointed notary public is revoked by the secretary of state, the secretary shall immediately notify the person through the mail. The notice shall state the cause of the revocation and shall inform the person of the right to a hearing on the revocation. The secretary of state shall adopt rules under chapter 17A to provide for a hearing for persons whose commission is revoked.

§ 77A.8. Discretion—limitation.

A notary public may exercise reasonable discretion in performing or declining to perform notarial services, but a notary shall not condition the performance of notarial services upon the requirement that the person served be a customer or client of the establishment by which the notary is employed.

The employer of a notary public shall not condition the performing of notarial services upon the requirement that the person served be a customer or client of the establishment by which the notary is employed.

§ 77A.9. Notarial acts.

1. In taking an acknowledgment, the notarial officer must determine, either from personal knowledge or from satisfactory evidence, that the person appearing before the notary and making the acknowledgment is the person whose true signature is on the instrument.

2. In taking a verification upon oath or affirmation, the notarial officer must determine, either from personal knowledge or from satisfactory evidence, that the person appearing before the officer and making the verification is the person whose true signature is on the statement verified.

3. In witnessing or attesting a signature, the notarial officer must determine, either from personal knowledge or from satisfactory evidence, that the signature is that of the person appearing before the officer and named on the instrument.

4. In certifying or attesting a copy of a document or other item, the notarial officer must determine that the copy is a full, true, and accurate transcription or reproduction of that which was copied.

5. In making or noting a protest of a negotiable instrument, the notarial officer must determine the matters set forth in section 554.3509.

6. A notarial officer has satisfactory evidence that a person is the person whose true signature is on a document in any of the following circumstances:

a. The person is personally known to the notarial officer.

b. The person is identified upon the oath or affirmation of a credible witness personally known to the notarial officer.

c. The person is identified on the basis of identification documents.

§ 77A.10. Notarial acts in this state.

1. A notarial act may be performed within this state by the following persons:

a. A notary public appointed by the secretary of state pursuant to section 77A.3.

b. A judge, clerk, or deputy clerk of a court of this state.

c. A person authorized by the law of this state to administer oaths.

d. Any other person authorized to perform the specific act by the law of this state.

2. Notarial acts performed within this state under federal authority have the same effect as if performed by a notarial officer of this state.

3. The signature and title of a person performing a notarial act are prima facie evidence that the signature is genuine and that the person holds the designated title.

§ 77A.11. Fees—certification.

The secretary of state shall collect the following fees, for use in offsetting the cost of administering this chapter:

1. For furnishing a certified copy of any document, instrument, or paper relating to a notary public, one dollar per page and five dollars for the certificate.

2. For furnishing an uncertified copy of any document, instrument, or paper relating to a notary public, one dollar per page.

3. For certifying, under seal of the secretary of state, a statement as to the status of a notary commission which would not appear from a certified copy of documents on file in the secretary of state's office, five dollars.

ADMINISTRATION OF OATHS

§ 78.1. General authority.

The following officers are empowered to administer oaths and to take affirmations:

1. Justices of the supreme court and judges of the court of appeals and district courts, including district associate judges and judicial magistrates.

2. Official court reporters of district courts in taking depositions under appointment or by agreement of counsel.

3. Clerks and deputy clerks of the supreme and district courts.

4. Notaries public.

5. Certified shorthand reporters.

§ 78.2. Limited authority.

The following officers and persons are empow-

ered to administer oaths and to take affirmations in any matter pertaining to the business of their respective office, position, or appointment.

1. Governor, secretary of state, secretary of agriculture, auditor of state, treasurer of state, attorney general.

2. Members of all boards, commissions, or bodies created by law.

3. All county officers other than those named in section 78.1.

4. Mayors and clerks of cities, precinct election officials, township clerks, assessors, and surveyors.

5. All duly appointed referees or appraisers.

6. All investigators for supplemental assistance as provided for under chapter 249.

7. The director and employees of the department of revenue and finance, as authorized by the director, and as set forth in chapters 421 and 422.

ACKNOWLEDGMENTS

§ 534.603. Acknowledgments by employees.

No public officer qualified to take acknowledgments or proofs of execution of written instruments shall by reason of the public officer's membership in or being an officer of or employment by a savings and loan association interested in such instrument be disqualified from taking and certifying to the acknowledgment or proof of execution of any written instrument in which such association is interested, and any such acknowledgment or proof heretofore taken or certified is hereby legalized and declared valid.

§ 558.20. Acknowledgments within state.

The acknowledgment of any deed, conveyance, or other instrument in writing by which real estate in this state is conveyed or encumbered, if made within this state, must be before some court having a seal, or some judge or clerk thereof, or some county auditor, or judicial magistrate or district associate judge within the county, or notary public within the state. Each of the officers above named is authorized to take and certify acknowledgments of all written instruments, authorized or required by law to be acknowledged.

§ 558.21. Acknowledgments outside of state.

When made out of the state but within the United States, it shall be before a judge of a court of record, or officer holding the seal thereof, or a commissioner appointed by the governor of this state to take the acknowledgment of deeds, or some notary public, or justice of the peace.

§ 558.22. Certificate of authenticity.

When made out of the state but within the United States and before a judge, or justice of the peace, a certificate, under the official seal of the clerk or other proper certifying officer of a court of record of the county or district, or of the secretary of state of the state or territory within which such acknowledgment was taken, under the seal of his office, of the official character of said judge, or justice, and of the genuineness of his signature, shall accompany said certificate of acknowledgment.

§ 558.23. Authorized foreign officials.

The proof or acknowledgment of any deed or other written instrument required to be proved or acknowledged in order to entitle the same to be recorded or read in evidence, when made by any person without this state and within any other state, territory, or district of the United States, may also be made before any officer of such state, territory, or district authorized by the laws thereof to take the proof and acknowledgment of deeds; and when so taken and certified as provided in section 558.24, may be recorded in this state, and read in evidence in the same manner and with like effect as proofs and acknowledgments taken before any of the officers named in section 558.21.

§ 558.24. Certificate of authenticity.

To entitle any conveyance or written instrument, acknowledged or proved under section 558.23, to be read in evidence or recorded in this state, there shall be subjoined or attached to the certificate of proof or acknowledgment signed by such officer a certificate of the secretary of state of the state or territory in which such officer resides, under the seal of such state or territory, or a certificate of the clerk of a court of record of such state, territory, or district in the county in which said officer resides or in which he took such proof or acknowledgment, under the seal of such court. Such certificate shall comply substantially with section 558.25.

§ 558.25. Form of authentication.

The following form of authentication of the proof or acknowledgment of a deed or other written instrument, when taken without this state and within any other state, territory, or district of the United States, or any form substantially in compliance with the foregoing provisions of this chapter, shall be used:

(Begin with a caption specifying the state, terri-

tory, or district, and county or place where the authentication is made.)

"I, _____, clerk of the _____ court in and for said county, which court is a court of record, having a seal (or I, _____, secretary of state of such state or territory), do hereby certify that _____, by and before whom the foregoing acknowledgment or proof was taken, was at the time of taking the same $\overline{\text{Name of office held}}$ residing or authorized to act in said county, and was duly authorized by the laws of said state, territory, or district to take and certify acknowledgments or proofs of deeds of land in said state, territory, or district, and that said conveyance and the acknowledgment thereof are in due form of law; and, further, that I am well acquainted with the handwriting of said _____, and that I verily believe that the signature to said certificate of acknowledgment or proof is genuine. In testimony whereof, I have hereunto set my hand and affixed the seal of the said court or state this _____ day of _____, A.D. 19__."

§ 558.26. Acknowledgments by military or naval officers.

In addition to the acknowledgment of instruments in the manner and form and as otherwise authorized by law, any person serving in or with the armed forces of the United States may acknowledge the same wherever located before any commissioned officer in active service of the armed forces of the United States with the rank of second lieutenant or higher in the army or marine corps, or ensign or higher in the navy or United States coast guard. Neither the instrument nor the acknowledgment shall be rendered invalid by the failure to state therein the place of execution or acknowledgment. No authentication of the officer's certificate shall be required, but the officer taking the acknowledgment shall indorse thereon or attach thereto a certificate substantially in the following form:

On this the _____ day of _____, 19__, before me, _____, the undersigned commissioned officer, personally appeared _____, (known to me, or satisfactorily proven) to be serving in or with the armed forces of the United States and to be the person whose name is subscribed to the within instrument and acknowledged that _____ he _____ executed the same as _____ voluntary act and deed.

_____

Signature of officer.

_____

Rank of officer and command to which attached.

Such acknowledgments executed according to

the above provisions shall be deemed of the same force and effect as acknowledgments executed before officers authorized to accept acknowledgments.

Any acknowledgments heretofore made by any person serving in or with the armed forces of the United States in the manner as prescribed by this section, or substantially so, are hereby legalized and considered sufficient.

§ 558.27. Acknowledgments outside United States.

When the acknowledgment is made without the United States, it may be before any ambassador, minister, secretary of legation, consul, vice-consul, charge d'affaires, consular agent, or any other officer of the United States in a foreign country who is authorized to issue certificates under the seal of the United States.

§ 558.28. Authorized foreign officials.

Said instruments may also be acknowledged or proved without the United States before any officer of a foreign country who is authorized by the laws thereof to certify to the acknowledgments of written documents.

§ 558.29. Certificate of authenticity.

The certificate of acknowledgment by a foreign officer must be authenticated by one of the above-named officers of the United States, whose official written statement that full faith and credit is due to the certificate of such foreign officer shall be deemed sufficient evidence of the qualification of said officer to take acknowledgments and certify thereto, and of the genuineness of his signature, and seal if he have any.

§ 558.30. Certificate of acknowledgment.

The court or officer taking the acknowledgment must indorse upon the deed or instrument a certificate setting forth the following particulars:

1. The title of the court or person before whom the acknowledgment was made.

2. That the person making the acknowledgment was known to the officer taking the acknowledgment to be the identical person whose name is affixed to the deed as grantor, or that such identity was proved by at least one credible witness, naming him.

3. That such person acknowledged the execution of the instrument to be his voluntary act and deed.

§ 558.31. Proof of execution and delivery in lieu of acknowledgment.

Proof of the due and voluntary execution and delivery of a deed or other instrument may be made before any officer authorized to take acknowledgments, by one competent person other than the vendee or other person to whom the instrument is executed, in the following cases:

1. If the grantor dies before making the acknowledgment.

2. If his attendance cannot be procured.

3. If, having appeared, he refuses to acknowledge the execution of the instrument.

§ 558.32. Contents of certificate.

The certificate indorsed by the officer upon a deed or other instrument thus proved must state:

1. The title of the officer taking the proof.

2. That it was satisfactorily proved that the grantor was dead, or that for some other reason his attendance could not be procured in order to make the acknowledgment, or that, having appeared, he refused to acknowledge the same.

3. The name of the witness by whom proof was made, and that it was proved by him that the instrument was executed and delivered by the person whose name is thereunto subscribed as a party.

§ 558.33. Subpoena.

An officer having power to take the proof hereinbefore contemplated may issue the necessary subpoenas, and compel the attendance of witnesses residing within the county, in the manner provided for the taking of depositions.

§ 558.34. Use of seal.

The certificate of proof or acknowledgment may be given under seal or otherwise, according to the mode by which the officer making the same usually authenticates his formal acts.

§ 558.35. Married women.

The acknowledgment of a married woman, when required by law, may be taken in the same form as if she were sole, and without any examination separate and apart from her husband.

§ 558.38. Officers of corporation.

If the acknowledgment is made by the officers of a corporation, the certificate shall show that such persons as such officers, naming the office of each person, acknowledged the execution of the instrument as provided in section 558.39.

§ 558.39. Forms of acknowledgment— Foreign acknowledgments.

The following forms of acknowledgment shall be sufficient in the cases to which they are respectively applicable. In each case where one of these forms is used, the name of the state and county where the acknowledgment is taken shall precede the body of the certificate, and the signature and official title of the officer shall follow it as indicated in the first form and shall constitute a part of the certificate, and the seal of the officer shall be attached when necessary under the provision of this chapter. No certificate of acknowledgment shall be held to be defective on account of the failure to show the official title of the officer making the certificate if such title appears either in the body of such certificate or in connection therewith, or with the signature thereto.

1. In the case of natural persons acting in their own right:

State of _____ }

} ss.

County of _____ }

On this _____ day of _____, A.D. 19___, before me, _____ (Insert title of acknowledging officer) personally appeared _____ to me known to be the person _____ named in and who executed the foregoing instrument, and acknowledged that _____ executed the name as _____ voluntary act and deed.

_____
Notary Public in the state of Iowa.

2. In the case of natural persons acting by attorney:

On this _____ day of _____, A.D. 19___, before me _____ (Insert title of acknowledging officer) personally appeared _____, to me known to be the person who executed the foregoing instrument in behalf of _____, and acknowledged that that person executed the same as the voluntary act and deed of said _____.

3. In the case of corporations or joint-stock associations:

On this _____ day of _____, A.D. 19___, before me, a _____ (Insert title of acknowledging officer) in and for said county, personally appeared _____, to me personally known, who being by me duly (sworn or affirmed) did say that that person is _____ (Insert title of executing officer) of said (corporation or association), that (the seal affixed to said instrument is the seal of said or no seal has been procured by the said) (corporation or association) and that said instrument was signed and sealed on behalf of the said (corporation or association) by authority of its board of (directors or trustees) and the said _____ acknowledged the execution of said instrument to be the voluntary act and deed of said (corporation or association) by it voluntarily executed.

4. In the case of partnerships:

On this _____ day of _____, A.D. 19___, before me, the undersigned, a Notary Public in and for the State of Iowa, personally appeared _____, to me personally known, who being by me duly sworn, did say that the person is one of the partners of _____, a partnership, and that the instrument was signed on behalf of the partnership by authority of the partners and the partner acknowledged the execution of the instrument to be the voluntary act and deed of the partnership by it and by the partner voluntarily executed.

5. In the case of an individual fiduciary:

On this _____ day of _____, A.D. 19___, before me, the undersigned, a Notary Public in and for the State of Iowa, personally appeared _____, to me known to be the identical person named in and who executed the foregoing instrument, and acknowledged that the person, as the fiduciary, executed the instrument as the voluntary act and deed of the person and of the fiduciary.

6. In the case of a corporate fiduciary:

On this _____ day of _____, A.D. 19___, before me, the undersigned, a Notary Public in and for the State of Iowa, personally appeared _____ and _____, to me personally known, who, being by me duly sworn, did say that they are the _____ and _____, respectively, of the corporation executing the foregoing instrument; that (no seal has been procured by) (the seal affixed thereto is the seal of) the corporation; that the instrument was signed (and sealed) on behalf of the corporation by authority of its Board of Directors; that _____ and _____ acknowledged the execution of the instrument to be the voluntary act and deed of the corporation and of the fiduciary, by it, by them and as the fiduciary voluntarily executed.

7. In the case of a limited partnership with corporate general partner:

On this _____ day of _____, A.D. 19___, before me, the undersigned, a Notary Public in and for the State of Iowa, personally appeared _____, to me personally known, who being by me duly sworn did say that the person is the _____ of _____, the General Partner of _____, a _____ limited partnership, executing the foregoing instrument, that no seal has been procured by the corporation; that the instrument was signed on behalf of the corporation as General Partner of _____, a _____ limited partnership, by authority of the corporation's Board of Directors; and that _____ as that officer acknowledged execution of the instrument to be the voluntary act and deed of the corporation and limited partnership by it and by the officer voluntarily executed.

8. In the case of a limited partnership with an individual general partner:

On this _____ day of _____, A.D. 19___, before me, the undersigned, a Notary Public in and for the State of Iowa, personally appeared _____, to me personally known, who, being by me duly sworn, did say that the person is (a) (the) General Partner of _____, an Iowa limited partnership, executing the foregoing instrument, that the instrument was signed on behalf of the limited partnership by authority of the limited partnership; and the general partner acknowledged the execution of the instrument to be the voluntary act and deed of the limited partnership, by it and by the general partner voluntarily executed.

9. In the case of joint ventures:

On this _____ day of _____, A.D. 19___, before me, the undersigned, a Notary Public in and for the State of Iowa, personally appeared _____ and _____, to me personally known, who, being by me duly sworn, did say that they are the _____ and _____, respectively, of _____, an Iowa corporation, a joint venturer of _____, a joint venture, executing the foregoing instrument, that (no seal has been procured by) (the seal affixed thereto is the seal of) the corporation; that the instrument was signed (and sealed) on behalf of the corporation as a joint venturer of _____, a joint venture, by authority of its Board of Directors; and that _____ and _____, as such officers, acknowledged the execution of the instrument to be the voluntary act and deed of the corporation and joint venture, by the corporation and joint venture and by them voluntarily executed.

10. In the case of municipalities:

On this _____ day of _____, A.D. 19___, before me, a Notary Public in and for the State of Iowa, personally appeared _____ and _____, to me personally known, and, who, being by me duly sworn, did say that they are the Mayor and City Clerk, respectively, of the City of _____, Iowa; that the seal affixed to the foregoing instrument is the corporate seal of the corporation, and that the instrument was signed and sealed on behalf of the corporation, by authority of its City Council, as contained in Ordinance No. _____ passed (the Resolution adopted) by the City Council, under Roll Call No. _____ of the City Council on the _____ day of _____, 19___, and that _____ and _____ acknowledged the execution of the instrument to be their voluntary act and deed and the voluntary act and deed of the corporation, by it voluntarily executed.

11. In the case of counties:

On this _____ day of _____, A.D. 19___, before me, _____, a Notary Public in and for the State of Iowa, personally appeared _____ and _____, to me personally known, and who, being by me duly sworn, did say that they are the Chairperson of the Board of Supervisors and County Auditor, respectively, of the County of _____, Iowa; that the seal affixed to the foregoing instrument is the corporate seal of the corporation, and that the instrument was signed and sealed on behalf of the corporation, by authority of its Board of Supervisors, as contained in Ordinance No. _____ passed (the Resolution adopted) by the Board of Supervisors, under Roll Call No. _____ of the Board of Supervisors on the _____ day of _____, 19___, and and _____ acknowledged the execution of the instrument to be their voluntary act and deed and the voluntary act and deed of the corporation, by it voluntarily executed.

12. In the case of natural persons acting as custodian pursuant to chapter 565B or any other Uniform Transfers to Minors Act:

On this _____ day of _____, A.D. 19___, before me, the undersigned, a Notary Public in and for said State, personally appeared _____, to me known to be the person named in and who executed the foregoing instrument, and acknowledged that the custodian executed the instrument as custodian for _____ (name of minor) _____, under the _____ Uniform Transfers to Minors Act, as the voluntary act and deed of the person and of the custodian.

13. In the case of corporations or national banking associations acting as custodians pursuant to chapter 565B or any other Uniform Transfers to Minors Act:

On this _____ day of _____, A.D. 19___, before me, the undersigned, a Notary Public in and for said State, personally appeared _____ and _____, to me known, who by me duly sworn, did say that they are the _____ and _____, respectively, of the Corporation executing the foregoing instrument; that (no seal has been procured by) (the seal affixed thereto is the seal of) the corporation; that the instrument was signed (and sealed) on behalf of the Corporation by authority of its Board of Directors; that _____ and _____ acknowledged the execution of the instrument as custodian of _____ (name of minor) _____, under the _____ Uniform Transfers to Minors Act, to be the voluntary act and deed of the person and of the custodian.

(In all cases add signature and title of the officer taking the acknowledgment, and strike from between the parentheses the word or clause not used, as the case may be.)

Any instrument affecting real estate situated in this state which has been or may be acknowledged or proved in a foreign state or country and in conformity with the laws of that foreign state or country, shall be deemed as good and valid in law as though acknowledged or proved in conformity with the existing laws of this state.

DEPOSITIONS

§ 622.84. Subpoenas—enforcing obedience.

1. When, by the laws of this or any other state or country, testimony may be taken in the form of depositions to be used in any of the courts thereof, the person authorized to take such depositions may issue subpoenas for witnesses, which must be served by the same officers and returned in the same manner as is required in district court, and obedience to the subpoenas may be enforced in the same way and to the same extent, or the person may report the matter to the district court who may enforce obedience as though the action was pending in the district court.

2. If a witness is located in any other state or country and refuses to voluntarily submit to the deposition, the court of jurisdiction in this state may, upon the application of any party, petition the court of competent jurisdiction in the foreign jurisdiction where the witness is located to issue subpoenas or make other appropriate orders to compel the witness' attendance at the deposition.

§ 622.102. Refusal to appear or testify.

Any witness who refuses to obey such subpoena or after appearance refuses to testify shall be reported by the officer or commissioner to the district court of the county where the subpoena was issued.

§ 622A.1. Definition.

As used in this chapter, "legal proceeding" means any action before any court, or any legal action preparatory to appearing before any court, whether civil or criminal in nature; and any administrative proceeding before any state agency or governmental subdivision which is quasi-judicial in nature and which has direct legal implications to any person.

§ 622A.2. Who entitled to interpreter.

Every person who cannot speak or understand the English language and who is a party to any legal proceeding or a witness therein, shall be entitled to an interpreter to assist such person throughout the proceeding.

[Iowa R. Civ. P.]

RULE 148. Conduct of oral examination.

(a) **Examination and cross-examination; record of examination; oath; objections.** Examination and cross-examination of witnesses may proceed as permitted at the trial. The officer before whom the deposition is to be taken shall put the witness on oath and shall personally, or by someone acting under his direction and in his presence, record the testimony of the witness. The testimony shall be taken stenographically or recorded by any other means ordered in accordance with rule 140 "b" (4). If requested by one of the parties, the testimony shall be transcribed. All objections made at the time of the examination to the qualifications of the officer taking the deposition, or to the manner of taking it, or to the evidence presented, or to the conduct of any party, and any other objection to the proceedings, shall be noted by the officer upon the deposition. Evidence objected to shall be taken subject to the objections. In lieu of participating in the oral examination, parties may serve written questions in a sealed envelope on the party taking the deposition and he shall transmit them to the officer, who shall propound them to the witness and record the answers verbatim.

(b) **Motion to terminate or limit examination.** At any time during the taking of the deposition, on motion of a party or of the deponent and upon a showing that the examination is being conducted in bad faith or in such manner as unreasonably to annoy, embarrass, or oppress the deponent or party, the court in which the action is pending or the court in the district where the deposition is being taken may order the officer conducting the examination to cease forthwith from taking the deposition, or may limit the scope and manner of the taking of the deposition as provided in rule 123. If the order made terminates the examination, it shall be resumed thereafter only upon the order of the court in which the action is pending. Upon demand of the objecting party or deponent, the taking of the deposition shall be suspended for the time necessary to make a motion for an order. The provisions of rule 134 "a" (4) apply to the award of expenses incurred in relation to the motion.

RULE 149. Reading and signing.

(a) No oral deposition reported and transcribed by an official court reporter or certified shorthand reporter of Iowa need be submitted to, read or signed by the deponent.

(b) **Submission to witness—changes, signing.** In other cases, when the testimony is fully transcribed the deposition shall be submitted to the witness for examination and shall be read to or by him, unless such examination and reading are waived by the witness and by the parties. Any changes in form or substance which the witness desires to make shall be entered upon the deposition by the officer with a statement of the reasons given by the witness for making them. If rule 149 "a" is not applicable, the deposition shall then be signed by the witness, unless the parties by stipulation waive the signing or the witness is ill or dead or cannot be found or refuses to sign. If the deposition is not signed by the witness within 30 days of its submission to him, the officer shall sign it and state on the record the fact of the waiver or of the illness, death, or absence of the witness or the fact of the refusal to sign together with the reason, if any, given therefor; and the deposition may then be used as fully as though signed unless on a motion to suppress under rule 158 "f" the court holds that the reasons given for the refusal to sign require rejection of the deposition in whole or in part.

RULE 151. Answers to interrogatories.

The party taking a deposition on written interrogatories shall promptly transmit a copy of the notice and all interrogatories to the officer designated in the notice. The officer shall promptly take deponent's answers thereto and complete the deposition, all as provided in rules 148 and 149, except that answers need not be taken stenographically.

RULE 152. Certification and return—copies.

(a) The officer shall certify on the deposition that the witness was duly sworn by him and that the deposition is a true record of the testimony given by the witness. He shall then securely seal the deposition in an envelope endorsed with the title of the action and marked "Deposition of (here insert name of witness)" and shall promptly file it with the court in which the action is pending or send it by registered or certified mail to the clerk thereof for filing. Documents and things produced for inspection during the examination of the witness shall, upon the request of a party, be marked for identification and annexed to and returned with the deposition, and may be inspected and copied by any party, except that

(1) the person producing the materials may substitute copies to be marked for identification, if he affords to all parties fair opportunity to verify the copies by comparison with the originals, and

(2) if the person producing the materials requests their return, the officer shall mark them, give each party an opportunity to inspect and copy them, and return them to the person producing them, and the materials may then be used in the same manner as if annexed to and returned with the deposition. Any party may move for an order that the

original be annexed to and returned with the deposition to the court, pending final deposition of the case.

(b) The clerk shall immediately give notice of the filing of all depositions to all parties who have appeared in the action.

(c) Upon payment of reasonable charges therefor, the officer shall furnish a copy of the deposition to any party or to the deponent.

RULE 153. Before whom taken.

(a) No deposition shall be taken before any party, or any person financially interested in the action, or an attorney or employee of any party, or any person related by consanguinity or affinity within the fourth degree to any party, his attorney, or an employee of either of them.

(b) Depositions within the United States or a territory or insular possession thereof may be taken before any person authorized to administer oaths, by the laws of the United States or of the place where the examination is held.

(c) Depositions in a foreign land may be taken before a secretary of embassy or legation, or a consul, vice-consul, consul-general or consular agent of the United States, or under rule 154.

(d) When the witness is in the military or naval service of the United States, his deposition may be taken before any commissioned officer under whose command he is serving, or any commissioned officer in the judge advocate general's department.

RULE 154. Letters rogatory.

A commission or letters rogatory to take depositions in a foreign land shall be issued only when convenient or necessary, on application and notice, and on such terms and with such directions as are just and appropriate. They shall specify the officer to take the deposition, by name or descriptive title, and may be addressed: "To the Appropriate Judicial Authority of (country)."

RULE 155. Subpoena.

(a) On application of any party, or proof of service of a notice to take depositions under rule 147 or rule 150, the clerk of court where the action is pending shall issue subpoenas for persons named in and described in said notice or application. Subpoenas may also be issued as provided by statute:

(b) No resident of Iowa shall be thus subpoenaed to attend out of the county where he resides, or is employed, or transacts his business in person.

(c) A subpoena may also command the person to whom it is directed to produce the books, papers, documents or tangible things designated therein; but the court, upon motion promptly made by the person to whom the subpoena is directed, or by any other person stating an interest in the documents affected, and in any event at or before the time specified in the subpoena for compliance therewith, may

(1) Quash or modify the subpoena if it is unreasonable and oppressive or

(2) Condition denial of the motion upon the advancement by the person in whose behalf the subpoena is issued of the reasonable cost of producing the books, papers, documents or tangible things.

LEGAL HOLIDAYS

[Iowa Code Ann.]

§ 33.1. Legal public holidays.

The following are legal public holidays:
1. New Year's Day, January 1.
2. Dr. Martin Luther King, Jr.'s Birthday, the third Monday in January.
3. Lincoln's Birthday, February 12.
4. Washington's Birthday, the third Monday in February.
5. Memorial Day, the last Monday in May.
6. Independence Day, July 4.
7. Labor Day, the first Monday in September.
8. Veterans Day, November 11.
9. Thanksgiving Day, the Fourth Thursday in November.
10. Christmas Day, December 25.

§ 31.4. Mother's Day—Father's Day.

The governor of this state is authorized and requested to issue annually a proclamation calling upon our state officials to display the American flag on all state and school buildings, and the people of the state to display the flag at their homes, lodges, churches, and places of business, on the second Sunday in May, known as Mother's Day, and on the third Sunday in June, known as Father's Day, as a public expression of reverence for the homes of our state, and to urge the celebration of Mother's Day and Father's Day in the proclamations in such a way as will deepen home ties, and inspire better homes and closer union between the commonwealth, its homes, and their children.

§ 31.5. Independence Sunday.

The governor is hereby authorized and requested to issue annually a proclamation, calling upon the citizens of Iowa to assemble themselves in their respective communities for the purpose of holding suitable religious-patriotic services and the display of the American colors, in commemoration of the signing of the Declaration of Independence, on In-

dependence Sunday, which is hereby established as the Sunday preceding the Fourth of July of each year, or on the Fourth when that date falls on Sunday.

§ 31.6. Columbus Day.

The governor of this state is hereby authorized and requested to issue annually a proclamation, calling upon our state officials to display the American flag on all state and school buildings and the people of the state to display the flag at their homes, lodges, churches, and places of business on the twelfth day of October, known as Columbus Day, to commemorate the life and history of Christopher Columbus and to urge that services and exercises be had in churches, halls and other suitable places expressive of the public sentiment befitting the anniversary of the discovery of America.

§ 31.7. Veterans' Day.

The governor is hereby authorized and requested to issue annually a proclamation designating the eleventh day of November as Veterans' Day and calling upon the people of Iowa to observe it as a legal holiday in honor of those who have been members of the armed forces of the United States, and urging state officials to display the American flag on all state and school buildings and the people of the state to display the flag at their homes, lodges, churches and places of business; that business activities be held to the necessary minimum; and that appropriate services and exercises be had expressive of the public sentiments befitting the occasion.

§ 31.8 Youth Honor Day.

The governor of this state is hereby requested and authorized to issue annually a proclamation designating the thirty-first day of October of each year as "Youth Honor Day".

§ 31.9. Herbert Hoover Day.

The Sunday which falls on or nearest the tenth day of August of each year is hereby designated as Herbert Hoover Day, which shall be a recognition day in honor of the late President Herbert Hoover. The governor is hereby authorized and requested to issue annually a proclamation designating such Sunday as Herbert Hoover Day and calling on the people and officials of the state of Iowa to commemorate the life and principles of Herbert Hoover, to display the American flag, and to hold appropriate services and ceremonies.

§ **31.10.** Dr. Martin Luther King, Jr. Day.

The third Monday of January of each year is designated as Dr. Martin Luther King, Jr. Day, which shall be a recognition day in honor of the late civil rights leader and Nobel Peace Prize recipient, Dr. Martin Luther King, Jr.

The governor is authorized and requested to issue annually a proclamation designating such Monday as Dr. Martin Luther King, Jr. Day and calling on the people and officials of the state of Iowa to commemorate the life and principles of Dr. King, to display the American flag, and to hold appropriate private services and ceremonies.

§ **541.202.** Negotiating instrument on holiday.

Nothing in any law of this state shall in any manner whatsoever affect the validity of, or render void or voidable, the payment, certification, or acceptance of a check or other negotiable instrument or any other transaction by a bank or trust company in this state because done or performed on any legal holiday or during any time other than regular banking hours, if such payment, certification, acceptance or other transaction could have been validly done or performed on any other day; provided that nothing herein shall be construed to compel any bank or trust company in this state, which by law or custom is entitled to close for the whole or any part of any legal holiday, to keep open for the transaction of business or to perform any of the acts or transactions aforesaid on any legal holiday except at its own option.

§ **617.8.** Holidays.

No person shall be held to answer or appear in any court on any day now or hereafter made a legal holiday.

KANSAS

NOTARIES PUBLIC

[KAN. STAT. ANN.]

§ 53-101. Appointment; term; qualifications; not state officer.

The secretary of state shall appoint notaries pub-lic, who may perform notarial acts in any part of this state for a term of not more than four years, unless sooner removed. Any person who is a citizen of the United States, who is at least 18 years of age and who is a resident of this state, or who is a resident of a state bordering on this state and who regularly carries on a business or profession in this state or is regularly employed in this state, shall be eligible to be appointed as a notary public as provided in this act. Notaries public shall not be considered as state officers.

§ 53-102. Application; oath; bond; filings required.

Every person, before entering upon the duties of a notary public, shall file with the secretary of state an application for appointment as a notary public, which shall also include an oath of office and a good and sufficient bond to the state of Kansas in the sum of $7,500, with one or more sureties to be approved by the secretary of state. The bond shall be conditioned upon the faithful performance of all notarial acts in accordance with law. Every person, before receiving appointment as a notary public, shall also file with the secretary of state the official signature and an impression of the seal to be used by the notary public.

§ 53-103. Forms for applications, bonds and oath.

Forms for applications, bonds and oath of office shall be furnished by the secretary of state.

§ 53-104. Filing and indexing application, bond, oath and record of appointment; fee.

Such application, bond, oath and record of appointment shall be filed in the office of the secretary of state and properly indexed in that office. The secretary of state shall receive a fee of $10 for such services. The secretary of state shall remit all moneys received under this section to the state treasurer, and the state treasurer shall deposit the same in the state treasury to the credit of the state general fund.

§ 53-105. Seal; statement of date of expiration of appointment.

Every notary public shall provide a notarial seal containing such notary's name exactly as it appears on the application for appointment as a notary public, and the words "notary public" and "state of

Kansas" or words of like import indicating state-wide notarial authority, approved by the secretary of state. Such seal shall authenticate all official acts, attestations and instruments therewith. Every notary public shall add to such notary's official signature the date of expiration of appointment as a notary public. The seal of every notary public shall be either a seal press and the impression thereof inked or blackened or a rubber stamp to be used with permanent ink so that any such seal may be legibly reproduced by photographic process. No notary public shall use either such seal unless an impression thereof has been filed in the office of secretary of state.

§ 53-105a. Certificate of appointment.

Upon receipt of a completed application with sufficient corporate bond, an oath of appointment, the correct fee, the official signature and an impression of the seal to be used by such notary public, the secretary of state, if satisfied the applicant is qualified to be appointed as a notary public, shall prepare a certificate of appointment for the applicant and forward the appointment to the applicant's residence. Each certificate of appointment shall contain at least the applicant's name and the date upon which the appointment shall expire.

§ 53-106. Penalty for failure to attach date of expiration of appointment.

If any notary public shall willfully neglect or refuse to attach to the notary's official signature the date of expiration of appointment, as provided in K.S.A. 53-105, the notary shall be deemed guilty of a class C misdemeanor.

§ 53-107. Powers and duties.

Notaries public shall have authority to: (1) Take acknowledgments; (2) administer oaths and affirmations; (3) take a verification upon oath or affirmation; (4) witness or attest a signature; (5) certify or attest a copy; (6) note a protest of a negotiable instrument; and (7) perform any other act permitted by law.

§ 53-109. Prohibited notarial acts; financial or beneficial interest.

(a) A notary public who has a direct financial or beneficial interest in a transaction shall not perform any notarial act in connection with such transaction;

(b) For purposes of this act, a notary public has a direct financial or beneficial interest in a transaction if the notary public:

(1) With respect to a financial transaction, is

named, individually, as a principal to the transaction;

(2) With respect to real property, is named, individually, as a grantor, grantee, mortgagor, mortgagee, trustor, trustee, beneficiary, vendor, vendee, lessor or lessee, to the transaction.

(c) For purposes of this act, a notary public has no direct financial or beneficial interest in a transaction when the notary public acts in the capacity of an agent, employee, insurer, attorney, escrow agent or lender for a person having a direct financial or beneficial interest in the transaction.

§ 53-113. Limitation of actions against notary and sureties.

No suit shall be instituted against any such notary or his or her securities more than three years after the cause of action accrues.

§ 53-114. Notary's change of name or seal; notification; new seal required.

(a) If a notary public changes name by any legal action, such notary shall obtain a new notary seal which meets the requirements established by K.S.A. 53-105, and the seal shall contain the new name of the notary. Prior to performing any acts as a notary public after such change, the notary shall mail or deliver to the secretary of state notice of the change of name which shall include a specimen of the new seal and a specimen of the notary's new official signature.

(b) If a notary public obtains a new seal for any reason, the notary shall mail or deliver to the secretary of state notice of the change of seal which shall include an impression of the new seal.

(c) Such notification, as provided for in subsections (a) and (b), shall be made on forms provided by the secretary of state within thirty (30) days after such change has occurred.

§ 53-115. Cancellation of notary public's bond; notice requirements.

No surety on a notary public's bond shall cancel such bond without giving written notice thereof to the secretary of state. Fourteen (14) days after receipt of such notice by the secretary of state, said surety shall no longer be liable on such bond.

Whenever the secretary of state receives notice of a surety's intention to cancel a notary's bond, said secretary of state shall notify the affected notary public that unless such notary files another good and sufficient surety bond with the secretary of state on or before the cancellation date of such notary public's surety bond, then such notary will no longer be authorized to perform notarial acts within this state.

§ 53-116. Resignation.

If a notary public no longer desires to be a notary public in this state, the notary shall send immediately by mail or deliver to the secretary of state a letter of resignation informing the secretary of state of the notary's desire to resign as a notary public in the state of Kansas. The appointment of the notary shall thereupon cease to be in effect.

§ 53-117. Reappointment.

No person may be automatically reappointed as a notary public. Every notary public who is an applicant for reappointment as a notary public shall comply with the provisions of K.S.A. 53-102.

§ 53-118. Appointment, refusal or revocation; grounds.

(a) The secretary of state may refuse to appoint any person as a notary public or may revoke the appointment of any notary public upon any of the following grounds:

(1) Substantial or material misstatement or omission in the application submitted to the secretary of state;

(2) Conviction of a felony or of a lesser offense involving moral turpitude or of a nature incompatible with the duties of a notary public. A conviction after a plea of nolo contendere is deemed to be a conviction within the meaning of this subsection;

(3) Revocation, suspension or denial of a professional license, if such revocation, suspension or denial was for misconduct, dishonesty or any cause substantially relating to the duties or responsibilities of a notary public;

(4) Cessation of United States citizenship;

(5) Incapacitation to such a degree that the person is incapable of reading or writing the English language;

(6) Failure to exercise the powers and duties of a notary public in accordance with this act.

(b) Any person whose notary public appointment has been removed, may not apply for an appointment until the expiration of four years from the date of removal of such appointment.

OATH

§ 54-106. Form of oath to be taken by officer.

All officers elected or appointed under any law of the state of Kansas shall, before entering upon the duties of their respective offices, take and subscribe an oath or affirmation, as follows:

"I do solemnly swear [or affirm, as the case may be] that I will support the constitution of the United States and the constitution of the state of Kansas, and faithfully discharge the duties of _____. So help me God."

ACKNOWLEDGMENTS

§ 58-2211. Acknowledgment of instrument relating to real estate.

All conveyances, and other instruments affecting real estate must be acknowledged before a person authorized by the uniform law on notarial acts to perform notarial acts or, if acknowledged within this state, by a county clerk, register of deeds or mayor or clerk of an incorporated city.

§ 58-2228. Validity of instruments acknowledged in other states.

All deeds, mortgages, powers of attorney and other instruments of writing for the conveyance or encumbrance of any lands, tenements or hereditaments situate within this state, executed and acknowledged or proved in any other state, territory, or country, in conformity with the laws of such state, territory, or country, or in conformity with the laws of this state, shall be as valid as if executed within this state in conformity with the provisions of this act.

§ 58-2229. Instruments as evidence.

Every instrument in writing, conveying or affecting real estate, which shall be acknowledged or proved and certified as hereinbefore prescribed, may, together with the certificates of acknowledgment or proof, be read in evidence without further proof.

DEPOSITIONS

§ 54-101. Officers authorized to administer oaths.

Notaries public, judges of courts in their respective jurisdictions, mayors of cities and towns in their respective cities and towns, clerks of courts of record, county clerks, and registers of deeds, are hereby authorized to administer oaths pertaining to all matters wherein an oath is required.

§ 54-102. How administered.

All oaths shall be administered by laying the right hand upon the Holy Bible, or by the uplifted right hand.

§ 54-103. Persons having conscientious scruples may affirm.

Any person having conscientious scruples against taking an oath, may affirm with like effect.

§ 54-104. Form of commencement and conclusion of oaths.

All oaths shall commence and conclude as follows: "You do solemnly swear," etc.; "So help you God."

Affirmation shall commence and conclude as follows: "You do solemnly, sincerely and truly declare and affirm," etc.; "And this you do under the pains and penalties of perjury."

§ 54-105. Falsifying oaths or affirmations.

All oaths and affirmations alike subject the party who shall falsify them to the pains and penalties of perjury.

§ 60-228. Persons before whom depositions may be taken.

(a) Within the United States. (1) Depositions may be taken in this state before any officer or person authorized to administer oaths by the laws of this state. (2) Without the state but within the United States, or within a territory or insular possession subject to the dominion of the United States, depositions shall be taken before an officer authorized to administer oaths by the laws of the place where the examination is held, or before a person appointed by the court in which the action is pending. A person so appointed has power to administer oaths and take testimony. (3) Any court of record of this state, or any judge thereof, before whom an action or proceeding is pending, is authorized to grant a commission to take depositions within or without the state. The commission may be issued by the clerk to a person or persons therein named, under the seal of the court granting the same.

(b) In foreign countries. In a foreign country, depositions may be taken (1) on notice before a person authorized to administer oaths in the place where the examination is held, either by the law of the United States or the law of that place, or (2) before a person appointed by commission, or (3) under letters rogatory. A person appointed by commission has power by virtue of his appointment to administer oaths and take testimony. A commission or letters rogatory shall be issued on application and notice, and on terms and directions that are just and appropriate. It is not requisite to the issuance of letters rogatory that the taking of the deposition by commission or on notice is impracticable

or inconvenient; and both a commission and letters rogatory may be issued in proper cases. A notice or commission may designate the person before whom the deposition is to be taken either by name or descriptive title. Letters rogatory may be addressed "To the Appropriate Judicial Authority in (here name the country)." Evidence obtained under letters rogatory shall not be excluded on the ground that it is not in the form of questions and answers or is not a verbatim transcript of the testimony.

(c) Disqualification for interest. No deposition shall be taken before a person who is a relative or employee or attorney or counsel of any of the parties, or is a relative or employee of such attorney or counsel, or is financially interested in the action.

(d) Depositions for use in foreign jurisdictions. Whenever the deposition of any person is to be taken in this state pursuant to the laws of another state or of the United States or of another country for use in proceedings there, the district court in the county where the deponent resides or is employed or transacts his business in person may, upon ex parte petition, make an order directing issuance of a subpoena as provided in section 60-245, in aid of the taking of the deposition, and may make any order in accordance with sections 60-230 (d), 60-237(a) or 60-237(b)(1).

LEGAL HOLIDAYS

§ 35-107. Legal public holidays designated.

(a) On and after January 1, 1976, the following days are declared to be legal public holidays and are to be observed as such:

New Year's Day, January 1;

Lincoln's Birthday, the twelfth day in February;

Washington's Birthday, the third Monday in February;

Memorial Day, the last Monday in May;

Independence Day, July 4;

Labor Day, the first Monday in September;

Columbus Day, the second Monday in October;

Veterans' Day, the eleventh day of November;

Thanksgiving Day, the fourth Thursday in November;

Christmas Day, December 25.

(b) Any reference in the laws of this state concerning observance of legal holidays shall on and after January 1, 1976, be considered as a reference to the day or days prescribed in subsection (a) hereof for the observance of such legal holiday or holidays.

§ 35-108. Commercial paper, agreements, written instruments and judicial proceedings not affected.

The provisions of this act shall not be construed to affect commercial paper, the making or execution of agreements or instruments in writing or interfere with judicial proceedings.

§ 52-717. Bank transactions on Saturday afternoon or holiday.

No provision of any law of this state shall be so construed as to prevent banks from paying checks, drafts, or other bills of exchange upon Saturday afternoon, or upon any legal holiday. Provided, Such payments would be legal if made at other times.

KENTUCKY

NOTARIES PUBLIC

[KY. REV. STAT. ANN.]

§ 423.010. Appointment, term, and qualifications of notaries; county clerk has powers of notary when acting in capacity as clerk.

(1) The Secretary of State may appoint as many notaries public as he deems necessary, who shall hold office for four (4) years. Any person desiring to be appointed a notary public shall make written application to the Secretary of State. The application shall be approved by the Circuit Judge, circuit clerk, county judge/executive, county clerk, justice of the peace, or a member of the General Assembly of the county of the residence of the applicant. No officer shall charge or accept any fee for approving the application. A notary public shall be eighteen (18) years of age, a resident of the county from which he makes his application, of good moral character, and capable of discharging the duties imposed upon him by this chapter, and the endorsement of the officer approving the application shall so state. The Secretary of State, in his certificate of appointment to the applicant, shall designate the limits within which the notary is to act. Before a notary acts, he shall take an oath before any person authorized to administer an oath as set forth in KRS 62.020 that he will honestly and diligently discharge the duties of his office. He shall in the same court give an obligation with good security for the proper discharge of the duties of his office. Every certificate of a notary public shall state the date of the expiration of his commission. The Secretary of State shall give to each notary appointed a certificate of his appointment under the seal of the Commonwealth of Kentucky in lieu of a commission heretofore required to be issued to the notary by the Governor of Kentucky, and receive a fee of ten dollars ($10) for the certificate.

(2) A county clerk shall have the powers of a notary public in the exercise of the official functions of the office of clerk within his county, and the

official actions of the county clerk shall not require the witness or signature of a notary appointed pursuant to subsection (1) of this section.

§ 423.020. Notary may act in any county; validity of instruments notarized; certification of notary's authority.

(1) A notary public may exercise all the functions of his office in any county of the state, by filing in the county clerk's office in such county his written signature and a certificate of the county clerk of the county for which he was appointed, setting forth the fact of his appointment and qualification as a notary public, and paying a fee of one dollar to the county clerk.

(2) When this has been done the instrument or instruments so proved or acknowledged and certified by the notary, whether prior or subsequent to this date, shall be entitled to be read as evidence or to be recorded in any county the same as if it were certified by a county clerk.

(3) The county clerk of a county in whose office any notary public has so filed his signature and certificate shall, when requested, subjoin to any certificate of proof or acknowledgment signed by the notary a certificate under his hand and seal, stating that such notary public has filed a certificate of his appointment and qualifications with his written signature in his office, and was at the time of taking such proof or acknowledgment duly authorized to take the same; that he is well acquainted with the handwriting of the notary public and believes that the signature to such proof or acknowledgment is genuine.

§ 423.030. Protests to be recorded; copies as evidence.

The notaries public shall record in a well bound and properly indexed book, kept by them for that purpose, all protests made by them for the nonacceptance or nonpayment of all bills of exchange, checks or promissory notes placed on the footing of bills of exchange, and on which a protest is required by law, or of which protest is evidence of dishonor. A copy of such protest certified by the notary public under his notarial seal is prima facie evidence in all the courts of this state.

§ 423.040. Notice of dishonor; to whom sent.

Notaries public shall upon protesting any instrument mentioned in KRS 423.030 give notice of the dishonor to such parties thereto as are required by law to be notified to fix their liability on such paper. When the residence of a party is unknown to the notary public, he shall send the notices to the

holders of the paper, shall state in his protest the names of the parties to whom he gave notice, and the time and manner of giving the same and such statement in such protest shall be prima facie evidence that notices were given as therein stated.

§ 423.050. Records of notary to be delivered to county clerk, when.

Upon the resignation of a notary public or the expiration of his term of office if he is not reappointed, he shall place his record book in the office of the county clerk in the county in which he was appointed, and if a notary dies, his representative shall deposit the record book with the clerk aforesaid. A copy of such record certified by the clerk in whose office it is filed shall be evidence in all the courts of this state.

§ 423.060. Foreign notary; when protest by is evidence.

If any commercial paper is protested in any other state of the United States in which it is made payable, and by the laws of that state a notary public or other officer authorized to protest the same is required to give notice of dishonor to the parties, or if the certificate of such notary or officer, or a copy thereof, stating that such notice was sent, is evidence in the courts of that state, then such protest, certificate or copy is admissible as evidence and shall have the same effect in the courts of this state as is given to such evidence in the courts of the other state.

§ 423.070. Commissioners of foreign deeds; appointment, term.

The governor may appoint and commission one or more commissioners of deeds in each state of the United States for a term of two years. Before entering on the duties of his office, each commissioner shall make and subscribe an affidavit, before an officer authorized to administer an oath, to well and truly execute and perform all the duties of his office. The affidavit must be filed in the office of the secretary of state of this state.

§ 423.080. Powers of commissioners.

Any commissioner of deeds appointed and qualified pursuant to KRS 423.070 may take the acknowledgment of proof of any instrument of writing, except wills, which instrument is required by the laws of this state to be recorded. The examination, acknowledgment or proof of any such instrument taken by a commissioner, and certified under his official seal, in the manner required by the laws of this state, shall authorize the instrument to be recorded in the proper office. A commissioner of deeds may administer any oath or take any affirmation necessary to discharge his official duties, and may take and certify depositions to be read on the trial of any action or proceeding in any of the courts of this state.

§ 423.990. Penalties.

For each failure to record his protest as required by KRS 423.030, a notary public shall forfeit all his fees and shall be fined five dollars.

ADDITIONAL AUTHORITY

[KY. CONST.]

§ 165. Incompatible offices.

No person shall, at the same time, be a state officer or a deputy officer or a member of the general assembly, and an officer of any county, city, town, or other municipality, or an employer thereof; and no person shall, at the same time, fill two municipal offices, either in the same or different municipalities, except as may be otherwise provided in this Constitution; but a notary public, or an officer of the militia, shall not be ineligible to hold any other office mentioned in this section.

[KY. REV. STAT. ANN.]

§ 62.050. Bonds, when to be given.

(1) No officer required by law to give bond shall enter upon the duties of his office until he gives the bond.

(2) Each person elected to an office who is required to give bond shall give the bond on or before the day the term of office to which he has been elected begins.

(3) Each person appointed to an office who is required to give bond shall give the bond within thirty (30) days after he receives notice of his appointment.

§ 289.241. Savings and loan association interest does not disqualify officer taking acknowledgment.

No public officer qualified to take acknowledgments or proofs of written instruments shall be disqualified from taking the acknowledgment or proof of any instrument in writing in which an [savings and loan] association is interested by reason of his membership in or employment by an association so interested, and any such acknowledgment or proofs heretofore taken are valid.

OATH

§ 62.020. Official oath, who may administer.

The official oath of any officer may be administered by any judge, county judge/executive, notary public, clerk of a court, or justice of the peace, within his district or county.

FEES

§ 14.090. Fees.

(1) The secretary of state shall charge and collect for the state the following fees:

For issuing commission with seal of Commonwealth attached and all necessary forms to a commissioner of foreign deeds $5.00
* * *

(2) No fee shall be collected for affixing the state seal to a commission issued to any public officer other than commissioner of foreign deeds or notary public, or to a grant, or to a pardon of a felony.

§ 64.300. Notaries public.

(1) The fees of notaries public for the following services shall be not more than set out in the following schedule:

Every attestation, protestation, or taking acknowledgment of any instrument of writing, and certifying the same under seal including, but not limited to, the notarization of votes of absentee voters $0.50

Recording same in book to be kept for that purpose .... .75

Each notice of protest .... .25

Administering oath and certificate thereof .... .20

(2) No fee or compensation shall be allowed or paid for affixing the jurat of a notary public to any application, affidavit, certificate or other paper necessary to be filed in support of any claim for the benefits of federal legislation for any person or his dependents who has served as a member of the army, navy, or marine corps of the United States.

OFFENSES

§ 62.990. Penalties.

(1) Any person who violates * * * or subsection (1) of KRS 62.050 [pertaining to when bonds are to be given] shall be fined not less than fifty nor more than one hundred dollars and removed from office by the judgment of conviction.

(2) If any person violates * * * or subsection (2) or (3) of KRS 62.050 [pertaining to when bonds are to be given], his office shall be considered vacant and he shall not be eligible for the same office for two years.

§ 514.040. Theft by deception.

(1) A person is guilty of theft by deception when he obtains property or services of another by deception with intent to deprive him thereof. A person deceives when he intentionally:

(a) Creates or reinforces a false impression, including false impressions as to law, value, intention or other state of mind;

(b) Prevents another from acquiring information which would affect his judgment of a transaction;

(c) Fails to correct a false impression which the deceiver previously created or reinforced or which the deceiver knows to be influencing another to whom he stands in a fiduciary or confidential relationship;

(d) Fails to disclose a known lien, adverse claim or other legal impediment to the enjoyment of property which he transfers or encumbers in consideration for the property obtained, whether such impediment is or is not valid or is or is not a matter of official record; or

(e) Issues or passes a check or similar sight order for the payment of money, knowing that it will be honored by the drawee.

(2) The term "deceive" does not, however, include falsity as to matters having no pecuniary significance or puffing by statements unlikely to deceive ordinary persons in the group addressed.

(3) Deception as to a person's intention to perform a promise shall not be inferred from the fact alone that he did not subsequently perform the promise.

(4) For purposes of subsection (1) of this section, an issuer of a check or similar sight order for the payment of money is presumed to know that the check or order, other than a postdated check or order, would not be paid, if:

(a) The issuer had no account with the drawee at the time the check or order was issued;

(b) Payment was refused by the drawee for lack of funds, upon presentation within thirty (30) days after issue, and the issuer failed to make good within ten (10) days after receiving notice of that refusal. An issuer makes good on a check or similar sight order for the payment of money by paying to the holder the face amount of the instrument, together with any fee to be imposed pursuant to subsection (4)(c) of this section; or

(c) If a county attorney issues notice to an issuer that a drawee has refused to honor an instrument due to a lack of funds as described in subsection (4)(b) of this section, the county attorney may charge a fee to the holder of five dollars ($5.00), if said instrument is paid.

(5) A person is guilty of theft by deception when he issues a check or similar sight order in payment of all or any part of any tax payable to the Commonwealth knowing that it will not be honored by the drawee.

(6) Theft by deception is a Class A misdemeanor unless the value of the property, service or the amount of the check or sight order referred to in subsection (5) of this section is one hundred dollars ($100) or more, in which case it is a Class D felony.

§ 516.030. Forgery in the second degree.

(1) A person is guilty of forgery in the second degree when, with intent to defraud, deceive or injure another, he falsely makes, completes or alters a written instrument which is or purports to be or which is calculated to become or to represent when completed:

(a) A deed, will, codicil, contract, assignment, commercial instrument, credit card or other instrument which does or may evidence, create, transfer, terminate or otherwise affect a legal right, interest, obligation or status; or

(b) A public record or an instrument filed or required or authorized by law to be filed in or with a public office or public employe; or

(c) A written instrument officially issued or created by a public office, public employe or governmental agency.

(2) Forgery in the second degree is a Class D felony.

§ 519.060. Tampering with public records.

(1) A person is guilty of tampering with public records when:

(a) He knowingly makes a false entry in or falsely alters any public record; or

(b) Knowing he lacks the authority to do so, he intentionally destroys, mutilates, conceals, removes or otherwise impairs the availability of any public records; or

(c) Knowing he lacks the authority to retain it, he refuses to deliver up a public record in his possession upon proper request of a public servant lawfully entitled to receive such record for examination or other purposes.

(2) Tampering with public records is a Class A misdemeanor.

§ 523.100. Unsworn falsification to authorities.

(1) A person is guilty of unsworn falsification to

authorities when, with an intent to mislead a public servant in the performance of his duty, he:

(a) Makes a material false written statement, which he does not believe, in an application for any pecuniary or other benefit or in a record required by law to be submitted to any governmental agency; or

(b) Submits or invites reliance on any writing which he knows to be a forged instrument, as defined in subsection (7) of KRS 516.010; or

(c) Submits or invites reliance on any sample, specimen, map, boundary mark or other object he knows to be false.

(2) Unsworn falsification to authorities is a Class B misdemeanor.

ACKNOWLEDGMENTS

§ 382.130. When deeds executed in this state to be admitted to record.

Deeds executed in this state may be admitted to record:

(1) On the acknowledgment, before the proper clerk, by the party making the deed;

(2) By the proof of two subscribing witnesses, or by the proof of one subscribing witness, who also proves the attestation of the other;

(3) By the proof of two witnesses that the subscribing witnesses are both dead; and also like proof of the signature of one of them and of the grantor;

(4) By like proof that both of the subscribing witnesses are out of the state, or that one is so absent and the other is dead; and also like proof of the signature of one of the witnesses and of the grantor; or

(5) On the certificate of a county clerk of this state, or any notary public, that the deed has been acknowledged before him by the party making the deed or proved before him in the manner required by subsection (2), (3) or (4).

§ 382.140. Recording of deeds executed out of state.

Deeds executed out of this state and within the United States or any of its dependencies may be admitted to record when certified, under the seal of his office or court, by a judge, clerk or deputy clerk of a court, or by a notary public, mayor of a city, secretary of state, commissioner authorized to take acknowledgment of deeds or justice of the peace, to have been acknowledged or proved before him in the manner required by KRS 382.130.

§ 382.150. Recording of deeds executed in foreign country.

Deeds not executed within the United States or any of its dependencies, may be admitted to record when certified, under his seal of office, by any foreign minister, officer in the consular service of the United States, secretary of legation of the United States, or by the secretary of foreign affairs or a notary public of the nation in which the acknowledgment is made, or by the judge or clerk of a superior court of the nation where the deed is executed, to have been acknowledged or proven before him in the manner prescribed by law.

§ 382.160. Certificate of acknowledgment or proof of deed.

(1) Where the acknowledgment of a deed is taken by an officer of this state or by an officer residing out of this state, he may simply certify that it was acknowledged before him, and when it was done.

(2) where a deed is proved by persons other than the subscribing witnesses, the officer shall state the name and residence of each person in his certificate.

Uniform Recognition of Acknowledgments Act

§ 423.110. Recognition of notarial acts performed outside this state.

For the purpose of KRS 423.110 to 423.190, "notarial acts" means acts which the laws and regulations of this state authorize notaries public of this state to perform, including the administering of oaths and affirmations, taking proof of execution and acknowledgments of instruments, and attesting documents. Notarial acts may be performed outside this state for use in this state with the same effect as if performed by a notary public of this state by the following persons authorized pursuant to the laws and regulations of other governments in addition to any other person authorized by the laws and regulations of this state:

(1) A notary public authorized to perform notarial acts in the place in which the act is performed;

(2) A judge, clerk, or deputy clerk of any court of record in the place in which the notarial act is performed;

(3) An officer of the foreign service of the United States, a consular agent, or any other person authorized by regulation of the United States department of state to perform notarial acts in the place in which the act is performed;

(4) A commissioned officer in active service with the armed forces of the United States and any other

person authorized by regulation of the armed forces to perform notarial acts if the notarial act is performed for one of the following or his dependents: a merchant seaman of the United States, a member of the armed forces of the United States, or any other person serving with or accompanying the armed forces of the United States;

(5) Any other person authorized to perform notarial acts in the place in which the act is performed; or

(6) A person, either a resident or a nonresident of Kentucky, who is appointed by the governor of Kentucky to perform notarial acts in or outside this state covering writings prepared for recordation in this state.

§ 423.120. Authentication of authority of officer.

(1) If the notarial act is performed by any of the persons described in subsection (1) to (4), inclusive, of KRS 423.110, other than a person authorized to perform notarial acts by the laws or regulations of a foreign country, the signature, rank, or title and serial number, if any, of the person are sufficient proof of the authority of a holder of that rank or title to perform the act. Further proof of his authority is not required.

(2) If the notarial act is performed by a person authorized by the laws or regulations of a foreign country to perform the act, there is sufficient proof of the authority of that person to act if:

(a) Either a foreign service officer of the United States resident in the country in which the act is performed or a diplomatic or consular officer of the foreign country resident in the United States certifies that a person holding that office is authorized to perform the act;

(b) The official seal of the person performing the notarial act is affixed to the document; or

(c) The title and indication of authority to perform notarial acts of the person appears either in a digest of foreign law or in a list customarily used as a source of such information.

(3) If the notarial act is performed by a person other than one described in subsections (1) and (2) of this section, there is sufficient proof of the authority of that person to act if the clerk of a court of record in the place in which the notarial act is performed certifies to the official character of that person and to his authority to perform the notarial act.

(4) The signature and title of the person performing the act are prima facie evidence that he is a person with the designated title and that the signature is genuine.

§ 423.130. Certificate of person taking acknowledgment.

The person taking an acknowledgment shall certify that:

(1) The person acknowledging appeared before him and acknowledged he executed the instrument; and

(2) The person acknowledging was known to the person taking the acknowledgment or that the person taking the acknowledgment had satisfactory evidence that the person acknowledging was the person described in and who executed the instrument.

§ 423.140. Recognition of certificate of acknowledgment.

The form of a certificate of acknowledgment used by a person whose authority is recognized under KRS 423.110 shall be accepted in this state if:

(1) The certificate is in a form prescribed by the laws or regulations of this state;

(2) The certificate is in a form prescribed by the laws or regulations applicable in the place in which the acknowledgment is taken; or

(3) The certificate contains the words "acknowledged before me," or their substantial equivalent.

§ 423.150. Certificate of acknowledgment.

The words "acknowledged before me" mean:

(1) That the person acknowledging appeared before the person taking the acknowledgment;

(2) That he acknowledged he executed the instrument;

(3) That, in the case of:

(a) A natural person, he executed the instrument for the purposes therein stated;

(b) A corporation, the officer or agent acknowledged he held the position or title set forth in the instrument and certificate, he signed the instrument on behalf of the corporation by proper authority, and the instrument was the act of the corporation for the purpose therein stated;

(c) A partnership, the partner or agent acknowledged he signed the instrument on behalf of the partnership by proper authority and he executed the instrument as the act of the partnership for the purpose therein stated;

(d) A person acknowledging as principal by an attorney in fact, he executed the instrument by proper authority as the act of the principal for the purposes therein stated;

(e) A person acknowledging as a public officer, trustee, administrator, guardian, or other representative, he signed the instrument by proper authority and he executed the instrument in the capacity and for the purposes therein stated; and

(4) That the person taking the acknowledgment either knew or had satisfactory evidence that the person acknowledging was the person named in the instrument or certificate.

§ **423.160.** Short forms of acknowledgment.

The forms of acknowledgment set forth in this section may be used and are sufficient for their respective purposes under any law of this state. The forms shall be known as "Statutory Short Forms of Acknowledgment" and may be referred to by that name. The authorization of the forms in this section does not preclude the use of other forms.

(1) For an individual acting in his own right:
State of ....
County of ....
The foregoing instrument was acknowledged before me this (date) by (name of person acknowledged).
 (Signature of person taking acknowledgment)
 (Title or rank)
 (Serial number, if any)

(2) For a corporation:
State of ....
County of ....
The foregoing instrument was acknowledged before me this (date) by (name of officer or agent, title of officer or agent) of (name of corporation acknowledging) a (state or place of incorporation) corporation, on behalf of the corporation.
 (Signature of person taking acknowledgment)
 (Title or rank)
 (Serial number, if any)

(3) For a partnership:
State of ....
County of ....
The foregoing instrument was acknowledged before me this (date) by (name of acknowledging partner or agent), partner (or agent) on behalf of (name of partnership), a partnership.
 (Signature of person taking acknowledgment)
 (Title or rank)
 (Serial number, if any)

(4) For an individual acting as principal by an attorney in fact:
State of ....
County of ....
The foregoing instrument was acknowledged before me this (date) by (name of attorney in fact) as attorney in fact on behalf of (name of principal).
 (Signature of person taking acknowledgment)
 (Title or rank)
 (Serial number, if any)

(5) By any public officer, trustee, or personal representative:
State of ....
County of ....
The foregoing instrument was acknowledged before me this (date) by (name and title of position).
 (Signature of person taking acknowledgment)
 (Title or rank)
 (Serial number, if any)

§ **423.170.** Acknowledgments not affected by KRS 423.110 to 423.190.

A notarial act performed prior to July 1, 1970, is not affected by KRS 423.110 to 423.190. KRS 423.110 to 423.190 provide an additional method of proving notarial acts. Nothing in KRS 423.110 to 423.190 diminishes or invalidates the recognition accorded to notarial acts by other laws or regulations of this state.

§ **423.180** Uniformity of interpretation.

KRS 423.110 to 423.190 shall be so interpreted as to make uniform the laws of those states which enact it.

§ **423.190** Short title.

KRS 423.110 to 423.190 may be cited as the "Uniform Recognition of Acknowledgments Act."

§ **423.200.** Admission of documents to the public record.

Notwithstanding any other provision of law, any certificate of an acknowledgment given and certified as provided by KRS 423.110 to 423.190 or as provided by those sections and other provisions of law, together with the instrument acknowledged, may be admitted to the public record provided for the type of instrument so acknowledged, and any instrument required to be sworn to or affirmed in order to be recorded may be admitted to record upon a jurat recognized under the provisions of KRS 423.110 to 423.190.

DEPOSITIONS

[KY. R. CIV. P.]

RULE 28. Persons before whom depositions may be taken.

28.01. Within the state.

Depositions taken in this state, to be used in its courts, shall be taken before an examiner; a judge, clerk, commissioner or official reporter of a court;

a notary public; or before such other persons and under such other circumstances as shall be authorized by law.

28.02. Without the state.

Depositions may be taken out of this state before a commissioner appointed by the governor of the state where taken; or before any person empowered by a commission directed to him by consent of the parties or by order of the court; or before a judge of a court, a justice of the peace, mayor of a city, or notary public; or before such persons and under such other circumstances as shall be authorized by the law of this state or the place where the deposition was taken.

28.03. Depositions to be used in other states.

A party desiring to take depositions in this state to be used in proceedings outside this state, may produce to a judge of the district court of the district in which the witness resides a commission authorizing the taking of such depositions or proof of notice duly served; whereupon it shall be the duty of the judge to issue, pursuant to Rule 45, the necessary subpoenas. Orders of the character provided in Rule 45.02 may be made upon proper application therefor by the person to whom such a subpoena is directed. Failure by any person without adequate excuse to obey a subpoena served upon him pursuant to this rule may be deemed a contempt of the court from which the subpoena issued.

LEGAL HOLIDAYS

[KY. REV. STAT. ANN.]

§ 2.110. Holidays.

(1) The 1st day of January (New Year's Day), the third Monday of January (Birthday of Martin Luther King, Jr.), the 19th day of January (Robert E. Lee Day), the 30th day of January (Franklin D. Roosevelt Day), the 12th day of February (Lincoln's Birthday), the third Monday in February (Washington's Birthday), the last Monday in May (Memorial Day), the 3rd day of June (Confederate Memorial Day, and Jefferson Davis Day), the 4th day of July (Independence Day), the first Monday in September (Labor Day), the second Monday in October (Columbus Day), the 11th day of November (Veterans Day), the 25th day of December (Christmas Day) of each year, and all days appointed by the President of the United States or by the governor as days of thanksgiving are holidays, on which all the public offices of this Commonwealth may be closed; and, subject to the provi-

sions of subsection (2) of this section, shall be considered as Sunday for all purposes regarding the presenting for payment or acceptance, and of protesting for and giving notice of the dishonor of bills of exchange, bank checks and promissory notes, placed by law upon the footing of bills of exchange. If any of the days named as holidays occur on Sunday, the next day thereafter shall be observed as a holiday but bills of exchange or other papers may be presented for payment or acceptance on the Saturday preceding the holiday and proceeded on accordingly.

(2) Any bank, trust company, or combined bank and trust company, may, at its option, either close or remain open for business on the third Monday of January (Birthday of Martin Luther King, Jr), the 19th day of January (Robert E. Lee Day), the 30th day of January (Franklin D. Roosevelt Day), the 12th day of February (Lincoln's Birthday), the third Monday in February (Washington's Birthday), the 3rd day of June (Confederate Memorial Day, and Jefferson Davis Day), the second Monday in October (Columbus Day), and the 11th day of November (Veterans Day), provided that any bank, trust company or combined bank and trust company electing to close on any of the above holidays may provide fifteen (15) days' notice to the public of such closing by posting a statement to such effect in some conspicuous place in said institution. Any bank, trust company, or combined bank and trust company electing to remain open on such of the above mentioned holidays may do so and as to such bank, trust company, or combined bank and trust company such day or days shall not constitute a holiday within the meaning of the provisions of the Uniform Commercial Code or any other law of the Commonwealth and such bank, trust company, or combined bank and trust company shall incur no liability by reason of remaining open on such holiday. If any such bank, trust company, or combined bank and trust company elects to close on such holidays, any act authorized, required or permitted to be performed at or by such bank, trust company, or combined bank and trust company, may be performed on the next succeeding business day and no liability or loss of rights of any kind shall result from remaining closed notwithstanding the provisions of any law of this Commonwealth to the contrary. The provisions of this section shall not operate to invalidate or prohibit the doing on any of the aforementioned holidays of any act by any person or bank or trust company, or combined bank and trust company, and nothing in this section shall, in any manner whatsoever affect the validity of or render void or voidable the payment, certification or acceptance of a check or any other negotiable instrument or any other transaction by any person or bank or trust company or combined bank and trust company be-

cause done or performed during any of the aforesaid holidays, notwithstanding the provisions of any other law of this Commonwealth to the contrary.

(3) No person shall be compelled to labor on the first Monday in September (Labor Day) by any person.

LOUISIANA

NOTARIES PUBLIC AND COMMISSIONERS

General Provisions

[La. Rev. Stat. Ann.]

35:1. Appointment of notaries public.

The governor may appoint, by and with the advice and consent of the Senate, and upon a certificate of competency by the appropriate district court as provided in R.S. 35:191(C)(2)(d), notaries public in the different parishes.

35:2. General powers; administration of certain oaths in any parish.

A. (1) Notaries public have power within their several parishes:

(a) To make inventories, appraisements, and partitions;

(b) To receive wills, make protests, matrimonial contracts, conveyances, and generally, all contracts and instruments of writing;

(c) To hold family meetings and meetings of creditors;

(d) To receive acknowledgments of instruments under private signature;

(e) To make affidavits of corrections;

(f) To affix the seals upon the effects of deceased persons and to raise the same.

(2) All acts executed by a notary public, in conformity with the provisions of Civil Code Art. 2234, shall be authentic acts.

(3) Notwithstanding any provision in the law to the contrary, a notary public shall have power, within the parish or parishes in which he is authorized, to exercise all of the functions of a notary public and to receive wills in which he is named as administrator, executor, trustee, attorney for the administrator, attorney for the executor, attorney for the trustee, attorney for a legatee, attorney for an heir, or attorney for the estate.

B. However, each notary public of this state shall have authority to administer oaths to parties appearing before such notary in any parish of the state for the taking or execution of depositions, interrogatories, and statements to be used in courts of record of this state. Such oaths, and the certificates issued by such notaries shall be received in the courts of this state and shall have legal efficacy, including legal efficacy for purposes of the laws on perjury.

35:2.1. Affidavit of corrections.

A. A clerical error in a notarial act affecting movable or immovable property or any other rights, corporeal or incorporeal, may be corrected by an act of correction executed by the notary before whom the act was passed. The act of correction shall be executed by the notary before two witnesses and another notary public.

B. The act of correction executed in compliance with this Section shall be given retroactive effect to the date of recordation of the original act. However, the act of correction shall not prejudice the rights acquired by any third person before the act of correction is recorded where the third person reasonably relied on the original act. The act of correction shall not alter the true agreement and intent of the parties.

C. A certified copy of the act of correction executed in compliance with this Section shall be deemed to be authentic for purposes of executory process.

35:3. Oaths and acknowledgments.

Oaths and acknowledgments, in all cases, may be taken or made by or before any notary public duly appointed and qualified in this state.

35:4. Notaries connected with banks and other corporations; powers.

It is lawful for any notary public who is a stockholder, director, officer, or employe of a bank or other corporation to take the acknowledgment of any party to any written instrument executed to or by such corporation, or to administer an oath to any other stockholder, director, officer, employe, or agent of such corporation, or to protest for non-acceptance or nonpayment of bills of exchange, drafts, checks, notes, and other negotiable instruments which may be owned or held for collection by such corporation. It is unlawful for any notary public to take the acknowledgment of an instrument by or to a bank or other corporation of which he is a stockholder, director, officer or employe, where the notary is a party to such instrument, either individually or as a representative of such corporation, or to protest any negotiable instrument owned or held for collection by the corporation, where the notary is individually a party to the instrument.

35:5. Foreign notaries; oaths, acts, and acknowledgments; effect.

Oaths, acts, and acknowledgments taken, made, or executed by or before any person purporting to be a notary public, duly appointed and duly qualified in any other state, territory of the United States, or the District of Columbia shall have the same force and effect without further proof of the signatures as if taken, made, or executed by or before a notary public in Louisiana. This Section is remedial and shall be retroactive. All oaths, acts, and acknowledgments heretofore made in compliance with the provisions of this Section are hereby validated.

35:6. Foreign notaries; acts and other instruments, effect.

All acts passed before any notary public and two witnesses in the District of Columbia, or any state of the United States other than Louisiana shall be authentic acts and shall have the same force and effect as if passed before a notary public in Louisiana.

35:7. Acts before military officers; force and effect.

Every mortgage, sale, lease, transfer, assignment, power of attorney or other instrument, heretofore or hereafter executed before any commissioned officer in the active service of the armed forces or the Coast Guard of the United States, and bearing the signature of such officer and the proper designation of his rank and branch of service or subdivision thereof, shall be admissible in evidence and eligible to record in this state, and shall have the same force and effect of an authentic act executed in Louisiana; and any oath, affirmation,

deposition, or affidavit, executed before any commissioned officer in the active service of the armed forces or the Coast Guard of the United States as herein provided, shall have the same force and effect as if made or executed before a notary in Louisiana. The provisions of this Section shall not apply to any such instrument executed in any state of the United States or in the District of Columbia, by persons not serving in or with the armed forces or the Coast Guard of the United States.

35:8. Recorder's copies of instruments before military officers; effect.

Whenever any original instrument executed pursuant to R.S. 35:7, has been deposited in the office of a parish recorder of this state, the recorder is authorized to make copies of the same which shall have the same force and effect of authentic acts executed in this state.

35:9. Instruments, before ambassadors and consular officials.

Every mortgage, sale, lease, transfer, assignment, power of attorney, or other instrument, and every oath or affirmation, made or taken in any foreign country, before any ambassador, minister, charge d'affaires, secretary of legation, consul general, consul, vice-consul, or commercial agent, or before one of the following officers commissioned or accredited to act at the place where the act is made or taken, and having an official seal, to wit: any officer of the United States, any notary public, or any commissioner or other agent of this state having power to take acknowledgments, and every acknowledgment, attestation or authentication of such instruments, oaths or affirmations made by any of these officers under their official seals and signatures, shall have the full force and effect of an authentic act executed in this state; and it shall not be necessary that the officer be assisted by two witnesses, as in the case of a notary executing an authentic act in this state, but the attestation, seal and signature of the officer shall of themselves be sufficient; nor shall it be necessary that the person appearing before the officer to execute any of these instruments, or to take any oath or affirmation, be a resident of the place where the officer is located. Whenever any such original instrument, oath, or affirmation has been deposited in the office of a notary in this state, the notary is authorized to make copies of the same, which shall have the same force and effect as copies of authentic acts executed in this state.

35:10. Place of executing notarial acts.

All notarial acts shall be made and executed at

any place within the jurisdictional limits of the notary.

35:11. Marital status of parties to be given; family home declaration.

A. Whenever notaries pass any acts they shall give the marital status of all parties to the act, viz: If either or any party or parties are men, they shall be described as single, married, or widower. If married or widower the Christian and family name of wife shall be given. If either or any party or parties are women, they shall be described as single, married or widow. If married or widow, their Christian and family name shall be given, adding that she is the wife of or widow of . . . the husband's name.

B. A declaration as to one's marital status in an acquisition of immovable property by the person acquiring the property creates a presumption that the marital status as declared in the act of acquisition is correct and, except as provided in Subsection C of this Section, any subsequent alienation, encumbrance, or lease of the immovable by onerous title shall not be attacked on the ground that the marital status was not as stated in the declaration.

C. Any person may file an action to attack the subsequent alienation, encumbrance, or lease on the ground that the marital status of the party as stated in the initial act of acquisition is false and incorrect; however, such action to attack the alienation, encumbrance, or lease shall not affect any right or rights acquired by a third person acting in good faith.

D. The presumption provided in Subsection B of this Section is hereby declared to be remedial and made retroactive to any alienation, encumbrance, or lease made prior to September 1, 1987. Any person who has a right as provided in Subsection C of this Section, which right has not prescribed or otherwise been extinguished or barred upon September 1, 1987 and who is adversely affected by the provisions of Subsection C of this Section shall have six months from September 1, 1987 to initiate an action to attack the transaction or otherwise be forever barred from exercising his right or cause of action.

35:12. Christian names to be given in full, together with parties' permanent mailing addresses.

Notaries shall insert in their acts the Christian names of the parties in full and not their initial letters alone, together with the permanent mailing addresses of the parties, and shall print or type the full names of the witnesses and of themselves under their respective signatures.

35:14. Disbarred or suspended attorney prohibited from exercising notarial functions.

Any attorney at law, or person who was an attorney at law, who is disbarred or suspended from the practice of law due to charges filed by the Committee on Professional Responsibility of the Louisiana State Bar Association or who has consented to disbarment shall not be qualified or eligible nor shall he exercise any functions as a notary public in any parish of the state of Louisiana as long as he remains disbarred or suspended from the practice of law in Louisiana. Provided, however, that nothing in this Section shall apply to any action taken against an attorney at law for failure to pay annual dues.

35:15.1. Ex officio notaries public for the Department of Justice.

A. Notwithstanding any provisions of the law relative to qualifications for and limitations on the number of notaries public, the governor is authorized to appoint, upon recommendation by the attorney general, investigators in the Department of Justice as ex officio notaries public. Each ex officio notary public appointed under the provisions of this Section shall be submitted to the Senate for confirmation.

B. Such an ex officio notary public may exercise the functions of a notary public only to administer oaths and receive sworn statements and shall otherwise be limited to matters within the official functions of the Department of Justice.

C. All acts performed by such an ex officio notary public authorized by this Section shall be performed without charge or other compensation.

D. The attorney general may suspend or terminate any appointment made pursuant to this Section at any time, and separation from the employ of the Department of Justice shall automatically terminate the powers of such an ex officio notary public.

35:15.2. Ex officio notaries public for the Department of State.

A. Notwithstanding any provisions of the law relative to qualifications for notaries public, the secretary of state is authorized to appoint not more than six essential employees within the Department of State as ex officio notaries public.

B. Such ex officio notaries public may exercise the functions of a notary public only to administer oaths and receive sworn statements and shall be limited to matters within the official functions of the Department of State. They shall use the official seal of the department.

C. All acts performed by such ex officio notaries

public authorized by this Section shall be performed without charge or other compensation.

35:15.3. Ex officio notaries public for the Governor's Consumer Protection Division.

A. Notwithstanding any provisions of the law relative to qualifications for and limitations on the number of notaries public, the governor is authorized to appoint, upon recommendation by the director of the Governor's Consumer Protection Division, investigative staff members in the Governor's Consumer Protection Division as ex officio notaries public. Each ex officio notary public appointed under the provisions of this Section shall be submitted to the Senate for confirmation.

B. Such ex officio notaries public may exercise the functions of a notary public only to administer oaths and receive sworn statements and shall otherwise be limited to matters within the official functions of the Governor's Consumer Protection Division as set forth in R.S. 51:1404.

C. All acts performed by such ex officio notary public authorized by this Section shall be performed without charge or other compensation.

D. The director of the Governor's Consumer Protection Division may suspend or terminate any appointment made pursuant to this Section at any time, and separation from the employ of the Governor's Consumer Protection Division shall automatically terminate the powers of such an ex officio notary public.

35:15.4. Ex officio notaries public for the Louisiana State Racing Commission.

A. Notwithstanding any provisions of the law relative to qualifications for notaries public, the governor, upon the recommendation of the chairman of the Louisiana State Racing Commission, shall appoint not more than two of its employees at each racing commission office as ex officio notaries public.

B. Such ex officio notaries public may exercise the functions of a notary public only to administer oaths and receive sworn statements and shall be limited to matters within the official duties of R.S. 4:150(B)(11).

C. All acts performed by such ex officio notary public authorized by this Section shall be performed without charge or other compensation.

D. The provisions of this Section shall not cause any additional cost to the state.

35:16. Ex officio notaries for district attorneys.

A. Notwithstanding any provisions of the law relative to qualifications for and limitations on the number of notaries public, each district attorney may designate an investigator in his office as administrative assistant and appoint him as an ex officio notary public.

B. Such an ex officio notary public may exercise, in the judicial district which the district attorney serves, the functions of a notary public only to administer oaths and execute affidavits, acknowledgments, and other documents, all limited to matters within the official functions of the office of district attorney.

C. Such ex officio notary public shall fulfill the same bond requirements as provided by law in the parish or parishes comprising the district which the district attorney serves, provided the total amount of the bond shall not exceed the amount required to exercise the functions of notary public in a single parish.

D. All acts performed by such an ex officio notary public authorized by this Section shall be performed without charge or other compensation.

E. The district attorney may suspend or terminate an appointment made pursuant to this Section at any time, and separation from the employ of the district attorney shall automatically terminate the powers of such an ex officio notary public.

F. The district attorney shall pay as an expense of his office the costs of the notarial seal, the notarial bond, and any fees required for filing the bond.

35:16.1. Ex officio notaries for police departments.

A. Notwithstanding any provisions of the law relative to qualifications of notaries public, each chief of police may designate officers in his office and appoint them as ex officio notaries public.

B. Each officer so appointed may exercise, in the municipality that the police department serves, the functions of a notary public only to administer oaths and execute affidavits, acknowledgments, and other documents, all limited to matters within the official functions of the police department for the enforcement of the provisions of Title 14 and Title 32 of the Louisiana Revised Statutes of 1950 and of the municipal ordinances which the police department is charged with enforcing.

C. Each ex officio notary public shall fulfill the same bond requirements as provided by law for notaries in the parish in which the municipality is located. The municipality shall pay as an expense of the office of the chief of police the costs of the notarial seal, the notarial bond, and any fees required for filing the bond.

D. All acts performed by each ex officio notary public authorized by this Section shall be performed without charge or other compensation.

E. The chief of police may suspend or terminate an appointment made pursuant to this Section at any time, and separation from the employ of the police department shall automatically terminate the powers of the ex officio notary public.

35:16.2. Ex officio notaries public for the United States Forest Service.

A. Notwithstanding any provisions of the law relative to qualification for and limitations on the number of notaries public, the governor is authorized to appoint, upon recommendation by the Forest Supervisor, realty specialists in the United States Forest Service as ex officio notaries public.

B. This ex officio notary public may exercise the functions of a notary public only to administer oaths and execute affidavits, acknowledgments, and other documents, all limited to matters within the official functions of his employment with the United States Forest Service.

C. All acts performed by an ex officio notary public authorized by this Section may be performed in any parish where national forest lands are administered, and shall be performed without charge or other compensation.

D. Separation from the employ of the United States Forest Service shall automatically terminate the powers of this ex officio notary public.

35:16.3. Ex officio notary public for the Sabine River Authority.

A. Notwithstanding any provisions of the law relative to qualification for notaries public, the director of the Sabine River Authority may appoint one employee of the Sabine River Authority as an ex officio notary public.

B. Such ex officio notary public may exercise the functions of a notary public only to administer oaths, receive sworn statements, and execute affidavits, acknowledgments, and other documents, and shall be limited to matters within the official functions of the Sabine River Authority.

C. All acts performed by such ex officio notary public authorized by this Section may be performed only in the parishes of Sabine, DeSoto, Beauregard, Calcasieu, Cameron, and Vernon and shall be performed without charge or other compensation.

D. The director of the Sabine River Authority may suspend or terminate any appointment made pursuant to this Section at any time and separation from the employ of the Sabine River Authority shall automatically terminate the powers of such ex officio notary public.

35:17. Municipal number or address to be included; immovable property.

Each person passing an act by which immovable property is conveyed, transferred, leased, or encumbered shall recite in the description of the property the municipal number or address thereof, if such number or address is applicable at the time of execution of the act; provided, that the failure to recite the municipal number or address shall not affect the validity of the act.

Bonds of Notaries Public Generally

35:71. Suspension of notaries; renewal of bonds; penalty.

A. All notaries may be suspended by any court of competent jurisdiction for failure to pay over money entrusted to them in their professional character, for failure to satisfy any final judgment rendered against them in such capacity, or for other just cause.

B. All notaries shall renew their bonds every five years except those notaries who are bonded with a personal surety, as provided in R.S. 35:75. Notaries with a personal surety bond shall renew their bonds upon the death of the personal surety in accordance with the provisions of this Chapter.

C. A qualified notary, other than a licensed attorney at law, who fails to renew his notarial bond timely shall be assessed a penalty of fifty dollars by the secretary of state. This penalty shall be in addition to the filing fee required for renewal of the bond.

D. Prior to the assessment of the penalty as provided for in Subsection C, the secretary of state shall, by certified mail, notify the notary of the penalty. The notary shall be given sixty days from the date on which said notification is postmarked to avoid the penalty by filing his notarial bond in accordance with law.

E. The secretary of state shall be authorized to institute collection of the penalty.

F. The secretary of state shall be authorized to promulgate rules and regulations, where necessary, for implementation of this Section, in accordance with the Administrative Procedure Act.

35:72. Bonds; elimination of requirement.

Notwithstanding any provision of law to the contrary, after August 1, 1988, no notary, who is a licensed attorney at law, shall be required to post a bond of any kind.

35:73. Bond not mortgage until suit filed and notice of lis pendens recorded.

The official notarial bond, given by any notary public shall not, when recorded as provided by law, operate as a mortgage either against the property of the principal or of the surety or sureties thereon, unless and until a suit has been filed against the notary to recover on the bond, and a notice of lis pendens has been placed of record against the notary in connection with the suit in the parish where the bond is recorded, in which case the bond shall then operate as a mortgage against the property of both the principal and surety, or sureties, thereon.

35:74. Inclusion of bonds in mortgage certificates.

The clerks of court in preparing mortgage certificates shall not include notarial bonds thereon unless an action has been commenced on the bond and a notice of lis pendens has been filed in connection therewith as provided in R.S. 35:73.

35:75. Substituted notarial bond with personal surety.

In all cases where notaries public throughout the State of Louisiana have filed or recorded, or may hereafter file and record, bonds in the offices of the several clerks of court and ex officio recorder of conveyances and mortgages, and the register of conveyances and mortgages of the parish of Orleans, with any surety company authorized to do business in the State of Louisiana as surety, as permitted by existing laws, may, in lieu of such bonds of any surety company aforesaid, substitute a bond with personal surety acceptable to the presiding judge of the parish for which the notary is commissioned. The Secretary of State shall accept said substituted notarial bond with personal surety in lieu of notarial bond with surety company as surety.

35:76. Release of surety company upon acceptance of personal surety bond.

The Secretary of State for the State of Louisiana, upon filing and recordation of a notarial bond with the Secretary of State, with personal surety in lieu of a surety company, shall upon request execute a release of the surety company effective as of the date of the acceptance of the personal surety bond in lieu thereof.

35:77. Cancellation of surety company bond.

Upon presentation of such personal surety bond containing a certificate of its sufficiency by the presiding judge of the parish of the state for which the notary was commissioned, and certificate of approval by the Secretary of State to any clerk of court and ex officio recorder of conveyances and mortgages, and the register of conveyances and

mortgages of the parish of Orleans, the said clerk, register or recorder of mortgages, shall upon application by any interested party cancel and erase in full from the records of his office said notarial bond with surety company as surety now or hereafter recorded in the conveyance or mortgage records of his office.

Leaves of Absence

35:131. Grant of leave of absence; designation of substitute notary; suspension of prescription.

A. The governor may grant leave of absence to notaries public for a period not exceeding thirty-six months, to date from the day of the permission granted by the governor.

B. Notaries public permitted to absent themselves shall be required to name and designate another notary public to represent them during their absence.

C. Absence from the state suspends the running of prescription against the notary.

35:132. Notaries in military service, leave of absence.

A leave of absence may be granted by the governor to any notary public upon his application to the governor in writing certifying that he is a member of the Army, Navy, Marine Corps or any other branch of the military service of the United States, or of the State of Louisiana, and stating the expiration date of his bond; if the notary so desires, he may name and designate another notary to represent him during his absence, but the representation shall cease upon the expiration of the absent notary's bond.

35:133. Notaries in military service, period of leave.

The period of the leaves of absence granted in accordance with R.S. 35:132 shall date from the day of the permission granted by the governor and shall terminate sixty days after the date of discharge of the notary from the military service of the United States or the State of Louisiana.

35:134. Expiration of bond during military service; renewal.

When the notarial bond of a notary public expires during the term of military service, the notary shall have sixty days from the date of his discharge from military service in which to apply for a new bond.

Appointment, Qualifications, and
Bonds of Notaries

35:191. Appointment; qualifications and bond; examination; examiners.

A. Any resident citizen or alien of the state, eighteen years of age or older, may be appointed a notary public in and for the parish in which he resides and in and for any one other parish in which he maintains an office, provided that he meets the requirements established by law for each parish in which he applies.

B. A resident citizen seeking to be appointed notary public in the parish of his residence or possessing a valid notarial commission in and for a parish based on his residence must be a registered voter of that parish.

C. Each applicant, otherwise qualified, may be appointed a notary public in and for a parish upon meeting all of the following conditions:

(1) Submitting an application to be appointed a notary public to the appropriate district court together with a certificate establishing his age, residence, location of his office when the applicant seeks to be appointed a notary based on such office, location of the office which was the basis for a current appointment as a notary in any other parish, if any, and a statement as to the applicant's good moral character, integrity, competency, and sober habits, sworn to and subscribed by two reputable citizens of the parish.

(2)(a) Taking and passing a written examination administered by an examining committee composed of three notaries appointed by the district court having jurisdiction in the parish, or in Orleans Parish the custodian of notarial records, and one attorney, and one notary public who is not an attorney. Two of the notaries shall be attorneys and one a notary public who is not an attorney. However, if no person within the parish who is a non-attorney notary will accept such appointment, the district court having jurisdiction in the parish shall appoint an additional attorney to serve on the examining committee.

(b) The examining committee members shall be appointed to serve a term of two years beginning October 1, 1977, and every two years thereafter. Examinations shall be given on the second Monday in July and the second Monday in December of each calendar year beginning in December, 1977, and may be given at such other times as the examining committee shall determine. Application to take such examination must be filed with the district court no later than thirty days prior to the date as fixed herein for such examination. Results of the examination shall be announced to each applicant within forty-five days following the examination. If the examining committee fails to sched-

ule and give the examinations as herein directed, then the said committee shall automatically be discharged and a new committee shall be appointed to fulfill the unexpired terms in accordance with the above provisions.

(c) In Orleans Parish, the examination shall be administered at the office of the custodian of notarial records.

(d) If found competent and possessed of the necessary qualifications, the court shall issue to the applicant an appropriate certificate, signed by a judge of the court.

(e) The examination provided for in this Paragraph may be dispensed with by the court if the applicant has been duly admitted to practice law in this state or holds a valid notarial commission in this state.

(3) Giving bond, with good and solvent security, in the sum of five thousand dollars conditioned for the faithful performance of all duties required by law toward all persons who may employ him in his profession of notary.

D. Notwithstanding any other provision of law to the contrary, any person who is validly appointed notary public in and for the parish of Orleans, the parish of St. Bernard, or the parish of Jefferson is hereby authorized and deemed eligible and qualified to exercise any and all of the functions of a notary public in the parishes of Orleans, St. Bernard, and Jefferson.

E. Notwithstanding any other provision of law to the contrary, any person who has been a validly appointed notary public in or for any parish for a period of five years and who changes his residence to another parish, and in the parish of his new residence complies with the laws governing notaries public in said parish, except taking and passing an examination, shall be issued a notarial commission for the parish of his new residence by the governor without advice and consent of the Senate and may exercise the functions of notary public in that parish.

F. Notwithstanding any other provision of law to the contrary, any person who is validly appointed notary public in and for any of the parishes of Tangipahoa, Livingston or St. Helena is hereby authorized and deemed eligible and qualified to exercise any and all of the functions a notary public in the parishes of Tangipahoa, Livingston and St. Helena.

G. Notwithstanding any other provision of law to the contrary, any person who is validly appointed notary public in and for any of the parishes of Bienville, Caldwell, East Carroll, Franklin, Jackson, Lincoln, Madison, Morehouse, Ouachita, Richland, Union, or West Carroll is hereby authorized and deemed eligible and qualified to exercise any and all of the functions of a notary public in the parishes of Bienville, Caldwell, East Carroll,

Franklin, Jackson, Lincoln, Madison, Morehouse, Ouachita, Richland, Union, or West Carroll.

H. Notwithstanding any other provision of law to the contrary, any person who is validly appointed notary public in and for either of the parishes of Caddo or Bossier is hereby authorized and deemed eligible and qualified to exercise any and all of the functions of a notary public in the parishes of Caddo and Bossier.

I. Notwithstanding any other provision of law to the contrary, any person who is validly appointed notary public in and for either of the parishes of Catahoula or Concordia is hereby authorized and deemed eligible and qualified to exercise any and all of the functions of a notary public in the parishes of Catahoula and Concordia.

J. Notwithstanding any other provision of law to the contrary, any person who is a validly appointed notary public in and for either of the parishes of Iberia or St. Mary is hereby authorized and deemed eligible and qualified to exercise any and all of the functions of a notary public in the parishes of Iberia and St. Mary.

K. Notwithstanding any other provision of law to the contrary, any person who is validly appointed notary public in and for any of the parishes of Allen, Beauregard, Calcasieu, Cameron, Vernon, or Jefferson Davis is hereby authorized and deemed eligible and qualified to exercise any and all functions of a notary public in the parishes of Allen, Beauregard, Calcasieu, Cameron, Vernon, and Jefferson Davis. No additional bonding or further application or examination shall be required due to the expanded jurisdictional limits authorized by this Subsection.

L. Any notary public in and for the parish of Acadia, Lafayette, or Vermillion is hereby authorized and qualified to exercise all of the functions of a notary public in and for any of said parishes. No additional bonding or further application or examination shall be required due to the expanded jurisdictional limits authorized by this Subsection.

M. Any notary public appointed in and for the parish of Iberia or Vermillion is hereby authorized and qualified to exercise any and all functions of a notary public in both parishes. No additional bonding or further application or examination shall be required due to the expanded jurisdictional limits authorized by this Subsection.

N. Any notary public appointed in and for the parish of Ascension, East Baton Rouge, East Feliciana, Livingston, Pointe Coupee, West Baton Rouge, or West Feliciana is hereby authorized and qualified to exercise all of the functions of a notary public in and for any of said parishes. No additional bonding or further application or examination shall be required due to the expanded jurisdictional limits authorized by this Subsection.

O. Notwithstanding any other provision of law to the contrary, any person who is validly appointed notary public in and for any of the parishes of Acadia, Evangeline, or St. Landry is hereby authorized and deemed eligible and qualified to exercise any and all of the functions of a notary public in the parishes of Acadia, Evangeline, and St. Landry. No additional bonding or further application or examination shall be required due to the expanded jurisdictional limits authorized by this Subsection.

P. Notwithstanding any other provision of law to the contrary, each person who is licensed to practice law in this state who is a notary public in and for any parish in this state may exercise the functions of a notary public in every parish in this state. The expanded jurisdictional limits authorized by this Subsection are additional to other provisions of law. No additional bonding or further application or examination shall be required due to the expanded jurisdictional limits authorized by this Subsection.

Q. Notwithstanding any other provision of law to the contrary, any person who is validly appointed notary public in and for either of the parishes of Lafayette or St. Landry is hereby authorized and qualified to exercise all of the functions of a notary public in and for both parishes. No additional bonding or further application or examination shall be required due to the expanded jurisdictional limits authorized by this Subsection.

35:192. Execution and recordation of bond; filing of certificate of competency.

A. The bond required of notaries by R.S. 35:191 shall be submitted to the clerk of court and ex officio recorder of mortgages for the parish where the notary will exercise the functions of his office, and, together with the certificate of competency above provided for, shall be filed in the office of the secretary of state. The bond shall be subscribed in favor of the governor; approved by the clerk, except in Orleans Parish; and if secured by personal surety, recorded in the mortgage office of the said parish in a special book kept for that purpose. In Orleans Parish, the bond shall be approved by the custodian of notarial records.

B. The provisions of Subsection A of this Section shall not affect the validity of bonds given or recorded in the mortgage or conveyance office of any parish prior to September 9, 1977.

35:193. Original surety company bond; necessity for recordation.

In all cases where notaries public furnish bond for the faithful performance of their duties, signed by a surety company, authorized to do business in this state, it shall not be necessary to record the bond in the office of the recorder of mortgages of the parish where the notary performs his duties, and in all cases, when existing bonds or future bonds of this character are filed and recorded in the mortgage office, they shall not operate as mortgages upon the property of the principal.

35:194. Substitution of personal surety bond or special mortgage.

In all cases where notaries public throughout the state have filed or recorded bonds in the offices of the several clerks of court and ex officio recorders of mortgages, with personal or individual surety, or who have executed and recorded a special mortgage on immovable property, as permitted by existing law, may, in lieu of such bonds, and in lieu of such special mortgages, substitute a bond in the same sum with any surety company authorized to do business in the state as surety.

35:195. Cancellation of personal surety bond or special mortgage.

Upon presentation of the surety bond provided for in R.S. 35:194 to any clerk of court and ex officio recorder of mortgages, the clerk shall file the bond, and upon application by any interested party, shall cancel and erase in full from the records of his office any bond with personal surety recorded in the mortgage records of his office, and likewise any special mortgage executed and recorded by any notary public, conditioned for the faithful performance of his duties as notary.

35:196. Substituted surety company bond; necessity for recordation.

The surety bond provided for in R.S. 35:194 shall not be recorded in the mortgage records of the clerks of court and ex-officio recorders of mortgages and shall not in any event be an encumbrance against the property of any notary making and executing such bond.

35:198. Liability of notary and surety; effect of surety company bond; cancellation of bond for nonpayment.

A. Nothing contained in R.S. 35:193 shall in any way affect the liablity of a notary for the failure to perform his duties, nor the liability of his surety for any neglect thereof, or in any way alter the requirements of the recording of bonds not signed by a surety company, or their legal effect when so recorded.

B. When the notary in Orleans Parish has given bond with a surety company, the surety has the right to cancel the bond for nonpayment of the premium by giving notice through registered mail to the custodian of notarial records for the parish of Orleans. This notice must be given thirty days prior to any anniversary date of the bond, after which anniversary date the liability of the surety company on the bond shall cease.

35:199. Acts affecting property in Orleans Parish; filing acts; penalty for violation.

Notaries outside the Parish of Orleans who pass acts of sale and acts of mortgage affecting property located in the Parish of Orleans shall, within fifteen days after the passage of such acts, deposit them in the office of the Custodian of Notarial Records of the Parish of Orleans, who shall receive and file them. The custodian may charge a filing fee of not more than twenty-five cents for each act filed.

Any notary who violates the provisions of this Section is guilty of a misdemeanor and shall be fined not more than twenty-five dollars, at the discretion of the court.

35:200. Limitation on actions.

Actions against sureties on said bonds shall prescribe in ten years from date of act of commission or omission.

35:201. Granting of commission; prerequisites.

A. Before the governor shall issue to the applicant a commission of notary public for any parish, he shall require of him the production of:

(1) The certificate provided by R.S. 35:191 (C)(2)(d);

(2) His oath of office;

(3) His bond, properly executed, approved and registered as provided in R.S. 35:192; and

(4) His official signature.

B. Upon the issuing of the commission, all of the above shall be deposited in the office of the secretary of state and annexed in the margin of a book to be kept for that purpose by the secretary of state; provided however, for the parish of Orleans, the secretary of state shall keep a book to be styled "The Notarial Book of Orleans Parish."

Notaries in Orleans Parish

35:281. Act evidencing transfer of real property; filing with board of assessors.

Whenever an act of sale or any other act evidencing a transfer of real property situated in the

Parish of Orleans is passed before a notary public, it shall be the duty of the notary to file a copy of any such act with the board of assessors for the Parish of Orleans within fifteen days from the date of sale or transfer.

35:282. Duplicate copy of sketch, blueprint, or survey.

Whenever there is annexed to any act of sale or other act of transfer of real estate any sketch, blue print, or survey which forms part of the act of sale or transfer, the notary public shall have attached to the copy of such act, a duplicate copy of the sketch, blue print, or survey.

35:283. Obligations under existing laws not affected.

Nothing contained in R.S. 35:281 and R.S. 35:282 shall be construed as relieving notaries public from the obligations imposed upon them to file copies of their acts with other officials or in other offices.

35:284. Violations.

Whoever violates the provisions of R.S. 35:281 or R.S. 35:282 shall be fined not more than fifty dollars or imprisoned in the parish jail for not more than sixty days, or both.

35:285. Deposit of original acts when property affected situated outside New Orleans.

Notaries public within the Parish of Orleans shall deposit in the office of the clerk and recorder of the parish in which the property is situated, whenever the property affected is situated in this state outside the Parish of Orleans, within fifteen days after the same shall have been passed, the original of all acts of sale, exchange, donation and mortgage of immovable property, passed before them, together with all resolutions, powers of attorney and other documents annexed to or made part of the acts, and in the order of their respective dates, first making a careful record of the acts in record books to be kept for that purpose.

35:286. Violations.

Notaries who contravene the provisions of R.S. 35:285 [concerning the deposit of original acts when the property affected is situated outside New Orleans] are liable to a fine of one hundred dollars for each infraction to be recovered before any court of competent jurisdiction, one-half for the benefit of the informer, as well as for all such damages as the parties may suffer thereby.

35:287. Deputies.

Every notary public in the Parish of Orleans may appoint one or more deputies to assist him in the making of protests and delivery of notices of protests of bills of exchange and promissory notes. Each notary shall be personally responsible for the acts of each deputy employed by him. Each deputy shall take an oath faithfully to perform his duties as such. The certificate of notice of protest shall state by whom made or served.

35:321. Terms defined.

As used in this Part, the terms defined in this Section shall have the meanings here given to them, except where the context clearly indicates otherwise.

1. "Notary" or "Notary Public" shall mean a "Notary Public in and for the Parish of Orleans;"
2. "Custodian" means "Custodian of Notarial Records in and for the Parish of Orleans."

35:322. Appointment and qualifications; vacancies.

The governor by and with the advice and consent of the senate, shall appoint a custodian of notarial records, whose term of office shall be for four years, and run concurrent with the governor. In the event of a vacancy in said office, the governor by and with the advice and consent of the senate shall appoint a custodian for the unexpired term.

The custodian shall be a duly licensed and practicing attorney at law and notary public in the parish of Orleans, and shall be a member in good standing of the Louisiana State Bar Association.

35:323. Central office, preservation of notarial records; permanent volumes.

A. The custodian shall maintain a central office in the city of New Orleans in the civil District Court Building in quarters presently provided by the city of New Orleans or other quarters in said courthouse to be provided in the city of New Orleans. The custodian shall demand, take possession of, collect, keep and preserve in this office the notarial records of notaries in the parish of Orleans who have ceased to be such, either by death, removal or otherwise, and shall hereafter classify these records according to their date, serial number, and in such a manner as will most facilitate access to them.

B. (1) Every authentic act except chattel mortgages and acts relating to real property outside of Orleans Parish, passed before a notary public in Orleans Parish, and also every act, contract and instrument except money judgments and chattel mortgages filed for record in the office of either the recorder of mortgages or the register of conveyances for the parish of Orleans shall, as a condition precedent to such filing in the office of the recorder of mortgages or the register of conveyances for the parish of Orleans be first filed in the office of the custodian of notarial records for the parish of Orleans. The custodian shall endorse on each act, contract or instrument filed in his office, the date of such filing, a serial number, and shall attach to such act, contract or instrument a certificate of its filing, date and serial number. Such act, contract or instrument so endorsed, shall thereafter be filed for record, if otherwise required by law, with the recorder of mortgages or the register of conveyances for the parish of Orleans, or both, and shall be registered and/or recorded with the serial number furnished by the custodian, provided, however, that nothing herein be deemed to impose upon the custodian any obligation to file any act, contract or instrument with either the recorder of mortgages or the register of conveyances. The recorder of mortgages and register of conveyances for the parish of Orleans shall thereafter return said act, contract or instrument to the custodian, showing the date of filing and time, by the recorder of mortgages and the book and folio number, and the custodian shall thereupon have permanent custody of the said act, contract or instrument, which shall then be filed in his office according to the serial number endorsed thereon by the custodian. The recorder of mortgages and register of conveyances for the parish of Orleans shall endorse upon the certificate issued by the custodian for each act, contract or instrument the date and time, by the recorder of mortgages, book and folio number of its recordation or registry, and shall furnish such certificate to the notary public or other person who caused the same to be filed with the custodian.

(2) It shall be the duty of all notaries public filing acts for registration and/or recordation pursuant hereto to deposit with the custodian all certificates, tax researches, surveys and documents pertaining to any act passed before them and this deposit must be made within sixty days of the date of registration and/or recordation. It shall be the duty of the custodian to file in permanent form, according to serial number, all acts, contracts and instruments filed with him and all certificates, tax researches and documents furnished him pertaining to all such acts.

C. (1) The custodian of notarial records shall charge the sum of five dollars for each act, contract, or other instrument thus filed and deposited in his office, with all such sums to be used only for the expenses and maintenance of said office.

(2) Notwithstanding the provisions of this subsection, all veterans of the armed forces of the United States of America shall be exempt from paying any fee for the filing and depositing of their discharge certificates or other evidence of honorable separation from the armed forces with the custodian of notarial records.

D. Every notary public for the parish of Orleans shall deliver for deposit to the office of the custodian, for permanent preservation, all acts executed before such notaries public prior to January 1, 1966, and the deposit of such acts shall not be optional, but shall be mandatory on the part of each notary public for the parish of Orleans. No charge shall be made by the custodian for the deposit of bound volumes of such acts. For the deposit of unbound acts, the custodian shall charge in accordance with the provisions of Subsection C of this section. The deposit of such acts shall be made not later than December 31, 1972. Whenever any notary public for the parish of Orleans shall fail to comply with the provisions aforestated then the custodian shall institute proceedings in accordance with the provisions of Subsection F of this section.

E. Every living, qualified notary public is authorized to certify true copies of any authentic act or any instrument under private signature hereafter or heretofore passed before him or acknowledged before him, and to make and certify copies, by any method, of any certificate, research, resolution, survey or other document annexed to the original of any authentic acts passed before him, and may certify such copies as true copies of the original document attached to the original passed before him.

F. Whenever any notary public for the parish of Orleans shall fail to comply with the provisions of this section then it shall be the duty of the custodian of notarial records to institute proceedings by rule in the Civil District Court for the parish of Orleans to require said notary public to show cause why his notarial commission should not be forfeited and why he should not be ordered to turn over all his notarial archives and records to the custodian of notarial records and pay all costs of said proceedings.

G. The indexing, binding and depositing of acts, contracts and instruments of writing executed before notaries public for the parish of Orleans, referred to in this section shall constitute an exception to the requirements of R.S. 35:329, and nothing contained in this section or in R.S. 35:329 shall be construed as requiring any notary public for the parish of Orleans to have an act executed before him in multiple originals.

35:323.1. Microfilm records; use; separate location.

A. Permission is hereby granted to the custodian to install and use microfilm machinery and apparatus in the recordation, filing, preservation and reproduction of all records and documents filed or deposited with the custodian prior to July 29, 1970, and subsequent thereto.

B. Such microfilm records and documents may be used only in emergency situations arising from fire, storm, theft, loss or any other emergency circumstances which may render the original record or document useless. Such microfilm records and documents shall be kept at a separate location from the original records and documents filed with the custodian.

C. Such microfilm copy shall be deemed to be an original record for all purposes, and shall be admissible in evidence in all courts or administrative agencies. A facsimile, exemplification or certified copy thereof shall for all purposes be deemed to be a transcript, exemplification or certified copy of the original.

D. Nothing contained herein shall in any manner be construed to permit the destruction of any notarial records presently in the possession of, or which may hereafter come into the possession of, the custodian of notarial records.

35:324. Bond of custodian.

The custodian shall give bond, in addition to his notarial bond, in the amount of ten thousand dollars in favor of the governor, with one or more good and solvent sureties approved by the presiding judge of the Civil District Court of the Parish of Orleans, conditioned upon the faithful performance of his duties as custodian. This bond shall be filed in the office of the Secretary of State.

35:325. List of notaries.

The custodian shall keep an accurate alphabetical list of all notaries public in and for the Parish of Orleans, showing their business and residence addresses and the expiration date of their bonds; he shall keep this list at all times open to public inspection during his office hours, and furnish the Secretary of State and the district attorney in and for the Parish of Orleans, annually on or before October 1st, a certified list of all notaries in and for the Parish of Orleans, showing the number of notaries and the number and names of those who have ceased to be notaries, and the number and names of those whose bonds have expired.

He shall diligently, by every means in his power, keep the list accurate and up to date at all times, and shall immediately notify the governor and the Secretary of State of each vacancy caused by death, resignation, removal from Orleans Parish, or any other cause, as soon as such facts are ascertained by him.

35:326. Statement furnished custodian by notaries.

Each notary shall, annually, before September 1st, furnish to the custodian a statement showing his office and residence address, the date of his bond and the surety or sureties thereon, and their addresses. Failure to furnish this statement shall be cause for the revocation of the commission of the notary.

35:327. Fee payable to custodian by notaries.

Each notary shall pay an annual fee of fifteen dollars, on or before September first of each year, to the custodian, the said fees to be used by the custodian for expenses of his office.

35:328. Testing sureties on bonds; new bond; forfeiture of commission for failure to give.

The custodian shall institute proceedings by rule in the Civil District Court of the Parish of Orleans at least once every twelve months, and oftener if he deem it proper and necessary, without the payment of costs by the custodian, on all notaries in the parish to test the surety on their official bonds, and should the sureties on the official bonds so tested, be judicially declared not good and solvent as required by law, the notary whose surety has been so declared shall pay the costs of the rule, and shall be allowed thirty days within which to give a new bond, and on his failure to do so within that time, shall forfeit his commission and turn over his notarial archives and records to the custodian, upon the payment of all costs which have been assessed against him in any proceeding filed by the custodian under the provisions of this Part. Whenever the notary's commission is revoked for failure to comply with the requirements of this Part, no judgment of any court reinstating the notary rendered after the expiration of thirty days as hereinabove provided for, shall be valid.

Provided, that he shall not be entitled to act as a notary during the period of thirty days; and

Provided, further, that should anyone ceasing by removal or otherwise to be a notary subsequently again be appointed to that office he shall be entitled to recover and obtain his notarial records and archives from the custodian.

35:329. Preservation by notaries of acts, contracts and instruments; binding and indexing; duties of custodian.

Every notary shall keep and preserve in his office and under his custody, the original of all acts, contracts and instruments of writing executed before him, with the exception only of affidavits and instruments under private signature, which may be acknowledged or proved before him, depositions of witnesses, and all acts of or in connection with the voluntary surrender of children under R.S. 9:401 through 9:405 and all acts amendatory thereto, and he shall cause these acts, contracts and instruments of writing, subject to the exceptions set forth above, to be bound in separate, permanent book form volumes for each year, with complete indices attached to each volume.

If the number of acts passed by a notary do not exceed fifty in any one year, he may wait until the end of the subsequent year to have them bound, but regardless of number, at the end of the subsequent year his acts for each of those years shall be bound as aforesaid. These acts together with protests made by him, will constitute the archives of his office. The custodian shall, at the time of trial of the rule provided in R.S. 35:328, require evidence from each notary that he has caused his acts to be bound and indexed in the manner aforesaid, and in case it should then appear that any notary public has neglected to comply with R.S. 35:321 through 35:335, the court shall allow the notary thirty days within which to index and bind his acts; and on his failure so to do within that time he shall forfeit his commission and turn over his notarial acts and records to the custodian in the same manner as provided in R.S. 35:328 for failure to furnish a proper bond.

35:330. Proceedings by custodian against absent notaries.

Should the proper official be unable to find any notary upon whom he desires to make service of process in any cause brought by the custodian under the authority of this Part, the custodian shall advertise such cause at least three times at intervals of not less than seven or more than ten days, in the official journal of the Parish of Orleans, and if no appearance has been made by the defendant notary in said cause, the custodian shall proceed against him as against an absent defendant, as provided by law.

35:331. Revocation of notary's commission for failure to furnish bond.

Failure of any notary to furnish proper surety bond shall be just cause for revocation of his notarial commission by a court of proper jurisdiction.

35:332. Notice by custodian of expiration date of bond.

It is the duty of the custodian to notify each notary of the expiration date of his bond, within sixty and not less than thirty days of the date of expiration; but the failure of the custodian to give such notice shall not prevent the custodian from proceeding to cancel the notary's commission as provided herein, nor shall it relieve the notary of any duties prescribed by law.

35:333. Rule to revoke notary's commission.

Should any notary fail or refuse to pay the annual fee fixed by R.S. 35:327, or fail or refuse to furnish the information required, or fail to provide the proper bond as required by law, the custodian shall promptly file a rule in the civil district court in and for the Parish of Orleans, or any other court of proper jurisdiction, to have the notary's commission revoked, and the notary shall pay all costs of the proceeding.

35:334. Misdemeanor to act after expiration of bond or after surety cancelled.

It is a misdemeanor, punishable as provided in R.S. 35:335, for any notary knowingly to act as such after the expiration of his bond, or after the surety on his bond has been cancelled as provided by law.

35:335. Willful violations.

The custodian or notary willfully violating the provisions of this Part shall be fined not less than fifty dollars nor more than five hundred dollars, or imprisoned for not less than ten days nor more than six months.

35:336. Deputies of custodian; appointment of archivist.

A. The custodian may appoint two deputies, who shall be sworn according to law, and such deputies, when appointed and sworn, shall have power to certify copies of acts and records of all kinds in the office. The deputies appointed by the custodian shall devote full time to the duties of that office and not receive a salary that exceeds thirty-five thousand dollars per annum.

B. (1) The custodian shall employ on a part-time basis a professional archivist to assist the custodian with the responsibilities of the office and to insure the adequate preservation of records and documents, whose salary shall not exceed twenty thousand dollars per annum.

(2) The archivist shall possess a baccalaureate degree in either history, political science, philosophy, anthropology, historical geography, archeology, French, Spanish or fine arts, and have either:

(a) At least two years of professional level experience in historical research or college level teaching in the above academic fields; or

(b) At least two years of experience in archival operations, records management, records preservation or other work involving locating, selecting, acquiring, and preserving documents or other valuable papers and materials.

35:337. Fees, salary, and excess funds of custodian.

A. The custodian may charge and receive the same fees of office as are allowed by law to other notaries for the making and certifying of copies. The compensation of the custodian shall not exceed thirty-five thousand dollars per annum and any remainder of fees shall be used solely to operate and maintain the functions of the office of notarial records.

B. Any unexpended or unencumbered funds remaining at the end of the fiscal year to the credit of the account of monies, fees, or sums collected by the custodian of notarial records shall be transferred by the custodian to the general fund of the city of New Orleans.

35:338. Annual budget; submission to enumerated entities.

The custodian of notarial records shall prepare a detailed annual budget at the end of its fiscal year and submit a copy of that budget to the legislative auditor pursuant to R.S. 24:513 et seq., and the Joint Legislative Committee on the Budget and publish a copy, at its own expense, in the official journal of the parish of Orleans, at his own expense commencing January 1, 1989.

ADDITIONAL AUTHORITY

6:785. Directors, employees and members not disqualified to make acknowledgments.

No public officer qualified to take acknowledgments or proof of written instruments shall be disqualified from taking the acknowledgment or proof of any instrument in writing in which an association is interested by reason of his membership in or employment by an association so interested, and any such acknowledgment or proof heretofore taken are hereby validated.

9:51. Civil rights and duties.

Women have the same rights, authority, privileges, and immunities, and shall perform the same obligations and duties as men in the holding of office including the civil functions of tutor, under tutor, curator, under curator, administrator, executor, arbitrator, and notary public.

37:212. "Practice of law" defined.

A. The practice of law means and includes:

(1) In a representative capacity, the appearance as an advocate, or the drawing of papers, pleadings or documents, or the performance of any act in connection with pending or prospective proceedings before any court of record in this state; or

(2) For a consideration, reward, or pecuniary benefit, present or anticipated, direct or indirect;

(a) The advising or counseling of another as to secular law;

(b) In behalf of another, the drawing or procuring, or the assisting in the drawing or procuring of a paper, document, or instrument affecting or relating to secular rights;

(c) The doing of any act, in behalf of another, tending to obtain or secure for the other the prevention or the redress of a wrong or the enforcement or establishment of a right; or

(d) Certifying or giving opinions as to title to immovable property or any interest therein or as to the rank or priority or validity of a lien, privilege or mortgage as well as the preparation of acts of sale, mortgages, credit sales or any acts or other documents passing titles to or encumbering immovable property.

B. Nothing in this Section prohibits any person from attending to and caring for his own business, claims, or demands, or from preparing abstracts of title; or from insuring titles to property, movable or immovable, or an interest therein, or a privilege and encumbrance thereon, but every title insurance contract relating to immovable property must be based upon the certification or opinion of a licensed Louisiana attorney authorized to engage in the practice of law. Nothing in this Section prohibits any person from performing as a notary public, any act necessary or incidental to the exercise of the powers and functions of the office of notary public, as those powers are delineated in Louisiana Revised Statutes of 1950, Title 35, Section 1, et seq.

C. Nothing in this Section shall prohibit any partnership, corporation, or other legal entity from asserting any claim, not exceeding two thousand dollars, or defense pertaining to an open account or promissory note, or suit for eviction of tenants on its own behalf in the courts of limited jurisdiction on its own behalf through a duly authorized partner, shareholder, officer, employee, or duly authorized agent or representative. No partnership, corporation, or other entity may assert any claim on behalf of another entity or any claim assigned to it.

D. Nothing in Article V, Section 24, of the Constitution of Louisiana or this Section shall prohibit justices or judges from performing all acts necessary or incumbent to the authorized exercise of duties as judge advocates or legal officers.

37:2554. Qualifications; examinations; certificates.

A. The board shall determine the qualifications of persons applying for examination under this Chapter, make rules for the examination of applicants and the issuance of certificates herein provided for which shall be subject to legislative oversight review pursuant to the Administrative Procedure Act, and shall grant certificates to such applicants as may, upon examination, be qualified in professional shorthand reporting and in such other subjects as the board may deem advisable.

B. The board may, at its discretion, waive regular examination of any person duly holding a comparable C.S.R. certificate from another state and desiring to move to Louisiana as a verbatim reporter.

C. No certificate holder shall be restricted from changing to any other shorthand system as defined in R.S. 37:2555, if he has at least five years previous experience as a verbatim reporter.

D. The board shall in no way restrict the use of electronic equipment to certificate holders hereunder in the performance of their duties, but shall exclude the use of all electronic recording equipment, except stenomask, to all applicants at the time and place of examination.

E. Every certificate holder hereunder shall be deemed a certified shorthand reporter, entitled to use the abbreviation "C.S.R." after his name, and at his expense shall receive from the board, and may keep while his certificate remains in effect, a metal seal imprinting his name and "Certified Shorthand Reporter of the State of Louisiana." Such certificate and seal shall authorize the holder thereof to issue affidavits with respect to his regular duties, to subpoena witnesses for depositions, to administer oaths and affirmations and to take depositions and sworn statements.

F. Within six months after January 1, 1987, the board shall accept, upon payment of a fee fixed by the board, applications for certified shorthand reporter certificates without an examination from any person furnishing due proof that his principal occupation in this state during the year prior to January 1, 1987, was that of a verbatim shorthand reporter proficiently taking and transcribing depositions, investigations, conventions, court proceedings, or hearings.

37:2555. Shorthand reporting defined.

A. The practice of shorthand reporting is defined as the making, by written symbols or abbreviations in shorthand or machine writing, or stenomask voice recording of a verbatim record of any oral court proceeding, public hearing, deposition, or proceeding.

B. There shall be two classifications of shorthand reporting which are designated and defined as follows:

(1) Official court reporters: any person appointed to serve as the official reporter for any court of record either as a permanent or temporary employee; and

(2) General reporting or free-lance reporting: Any person engaged in the reporting of depositions, sworn statements, public hearings or proceedings, whether self-employed or through any business, firm, corporation or agency, engaged in the reporting of depositions, sworn statements, or public hearings or proceedings.

[LA. CIV. CODE ANN.]

Art. 1833. Authentic act.

An authentic act is a writing executed before a notary public or other officer authorized to perform that function, in the presence of two witnesses, and signed by each party who executed it, by each witness, and by each notary public before whom it was executed.

To be an authentic act, the writing need not be executed at one time or place, or before the same notary public or in the presence of the same witnesses, provided that each party who executes it does so before a notary public or other officer authorized to perform that function, and in the presence of two witnesses and each party, each witness, and each notary public signs it.

If a party is unable or does not know how to sign his name, the notary public must cause him to affix his mark to the writing.

FEES

[LA. REV. STAT. ANN.]

9:1423. Fees of experts and appraisers.

The fees allowed to experts, notary publics and appraisers appointed to assist in taking inventories of successions, tutorships, interdictions, and other proceedings requiring the taking of inventories, shall be fixed by the court appointing such experts, notary publics and appraisers, and shall be taxed as costs in those proceedings in which the taking of an inventory is required.

ACKNOWLEDGMENTS

Within State

35:511. Forms of acknowledgment.

Either the forms of acknowledgment now in use in this State, or the following, may be used in the case of conveyances or other written instruments, whenever such acknowledgment is required or authorized by law for any purpose:

(Begin in all cases by a caption specifying the state and place where the acknowledgment is taken.)

1. In the case of natural persons acting in their own right:

On this _____ day of _____, 19__, _____ before me personally appeared AB (or AB and CD), to me known to be the person (or persons) described in and who executed the foregoing instrument, and acknowledged that he (or they) executed it as his (or their) free act and deed.

2. In the case of natural persons acting by attorney:

On this _____ day of _____, 19__, before me personally appeared AB, to me known to be the person who executed the foregoing instrument in behalf of CD, and acknowledged that he executed it as the free act and deed of said CD.

3. In the case of corporations or joint stock associations:

On this _____ day of _____, 19__, before me appeared AB, to me personally known, who, being by me duly sworn (or affirmed) did say that he is the president (or other officer or agent of the corporation or association), of (describing the corporation or association), and that the seal affixed to said instrument is the corporate seal of said corporation (or association) and that the instrument was signed and sealed in behalf of the corporation (or association) by authority of its Board of Directors (or trustees) and that AB acknowledged the instrument to be the free act and deed of the corporation (or association).

(In case the corporation or association has no corporate seal, omit the words "the seal affixed to said instrument is the corporate seal of the corporation (or association), and that" and add, at the end of the affidavit clause, the words "and that the corporation (or association) has no corporate seal").

(In all cases add signature and title of the officer taking the acknowledgment.)

35:512. Married women, acknowledgment by.

The acknowledgment of a married woman when required by law may be taken in the same form as if she were sole and without any examination separate and apart from her husband.

35:513. Officers before whom proof or acknowledgment taken in other states.

The proof or acknowledgment of any deed or other written instrument required to be proved or acknowledged in order to enable the same to be recorded or read in evidence, when made by any person without this state and within any other state, territory, or district of the United States, may be made before any officer of such state, territory or district, authorized by the laws thereof to take the proof and acknowledgment of deeds, and when so taken and certified under his official seal, shall be entitled to be recorded in this state, and may be read in evidence in the same manner and with like effect as proofs and acknowledgments taken before any of the officers now authorized by law to take such proofs and acknowledgments, and whose authority so to do is not intended to be hereby affected.

Foreign

35:551. Officers before whom made.

All instruments requiring acknowledgment, if acknowledged without the United States, shall be acknowledged before an ambassador, minister, envoy or charge d'affaires of the United States, in the country to which he is accredited, or before one of the following officers commissioned or accredited to act at the place where the acknowledgment is taken, and having an official seal, viz.:—any officer of the United States; a notary public; or a commissioner or other agent of this state having power to take acknowledgments.

35:552. Form of certificate of acknowledgment.

Every certificate of acknowledgment, made without the United States, shall contain the name or names of the person or persons making the acknowledgment, the date when and the place where made, a statement of the fact that the person or persons making the acknowledgment knew the contents of the instrument, and acknowledged it to be his, her or their act; the certificate shall also contain the name of the person before whom made, his official title, and be sealed with his official seal and may be substantially in the following form:

_____ (name of country).

_____ (name of city, province or other political subdivision). Before the undersigned _____ (naming the officer and designating his official title) duly commissioned (or appointed) and qualified, this day personally appeared at the place above named _____ (naming the person or persons acknowledging) who declared that he (she or they) knew the contents of the foregoing instrument, and acknowledged it to be his (her or their) act.

Witness my hand and official seal this _____ day of _____, 19___.

_____ (name of officer).
_____ (official title).

(seal)

When the seal affixed shall contain the names or the official style of the officer, any error in stating, or failure to state otherwise the name or the official style of the officer, shall not render the certificate defective.

35:553. Acknowledgments in form used in state.

A certificate of acknowledgment of a deed or other instrument acknowledged without the United States before any officer mentioned in R.S. 35:551 shall also be valid if in the same form as now is or hereafter may be required by law, for an acknowledgment within this state.

35:554. Interpretation and construction.

This Part shall be so interpreted and construed as to effectuate its general purpose to make uniform the law of those states which enact it.

35:555. Force and effect.

Every acknowledgment or proof of any legal instrument and any oath or affirmation, taken or made before a commissioner, ambassador, minister, charge d'affaires, secretary of legation, consul general, consul, or vice consul, and every attestation or authentication made by them, when duly certified as above provided, shall have the force and effect of an authentic act executed in this state.

DEPOSITIONS

[La. Code Civ. Proc. Ann.]

Art. 1434. Person before whom deposition taken.

A deposition shall be taken before an officer authorize to administer oaths, who is not an employee or attorney of any of the parties or otherwise interested in the outcome of the case.

LEGAL HOLIDAYS

[La. Rev. Stat. Ann.]

1:55. Days of public rest, legal holidays and half holidays.

A. The following shall be days of public rest and legal holidays and half-holidays:

(1) The following shall be days of public rest and legal holidays: Sundays; January 1, New Year's Day; January 8, Battle of New Orleans; the third Monday in January, Dr. Martin Luther King, Jr.'s Birthday; January 19, Robert E. Lee Day; third Monday in February, Washington's Birthday; Good Friday; the last Monday in May, National Memorial Day; June 3, Confederate Memorial Day; July 4, Independence Day; August 30, Huey P. Long Day; the first Monday in September, Labor Day; the second Monday in October, Christopher Columbus Day; November 1, All Saints' Day; November 11, Veterans' Day; the fourth Thursday in November, Thanksgiving Day; December 25, Christmas Day; Inauguration Day in the city of Baton Rouge; provided, however, that in the parish of Orleans, the city of Baton Rouge, in each of the parishes comprising the second and sixth congressional districts, except the parish of Ascension, and in each of the parishes comprising the fourteenth and thirty-first judicial districts of the state, the whole of every Saturday shall be a legal holiday, and in the parishes of Catahoula, Caldwell, West Carroll, Concordia, East Carroll, Franklin, Madison, Morehouse, Ouachita, Richland, Tensas, Union, Jackson, Avoyelles, West Feliciana, Rapides, Natchitoches, Grant, LaSalle, Winn, Lincoln, and East Baton Rouge, the whole of every Saturday shall be a holiday for all banking institutions, and in the parishes of Sabine and Vernon each Wednesday and Saturday, from 12:00 o'clock noon until 12:00 o'clock midnight, shall be a half-holiday for all banking institutions. All banks and trust companies, however, may, each at its option, remain open and exercise all of its regular banking functions and duties upon January 8; Dr. Martin Luther King, Jr.'s Birthday; January 19; Washington's Birthday; Good Friday; National Memorial Day; June 3; August 30; Christopher Columbus Day; November 1; and Veterans' Day; and all banks and trust companies located in Ward 1 of the parish of Avoyelles may, each at its option, remain open and exercise all of its regular banking functions and duties until 12 o'clock noon on Saturdays; however, when on any of said last named days any bank or trust company does actually remain open it shall, as to transactions on such day, to exactly the same extent as if such day were not otherwise a legal holiday, be not subject to any of the provisions of R.S. 7:85 and R.S. 7:251 or any other laws of Louisiana covering the matters of ma-

turity of negotiable instruments and demand, notice, presentment, acceptance, or protest thereof on legal holidays and half holidays, and all instruments payable to or at such bank upon such day shall become due on such day; and provided, further, that the option of remaining open shall not, except as otherwise provided in this Paragraph, apply to Saturdays of Wednesdays which are holidays or half-holidays, or to Mardi Gras when the same has been declared a legal holiday; and provided still further that nothing in any law of this state shall in any manner whatsoever affect the validity of or render void or voidable the payment, certification, or acceptance of a check or other negotiable instrument or any other transaction by a bank in Louisiana because done on any holiday or half-holiday or because done on any day upon which such bank, if remaining open because of the option given it herein, if the payment, certification, acceptance, or other transaction could have been validly done on any other day.

(2) In all parishes of the state the governing authorities thereof shall have the option to declare the whole of every Saturday a holiday, and until the whole of Saturday is so declared a holiday in any parish, Saturday from 12 o'clock noon until 12 o'clock midnight shall be a half-holiday; provided that in the city of Baton Rouge and in the Parish of Orleans the whole of every Saturday is a holiday; provided further, that the governing authority of the Parish of Washington may declare the whole of Wednesday or the whole of Saturday a holiday, and if the Parish of Washington declares the whole or Wednesday a holiday, no part of Saturday shall be a holiday in that parish. In no parish shall the whole of Wednesday be a holiday when the immediately preceding day is a holiday.

(3) In the parishes of Orleans, St. Bernard, Jefferson, Plaquemines, St. Charles, St. James, St. John the Baptist, East Baton Rouge, Lafayette, St. Tammany, Iberia, St. Martin, Ascension, Washington, Calcasieu, Jefferson Davis, St. Landry, Evangeline, Cameron, Assumption, St. Mary, Acadia, Vermilion, Iberville, Pointe Coupee, West Baton Rouge, Lafourche, East Feliciana, and West Feliciana, and in all municipalities, Mardi Gras shall be a holiday when the governing authorities so declare by ordinance. The school boards of the parishes of Acadia and Lafayette may declare Mardi Gras and the International Rice Festival in Crowley a holiday for public school children of those parishes. In the parish of Washington, the Friday of the Washington Parish Free Fair shall be a legal holiday for the purpose of authorizing the clerk of court for the parish of Washington to close his office on that day.

(4) Whenever December 25, January 1, or July 4 falls on a Sunday, the next day is a holiday. When December 25, January 1, or July 4 falls on a Saturday, the preceding Friday is a holiday when the governing authorities so declare by ordinance, and if the local governing authorities declare the Friday preceding January 1st a legal holiday, such holiday shall be an optional holiday for banking institutions, and each bank may, each at its option remain open and exercise all of its regular banking functions under conditions set forth in Paragraph (1) of Subsection A of this Section.

(5) The governing authorities of all parishes in the state shall have the option to declare the second Friday of Holiday in Dixie a legal holiday. The school boards in all parishes shall have the option to declare such day a holiday for public school children.

B. Legal holidays shall be observed by the departments of the state as follows:

(1) In so far as may be practicable in the administration of the government, no employee shall work on New Year's Day, Mardi Gras Day, Good Friday, Independence Day, Labor Day, Veterans' Day, Thanksgiving Day, Christmas Day, Inauguration Day once in every four years in the city of Baton Rouge, or General Election Day every two years.

(2) Dr. Martin Luther King, Jr.'s Birthday, Robert E. Lee Day, Washington's Birthday, National Memorial Day, Confederate Memorial Day, and Huey P. Long Day shall be observed only in such manner as the governor may proclaim, considering the pressure of the state's business, provided, however, that not more than two such legal holidays shall be proclaimed in any one year, one of which shall be National Memorial Day. The governor shall call as a state holiday at least once every two years the birthday of Dr. Martin Luther King, Jr.

(3) The governor, by executive proclamation, may authorize the observance of such other holidays and half-holidays as he may deem in keeping with efficient administration. Whenever, in accordance with this Paragraph, the governor declares the fourth Friday in November a holiday, such holiday shall be designated as Acadian Day and shall be observed in commemoration of the arrival in Louisiana of the Acadian people from the French colony Acadie following the ceding of that colony to England in 1713 and in recognition of the fact that much of the early economic and political development of Louisiana is directly attributable to the industry of the Acadian people, through cultivation of land, utilization of Louisiana's natural resources, and the interest of the Acadian people in political self-determination and American democracy.

(4) When one or more holidays or half-holidays fall on a full-time employee's regular day off, his holiday shall be the closest regularly scheduled workday preceding or following the legal holiday, as designated by the head of the agency. Employees

whose regular work hours do not fall in the time period, or fall only partly within the time period, of the holiday shall receive a number of hours equivalent to the holiday through compensatory time or over-time. Part-time employees having a regular work schedule will receive benefits in a similar manner as full-time employees except that their benefits will be prorated to the number of hours normally worked.

(5) When time off is declared in case of natural emergencies, only those persons actually scheduled to work during the time period of the declaration shall receive the time off. Those persons who are scheduled to work during those hours and, because of the requirements of their job, do in fact work shall be entitled to compensatory time for those hours.

C. It shall be lawful to file and record suits, deeds, mortgages and liens, to issue and serve citations, to make sheriff's sales by virtue of any execution, and to take and to execute all other legal proceedings on Wednesday and Saturday holidays and half-holidays.

D. Notwithstanding the provisions of R.S. 6:65 or any other law to the contrary, all banking institutions and savings and loan associations located within the parishes of Terrebonne, Lafourche, Iberia, Pointe Coupee, West Baton Rouge, St. Mary, and Iberville, and all banking institutions located within the parishes of Lafayette and St. Landry, shall be closed during any year on Saturdays, Sundays, New Year's Day, Mardi Gras, Independence Day, Labor Day, Thanksgiving and Christmas; provided, however, that when New Year's Day, Independence Day or Christmas fall on a Sunday, said banking institutions and savings and loan associations shall be closed on the next day, and said financial institutions may, each at its option, remain open and exercise all of its regular functions and duties upon January eighth; January nineteenth; the third Monday in February, Washington's Birthday; Good Friday; the last Monday in May, National Memorial Day; June third; August thirtieth; the second Monday in October, Christopher Columbus Day; November first; and November eleventh, Veterans' Day; and further provided that when on any of said last named days any said financial institution does actually remain open it shall, as to transactions on such day, to exactly the same extent as if such day were not otherwise a legal holiday, be not subject to any of the provisions of R.S. 7:85 and R.S. 7:251, or any other laws of Louisiana, covering the matters of maturity of negotiable instruments and demands, notice, presentment, acceptance or protest thereof on legal holidays and half-holidays, and all instruments payable to or at such bank upon such day shall become due on such day; and provided further that the option of remaining open shall not apply to Sat-

urdays or Wednesdays which are holidays or half-holidays, or to Mardi Gras when the same has been declared a legal holiday; and provided further that nothing in any law of this state shall in any manner whatsoever affect the validity of, or render void or voidable, the payment, certification of acceptance of a check or other negotiable instrument, or any other transaction by a bank in Louisiana because done on any holiday or half-holiday or because done on any day upon which such financial institution if remaining open because of the option given it herein, if the payment, certification, acceptance, or other transaction could have been validly done on any other day, provided, however, that in the parishes of Beauregard, Sabine, Vernon, Evangeline and DeSoto the banking institutions may elect to make the whole of Saturdays holidays and close, in lieu of half-holidays on Wednesdays and half-holidays on Saturdays.

(E)(1)(a) Each clerk of a district court, parish court, and city court shall close his office on the following days: New Year's Day, January first; Washington's Birthday, the third Monday in February; Good Friday; Memorial Day, the last Monday in May; the Fourth of July; Labor Day, the first Monday in September; All Saints' Day, November first; Veterans' Day, November eleventh; Thanksgiving Day and the following day, the fourth Thursday and Friday in November; Christmas Eve Day; Christmas Day; and New Year's Eve Day, December thirty-first. Whenever New Year's Day, the Fourth of July, or Christmas Day falls on a Saturday, the preceding Friday shall be a holiday. Whenever New Year's Day, the Fourth of July, or Chrismas Day falls on a Sunday, the following Monday shall be a holiday. In addition, in the City Court of Hammond, Mardi Gras and the day on which the national observance of Martin Luther King, Jr.'s birthday is celebrated shall be legal holidays and the clerk of court shall close his office on these days.

(b) In addition, each clerk of a district court shall close his office on the day upon which the governor has proclaimed Dr. Martin Luther King, Jr.'s birthday as a legal holiday pursuant to R.S. 1:55(B)(2), and, notwithstanding the provisions of Paragraph (2) of this Subsection, shall close his office on any day an emergency situation has been declared by the governor or the local governing authority and governmental entities, including the courthouse, have been ordered to close.

(2) If an emergency situation develops which, in the judgment of the clerk of court, renders it hazardous or otherwise unsafe for employees of the office of the clerk to continue in the performance of their official duties or for the general public to conduct business with the clerk's office, the clerk, with prior approval from the clerk's chief judge or other person authorized to exercise his authority, may or-

der the closing of his office for the duration of the hazardous or unsafe condition. No such closure shall be effective nor shall such period of closing be considered a legal holiday unless prior written approval or written confirmation from such chief judge or person acting on his behalf is received by the clerk of court. When the office is reopened, the clerk shall have published as soon as possible a legal notice in all of the official parish journals of the parishes within the district setting forth the dates of closure, the hour of closure if applicable, the reasons for closure, and a statement that, pursuant to R.S. 1:55(E)(3), these days or parts of days were legal holidays. The clerk shall attach a similar statement to every document, petition, or pleading filed in the office of the clerk on the first day or part of a day his office is open after being closed under the provisions of this Paragraph, whenever the petition or document relates to a cause of action, right of appeal, or other matter against which prescription could have run or time periods imposed by law could have expired.

(3) Only the enumerated holidays in Paragraph (1) of this Subsection, days of closure under Paragraph (2) of this Subsection, Mardi Gras only in those parishes in which the governing authority of the parish declares a holiday under authority of Subsection A(3) of this Section, and all Saturdays and Sundays shall be considered as legal holidays for the purposes of Article 5059 of the Louisiana Code of Civil Procedure.

MAINE

NOTARIES PUBLIC

[ME. REV. STAT. ANN.]

Tit. 4, § 951. Seal; authority to administer oaths.

A notary public may keep a seal of office, whereon is engraven the notary public's name and the words "Notary Public" and "Maine" or its abbreviation "Me.," with the arms of state or such other device as the notary public chooses. When authorized by the laws of this State or of any other state or country to do any official act, the notary public may administer any oath necessary to the completion or validity thereof.

Tit. 4, § 952. Protests of losses; record and copies.

When requested, every notary public shall enter on record all losses or damages sustained or apprehended by sea or land, and all averages and such other matters as, by mercantile usage, appertain to his office, grant warrants of survey on vessels, and all facts, extracts from documents and circumstances so noted shall be signed and sworn to by all the persons appearing to protest. He shall note, extend and record the protest so made, and grant authenticated copies thereof, under his signature and notarial seal, to those who request and pay for them.

Tit. 4, § 953. Demand and notice on bills and notes.

Any notary public may, in behalf of any person interested, present any bill of exchange or other negotiable paper for acceptance or payment to any party liable therefor, notify indorsers or other parties thereto, record and certify all contracts usually recorded or certified by notaries, and in general, do all acts which may be done by notaries public according to the usages of merchants and authorized by law. He shall record all mercantile and marine protests by him noted and done in his official capacity.

Tit. 4, § 954. Acts of notary who is interested in corporation.

Any notary public who is a stockholder, director, officer or employee of a bank or other corporation may take the acknowledgment of any party to any written instrument executed to or by such corporation, or may administer an oath to any other stockholder, director, officer, employee or agent of such corporation, or may protest for nonacceptance or nonpayment bills of exchange, drafts, checks, notes and other negotiable instruments which may be owned or held for collection by such bank or other corporation. It shall be unlawful for any notary public to take the acknowledgment of an instrument by or to a bank or other corporation of which he is a stockholder, director, officer or employee where such notary is a party to such instrument, either individually or as a representative of such bank or other corporation, or to protest any negotiable instrument owned or held for collection by such bank or other corporation, where such notary is individually a party to such instrument.

Tit. 4, § 954-A. Conflict of interest if notary related.

A notary public shall not perform any notarial act for any person if that person is the notary public's spouse, parent, sibling, child, spouse's parent or child's spouse, except that a notary public may solemnize the marriage of the notary public's parent, sibling, child or spouse's parent if the ceremony is witnessed and the marriage certificate signed by another notary public unrelated by marriage or blood to the parties. This section does not affect or apply to notarial acts performed before the effective date of this section.

Tit. 4, § 955. Copies; evidence.

The protest of any foreign or inland bill of exchange, promissory note or order, and all copies or certificates by him granted shall be under his hand and shall be received in all courts as legal evidence of the transactions and as to the notice given to the drawer or indorser and of all facts therein contained.

Tit. 4, § 955-A. Removal from office.

1. **Complaint by Secretary of State.** The Secretary of State may file a complaint with the Administrative Court to have a notary public removed from office.
2. **Action by Administrative Court.** If the Administrative Court, upon complaint by the Secretary of State, finds that the notary public has performed in an improper manner any duty imposed

upon the notary public by law, or has performed acts not authorized by law, the Administrative Court may remove the notary public from office.

Tit. 4, § 955-B. Maintenance of records.

The Secretary of State shall recommend that every notary public keep and maintain records of all notarial acts performed.

Tit. 4, § 956. Resignation or removal; deposit of records.

On the resignation or removal from office of any notary public, his records shall be deposited with the clerk of the judicial courts in the county for which he was appointed. Any notary public who shall, for a period of 3 months, neglect to comply with such requirement and any administrator or executor representing a deceased notary public who shall, for a period of 3 months, neglect to comply with such requirement shall forfeit not less than $50 nor more than $500.

Tit. 4, § 957. Injury or concealment of records.

Whoever knowingly destroys, defaces or conceals such record forfeits not less than $200 nor more than $1,000, and is liable for damages to any person injured in a civil action.

Tit. 4, § 958. Fees for protest.

For each protest of a bill or note, notifying parties, making his certificate thereof in due form and recording his proceedings, a notary public shall receive $1.50.
* * *

ADDITIONAL AUTHORITY

[ME. CONST.]

Art. 5, pt. 1, § 8. To appoint officers; procedure for confirmation; affirmative vote of 2/3 of members required; Governor or President of Senate may call Senate into session; nomination by Governor made 7 days prior to appointment of nominee.

Section 8. The Governor shall nominate, and, subject to confirmation as provided herein, appoint all judicial officers, except judges of probate and justices of the peace if their manner of selection is otherwise provided for by this Constitution or by law, and all other civil and military officers whose appointment is not by this Constitution, or shall not by law be otherwise provided for.

The procedure for confirmation shall be as follows: an appropriate legislative committee comprised of members of both houses in reasonable proportion to their membership as provided by law shall recommend confirmation or denial by majority vote of committee members present and voting. The committee recommendation shall be reviewed by the Senate and upon review shall become final action of confirmation or denial unless the Senate by vote of ⅔ of those members present and voting overrides the committee recommendation. The Senate vote shall be by the yeas and nays.

All statutes enacted to carry out the purposes of the second paragraph of this section shall require the affirmative vote of ⅔ of the members of each House present and voting.

Either the Governor or the President of the Senate shall have the power to call the Senate into session for the purpose of voting upon confirmation of appointments.

Every nomination by the Governor shall be made 7 days at least prior to appointment of the nominee.

[ME. REV. STAT. ANN.]

Tit. 4, § 202. Oaths and acknowledgments.

All oaths required to be taken by personal representatives, trustees, guardians, conservators, or of any other persons in relation to any proceeding in the probate court, or to perpetuate the evidence of the publication of any order of notice, may be administered by the judge or register of probate or any notary public. A certificate thereof, when taken out of court, shall be returned into the registry of probate and there filed. When any person of whom such oath is required, including any parent acknowledging consent to an adoption, resides temporarily or permanently without the State, the oath or acknowledgment may be taken before and be certified by a notary public without the State, a commissioner for the State of Maine or a United States Consul.

Tit. 4, § 1056. Powers of attorneys.

Attorneys at law duly admitted and eligible to practice in the courts of the State shall have all of the powers of notaries public and be authorized to do all acts which may be done by notaries public with the same effect thereof and have the same territorial jurisdiction.

FEES

Tit. 5, § 87. Fees payable by public officers.

A fee of $25 shall be paid to the Secretary of State by any person appointed to the office of notary public, commissioner to take depositions and disclosures, disclosure commissioner and commissioner appointed under Title 33, section 251, before the person enters upon the discharge of official duties.

OFFENSES

Tit. 17-A, § 701. Definitions.

As used in sections 702 and 703:

1. A person "falsely alters" a written instrument when, without the authority of anyone entitled to grant it, he changes a written instrument, whether it be in complete or incomplete form, by means of erasure, obliteration, deletion, insertion of new matter, transposition of matter, or in any other manner, so that such instrument in its thus altered form appears or purports to be in all respects an authentic creation of, or fully authorized by, its ostensible holder, author, maker or drawer;

2. A person "falsely completes" a written instrument when, by adding, inserting or changing matter, he transforms an incomplete written instrument into a complete one, without the authority of anyone entitled to grant it, so that such complete instrument appears or purports to be in all respects an authentic creation of, or fully authorized by, its ostensible author, maker or drawer;

3. A person "falsely makes" a written instrument when he makes or draws a complete written instrument in its entirety or an incomplete written instrument, which purports to be an authentic creation of its ostensible author, maker or drawer, but which is not such, either because the ostensible maker or drawer is fictitious or because, if real, he did not authorize the making or drawing thereof;

4. "Written instrument" includes any token, coin, stamp, seal, badge, trademark, credit card, absentee ballot application, absentee ballot envelope, other evidence or symbol of value, right, privilege or identification, and any paper, document or other written instrument containing written or printed matter or its equivalent;

5. "Complete written instrument" means a written instrument which purports to be a genuine written instrument fully drawn with respect to every essential feature thereof; and

6. "Incomplete written instrument" means a written instrument which contains some matter by way of content or authentication but which re-

quires additional matter in order to render it a complete written instrument.

Tit. 17-A, § 702. Aggravated forgery.

1. A person is guilty of aggravated forgery if, with intent to defraud or deceive another person or government, he falsely makes, completes, endorses or alters a written instrument, or knowingly utters or possesses such an instrument, and the instrument is:

A. Part of an issue of money, stamps, securities or other valuable instruments issued by a government or governmental instrumentality;

B. Part of an issue of stocks, bonds or other instruments representing interests in or claims against an organization or its property;

C. A will, codicil or other instrument providing for the disposition of property after death;

D. A public record or an instrument filed or required or authorized by law to be filed in or with a public office or public employee; or

2. Aggravated forgery is a Class B crime.

Tit. 17-A, § 703. Forgery.

1. A person is guilty of forgery if, with the intent to defraud or deceive another person or government, he:

A. Falsely makes, completes, endorses or alters a written instrument, or knowingly utters or possesses such an instrument; or

B. Causes another, by deception, to sign or execute a written instrument, or utters such an instrument.

2. Violation of this section is:

A. A Class B crime if the face value of the written instrument or the aggregate value of instruments exceeds $5,000;

B. A Class C crime if:

(1) The face value of the written instrument or the aggregate value of instruments exceeds $1,000 but does not exceed $5,000; or

(2) The actor has 2 prior convictions for any combination of theft, violation or attempted violation of this section, violation or attempted violation of section 702 or 708 or any violation or attempted violation of section 401 if the intended crime within the structure is theft, or any violation or attempted violation of section 651. Determination of whether a conviction constitutes a prior conviction for purposes of this subsection shall be pursuant to section 362, subsection 3–A; or

C. Except as provided in paragraphs A and B, forgery is a Class D crime.

3. Amounts of value involved in forgeries may be aggregated in the same manner as provided in section 352, subsection 5, paragraph E. Prosecution of an aggregated forgery may be brought in any venue in which one of the aggregated forgeries was committed.

ACKNOWLEDGMENTS

Tit. 33, § 203. Need for acknowledgment.

Deeds and all other written instruments before recording in the registries of deeds, except those issued by a court of competent jurisdiction and duly attested by the proper officer thereof, and excepting plans and notices of foreclosure of mortgages and certain financing statements as provided in Title 11, section 9–401, and excepting notices of liens for internal revenue taxes and certificates discharging such liens as provided in section 664, shall be acknowledged by the grantors, or by the persons executing any such written instruments, or by one of them, or by their attorney executing the same, or by the lessor in a lease or one of the lessors or his attorney executing the same, before a notary public in the State, or before an attorney-at-law duly admitted and eligible to practice in the courts of the State, if within the State; or before any clerk of a court of record having a seal, notary public or commissioner appointed by the Governor of this State for the purpose, or a commissioner authorized in the State where the acknowledgment is taken, within the United States; or before a minister, vice-consul or consul of the United States or notary public in any foreign country.

Any person who is in the Armed Forces of the United States, and who executes a general or special power of attorney, deed, lease, contract or any instrument that is required to be recorded, may acknowledge the same as his true act and deed before any lieutenant or officer of senior grade thereto in the Army, U.S. Marine Corps or Air Force or before any ensign or officer of senior grade thereto in the Navy or Coast Guard and the record of such acknowledgment by said officers shall be received and have the same force and effect as acknowledgments under the other provisions of this section, and all such instruments heretofore executed are hereby validated as to acknowledgment and authenticity. Powers of attorney and other instruments requiring seals executed by such members of the armed forces may be accepted for recordation in registries of deeds and other offices of record in cases where no seal is affixed after the name of the person or persons executing the instrument with like force and effect as though seals were affixed thereto.

Any notary public who is a stockholder, director, officer or employee of a bank or other corporation may take the acknowledgment of any party to any written instrument executed to or by such corporation, provided such notary public is not a party to such instrument either individually or as a representative of such bank or other corporation.

This section shall not be construed as invalidating any instrument duly executed in accordance with the statutes heretofore in effect or made valid by any such statute. All such instruments may be admitted to record which at the time of their execution or subsequent validation could be so recorded.

Notwithstanding any of the requirements in this section, an instrument with an acknowledgment conforming to the requirements of the Uniform Recognition of Acknowledgments Act, Title 4, section 1011 et seq., shall be accepted for recording purposes.

Tit. 33, § 207. Recording master form.

An instrument containing a form or forms of covenants, conditions, obligations, powers and other clauses of a mortgage, or deed of trust, may be recorded in the registry of deeds of any county and the recorder of such county, upon the request of any person, on tender of the lawful fees therefor, shall record the same in his registry. Every such instrument shall be entitled on the face thereof as a "Master form recorded by _____" (name of person causing the instrument to be recorded). Such instrument need not be acknowledged to be entitled to record.

Tit. 33, § 306. Indorsement of certificate of acknowledgment.

A certificate of acknowledgment or proof of execution must be indorsed on or annexed to the deed, and then the deed and certificate may be recorded in the registry of deeds. No deed can be recorded without such certificate.

Tit. 33, § 351. Acknowledgments after commission expired.

When a person authorized to take acknowledgments takes and certifies one in good faith after the expiration of his commission, not being aware of it, such acknowledgment is as valid as if done before such expiration.

Uniform Recognition of Acknowledgments Act

Tit. 4, § 1011. Recognition of notarial acts performed outside this State.

For the purposes of this Act, "notarial acts" means acts which the laws and regulations of this State authorize notaries public of this State to perform, including the administering of oaths and affirmations, taking proof of execution and acknowledgments of instruments, and attesting documents. Notarial acts may be performed outside this State for use in this State with the same effect as if performed by a notary public of this State by the following persons authorized pursuant to the laws and regulations of other governments in addition to any other person authorized by the laws and regulations of this State:

1. **Notary public.** A notary public authorized to perform notarial acts in the place in which the act is performed;

2. **Judge; clerk.** A judge, clerk or deputy clerk of any court of record in the place in which the notarial act is performed;

3. **Foreign service.** An officer of the foreign service of the United States, a consular agent or any other person authorized by regulation of the United States Department of State to perform notarial acts in the place in which the act is performed;

4. **Officer in Armed Forces.** A commissioned officer in active service with the Armed Forces of the United States and any other person authorized by regulation of the Armed Forces to perform notarial acts if the notarial act is performed for one of the following or his dependents: A merchant seaman of the United States, a member of the Armed Forces of the United States or any other person serving with or accompanying the Armed Forces of the United States; or

5. **Others.** Any other person authorized to perform notarial acts in the place in which the act is performed.

Tit. 4, § 1012. Authentication of authority of officer.

1. **Proof.** If the notarial act is performed by any of the persons described in section 1011, subsections 1 to 4, other than a person authorized to perform notarial acts by the laws or regulations of a foreign country, the signature, rank or title and serial number, if any, of the person are sufficient proof of the authority of a holder of that rank or title to perform the act. Further proof of his authority is not required.

2. **—other.** If the notarial act is performed by a person authorized by the laws or regulations of a foreign country to perform the act, there is sufficient proof of the authority of that person to act if:

A. Either a foreign service officer of the United States resident in the country in which the act is performed or a diplomatic or consular officer of the foreign country resident in the United States certifies that a person holding that office is authorized to perform the act;

B. The official seal of the person performing the notarial act is affixed to the document; or

C. The title and indication of authority to perform notarial acts of the person appears either in a digest of foreign law or in a list customarily used as a source of such information.

3. —other persons. If the notarial act is performed by a person other than one described in subsections 1 and 2, there is sufficient proof of the authority of that person to act if the clerk of a court of record in the place in which the notarial act is performed certifies to the official character of that person and to his authority to perform the notarial act.

4. Signature and title. The signature and title of the person performing the act are prima facie evidence that he is a person with the designated title and that the signature is genuine.

Tit. 4, § 1013. Certificate of person taking acknowledgment.

The person taking an acknowledgment shall certify that:

1. Appearance. The person acknowledging appeared before him and acknowledged he executed the instrument; and

2. Person known. The person acknowledging was known to the person taking the acknowledgment or that the person taking the acknowledgment had satisfactory evidence that the person acknowledging was the person described in and who executed the instrument.

Tit. 4, § 1014. Recognition of certificate of acknowledgment.

The form of a certificate of acknowledgment used by a person whose authority is recognized under section 1011 shall be accepted in this State if:

1. Laws of the State. The certificate is in a form prescribed by the laws or regulations of this State;

2. Laws of state where acknowledged. The certificate is in a form prescribed by the laws or regulations applicable in the place in which the acknowledgment is taken; or

3. Certain words. The certificate contains the words "acknowledged before me," or their substantial equivalent.

Tit. 4, § 1014-A. Presumption of compliance.

For the purposes of section 1014, subsection 2, a certificate of acknowledgment taken in a state other than Maine shall be presumed to be in a form prescribed by the laws or regulations applicable in the place in which the acknowledgment is taken if upon that certificate appears, in stamped, printed or embossed form, either separately or together:

1. Notary public. The words "notary public;"

2. Name. The name of the notary public; and

3. State. The name of the state, or an abbreviation of the name of the state, in which the acknowledgment was taken.

Tit. 4, § 1015. Certificate of acknowledgment.

1. Definition. The words "acknowledged before me" means:

A. That the person acknowledging appeared before the person taking the acknowledgment;

B. That he acknowledged he executed the instrument;

C. That, in the case of:

(1) A natural person, he executed the instrument for the purposes therein stated;

(2) A corporation, the officer or agent acknowledged he held the position or title set forth in the instrument and certificate, he signed the instrument on behalf of the corporation by proper authority, and the instrument was the act of the corporation for the purpose therein stated;

(3) A partnership, the partner or agent acknowledged he signed the instrument on behalf of the partnership by proper authority and he executed the instrument as the act of the partnership for the purposes therein stated;

(4) A person acknowledging as principal by an attorney in fact, he executed the instrument by proper authority as the act of the principal for the purposes therein stated;

(5) A person acknowledging as a public officer, trustee, administrator, guardian or other representative, he signed the instrument by proper authority and he executed the instrument in the capacity and for the purposes therein stated; and

D. That the person taking the acknowledgment either knew or had satisfactory evidence that the person acknowledging was the person named in the instrument or certificate.

Tit. 4, § 1016. Short forms of acknowledgment.

The forms of acknowledgment set forth in this section may be used and are sufficient for their respective purposes under any law of this State. The forms shall be known as "Statutory Short Forms of Acknowledgment" and may be referred to by that name. The authorization of the forms in this section does not preclude the use of other forms.

1. Individual. For an individual acting in his own right:

State of _____

County of _____

The foregoing instrument was acknowledged before me this (date) by (name of person acknowledged).

> (Signature of person taking acknowledgment)
> (Title or rank)
> (Serial number, if any)

2. Corporation. For a corporation:

State of _____

County of _____

The foregoing instrument was acknowledged before me this (date) by (name of officer or agent, title of officer or agent) of (name of corporation acknowledging) a (state or place of incorporation) corporation, on behalf of the corporation..

> (Signature of person taking acknowledgment)
> (Title or rank)
> (Serial number, if any)

3. Partnership. For a partnership:

State of _____

County of _____

The foregoing instrument was acknowledged before me this (date) by (name of acknowledging partner or agent), partner (or agent) on behalf of (name of partnership), a partnership.

> (Signature of person taking acknowledgment)
> (Title or rank)
> (Serial number, if any)

4. Principal. For an individual acting as principal by an attorney in fact:

State of _____

County of _____

The foregoing instrument was acknowledged before me this (date) by (name of attorney in fact) as attorney in fact on behalf of (name of principal).

> (Signature of person taking acknowledgment)
> (Title or rank)
> (Serial number, if any)

5. Public Officer. By any public officer, trustee or personal representative:

State of _____

County of _____

The foregoing instrument was acknowledged before me this (date) by (name and title of position).

> (Signature of person taking acknowledgment)
> (Title or rank)
> (Serial number, if any)

Tit. 4, § 1017. Acknowledgments not affected by this Act.

A notarial act performed prior to October 1, 1969 is not affected by this Act. This Act provides an additional method of proving notarial acts. Nothing in this Act diminishes or invalidates the recognition accorded to notarial acts by other laws or regulations of this State.

Tit. 4, § 1018. Uniformity of interpretation.

This Act shall be so interpreted as to make uniform the laws of those states which enact it.

Tit. 4, § 1019. Short title.

This Act may be cited as the Uniform Recognition of Acknowledgments Act.

DEPOSITIONS

[ME. R. CIV. P.]

RULE 28. Persons before whom depositions may be taken.

(a) Within the State. Within the state depositions shall be taken before a justice of the peace or notary public or a person appointed by the court. A person so appointed has power to administer oaths and take testimony.

(b) Outside the State. Within another state, or within a territory or insular possession subject to the dominion of the United States, or in a foreign country, depositions may be taken (1) on notice before a person authorized to administer oaths in the place in which the examination is held, either by the law thereof or by the law of the United States, or (2) before a person appointed or commissioned by the court, and such a person shall have the power by virtue of his appointment or commission to administer any necessary oath and take testimony, or (3) pursuant to a letter rogatory. A commission or a letter rogatory shall be issued on application and notice and on terms that are just and appropriate. It is not requisite to the issuance of a commission or a letter rogatory that the taking of the deposition in any other manner is impracticable or inconvenient; and both a commission and a letter rogatory may be issued in proper cases. A notice or commission may designate the person before whom the deposition is to be taken either by name or descriptive title. A letter rogatory may be addressed "To the Appropriate Authority in (here name the state, territory or country)." Evidence obtained in a foreign country in response to a letter rogatory need not be excluded merely for the reason that it is not a verbatim transcript or that the testimony was not taken under oath or for any similar departure from the requirements for depositions taken within the United States under these rules.

(c) Disqualification for Interest. No deposition shall be taken before a person who is a relative or employee or attorney or counsel of any of the parties, or is a relative or employee of such attorney or counsel, or is financially interested in the action.

(d) Depositions for Use in Foreign Jurisdictions. Whenever the deposition of any person is to be taken in this state pursuant to the laws of another state or of the United States or of another country for use in proceedings there, the Superior Court in the county where the deponent resides or is employed or transacts his business in person may, upon petition, make an order directing issuance of a subpoena as provided in Rule 45, in aid of the taking of the deposition, and may make any order in accordance with Rule 30(d), 37(a) or 37(b)(1).

COMMISSIONER OF DEEDS

[ME. REV. STAT. ANN.]

Tit. 33, § 251. Appointment; powers.

The Governor may appoint one or more commissioners in any other of the United States and in any foreign country, who shall continue in office during his pleasure; and have authority to take the acknowledgment and proof of the execution of any deed, other conveyance or lease of lands lying in this State; and of any contract, letter of attorney or any other writing, under seal or not, to be used or recorded in this State.

Tit. 33, § 252. Legal effect of official acts.

The acknowledgment or proof, taken according to the laws of this State and certified by any such commissioner under his seal of office, annexed to or indorsed on such instrument, shall have the same force and effect as if done by an officer authorized to perform such acts within this State.

Tit. 33, § 253. Administration of oaths and depositions.

Every commissioner appointed under section 251 may administer any oath lawfully required in this State to any person willing to take it; and take and duly certify all depositions to be used in any of the courts in this State, in conformity to the laws thereof, on interrogatories proposed under commission from a court of this State, by consent of parties or on legal notice given to the opposite party. All such acts shall be as valid as if done and certified according to law by a judicial officer or notary public in this State.

Tit. 33, § 254. Qualifications and seal.

Every commissioner appointed under section 251, before performing any duty or exercising any power by virtue of his appointment, shall take and subscribe an oath or affirmation, before a judge or clerk of one of the superior courts of the state or country in which he resides, well and faithfully to execute and perform all his official duties under the laws of this State; which oath and a description of his seal of office shall be filed in the office of the Secretary of State.

LEGAL HOLIDAYS

Tit. 4, § 1051. Legal holidays.

No court may be held on Sunday or any day designated for the annual Thanksgiving; New Year's Day, January 1st; Martin Luther King, Jr., Day, the 3rd Monday in January; Washington's Birthday, the 3rd Monday in February; Patriot's Day, the 3rd Monday in April; Memorial Day, the last Monday in May, but if the Federal Government designates May 30th as the date for observance of Memorial Day, the 30th of May; the 4th of July; Labor Day, the first Monday of September; Columbus Day, the 2nd Monday in October; Veterans' Day, November 11th; or on Christmas Day. The Chief Justice of the Supreme Judicial Court may order that court be held on a legal holiday when he finds that the interests of justice and judicial economy in any particular case will be served. The public offices in county buildings may be closed to business on the holidays named in this section. When any one of the holidays named in this section falls on Sunday, the Monday following shall be observed as a holiday, with all the privileges applying to any of the days named in this section.

MARYLAND

NOTARIES PUBLIC

[MD. ANN. CODE]

Art. 68, § 1. Appointment, qualifications, application, term, commission and fees.

(a) Appointment. — (1) The Governor, on approval of the application by a senator representing the senatorial district and subdistrict in which the applicant resides, shall appoint and commission in his discretion and judgment any number of persons as notaries public, as provided herein.

(2) The Governor, on approval of the application by the Secretary of State, shall appoint and commission out-of-state court reporters as notaries public, as provided in this article.

(b) Qualifications. — (1) Every person appointed shall be at least 18 years of age, of good moral character and integrity, a resident in this State for a period of 1 year prior to appointment, and a resident of the senatorial district from which he or she is appointed.

(2) The residence requirements shall not apply to persons having an appointment as an official court reporter by any court of any county or Baltimore City.

(3) The residence requirements do not apply to out-of-state court reporters applying for appointment as a notary public in this State; however, an out-of-state court reporter shall be deemed to have irrevocably appointed the Secretary of State as his or her agent upon whom may be served any sum-

mons, subpoena, subpoena duces tecum, or other process.

(4) Notwithstanding the provisions of paragraphs (1) and (2) of this subsection, and subject to the provisions of this subtitle, a notary commissioned in a state other than the State of Maryland who moves to this State shall be a resident of this State for a period of 6 months prior to appointment as notary public in this State.

(c) *Application; notice of appointment.* — Applications for original appointment as a notary public shall be made on forms prepared by the Secretary of State and shall be sworn to by the applicant, and must bear thereon or be accompanied by the written approval of a senator representing the senatorial district and subdistrict in which the applicant resides. An out-of-state court reporter shall make an application for original appointment as a notary public as described above through a Maryland State Senator. Completed applications shall be filed with the Secretary of State. When the appointment is made by the Governor, the Secretary of State shall so notify the applicant.

(d) *Term.* — The term of a notary public commission is 4 years.

(2) The Secretary of State shall adopt, by regulation, a staggered system for the expiration and renewal of notary public commissions.

(e) *Renewal of commission; qualifying; revocation and reinstatement.* — Notary public commissions may be renewed from term to term, and the Secretary of State shall issue an application of renewal to the notary public at or prior to the expiration of the term of the existing commission. Upon receipt of a satisfactory application of renewal from the notary public, the Secretary shall issue notice of renewal to the notary public. Within thirty (30) days after the issuance by the Secretary of State of notice of appointment or renewal the notary public shall qualify before the appropriate clerk of the court and pay the fees herein prescribed. An out-of-state court reporter commissioned as a notary public shall qualify before the clerk of the circuit court in any county or Baltimore City and pay the fees prescribed. The appointment and commission of any notary public who fails to qualify and pay the fees within said time shall stand revoked, and in such case the court clerk shall return the commission of the notary public to the Secretary of State with a certification that the notary public failed to qualify and pay the fees within the required time, but the Secretary of State for good cause shown may reinstate the appointment and commission.

(f) *Fees.* At the time the notice of appointment by the Governor or the notice of renewal is issued, the Secretary of State shall forward to the clerk of the circuit court of the county in which the notary public resides or in the case of the notary public who is an out-of-state court reporter, to the clerk of the circuit court in the county or Baltimore City where the notary is to qualify, a commission signed by the Governor and Secretary of State under the great seal of the State. The clerk of the court shall deliver the commission to the notary public upon qualification and payment of the prescribed fees by the notary public. Each notary public shall pay to the clerk a fee of one dollar ($1.00) for qualifying the notary public and registering his name, address, and commission expiration date of the notary public, and a fee of ten dollars ($10.00) or such lesser amount as may be prescribed by the Secretary of State for the commission issued. The fee shall be paid by the clerk to the treasury of the State of Maryland. The Secretary of State may fix such other reasonable fees as may be required for the processing of applications and the issuance and renewal of notarial commissions.

(g) *Forms.* The Secretary of State may prepare and adopt forms as required under this section, including the form of original and renewal applications, the form of commissions, and forms for renewal of commissions.

Art. 68, § 2. Removal.

Any notary public may be removed from office by the Governor for good cause either in his own initiative or upon a request made to him in writing by the Senator who approved the appointment. After notice to the notary and the opportunity for a hearing before the Secretary of State, the Secretary of State shall submit his recommendation to the Governor for action as the Governor determines to be required in the case.

Art. 68, § 3. Administration of oaths; certificate under seal as evidence.

Each notary public shall have the power of administering oaths according to law in all matters and cases of a civil nature in which a justice of the peace might have administered an oath prior to July 5, 1971, and with the same effect; and a certificate under the notarial seal of a notary public shall be sufficient evidence of his having administered such oath in his character as notary public.

Art. 68, § 4. Acknowledgments; protests and declarations.

A notary shall have power to receive the proof or acknowledgment of all instruments of writing relating to commerce or navigation and such other writings as have been usually proved and acknowledged before notaries public; and to make protests and declarations and testify the truth thereof under his seal of office concerning all matters done by him in virtue of his office.

Art. 68, § 5. Register; certified copies of record.

Each notary shall keep a fair register of all protests and other official acts by him done in virtue of his office and shall, when required, give a certified copy of any record in his office to any person applying for the same, the said person paying the usual fees therefor.

Art. 68, § 6. Notary to have seal or stamp.

(a) *In general.* — Every notary shall provide a public notarial seal or stamp with which he shall authenticate his acts, instruments and attestations, on which seal or stamp shall be shown such device as he may think proper and for legend shall have the name, surname and office of the notary and the place of his residence, which shall be designated by the county of his residence or if the notary is a resident of the City of Baltimore, by the City of Baltimore.

(b) *Where notary is out-of-state court reporter.* — If the notary is an out-of-state court reporter, the legend shall have the name, surname, office of the notary, and the county where the notary qualified.

(c) *Inclusion of expiration date of notary's commission.* — Every notary shall include on each act, instrument, or attestation the expiration date of the notary's commission as a notary public.

Art. 68, § 7. Acting outside of county or city for which appointed.

A notary may exercise all functions of the office of notary in any other county or city than the county or city for which he may be appointed, with the same power and effect in all respects as if the same were exercised in the county or city for which he may be appointed.

Art. 68, § 8. Form of protest.

It shall not be lawful for any notary public to sign and issue any protest except in the form prescribed by the Comptroller.

Art. 68, § 10. When notaries may not take acknowledgments and protests.

It shall be lawful for any notary public who is a stockholder, director, officer or employee of a bank or other corporation to take the acknowledgment of any party to any written instrument executed to or by such corporation, or to administer an oath to any other stockholder, director, officer, employee or agent of such corporation, or to protest for non-acceptance or nonpayment bills of exchange, drafts, checks, notes and other negotiable instruments which may be owned or held for collection of such corporation; provided, it shall be unlawful for any notary public to take the acknowledgment of an instrument by or to a bank or other corporation of which he is a stockholder, director, officer or employee, where such notary is a party to such instrument, either individually or as a representative of such corporation, or to protest any negotiable instrument owned or held for collection by such corporation, where such notary is individually a party to such instrument.

Art. 68, § 11. Out-of-state court reporter commissioned as notary public—Limitation of powers.

An out-of-state court reporter commissioned as a notary public has powers limiteds to swearing in witnesses and taking depositions.

Art. 68, § 12. Same—Charging of fees.

An out-of-state court reporter commissioned as a notary public may charge the fees provided in Article 36, § 23 of the Code for the services the out-of-state notary has the power to perform.

Art. 68, § 13. Same—Reciprocity in issuance of commissions thereto.

Subject to the provisions of this section, limited notary public commissions for out-of-state reporters shall be issued only to persons residing in states, or the District of Columbia, which allow similar certification for Maryland resident notaries public.

ADDITIONAL AUTHORITY

[MD. CONST.]

Art. IV, § 45. Notaries Public.

Notaries Public may be appointed for each county, and the city of Baltimore, in the manner, for the purpose, and with the powers now fixed, or which may hereafter be prescribed by Law.

[MD. CONST., DECLARATION OF RIGHTS]

Art. 35. Holding more than one office prohibited; persons in public trust not to receive presents from other states, etc.; position of notary public not an office of profit.

That no person shall hold, at the same time, more than one office of profit, created by the Constitution or Laws of this State; nor shall any person in public trust receive any present from any foreign Prince or State, or from the United States, or any of them, without the approbation of this State. The position of Notary Public shall not be considered an office of profit within the meaning of this Article....

FEES

[MD. ANN. CODE]

Art. 36, § 23. Fees and expenses.

(a) *Fees.* — The Secretary of State shall adopt rules and regulations to establish fees, not to exceed $2 for an original notarial act, and an appropriate lesser amount for the repetition of that original notarial act or to make a copy of the matter addressed by that original notarial act.

(b) *Mileage expenses.* — A notary public may charge 19 cents per mile, or a higher amount set by regulation of the Secretary of State, as compensation for travel required for the performance of a notarial act.

ACKNOWLEDGMENTS

Uniform Acknowledgments Act

Art. 18, § 1. Acknowledgments to conform to subtitle.

Any instrument may be acknowledged in the manner and form now provided by the laws of this State, or as provided by this subtitle.

Art. 18, § 2. Acknowledgment within the State.

The acknowledgment of any instrument may be made in this State before:

(1) A judge of a court of record;

(2) A clerk or deputy clerk of a court having a seal;

(3) A notary public; or

(4) A master in chancery.

Art. 18, § 3. Acknowledgment within the United States.

The acknowledgment of any instrument may be made without the State but within the United States or a territory or insular possession of the United States or the District of Columbia and within the jurisdiction of the officer, before:

(1) A clerk or deputy clerk of any federal court;

(2) A clerk or deputy clerk of any court of record of any state or other jurisdiction;

(3) A notary public.

Art. 18, § 4. Acknowledgment without the United States.

The acknowledgment of any instrument may be made without the United States before:

(1) An ambassador, minister, charge d'affaires, counselor to or secretary of a legation, consul general, counsul, vice-consul, commercial attache, or consular agent of the United States accredited to the country where the acknowledgment is made.

(2) A notary public of the country where the acknowledgment is made.

(3) A judge or clerk of a court of record of the country where the acknowledgment is made.

Art. 18, § 5. Requisites of acknowledgment.

The officer taking the acknowledgment shall know or have satisfactory evidence that the person making the acknowledgment is the person described in and who executed the instrument.

Art. 18, § 6. Acknowledgment by a married woman.

An acknowledgment of a married woman may be made in the same form as though she were unmarried.

Art. 18, § 7. Forms of certificates.

An officer taking the acknowledgment shall endorse thereon or attach thereto a certificate substantially in one of the following forms:

(a) *By individuals.*

State of ....

County of ....

On this the ...... day of ......, 19. .., before me, ..., the undersigned officer, personally appeared ......, known to me (or satisfactorily proven) to be the person whose name . . . . . . subscribed to the within instrument and acknowledged that ...... he . . . executed the same for the purposes therein contained.

In witness whereof I hereunto set my hand and official seal.

....
....
Title of officer.

(b) By a corporation.

State of ....
County of ....

On this the ...... day of ......, 19. .., before me, ..., the undersigned officer, personally appeared ......, who acknowledged himself to be the ...... of ......, a corporation, and that he, as such ......, being authorized so to do, executed the foregoing instrument for the purposes therein contained, by signing the name of the corporation by himself as ......

In witness whereof I hereunto set my hand and official seal.

....
....
Title of officer.

(c) By an attorney in fact.

State of ....
County of ....

On this the ...... day of ......, 19. .., before me, ..., the undersigned officer, personally appeared ......, known to be (or satisfactorily proven) to be the person whose name is subscribed as attorney in fact for ......, and acknowledged that he executed the same as the act of his principal for the purposes therein contained.

In witness whereof I hereunto set my hand and official seal.

....
....
Title of officer.

(d) By any public officer or deputy thereof; or by any trustee, administrator, guardian, or executor.

State of ....
County of ....

On this the ...... day of ......, 19. .., before me, ..., the undersigned officer, personally appeared ......, of the State (county or city as the case may be) of ......, known to me (or satisfactorily proven) to be the person described in the foregoing instrument, and acknowledged that he executed the same in the capacity therein stated and for the purposes therein contained.

In witness whereof I hereunto set my hand and official seal.

....
....
Title of officer.

Art. 18, § 8. Execution of certificate.

The certificate of the acknowledging officer shall be completed by his signature, his official seal if he has one, the title of his office, and if he is a notary public, the date his commission expires.

Art. 18, § 9. Authentication of acknowledgments.

(a) If the acknowledgment is taken within this State or is made without the United States by an officer of the United States no authentication shall be necessary.

(b) If the acknowledgment is taken without this State, but in the United States, a territory or insular possession of the United States, or the District of Columbia, no authentication shall be necessary. The certificate may, however, be authenticated by a certificate as to the official character of such officer, executed, if the acknowledgment is taken by a clerk or deputy clerk of a court, by the presiding judge of the court, or, if the acknowledgment is taken by a notary public, by a clerk of a court of record of the county, parish or district in which the acknowledgment is taken. The signature to such authenticating certificate may be a facsimile printed, stamped, photographed or engraved thereon when the certificate bears the seal of the authenticating officer.

(c) If the acknowledgment is made without the United States and by a notary public or a judge or clerk of a court of record of the country where the acknowledgment is made, the certificate shall be authenticated by a certificate under the great seal of state of the country, affixed by the custodian of such seal, or by a certificate of a diplomatic, consular or commercial officer of the United States accredited to that country, certifying as to the official character of such officer.

Art. 18, § 10. Acknowledgments under laws of other states.

Notwithstanding any provision in this subtitle contained, the acknowledgment of any instrument without this State in compliance with the manner and form prescribed by the laws of the place of its execution, if in a state, a territory or insular possession of the United States, or in the District of Columbia, verified by the official seal of the officer before whom it is acknowledged, shall have the same effect as an acknowledgment in the manner and form prescribed by the laws of this State for instruments executed within the State.

Art. 18, § 11. Acknowledgments by persons serving in or with the armed forces of the United States and their spouses or dependents within or without the United States.

In addition to the acknowledgment of instruments in the manner and form and as otherwise authorized by this subtitle, any person serving in or with the armed forces of the United States and their respective spouses or their dependents, may acknowledge the same wherever located before any commissioned officer in active service of the armed forces of the United States with the rank of second lieutenant or higher in the Army, Air Force or Marine Corps, or ensign or higher in the Navy or United States Coast Guard. The instrument shall not be rendered invalid by the failure to state therein the place of execution or acknowledgment. No authentication of the officers' certificate of acknowledgment shall be required but the officer taking the acknowledgment shall endorse thereon or attach thereto a certificate substantially in the following form:

On this the . . . . . . day of . . . . . ., 19. . ., before me, ..., the undersigned officer, personally appeared . . . ., known
(Serial No.) (if any)
to me (or satisfactorily proven) to be (serving in or with the armed forces of the United States) the spouse of) (a dependent of) . . . .,
(Serial No.) (if any)
a person serving in or with the armed forces of the United States and to be the person whose name is subscribed to the within instrument and acknowledged that . . . . . . he . . . . . . executed the same for the purpose therein contained. And the undersigned does further certify that he is at the date of this certificate a commissioned officer of the rank stated below and is in the active service of the armed forces of the United States.

. . . .
Signature of officer.

. . . .
Rank and Serial No. of Officer and Command to Which Attached.

Art. 18, § 12. Acknowledgments not affected by this subtitle.

No acknowledgment heretofore taken shall be affected by anything contained herein.

Art. 18, § 13. Uniformity of interpretation.

This subtitle shall be so interpreted as to make uniform the laws of those states which enact it.

Art. 18, § 14. Name of act.

This subtitle may be cited as the Uniform Acknowledgments Act.

Notarial Acts Before Commissioned Officers

Art. 18, § 15. Performance of notarial acts before commissioned officers.

(a) *When authorized.* — In addition to the acknowledgment of instruments and the performance of other notarial acts in the manner and form and as otherwise authorized by law, instruments may be acknowledged, documents attested, oaths and affirmations administered, depositions and affidavits executed, and other notarial acts performed, before or by any commissioned officer in active service of the armed forces of the United States with the rank of second lieutenant or higher in the Army or Marine Corps, or with the rank of ensign or higher in the Navy or Coast Guard, or with equivalent rank in any other component part of the armed forces of the United States, by any person who either (1) is a member of the armed forces of the United States, or (2) is serving as a merchant seaman outside the limits of the United States included within the forty-eight states and the District of Columbia; or (3) is outside said limits by permission, assignment or direction of any department or official of the United States government, in connection with any activity pertaining to the prosecution of any war in which the United States is then engaged.

(b) *Validation of such acts heretofore done.* — Such acknowledgment of instruments, attestation of documents, administration of oaths and affirmations, execution of depositions and affidavits, and performance of other notarial acts, heretofore or hereafter made or taken, are hereby declared legal, valid and binding, and instruments and documents so acknowledged, authenticated, or sworn to shall be admissible in evidence and eligible to record in this State under the same circumstances, and with the same force and effect as if such acknowledgment, attestation, oath, affirmation, deposition, affidavit, or other notarial act, had been made or taken within this State before or by a duly qualified officer or official as otherwise provided by law.

(c) *What certificate to show.* — In the taking of acknowledgments and the performing of other notarial acts requiring certification, a certificate endorsed upon or attached to the instrument or document, which shows the date of the notarial act and which states, in substance, that the person appearing before the officer acknowledged the instrument as his act or made or signed the instrument or document under oath, shall be sufficient for all intents and purposes. The instrument or document shall not be rendered invalid by the failure to state the place of execution or acknowledgment.

(*d*) *Prima facie evidence of authority.* — If the signature, rank, and branch of service or subdivision thereof, of any such commissioned officer appear upon such instrument or document or certificate, no further proof of the authority of such officer so to act shall be required and such action by such commissioned officer shall be prima facie evidence that the person making such oath or acknowledgment is within the purview of this section.

Art. 18, § 16. Validation of certain acknowledgments.

Any legal instrument which has been properly acknowledged within the two years next preceding June 1, 1953, according to the laws and practices then existing, shall not be construed to be defective or wrongfully acknowledged by reason of any provision contained in Chapter 404, Acts 1953, but the same shall be construed and treated as properly acknowledged for all the purposes of said chapter.

Corporations and Associations

[Md. Corps. & Ass'ns Code Ann.]

§ 1-303. Corporate acknowledgments.

(*a*) *By attorney.* — A corporation may acknowledge by its appointed attorney any document required by law to be acknowledged and the appointment may be in the document.

(*b*) *By president or vice-president.* — The document may be acknowledged by the president or a vice-president of the corporation without any appointment.

DEPOSITIONS

Uniform Foreign Depositions Act

[Md. Cts. & Jud. Proc. Code Ann.]

§ 9-401. Authority to act.

Whenever any mandate, writ, or commission is issued out of any court of record in any other state, territory, district, or foreign jurisdiction, or whenever upon notice or agreement it is required to take the testimony of a witness or witnesses in the State, witnesses may be compelled to appear and testify in the same manner and by the same process and proceeding as may be employed for the purpose of taking testimony in proceedings pending in the State.

§ 9-402. Uniformity of interpretation.

This act shall be so interpreted and construed as to effectuate its general purposes to make uniform the law of those states which enact it.

§ 9-403. Short title.

This act may be cited as the Maryland Uniform Foreign Depositions Act.

Rules of Civil Procedure, Circuit Court

RULE 2-414. Deposition—Officer before whom taken.

(a) **In This State.** — In this State, a deposition shall be taken before any person authorized to administer an oath.

(b) **In Other States.** — In any other state of the United States or in a territory, district, or possession of the United States, a deposition shall be taken before any person authorized to administer an oath by the laws of the United States or by the laws of the place where the deposition is taken or before any person appointed by the court in which the action is pending. The person appointed has the power to administer an oath and take testimony.

(c) **In Foreign Countries.** — In a foreign country, a deposition may be taken (1) on notice before any person authorized to administer an oath in the place in which the deposition is taken, either by the laws of that place or by the laws of the United States, or (2) before any person commissioned by the court, which person has the power by virtue of the commission to administer an oath and take testimony, or (3) pursuant to a letter rogatory. A commission or a letter rogatory shall be issued on motion and notice and on terms that are just and appropriate. It is not necessary to the issuance of a commission or a letter rogatory that the taking of the deposition in any other manner is impracticable or inconvenient, and both a commission and a letter rogatory may be issued in proper cases. A notice or commission may designate the person before whom the deposition is to be taken either by name or descriptive title. A letter rogatory may be addressed "To the Appropriate Authority in (here name the country)." Evidence obtained in response to a letter rogatory need not be excluded merely for the reason that it is not a verbatim transcript or that the testimony was not taken under oath or for any similar departure from the requirements for depositions taken within the United States under these rules.

(d) **Disqualification for Interest.** — A deposition shall not be taken before a person who is a relative or employee or attorney of a party, or is a relative or employee of an attorney of a party, or is financially interested in the action.

(e) **Objections.** — Any objection to the taking of a deposition because of the disqualification of the officer is waived unless made before the deposition begins or as soon thereafter as the disqualification becomes known or could be discovered with reasonable diligence.

LEGAL HOLIDAYS

[MD. ANN. CODE]

Art. 1, § 27. Legal holidays.

(a) *"Legal holiday" defined.* — In this Code and any rule, regulation, or directive adopted under it, "legal holiday" means:

(1) January 1, for New Year's Day;

(2) January 15, for Dr. Martin Luther King, Jr.'s birthday;

(3) February 12, for Lincoln's birthday;

(4) The third Monday in February, for Washington's birthday;

(5) March 25, for Maryland Day;

(6) Good Friday;

(7) May 30, for Memorial Day, unless the United States Congress designates another day for observance of that legal holiday, in which case, the day designated by the United States Congress;

(8) July 4, for Independence Day;

(9) The first Monday in September, for Labor Day;

(10) September 12, for Defenders' Day;

(11) October 12, for Columbus Day, unless the United States Congress designates another day for observance of that legal holiday, in which case, the day designated by the United States Congress;

(12) November 11, for Veterans' Day;

(13) The fourth Thursday in November, for Thanksgiving Day;

(14) December 25, for Christmas Day;

(15) Each statewide general election day in this State; and

(16) Each other day that the President of the United States or the Governor designates for general cessation of business.

Bank Holidays

[MD. FIN. INST. CODE ANN.]

§ 5-701. Definitions.

(a) *In general.* — In this subtitle the following words have the meanings indicated.

(b) *Federal holiday.* — "Federal holiday" means as to each corresponding legal holiday, the date that the federal government designates for observance of the holiday.

(c) *Optional bank holiday.* — "Optional bank holiday" means a day on which a banking institution is authorized to be closed.

§ 5-702. Scope of subtitle.

For the purposes of this subtitle, the operation of an electronic terminal or the conduct of internal operations by a banking institution does not constitute being open for business.

§ 5-703. Required business days.

A banking institution shall be open for business on each day during the year except for the days on which the banking institution is required or authorized by this subtitle to be closed.

§ 5-704. Sundays.

Each banking institution shall be closed on Sunday.

§ 5-705. Legal holidays.

(a) *Mandatory bank holidays.* — (1) Subject to paragraph (2) of this subsection, each banking institution shall be closed on the following legal holidays:

(i) New Year's Day;

(ii) Dr. Martin Luther King, Jr.'s Birthday;

(iii) Washington's Birthday;

(iv) Good Friday;

(v) Memorial Day;

(vi) Independence Day;

(vii) Labor Day;

(viii) Columbus Day;

(ix) Veterans' Day;

(x) Thanksgiving Day; and

(xi) Christmas Day.

(2) When a legal holiday differs from the corresponding federal holiday, a banking institution:

(i) May be closed on both holidays; and

(ii) Shall be closed on one of the holidays.

(b) *Optional bank holidays.* — (1) Each legal holiday that is not listed in subsection (a) of this section is an optional bank holiday.

(2) When, as to any optional bank holiday, the legal holiday differs from the corresponding federal holiday, a banking institution may be closed on:

(i) Both holidays;

(ii) The legal holiday; or

(iii) The federal holiday.

§ 5-706. Saturdays.

(a) *In general.* — Saturday is an optional bank holiday.

(b) *Partial business day.* — A banking institution

that opens for business on Saturday may close at noon.

§ 5-707. Emergencies.

(a) *"Emergency" defined.* — In this section, "emergency" has the meaning stated in Article 41, § 2-103 of the Code.

§ 5-708. Action by directors.

A banking institution shall be open for business or shall be closed on optional bank holidays, as the directors of the banking institution may specify by resolution.

MASSACHUSETTS

NOTARIES PUBLIC

[MASS. CONST.]

Am. Art. IV, § 106. Appointment, tenure, etc., of notaries public.

Notaries public shall be appointed by the governor in the same manner as judicial officers are appointed, and shall hold their offices during seven years, unless sooner removed by the governor with the consent of the council, [upon the address of both houses of the legislature]. Women shall be eligible to appointment as notaries public. Upon the change of name of any woman, she shall re-register under her new name and shall pay such fee therefor as shall be established by the general court.

Am. Art. XXXVII, § 139. Removal of certain officers.

The governor, with the consent of the council, may remove justices of the peace and notaries public.

[MASS. ANN. LAWS]

Ch. 9, § 15. Notice of expiration of commissions.

The secretary shall send by first class mail to every justice of the peace or notary public a notice of the time of expiration of his commission, not more than thirty nor less than fourteen days before such expiration.

Ch. 9, § 15A. Validation of acts performed by notary public, etc., after change of name or expiration of commission.

If a notary public, whose name has been changed by marriage or decree of court and who has failed to re-register as required by law, or a notary public or justice of the peace whose commission has expired, continues to act as such after such change of name or expiration the state secretary, upon the application of such person and the payment of a fee of five dollars, may issue a certificate validating all such acts done after such change of name or expiration.

Ch. 30, § 12. Failure to qualify.

A person appointed to an office by the governor with or without the advice and consent of the council shall be notified of his appointment by the state secretary and his commission delivered to him upon qualification, and if he does not, within three months after the date of such appointment, take and subscribe the oaths of office, his appointment shall be void, and the secretary shall forthwith notify him thereof, and shall also certify said facts to the governor. This section shall be printed on every such commission.

Ch. 30, § 13. Fees for certain commissions, etc.

Before the delivery of a commission to a person appointed commissioner under section three or four of chapter two hundred and twenty-two, master in chancery or justice of the peace, he shall pay to the state secretary a fee to be determined annually by the commissioner of administration under the pro-

vision of section three B of chapter seven. Before the delivery of a commission to a person appointed a notary public he shall pay to the state secretary a fee as determined annually under the aforementioned provision. Upon the change of name of any woman who has been appointed and qualified as a notary public, she shall re-register under her new name and shall pay to the state secretary a fee as determined annually under the aforementioned provision.

Ch. 222, § 1. Justices of the peace and notaries public; appointment and jurisdiction.

Justices of the peace and notaries public shall be appointed, and their commissions shall be issued, for the commonwealth, and they shall have jurisdiction throughout the commonwealth when acting under the sole authority of such a commission. Unless otherwise expressly provided they may administer oaths or affirmations in all cases in which an oath or affirmation is required, and take acknowledgments of deeds and other instruments.

Ch. 222, § 8. Justices of the peace, etc., to print, etc., name and affix date of expiration of commission.

A justice of the peace or notary public, when taking acknowledgment of an instrument provided by law to be recorded, shall print or type his name directly below his signature and affix thereto the date of the expiration of his commission in the following language: "My commission expires _____." Failure to comply with this action shall not affect the validity of any instrument, or the record thereof.

Ch. 222, § 8A. Same subject.

A justice of the peace, notary public or other person duly authorized, when taking an acknowledgment or administering an oath with relation to an instrument filed in a proceeding in the probate court shall print or type his name directly below his signature thereon. Failure to comply with this section shall not affect the validity of any instrument or the record thereof.

SEAL

Ch. 59, § 31. Lists to be verified by oath.

The assessors shall in all cases require a person bringing in a list to make oath that it is true. The oath may be administered by any of the assessors or by their secretary or head clerk, or by any notary public, whose jurat shall be duly authenticated by his seal, or, in this commonwealth, by a justice of the peace. So much of this section as relates to administering the oath shall not apply to Boston.

FEES

Ch. 262, § 41. Notaries public.

The fees of notaries public shall be as follows:

For the protest of a bill of exchange, order, draft or check for non-acceptance or non-payment, or of a promissory note for non-payment, if the amount thereof is five hundred dollars or more, one dollar; if it is less than five hundred dollars, fifty cents; for recording the same, fifty cents; for noting the non-acceptance or non-payment of a bill of exchange, order, draft or check or the non-payment of a promissory note, seventy-five cents; and for each notice of the non-acceptance or non-payment of a bill, order, draft, check or note, given to a party liable for the payment thereof, twenty-five cents; but the whole cost of protest, including necessary notices and the record, if the bill, order, draft, check or note is of the amount of five hundred dollars or more, shall not exceed two dollars, and if it is less than five hundred dollars, shall not exceed one dollar and fifty cents; and the whole cost of noting, including recording and notices, shall in no case exceed one dollar and twenty-five cents.

OFFENSES

Ch. 222, § 9. Penalty for acting as justice of the peace, etc., after expiration of commission.

Whoever presumes to act as a justice of the peace or notary public after the expiration of his commission, and after receiving notice of such expiration, shall be punished by a fine of not less than one hundred nor more than five hundred dollars.

Ch. 222, § 10. Penalty for destroying records of notary public.

Whoever knowingly destroys, defaces or conceals the records or official papers of a notary public shall forfeit not more than one thousand dollars and be liable for damages to any person injured thereby.

Ch. 267, § 1. Forgery of records, certificates, etc.

Whoever, with intent to injure or defraud, falsely makes, alters, forges or counterfeits a public record, or a certificate, return or attestation of a clerk or register of a court, public register, notary public, justice of the peace, town clerk or any other public officer, in relation to a matter wherein such certificate, return or attestation may be received as legal proof, or a charter, deed, will, testament, bond or writing obligatory, power of attorney, policy of insurance, bill of lading, bill of exchange or promissory note; or an order, acquittance or discharge for money or other property or a credit card or an instrument described as a United States Dollar Traveller's Check or Cheque, purchased from a bank or other financially responsible institution, the purpose of which is a source of ready money on cashing the instrument without identification other than the signature of the purchaser; or an acceptance of a bill of exchange, or an endorsement or assignment of a bill of exchange or promissory note for the payment of money; or an accountable receipt for money, goods or other property; or a stock certificate, or any evidence or muniment of title to property; or a certificate of title, duplicate certificate of title, certificate issued in place of a duplicate certificate, the registration book, entry book, or any indexes provided for by chapter one hundred and eighty-five, or the docket of the recorder; shall be punished by imprisonment in the state prison for not more than ten years or in jail for not more than two years.

Ch. 268, § 33. Falsely assuming to be justice of the peace or certain public officers.

Whoever falsely assumes or pretends to be a justice of the peace, notary public, sheriff, deputy sheriff, medical examiner, associate medical examiner, constable, police officer, probation officer, or examiner, investigator or other officer appointed by the registrar of motor vehicles, or inspector, investigator or examiner of the department of public utilities, or investigator or other officer of the alcoholic beverages control commission, or investigator or other official of the bureau of special investigations, or examiner, investigator or other officer of the department of revenue, and acts as such or requires a person to aid or assist him in a matter pertaining to the duty of such officer, shall be punished by a fine of not more than four hundred dollars or by imprisonment for not more than one year.

SAFE DEPOSIT BOXES

Ch. 158, § 17. Proceedings if rent of safe deposit boxes not paid.

As herein used, "bank" shall mean any bank as defined in section one of chapter one hundred and sixty-seven, any national banking association doing business in the commonwealth and any domestic corporation organized under general or special laws of the commonwealth for the purpose of carrying on the business of a safe deposit company; "safe deposit box" shall mean a box or safe in the vaults of any bank; "lessee" shall mean the person or persons in whose name or names a safe deposit box stands on the books of a bank; and "rent" shall mean the amount due to a bank for the rental or use of a safe deposit box.

Any bank which leases a safe deposit box for rent shall advise the lessee in writing that insurance coverage for the contents of such safe deposit box is not provided by such bank, but that the lessee may, at his own expense, insure said contents with an insurance company of his own selection. The commissioner and banks shall establish such rules and regulations as he deems necessary to carry out the purposes of this paragraph. (Added by 1980, 484, approved July 11, 1980, effective 90 days thereafter.)

If the rent for a safe deposit box in a bank has not been paid for one year after being due, the bank may mail, postpaid, to the lessee at his address shown on the books of said bank, a notice stating that if the rent for such safe deposit box is not paid within sixty days from the date of such notice, the bank may cause such safe deposit box to be opened and the contents disposed of in accordance with the terms of this section. Upon the expiration of sixty days from the date of such notice, if the lessee has failed to pay the rent for such safe deposit box in full to the date of such notice, all rights of the lessee in the safe deposit box and of access thereto shall cease, and such bank may, at any time thereafter in the presence of one of its officers and of a notary public not in the general employ of such bank, cause such safe deposit box to be opened, and such notary public shall remove the contents thereof, list the same and seal such contents in a package, marking thereon the name of the lessee and his address as shown on the books of the bank. An affidavit setting forth the facts concerning the entry, listing the contents of the safe deposit box and signed by the bank officer and the notary public shall be retained by the bank. Such affidavit shall be prima facie evidence of the facts therein set forth in all proceedings at law and equity wherein evidence of such facts would be competent. (Amended by 1983, 620, approved December 17, 1983, effective 90 days thereafter.)

The package containing the contents of any safe deposit box opened as aforesaid shall be retained on special deposit by the bank, subject to payment of rent due for such safe deposit box, all expenses incurred in connection with opening said safe deposit box and charges for safekeeping of such package. If such package remains unclaimed for seven years

and the amounts due as above provided remain unpaid the bank may mail, postpaid, to the person or persons to whom, and at the address at which, the notice provided for above was mailed, a notice stating that if such amounts shall not be paid within sixty days from the date of such notice, the bank will turn over the contents less the rental charges to the state treasurer as abandoned property, to be held by him subject to the provisions of chapter two hundred A. The bank may sell, assign or deliver so much of the contents of such package, at either public or private sale, as will enable it to realize such amount as will compensate for said charges.

The affidavit required by this section may be in the following form:—

COMMONWEALTH OF MASSACHUSETTS

County of

We, _____ an authorized official of _____ and _____ a notary public not in the general employ of said bank, hereby certify that on the _____ day of _____, 19__, we were present and witnessed the forcible opening of Safe No. _____ leased in the name of _____ in the vaults of the _____ office of said bank; that the contents of said safe were removed, examined, listed and then enclosed in a package and sealed in our presence. We further certify that the following is a true and complete list of all the contents removed from said safe.

(Allow space here for listing of contents.)

....

Signature of officer.   Title.

....

Name of Bank.

....

Signature of notary public not in the general employ of said bank.

Ch. 167, § 32. Property in possession of, or deposited with, bank; written notice; disposition.

Should any bank, at the time when the commissioner takes possession thereof, have in its possession for safe keeping and storage, any jewelry, plate, money, securities, valuable papers or other valuable personal property, or should to have rented any box, safes, or safe deposit boxes, or any part thereof, for the storage of property of any kind, the commissioner may at any time after taking possession as aforesaid cause to be mailed to the person claiming or appearing upon the books of the bank to be the owner of such property, or to the person in whose name the safe, vault, or box stands, a written notice in a securely closed postpaid, registered letter, directed to such person at his post office address as recorded upon the books of the bank, notifying such person to remove, within a period fixed by said notice and not less than sixty days from the date thereof, all such personal property; and upon the date fixed by said notice, the contract, if any, between such persons and the bank for the storage of such property, or for the use of said safe, vault or box, shall cease and determine, and the amount of unearned rent or charges, if any, paid by such person shall become debt of the bank to such person. If the property be not removed within the time fixed by the notice, the commissioner may make such disposition of said property as the supreme judicial court, upon application thereto, may direct; and thereupon the commissioner may cause any safe, vault or box to be opened in his presence, or in the presence of one of his special agents and a notary public not an officer or employee of the bank, or of the commissioner, and the contents thereof, if any, to be sealed up by such notary public in a package upon which the notary public shall distinctly mark the name and address of the person in whose name such safe, vault or box stands upon the books of the bank, and shall attach thereto a list and description of the property therein. The package so sealed and addressed, together with the list and description, may be kept by the commissioner in one of the general safes for boxes of the bank until delivered to the person whose name it bears, or may otherwise be disposed of as directed by the court.

ACKNOWLEDGMENTS

Ch. 183, § 30. Acknowledgment, how made.

The acknowledgment of a deed or other written instrument required to be acknowledged shall be by one or more of the grantors or by the attorney executing it. The officer before whom the acknowledgment is made shall endorse upon or annex to the instrument a certificate thereof. Such acknowledgment may be made—

(a) If within the commonwealth, before a justice of the peace or notary public.

(b) If without the commonwealth, in any state, territory, district or dependency of the United States, before a justice of the peace, notary public, magistrate or commissioner appointed therefor by the governor of this commonwealth, or, if a certificate of authority in the form prescribed by section thirty-three is attached thereto, before any other officer therein authorized to take acknowledgment of deeds.

(c) If without the United States or any dependency thereof, before a justice of the peace, notary, magistrate or commissioner as above provided, or before an ambassador, minister, consul, vice con-

sul, charge d'affaires or consular officer or agent of the United States accredited to the country where the acknowledgment is made; if made before an ambassador or other official of the United States, it shall be certified by him under his seal of office.

Ch. 183, § 31. Acknowledgment by married woman.

The acknowledgment by a married woman may be taken in the same form as if she were sole, and without any examination separate and apart from her husband.

Ch. 183, § 32. Acknowledgment of powers of attorney to convey real estate.

The law relative to the acknowledgment and recording of deeds shall apply to letters of attorney for the conveyance of real estate.

Ch. 183, § 33. Certificate of authority of officer.

Whenever, under clause (b) of section thirty or under section forty-one, a certificate of authority is required to be attached, there shall be subjoined or attached to the certificate of proof or acknowledgment a certificate of the secretary of state of the state where the officer taking the acknowledgment resides, under the seal of such state, or a certificate of the clerk of a court of record of such state in the county where said officer resides or where he took such proof or acknowledgment, under the seal of the court, stating that said officer was, at the time of taking such proof or acknowledgment, duly authorized thereto in said state, and that said secretary of state or clerk of court is well acquainted with his handwriting and verily believes the signature affixed to such certificate of proof or acknowledgment is genuine.

Ch. 183, § 34. Proof of execution if grantor is dead or non-resident.

If the grantor dies or removes from the commonwealth without having acknowledged his deed, the due execution thereof may be proved before any court of record in this commonwealth by the testimony of a subscribing witness thereto.

Ch. 183, § 35. Proof if witnesses are dead or non-resident.

If all the subscribing witnesses to the deed are also dead or out of the commonwealth, the due execution thereof may be proved before such court by proving the handwriting of the grantor and of a subscribing witness.

Ch. 183, § 39. Unwitnessed deeds not to be so proved.

The execution of a deed shall not be proved in the manner before provided unless it has at least one subscribing witness.

Ch. 183, § 40. Endorsement of certificate of proof.

A certificate of proof of the execution of a deed shall be endorsed upon it or annexed thereto by the clerk or register of the court or by the judge before whom such proof is made, and the certificate shall state whether the grantor was present at the hearing.

Ch. 183, § 41. Proof of deed outside the commonwealth.

The proof of a deed or other instrument, if made without the commonwealth in some state, territory, district or dependency of the United States, may be made before any of the persons enumerated in clause (b) of section thirty; provided, however, that a certificate of authority as provided in section thirty-three shall be attached thereto; if without the United States or any dependency thereof, such may be made before any of the persons enumerated in clause (c) of said section thirty.

Ch. 183, § 42. Forms of acknowledgment, etc.

The forms set forth in the appendix to this chapter for taking acknowledgments to deeds and other instruments and for certifying the authority of officers taking proofs for acknowledgments may be used, but shall not prevent the use of any other form heretofore lawfully used.

Appendix

FORMS OF ACKNOWLEDGMENTS, ETC.

(13) *Acknowledgment of Individual Acting in his Own Right*

(Caption specifying the state and place where the acknowledgment is taken.)

On this _____ day of _____ 19___, before me personally appeared A B (or A B and C D), to me known to be the person (or persons) described in and who executed the foregoing instrument, and acknowledged that he (or they) executed the same as his (or their) free act and deed.

(Signature and title of officer taking acknowledgment. Seal, if required.)

(14) *Acknowledgment of Individual Acting by Attorney*

(Caption specifying the state and place where the acknowledgment is taken.)

On this _____ day of _____, 19___, before me personally appeared A B, to me known to be the person who executed the foregoing instrument in behalf of C D, and acknowledged that he executed the same as the free act and deed of said C D.

(Signature and title of officer taking acknowledgment. Seal, if required.)

(15) *Acknowledgment of a Corporation or Joint Stock Association*

(Caption specifying the state and place where the acknowledgment is taken.)

On this _____ day of _____, 19___, before me personally appeared A B, to me personally known, who, being by me duly sworn (or affirmed), did say that he is the president (or other officer or agent of the corporation or association) of (describing the corporation or association) and that the seal affixed to said instrument is the corporate seal of said corporation (or association), and that said instrument was signed and sealed in behalf of said corporation (or association) by authority of its board of directors (or trustees), and said A B acknowledged said instrument to be the free act and deed of said corporation (or association).

(Signature and title of officer taking acknowledgment. Seal, if required.)

[If the corporation or association has no corporate seal, the words "the seal affixed to said instrument is the corporate seal of said corporation (or association), and that" shall be omitted, and at the end of the affidavit shall be added the words "and that said corporation (or association) has no corporate seal."]

(16) *Certificate of Authority of Officer Taking Acknowledgment*

(Caption specifying the state, county or place where the authentication is made.)

I, _____, clerk of the _____ in and for said county, which court is a court of record having a seal (or, I, _____, the secretary of state of such state or territory), do hereby certify that _____, by and before whom the foregoing acknowledgment (or proof) was taken, was, at the time of taking the same, a notary public (or other officer) residing (or authorized to act) in said county, and was duly authorized by the laws of said state (territory or district) to take and certify acknowledgments or proofs of deeds of land in said state (territory or district), and further that I am well acquainted with the handwriting of said _____, and that I verily believe that the signature to said certificate of acknowledgment (or proof) is genuine. In testimony whereof, I have hereunto set my hand and affixed the seal of the said court (or state) this _____ day of _____, 19___.

    (Signature and title of officer certifying. Seal.)

Ch. 222, § 11. Acknowledgment of written instruments by persons serving in or with the armed forces of the United States or their dependents.

Persons serving in or with the armed forces of the United States or their dependents, wherever located, may acknowledge any instrument, in the manner and form required by the laws of this commonwealth, before any commissioned officer in the active service of the armed forces of the United States with the rank of second lieutenant or higher in the army, air force or marine corps, or ensign or higher in the navy or United States Coast Guard. Any such instrument shall contain a statement that the person executing the instrument is serving in or with the armed forces of the United States or is a dependent of a person serving in or with the armed forces of the United States, and in either case the statement shall include the serial number of the person so serving. No such instrument shall be rendered invalid by the failure to state therein the place of execution or acknowledgment.

No authentication of the officer's certificate of acknowledgment shall be required.

Instruments so acknowledged outside of the commonwealth, if otherwise in accordance with law, shall be received and may be used in evidence, or for any other purpose, in the same manner as if taken before a commissioner of the commonwealth appointed to take depositions in other states.

DEPOSITIONS

State Administrative Procedure

Ch. 30A, § 12. Subpoenas in adjudicatory proceedings.

In conducting adjudicatory proceedings, [state administrative] agencies shall issue, vacate, modify and enforce subpoenas in accordance with the following provisions:—

    * * *

(3) Any party to an adjudicatory proceeding shall be entitled as of right to the issue of subpoenas in the name of the agency conducting the proceeding. The party may have such subpoenas issued by a notary public or justice of the peace, or he may make written application to the agency, which shall forthwith issue the subpoenas requested. However issued, the subpoena shall show on its face the name and address of the party at whose request the subpoena was issued. Unless otherwise provided by any law, the agency need not pay fees for attendance and travel to witnesses summoned by a party.

    * * *

Depositions Taken Outside of State

Ch. 223A, § 10. Taking of depositions outside of commonwealth to obtain evidence in action pending in commonwealth; issuance of commission or letter rogatory.

(a) A deposition to obtain testimony or documents or other things in an action pending in this commonwealth may be taken outside this commonwealth:

(1) On reasonable notice in writing to all parties, setting forth the time and place for taking the deposition, the name and address of each person to be examined, if known, and if not known, a general description sufficient to identify him or the particular class or group to which he belongs and the name or descriptive title of the person before whom the deposition will be taken. The deposition may be taken before a person authorized to administer oaths in the place in which the deposition is taken by the law thereof or by the law of this commonwealth or the United States.

(2) Before a person commissioned by the court. The person so commissioned shall have the power by virtue of his commission to administer any necessary oath.

(3) Pursuant to a letter rogatory issued by the court. A letter rogatory may be addressed "To the Appropriate Authority in (here name the state or country)."

(4) In any manner before any person, at any time or place, or upon any notice stipulated by the parties. A person designated by the stipulation shall have the power by virtue of his designation to administer any necessary oath.

(b) A commission or a letter rogatory shall be issued after notice and application to the court, and on terms that are just and appropriate. It shall not be requisite to the issuance of a commission or a letter rogatory that the taking of the deposition in any other manner is impracticable or inconvenient, and both a commission and a letter rogatory may be issued in proper cases. Evidence obtained in a foreign country in response to a letter rogatory need not be excluded merely for the reason that it is not a verbatim transcript or that the testimony was not taken under oath or for any similar departure from the requirements for depositions taken within this commonwealth.

Depositions for Foreign Proceedings

Ch. 223A, § 11. Compelling production of evidence to be used in proceeding in tribunal outside of commonwealth; application for order; practice and procedure.

A court of this commonwealth may order a person who is domiciled or is found within this commonwealth to give his testimony or statement or to produce documents or other things for use in a proceeding in a tribunal outside this commonwealth. The order may be made upon the application of any interested person or in response to a letter rogatory and may prescribe the practice and procedure, which may be wholly or in part the practice and procedure of the tribunal outside this commonwealth, for taking the testimony or statement or producing the documents or other things. To the extent that the order does not prescribe otherwise, the practice and procedure shall be in accordance with that of the court of this commonwealth issuing the order. The order may direct that the testimony or statement be given, or document or other thing produced, before a person appointed by the court. The person appointed shall have power to administer any necessary oath.

Witnesses

Ch. 233, § 1. Witnesses, how summoned.

A clerk of a court of record, a notary public or a justice of the peace may issue summonses for witnesses in all cases pending before courts, magistrates, auditors, referees, arbitrators or other persons authorized to examine witnesses, and at all hearings upon applications for complaints wherein a person may be charged with the commission of a crime; but a notary public or a justice of the peace shall not issue summonses for witnesses in criminal cases except upon request of the attorney general, district attorney or other person who acts in the case in behalf of the commonwealth or of the defendant. If the summons is issued at the request of the defendant that fact shall be stated therein. The summons shall be in the form heretofore adopted and commonly used, but may be altered from time to time like other writs.

Ch. 233, § 30. Deponent, how sworn and examined; use of recording devices.

The deponent shall be sworn or affirmed to tes-

tify the truth, the whole truth and nothing but the truth, relative to the cause for which the deposition is taken. The deponent shall then be examined by the justice or notary, and may be examined by the parties, and the testimony may be taken in writing or by any recording device, including an electronic device, which will accurately preserve such testimony.

Ch. 233, § 31. Order of examination.

The party producing the deponent shall be allowed first to examine him, either upon verbal or written interrogatories, on all the points which he considers material; the adverse party may then examine him in like manner, after which either party may propose further interrogatories.

Ch. 233, § 32. Manner of taking depositions.

The deposition shall be written by the justice or notary or deponent or by a disinterested person in the presence and under the direction of the justice or notary, shall be carefully read to or by the deponent, and then subscribed by him.

Ch. 233, § 33. Certificate to be annexed.

The justice or notary shall annex to the deposition a certificate of the time and manner of taking it, the person at whose request and the cause in which it was taken, the reason for taking it, and that the adverse party attended, or if he did not attend what notice was given to him.

Ch. 233, § 34. Depositions to be delivered to court, etc.

The deposition shall be delivered by the justice or notary to the court, arbitrators, referees or other persons before whom the cause is pending, or shall be enclosed and sealed by him and directed to it or them, and shall remain sealed until opened by it or them.

Ch. 233, § 38. Compelling deponent to testify.

A person may be summoned and compelled to give his deposition at a place within twenty miles of his place of abode, in like manner and under the same penalties as are provided for a witness before a court.

FORM 1

Subpoena to Appear Before Notary Public on Taking of Deposition

[*Title of Court and Cause*]
Commonwealth of Massachusetts
County of __1_____   ss.
  To __2_____

We command you that, all business and excuses being set aside, you appear and attend before __3_____, a notary public in and for the County of __4_____, Commonwealth of Massachusetts, at __5_____ [his *or* her] office at __6_____ [*address*], City of __7_____, County of __8_____, Commonwealth of Massachusetts, on __9_____, 19__10__, at __11_____ o'clock __12__m., then and there to testify in the above entitled cause now pending in the __13_____ Court, County of __14_____, Commonwealth of Massachusetts, on the part of plaintiff therein. For failure to attend you will be deemed guilty of contempt of court and liable to pay all damages sustained thereby to the parties aggrieved, and to forfeit in addition the sum of $__15__.
Dated __16_____, 19__17__.

[*Seal*]   [*Signature*]

FORM 2

Subpoena to Witness to Take Deposition

[*Title of Court and Cause*]
Commonwealth of Massachusetts
County of __1_____   ss.
  To: __2_____

You are hereby ordered to appear and attend as a witness before __3_____, a __4_____ [notary public *or as the case may be*], at the office of __5_____ at __6_____ [*address*], City of __7_____, County of __8_____, Commonwealth of Massachusetts, on __9_____, 19__10__, at __11_____ o'clock __12__m., in order to testify in the above entitled cause on the part of __13_____, __14_____ [plaintiff *or* defendant].

For failure to attend or answer as a witness you will be deemed guilty of contempt of court, and liable to pay all losses and damages sustained thereby by the parties aggrieved and forfeit the sum of $__15__.
Dated __16_____, 19__17__.

[*Seal*]   [*Signature*]

Ch. 233, § 40. Courts may make rules for depositions.

The courts may make rules regulating the time and manner of opening, filing and safe keeping of depositions, and the taking and use thereof.

Ch. 233, § 41. Depositions of Persons Outside Commonwealth.

The deposition of a person without the commonwealth may be taken under a commission issued to one or more competent persons in another state or country by the court in which the cause is pending, or it may be taken before a commissioner appointed by the governor for that purpose, and in either case the deposition may be used in the same manner and subject to the same conditions and objections as if it had been taken in the commonwealth.

Ch. 233, § 42. Written interrogatories, etc.

Unless the court otherwise orders, a deposition taken before commissioners shall be taken upon written interrogatories, which shall be filed in the clerk's office and notice thereof given to the adverse party or his attorney, and upon cross interrogatories, if any are filed by him. But if the defendant does not enter his appearance in the action within the time required by law, no notice to him shall be required. The court may in any case order depositions to be taken before the commissioners, in the manner provided by law for taking the depositions of witnesses within the commonwealth in actions at law, or in such manner as the court orders, and in such cases shall determine what notice shall be given to the adverse party, his agent or attorney, and the manner of service thereof, may authorize the taking of depositions of witnesses not specifically named in the commission, and may limit the extent of the inquiry. The court may order the production before the commissioner of any books, instruments or papers relative to any matter in issue.

Ch. 233, § 73. Oaths before a notary of another state or country.

All oaths and affidavits administered or taken by a notary public, duly commissioned and qualified by authority of any other state or government, within the jurisdiction for which he is commissioned, and certified under his official seal, shall be as effectual in this commonwealth as if administered or taken and certified by a justice of the peace therein.

Civil Procedure

[Mass. R. Civ. P.]

RULE 28. Persons before whom depositions may be taken.

(a) Within the United States. Within the United States or within a territory or insular possession subject to the jurisdiction of the United States, depositions shall be taken before an officer authorized to administer oaths by the laws of the United States or of the place where the examination is held, or before a person appointed by the court in which the action is pending. A person so appointed has power to administer oaths and take testimony. The term officer as used in Rules 30, 31 and 32 includes a person appointed by the court or designated by the parties under Rule 29.

(b) In Foreign Countries. In a foreign country, depositions may be taken (1) on notice before a person authorized to administer oaths in the place in which the examination is held, either by the law thereof or by the laws of the United States, or (2) before a person commissioned by the court, and a person so commissioned shall have the power by virtue of his commission to administer any necessary oath and take testimony, or (3) pursuant to a letter rogatory. A commission or a letter rogatory shall be issued on application and notice and on terms that are just and appropriate. It is not requisite to the issuance of a commission or a letter rogatory that the taking of the deposition in any other manner is impracticable or inconvenient; and both a commission and a letter rogatory may be issued in proper cases. A notice or commission may designate the person before whom the deposition is to be taken either by name or descriptive title. A letter rogatory may be addressed "To the Appropriate Authority in [here name the country]." Evidence obtained in response to a letter rogatory need not be excluded merely for the reason that it is not a verbatim transcript or that the testimony was not taken under oath or for any similar departure from the requirements for depositions taken within the United States under these rules.

(c) Disqualification for Interest. No deposition shall be taken before a person who is a relative or employee or attorney or counsel of any of the parties, or is a relative or employee of such attorney or counsel, or is financially interested in the action.

COMMISSIONERS

[Mass. Ann. Laws]

Ch. 222, § 3. Commissioners to qualify public officers; appointment and returns; certain fees prohibited.

The governor, with the advice and consent of the council, shall appoint commissioners to administer to public officers the oaths of office required by the constitution. Upon administering such oaths, the commissioners shall forthwith make return thereof, with the date of the same, to the state secretary. Neither the state secretary, nor any officer or employee in his department acting as such a commissioner, shall charge any fee for administering such an oath.

Ch. 222, § 4. Commissioners in other states and countries.

The governor, with the advice and consent of the council, may appoint commissioners in the states, territories, districts and dependencies of the United States, and one or more commissioners in every foreign country, to hold office for three years from the date of their respective appointments.

Ch. 222, § 5. Oath, signature, seal, etc.

A person appointed commissioner in a state, territory, district or dependency of the United States shall, within three months after his appointment, take and subscribe an oath before a justice of the peace or other magistrate of the town or county where he resides, or before a clerk of a court of record within the state, territory, district or dependency where he resides, faithfully to perform the duties of his office, and shall cause an official seal to be prepared, upon which shall appear his name, the words "Commissioner for Massachusetts" and the name of the state, territory, district or dependency, and town or county where he resides. A person appointed commissioner in a foreign country shall, before performing any duty of his office, take and subscribe an oath before a judge or clerk of a court of record of the county where he resides or before an ambassador, minister or consul of the United States, accredited to such country, faithfully to perform the duties of his office. In each case, a certificate of the commissioner's oath of office and his signature and an impression of his official seal shall be forthwith transmitted to and filed in the office of the state secretary.

Ch. 222, § 6. Powers and duties.

A commissioner may, in his state, territory, district, dependency or country, administer oaths and take depositions, affidavits and acknowledgments of deeds and other instruments, to be used or recorded in this commonwealth, and the proof of such deeds, if the grantor refuses to acknowledge the same, all of which shall be certified by him under his official seal.

Ch. 222, § 7. Instructions, etc.

The state secretary shall prepare and forward to each commissioner appointed under section four, instructions and forms in conformity to law, and a copy of the three preceding sections.

Ch. 262, § 42. Commissioners in other states, etc.

The fees of commissioners appointed under section four of chapter two hundred and twenty-two shall be as follows:

For administering oaths and certifying the same under their official seals, one dollar for each; for taking acknowledgments of deeds and other instruments and certifying the same under their official seals, one dollar for each; for each written page contained in any deposition or affidavit taken by them, fifty cents; for administering the oath or affirmation to each deponent, one dollar; for authenticating, sealing up and directing each deposition, one dollar; for services not hereinbefore specified, the same fees as are allowed to justices of the peace in this commonwealth for like services; but the court to which a deposition is returnable shall order further allowance therefor if it appears proper to do so.

LEGAL HOLIDAYS

Ch. 4, § 7. Legal holiday.

* * *

Eighteenth, "Legal holiday" shall include January first, July fourth, November eleventh, and Christmas Day, or the day following when any of said days occurs on Sunday, and the third Monday in January, the third Monday in February, the third Monday in April, the last Monday in May, the first Monday in September, the second Monday in October, and Thanksgiving Day. "Legal holiday" shall also include, with respect to Suffolk county only, March seventeenth and June seventeenth, or the day following when said days occur on Sunday; provided, however, that the words "legal holiday" as used in section forty-five of chapter one hundred and forty-nine shall not include March seventeenth, or the day following when said day occurs on Sunday. Eighteenth A, "Commemoration day" shall include March fifteenth, in honor of Peter Francisco day, May twentieth, in honor of General Marquis de Lafayette and May twenty-ninth, in honor of the birthday of President John F. Kennedy. The governor shall issue a proclamation in connection with each such commemoration day.

MICHIGAN

NOTARIES PUBLIC

[MICH. COMP. LAWS ANN.]

§ 55.103 Transfer of notary public functions to department of state.

WHEREAS, Section 107 of the Revised Statutes of 1846, as amended, being Sections 55.107 of the Compiled Laws of 1970, assigns certain functions with respect to notaries public to the Governor; and

WHEREAS, all or any portion of those functions may be delegated by Executive Order to the Department of State pursuant to Section 33, Act 380 of the Public Acts of 1965, being Section 16.133 of the Michigan Compiled Laws of 1970; and

WHEREAS, all ministerial and clerical duties and functions relative to processing applications for notaries public were transferred and delegated to the Department of State by Executive Order 1970-3 on February 9, 1970; and

WHEREAS, all remaining powers, duties, and functions of the Governor with respect to notaries public, being those vested by Sections 55.107 through 55.117 inclusive, of the Michigan Compiled Laws of 1970, except the appointment authority of the Governor set forth in the first sentence of Section 55.107, were transferred and delegated to the Department of State by Executive Order 1976-11 on November 2, 1976,

NOW, WHEREFORE, I, WILLIAM G. MILLIKEN, Governor of the State of Michigan, pursuant to Section 33, Act 380 of the Public Acts of 1965, do hereby revoke Executive Order 1970-3 [55.101] and Executive Order 1976-11 [55.102].

I further hereby delegate to the Department of State all powers, duties, and functions of the Governor with respect to notaries public, being those vested by Sections 55.107 through 55.117 inclusive, of the Michigan Compiled Laws of 1970, reserving none of these powers, duties, and functions.

This delegation and transfer shall become effective August 15, 1980.

§ 55.107. Appointment, term, eligibility; application; revocation; fees; indorsement of application in blank; deposit of fees.

The governor may appoint 1 or more persons notaries public in each county of this state, who shall hold their offices respectively for 4 years from the date of their appointment, unless sooner removed by the governor. No person shall be eligible to receive such an appointment unless he or she shall be, at the time of making application for appointment, of the age of 18 years, a resident of the county of which he or she desires to be appointed notary public, and a citizen of this state. The person desiring to be appointed shall make a written application on an official form distributed by the county clerk of each county, stating the age of the applicant, which application shall be indorsed by a member of the legislature, or some circuit or probate judge of the county, district or circuit of which the applicant is a resident, and be presented to the governor, accompanied by a fee of * * *. Effective April 1, 1972 the fee shall be $3.00. Under no circumstances shall such application form be indorsed in blank, prior to completion and signature by the applicant. The governor may revoke a commission issued to a notary public upon presentation to him of satisfactory evidence of official misconduct or incapacity. The governor shall revoke the commission issued to a notary public upon presentation to him of satisfactory evidence of the notarization of a paper or document prior to completion by the person whose signature is notarized. On the last days of March, June, September and December of each

year, the governor shall deposit all fees so received by him during the last preceding quarter with the state treasurer, which shall be placed in the general fund.

Any notary public whose name has been changed pursuant to law subsequent to the issuance of a commission shall continue to use the name set forth in the commission for all purposes authorized under such commission until the expiration thereof.

§ 55.108. Commission transmitted, notice.

Whenever the governor shall appoint a notary public, the secretary of state shall transmit his commission to the clerk of the county for which such notary was appointed; and the county clerk, on receiving such commission, shall give notice thereof to the person so appointed.

§ 55.109. Oaths; quarterly lists; fees.

(1) Before performing the duties of office and within 90 days after receiving notice of appointment from the county clerk, a person appointed as a notary public shall take and file with the county clerk the oath prescribed by the constitution. The county clerk shall file the oath thus taken in the clerk's office and, on the last day of December, March, June, and September in each year, shall transmit to the secretary of state a written list containing the names of all persons to whom, during each preceding quarter, the county clerk has delivered commissions, the date of filing their oaths and bonds, and their respective addresses with the clerk's certificate that such persons have fully complied with the provisions of law in regard to their qualification for the discharge of the duties of the office of notary public.

(2) The county clerk, for all services required by this act, shall be entitled to receive the sum of $1.00 from each person qualifying. A charter county with a population of more than 2,000,000 may impose by ordinance a fee for the county clerk's services different in amount than the fee prescribed by this subsection. A charter county shall not impose a fee which is greater than the cost of the service for which the fee is charged.

(3) If the county clerk of any county is appointed to the office of notary public, the oath of office required by the constitution shall be filed with the judge of probate of that county.

§ 55.110. Bond, approval.

Each notary public shall, before entering upon the duties of his or her office, and within the time limited for the filing of the official oath, give bond to the people of this state, with 1 or more sureties, to be approved by the county clerk, in the penal sum of $10,000.00. The condition of the bond shall be that the notary public shall duly and faithfully discharge the duties of office. The notary public shall file the bond with the county clerk. If the county clerk of any county is appointed to the office of notary public, the bond required by this section shall be approved by, and filed with the judge of the probate court for that county.

§ 55.111. Delivery of commission; notice to secretary of state.

Upon the filing of the official oath and bond, as required in the 2 next preceding sections, the clerk shall deliver to the person so appointed the commission received by him for such person: Provided, That where such oath and bond shall have been filed with the judge of probate, as provided in the 2 next preceding sections, he shall give the same notice thereof to the secretary of state as is required in this section to be given by the county clerk.

§ 55.112. Notary's powers.

Notaries public shall have authority to take the proof and acknowledgment of deeds; to administer oaths, and take affidavits in any matter or cause pending, or to be commenced or moved in any court of this state; to demand acceptance of foreign and inland bills of exchange, and of promissory notes, and to protest the same for non-acceptance, or non-payment, as the case may require; and to exercise such other powers and duties, as by the law of nations, and according to commercial usage, or by the laws of any other state, government or country, may be performed by notaries public.

§ 55.113. Certificate as presumptive evidence; exception.

In all the courts of this state the certificate of a notary public, under his hand and seal of office, of official acts done by him as such notary, shall be received as presumptive evidence of the facts contained in such certificate; but such certificate shall not be evidence of notice of non-acceptance or non-payment in any case in which a defendant shall annex to his plea, an affidavit denying the fact of having received such notice.

§ 55.114. Office vacated, disposition of records; penalty, neglect.

Whenever the office of any notary public shall become vacant, the records of such notary and all the papers relating to his office, shall be deposited in the office of the clerk of the proper county; and

any notary, who, on his resignation or removal from office, shall neglect for the space of 3 months, to deposit such records and papers, and any executor or administrator of any deceased notary public, who shall neglect for the space of 3 months after his appointment, to deposit with said clerk all such records and papers as shall come to his hands, shall forfeit and pay a sum not less than 50 dollars, nor more than 200 dollars.

§ 55.115. Destruction or concealment of papers, penalty, civil liability.

If any person shall knowingly destroy, deface, or conceal any records or papers belonging to the office of a notary public, he shall forfeit and pay a sum not exceeding 500 dollars; and such person shall also be liable to an action for damages at the suit of the party injured.

§ 55.116. Records kept by county clerk; copies, fees.

The county clerk shall receive and safely keep all the records and papers of notaries public, directed to be deposited in his office, and shall give certified copies of such records and papers, under his hand and seal, when required; and for such copies he shall receive the same fees as are by law allowed to notaries public; and copies so given by said clerk shall be as valid and effectual as if given by a notary public.

§ 55.117. Notary's residence; jurisdiction, fees.

Notaries public shall reside in the county for which they are appointed, but they may act as such notaries in any part of this state; and they shall receive for their services such fees as are provided by law.

§ 55.221. Notaries public; typing, etc., name, etc., on affidavit, deposition, etc.; expiration date of commission; validity of instrument.

Notaries public shall legibly type, print or stamp on each affidavit, deposition, certificate and acknowledgment given or taken by them, and to all other instruments signed notarially, the date upon which their commissions shall expire, their commissioned names and the name of the county in which they are authorized to officiate: Provided, however, That where any such instrument has been heretofore or shall be hereafter recorded in the office of the register of deeds of any county without the date upon which said notary commission expires being affixed thereto, or shown on the record of such instrument, a certificate by a county clerk may be recorded in such register's office. Upon the recording of such certificate, showing that such person taking such acknowledgment was actually a notary public of such county on the date of such acknowledgment and giving the date on which his commission would expire, the record of such certificate and the record of such instrument shall be effectual for all purposes of a legal record, and the record of such instrument and such certificate or a transcript thereof may be given in evidence as in other cases, and such instrument shall be construed to be as valid and effectual as if such instrument had been in such respect duly executed.

§ 55.251. Notary connected with bank or corporation, limited powers.

It shall be lawful for any notary public who is a stockholder, director, officer or employe of a bank or other corporation to take the acknowledgment of any party to any written instrument executed to or by such corporation, or to administer an oath to any other stockholder, director, officer, employe or agent of such corporation, or to protest for non-acceptance or non-payment bills of exchange, drafts, checks, notes and other negotiable instruments which may be owned or held for collection by such bank or other corporation: Provided, It shall not be lawful for any notary public to take the acknowledgment of an instrument by or to a bank or other corporation of which he is a stockholder, director, officer or employe, where such notary is named as a party to such instrument, either individually or as a representative of such bank or other corporation, or to protest any negotiable instrument owned or held for collection by such bank or other corporation, where such notary is individually a party to such instrument.

ADDITIONAL AUTHORITY

§ 4.121. Oaths, depositions, acknowledgments; power of legislators.

During his term of office, every senator and representative in the state legislature is hereby authorized, by virtue of his office to administer oaths, take depositions and acknowledgments.

§ 16.133. Certain powers, duties and functions of governor; transfer.

All or any portion of the powers, duties and functions of governor under section 107 of chapter 14 of the Revised Statutes of 1846, as amended, being section 55.107 of the Compiled Laws of 1948, relating to notaries public, may be delegated by executive order to the department of state.

FEES

§ 600.2564. Fees of notaries public.

Notaries public shall be entitled to the following fees, which are not taxable as costs:

(1) For drawing and copy of protest of the nonpayment of a promissory note or bill of exchange, or of the nonacceptance of such bill, 50 cents, in cases where by law, such protest is necessary, but in no other case.

(2) For drawing and copy of every other protest, 25 cents.

(3) For drawing, copy, and serving every notice of nonpayment of a note, or nonacceptance of a bill, 25 cents.

(4) For drawing any affidavit, or other paper or proceeding, for which provision is not herein made, 20 cents for each folio, and for copying the same, 6 cents for each folio.

(5) For taking the acknowledgment of deeds, and for other services authorized by law, the same fees as are allowed to other officers for similar services.

OFFENSES

§ 750.248. Forgery of records and other instruments, venue.

(1) Any person who shall falsely make, alter, forge or counterfeit any public record, or any certificate, return or attestation of any clerk of a court, public register, notary public, justice of the peace, township clerk, or any other public officer, in relation to any matter wherein such certificate, return or attestation may be received as legal proof, or any charter, deed, will, testament, bond or writing obligatory, letter of attorney, policy of insurance, bill of lading, bill of exchange, promissory note, or any order, acquittance of discharge for money or other property, or any waiver, release, claim or demand, or any acceptance of a bill of exchange, or indorsement, or assignment of a bill of exchange or promissory note for the payment of money, or any accountable receipt for money, goods or other property, with intent to injure or defraud any person, shall be guilty of a felony, punishable by imprisonment in the state prison not more than 14 years.

(2) The venue in a prosecution under this section may be either in the county in which the forgery was performed, or in a county in which any false, forged, altered or counterfeit record, deed, instrument or other writing is uttered and published with intent to injure or defraud.

§ 750.249. Same; uttering and publishing.

UTTERING AND PUBLISHING FORGED INSTRUMENTS— Any person who shall utter and publish as true, any false, forged, altered or counterfeit record, deed, instrument or other writing mentioned in the preceding section, knowing the same to be false, altered, forged or counterfeit, with intent to injure or defraud as aforesaid, shall be guilty of a felony, punishable by imprisonment in the state prison not more than 14 years.

§ 750.504. Punishment of misdemeanors when not fixed by statute.

A person convicted of a crime declared in this or any other act of the state of Michigan to be a misdemeanor, for which no other punishment is specially prescribed by any statute in force at the time of the conviction and sentence, shall be punished by imprisonment in the county jail for not more than 90 days or by a fine of not more than 100 dollars, or by both such fine and imprisonment.

ACKNOWLEDGMENTS

§ 565.8. Execution of deed; witnesses, acknowledgment; validation of certain acknowledgments; deeds not properly witnessed, use in evidence.

Deeds executed within this state of lands, or any interest in lands, shall be executed in the presence of 2 witnesses, who shall subscribe their names to the deed as such and the persons executing the deeds may acknowledge the execution before any judge, clerk of a court of record, or notary public within the state. The officer taking the acknowledgment shall endorse on the deed a certificate of the acknowledgment, and the true date of taking the acknowledgment, under his or her hand. Any deed which was acknowledged before any county clerk or clerk of any circuit court, before September 18, 1903, and the acknowledgment of the deed, and, if recorded, the record of the deed, shall be as valid for all purposes so far as the acknowledgment and record are concerned, as if the deed had been acknowledged before any other officer named in this section, and the legality of the acknowledgment and record shall not be questioned in any court or place. If a deed has been recorded which lacks 1 or more witnesses and the deed has been of record for a period of 10 years or more, and is otherwise eligible to record, the record of the deed shall be effectual for all purposes of a legal record and the record of the deed or a transcript thereof may be given in evidence in all cases and the deed shall be as valid and effectual as if it had been duly executed in compliance with this section.

§ 565.9. Execution of deed in another state; governing law, acknowledgment.

If any such deed shall be executed in any other state, territory or district of the United States, such deed may be executed according to the laws of such state, territory or district, and the execution thereof may be acknowledged before any judge of a court of record, notary public, justice of the peace, master in chancery or other officer authorized by the laws of such state, territory or district to take the acknowledgment of deeds therein, or before any commissioner appointed by the governor of this state for such purpose.

§ 565.10. Same; acknowledgment; seal of officer, certificate; record of prior deeds as evidence.

In the cases provided for in the last preceding section unless the acknowledgment be taken before a commissioner appointed by the governor of this state for that purpose the officer taking such acknowledgment shall attach thereto the seal of his office, and if such acknowledgment be taken before a justice of the peace or other officer having no seal of office, such deed or other conveyance or instrument shall have attached thereto a certificate of the clerk or other proper certifying officer of a court of record of the county or district, or of the secretary of state of the state or territory within which such acknowledgment was taken under the seal of his office, that the person whose name is subscribed to the certificate of acknowledgment was, at the date thereof, such officer as he is therein represented to be, and that he believes the signature of such person to such certificate of acknowledgment to be genuine, and that the deed is executed and acknowledged according to the laws of such state, territory or district. Whenever any deed or other instrument effecting [affecting] the title to land, executed, acknowledged and authenticated in accordance with this section and the last preceding section, has been heretofore recorded in the proper county, such record, or a certified transcript thereof shall be prima facie evidence of the due execution of such instrument to the same extent as if it had been authenticated as required by the statute in force at the time such instrument was recorded.

§ 565.11. Execution of deed in foreign country; governing law; acknowledgment; certificate, seal; validation of certain deeds, record as evidence.

If such deed be executed in any foreign country

it may be executed according to the laws of such country, and the execution thereof may be acknowledged before any notary public therein or before any minister plenipotentiary, minister extraordinary, minister resident, charge d'affaires, commissioner, or consul of the Untied States, appointed to reside therein; which acknowledgment shall be certified thereon by the officer taking the same under his hand, and if taken before a notary public his seal of office shall be affixed to such certificate: Provided, That all deeds of land situated within this state, heretofore or hereafter made in any foreign country, and executed in the presence of 2 witnesses, who shall have subscribed their names to the same as such, and the execution thereof shall have been acknowledged by the persons executing the same before any 1 of the officers authorized by this section to take such acknowledgment, and such acknowledgment shall have been certified thereon, as above required, shall be deemed between the parties thereto and all parties claiming under or through them, as valid and effectual to convey the legal estate of the premises therein described; and whenever such deed has been recorded in the office of the register of deeds of the proper county such record shall be effectual for all purposes of a legal record, and the record of such deed, or a transcript thereof, may be given in evidence as in other cases: Provided, That nothing herein contained shall impair the rights of any person under a purchase heretofore made in good faith and on valuable consideration.

§ 565.16. Refusal to acknowledge deed; application to justice, summons to grantor.

If any grantor residing in this state, shall refuse to acknowledge his deed, the grantee or any person claiming under him, may apply to any justice of the peace in the county where the land lies, or where the grantor or any subscribing witness to the deed resides, who shall thereupon issue a summons to the grantor to appear at a certain time and place before the said justice, to hear the testimony of the subscribing witnesses to the deed; and the said summons with a copy of the deed annexed, shall be served at least 7 days before the time therein assigned for proving the deed.

Uniform Recognition of Acknowledgments Act

§ 565.261. Short title.

This act shall be known and may be cited as the "uniform recognition of acknowledgments act."

§ 565.262. Notarial acts, definition; persons performing out of state.

For the purposes of this act, "notarial acts" means acts which the laws of this state authorize notaries public of this state to perform, including the administering of oaths and affirmations, taking proof of execution and acknowledgments of instruments, and attesting documents. Notarial acts may be performed outside this state for use in this state with the same effect as if performed by a notary public of this state by the following persons authorized pursuant to the laws and regulations of other governments in addition to any other person authorized by the laws of this state:

(a) A notary public authorized to perform notarial acts in the place in which the act is performed.

(b) A judge, clerk or deputy clerk of any court of record in the place in which the notarial act is performed.

(c) An officer of the foreign service of the United States, a consular agent or any other person authorized by regulation of the United States department of state to perform notarial acts in the place in which the act is performed.

(d) A commissioned officer in active service with the armed forces of the United States and any other person authorized by regulation of the armed forces to perform notarial acts if the notarial act is performed for 1 of the following or his dependents: a merchant seaman of the United States, a member of the armed forces of the United States or any other person serving with or accompanying the armed forces of the United States.

(e) Any other person authorized to perform notarial acts in the place in which the act is performed.

§ 565.263. Authority of officer, authentication.

(1) If the notarial act is performed by any of the persons described in subdivisions (a) to (d) of section 2, other than a person authorized to perform notarial acts by the laws or regulations of a foreign country, the signature, rank or title and serial number, if any, of the person are sufficient proof of the authority of a holder of that rank or title to perform the act. Further proof of his authority is not required.

(2) If the notarial act is performed by a person authorized by the laws or regulations of a foreign country to perform the act, there is sufficient proof of the authority of that person to act if any of the following exist:

(a) Either a foreign service officer of the United States resident in the country in which the act is performed or a diplomatic or consular officer of the foreign country resident in the United States certifies that a person holding that office is authorized to perform the act.

(b) The official seal of the person performing the notarial act is affixed to the document.

(c) The title and indication of authority to perform notarial acts of the person appears either in a digest of foreign law or in a list customarily used as a source of such information.

(3) If the notarial act is performed by a person other than 1 described in subsections (1) and (2), there is sufficient proof of the authority of that person to act if the clerk of a court of record in the place in which the notarial act is performed certifies to the official character of that person and to his authority to perform the notarial act.

(4) The signature and title of the person performing the act are prima facie evidence that he is a person with the designated title and that the signature is genuine.

§ 565.264. Certificate of person taking acknowledgment.

The person taking an acknowledgment shall certify that the person acknowledging appeared before him and acknowledged he executed the instrument; and the person acknowledging was known to the person taking the acknowledgment or that the person taking the acknowledgment had satisfactory evidence that the person acknowledging was the person described in and who executed the instrument.

§ 565.265. Form of certificate of acknowledgment.

The form of a certificate of acknowledgment used by a person whose authority is recognized under section 2 shall be accepted in this state if 1 of the following is true:

(a) The certificate is in a form prescribed by the laws or regulations of this state.

(b) The certificate is in a form prescribed by the laws applicable in the place in which the acknowledgment is taken.

(c) The certificate contains the words "acknowledged before me", or their substantial equivalent.

§ 565.266. Acknowledged before me, meaning.

The words "acknowledged before me" means:

(a) That the person acknowledging appeared before the person taking the acknowledgment.

(b) That he acknowledged he executed the instrument.

(c) That, in the case of:

(i) A natural person, he executed the instrument for the purposes therein stated.

(ii) A corporation, the officer or agent acknowledged he held the position or title set forth in the instrument and certificate, he signed the instrument on behalf of the corporation by proper authority and the instrument was the act of the corporation for the purpose therein stated.

(iii) A partnership, the partner or agent acknowledged he signed the instrument on behalf of the partnership by proper authority and he executed the instrument as the act of the partnership for the purposes therein stated.

(iv) A person acknowledging as principal by an attorney in fact, he executed the instrument by proper authority as the act of the principal for the purposes therein stated.

(v) A person acknowledging as a public officer, trustee, administrator, guardian or other representative, he signed the instrument by proper authority and he executed the instrument in the capacity and for the purposes therein stated.

(d) That the person taking the acknowledgment either knew or had satisfactory evidence that the person acknowledging was the person named in the instrument or certificate.

§ 565.267. Statutory short forms of acknowledgment.

(1) The forms of acknowledgment set forth in this section may be used and are sufficient for their purposes under any law of this state. The forms shall be known as "statutory short forms of acknowledgment" and may be referred to by that name. The authorization of the forms in this section does not preclude the use of other forms.

(2) For an individual acting in his own right:

State of _____

County of _____

The foregoing instrument was acknowledged before me this (date) by (name of person acknowledged).

(Signature of person taking acknowledgment)

(Title or rank)

(Serial number, if any)

(3) For a corporation:

State of _____

County of _____

The foregoing instrument was acknowledged before me this (date) by (name of officer or agent, title or officer or agent) of (name of corporation acknowledging) a (state or place of incorporation) corporation, on behalf of the corporation.

(Signature of person taking acknowledgment)

(Title or rank)

(Serial number, if any)

(4) For a partnership:

State of _____

County of _____

The foregoing instrument was acknowledged before me this (date) by (name of acknowledging partner or agent), partner (or agent) on behalf of (name of partnership), a partnership.

(Signature of person taking acknowledgment)

(Title or rank)

(Serial number, if any)

(5) For an individual acting as principal by an attorney in fact:

State of _____

County of _____

The foregoing instrument was acknowledged before me this (date) by (name of attorney in fact) as attorney in fact on behalf of (name of principal).

(Signature of person taking acknowledgment)

(Title or rank)

(Serial number, if any)

(6) By any public officer, trustee, or personal representative:

State of _____

County of _____

The foregoing instrument was acknowledged before me this (date) by (name and title of position).

(Signature of person taking acknowledgment)

(Title or rank)

(Serial number, if any)

§ 565.268. Prior notarial acts unaffected.

A notarial act performed prior to the effective date of this act is not affected by this act. This act provides an additional method of proving notarial acts. Nothing in this act diminishes or invalidates the recognition accorded to notarial acts by other laws of this state.

§ 565.269. Uniform interpretation.

This act shall be so interpreted as to make uniform the laws of those states which enact it.

§ 565.270. Repealed.

Act No. 185 of the Public Acts of 1895, being sections 565.251 to 565.256 of the Compiled Laws of 1948, is repealed.

By Married Women

§ 565.281. Acknowledgment by married woman.

That hereafter the acknowledgment of any married woman to a deed of conveyance or other instrument affecting real property, may be taken in the same manner as if she were sole.

DEPOSITIONS

§ 600.1432. Oath, mode of administration.

The usual mode of administrating oaths now practiced in this state, by the person, who swears holding up the right hand, shall be observed in all cases in which an oath may be administered by law except in the cases herein otherwise provided. The oath should commence, "You do solemnly swear or affirm."

§ 600.1442. Persons before whom oaths, affidavits, and depositions may be taken * * * court appointee; stipulation.

Oaths, affidavits and depositions in any cause, matter or proceeding in any court of record, may also be taken before any person appointed by the court for that purpose or before any person upon whom the parties agree by stipulation in writing or on the record.

§ 600.1725. Witness, refusal to testify, penalty.

If any witness attending pursuant to a subpoena, or brought before any court, judge, officer, commissioner, or before any person before whom depositions may be taken, refuses without reasonable cause

(1) to be examined, or

(2) to answer any legal and pertinent question, or

(3) to subscribe his deposition after it has been reduced to writing, the officer issuing the subpoena shall commit him, by warrant, to the common jail of the county in which he resides. He shall remain there until he submits to be examined, or to answer, or to subscribe his deposition, as the case may be, or until he is discharged according to law.

§ 600.1852. Foreign proceedings; service of process; letters rogatory; foreign orders, judgments, or decrees, recognition or enforcement; orders to testify or produce documents; procedure.

(1) Any court of record of this state as provided in subsection (2) may order service upon any person who is domiciled or can be found within this state of any document issued in connection with a proceeding in a tribunal outside this state. The order may be made upon application of any interested person or in response to a letter rogatory issued by a tribunal outside this state and shall direct the manner of service. Service in connection with a proceeding in a tribunal outside this state may be

made within this state without an order of court. Service under this section does not, of itself, require the recognition or enforcement of an order, judgment or decree rendered outside this state.

(2) Any court of record of this state may order a person who is domiciled or is found within this state to give his testimony or statement or to produce documents or other things for use in a proceeding in a tribunal outside this state. The order may be made upon the application of any interested person or in response to a letter rogatory and may prescribe the practice and procedure, which may be wholly or in part the practice and procedure of the tribunal outside this state, for taking the testimony or statement or producing the documents or other things. The order shall be issued upon petition to a court of record in the county in which the deponent resides or is employed or transacts his business in person or is found for a subpoena to compel the giving of testimony by him. The court may hear and act upon the petition with or without notice as the court directs. To the extent that the order does not prescribe otherwise, the practice and procedure shall be in accordance with that of the court of this state issuing the order. The order may direct that the testimony or statement be given, or document or other thing produced, before a person appointed by the court. The person appointed shall have power to administer any necessary oath. A person within this state may voluntarily give his testimony or statement or produce documents or other things for use in a proceeding before a tribunal outside this state.

§ 767.77. Commission to examine out-of-state witness; granting on application of defendant.

When an issue of fact shall be joined upon any indictment, the court in which the same is pending may, on application of the defendant, grant a commission to examine any material witnesses residing out of this state, in the same manner as in civil cases.

§ 767.78. Same; interrogatories, reading of deposition.

Interrogatories to be annexed to such commission shall be settled and such commission shall be issued, executed and returned in the manner prescribed by law in respect to commissions in civil cases, and the deposition taken thereon and returned shall be read in the same cases, and with like effect in all respects, as in civil suits.

[MICH. GEN. CT. R.]

RULE 304. Persons before whom depositions may be taken.

1. Within the United States. Within the United States or within a territory or insular possession subject to the dominion of the United States, depositions shall be taken (1) before a person authorized to administer oaths by the laws of this state or of the United States or of the place where the examination is held, or (2) before such person as may be appointed by the court in which the action is pending, or (3) before any person upon whom the parties agree by stipulation in writing or on the record. A person so appointed or agreed to shall have the power to administer oaths, take testimony, and do all other acts necessary to take an effective deposition.

2. In Foreign Countries. In a foreign state or country depositions shall be taken (1) before a secretary of embassy or legation, consul general, consul, vice consul, or consular agent of the United States, or (2) before such person as may be appointed by commission or under letters rogatory, or (3) before any person upon whom the parties agree by stipulation in writing or on the record. Such persons have the power to administer oaths, take testimony, and do all other acts necessary to take an effective deposition. A commission or letters rogatory shall be issued only when necessary or convenient, on application or notice, and on such terms and with such directions as are just and appropriate. Persons may be designated in notices or commissions either by name or descriptive title and letters rogatory may be addressed "To the Appropriate Judicial Authority in (here name the country)."

3. Disqualifications for Interest. No deposition shall be taken before a person who is a relative or employee or attorney or counsel of any of the parties, or is a relative or employee of such attorney or counsel, or is financially interested in the action unless the parties agree by stipulation in writing or on the record to the contrary.

LEGAL HOLIDAYS

[MICH. COMP. LAWS ANN.]

§ 435.101. Public holidays for bills and notes; transaction of business, holding of courts, adjournment of cases; Saturdays.

The following days namely: January 1, New Year's day; the third Monday in January in conjunction with the federal holiday, Martin Luther King, Jr. day; February 12, Lincoln's birthday; the third Monday of February, Washington's birthday;

the last Monday of May, Memorial or Decoration day; July 4; the first Monday in September, Labor day; the second Monday in October, Columbus day; November 11, Veterans' day; December 25, Christmas day; every Saturday from 12 noon until 12 midnight, which is designated a half holiday; and the fourth Thursday of November, Thanksgiving day, for all purposes regarding the presenting for payment or acceptance, and the protesting and giving notice of the dishonor of bills of exchange, bank checks, and promissory notes, also for the holding of courts, except as otherwise provided in this act, shall be treated and considered as the first day of the week, commonly called Sunday, and as public holidays or half holidays. Bills, checks, and notes otherwise presentable for acceptance of payment on these days shall be considered as payable and presentable for acceptance or payment on the next secular or business day following the holiday or half holiday. A law in this state shall not affect the validity of, or render void or voidable, the payment, certification, or acceptance of a check or other negotiable instrument or any other transaction by a bank in this state, because done or performed on a Saturday between 12 noon and midnight, if the payment, certification, acceptance, or other transaction would be valid if done or performed before 12 noon on that Saturday. This act does not compel a bank, savings and loan association, or building and loan association in this state, which by law or custom is entitled to close at 12 noon on a Saturday, to keep open for the transaction of business or to perform the acts or transactions described in this section, on a Saturday after that hour except at its own option. In construing this section, every Saturday, unless a whole holiday, shall for the holding of court and the transaction of business authorized by the laws of this state be considered a secular or business day. If the return or adjourn day in an action, matter, or hearing before a court, officer, referee, or arbitrators, falls on any of the days mentioned in this section except Sunday, then that action, matter, or proceeding, commenced or adjourned, shall not, by reason of coming on any of those days except Sunday, abate, but shall stand continued on the next succeeding day, at the same time and place unless the next day is the first day of the week, or a holiday, in which case it shall stand continued to the day succeeding the first day of the week or holiday, at the same time and place. When the first day of the general term of a circuit court, as fixed by the order of a circuit judge, falls upon either of the days mentioned in this section or when a circuit court is adjourned to a day mentioned in this section, that court may be adjourned to the following secular day. This act shall not prevent or invalidate the entry, issuance, service, or execution of a writ, summons, or confession of judgment, or other legal process, the holding courts or the transaction of lawful business except banking on any of the Saturday afternoons designated in this act as half holidays, nor shall this act prevent a bank, savings and loan association, or building and loan association from keeping its doors open or transacting its business on Saturday afternoons, if by vote of its directors it elects to do so. The legislative body of a county or city may, by ordinance or resolution, provide for the closing of county or municipal offices for any or for all purposes on every Saturday. This act shall not affect state employees working on a Sunday in accordance with their employment as construed by the civil service commission.

§ 435.102. Holiday on Sunday, observance on Monday.

Whenever January 1; February 12; July 4; November 11; or December 25 shall fall upon Sunday, the next Monday following shall be deemed a public holiday for any or all of the purposes aforesaid. In such cases all bills of exchange, checks, and promissory notes made after the passage of this act which would otherwise be presentable for acceptance or payment on such Monday shall be deemed to be presentable for acceptance or payment on the secular business day next succeeding the holiday.

§ 435.103. Saturday closing for banks, savings and loan associations, building and loan associations.

In addition to the holidays and half-holidays designated in section 1 of this act, and notwithstanding the provisions of any other law of this state to the contrary, any one or more Saturdays up to 12 o'clock noon upon which a bank, savings and loan association, and building and loan association, as hereinafter defined, may desire to close as hereinafter provided, is hereby designated a holiday for such bank, savings and loan association, and building and loan association for such period and shall for all purposes whatever as regards the presenting for payment or acceptance, and the protesting and giving notice of the dishonor of bills of exchange, bank checks and promissory notes, after this act shall take effect, but for no other purpose be treated and considered as the first day of the week, commonly called Sunday. All such bills, checks and notes otherwise presentable for acceptance or payment on any such holiday shall be deemed to be payable and presentable for acceptance or payment on the secular or business day next succeeding such holiday.

The terms "bank", "savings and loan association" or "building and loan association" as used in this section shall mean any bank, savings and loan association or building and loan association organized under the laws of this state, any partnership or individual conducting a legally authorized private banking business, any national bank or federal savings and loan association and any federal reserve bank or branch thereof.

Any bank, savings and loan association or building and loan association desiring to close as aforesaid shall install a night depository before so doing.

Any bank, savings and loan association or building and loan association desiring to close as aforesaid shall adopt a resolution to that effect concurred in by a majority of its board of directors, or if a private bank by a majority of its partners or by all of them if there be no more than 2 partners, notice of which shall be posted in its banking house or place of doing business for not less than 15 days before the taking effect thereof.

§ 435.131. Seventh Day Adventists; application of Sunday laws.

Whenever in the statutes of this state, rights, privileges, immunities or exemptions are given or duties and responsibilities are imposed on persons who conscientiously believe the seventh day of the week ought to be observed as the sabbath, said sabbath or seventh day shall mean and be construed in accordance with the worship and belief of such persons to include the period from sunset on Friday evening to sunset on Saturday evening.

MINNESOTA

NOTARIES PUBLIC

[MINN. STAT. ANN.]

§ 359.01. Commission.

Subdivision 1. Resident notaries. The governor may appoint and commission as notaries public, by and with the advice and consent of the senate, as many citizens of this state or resident aliens, over the age of 18 years, resident in the county for which appointed, as the governor deems necessary.

Subdivision 2. Nonresident notaries. Notwithstanding the provisions of subdivision 1, the governor may appoint as notary public, by and with the advice and consent of the senate, a person who is not a resident of this state and who is not a resident of the county for which appointment is sought if:

(1) the person is a resident of Wisconsin, Iowa, North Dakota, or South Dakota, and of a county that shares a boundary with this state;

(2) the person designates the court administrator of the district court of a county of this state that shares a boundary with the county of residence as agent for the service of process for all purposes relating to notarial acts and for receipt of all correspondence relating to notarial acts.

Subdivision 3. Fees. The fee for each commission shall not exceed $10.

§ 359.02. Term, bond, oath, reappointment.

A notary commissioned under section 359.01 holds office for six years, unless sooner removed by the governor or the district court. Before entering upon the duties of office, a newly commissioned notary shall file the notary's oath of office with the secretary of state. Within 30 days before the expiration of the commission a notary may be reappointed for a new term to commence and to be designated in the new commission as beginning upon the day immediately following the date of expiration. The reappointment takes effect and is valid although the appointing governor may not be in the office of the governor on the effective day.

§ 359.03. Seal; register.

Subdivision 1. Every notary shall get an official seal, with which to authenticate official acts, and upon which shall be engraved the arms of this state, the words "notarial seal," and the name of the county for which appointed. Such seal, with the notary's official register, shall be exempt from execution, and, on death or removal from office, such register shall be deposited with the court administrator of the district court of the notary's county.

* * *

Subdivision 3. The seal of every notary public after January 1, 1972, may be affixed by a stamp that will print a seal which legibly reproduces under photographic methods the seal of the state of

Minnesota, the name of the notary, the words "Notary Public," the name of the county for which appointed, and the words "My commission expires . . . . ," with the expiration date shown thereon. The seal shall be a rectangular form of not more than three-fourths of an inch vertically by 2-1/2 inches horizontally, with a serrated or milled edge border, and shall contain the information required by this subdivision.

§ 359.04. Powers.

Every such notary shall have power throughout the state, to administer all oaths required or authorized by law, to take and certify depositions, acknowledgments of deeds, and other instruments, and to receive, make out and record notarial protests.

§ 359.05. Date of expiration of commission and name to be endorsed.

Each notary public so appointed, commissioned, and qualified, shall have power throughout this state to administer all oaths required or authorized to be administered in this state; to take and certify all depositions to be used in any of the courts of this state; to take and certify all acknowledgments of deeds, mortgages, liens, powers of attorney, and other instruments in writing, and to receive, make out, and record notarial protests.

Every notary public, except in cases provided in section 359.03, subdivision 3, taking an acknowledgment of an instrument, taking a deposition, administering an oath, or making a notarial protest, shall, immediately following the notary's signature to the jurat or certificate of acknowledgment, endorse the date of the expiration of the commission; such endorsement may be legibly written, stamped, or printed upon the instrument, but must be disconnected from the seal, and shall be substantially in the following form: "My commission expires . . . ., 19. . ." Except in cases provided in section 359.03, subdivision 3, every notary public, in addition to signing the jurat or certificate of acknowledgment, shall, immediately following the signature and immediately preceding the official description, endorse thereon the notary's name with a typewriter or print the same legibly with a stamp or with pen and ink; provided that the failure so to endorse or print the name shall not invalidate any jurat or certificate of acknowledgment.

§ 359.061. Record of commission; certificate.

The commission of every notary shall be recorded in the office of the court administrator of the district court of the county of appointment, in a record kept for that purpose. The court administrator, when requested, shall certify to official acts in the manner and for the fees prescribed by statute or court rule.

§ 359.07. Notary in detached county.

Subdivision 1. Powers. In any county which has heretofore been detached from another county of this state, and which has been newly created and organized, any notary public residing in such newly created and organized county, who was a resident of the county from which the new county was detached and created, shall have the same powers during the unexpired term of appointment as such notary public was authorized by law to exercise under the commission issued to the notary as a resident of the county from which the new county was detached and created and within which the original appointment as notary public was made; and all acts heretofore done by any such notary public, while residing in the newly created and organized county, otherwise in conformity of law, are hereby declared to be legal and valid and to the same effect as if the notary public had been originally commissioned as a resident of the newly created and organized county.

Subdivision 2. Record of commission. Such notary public so residing in the newly created and organized county shall have the commission as such notary public recorded by the court administrator of the district court of the newly created and organized county of residence, or of the county to which the newly created county is attached for judicial purposes, as provided in section 359.061, and when so recorded shall be entitled to the same certificate of and from the court administrator of the district court as provided in section 359.061.

Subdivision 3. Seal. Such notary shall, immediately upon the adoption of this section, get an official seal, as provided in and in conformity with section 359.03.

§ 359.071. Change of residence.

A notary public who, during a term of office, establishes residency in a county of this state other than the county for which appointed, may file with the secretary of state an affidavit identifying the county of current residency, the county of appointment as notary public, and the date of change of residency. If the affidavit is properly filed, the notary continues to have the same powers during the unexpired term of appointment as if there were no change of residence. The notary public may use the official seal for the remainder of the term.

§ 359.08. Misconduct.

Any notary who shall exercise the duties of his office after the expiration of his term, or when otherwise disqualified, shall be guilty of a misdemeanor.

§ 359.11 Taking depositions.

In taking depositions, the notary shall have the power to compel the attendance of and to punish witnesses for refusing to testify as provided by statute or court rule. All sheriffs and constables shall serve and return all process issued by any notary in taking depositions.

§ 359.12. Removal from office.

Every notary who shall charge or receive a fee or reward for any act or service done or rendered by him under this chapter greater than the amount allowed by law, or who dishonestly or unfaithfully discharges his duties as notary, shall, on complaint filed and substantiated as in other civil cases in the district court of the county in which he resides, be removed from office by such court. The fact of such removal shall thereupon be certified by the clerk to the governor, and the person so removed shall thereafter be ineligible to such office.

ADDITIONAL AUTHORITY

[MINN. CONST.]

Art. 5, § 3. Powers and duties of governor.

Section 3. The governor shall communicate by message to each session of the legislature information touching the state and country. He is commander-in-chief of the military and naval forces and may call them out to execute the laws, suppress insurrection and repel invasion. He may require the opinion in writing of the principal officer in each of the executive departments upon any subject relating to his duties. With the advice and consent of the senate he may appoint notaries public and other officers provided by law. He may appoint commissioners to take the acknowledgment of deeds or other instruments in writing to be used in the state. He shall take care that the laws be faithfully executed. He shall fill any vacancy that may occur in the offices of secretary of state, treasurer, auditor, attorney general and the other state and district offices hereafter created by law until the end of the term for which the person who had vacated the office was elected or the first Monday in January following the next general election, whichever is sooner, and until a successor is chosen and qualified.

[MINN. STAT. ANN.]

§ 51A.52. Directors, employees, members, and stockholders of association may acknowledge instruments to which it is a party.

No public officer qualified to take acknowledgments or proofs of written instruments shall be disqualified from taking the acknowledgment or proof of any instrument in writing in which an association is interested by reason of membership in, stockholder interest in, or employment by an association so interested, and any acknowledgments or proofs heretofore taken are hereby validated.

§ 358.07. Forms of oath in various cases.

An oath substantially in the following forms shall be administered to the respective officers and persons hereinafter named:

* * *

(7) To witnesses:
"You do swear that the evidence you shall give relative to the cause now under consideration shall be the whole truth, and nothing but the truth. So help you God."

(8) To interpreters:
"You do swear that you will truly and impartially interpret to this witness the oath about to be administered to him, and the testimony he shall give relative to the cause now under consideration. So help you God."

* * *

(10) To affiants:
"You do swear that the statements of this affidavit, by you subscribed, are true. So help you God."

§ 358.08. Affirmation in lieu of oath.

If any person of whom an oath is required shall declare that he has religious scruples against taking the same, the word "swear" and the words "so help you God" may be omitted from the foregoing forms, and the word "affirm" and the words "and this you do under the penalties of perjury" shall be substituted therefor, respectively, and such person shall be considered, for all purposes, as having been duly sworn.

§ 358.09. By whom and how administered.

Any officer authorized by this chapter to take and certify acknowledgments may administer an oath, and, if the same be in writing, may certify the same under his official signature, and the seal of his office, if there be one, in the following form: "Subscribed and sworn to before me this . . . . . . day of . . . . . ., 19. . ." The mode of administering an oath commonly practiced in the place where it is taken shall be followed, including, in this state, the ceremony of uplifting the hand.

§ 358.14. Married persons.

No separate examination of each spouse shall be required, but if husband and wife join in and acknowledge the execution of any instrument, they shall be described in the certificate of acknowledgment as husband and wife; and, if they acknowledge it before different officers, or before the same officer at different times, each shall be described in the certificate as the spouse of the other.

§ 358.15. Ex officio notary public.

The following officers have the powers of a notary public within the state:

(1) every member of the legislature, while still a resident in the district from which elected; but no fee or compensation may be received for exercising these powers. The form of the official signature in these cases is: "A. B., Representative (or Senator), ... District, Minnesota, ex officio notary public. My term expires January 1, 19. . . . .;"

(2) the clerks or recorders of towns, and cities; and

(3) court commissioners, county recorders, and county auditors, and their several deputies, and county commissioners, all within their respective counties.

§ 358.25. Power given for taking acknowledgments for protesting bills of exchange.

Any person authorized to take acknowledgments or administer oaths, who is at the same time an officer, director or stockholder of a corporation, is hereby authorized to take acknowledgments of instruments wherein such corporation is interested, and to administer oaths to any officer, director, or stockholder of such corporation as such, and to protest for non-acceptance or non-payment bills of exchange, drafts, checks, notes and other negotiable or non-negotiable instruments which may be owned or held for collection by such corporation, as fully and effectually as if he were not an officer, director, or stockholder of such corporation.

FEES

§ 357.17. Notaries public.

The maximum fees to be charged and collected by a notary public shall be as follows:

(1) For protest of nonpayment of note or bill of exchange or of nonacceptance of such bill, where protest is legally necessary, and copy thereof, $1;

(2) For every other protest and copy, $1;

(3) For making and serving every notice of nonpayment of note or nonacceptance of bill and copy thereof, $1;

(4) For any affidavit or paper for which provision is not made herein, $1 per folio, and 20 cents per folio for copies;

(5) For each oath administered, $1;

(6) For acknowledgments of deeds and for other services authorized by law, the legal fees allowed other officers for like services;

(7) For recording each instrument required by law to be recorded by the notary, $1 per folio.

OFFENSES

§ 609.03. Punishment when not otherwise fixed.

If a person is convicted of a crime for which no punishment is otherwise provided the person may be sentenced as follows:

* * *

(3) If the crime is a misdemeanor, to imprisonment for not more than 90 days or to payment of a fine of not more than $700, or both; or

* * *

§ 609.65. False certification by notary public.

Whoever, when acting or purporting to act as a notary public or other public officer, certifies falsely that an instrument has been acknowledged or that any other act was performed by a party appearing before the actor or that as such notary public or other public officer the actor performed any other official act may be sentenced as follows:

(1) If the actor so certifies with intent to injure or defraud, to imprisonment for not more than three years or to payment of a fine of not more than $5,000, or both; or

(2) In any other case, to imprisonment for not more than 90 days or to payment of a fine of not more than $700, or both.

UNIFORM LAW ON NOTARIAL ACTS

§ 358.41. Definitions.

As used in sections 358.41 to 358.49:

(1) "Notarial act" means any act that a notary public of this state is authorized to perform, and includes taking an acknowledgment, administering

an oath or affirmation, taking a verification upon oath or affirmation, witnessing or attesting a signature, certifying or attesting a copy, and noting a protest of a negotiable instrument.

(2) "Acknowledgment" means a declaration by a person that the person has executed an instrument for the purposes stated therein and, if the instrument is executed in a representative capacity, that the person signed the instrument with proper authority and executed it as the act of the person or entity represented and identified therein.

(3) "Verification upon oath or affirmation" means a declaration that a statement is true made by a person upon oath or affirmation.

(4) "In a representative capacity" means:

(i) for and on behalf of a corporation, partnership, trust, or other entity, as an authorized officer, agent, partner, trustee, or other representative;

(ii) as a public officer, personal representative, guardian, or other representative, in the capacity recited in the instrument;

(iii) as an attorney in fact for a principal; or

(iv) in any other capacity as an authorized representative of another.

(5) "Notarial officer" means a notary public or other officer authorized to perform notarial acts.

§ 358.42. Notarial acts.

(a) In taking an acknowledgment, the notarial officer must determine, either from personal knowledge or from satisfactory evidence, that the person appearing before the officer and making the acknowledgment is the person whose true signature is on the instrument.

(b) In taking a verification upon oath or affirmation, the notarial officer must determine, either from personal knowledge or from satisfactory evidence, that the person appearing before the officer and making the verification is the person whose true signature is on the statement verified.

(c) In witnessing or attesting a signature the notarial officer must determine, either from personal knowledge or from satisfactory evidence, that the signature is that of the person appearing before the officer and named therein.

(d) In certifying or attesting a copy of a document or other item, the notarial officer must determine that the proffered copy is a full, true, and accurate transcription or reproduction of that which was copied.

(e) In making or noting a protest of a negotiable instrument the notarial officer must determine the matters set forth in section 336.3-509.

(f) A notarial officer has satisfactory evidence that a person is the person whose true signature is on a document if that person (i) is personally known to the notarial officer, (ii) is identified upon the oath or affirmation of a credible witness personally known to the notarial officer, or (iii) is identified on the basis of identification documents.

§ 358.43. Notarial acts in this state.

(a) A notarial act may be performed within this state by the following persons:

(1) a notary public of this state,

(2) a judge, clerk or court administrator, or deputy clerk or court administrator of any court of this state,

(3) a person authorized by the law of this state to administer oaths, or

(4) any other person authorized to perform the specific act by the law of this state.

(b) Notarial acts performed within this state under federal authority as provided in section 358.45 have the same effect as if performed by a notarial officer of this state.

(c) The signature and title of a person performing a notarial act are prima facie evidence that the signature is genuine and that the person holds the designated title.

§ 358.44. Notarial acts in other jurisdictions of the United States.

(a) A notarial act has the same effect under the law of this state as if performed by a notarial officer of this state, if performed in another state, commonwealth, territory, district, or possession of the United States by any of the following persons:

(1) a notary public of that jurisdiction;

(2) a judge, clerk, or deputy clerk of a court of that jurisdiction; or

(3) any other person authorized by the law of that jurisdiction to perform notarial acts.

(b) Notarial acts performed in other jurisdictions of the United States under federal authority as provided in section 358.45 have the same effect as if performed by a notarial officer of this state.

(c) The signature and title of a person performing a notarial act are prima facie evidence that the signature is genuine and that the person holds the designated title.

(d) The signature and indicated title of an officer listed in subsection (a)(1) or (a)(2) conclusively establish the authority of a holder of that title to perform a notarial act.

§ 358.45. Notarial acts under federal authority.

(a) A notarial act has the same effect under the law of this state as if performed by a notarial officer of this state if performed anywhere by any of the following persons under authority granted by the law of the United States:

(1) a judge, clerk, or deputy clerk of a court;

(2) a commissioned officer on active duty in the military service of the United States;

(3) an officer of the foreign service or consular officer of the United States; or

(4) any other person authorized by federal law to perform notarial acts.

(b) The signature and title of a person performing a notarial act are prima facie evidence that the signature is genuine and that the person holds the designated title.

(c) The signature and indicated title of an officer listed in subsection (a)(1), (a)(2), or (a)(3) conclusively establish the authority of a holder of that title to perform a notarial act.

§ 358.46. Foreign notarial acts.

(a) A notarial act has the same effect under the law of this state as if performed by a notarial officer of this state if performed within the jurisdiction of and under authority of a foreign nation or its constituent units or a multinational or international organization by any of the following persons:

(1) a notary public or notary;

(2) a judge, clerk, or deputy clerk of a court of record; or

(3) any other person authorized by the law of that jurisdiction to perform notarial acts.

(b) An "Apostille" in the form prescribed by the Hague Convention of October 5, 1961, conclusively establishes that the signature of the notarial officer is genuine and that the officer holds the indicated office.

(c) A certificate by a foreign service or consular officer of the United States stationed in the nation under the jurisdiction of which the notarial act was performed, or a certificate by a foreign service or consular officer of that nation stationed in the United States, conclusively establishes any matter relating to the authenticity or validity of the notarial act set forth in the certificate.

(d) An official stamp or seal of the person performing the notarial act is prima facie evidence that the signature is genuine and that the person holds the indicated title.

(e) An official stamp or seal of an officer listed in subsection (a)(1) or (a)(2) is prima facie evidence that a person with the indicated title has authority to perform notarial acts.

(f) If the title of office and indication of authority to perform notarial acts appears either in a digest of foreign law or in a list customarily used as a source for that information, the authority of an officer with that title to perform notarial acts is conclusively established.

§ 358.47. Certificate of notarial acts.

(a) A notarial act must be evidenced by a certificate signed and dated by a notarial officer. The certificate must include identification of the jurisdiction in which the notarial act is performed and the title of the office of the notarial officer and may include the official stamp or seal of office. If the officer is a notary public, the certificate must also indicate the date of expiration, if any, of the commission of office, but omission of that information may subsequently be corrected. If the officer is a commissioned officer on active duty in the military service of the United States, it must also include the officer's rank.

(b) A certificate of a notarial act is sufficient if it meets the requirements of subsection (a) and it:

(1) is in the short form set forth in section 358.48;

(2) is in a form otherwise prescribed by the law of this state;

(3) is in a form prescribed by the laws or regulations applicable in the place in which the notarial act was performed; or

(4) sets forth the actions of the notarial officer and those are sufficient to meet the requirements of the designated notarial act.

(c) By executing a certificate of a notarial act, the notarial officer certifies that the officer has made the determinations required by section 358.42.

§ 358.48. Short forms.

The following short form certificates of notarial acts are sufficient for the purposes indicated, if completed with the information required by section 358.47, subsection (a):

(1) For an acknowledgment in an individual capacity;

State of . . . .

County of . . . .

This instrument was acknowledged before me on . . . .(date) by . . . . (name(s) of person(s)).

. . . .
(Signature of notarial officer)

(Seal, if any)

. . . .
Title (and Rank)
My commission expires: . . . .

(2) For an acknowledgment in a representative capacity:

State of . . . .

County of . . . .

This instrument was acknowledged before me on . . . .(date) by . . . .(name(s) of person(s)) as . . . .(type of authority, e.g., officer, trustee, etc.) of . . . .

. . . .(name of party on behalf of whom the instrument was executed).

. . . .
(Signature of notarial officer)
(Seal, if any)

. . . .
Title (and Rank)
My commission expires: . . . .

(3) For a verification upon oath or affirmation:
State of . . . .
County of . . . .
Signed and sworn to (or affirmed) before me on
. . . . (date) by (name(s) of person(s)
making statement).

. . . .
(Signature of notarial officer)
(Seal, if any)

. . . .
Title (and Rank)
My commission expires: . . . .

(4) For witnessing or attesting a signature:
State of . . . .
County of . . . .
Signed or attested before me on . . . .
(date) by . . . .(name(s) of person(s)).

. . . .
(Signature of notarial officer)
(Seal, if any)

. . . .
Title (and Rank)
My commission expires: . . . .

(5) For attestation of a copy of a document:
State of . . . .
County of . . . .
I certify that this is a true and correct copy of a document in the possession of . . . .
Dated: . . . .

. . . .
(Signature of notarial officer)
(Seal, if any)

. . . .
Title (and Rank)
My commission expires: . . . .

§ 358.49. Short title.

Sections 358.41 to 358.49 may be cited as the uniform law on notarial acts.

§ 358.50. Effect of acknowledgment.

An acknowledgment made in a representative capacity for and on behalf of a corporation, partner-ship, trust, or other entity and certified substantially in the form prescribed in this chapter is prima facie evidence that the instrument was executed and delivered with proper authority.

DEPOSITIONS

[MINN. R. CIV. P.]

RULE 28. Persons before whom depositions may be taken.

28.01. Within the United States.

Within the United States or within a territory or insular possession subject to the jurisdiction of the United States, depositions shall be taken before an officer authorized to administer oaths by the laws of the United States or of the place where the examination is held, or before a person appointed by the court in which the action is pending. The term "officer" as used in Rules 28, 30, 31 and 32 includes a person appointed by the court or designated by the parties pursuant to Rule 29. A person so appointed has power to administer oaths and take testimony.

28.02. In Foreign Countries.

In a foreign country, depositions may be taken (1) on notice before a person authorized to administer oaths in the place in which the examination is held, either by the law thereof or by the law of the United States, or (2) before a person commissioned by the court, and a person so commissioned shall have the power by virtue of the commission to administer any necessary oath and take testimony, or (3) pursuant to a letter rogatory. A commission or a letter rogatory shall be issued on application and notice, and on terms that are just and appropriate. It is not requisite to the issuance of a commission or a letter rogatory that the taking of the deposition in any other manner is impracticable or inconvenient; and both a commission and a letter rogatory may be issued in proper cases. A notice or commission may designate the person before whom the deposition is to be taken either by name or descriptive title. A letter rogatory may be addressed "To the Appropriate Authority in (here name the country)." Evidence obtained in response to a letter rogatory need not be excluded merely for the reason that it is not a verbatim transcript or that the testimony was not taken under oath or for any similar departure from the requirements for deposition taken within the United States pursuant to these rules.

28.03. Disqualification for Interest.

No deposition shall be taken before or reported by any person who is a relative or employee or attorney or counsel of any of the parties, or is a relative or employee of such attorney or counsel, or is financially interested in the action, or who has a contract with the party, attorney, or person with an interest in the action that affects or has a substantial tendency to affect impartiality.

LEGAL HOLIDAYS

[MINN. STAT. ANN.]

§ 645.44. Holidays

* * *

Subdivision 5. Holidays. "Holiday" includes New Year's Day, January 1; Martin Luther King's Birthday, the third Monday in January; Washington's and Lincoln's Birthday, the third Monday in February; Memorial Day, the last Monday in May; Independence Day, July 4; Labor Day, the first Monday in September; Christopher Columbus Day, the second Monday in October; Veterans Day, November 11; Thanksgiving Day, the fourth Thursday in November; and Christmas Day, December 25; provided, when New Year's Day, January 1; or Independence Day, July 4; or Veterans Day, November 11; or Christmas Day, December 25; falls on Sunday, the following day shall be a holiday and, provided, when New Year's Day, January 1; or Independence Day, July 4; or Veterans Day, November 11; or Christmas Day, December 25; falls on Saturday, the preceding day shall be a holiday. No public business shall be transacted on any holiday, except in cases of necessity and except in cases of public business transacted by the legislature, nor shall any civil process be served thereon. However, for the executive branch of the state of Minnesota, "holiday" also includes the Friday after Thanksgiving but does not include Christopher Columbus Day. Other branches of state government and political subdivisions shall have the option of determining whether Christopher Columbus Day and the Friday after Thanksgiving shall be holidays. Where it is determined that Columbus Day or the Friday after Thanksgiving is not a holiday, public business may be conducted thereon.

Any agreement between a public employer and an employee organization citing Veterans Day as the fourth Monday in October shall be amended to cite Veterans Day as November 11.

* * *

MISSISSIPPI

NOTARIES PUBLIC

[Miss. Code Ann.]

§ 25-33-1. Appointment, bond and oath.

The Governor may appoint notaries public who may serve in any or all counties of this state. A notary public shall hold office for a term of four (4) years. Notaries public who are appointed and commissioned after July 1, 1988, shall give bond, with sufficient sureties, in the penalty of Five Thousand Dollars ($5,000.00). All such bonds shall be conditioned and approved as bonds of state officers are required to be, except that notaries public shall not otherwise be considered as state officers. Each notary public shall take the oath of office prescribed by Section 268 of the Constitution. A notary public shall qualify by filing the oath and bond in the office of the Secretary of State.

The bond requirements, unexpired appointments and commissions of notaries public issued prior to July 1, 1988, shall be sufficient, regardless of any jurisdictional limitations, to authorize notaries public appointed and commissioned prior to July 1, 1988, to serve any or all counties of this state. Any notary public commission containing language limiting the jurisdiction of a notary public may be returned to the Secretary of State. The Secretary of State shall then issue a new certificate indicating that such notary public may serve in any and all counties of this state.

§ 25-33-3. To procure seals.

Every notary public appointed and commissioned shall, at his own expense, procure a suitable notarial seal. Each seal shall have the name of the county of the notary's residence with that of the state and his own name on the margin thereof, and the words "notary public" across the center; and his official acts shall be attested by his seal of office.

The failure of such seal to conform to the provisions of this section shall not invalidate any official act or certificate of such notary public.

It shall be the duty of the Secretary of State to have printed a suitable number of copies of this section and to deliver to each notary public hereafter appointed a copy at the time of the issuance of his commission.

§ 25-33-5. Register of official acts.

Every notary public shall keep a fair register of all his official acts, and shall give a certified copy of his record, or any part thereof, to any person applying for it and paying the legal fees therefor.

§ 25-33-7. Disposal of register and papers.

In the case of the death, resignation, disqualification or expiration of the term of office of any notary public, his registers and other public papers shall, within thirty (30) days, be lodged in the office of the clerk of the circuit court of the county of his residence; and the clerk of that county may maintain an action for them.

§ 25-33-9. Administer oaths.

Every notary public shall have the power of administering oaths and affirmations in all matters incident to his notarial office, and he shall be further qualified and empowered to administer oaths and affirmations for the purpose of taking oral testimony under oath or affirmation within the state at large.

§ 25-33-11. Powers and duties.

Every notary public shall have power to receive the proof or acknowledgment of all instruments of writing relating to commerce or navigation, such as bills of sale, bottomries, mortgages, and hypothecations of ships, vessels or boats, charter parties of affreightment, letters of attorney, and such other writings as are commonly proved or acknowledged before notaries; and to perform all other duties required of notaries by commercial usage, and also to make declarations and certify the truth thereof, under his seal of office, concerning all matters done by him in virtue of his office.

§ 25-33-13. Affixation of expiration date of commission.

Every notary public, holding commission as such through appointment by the governor, shall be required to affix to any written or printed certificate of acknowledgment by him, in addition to his official seal and signature a written or printed recital of the date at which his commission expires. The failure of such notary public to affix such recital of date at which his commission expires shall not invalidate the acknowledgment of such instrument or such certificate of acknowledgment, or otherwise affect the validity or recording of any instrument.

In case of the failure hereafter on the part of any notary public, so holding commission, to comply with the requirement of this section, his commission may be revoked by the governor.

§ 25-33-15. Record of protest of bill or note.

When any notary public, court judge, or clerk shall protest any bill of exchange or promissory note, he shall make a full and true record in his register or book kept for that purpose of all his proceedings in relation thereto, and shall note thereon whether demand of the sum of money therein mentioned was made, of whom, when, and where; whether he presented such bill or note; whether no-

tices were given, to whom, and in what manner; where the same was mailed, and when and to whom and where directed; and of every other fact touching the same.

§ 25-33-17. Ex officio notaries public.

All justice court judges and clerks, clerks of the circuit and chancery courts and assistant secretaries of state are notaries public by virtue of their office, and shall possess all the powers and discharge all the duties belonging to the office of notary public, and may authenticate all their acts, instruments and attestations by the common seal of office; and all acts done by them of a notarial character shall receive the same credit and legal effect as are attached to the acts of notaries public.

§ 25-33-19. Common seal of such officers.

The board of supervisors of every county shall provide a notarial seal, with the inscription "notary public" around the margin and the image of an eagle in the center, which seal shall be kept in the office of the clerk of the circuit court; and all ex-officio notaries public may at all times have access to and use such seal for the authentication of any notarial act necessary to be so authenticated.

§ 25-33-21. Acknowledgment by notary public as stockholder.

It shall be lawful for any notary public who is a stockholder, director, officer, or employee of a bank or other corporation to take the acknowledgment of any party to any written instrument to or by such corporation, or to administer an oath to any other stockholder, director, officer, employee, or agent of such corporation, or to protest for nonacceptance or nonpayment bills of exchange, drafts, checks, notes, and other negotiable instruments which may be owned or held for collection by such corporation; provided, it shall be unlawful for any notary public to take the acknowledgment of an instrument by or to a bank or other corporation of which he is a stockholder, director, officer, or employee, where such notary is a party to such instrument, either individually or as a representative of such corporation, or to protest any negotiable instrument owned or held for collection by such corporation, where such notary is individually a party to such instrument.

§ 25-33-23. Notarial acts of commissioned officers of United States armed forces.

In addition to the acknowledgment of instruments and the performance of other notarial acts in the manner and form and as otherwise authorized by law, instruments may be acknowledged, documents attested, oaths and affirmations administered, depositions and affidavits executed, and other notarial acts performed before or by any commissioned officer in active service of the armed forces of the United States with the rank of second lieutenant or higher in the army or marine corps, or with the rank of ensign or higher in the navy or coast guard, or with equivalent rank in any other component part of the armed forces of the United States, by any person who either (a) is a member of the armed forces of the United States or the husband or wife of a member of the armed forces of the United States; or (b) is serving as a merchant seaman outside the limits of the United States included within the 48 states and the District of Columbia; or (c) is outside said limits by permission, assignment, or direction of any department or official of the United States government, in connection with any activity pertaining to the prosecution of any war in which the United States is then engaged.

Such acknowledgments of instruments, attestation of documents, administration of oaths and affirmations, executions of depositions and affidavits, and performance of other notarial acts, heretofore or hereafter made or taken, are hereby declared legal, valid, and binding, and instruments and documents so acknowledged, authenticated, or sworn to shall be admissible in evidence and eligible to record in this state under the same circumstances and with the same force and effect as if such acknowledgment, attestation, oath, affirmation, deposition, affidavit, or other notarial act had been made or taken within this state before or by a duly qualified officer or official as otherwise provided by law.

In the taking of acknowledgments and the performing of other notarial acts requiring certification, a certificate endorsed upon or attached to the instrument or documents, which shows the date of the notarial act and which state, in substance, that the person appearing before the officer acknowledged the instrument as his act or made or signed the instrument or document under oath, shall be sufficient for all intents and purposes. The instrument or document shall not be rendered invalid by the failure to state the place of execution or acknowledgment.

If the signature, rank, and branch of service or subdivision thereof, of any such commissioned officer appear upon such instrument or document or certificate, no further proof of the authority of such officer so to act shall be required, and such action by such commissioned officer shall be prima facie evidence that the person making such oath or acknowledgment is within the purview of this section.

ADDITIONAL AUTHORITY

[MISS. CONST.]

Art. 12, § 250.

All qualified electors and no others shall be eligible to office, except as otherwise provided in this Constitution; provided, however, that as to an office where no other qualification than that of being a qualified elector is provided by this Constitution, the legislature may, by law, fix additional qualifications for such office.

Art. 14, § 266.

No person holding or exercising the rights or powers of any office of honor or profit, either in his own right or as a deputy, or while otherwise acting for or in the name or by the authority of another, under any foreign government, or under the government of the United States, shall hold or exercise in any way the rights and powers of any office of honor or profit under the laws or authority of this state, except notaries, commissioners of deeds, and United States commissioners.

FEES

[MISS. CODE ANN.]

§ 25-7-29. Notaries public.

Notaries public shall charge the following fees:
(a) For protesting bill or note for non-acceptance or non-payment, and giving notice..........$1.00
(b) Registering such protest and making record
.... .50
(c) Attesting letters of attorney and seal ... .50
(d) Notarial affidavit to an account or other writing and seal .... .50
(e) Each oath or affirmation and seal ..... .50
(f) Notarial procuration and seal 1.00
(g) Certifying sales at auction and seal .... .50
(h) Taking proof of debts to be sent abroad .50
(i) Protest in insurance cases and seal 1.00
(j) Copy of record and affidavit 1.00

OFFENSES

§ 97-11-25. Embezzlement—officers, trustees and public employees, converting property to own use.

If any state officer or any county officer, or an officer in any district or subdivision of a county, or an officer of any city, town or village, or a notary public, or any other person holding any public office or employment, or any executor, administrator or guardian, or any trustee of an express trust, any master or commissioner or receiver, or any attorney at law or solicitor, or any bank or collecting agent, or other person engaged in like public employment, or any other person undertaking to act for others and intrusted by them with business of any kind, or with money, shall unlawfully convert to his own use any money or other valuable thing which comes to his hands or possession by virtue of his office or employment, or shall not, when lawfully required to turn over such money or deliver such thing, immediately do so according to his legal obligation, he shall, on conviction, be committed to the department of corrections for not more than twenty (20) years, or be fined not more than five thousand dollars ($5,000.00).

ACKNOWLEDGMENTS

§ 89-3-3. Acknowledgment and proof.

Every conveyance, contract or agreement proper to be recorded, may be acknowledged or proved before any judge of the United States court, any judge of the supreme court, any judge of the circuit court, or any chancellor, or any judge of the county court, or before any clerk of a court of record or notary public, who shall certify such acknowledgment or proof under the seal of his office, or before any justice of the peace, or police justice, or mayor of any city, town, or village, or clerk of a municipality, or member of the board of supervisors, whether the property conveyed be within his county or not.

§ 89-3-5. Acknowledgments before commissioned officers of United States armed forces.

In all cases where a conveyance, contract, agreement or other instrument of writing has heretofore been acknowledged or proved before any commissioned officer in the services of the United States armed forces, such acknowledgment or affidavit is hereby declared to be good, valid and binding to the same extent and with like effect as though such conveyance, contract, agreement, or other instrument of writing had been acknowledged or proved before any officer authorized by law to take acknowledgments in the State of Mississippi.

§ 89-3-7. Forms of acknowledgment.

The following forms of acknowledgment may be used in the case of conveyances or other written instruments affecting real estate or personal property; and any acknowledgment so taken and certified shall be sufficient to satisfy all requirements of law:

(a) In the case of natural persons acting in their own right:

"STATE OF _____
COUNTY OF _____

Personally appeared before me, the undersigned authority in and for the said county and state, on this _____ day of _____, 19___, within my jurisdiction, the within named _____, who acknowledged that (he)(she)(they) executed the above and foregoing instrument.

_____ (NOTARY PUBLIC)

My commission expires:
_____ "

(Affix official seal, if applicable)

(b) In the case of corporations:

"STATE OF _____
COUNTY OF _____

Personally appeared before me, the undersigned authority in and for the said county and state, on this _____ day of _____, 19___, within my jurisdiction, the within named _____, who acknowledged that (he)(she) is _____ of _____, a _____ corporation,and that for and on behalf of the said corporation, and as its act and deed (he)(she) executed the above and foregoing instrument, after first having been duly authorized by said corporation so to do.

_____(NOTARY PUBLIC)

My commission expires:
_____ "

(Affix official seal, if applicable)

(c) In the case of persons acting in representative capacities:

"STATE OF _____
COUNTY OF _____

Personally appeared before me, the undersigned authority in and for the said county and state, on this _____ day of _____, 19___, within my jurisdiction, the within named _____, who acknowledged that (he)(she) is _____ of _____ and that in said representative capacity (he)(she) executed the above and foregoing instrument, after first having been duly authorized so to do.

_____(NOTARY PUBLIC)

My commission expires:
_____ "

(Affix official seal, if applicable)

(d) In the case of proof of execution of the instrument made by a subscribing witness:

"STATE OF _____
COUNTY OF _____

Personally appeared before me, the undersigned authority in and for the said county and state, on this _____ day of _____, 19___, within my jurisdiction, CD, one of the subscribing witnesses to the above and foregoing instrument, who, being first duly sworn, states that (he)(she) saw the within (or above) named AB, whose name is subscribed thereto, sign and deliver the same to EF (or that (he)(she) heard AB acknowledge that (he)(she) signed and delivered the same to EF); and that the affiant subscribed (his)(her) name as witness thereto in the presence of AB.

_____(NOTARY PUBLIC)

My commission expires:

_____"

(Affix official seal, if applicable)

§ 89-3-9. Acknowledgment or proof in another state.

If the party who shall execute any conveyance of lands or personal property situated in this state, or if the witnesses thereto reside or be in some other state, territory in the Union, the District of Columbia, or in any possession of the United States, or land over which the United States has sovereign power, then the acknowledgment or proof may be made before and certified by the chief justice of the United States, or an associate justice of the Supreme Court of the United States, or a circuit or district judge of the United States, or any other United States judge, or any judge or justice of the supreme or superior court of any such state, territory, District of Columbia, or possession of the United States, or land over which the United States has sovereign power, or any justice of the peace of such state, territory, District of Columbia, possession, or land over which the United States has sovereign power, whose official character shall be certified under the seal of some court of record in his country, parish or other named official jurisdiction, or before any commissioner residing in such state, territory, District of Columbia, possession, or land over which the United States has sovereign power, who may be appointed by the governor of this state to take acknowledgments and proof of conveyances, or any notary public or a clerk of a court of record having a seal of office in said state, territory, District of Columbia, possession, or land over which the United States has sovereign power, and shall be as good and effectual as if the certificate of acknowledgment or proof had been made by a competent officer in this state.

§ 89-3-13. Acknowledgment or proof in foreign country.

If the party who shall execute any conveyance of lands or personal property situated in this state, or if the witnesses thereto, reside or be in a foreign country, the acknowledgment or proof of the execution of such conveyance may be made before any court of record, or the mayor or chief magistrate of any city, borough, or corporation of such foreign country in which the party or witness resides or

may be; or before any commissioner residing in such country who may be appointed by the Governor, or before any ambassador, foreign minister, secretary of legation, or consul of the United States to the foreign country in which the party or witness may reside or be; or before any notary public commissioned by the government of the foreign country or any other person authorized by said government to take oaths or acknowledgments; but the certificate shall show that the party, or the party and witness, were identified before the officer, and that the party acknowledged the execution of the instrument, or that the execution was duly proved by the witness, and it shall be as good and effectual as if made and certified by a competent officer of this state.

§ 89-3-15. Grantor and witness dead or absent, how proved.

If the grantor and witness or witnesses of any instrument of writing be dead or absent, so that the personal attendance of neither can be had, it may be established by the oath of any person who, on examination before an officer competent to take acknowledgments, can prove the handwriting of the deceased or absent witness or witnesses; or when such proof cannot be had, then the handwriting of the grantor may be proved, and the officer before whom such proof is made shall certify accordingly, and such certificate shall be deemed equivalent to an acknowledgment by the grantor or proof by a subscribing witness, and entitle the instrument to be recorded.

DEPOSITIONS

§ 13-1-227. Depositions before action or pending appeal.

(a) Before action. (1) Petition. A person who desires to perpetuate his own testimony or that of another person regarding any matter that may be cognizable in any court of this state may file a verified petition in the circuit or chancery court in the county of the residence of any expected adverse party. The petition shall be entitled in the name of the petitioner and shall show: (1) that the petitioner expects to be a party to an action cognizable in a court of this state but is presently unable to bring it or cause it to be brought, (2) the subject matter of the expected action and his interest therein, (3) the facts which he desires to establish by the proposed testimony and his reasons for desiring to perpetuate it, (4) the names or a description of the persons he expects will be adverse parties and their addresses so far as known, and (5) the names and addresses of the persons to be examined and the substance of the testimony which he expects to elicit from each, and shall ask for an order authorizing the petitioner to take the depositions of the persons to be examined named in the petition, for the purpose of perpetuating their testimony.

(2) **Notice and service.** The petitioner shall thereafter serve a notice upon each person named in the petition as an expected adverse party, stating that the petitioner will apply to the court, at a time and place named therein, for the order described in the petition. At least twenty (20) days before the date of hearing the notice shall be served in the same manner of service of summons; but if such service cannot with due diligence be made upon any expected adverse party named in the petition, the court may make such order as is just for service by publication or otherwise, and shall appoint, for persons not served in the manner provided by law, an attorney who shall represent them, and, in case they are not otherwise represented, shall cross-examine the deponent.

(3) **Order and examination.** If the court is satisfied that the perpetuation of the testimony may prevent a failure or delay of justice, it shall make an order designating or describing the persons whose depositions may be taken and specifying the subject matter of the examination and whether the depositions shall be taken upon oral examination or written interrogatories. The depositions may then be taken in accordance with sections 13-1-201, 13-1-226 through 13-1-237, 13-1-241, and 13-1-243; and the court may make orders of the character provided for by section 13-1-234. For the purpose of applying sections 13-1-201, 13-1-226 through 13-1-237, 13-1-241, and 13-1-243, to depositions for perpetuating testimony, each reference therein to the court in which the action is pending shall be deemed to refer to the court in which the petition for such deposition was filed.

(4) **Use of deposition.** If a deposition to perpetuate testimony is taken under sections 13-1-201, 13-1-226 through 13-1-237, 13-1-241, 13-1-243, it may be used in any action involving the same subject matter subsequently brought in a circuit, chancery or county court in accordance with section 13-1-232(a).

(b) **Pending appeal.** If an appeal has been taken from a judgment of a court or before the taking of an appeal if the time therefor has not expired, the court in which the judgment was rendered may allow the taking of the depositions of witnesses to perpetuate their testimony for use in the event of further proceedings in the court. In such case the party who desires to perpetuate the testimony may make a motion in the court for leave to take the depositions, upon the same notice and service thereof as if the action was pending in the court. The motion shall show (1) the names and addresses of persons to be examined and the substance of the

testimony which he expects to elicit from each; (2) the reasons for perpetuating their testimony. If the court finds that the perpetuation of the testimony is proper to avoid a failure or delay of justice, it may make an order allowing the depositions to be taken and may make orders of the character provided for by section 13-1-234, and thereupon the depositions may be taken and used in the same manner and under the same conditions as are prescribed in sections 13-1-201, 13-1-226 through 13-1-237, 13-1-241, and 13-1-243, for depositions taken in actions pending in the court.

(c) **Perpetuation by action.** This section does not limit the power of a court to entertain an action to perpetuate testimony.

§ 13-1-228. Persons before whom depositions may be taken.

(a) **Within the United States.** Within the United States or within a territory or insular possession subject to the dominion of the United States, depositions shall be taken before an officer authorized to administer oaths by the laws of the United States or of the place where the examination is held, or before a person appointed by the court in which the action is pending. A person so appointed has power to administer oaths and take testimony.

(b) **In foreign countries.** In a foreign country, depositions may be taken (1) on notice before a person authorized to administer oaths in the place in which the examination is held, either by the law thereof or by the law of the United States, or (2) before a person commissioned by the court, and a person so commissioned shall have the power by virtue of his commission to administer any necessary oath and take testimony, or (3) pursuant to a letter rogatory. A commission or a letter rogatory shall be issued on application and notice and on terms that are just and appropriate. It is not requisite to the issuance of a commission or a letter rogatory that the taking of the deposition in any other manner is impracticable or inconvenient; and both a commission and a letter rogatory may be issued in proper cases. A notice or commission may designate the person before whom the deposition is to be taken either by name or descriptive title. A letter rogatory may be addressed "To the Appropriate Authority in (here name the country)." Evidence obtained in response to a letter rogatory need not be excluded merely for the reason that it is not a verbatim transcript or that the testimony was not taken under oath or for any similar departure from the requirements for depositions taken within the United States under sections 13-1-201, 13-1-226, through 13-1-237, 13-1-241, and 13-1-243.

(c) **Disqualification for interest.** No deposition shall be taken before a person who is a relative or employee or attorney or counsel of any of the parties, or is a relative or employee of such attorney or counsel, or is financially interested in the action.

§ 13-1-229. Stipulations regarding discovery procedure.

Unless the court orders otherwise, the parties may by written stipulation (1) provide that depositions may be taken before any person, at any time or place, upon any notice, and in any manner and when so taken may be used like other depositions, and (2) modify the procedures provided by sections 13-1-201, 13-1-226 through 13-1-237, 13-1-241, and 13-1-243, for other methods of discovery, except that stipulations extending the time provided in sections 13-1-233, 13-1-234 and 13-1-236 for responses to discovery may be made only with the approval of the court.

§ 13-1-230. Depositions upon oral examination.

(a) **When depositions may be taken.** After commencement of the action, any party may take the testimony of any person, including a party by deposition upon oral examination. Leave of court, granted with or without notice, must be obtained only if the plaintiff seeks to take a deposition prior to the expiration of thirty (30) days after service of the summons upon any defendant, except that leave is not required (1) if a defendant has served a notice of taking deposition or otherwise sought discovery, or (2) if special notice is given under subsection (b)(2) of this section. The attendance of witnesses may be compelled by subpoena. The deposition of a person confined in prison may be taken only by leave of court on such terms as the court prescribes.

(b) **Notice of examination: general requirements; special notice; nonstenographic recording; production of documents and things; deposition of organization.** (1) A party desiring to take the deposition of any person upon oral examination shall give reasonable notice in writing to every other party to the action. Reasonable notice shall mean at least five (5) days in advance of the proposed examination. The notice shall state the time and place for taking the deposition and the name and address of each person to be examined, if known, and, if the name is not known, a general description sufficient to identify him or the particular class or group to which he belongs. If a subpoena duces tecum is to be served on the person to be examined, the designation of the materials to be produced as set forth in the subpoena shall be attached to or included in the notice.

(2) Leave of court is not required for the taking of a deposition by plaintiff if the notice (A) states that the person to be examined is about to go out of the state and will be unavailable for examination unless his deposition is taken before expiration of the thirty-day period, and (B) sets forth facts to support the statement. The plaintiff's attorney shall sign the notice, and his signature constitutes a certification by him that to the best of his knowledge, information and belief the statement and supporting facts are true.

If a party shows that when he was served with notice under this subsection (b)(2) he was unable through the exercise of diligence to obtain counsel to represent him at the taking of the deposition, the deposition may not be used against him.

(3) The court may for cause shown enlarge or shorten the time for taking the deposition.

(4) The court may upon motion order that the testimony at a deposition be recorded by other than stenographic means, in which event the order shall designate the manner of recording, preserving, and filing the deposition, and may include other provisions to assure that the recorded testimony will be accurate and trustworthy. If the order is made, a party may nevertheless arrange to have a stenographic transcription made at his own expense.

(5) The notice to a party deponent may be accompanied by a request made in compliance with section 13-1-234 for the production of documents and tangible things at the taking of the deposition. The procedure of section 13-1-234 shall apply to the request.

(6) A party may in his notice and in a subpoena name as the deponent a public or private corporation or a partnership or association or governmental agency and describe with reasonable particularity the matters on which examination is requested. In that event, the organization so named shall designate one or more officers, directors, or managing agents, or other persons who consent to testify on its behalf, and may set forth, for each person designated, the matters on which he will testify. A subpoena shall advise a nonparty organization of its duty to make such a designation. The persons so designated shall testify as to matters known or reasonably available to the organization. This subsection (b)(6) does not preclude taking a deposition by any other procedure authorized in sections 13-1-201, 13-1-226 through 13-1-237, 13-1-241, and 13-1-243.

(c) **Examination and cross-examination; record of examination; oath; objections.** Examination and cross-examination of witnesses may proceed as permitted at trial. The officer before whom the deposition is to be taken shall put the witness on oath and shall personally, or by someone acting under his direction and in his presence, record the testimony of the witness. The testimony shall be taken stenographically or recorded by any other means ordered in accordance with subsection (b)(4) of this section. If requested by one of the parties, the testimony shall be transcribed.

All objections made at time of the examination to the qualifications of the officer taking the deposition, or to the manner of taking it, or to the evidence presented, or to the conduct of any party, and any other objection to the proceedings, shall be noted by the officer upon the deposition. Evidence objected to shall be taken subject to the objections. In lieu of participating in the oral examination, parties may serve written questions in a sealed envelope on the party taking the deposition and he shall transmit them to the officer, who shall propound them to the witness and record the answers verbatim.

(d) **Motion to terminate or limit examination.** At any time during the taking of the deposition, on motion of a party or of the deponent and upon a showing that the examination is being conducted in bad faith or in such manner as unreasonably to annoy, embarrass, or oppress the deponent or party, the court in which the action is pending may order the officer conducting the examination to cease forthwith from taking the deposition or may limit the scope and manner of the taking of the deposition as provided in section 13-1-226(c). If the order made terminates the examination, it shall be resumed thereafter only upon the order of the court in which the action is pending. Upon demand of the objecting party or deponent, the taking of the deposition shall be suspended for the time necessary to make a motion for an order. Section 13-1-237(a)(4) applies to the award of expenses incurred in relation to the motion.

(e) **Submission to witness; changes; signing.** When the testimony is fully transcribed the deposition shall be submitted to the witness for examination and shall be read to or by him, unless such examination and reading are waived by the witness and by the parties. Any changes in form or substance which the witness desires to make shall be entered upon the deposition by the officer with a statement of the reasons given by the witness for making them. The deposition shall then be signed by the witness, unless the parties by stipulation waive the signing or the witness is ill or cannot be found or refuses to sign. If the deposition is not signed by the witness within thirty (30) days of its submission to him, the officer shall sign it and state on the record the fact of the waiver or of the illness or absence of the witness or the fact of the refusal to sign, together with the reason, if any, given therefor; and the deposition may then be used as fully as though signed unless on a motion to suppress under section 13-1-232(d)(4) the court holds that the reasons given for the refusal to sign require rejection of the deposition in whole or in part.

(f) **Certification and filing by officer; exhibits; copies; notice of filing.** (1) The officer shall certify on the deposition that the witness was duly sworn by him and that the deposition is a true record of the testimony given by the witness. He shall then securely seal the deposition in an envelope indorsed with the title of the action and marked "Deposition of (here insert name of witness)" and shall promptly file it with the court in which the action is pending or send it by registered or certified mail to the clerk thereof for filing.

Documents and things produced for inspection during the examination of the witness shall, upon the request of a party, be marked for identification and annexed to and returned with the deposition, and may be inspected and copied by any party, except that (A) the person producing the materials may substitute copies to be marked for identification, if he affords to all parties fair opportunity to verify the copies by comparison with the originals, and (B) if the person producing the materials requests their return, the officer shall mark them, give each party an opportunity to inspect and copy them, and return them to the person producing them, and the materials may then be used in the same manner as if annexed to and returned with the deposition. Any party may move for an order that the original be annexed to and returned with the deposition to the court, pending final deposition of the case.

(2) Upon payment of reasonable charges therefor, the officer shall furnish a copy of the deposition to any party or to the deponent.

(3) The party taking the deposition shall give prompt notice of its filing to all other parties.

(g) **Failure to attend or to serve subpoena; expenses.** (1) If the party giving the notice of the taking of a deposition fails to attend and proceed therewith and another party attends in person or by attorney pursuant to the notice, the court may order the party giving the notice to pay to such other party the reasonable expenses incurred by him and his attorney in attending, including reasonable attorney's fees.

(2) If the party giving the notice of the taking of a deposition of a witness fails to serve a subpoena upon him and the witness because of such failure does not attend, and if another party attends in person or by attorney because he expects the deposition of that witness to be taken, the court may order the party giving the notice to pay to such other party the reasonable expenses incurred by him and his attorney in attending, including reasonable attorney's fees.

§ 13-1-231. Depositions upon written questions.

(a) **Serving the questions; notice.** After commencement of the action, any party may take the testimony of any person, including a party, by deposition upon written questions. The attendance of witnesses may be compelled by the use of subpoena as provided by law. The deposition of a person confined in prison may be taken only by leave of court on such terms as the court prescribes.

A party desiring to take a deposition upon written questions shall serve them upon every other party with a notice stating (1) the name and address of the person who is to answer them, if known, and if the name is not known, a general description sufficient to identify him or the particular class or group to which he belongs, and (2) the name or descriptive title and address of the officer before whom the deposition is to be taken. A deposition upon written questions may be taken of a public or private corporation or a partnership or association or governmental agency in accordance with section 13-1-230(b)(6).

Within thirty (30) days after the notice and written questions are served, a party may serve cross questions upon all other parties. Within ten (10) days after being served with cross questions, a party may serve redirect questions upon all other parties. Within ten (10) days after being served with redirect questions, a party may serve recross questions upon all other parties. The court may for cause shown enlarge or shorten the time.

(b) Officer to take responses and prepare record. A copy of the notice and copies of all questions served shall be delivered by the party taking the deposition to the officer designated in the notice, who shall proceed promptly, in the manner provided by section 13-1-230(c), (e), and (f), to take the testimony of the witness in response to the questions and to prepare, certify and file or mail the deposition, attaching thereto the copy of the notice and the questions received by him.

(c) Notice of filing. When the deposition is filed, the party taking it shall promptly give notice thereof to all other parties.

§ 13-1-232. Use of depositions in court proceedings.

(1) Use of depositions. At the trial or upon the hearing of a motion or an interlocutory proceeding, any part or all of a deposition, so far as admissible under the rules of evidence applied as though the witness were then present and testifying, may be used against any party who was present or represented at the taking of the deposition or who had reasonable notice thereof, in accordance with any of the following provisions:

(a) Any deposition may be used by any party for the purpose of contradicting or impeaching the testimony of deponent as a witness.

(b) The deposition of a party or of anyone who at the time of taking the deposition was an officer, director or managing agent, or a person designated

under sections 13-1-230(b)(6) or 13-1-231(a) to testify on behalf of a public or private corporation, partnership or association or governmental agency which is a party may be used by an adverse party for any purpose.

(c) The deposition of a witness, whether or not a party, may be used by any party for any purpose if the court finds: (A) that the witness is dead; or (B) that the witness is at a greater distance than one hundred (100) miles from the place of trial or hearing, or is out of the state, unless it appears that the absence of the witness was procured by the party offering the deposition; or (C) that the witness is unable to attend or testify because of age, illness, infirmity, or imprisonment; or (D) that the party offering the deposition has been unable to procure the attendance of the witness by subpoena; or (E) upon application and notice, that such exceptional circumstances exist as to make it desirable, in the interest of justice and with due regard to the importance of presenting the testimony of witnesses orally in open court, to allow the deposition to be used.

(d) If only part of a deposition is offered in evidence by a party, an adverse party may require him to introduce any other part which ought in fairness to be considered with the part introduced, and any party may introduce any other parts.

Substitution of parties does not affect the right to use depositions previously taken; and, when an action in any court has been dismissed and another action involving the same subject matter is afterward brought between the same parties or their representatives or successors in interest, all depositions lawfully taken and duly filed in the former action may be used in the latter as if originally taken therefor.

(2) Objections to admissibility. Subject to the provisions of section 13-1-228(b) and subsection (4)(c) of this section, objection may be made at the trial or hearing to receiving in evidence any deposition or part thereof for any reason which would require the exclusion of the evidence if the witness were then present and testifying.

(3) Effect of taking or using depositions. A party does not make a person his own witness for any purpose by taking his deposition. The introduction in evidence of the deposition or any part thereof for any purpose other than that of contradicting or impeaching the deponent makes the deponent the witness of the party introducing the deposition, but this shall not apply to the use by an adverse party of a deposition under subsection (a)(2) of this section. At the trial or hearing any party may rebut any relevant evidence contained in a deposition whether introduced by him or by any other party.

(4) Effect of errors and irregularities in depositions. (a) As to notice. All errors and irregularities in the notice for taking a deposition are waived unless written objection is promptly served upon the party giving the notice.

(b) As to disqualification of officer. Objection to taking a deposition because of disqualification of the officer before whom it is to be taken is waived unless made before the taking of the deposition begins or as soon thereafter as the disqualification becomes known or could be discovered with reasonable diligence.

(c) As to taking of deposition. (i) Objections to the competency of a witness or to the competency, relevancy, or materiality of testimony are not waived by failure to make them before or during the taking of the deposition, unless the ground of the objection is one which might have been obviated or removed if presented at that time.

(ii) Errors and irregularities occurring at the oral examination in the manner of taking the deposition, in the form of the questions or answers, in the oath or affirmation, or in the conduct of parties, and errors of any kind which might be obviated, removed, or cured if promptly presented, are waived unless seasonable objection thereto is made at the taking of the deposition.

(iii) Objections to the form of written questions submitted under section 13-1-231 are waived unless served in writing upon the party propounding them within the time allowed for serving the succeeding cross or other questions and within five (5) days after service of the last questions authorized.

(d) As to completion and return of deposition. Errors and irregularities in the manner in which the testimony is transcribed or the deposition is prepared, signed, certified, sealed, indorsed, transmitted, filed, or otherwise dealt with by the officer under sections 13-1-230 and 13-1-231 are waived unless a motion to suppress the deposition or some part thereof is made with reasonable promptness after such defect is, or with due diligence might have been, ascertained.

COMMISSIONERS

§ 7-1-17. Commissioners for other states.

The governor may appoint one or more commissioners, residing in each of the states and territories of the United States and in the District of Columbia or in any foreign country, who shall hold their office for the term of four years from the date of their commissions. They shall have full power to administer oaths and affirmations, to take and certify depositions and affidavits to be used in this state, and to take and certify the acknowledgment and proof of all instruments of writing to be recorded in this state; and their acts shall be as effectual in law as if done and certified by any officer thereunto duly authorized in this state. Before any

commissioner so appointed shall proceed to perform any of the duties of his office, he shall take and subscribe an oath, before an officer authorized to administer oaths in the state or county for which such commissioner may be appointed, that he will faithfully discharge all the duties of the office, which oath shall be filed in the office of the secretary of state within six months after the taking and subscribing of the same.

LEGAL HOLIDAYS

§ 3-3-7. Legal holidays.

The following are declared to be legal holidays, viz: the first day of January (New Year's Day); the third Monday of January (Robert E. Lee's birthday and Dr. Martin Luther King, Jr.'s birthday); the third Monday of February (Washington's birthday); the last Monday of April (Confederate Memorial Day); the last Monday of May (National Memorial Day and Jefferson Davis' birthday); the fourth day of July (Independence Day); the first Monday of September (Labor Day); the eleventh day of November (Armistice or Veterans' Day); the day fixed by proclamation by the Governor of Mississippi as a day of Thanksgiving, which shall be fixed to correspond to the date proclaimed by the President of the United States (Thanksgiving Day); and the twenty-fifth day of December (Christmas Day). Provided however, that in the event any holiday hereinbefore declared legal shall fall on Sunday, then the next following day shall be a legal holiday.

August 16 is declared to be Elvis Aaron Presley Day in recognition and appreciation of Elvis Aaron Presley's many contributions, international recognition and the rich legacy left to us by Elvis Aaron Presley. This day shall be a day of recognition and observation and shall not be recognized as a legal holiday.

May 8 is declared to be Hernando de Soto Day in recognition, observation and commemoration of Hernando de Soto, who led the first and most imposing expedition ever made by Europeans into the wilds of North America and the State of Mississippi, and in further recognition of the Spanish explorer's 187-day journey from the Tombigbee River basin on our state's eastern boundary, westward to the place of discovery of the Mississippi River on May 8, 1541. This day shall be a day of commemoration, recognition and observation of Hernando de Soto and European exploration and shall not be recognized as a legal holiday.

Insofar as possible, Armistice Day shall be observed by appropriate exercises in all the public schools in the State of Mississippi at the eleventh hour in the morning of the eleventh day of the eleventh month of the year.

MISSOURI

NOTARIES PUBLIC

[Mo. Ann. Stat.]

§ 486.200. Definitions.

As used in sections 486.200 to 486.405

(1) **"County"** means any of the several counties of this state or the city of St. Louis;

(2) **"County clerk"** means any of the several county clerks of this state or the clerk of the circuit court in the city of St. Louis;

(3) **"Facsimile"** means an exact copy preserving all the written or printed marks of the original;

(4) **"Notarization"** means the performance of a notarial act;

(5) **"Notary public"** and **"notary"** means any person appointed and commissioned to perform notarial acts;

(6) **"Official misconduct"** means the wrongful exercise of a power or the wrongful performance of a duty. The term **"wrongful"** as used in the definition of official misconduct means unauthorized, unlawful, abusive, negligent, reckless, or injurious.

§ 486.205. Notary public, how appointed.

Upon application, the secretary of state may appoint and commission individual persons as notaries public in each of the several counties in this state. The secretary of state may not appoint and commission as a notary public any person who submits an application containing substantial and material misstatement or omission of fact.

§ 486.210. Notary's authority to be statewide.

Each notary public may perform notarial acts anywhere within this state.

§ 485.215. Term of office.

Each notary public may perform notarial acts for a term of four years from the date of his commission, unless sooner removed.

§ 486.220. Qualifications for notary.

1. Each person appointed and commissioned as a notary public shall, except as provided for in subsection 2 of this section:

(1) Be a citizen of the United States and at least eighteen years of age;

(2) Be a registered voter of the county within and for which he is commissioned;

(3) Have a residence address in the county within and for which he is commissioned;

(4) Be a resident of the state for one year preceding the date of his commission;

(5) Be able to read and write the English language; and

(6) Not have had his commission revoked during the past ten years.

2. Any person who does not qualify under subsection 1 of this section may nonetheless be appointed and commissioned as a notary public provided that person:

(1) Is a citizen of the United States and at least eighteen years of age;

(2) Works in Missouri and will use the notary seal in the course of his employment in Missouri;

(3) Has a work address in the county within and for which he is commissioned for one year preceding the date of his commission;

(4) Is able to read and write the English language;

(5) Has not had a notary commission revoked in any state during the past ten years; and

(6) Authorizes the secretary of state as the agent and representative of such person to accept service of process or service of any notice or demand required or permitted by law to be served upon such person.

3. A notary public is not a public officer within the meaning of article VII of the Missouri Constitution.

§ 486.225. Application, form of, fee.

1. Upon a form prepared by the secretary of state, each applicant for appointment and commission as a notary public shall swear, under penalty of perjury, that the answers to all questions on the application are true and complete to the best of his knowledge and that he is qualified to be appointed and commissioned as a notary public. The completed application form shall be filed with the secretary of state.

2. With his application, each applicant for appointment and commission as a notary public shall submit to the secretary of state endorsements from two registered voters of this state in substantially the following form:

I, ... (name of endorser), a registered voter of this state and . . . . County, believe to the best of my knowledge, the applicant is a person of good moral character and integrity and capable of performing notarial acts.

. . . .
(Endorser's signature and residence address)

3. With his application, each applicant for appointment and commission as a notary public shall submit to the secretary of state, payable to the director of revenue, a commission fee of fifteen dollars.

§ 486.230. Commission to be issued, when—contents.

Upon receipt of a completed application, proper endorsements and the correct fee, the secretary of state, if satisfied the applicant is qualified to be appointed and commissioned as a notary public, shall prepare a notary commission for the applicant and forward the commission to the county clerk in the county of the applicant's residence. Each commission shall contain the applicant's name, the county within and for which he is to be commissioned, the date upon which the commission takes effect and the date upon which it expires.

§ 486.235. Bond required—oath, form of.

1. During his term of office each notary public shall maintain a surety bond in the sum of ten thousand dollars with, as surety thereon, a company qualified to write surety bonds in this state. The bond shall be conditioned upon the faithful performance of all notarial acts in accordance with this chapter. Each notary public shall notify the secretary of state of changes on or riders to the bond.

2. Before receiving his commission, each applicant shall submit to the county clerk of the county within and for which he is to be commissioned, an executed bond commencing at least thirty days after the date he submitted his application to the secretary of state with a term of four years.

3. Before receiving his commission, each applicant shall take the following oath in the presence of the county clerk:

I, ... (name of applicant), solemnly swear, under the penalty of perjury, that I have carefully read the notary law of this state, and if appointed and commissioned as a notary public, I will uphold the Constitution of the United States and of this state and will faithfully perform to the best of my ability all notarial acts in conformance with the law.

. . . . (signature of applicant)

Subscribed and sworn to before me this . . . . day of . . . ., 19. . .

. . . . (signature of county clerk)

4. Before receiving his commission, each applicant shall submit to the county clerk a handwritten specimen of his official signature which contains his surname and at least the initial of his first name.

5. Immediately after receiving the bond and official signature and witnessing the oath, the county clerk shall award to the applicant his commission as a notary public.

§ 486.240. Failure of applicant to appear and qualify, effect of.

If the person for whom a commission is issued fails to appear and qualify within ninety days after the commission is issued, the county clerk shall note the failure on the commission and return it to the secretary of state. The secretary of state shall immediately cancel and annul the commission.

§ 486.245. Register of notaries to be kept—bond, signature and oath to secretary of state.

The county clerk shall keep a register, listing the name and address of each person to whom he awards a notary commission and the date upon which he awards the commission. Within thirty days after receiving a bond, signature and oath, the county clerk shall forward the bond, signature and oath to the secretary of state by certified mail. All such bonds, signatures and oaths shall be preserved permanently by the secretary of state.

§ 486.250. Powers of notary.

Each notary public is empowered to
(1) Take acknowledgments;
(2) Administer oaths and affirmations;
(3) Certify that a copy of a document is a true copy of another document; and
(4) Perform any other act permitted by law.

§ 486.255. Notary disqualified, when.

1. For the purposes of this chapter, a notary public has a disqualifying interest in a transaction in connection with which notarial services are requested if he is named, individually, as a party to the transaction.

2. No notary who has a disqualifying interest in a transaction may legally perform any notarial act in connection with the transaction.

§ 486.260. Notary to keep journal.

Each notary public shall provide and keep a permanently bound journal of his notarial acts containing numbered pages.

§ 486.265. Certified copy of notary record, when given, fee—minute book to be kept.

Every notary shall keep a true and perfect record of his official acts, except those connected with judicial proceedings, and those for whose public record the law provides, and if required, shall give a certified copy of any record in his office, upon the payment of the fees therefor. Every notary shall make and keep an exact minute, in a book kept by him for that purpose, of each of his official acts, except as herein provided.

§ 486.270. Copies of notarial acts furnished on court order—fee.

Each notary public, upon written court order, shall furnish facsimiles of entries made in his journal of notarial acts or any other papers or copies relating to his notarial acts, upon receipt of a fee of one dollar per 8½ x 11 inch paper or part of a page.

§ 486.275. Signature of notary required, when.

At the time of notarization a notary public shall sign his official signature on each notary certificate.

§ 486.280. Printed information required on notary certificate.

On every notary certificate, a notary public shall indicate clearly and legibly by means of rubber stamp, typewriting or printing, so that it is capable of photographic reproduction:

(1) His name exactly as it appears on his commission;

(2) The words "Notary Public," "State of Missouri," and "My commission expires . . (commission expiration date);"

(3) The name of the county within which he is commissioned.

§ 486.285. Seal, words required on—seal, how applied.

1. Each notary public shall provide, keep, and use a seal embosser engraved to show the words "Notary Seal," his name, "Notary Public," and "State of Missouri."

2. The indentations made by the seal embosser shall not be applied on the notarial certificate or document to be notarized in a manner that will render illegible or incapable of photographic reproduction any of the printed marks or writing on the certificate or document.

§ 486.290. Illegibility of certificate, effect of.

The illegibility of any of the information required by sections 486.280, 486.285, and 486.290 does not affect the validity of the transaction.

§ 486.295. Change of address, notice of, effect of.

Any notary public who changes the address of his residence in the county within and for which he is commissioned shall forthwith mail or deliver a notice of the fact to the secretary of state including his old address and his current address. The secretary of state shall notify the county clerk of the change of address. The notary's commission shall remain in effect until its expiration date, unless sooner revoked.

§ 485.300. Change of name by notary, notice to secretary of state, procedure, fee—signature, how signed.

Any notary who lawfully changes his name shall forthwith request an amended commission from the secretary of state and shall send him five dollars, his current commission, and a notice of change form provided by the secretary of state, which shall include his new name and contain a specimen of his official signature. The secretary of state shall issue an amended commission to him in his new name and shall notify the clerk of the county within and for which the notary is commissioned. After requesting an amended commission, the notary may continue to perform notarial acts in his former name, until he receives the amended commission.

§ 486.305. Loss of seal or journal, notice to secretary of state.

Any notary public who loses or misplaces his journal of notarial acts or official seal shall forthwith mail or deliver notice of the fact to the secretary of state.

§ 486.310. Resignation, how effective.

If any notary public no longer desires to be a notary public, he shall forthwith mail or deliver to the secretary of state a letter of resignation, and his commission shall thereupon cease to be in effect.

§ 486.315. Removal from county of residence, effect of—amended commission, when, procedure, fee.

If a notary public has ceased to have a residence address in the county within and for which he is commissioned, his commission shall thereupon cease to be in effect, unless the secretary of state issues an amended commission. When a notary public, who has established a residence address in a county of the state other than the county in which he was first commissioned, requests an amended commission, delivers his current commission, notice of change form, and five dollars to the secretary of state, the secretary of state shall issue an amended commission to him, for the county in which his new residence is located and shall notify the county clerk of the county where the notary's new address is located. After requesting an amended commission, the notary may continue to perform notarial acts with certificates showing the county within and for which he is commissioned, until he receives his amended commission.

§ 486.320. Notice of revocation of commission, compliance with.

If any notary public receives notice from the secretary of state that his commission has been revoked, the person whose commission is revoked shall forthwith mail or deliver to the secretary of state his commission.

§ 486.325. Automatic reappointment prohibited.

1. No person may be automatically reappointed as a notary public.
2. Each notary public who is an applicant for reappointment as a notary public shall re-comply with the provisions of sections 486.225 and 486.235.

§ 486.330. Form of acknowledgments.

Except as otherwise provided in section 442.210, RSMo, certificates of acknowledgment shall be in substantially the following form:

(1) By an individual.

State of . . . ., County (and/or City) of . . . . . On this . . . . day of . . . . in the year . . . . before me, ... (name of notary), a Notary Public in and for said state, personally appeared . . . . . (name of individual), known to me to be the person who executed the within . . . . (type of document), and acknowledged to me that . . . . (he) executed the same for the purposes therein stated.

(2) By a Partner.

State of . . . ., County (and/or City) of . . . . . On this . . . . day of . . . . in the year . . . . before me, ... (name of notary), a Notary Public in and for said state, personally appeared . . . . . (name of partner) of . . . . (name of partnership), known to me to be the person who executed the within . . . . (type of document) in behalf of said partnership and acknowledged to me that he executed the same for the purposes therein stated.

. . . . . (official signature and official seal of notary.)

(3) By a Corporate Officer.

State of . . . ., County (and/or City) of . . . . On this . . . . day of . . . . in the year . . . . before me, . . . (name of notary), a Notary Public in and for said state, personally appeared . . . . . (name of officer), ... (title of person, president, vice president, etc.), ... (name of corporation), known to me to be the person who executed the within . . . . (type of document) in behalf of said corporation and acknowledged to me that he executed the same for the purposes therein stated.

. . . . . (official signature and official seal of notary.)

(4) By an Attorney in Fact for Principal or Surety.

State of . . . ., County (and/or City) of . . . . On this . . . . day of . . . . in the year . . . . before me, ... (name of notary), a Notary Public in and for said state, personally appeared . . . . . (name of attorney in fact), Attorney in Fact for . . . . (name of principal or surety), known to me to be the person who executed the within . . . . (type of document), in behalf of said principal (or surety), and acknowledged to me that he executed the same for the purposes therein stated.

. . . . . (official signature and official seal of notary.)

(5) By a Public Officer, Deputy, Trustee, Administrator, Guardian or Executor.

State of . . . ., County (and/or City) of . . . . On this . . . . day of . . . . in the year . . . . before me, ... (name of notary), a Notary Public in and for said state, personally appeared . . . . . (name of person), ..., (person's official title) known to me to be the person who executed the within . . . . (type of document) in behalf of . . . . . (public corporation, agency, political subdivision or estate) and acknowledged to me that he executed the same for the purposes therein stated.

. . . . . (official signature and official seal of notary.)

(6) By a United States Citizen Who is Outside the United States. (description or location of place where acknowledgment is taken)

On this . . . . day of . . . ., in the year . . . ., before me . . . . . . (name and title of person acting as a notary and refer to law or authority granting power to act as a notary), personally appeared . . . . . (name of citizen) known to me to be the person who executed the within . . . . (type of document) and acknowledged to me that . . . . (he) executed the same for the purposes therein stated.

. . . . . . (official signature and official seal of person acting as a notary and refer to law or authority granting power to act as a notary).

(7) By An Individual Who Cannot Write His Name.

State of . . . ., County (and/or City) of . . . . . On this . . . . day of . . . . in the year . . . . before me, ... (name of notary), a Notary Public in and for said state, personally appeared . . . . . (name of individual), known to me to be the person who, being unable to write his name, made his mark in my presence. I signed his name at his request and in his presence on the within . . . . (type of document) and he acknowledged to me that he made his mark on the same for the purposes therein stated.

. . . . . (official signature and official seal of notary.)

§ 486.335. Affirmations, form of.

Affirmations shall be in substantially the following form:

(1) If the affirmation to be administered by the notary public is in writing and the person who took the affirmation has signed his name thereto, the notary public shall write or print under the text of the affirmation the following:

"Subscribed and affirmed before me this . . . . . day of . . . . . ., 19. . . ."

. . . . . . (official signature and official seal of notary.)

(2) If the affirmation to be administered by the notary public is not in writing, the notary public shall address the affirmant substantially as follows:

"You do solemnly affirm, under the penalty of perjury, that the testimony you shall give in the matter in issue, pending between . . . . and . . . ., shall be the truth, the whole truth, and nothing but the truth."

§ 486.340. Executing witness defined—form of affidavit of executing witness.

1. As used in this section, the words "executing witness" means an individual who acts in the place of a notary.

2. An executing witness may not be related by blood or marriage or have a disqualifying interest as defined in section 486.255.

3. The affidavit of executing witness for acknowledgment by an individual who does not appear before a notary shall be in substantially the following form:

I, ... (name of executing witness), do solemnly affirm under the penalty of perjury, that . . . . (name of person who does not appear before a notary), personally known to me, has executed the within . . . . . (type of document) in my presence,

and has acknowledged to me that . . . . . (he) executed the same for the purposes therein stated and requested that I sign my name on the within document as an executing witness. . . . . (signature of executing witness)

Subscribed and affirmed before me this . . . . day of . . . ., 19. . . .

. . . . . (official signature and official seal of notary.)

§ 486.345. Facsimile may be certified—form of certification.

1. A notary public may certify a facsimile of a document if he receives a signed written request stating that a certified copy or facsimile, preparation of a copy, or certification of a copy of the document does not violate any state or federal law.

2. Each notary public shall retain a facsimile of each document he has certified as a facsimile of another document, together with other papers or copies relating to his notarial acts.

3. The certification of a facsimile shall be in substantially the following form:

State of . . . . . . County (and/or City) of . . . . I, ... (name of notary), a Notary Public in and for said state, do certify that on . . . . . . (date) I carefully compared the attached facsimile of . . . . (type of document) and the facsimile I now hold in my possession. They are complete, full, true and exact facsimiles of the document they purport to reproduce.

. . . . (official signature and official seal of notary.)

§ 486.350. Maximum fees—overcharges or charge for absentee ballots, effect of.

1. The maximum fee in this state for notarization of each signature and the proper recording thereof in the journal of notarial acts is two dollars for each signature notarized.

2. The maximum fee in this state for certification of a facsimile of a document, and the proper recordation thereof in the journal of notarial acts is two dollars for each 8½ x 11 inch paper retained in the notary's file.

3. The maximum fee in this state is one dollar for any other notarial act performed.

4. No notary shall charge or collect a fee for notarizing the signature on any absentee ballot or absentee voter registration.

5. A notary public who charges more than the maximum fee specified or who charges or collects a fee for notarizing the signature on any absentee ballot or absentee voter registration is guilty of official misconduct.

§ 486.355. Liable in damages, when.

A notary public and the surety or sureties on his bond are liable to the persons involved for all damages proximately caused by the notary's official misconduct.

§ 486.360. Employer of a notary public liable, when.

The employer of a notary public is also liable to the persons involved for all damages proximately caused by the notary's official misconduct, if:

(1) The notary public was acting within the scope of his employment at the time he engaged in the official misconduct; and

(2) The employer consented to the notary public's official misconduct.

§ 486.365. Sole cause not necessary to establish notary's liability.

It is not essential to a recovery of damages that a notary's official misconduct be the only proximate cause of the damages.

§ 486.370. Penalty for notary's misconduct.

1. A notary public who knowingly and willfully commits any official misconduct is guilty of a misdemeanor and is punishable upon conviction by a fine not exceeding five hundred dollars or by imprisonment for not more than six months or both.

2. A notary public who recklessly or negligently commits any official misconduct is guilty of a misdemeanor and is punishable upon conviction by a fine not exceeding one hundred dollars.

§ 486.375. Impersonation of a notary, penalty for.

Any person who acts as, or otherwise willfully impersonates, a notary public while not lawfully appointed and commissioned to perform notarial acts is guilty of a misdemeanor and punishable upon conviction by a fine not exceeding five hundred dollars or by imprisonment for not more than six months or both.

§ 486.380. Unlawful possession of notary seal, journal or papers a misdemeanor, penalty.

Any person who unlawfully possesses a notary's journal, official seal or any papers or copies relating to notarial acts, is guilty of a misdemeanor and is punishable upon conviction by a fine not exceeding five hundred dollars.

§ 486.385. Grounds for revocation of commission.

1. The secretary of state may revoke the commission of any notary public who during the current term of appointment:

(1) Submits an application for commission and appointment as a notary public which contains substantial and material misstatement of facts;

(2) Is convicted of any felony or official misconduct under this chapter;

(3) Fails to exercise the powers or perform the duties of a notary public in accordance with this chapter;

(4) Is adjudged liable or agrees in a settlement to pay damages in any suit grounded in fraud, misrepresentation, impersonation, or violation of the state regulatory laws of this state, if his liability is not solely by virtue of his agency or employment relationship with another who engaged in the act for which the suit was brought;

(5) Uses false or misleading advertising wherein he represents or implies, by virtue of his title of notary public, that he has qualifications, powers, duties, rights, or privileges that he does not possess by law;

(6) Engages in the unauthorized practice of law;

(7) Ceases to be a citizen of the United States;

(8) Ceases to be a registered voter of the county within and for which he is commissioned;

(9) Ceases to have a residence address in the county within and for which he is commissioned, unless he has been issued an amended commission;

(10) Becomes incapable of reading or writing the English language;

(11) Fails to maintain the surety bond required by section 486.235.

2. A notary's commission may be revoked under the provisions of this section only if action is taken subject to the rights of the notary public to notice, hearing, adjudication and appeal.

§ 486.390. Unauthorized practice of law by notary, remedy for.

1. Upon his own information or upon complaint of any person, the attorney general, or his designee, may maintain an action for injunctive relief in the circuit court of Cole County against any notary public who renders, offers to render, or holds himself out as rendering any service constituting the unauthorized practice of the law. Any organized bar association in this state may intervene in the action, at any stage of the proceeding, for good cause shown. The action may also be maintained by an organized bar association in this state.

2. The remedies provided in subsection 1 of this section are in addition to, and not in substitution for, other available remedies.

§ 486.395. Certification of notary's authority by the secretary of state, fee, form.

Upon the receipt of a written request, the notarized document and a fee of ten dollars payable to the director of revenue, the secretary of state shall provide a certificate of authority in substantially the following form:

I, ... (appointing state official, or local or district office designated by appointing state official, name and title) of the State of (name of state) which office is an office of record having a seal, certify that . . . . (notary's name), by whom the foregoing or annexed document was notarized, was, at the time of the notarization of the same, a Notary Public authorized by the laws of this State to act in this State and to notarize the within . . . . (type of document), and I further certify that the Notary's signature on the document is genuine to the best of my knowledge, information, and belief and that such notarization was executed in accordance with the laws of this State.

In testimony whereof, I have affixed my signature and seal of this office this . . . . . day of . . . . . , 19. . . .

. . . .
(secretary of state's signature, title, jurisdiction, address and the seal affixed near the signature.)

§ 486.405. Term of notary not to be diminished, exception.

Nothing in sections 486.200 to 486.405 shall be construed in any way as interfering with or discontinuing the term of office of any person now serving as a notary public until the term for which he was commissioned has expired, or until he has been removed pursuant to the provisions of sections 486.200 to 486.405.

ADDITIONAL AUTHORITY

§ 490.560. Notary's certificate of protest.

The certificate of a notary public, protesting a bill of exchange or negotiable promissory note, without as well as within this state, setting forth the demand of payment, refusal, protest therefor, and notice of dishonor to parties thereto, and the manner of each of said acts, and verified by his affidavit, shall, in all courts in this state, be prima facie evidence of such acts; provided, such certificate be filed in the cause for at least fifteen days before the trial thereof.

§ 491.090. Summons of witnesses—procedure—consequences of failure to appear.

1. In all cases where witnesses are required to attend the trial in any cause in any court of record, a summons shall be issued by the clerk of the court wherein the matter is pending, or by some notary public of the county wherein such trial shall be had, stating the day and place when and where the witnesses are to appear.

2. The witness shall be required to attend a trial from time to time, and from term to term, until the case be disposed of or the witness is finally discharged by the court. The witness shall be liable to attachment for any default or failure to appear as a witness at the trial and adjudged to pay the costs. Costs shall not be allowed for any subsequent recognizance or subpoena for the witness.

§ 491.100. Summons, form—how issued—subpoena for property, court's authority to quash, when exercised.

1. Such summons shall be in the form of a subpoena, shall state the name of the court and the title of the action, the names, addresses and telephone numbers of the attorneys for the respective parties and identifying the attorney or party requesting the attendance of the witness and shall command each person to whom it is directed to attend and give testimony at a time and place therein specified or shall otherwise advise the witness of the name and telephone number of a person who can direct the witness of the time and place his appearance is required. The clerk of the court wherein the matter is pending, or the notary public of the county wherein such trial shall be had, shall issue a subpoena, or a subpoena for the production of objects and documentary evidence, signed and sealed but otherwise in blank, to a party requesting it, who shall fill it in before service.

2. The court may, on application of the party causing the subpoena to be issued, order that the witness shall appear, from time to time until the case is disposed of or he is otherwise excused by the court.

3. Where a subpoena commands the person to whom it is directed to produce the objects, books, papers, or documents designated therein, the court upon motion may, promptly, and in any event at or before the time specified in the subpoena for compliance therewith, quash the subpoena if it is unreasonable and oppressive or condition denial of the motion upon the advancement by the person in whose behalf the subpoena is issued of the reasonable cost of producing the objects, books, papers, or documents.

FEES

Art. 6, § 12. Officers compensated only by salaries in certain counties.

All public officers in the city of St. Louis and all state and county officers in counties having 100,000 or more inhabitants, excepting public administrators and notaries public, shall be compensated for their services by salaries only.

28.160. State entitled to certain fees.

The state shall be entitled to fees for services to be rendered by the secretary of state as follows:

For issuing commission to notary public . .$15.00
For countersigning and sealing certificates
of official character 10.00
For all other certificates. 5.00
For copying records, papers or documents,
for pages 8½ X 14 inches
and smaller. 50
For duplicating microfilm, for each roll 5.00
For certifying copies of records and papers
or documents. 5.00
For causing service of process to be made . .10.00
For electronic telephone transmittal,
per page. 2.00
For copies of computer printouts, per page. .2.00

OFFENSES

§ 570.090. Forgery.

1. A person commits the crime of forgery if, with the purpose to defraud, he

(1) Makes, completes, alters or authenticates any writing so that it purports to have been made by another or at another time or place or in a numbered sequence other than was in fact the case or with different terms or by authority of one who did not give such authority; or

(2) Erases, obliterates or destroys any writings; or

(3) Makes or alters anything other than a writing, so that it purports to have a genuineness, antiquity, rarity, ownership or authorship which it does not possess; or

(4) Uses as genuine, or possesses for the purpose of using as genuine, or transfers with the knowledge or belief that it will be used as genuine, any writing or other thing which the actor knows has been made or altered in the manner described in this section.

2. Forgery is a class C felony.

§ 570.100. Possession of a forging instrumentality.

1. A person commits the crime of possession of a forging instrumentality if, with the purpose of committing forgery, he makes, causes to be made or possesses any plate, mold, instrument or device for making or altering any writing or anything other than a writing.

2. Possession of a forging instrumentality is a class C felony.

§ 570.110. Issuing a false instrument or certificate.

1. A person commits the crime of issuing a false instrument or certificate when, being authorized by law to take proof or acknowledgment of any instrument which by law may be recorded, or being authorized by law to make or issue official certificates or other official written instruments, he issues such an instrument or certificate, or makes the same with the purpose that it be issued, knowing:

(1) That it contains a false statement or false information; or

(2) That it is wholly or partly blank.

2. Issuing a false instrument or certificate is a class A misdemeanor.

§ 575.060. False declarations.

1. A person commits the crime of making a false declaration if, with the purpose to mislead a public servant in the performance of his duty, he:

(1) Submits any written false statement, which he does not believe to be true

(a) In an application for any pecuniary benefit or other consideration; or

(b) On a form bearing notice, authorized by law, that false statements made therein are punishable; or

(2) Submits or invites reliance on

(a) Any writing which he knows to be forged, altered or otherwise lacking in authenticity; or

(b) Any sample, specimen, map, boundary mark, or other object which he knows to be false.

2. The falsity of the statement or the item under subsection 1 of this section must be as to fact which is material to the purposes for which the statement is made or the item submitted; and the provisions of subsections 2 and 3 of section 575.040 shall apply to prosecutions under subsection 1 of this section.

3. It is a defense to a prosecution under subsection 1 of this section that the actor retracted the false statement or item but this defense shall not apply if the retraction was made after:

(1) The falsity of the statement or item was exposed; or

(2) The public servant took substantial action in reliance on the statement or item.

4. The defendant shall have the burden of injecting the issue of retraction under subsection 3 of this section.

5. Making a false declaration is a class B misdemeanor.

ACKNOWLEDGMENTS

§ 442.150. Proof or acknowledgment, by whom taken.

The proof or acknowledgment of every conveyance or instrument in writing affecting real estate in law or equity, including deeds of married women, shall be taken by some one of the following courts or officers:

(1) If acknowledged or proved within this state, by some court having a seal, or some judge, justice or clerk thereof, or a notary public; or

(2) If acknowledged or proved without this state and within the United States, by any notary public or by any court of the United States, or of any state or territory, having a seal, or the clerk of any such court or any commissioner appointed by the governor of this state to take the acknowledgment of deeds;

(3) If acknowledged or proved without the United States, by any court of any state, kingdom or empire having a seal or the mayor or chief officer of any city or town having an official seal or by any minister or consular officer of the United States or notary public having a seal.

§ 442.160. Acknowledgments of instruments by persons in military service—form—instruments previously acknowledged validated, when.

1. Any commissioned officer, other than a commissioned warrant officer, of any of the armed forces of the United States, on active duty, shall have the power and authority to take proof or acknowledgment of any instrument in writing, of any member of any of the armed forces of the United States, on active duty, with like effect as if the same were taken within the state of Missouri by a notary public. If any instrument in writing so acknowledged by such member of the armed forces of the United States be of such a nature as to require a joint or separate acknowledgment of his or her spouse, said officers shall have the power and authority to take the acknowledgment of such spouse.

2. Said officer shall certify the act, stating the time and place thereof, over his signature, setting forth his grade, serial number, branch of service (army, navy, etc.), and permanent mailing address.

If said officer shall omit from his certificate the place thereof, serial number, branch of service, and permanent mailing address, or any of them, it shall be deemed to have been done for reasons of security and shall not invalidate said certificate. The signature of any such officer, together with his grade, shall be prima facie evidence of his authority.

3. Any form of acknowledgment complying with the requirements of this section may be used, and the following form shall be taken to satisfy all requirements of this section:

With the Armed Forces   }
of the United States   } ss
at _____   }

On this _____ day of _____, A.D. 19 __, before me, a commissioned officer of the the armed forces of the United States, on active duty therewith, personally appeared _____, a member of the armed forces of the United States, on active duty therewith, (and _____ (his wife, her husband),) to me known to be the person described in and who executed the foregoing instrument, and acknowledged that _____ executed the same as _____ free act and deed. (The said _____ declared _____ to be single and unmarried.)

IN TESTIMONY WHEREOF, I have hereunto set my hand and grade (serial number, branch of service, and permanent mailing address).

(Signature)   Serial Number
_____

(Grade)(Branch of Service: Army, Navy, etc.)
_____

(Permanent mailing address)
_____

4. All such proof or acknowledgment of any instrument in writing heretofore made and which was not in conformity with the requirements of the laws at that time, but are in conformity with the requirements of this section, are hereby validated and legalized for all purposes from and after the effective date of this section. It shall not be necessary to rerecord any such instrument.

§ 442.180. Certificate to be endorsed on conveyance.

Every court or officer taking the proof or acknowledgment of any conveyance or instrument of writing affecting real estate, or the relinquishment of the dower of a married woman, shall grant a certificate thereof, and cause the same to be endorsed on such conveyance or instrument or writing.

§ **442.190.** Certificate, how made.

Such certificate shall be

(1) When granted by a court, under the seal of the court;

(2) When granted by the clerk of the court, under the hand of the clerk and seal of the court of which he is clerk;

(3) When granted by an officer who has a seal of office, under the hand and official seal of such officer;

(4) When granted by an officer who has no seal of office, under the hand of such officer.

§ **442.200.** Identity of persons making acknowledgments, how ascertained.

No acknowledgment of any instrument in writing conveying real estate, or whereby any real estate may be affected, shall be taken unless the persons offering to make such acknowledgment shall be personally known to at least one judge of the court, or to the officer taking the same, to be the person whose name is subscribed to such instrument as a party thereto, or shall be proved to be such by at least two credible witnesses.

§ **442.210.** Certificate of acknowledgment—contents.

1. The certificate of acknowledgment shall state the act of acknowledgment, and that the person making the same was personally known to at least one judge of the court, or to the officer granting the certificate, to be the person whose name is subscribed to the instrument as a party thereto, or was proved to be such by at least two witnesses, whose names and places of residence shall be inserted in the certificate; and the following forms of acknowledgment may be used in the case of conveyances or other written instruments affecting real estate; and any acknowledgment so taken and certified shall be sufficient to satisfy all requirements of law relating to the execution or recording of such instruments (begin in all cases by a caption, specifying the state and place where the acknowledgment is taken):

(1) In case of natural persons acting in their own right

On this _____ day of _____, 19__, before me personally appeared A B (or A B and C D), to me known to be the person (or persons) described in and who executed the foregoing instrument, and acknowledged that he (or they) executed the same as his (or their) free act and deed.

(2) In the case of natural persons acting by attorney

On this _____ day of _____, 19__, before me personally appeared A B, to me known to be the person who executed the foregoing instrument in behalf of C D, and acknowledged that he executed the same as the free act and deed of C D.

(3) In the case of corporations or joint stock associations

On this _____ day of _____[,] 19__, before me appeared A B, to me personally known, who, being by me duly sworn (or affirmed) did say that he is the president (or other officer or agent of the corporation or association), of (describing the corporation or association), and that the seal affixed to foregoing instrument is the corporate seal of said corporation (or association), and that said instrument was signed and sealed in behalf of said corporation (or association) by authority of its board of directors (or trustees), and said A B acknowledged said instrument to be the free act and deed of said corporation (or association).

2. In case the corporation or association has no corporate seal, omit the words "the seal affixed to said instrument is the corporate seal of said corporation (or association), and that," and add at the end of the affidavit clause the words "and that said corporation (or association) has no corporate seal."

3. (In all cases add signature and title of the officer taking the acknowledgment).

4. When a married woman unites with her husband in the execution of any such instrument, and acknowledges the same in one of the forms above sanctioned, she shall be described in the acknowledgment as his wife, but in all other respects her acknowledgment shall be taken and certified as if she were sole; and no separate examination of a married woman in respect to the execution of any release or dower, or other instrument affecting real estate, shall be required.

DEPOSITIONS

§ **492.010.** Officers and notary public authorized to admininster oaths.

Every court and judge, justice and clerk thereof, notaries public, certified court reporters and certified shorthand reporters, shall respectively have power to admininster oaths and affirmations to witnesses and others concerning any thing or proceeding pending before them, respectively, and to administer oaths and take affidavits and depositions within their respective jurisdictions, in all cases where oaths and affirmations are required by law to be taken.

§ **492.090.** Officers authorized to take depositions.

Depositions may be taken by some one of the following officers:

(1) If taken within this state, by some judge, jus-

tice, magistrate, notary public or clerk of any court having a seal, in vacation of court, mayor or chief officer of a city or town having a seal of office;

(2) If taken without this state, by some officer out of this state appointed by authority of the laws of this state to take depositions, or by some consul or commercial or diplomatic representative of the United States, having a seal, or mayor or chief officer of any city, town or borough, having a seal of office, or by some judge, justice of the peace, or other judicial officer, or by some notary public, within the government where the witness may be found.

§ 492.290. Witnesses to be examined on oath.

Every witness examined, in pursuance of sections 492.080 to 492.400 shall be sworn or affirmed to testify the whole truth, and his examination shall be reduced to writing, or taken in shorthand and transcribed, in writing, in the presence of the person or officer before whom the same shall be taken.

§ 492.320. Residence of witness certified by officer.

When the officer taking depositions in virtue of this law shall, in his certificate, state the place of residence of the witness, such statement shall be prima facie evidence of the facts.

§ 492.340. Deposition shall be submitted to witness for examination—signing of deposition.

When the testimony is fully transcribed the deposition shall be submitted to the witness for examination and shall be read to or by him, unless such examination and reading are waived by the witness and by the parties. Any changes in form or substance which the witness desires to make shall be entered upon the deposition by the officer with a statement of the reasons given by the witness for making them. The deposition shall then be signed by the witness, unless the parties by stipulation waive the signing or the witness is ill or cannot be found, or is dead or refuses to sign. If the deposition is not signed by the witness, the officer shall sign it and state on the record the fact of the waiver or of the illness, or death or absence of the witness or the fact of the refusal to sign together with the reason, if any, given therefor; and the deposition may then be used as fully as though signed, unless on a motion to suppress the court holds that the reasons given for the refusal to sign requires rejection of the deposition in whole or in part.

§ 492.350. Certificate of officer taking depositions.

To every deposition or examination, taken by virtue of sections 492.080 to 492.400 shall be appended the certificate of the person or officer by or before whom the same shall be taken, showing that the deposition or examination was reduced to writing in his presence, and was subscribed and sworn to by the witnesses, and the place at which, and the days, and within the hours, when the same was taken.

§ 492.360. Exhibits to be enclosed with depositions and directed to clerk.

Depositions or examinations taken by virtue of any of the provisions of sections 492.080 to 492.400 and all exhibits produced to the person or officer taking such examinations or depositions, and proved or referred to by any witness, together with the commission and interrogatories, if any, shall be enclosed, sealed up, and directed to the clerk of the court in which or the magistrate before whom the action is pending.

[Mo. R. Civ. P.]

RULE 57.03. Depositions upon oral examination.

(a) **When Depositions May Be Taken.** After commencement of the action, any party may take the testimony of any person, including a party, by deposition upon oral examination. Leave of court, granted with or without notice, must be obtained only if the plaintiff seeks to take a deposition prior to the expiration of 30 days after service of the summons and petition upon any defendant, except that leave is not required if a defendant has served a notice of taking deposition or otherwise sought discovery. The attendance of witnesses may be compelled by subpoena as provided in Rule 57.09. The attendance of a party is compelled by notice as provided in subdivision (b) of this Rule. The deposition of a person confined in prison may be taken only by leave of court on such terms as the court describes.

(b) **Notice of Examination: General Requirements; Special Notice; Production of Documents and Things; Deposition of Organization.**

(1) A party desiring to take the deposition of any person upon oral examination shall give not less than 7 days notice in writing to every other party to the action. The notice shall state the time and place for taking the deposition and the name and address of each person to be examined, if known, and, if the name is not known, a general description sufficient to identify him or the particular class or group to which he belongs. If a subpoena duces tecum is to be served on the person to be examined, the des-

ignation of the materials to be produced as set forth in the subpoena shall be attached to or included in the notice.

(2) The court may for cause shown enlarge or shorten the time for taking the deposition.

(3) The notice to a party deponent may be accompanied by a request made in compliance with Rule 58.01 for the production of documents and tangible things at the taking of the deposition. The procedure of Rule 58.01 shall apply to the request.

(4) A party may in his notice and in a subpoena name as the deponent a public or private corporation or a partnership or association or governmental agency and describe with reasonable particularity the matters on which examination is requested. In that event, the organization so named shall designate one or more officers, directors, or managing agents, or other persons who consent to testify on its behalf and may set forth, for each person designated, the matters on which he will testify. A subpoena shall advise a nonparty organization of its duty to make such a designation. The persons so designated shall testify as to matters known or reasonably available to the organization. This subdivision (b)(4) does not preclude taking a deposition by any other procedure authorized in these Rules.

(5) When the party causing a deposition or depositions to be taken under a notice shall have completed the taking thereof, any other party may, before the same or any other officer authorized to take depositions, and at the same place, proceed immediately, or on the next day, to take any depositions he may desire to be taken in the civil action, and may continue the taking thereof from day to day, at said place, until he shall have taken all he desires; but to do so, he shall, before or during the time of the taking of the depositions on behalf of the other party, give all other parties, or the attorneys representing them, notice in writing of his intention to do so, the name and address of each person to be examined, if known, and, if the name is not known, a general description sufficient to identify him or the particular class or group to which he belongs. If a subpoena duces tecum is to be served on the person to be examined, the designation of the materials to be produced as set forth in the subpoena shall be attached to or included in the notice.

(c) Non-Stenographic Recording—Video Tape. Depositions may be recorded by the use of video tape or similar methods. The recording of the deposition by video tape shall be in addition to a usual recording and transcription method unless the parties otherwise agree:

(1) If the deposition is to be recorded by video tape every notice or subpoena for the taking of the deposition shall state that it is to be video taped and shall state the name, address and employer of the recording technician. If a party upon whom notice for the taking of a deposition has been served desires to have the testimony additionally recorded by other than stenographic means, he shall serve notice on the opposing party and the witness that the proceedings are to be video taped. Such notice must be served not less than 3 days prior to the date designated in the original notice for the taking of the depositions and shall state the name, address and employer of the recording technician.

(2) Where the deposition has been recorded only by video tape and if the witness and parties do not waive signature, a written transcription of the audio shall be prepared to be submitted to the witness for signature as provided in Rule 57.03(f).

(3) The witness being deposed shall be sworn as a witness on camera by an authorized person.

(4) More than one camera may be used, either in sequence or simultaneously.

(5) The attorney for the party requesting the video taping of the deposition shall take custody of and be responsible for the safeguarding of the video tape and shall, upon request, permit the viewing thereof by the opposing party and if requested, shall provide a copy of the video tape at the cost of the requesting party.

(6) Unless otherwise stipulated to by the parties, the expense of video taping is to be borne by the party utilizing it and shall not be taxed as costs.

(d) Record of Examination; Oath; Objections. The officer before whom deposition is to be taken shall put the witness on oath or affirmation and shall personally, or by someone acting under his direction and in his presence, record the testimony of the witness. The testimony shall be taken stenographically or recorded by any other means ordered in accordance with subdivision (c) of this Rule. If requested by one of the parties, the testimony shall be transcribed.

All objections made at the time of the examination to the qualifications of the officer taking the deposition, or to the manner of taking it, or to the evidence presented, or to the conduct of any party, or any other objection to the proceedings, shall be noted by the officer upon the deposition. Evidence objected to shall be taken subject to the objections. In lieu of participating in the oral examination, parties may serve written questions in a sealed envelope on the party taking the deposition and he shall transmit them to the officer before whom the deposition is to be taken, who shall propound them to the witness and the questions and answers there to shall be recorded.

(e) Motion to Terminate or Limit Examination. At any time during the taking of the deposition, on motion of a party or of the deponent and upon a showing that the examination is being conducted in bad faith or in such manner as unreasonably to annoy, embarrass, or oppress the deponent or party, the court in which the action is pending or a court having general jurisdiction in the place where the deposition is being taken may order the officer conducting the examination to cease forthwith from taking the deposition, or may limit the scope and manner of the taking of the deposition as provided in Rule 56.01(c). If the order made terminates the examination, it shall be resumed thereafter only upon the order of the court in which the action is pending. Upon demand of the objecting party or deponent, the taking of the deposition shall be suspended for the time necessary to make a motion for an order. The provisions of Rule 61.01(g) apply to the award of expenses incurred in relation to the motion.

(f) **Submission to Witness; Changes; Signing.** When the testimony is fully transcribed, the deposition shall be submitted by the officer to the witness for examination and shall be read to or by him, unless such examination and reading are waived by the witness and by the parties. Any changes in form or substance which the witness desires to make shall be entered upon the deposition by the officer with a statement of the reasons given by the witness for making them; provided, however, that the answers or responses as originally given, together with the changes made and reasons given therefor, shall be considered as a part of the deposition. The deposition shall then be signed by the witness, unless the parties by stipulation waive the signing or the witness is ill or cannot be found, or is dead or refuses to sign. If the deposition is not signed by the witness, the officer shall sign it and state on the record the fact of the waiver or of the illness, or death or absence of the witness or the fact of the refusal to sign together with the reasons, if any, given therefor; and the deposition may then be used as fully as though signed, unless, on a motion to suppress, the court holds that the reasons given for the refusal to sign require rejection of the deposition in whole or in part.

(g) **Certification and Filing by Officers; Exhibits; Copies.**

(1) The officer shall certify on the deposition that the witness was duly sworn by him and that the deposition is a true record of the testimony given by the witness. He shall then securely seal the deposition in an envelope endorsed with the title of the action and marked "Deposition of [here insert name of witness]" and shall promptly file it with the court in which the civil action is pending or send it by registered or certified mail to the clerk thereof for filing.

Documents and things produced for inspection during the examination of the witness, shall, upon the request of a party, be marked for identification and annexed to and returned with the deposition, and may be inspected and copied by any party, except that (A) the person producing the materials may substitute copies to be marked for identifica-

tion, if he affords to all parties fair opportunity to verify the copies by comparison with the originals, and (B) if the person producing the materials requests their return, the officer shall mark them, give each party an opportunity to inspect and copy them, and return them to the person producing them, and the materials may then be used in the same manner as if annexed to and returned with the deposition. Any party may move for an order that the original be annexed to and returned with the deposition to the court pending final disposition of the civil action.

(2) Upon payment of reasonable charges therefor, the officer shall furnish a copy of the deposition to any party or to the deponent.

(h) **Failure to Attend or to Serve Subpoena; Expenses.**

(1) If the party giving the notice of the taking of a deposition fails to attend and proceed therewith and another party attends in person or by attorney pursuant to the notice, the court may order the party giving notice to pay to such other party the reasonable expenses incurred by him and his attorney in attending, including reasonable attorney's fees.

(2) If a witness fails to appear for a deposition and the party giving the notice of the taking of the deposition has not complied with these Rules to compel the attendance of the witness, the court may order the party giving the notice to pay to any party attending in person or by attorney the reasonable expenses incurred by him and by his attorney in attending, including reasonable attorney's fees.

RULE 57.04. Depositions upon written questions.

(a) **Serving Questions; Notice.** After commencement of the action, any party may take the testimony of any person, including a party, by deposition upon written questions. The attendance of witnesses may be compelled by the use of subpoena as provided in Rule 57.09. The deposition of a person confined in prison may be taken only by leave of court on such terms as the court prescribes.

A party desiring to take a deposition upon written questions shall serve them upon every other party with a notice stating (1) the name and address of the person who is to answer them, if known, and if the name is not known, a general description sufficient to identify him or the particular class or group to which he belongs, and (2) the name or descriptive title and address of the officer before whom the deposition is to be taken. A deposition upon written questions may be taken of a public or private corporation or a partnership or association or governmental agency in accordance with the provisions of Rule 57.03(b)(4).

Within 30 days after the notice and written questions are served, a party may serve cross questions upon all other parties. Within 10 days after being served with cross questions, a party may serve redirect questions upon all other parties. Within 10 days after being served with redirect questions, a party may serve recross questions upon all other parties. The court may for cause shown enlarge or shorten the time.

(b) Officer to Take Responses and Prepare Record. A copy of the notice and copies of all questions served shall be delivered by the party taking the deposition to the officer designated in the notice, who shall proceed promptly, in the manner provided by Rule 57.03(d), (f), and (g), to take the testimony of the witness in response to the questions and to prepare, certify, and file or mail the deposition, attaching thereto the copy of the notice and the questions received by him.

(c) Notice of Filing. When the deposition is filed the party taking it shall promptly give notice thereof to all other parties.

RULE 57.05. Persons before whom depositions may be taken.

(a) In Missouri. Within the State of Missouri, depositions shall be taken before an officer authorized by the laws of this State to admininster oaths, or before a person appointed by the court in which the action is pending. A person so appointed has power to administer oaths and take testimony.

(b) Elsewhere in the United States. Within other States of the United States or within a territory or insular possession subject to the dominion of the United States, depositions shall be taken before a person authorized to admininster oaths by the laws of the United States or of the place where the examination is held, or before a person appointed by the court in which the action is pending. A person so appointed has power to admininster oaths and take testimony.

(c) In Foreign Countries. In a foreign country, a deposition may be taken:

(1) On notice before a person authorized to admininster oaths in the place in which the examination is held, either by the law thereof or by the law of the United States, or

(2) Before a person commissioned by the court, and a person so commissioned has the power by virtue of his commission to administer any necessary oath and take testimony, or

(3) *Pursuant to Letter Rogatory.* A commission or a letter rogatory shall be issued on application and notice and on terms that are just and appropriate. It is not requisite to the issuance of a commission or a letter rogatory that the taking of the deposition in any other manner is impracticable or inconvenient; and both a commission and a letter rogatory may be issued in proper cases. A notice or commission may designate the person before whom the deposition is to be taken either by name or descriptive title. A letter rogatory may be addressed "To the Appropriate Authority in [here name the country]". Evidence obtained in response to a letter rogatory need not be excluded merely for the reason that it is not a verbatim transcript or that the testimony was not taken under oath or for any similar departure from the requirements for depositions taken within the United States under these rules.

(d) Disqualification for Interest. No deposition shall be taken before a person who is a relative or employee or attorney or counsel of any of the parties, or is a relative or employee of such attorney or counsel, or is financially interested in the action.

COMMISSIONERS

[Mo. Ann. Stat.]

§ 486.100. Appointment—powers generally.

The governor may appoint and commission in any other state, in the District of Columbia, in each of the territories of the United States, and in any foreign country, one or more commissioners, who shall continue in office during the pleasure of the governor, and shall have the authority to take relinquishments of dower of married women, the acknowledgment or proof of the execution of any deed or other conveyance, or lease of any lands lying in this state, or of any contract, letters of attorney, or of any other writing, under seal or note, to be used and recorded in this state; and such commissioners appointed for any foreign country shall also have authority to certify to the official character, signature or seal of any officer within their district, who is authorized to take acknowledgments or declarations under oath.

§ 486.110. Official oath.

Every such commissioner, before performing any duty or exercising any power in virtue of his appointment, shall take and subscribe an oath or affirmation before some judge or clerk of any United States court of record or before some judge or clerk of any court of record in and of the state of Missouri, or before a judge or clerk of one of the courts of record of the district, territory, state or county in which said commissioner shall reside, well and faithfully to execute and perform all the duties of such commissioner, under and by virtue of the laws of the state of Missouri; which oath, and a description of his seal of office, if there be one, together with his signature thereto, shall be filed in the office of the secretary of state of this state within six months after the date of his appointment.

§ 486.120. Effect of authentication by commissioner.

An acknowledgment or proof so taken according to the laws of this state, and certified to by any such commissioner, under his seal of office, if there is one annexed to or indorsed on the instrument, has the same force and effect as if the same had been made before a judge or magistrate, or any other officer authorized to perform the act in this state.

§ 486.130. Additional powers—oaths-depositions.

Every commissioner shall have power to administer any oath which may be lawfully required in this state, to any person willing to take it; and to take and certify all depositions to be used in any of the courts of this state, in conformity to the laws thereof, either on interrogatories proposed under commission from a court of this state, or by consent of parties, or on legal notice given to the opposite party; and all such acts may be as valid as if done and certified according to law by a magistrate in this state.

§ 486.140. Fees.

Commissioners shall for like services be allowed the same fees as clerks of courts of record.

PUBLIC HOLIDAYS

§ 9.010. Public holidays.

The first day of January, the third Monday of January, the twelfth day of February, the third Monday in February, the eighth day of May, the last Monday in May, the fourth day of July, the first Monday in September, the second Monday in October, the eleventh day of November, the fourth Thursday in November, and the twenty-fifth of December, are declared and established public holidays; and when any of such holidays falls upon Sunday, the Monday next following shall be considered the holiday. There shall be no holiday for state employees on the fourth Monday of October.

§ 9.020. Designation of certain holidays.

In each year the third Monday of January is known as "Martin Luther King Day" and the twelfth day of February is known as "Lincoln Day" and the thirteenth day of April is known as "Jefferson Day" and the second Monday in October is known as "Columbus Day".

MONTANA

NOTARIES PUBLIC

[MONT. CODE ANN.]

§ 1-5-401. Appointment.

The governor may appoint and commission as many notaries public for the state of Montana as in his judgment may be deemed best.

§ 1-5-402. Qualifications—residence.

Every person appointed as notary public must, at the time of his appointment, be a citizen of the United States and of the state of Montana for at least 1 year preceding his appointment and must continue to reside within the state of Montana. Removal from the state vacates his office and is equivalent to resignation.

§ 1-5-403. Term of office.

The term of office of a notary public is 3 years from and after the date of his commission.

§ 1-5-404. Revocation of commission.

Upon 10 days' notice, the governor may revoke the commission of any notary public for any cause he may deem sufficient.

§ 1-5-405. Bond and commission.

Each notary public must give an official bond in the sum of $5,000. The bond must be approved by the secretary of state. Upon the approval of the bond and the filing in the office of the secretary of state of the official oath of such notary public, the governor may issue a commission.

§ 1-5-406. Liabilities on official bond.

For the official misconduct or neglect of a notary public, he and the sureties on his official bond are liable to the parties injured thereby for all damages sustained.

§ 1-5-407. Certifying the official character of a notary.

The secretary of state may certify to the official character of such notary public. Any notary public may file a copy of his commission in the office of any county clerk of any county in the state, and thereafter said county clerk may certify to the official character of such notary public.

§ 1-5-408. Fees for filing commission and issuing certificates.

The secretary of state shall receive for each certificate of official character issued, with seal attached, $2. The county clerk of any county in this state shall receive a fee as provided in 7-4-2631 for filing a copy of the commission and certifying to the official character.

§ 1-5-409. Information to be filed.

A person appointed as a notary public shall file his address and telephone number with the office of the secretary of state. If the notary public changes his address or telephone number during his term of commission, he shall notify the office of the change.

§ 1-5-410. through 1-5-414. Reserved.

§ 1-5-415. Statewide jurisdiction.

The jurisdiction of notaries public shall be coextensive with the boundaries of the state, irrespective of their place of residence within the state. Every person receiving a commission as notary public shall have jurisdiction to perform his official duties and acts in every county of the state of Montana.

§ 1-5-416. Powers and duties.

A notary public shall:

(1) take the acknowledgment or proof of any power of attorney, mortgage, deed, grant, transfer, or other instrument executed by any person and give a certificate of such proof or acknowledgment, endorsed on or attached to the instrument;

(2) take depositions and affidavits and administer oaths and affirmations in all matters incident to the duties of his office or to be used before any court, judge, officer, or board in this state;

(3) whenever requested and upon payment of his fees therefor, make and give a certified copy of any record in his office;

(4) provide and keep an official seal, upon which must be engraved the name of the state of Montana and the words "Notarial Seal", with the surname of the notary and at least the initials of his given name;

(5) authenticate with his official seal all official acts. Whenever the notary public signs his name officially as a notary public, he shall add to his signature the words "Notary Public for the State of Montana, residing at.... (stating the name of his post office)" and shall endorse upon the instrument the date of the expiration of his commission.

§ 1-5-417. Authority of notaries who are stockholders, officers, or employees of corporations.

It shall be lawful for any notary public who is a stockholder, director, officer, or employee of a bank or other corporation to take the acknowledgment of any party to any written instrument executed to or by such corporation, to administer an oath to any other stockholder, director, officer, employee, or agent of such corporation, or to protest for nonacceptance or nonpayment bills of exchange, drafts, checks, notes, and other negotiable instruments which may be owned or held for collection by such bank or other corporation; provided, it shall be unlawful for any notary public to take the acknowledgment of an instrument by or to a bank or other corporation of which he is a stockholder, director, officer, or employee where such notary is a party to such instrument, either individually or as a representative of such bank or other corporation, or to protest any negotiable instrument owned or held for collection by such bank or other corporation where such notary is individually a party to such instrument.

§ 1-5-418. Fees of notaries.

Fees of notaries public are as follows:
(1) for drawing an affidavit, deposition, or other

paper for which provision is not herein made, $3.50 per page;

(2) for taking an acknowledgment or proof of a deed or other instrument, to include the seal and the writing of the certificate, for the first signature, $1;

(3) for each additional signature, 50 cents;

(4) for administering an oath or affirmation, $1;

(5) for certifying an affidavit, with or without seal, including oath, $1.

§ 1-5-419. Transfer of records upon termination of office.

It is the duty of every notary public on his resignation or removal from office or at the expiration of his term and, in case of his death, of his legal representative to forthwith deposit all the records kept by him in the office of the county clerk of the county in which he was resident. On failure to do so, the person so offending is liable to damages to any person injured thereby.

§ 1-5-420. Powers and duties of clerk with whom records deposited.

It is the duty of each clerk aforesaid to receive and safely keep all such records and papers of the notary in the case above named and to give attested copies of them under his seal, for which he may demand such fees as by law may be allowed to the notaries, and such copies shall have the same effect as if certified by the notary.

AFFIDAVITS

§ 26-1-1001. Affidavit defined.

An "affidavit" is a written declaration under oath, made without notice to the adverse party.

§ 26-1-1002. Permissible uses for affidavits.

An affidavit may be used:

(1) to verify a pleading or a paper in a special proceeding;

(2) to prove the service of a summons, notice, or other paper in an action or special proceeding;

(3) to obtain a provisional remedy, the examination of a witness, or a stay of proceedings;

(4) upon a motion; and

(5) in any other case expressly permitted by some other provision of this code.

§ 26-1-1003. Affidavits made in this state—before whom taken.

An affidavit to be used before any court, judge, or officer of this state may be taken before any judge or clerk of any court or any justice of the peace, county clerk, or notary public in this state.

§ 26-1-1004. Affidavits made in another state—before whom taken.

An affidavit taken in another state of the United States to be used in this state may be taken before a commissioner appointed by the governor of this state to take affidavits and depositions in such other state, before any notary public in another state, or before any judge or clerk of a court of record having a seal.

ACKNOWLEDGMENTS

§ 1-5-101. By whom and where acknowledgments may be taken.

(1) The proof of acknowledgment of an instrument may be made at any place within this state before a justice or clerk of the supreme court or a judge of the district court.

(2) The proof of acknowledgment of an instrument may be made in this state within the city, county, or district for which the officer was elected or appointed, before either:

(a) a clerk of a court of record;

(b) a county clerk;

(c) a notary public authorized by any jurisdiction to perform notarial acts;

(d) a justice of the peace; or

(e) a United States commissioner.

§ 1-5-102. Acknowledgments of notarial acts.

The proof of acknowledgment of an instrument may be performed for use in this state with the same effect as if performed by a notary public in this state before:

(1) a justice, judge, or clerk of any court of record of the United States;

(2) a justice, judge, or clerk of any court of record of any state or territory;

(3) a notary public authorized by any jurisdiction to perform notarial acts; or

(4) any other officer of the state or territory where the acknowledgment is made, authorized by its laws to take such proof or acknowledgment.

§ 1-5-103. Proofs and acknowledgments taken outside the United States.

The proof or acknowledgment of an instrument may be made without the United States before either:

(1) a minister, commissioner, or charge d'affaires of the United States, resident and accredited in the country where the proof or acknowledgment is made;

(2) a consul, vice consul, or consular agent of the United States, resident in the country where the proof or acknowledgment is made;

(3) a judge of a court of record of the country where the proof or acknowledgment is made;

(4) commissioners appointed for such purposes by the governor of the state pursuant to special statutes; or

(5) a notary public.

§ 1-5-104. Proofs and acknowledgments by deputy officers.

When any of the officers mentioned in 1-5-101 through 1-5-103 are authorized by law to appoint a deputy, the acknowledgment of proof may be taken by such deputy in the name of his principal.

§ 1-5-105. Notarial acts by officers in the armed services.

(1) In addition to the acknowledgment of instruments and the performance of other notarial acts in the manner and form otherwise authorized by law, instruments may be acknowledged, documents attested, oaths and affirmations administered, depositions and affidavits executed, and other notarial acts performed before or by any commissioned officer in active service of the armed forces of the United States with the rank of second lieutenant or higher in the army or marine corps, with the rank of ensign or higher in the navy or coast guard, or with equivalent rank in any other component part of the armed forces of the United States, at the request of any person who:

(a) is a member of the armed forces of the United States;

(b) is serving as a merchant seaman outside the limits of the continental United States, excluding Alaska; or

(c) is outside the limits of the United States of America by permission, assignment, or direction of any department or official of the United States government in connection with any activity pertaining to the prosecution of any war in which the United States is then engaged.

(2) Such acknowledgment of instruments, attestation of documents, administration of oaths and affirmations, execution of depositions and affidavits, and performance of other notarial acts, heretofore or hereafter made or taken, are valid and binding; and instruments and documents so acknowledged, authenticated, or sworn to are admissible in evidence and eligible to be recorded in this state under the same circumstances and with the same effect as if such acknowledgment, attestation, oath, affirmation, deposition, affidavit, or other notarial act had been made or taken within this state before or by a duly qualified officer or official as otherwise provided by law.

(3) In the taking of acknowledgments and the performing of other notarial acts requiring certification, a certificate endorsed upon or attached to the instrument which shows the date of the notarial act and which states, in substance, that the person appearing before the officer acknowledged the instrument as his act or made or signed the instrument under oath is sufficient for all purposes. The instrument is not rendered invalid by the failure to state the place of execution or acknowledgment.

(4) The signature, rank, and branch of service or subdivision thereof of any such commissioned officer must appear upon the instrument or certificate, and no further proof of the authority of the officer to so act is required. Such action by the commissioned officer is prima facie evidence that the person making the oath or acknowledgment is within the purview of this section.

§ 1-5-106. Officers to authenticate certificate.

Officers taking and certifying acknowledgments or proof of instruments for record must authenticate their certificates by affixing their signatures, followed by the names of their offices, also their seals of office if, by the laws of the state or country where the acknowledgment or proof is taken or by authority of which they are acting, they are required to have official seals.

§ 1-5-107. Certificate of clerk authenticating justice of the peace's certificate.

The certificate of proof or acknowledgment, if made before a justice of the peace, when used in any county other than that in which he resides, must be accompanied by a certificate under the hand and seal of the clerk of the county in which the justice resides, setting forth that such justice, at the time of making such proof or acknowledgment, was authorized to take the same and that the clerk is acquainted with his handwriting and believes that the signature to the original certificate is genuine.

§ **1-5-108.** Action to correct defective certificate.

When the acknowledgment or proof of the execution of an instrument is properly made but defectively certified, any party interested may have an action in the district court to obtain a judgment correcting the certificate.

§ **1-5-109.** Action for judgment proving an instrument.

Any person interested under an instrument entitled to be proved for record may institute an action in the district court against the proper parties to obtain a judgment proving such instrument.

§ **1-5-110.** Effect of judgment correcting defect or proving instrument.

A certified copy of the judgment in a proceeding instituted under 1-5-108 or 1-5-109 showing the proof of the instrument and attached thereto entitles such instrument to record with the like effect as if acknowledged.

§ **1-5-201.** Requirement that officer have evidence of authority of person making acknowledgment.

The acknowledgment of an instrument must not be taken unless the officer taking it knows or has satisfactory evidence that the person making such acknowledgment is the individual who is described in and who executed the instrument or, if executed by a corporation, that the person making such acknowledgment is the president, vice-president, secretary, or assistant secretary of such corporation or other person duly authorized by resolution of such corporation, who executed it on its behalf.

§ **1-5-202.** Officer to certify acknowledgment.

An officer taking the acknowledgment of an instrument must endorse thereon or attach thereto a certificate substantially in the forms prescribed in this part.

§ **1-5-203.** General form of certificate of acknowledgment.

The certificate of acknowledgment, unless it is otherwise in this part provided, must be substantially in the following form:
State of ....
County of ...
On this .... day of .... in the year ...., before me (here insert the name and quality of the officer), personally appeared ...., known to me (or proved to me on the oath of ....) to be the person whose name is subscribed to the within instrument, and acknowledged to me that he (she or they) executed the same.

§ **1-5-204.** Form of certificate of acknowledgment by corporation.

The certificate of acknowledgment of an instrument executed by a corporation must be substantially in the following form:
State of ....
County of ...
On this .... day of .... in the year ...., before me (here insert the name and quality of the officer), personally appeared ...., known to me (or proved to me on the oath of ....) to be the president (or vice-president, secretary, or assistant secretary) of the corporation that executed the within instrument [where, however, the instrument is executed in behalf of the corporation by someone other than the president, vice-president, secretary, or assistant secretary, insert: known to me (or proved to me on the oath of ....) to be the person who executed the within instrument on behalf of the corporation therein named], and acknowledged to me that such corporation executed the same.

§ **1-5-205.** Form of certificate of acknowledgment by attorney-in-fact.

The certificate of acknowledgment by an attorney-in-fact must be substantially in the following form:
State of ....
County of ...
On this .... day of .... in the year ...., before me (here insert the name and quality of the officer), personally appeared ...., known to me (or proved to me on the oath of ....) to be the person whose name is subscribed to the within instrument as the attorney-in-fact of ...., and acknowledged to me that he subscribed the name of .... thereto as principal and his own name as attorney-in-fact.

§ **1-5-206.** Acknowledgment by married person.

(1) The acknowledgment of a married person to an instrument purporting to be executed by such person must be taken the same as that of any other person.

(2) A conveyance by a married person has the same effect as if such person were unmarried and may be acknowledged in the same manner.

§ 1-5-207. Form of certificate of acknowledgment by married person.

The certificate of acknowledgment by a married person must be substantially in the form prescribed in 1-5-203.

§ 1-5-208. Effect of acknowledgment taken in accordance with another state's laws.

Notwithstanding any provision contained in this chapter, the acknowledgment of any instrument without this state in compliance with the manner and form prescribed by the laws of the place of its execution, if in a state, territory, or insular possession of the United States or in the District of Columbia, verified by the official seal of the officer before whom it is acknowledged, shall have the same effect as an acknowledgment in the manner and form prescribed by the laws of this state for instruments executed within the state.

§ 1-5-301. Who may prove execution of instrument.

Proof of the execution of an instrument which has not been acknowledged may be made by:

(1) all of the parties who executed it or any one of them;

(2) a subscribing witness; or

(3) other witnesses in cases mentioned in 1-5-302.

§ 1-5-302. When execution may be proved by handwriting.

The execution of an instrument may be established by proof of the handwriting of the party and of a subscribing witness, if there is one, in the following cases:

(1) when the parties and all the subscribing witnesses are dead;

(2) when the parties and all the subscribing witnesses are nonresidents of the state;

(3) when the place of their residence is unknown to the party desiring the proof and cannot be ascertained by the exercise of due diligence;

(4) when the subscribing witness conceals himself or cannot be found by the officer by the exercise of due diligence in attempting to serve the subpoena or attachment; or

(5) in case of the continued failure or refusal of the witness to testify for the space of 1 hour after his appearance.

§ 1-5-303. Facts which must be shown when offering proof of handwriting.

The evidence taken under 1-5-302 must satisfactorily prove to the officer the following facts:

(1) the existence of one or more of the conditions mentioned in 1-5-302;

(2) that the witness testifying knew the person whose name purports to be subscribed to the instrument as a party and is well acquainted with his signature;

(3) that the witness testifying personally knew the person who subscribed the instrument as a witness and is well acquainted with his signature;

(4) that the signature or signatures in question are genuine; and

(5) the place of residence of the witness.

§ 1-5-304. Powers of officer taking proof of execution.

Officers authorized to take the proof of instruments are authorized in such proceedings to:

(1) administer oaths or affirmations as prescribed by law;

(2) employ and swear interpreters; and

(3) issue subpoenas as prescribed by law.

§ 1-5-305. Contents of certificate of proof.

An officer taking proof of the execution of any instrument must, in his certificate endorsed thereon or attached thereto, set forth all the matters required by law to be done or known by him or proved before him on the proceeding, together with the names of all the witnesses examined before him, their places of residence respectively, and the substance of their testimony.

§ 70-20-106. Grant by married person— how acknowledged.

No estate in the real property of a married person passes by any grant purporting to be executed or acknowledged by such person unless the grant or instrument is acknowledged by the grantor in the manner prescribed by 1-5-206 and 1-5-207.

§ 70-20-107. Power of attorney of married person—how acknowledged.

A power of attorney of a married person, authorizing the execution of an instrument transferring an estate in his separate real property, has no validity for that purpose unless acknowledged by him in the manner provided in 1-5-206 and 1-5-207.

§ 70-20-108. Attorney-in-fact—how must execute for principal.

When an attorney-in-fact executes an instrument transferring an estate in real property, he must subscribe the name of his principal to it and his own name as attorney-in-fact.

DEPOSITIONS

§ 1-1-202. Terms relating to procedure and the judiciary.

Unless the context requires otherwise, the following definitions apply in the Montana Code Annotated:

(1) A "deposition" is a written declaration under oath or affirmation, made upon notice to the adverse party for the purpose of enabling him to attend and cross-examine.

* * *

§ 1-6-101. Officers who may administer oaths.

Every court, judge, clerk of any court, justice, notary public, and officer or person authorized to take testimony in any action or proceeding or to decide upon evidence has power to administer oaths or affirmations.

§ 1-6-102. Form of ordinary oath.

An oath or affirmation in an action or proceeding may be administered as follows: the person who swears or affirms expressing his assent when addressed in the following form, "You do solemnly swear (or affirm, as the case may be) that the evidence you shall give in this issue (or matter), pending between .... and ...., shall be the truth, the whole truth, and nothing but the truth, so help you God".

§ 1-6-103. Variation of oath to suit witness's belief.

The court shall vary the mode of swearing or affirming to accord with the witness's beliefs whenever it is satisfied that the witness has a distinct mode of swearing or affirming.

§ 1-6-104. Affirmation or declaration in lieu of oath.

Any person who desires it may, at his option, instead of taking an oath make his solemn affirmation or declaration by assenting when addressed in the following form: "You do solemnly affirm (or declare), etc.", as in 1-6-102.

[Mont. R. Civ. P.]

Rule 28. Persons before whom depositions may be taken.

Rule 28(a). Within the United States. Within the state of Montana, depositions shall be taken before a person authorized by the laws of this state to administer oaths; without the state, but within the United States, or within a territory or insular possession subject to the dominion of the United States, depositions shall be taken before a person authorized to administer oaths by the laws of this state, the United States, or of the place where the examination is held; within or without the state of Montana, depositions may also be taken before a person appointed by the court in which the action is pending, which persons so appointed shall have the power to administer oaths and take testimony.

Rule 28(b). In foreign countries. In a foreign country, depositions may be taken (1) on notice before a person authorized to administer oaths in the place in which the examination is held, either by the law thereof or by the law of the United States, or (2) before a person commissioned by the court, and a person so commissioned shall have the power by virtue of his commission to administer any necessary oath and take testimony, or (3) pursuant to letter rogatory. A commission or a letter rogatory shall be issued on application and notice, and on terms that are just and appropriate. It is not requisite to the issuance of a commission or a letter rogatory that the taking of the deposition in any other manner is impracticable or inconvenient; and both a commission and a letter rogatory may be issued in proper cases. A notice or commission may designate the person before whom the deposition is to be taken either by name or descriptive title. A letter rogatory may be addressed "To the Appropriate Authority in [here name the country]." Evidence obtained in response to a letter rogatory need not be excluded merely for the reason that it is not a verbatim transcript or that the testimony was not taken under oath or for any similar departure from the requirements for depositions taken within the United States under these rules.

Rule 28(c). Disqualification for interest. No deposition shall be taken before a person who is a relative or employee or attorney or counsel of any of the parties, or is a relative or employee of such attorney or counsel, or is financially interested in the action.

Rule 28(d). Depositions to be used in other states. Whenever the deposition of any person is to be taken in this state pursuant to the laws of another state or the United States or of another country for use in proceedings there, the district court of the county where the witness is to be served, upon proof that notice has been duly served, may issue, pursuant to Rule 45(d), the necessary subpoenas.

Rule 28(e). Deposition to be taken in sister states and foreign countries for use in this state. Whenever the deposition of any person is to be taken in a sister state or a foreign country, or any other jurisdiction, foreign or domestic, for use in this state, pursuant either to notice or stipulation, the clerk or equivalent officer of any court having jurisdiction at the place where the witness is to be served or the deposition taken, upon proof that notice has been duly served for taking of the deposition or that the parties have stipulated to such taking, may issue the necessary subpoenas or equivalent court instruments to require such witness to attend for the taking of the deposition at the time and place in the sister state or foreign country, or any other jurisdiction, foreign or domestic, designated in the notice or stipulation.

LEGAL HOLIDAYS

[Mont. Code Ann.]

§ 1-1-216. Legal holidays and business days.

(1) The following are legal holidays in the state of Montana:

(a) Each Sunday;

(b) New Year's Day, January 1;

(c) Lincoln's and Washington's Birthdays, the third Monday in February;

(d) Memorial Day, the last Monday in May;

(e) Independence Day, July 4;

(f) Labor Day, the first Monday in September;

(g) Columbus Day, the second Monday in October;

(h) Veterans' Day, November 11;

(i) Thanksgiving Day, the fourth Thursday in November;

(j) Christmas Day, December 25;

(k) State general election day;

(l) Heritage Day, to be observed annually on a date determined by the governing body of each political subdivision for the purposes of that political subdivision and by the governor for the executive, legislative, and judicial branches of state government, including the Montana university system.

(2) If any of the above-enumerated holidays (except Sunday) fall upon a Sunday, the Monday following is a holiday. All other days are business days.

§ 32-1-482. Transaction on holidays.

Nothing in any law of this state shall in any manner whatsoever affect the validity of, or render void or voidable, the payment, certification or acceptance of a check or other negotiable instrument, or any other transaction by a bank in this state, because done or performed during any time other than regular banking hours or on a legal holiday; provided, that nothing shall be construed herein to compel any bank in this state, which by law or custom is entitled to close at twelve noon on any Saturday, or for the whole or part of any legal holiday, to keep open for transaction of business, or to perform any of the acts or transactions aforesaid on any Saturday after such hour or on any legal holiday except at its option.

NEBRASKA

NOTARIES PUBLIC

[NEB. REV. STAT.]

§ 64-101. Notary public; appointment; qualifications; term.

(1) The Governor is hereby authorized to appoint and commission such number of persons to the office of notary public as he shall deem necessary. (2) There shall be one class of such appointments which shall be valid in the entire state and referred to as general notaries public. (3) The term effective date, as used with reference to a commission of a notary public, shall mean the date of the commission unless the commission shall state when it goes into effect, in which event that date shall be the effective date. (4) A general commission may refer to the office as notary public and shall contain a provision showing that the person therein named is authorized to act as a notary public anywhere within the State of Nebraska or, in lieu thereof, may contain the word general or refer to the office as general notary public. (5) No person shall be appointed a notary public unless his or her application is accompanied by the petition of at least twenty-five legal voters of the county in which he or she resides. (6) No appointment shall be made until such applicant shall have attained the age of twenty years nor unless such applicant shall certify to the Governor under oath that he or she has care-

317

fully read and understands the laws relating to the duties of notaries public and will, if commissioned, faithfully discharge the duties pertaining to said office and keep records according to law. (7) Each person appointed a notary public shall hold office for a term of four years from the effective date of his or her commission unless sooner removed.

§ 64-102. Commission; how obtained; bond.

Any person may apply for a commission authorizing the applicant to act as a notary public anywhere in the State of Nebraska, and thereupon the Governor may, at his discretion, issue a commission authorizing such notary public to act as such anywhere in the State of Nebraska. A general commission shall not authorize the holder thereof to act as a notary public anywhere in the State of Nebraska until a bond in the sum of four thousand dollars, with an incorporated surety company as surety, has been executed and approved by and filed in the office of the Secretary of State. Upon the filing of such bond with the Secretary of State and the issuance of such commission, such notary public shall be authorized and empowered to perform any and all the duties of a notary public in any and all the counties in the State of Nebraska. Such bond shall be conditioned for the faithful performance of the duties of such office. Such person so appointed to the office of notary public shall make oath or affirmation, to be endorsed on such bond, and subscribed by him before some officer authorized by law to administer oaths, and by him certified thereon, that he will support the Constitution of the United States and the Constitution of the State of Nebraska, and will faithfully and impartially discharge and perform the duties of the office of notary public.

§ 64-103. Commission; signature; sealing; filing and approval of bond; delivery of commission.

When any person shall be appointed to the office of notary public, the Governor shall cause his signature or a facsimile thereof to be affixed to the commission and deliver the same to the Secretary of State. Upon the receipt of the commission by the secretary, he shall affix thereto the great seal of state. Upon the filing and approval of the bond, as provided for in section 64-102, the Secretary of State shall mail or deliver the commission to the applicant.

§ 64-107. Notary public; powers and duties; certificate or records; receipt in evidence.

A notary public is authorized and empowered, within the state: (1) To administer oaths and affirmations in all cases; (2) to take depositions, acknowledgments, and proofs of the execution of deeds, mortgages, powers of attorney, and other instruments in writing, to be used or recorded in this or another state; (3) to demand acceptance or payment of any foreign, inland, domestic bill of exchange, promissory note or other obligation in writing, and to protest the same for nonacceptance or nonpayment, as the case may be, and give notice to endorsers, makers, drawers or acceptors of such demand or nonacceptance or nonpayment; and (4) to exercise and perform such other powers and duties as by the law of nations, and according to commercial usage, or by the laws of the United States, or of any other state or territory of the United States, or of any other government or country, may be exercised and performed by notaries public. Over his signature and official seal, he shall certify the performance of such duties so exercised and performed under the provisions of this section, which certificate shall be received in all courts of this state as presumptive evidence of the facts therein certified to.

§ 64-108. Summons; issuance, when authorized; contempt, power to punish.

Every notary public, when notice by a party to any civil suit pending in any court of this state upon any adverse party for the taking of any testimony of witnesses by deposition, or any commission to take testimony of witnesses to be preserved for use in any suit thereafter to be commenced, has been deposited with him, or when a special commission issued out of any court of any state or country without this state, together with notice for the taking of testimony by depositions or commissions, has been deposited with him, is empowered to issue summons and command the presence before him of witnesses, and to punish witnesses for neglect or refusal to obey such summons, or for refusal to testify when present, by commitment to the jail of the county for contempt. All sheriffs and constables in this state are required to serve and return all process issued by notaries public in the taking of testimony of witnesses by commission or deposition.

§ 64-109. Civil liability of notary public; actions.

If any person shall be damaged or injured by the unlawful act, negligence or misconduct of any notary public in his official capacity, the person damaged or injured may maintain a civil action on the official bond of such notary public against such notary public, and his sureties, and a recovery in such action shall not be a bar to any future action for other causes to the full amount of the bond.

§ 64-112. Removal from state; termination; notice to Secretary of State.

Every notary public removing from the State of Nebraska shall notify the Secretary of State of such removal. Such a removal shall terminate the term of his office.

§ 64-113. Notary public; removal; grounds; procedure; penalty.

Whenever charges of malfeasance in office shall be preferred to the Governor against any notary public in this state, or whenever the Governor shall have reasonable cause to believe any notary public in this state is guilty of acts of malfeasance in office, he may appoint any disinterested person, not related by consanguinity to either the notary public or person preferring the charges, and authorized by law to take testimony of witnesses by deposition, to notify such notary public to appear before him on a day and at an hour certain, after at least ten days from the day of service of such notice. He may summon witnesses, in the manner provided by section 64-108, to appear before him at the time specified in said notice, and he may take the testimony of such witnesses in writing, in the same manner as is by law provided for taking depositions, and certify the same to the Governor. The notary public may appear, at such time and place, and cross-examine witnesses, and produce witnesses in his behalf, which cross-examination and testimony shall be likewise certified to the Governor. Upon the receipt of such examination, duly certified in the manner prescribed for taking depositions to be used in suits in the district courts of this state, the Governor shall examine the same, and if therefrom he shall be satisfied that the charges are substantially proved, he may remove the person charged from the office of notary public. Within thirty days from such removal and notice thereof, such notary public shall deposit, with the Secretary of State, his commission as notary public. The commission shall be cancelled by the Secretary of State. Thereafter such person so removed from office shall be forever disqualified from holding the office of notary public. The fees for taking such testimony shall be paid by the state at the same rate as fees for taking depositions by notaries public. The failure of the notary public to deposit his commission with the Secretary of State as required by this section shall subject him to a penalty of two hundred dollars, to be recovered in the name of the state.

§ 64-114. Notary public; change of name; continue to act.

Any person, whose name is legally changed after a commission as a notary public is issued to him or her, may continue to act as such notary public and use the original commission, seal, and name until the expiration or termination of such commission. The bond given by such notary public shall continue in effect, regardless of such legal change of name of such notary public, if the notary public uses the name under which the commission is issued.

§ 64-116. Notary public; commission; renewal; procedure.

Commissions for general notaries public may be renewed within thirty days prior to the date of expiration by filing a renewal application along with the payment of a fee of five dollars and a new bond with the Secretary of State. The bond required for a renewal of such commission shall be in the same manner and form as provided in section 64-102. The renewal application shall be in the manner and form as prescribed by the Secretary of State. Such renewal application made prior to the date of the expiration of any general notary public commission need not be accompanied by any petition. Any renewal application for such commission made after the date of expiration of the commission shall be made in the same manner as a new application for such commission as a general notary public.

ADDITIONAL AUTHORITY

§ 25-1213. Notarial protest as evidence of dishonor.

The usual protest by a notary public, without proof of his signature or notarial seal, is evidence of the dishonor and notice of a bill of exchange or promissory note.

FEES

§ 33-102. Notary public commission; fees.

The Secretary of State shall be entitled, for receiving, affixing the great seal to, and forwarding the commission of a notary public, to the sum of ten dollars and the additional sum of ten dollars for filing and approving the bond of a notary public.

§ 33-133. Notaries public; fees.

Notaries public may charge and collect fees as follows: For each protest, one dollar; for recording the same, fifty cents; for each notice of protest, twenty-five cents; for taking affidavits and seal, twenty-five cents; for administering oath or affirmation, five cents; for taking deposition, for each one hundred words contained in such deposition and in the certificate, ten cents and no more; for each certificate and seal, twenty-five cents; for taking acknowledgment of deed or other instrument, fifty cents; and for each mile traveled in serving notice, mileage at the rate provided in section 81-1176 for state employees.

ACKNOWLEDGMENTS

§ 25-1222. Private writing; when admissible without proof.

Every private writing, except a last will and testament, after being acknowledged or proved and certified in the manner prescribed for the proof or acknowledgment of conveyances of real property, may be read in evidence without further proof.

Uniform Recognition of Acknowledgments Act

§ 64-201. Notarial acts, defined; performed.

For the purposes of section 64-201 to 64-210, unless the context otherwise requires: Notarial acts means acts which the laws and regulations of this state authorize notaries public of this state to perform, including the administering of oaths and affirmations, taking proof of execution and acknowledgments of instruments, and attesting documents. Notarial acts may be performed outside this state for use in this state with the same effect as if performed by a notary public of this state by the following persons authorized pursuant to the laws and regulations of other governments in addition to any other person authorized by the laws and regulations of this state:

(1) A notary public authorized to perform notarial acts in the place in which the act is performed;

(2) A judge, clerk, or deputy clerk of any court of record in the place in which the notarial act is performed;

(3) An officer of the foreign service of the United States, a consular agent, or any other person authorized by regulation of the United States Department of State to perform notarial acts in the place in which the act is performed;

(4) A commissioned officer in active service with the armed forces of the United States and any other person authorized by regulation of the armed forces to perform notarial acts if the notarial act is performed for one of the following or his dependents: a merchant seaman of the United States, a member of the armed forces of the United States, or any other person serving with or accompanying the armed forces of the United States; or

(5) Any other person authorized to perform notarial acts in the place in which the act is performed.

§ 64-202. Notarial act; performance; proof of authority.

(a) If the notarial act is performed by any of the persons described in paragraphs 1 to 4, inclusive of section 64-201, other than a person authorized to perform notarial acts by the laws or regulations of a foreign country, the signature, rank, or title and serial number, if any, of the person are sufficient proof of the authority of a holder of that rank or title to perform the act. Further proof of his authority is not required.

(b) If the notarial act is performed by a person authorized by the laws or regulations of a foreign country to perform the act, there is sufficient proof of the authority of that person to act if:

(1) Either a foreign service officer of the United States resident in the country in which the act is performed or a diplomatic or consular officer of the foreign country resident in the United States certifies that a person holding that office is authorized to perform the act;

(2) The official seal of the person performing the notarial act is affixed to the document; or

(3) The title and indication of authority to perform notarial acts of the person appears either in a digest of foreign law or in a list customarily used as a source of such information.

(c) If the notarial act is performed by a person other than one described in subsections (a) and (b), there is sufficient proof of the authority of that person to act if the clerk of a court of record in the place in which the notarial act is performed certifies to the official character of that person and to his authority to perform the notarial act.

(d) The signature and title of the person performing the act are prima facie evidence that he is a person with the designated title and that the signature is genuine.

§ 64-203. Certificate; contents.

The person taking an acknowledgment shall certify that:

(1) The person acknowledging appeared before him and acknowledged he executed the instrument; and

(2) The person acknowledging was known to the person taking the acknowledgment or that the person taking the acknowledgment had satisfactory evidence that the person acknowledging was the person described in and who executed the instrument.

§ 64-204. Certificate of acknowledgment; form; acceptance.

The form of a certificate of acknowledgment used by a person whose authority is recognized under section 64-201 shall be accepted in this state if:

(1) The certificate is in a form prescribed by the laws or regulations of this state;

(2) The certificate is in a form prescribed by the laws or regulations applicable in the place in which the acknowledgment is taken; or

(3) The certificate contains the words acknowledged before me, or their substantial equivalent.

§ 64-205. Acknowledgment, defined.

The words acknowledged before me means

(1) That the person acknowledging appeared before the person taking the acknowledgment,

(2) That he acknowledged he executed the instrument,

(3) That, in the case of:

(i) A natural person, he executed the instrument for the purposes therein stated;

(ii) A corporation, the officer or agent acknowledged he held the position or title set forth in the instrument and certificate, he signed the instrument on behalf of the corporation by proper authority, and the instrument was the act of the corporation for the purpose therein stated;

(iii) A partnership, the partner or agent acknowledged he signed the instrument on behalf of the partnership by proper authority and he executed the instrument as the act of the partnership for the purposes therein stated;

(iv) A person acknowledging as principal by an attorney in fact, he executed the instrument by proper authority as the act of the principal for the purposes therein stated;

(v) A person acknowledging as a public officer, trustee, administrator, guardian, or other representative, he signed the instrument by proper authority and he executed the instrument in the capacity and for the purposes therein stated; and

(4) That the person taking the acknowledgment either knew or had satisfactory evidence that the person acknowledging was the person named in the instrument or certificate.

§ 64-206. Statutory short forms of acknowledgment; use of other forms.

The forms of acknowledgment set forth in this section may be used and are sufficient for their respective purposes under any law of this state. The forms shall be known as Statutory Short Forms of Acknowledgment and may be referred to by that name. The authorization of the forms in this section does not preclude the use of other forms.

(1) For an individual acting in his own right:
State of ....
County of ....
The foregoing instrument was acknowledged before me this (date) by (name of person acknowledged).
(Signature of Person Taking Acknowledgment)
(Title or Rank)
(Serial Number, if any)

(2) For a corporation:
State of ....
County of ....
The foregoing instrument was acknowledged before me this (date) by (name of officer or agent, title of officer or agent) of (name of corporation acknowledging) a (state or place of incorporation) corporation, on behalf of the corporation.
(Signature of Person Taking Acknowledgment)
(Title or Rank)
(Serial Number, if any)

(3) For a partnership:
State of ....
County of ....
The foregoing instrument was acknowledged before me this (date) by (name of acknowledging partner or agent), partner (or agent) on behalf of (name of partnership), a partnership.
(Signature of Person Taking Acknowledgment)
(Title or Rank)
(Serial Number, if any)

(4) For an individual acting as principal by an attorney in fact:
State of ....
County of ....
The foregoing instrument was acknowledged before me this (date) by (name of attorney in fact) as attorney in fact on behalf of (name of principal).
(Signature of Person Taking Acknowledgment)
(Title or Rank)
(Serial Number, if any)

(4) By any Public Officer, trustee, or personal representative:
State of ....
County of ....
The foregoing instrument was acknowledged before me this (date) by (name and title of position).
(Signature of Person Taking Acknowledgment)
(Title or Rank)
(Serial Number, if any)

§ 64-207. Prior notarial acts; effect.

A notarial act performed prior to August 25, 1969, is not affected by sections 64-201 to 64-210. Sections 64-201 to 64-210 provide an additional method of proving notarial acts. Nothing in sections 64-201 to 64-210 diminishes or invalidates the recognition accorded to notarial acts by other laws or regulations of this state.

§ 64-208. Sections, how interpreted.

Sections 64-201 to 64-210 shall be so interpreted as to make uniform the laws of those states which enact it.

§ 64-209. Act, how cited.

Sections 64-201 to 64-210 may be cited as the Uniform Recognition of Acknowledgments Act.

§ 64-210. Seal; contents; ink stamp.

(1) Each notary public, before performing any duties of his office, shall provide himself with an official seal on which shall appear the words State of Nebraska, General Notary or State of Nebraska, General Notarial, and his name, and in addition, at his option, the date of expiration of his commission; *Provided*, a notary public may use the initial letters of his first name and middle name. A notary public shall authenticate all his official acts with such seal. Under his official signature, on all certificates of authentication made by him, he shall write, stamp, or otherwise show the date when his term of office as such notary public will expire if such date of expiration is not engraved on the seal.

(2) The official seal of a notary public may be either an engraved or ink stamp seal with which he shall authenticate all of his official acts; *Provided*, that every notary who receives a commission, either new or renewal, on or after January 1, 1972, shall use an ink stamp seal to authenticate any instrument.

§ 64-212. Acknowledgment; insurance companies; cooperative credit associations; credit unions; by officer, agents and servants; authorized.

It shall be lawful for a member or shareholder, an appointive officer, elective officer, agent, director, or employee of an insurance company, a cooperative credit association, or a credit union who is a notary public and is not a director or elected officer of such association, insurance company, or credit union, to take the acknowledgment of any person to any written instrument executed to or by said association, insurance company, or credit union and to administer an oath to any shareholder, director, elected or appointive officer, employee, or agent of such association, insurance company, or credit union.

§ 64-214. Acknowledgments; banks; by stockholders, officers and directors; authorized.

(1) It shall be lawful for any stockholder, officer, or director of a bank, who is a notary public, to take the acknowledgment of any person to any written instrument given to or by the bank and to administer an oath to any other stockholder, director, officer, employee or agent of the bank.

(2) * * *

§ 64-215. Acknowledgments; savings and loan associations; industrial loan and investment companies; by shareholders, directors, officers, agents, and servants; authorized; prior acknowledgments validated.

It shall be lawful for any shareholder, director, employee, agent, or any elected or appointed officer of a savings and loan association or industrial loan and investment company, who is a notary public, (1) to take the acknowledgment of any person to any written instrument given to or by the savings and loan association or industrial loan and investment company and (2) to administer an oath to any other shareholder, director, officer, employee, or agent of the savings and loan association or industrial loan and investment company. ***.

§ 76-217.01. Acknowledgment; defective seal; validity.

No deed, mortgage, affidavit, power of attorney or other instrument in writing shall be invalidated because of any defects in the wording of the seal of the notary public attached thereto.

§ 76-218. Acknowledgment and recording of instruments; violations; penalty.

Every officer within this state authorized to take the acknowledgment or proof of any conveyance, and every county clerk, who shall be guilty of knowingly stating an untruth, or guilty of any malfeasance or fraudulent practice in the execution of the duties prescribed for them by law, in relation to the taking or the certifying of the proof or acknowledgment, or the recording or certifying of any record of any such conveyance, mortgage or instrument in writing, or in relation to the canceling of any mortgage, shall upon conviction be adjudged guilty of a misdemeanor, and be subject to punishment by fine not exceeding five hundred dollars, and imprisonment not exceeding one year, and shall also be liable in damages to the party injured.

§ 76-219. Acknowledgment; before whom taken in any other state or territory.

If the instrument is executed and acknowledged or proved in any other state, territory or district of the United States, it must be executed and acknowledged or proved either according to the laws of such state, territory or district or in accordance with the law of this state, and if acknowledged out of this state it must be before some court of record or clerk or officer holding the seal thereof, or before some commissioner to take the acknowledgment of deeds, appointed by the Governor of this state, or before some notary public.

§ 76-226. Deeds; execution in foreign country; laws governing; acknowledgment.

If such deed be executed in a foreign country, it may be executed according to the laws of such country, and the execution thereof may be acknowledged before any notary public therein, or before any minister plenipotentiary, minister extraordinary, minister resident, charge d'affaires, commissioner, commercial agent, or consul of the United States appointed to reside therein, which acknowledgment shall be certified thereon by the officer taking the same, under his hand, and if taken before a notary public, his seal of office shall be affixed to such certificate.

§ 76-227. Acknowledgment before army officers; validity.

The acknowledgment of legal instruments, the attestation of documents, the administration of oaths and other notarial acts, heretofore or hereafter taken before any duly commissioned officer of the army, navy, marine corps, coast guard, or any other component part of the armed forces of the United States are hereby declared legal, valid and binding, and such instrument and documents shall be admissible in evidence and eligible to record in this state under the same circumstances, and with the same force and effect as if such acknowledgment, attestation, oath, affidavit, or other notarial act had been made or taken before a notary public within this state. If the signature, rank and branch of service of any such officer appear upon such instrument or document, no further proof of the authority of such officer to so act shall be required.

§ 76-241. Deeds and other instruments; when not lawfully recorded.

All deeds, mortgages and other instruments of writing shall not be deemed lawfully recorded unless they have been previously acknowledged or proved in the manner prescribed by statute.

§ 76-242. Conveyances; acknowledged in another state; recording; what constitutes sufficient authentication.

In all cases provided for in section 76-219, if such acknowledgment or proof is taken before a notary public or other officer using an official seal, except a commissioner appointed by the Governor of this state, the instrument thus acknowledged or proved shall be entitled to be recorded without further authentication. In all other cases the deed or other instrument shall have attached thereto a certificate of the clerk of a court of record, or other proper certifying officer of the county, district or state within which the acknowledgment or proof was taken, under the seal of his office, showing that the person, whose name is subscribed to the certificate of acknowledgment, was at the date thereof such officer as he is therein represented to be; that he is well acquainted with the handwriting of such officer; that he believes the signature of such officer to be genuine; and that the deed or other instrument is executed and acknowledged according to the laws of such state, district or territory.

DEPOSITIONS

§ 25-1229. Subpoena; disobedience; refusal to testify or sign deposition; contempt.

Disobedience of a subpoena, or a refusal to be sworn, or to answer as a witness, or to subscribe a deposition, when lawfully ordered, may be punished as a contempt of the court or officer by whom his attendance or testimony is required.

§ 25-1231. Subpoena; disobedience; refusal to testify or sign deposition; punishment of witness for contempt.

The punishment for the contempt mentioned in section 25-1229 shall be as follows: When the witness fails to attend in obedience to the subpoena, except in case of a demand and failure to pay his fees, the court or officer may fine the witness in a sum not exceeding fifty dollars. In other cases, the court or officer may fine the witness in a sum not exceeding fifty dollars nor less than five dollars, or may imprison him in the county jail, there to remain until he shall submit to be sworn, to testify or give his deposition. The fine imposed by the court shall be paid into the county treasurer, and that imposed by the officer shall be for the use of the party for whom the witness was subpoenaed. The witness shall also be liable to the party injured for any damages occasioned by his failure to attend, or his refusal to be sworn, to testify or give his deposition.

§ 25-1242. Deposition, defined.

A deposition is a written declaration under oath or a videotape taken under oath in accordance with procedures provided by law, made upon notice to the adverse party for the purpose of enabling him to attend and cross-examine, or made upon written interrogatories.

LEGAL HOLIDAYS

§ 62-301. Holidays, enumerated; federal holiday schedule observed; exceptions; bank holidays.

(1) For the purposes of the Uniform Commercial Code and section 62-301.01, the following days shall be holidays: New Year's Day, January 1; Birthday of Martin Luther King, Jr., the third Monday in January; President's Day, the third Monday in February; Arbor Day, April 22; Memorial Day, the last Monday in May; Independence Day, July 4; Labor Day, the first Monday in September; Columbus Day, the second Monday in October; Veterans Day, November 11, and the federally recognized holiday therefor, or either of them; Thanksgiving Day, the fourth Thursday in November; the day after Thanksgiving; and Christmas Day, December 25. If any of such dates fall on Sunday, the following Monday shall be a holiday. If the date designated by the state for observance of any legal holiday enumerated in this section, except Veterans Day, is different from the date of observance of such holiday pursuant to a federal holiday schedule, the federal holiday schedule shall be observed.

(2) Any bank doing business in this state may, by a brief written notice at, on, or near its front door, fully dispense with or restrict, to such extent as it may determine, the hours within which it will be open for business.

(3) Any bank may close on Saturday if it states such fact by a brief written notice at, on, or near its front door. Where such bank shall, in observance of such a notice, not be open for general business, such day shall, with respect to the particular bank, be the equivalent of a holiday, as fully as if such day were listed in subsection (1) of this section, and any act authorized, required, or permitted to be performed at, by, or with respect to such bank which shall, in observance of such notice, not be open for general business, acting in its own behalf or in any capacity whatever, may be performed on the next succeeding business day and no liability or loss of rights on the part of any person shall result from such delay.

(4) Any bank which, by the notice provided by subsection (3) of this section, has created the holi-day for such bank may, without destroying the legal effect of the holiday for it and solely for the convenience of its customers, remain open all or part of such day in a limited fashion by treating every transaction with its customers on such day as though the transaction had taken place immediately upon the opening of such bank on the first following business day.

(5) Whenever the word bank is used in this section it shall include industrial loan and investment company, building and loan association, savings and loan association, credit union, savings bank, trust company, investment company, cooperative credit association, and any other type of financial institution.

§ 62-301.01. Holidays; transactions with bank; validity.

Nothing in any law of this state shall in any manner affect the validity of, or render void or voidable any transaction by a bank in this state because done or performed during any time other than regular banking hours; *Provided*, that nothing herein shall be construed to compel any bank in this state which by law or custom is entitled to close at a fixed hour on any day or for the whole or any part of any holiday, to keep open for the transaction of business on any day after such hour, or on any holiday, except at its own option.

§ 84-104.01. Veterans Day; proclamation by Governor; prohibition of transaction of business by state departments; manner of observance.

The Governor shall issue his proclamation each year designating Veterans Day and calling upon the public schools and citizens of Nebraska to observe such day as a patriotic day. Veterans Day shall be November 11, annually, unless such date falls on Saturday, or Sunday, in which event the Governor may declare the preceding Friday or the following Monday as Veterans Day. No business shall be transacted on that day at any department of the State of Nebraska, except for necessary maintenance, highway construction inspection or in case of emergency. In pursuance to such proclamation, suitable exercises having reference to the wars and military campaigns of the United States, of Nebraska's role therein, and honoring the veterans of such wars and campaigns may be held in all schools of the state, both public and private.

NEVADA

NOTARIES PUBLIC

[Nev. Rev. Stat.]

§ 240.010. Appointment by secretary of state.

1. The secretary of state may appoint notaries public in this state.

2. The secretary of state may not appoint as a notary public any person who submits an application containing any substantial and material misstatement or omission of fact.

§ 240.015. Qualifications.

Each person appointed as a notary public must be:

1. A citizen of the United States or lawfully admitted for permanent residency in the United

States as verified by the Immigration and Naturalization Service.

2. At least 18 years of age.

§ 240.017. Regulations.

The secretary of state may adopt regulations prescribing the procedure for the appointment of a notary public.

§ 240.020. Notaries may act in any part of state; term of office.

Notaries public may perform notarial acts in any part of this state for a term of 4 years, unless sooner removed.

§ 240.030. Application for appointment; fees; oath and bond; duplicate or amended certificates.

1. Each person applying for appointment as a notary public shall:

(a) At the time he submits his application, pay to the secretary of state $35.

(b) Take and subscribe to the oath set forth in section 2 of article 15 of the constitution of the State of Nevada as if he were a public officer.

(c) Enter into a bond to the State of Nevada in the sum of $10,000, to be approved by the clerk of the county in which the applicant resides.

2. In completing an application, bond, oath or other document necessary to apply for appointment as a notary public, an applicant who is employed as a peace officer and is required to be a notary public as a condition of that employment must not be required to disclose his residential address or telephone number on any such document which will become available to the public.

3. The bond, together with the oath, must be filed and recorded in the office of the county clerk of the county in which the applicant resides when he applies for his appointment. On a form provided by the secretary of state, the county clerk shall immediately certify to the secretary of state that the bond and oath have been filed and recorded. Upon receipt of the application, fee and certification that the bond and oath have been filed and recorded, the secretary of state shall issue a certificate of appointment as a notary public to the applicant.

4. The secretary of state shall charge a fee of $10 for each duplicate or amended certificate of appointment which is issued to a notary.

§ 240.040. Authentication of acts; use of rubber or mechanical stamp; seal not required.

1. Each notary public shall authenticate all his acts, including any acknowledgment, jurat, verification or other certificate, by setting forth the following:

(a) The venue;

(b) His signature; and

(c) A statement imprinted in black ink with a rubber or other mechanical stamp setting forth his name, the phrase "Notary Public, State of Nevada" and the date on which his appointment expires.

2. After July 1,1965, a notarial seal is not required on notarized documents.

§ 240.060. Powers and duties of notary public.

1. Each notary public may:

(a) Administer oaths or affirmations;

(b) Take acknowledgments and depositions;

(c) Certify copies;

(d) Execute jurats; and

(e) Perform such other duties as may be prescribed by specific statute.

2. A notary public shall perform notarial acts in lawful transactions for a person who requests the act and tenders the appropriate fee.

§ 240.065. Restrictions on powers of notary public.

A notary public may not perform any act authorized by NRS 240.060 if he:

1. Executed or is named in the instrument acknowledged or sworn to;

2. Will receive directly from a transaction relating to the instrument any commission, fee, advantage, right, title, interest, property or other consideration in excess of the authorized fees; or

3. Is related to the person whose signature is to be acknowledged or sworn to as a spouse, sibling or lineal ancestor or descendant.

§ 240.075. Prohibited acts.

A notary public shall not:

1. Influence a person to enter or not enter into a lawful transaction involving a notarial act performed by the notary public.

2. Certify an instrument containing a statement known by him to be false.

3. Perform any act as a notary public with intent to deceive or defraud.

4. Endorse or promote any product, service or offering if his appointment as a notary public is used in the endorsement or promotional statement.

§ 240.085. Advertisements in language other than English to contain notice if notary public is not an attorney; penalties.

1. Every notary public who is not an attorney licensed to practice law in this state and who advertises his services as a notary public in a language other than English by any form of communication, except a single plaque on his desk, shall post or otherwise include with the advertisement a notice in the language in which the advertisement appears. The notice must be of a conspicuous size, if in writing, and must appear in substantially the following form:

I AM NOT AN ATTORNEY IN THE STATE OF NEVADA. I AM NOT LICENSED TO GIVE LEGAL ADVICE. I MAY NOT ACCEPT FEES FOR GIVING LEGAL ADVICE.

2. If the secretary of state finds a notary public guilty of violating the provisions of subsection 1, he shall:

(a) Suspend the appointment of the notary public for not less than 1 year.

(b) Revoke the appointment of the notary public for a third or subsequent offense.

3. A notary public who is found guilty in a criminal prosecution of violating subsection 1 shall be punished by a fine of not more than $2,000.

§ 240.100. Fees.

1. Except as provided in subsection 3, a notary public may charge the following fees and no more:

For taking an acknowledgment, for the first signature $1.00
For each additional signature 50
For administering an oath or affirmation without a signature 0.25
For a certified copy, each page 50
For a jurat, for each signature on the affidavit 1.00

2. All fees prescribed in this section are payable in advance, if demanded.

3. A notary public may charge an additional fee for traveling to perform a notarial act if:

(a) He explains to the person requesting the notarial act that the fee is in addition to the fee authorized in subsection 1 and is not required by law; and

(b) The person requesting the notarial act agrees in advance upon the amount of the additional fee.

§ 240.110. Posting of table of fees; penalty.

1. Every notary public shall publish and set up in some conspicuous place in his office a table of his fees, according to this chapter, for the inspection of all persons who have business in his office. The schedule must not be printed in smaller than 1/2-inch type.

2. For each day's failure to comply with the provisions of subsection 1, he shall forfeit a sum not exceeding $20 with costs, which may be recovered by any person by an action before any justice of the peace of the same county.

§ 240.120. Book of fees; penalty.

1. Each notary public shall keep a fee book in his office in which he shall enter:

(a) The fees charged, in detail.

(b) The title of the matter, proceeding or action on which they are charged.

2. The fee book shall be open to public inspection.

3. Any notary public who shall violate any of the provisions of this section shall be fined not more than $1,000.

§ 240.130. No other fees to be charged; penalty.

1. No other fees shall be charged than those specially set forth in this chapter, nor shall fees be charged for any other services than those mentioned in this chapter.

2. Any notary public who shall violate any of the provisions of this section shall be fined not more than $1,000.

§ 240.140. Penalties for taking larger fee than authorized.

If any notary public takes more or greater fees than are allowed in this chapter, he shall be fined not more than $1,000, and his appointment must be revoked.

§ 240.150. Penalties for misconduct or neglect.

For any misconduct or neglect in any of the cases in which any notary public appointed under the authority of this state, may act, either by the law of this state, or of any state, territory or country, or by the law of nations, or by commercial usage, he is liable on his official bond to the parties injured thereby, for all the damages sustained; and for any willful violation or neglect of duty, a notary public shall be fined not more than $2,000, and his appointment must be revoked.

§ 240.160. Revocation of appointment.

The secretary of state may at any time, for cause, revoke the appointment of a notary public.

OFFENSES

§ 205.120. False certificate to certain instruments punishable as forgery.

Every officer authorized to take a proof or acknowledgment of an instrument which by law may be recorded, who shall willfully certify falsely that the execution of such instrument was acknowledged by any party thereto, or that the execution thereof was proved, shall be guilty of a felony, and shall be punished the same as persons who are guilty of forgery.

SAFE-DEPOSIT BOXES

§ 663.085. Safe-deposit boxes: Unpaid rentals; notice to lessee; disposition of contents.

1. If the rental due on a safe-deposit box has not been paid for 90 days, the lessor may send a notice by registered or certified mail to the last known address of the lessee stating that the safe-deposit box will be opened and its contents stored at the expense of the lessee unless payment of the rental is made within 30 days. If the rental is not paid within 30 days from the mailing of the notice, the box may be opened in the presence of any officer of the lessor and a notary public. The contents must be sealed in a package by the notary public, who shall write on the outside the name of the lessee and the date of the opening in the presence of the officer. The notary public and the officer shall execute a certificate reciting the name of the lessee, the date of the opening of the box and a list of its contents. The certificate must be included in the package and a copy of the certificate must be sent by registered or certified mail to the last known address of the lessee. The package must then be placed in the general vaults of the lessor at a rental not exceeding the rental previously charged for the box.

2. If the contents of the safe-deposit box have not been claimed within 6 months of the mailing of the certificate, the lessor may send another notice to the last known address of the lessee stating that, unless the accumulated charges are paid within 30 days, the contents of the box will be sold at public or private sale at a specified time and place, or, in the case of securities listed on a stock exchange, will be sold upon the exchange on or after a specified date. The time, place and manner of sale must also be posted conspicuously on the premises of the lessor and advertised once in a newspaper of general circulation in the community. Except as otherwise provided in subsection 3, if the articles are not claimed, they may then be sold in accordance with the notice.

3. Any document which has legal significance, including a will, codicil, deed, mortgage, policy of insurance, certificate of birth, marriage or death, contract or other evidence of indebtedness must be retained by the lessor or subsequent custodian, unless claimed by the owner, for 8 years after the box is opened pursuant to subsection 1. After that time, they may be destroyed. Any other documents or writings of a private nature, if they have little or no apparent value, need not be offered for sale, but must be retained, unless claimed by the owner, for 6 months, after which they may be destroyed.

4. The balance of the proceeds, after deducting accumulated charges, including the expense of advertising and conducting the sale, together with any money discovered in the box must be deposited to the credit of the lessee in any account maintained by him, or if none, must be deposited in a deposit account with the bank operating the safe-deposit facility, or in the case of a subsidiary safe-deposit company, a bank owning stock therein, and must be identified on the books of the bank as arising from the sale of contents of a safe-deposit box.

ACKNOWLEDGMENTS

§ 1.180. Documents to which seal affixed.

The seal of the court need not be affixed to any proceedings therein except:

1. To a summons, writ or commission to take testimony.

* * *

4. To certificate of acknowledgment and all final process.

§ 111.240. Acknowledgment of conveyances.

Every conveyance in writing whereby any real property is conveyed or may be affected shall be acknowledged or proved and certified in the manner provided in this chapter.

§ 111.245. Acknowledgment of married woman.

Any officer authorized by this chapter to take the proof or acknowledgment of any conveyance whereby any real property is conveyed, or may be affected, may take and certify the acknowledgment of a married woman to any such conveyance of real property.

§ 111.250. Endorsement or annexation of certificate.

1. Every person who takes the proof or acknowledgment of any conveyance affecting any real property shall grant a certificate thereof and cause the certificate to be endorsed or annexed to the conveyance.

2. The certificate must be:

(a) When granted by a judge, justice of the peace or clerk, under the hand of the judge, justice of the peace or clerk, and the seal of the court.

(b) When granted by an officer who has a seal of office, under the hand and official seal of the officer.

§ 111.255. Proof of identity of person making acknowledgment required.

No acknowledgment of any conveyance whereby any real property is conveyed, or may be affected, may be taken unless the person offering to make the acknowledgment is personally known to the person taking the acknowledgment to be the person whose name is subscribed to the conveyance as a party to it, or is proved to be that person.

§ 111.260. Contents of certificate of acknowledgment.

The certificate of the acknowledgment must state the fact of acknowledgment, and that the person making the acknowledgment was personally known to the person granting the certificate to be the person whose name is subscribed to the conveyance as a party or was proved to be that person.

§ 111.265. Persons authorized to take acknowledgment or proof within state.

The proof or acknowledgment of every conveyance affecting any real property, if acknowledged or proved within this state, must be taken by one of the following persons:

1. A judge or a clerk of a court having a seal.
2. A notary public.
3. A justice of the peace.

§ 111.270. Form of certificate made within state for natural person, corporation or partnership.

1. A certificate, when made for an acknowledgment by a natural person, corporation or partnership, must be in substantially the following form:

State of Nevada]
]SS.
County of ....]
On .... (date) personally appeared before me, a notary public (or judge or other authorized person, as the case may be), ..., personally known (or proved) to me to be the person whose name is subscribed to the above instrument who acknowledged that he executed the instrument.

....
(Signature)

2. Any acknowledgment made before July 1, 1967, which is in a form substantially the same as that contained in subsection 1, is a valid acknowledgment.

§ 111.280. Form of certificate made within state for attorney in fact.

A certificate, when made for an acknowledgment by an attorney in fact, must be in substantially the following form:

State of Nevada]
]SS.
County of ....]
On this ...... day of ......, A.D. ......, personally appeared before me, a notary public (or judge or other authorized person, as the case may be), in and for .... County, A.B., known (or proved) to me to be the person whose name is subscribed to the within instrument as the attorney in fact of ...., and acknowledged to me that he subscribed his own name as attorney in fact.

§ 111.290. Persons authorized to take acknowledgment or proof outside state.

The proof or acknowledgment of every conveyance affecting any real property, taken without this state but within the United States, must be taken by one of the following:

1. A judge or a clerk of a court having a seal.
2. A notary public.
3. A justice of the peace.
4. A commissioner appointed by the governor of this state for that purpose.

§ 111.295. Form of acknowledgment made outside state.

Any acknowledgment heretofore or hereafter taken, or certificate thereof made, without this state, either in accordance with the laws of this state or in accordance with the laws of the place where the acknowledgment is taken, shall be sufficient in this state.

§ 111.300. Who may take acknowledgment outside United States: Form of certificate.

1. All deeds or other instruments requiring acknowledgment, if acknowledged without the United States, shall be acknowledged:

(a) Before an ambassador, minister, envoy or charge d'affaires of the United States, in the country to which he is accredited; or

(b) Before one of the following persons commissioned or credited to act at the place where the acknowledgment is taken, and having an official seal:

(1) Any consular officer of the United States.

(2) A notary public.

(3) A commissioner or other agent of this state having power to take acknowledgments to deeds.

2. Every certificate of acknowledgment made without the United States shall contain:

(a) The name or names of the person or persons making the acknowledgment.

(b) The date when and the place where made.

(c) A statement of the fact that the person or persons making the acknowledgment knew the contents of the instrument and acknowledged the same to be his, her or their act.

(d) The name of the person before whom made, his official title, and be sealed with his official seal. When the seal affixed shall contain the name or the official style of the person, any error in stating, or failure to state otherwise the name or the official style of the person, shall not render the certificate defective.

3. The certificate may be substantially in the following form:

.... (Name of country)

.... (Name of city, province or other
               political subdivision)

Before the undersigned, ... (naming the person and designating his official title), duly commissioned (or appointed) and qualified, this day personally appeared at the place above named .... (naming the person or persons acknowledging), who declared that he (she or they) knew the contents of the foregoing instrument, and acknowledged the same to be his (her or their) act.

Witness my hand and official seal this ...... day of ......, 19....

(Seal)   .... (Name of person before
                       whom made)
                 .... (Official title)

4. A certificate of acknowledgment of a deed or other instrument acknowledged without the United States before any person mentioned in subsection 1 shall also be valid if in the same form as now is or hereafter may be required by law, for an acknowledgment within this state.

§ 111.305. Acknowledgments of members of and persons present with Armed Forces: Form of certificates; retroactive provisions.

1. In addition to the acknowledgment of instruments in the manner and form and as otherwise authorized by the laws of the State of Nevada, any person serving in or with the Armed Forces of the United States or any person whose duties require his presence with the Armed Forces of the United States may acknowledge the same wherever located, whether within or without the United States, before any commissioned officer in active service of the Armed Forces of the United States with the rank of second lieutenant or higher in the army, air force or marine corps, or ensign or higher in the navy or United States Coast Guard. The instrument shall not be rendered invalid by the failure to state therein the place of execution or acknowledgment.

2. No authentication of the officer's certificate of acknowledgment shall be required, but the officer taking the acknowledgment shall endorse thereon or attach thereto a certificate substantially in the following form:

On this, the ...... day of ......, 19...., before me, ..., the undersigned officer, personally appeared ...., known to me (or satisfactorily proven) to be serving in or with the Armed Forces of the United States, or known to me (or satisfactorily proven) to be a person whose duties require his presence with the Armed Forces of the United States, and to be the person whose name is subscribed to the within instrument, and acknowledged that he executed the same freely and voluntarily for the purposes therein mentioned. And the undersigned does further certify that he is at the date of this certificate a commissioned officer of the rank stated below and is in the active service of the Armed Forces of the United States.

....
Signature of officer.

....
Rank of officer and
command to
which attached.

3. Any officer mentioned in subsection 1 shall have power to administer oaths or affirmations to any person serving in or with the Armed Forces of the United States, or to any person whose duties require his presence with the Armed Forces of the United States, wherever located, whether within or without the United States, with the same force and effect as if the same were administered by any other officer now authorized by the laws of the State of Nevada to administer oaths or affirmations.

4. The provisions of this section are expressly made retroactive to and including September 8, 1939, and all acknowledgments taken and oaths administered in conformity with the provisions of this section since September 8, 1939, and prior to March 24, 1943, shall be and are hereby declared to be as effective as though taken after March 24, 1943.

§ 111.310. Instruments entitled to recordation; patents need not be acknowledged.

1. A certificate of the acknowledgment of any conveyance or other instrument in any way affecting the title to real or personal property, or the proof of the execution thereof, as provided in this chapter, signed by the officer taking the same, and under the seal or stamp of such officer, if such officer is required by law to have a seal or stamp, shall entitle such conveyance or instrument, with the certificate or certificates, to be recorded in the office of the recorder of any county in this state.

2. Any state or United States contract or patent for land may be recorded without any acknowledgment or proof.

§ 281.180. Records of official acts of officers taking acknowledgments; liabilities and penalties.

1. Each officer authorized by law to take the proof or acknowledgment of the execution of conveyances of real property, or other instrument required by law to be proved or acknowledged, shall keep a record of all his official acts in relation thereto in a book to be provided by him for that purpose. There shall be entered in the book:

(a) The date of the proof or acknowledgment thereof.

(b) The date of the instrument.

(c) The name or character of the instrument proved or acknowledged.

(d) The names of each of the parties thereto, as grantor, grantee or otherwise.

During business hours, the record shall be open to public inspection without fee or reward.

2. Any officer mentioned in subsection 1 who refuses or neglects to comply with the requirements of this section shall:

(a) Be punished by a fine of not more than $500; and

(b) Be liable on his official bond in damages to any person injured by such refusal or neglect to the extent of the injury sustained by reason of the refusal or neglect mentioned in this subsection.

DEPOSITIONS

Affidavits

§ 53.010. Persons before whom affidavits may be taken for use in this state.

An affidavit to be used before any court, judge or officer of this state may be taken before any justice, judge or clerk of any court, or any justice of the peace or notary public in this state.

§ 53.020. Taking of affidavits in other states and territories for use in this state.

An affidavit taken in another state or in a territory of the United States to be used in this state shall be taken before a commissioner appointed by the governor of this state to take affidavits and depositions in such other state or territory, or before any notary public or judge of a court of record having a seal.

§ 53.030. Certification of signature of officer to affidavit taken in another state or territory.

When an affidavit is taken before a judge of a court in another state or in a territory of the United States, the genuineness of the signature of the judge, the existence of the court, and the fact that such judge is a member thereof shall be certified by the clerk of the court, under the seal thereof.

§ 53.040. Taking of affidavits in foreign countries.

An affidavit taken in a foreign country to be used in this state shall be taken before an ambassador, minister, consul, vice consul or other consular agent of the United States, or any notary public or other person authorized by the laws of such country to administer oaths, or before any judge of a court of record of such foreign country, with the seal of the court attached, if there be one, and if there be none, then with a statement attached by the judge or clerk of the court to the effect that the court has no seal.

Uniform Foreign Depositions Act

§ 53.050. Short title.

NRS 53.050 to 53.070, inclusive, may be cited as the Uniform Foreign Depositions Act.

§ 53.060. Authority to act.

Whenever any mandate, writ or commission is issued out of any court of record in any other state, territory, district or foreign jurisdiction, or whenever upon notice or agreement it is required to take the testimony of a witness or witnesses in this state, witnesses may be compelled to appear and testify in the same manner and by the same process and proceeding as may be employed for the purpose of taking testimony in proceedings pending in this state.

§ 53.070. Uniformity of interpretation.

NRS 53.050 to 53.070, inclusive, shall be so interpreted and construed as to effectuate their general purposes to make uniform the law of those states which enact them.

Justices' Courts
[Nev. Justices' Ct. R. Civ. P.]

Rule 1. Scope and application of rules.

These rules govern the procedure in the justices' courts in all suits of a civil nature, with the exceptions stated in Rule 81. They shall be construed to secure the just, speedy and inexpensive determination of every action. Whenever it is made to appear to the court that a particular situation does not fall within any of these rules or that the literal application of a rule would work hardship or injustice in a particular situation, the court shall make such order as the interests of justice require. Rules 1 and 3 through 87 also apply to civil proceedings in municipal courts to the extent practicable.

Rule 28. Persons before whom depositions may be taken.

(a) **Within the United States.** Within the United States or within a territory or insular possession subject to the dominion of the United States, depositions shall be taken before an officer authorized to administer oaths by the laws of the United States or of the place where the examination is held, or before a person appointed by the court in which the action is pending. A person so appointed has power to administer oaths and take testimony. Upon proof that the notice to take a deposition outside the State of Nevada has been given as provided in these rules, the clerk shall issue a commission or letters rogatory in the form prescribed by the jurisdiction in which the deposition is to be taken, such form to be presented by the party seeking the deposition. Any error in the form or in the commission or letters is waived unless objection thereto be filed and served on or before the time fixed in the notice. The term "officer" as used in Rules 30, 31 and 32 includes a person appointed by the court or designated by the parties under Rule 29.

(b) **In Foreign Countries.** In a foreign country, depositions may be taken (1) on notice before a person authorized to administer oaths in the place in which the examination is held, either by the law thereof or by the law of the United States, or (2) before a person commissioned by the court, and a person so commissioned shall have the power by virtue of his commission to administer any necessary oath and take testimony, or (3) pursuant to a letter rogatory. A commission or a letter rogatory shall be issued on application and notice and on terms that are just and appropriate. It is not requisite to the issuance of a commission or a letter rogatory that the taking of the deposition in any other manner is impracticable or inconvenient; and both a commission and a letter rogatory may be issued in proper cases. A notice or commission may designate the person before whom the deposition is to be taken either by name or descriptive title. A letter rogatory may be addressed "To the Appropriate Authority in [here name the country]." Evidence obtained in response to a letter rogatory need not be excluded merely for the reason that it is not a verbatim transcript or that the testimony was not taken under oath or for any similar departure from the requirements for depositions taken within the United States under these rules.

(c) **Disqualification for Interest.** No disposition shall be taken before a person who is a relative or employee or attorney or counsel of any of the parties, or is a relative or employee of such attorney or counsel, or is financially interested in the action.

District Courts
[Nev. Dist. Ct. R. Civ. P.]

Rule 1. Scope of rules.

These rules govern the procedure in the district courts in all suits of a civil nature whether cognizable as cases at law or in equity, with the exceptions stated in Rule 81. They shall be construed to secure the just, speedy and inexpensive determination of every action.

Rule 28. Persons before whom depositions may be taken.

(a) **Within the United States.** Within the United States or within a territory or insular possession subject to the dominion of the United States, depositions shall be taken before an officer authorized to administer oaths by the laws of the United States or of the place where the examination is held, or before a person appointed by the court in which the action is pending. A person so appointed has power to administer oaths and take testimony. Upon proof that the notice to take a deposition outside the State of Nevada has been given as provided in these rules, the clerk shall issue a commission or letters rogatory in the form prescribed by the jurisdiction in which the deposition is to be taken, such form to be presented by the party seeking the deposition. Any error in the form or in the commission or letters is waived unless objection thereto be filed and served on or before the time fixed in the notice. The term "officer" as used in Rules 30, 31 and 32 includes a person appointed by the court or designated by the parties under Rule 29.

(b) In Foreign Countries. In a foreign country, depositions may be taken (1) on notice before a person authorized to administer oaths in the place in which the examination is held, either by the law thereof or by the law of the United States, (2) before a person commissioned by the court, and a person so commissioned shall have the power by virtue of his commission to administer any necessary oath and take testimony, or (3) pursuant to a letter rogatory. A commission or a letter rogatory shall be issued on application and notice and on terms that are just and appropriate. It is not requisite to the issuance of a commission or a letter rogatory that the taking of the deposition in any other manner is impracticable or inconvenient; and both a commission and a letter rogatory may be issued in proper cases. A notice or commission may designate the person before whom the deposition is to be taken either by name or descriptive title. A letter rogatory may be addressed "To the Appropriate Authority in [here name the country]." Evidence obtained in response to a letter rogatory need not be excluded merely for the reason that it is not a verbatim transcript or that the testimony was not taken under oath or for any similar departure from the requirements for depositions taken within the United States under these rules.

(c) Disqualification for Interest. No deposition shall be taken before a person who is a relative or employee or attorney or counsel of any of the parties, or is a relative or employee of such attorney or counsel, or is financially interested in the action.

COMMISSIONERS

[Nev. Rev. Stat.]

§ 240.170. Appointment and term.

The governor may, when in his judgment it may be necessary, appoint in each of the United States, and in each of the territories and districts thereof, and in each foreign state, kingdom, province, territory and colony, one or more commissioners of deeds, to continue in office 4 years, unless sooner removed by him.

§ 240.180. Fee for commission.

Before any commission is delivered to any appointee under the provisions of NRS 240.170 to 240.220, inclusive, a fee of $25 on the commission, exclusive of other legal charges thereon, shall be paid therefor to the secretary of state.

§ 240.190. Oath of office.

Before any appointed commissioner shall proceed to perform any of the duties of his office, he shall take and subscribe an oath that he will faithfully perform and discharge all of the duties of his office. The oath shall be filed in the office of the secretary of State of Nevada within 6 months after being taken and subscribed.

§ 240.200. Commission and copy of law transmitted to appointee.

The secretary of state shall transmit a copy of NRS 240.170 to 240.220, inclusive, with the commission to each person appointed under the provisions of NRS 240.170 to 240.220, inclusive.

§ 240.210. Powers of commissioners.

Every commissioner of deeds appointed by the governor shall have power:

1. To administer oaths.
2. To take and certify depositions and affidavits to be used in this state.
3. To take the acknowledgment or proof of any deed or other instrument to be recorded in this state, and duly certify the same under his hand and official seal.

§ 240.220. Legality of acts of commissioner.

All oaths administered by commissioners of deeds, all depositions and affidavits taken by them, and all acknowledgments and proofs of deeds and other instruments, taken and certified by them under their seals as commissioners of deeds, shall have the same force and effect in law, for all purposes whatever, as if done and certified by any notary public or officer, in and for this state, who is now or hereafter may be authorized by law to perform such act.

§ 240.230. Compensation of commissioners of deeds acting in Nevada; penalties.

1. Commissioners of deeds appointed by the governors of any of the states of the United States of America, or of any of the territories thereof, to reside in the State of Nevada, may receive for services rendered in this state the following compensation, and none other:

For drawing an affidavit, deposition or other paper, for each folio $0.30
For administering an oath or affirmation . .25
For putting his seal to such instruments .. .50
For taking an acknowledgment or proof of deed or other instrument, to include the seal and the writing of the certificate, for the first signature 1.00
For each additional signature .... .50

2. Each commissioner of deeds residing in this

state shall be subject to all the penalties for official delinquency or extortions as are provided by law for official misconduct.

LEGAL HOLIDAYS

§ 1.130. Nonjudicial days; transaction of judicial business.

1. No court except a justice's court or a municipal court shall be opened nor shall any judicial business be transacted except by a justice's court or municipal court on Sunday, or on any day declared to be a legal holiday according to the provisions of NRS 236.015, except for the following purposes:

(a) To give, upon their request, instructions to a jury then deliberating on their verdict.

(b) To receive a verdict or discharge a jury.

(c) For the exercise of the power of a magistrate in a criminal action or in a proceeding of a criminal nature.

(d) For the issue of a writ of attachment, which may be issued on each and all of the days above enumerated upon the plaintiff, or some person in his behalf, setting forth in the affidavit required by law for obtaining the writ the additional averment as follows: That the affiant has good reason to believe, and does believe, that it will be too late for the purpose of acquiring a lien by the writ to wait until subsequent day for the issuance of the same. All proceedings instituted, and all writs issued, and all official acts done on any of the days above specified, under and by virtue of this section, shall have all the validity, force and effect of proceedings commenced on other days, whether a lien be obtained or a levy made under and by virtue of the writ.

2. Nothing herein contained shall affect private transactions of any nature whatsoever.

§ 10.165. Performance of secular acts.

Whenever any act of a secular nature, other than a work of necessity or mercy, is appointed by law or contract to be performed upon a particular day, which day falls upon a holiday or a nonjudicial day, it may be performed upon the next business day with the same effect as if it had been performed upon the day appointed; and if such act is to be performed at a particular hour it may be performed at the same hour of the next business day.

§ 236.015. Legal holidays; closing of state, county and city offices, courts, banks, savings and loan associations, public schools and University of Nevada System.

1. The following days are declared to be legal holidays for state, county and city governmental offices:

January 1 (New Year's Day)

Third Monday in January (Martin Luther King, Jr.'s Birthday)

Third Monday in February (Washington's Birthday)

Last Monday in May (Memorial Day)

July 4 (Independence Day)

First Monday in September (Labor Day)

October 31 (Nevada Day)

November 11 (Veterans' Day)

Fourth Thursday in November (Thanksgiving Day)

Friday following the fourth Thursday in November (Family Day)

December 25 (Christmas Day)

Any day that may be appointed by the President of the United States for public fast, thanksgiving or as a legal holiday except for any Presidential appointment of the fourth Monday in October as Veterans' Day.

2. All state, county and city offices, courts, banks, savings and loan associations, public schools and the University of Nevada System must close on the legal holidays enumerated in subsection 1 unless in the case of appointed holidays all or a part thereof are specifically exempted.

3. If January 1, July 4, October 31, November 11 or December 25 falls upon a:

(a) Sunday, the Monday following must be observed as a legal holiday.

(b) Saturday, the Friday preceding must be observed as a legal holiday.

4. To celebrate the 500th anniversary of the arrival of Cristoforo Columbo in the New World, October 12, 1992, is hereby declared to be a legal holiday for state, county and city governmental offices. All state, county and city offices, courts, banks, savings and loan associations, public schools and the University of Nevada System must close on this day.

NEW HAMPSHIRE

NOTARIES PUBLIC

[N.H. REV. STAT. ANN.]

§ 455:1. Appointment.

Notaries public shall be appointed by the governor, with advice and consent of the executive council, and shall be commissioned for 5 years.

§ 455:2. Application.

Any person applying to be a notary public shall have been a registered voter in this state for at least 3 years immediately preceding the date of application. The applicant shall sign a written statement under oath as to whether he has ever been arrested or convicted of a crime that has not been annulled by a court, other than minor traffic violations. The applicant shall be endorsed for appointment by 2 notaries public and a registered voter of this state.

§ 455:2-a Competency.

It shall be lawful for any notary public or any other officer authorized to administer an oath or take an acknowledgment or proof of an instrument or make protest, who is a stockholder, director, officer or employee of a bank or other corporation, to take the acknowledgment of any party to any written instrument executed to or by such corporation, or to administer an oath to any other stockholder, director, officer, employee or agent of such corporation, or to protest for nonacceptance or nonpayment bills of exchange, drafts, checks, notes and other negotiable instruments which may be owned or held for collection by such corporation; provided it shall be unlawful for any notary public or other officer authorized to administer an oath or take an acknowledgment or proof of an instrument or make protest, to take the acknowledgment of an instrument executed by or to a bank or other corporation of which he is a stockholder, director, officer or employee, where such notary or other officer is a party to such instrument, either individually or as a representative of such corporation, or to protest any negotiable instrument owned or held for collection by such corporation, where such notary or other officer is individually a party to such instrument. No person acting in the capacity of notary public shall notarize his or her own signature. This section shall not be construed to imply that the acts herein made lawful may heretofore have been unlawful, and no instrument heretofore acknowledged or notarized before a notary public or other officer who would have been competent to act under the terms hereof shall hereafter be impugned or invalidated on the grounds that such notary public or other officer was incompetent to act.

§ 455:3. Powers.

Every notary public, in addition to the usual powers of the office, shall have the same powers as a justice of the peace in relation to depositions and the acknowledgment of deeds and other instruments and the administering of oaths. All acknowledgments made by a notary public shall be under an official seal.

§ 455:4. Protest as evidence.

The protest of a bill of exchange, note or order, duly certified by a notary public under his hand and official seal, shall be evidence of the facts stated in the protest and of the notice given to the drawer or indorsers.

§ 455:5. Deposit of records.

Whenever a notary shall remove from the state, resign or from any cause cease to act in that capacity, he shall, within 3 months thereafter, deposit all his notarial records and all papers filed in his office in the office of the secretary of state.

§ 455:6. Notary's death or insanity.

If a notary shall die or become insane it shall be the duty of his administrator, executor or guardian to deposit his records and papers in the manner aforesaid.

§ 455:7. Demand for records.

The secretary of state may demand and receive any such records and papers of any person in whose possession the same may be.

§ 455:8. —Penalty for nondelivery.

If any person in whose possession any such records or papers may be shall neglect or refuse to deliver the same to the secretary, or upon his order on demand, or shall knowingly destroy or conceal any such records, he shall be guilty of a misdemeanor if a natural person, or guilty of a felony if any other person, and shall also be liable for damages to any person injured, in an action on the case.

§ 455:9. Custody of records.

All notarial records and papers shall be kept by the secretary of state safely and in such manner that reference thereto may easily be had for a period of 3 years. These records shall be open to the examination of any person interested therein.

§ 455:10. Copies of records.

The secretary of state shall make out and certify copies of any such records and papers, upon payment or tender of the fees therefor, and his certificate shall have the same validity as if made by such notary himself.

§ 455:11. Protests, certificates, etc.

Notaries public shall be entitled to the following fees:

For every protest under seal, fifty cents; every certificate under seal, twenty-five cents.

For waiting on a person to demand payment, or to witness any matter, and certifying the same under seal, fifty cents.

For every notice of nonpayment to any party to a bill or note, twenty-five cents.

For services relating to the taking of depositions, the same fees as justices are entitled to receive.

For administering and certifying oaths, except the oaths of office of town officers, one dollar.

FEES

§ 5:10. Office fees.

Except as otherwise provided, the following fees shall be paid to the secretary of state for the use of the state: For every commission issued to a justice of the peace or to a notary public, $30; for every certificate pertaining to the existence of a corporation, trade name, or other business entity, or writ served on the same, $5; for every such certificate in long form, $10; for every other certificate under seal of the state, $1; for engrossing private acts, $1 for each page of 240 words.

OFFENSES

§ 638:1. Forgery.

I. A person is guilty of forgery if, with purpose to defraud anyone, or with knowledge that he is facilitating a fraud to be perpetrated by anyone, he:

(a) Alters any writing of another without his authority or utters any such altered writing; or

(b) Makes, completes, executes, authenticates, issues, transfers, publishes or otherwise utters any writing so that it purports to be the act of another, or purports to have been executed at a time or place or in a numbered sequence other than was in fact the case, or to be a copy of an original when no such original existed.

II. As used in this section, "writing" includes printing or any other method of recording information, checks, tokens, stamps, seals, credit cards, badges, trademarks, and other symbols of value, right, privilege, or identification.

III. Forgery is a class B felony if the writing is or purports to be

(a) A security, revenue stamp, or any other instrument issued by a government, or any agency thereof; or

(b) A check, an issue of stocks, bonds, or any other instrument representing an interest in or a claim against property, or a pecuniary interest in or claim against any person or enterprise.

IV. All other forgery is a misdemeanor.

V. A person is guilty of a misdemeanor if he knowingly possesses any writing that is a forgery under this section or any device for making any such writing. It is an affirmative defense to prosecution under this paragraph that the possession was without an intent to defraud.

§ 638:2. Fraudulent handling of recordable writings.

A person is guilty of a class B felony if, with a purpose to deceive or injure anyone, he falsifies, destroys, removes or conceals any will, deed, mortgage, security instrument or other writing for which the law provides public recording.

§ 651:2. Sentences and limitations.

I. A person convicted of a felony or misdemeanor may be sentenced to imprisonment, probation, conditional or unconditional discharge, or a fine.

II. If a sentence of imprisonment is imposed, the court shall fix the maximum thereof which is not to exceed:

(a) Fifteen years for a class A felony,

(b) Seven years for a class B felony,

(c) One year for a misdemeanor,

(d) Life imprisonment for murder in the second degree,

and in the case of a felony only, a minimum which is not to exceed 1/2 of the maximum, or if the maximum is life imprisonment, such minimum term as the court may order.

II-a. A person convicted of murder in the first degree shall be sentenced as provided in RSA 630:1-a.

II-b. A person convicted of the felonious use of a firearm, as provided in RSA 650-A:1, shall, in addition to any punishment provided for the underlying felony, be given a minimum mandatory sentence of one year imprisonment for a first offense and a minimum mandatory sentence of 3 years' imprisonment for any subsequent offense. Neither the whole nor any part of the additional sentence of imprisonment hereby provided shall be served concurrently with any other term nor shall the whole or any part of such additional term of imprisonment be suspended. No action brought to enforce sentencing under this section shall be continued for sentencing, nor shall the provisions of RSA 651-A relative to parole apply to any sentence of imprisonment imposed.

II-c. A person convicted of attempted murder shall be sentenced to a term of not more than 30 years imprisonment.

II-d. A person convicted of manslaughter shall be sentenced as provided in RSA 630:2, II.

II-e. To the minimum sentence of every person who is sentenced to imprisonment for a maximum of more than one year shall be added a disciplinary period equal to 150 days for each year of the minimum term of his sentence, to be prorated for any part of the year. The presiding justice shall certify, at the time of sentencing, the minimum term of the sentence and the additional disciplinary period required under this paragraph. This additional disciplinary period may be reduced for good conduct as provided in RSA 651-A:22. There shall be no addition to the sentence under this section for the period of pre-trial confinement for which credit against the sentence is awarded pursuant to RSA 651-A:23.

II-f. A person convicted of violating RSA 159:3-a, I shall be sentenced as provided in RSA 159:3-a, II and III. [Added 1989, 295:2, eff. Jan. 1, 1990.]

III. A person convicted of a violation may be sentenced to probation, conditional or unconditional discharge, or a fine.

IV. A fine may be imposed in addition to any sentence of imprisonment, probation, or conditional discharge. The limitations on amounts of fines authorized in subparagraphs (a) and (b) shall not include the amount of any civil penalty, the imposition of which is authorized by statute or by a properly adopted local ordinance, code, or regulation. The amount of any fine imposed on: [Amended 1988, 19:4, eff. Jan. 1, 1989.]

(a) Any individual may not exceed $2,000 for a felony, $1,000 for a misdemeanor, and $500 for a violation.

(b) A corporation or unincorporated association may not exceed $50,000 for a felony, $10,000 for a misdemeanor and $500 for a violation. A writ of execution may be issued by the court against the corporation or unincorporated association to compel payment of the fine, together with costs and interest.

(c) If a defendant has gained property through the commission of any felony, then in lieu of the amounts authorized in paragraphs (a) and (b), the fine may be an amount not to exceed double the amount of that gain.

V. A person may be placed on probation if the court finds he is in need of the supervision and guidance that the probation service can provide under such conditions as the court may impose. The period of probation shall be for a period to be fixed by the court not to exceed 5 years for a felony, 2 years for a misdemeanor and one year for a violation. Upon petition of the probation officer or the probationer, the period may be terminated sooner by the court if the conduct of the probationer warrants it. In cases of persons convicted of felonies or misdemeanors, the sentence may include, as a condition of probation, confinement to a person's place of residence for not more than one year in case of a misdemeanor or more than 5 years in case of a felony. Such home confinement may be monitored by a probation officer and supplemented, as determined by the department of corrections, by electronic monitoring to verify compliance. Upon rec-

ommendation by the department of corrections, the court may, as a condition of probation, order a prison-bound offender placed in an intensive supervision program as an alternative to incarceration, under requirements and restrictions established by the department of corrections. Upon recommendation by the department of corrections, the court may sentence a prison-bound offender to a special alternative incarceration program involving short term confinement followed by intensive community supervision. The department of corrections shall adopt rules governing eligibility for such programs. Any offender placed in either the home confinement, intensive supervision or special alternative incarceration program who violates the conditions or restrictions of his probation shall be subject to immediate arrest by a probation officer or any authorized law enforcement officer and brought before the court for an expeditious hearing pending further disposition.

V. A person may be placed on probation if the court finds he is in need of the supervision and guidance that the probation service can provide. The period of probation shall be for a period to be fixed by the court not to exceed 5 years for a felony, 2 years for a misdemeanor, and one year for a violation. Upon petition of the probation officer or the probationer the period may be terminated sooner by the court if the conduct of the probationer warrants it.

VI. A person may be sentenced to a period of conditional discharge if he is not imprisoned and the court is of the opinion that probationary supervision is unnecessary, but that the defendant should conduct himself according to conditions determined by the court. Such conditions may include (a) restrictions on the defendant's travel, association, place of abode, such as will protect the victim of the crime or insure the public peace; (b) an order requiring the defendant to attend counseling or any other mode of treatment the court deems appropriate; and (c) restitution to the victim. The period of a conditional discharge shall be 3 years for a felony and one year for a misdemeanor or violation. However, if the court has required as a condition that the defendant make restitution or reparation to the victim of his offense and that condition has not been satisfied, the court may, at any time prior to the termination of the above periods, extend the period for a felony by no more than 2 years and for a misdemeanor or violation by no more than one year in order to allow the defendant to satisfy the condition. During any period of conditional discharge the court may, upon its own motion or on petition of the defendant, discharge the defendant unconditionally if the conduct of the defendant warrants it. The court is not required to revoke a conditional discharge if the defendant commits an additional offense or violates a condition.

VI-a. A person convicted of a violation of RSA 634:2 or of RSA 644:3 may be required as a condition of discharge under paragraph VI to perform not more than 50 hours of uncompensated public service under the supervision of an elected or appointed official of the city or town in which the offense occurred, such service being of a sort that in the opinion of the court will foster respect for those interests violated by the defendant's conduct.

VII. When a probation or a conditional discharge is revoked, the defendant may be fined, as authorized by paragraph IV, if a fine was not imposed in addition to the probation or conditional discharge. Otherwise the defendant shall be sentenced to imprisonment as authorized by paragraph II.

VIII. A person may be granted an unconditional discharge if the court is of the opinion that no proper purpose would be served by imposing any condition or supervision upon the defendant's release. A sentence of unconditional discharge is for all purposes a final judgment of conviction.

SAFE DEPOSIT BOXES

§ 385:1. Rent unpaid, procedure.

If the amount due for the rent or use of a box or safe in the vaults of a domestic corporation authorized to engage in the business of letting vaults, safes, and other receptacles shall not have been paid for six months, such corporation may cause to be mailed, postpaid, to the person in whose name such safe or box stands upon the books of such corporation and at his address as stated on said books, a notice stating that if the amount then due for the use or rent of such safe or box shall not be paid within sixty days from the date of such notice such corporation will cause the safe or box to be opened in the presence of its president, treasurer, or superintendent and of a notary public, and the contents thereof, if any, to be sealed up in a package and placed in one of the storage vaults of such corporation.

§ 385:2. Box to be opened, etc.

If, upon the expiration of said sixty days from the date of such notice, such person shall have failed to pay the amount due for the use or rent of such safe or box in full to the date of such notice, all right of such person in such safe or box and of access thereto shall cease, and such corporation may in the presence of its president, treasurer, or superintendent and of a notary public not an officer or in the general employ of such corporation,

cause such safe or box to be opened, and such notary public shall remove the contents thereof, make a list of the same and shall seal up such contents in a package and shall mark thereon the name of the person in whose name such safe or box stood on the books of such corporation and his address as stated on said books, and such package shall in the presence of said notary public and of said president, treasurer, or superintendent be placed in one of the storage vaults of such corporation; and the proceedings of such notary public, including said list of the contents of said safe or box and his estimate of the total value of said contents, shall be set forth by him in his own handwriting and under his official seal in a book kept by such corporation for the purpose. The officer of such corporation who sent said written notice shall in the same book state his proceedings relative thereto, setting forth a copy of said notice. Both of said statements shall be sworn to by such notary public and officer, respectively, before a justice of the peace, who shall make certificate thereof in said book.

§ 385:3. Statement of proceedings as evidence.

Said written statements shall be prima facie evidence of the facts therein set forth in all proceedings at law and in equity wherein evidence of such facts would be competent. The provisions hereof shall not impair any right relative to such safes or boxes or their contents which such corporation would otherwise have.

§ 385:4. Delivery to state.

At the expiration of five years after the removal of the contents of such safe or box, the corporation shall sell all the property or articles of value set out in said written statements at public auction, provided that a notice of the time and place of sale has been published once weekly for three consecutive weeks, the last such publication being no less than ten days before said public auction, in a newspaper published in the place where the sale is held, or having a general circulation in such place.

§ 385:5. Disposition of proceeds.

From the proceeds of said sale the corporation shall deduct all its charges for rental up to the time of opening said box or safe, the cost of opening, further cost of safekeeping all its contents and any costs of said public auction and shall hold the net cash proceeds from such public auction subject to the provisions of RSA 471-C. The corporation shall maintain a statement of all charges deducted from the proceeds of said auction which shall be signed by the president, treasurer or superintendent of said corporation and verified before a notary public or justice of the peace.

ACKNOWLEDGMENTS

§ 477:3. Execution.

Every deed or other conveyance of real estate shall be signed by the party granting the same and acknowledged by the grantor before a justice, notary public or commissioner and shall show the mailing address of the grantee.

§ 477:4. Acknowledgments.

Acknowledgments may be taken outside the United States before an ambassador, minister, envoy or charge d'affaires of the United States, in the country to which he is accredited, or before any consular officer of the United States, a notary public, or a commissioner or other agent of this state having an official seal and power to take acknowledgments at such place.

§ 477:5. Certificate of acknowledgment.

A certificate of an acknowledgment taken outside the United States before any authorized officer shall be valid if in the form required by law for an acknowledgement taken within the state.

§ 477:6. —Fee for certificate.

The fee for taking and certifying the acknowledgment of a deed or other instrument by one or more persons at one time shall be seventeen cents.

§ 477:7. Validity.

No deed of bargain and sale, mortgage nor other conveyance of real estate, nor any lease for more than 7 years from the making thereof, shall be valid to hold the same against any person but the grantor and his heirs only, unless such deed or lease be acknowledged and recorded, according to the provisions of this chapter. All deeds which have been acknowledged and recorded according to the provisions of this chapter since August 15, 1981, but which were not attested to, shall be considered valid under this section.

§ 477:7-a. Notice of lease.

Notwithstanding the provisions of RSA 477:7, a notice of lease consisting of an instrument in writing executed, witnessed and acknowledged by all persons who are parties to the lease, and containing the following information with reference to such lease shall be sufficient compliance with the provisions of this chapter:

I. The names and addresses of each party to the lease;

II. The date of execution of the lease;

III. A description of the demised premises as it appears in the lease;

IV. The term of such lease; and

V. The date of commencement of such term and all rights of extension or renewal.

Uniform Acknowledgment Act

§ 456:1. Acknowledgment of instruments.

Any instrument may be acknowledged in the manner and form as otherwise provided by the laws and customs of this state, or as provided by this chapter.

§ 456:2. Validity of earlier acknowledgments.

All acknowledgments of written instruments made since March 30, 1943, pursuant to existing custom in this state are hereby declared to be valid.

§ 456:3. Acknowledgment within the United States.

The acknowledgments of any instrument may be made without the state but within the United States or a territory or insular possession of the United States or the District of Columbia or the Philippine Islands and within the jurisdiction of the officer before:

I. A clerk or deputy clerk of any federal court;

II. A clerk or deputy clerk of any court of record of any state or other jurisdiction;

III. A notary public; or

IV. A commissioner or register of deeds.

§ 456:4. Acknowledgment within the state.

The acknowledgment of any instrument may be made in this state before:

I. A judge of the supreme court, superior court, probate court or municipal court;

II. A clerk or deputy clerk of a court having a seal;

III. A commissioner or register of deeds;

IV. A notary public; or

V. A justice of the peace.

§ 456:5. Acknowledgment without the United States.

The acknowledgment of any instrument may be made without the United States before:

I. An ambassador, minister, charge d'affaires,

counselor to or secretary of a legation, consul general, consul, vice-consul, commercial attache, or consular agent of the United States accredited to the country where the acknowledgment is made;

II. A notary public of the country where the acknowledgment is made;

III. A judge or clerk of a court of record of the country where the acknowledgment is made.

§ 456:6. Requisites of acknowledgment.

The officer taking the acknowledgment shall know or have satisfactory evidence that the person making the acknowledgment is the person described in and who executed the instrument.

§ 456:7. Married woman.

An acknowledgment of a married woman may be made in the same form as though she were unmarried.

§ 456:8. Forms of certificates.

An officer taking the acknowledgment shall endorse thereon or attach thereto a certificate substantially in one of the following forms:

I. By individuals:
State of ....
County of ....
On this the .... day of ...., 19....., before me, ..., the undersigned officer, personally appeared ...., known to me (or satisfactorily proven) to be the person whose name .... subscribed to the within instrument and acknowledged that .... he .... executed the same for the purposes therein contained.

In witness whereof I hereunto set my hand and official seal.

....
....
Title of Officer.

II. By a corporation:
State of ....
County of ....
On this the .... day of ...., 19....., before me, ..., the undersigned officer, personally appeared ...., who acknowledged himself to be the .... of ...., a corporation, and that he, as such ...., being authorized so to do, executed the foregoing instrument for the purposes therein contained, by signing the name of the corporation by himself as ....

In witness whereof I hereunto set my hand and official seal.

....
....
Title of Officer.

III. By an attorney in fact:
State of ....
County of ....
On this the .... day of ...., 19....., before me, ..., the undersigned officer, personally appeared ...., known to me (or satisfactorily proven) to be the person whose name is subscribed as attorney in fact for ...., and acknowledged that he executed the same as the act of his principal for the purposes therein contained.

In witness whereof I hereunto set my hand and official seal.

....
....
Title of Officer.

IV. By any public officer or deputy thereof, or by any trustee, administrator, guardian, or executor:
State of ....
County of ....
On this the .... day of ...., 19....., before me, ..., the undersigned officer, personally appeared .... of the state (county, city, or town as the case may be) of ...., known to me (or satisfactorily proven) to be the person described in the foregoing instrument, and acknowledged that he executed the same in the capacity therein stated and for the purposes therein contained.

In witness whereof I hereunto set my hand and official seal.

....
....
Title of Officer.

§ 456:9. Execution of certificate.

The certificate of the acknowledging officer shall be completed by his signature, his official seal if he has one, the title of his office, and if he is a notary public, the date his commission expires.

§ 456:10. Authentication of acknowledgments.

I. If the acknowledgment is taken within this state or is made without the United States by an officer of the United States no authentication shall be necessary.

II. If the acknowledgment is taken without this state, but in the United States, or a territory or insular possession of the United States, the certificate shall be authenticated by certificate as to the official character of such officer, executed, if the acknowledgment is taken by a clerk or deputy clerk of a court, by the presiding judge of the court or, if the acknowledgment is taken by a notary public, or any other person authorized to take acknowledgments, by a clerk of a court of record of the county in which the acknowledgment is taken. The signature to such authenticating certificate may be a facsimile printed, stamped, photographed or engraved thereon when the certificate bears the seal of the authenticating officer. A judge or clerk authenticating an acknowledgment shall endorse thereon or attach thereto a certificate in substantially the following form:

State of New Hampshire ....
County of ....
I .... - judge - clerk - of the
.... court in and for said county, which court is a court of record, having a seal, do hereby certify that .... by and before whom the foregoing - annexed - acknowledgment was taken, was at the time of taking the same a notary public (or other officer as the case may be) authorized to act in said county, and was authorized by the laws of said state to take and certify acknowledgments in said state, and, further, that I am acquainted with his handwriting and that I believe that the signature to the certificate of acknowledgment is genuine.

In testimony whereof I have hereunto set my hand and affixed the seal of this court this .... day of ...., 19.....

III. If the acknowledgment is taken without the United States and by a notary public or a judge or clerk of a court of record of the country where the acknowledgment is taken, the certificate shall be authenticated by a certificate under the great seal of state of the country, affixed by the custodian of such seal, or by a certificate of a diplomatic, consular or commercial officer of the United States accredited to that country, certifying as to the official character of such officer. The officer authenticating an acknowledgment shall endorse thereon or attach thereto a certificate in substantially the form prescribed in paragraph II of this section.

§ 456:11. Acknowledgments under laws of other states.

Notwithstanding any provision of this chapter contained, the acknowledgment of any instrument without this state in compliance with the manner and form prescribed by the laws of the place of its execution, if in a state, a territory or insular possession of the United States, or in the District of Columbia, or in the Philippine Islands, verified by the official seal of the officer before whom it is acknowledged, and authenticated in the manner provided by RSA 456:10, II, shall have the same effect as an acknowledgment in the manner and form prescribed by the laws of this state for instruments executed within the state.

§ 456:12. Acknowledgment by persons serving in or with the Armed Forces of the United States or their dependents, within or without the United States.

In addition to the acknowledgment of instruments in the manner and form and as otherwise authorized by this chapter, persons serving in or with the armed forces of the United States or their dependents, wherever located, may acknowledge the same before any commissioned officer in active service of the armed forces of the United States with the rank of second lieutenant or higher in the army, air force, or marine corps, or ensign or higher in the navy or coast guard. The instrument shall not be rendered invalid by the failure to state therein the place of execution or acknowledgment. No authentication of the officer's certificate of acknowledgment shall be required but the officer taking the acknowledgment shall indorse thereon or attach thereto a certificate substantially in the following form:

On this the .... day of ...., 19....., before me, ..., the undersigned officer, personally appeared ...., Serial No. ...., known to me (or satisfactorily proven) to be (serving in or with the armed forces of the United States) (a dependent of ...., Serial No. ...., a person serving in or with the armed forces of the United States) and to be the person whose name is subscribed to the within instrument and acknowledged that .... he .... executed the same for the purposes therein contained. And the undersigned does further certify that he is at the date of this certificate a commissioned officer of the rank stated below and is in the active service of the armed forces of the United States.

....
Signature of the Officer.
....
Rank and Serial No.
of Officer and Command
to which attached

§ 456:13. Acknowledgments not affected by this chapter.

No acknowledgment heretofore taken shall be affected by anything contained herein.

§ 456:14. Uniformity of interpretation.

This chapter shall be so interpreted as to make uniform the laws of those states which enact it.

§ 456:15. Short title.

This chapter may be cited as the Uniform Acknowledgment Act.

Uniform Recognition of Acknowledgments Act

§ 456-A:1. Recognition of notarial acts performed outside this state.

For the purposes of this chapter, "notarial acts" means acts which the laws and regulations of this state authorize notaries public of this state to perform, including the administering of oaths and affirmations, taking proof of execution and acknowledgments of instruments, and attesting documents. Notarial acts may be performed outside this state for use in this state with the same effect as if performed by a notary public of this state by the following persons authorized pursuant to the laws and regulations of other governments in addition to any other person authorized by the laws and regulations of this state:

I. A notary public authorized to perform notarial acts in the place in which the act is performed;

II. A judge, clerk, or deputy clerk of any court of record in the place in which the notarial act is performed;

III. An officer of the foreign service of the United States, a consular agent, or any other person authorized by regulation of the United States department of state to perform notarial acts in the place in which the act is performed;

IV. A commissioned officer in active service with the armed forces of the United States and any other person authorized by regulation of the armed forces to perform notarial acts if the notarial act is performed for one of the following or his dependents: a merchant seaman of the United States, a member of the armed forces of the United States, or any other person serving with or accompanying the armed forces of the United States; or

V. Any other person authorized to perform notarial acts in the place in which the act is performed.

§ 456-A:2. Authentication of authority of officer.

I. If the notarial act is performed by any of the persons described in RSA 456-A:1, I-IV, inclusive, other than a person authorized to perform notarial acts by the laws or regulations of a foreign country, the signature, rank, or title and serial number, if any, of the person are sufficient proof of the authority of a holder of that rank or title to perform the act. Further proof of his authority is not required.

II. If the notarial act is performed by a person authorized by the laws or regulations of a foreign country to perform the act, there is sufficient proof of the authority of that person to act if:

(a) Either a foreign service officer of the United States resident in the country in which the act is performed or a diplomatic or consular officer of the foreign country resident in the United States certifies that a person holding that office is authorized to perform the act;

(b) The official seal of the person performing the notarial act is affixed to the document; or

(c) The title and indication of authority to perform notarial acts of the person appears either in a digest of foreign law or in a list customarily used as a source of such information.

III. If the notarial act is performed by a person other than one described in paragraphs I and II, there is sufficient proof of the authority of that person to act if the clerk of a court of record in the place in which the notarial act is performed certifies to the official character of that person and to his authority to perform the notarial act.

IV. The signature and title of the person performing the act are prima facie evidence that he is a person with the designated title and that the signature is genuine.

§ 456-A:3. Certificate of person taking acknowledgment.

The person taking an acknowledgment shall certify that:

I. The person acknowledging appeared before him and acknowledged he executed the instrument; and

II. The person acknowledging was known to the person taking the acknowledgment or that the person taking the acknowledgment had satisfactory evidence that the person acknowledging was the person described in and who executed the instrument.

§ 456-A:4. Recognition of certificate of acknowledgment.

The form of a certificate of acknowledgment used by a person whose authority is recognized under RSA 456-A:1 shall be accepted in this state if:

I. The certificate is in a form prescribed by the laws or regulations of this state;

II. The certificate is in a form prescribed by the laws or regulations applicable in the place in which the acknowledgment is taken; or

III. The certificate contains the words "acknowledged before me," or their substantial equivalent.

§ 456-A:5. Certificate of acknowledgment.

The words "acknowledged before me" means:

I. That the person acknowledging appeared before the person taking the acknowledgment,

II. That he acknowledged he executed the instrument,

III. That, in the case of:

(a) A natural person, he executed the instrument for the purposes therein stated;

(b) A corporation, the officer or agent acknowledged he held the position or title set forth in the instrument and certificate, he signed the instrument on behalf of the corporation by proper authority, and the instrument was the act of the corporation for the purpose therein stated;

(c) A partnership, the partner or agent acknowledged he signed the instrument on behalf of the partnership by proper authority and he executed the instrument as the act of the partnership for the purposes therein stated;

(d) A person acknowledging as principal by an attorney in fact, he executed the instrument by proper authority as the act of the principal for the purposes therein stated;

(e) A person acknowledging as a public officer, trustee, administrator, guardian, or other representative, he signed the instrument by proper authority and he executed the instrument in the capacity and for the purposes therein stated; and

IV. That the person taking the acknowledgment either knew or had satisfactory evidence that the person acknowledging was the person named in the instrument or certificate.

§ 456-A:6. Short forms of acknowledgment.

The forms of acknowledgment set forth in this section may be used and are sufficient for their respective purposes under any law of this state. The forms shall be known as "statutory short forms of acknowledgment" and may be referred to by that name. The authorization of the forms in this section does not preclude the use of other forms.

I. For an individual acting in his own right:

State of ....

County of ....

The foregoing instrument was acknowledged before me this (date) by (name of person acknowledged).

> (Signature of Person Taking
> Acknowledgment)
> (Title or Rank)
> (Serial Number, if any)

II. For a corporation:

State of ....

County of ....

The foregoing instrument was acknowledged before me this (date) by (name of officer or agent, title of officer or agent) of (name of corporation acknowledging) a (state or place of incorporation) corporation, on behalf of the corporation.

> (Signature of Person Taking
> Acknowledgment)
> (Title or Rank)

> (Serial Number, if any)

III. For a partnership:

State of ....

County of ....

The foregoing instrument was acknowledged before me this (date) by (name of acknowledging partner or agent), partner (or agent) on behalf of (name of partnership), a partnership.

> (Signature of Person Taking
> Acknowledgment)
> (Title or Rank)
> (Serial Number, if any)

IV. For an individual acting as principal by an attorney in fact:

State of ....

County of ....

The foregoing instrument was acknowledged before me this (date) by (name of attorney in fact) as attorney in fact on behalf of (name of principal).

> (Signature of Person Taking
> Acknowledgment)
> (Title or Rank)
> (Serial Number, if any)

V. By any public officer, trustee, or personal representative:

State of ....

County of ....

The foregoing instrument was acknowledged before me this (date) by (name and title of position).

> (Signature of Person Taking
> Acknowledgment)
> (Title or Rank)
> (Serial Number, if any)

§ 456-A:7. Acknowledgments not affected by this chapter.

A notarial act performed prior to August 2, 1969, is not affected by this chapter. This chapter provides an additional method of proving notarial acts. Nothing in this chapter diminishes or invalidates the recognition accorded to notarial acts by other laws or regulations of this state.

§ 456-A:8. Uniformity of interpretation.

This chapter shall be so interpreted to make uniform the laws of those states which enact it.

§ 456-A:9. Short title.

This chapter may be cited as the Uniform Recognition of Acknowledgments Act.

DEPOSITIONS
Witnesses

§ 516:4. Issue [of summonses] for depositions.

Any justice or notary may issue such writs [summonses] for witnesses to appear before himself or any other justice or notary, to give depositions in any matter or cause in which the same may be lawfully taken.

§ 516:7. Penalty [for neglect to attend].

Every court, justice and notary, before whom a person has been summoned to appear and testify or to give a deposition, may bring the person neglecting or refusing to appear or to testify or to give his deposition, by attachment, before them, and if, on examination, he has no reasonable excuse, may find him guilty of a violation, and may order him to pay costs.

§ 516:23. Party deponent.

No party shall be compelled, in testifying or giving a deposition, to disclose the names of the witnesses by whom nor the manner in which he proposes to prove his case, nor, in giving a deposition, to produce any writing which is material to his case or defense, unless the deposition is taken in his own behalf.

Civil Cases

§ 517:2. Before whom.

Any justice or notary public in the state, any commissioner appointed under the laws of the state to take depositions in other states, any judge or justice of the peace or notary public in any other state or country, may take such deposition.

§ 517:3. Disqualifications.

No person shall write the testimony of a witness, or act as magistrate in taking same, who would be disqualified to act as juror on the trial of the cause, for any reason except exemption from service as a juror.

§ 517:7. Signing; oath.

Every witness shall subscribe his deposition, and shall make oath that it contains the truth, the whole truth and nothing but the truth, relative to the cause for which it was taken.

§ 517:8. Caption.

The magistrate taking the deposition shall certify such oath, with the time and place of taking the deposition, the case and court in which it is to be used, that the adverse party was or was not present, was or was not notified, and that he did or did not object.

§ 517:9. Annexing copy of notice.

A copy of the notice left with the adverse party, his agent or attorney, with the return of the officer or affidavit of the person leaving such notice thereon, stating the time of leaving it, shall be annexed to the caption of the deposition, when the adverse party does not attend.

§ 517:10. Sealing.

Depositions so taken shall be sealed up by the magistrate taking the same, directed to the court or justice before whom they are to be used, with a brief description of the case, and shall be so delivered into court.

Criminal Cases

§ 517:14-e. Record.

The justice presiding at a deposition taken [by the prosecution in a criminal case] shall cause a record to be made of the proceedings and shall cause a copy thereof to be furnished to the defendant. Such record or a copy thereof may be used in the trial of the case whenever in the discretion of the court the use thereof shall be deemed necessary for the promotion of justice.

Commissioners

§ 517:15. Appointment.

Upon petition the superior court may appoint some suitable person as commissioner to take depositions outside this state, for use in causes pending in or returnable to said court.

§ 517:16. Procedure.

After the appointment of such commissioner, the notice of the time and place of taking depositions before him, the proceedings in taking such depositions, the certificates to be made by him, and all other formalities with reference to taking, filing and using such depositions shall be the same, so far as applicable, as for taking other depositions in civil causes.

§ 517:17. Powers.

Said commissioner shall have and exercise all the powers conferred by the laws of other states, territories and foreign countries upon commissioners or other persons authorized to take depositions in said other states, territories and foreign countries for use in causes pending in this state.

§ 517:18. Foreign.

A commissioner or other person appointed by any court of record of any other state, territory or foreign country, for the purpose of taking depositions in this state for use in causes pending in such court of record, shall have the same powers of procuring the attendance of witnesses to give depositions before him, and of requiring the production of papers and the giving of such depositions, as justices of the peace within this state with reference to depositions for use in civil causes pending within the courts of this state.

Fees

§ 517:19. Officials.

Justices of the peace or other officers shall be allowed:

For a blank writ of summons; ten cents.

For swearing each witness and caption of deposition, thirty-four cents.

For writing a deposition, each page, seventeen cents.

For travel to swear witnesses, each mile, six cents.

§ 517:20. Stenographers.

When by agreement of the parties depositions are taken in shorthand and thereafter transcribed, or are taken down by the use of a typewriter, the court may allow as costs the whole or any part of the expense thereof, as justice may require.

COMMISSIONERS

§ 455:12. Appointment.

The governor, with advice and consent of the executive council, may appoint, in each state, district and territory of the United States, and in each foreign country to which the United States sends a representative, a commissioner or commissioners, to continue in office 5 years.

§ 455:13. Oath.

Before any commissioner shall perform any duty

of his office, he shall take and subscribe an oath, before a judge of some court of record, that he will well and faithfully perform all the duties of the office, which oath shall be filed by him in the office of the secretary of state within 3 months after taking the same.

§ 455:14. Powers.

Such commissioner may, both within and without this state, administer oaths, take depositions and affidavits to be used in this state and notify parties of the time and place thereof, and take the acknowledgment of deeds or instruments to be used or recorded in this state, in the same manner and with the same effect as a justice of the peace of this state may do within the state.

§ 455:15. For other states; by court appointment.

Any commissioner for any other state who is authorized to take depositions, administer oaths and affirmations and take the acknowledgment of deeds within this state, to be used in such other state, and any commissioner appointed by the supreme or superior court or any justice thereof, shall have the power to administer oaths and affirmations, to issue writs of summons to a witness, to proceed against such witness upon his neglect to appear and give his deposition, and in all proceedings under his commission, that is vested in justices of the peace in like cases.

LEGAL HOLIDAYS

§ 288:1. Holidays.

Thanksgiving Day whenever appointed, the fourth Monday in April known as Fast Day, the first Monday in September known as Labor Day, the day on which the biennial election is held, January first, the third Monday in February known as Washington's Birthday, the thirtieth day in May known as Memorial Day, July fourth, the second Monday in October known as Columbus Day, the eleventh day in November known as Veterans Day and Christmas Day are legal holidays.

§ 288:2. —Falling on Sunday.

When any holiday listed in RSA 288:1 falls on Sunday, the following day shall be observed as a holiday.

§ **288:3.** Banking organizations, closing on Saturdays.

Any banking organization which for the purposes of this section shall include not only state banks, savings banks, trust companies, and other companies, associations and businesses described in section 1 of chapter 384, RSA, but also any national banking association, federal savings and loan association or federal credit union doing business in this state, may remain closed on any or all Saturdays as it may determine from time to time. Any Saturday on which a banking organization remains closed shall be with respect to such banking organization a holiday and not a business day. Any act authorized, required or permitted to be performed at or by or with respect to any banking organization as herein defined, on a Saturday, may be so performed on the next succeeding business day, and no liability or loss or rights of any kind shall result from such delay.

NEW JERSEY

NOTARIES PUBLIC

[N.J. Stat. Ann.]

§ 52:7-10. Short title.

This act shall be known and may be cited as the "Notaries Public Act of 1979."

§ 57:7-11. Appointment; term; removal; application; renewals.

a. The Secretary of State shall appoint so many notaries public as the Secretary of State shall deem necessary to commission, who shall hold their respective offices for the term of five years, but may be removed from office at the pleasure of the Secretary of State.

b. A person desiring to be appointed and commissioned a notary public shall make application to the Secretary of State on a form prescribed by the Secretary of State and endorsed by a member of the Legislature or the Secretary of State or Assistant Secretary of State. Renewals thereof shall be made in the same manner as the original application.

c. The fee to be collected by the Secretary of State for that appointment or renewal shall be $25.00.

§ 57:7-12. Minimum age.

No person shall be appointed a notary public unless he is 18 years of age or older.

§ 52:7-13. Appointment of nonresidents; requirements.

No person shall be denied appointment as a notary public on account of residence outside of this State, provided such person resides in a State adjoining this State and maintains, or is regularly employed in, an office in this State. Before any such nonresident shall be appointed and commissioned as a notary public, he shall file with the Secretary of State an affidavit setting forth his residence and the address of his office or place of employment in this State. Any such nonresident notary public shall file with the Secretary of State a certificate showing any change of residence or of his office or place of employment address in this State.

§ 52:7-14. Oath; filing; certificate of commission and qualification.

a. Within 3 months of the receipt of his commission, each notary public shall take and subscribe an oath before the clerk of the county in which he resides, faithfully and honestly to discharge the duties of his office, and that he will make and keep a true record of all such matters as are required by law, which oath shall be filed with said clerk. The oath of office of a nonresident notary public shall be taken and subscribed before the clerk of the county in which he maintains his office or is employed in this State.

b. Upon the administration of said oath, the said clerk shall cause the notary public to indorse a certificate of commission and qualification and shall transmit said certificate to the Secretary of State within 10 days of the administration of said oath.

c. The Secretary of State shall cancel and revoke the appointment of any notary public who fails to take and subscribe said oath within 3 months of the receipt of his commission and any appointment so canceled and revoked shall be null, void and of no effect.

§ 52:7-15. State-wide authority; filing certificates of commission and qualification with county clerks.

a. A notary public who has been duly commissioned and qualified is authorized to perform his duties throughout the State.

b. Any notary public, after having been duly commissioned and qualified, shall, upon request, receive from the clerk of the county where he has qualified, as many certificates of his commission and qualification as he shall require for filing with other county clerks of this State, and upon receipt of such certificates the notary public may present the same, together with his autograph signature, to such county clerks as he may desire, for filing.

§ 52:7-16. County clerk to attach certificate of authority to notaries' certificates of proof, acknowledgments or affidavits.

The county clerk of the county in which a notary public resides or the county clerk of any county where such notary public shall have filed his autograph signature and certificate, as provided in section 6 of this act, shall, upon request, subjoin to any certificate of proof, acknowledgment or affidavit signed by the notary public, a certificate under the clerk's hand and seal stating that the notary public was at the time of taking such proof, acknowledgment or affidavit duly commissioned and sworn and residing in this State, and was as such an officer of this State duly authorized to take and certify said proof, acknowledgment or affidavit as well as to take and certify the proof or acknowledgment of deeds for the conveyance of lands, tenements or hereditaments and other instruments in writing to be recorded in this State; that said proof, acknowledgment or affidavit is duly executed and taken according to the laws of this State; that full faith and credit are and ought to be given to the official acts of the notary public, and that the county clerk is well acquainted with the handwriting of the notary public and believes the signature to the instrument to which the certificate is attached is his genuine signature.

§ 52:7-17. Fee.

The Secretary of State shall, by regulation, fix a fee to be charged to each notary for the costs of printing and distribution to each applicant of a manual prescribing the powers, duties and responsibilities of a notary.

§ 52:7-18. Statement by notary public after change in name; filing; evidence of continuance of powers and privileges.

After a notary public adopts a name different from that which he used at the time he was commissioned, and before he signs his name to any document which he is authorized or required to sign as notary public, he shall make and sign a statement in writing and under oath, on a form prescribed and furnished by the Secretary of State, setting out the circumstances under which he has adopted the new name. The statement shall set forth whether the new name has been adopted through marriage or by a change of name proceeding or otherwise, and such other information as the Secretary of State shall require.

The statement shall be filed in the office of the Secretary of State and in the office of the clerk of the county where he qualified as a notary public and in the office of the clerk of any county in which he may have filed a certificate of his commission and qualification.

Such statement, or a certified copy thereof, shall be evidence of the right of said notary public to continue to exercise the powers and privileges and perform the duties of a notary public in his changed and new name.

§ 52:7-19. Affixation of name.

Each notary public, in addition to subscribing his autograph signature to any jurat upon the administration of any oath or the taking of any acknowledgment or proof, shall affix thereto his name in such a manner and by such means, including, but not limited to, printing, typing, or impressing by seal or mechanical stamp, as will enable the Secretary of State easily to read said name.

§ 52:7-20. Conviction of offense involving dishonesty or crime of second degree; prohibition of appointment.

No person shall be appointed a notary public if he has been convicted under the laws of this State of an offense involving dishonesty or of a crime of the second degree or above, but nothing in this section shall be deemed to supersede P.L. 1968, c. 282 (C. 2A:168A-1 et seq.).

§ 52:7-21. Conviction under laws of another state or United States; prohibition of appointment.

No person shall be appointed a notary public if he has been convicted under the laws of another state, or of the United States, of an offense or crime involving dishonesty or which, if committed in this State, would be a crime of the second degree or above, but nothing in this section shall be deemed to supersede P.L. 1968, c. 282 (C. 2A:168A-1 et seq.).

ADDITIONAL AUTHORITY

§ 2A:82-7. Certificate of protest as evidence.

The certificate of a notary public of this state or of any other state of the United States, under his hand and official seal accompanying any bill of exchange or promissory note which has been protested by such notary for nonacceptance or nonpayment, shall be received in all the courts of this state as competent evidence of the official character of such notary, and also of the facts therein certified as to the presentment and dishonor of such bill or note and of the time and manner of giving or sending notice of dishonor to the parties to such bill or note.

§ 41:2-1. Before whom [oaths, affirmations, and affidavits] taken.

All oaths, affirmations and affidavits required to be made or taken by law of this State, or necessary or proper to be made, taken or used in any court of this State, or for any lawful purpose whatever, may be made and taken before any one of the following officers:

* * *

Notaries public;
Commissioners of deeds;

* * *

This section shall not apply to official oaths required to be made or taken by any of the officers of this State, nor to oaths or affidavits required to be made and taken in open court.

§ 41:2-3. Oaths administered by notaries public in bank matters.

A notary public who is a stockholder, director,

officer, employee or agent of a bank or other corporation may administer an oath to any other stockholder, director, officer, employee or agent of the corporation.

SEAL

§ 41:1-7. Seal not necessary to validity of oath or affidavit.

It shall not be necessary to the validity or sufficiency of any oath, affirmation or affidavit, made or taken before any of the persons named in section 41:2-1 of this title [which includes, among others, "Notaries public" and "Commissioners of deeds"], that the same shall be certified under the official seal of the officer before whom made.

FEES

§ 22A:2-29. Fees for filing, indexing, entering or recording certain documents or papers in office of county clerk or deputy clerk of Superior Court.

Upon the filing, indexing, entering or recording of the following documents or papers in the office of the county clerk or deputy clerk of the Superior Court, such parties, filing or having the same recorded or indexed in the county clerk's office or with the deputy clerk of the Superior Court in the various counties in this State, shall pay the following fees in lieu of the fees heretofore provided for the filing, recording or entering of such documents or papers:

* * *

Commissions and oaths—

Administering oaths to notaries public and commissioners of deeds . . . . $ 7.50

For issuing certificate of authority of notary to take proof, acknowledgment of affidavit . . . . $ 3.00

For issuing each certificate of the commission and qualification of notary public for filing with other county clerks . . . . $ 6.00

For filing each certificate of the commission and qualification of notary public, in office of county clerk of county other than where such notary has qualified . . . . $ 6.00

§ 22A:4-13. Demand or protest of negotiable instruments.

A notary public for performing the services herein enumerated shall be entitled to receive the following fees:

For making demand for payment or acceptance

of a promissory note, bill of exchange, draft or check, protesting the same and registering protest of the same, two dollars ($2.00).

For making and serving each and every notice of protest to be served on the persons entitled thereto, in addition to the cost of postage for each notice if sent by mail, for each of said notices so made and served, ten cents ($0.10).

If a notary charges any greater fees for the services mentioned than are herein allowed he shall forfeit and pay to the party from whom he has taken the same the sum of twenty-five dollars ($25.00), to be recovered in a civil action, with costs, before a court of competent jurisdiction.

§ 22A:4-14. Acknowledgments, proof, affidavits and oaths.

For a service specified in this section, commissioners of deeds, foreign commissioners of deeds, notaries public, judges and other officers authorized by law to perform such service, shall receive a fee as follows:

For administering an oath or taking an affidavit, $0.50.

For taking proof of a deed, $1.00.

For taking all acknowledgments, $1.00.

OFFENSES

§ 2C:28-8. Impersonating a public servant.

A person commits a disorderly persons offense if he falsely pretends to hold a position in the public service with purpose to induce another to submit to such pretended official authority or otherwise to act in reliance upon that pretense.

§ 2C:43-3. Fines and restitutions.

A person who has been convicted of an offense may be sentenced to pay a fine, to make restitution, or both, such fine not to exceed:

* * *

c. $1,000.00, when the conviction is of a disorderly persons offense;

* * *

e. Any higher amount equal to double the pecuniary gain to the offender or loss to the victim caused by the conduct constituting the offense by the offender. In such case the court shall make a finding as to the amount of the gain or loss, and if the record does not contain sufficient evidence to support such a finding the court may conduct a hearing upon the issue. For purposes of this section the terms "gain" means the amount of money or the value of property derived by the offender and "loss" means the amount of value separated from the victim. The term "gain" shall also mean, where appropriate, the amount of any tax, fee, penalty, and interest avoided, evaded, or otherwise unpaid or improperly retained or disposed of;

*   *   *

The restitution ordered paid to the victim shall not exceed his loss, except that in any case involving the failure to pay any State tax, the amount of restitution to the State shall be the full amount of the tax avoided or evaded, including full civil penalties and interest as provided by law. In any case where the victim of the offense is any department or division of State government, the court shall order restitution to the victim. Any restitution imposed on a person shall be in addition to any fine which may be imposed pursuant to this section.

ACKNOWLEDGMENTS

§ 2A:82-17. Certificates of acknowledgment or proof of instruments as evidence of execution thereof.

If any instrument heretofore made and executed or hereafter to be made and executed shall have been acknowledged, by any party who shall have executed it, or the execution thereof by such party shall have been proved by one or more of the subscribing witnesses to such instrument, in the manner and before one of the officers provided and required by law for the acknowledgment or proof of instruments in order to entitle them to be recorded, and, when a certificate of such acknowledgment or proof shall be written upon or under, or be annexed to such instrument and signed by such officer in the manner prescribed by law, such certificate of acknowledgment or proof shall be and constitute prima facie evidence of the due execution of such instrument by such party. Such instrument shall be received in evidence in any court or proceeding in this state in the same manner and to the same effect as though the execution of such instrument by such party had been proved by other evidence.

§ 46:14-1. Acknowledgments by married women.

From and after March seventeenth, one thousand nine hundred and sixteen, any instrument of the nature or description set forth in section 46:16-1 of this title, may be executed and delivered by any married woman of the age of twenty-one years without a private examination apart from her husband, and without an acknowledgment made by her that she signed, sealed and delivered the same as her voluntary act and deed, freely, without any

fear, threats or compulsion of her husband; and any such deed or instrument shall be sufficiently acknowledged by such married woman if she shall acknowledge the same manner as if she were feme sole, and to which the officer taking such acknowledgment shall certify in like manner as in the case of a feme sole.

§ 46:14-2. Acknowledgment by corporation.

Whenever any president, vice-president or other presiding officer, or any secretary, assistant secretary or other recording officer, or any treasurer or assistant treasurer of any corporation, or in the case of a corporation dissolved in any manner, the trustee or trustees in dissolution thereof, who shall have signed the same as such officer or as such trustee or trustees shall acknowledge that any deed, paper or other instrument in writing, made by any corporation and sealed with its corporate seal, is the voluntary act and deed of such corporation, made by virtue of authority from its board of directors, board of trustees, or other similar body, and such acknowledgment is made before any officer authorized by the laws of this State to take acknowledgment of deeds for real estate in this State, in order to entitle the same to be recorded, and there shall be indorsed on or attached to such deed, paper or other instrument in writing a certificate of such acknowledgment signed by the officer before whom the same was made, it shall be as good and effectual in law as if it had been made, executed and acknowledged by a natural person.

§ 46:14-4. Proof of instruments not acknowledged or proved when witnesses dead, insane or nonresident; application to County Court; notice; certificate of proof.

If the grantor or any of the grantors of any deed or instrument of the nature or description set forth in section 46:16-1 of this Title, made and executed, but not acknowledged or proved according to law, and the subscribing witnesses thereto are dead, of unsound mind or resident without the United States, such deed or instrument may be proved before the County Court of the county in which the real estate or property affected thereby, or some part thereof, is situate, by proving the handwriting of such grantor or grantors, to the full satisfaction of such court, which proof may be made by affidavits in writing, taken before any officer in this State authorized by law to take the acknowledgment and proof of deeds, and annexed to such deed or instrument. The proofs shall be certified on or under such deed or instrument in open court by the judge holding such court.

Before any proof shall be taken as herein provided, notice of the application to the County Court for that purpose, describing the deed or instrument and the real estate or property contained therein or affected thereby, and the time and place of such application, shall be given by advertisements, signed by the person making the application, and set up in at least five of the public places in the county, one of which such places shall be in the municipality in which such real estate or property is situate at least four weeks before making the application, and also by a publication four times during four consecutive calendar weeks, once in each week, in a newspaper printed in such county, if any be printed therein, and, if not, in a newspaper circulating in such county and printed in an adjacent county. Due proof, by affidavit annexed to such deed or instrument, of the notice herein required shall be made to the court, and certified by the judge thereof in the certificate of proof herein required.

§ 46:14-5. Proof of assignments of mortgages not acknowledged or proved; record thereof.

If the assignor of any mortgage upon real estate in this State, heretofore or hereafter made and executed but not acknowledged or proved according to law and the subscribing witnesses thereto be dead, of unsound mind, nonresidents of this State or not to be found within this State, the deed of assignment may be proved before a judge of the Superior Court, by proving the handwriting of such witnesses to the satisfaction of the judge, and, upon the certificate of such judge indorsed on or annexed to such assignment that such proof has been made before him, such assignment may be recorded the same as if it were acknowledged according to law.

§ 46:14-6. Officers of state before whom deeds or instruments may be acknowledged or proved; methods; certificates.

If any deed or instrument of the nature or description set forth in section 46:16-1 of this Title shall have been or shall be acknowledged by a party executing the same, such party being in this State, whether residing in this State or elsewhere, before any one of the officers herein named, whether such officer was or is appointed for, or whether he was or is in the county where the affected real estate is situate or where such acknowledgment was or is taken, or not, such officer being satisfied that such party is the grantor, vendor, vendee, lessor or lessee in such deed or instrument, of all of which such officer shall make his certificate on, under or annexed to such deed or instrument, or if such deed or instrument shall have been or shall be proved before any such officer anywhere

in this State by one or more of the subscribing witnesses thereto, such witness or witnesses being within this State, whether residing in this State or elsewhere, that such party (the grantor, vendor, vendee, lessor or lessee), signed, sealed and delivered such deed or instrument as his act and deed, and a certificate of such proof signed by such officer, shall be written upon, or under or be annexed to, such deed or instrument, every such deed or instrument, so acknowledged or proved, shall be deemed to be duly acknowledged or proved.

The officers of this State authorized to take acknowledgments or proofs in this State under authority of this section are a justice of the Supreme Court; a judge of the Superior Court; a judge of the County Court of any county; a master of the Superior Court by such designation, or by the designation of master-in-chancery or master of the court of chancery of New Jersey; an attorney-at-law; a counsellor-at-law; a notary public; a commissioner of deeds appointed for any county; a county clerk of any county; a deputy county clerk; a surrogate or deputy surrogate of any county; and a register of deeds and mortgages or deputy register of any county.

§ 46:14-7. Officers without state but within United States before whom deeds or instruments may be acknowledged or proved; methods; certificates.

If the party who shall have executed or who shall execute any deed or instrument of the description or nature set forth in section 46:16-1 of this Title, or the witnesses thereto, shall have happened or shall happen to be in some other state of the United States or territory thereof, or in the District of Columbia, whether resident in this State, or in such state, territory or district, or elsewhere, an acknowledgment or proof of such as is prescribed by section 46:14-6 of this Title, made before and certified by any one of the officers herein named, shall be as good and effectual as if the same had been made in this State before an officer authorized to take acknowledgments or proofs within the State and had been certified by him, as provided in section 46:16-6.

The officers authorized to take acknowledgments and proofs under authority of this section are:

a. The Chief Justice or any associate justice of the Supreme Court of the United States, or a master of the Superior Court of New Jersey or attorney-at-law of New Jersey, at any place without the State but within the territorial limits of the United States.

b. At any place without this State but within the territorial limits of the United States and within the territorial limits of the jurisdiction of such officer or of his court, by

(1) A judge of any of the United States courts other than the Supreme Court;

(2) The Chancellor of any state of the United States or territory thereof;

(3) Any judge or justice of the Supreme Court or Superior Courts of any state of the United States or territory thereof, or the District of Columbia;

(4) Any foreign commissioner of deeds for New Jersey, when his certificate of acknowledgment or proof is duly certified under his official seal;

(5) The mayor or other chief magistrate of any city, borough or corporation, when his certificate of acknowledgment or proof is duly certified under the seal of the city, borough or corporation of which he was or is the mayor or chief magistrate;

(6) A judge of a court of record of any state of the United States or territory thereof, or of the District of Columbia when his certificate of acknowledgment or proof is duly certified that he was or is such judge under the great seal of such state, territory or district, or under the seal of a court of record of the state, county, city or district in which the acknowledgment or proof was or is made and in and for which he was or is such judge; or

(7) Any notary public of any such state, territory or district, then residing or being anywhere therein, and a recital in his certificate of acknowledgment or proof that he is such notary with his official designation annexed to his signature and attested under his official seal, if such seal is required within the jurisdiction wherein he holds the office of notary public, shall be sufficient proof that the person before or by whom such acknowledgment or proof was taken is such notary.

(8) Any officer of any such state, territory or district, then residing and being anywhere in such state, territory or district, authorized at the time of such acknowledgment or proof by the laws of such state, territory or district to take acknowledgments and proofs, when his certificate of acknowledgment or proof is accompanied by a certificate under the great seal of such state, territory or district, or under the seal of some court of record in or county clerk of the state, county, city or district in which the acknowledgment or proof was or shall be made, and that such officer was, at the time of the taking of such acknowledgments or proofs, authorized by the laws of such state, territory or district to take acknowledgments and proofs.

§ 46:14-8. Officers without United States before whom deeds or instruments may be acknowledged or proved: methods; certificates; proof of authority.

If the party who shall have executed or who shall execute any deed or instrument of the description or nature set forth in section 46-16-1 of this Title, or the witnesses thereto, shall have happened or

shall happen to be in any foreign kingdom, State, nation or colony, whether resident in this State, or in such foreign kingdom, State, nation or colony, or elsewhere, an acknowledgment or proof such as is prescribed by section 46:14-6 of this Title, made before and certified by any one of the officers herein named, shall be as good and effectual as if the same had been made within this State before an officer authorized to take acknowledgments or proofs within the State and had been certified by him, as provided in section 46:14-6.

The officers authorized to take acknowledgments or proofs under authority of this section are:

(a) Any master of the Superior Court or attorney-at-law of New Jersey;

(b) Any public ambassador, minister, consul, vice-consul, consular agent, charge d'affaires or other representative of the United States for the time being, to or at any such foreign kingdom, State, nation or colony;

(c) Any court of law of such foreign kingdom, State, nation or colony;

(d) Any notary, notary public, commissioner for oaths, mayor or other chief magistrate, of and then having been or being within any city, borough, or corporation of such foreign kingdom, State, nation or colony, in which city, borough or corporation such party or witnesses may have happened or may happen to be.

Acknowledgments or proofs taken or made by a court of law, a notary, notary public, commissioner for oaths, or a mayor or other chief magistrate under authority of this section shall be certified if taken by said court under the official seal of said court, and the hand of the judge or clerk thereof, or under the official seal, if any, and the hand of any other person hereby authorized to take acknowledgments or proofs; and such certificate of acknowledgment or proof shall be sufficient proof as to the existence and authority of said court, mayor, notary or other officer.

DEPOSITIONS

§ 41:2-17. Officers authorized to administer or take [oaths, affirmations or affidavits out of state]; jurat; certificate.

Any oath, affirmation or affidavit required or authorized to be taken in any suit or legal proceeding in this state, or for any lawful purpose whatever, except official oaths and depositions required to be taken upon notice, when taken out of this state, may be taken before any notary public of the state, territory, nation, kingdom or country in which the same shall be taken, or before any officer who may be authorized by the laws of this state to take the acknowledgment of deeds in such state, territory, nation, kingdom or country; and a recital that he is such notary or officer in the jurat or certificate of such oath, affirmation or affidavit, and his official designation annexed to his signature, and attested under his official seal, shall be sufficient proof that the person before whom the same is taken is such notary or officer. When, however, any other certificate is required by law to be annexed to the certificate of such officer, other than a notary public, for the recording of a deed acknowledged before him, a like certificate shall be annexed to his certificate of the taking of such oath.

Civil Practice

Superior Court, County Courts and
Surrogate's Courts

[N.J. R. Civ. Prac.]

Rule 4:12. Persons before whom depositions may be taken; authority.

4:12-1. Within the state.

Within this State, depositions shall be taken before a person authorized by the laws of this State to administer oaths.

4:12-2. Without the state but within the United States.

Outside this State but within the United States or within a territory or insular possession subject to the dominion of the United States, depositions shall be taken before a person authorized to administer oaths by the laws of this State, of the United States or of the place where the examination is held.

4:12-3. In foreign countries.

In a foreign country depositions shall be taken (a) on notice before a secretary of embassy or legation, consul general, consul, vice consul, or consular agent of the United States, or (b) before such person or officer as may be appointed by commission or under letters rogatory. A commission or letters rogatory shall be issued only when necessary or convenient, on application and notice, and on such terms and with such directions as are appropriate. Officers may be designated in notices or commissions either by name or descriptive title and letters rogatory may be addressed "To the Appropriate Judicial Authority in (here name the country)."

4:12-4. Disqualification for interest.

No deposition shall be taken before or by a person who is a relative, employee or attorney of a party or a relative or employee of such attorney or is financially interested in the action.

Criminal Practice

Superior Court and County Courts

Other Courts

[N.J. R. Crim. Prac.]

Rule 3:13-2. Depositions.

(a) **When and how taken.** If it appears to the judge of the court in which the indictment or accusation is pending, that a material witness may be unable to attend or may be prevented from attending the trial of the indictment or accusation, or any hearing in connection therewith, the court, to prevent injustice, may upon motion and notice to the parties order that the testimony of such witness be taken orally by deposition as provided in civil actions and that any designated books, papers, documents or tangible objects, not privileged, be produced at the same time and place. If a witness is committed for failure to give bail to appear to testify at a trial or hearing, the court on written motion of the witness and upon notice to the parties may direct that his deposition be taken, and after the deposition has been subscribed the court may discharge the witness. The transcript of all depositions shall be filed with the county clerk as provided in civil actions.

(b) **Use.** [Omitted.]

(c) **Objections to admissibility.** Objections to receiving a deposition or part thereof in evidence may be made as provided in civil actions.

COMMISSIONERS

[N.J. Stat. Ann.]

§ 52:6-12. Appointment; number; designation and description; application; fees.

a. The Secretary of State may appoint such number of commissioners resident in each of the States and territories of the United States and the District of Columbia as he may deem expedient, except where the appointments are incompatible with the laws of the jurisdiction wherein the commissioners reside. Persons thus appointed shall be commissioned by the Governor.

b. Each commissioner so appointed shall be designated a "foreign commissioner of deeds for New Jersey," and may be so described in his appointment and commission or as a "commissioner for taking the acknowledgment or proof of deeds for New Jersey in (such State, territory or district)." He may use either of these designations in his certificates.

c. A person desiring to be appointed and commissioned a foreign commissioner of deeds shall make application to the Secretary of State on a form prescribed by him and endorsed by a member of the Legislature or the Secretary of State or the Assistant Secretary of State. Renewals shall be made in the same manner as the original application. The fees required to be paid for the issuance of any commission to a person appointed as foreign commissioner of deeds for New Jersey shall be paid to the Secretary of State, who shall account to the State Treasurer for the same.

§ 52:6-13. Terms of office; removal by governor.

Commissioners appointed by virtue of section 52:6-12 of this title shall hold office for a term of three years. They may be removed from office at the pleasure of the governor, and shall be removed if it is made to appear to the governor that they have been or are charging more or greater fees than are allowed by law.

§ 52:6-14. Removal from residence as vacating appointment.

Except as provided in section 52:6-15 of this title, if a foreign commissioner removes out of the state, territory or district in which he resides at the time of his appointment, his commission shall thereupon be void.

§ 52:6-15. Foreign commissioner of deeds for adjoining states.

No person shall be denied appointment as a foreign commissioner of deeds of an adjoining state on account of residence outside of that State, provided such person resides in this State. The official acts of such a commissioner resident in this State and performed in an adjoining state shall be as valid and effectual as if he had resided in the adjoining state.

§ 52:6-16. Fee to accompany application for commission.

Each applicant for a commission as a foreign commissioner of deeds for New Jersey shall inclose with his application the fee required by section [22A:4-1]* of the title Fees and Costs, which shall be returned if a commission is not issued to him.

(*) The statute says "section 22:4-1." That former section has been transferred and renumbered as § 22A:4-1.

§ 52:6-17. Official oath; by whom administered.

Each foreign commissioner of deeds shall, before

he enters upon the duties of his office, take and subscribe an oath to perform well and faithfully the duties of his office in accordance with the laws of this State. The oath may be administered by any person authorized to do so under R.S. 41:2-1 or R.S. 41:2-17.

§ 52:6-18. Seal; impression of filed with secretary of state.

Each foreign commissioner of deeds shall attest his official acts by an official seal, an impression of which, in wax or other appropriate substance shall, with his official oath, be filed in the office of the secretary of state of this state.

§ 52:6-20. Use and effect of official certificates.

The official certificates of a foreign commissioner of deeds attested by his official seal may be indorsed upon or annexed to any instrument of writing for use or record in this state, and shall be entitled to full faith and credit.

§ 52:6-21. Manual; provision to applicants.

The secretary of state shall provide to each applicant a manual prescribing the powers and duties of a foreign commissioner of deeds.

§ 52:6-22. List of foreign commissioners of deeds.

The secretary of state shall maintain a list of all foreign commissioners of deeds including the dates of their appointment and the expiration of their terms.

LEGAL HOLIDAYS

§ 36:1-1. Presentation for payment of bills; checks and notes, transaction of public business; state and county offices closed.

The following days in each year shall, for all purposes whatsoever as regards the presenting for payment or acceptance, and of the protesting and giving notice of dishonor, of bills of exchange, bank checks and promissory notes be treated and considered as the first day of the week, commonly called Sunday, and as public holidays: January 1, known as New Year's Day; the third Monday in January, known as Martin Luther King's Birthday; February 12, known as Lincoln's Birthday; the third Monday in February, known as Washington's Birthday; the day designated and known as Good Friday; the last

Monday in May, known as Memorial Day; July 4, known as Independence Day; the first Monday in September, known as Labor Day; the second Monday in October, known as Columbus Day; November 11, known as Armistice Day or Veterans' Day; the fourth Thursday in November, known as Thanksgiving Day; December 25, known as Christmas Day; any general election day in this State; every Saturday; and any day heretofore or hereafter appointed, ordered or recommended by the Governor of this State, or the President of the United States, as a day of fasting and prayer, or other religious observance, or as a bank holiday or holidays. All such bills, checks and notes, otherwise presentable for acceptance or payment on any of the days herein enumerated, shall be deemed to be payable and be presentable for acceptance or payment on the secular or business day next succeeding any such holiday.

Whenever any of the days herein enumerated can and shall fall on a Sunday, the Monday next following shall, for any of the purposes herein enumerated be deemed a public holiday; and bills of exchange, checks and promissory notes which otherwise would be presentable for acceptance or payment on such Monday shall be deemed to be presentable for acceptance or payment on the secular or business day next succeeding such holiday.

In construing this section, every Saturday shall, until 12 o'clock noon, be deemed a secular or business day, except as hereinbefore provided in regard to bills of exchange, bank checks and promissory notes, and the days herein enumerated except bank holidays and Saturdays shall be considered as the first day of the week, commonly called Sunday, and public holidays, for all purposes whatsoever as regards the transaction of business in the public offices of this State, or counties of this State; but on all other days or half days, except Sunday or as otherwise provided by law, such offices shall be kept open for the transaction of business.

§ 36:1-1.2 Legal holiday on Saturday; preceding Friday deemed to be holiday.

Whenever any legal holiday enumerated in R.S. 36:1-1 other than Saturday can and shall fall on a Saturday, the preceding Friday shall be deemed to

be said holiday for State employees, and the public offices of the State government shall be closed for the transaction of business.

§ 36:1-2. Transaction of business on holidays.

Any person or corporation, including without limitation a bank, trust company, banking institution and savings and loan association, may transact either private or public business in this State on any designated holiday, in the same manner as on any other day of the week on which it is lawful to transact such business.

§ 36:1-3. Sales of real and personal property on designated holidays.

Any sale of real or personal property made by any public officer, or by any citizen of this State, on any designated holiday, shall be as valid as though such sale was made on any other day of the week on which it is lawful to sell and transfer real or personal property.

§ 36:1-4. Transactions by certain financial institutions after 12 o'clock noon on Saturdays and public holidays.

The payment, certification or acceptance of any check or other negotiable instrument or any other transaction by any bank or trust company, banking institution or savings and loan association shall not be void or voidable or invalid because done or performed on a day designated in R.S. 36:1-1 as a public holiday, including Saturday between 12 o'clock noon and midnight, if such payment, certification, acceptance or other transaction would be valid if done or performed at a time or on a day which is not designated as a public holiday. Nothing herein contained shall be construed to compel any bank or trust company, banking institution or savings and loan association to keep open, or to perform any of the acts or transactions aforesaid, on any Saturday after 12 o'clock noon or on any day designated as a public holiday except at its own option.

NEW MEXICO

NOTARIES PUBLIC

[N.M. Stat. Ann.]

§ 14-12-1. Notaries; powers and duties.

The office of "notary public" is established. At any place within the state, a notary public may:

A. administer oaths;

B. take and certify acknowledgments of instruments in writing;

C. take and certify depositions;

D. make declarations and protests; and

E. perform other duties as provided by law.

§ 14-12-2. Notaries; qualifications.

Each notary public shall:

A. be a resident of New Mexico;

B. be at least eighteen years of age;

C. be able to read and write the English language;

D. not have been convicted of a felony; and

E. not have had a notary public commission revoked during the past five years.

§ 14-12-3. Notaries; application.

Each applicant for appointment as a notary public shall submit to the secretary of state:

A. an application for appointment on a form prescribed by the secretary of state which includes a statement of the applicant's qualification and contains evidence of his good moral character as shown by signatures of two citizens of this state;

B. the oath prescribed by the constitution for state officers and an official bond to the state, with two sureties, in the amount of five hundred dollars ($500) conditioned for the faithful discharge of duties as a notary public;

C. an application which is made by and signed by the applicant using his surname and one given name, plus an initial or additional name, if he so desires, or surname and at least two initials; and

D. an application fee in the amount of ten dollars ($10.00).

§ 14-12-4. Notaries; appointment; term.

Upon receipt of the completed application for appointment and the application fee, and upon approval of the applicant's bond, the secretary of state shall notify the governor who shall appoint the applicant as a notary public for a term of four years from the date of appointment unless sooner removed by the governor. The secretary of state shall issue a commission to each notary public appointed by the governor.

§ 14-12-5. Notaries; seal or stamp.

Each notary shall provide himself with a notarial seal or stamp containing his name and the words "NOTARY PUBLIC—STATE OF NEW MEXICO," and shall authenticate his official acts and acknowledgments with the seal or stamp.

§ 14-12-6. Notarial seal.

Each notary shall authenticate his official acts and acknowledgments with a notarial seal or stamp which, if a seal, shall contain his name and the words "NOTARY PUBLIC—STATE OF NEW MEXICO," and which if a stamp, shall be in substantially the following form:
"SEAL
STATE OF
NEW MEXICO

OFFICIAL SEAL

....
(name of notary printed)
NOTARY PUBLIC—STATE OF NEW MEXICO
My Commission Expires ...."
(date)

§ 14-12-7. Notaries; certification.

Upon request, the secretary of state shall certify to official acts of a notary public.

§ 14-12-8. Notaries; action on bond.

Any person damaged by an unlawful act, negligence or misconduct of a notary public in his official capacity may bring a civil action on the notary public's official bond.

§ 14-12-9. Notaries; reappointment.

At least thirty days before expiration of each notary public term, the secretary of state shall mail a notice of the expiration to the notary public's address of record. A notary public may be reappointed upon making application in the same manner as required for an original application.

§ 14-12-10. Protesting bills and notes; notice.

Each notary public when any bill of exchange, promissory note or other written instrument shall be by such notary protested for nonacceptance or nonpayment shall give notice in writing thereof to the maker and to each and every endorser of such bill of exchange, and to the maker of each security, or the endorsers of any promissory note or other written instrument, immediately after such protest shall have been made.

§ 14-12-11. Service of notice of protest.

Each notary public may serve notice personally upon each person protested against by delivering to such person a notice in writing, or he may make such service by placing such notice in a sealed envelope with sufficient postage thereon addressed to the person to be charged, at his last place of residence, according to the best information that the person giving the notice may obtain, and by depositing such envelope containing such notice in the United States mail or post office.

§ 14-12-12. Recording protest notices; use as evidence.

Each notary public shall keep record of all protest notices and of the time and manner in which the same were served and of the names of all persons to whom the same were directed. Also the description and the amount of the instrument protested, which record, or a copy thereof certified by the notary public under seal, shall at all times be competent evidence to prove such notice in any court of this state.

§ 14-12-13. Notaries; removal from office.

A. The governor may revoke the commission of any notary public who:
(1) submits an application for appointment as a notary public which contains a false statement;
(2) is or has been convicted of any felony or of a misdemeanor arising out of a notarial act performed by him;
(3) engages in the unauthorized practice of law;
(4) ceases to be a New Mexico resident; or
(5) commits a malfeasance in office.
B. A notary's commission may be revoked under the provisions of this section only if action is taken subject to the rights of the notary public to notice, hearing, adjudication and appeal.

§ 14-12-14. Notaries; change of address.

Each notary public shall promptly notify the secretary of state of any change of his mailing address.

§ 14-12-15. Notaries; change of name.

Upon any change of his name, a notary public shall promptly make application to the secretary of state for issuance of a corrected commission. The application shall be on a form prescribed by the secretary of state. Upon receipt of the completed application, the secretary of state shall issue a corrected commission showing the notary public's new name. The corrected commission expires on the same date as the original certificate it replaces.

§ 14-12-16. Endorsing expiration date of commission.

Every notary public certifying to any acknowledgment, oath or other matter shall, immediately opposite or following his signature to the jurat or certificate of acknowledgment, endorse the date of the expiration of such commission; such endorsement may be legibly written, stamped or printed upon the instrument, but must be disconnected from the seal and shall be substantially in the following form:

"My commission expires (stating date of expiration of commission)."

§ 14-12-17. Disqualified notary exercising powers; penalty.

Any notary public who exercises the duties of his office with the knowledge that his commission has expired or that he is otherwise disqualified, is guilty of a misdemeanor, and upon conviction thereof shall be punished by a fine of one hundred dollars [($100)] and shall be removed from office by the governor.

§ 14-12-18. False certificate; authenticating documents in absence of proper party; penalty.

If any notary public, or any other officer authorized by law to make or give any certificate or other writing shall make or deliver as true any certificate or writing containing statements which he knows to be false, or appends his official signature to acknowledgments or other documents when the parties executing same have not appeared in person before him shall be deemed guilty of a misdemeanor and upon conviction shall be punished by a fine not exceeding two hundred dollars [($200)], or by imprisonment for a period not exceeding three months, or both such fine and imprisonment.

§ 14-12-19. Fees.

A. Every notary public in this state shall be entitled to collect the following fees for his services:

(1) for each act of protest and certificate thereof
.... $2.00

(2) for each notice of protest prepared and mailed to the parties in interest .... .25

(3) for any certificate under seal 1.00

(4) for each acknowledgment to deed or other document 1.00

(5) for administering or certifying to any oath
.... 1.00

B. Whenever a notary shall be authorized by proper process to take testimony or depositions and report the same to the proper authority without making findings of fact or law, such notary public shall be entitled to collect the following fees for his services:

(1) for noting each meeting to take testimony
.... $1.00

(2) for noting each adjournment from one day to another 1.00

(3) for swearing each witness .... .25

(4) for certifying and transmitting the record
.... 1.50

(5) for transcribing or reducing to writing testimony, per folio of one hundred words, original
.... .15

(6) for each additional copy of same, per folio
.... .05

And every notary in addition to collecting fees when called from his office shall be entitled to ten cents ($.10) per mile.

§ 14-12-20. Notary affiliated with bank or corporation; power restricted.

It shall be lawful for any notary public who is a stockholder, director, officer or employee of a bank or other corporation to take the acknowledgment of any party to any written instrument executed to or by such corporation, or to administer an oath to any other stockholder, director, officer, employee or agent of such corporation or to protest for non-acceptance or nonpayment bills of exchange, drafts, checks, notes and other negotiable instruments which may be owned or held for collection by such corporation; provided, it shall be unlawful for any notary public to take the acknowledgment of an instrument by or to a bank or other corporation of which he is stockholder, director, officer or employee, where such notary is a party to such instrument, either individually or as a representative of such corporation, or to protest any negotiable instrument owned or held for collection by such corporation, where such notary is individually a party to such instrument.

ACKNOWLEDGMENTS AND OATHS

§ 14-13-1. Administration of oath.

Whenever any person shall be required to take an oath before he enters upon the discharge of any office, place or business, or on any lawful occasion, any person administering the oath shall do so in the following form, viz: the person swearing shall, with his right hand uplifted, follow the words required in the oath as administered, beginning: I do solemnly swear, and closing: so help me God.

§ 14-13-2. Administration of affirmation in lieu of oath.

Whenever any person is required to take or subscribe an oath and shall have conscientious scruples against taking the same, he shall be permitted, instead of such oath, to make a solemn affirmation, with uplifted right hand, in the following form, viz: you do solemnly, sincerely and truly declare and affirm, and close with: and this I do under the pains and penalties of perjury, which affirmation shall be equally valid as if such person had taken an oath in the usual form; and every person guilty of falsely, willfully or corruptly declaring as aforesaid, shall be liable to punishment for the same as for perjury.

§ 14-13-3. Oaths; power to administer.

The secretary of state of New Mexico, county clerks, clerks of probate courts, clerks of district courts, clerks of magistrate courts if the magistrate court has a seal, and all duly commissioned and acting notaries public, are hereby authorized and empowered to administer oaths and affirmations in all cases where magistrates and other officers within the state authorized to administer oaths may do so, under existing laws, and with like effect.

§ 14-13-4. Officers authorized to take acknowledgments.

The acknowledgment of any instrument of writing may be made within this state before either:

A. a clerk of the district court;

B. a judge or clerk of the probate court, using the probate seal;

C. a notary public;

D. a justice of the peace [magistrate];

E. a county clerk, using the county clerk seal.

§ 14-13-5. Acknowledgments outside state.

The acknowledgment of any instrument of writ-

ing may be made without this state, but within the United States or their territories, before either:

A. a clerk of some court of record having a seal;

B. a commissioner of deeds duly appointed under the laws of this state;

C. a notary public having a seal.

§ 14-13-6. Acknowledgments in foreign countries.

The acknowledgment of any instrument of writing may be made without the United States before either:

A. a minister, commissioner or charge d'affaires of the United States, resident and accredited in the country where the acknowledgment is made;

B. a consul general, consul, vice consul, deputy consul or consular agent of the United States resident in the country where the acknowledgment is made, having a seal;

C. a notary public having a seal;

D. a commissioner of deeds duly appointed under the laws of this state.

§ 14-13-7. Military officers; power to take acknowledgments and administer oaths.

In addition to the acknowledgment of instruments and the performance of other notarial acts in the manner and form as otherwise authorized by law, instruments may be acknowledged, documents attested, oaths and affirmations administered, depositions and affidavits executed, and all notarial acts, authorized under the laws of the state of New Mexico to be performed by notaries public, may be performed before or by any commissioned officer in active service of the armed forces of the United States with the rank of second lieutenant or higher in the army or marine corps, or with the rank of ensign or higher in the navy or coast guard or with equivalent rank in any other component part of the armed forces of the United States, for any person who either:

A. is a member of the armed forces of the United States or the spouse of a member of the armed forces of the United States; or

B. is serving as a merchant seaman outside the limits of the United States included within the fifty states and the District of Columbia; or

C. is outside said limits by permission, assignment or direction of any department or official of the United States government, in connection with any activity pertaining to the prosecution of any war in which the United States is then engaged.

Such acknowledgment of instruments, attestation of documents, administration of oaths and affirmations, execution of depositions and affidavits and performance of other notarial acts, heretofore or hereafter made or taken, are hereby declared legal, valid and binding, and instruments and documents so acknowledged, authenticated or sworn to shall be admissible in evidence and eligible to record in this state under the same circumstances, and with the same force and effect as if such acknowledgment, attestation, oath, affirmation, deposition, affidavit or other notarial act, had been made or taken within this state before or by a duly qualified officer or official as otherwise provided by law.

In the taking of acknowledgments and the performing of other notarial acts requiring certification, a certificate endorsed upon or attached to the instruments or documents, which shows the date of the notarial act, and which states, in substance, that the person appearing before the officer acknowledged the instrument as his act or made or signed the instrument or document under oath, shall be sufficient for all intents and purposes. The instrument or document shall not be rendered invalid by the failure to state the place of execution or acknowledgment.

If the signature, rank and branch of service, or subdivision thereof, of any such commissioned officer appear upon such instrument or document or certificate, no further proof of the authority of such officer so to act shall be required and such action by such commissioned officer shall be prima facie evidence that the person making such oath or acknowledgment is within the purview of this act [section], and that the signature of such person is genuine.

§ 14-13-8. Contents of certificate of acknowledgment.

The certificate of acknowledgment shall express the fact of the acknowledgment being made, and also, that the person making the same was personally known to at least one of the judges of the court, or to the officer granting the certificate, to be the person whose name is subscribed to the writing or a party to it, or that it was proven to be such person by the testimony of at least two reliable witnesses.

§ 14-13-9. Forms; instruments affecting real estate.

That the following forms of acknowledgment may be used in the case of conveyances or other written instruments affecting real estate, and any acknowledgment so taken and certified shall be sufficient to satisfy all requirements of law relating to the execution or recording of such instruments:

A. in case of natural persons acting in their own right:
State of New Mexico,
County of ....

On this .... day of .... 19...., before me personally appeared A. B. (or A. B. and C. D.) to me known to be the person (or persons) described in and who executed the foregoing instrument, and acknowledged that he (or they) executed the same as his (or their) free act and deed;

B. in the case of natural persons acting by attorney:
State of New Mexico,
County of ....

On this .... day of .... 19...., before me personally appeared A. B., to me known to be the person who executed the foregoing instrument in behalf of C. D., and acknowledged that he executed the same as the free act and deed of said C. D.;

C. in case of corporations or joint stock associations:
State of New Mexico,
County of ....

On this .... day of .... 19...., before me appeared A. B., to me personally known, who, being by me duly sworn (or affirmed) did say that he is the president(or other officer or agent of the corporation or association) of (describing the corporation or association), and that the seal affixed to said instrument is the corporate seal of said corporation (or association) and that said instrument was signed and sealed in behalf of said corporation (or association) by authority of its board of directors (or trustees), and said A. B. acknowledged said instrument to be the free act and deed of said corporation (or association).

In case the corporation or association has no corporate seal, omit the words: "the seal affixed to said instrument is the corporate seal of such corporation (or association), and that," and add at the end of the affidavit clause the words: "and that said corporation (or association) has no corporate seal."

In all cases add signature and title of the officer taking the acknowledgment.

§ 14-13-10. Acknowledgment by married woman.

When a married woman unites with her husband in the execution of any such instrument and acknowledges the same in one of the forms sanctioned, she shall be described in the acknowledgment as his wife, but in all other respects her acknowledgment shall be taken and certified as if she were sole.

§ 14-13-11. Wage and salary assignments.

A. All assignments of wages or salaries due or to become due to any person, in order to be valid, shall be acknowledged by the party making the assignment before a notary public or other officer authorized to take acknowledgments. The assignment shall be recorded in the office of the county clerk of the county in which the money is to be paid and a copy served upon the employer or person who is to make payment.

B. Any assignment of wages or salary is void if it provides for an assignment of more than twenty-five percent of the assignor's disposable earnings for any pay period. As used in this section, "disposable earnings" means that part of the assignor's wage or salary remaining after deducting the amounts which are required by law to be withheld.

§ 14-13-12. Instrument needs no acknowledgment in absence of statutory requirement.

An acknowledgment of an instrument of writing shall not be necessary to its execution unless expressly so provided by statute.

§ 14-13-13. Validation of former acknowledgments; 1951 act.

All acknowledgments taken outside the state of New Mexico prior to the passage and approval of this act [this section], before any officer authorized by the laws of this state to take such acknowledgments, under the seal of such officer, and all acknowledgments taken within this state before the passage and approval of this act, before any officer authorized by law to take acknowledgments, notwithstanding any defect in the form of a certificate of acknowledgment or the failure to show the date of the expiration of the commission of the officer before whom such acknowledgment was taken or the failure to show that the seal of said officer was affixed to the instrument acknowledged and/or notwithstanding the failure of such acknowledgment to comply with the provisions of Section 14-13-10 NMSA 1978, if the marital status of any married woman uniting with her husband in the execution of any instrument may otherwise appear from the body of the instrument so acknowledged, and the record thereof in the office of the county clerk, are hereby confirmed and made valid to the extent as though said certificate of acknowledgment and the record thereof had been in the form prescribed by law.

§ 14-13-14. Validation of former acknowledgments; 1957 act.

All acknowledgments taken outside the state of New Mexico prior to the passage and approval of this act [this section], before any officer authorized by the laws of this state to take such acknowledg-

ments, under the seal of such officer, and all acknowledgments taken within this state before the passage and approval of this act, before any officer authorized by law to take acknowledgments, notwithstanding any defect in the form of a certificate of acknowledgment or the failure to show the date of the expiration of the commission of the officer before whom such acknowledgment was taken or the failure to show that the seal of said officer was affixed to the instrument acknowledged and/or notwithstanding the failure of such acknowledgment to comply with the provisions of Section 14-13-10 NMSA 1978, if the marital status of any married woman uniting with her husband in the execution of any instrument may otherwise appear from the body of the instrument so acknowledged, and the record thereof in the office of the county clerk, are hereby confirmed and made valid to the extent as though said certificate of acknowledgment and the record thereof has been in the form prescribed by law.

§ 14-13-15. Validation of former acknowledgments; 1965 act.

All acknowledgments taken outside the state of New Mexico prior to the passage and approval of this act [this section], before any officer authorized by the laws of this state to take such acknowledgments, under the seal of such officer, and all acknowledgments taken within this state before the passage and approval of this act, before any officer authorized by law to take acknowledgments, notwithstanding any defect in the form of a certificate of acknowledgment or the failure to show the date of the expiration of the commission of the officer before whom such acknowledgment was taken or the failure to show that the seal of said officer was affixed to the instrument acknowledged and/or notwithstanding the failure of such acknowledgment to comply with the provisions of Section 14-13-10 NMSA 1978, if the marital status of any married woman uniting with her husband in the execution of any instrument may otherwise appear from the body of the instrument so acknowledged, and the record thereof in the office of the county clerk, are hereby confirmed and made valid to the extent as though said certificate of acknowledgment and the record thereof has been in the form prescribed by law.

§ 14-13-16. Validation of former acknowledgments; 1967 act.

All acknowledgments taken outside the state of New Mexico prior to the passage and approval of this act [this section], before any officer authorized by the laws of this state to take such acknowledgments, under the seal of such officer, and all acknowledgments taken within this state before the passage and approval of this act, before any officer authorized by law to take acknowledgments, notwithstanding any defect in the form of a certificate of acknowledgment or the failure to show the date of the expiration of the commission of the officer before whom such acknowledgment was taken or the failure to show that the seal of said officer was affixed to the instrument acknowledged and/or notwithstanding the failure of such acknowledgment to comply with the provisions of Section 14-13-10 NMSA 1978, if the marital status of any married woman uniting with her husband in the execution of any instrument may otherwise appear from the body of the instrument so acknowledged, and the record thereof in the office of the county clerk, are hereby confirmed and made valid to the extent as though said certificate of acknowledgment and the record thereof has been in the form prescribed by law.

§ 14-13-17. Validation of former acknowledgments; 1971 act.

All acknowledgments taken outside the state of New Mexico prior to the passage and approval of this act [this section], before any officer authorized by the laws of this state to take such acknowledgments, under the seal of such officer, and all acknowledgments taken within this state before the passage and approval of this act, before any officer authorized by law to take acknowledgments, notwithstanding any defect in the form of a certificate of acknowledgment or the failure to show the date of the expiration of the commission of the officer before whom such acknowledgment was taken or the failure to show that the seal of said officer was affixed to the instrument acknowledged and/or notwithstanding the failure of such acknowledgment to comply with the provisions of Section 14-13-10 NMSA 1978, if the marital status of any married woman uniting with her husband in the execution of any instrument may otherwise appear from the body of the instrument so acknowledged, and the record thereof in the office of the county clerk, are hereby confirmed and made valid to the extent as though said certificate of acknowledgment and the record thereof has been in the form prescribed by law.

§ 14-13-18. Validation of former acknowledgments; 1975 act.

All acknowledgments taken outside the state of New Mexico prior to the passage and approval of this act [this section], before any officer authorized by the laws of this state to take such acknowledgments, under the seal of such officer, and all acknowledgments taken within this state before the

passage and approval of this act, before any officer authorized by law to take acknowledgments, notwithstanding any defect in the form of a certificate of acknowledgment or the failure to show the date of the expiration of the commission of the officer before whom such acknowledgment was taken or the failure to show that the seal of said officer was affixed to the instrument acknowledged and/or notwithstanding the failure of such acknowledgment to comply with the provisions of Section 14-13-10 NMSA 1978, if the marital status of any married woman uniting with her husband in the execution of any instrument may otherwise appear from the body of the instrument so acknowledged, and the record thereof in the office of the county clerk, are hereby confirmed and made valid to the extent as though said certificate of acknowledgment and the record thereof has been in the form prescribed by law.

§ 14-13-19. Short forms for acknowledgments authorized.

The forms of acknowledgment set forth in the appendix [14-13-23 NMSA 1978] to this act may be used and shall be sufficient for their respective purposes. They shall be known as "statutory forms of acknowledgment" and may be referred to as such. They may be altered as circumstances require; and the authorization of such forms shall not prevent the use of other forms. Marital status or other status of a person or persons may be shown if desired after the name of such person or persons.

§ 14-13-20. Application of act.

For the purpose of avoiding the unnecessary use of words in acknowledgments whether said statutory form or other form is used, the rules and definitions contained in this act [14-13-19 to 14-13-23 NMSA 1978] shall apply to all instruments executed or delivered on or after the effective date of this act.

§ 14-13-21. Definition.

In the forms of acknowledgment provided by Sections 14-13-19 through 14-12-23 NMSA 1978, the words "was acknowledged" shall mean:

A. in the case of a natural person acknowledging that such person personally appeared before the officer taking the acknowledgment and acknowledged that he executed the acknowledged instrument as his free act and deed for the uses and purposes therein set forth;

B. in the case of a person acknowledging as principal by an attorney-in-fact, that such attorney-in-fact appeared personally before the officer taking the acknowledgment and that the attorney-in-fact acknowledged that he executed the acknowledged instrument as the free act and deed of the principal for the uses and purposes therein set forth;

C. in the case of a partnership acknowledging by a partner or partners, that such partner or partners personally appeared before the officer taking the acknowledgment and that he or they acknowledged that he or they executed the acknowledged instrument as the free act and deed of the partnership for the uses and purposes therein set forth;

D. in the case of a limited partnership acknowledging by a general partner or general partners, that such partner or partners appeared before the officer taking the acknowledgment and that he or they acknowledged that he or they executed the acknowledged instrument as the free act and deed of the limited partnership for the uses and purposes therein set forth; and

E. in the case of a corporation or incorporated association acknowledging by an officer or agent of the corporation or incorporated association, that such acknowledging officer or agent personally appeared before the officer taking the acknowledgment; that the seal affixed to the instrument is the corporate seal of the corporation or association, that the instrument was signed and sealed on behalf of the corporation or association by authority of its board of directors, and that the acknowledging officer or agent acknowledged that the acknowledged instrument was the free act and deed of such corporation or association for the uses and purposes therein set forth. In case a corporation or association has no corporate seal, this fact can be indicated by adding to the form provided for in Subsection E of Section 14-13-23 NMSA 1978 the words "The corporation (or association) has no corporate seal."

§ 14-13-22. Prima facie evidence of execution.

Any acknowledgment taken and certified as provided by law shall be prima facie evidence of the execution of the instrument by the parties acknowledging the same, in all of the courts of this state.

§ 14-13-23. Short forms of acknowledgment.

A. For a natural person acting in his own right:
State of ....
County of ....
The foregoing instrument was acknowledged before me this (date) by (name or names of person or persons acknowledging).

Signature of officer

....
(Title of Officer)

My commission expires:

B. For a natural person as principal acting by attorney-in-fact:
State of ....
County of ....
The foregoing instrument was acknowledged before me this (date) by (name of attorney-in-fact) as attorney-in-fact on behalf of (name of principal).

Signature of officer

....
(Title of Officer)

My commission expires:

C. For a partnership acting by one or more partners:
State of ....
County of ....
The foregoing instrument was acknowledged before me this (date) by (name of acknowledging partner or partners), partner(s) on behalf of (name of partnership), a partnership.

Signature of officer

....
(Title of Officer)

My commission expires:

D. For limited partnership acting by one or more general partners:
State of ....
County of ....
The foregoing was acknowledged before me this (date) by (name of acknowledging general partner or partners), partner(s) on behalf of (name of limited partnership), a limited partnership.

Signature of officer

....
(Title of Officer)

My commission expires:

E. For a corporation or incorporated association:
State of ....
County of ....
The foregoing instrument was acknowledged before me this (date) by (name of officer), (title of officer) of (name of corporation acknowledging), a (state or county of incorporation) corporation, on behalf of the corporation.

Signature of officer

....
(Title of Officer)

My commission expires:

§ 14-13-24. Validation of certain prior acknowledgments.

All acknowledgments taken outside the state of New Mexico prior to the passage and approval of this act [14-13-21, 14-13-23, 14-13-24 NMSA 1978], before any officer authorized by either the laws of the jurisdiction where taken or the laws of this state to take such acknowledgments, and all acknowledgments taken within this state before the passage and approval of this act, before any officer authorized by law to take acknowledgments, notwithstanding the form of the certificate of acknowledgment or the failure to show the date of the expiration of the commission of the officer before whom such acknowledgment [acknowledgment] was taken or the failure to show that the seal of said officer was affixed to the instrument acknowledged and/or notwithstanding the failure of such acknowledgment to comply with the provisions of Section 14-13-10 NMSA 1978, if the marital status of any married woman uniting with her husband in the execution of any instrument may otherwise appear from the body of the instrument so acknowledged, and the record thereof in the office of the county clerk, are hereby confirmed and made valid to the extent as though said certificate of acknowledgment and the record thereof has been in the form prescribed by law.

DEPOSITIONS

[N.M. R. Civ. P.]

Rule 1-028. Persons before whom depositions may be taken.

A. **Within the United States.** Within the United States or within a territory or insular possession subject to the dominion of the United States, depositions shall be taken before an officer authorized to administer oaths by the laws of the United States or of the place where the examination is held, or before a person appointed by the court in which the action is pending. A person so appointed has power to administer oaths and take testimony.

B. **In foreign countries.** In a foreign country, depositions may be taken:

(1) on notice before a person authorized to administer oaths in the place in which the examination is held, either by the law thereof or by the law of the United States; or

(2) before a person commissioned by the court, and a person so commissioned shall have the power by virtue of his commission to administer any necessary oath and take testimony; or

(3) pursuant to a letter rogatory. A commission or a letter rogatory shall be issued on application and notice and on terms that are just and appropriate. It is not requisite to the issuance of a commission or a letter rogatory that the taking of the deposition in any other manner is impracticable or inconvenient; and both a commission and a letter rogatory may be issued in proper cases. A notice or commission may designate the person before whom the deposition is to be taken either by name or descriptive title. A letter rogatory may be addressed

"To the Appropriate Authority in (*here name the country*)." Evidence obtained in response to a letter rogatory need not be excluded merely for the reason that it is not a verbatim transcript or that the testimony was not taken under oath or for any similar departure from the requirements for depositions taken within the United States under these rules.

C. **Disqualification for interest.** No deposition shall be taken before a person who is a relative or employee or attorney or counsel of any of the parties, or is a relative or employee of such attorney or counsel, or is financially interested in the action.

Rule 5-503. Depositions; statements.

* * *

E. **Persons before whom depositions may be taken.**

(1) Within the State of New Mexico, depositions shall be taken by an official court reporter, by a tape monitor, by anyone agreed to by the parties or, in the case of an emergency, by anyone designated by the trial court.

(2) Within the United States or within a territory or insular possession subject to the dominion of the United States, depositions shall be taken before an officer authorized to administer oaths by the laws of the United States or of the place where the examination is held, or before a person appointed by the court in which the action is pending. A person so appointed has power to administer oaths and take testimony.

(3) In a foreign country, depositions may be taken:

(a) on notice before a person authorized to administer oaths in the place in which the examination is held, either by the law thereof or by the law of the United States;

(b) before a person commissioned by the court, and a person so commissioned shall have the power by virtue of his commission to administer any necessary oath and take testimony; or

(c) pursuant to a letter rogatory. A commission or a letter rogatory shall be issued on application and notice and on terms that are just and appropriate. It is not requisite to the issuance of a commission or a letter rogatory that the taking of the deposition in any other manner is impracticable or inconvenient; and both a commission and a letter rogatory may be issued in proper cases. A notice or commission may designate the person before whom the deposition is to be taken either by name or descriptive title. A letter rogatory may be addressed "To the Appropriate Authority in (*here name the country*)." Evidence obtained in response to a letter rogatory need not be excluded merely for the reason that it is not a verbatim transcript or that the testimony was not taken under oath or for any similar departure from the requirements for depositions taken within the United States under these rules.

(4) No deposition shall be taken before a person who is a relative, employee, attorney or counsel of any of the parties, or is a relative or employee of such attorney or counsel, or is interested in the action.

F. Depositions; notice of examination; nonstenographic recording.

(1) A party desiring to take the deposition of any person upon oral examination shall give notice in writing to every other party to the action. The notice shall state the time and place set for taking the deposition and the name and address of each person to be examined.

(2) The court may for cause shown enlarge or shorten the time previously set for taking the deposition.

(3) Depositions shall be taken on an audio recording device or a videotape recorder.

G. Record of examination. The officer before whom the deposition is to be taken shall put the person on oath and shall personally, or by someone acting under his direction and in his presence, record the testimony of the witness.

* * *

LEGAL HOLIDAYS

[N.M. Stat. Ann.]

§ 12-5-2. Legal holidays; designation.

Legal public holidays in New Mexico are:

A. New Year's day, January 1;

B. Martin Luther King, Jr.'s birthday, third Monday in January;

C. Washington's and Lincoln's birthday, President's day, third Monday in February;

D. Memorial day, last Monday in May;

E. Independence day, July 4;

F. Labor day, first Monday in September;

G. Columbus day, second Monday in October;

H. Armistice day and Veterans' day, November 11;

I. Thanksgiving day, fourth Thursday in November; and

J. Christmas day, December 25.

§ 12-5-3. Legal holidays; Sundays; effect on commercial paper.

A. Whenever a legal public holiday falls on Sunday, the following Monday is a legal public holiday.

B. Any bill, check or note presentable for acceptance or payment on a legal public holiday or on a Sunday is payable and presentable for acceptance or payment on the next business day after the legal public holiday or Sunday.

NEW YORK

NOTARIES PUBLIC

[N.Y. Exec. Law]

§ 130. Appointment of notaries public.

The secretary of state may appoint and commission as many notaries public for the state of New York as in his judgment may be deemed best, whose jurisdiction shall be co-extensive with the boundaries of the state. The appointment of a notary public shall be for a term of two years. An application for an appointment as notary public shall be in form and set forth such matters as the secretary of state shall prescribe. Every person appointed as notary public must, at the time of his appointment, be a citizen of the United States and either a resident of the state of New York or have an office or place of business in New York state. A notary public who is a resident of the state and who moves out of the state but still maintains a place of business or an office in New York state does not vacate his office as a notary public. A notary public who is a nonresident and who ceases to have an office or place of business in this state, vacates his office as a notary public. A notary public who is a resident of New York state and moves out of the state and who does not retain an office or place of business in this state shall vacate his office as a notary public. A non-resident who accepts the office as a notary public in this state thereby appoints the secretary of state as the person upon whom process can be served on his behalf. Before issuing to any applicant a commission as notary public, unless he be an attorney and counsellor at law duly admitted to practice in this state, the secretary of state shall satisfy himself that the applicant is of good moral character, has the equivalent of a common school education and is familiar with the duties and responsibilities of a notary public; provided, however, that where a notary public applies, before the expiration of his term, for a reappointment or where a person whose term as notary public shall have expired applies within six months thereafter for appointment as a notary public, such qualifying requirements may be waived by the secretary of state, and further, where an application for reappointment is filed after the expiration of the aforementioned renewal period by a person who failed or was unable to reapply by reason of his induction or enlistment in the armed forces of the United States, such qualifying requirements may also be waived by the secretary of state, provided such application for reappointment is made within a period of one year after the military discharge of the applicant under conditions other than dishonorable. In any case, the appointment or reappointment of any applicant is in the discretion of the secretary of state. The secretary of state may suspend or remove from office, for misconduct, any notary public appointed by him but no such removal shall be made unless the person who is sought to be removed shall have been served with a copy of the charges against him and have an opportunity of being heard. No person shall be appointed as a notary public under this article who has been convicted, in this state or any other state or territory, of a felony or any of the following offenses, to wit:

(a) Illegally using, carrying or possessing a pistol or other dangerous weapon; (b) making or possess-

ing burglar's instruments; (c) buying or receiving or criminally possessing stolen property; (d) unlawful entry of a building; (e) aiding escape from prison; (f) unlawfully possessing or distributing habit forming narcotic drugs; (g) violating sections two hundred seventy, two hundred seventy-a, two hundred seventy-b, two hundred seventy-c, two hundred seventy-one, two hundred seventy-five, two hundred seventy-six, five hundred fifty, five hundred fifty-one, five hundred fifty-one-a and subdivisions six, eight, ten or eleven of section seven hundred twenty-two of the former penal law as in force and effect immediately prior to September first, nineteen hundred sixty-seven, or violating sections 165.25, 165.30, subdivision one of section 240.30, subdivision three of section 240.35 of the penal law, or violating sections four hundred seventy-eight, four hundred seventy-nine, four hundred eighty, four hundred eighty-one, four hundred eighty-four, four hundred eighty-nine and four hundred ninety-one of the judiciary law; or (h) vagrancy or prostitution, and who has not subsequent to such conviction received an executive pardon therefor or a certificate of good conduct from the parole board to remove the disability under this section because of such conviction.

A person regularly admitted to practice as an attorney and counsellor in the courts of record of this state, whose office for the practice of law is within the state, may be appointed a notary public and retain his office as such notary public although he resides in or removes to an adjoining state. For the purpose of this and the following sections of this article such person shall be deemed a resident of the county where he maintains such office.

§ 131. Procedure of appointment; fees and commissions.

1. Upon being satisfied of the competency and good character of the applicant for appointment as notary public, the secretary of state shall issue a commission to such person. The secretary of state shall receive a non-refundable examination fee of fifteen dollars from each person who takes an examination to qualify for application of licensure pursuant to this section and section one hundred thirty of this article.

2. The secretary of state shall receive a non-refundable application fee of twenty dollars from applicants for appointment or reappointment, which fee shall be submitted together with the application. No further fee shall be paid for the issuance of the commission after approval of such application. Notwithstanding the provisions of section one hundred thirty of this article, after January first, nineteen hundred eighty-six, the secretary of state shall assign staggered expiration dates for outstanding

appointments that have been previously renewed on March thirtieth of each year and such appointments shall thereafter expire two years from the assigned date unless renewed. If the assigned date results in a term that exceeds twenty-four months, the applicant shall pay an additional prorated adjustment together with the regular renewal fee. The secretary of state shall assign dates to existing appointments in a manner which shall result in a term of not less than two years.

3. The commission, duly dated, shall be transmitted by the secretary of state to the county clerk of the county in which the appointee resides. Upon receiving such commission, the county clerk shall forthwith notify each person so appointed to qualify by filing with him his oath of office, duly executed before any person authorized to administer an oath, together with his official signature, within thirty days from the date of such notice.

3-a. The county clerk may designate from among the members of his staff, by a certificate filed in his office, any assistant to administer oaths of office to persons appointed notaries public by the secretary of state who appear at the county clerk's office for the purpose of executing such oaths.

4. The county clerk shall make proper index of commissions and official signatures filed with him. For filing and indexing the commission of appointment and official signature, the county clerk shall be paid a fee of one dollar by the appointee, which fee shall include the administration of the oath by the county clerk, should he administer the same.

5. If a person appointed notary public shall not file his oath of office as such notary public, in the office of the clerk of the county of his residence, within thirty days after the notice of his appointment as above provided, his appointment is deemed revoked and the fee filed with his application forfeited. However, after such revocation, any such notary public may reapply for a new appointment, but shall not be required to take and pass another examination during the term for which he was previously certified.

6. Each county clerk on or before the tenth day of each month shall make a report to the secretary of state for the preceding month, indicating the name and date of the qualification of each notary public and also the name of each notary public whose appointment was revoked and fee forfeited by his failure to qualify.

7. Except for changes made in an application for reappointment, the secretary shall receive a nonrefundable fee of ten dollars for changing the name or address of a notary public.

8. A duplicate identification card may be issued to a notary public for one lost, destroyed or damaged upon application therefor on a form prescribed by the secretary of state and upon payment of a non-refundable fee of ten dollars. Each such duplicate identification card shall have the word "duplicate" stamped across the face thereof and shall bear the same number as the one it replaces.

§ 132. Certificates of official character of notaries public.

The secretary of state or the county clerk of the county in which the commission of a notary public is filed may certify to the official character of such notary public and any notary public may file his autograph signature and a certificate of official character in the office of any county clerk of any county in the state and in any register's office in any county having a register and thereafter such county clerk may certify as to the official character of such notary public. The secretary of state shall collect for each certificate of official character issued by him the sum of one dollar. The county clerk and register of any county with whom a certificate of official character has been filed shall collect for filing the same the sum of one dollar. For each certificate of official character issued, with seal attached, by any county clerk, the sum of one dollar shall be collected by him.

§ 133. Certification of notarial signatures.

The county clerk of a county in whose office any notary public has qualified or has filed his autograph signature and a certificate of his official character, shall, when so requested and upon payment of a fee of fifty cents affix to any certificate of proof or acknowledgment or oath signed by such notary anywhere in the state of New York, a certificate under his hand and seal, stating that a commission or a certificate of his official character with his autograph signature has been filed in his office, and that he was at the time of taking such proof or acknowledgment or oath duly authorized to take the same; that he is well acquainted with the handwriting of such notary public or has compared the signature on the certificate of proof or acknowledgment or oath with the autograph signature deposited in his office by such notary public and believes that the signature is genuine. An instrument with such certificate of authentication of the county clerk affixed thereto shall be entitled to be read in evidence or to be recorded in any of the counties of this state in respect to which a certificate of a county clerk may be necessary for either purpose.

§ 134. Signature and seal of county clerk.

The signature and seal of a county clerk, upon a certificate of official character of a notary public or the signature of a county clerk upon a certificate of authentication of the signature and acts of a notary public or commissioner of deeds, may be a facsimile, printed, stamped, photographed or engraved thereon.

§ 135. Powers and duties; in general; of notaries public who are attorneys at law.

Every notary public duly qualified is hereby authorized and empowered within and throughout the state to administer oaths and affirmations, to take affidavits and depositions, to receive and certify acknowledgments or proof of deeds, mortgages and powers of attorney and other instruments in writing; to demand acceptance or payment of foreign and inland bills of exchange, promissory notes and obligations in writing, and to protest the same for non-acceptance or non-payment, as the case may require, and, for use in another jurisdiction, to exercise such other powers and duties as by the laws of nations and according to commicial usage, or by the laws of any other government or country may be exercised and performed by notaries public, provided that when exercising such powers he shall set forth the name of such other jurisdiction.

A notary public who is an attorney at law regularly admitted to practice in this state may, in his discretion, administer an oath or affirmation to or take the affidavit or acknowledgment of his client in respect of any matter, claim, action or proceeding.

For any misconduct by a notary public in the performance of any of his powers such notary public shall be liable to the parties injured for all damages sustained by them.

A notary public shall not, directly or indirectly, demand or receive for the protest for the non-payment of any note, or for the non-acceptance or non-payment of any bill of exchange, check or draft and giving the requisite notices and certificates of such protest, including his notarial seal, if affixed thereto, any greater fee or reward than seventy-five cents for such protest, and ten cents for each notice, not exceeding five, on any bill or note. Every notary public having a seal shall, except as otherwise provided, and when requested, affix his seal to such protest free of expense.

§ 135-a. Notary public or commissioner of deeds; acting without appointment; fraud in office.

1. Any person who holds himself out to the public as being entitled to act as a notary public or commissioner of deeds, or who assumed, uses or advertises the title of notary public or commissioner of deeds, or equivalent terms in any language, in such a manner as to convey the impression that he is a notary public or commissioner of deeds without having first been appointed as notary public or commissioner of deeds, or

2. A notary public or commissioner of deeds, who in the exercise of the powers, or in the performance of the duties of such office shall practice any fraud or deceit, the punishment for which is not otherwise provided for by this act, shall be guilty of a misdemeanor.

§ 136. Notarial fees.

A notary public shall be entitled to the following fees:

1. For administering an oath or affirmation, and certifying the same when required, except where another fee is specifically prescribed by statute, twenty-five cents.

2. For taking and certifying the acknowledgment or proof of execution of a written instrument, by one person, twenty-five cents, and by each additional person, twenty-five cents, for swearing each witness thereto, twenty-five cents.

§ 137. Statement as to authority of notaries public.

In exercising his powers pursuant to this article, a notary public, in addition to the venue of his act and his signature, shall print, typewrite, or stamp beneath his signature in black ink, his name, the words "Notary Public State of New York," the name of the county in which he originally qualified, and the date upon which his commission expires and, in addition, wherever required, a notary public shall also include the name of any county in which his certificate of official character is filed, using the words "Certificate filed .... County." A notary public who is duly licensed as an attorney and counsellor at law in this state may in his discretion, substitute the words "Attorney and Counsellor at Law" for the words "Notary Public." A notary public who has qualified or who has filed a certificate of official character in the office of the clerk in a county or counties within the city of New York must also affix to each instrument his official number or numbers in black ink, as given to him by the clerk or clerks of such county or counties at the time such notary qualified in such county or counties and, if the instrument is to be recorded in an office of the register of the city of New York in any county within such city and the notary has been given a number or numbers by such register or his predecessors in any county or counties, when his autographed signature and certificate are filed in such office or offices pursuant to this chapter, he shall also affix such number or numbers. No official act of such notary public shall be held invalid on account of the failure to comply with these provisions. If any notary public shall wilfully fail to comply with any of the provisions of this section, he shall be subject to disciplinary action by the secretary of state. In all the courts within this state the certificate of a notary public, over his signature, shall be received as presumptive evidence of the facts contained in such certificate; provided, that any person interested as a party to a suit may contradict, by other evidence, the certificate of a notary public.

§ 138. Powers of notaries public or other officers who are stockholders, directors, officers or employees of a corporation.

A notary public, justice of the supreme court, a judge, clerk, deputy clerk, or special deputy clerk of a court, an official examiner of title, or the mayor or recorder of a city, a justice of the peace, surrogate, special surrogate, special county judge, or commissioner of deeds, who is a stockholder, director, officer or employee of a corporation may take the acknowledgment or proof of any party to a written instrument executed to or by such corporation, or administer an oath to any other stockholder, director, officer, employee or agent of such corporation, and such notary public may protest for non-acceptance or non-payment, bills of exchange, drafts, checks, notes and other negotiable instruments owned or held for collection by such corporation; but none of the officers above named shall take the acknowledgment or proof of a written instrument by or to a corporation of which he is a stockholder, director, officer or employee, if such officer taking such acknowledgment or proof be a party executing such instrument, either individually or as a representative of such corporation, nor shall a notary public protest any negotiable instruments owned or held for collection by such corporation, if such notary public be individually a party to such instrument, or have a financial interest in the subject of same. All such acknowledgments or proofs of deeds, mortgages or other written instruments, relating to real property heretofore taken before any of the officers aforesaid are confirmed. This act shall not affect any action or legal proceeding now pending.

ADDITIONAL AUTHORITY

[N.Y. Pub. Off. Law]

§ 3. Qualifications for holding office.

* * *

3. Nothing herein contained shall operate to prevent a person regularly admitted to practice as an attorney and counsellor in the courts of record of this state, whose office for the practice of law is within the state, from accepting or retaining an appointment as a notary public, as provided in section one hundred thirty of the executive law, al-

though he resides in or removes to an adjoining state. For the purposes of accepting and retaining an appointment as a notary public such person shall be deemed a resident of the county where he maintains such office for the practice of law.

3-a. Nothing herein contained shall operate to prevent a person regularly admitted to practice as an attorney and counsellor in the courts of record of this state, whose office for the practice of law is within the city of New York, from accepting or retaining an appointment as a commissioner of deeds in and for the city of New York, as provided in section one hundred forty of the executive law, although he resides in or removes to another city in this state or to an adjoining state. For the purposes of accepting and retaining an appointment as a commissioner of deeds in and for the city of New York, such person shall be deemed a resident of the county where he maintains such office.

* * *

7. Nothing herein contained shall operate to prevent a person regularly admitted to practice as an attorney and counsellor in the courts of record of this state, whose office for the practice of law is within the state, from accepting or retaining an appointment as a commissioner of deeds in and for the city of New York, as provided in section one hundred forty of the executive law, although he resides in or removes to any other county in the state or an adjoining state. For the purposes of accepting and retaining an appointment as a commissioner of deeds such person shall be deemed a resident of the county where he maintains such office for the practice of law.

* * *

§ 8. Commissions of officers.

*** Commissions of notaries public shall be signed by the secretary of state, or by a person or persons in the department of state designated by the secretary of state, and shall be sent to the county clerk of the county in which such notaries public respectively reside. Commissions of commissioners of deeds in other states, territories and foreign countries, shall be signed by the secretary of state, or by a person or persons in the department of state designated by secretary of state. *** Every such written appointment shall be deemed the commission of the officer appointed, and if of a state officer, a duplicate or a certified copy thereof shall be recorded in the office of the department of state; if of a local officer it shall be sent to the clerk of the county in which the officer appointed shall then reside, who shall file the same in his office, and notify the officer appointed of his appointment.

§ 10.   Official oaths.

Every officer shall take and file the oath of office required by law, and every judicial officer of the unified court system, in addition, shall file a copy of said oath in the office of court administration, before he shall be entitled to enter upon the discharge of any of his official duties. An oath of office may be administered by a judge of the court of appeals, the attorney general, or by any officer authorized to take, within the state, the acknowledgment of the execution of a deed of real property, or by an officer in whose office the oath is required to be filed or by his duly designated assistant, or may be administered to any member of a body of officers, by a presiding officer or clerk, thereof, who shall have taken an oath of office. An oath of office may be administered to any state or local officer who is a member of the armed forces of the United States by any commissioned officer, in active service, of the armed forces of the United States. In addition to the requirements of any other law, the certificate of the officer in the armed forces administering the oath of office under this section shall state (a) the rank of the officer administering the oath, and (b) that the person taking the oath was at the time, enlisted, inducted, ordered or commissioned in or serving with, attached to or accompanying the armed forces of the United States. The fact that the officer administering the oath was at the time duly commissioned and in active service with the armed forces, shall be certified by the secretary of the army, secretary of the air force or by the secretary of the navy, as the case may be, of the United States, or by a person designated by him to make such certifications, but the place where such oath was administered need not be disclosed. The oath of office of a notary public or commissioner of deeds shall be filed in the office of the clerk of the county in which he shall reside. The oath of office of every state officer shall be filed in the office of the secretary of state; of every officer of a municipal corporation, including a school district, with the clerk thereof; and of every other officer, including the trustees and officers of a public library and the officers of boards of cooperative educational services, in the office of the clerk of the county in which he shall reside, if no place be otherwise provided by law for the filing thereof.

FEES

[N.Y. Civ. Prac. L. & R.]

§ 8009.   Oaths; acknowledgments; certification or exemplification.

Any authorized officer is entitled, for the services specified, to the following fees:

1. for administering an oath or affirmation, and certifying it when required, except where another fee is specifically prescribed by statute, in the counties within the city of New York, one dollar, and in all other counties, twenty-five cents.

2. for taking and certifying the acknowledgment or proof of the execution of a written instrument, twenty-five cents for one person and twenty-five cents for each additional person, and twenty-five cents for swearing each witness thereto; and

3. for certifying or exemplifying a typewritten or printed copy of any document, paper, book or record in his custody, except in the counties within the city of New York, three cents for each folio with a minimum fee of twenty-five cents.

[N.Y. Pub. Of. Law]

§ 68-a.   Fees for oath or acknowledgment.

Any officer, authorized to perform the services specified in this section, and to receive fees therefor, is entitled to the following fees:

1. For administering an oath or affirmation, and certifying the same when required, except where another fee is specially prescribed by statute, twenty-five cents.

2. For taking and certifying the acknowledgment or proof of the execution of a written instrument; by one person, twenty-five cents; and by each additional person, twenty-five cents; for swearing each witness thereto, twenty-five cents.

§ 69.   Fee for administering certain official oaths prohibited.

An officer is not entitled to a fee, for administering the oath of office to a member of the legislature, to any military officer, to an inspector of election, clerk of the poll, or to any other public officer or public employee.

OFFENSES

[N.Y. Penal Law]

§ 55.10.   Designation of offenses.

* * *

2. Misdemeanors.

* * *

(b) Any offense defined outside this chapter which is declared by law to be a misdemeanor without specification of the classification thereof or of the sentence therefor shall be deemed a class A misdemeanor.

* * *

§ 70.15. Sentences of imprisonment for misdemeanors and violation.

1. Class A misdemeanor. A sentence of imprisonment for a class A misdemeanor shall be a definite sentence. When such a sentence is imposed the term shall be fixed by the court, and shall not exceed one year; provided, however, that a sentence of imprisonment imposed upon a conviction to criminal possession of a weapon in the fourth degree as defined in subdivision one of section 265.01 must be for a period of no less than one year when the conviction was the result of a plea of guilty entered in satisfaction of an indictment or any count thereof charging the defendant with the class D violent felony offense of criminal possession of a weapon in the third degree as defined in subdivision four of section 265.02, except that the court may impose any other sentence authorized by law upon a person who has not been previously convicted in the five years immediately preceding the commission of the offense for a felony or a class A misdemeanor defined in this chapter, if the court having regard to the nature and circumstances of the crime and to the history and character of the defendant, is of the opinion that such sentence would be unduly harsh.

* * *

§ 80.05. Fines for misdemeanors and violation.

1. Class A misdemeanor. A sentence to pay a fine for a class A misdemeanor shall be a sentence to pay an amount, fixed by the court, not exceeding one thousand dollars, provided, however, that a sentence imposed for a violation of section 215.80 of this chapter may include a fine in an amount equivalent to double the value of the property unlawfully disposed of in the commission of the crime.

* * *

SAFE DEPOSIT BOXES

[N.Y. BANKING LAW]

§ 335. Special remedies where rental of safe deposit box is not paid or when safe deposit box is not vacated on termination of lease.

Every lessor shall be entitled to the following special remedies:

1. (a) If the amount due for the rental of any safe deposit box let by any lessor shall not have been paid for one year, or if the lessee thereof shall not have removed the contents thereof within thirty days from the termination of the lease therefore for any reason other than for nonpayment of rent, the lessor may, at the expiration of such period, send to the lessee of such safe deposit box, by registered or certified mail, return receipt requested, a notice in writing in a securely closed postpaid letter, directed to such person at his last known post-office address, as recorded upon the books of the lessor, notifying such lessee that if the amount due for the rental of such safe deposit box is not paid within thirty days from date, and/or if the contents thereof are not removed within thirty days from date, the lessor may, at any time thereafter, cause such safe deposit box to be opened, and the contents thereof to be inventoried and removed from such safe deposit box.

(b) At any time after the expiration of thirty days from the date of mailing such notice, and the failure of the lessee of the safe deposit box to pay the amount due for the rental thereof to the date of payment, and/or remove the contents thereof, the lessor may, in the presence of a notary public and of any officer of the lessor or any other employee of the lessor designated for such purpose by the lessor, cause such safe deposit box to be opened, and the contents thereof, if any, to be removed and inventoried. Such contents shall be retained by the lessor for safe-keeping for a period of not less than two years unless sooner removed by the lessee of the safe deposit box so opened. The charge for such safe-keeping shall not exceed the original rental of the safe deposit box so opened. The notary public shall file with the lessor a certificate under seal, which shall fully set out the date of the opening of such safe deposit box, the name of the lessee of such safe deposit box and a list of the contents, if any.

* * *

§ 605. Voluntary liquidation; sale of assets; forfeiture of charter by non-user.

1. Any corporate banking organization, the assets of which have a value at least equal to its liabilities, exclusive of any liability to shareholders or stockholders, as such, may voluntarily wind up its affairs; but no banking organization of which the superintendent has taken possession in accordance with the provisions of section six hundred six of this chapter shall take any steps for such voluntary dissolution until it has received the written approval of the superintendent.

2. To effect a voluntary dissolution a meeting of the stockholders or shareholders of any corporation shall be held upon not less than twenty days' written notice to each such stockholder or shareholder, either served personally or mailed to him at the address appearing upon the books of the corporation, and containing a statement of the purpose for which such meeting is called. Proof by affidavit of due service of such notice shall be filed in the office

of the corporation before or at the time of such meeting.

In the case of mutual savings bank, a meeting of its board of trustees shall be held upon like notice. Proof by affidavit of due service of such notice shall be filed in the office of the savings bank before or at the time of such meeting.

3. At such a meeting of stockholders or mutual shareholders, such stockholders or mutual shareholders may, by a vote of the owners of at least two-thirds in amount of the entire capital stock or capital of such corporation, direct that the corporation be closed and its business wound up. The proceedings of such meeting shall be entered in the minutes of such corporation.

At such a meeting of the board of trustees of a savings bank, the trustees may by vote of not less than two-thirds of their whole number, direct by resolution that the savings bank be closed and its business wound up. The vote on such resolution shall be recorded with the resolution in the minutes of the board of trustees.

A copy of the minutes of such meeting of stockholders or mutual shareholders or board of trustees, verified by the presiding officer and by the secretary of such meeting, shall be filed in the office of the superintendent within five days after the date of such meeting.

4. Within three months after the date of any such meeting, application may be made to the supreme court, after due notice to the superintendent, for an order declaring the business of such corporation closed. In a proper case the court shall make such order which shall prescribe the notice to be given to creditors and depositors to present their claims to the corporation for payment. Within five days after the making of such order, a certified copy thereof shall be filed in the office of the superintendent. Upon the entry of such order such corporation shall cease to do business and shall wind up it affairs, pay its creditors and depositors, if any, and, except in the case of a mutual savings bank, distribute any remaining assets among its shareholders or stockholders according to their respective rights and interests. Any petition, application, or motion to vacate, set aside, modify or amend such order so as to permit the corporation to resume business shall have incorporated therein a certificate of the superintendent certifying that after investigation the superintendent has found, and the banking board by a three-fifths vote of all its members has found, that the public convenience and advantage will be promoted by the granting of said petition, application or motion.

4-a. (a) Such corporation may, at any time after entry of the order described in subdivision four of this section, cause to be mailed to each person claiming to be, or appearing upon the books of such corporation to be

(1) the owner of any personal property in the custody or possession of such corporation as bailee or depositary for hire or otherwise, including the contents of any safe, vault or box theretofore opened for non-payment of rental in accordance with the provisions of this chapter, or

(2) the lessee of any safe, vault or box, a notice in writing directed by registered mail to such person at his last address as the same appears on the books of such corporation or at his last known address if no address appears on such books, notifying such person to remove all such property or the contents of any such safe, vault or box, within a period stated in said notice, which period shall be not less than sixty days from the date of such notice, and further notifying such person of the terms and provisions of this subdivision. The contract of bailment or of deposit for hire, or lease of safe, vault or box, if any, between the person to whom such notice is mailed and such corporation shall cease and determine upon the date for removal fixed in such notice. Such person shall have a claim against such corporation for the amount of the unearned rent or charges, if any, paid by such person from the date fixed in such notice, if the property or contents is removed on or before such date, or from the date of actual removal, if the property or contents is removed after such date.

(b) If such property or contents shall not be removed, and all rent or storage and other charges theretofore accrued, if any, shall not be paid, within the time fixed by such notice, such corporation shall, within thirty days thereafter, cause such property to be inventoried, or such safe, vault or box, or any package, parcel or receptacle in the custody or possession of such corporation as bailee or depositary for hire or otherwise, to be opened and the contents, if any, to be removed and inventoried, in the presence of an officer of such corporation and of a notary public, not an officer or employee thereof. Such property or contents shall thereupon be sealed up by such notary public in a package distinctly marked by him with the name of the person in whose name such property or such safe, vault, box, package, parcel or receptacle stands upon the books of such corporation, and a copy of the inventory of the property therein shall be certified and attached thereto by such notary public. Such package may be kept in such place as the corporation, with the approval of the superintendent, may determine, at the expense and risk of the person in whose name it stands until delivered to such person or until sold, destroyed or otherwise disposed of as hereinafter provided. Such package may, from time to time, pending final disposition of its contents, be opened in the presence of an officer of such corporation and of a notary public, not an officer or employee thereof, for inspection or appraisal, or to enable such corporation to exercise any of the powers conferred or duties imposed by this article. Whenever such package is opened, the notary shall endorse on the outside thereof the date of the opening and re-sealing, and shall certify and attach thereto a list of the articles, if any, removed therefrom, or placed or replaced therein, and an affidavit of the officer in whose presence it was opened showing the reason for opening the same.

(c) At any time prior to the sale, destruction or other disposition of the contents thereof, the person in whose name such package stands may require the delivery thereof upon payment of all rental or storage charges accrued, and all other charges or expenses paid or incurred to the date of delivery with respect to such package or the contents thereof, including the cost of inventorying or of opening and inventorying, the fees of the notary public, the cost of preparing and mailing the notice, and advertising, if any. If the principal of, or interest, income, or dividends on any bonds, stock certificates, promissory notes, choses in action or other securities contained in such package, is or becomes due and payable while it is in the possession of such corporation, it may at it election collect such principal, interest, income or dividends, and from the proceeds thereof may deduct all such sums due for rental and other charges, until the time of such collection. The balance, if any, of the amount or amounts so collected shall be disposed of as hereafter in paragraph (e) of this subdivision and in subdivision five hereof provided.

(d) After the expiration of one year from the time of mailing the notice in paragraph (a) of this subdivision described, such corporation may apply to the supreme court for an order authorizing such corporation to sell, destroy or otherwise dispose of the contents of such package. In a proper case, the court shall make such order upon such terms and conditions as justice may require. The application for an order of the supreme court pursuant to this paragraph shall be made upon an order to show cause, which shall provide that notice thereof to the person in whose name such package stands and to any other person claiming or appearing to have an interest therein, shall be published, mailed or given in such other manner as the court may prescribe. Whenever, pursuant to the provisions of this paragraph, a corporation is given the power to sell the contents of any package, such power to sell shall be deemed a power to sell in satisfaction of a lien or a non-payment of rental or storage charges accrued, and all other charges and expenses paid or incurred to the date of sale with respect to such package and the contents thereof, including the charges and expenses described in paragraph (c) hereof. Such power to sell, or the power to destroy or otherwise dispose of, when authorized pursuant to the provisions of this paragraph, shall be deemed to include the power to see, destroy or otherwise

dispose of, as the case may be, any bonds, stock certificates, promissory notes, choses in action, or other securities, and any other tangible or intangible property contained in any package, regardless of whether or not it shall appear from such securities or properties that the person in whose name the package stands, possesses title to or interest in such securities or other properties, or power to transfer such title or interest, and any sale of such securities or properties, pursuant to this paragraph, shall vest good title thereto in the purchaser thereof.

(e) From the proceeds of any sale, such corporation shall deduct all rental or storage charges accrued, and all other charges and expenses paid or incurred to the date of sale, including the charges and expenses described in paragraph (c) hereof, and the expenses of sale. The balance of such proceeds, if any, shall be credited to the person in whose name such package stood and, unless sooner paid over to the superintendent pursuant to subdivision five hereof, shall be paid over to such person, his assignee or legal representative on satisfactory evidence of identity.

(f) The provisions of this subdivision do not affect or preclude any other remedy by action or otherwise for the enforcement of the claims or rights of such corporation against the person in whose name any property, or any safe, vault, box, package, parcel or receptacle stands, nor affect, nor bar the right of such corporation to recover, before sale, any debt or claim due it or, after sale, so much of the debt or claim as shall not be paid by the proceeds of the sale.

(g) The procedure prescribed in this subdivision may be followed by any corporation winding up its affairs in accordance with the provisions of this section, notwithstanding the fact that such corporation may have commenced proceedings to open, or may have opened, any safe, vault or box for nonpayment of rental in accordance with other provisions of this chapter and notwithstanding the contents of any notice that may have been given by such corporation in accordance with any requirement of this section.

* * *

OATHS AND AFFIRMATIONS

[N.Y. Civ. Prac. L. & R.]

§ **2309.** Oaths and affirmations.

(a) **Persons authorized to administer.** Unless otherwise provided, an oath or affirmation may be administered by any person authorized to take acknowledgments of deeds by the real property law. Any person authorized by the laws of this state to receive evidence may administer an oath or affirmation for that purpose. An oath to a juror or jurors may be administered by a clerk of court and his deputies. This section shall not apply to an oath of office.

(b) Form. An oath or affirmation shall be administered in a form calculated to awaken the conscience and impress the mind of the person taking it in accordance with his religious or ethical beliefs.

(c) Oaths and affirmations taken without the state. An oath or affirmation taken without the state shall be treated as if taken within the state if it is accompanied by such certificate or certificates as would be required to entitle a deed acknowledged without the state to be recorded within the state if such deed had been acknowledged before the officer who administered the oath or affirmation.

(d) Form of certificate of oath or affirmation administered by officer of the armed forces of the United States. The certificate of an oath or affirmation administered within or without the state or the United States, by an officer of the armed forces of the United States authorized by the real property law to take acknowledgment of deeds, shall state:

1. the rank and serial number of the officer before whom the oath or affirmation is taken and the command to which he is attached;

2. that the person taking the oath or affirmation was, at the time of taking it, a person enlisted or commissioned in or serving in or with the armed forces of the United States or the dependent of such a person, or a person attached to or accompanying the armed forces of the United States; and

3. the serial number of the person who takes, or whose dependent takes the oath or affirmation, if such person is enlisted or commissioned in the armed forces of the United States. The place where such oath or affidavit is taken need not be disclosed.

ACKNOWLEDGMENTS

[N.Y. REAL PROP. LAW]

§ 298. Acknowledgments and proofs within the state.

The acknowledgment or proof, within the state, of a conveyance of real property situate in this state may be made: 1. At any place within the state, before (a) a justice of the supreme court; (b) an official examiner of title; (c) an official referee; or (d) a notary public.

2. Within the district wherein such officer is authorized to perform official duties, before (a) a judge or clerk of any court of record; (b) a commissioner of deeds outside of the city of New York, or a commissioner of deeds of the city of New York within the five counties comprising the city of New York; (c) the mayor or recorder of a city; (d) a surrogate, special surrogate, or special county judge;

or (e) the county clerk or other recording officer of a county.

3. Before a justice of the peace, town councilman, village police, justice or a judge of any court of inferior local jurisdiction, anywhere within the county containing the town, village or city in which he is authorized to perform official duties.

§ 299. Acknowledgments and proofs without the state, but within the United States or any territory, possession, or dependency thereof.

The acknowledgment or proof of a conveyance of real property situate in this state, if made (a) without the state but within the United States, (b) within any territory, possession, or dependency of the United States, or (c) within any place over which the United States, at the time when such acknowledgment or proof is taken, has or exercises jurisdiction, sovereignty, control, or a protectorate, may be made before any of the following officers acting within his territorial jurisdiction or within that of the court of which he is an officer:

1. A judge or other presiding officer of any court having a seal, or the clerk or other certifying officer thereof.

2. A mayor or other chief civil officer of any city or other political subdivision.

3. A notary public.

4. A commissioner of deeds appointed pursuant to the laws of this state to take acknowledgments or proofs without this state.

5. Any person authorized, by the laws of the state, District of Columbia, territory, possession, dependency, or other place where the acknowledgment or proof is made, to take the acknowledgment or proof of deeds to be recorded therein.

§ 299-a. Acknowledgment to conform to law of New York or of place where taken; certificate of conformity.

An acknowledgment or proof made pursuant to the provisions of section two hundred ninety-nine of this chapter may be taken in the manner prescribed either by the laws of the state of New York or by the laws of the state, District of Columbia, territory, possession, dependency, or other place where the acknowledgment or proof is taken. The acknowledgment or proof, if taken in the manner prescribed by such state, District of Columbia, territory, possession, dependency, other place, must be accompanied by a certificate to the effect that it conforms with such laws. Such certificate may be made by

(a) An attorney-at-law admitted to practice in the state of New York, resident in the place where the acknowledgment or proof is taken, or by

(b) An attorney-at-law admitted to practice in

the state, District of Columbia, territory, possession, dependency, or other place where the acknowledgment or proof is taken, or by

(c) Any other person deemed qualified by any court of the state of New York, if, in any action, proceeding, or other matter pending before such court, it be necessary to determine that such acknowledgment or proof conforms with the laws of such state, District of Columbia, territory, possession, dependency, or other place; or by the supreme court of the state of New York, on application for such determination. The justice, judge, surrogate, or other presiding judicial officer shall append to the instrument so acknowledged or proved his signed statement that he deemed such person qualified to make such certificate.

2. (a) The signature to such a certificate of conformity shall be presumptively genuine, and the qualification of the person whose name is so signed as a person authorized to make such certificate shall be presumptively established by the recital thereof in the certificate.

(b) The statement of a judicial officer appended to the instrument that he deemed the person making such certificate qualified shall establish the qualification of the person designated therein to make such certificate; and the recording, filing, registering or use as evidence of the instrument shall not depend on the power of the court to make the statement and proof shall not be required of any action, proceeding, matter or application in which or in connection with which the statement is made.

(c) When an instrument so acknowledged or proved is accompanied by the certificate of conformity and the statement of a judicial officer, if any be required, the acknowledgment or proof of the instrument, for the purpose of recording, filing or registering in any recording or filing office in this state or for use as evidence, shall be equivalent to one taken or made in the form prescribed by law for use in this state; and if the acknowledgment or proof is properly authenticated, where authentication is required by law, and if the instrument be otherwise entitled to record, filing or registering, such instrument, together with the acknowledgment or proof, the certificate of conformity and any certificate of authentication or statement of a judicial officer, may be recorded, filed or registered in any recording or filing office in this state, and shall be so recorded, filed or registered upon payment or tender of lawful fees therefor. In fixing the fees of a recording, filing or registering officer, the certificate of conformity and the statement of a judicial officer appended, if any, shall be treated as certificates of authentication required by other provisions of this chapter.

§ 300. Acknowledgment and proofs by persons in or with the armed forces of the United States.

The acknowledgment or proof of a conveyance of real property situate in this state, if made by a person enlisted or commissioned in or serving in or with the armed forces of the United States or by a dependent of any such person, wherever located, or by a person attached to or accompanying the armed forces of the United States, whether made within or without the United States, may be made before any commissioned officer in active service of the armed forces of the United States with the rank of second lieutenant or higher in the Army, Air Force or Marine Corps, or ensign or higher in the Navy or Coast Guard, or with equivalent rank in any other component part of the armed forces of the United States.

In addition to the requirements of sections three hundred and three, three hundred and four, and three hundred and six of this chapter, the certificate of an acknowledgment or proof taken under this section shall state (a) the rank and serial number of the officer taking the same, and the command to which he is attached, (b) that the person making such acknowledgment or proof was, at the time of making the same, enlisted or commissioned in or serving in or with the armed forces of the United States or the dependent of such a person, or a person attached to or accompanying the armed forces of the United States, and (c) the serial number of the person who makes, or whose dependent makes the acknowledgment or proof if such person is enlisted or commissioned in the armed forces of the United States. The place where such acknowledgment or proof is taken need not be disclosed.

No authentication of the officer's certificate of acknowledgment or proof shall be required.

Notwithstanding any of the provisions of this section, the acknowledgment or proof of a conveyance of real property situate in this state may also be made as provided in sections two hundred ninety-eight, two hundred ninety-nine, two hundred ninety-nine-a, three hundred one, and three hundred one-a, of this chapter.

§ 301. Acknowledgments and proofs in foreign countries.

The acknowledgment or proof of a conveyance of real property situate in this state may be made in foreign countries before any of the following officers acting within his territorial jurisdiction or within that of the court of which he is an officer:

1. An ambassador, envoy, minister, charge d'affaires, secretary of legation, consul-general, consul, vice-consul, consular agent, vice-consular agent, or any other diplomatic or consular agent or repre-

sentative of the United States, appointed or accredited to, and residing within, the country where the acknowledgment of proof is taken.

2. A judge or other presiding officer of any court having a seal, or the clerk or other certifying officer thereof.

3. A mayor or other chief civil officer of any city or other political subdivision.

4. A notary public.

5. A commissioner of deeds appointed pursuant to the laws of this state to take acknowledgments or proofs without this state.

6. A person residing in, or going to, the country where the acknowledgment or proof is to be taken, and specially authorized for that purpose by a commission issued to him under the seal of the supreme court of the state of New York.

7. Any person authorized, by the laws of the country where the acknowledgment or proof is made, to take acknowledgments of conveyances of real estate or to administer oaths in proof of the execution thereof.

§ 301-a. Acknowledgment to conform to law of New York or of foreign country; certificate of conformity.

1. An acknowledgment or proof made pursuant to the provisions of section three hundred one of this chapter may be taken in the manner prescribed either by laws of the state of New York or by the laws of the country where the acknowledgment or proof is taken. The acknowledgment or proof, if taken in the manner prescribed by the laws of such foreign country, must be accompanied by a certificate to the effect that it conforms with such laws. Such certificate may be made by

(a) An attorney-at-law admitted to practice in the state of New York, resident in such foreign country, or by

(b) A consular officer of the United States, resident in such foreign country, under the seal of his office, or by

(c) A consular officer of such foreign country, resident in the state of New York, under the seal of his office, or by

(d) Any other person deemed qualified by any court of the state of New York, if, in any action, proceeding, or other matter pending before such court, it be necessary to determine that such acknowledgment or proof conforms with the laws of such foreign country; or by the supreme court of the state of New York, on application for such determination.

The justice, judge, surrogate, or other presiding judicial officer shall append to the instrument so acknowledged or proved his signed statement that he deemed such person qualified to make such certificate.

2. (a) The signature to such a certificate of conformity shall be presumptively genuine, and the qualification of the person whose name is so signed as a person authorized to make such certificate shall be presumptively established by the recital thereof in the certificate.

(b) The statement of a judicial officer appended to the instrument that he deemed the person making such certificate qualified shall establish the qualification of the person designated therein to make such certificate; and the recording, filing, registering or use as evidence of the instrument shall not depend on the power of the court to make the statement and proof shall not be required of any action, proceeding, matter or application in which or in connection with which the statement is made.

(c) When an instrument so acknowledged or proved is accompanied by the certificate of conformity and the statement of a judicial officer, if any be required, the acknowledgment or proof of the instrument, for the purpose of recording, filing or registering in any recording or filing office in this state or for use as evidence, shall be equivalent to one taken or made in the form prescribed by law for use in this state; and if the acknowledgment or proof is properly authenticated, where authentication is required by law, and if the instrument be otherwise entitled to record, filing or registering, such instrument, together with the acknowledgment or proof, the certificate of conformity and any certificate of authentication or statement of a judicial officer, may be recorded, filed or registered in any recording or filing office in this state, and shall be so recorded, filed or registered upon payment or tender of lawful fees therefor. In fixing the fees of a recording, filing or registering officer, the certificate of conformity and the statement of a judicial officer appended, if any, shall be treated as certificates of authentication required by other provisions of this chapter.

§ 302. Acknowledgments and proofs by married women.

The acknowledgment or proof of a conveyance of real property, within the state, or of any other written instrument, may be made by a married woman the same as if unmarried.

§ 303. Requisites of acknowledgments.

An acknowledgment must not be taken by any officer unless he knows or has satisfactory evidence, that the person making it is the person described in and who executed such instrument.

§ 304. Proof of subscribing witness.

When the execution of a conveyance is proved by a subscribing witness, such witness must state his own place of residence, and if his place of residence is in a city, the street and street number, if any thereof, and that he knew the person described in and who executed the conveyance. The proof must not be taken unless the officer is personally acquainted with such witness, or has satisfactory evidence that he is the same person, who was a subscribing witness to the conveyance.

§ 305. Compelling witnesses to testify.

On the application of a grantee in a conveyance, his heir or personal representative, or a person claiming under either of them, verified by the oath of the applicant, stating that a witness to the conveyance, residing in the county where the application is made, refuses to appear and testify concerning its execution, and that such conveyance can not be proved without his testimony, any officer authorized to take, within the state, acknowledgment or proof of conveyance of real property may issue a subpoena, requiring such witness to attend and testify before him concerning the execution of the conveyance. A subpoena issued under his section shall be regulated by the civil practice law and rules.

§ 306. Certificate of acknowledgment or proof.

A person taking the acknowledgment or proof of a conveyance must indorse thereupon or attach thereto, a certificate, signed by himself, stating all the matters required to be done, known, or proved on the taking of such acknowledgment or proof; together with the name and substance of the testimony of each witness examined before him, and if a subscribing witness, his place of residence.

Any conveyance which has heretofore been recorded, or which may hereafter be recorded, shall be deemed to have been duly acknowledged or proved and properly authenticated, when ten years have elapsed since such recording; saving, however, the rights of every purchaser in good faith and for a valuable consideration deriving title from the same vendor or grantor, his heirs or devisees, to the same property or any portion thereof, whose conveyances shall have been duly recorded before the said period of ten years shall have elapsed.

§ 307. When certificate to state time and place.

When the acknowledgment or proof is taken by a commissioner of deeds appointed pursuant to the laws of this state to take acknowledgments or proofs without this state, whether within or without the United States, the certificate must also state the day on which, and the city or other political subdivision, and the state or country or other place in which, the same was taken.

§ 308. When certificate must be under seal.

1. When a certificate of acknowledgment or proof is made without this state, whether within or without the United States, (a) if made by a judge or other presiding officer of a court having a seal, or by the clerk or other certifying officer thereof, such certificate must be under the seal of such court; (b) if made by a commissioner of deeds appointed pursuant to the laws of this state to take acknowledgments or proofs without this state, such certificate must be under his seal of office; (c) if made by any officer specified in subdivision one of section three hundred one of this chapter, such certificate must be under the seal of the legation or consulate to which such officer is attached.

2. Any certificate, required by the provisions of section three hundred eleven of this chapter to be authenticated, must be so authenticated, in addition to being under seal as provided in this section.

§ 309. Acknowledgment by corporation and form of certificate.

The acknowledgment of a conveyance or other instrument by a corporation, must be made by some officer, or in case of a dissolved corporation, by some officer or director thereof authorized to execute the same by the board of directors of said corporation. The certificate of acknowledgment must conform substantially with one of the following alternative forms, the blanks being properly filled:

State of New York]
                    ] ss.:
County of ......]

On the .... day of .... in the year .... before me personally came .... to me known, who, being by me duly sworn, did depose and say that he resides in .... (if the place of residence is in a city, include the street and street number, if any, thereof); that he is the (president or other officer or director) of the (name of corporation), the corporation described in and which executed the above instrument; that he knows the seal of said corporation; that the seal affixed to said instrument is such corporate seal; that it was so affixed by order of the board of directors of said corporation, and that he signed his name thereto by like order.

(Signature and office of
person taking acknowledgment.)

State of New York]
           ] ss.:
County of .....]

On the .... day of .... in the year .... before me personally came .... to me known, who, being by me duly sworn, did depose and say that he resides in .... (if the place of residence is in a city, include the street and street number, if any, thereof); that he is the (president or other officer or director) of the (name of corporation), the corporation described in and which executed the above instrument; and that he signed his name thereto by order of the board of directors of said corporation.

(Signature and office of
person taking acknowledgment.)

§ 310. Authentication of acknowledgments and proofs made within the state.

1. When a certificate of acknowledgment or proof is made, within this state, by a commissioner of deeds, a justice of the peace, town councilman, village police justice, or a judge of any court of inferior local jurisdiction, such certificate does not entitle the conveyance so acknowledged or proved to be read in evidence or recorded in any county of this state except a county in which the officer making such certificate is authorized to act at the time of making the same, unless such certificate is authenticated by a certificate of the clerk of such county; provided, however, that all certificates of acknowledgment or proof, made by a commissioner of deeds of the city of New York residing in any part therein, shall be authenticated by the clerk of any county within said city, in whose office such commissioner of deeds shall have filed a certificate under the hand and seal of the city clerk of said city, showing the appointment and term of office of such commissioner; and no other certificates shall be required from any other officer to entitle such conveyance to be read in evidence or recorded in any county of this state.

2. Except as provided in this section, no certificate of authentication shall be required to entitle a conveyance to be read in evidence or recorded in this state when acknowledged or proved before any officer designated in section two hundred ninety-eight of this article to take such acknowledgment or proof, nor shall such authentication be required for recording in the office of the city register of the city of New York of such acknowledgment or proof by a commissioner of deeds of the city of New York.

§ 311. Authentication of acknowledgments and proofs made without the state.

1. When a certificate of acknowledgment or proof is made, either within or without the United States, by a commissioner of deeds appointed pursuant to the laws of this state to take acknowledgments or proofs without this state, the conveyance so acknowledged or proved is not entitled to be read in evidence or recorded in this state, except as provided in subdivision five of section one hundred eight of the executive law, unless such certificate is authenticated by the certificate of the secretary of state of the state of New York.

2. When a certificate of acknowledgment or proof is made by a notary public in a foreign country other than Canada, the conveyance so acknowledged or proved is not entitled to be read in evidence or recorded in this state unless such certificate is authenticated (a) by the certificate of the clerk or other certifying officer of a court in the district in which such acknowledgment or proof was made, under the seal of such court, or (b) by the certificate of the clerk, register, recorder, or other recording officer of the district in which such acknowledgment or proof was made, or (c) by the certificate of the officer having charge of the official records of the appointment of such notary, or having a record of the signature of such notary, or (d) by the certificate of a consular officer of the United States resident in such country.

3. When a certificate of acknowledgment or proof, made by the mayor or other chief civil officer of a city or other political subdivision, is not under the seal of such city or other political subdivision, the conveyance so acknowledged or proved is not entitled to be read in evidence or recorded in this state unless such certificate is authenticated by the certificate of the clerk of such city or other political subdivision, or by the certificate of a consular officer of the United States resident in the country where the acknowledgment or proof was made.

4. When a certificate of acknowledgment or proof is made pursuant to the provisions of subdivision five of section two hundred ninety-nine or of subdivision seven of section three hundred one of this chapter by an officer or person not elsewhere in either of said sections specifically designated to take acknowledgments or proofs, the conveyance so acknowledged or proved is not entitled to be read in evidence or recorded within this state unless such certificate is authenticated (a) by the certificate of the secretary of state of a state, or of the secretary of a territory, of the United States, or (b) by the certificate of any officer designated in subdivision three of this section to authenticate certificates of acknowledgment or proof, or (c) by the certificate of any officer designated in clauses (a) or (b) of

subdivision two of this section to authenticate certificates of acknowledgment or proof, or (d) by the certificate of the officer having charge of the official records showing that the person taking the acknowledgment or proof is such officer as he purports to be, or having a record of the signature of such person.

5. Except as provided in this section, no certificate of authentication shall be required to entitle a conveyance to be read in evidence or recorded in this state when acknowledged or proved before any officer designated in section two hundred ninety-nine or in section three hundred one of this chapter to take such acknowledgment or proof.

§ 312. Contents of certificate of authentication.

1. An officer authenticating a certificate of acknowledgment or proof must subjoin or attach to the original certificate a certificate under his hand.

2. When the certificate of acknowledgment or proof is made by a notary public, without the state but within the United States or within any territory, possession, or dependency of the United States, or within any place over which the United States, at the time when such acknowledgment or proof is taken, has or exercises jurisdiction, sovereignty, control, or a protectorate, the certificate of authentication must state in substance that, at the time when such original certificate purports to have been made, the person whose name is subscribed to the certificate was such officer as he is therein represented to be.

In every other case the certificate of authentication must state in substance (a) that, at the time when such original certificate purports to have been made, the person whose name is subscribed to the original certificate was such officer as he is therein represented to be; (b) that the authenticating officer is acquainted with the handwriting of the officer making the original certificate, or has compared the signature of such officer upon the original certificate with a specimen of his signature filed or deposited in the office of such authenticating officer, or recorded, filed, or deposited, pursuant to law, in any other place, and believes the signature upon the original certificate is genuine; and (c), if the original certificate is required to be under seal, that the authenticating officer has compared the impression of the seal affixed thereto with a specimen impression thereof filed or deposited in his office, or recorded, filed, or deposited, pursuant to law, in any other place, and believes the impression of the seal upon the original certificate is genuine.

3. When such original certificate is made pursuant to subdivision five of section two hundred ninety-nine of this chapter, such certificate of au-

thentication must also specify that the person making such original certificate, at the time when it purports to have been made, was authorized, by the laws of the state, District of Columbia, territory, possession, dependency, or other place where the acknowledgment or proof was made, to take the acknowledgment or proof of deeds to be recorded therein.

4. When such original certificate is made pursuant to subdivision seven of section three hundred one of this chapter, such certificate of authentication must also specify that the person making such original certificate, at the time when it purports to have been made, was authorized, by the laws of the country where the acknowledgment or proof was made, to take acknowledgments of conveyances of real estate or to administer oaths in proof of the execution thereof.

§ 313. Notary public.

The term "notary public," as used in sections two hundred ninety-nine, three hundred one, three hundred eight, and three hundred eleven, of this chapter, includes any person appointed to perform notarial functions.

§ 330. Officers guilty of malfeasance liable for damages.

An officer authorized to take the acknowledgment or proof of a conveyance or other instrument, or to certify such proof or acknowledgment, or to record the same, who is guilty of malfeasance or fraudulent practice in the execution of any duty prescribed by law in relation thereto, is liable in damages to the person injured.

DEPOSITIONS

[N.Y. Civ. Prac. L. & R.]

RULE 3113. Conduct of the examination.

(a) **Persons before whom depositions may be taken.** Depositions may be taken before any of the following persons except an attorney, or employee of an attorney, for a party or prospective party and except a person who would be disqualified to act as a juror because of interest in the event or consanguinity or affinity to a party:

1. within the state, a person authorized by the laws of the state to administer oaths;

2. without the state but within the United States or within a territory or possession subject to the dominion of the United States, a person authorized to take acknowledgments of deeds outside of the state by the real property law of the state or to administer oaths by the laws of the United States or

of the place where the deposition is taken; and

3. in a foreign country, any diplomatic or consular agent or representative of the United States, appointed or accredited to, and residing within, the country, or a person appointed by commission or under letters rogatory, or an officer of the armed forces authorized to take the acknowledgment of deeds.

Officers may be designated in notices or commissions either by name or descriptive title and letters rogatory may be addressed "To the Appropriate Authority in (here name the state or country)."

(b) Oath of witness; recording of testimony; objections; continuous examination; written questions read by examining officer. The officer before whom the deposition is to be taken shall put the witness on oath and shall personally, or by someone acting under his direction, record the testimony. The testimony shall be recorded by stenographic or other means, subject to such rules as may be adopted by the appellate division in the department where the action is pending. All objections made at the time of the examination to the qualifications of the officer taking the deposition or the person recording it, or to the manner of taking it, or to the testimony presented, or to the conduct of any person, and any other objection to the proceedings, shall be noted by the officer upon the deposition and the deposition shall proceed subject to the right of a person to apply for a protective order. The deposition shall be taken continuously and without unreasonable adjournment, unless the court otherwise orders or the witness and parties present otherwise agree. In lieu of participating in an oral examination, any party served with notice of taking a deposition may transmit written questions to the officer, who shall propound them to the witness and record the answers.

(c) Examination and cross-examination. Examination and cross-examination of deponents shall proceed as permitted in the trial of actions in open court. When the deposition of a party is taken at the instance of an adverse party, the deponent may be cross-examined by his own attorney. Cross-examination need not be limited to the subject matter of the examination in chief.

RULE 3114. Examination of witness who does not understand the English language.

If the witness to be examined does not understand the English language, the examining party must, at his own expense, provide a translation of all questions and answers. Where the court settles questions, it may settle them in the foreign language and in English. It may use the services of one or more experts whose compensation shall be paid by the party seeking the examination and may be taxed as a disbursement.

RULE 3116. Signing deposition; physical preparation; copies.

(a) Signing. The deposition shall be submitted to the witness for examination and shall be read to or by him, and any changes in form or substance which the witness desires to make shall be entered at the end of the deposition with a statement of the reasons given by the witness for making them. The deposition shall then be signed by the witness before any officer authorized to administer an oath, except that a witness who is an adverse party shall not be required to sign such deposition upon thirty days prior written notice to return the examination signed. If a witness, other than an adverse party, fails to sign the deposition, the officer before whom the deposition was taken shall sign it and state on the record the fact of the witness' failure or refusal to sign, together with any reason given. The deposition may then be used as fully as though signed.

(b) Certification and filing by officer. The officer before whom the deposition was taken shall certify on the deposition that the witness was duly sworn by him and that the deposition is a true record of the testimony given by the witness. He shall list all appearances by the parties and attorneys. If the deposition was taken on written questions, he shall attach to it the copy of the notice and written questions received by him. He shall then securely seal the deposition in an envelope endorsed with the title of the action and the index number of the action, if one has been assigned, and marked "Deposition of (here insert name of witness)" and shall promptly file it with, or send it by registered or certified mail to the clerk of the court where the case is to be tried. The deposition shall always be open to the inspection of the parties, each of whom is entitled to make copies thereof. If a copy of the deposition is furnished to each party or if the parties stipulate to waive filing, the officer need not file the original but may deliver it to the party taking the deposition.

(c) Exhibits. Documentary evidence exhibited before the officer or exhibits marked for identification during the examination of the witness shall be annexed to and returned with the deposition. However, if requested by the party producing documentary evidence or on exhibit, the officer shall mark it for identification as an exhibit in the case, give each party an opportunity to copy or inspect it, and return it to the party offering it, and it may then be used in the same manner as if annexed to and returned with the deposition.

(d) Expenses of taking. Unless the court orders otherwise, the party taking the deposition shall bear the expense thereof.

(e) Errors of officer or person transcribing. Errors and irregularities of the officer or the person transcribing the deposition are waived unless a motion to suppress the deposition or some part thereof is made with reasonable promptness after such defect is, or with due diligence might have been, ascertained.

COMMISSIONERS

[N.Y. Exec. Law]

§ 96. Fees and refunds.

Except as otherwise provided by section ninety-six-a of this chapter, the department of state shall collect the following fees:

* * *

6. For a certificate as to the official character of a commissioner of deeds residing in another state or foreign country, one dollar.

* * *

§ 139. Commissioners of deeds within the state.

1. Commissioners of deeds in the cities of this state shall be appointed by the common councils of such cities respectively, and shall hold office for the term of two years from the date of their appointment, and until others are appointed in their places. A vacancy occurring during the term for which any commissioner shall be appointed, shall be filed by the common council. The common council of the several cities of this state, except in cities of this state situate in a county which has a population of not less than one hundred and eighty thousand, and not more than six hundred and fifty thousand, according to the last state or federal enumeration, shall at the end of every even numbered year, by resolution of the board, determine the number of commissioners of deeds to be appointed for such cities respectively.

2. The term of office of each commissioner of deeds appointed by the common council in cities of this state situate in a county which has a population of not less than one hundred and eighty thousand, and not more than six hundred and fifty thousand, according to the last state or federal enumeration, shall expire on the thirty-first of December of the even numbered year next after he shall be appointed. The common council of any such city shall in the month of November in every even numbered year, by resolution, determine the number of commissioners of deeds to be appointed in such cities, respectively, for the next succeeding two years.

3. Any person who resides in or maintains an office or other place of business in any such city and who resides in the county in which said city is situated shall be eligible to appointment. Such commissioners of deeds may be appointed by the common council by resolution, and the city clerk

shall immediately after such appointment, file a certificate thereof with the county clerk of the county in which such city is situate, specifying the term for which the said commissioners of deeds shall have been appointed; the county clerk shall thereupon notify such persons of their appointment, and such persons so appointed shall qualify by filing with him his oath of office, duly executed before such county clerk or before any person authorized to administer an oath, together with his official signature, within thirty days from the date of such notice.

4. The county clerk shall make a proper index of certificates of appointment and official signatures filed with him. For filing and indexing the certificate of appointment and official signature, the county clerk shall be paid a fee of one dollar by the appointee, which fee shall include the administration of the oath by the county clerk, should he administer the same.

5. If a person appointed commissioner of deeds shall not file his oath of office as such commissioner of deeds, in the office of the clerk of the county of his residence, within thirty days after the notice of his appointment as above provided, his appointment is deemed revoked and the fee filed with his application forfeited.

6. A commissioner of deeds may file his autograph signature and certificate of appointment in the office of any county clerk, and the county clerk of the county in which such city is located, upon request of any commissioner appointed under the provisions of this section and upon payment of twenty-five cents for each certificate, must make and deliver to such commissioner such number of certificates as may be required. Such certificates shall be issued under the hand and seal of the county clerk of the county in which such city is located, showing the appointment and term of office of such commissioner and stating the county in which he resides. Such a certificate may be filed in the office of any county clerk upon the payment of one dollar for such filing in each office. The clerks of the counties outside the city of New York, shall each keep a book or card index file in which shall be registered the signature of the commissioners so filing such certificates.

7. The county clerk of the county in which said city is located shall, upon demand and upon payment of the sum of fifty cents, authenticate a certificate of acknowledgment or proof of oath taken before such commissioner of deeds within such city, by subjoining or attaching to the original certificate of acknowledgment or proof of oath a certificate under his hand and official seal specifying that at the time of taking the acknowledgment or proof of oath the officer taking it was duly authorized to take the same; that the authenticating officer is acquainted with the former's handwriting, or has

compared the signature on the certificate of acknowledgment or proof of oath with the autograph signature deposited in his office by such officer, and that he verily believes the signature is genuine.

8. Any instrument or paper sworn to, proved or acknowledged before a commissioner of deeds within a city and authenticated as hereinbefore provided by the clerk of a county within which such city is located shall be recorded and read in evidence in any county in this state without further proof; provided, however, that a county clerk's certificate of authentication shall not be necessary to entitle any deed or other instrument or paper so proved or acknowledged to be recorded in any office where such commissioner has filed his autograph signature and certificate of appointment or to be read in evidence in any county in which such commissioner has filed with the county clerk his autograph signature and certificate of appointment, as herein provided.

9. The foregoing provisions of this section shall not apply in the city of New York.

§ 140. Commissioners of deeds in the city of New York.

1. The council of the city of New York is hereby authorized and is empowered to appoint commissioners of deeds in such city from time to time, who shall hold their offices for two years from the date of their appointment.

2. No person shall be appointed a commissioner of deeds except an attorney-at-law unless such person shall have submitted with his application proof of his ability to perform the duties of the office. Applicants serving clerkships in the offices of attorneys, and whose clerkship certificate is on file with proper officials, shall submit an affidavit to that effect. Other employees of attorneys shall submit an affidavit sworn to by a member of the firm of such attorneys that the applicant is a proper and competent person to perform the duties of a commissioner of deeds. Every other applicant shall furnish a certificate of the city clerk of such city stating that he has examined the applicant and believes such applicant to be competent to perform the duties of a commissioner of deeds; provided, however, that where a commissioner of deeds applies, before the expiration of his term, for a reappointment or where a person whose term as commissioner of deeds shall have expired applies within six months after such expiration for appointment as a commissioner of deeds, such examination shall not be required. Upon any such application for such renewal the city clerk shall furnish the applicant with a certificate stating that the applicant has theretofore qualified for appointment and indicate the date of the applicant's original appointment

thereon. The fee for issuing each such certificate shall be fifty cents.

3. Such appointment shall not require the approval of the mayor, and hereafter, at the time of subscribing or filing the oath of office, the city clerk shall collect from each person appointed a commissioner of deeds the sum of seven dollars and fifty cents, and he shall not administer or file such oath unless such fee has been paid.

4. The city clerk shall designate a commissioner of deeds clerk, whose duties shall be to enter the names of commissioners of deeds appointed in a book kept for that purpose, make out certificates of appointment and discharge such other duties as the city clerk may designate.

5. Any person hereafter appointed to the office of commissioner of deeds in and for the city of New York by the council, before entering upon the discharge of the duties of such office and within thirty days after such appointment, shall take and subscribe before the commissioner of deeds clerk in the office of the city clerk or before any person authorized to administer oaths the following oath of office: that the applicant is a citizen of the United States, and a resident of the State of New York, the city of New York and the county of (naming the county); that he will support the constitution of the United States and the constitution of the state of New York and faithfully discharge the duties of the office of commissioner of deeds. A person regularly admitted to practice as an attorney and counsellor in the courts of record of this state, whose office for the practice of law is within the city of New York, may be appointed a commissioner of deeds in and for the city of New York and may retain his office as such commissioner of deeds although he resides in or removes to another city in this state or to an adjoining state. For the purposes of this and the following sections of this article such person shall be deemed a resident of the county where he maintains such office.

5-a. A person regularly admitted to practice as an attorney and counsellor in the courts of record of this state, whose office for the practice of law is within the city of New York, may be appointed a commissioner of deeds in and for the city of New York and may retain his office as such commissioner of deeds although he resides in or removes to any other county in this state or to an adjoining state. For the purposes of this article such person shall be deemed a resident of the county where he maintains such office.

6. Any commissioner of deeds who may remove from the city of New York during his term of office vacates his office and is hereby required to notify the city clerk of such removal, and immediately upon the receipt of such notice of removal the city clerk shall cause the name of such commissioner to

be stricken from the roll of commissioners of deeds of the city.

7. Any person appointed to the office of commissioner of deeds under the provisions of this section, upon qualifying as above provided, may administer oaths and take acknowledgments or proofs of deeds and other instruments in any part of the city of New York.

8. A commissioner of deeds may file his autograph signature and certificate of appointment in the office of any county clerk in the city; and the city clerk, upon request of any commissioner appointed under the provisions of this section and upon payment of twenty-five cents for each certificate, must make and deliver to such commissioner such number of certificates as such commissioner may require. Such certificates shall be issued under the hand and official seal of the city clerk, showing the appointment and term of office of such commissioner and stating the county in which he resides, which certificates may be filed in the offices of the several county clerks in the city upon payment of one dollar in each office for filing.

9. The clerks of the counties of New York, Kings, Queens, Richmond and Bronx shall each keep a book or card index file in which shall be registered the signature of the commissioners so filing such certificates; and the county clerk of any county in the city with whom such commissioner has filed a certificate of appointment shall, upon demand and upon payment of the sum of fifty cents, authenticate a certificate of acknowledgment or proof of oath taken before such commissioner of deeds, without regard to the county in the city in which such acknowledgment or proof was taken or oath administered, by subjoining or attaching to the original certificate of acknowledgment or proof or oath a certificate under his hand and official seal specifying that at the time of taking the acknowledgment or proof or oath the officer taking it was duly authorized to take the same; that the authenticating officer is acquainted with the former's handwriting, or has compared the signature on the certificate of acknowledgment, proof or oath with the autograph signature deposited in his office by such officer, and that he verily believes the signature is genuine.

10. Any instrument or paper sworn to, proved or acknowledged before a commissioner of deeds within the city of New York and authenticated as herinbefore provided by the clerk of any county within the city with whom such commissioner has filed his autograph signature and certificate of appointment shall be recorded and read in evidence in any county in this sate without further proof; provided, however, that a county clerk's certificate of authentication shall not be necessary to entitle any deed or other instrument or paper so proved or acknowledged to be recorded or read in evidence in

any office of the county clerks within the city of New York or the office of the register of the city of New York.

11. A commissioner of deeds must affix, in black ink, to each instrument sworn to, acknowledged or proved, in addition to his signature, the date when his term expires and his official number as given to him by the city clerk, and must print, typewrite or stamp his name in black ink beneath his signature.

12. The mayor of the city of New York may remove any commissioner of deeds appointed under the provisions of this section for cause shown; but no such commissioner shall be removed until charges have been duly made against him to the mayor and the commissioner shall have had an opportunity to answer the same. At any proceedings held before the mayor for the removal of such commissioner of deeds the mayor shall have power to subpoena witnesses and to compel the attendance of the same, and to administer oaths, and to compel the production of books and papers, and upon the termination of such proceedings shall make his decision thereon in writing and cause the same to be filed in the office of the city clerk of the city of New York, provided, however, that the mayor may, whenever a hearing is granted by him on complaint against a commissioner of deeds, designate an assistant corporation counsel to preside who shall have power to subpoena witnesses and to compel the attendance of the same, administer oaths, compel the production of books and papers and receive exhibits; such assistant shall, upon the termination of such proceedings, certify a copy of the stenographer's minutes of such hearing and such exhibits as may be received in evidence, together with his recommendations on the issues presented, whereupon the mayor shall render a decision on all matters presented on such hearing.

13. In case such commissioner shall be removed from office the city clerk, immediately upon the receipt by him of the order of removal signed by the mayor, shall cause the name of such commissioner so removed to be stricken from the roll of commissioners of deeds of the city.

14. No person who has been removed from office as a commissioner of deeds for the city of New York, as herein before provided, shall thereafter be eligible again to be appointed as such commissioner nor, shall he be eligible thereafter to appointment to the office of notary public.

15. Any person who has been removed from office as aforesaid, who shall, after knowledge of such removal, sign or execute an instrument as a commissioner of deeds or notary public shall be deemed guilty of a misdemeanor.

16. In case of the removal for cause, or removal from the city or resignation of a commissioner of deeds, the city clerk shall immediately notify each

county clerk and the register of the city of New York of such removal or resignation.

§ 141. Commissioners of deeds in other states, territories and foreign countries.

The secretary of state may, in his discretion, appoint and commission in any other state, territory or dependency, or in any foreign country, such number of commissioners of deeds as he may think proper, each of whom shall be a resident of or have his place of business in the city, county, municipality or other political subdivision from which chosen, and shall hold office for the term of four years, unless such appointment shall be sooner revoked by the secretary of state, who shall have power to revoke the same. A person applying for appointment as a commissioner of deeds shall state in his application the city, county, muinicipality or other political subdivision for which he desires to be appointed, and shall enclose with his application the sum of ten dollars, which sum, if a commission shall be granted, shall be paid by the secretary of state into the state treasury, and if such commission shall not be granted, then the same shall be returned to the person making the application. Each commissioner, before performing any of the duties or exercising any of the powers of his office, shall take the constitutional oath of office, if appointed for a city or county within the United States, before a justice of the peace or some other magistrate in such city or county; and if for a territory or dependency, before a judge of a court of record in such territory or dependency; and if for a city, municipality or other political subdivision in a foreign country, before a person authorized by the laws of this state to administer an oath in such country, or before a clerk or judge of a court of record in such foreign country; and shall cause to be prepared an official seal on which shall be designated his name, the words, "commissioner of deeds for the state of New York," and the name of the city or county, and the state, country, municipality or other political subdivision from which appointed, and shall file a clear impression of such seal, his written signature and his oath certified by the officer before whom it was taken, in the office of the department of state. The secretary of state upon receipt of such impression, signature and oath, shall forward to such commissioner instructions and forms, and a copy of the appropriate sections of this chapter.

§ 142. Powers of such commissioners.

Every such commissioner shall have authority, within the city, county, municipality or other political subdivision for which he is appointed, and in the manner in which such acts are performed by authorized officers within the state:

1. To take the acknowledgment or proof of the execution of a written instrument, except a bill of exchange, promissory note or will, to be read in evidence or recorded in this state.

2. To administer oaths.

3. If such commissioner is also an attorney at law regularly admitted to practice in this state, in his discretion, to the extent authorized by this section, to administer an oath to or take the acknowledgment of or proof of the execution of an instrument by his client with respect to any matter, claim, action or proceeding.

4. If appointed for a foreign country, to certify to the existence of a patent, record or other document recorded in a public office or under official custody in such foreign country, and to the correctness of a copy of such patent, record or document, or to the correctness of a copy of a certified copy of such patent, record or other document, which has been certified according to the form in use in such foreign country.

5. A written instrument acknowledged or proved, an oath administered, or a copy of a certified copy of a patent, record or other document certified, as heretofore provided in this section, may be read in evidence or recorded within this state, the same as if taken, administered or certified within the state before an officer authorized to take the acknowledgment or proof of a written instrument, to administer oaths, or to certify to the correctness of a public record, if there shall be annexed or subjoined thereto, or indorsed thereon a certificate of the commissioner before whom such acknowledgment or proof was taken, by whom the oath was administered, or by whom the correctness of such copy is certified, under his hand and official seal. Such certificate shall specify the day on which, and the city or other political subdivision, and the state or country or other place in which, the acknowledgment or proof was taken, or the oath administered, without which specification the certificate shall be void. Except as provided in subdivision five of this section, such certificate shall be authenticated by the certificate of the secretary of state annexed or subjoined to the certificate of such commissioner, that such commissioner was, at the time of taking such acknowledgment or proof, of administering such oath, or of certifying to such patent record or document, or copy thereof, duly authorized therefor, that he is acquainted with the handwriting of such commissioner, or has compared the signature upon the certificate with the signature of such commissioner deposited in his office, that he has compared the impression of the seal affixed to such certificate with the impression of the seal of such commissioner deposited in his office, and that he believes the signature and the impression of the seal upon such certificate to be genuine. The certificate of a commissioner as to the

correctness of a copy of a certified copy of a patent, record or other document, as provided by this section, shall be presumptive evidence that it was certified according to the form in use in such foreign country.

6. A commissioner of deeds appointed pursuant to the preceding section may during his term of office procure from the secretary of state, on payment to him of a fee of two dollars, a certificate of his appointment, prescribed by the secretary of state, stating among other things, the date of his appointment, the date of expiration thereof and the city, county, municipality or other political subdivision for which he is appointed, and containing the signature of the commissioner in his own handwriting and his official seal, and certifying that he has compared the signature on such certificate with the signature of such commissioner deposited in his office, that he has compared the impression of the seal affixed to such certificate with the impression of the seal of such commissioner deposited in his office and that he believes the signature and the impression of the seal upon such certificate to be genuine. Such a certificate may be filed by such commissioner in the office of any county clerk or register in the state upon the payment to such county clerk or register of a fee of two dollars. Upon the filing of such certificate in the office of a county clerk or register in this state, a written instrument certified copy of a patent, record or other document certified, by a commissioner pursuant to this section, shall be entitled to be read in evidence and shall be accepted for filing or recording and filed or recorded, as the case may be, in the office of such county clerk or register, on tender or payment of the lawful fees therefor, without having annexed or subjoined to the certificate of such commissioner contained thereon the authenticating certificate of the secretary of state as required by subdivision five of this section or by subdivision one of section three hundred eleven of the real property law or by any other provision of law.

§ 142-a. Validity of acts of notaries public and commissioners of deeds notwithstanding certain defects.

1. Except as provided in subdivision three of this section, the official certificates and other acts heretofore or hereafter made or performed of notaries public and commissioners of deeds heretofore or hereafter and prior to the time of their acts appointed or commissioned as such shall not be deemed invalid, impaired or in any manner defective, so far as they may be affected, impaired or questioned by reason of defects described in subdivision two of this section.

2. This section shall apply to the following defects:

(a) ineligibility of the notary public or commissioner of deeds to be appointed or commissioned as such;

(b) misnomer or misspelling of name or other error made in his appointment or commission;

(c) omission of the notary public or commissioner of deeds to take or file his official oath or otherwise qualify;

(d) expiration of his term, commission or appointment;

(e) vacating of his office by change of his residence, by acceptance of another public office, or by other action on his part;

(f) the fact that the action was taken outside the jurisdiction where the notary public or commissioner of deeds was authorized to act.

3. No person shall be entitled to assert the effect of this section to overcome a defect described in subdivision two if he knew of the defect or if the defect was apparent on the face of the certificate of the notary public or commissioner of deeds; provided however, that this subdivision shall not apply after the expiration of six months from the date of the act of the notary public or commissioner of deeds.

4. After the expiration of six months from the date of the official certificate or other act of the commissioner of deeds, subdivision one of this section shall be applicable to a defect consisting in omission of the certificate of a commissioner of deeds to state the date on which and the place in which an act was done, or consisting of an error in such statement.

5. This section does not relieve any notary public or commissioner of deeds from criminal liability imposed by reason of his act, or enlarge the actual authority of any such officer, nor limit any other statute or rule of law by reason of which the act of a notary public or commissioner of deeds, or the record thereof, is valid or is deemed valid in any case.

§ 143. Fees of such commissioners.

The fees of such commissioners shall be as follows:

1. If appointed for another state, territory or dependency, not to exceed four times the amount allowed by the laws of such state, territory or dependency for like services, and not to exceed in any case one dollar for taking the proof or acknowledgment of a written instrument, or administering an oath;

2. If appointed for Great Britain or Ireland, for administering or certifying an oath, one shilling sterling, and for taking the proof or acknowledgment of a written instrument, or for certifying to

the existence or correctness of a copy of a patent, record or document, four shillings sterling;

3. If appointed for France or any other foreign country, for administering and certifying an oath, one franc and twenty-five centimes, and for taking the proof or acknowledgment of a written instrument, or for certifying to the existence or correctness of a copy of a patent, record or document, five francs.

§ 144. Saving clause.

In case it be judicially determined that any phrase, clause, part, paragraph or section of any of the provisions of sections one hundred thirty, one hundred thirty-one, one hundred thirty-two, one hundred thirty-three, one hundred thirty-five, one hundred thirty-six, one hundred thirty-seven and one hundred thirty-eight is unconstitutional or otherwise invalid, such determination shall not affect the validity or effect of the remaining provisions of the aforementioned sections. All persons heretofore appointed and still holding office as notaries public shall continue in such office after the effective date of this article, with the same powers and duties as herein provided until the expiration of the term for which they were appointed.

PUBLIC HOLIDAYS

[N.Y. GEN. CONSTR. LAW]

§ 24. Public holidays; half-holidays.

The term public holiday includes the following days in each year: the first day of January, known as New Year's day; the third Monday of January, known as Dr. Martin Luther King, Jr. day; the twelfth day of February, known as Lincoln's birthday; the third Monday in February, known as Washington's birthday; the last Monday in May, known as Memorial day; the second Sunday in June, known as Flag day; the fourth day of July, known as Independence day; the first Monday in September, known as Labor day; the second Monday in October, known as Columbus day; the eleventh day of November, known as Veterans' day; the fourth Thursday in November, known as Thanksgiving day; and the twenty-fifth day of December, known as Christmas day, and if any of such days except Flag day is Sunday, the next day thereafter; each general election day, and each day appointed by the president of the United States or by the governor of this state as a day of general thanksgiving, general fasting and prayer, or other general religious observances. The term half-holiday includes the period from noon to midnight of each Saturday which is not a public holiday.

§ 25. Public holiday, Saturday or Sunday in contractual obligations; extension of time where performance of act authorized required by contract is due on Saturday, Sunday or public holiday.

1. Where a contract by its terms authorizes or requires the payment of money or the performance of a condition on a Saturday, Sunday or a public holiday, or authorizes or requires the payment of money or the performance of a condition within or before or after a period of time computed from a certain day, and such period of time ends on a Saturday, Sunday or a public holiday, unless the contract expressly or impliedly indicates a different intent, such payment may be made or condition performed on the next succeeding business day, and if the period ends at a specified hour, such payment may be made or condition performed, at or before the same hour of such next succeeding business day, with the same force and effect as if made or performed in accordance with the terms of the contract.

2. Where time is extended by virtue of the provisions of this section, such extended time shall not be included in the computation of interest unless the contract so provides, except that when the period is specified as a number of months, such extended time shall be included in the computation of interest unless the contract otherwise provides.

3. Notwithstanding any other provision of law, all time deposits and certificates of deposit of banking organizations that mature on a Saturday, Sunday or bank holiday shall continue to accrue interest at the same rate fixed for the term of the deposit or certificate until the first banking day next succeeding the date of maturity, at which the principal and all accrued interest may be withdrawn, unless sooner withdrawn by the depositor.

NORTH CAROLINA

52-10. Contracts between husband and wife generally; releases.

DEPOSITIONS

8-74. Depositions for defendant in criminal actions.
8-76. Depositions before municipal authorities.
8-77. Depositions in quo warranto proceedings.
8-78. Commissioner may subpoena witness and punish for contempt.
8-79. Attendance before commissioner enforced.
8-80. Remedies against defaulting witness before commissioner.

LEGAL HOLIDAYS

103-4. Dates of public holidays.
103-5. Acts to be done on Sunday or holidays.

NOTARIES PUBLIC

[N.C. GEN. STAT.]

§ 10-1. Appointment and commission; term of office; revocation of commission.

The Secretary of State may, from time to time, at his discretion, appoint one or more fit persons in every county to act as notaries public and shall issue to each a commission upon payment of a fee of fifteen dollars ($15.00). The commission shall show that it is for a term of five years and shall show the effective date and the date of expiration. The term of the commission shall be computed by including the effective date and shall end at midnight of the day preceding the anniversary of the effective date, five years thereafter. The commission shall be sent to the register of deeds of the county in which the appointee lives and a copy of the letter of transmittal to the register of deeds shall be sent to the appointee concerned. The commission shall be retained by the register of deeds until the appointee has qualified in the manner provided in G.S. 10-2.

Any commission so issued by the Secretary of State or his predecessor, shall be recoverable by him in his discretion upon complaint being made against such notary public and when he shall be satisfied that the interest of the public will be best served by the revocation of said commission. Whenever the Secretary of State shall have revoked the commission of any notary public appointed by him, or his predecessor in office, it shall be his duty to file with the register of deeds in the county of such notary public a copy of said order and mail a copy of same to said notary public. The Secretary of State may revoke the commission of a notary who in the performance of his duties fails to comply with the laws of the State.

Any person holding himself out to the public as a notary public, or any person attempting to act in such capacity after his commission shall have been revoked by the Secretary of State, shall be guilty of a misdemeanor and upon conviction shall be fined or imprisoned, or both, in the discretion of the court.

§ 10-1.1. Requirements for appointment.

(a) To be eligible for appointment as a notary public a person shall:

(1) Apply for appointment on a form to be provided by the Secretary of State to be made available at the office of the register of deeds of each county.

(2) Be 18 years of age or older and registered to vote in the State of North Carolina.

(3) Possess a high school diploma or its equivalent.

(4) Obtain a recommendation as to character and fitness from one publicly elected official in North Carolina.

(5) Satisfactorily complete a course of study approved by the Secretary of State which shall consist of not less than three hours nor more than six hours of classroom instruction; except that practicing attorneys at law shall be exempt from this requirement. Local bar associations shall be qualified to teach or conduct a course of instruction upon authorization by the Secretary of State.

(6) Purchase a manual approved by the Secretary of State that describes the duties, authority and ethical responsibilities of notaries public.

(b) The Secretary of State may waive the requirements in subdivisions (a)(3), (a)(4), (a)(5), and (a)(6) of this section when a person applies for a second or subsequent commission.

§ 10-2. To qualify before register of deeds; record of qualification.

Upon appearing before the register of deeds to which their commissions were delivered, the notaries shall be duly qualified by taking before the register an oath of office, and the oaths prescribed for officers. Following the administration of the oaths of office, the notary shall place his signature in a book designated as "The Record of Notaries Public." The Record of Notaries Public shall contain the name of the notary, the signature of the notary, the effective date and expiration date of the commission, the date the oath was administered, and the date of revocation if the commission is revoked by the Secretary of State. The information contained in The Record of Notaries Public shall constitute the official record of the qualification of notaries public, and the register of deeds shall deliver the commission to the notary following his qualification and notify the Secretary of State of such qualification.

§ 10-3. Clerks notaries ex officio; may certify own seals.

The clerks of the superior court may act as notaries public, in their several counties, by virtue of their offices as clerks, and may certify their notarial acts under the seals of their respective courts.

§ 10-5. Powers of notaries public.

(a) Subject to the exception stated in subsection (c), a notary public commissioned under the laws of this State acting anywhere in this State may:

(1) Take and certify the acknowledgment of a contract, release, or separation agreement between a husband or wife as prescribed by the provisions of G.S. 52-10 or 52-10.1, and take and certify the acknowledgment or proof of the execution or signing of any other instrument or writing;

(2) Take affidavits and depositions;

(3) Administer oaths and affirmations, including oaths of office, except when such power is expressly limited to some other public officer;

(4) Protest for nonacceptance or nonpayment, notes, bills of exchange and other negotiable instruments; and

(5) Perform such acts as the law of any other jurisdiction may require of a notary public for the purposes of that jurisdiction.

(b) Any act within the scope of subsection (a) performed in another jurisdiction by a notary public of that jurisdiction has the same force and effect in this State as fully as if such act were performed in this State by a notary public commissioned under the laws of this State.

(c) A notary public who, individually or in any fiduciary capacity, is a party to any instrument, cannot take the proof or acknowledgment of himself in such fiduciary capacity or of any other person thereto.

(d) A notary public who is a stockholder, director, officer, or employee of a corporation is not disqualified to exercise any power, which he is authorized by this section to exercise, with respect to any instrument or other matter to which such corporation is a party or in which it is interested unless he is individually a party thereto.

§ 10-6. May exercise powers in any county.

Notaries public have full power and authority to perform the functions of their office in any and all counties of the State, and full faith and credit shall be given to any of their official acts wheresoever the same shall be made and done.

§ 10-7. Certificates of official character.

The Secretary of State and the register of deeds in the county in which the notary public qualified may certify to the official character and authority of such notary public.

§ 10-8. Fees of notaries.

(a) Notaries public shall be allowed the following fees:

(1) Taking and certifying the acknowledgment or proof of the execution or signing of any instrument or writing $1.00

(2) Taking affidavits 1.00

(3) Administering oaths (except that oaths of office shall be administered to public officials without charge) 1.00

(b) Notwithstanding the above schedule, notary fees for acknowledging signatures on documents required by the Division of Motor Vehicles shall be in accordance with the schedule of fees set forth in G.S. 20-42(a).

§ 10-9. Official acts of notaries public; signatures; appearance of names; notarial stamps or seals; expiration of commissions.

Official acts of notaries public in the State of North Carolina shall be attested:

(1) By their proper signatures;

(2) By the readable appearance of their names, either from their signatures or otherwise;

(3) By the clear and legible appearance of their notarial stamps or seals;

(4) By a statement of the date of expiration of their commissions;

provided, that the failure to comply with the provisions of subdivision (2) and (4) shall not invalidate their official acts.

§ 10-10. Notarial stamp or seal.

A notary public shall provide and keep an official stamp or seal which shall clearly show and legibly reproduce under photographic methods, when embossed, stamped, impressed or affixed to a document, the name of the notary, the name of the county in which appointed and qualified, the words "North Carolina" or an abbreviation thereof, and the words "Notary Public." It shall be the duty of a notary public to replace a seal which has become so worn that it can no longer clearly show or legibly reproduce under photographic methods the information required by this section. Provided, that a notary public appointed prior to July 1, 1973, who has adopted and is using a seal which does not meet the requirements of this section, shall be entitled to continue to use such seal until the expiration of his current commission.

§ 10-11. Acts of minor notaries validated.

All acts of notaries public for the State of North Carolina who were not yet 21 years of age at the time of the performance of such acts are hereby validated; and in every case where deeds or other instruments have been acknowledged before such notary public who was not yet 21 years of age at the time of taking of said acknowledgment, such acknowledgment taken before such notary public is hereby declared to be sufficient and valid.

§ 10-12. Acts of certain notaries prior to and after qualification and whose commissions have expired validated.

(a) All acknowledgments taken and other official acts done by any person who has heretofore been appointed or reappointed as a notary public, but who at the time of acting had failed to qualify as provided by law, shall, notwithstanding, be in all respects valid and sufficient; and property conveyed by instruments in which the acknowledgments were taken by such notary public are hereby validated and shall convey the properties therein purported to be conveyed as intended thereby.

(b) All acknowledgments taken and other official acts done by any person who has heretofore been appointed as a notary public, but whose commission has expired at the time of acting, shall be in all respects valid and sufficient. Instruments conveying property acknowledged by this notary public are validated and convey the properties they purport to convey.

(c) All acknowledgments taken and other official acts done by any person who has heretofore been appointed or reappointed and who has qualified as a notary public, but who, prior to the expiration of the commission, fails to continue to satisfy voting registration or residence requirements promulgated by the Secretary of State shall, notwithstanding, be in all respects valid and sufficient; and property conveyed by instruments in which the acknowledgments were taken by such notary public are hereby validated and shall convey the properties therein purported to be conveyed as intended thereby.

(d) This section shall apply to notarial acts prior to April 1, 1989.

§ 10-13. Acts of notaries public in certain instances validated.

The acts of any person heretofore performed after appointment as a notary public and prior to qualification as a notary public or upon reappointment and prior to qualification:

(1) In taking any acknowledgment, or
(2) In notarizing any instrument,
are all hereby declared to be valid and of the same legal effect as if such person had qualified as a notary public prior to performing any such acts.

§ 10-14. Validation of acknowledgment wherein expiration of notary's commission erroneously stated.

All deeds, deeds of trust, mortgages, conveyances, affidavits, and all other paper writings similar or dissimilar to those enumerated herein, whether or not permitted or required to be recorded or filed under the laws of this State heretofore or hereafter executed, bearing an official act of a notary public in which the date of the notary's commission is erroneously stated, are, together with all subsequent acts or actions taken thereon, including but not limited to probate and registration, hereby declared in all respects to be valid to the extent as if the correct expiration date had been stated and shall be binding on the parties of such paper writings and their privies; and such paper writings, together with their certificates may, if otherwise competent, be read in evidence as a muniment of title for all intents and purposes in any of the courts of this State: provided, that at the date of such official act the notary's commission was actually in force.

§ 10-15. Validation of instruments which do not contain readable impression of notary's name.

All deeds, deeds of trust, mortgages, conveyances, affidavits and all other paper writings similar or dissimilar to those enumerated herein, whether or not permitted or required to be recorded or filed under the laws of this State heretofore executed, bearing the official act of a notary public as attested by his notarial seal, but which seal does not contain a readable impression of the notary's name are, together with all subsequent acts or actions taken thereon, including but not limited to probate and registration, hereby declared in all respects to be valid to the same extent as if the seal containing a readable impression of the notary's name had been affixed thereto, and shall be binding on the parties of such paper writings and their privies; and such paper writings, together with their certificates, if otherwise competent, may be read in evidence as a muniment of title for all intents and purposes in any of the courts of this State.

§ 10-16. Acts of notaries with seal containing name of another state validated.

The notarial acts of any person heretofore duly commissioned as a notary public in this State, who used in performing such acts a seal correctly containing the name of the notary and the proper county but mistakenly containing the abbreviation for the State of Georgia instead of North Carolina, are hereby validated and given the same legal effect as if such misprint or incorrect designation of the State had not appeared on the seal or seal imprint so used.

§ 10-16.1. Act of notaries with seal omitting name of this State validated.

The notarial acts of any person heretofore duly commissioned as a notary public in this State, who used in performing such acts a seal correctly containing the name of the notary, but the words "North Carolina" or an abbreviation "N. C." were omitted, are hereby validated and given the same legal effect as if such correct designation of the State had appeared on the seal or seal imprints so used. This section shall apply to notarial acts prior to April 1, 1985.

§ 10-17. Validation of certain instruments acknowledged prior to January 1, 1945.

Where any person has taken an acknowledgment as a notary public of a person acting through another by virtue of the execution of a power of attorney and by said person acting in his individual capacity and said notary public has failed to include within his certificate the acknowledgment of said person in his capacity as attorney-in-fact, and such acknowledgment has been otherwise duly probated and recorded, then such acknowledgment is hereby declared to be sufficient and valid: provided, this section shall apply only to those deeds and other instruments acknowledged prior to January 1, 1945.

OATHS

§ 11-1. Oaths and affirmations to be administered with solemnity.

Whereas, lawful oaths for discovery of truth and establishing right are necessary and highly conducive to the important end of good government; and being most solemn appeals to Almighty God, as the omniscient witness of truth and the just and omnipotent avenger of falsehood, and whereas, lawful affirmations for the discovery of truth and establishing right are necessary and highly conducive to the important end of good government, therefore, such oaths and affirmations ought to be taken and administered with the utmost solemnity.

§ 11-2. Administration of oaths.

Judges and other persons who may be empowered to administer oaths, shall (except in the cases in this Chapter excepted) require the party to be sworn to lay his hand upon the Holy Scriptures, in token of his engagement to speak the truth and in further token that, if he should swerve from the truth, he may be justly deprived of all the blessings of that holy book and made liable to that vengeance which he has imprecated on his own head.

§ 11-3. Administration of oath with uplifted hand.

When the person to be sworn shall be conscientiously scrupulous of taking a book oath in manner aforesaid, he shall be excused from laying hands upon, or touching the Holy Gospel; and the oath required shall be administered in the following manner, namely: He shall stand with his right hand lifted up towards heaven, in token of his solemn appeal to the Supreme God, and also in token that if he should swerve from the truth he would draw down the vengeance of heaven upon his head, and shall introduce the intended oath with these words, namely:

I, A. B., do appeal to God, as a witness of the truth and the avenger of falsehood, as I shall answer the same at the great day of judgment, when the secrets of all hearts shall be known (etc., as the words of the oath may be).

§ 11-4. Affirmation in lieu of oath.

When a person to be sworn shall have conscientious scruples against taking an oath in the manner prescribed by G.S. 11-2, 11-3, or 11-7, he shall be permitted to be affirmed. In all cases the words of the affirmation shall be the same as the words of the prescribed oath, except that the word "affirm" shall be substituted for the word "swear" and the words "so help me God" shall be deleted.

§ 11-7. Oath of affirmation to support Constitutions; all officers to take.

Every member of the General Assembly and every person elected or appointed to hold any office of trust or profit in the State shall, before taking office or entering upon the execution of the office, take and subscribe to the following oath:

"I, ..., do solemnly and sincerely swear that I will support the Constitution of the United States; that I will be faithful and bear true allegiance to the State of North Carolina, and to the constitutional powers and authorities which are or may be established for the government thereof; and that I will endeavor to support, maintain and defend the Constitution of said State, not inconsistent with the Constitution of the United States, to the best of my knowledge and ability; so help me God."

§ 11-7.1. Who may administer oaths of office.

(a) Except as otherwise specifically required by statute, an oath of office may be administered by:

(1) A justice, judge, magistrate, clerk, assistant clerk, or deputy clerk of the General Court of Justice, a retired justice or judge of the General Court of Justice, or any member of the federal judiciary;

(2) The Secretary of State;

(3) A notary public;

(4) A register of deeds;

(5) A mayor of any city, town, or incorporated village;

(6) The chairman of a committee of the House or Senate of the General Assembly, or either of the cochairmen of a joint committee;

(7) The clerk of any county, city, town or incorporated village.

(b) The administration of an oath by any judge of the Court of Appeals prior to March 7, 1969, is hereby validated.

FEES

§ 147-15.1. Fees collected by private secretary.

The secretary to the Governor shall charge and collect the following fees, to be paid by the person for whom the services are rendered: for the commission of a notary public, ten dollars ($10.00); for the commission of a special policeman, five dollars ($5.00). All fees collected by the secretary shall be paid into the State treasury.

OFFENSES

§ 14-3. Punishment of misdemeanors, infamous offenses, offenses committed in secrecy and malice or with deceit and intent to defraud.

(a) Except as provided in subsection (b), every person who shall be convicted of any misdemeanor for which no specific punishment is prescribed by statute shall be punishable by fine, by imprisonment for a term not exceeding two years, or by both, in the discretion of the court.

(b) If a misdemeanor offense as to which no specific punishment is prescribed be infamous, done in secrecy and malice, or with deceit and intent to defraud, the offender shall, except where the of-

fense is a conspiracy to commit a misdemeanor, be guilty of a Class H felony.

§ 14-76. Larceny, mutilation, or destruction of public records and papers.

If any person shall steal, or for any fraudulent purpose shall take from its place of deposit for the time being, or from any person having the lawful custody thereof, or shall unlawfully and maliciously obliterate, injure or destroy any record, writ, return, panel, process, interrogatory, deposition, affidavit, rule, order or warrant of attorney or any original document whatsoever, of or belonging to any court of record, or relating to any matter, civil or criminal, begun, pending or terminated in any such court, or any bill, answer, interrogatory, deposition, affidavit, order or decree or any original document whatsoever, of or belonging to any court or relating to any cause or matter begun, pending or terminated in any such court, every such offender shall be guilty of a misdemeanor; and in any indictment for such offense it shall not be necessary to allege that the article, in respect to which the offense is committed, is the property of any person or that the same is of any value. If any person shall steal or for any fraudulent purpose shall take from the register's office, or from any person having the lawful custody thereof, or shall unlawfully and willfully obliterate, injure or destroy any book wherein deeds or other instruments of writing are registered, or any other book of registration or record required to be kept by the register of deeds or shall unlawfully destroy, obliterate, deface or remove any records of proceedings of the board of county commissioners, or unlawfully and fraudulently abstract any record, receipt, order or voucher or other paper writing required to be kept by the clerk of the board of commissioners of any county, he shall be guilty of a misdemeanor.

SAFE-DEPOSIT BOXES

§ 53-43.7. Safe-deposit boxes; unpaid rentals; procedure; escheats.

(a) If the rental due on a safe-deposit box has not been paid for one year, the lessor may send a notice by registered mail to the last known address of the lessee stating that the safe-deposit box will be opened and its contents stored at the expense of the lessee unless payment of the rental is made within 30 days. If the rental is not paid within 30 days from the mailing of the notice, the box may be opened in the presence of an officer of the lessor and of a notary public who is not a director, officer, employee or stockholder of the lessor. The contents shall be sealed in a package by the notary public who shall write on the outside the name of the lessee and the date of the opening. The notary public shall execute a certificate reciting the name of the lessee, the date of the opening of the box and a list of its contents. The certificate shall be included in the package and a copy of the certificate shall be sent by registered mail to the last known address of the lessee. The package shall then be placed in the general vaults of the lessor at a rental not exceeding the rental previously charged for the box.

(b) Any property, including documents or writings of a private nature, which has little or no apparent value, need not be sold but may be destroyed by the Treasurer or by the lessor, if retained by the lessor pursuant to a determination by the Treasurer under G.S. 116B-31(c).

(c) If the contents of the safe-deposit box have not been claimed within two years of the mailing of the certificate, the lessor may send a further notice to the last known address of the lessee stating that, unless the accumulated charges are paid within 30 days, the contents of the box will be delivered to the State Treasurer as abandoned property under the provisions of Chapter 116B.

(d) The lessor shall submit to the Treasurer a verified inventory of all of the contents of the safe-deposit box upon delivery of the contents of the box or such part thereof as shall be required by the Treasurer under G.S. 116B-319(c); but the lessor may deduct from any cash of the lessee in the safe-deposit box an amount equal to accumulated charges for rental and shall submit to the Treasurer a verified statement of such charges and deduction. If there is no cash, or insufficient cash to pay accumulated charges, in the safe-deposit box, the lessor may submit to the Treasurer a verified statement of accumulated charges or balance of accumulated charges due, and the Treasurer shall remit to the lessor the charges or balance due, up to the value of the property in the safe-deposit box delivered to him, less any costs or expenses of sale; but if the charges or balance due exceeds the value of such property, the Treasurer shall remit only the value of the property, less costs or expenses of sale. Any accumulated charges for safe-deposit box rental paid by the Treasurer to the lessor shall be deducted from the value of the property of the lessee delivered to the Treasurer.

(e) Repealed by Session Laws 1979, 2nd Session, c. 1311, s. 5.

(f) A copy of this section shall be printed on every contract for rental of a safe-deposit box.

ACKNOWLEDGMENTS

§ 47-1. Officials of State authorized to take probate.

The execution of all deeds of conveyance, contracts to buy, sell or convey lands, mortgages, deeds of trust, instruments modifying or extending the terms of morgages or deeds of trust, assignments, powers of attorney, covenants to stand seized to the use of another, leases for more than three years, releases, affidavits concerning land titles or family history, any instruments pertaining to real property, and any and all instruments and writings of whatever nature and kind which are required or allowed by law to be registered in the office of the register of deeds or which may hereafter be required or allowed by law to be so registered, may be proved or acknowledged before any one of the following officials of this State: The justices, judges, magistrates, clerks, assistant clerks, and deputy clerks of the General Court of Justice, and notaries public.

§ 47-2. Officials of the United States, foreign countries, and sister states.

The execution of all such instruments and writings as are permitted or required by law to be registered may be proved or acknowledged before any one of the following officials of the United States, of the District of Columbia, of the several states and territories of the United States, of countries under the dominion of the United States and of foreign countries: Any judge of a court of record, any clerk of a court of record, any notary public, any commissioner of deeds, any commissioner of oaths, any mayor or chief magistrate of an incorporated town or city, any ambassador, minister, consul, vice-consul, consul general, vice-consul general, or commercial agent of the United States, any justice of the peace of any state or territory of the United States, any officer of the army or air force of the United States or United States marine corps having the rank of warrant officer or higher, any officer of the United States navy or coast guard having the rank of warrant officer, or higher, or any officer of the United States merchant marine having the rank of warrant officer, or higher. No official seal shall be required of said military, naval or merchant marine official, but he shall sign his name, designate his rank, and give the name of his ship or military organization and the date, and for the purpose of certifying said acknowledgment, he shall use a form in substance as follows:

On this _____ day of _____, 19___, before me _____, the undersigned officer, personally appeared _____, known to me (or satisfactorily proven) to be accompanying or serving in or with the armed forces of the United States (or to be the spouse of a person accompanying or serving in or with the armed forces of the United States) and to be the person whose name is subscribed to the within instruments and acknowledged that _____ he _____ executed the same for the purposes therein contained. And the undersigned does further certify that he is at the date of this certificate a commissioned officer of the rank stated below and is in the active service of the armed forces of the United States.

_____
Signature of Officer

_____
Rank of Officer and command to which attached.

If the proof or acknowledgment of the execution of an instrument is had before a justice of the peace of any state of the United States other than this State or of any territory of the United States, the certificate of such justice of the peace shall be accompanied by a certificate of the clerk of some court of record of the county in which such justice of the peace resides, which certificate of the clerk shall be under his hand and official seal, to the effect that such justice of the peace was at the time the certificate of such justice bears date an acting justice of the peace of such county and state or territory and that the genuine signature of such justice of the peace is set to such certificate.

§ 47-2.2. Notary public of sister state; lack of seal or stamp or expiration date of commission.

If the proof or acknowledgment of any instrument is had before a notary public of any state other than North Carolina and the instrument does not show the seal or stamp of the notary public and the expiration date of the commission of the notary public, the certificate of proof or acknowledgment made by such notary public shall be accompanied by the certificate of the county official before whom the notary qualifies for office, stating that such notary public was at the time his certificate bears date an acting notary public of such state, and that such notary's genuine signature is set to his certificate. The certificate of the official herein provided for shall be under his hand and official seal.

§ 47-5. When seal of officer necessary to probate.

When proof or acknowledgment of the execution of any instrument by any maker of such instrument, whether a person or corporation, is had before any official authorized by law to take such proof and acknowledgment, and such official has an official seal, he shall set his official seal to his certificate. If the official before whom the instrument is proved or acknowledged has no official seal he shall certify under his hand, and his private seal shall not be essential. When the instrument is proved or acknowledged before the register of deeds of the county in which the instrument is to be registered, the official seal shall not be necessary.

§ 47-8. Attorney in action not to probate papers therein.

No practicing attorney-at-law has power to administer any oaths to a person to any paper-writing to be used in any legal proceedings in which he appears as attorney.

§ 47-9. Probates before stockholders in building and loan associations.

No acknowledgment or proof of execution of any mortgage or deed of trust executed to secure the payment of any indebtedness to any building and loan association shall hereafter be held invalid by reason of the fact that the officer taking such acknowledgment or proof is a stockholder in said building and loan association. This section does not authorize any officer or director of a building and loan association to take acknowledgments or proofs. The provisions of this section shall apply to federal savings and loan associations having their principal offices in this State. Acknowledgments and proofs of execution, including private examinations of any married woman taken before March 20, 1939, by an officer who is or was a stockholder in any federal savings and loan association, are hereby validated.

§ 47-14.1. Repeal of laws requiring private examination of married women.

All deeds, contracts, conveyances, leaseholds or other instruments executed from and after February 7, 1945, shall be valid for all purposes without the separate, privy, or private examination of a married woman where she is a party to or a grantor in such deed, contract, conveyance, leasehold or other instrument, and it shall not be necessary nor required that the separate or privy examination of such married woman be taken by the certifying officer. From and after February 7, 1945, all laws and clauses of laws contained in any section of the General Statutes requiring the privy or private examination of a married woman are hereby repealed.

§ 47-38. Acknowledgment by grantor.

Where the instrument is acknowledged by the

grantor or maker, the form of acknowledgment shall be in substance as follows:

North Carolina, ... County.

I (here give the name of the official and his official title), do hereby certify that (here give the name of the grantor or maker) personally appeared before me this day and acknowledged the due execution of the foregoing instrument. Witness my hand and (where an official seal is required by law) official seal this the .... (Official seal.) day of .... (year).

....
(Signature of officer.)

§ 47-40. Husband's acknowledgment and wife's acknowledgment before the same officer.

Where the instrument is acknowledged by both husband and wife or by other grantor before the same officer the form of acknowledgment shall be in substance as follows:

I (here give name of official and his official title), do hereby certify that (here give names of the grantors whose acknowledgment is being taken) personally appeared before me this day and acknowledged the due execution of the foregoing (or annexed) instrument.

§ 47-41. Corporate conveyances.

The following forms of probate for deeds and other conveyances executed by a corporation shall be deemed sufficient, but shall not exclude other forms of probate which would be deemed sufficient in law. If the deed or other instrument is executed by the president, any vice-president, assistant vice-president, manager, comptroller, treasurer, assistant treasurer, trust officer or assistant trust officer, or chairman or vice-chairman of such corporation signing the name of such corporation by him as such officer, is sealed with its common or corporate seal, and is attested by its secretary or assistant secretary, trust officer, assistant trust officer, associate trust officer, or, in case of a bank, by its secretary, assistant secretary, cashier or assistant cashier, the following form of acknowledgment is sufficient:

....
(State and county, or other description of place where acknowledgment is taken)

I, ..., ...,
(Name of officer taking   (Official title of officer
acknowledgment)   taking acknowledgment)

certify that .... personally came before
(Name of secretary,
assistant secretary,
cashier or assistant
cashier)

me this day and acknowledged that he (or she) is

....
(Secretary, assistant secretary,
cashier or assistant cashier)

of ...., a corporation, and that by
(Name of corporation)

authority duly given and as the act of the corporation, the foregoing instrument was signed in its name by its ....,
(President or vice-president)

sealed with its corporate seal, and attested by himself (or herself) as its ....
(Secretary, assistant secretary,
cashier or assistant cashier)

My commission expires ....
(Date of expiration of commission
as notary public)

Witness my hand and official seal, this the ....
day of ....,
(Month)

....
(Year)

....
(Signature of officer taking acknowledgment)
(Official seal, if officer taking acknowledgment has one)

(1) The words "a corporation" following the blank for the name of the corporation may be omitted when the name of the corporation ends with the word "Corporation" or "Incorporated."

(2) The words "My commission expires" and the date of expiration of the notary public's commission may be omitted except when a notary public is the officer taking the acknowledgment.

(3) The words "and official seal" and the seal itself may be omitted when the officer taking the acknowledgment has no seal or when such officer is the clerk, assistant clerk or deputy clerk of the superior court of the county in which the deed or other instrument acknowledged is to be registered.

If the instrument is executed by the president or presiding member or trustee and two other members of the corporation, and sealed with the common seal, the following form shall be sufficient:

North Carolina, ... County.

This ...... day of ......, A.D. ......, personally came before me (here give the name and official title of the officer who signs this certificate) A.B. (here give the name of the subscribing witness), who, being by me duly sworn, says that he knows the common seal of the (here give the name of the corporation), and is also acquainted with C.D., who is the president (or presiding member or trustee), and also with E.F. and G.H., two other members of said corporation; and that he, the said A.B., saw the said president (or presiding member or trustee) and the two said other members sign the said instrument, and saw the said president (or presiding member or trustee) affix the said common seal of said corporation thereto, and that he, the said subscribing witness, signed his name as such subscribing witness thereto in their presence. Witness my hand and (when an official seal is required by law) official seal, this ..... day of ..... (year).

(Official seal.)

....
(Signature of officer.)

If the deed or other instrument is executed by the president, presiding member or trustee of the corporation, and sealed with the common seal, the following forms of proof and certificate thereof shall be deemed sufficient:

North Carolina, ... County.

This ...... day of ......, A.D. ......, personally came before me (here give the name and official title of the officer who signs the certificate) A.B. (here give the name of the attesting secretary or assistant secretary), who, being by me duly sworn, says that he knows the common seal of (here give the name of the corporation), and is acquainted with C.D., who is the president of said corporation, and that he, the said A.B., is the secretary (or assistant secretary) of the said corporation, and saw the said common seal of said corporation of said instrument by said president (or that he, the said A.B., secretary or assistant secretary as aforesaid, affixed said seal to said instrument), and that he, the said A.B., signed his name in attestation of the execution of said instrument in the presence of said president of said corporation. Witness my hand and (when an official seal is required by law) official seal, this the ..... day of ..... (year).

(Official seal.)

....
(Signature of officer.)

North Carolina, ... County.

This is to certify that on the ...... day of ......, 19......, before me personally came .... (president, vice-president, secretary or assistant secretary, as the case may be), with whom I am personally acquainted, who, being by me duly sworn, says that .... is the president (or vice-president), and .... is the secretary (or assistant secretary) of the ...., the corporation described in and which executed the foregoing instrument; that he knows the common seal of said corporation; that the seal affixed to the foregoing instrument is said common seal, and the name of the corporation was subscribed thereto by the said president (or vice-president), and that said president (or vice-president) and secretary (or assistant secretary) subscribed their names thereto, and said common seal was affixed, all by order of the board of directors of said corporation, and that the said instrument is the act and deed of said corporation. Witness my hand and

(when an official seal is required by law) official seal, this the ..... day of ..... (year).

(Official seal.)

....
(Signature of officer.)

If the deed or other instrument is executed by the signature of the president, vice-president, presiding member or trustee of the corporation, and sealed with its common seal and attested by its secretary or assistant secretary, the following form of proof and certificate thereof shall be deemed sufficient:

This ...... day of ......, A.D. ...., personally came before me (here give name and official title of officer who signs the certificate) A.B., who, being by me duly sworn, says that he is president (vice-president, presiding member or trustee) of the .... Company, and that the seal affixed to the foregoing (or annexed) instrument in writing is the corporate seal of said company, and that said writing was signed and sealed by him in behalf of said corporation by its authority duly given. And the said A.B. acknowledged the said writing to be the act and deed of said corporation.

(Official seal.)

....
(Signature of officer.)

If the officer before whom the same is proven be the clerk or deputy clerk of the superior court of the county in which the instrument is offered for registration, he shall add to the foregoing certificate the following: "Let the instrument with the certificate be registered."

All corporate conveyances probated and recorded prior to February 14, 1939, wherein the same was attested by the assistant secretary, instead of the secretary, and otherwise regular, are hereby validated as if attested by the secretary of the corporation.

The following forms of probate for contracts in writing for the purchase of personal property by corporations providing for a lien on the property or the retention of a title thereto by the vendor as security for the purchase price or any part thereof, or chattel mortgages, chattel deeds of trust and conditional sales of personal property executed by a corporation shall be deemed sufficient but shall not exclude other forms of probate which would be deemed sufficient in law:

North Carolina

.... County

I, ..., do hereby certify that ...., personally came before me
(name of president,
secretary or treasurer)

this day and acknowledged that he is ....
(president,
secretary
or
treasurer)
of .... and acknowledged,
(name of corporation)
on behalf of ...., the
(name of corporation)
grantor, the due execution of the foregoing instrument.

Witness my hand and official seal, this ...... day of ....., 19 .....
(Official Seal)

....
(Title of officer)
....
(Name of state)
....
(County)
I, ...,
(Name of officer taking proof)
.... of
(Official title of officer taking proof)
........................, ...,
(County)   (Name of state)
certify that ....
(Name of subscribing witness)
personally appeared before me, and being duly sworn, stated that in his presence ....
(Name of president, secretary or treasurer of maker)
(signed the foregoing instrument) (acknowledged the execution of the foregoing instrument.) (Strike out the words not applicable.)

WITNESS my hand and official seal, this .....
day of ...., 19.......
(Month)   (Year)
....
(Signature of official taking proof)
....
(Official title of official taking proof)
My commission expires ....
(Date of expiration of official's commission)

All deeds and other conveyances heretofore executed by any of the aforementioned corporate officers are hereby validated to the extent that such deeds or other conveyances were otherwise properly executed, probated, and recorded.

§ 47-42. Attestation of bank conveyances by secretary or cashier.

(a) In all forms of proof and certificates for deeds and conveyances executed by banking corpora-

tions, either the secretary or the cashier of said banking corporation shall attest such instruments.

* * *

§ 47-43. Form of certificate of acknowledgment of instrument executed by attorney in fact.

When an instrument purports to be signed by parties acting through another by virtue of the execution of a power of attorney, the following form of certificate shall be deemed sufficient, but shall not exclude other forms which would be deemed sufficient in law:

North Carolina, _____ County.

I (here give name of the official and his official title), do hereby certify that (here give name of attorney in fact), attorney in fact for (here give names of parties who executed the instrument through attorney in fact), personally appeared before me this day, and being by me duly sworn, says that he executed the foregoing and annexed instrument for and in behalf of (here give names of parties who executed the instrument through attorney in fact), and that his authority to execute and acknowledge said instrument is contained in an instrument duly executed, acknowledged, and recorded in the office of (here insert name of official in whose office power of attorney is recorded, and the county and state of recordation), on the (day of month, month, and year of recordation), and that this instrument was executed under and by virtue of the authority given by said instrument granting him power of attorney; that the said (here give name of attorney in fact) acknowledged the due execution of the foregoing and annexed instrument for the purposes therein expressed for an in behalf of the said (here give names of parties who executed the instrument through attorney in fact).

WITNESS my hand and official seal, this _____ day of _____, (year) _____.
(Official seal.)

_____
Signature of Officer

§ 47-43.1. Execution and acknowledgment of instruments by attorneys or attorneys in fact.

When an instrument purports to be executed by parties acting through another by virtue of a power of attorney, it shall be sufficient if the attorney or attorney in fact signs such instrument either in the name of the principal by the attorney or attorney in fact or signs as attorney or attorney in fact for the principal; and if such instrument purports to be under seal, the seal of the attorney in fact shall be sufficient. For such instrument to be executed under seal, the power of attorney must have been executed under seal.

§ 47-43.2. Officer's certificate upon proof of instrument by subscribing witness.

When the execution of an instrument is proved by a subscribing witness as provided by G.S. 47-12, the certificate required by G.S. 47-13.1 shall be in substantially the following form:

STATE OF _____ (Name of state)
_____ COUNTY
I, _____ (Name of officer taking proof), a _____ (Official title of officer taking proof) of _____ COUNTY, _____ (Name of state), certify that _____ (Name of subscribing witness) personally appeared before me this day, and being duly sworn, stated that in his presence _____ (Name of maker) signed the foregoing instrument) (acknowledged the execution of the foregoing instrument.) (Strike out the words not applicable.)

WITNESS my hand and official seal, this the _____ day of _____ (Month), 19__ (Year).

_____
(Signature of officer taking proof)
_____
(Official title of officer taking proof)
My commission expires _____ (Date of expiration of officer's commission).

* * *

§ 47-43.3. Officer's certificate upon proof of instrument by proof of signature of maker.

When the execution of an instrument is proved by proof of the signature of the maker as provided by G.S. 47-12.1 or as provided by G.S. 47-13, the certificate required by G.S. 47-13.1 shall be in substantially the following form:

STATE OF _____ (Name of state)
_____ COUNTY
I, _____ (Name of officer taking proof), a _____ (Official title of officer taking proof) of _____ COUNTY, _____ (Name of state), certify that _____ (Name of person familiar with maker's handwriting) personally appeared before me this day, and being duly sworn, stated that he knows the handwriting of _____ (Name of maker) and that the signature of the foregoing instrument is the signature of _____ (Name of maker).

WITNESS my hand and official seal, this the

_____ day of _____ (Month), 19__ (Year).

_____
(Signature of officer taking proof)
_____
(Official title of officer taking proof)
My commission expires _____ (Date of expiration of officer's commission).

§ 47-43.4. Officer's certificate upon proof of instrument by proof of signature of subscribing witness.

When the execution of an instrument is proved by proof of the signature of a subscribing witness as provided by G.S. 47-12.1, the certificate required by G.S. 47-13.1 shall be in substantially the following form:

STATE OF _____ (Name of state)
_____ COUNTY
I, _____ (Name of officer taking proof), a _____ (Official title of officer taking proof) of _____ COUNTY, _____ (Name of state), certify that _____ (Name of person familiar with handwriting of subscribing witness) personally appeared before me this day, and being duly sworn, stated that he knows the handwriting of _____ (Name of subscribing witness) and that the signature of _____ (Name of subscribing witness), as a subscribing witness to the foregoing instrument is the signature of _____ (Name of subscribing witness).

WITNESS my hand and official seal, this the _____ day of _____ (Month), 19__ (Year).

_____
(Signature of officer taking proof)
_____
(Official title of officer taking proof)
My commission expires _____ (Date of expiration of officer's commission).

§ 47-44. Clerk's certificate upon probate by justice of peace or magistrate.

When the proof or acknowledgment of any instrument is had before a justice of the peace of some other state or territory of the United States, or before a magistrate of this State, but of a county different from that in which the instrument is offered for registration, the form of certificate as to his official position and signature shall be substantially as follows:

North Carolina _____ County.

I, A.B. (here give name and official title of a clerk of a court of record), do hereby certify that C.D. (here give the name of the justice of the peace or magistrate taking the proof, etc.), was at the time of signing the foregoing (or annexed) certificate an acting justice of the peace or magistrate in and for the county of _____ and State (or territory) of _____, and that his signature thereto is in his own proper handwriting.

In witness whereof, I hereunto set my hand and official seal, this _____ day of _____ , A.D. _____.

(Official seal.)

_____
(Signature of officer.)

§ 47-53. Probates omitting official seals, etc.

In all cases where the acknowledgment, private examination, or other proof of the execution of any deed, mortgage, or other instrument authorized or required to be registered has been taken or had by or before any commissioner of affidavits and deeds of this State, or clerk or deputy clerk of a court of record, or notary public of this or any other state, territory, or district, and such deed, mortgage, or other instrument has heretofore been recorded in any county in this State, but such commissioner, clerk, deputy clerk, or notary public has omitted to attach his or her official or notarial seal thereto, or if omitted, to insert his or her name in the body of the certificate, or if omitted, to sign his or her name to such certificate, if the name of such officer appears in the body of said certificate or is signed thereto, or it does not appear of record that such seal was attached to the original deed, mortgage, or other instrument, or such commissioner, clerk, deputy clerk, or notary public has certified the same as under his or her "official seal," or "notarial seal," or words of similar import, and no such seal appears of record or where the officer uses "notarial" in his or her certificate and signature shows that "C.S.C.," or "clerk of superior court," or similar exchange of capacity, and the word "seal" follows the signature, then all such acknowledgments, private examinations or other proofs of such deeds, mortgages, or other instruments, and the registration thereof, are hereby made in all respects valid and binding. The provisions of this section apply to acknowledgments, private examinations, or proofs taken prior to April 1, 1989: Provided, this section does not apply to pending litigation.

§ 47-53.1. Acknowledgment omitting seal of notary public.

Where any person has taken an acknowledgment as a notary public and has failed to affix his seal

and such acknowledgment has been otherwise duly probated and recorded then such acknowledgment is hereby declared to be sufficient and valid: Provided this shall apply only to those deeds and other instruments acknowledged prior to April 1, 1989.

§ 47-62. Probates before interested notaries.

The proof and acknowledgment of instruments required by law to be registered in the office of the register of deeds of a county, and all privy examinations of a feme covert to such instruments made before any notary public on or since March 11, 1907, are hereby declared valid and sufficient, notwithstanding the notary may have been interested as attorney, counsel or otherwise in such instruments.

§ 47-63. Probate before officer of interested corporation.

In all cases when acknowledgment or proof of any conveyance has been taken before a clerk of superior court, magistrate or notary public, who was at the time a stockholder or officer in any corporation, bank or other institution which was a party to such instrument, the certificates of such clerk, magistrate, or notary public shall be held valid, and are so declared.

§ 47-77. Before notaries and clerks in other states.

All deeds and conveyances made for lands in this State which have, previous to February 15, 1883, been proved before a notary public or clerk of a court of record, or before a court of record, not including mayor's court, of any other state, where such proof has been duly certified by such notary or clerk under his official seal, or the seal of the court, or in accordance with the act of Congress regulating the certifying of records of the courts of one state to another state, or under the seal of such courts, and such deed or conveyance, with the certificate, has been registered in the office of register of deeds in the book of records thereof for the county in which such lands were situate at the time of such registration, are declared to be validly registered, and the proof and registration is adjudged valid. All deeds and conveyances so proved, certified and registered, or certified copies of the same, may be used as evidence of title for the lands on the trial of any suit in any courts where title to the lands come into controversy.

§ 47-78. Acknowledgment by resident taken out-of-state.

When prior to the ninth day of March, 1895, a deed or mortgage executed by a resident of this State has been proved or acknowledged by the maker thereof before a notary public of any other state of the United States, and has been ordered to be registered by the clerk of the superior court of the county in which the land conveyed is situated, and said deed or mortgage has been registered, such registration is valid.

§ 47-90. Validation of acknowledgments taken by notaries public holding other office.

In every case where deeds or other instruments have been acknowledged before a notary public, when the notary public, at the time was also holding some other office, and the deed or other instrument has been duly probated and recorded, such acknowledgment taken by such notary public is hereby declared to be sufficient and valid.

§ 47-95. Acknowledgments taken by notaries interested as trustee or holding other office.

In every case where deeds and other instruments have been acknowledged and privy examination of wives had before notaries public, or justices of the peace, prior to January 1, 1975, when the notary public or justice of the peace at the time was interested as trustee in said instrument or at the time was also holding some other office, and the deed or other instrument has been duly probated and recorded, such acknowledgment and privy examination taken by such notary public or justice of the peace is hereby declared to be sufficient and valid.

§ 47-102. Absence of notarial seal.

Any deed executed prior to the first day of January, 1945, and duly acknowledged before a North Carolina notary public, and the probate recites "witness my hand and notarial seal," or words of similar import, and no seal was affixed to the said deed, shall be ordered registered by the clerk of the superior court of the county in which the land lies, upon presentation to him: Provided, the probate is otherwise in due form.

§ 47-103. Deeds probated and registered with notary's seal not affixed, validated.

Any deed conveying or affecting real estate executed prior to January 1, 1932, and ordered registered and recorded in the county in which the land lies prior to said date, from which deed and the acknowledgment and privy examination thereof the seal of the notary public taking the acknowledgment or privy examination of the grantor or grantors thereof was omitted, is hereby declared to be sufficient and valid, and the probate and registration thereof are hereby in all respects validated and confirmed to the same effect as if the seal of said notary was affixed to the acknowledgment or privy examination thereof.

§ 47-104. Acknowledgments of notary holding other office.

In every case where deeds or other instruments have been acknowledged before a notary public, when the notary public at the time was also holding some other office, and the deed or other instrument has been duly probated and recorded, such acknowledgment taken by such notary public is hereby declared to be sufficient and valid.

§ 47-108. Acknowledgments before notaries under age.

All acts of notaries public for the State of North Carolina who were not yet 21 years of age at the time of performance of such acts are hereby validated; and in every case where deeds or other instruments have been acknowledged before such notary public who was not yet 21 years of age at the time of taking of said acknowledgment, such acknowledgment taken before such notary public is hereby declared to be sufficient and valid.

§ 47-108.2. Acknowledgments and examinations before notaries holding some other office.

In every case where deeds or other instruments have been acknowledged, and where privy examination of wives had, before a notary public, when the notary public at the time was also holding some other office, and the deed or other instrument has been otherwise duly probated and recorded, such acknowledgment taken by, and such privy examination had before such notary public is hereby declared to be sufficient and valid.

§ 47-108.3. Validation of acts of certain notaries public prior to November 26, 1921.

In all cases where prior to November 26, 1921, instruments by law, or otherwise, required, permitted or authorized to be registered, certified, probated, recorded or filed with certificates of notaries public showing the acknowledgments or proofs of execution thereof as required by the laws of the State of North Carolina have been registered, certified, probated, recorded or filed, such registration, certifications, probates, recordations and filings are hereby validated and made as good and sufficient as though such instruments had been in all respects properly registered, certified, probated, recorded or filed, notwithstanding there are no records in the office of the Governor of the State of North Carolina or in the office of the clerk of the superior court of the county in which such notaries public had ever been appointed or subscribed written oaths or received any certificates or commissions or were qualified as notaries public at the time of the performance of the acts hereby validated.

§ 47-108.11. Validation of recorded instruments where seals have been omitted.

In all cases of any deed, deed of trust, mortgage, lien or other instrument authorized or required to be registered in the office of the register of deeds of any county in this State where it appears of record or it appears that from said instrument, as recorded in the office of the register of deeds of any county in the State, there has been omitted from said recorded or registered instrument the word "seal," "notarial seal" and that any of said recorded or registered instruments shows or recites that the grantor or grantors "have hereunto fixed or set their hands and seals" and the signature of the grantor or grantors appears without a seal thereafter or on the recorded or registered instrument or in all cases where it appears there is an attesting clause which recites "signed, sealed and delivered in the presence of," and the signature of the grantor or grantors appears on the recorded or registered instrument without any seal appearing thereafter or of record, then all such deeds, mortgages, deeds of trust, liens or other instruments, and the registration of same in the office of the register of deeds, are hereby declared to be in all respects valid and binding and are hereby made in all respects valid and binding to the same extent as if the word "seal" or "notarial seal" had not been omitted, and the registration and recording of such instruments in the office of the register of deeds in any county in this State are hereby declared to be valid, proper, legal and binding registrations.

This section shall not apply in any respect to any instrument recorded or registered subsequent to April 1, 1989, or to pending litigation or to any such instruments now directly or indirectly involved in pending litigation.

§ 47-108.18. Registration of certain instruments containing a notarial jurat validated.

A notarial jurat constitutes an acknowledgment in due form for all plats or maps that have theretofore been accepted for filing and registration under G.S. 47-30 as amended. No plat or map heretofore accepted for filing and registration, that contains a notarial jurat instead of an acknowledgment may be held to be improperly registered solely for lack of a proper acknowledgment.

§ 52-7. Validation of certificates of notaries public as to contracts or conveyances between husband and wife.

Any contract between husband and wife coming within the provisions of G.S. 52-6, executed prior to the first day of January, 1955, acknowledged before a notary public and containing a certificate of the notary public of his conclusions and findings of fact that such conveyance is not unreasonable or injurious to the wife, is hereby in all respects validated and confirmed, to the same extent as though said certifying officer were one of the officers named in G.S. 52-6.

§ 52-10. Contracts between husband and wife generally; releases.

(a) Contracts between husband and wife not inconsistent with public policy are valid, and any persons of full age about to be married and married persons may, with or without a valuable consideration, release and quitclaim such rights which they might respectively acquire or may have acquired by marriage in the property of each other; and such releases may be pleaded in bar of any action or proceeding for the recovery of the rights and estate so released. No contract or release between husband and wife made during their coverture shall be valid to affect or change any part of the real estate of either spouse, or the accruing income thereof for a longer time than three years next ensuing the making of such contract or release, unless it is in writing and is acknowledged by both parties before a certifying officer.

(b) Such certifying officer shall be a notary public, or a justice, judge, magistrate, clerk, assistant clerk or deputy clerk of the General Court of Justice, or the equivalent or corresponding officers of the state, territory or foreign country where the acknowledgment is made. Such officer must not be a party to the contract.

(c) This section shall not apply to any judgment of the superior court or other State court of competent jurisdiction, which, by reason of its being consented to by a husband and wife, or their attorneys, may be construed to constitute a contract or release between such husband and wife.

DEPOSITIONS

§ 8-74. Depositions for defendant in criminal actions.

In all criminal actions, hearings and investigations it shall be lawful for the defendant in any such action to make affidavit before the clerk of the superior court of the county in which said action is pending, that it is important for the defense that he have the testimony of any person, whose name must be given, and that such person is so infirm, or otherwise physically incapacitated, or non-resident of this State, that he cannot procure his attendance at the trial or hearing of said cause. Upon the filing of such affidavit, it shall be the duty of the clerk to appoint some responsible person to take the deposition of such witness, which deposition may be read in the trial of such criminal action under the same rules as now apply by law to depositions in civil actions: provided, that the district attorney or prosecuting attorney of the district, county or town in which such action is pending have 10 days' notice of the taking of such deposition, who may appear in person or by representative to conduct the cross-examination of such witness.

§ 8-76. Depositions before municipal authorities.

Any board of alderman, board of town or county commissioners or any person interested in any proceeding, investigation, hearing or trial before such board, may take the depositions of all persons whose evidence may be desired for use in said proceeding, investigation, hearing or trial; and to do so, the chairman of such board or such person may apply in person or by attorney to the superior court clerk of that county in which such proceeding, investigation, hearing or trial is pending, for a commission to take the same, and said clerk, upon such application, shall issue such commission, or such deposition may be taken by a notary public of this State or of any other state or foreign country without a commission issuing from the court; and the notice and proceedings upon the taking of said depositions shall be the same as provided for in civil actions; and if the person upon the notice of the taking of such deposition is to be served is absent from or cannot after due diligence be found within this State, but can be found within the county in which the deposition is to be taken, then, and in that case, said notice shall be personally served on such person by the commissioner appointed to take such deposition or by the notary taking such deposition, as the case may be; and when any such deposition is returned to the clerk it shall be opened and passed upon by him and delivered to such board, and the reading and using of such deposi-

tion shall conform to the rules of the superior court.

§ 8-77. Depositions in quo warranto proceedings.

In all actions for the purpose of trying the title to the office of clerk of the superior court, register of deeds, county treasurer or sheriff of any county, it shall be competent and lawful to take the deposition of witnesses before a commissioner or commissioners to be appointed by the judge of the district wherein the case is to be tried, or the judge holding the court of said district, or the clerk of the court wherein the case is pending, or a notary public, under the same rules as to time of notice and as to the manner of taking and filing the same as is now provided by law for the taking of depositions in other cases; and such depositions, when so taken, shall be competent to be read on the trial of such action, without regard to the place of residence of such witness or distance of residence from said place of trial: Provided that the provisions of this section shall not be construed to prevent the oral examination, by either party on the trial, of such witness as they may summon in their behalf.

§ 8-78. Commissioner may subpoena witness and punish for contempt.

Commissioners to take depositions appointed by the courts of this state, or by the courts of the states or territories of the United States, arbitrators, referees, and all persons acting under a commission issuing from any court of record in this state, are hereby empowered, they or the clerks of the courts respectively in this State, to which such commission shall be returnable, to issue subpoenas, specifying the time and place for the attendance of witnesses before them, and to administer oaths to said witnesses, to the end that they may give their testimony. And any witness appearing before any of the said persons and refusing to give his testimony on oath touching such matters as he may be lawfully examined unto shall be committed, by warrant of the person before whom he shall so refuse, to the common jail of the county, there to remain until he may be willing to give his evidence; which warrant of commitment shall recite what authority the person has to take the testimony of such witness, and the refusal of the witness to give it.

§ 8-79. Attendance before commissioner enforced.

The sheriff of the county where the witness may be shall execute all such subpoenas, and make due return thereof before the commissioner, or other person, before whom the witness is to appear, in the same manner, and under the same penalties, as in case of process of a like kind returnable to court; and when the witness shall be subpoenaed five days before the time of his required attendance, and shall fail to appear according to the subpoena and give evidence, the default shall be noted by the commissioner, arbitrator, or other person aforesaid; and in case the default be made before a commissioner acting under authority from courts without the State, the defaulting witness shall forfeit and pay to the party at whose instance he may be subpoenaed fifty dollars, and on the trial for such penalty the subpoena issued by the commissioner, or other person, as aforesaid, with the indorsement thereon of due service by the officer serving the same, together with the default noted as aforesaid and indorsed on the subpoena, shall be prima facie evidence of the forfeiture, and sufficient to entitle the plaintiff to judgment for the same, unless the witness may show his incapacity to have attended.

§ 8-80. Remedies against defaulting witness before commissioner.

But in case the default be made before a commissioner, arbitrator, referee or other person, acting under a commission or authority from any of the courts of this State, then the same shall be certified under his hand, and returned with the subpoena to the court by which he was commissioned or empowered to take the evidence of such witness; and thereupon the court shall adjudge the defaulting witness to pay to the party at whose instance he was summoned the sum of forty dollars ($40.00); but execution shall not issue therefor until the same be ordered by the court, after such proceedings had as shall give said witness an opportunity to show cause, if he can, against the issuing thereof.

LEGAL HOLIDAYS

§ 103-4. Dates of public holidays.

(a) The following are declared to be legal public holidays:

(1) New Year's Day, January 1.

(1a) Martin Luther King, Jr.'s, Birthday, the third Monday in January.

(2) Robert E. Lee's Birthday, January 19.

(3) Washington's Birthday, the third Monday in February.

(3a) Greek Independence Day, March 25.

(4) Anniversary of signing of Halifax Resolves, April 12.

(5) Confederate Memorial Day, May 10.

(6) Anniversary of Mecklenburg Declaration of Independence, May 20.

(7) Memorial Day, the last Monday in May.

(8) Good Friday.

(9) Independence Day, July 4.

(10) Labor Day, the first Monday in September.

(11) Columbus Day, the second Monday in October.

(11a) Yom Kippur.

(12) Veterans' Day, November 11.

(13) Tuesday after the first Monday in November in years in which a general election is to be held.

(14) Thanksgiving Day, the fourth Thursday in November.

(15) Christmas Day, December 25.

§ 103-5. Acts to be done on Sunday or holidays.

Where the day or the last day for doing an act required or permitted by law to be done falls on Sunday or a holiday the act may be done on the next succeeding secular or business day and where the courthouse in any county is closed on Saturday or any other day by order of the board of county commissioners of said county and the day or the last day required for filing an advance bid or the filing of any pleading or written instrument of any kind with any officer having an office in the courthouse, or the performance of any act required or permitted to be done in said courthouse falls on Saturday or other day during which said courthouse is closed as aforesaid, then said Saturday or other day during which said courthouse is closed as aforesaid shall be deemed a holiday; and said advance bid, pleading or other written instrument may be filed, and any act required or permitted to be done in the courthouse may be done on the next day during which the courthouse is open for business.

NORTH DAKOTA

NOTARIES PUBLIC

[N.D. Cent. Code]

§ 44-06-01. Appointment and qualification of notaries public.

The secretary of state shall appoint in each county in this state one or more notaries public, who shall hold office for six years unless sooner removed by the secretary of state. Each notary shall have power and authority anywhere in the state to administer oaths and perform all other duties required by law. A person, to be eligible to such appointment, at the time of appointment, must have the qualifications of an elector as to age and residence.

§ 44-06-02. Commission—record—fee—notice.

The secretary of state shall issue a commission to each notary public appointed by the secretary of state which shall be posted by such notary in a conspicuous place in his office. The secretary of state shall collect twenty dollars for the issuance of such commission. Such sum shall be paid into the state treasury and credited to the general fund. The secretary of state shall keep in his office a record of such appointments and the date of the expiration of the same, and shall notify each notary public by mail at least thirty days before the expiration of his term of the date upon which his commission will expire. Such notice shall be addressed to such notary public at his last known place of residence.

§ 44-06-03. Oath and bond of notary public—approval of bond.

Each notary public, before entering upon the duties of the office, shall take the oath prescribed for civil officers and give to the state a bond in the penal sum of seven thousand five hundred dollars conditioned for the faithful discharge of the duties of the office. Such bond may be furnished by a surety or bonding company authorized to do business in this state or by one or more sureties, and is subject to approval by the secretary of state.

§ 44-06-03.1. Notice by surety to secretary of state of claim against bond.

If a surety or bonding company giving a bond under section 44-06-03 receives a claim against that bond with respect to a notary public, that surety or bonding company shall notify the secretary of state of the outcome of said claim.

§ 44-06-04. Deposit of oath, bond, and impression of notarial seal.

Each notary public, before entering upon the duties of such office, shall provide himself with an official seal bearing his name and shall deposit a legible impression of such seal, together with his oath and bond, in the office of the secretary of state.

§ 44-06-05. Vacancy—disposition of records.

Whenever the office of any notary public shall become vacant, the record of such notary together with all papers relating to the office must be deposited in the office of the secretary of state. Any notary public who, on resignation or removal from office, or any executor or administrator of the estate of any deceased notary public who neglects to deposit such records and papers as aforesaid for the space of three months, or any person who knowingly destroys, defaces, or conceals any records or papers of any notary public, shall forfeit and pay a sum of not less than fifty dollars nor more than five

hundred dollars, and he also shall be liable in a civil action for damages to any party injured.

§ 44-06-06. Duty of notary as to instrument protested by him.

Each notary public, when any bill of exchange, promissory note, or other written instrument, shall be by him protested for nonacceptance or nonpayment, shall give notice thereof in writing to the maker, to each and every endorser of such bill of exchange, and to the maker of each security or the endorsers of any promissory note or other written instrument, immediately after such protest shall have been made.

§ 44-06-07. Service of notice by notary public.

Each notary public shall serve notice personally upon each person protested against, or by properly folding the notice, directing it to the person to be charged at his place of residence according to the best information that the person giving the notice can obtain, depositing it in the United States mail or post office most conveniently accessible, and prepaying the postage thereon.

§ 44-06-08. Record of notices—certified copy—competent evidence.

Each notary public shall keep a record of all notices, of the time and manner in which the same were served, the names of all the persons to whom the same were directed, and the description and amount of the instrument protested. Such record, or a copy thereof, certified by the notary under seal, at all times shall be competent evidence to prove such notice in any court of this state.

§ 44-06-09. Secretary of state—preservation of records.

The secretary of state shall receive and keep safely all the records and papers directed by this chapter to be deposited in his office and shall furnish certified copies thereof when required. Such copies shall have the same force and effect as if the same were certified by the notary public by whom the record was made.

§ 44-06-11. Revocation of notary commission—notice.

In case the commission of any person appointed as a notary is revoked, the secretary of state shall give notice thereof by mail to such person immediately and to the clerk of the district court of the proper county.

§ 44-06-12. Notary public commission—date of expiration.

Every notary public taking an acknowledgment to any instrument, immediately following his signature to the jurat or certificates of acknowledgment, shall legibly print, stamp, or type his name and shall endorse the date of the expiration of such commission. Such endorsement may be written legibly, stamped, or printed upon the instrument either connected to or disconnected from the seal, and shall be substantially in the following form:

My commission expires _____, 19___.

§ 44-06-13. Acting as notary when disqualified—penalty.

Any notary public who exercises the duties of his office with knowledge that this commission has expired or has been canceled or that he is disqualified otherwise is guilty of an infraction, and, if appropriate, his commission shall be canceled by the secretary of state.

§ 44-06-13.1. Wrongfully notarizing document—penalty.

Any notary public who appends his official signature to any document when the parties thereto have not executed the document in his presence is guilty of an infraction and his commission shall be canceled by the secretary of state, who shall give written notice of such cancellation to the notary public.

§ 44-06-14. Fees to be charged by notaries public.

A notary public is entitled to charge and receive the following fees:

1. For each protest, fifty cents.
2. For recording the same, twenty-five cents.
3. For each notice of protest completed and served, twenty-five cents and postage for mailing the notice.
4. For taking affidavit and seal, one dollar and fifty cents.
5. For administering an oath or affirmation, ten cents.
6. For taking a deposition, each ten words, one and one-half cents.
7. For each certificate and seal, one dollar and fifty cents.
8. For taking proof of acknowledgment, one dollar and fifty cents.

OATHS

§ 44-05-01. Officers authorized to administer oaths.

The following officers are authorized to administer oaths:

1. Each justice of the supreme court, each judge of the district court, the clerk of the supreme court, and the clerk's deputy.
2. Judge of the county court, clerk of the district court, clerk of the county court, county auditor, register of deeds, and the deputy of each such officer within that officer's county.
3. Each county commissioner and public administrator within that officer's county.
4. Notary public anywhere in the state, upon complying with section 44-06-04.
5. Each city auditor, municipal judge, and township clerk, within that officer's own city or township.
6. Each sheriff and the deputy sheriff within the sheriff's county in the cases prescribed by law.
7. Other offices in the cases prescribed by law or by rule of the supreme court.

§ 44-05-02. Person may affirm.

A person conscientiously opposed to swearing may affirm and shall be subject to the penalties of perjury as in case of swearing.

§ 44-05-03. Fee for taking acknowledgment and administering an oath.

Any officer authorized by law to take and certify acknowledgment of a deed or other instrument is entitled to charge and receive not more than one dollar.

ACKNOWLEDGMENTS

§ 47-19-13. Acknowledgment and proof—persons authorized to make—state-wide jurisdiction.

The proof or acknowledgment of an instrument may be made at any place within this state before a judge, or the clerk, of the supreme court, or a notary public.

§ 47-19-14. Acknowledgment and proof—limited to district of officer.

The proof or acknowledgment of an instrument may be made in this state within the judicial district, county, subdivision, or city for which the officer was elected or appointed, before:

1. A judge or clerk of a court of record;
2. A mayor of a city;
3. A register of deeds;
4. A United States commissioner;
5. A county auditor; or
6. A township clerk or a city auditor.

Uniform Recognition of Acknowledgments Act

§ 47-19-14.1. Recognition of notarial acts.

For the purposes of this section and sections 47-19-14.2 and 47-19-14.7, "notarial acts" mean acts which the laws and regulations of this state authorize notaries public of this state to perform, including the administering of oaths and affirmations, taking proof of execution and acknowledgments of instruments, and attesting documents. Notarial acts may be performed for use in this state with the same effect as if performed by a notary public of this state by the following persons authorized pursuant to the laws and regulations of other governments in addition to any other person authorized by the laws and regulations of this state:

1. A notary public authorized by any jurisdiction to perform notarial acts.
2. A justice, judge, clerk, or deputy clerk of any court of record in the place in which the notarial act is performed.
3. An officer of the foreign service of the United States, a consular agent, or any other person authorized by regulation of the United States department of state to perform notarial acts in the place in which the act is performed.
4. A commissioned officer or noncommissioned officer in active service with the armed forces of the United States and any other person authorized by regulation of the armed forces to perform notarial acts, if the notarial act is performed for one of the following, or his dependents: a merchant seaman of the United States, a member of the armed forces of the United States, or any other person serving with or accompanying the armed forces of the United States.
5. Any other person authorized to perform notarial acts in the place in which the act is performed.

§ 47-19-14.2. Authentication of authority of officer.

1. If the notarial act is performed by any of the persons described in subsections 1 through 4 of section 47-19-14.1, other than a person authorized to perform notarial acts by the laws or regulations of a foreign country, written indication of his title or rank and serial number, if any, is sufficient proof of the authority of a holder of that rank or title to perform the act. Further proof of his authority is not required.

2. If the notarial act is performed by a person authorized by the laws or regulations of a foreign country to perform the act, there is sufficient proof of the authority of that person to perform the act if:

a. Either a foreign service officer of the United States, resident in the country in which the act is performed, or a diplomatic or consular officer of the foreign country, resident in the United States, certifies that a person holding that office is authorized to perform the act;

b. The official seal of the person performing the notarial act is affixed to the document; or

c. The title of the person, and an indication of his authority to perform notarial acts appears either in a recognized digest of foreign law, or in a list customarily used as a source of such information.

3. If the notarial act is performed by a person other than one described in subsections 1 and 2, there is sufficient proof of the authority of that person to act, if the clerk of a court of record, in the place in which the notarial act is performed, certifies to the official character of that person, and to his authority to perform the notarial act.

4. The signature and title of the person performing the notarial acts are prima facie evidence that he is a person with the designated title and that the signature is genuine.

§ 47-19-14.3. Certification of person taking acknowledgment.

The person taking an acknowledgment shall certify that:

1. The person acknowledging appeared before him and acknowledged that he executed the instrument; and

2. The person acknowledging was known to the person taking the acknowledgment, or that the person taking the acknowledgment had satisfactory evidence that the person acknowledging was the person described in and who executed the instrument.

§ 47-19-14.4. Recognition of certificate of acknowledgment.

The form of a certificate of acknowledgment used by a person whose authority is recognized under section 47-19-14.2 shall be accepted in this state if:

1. The certificate is in a form prescribed by the laws or regulations of this state;

2. The certificate is in a form prescribed by the laws or regulations applicable in the place in which the acknowledgment is taken; or

3. The certificate contains the words "acknowledged before me" or their substantial equivalent.

§ 47-19-14.5. Certificate of acknowledgment.

The words "acknowledged before me," or their substantial equivalent, as used in a certificate of acknowledgment made by a person taking an acknowledgment outside this state shall mean:

1. That the person acknowledging appeared before the person taking the acknowledgment and acknowledged that he executed the instrument;

2. That, in the case of:

a. A corporation, the officer or agent acknowledged that he held the position or title set forth in the instrument and certificate; that he signed the instrument on behalf of the corporation by proper authority; and that the instrument was the act of the corporation;

b. A partnership, the partner or agent acknowledged that he signed the instrument on behalf of the partnership by proper authority and that the instrument was the act of the partnership;

c. A person acknowledging as attorney in fact for a principal, that he signed the instrument by proper authority as the act of the principal;

d. A person acknowledging as a public officer, trustee, administrator, guardian, or other representative, that he signed the instrument by proper authority and in the capacity stated in the instrument; and

3. That the person taking the acknowledgment either knew, or had satisfactory evidence, that the person acknowledging was the person named in the instrument or certificate.

§ 47-19-14.6. Short forms of acknowledgment.

The forms of acknowledgment set forth in this section may be used and are sufficient for their respective purposes under any law or regulation of this state. The forms shall be known as the "statutory short forms of acknowledgment," and may be referred to by that name. The authorization of the forms provided in this section does not preclude the use of other forms:

1. For an individual acting in his own right:
State of _____
County of _____
The foregoing instrument was acknowledged before me this (date) by (name of person acknowledging).
(Signature of person taking acknowledgment)
(Title or rank)
(Serial number, if any)

2. For a corporation:
State of _____
County of _____
The foregoing instrument was acknowledged before me this (date) by (name of officer or agent and title of officer or agent) of (name of corporation acknowledging), a (state or place of incorporation) corporation, on behalf of the corporation.
(Signature of person taking acknowledgment)
(Title or rank)
(Serial number, if any)

3. For a partnership:
State of _____
County of _____
The foregoing instrument was acknowledged before me this (date) by (name of acknowledging partner or agent), partner (or agent), on behalf of (name of partnership), a partnership.
(Signature of person taking acknowledgment)
(Title or rank)
(Serial number, if any)

4. For an individual acting as an attorney in fact for a principal:
State of _____
County of _____
The foregoing instrument was acknowledged before me this (date) by (name of attorney in fact) as attorney in fact on behalf of (name of principal).
(Signature of person taking acknowledgment)
(Title or rank)
(Serial number, if any)

5. For a public officer, trustee, guardian, personal representative or other representative:
State of _____
County of _____
The foregoing instrument was acknowledged before me this (date) by (name and title of position).
(Signature of person taking acknowledgment)
(Title or rank)
(Serial number, if any)

§ 47-19-14.7. Prior acknowledgments not affected.

A notarial act performed prior to the effective date of sections 47-19-14.1 through 47-19-14.8 shall not be affected by those sections. Sections 47-19-14.1 through 47-1-14.8 provide an additional method of proving notarial acts, and do not diminish or invalidate the recognition accorded to notarial acts by other laws or regulations of this state.

§ 47-19-14.8. Short title.

Sections 47-19-14.1 through 47-19-14.8 may be cited as the Uniform Recognition of Acknowledgments Act.

§ 47-19-20. Identity of person acknowledging—proof required.

The acknowledgment of an instrument must not be taken unless the officer taking it knows or has satisfactory evidence on the oath or affirmation of a credible witness that the person making the acknowledgment is the individual who is described in and who executed the instrument, or if executed by a corporation, that the officer making such acknowledgment is authorized to make it as provided in section 47-10-05.1.

§ 47-19-21. Proof of an unacknowledged instrument—method.

Proof of the execution of an instrument when not acknowledged may be made:

1. By the party executing it;

2. By a subscribing witness; or

3. By other witnesses in cases mentioned in sections 47-19-23 and 47-19-24.

§ 47-19-22. Knowledge required to officer of subscribing witness in taking proof.

If proof of the execution of an instrument is made by a subscribing witness, such witness must be known personally to the officer taking the proof to be the person whose name is subscribed to the instrument as a witness or must be proved to be such by the oath of a credible witness. The subscribing witness must prove that the person whose name is subscribed to the instrument as a party is the person described in it, that such person executed it, and that the witness subscribed his name thereto as a witness.

§ 47-19-23. Proof by handwriting—when received—requirements.

The execution of an instrument may be established by proof of the handwriting of the party and of a subscribing witness, if there is one, in the following cases:

1. When the parties and all the subscribing witnesses are dead;

2. When the parties and all the subscribing witnesses are nonresidents of the state;

3. When the place of their residence is unknown to the party desiring the proof and cannot be ascertained by the exercise of due diligence;

4. When the subscribing witness conceals himself, or cannot be found by the officer by the exercise of due diligence in attempting to serve a subpoena or attachment; or

5. In case of the continued failure or refusal of the witness to testify for the space of one hour after his appearance.

§ 47-19-24. Proof by handwriting—facts required.

The evidence taken under section 47-19-23 must prove to the officer satisfactorily the following facts:

1. The existence of one or more of the conditions mentioned therein;

2. That the witness testifying knew the person whose name purports to be subscribed to the instrument as a party, that he is well acquainted with his signature, and that it is genuine;

3. That the witness testifying personally knew the person who subscribed the instrument as a witness, that he is well acquainted with his signature, and that it is genuine; and

4. The place of residence of the witness testifying.

§ 47-19-25. Certificate of proof—contents.

An officer taking proof of the execution of an instrument must set forth in his certificate, endorsed thereon or attached thereto:

1. All the matters required by law to be done or known by him;

2. All the matters required by law to be proved before him on the proceeding;

3. The names of all the witnesses examined before him;

4. The place of residence of all witnesses examined before him; and

5. The substance of the evidence given by witnesses examined before him.

Forms

§ 47-19-26. Certificate of acknowledgment—forms.

An officer taking an acknowledgment of an instrument within this state must endorse thereon or attach thereto a certificate substantially in the forms prescribed in sections 47-19-27, 47-19-28, 47-19-29, and 47-19-30.

§ 47-19-27. General certificate of acknowledgment.

A certificate of acknowledgment, unless otherwise provided in this chapter, must be in substantially the following form:

STATE OF NORTH DAKOTA
County of _____
    On this _____ day of _____, in the year _____ before me personally appeared _____, known to me (or proved to me on oath of _____) to be the person who is described in and who executed the within instrument, and acknowledged to me that he (or they) executed the same.

§ 47-19-28. Certificate of acknowledgment executed by a corporation.

The certificate of acknowledgment of an instrument executed by a corporation must be substantially in the following form:

STATE OF NORTH DAKOTA
County of _____
    On this _____ day of _____, in the year _____ before me (here insert the name and quality of the officer), personally appeared _____, known to me (or proved to me on oath of _____) to be the president (or other officer or person) of the corporation that is described in and that executed the within instrument, and acknowledged to me that such corporation executed the same.

§ 47-19-29. Certificate of acknowledgment by an attorney in fact.

The certificate of acknowledgment by an attorney in fact must be substantially in the following form:

STATE OF NORTH DAKOTA
County of _____
    On this _____ day of _____, in the year _____ before me (here insert the name and quality of the officer), personally appeared _____, known to me (or proved to me on oath of _____) to be the person who is described in and whose name is subscribed to the within instrument as the attorney in fact of _____ and acknowledged to me that he subscribed the name of _____ thereto as principal and his own name as attorney in fact.

§ 47-19-30. Certificate of acknowledgment by deputy sheriff.

All acknowledgments of deeds or other instruments in writing made by any deputy sheriff of this state shall be made substantially in the following form:

STATE OF NORTH DAKOTA
County of _____
    On this _____ day of _____, in the year _____ before me, a _____, in and for said county, personally appeared _____, known to me to be the person who is described in and whose name is subscribed to the within instrument as deputy sheriff of said county and acknowledged to me that he subscribed the name of _____ thereto as sheriff of said county and his own name as deputy sheriff.

§ 47-19-32. Certification of acknowledgments or proof of instruments—officer's certificate—how authenticated.

An officer taking and certifying an acknowledgment or proof of an instrument for record must authenticate his certificate by affixing thereto:

1. His signature followed by the name of his office; and

2. His seal of office, if by the laws of the territory, state, or country where the acknowledgment or proof is taken, or by authority of which he is acting, he is required to have an official seal.

A judge or clerk of a court of record must authenticate his certificate by affixing thereto the seal of his court. A mayor of a city must authenticate his certificate by affixing thereto the seal of his city.

§ 47-19-33. Who shall not execute acknowledgments and affidavits.

No person heretofore or hereafter authorized by law to take or receive the proof or acknowledgment of the execution of an instrument or affidavit and to certify thereto shall take or receive such proof, acknowledgment, or affidavit or certify to the same, if he shall be a party to such instrument, or a member of any partnership which shall or may be a party to such instrument, nor if the husband or wife of such person or officer shall be a party to such instrument.

§ 47-19-34. Proof and acknowledgment of instruments as to corporations.

No provision in any of the laws of this state, relating to the proof and acknowledgment of instruments and the taking of affidavits, shall be construed to invalidate or affect the proof or acknowledgment, affidavit, or the certificate thereof, of any instrument to which a corporation may be a party and which shall have been or may be proven, acknowledged, sworn to before, or certified to by, an officer or person authorized by law, who may be an officer, director, employee, or stockholder of such corporation. No person otherwise qualified or authorized by law to take and receive the proof or acknowledgment of an instrument or affidavit and to certify thereto shall be disqualified by reason of being an officer, director, employee, or stockholder of any corporation which is a party to such instrument, and such proof, acknowledgment, and certificate thereof shall be valid for all purposes.

§ 47-19-35. Persons authorized to take acknowledgments and affidavits.

All officers and persons, authorized by law to take the proof or acknowledgment of an instrument or affidavit and to certify thereto, may take such proof or acknowledgment and certify to the same in any case not prohibited by this chapter.

§ 47-19-36. Authority of officers in taking proof.

Officers authorized to take the proof of instruments are authorized in such proceedings:

1. To administer oaths or affirmations;

2. To employ and swear interpreters; and

3. To issue subpoenas, obedience to which may be enforced as provided by title 28 [Judicial Procedure, Civil].

DEPOSITIONS

§ 27-10-23. Contempt of witness before notary public, officer, board, or tribunal.

If a witness fails to attend for examination when duly required to do so, or refuses to be sworn, or to answer as a witness, before a notary public or any other officer, board, or tribunal authorized by law to require his attendance for examination and to take testimony, such notary public, officer, board, or tribunal shall certify such fact to the judge of the district court of the county in which such witness resides or in which such witness may be present. Such judge, by order, then shall require such witness to attend before him for examination at a time and place specified in the order. Upon the return day of the order, the examination of the witness shall be conducted before the judge, and for the failure of such witness to attend, or to be sworn, or to answer as a witness, or for a refusal of such witness to do any act required of him by law, he may be punished as for a contempt in the manner provided in this chapter.

§ 31-04-02. "Affidavit" defined.

An affidavit is a written declaration under oath made without notice to the adverse party.

§ 31-04-03. "Deposition" defined.

A deposition is a written declaration under oath made upon notice to the adverse party for the purpose of enabling him to attend and cross-examine, or upon written interrogatories.

[N.D. R. Civ. P.]

RULE 28. Persons before whom depositions may be taken.

(a) **Within the United States.** Within the United States or within a territory or insular possession subject to the jurisdiction of the United States, depositions must be taken before an officer authorized to administer oaths by the laws of this state or of the United Sates or of the place where the examination is held, or before a person appointed by the court in which the action is pending. A person so appointed has power to administer oaths and take testimony. Depositions may also be taken before a person commissioned by the court or pursuant to a letter rogatory under subdivisions (b) and (c). The term officer as used in Rules 30, 31, and 32 includes a person appointed by the court or designated by the parties under Rule 29.

(b) **In foreign countries.** In a foreign country, depositions may be taken (i) on notice before a person authorized to administer oaths in the place in which the examination is held, either by the law thereof or by the law of the United States, or (ii) before a person commissioned by the court, and a person so commissioned has the power by virtue of the commission to administer any necessary oath and take testimony, or (iii) pursuant to a letter rogatory.

(c) **Commission or letter rogatory.** A commission or a letter rogatory must be issued on application and notice, and on terms that are just and appropriate. It is not requisite to the issuance of a commission or a letter rogatory that the taking of the deposition in any other matter is impracticable or inconvenient; and both a commission and a letter rogatory may be issued in proper cases. A notice or commission may designate the person before whom the deposition is to be taken either by name or descriptive title. A letter rogatory may be addressed "To the Appropriate Authority in [here name the state or country]." Evidence obtained in a foreign country pursuant to a commission or in response to a letter rogatory need not be excluded merely for the reason that it is not a verbatim transcript or that the testimony was not taken under oath or for any similar departure from the requirements for depositions taken under these rules.

(d) Disqualification for interest. No deposition may be taken before a person who is a relative, employee, or attorney or counsel of any of the parties, or who is a relative or employee of that attorney or counsel, or who is financially interested in the action.

[N.D. R. Crim. P.]

RULE 15. Depositions.

(a) When taken. At any time after the defendant has appeared, any party may take testimony of any person by deposition including audio-visual depositions taken as provided in Rule 30.1 of the civil rules, except:

(1) The defendant may not be deposed unless the defendant consents and the defendant's lawyer, if the defendant has one, is present or the defendant waives the lawyer's presence;

(2) A discovery deposition may be taken after the time set by the court only with leave of court;

(3) A deposition to perpetuate testimony may be taken only with leave of court, which shall be granted upon motion of any party if it appears that the deponent may be able to give material testimony but may be unable to attend a trial or hearing; and

(4) Upon motion of a party or of the deponent and upon a showing that the taking of the deposition does or will unreasonably annoy, embarrass, or oppress, or cause undue burden or expense to, the deponent or a party, the court in which the prosecution is pending or a court of the jurisdiction where the deposition is being taken may order that the deposition not be taken or continue or may limit the scope and manner of its taking. Upon demand of the objecting party or deponent, the taking of the deposition may be suspended for the time necessary to make the motion.

Attendance of witnesses and production of documentary evidence and objects may be compelled by subpoena under Rule 17.

(b) Witness who would not respond to subpoena. If a party is granted leave to take a deposition to perpetuate testimony, the court, upon motion of the party and a showing of probable cause to believe that the deponent would not respond to a subpoena, by order shall direct a law enforcement officer to take the deponent into custody and hold the deponent until the taking of the deposition commences but not to exceed six hours and to keep the deponent in custody during the taking of the deposition. If the motion is by the prosecuting attorney, the court, upon further motion by the prosecuting attorney and a showing of probable cause to believe that the defendant would not otherwise attend the taking of the deposition, may make the same order as to the defendant.

(c) Notice of taking. The party at whose instance the deposition is to be taken shall give all parties reasonable written notice of the name and address of each person to be examined, the time and place for the deposition, and the manner of recording. Upon motion of a party or of the deponent the court may change the time, place, or manner of record.

(d) How taken. The deposition shall be taken in the manner provided in civil actions, except:

(1) If the deposition is taken at a place over which this state lacks jurisdiction, it may be taken instead in the manner provided by the law of that place;

(2) It shall be recorded by the means specified in the notice; and

(3) Upon motion of a party and a showing that a party or the deponent is engaging in serious misconduct at the taking of a deposition, the court by order of a designated officer, in which case the designated officer may preside over the remainder of the deposition's taking.

(e) Place of taking. The deposition shall be taken in a building where the trial may be held, at a place agreed upon by the parties, or at a place designated by special or general order of the court. If the defendant is in custody or subject to terms of release which prohibit leaving the state and does not appear before the court and understandingly and voluntarily waives the right to be present, a deposition to perpetuate testimony shall not be taken at a place which requires transporting the defendant within a jurisdiction which does not confer upon law enforcement officers of this state the right to transport prisoners within it.

(f) Presence of defendant.

(1) At discovery deposition. The defendant may be present at the taking of a discovery deposition, but if the defendant is in custody the defendant may be present only with leave of court.

(2) At deposition to perpetuate testimony. The defendant must be present at the taking of a deposition to perpetuate testimony, but if the defendant's counsel is present at the taking:

(i) The court may excuse the defendant from being present if the defendant appears before the court and understandingly and voluntarily waives the right to be present;

(ii) The taking of the deposition may continue if the defendant, present when it commenced, thereafter leaves voluntarily; or

(iii) If the deposition's taking is presided over by a judicial officer, the judicial officer may direct that the deposition's taking or part thereof be conducted in the defendant's absence if the judicial officer has justifiably excluded the defendant because of the defendant's disruptive conduct.

(3) Unexcused absence. If the defendant is not present at the commencement of the taking of a deposition to perpetuate testimony and the defendant's absence has not been excused:

(i) Its taking may proceed, in which case the deposition may be used only as a discovery deposition; or

(ii) If the deposition is taken at the instance of the prosecution, the prosecuting attorney may direct that the commencement of its taking be postponed until the defendant's attendance can be obtained, and the court, upon application of the prosecuting attorney, by order may direct a law enforcement officer to take the defendant into custody during the taking of the deposition.

(g) Payment of expenses. If the deposition is taken at the instance of the prosecution, the court may, and in all cases where the defendant is unable to bear the expense the court shall direct the state to pay the expense of taking the deposition, including the reasonable expenses of travel and subsistence of defense counsel and, if the deposition is to perpetuate testimony or if the court permits as to a discovery deposition, of the defendant in attending the deposition.

(h) Substantive use on grounds of unavailability. So far as otherwise admissible under the rules of evidence, a deposition to perpetuate testimony may be used as substantive evidence at the trial or upon any hearing if the deponent is unavailable as defined in Rule 804(a) of the North Dakota Rules of Evidence. A discovery deposition may then be so used if the court determines that the use is fair in light of the nature and extent of the total examination at the taking thereof, but it may be offered by the prosecution only if the defendant was present at its taking. If only a part of a deposition is offered in evidence by a party, an adverse party may require the offering of all of it that is relevant to the part offered.

(i) Objections to admissibility. Objections to receiving in evidence a deposition or part thereof may be made as provided in civil actions.

(j) Deposition by agreement not precluded. Nothing in this rule precludes the taking of a deposition, orally or upon written questions, or the use of a deposition, by agreement of the parties.

LEGAL HOLIDAYS

[N.D. CENT. CODE]

§ **1-03-01.** Holidays.

Holidays are as follows:

1. Every Sunday.
2. The first day of January, which is New Year's Day.
3. The third Monday in February, in recognition of the birthday of George Washington.

4. The Friday next preceding Easter Sunday and commonly known as Good Friday.
5. The last Monday in May, which is Memorial Day.
6. The fourth day of July, which is the anniversary of the Declaration of Independence.
7. The first Monday in September, which is Labor Day.
8. The eleventh day of November, which is Veterans' Day.
9. The fourth Thursday in November, which is Thanksgiving Day.
10. The twenty-fifth day of December, which is Christmas Day.
11. Every day appointed by the President of the United States or by the governor of this state for a public holiday.

Nothing in this section may be construed to prevent the holding of legislative sessions or the taking of final action on any legislative matter upon any of such holidays other than Sunday. Any action heretofore taken upon any legislative matter upon any such holiday is valid and legal for all purposes.

§ **1-03-01.1.** Closing of state offices— Christmas Eve.

State offices must be closed at twelve noon on December twenty-fourth, Christmas Eve day, unless it is a weekend or holiday pursuant to section 1-03-02.1.

§ **1-03-02.** When day following holiday shall be a holiday.

If the first day of January, the fourth day of July, the eleventh day of November, or the twenty-fifth day of December falls upon a Sunday, the Monday following shall be the holiday.

§ **1-03-02.1** When holiday falls on a Saturday.

If any of the holidays enumerated in section 1-03-02 fall on a Saturday, the Friday immediately before shall be the holiday.

§ **1-03-04.** Business days.

All days other than those mentioned in sections 1-03-01, 1-03-02, and 1-03-02.1 are to be deemed business days for all purposes. However, any bank may remain closed on any one business day of each week, as it may from time to time elect. Any day upon which a bank is so closed shall be, with respect to such bank, a holiday and not a business day. Any act authorized, required, or permitted to be performed at or by or with respect to such bank on such day, may be performed on the next succeeding business day, and no liability or loss of rights shall result from such delay.

Notice of intention on the part of any bank to remain closed on a business day of the week shall be posted in a conspicuous place in the lobby of the bank at least ten days prior to the establishment of such practice and similar notice shall be given when a bank elects to change the day of the week on which it remains closed. Any state bank establishing the practice, as hereinbefore provided, of closing one day a week shall give ten days' notice in writing to the commissioner of banking and financial institutions, in addition to posting the notice in the lobby. However, any bank may elect to remain closed on a business day of the week without any prior notice in the event of the following emergencies: any act of God, death of an officer, or a robbery.

§ 1-03-05. Act due on holiday performed on next day.

Whenever an act of a secular nature, other than a work of necessity or mercy, is appointed by law or contract to be performed upon a particular day, which falls upon a holiday, such act may be performed upon the next business day with the same effect as if it had been performed upon the day appointed.

OHIO

NOTARIES PUBLIC

[OHIO REV. CODE ANN.]

§ 147.01. Appointment and commission of notaries public.

The governor may appoint and commission as notaries public as many persons as he considers necessary, who are citizens of this state and are of the age of eighteen or over. A notary public shall be appointed and commissioned as a notary public for the state. The governor may revoke a commission issued to a notary public upon presentation of satisfactory evidence of official misconduct or incapacity.

§ 147.02. Certificate of qualifications.

Before the appointment of a notary public is made, the applicant shall produce to the governor a certificate from a judge of the court of common pleas, court of appeals, or supreme court, that he is of good moral character, a citizen of the county in which he resides, and, if it is the fact, that the applicant is an attorney at law qualified and admitted to practice in this state, and possessed of sufficient qualifications and ability to discharge the duties of the office of notary public. No judge shall issue such certificate until he is satisfied from his personal knowledge that the applicant possesses the qualifications necessary to a proper discharge of the duties of the office, or until the applicant has passed an examination under such rules and regulations as the judge may prescribe. If the applicant is admitted to the practice of law in this state, this fact shall also be certified by the judge in his certification.

§ 147.03. Term of office; oath.

Each notary public, except a citizen of this state

421

admitted to the practice of law by the Ohio supreme court, shall hold his office for the term of five years unless the commission is revoked. Before entering upon the duties of his office, he shall take and subscribe an oath to be indorsed on his commission.

A citizen of this state admitted to the practice of law by the Ohio supreme court shall hold his office as a notary public as long as such citizen is a resident of this state, is in good standing before the Ohio supreme court, and the commission is not revoked. Before entering upon the duties of his office he shall deposit with the secretary of state the certificate provided for in section 147.02 of the Revised Code and shall take and subscribe an oath to be indorsed on his commission.

A notary public who violates the oath required by this section shall be removed from office by the court of common pleas of the county in which he resides, upon complaint filed and substantiated in such court, and the court shall thereupon certify such removal to the governor. The person so removed shall be ineligible for reappointment to the office of notary public.

Each citizen of this state holding office as a notary public on October 24, 1961, shall continue in such office until the expiration of his term and he shall thereafter hold office pursuant to this section.

§ 147.04. Seal and register.

Before entering upon the discharge of his duties, a notary public shall provide himself with a seal of a notary public. The seal shall consist of the coat of arms of the state within a circle one inch in diameter and shall be surrounded by the words "notary public," "notarial seal," or words to that effect, the name of the notary public and the words "State of Ohio." The seal may be of either a type that will stamp ink onto a document or one that will emboss it. The name of the notary public may, instead of appearing on the seal, be printed, typewritten, or stamped in legible, printed letters near his signature on each document signed by him. A notary public shall also provide himself with an official register in which shall be recorded a copy of every certificate of protest and copy of note, which seal and record shall be exempt from execution. Upon the death, expiration of term without reappointment, or removal from office of any notary public, his official register shall be deposited in the office of the county recorder of the county in which he resides.

§ 147.05. Commission to be recorded; fee.

Before entering upon the duties of his office, a notary public shall leave his commission with the oath indorsed thereon with the clerk of the court of common pleas of the county in which he resides. The commission shall be recorded by the clerk in a

book kept for that purpose. The clerk shall indorse on the margin of the record and on the back of the commission the time he received it for record, and make a proper index to all commissions recorded by him. For recording and indexing such commission, the fee of the clerk shall be as provided for in division (S) of section 2303.20 of the Revised Code.

§ 147.06. Certified copy of commission to be evidence; fees.

Upon application, the clerk of the court of common pleas shall make a certified copy of a commission and the indorsements thereon, under the seal of the court, which certified copy shall be prima facie evidence of the matters and facts therein contained. For each certified copy of a commission the clerk shall be entitled to receive a fee of two dollars.

§ 147.07. Powers; jurisdiction.

A notary public may, throughout the state, administer oaths required or authorized by law, take and certify depositions, take and certify acknowledgments of deeds, mortgages, liens, powers of attorney, and other instruments of writing, and receive, make, and record notarial protests. In taking depositions, he shall have the power that is by law vested in judges of county courts to compel the attendance of witnesses and punish them for refusing to testify. Sheriffs and constables are required to serve and return all process issued by notaries public in the taking of depositions.

§ 147.08. Fees.

A notary public is entitled to the following fees:

(A) For the protest of a bill of exchange or promissory note, one dollar and actual necessary expenses in going beyond the corporate limits of a municipal corporation to make presentment or demand;

(B) For recording an instrument required to be recorded by a notary public, ten cents for each one hundred words;

(C) For taking and certifying acknowledgments of deeds, mortgages, liens, powers of attorney, and other instruments of writing, and for taking and certifying depositions and affidavits, administering oaths, and other official services, the same fees as are allowed by section 2319.27 of the Revised Code or by law to clerks of the courts of common pleas for like services.

§ 147.09. Protests are evidence.

The instrument of protest of a notary public appointed and qualified under the laws of this state or of any other state or territory of the United States, accompanying a bill of exchange or promissory note, which has been protested by such notary public for nonacceptance or for nonpayment constitutes prima-facie evidence of the facts therein certified. Such instrument may be contradicted by other evidence.

§ 147.10. Notary public acting after commission expires.

No notary public shall do or perform any act as a notary public knowing that his term of office has expired.

§ 147.11. Forfeiture.

A person appointed notary public who performs any act as such after expiration of his term of office, knowing that his term has expired, shall forfeit not more than five hundred dollars, to be recovered by an action in the name of the state. Such act shall render such person ineligible for reappointment.

§ 147.12. Acts done by notary public after term valid.

An official act done by a notary public after the expiration of his term of office is as valid as if done during his term of office.

§ 147.13. Removal for receiving excess fees.

A notary public who charges or receives for an act or service done or rendered by him a fee greater than the amount prescribed by law, or who dishonestly or unfaithfully discharges any of his duties as notary public, shall be removed from his office by the court of common pleas of the county in which he residues, upon complaint filed and substantiated in such court, and the court shall thereupon certify such removal to the governor. The person so removed shall be ineligible for reappointment to the office of notary public.

§ 147.14. Removal from office for certifying affidavit without administering oath.

No notary public shall certify to the affidavit of a person without administering the oath or affirmation to such person. A notary public who violates this section shall be removed from office by the court of common pleas of the county in which the conviction was had. The court shall thereupon certify such removal to the governor. The person so removed shall be ineligible to reappointment for a period of three years.

§ 147.32. Commissioners of the state for veterans' affairs.

Representatives of the United Spanish War Veterans, The Disabled American Veterans, The American Legion, Veterans of Foreign Wars of the United States, and other congressionally chartered veterans' organizations, who are recognized as such representatives by the administrator of the veterans' administration, and who are engaged in the preparation and prosecution of claims of veterans and their dependents before the rating agencies of the veterans' administration within the state, may be appointed as commissioners of the state. Such commissioners shall continue in office for a term of three years. Each of such commissioners shall, before performing any of his duties, take and subscribe to an oath of office before a judge of a court of record within this state. Such oath, with his signature thereto and an impression of his seal of office and his residence address, shall forthwith be transmitted by him to the governor, and filed by the governor in the office of the secretary of state.

Each of such commissioners shall procure and employ a seal of the dimensions and inscription set forth and prescribed for notaries public, in section 147.04 of the Revised Code, except that the words shall be: "Commissioner of the State of Ohio for Veterans' Affairs."

Such commissioners may, without fee and within the state, administer oaths, take acknowledgments, and attest the execution of any instruments of writing only in connection with or used before the veterans' administration.

§ 147.37. Fees for commissions.

Each person receiving a commission as a notary public, except a citizen of this state admitted to the practice of law by the Ohio supreme court, shall pay a fee of five dollars. Each person receiving a commission as a notary public who is a citizen of this state admitted to the practice of law by the Ohio supreme court, shall pay a fee of ten dollars.

§ 147.371. Fees for duplicate commissions.

Upon receipt of a fee of two dollars and an affidavit that the original commission has been lost or destroyed a duplicate commission as notary public shall be issued by the governor.

§ 147.39. Prior notarial acts by armed forces officers valid.

Any acknowledgment or proof of execution of a deed, mortgage, lease, power of attorney, or other instrument that was taken, and any other notarial act that was performed, by a commissioned officer in active service with the armed forces of the

United States for a person who was a member of the armed forces of the United States, for a person who was accompanying the armed forces of the United States, or for a person who was a dependent of either such category of persons, and that was taken or performed between January 1, 1941, and January 1, 1974, in conformity with the provisions of a prior statute that then was in effect is as valid as if the acknowledgment, proof of execution, or other notarial act was performed in conformity with the provisions of sections 147.51 to 147.58 of the Revised Code.

§ 147.40. Manner of taking depositions.

Depositions taken in pursuance of sections 147.07 and 147.51 to 147.58 of the Revised Code by a person described in division (D) of section 147.51 of the Revised Code shall be taken on written interrogatories, on a written notice being given by the party desiring to take such depositions, which notice shall contain the names of the parties plaintiff and defendant, the court or tribunal in which the action is pending, the number of the regiment or battalion to which the witness belongs, and the names of the witnesses. The notice shall be served upon the adverse party, or his agent or attorney of record, or left at his usual place of abode, with a copy of the interrogatories, at least twenty days prior to the taking of such depositions. If the party on whom such notice is served desires to file cross-interrogatories, a copy of them shall be served on the adverse party, or his agent or attorney of record, or left at his usual place of abode, within six days after the notice of taking depositions has been served, and the party giving the notice to take depositions, shall forward with his notice and interrogatories, the cross-interrogatories so served on him; and neither party, by himself, or his agent or attorney, shall be present at the time of taking such depositions.

§ 147.99. Penalties.

(A) Whoever violates section 147.10 of the Revised Code shall be fined not more than five hundred dollars.

(B) Whoever violates section 147.14 of the Revised Code shall be fined not more than one hundred dollars or imprisoned not more than thirty days, or both.

ADDITIONAL AUTHORITY

[OHIO CONST.]

§ Art. II, § 4. Eligibility.

No member of the general assembly shall, during the term for which he was elected, unless during such term he resigns therefrom, hold any public office under the United States, or this state, or a political subdivision thereof; but this provision does not extend to officers of a political party, notaries public, or officers of the militia or of the United States armed forces.

No member of the general assembly shall, during the term for which he was elected, or for one year thereafter, be appointed to any public office under this state, which office was created or the compensation of which was increased, during the term for which he was elected.

SEAL

[OHIO REV. CODE ANN.]

§ 5.04. Coat of arms of state.

* * *

The coat of arms of the state shall correspond substantially with the following design:

* * *

FEES

§ 2303.20. Fees.

The clerk of the court of common pleas shall charge the following fees and no more:

* * *

(S) One dollar for recording commission of mayor or notary public;

* * *

OFFENSES

§ 2921.13. Falsification.

(A) No person shall knowingly make a false statement, or knowingly swear or affirm the truth of a false statement previously made, when any of the following applies:

(1) The statement is made in any official proceeding.

* * *

(6) The statement is sworn or affirmed before a

notary public or other person empowered to administer oaths.

(7) The statement is in writing on or in connection with a report or return which is required or authorized by law.

* * *

(C) Where contradictory statements relating to the same fact are made by the offender within the period of the statute of limitations for falsification, it is not necessary for the prosecution to prove which statement was false, but only that one or the other was false.

(D)(1) Whoever violates division (A)(1), (2), (3), (4), (5), (6), (7), (8), (11), or (12) of this section is guilty of falsification, a misdemeanor of the first degree.

* * *

§ 2929.21. Penalties for misdemeanor.

(A) Except as provided in section 2929.23 of the Revised Code, whoever is convicted of or pleads guilty to a misdemeanor other than a minor misdemeanor shall be imprisoned for a definite term or fined, or both, which term of imprisonment and fine shall be fixed by the court as provided in this section.

* * *

(B) Terms of imprisonment for misdemeanor shall be imposed as follows:

(1) For a misdemeanor of the first degree, not more than six months;

* * *

(C) Fines for misdemeanor shall be imposed as follows:

(1) For a misdemeanor of the first degree, not more than one thousand dollars;

* * *

ACKNOWLEDGMENTS

Uniform Recognition of Acknowledgments Act

§ 147.51. Notarial acts.

For the purposes of sections 147.51 to 147.58 of the Revised Code, "notarial acts" means acts which the laws and regulations of this state authorize notaries public of this state to perform, including the administration of oaths and affirmations, taking proof of execution and acknowledgment of instruments, and attesting documents.

Notarial acts may be performed outside this state for use in this state with the same effect as if performed by a notary public of this state by the following persons authorized pursuant to the laws and regulations of other governments, in addition to

any other persons authorized by the laws and regulations of this state:

(A) A notary public authorized to perform notarial acts in the place in which the act is performed;

(B) A judge, clerk, or deputy clerk of any court of record in the place in which the notarial act is performed;

(C) An officer of the foreign service of the United States, a consular agent, or any other person authorized by regulation of the United States department of state to perform notarial acts in the place in which the act is performed;

(D) A commissioned officer in active service with the armed forces of the United States and any other person authorized by regulation of the armed forces to perform notarial acts if the notarial act is performed for one of the following or his dependents:

(1) A merchant seaman of the United States;

(2) A member of the armed forces of the United States;

(3) Any other person serving with or accompanying the armed forces of the United States;

(E) Any other person authorized to perform notarial acts in the place in which the act is performed.

§ 147.52. Notarial acts by authorized person.

(A) If the notarial act is performed by any of the persons described in divisions (A) to (D) of section 147.51 of the Revised Code, other than a person authorized to perform notarial acts by the laws or regulations of a foreign country, the signature, rank, or title and serial number, if any, of the person are sufficient proof of the authority of a holder of that rank or title to perform the act. Further proof of his authority is not required.

(B) If the notarial act is performed by a person authorized by the laws or regulations of a foreign country to perform the act, there is sufficient proof of the authority of that person to act if:

(1) Either a foreign service officer of the United States residing in the country in which the act is performed or a diplomatic or consular officer of the foreign country residing in the United States certifies that a person holding that office is authorized to perform the act;

(2) The official seal of the person performing the notarial act is affixed to the document; or

(3) The title and indication of authority to perform notarial acts of the person appears either in a digest of foreign law or in a list customarily used as a source of such information.

(C) If the notarial act is performed by a person other than one described in division (A) and (B) of this section, there is sufficient proof of the authority of that person to act if the clerk of a court of record in the place in which the notarial act is performed certifies to the official character of that person and to his authority to perform the notarial act.

(D) The signature and title of the person performing the act are prima-facie evidence that he is a person with the designated title and that the signature is genuine.

§ 147.53. Taking an acknowledgment.

The person taking an acknowledgment shall certify that:

(A) The person acknowledging appeared before him and acknowledged he executed the instrument;

(B) The person acknowledging was known to the person taking the acknowledgment, or that the person taking the acknowledgment had satisfactory evidence that the person acknowledging was the person described in and who executed the instrument.

§ 147.54. Recognized certificate of acknowledgment.

The form of a certificate of acknowledgment used by a person whose authority is recognized under section 147.51 of the Revised Code shall be accepted in this state if:

(A) The certificate is in a form prescribed by the laws or regulations of this state;

(B) The certificate is in a form prescribed by the laws or regulations applicable in the place in which the acknowledgment is taken; or

(C) The certificate contains the words "acknowledged before me," or their substantial equivalent.

§ 147.541. "Acknowledged before me" defined.

The words "acknowledged before me" means that:

(A) The person acknowledging appeared before the person taking the acknowledgment;

(B) He acknowledged he executed the instrument;

(C) In the case of:

(1) A natural person, he executed the instrument for the purposes therein stated;

(2) A corporation, the officer or agent acknowledged he held the position or title set forth in the instrument and certificate, he signed the instrument on behalf of the corporation by proper authority, and the instrument was the act of the corporation for the purpose therein stated;

(3) A partnership, the partner or agent acknowledged he signed the instrument on behalf of the partnership by proper authority and he executed

the instrument as the act of the partnership for the purposes therein stated;

(4) A person acknowledging as principal by an attorney in fact, he executed the instrument by proper authority as the act of the principal for the purposes therein stated;

(5) A person acknowledging as a public officer, trustee, administrator, guardian, or other representative, he signed the instrument by proper authority and he executed the instrument in the capacity and for the purposes therein stated; and

(D) The person taking the acknowledgment either knew or had satisfactory evidence that the person acknowledging was the person named in the instrument or certificate.

§ 147.55. Forms of acknowledgment.

The forms of acknowledgment set forth in this section may be used and are sufficient for their respective purposes under any section of the Revised Code. The forms shall be known as "statutory short forms of acknowledgment" and may be referred to by that name. The authorization of the forms in this section does not preclude the use of other forms.

(A) "For an individual acting in his own right:

State of ....

County of ....

The foregoing instrument was acknowledged before me this (date) by (name of person acknowledged.)

(Signature of person taking acknowledgment)
(Title or rank)
(Serial number, if any)"

(B) "For a corporation:

State of ....

County of ....

The foregoing instrument was acknowledged before me this (date) by (name of officer or agent, title of officer or agent) of (name of corporation acknowledging) a (state or place of incorporation) corporation, on behalf of the corporation.

(Signature of person taking acknowledgment)
(Title or rank)
(Serial number, if any)"

(C) "For a partnership:

State of ....

County of ....

The foregoing instrument was acknowledged before me this (date) by (name of acknowledging partner or agent), partner (or agent) on behalf of (name of partnership), a partnership.

(Signature of person taking acknowledgment)
(Title or rank)
(Serial number, if any)"

(D) "For an individual acting as principal by an attorney in fact:
State of ....
County of ....
The foregoing instrument was acknowledged before me this (date) by (name of attorney in fact) as attorney in fact on behalf of (name of principal).
(Signature of person taking acknowledgment)
(Title or rank)
(Serial number, if any)"

(E) "By any public officer, trustee, or personal representative:
State of ....
County of ....
The foregoing instrument was acknowledged before me this (date) by (name and title of position.)
(Signature of person taking acknowledgment)
(Title or rank)
(Serial number, if any)"

§ 147.56. Notarial acts performed prior to January 1, 1974.

A notarial act performed prior to January 1, 1974, is not affected by sections 147.51 to 147.58 of the Revised Code. These sections provide an additional method of proving notarial acts and do not diminish or invalidate the recognition accorded to notarial acts by other laws or regulations of this state.

§ 147.57. Uniformity of the law.

Sections 147.51 to 147.58 of the Revised Code shall be so interpreted as to make uniform the laws of those states which enact it.

§ 147.58. Uniform recognition of acknowledgments act.

Sections 147.51 to 147.58 of the Revised Code may be cited as the "Uniform Recognition of Acknowledgments Act."

§ 5301.01. Acknowledgment of deeds, mortgages, and leases.

A deed, mortgage, land contract ..., or lease or any interest in real property must be signed by the grantor, mortgagor, vendor, or lessor, and such signing must be acknowledged by the grantor, mortgagor, vendor, or lessor in the presence of two witnesses, who shall attest the signing and subscribe their names to the attestation. Such signing must be acknowledged by the grantor, mortgagor, vendor, or lessor before a judge of a court of record in this state or a clerk thereof, a county auditor, county engineer, notary public, mayor, or county court judge, who shall certify the acknowledgment and subscribe his name to the certificate of such acknowledgment.

§ 5301.06. Instruments executed according to law of place where made.

All deeds, mortgages, powers of attorney, and other instruments of writing for the conveyance or encumbrance of lands, tenements, or hereditaments situated within this state, executed and acknowledged, or proved, in any other state, territory, or country in conformity with the laws of such state, territory, or country, or in conformity with the laws of this state, are as valid as if executed within this state, in conformity with ... the Revised Code.

DEPOSITIONS

§ 2319.03. Use of affidavit.

An affidavit may be used to verify a pleading, to prove the service of the summons, notice, or other process in an action; or to obtain a provisional remedy, an examination of a witness, a stay of proceedings, or upon a motion, and in any other case permitted by law.

§ 2319.04. Before whom affidavit may be made.

An affidavit may be made in or out of this state before any person authorized to take depositions, and unless it is a verification of a pleading it must be authenticated in the same way as a deposition.

Such affidavit may be made before any person authorized to administer oaths whether an attorney in the case or not.

§ 2319.09. Uniform foreign depositions.

Whenever any mandate, writ, or commission is issued out of any court of record in any other state, territory, district, or foreign jurisdiction, or whenever upon notice or agreement it is required to take the testimony of a witness in this state, witnesses may be compelled to appear and testify in the same manner and by the same process and proceedings as are employed for the purpose of taking testimony in proceedings pending in this state.

This section shall be so interpreted and construed as to effectuate its general purpose to make the law of this state uniform with those states which enact similar legislation.

§ 2319.27. Fees for taking depositions; lien.

Except as section 147.08 of the Revised Code governs the fees chargeable by a notary public for services rendered in connection with depositions, the fees and expenses chargeable for the taking and certifying of a deposition by a person who is authorized to do so in this state, including, but not limited to, a shorthand reporter, stenographer, or person described in Civil Rule 28, may be established by that person subject to the qualification specified in this section, and may be different than the fees and expenses charged for the taking and certifying of depositions by similar persons in other areas of this state. Unless, prior to the taking and certifying of a deposition, the parties who request it agree that the fees or expenses to be charged may exceed the usual and customary fees or expenses charged in the particular community for similar services, such a person shall not charge fees or expenses in connection with the taking and certifying of the deposition that exceed those usual and customary fees and expenses.

The person taking and certifying a deposition may retain the deposition until the fees and expenses that he charged are paid. He also shall tax the costs, if any, of a sheriff or other officer who serves any process in connection with the taking of a deposition and the fees of the witnesses, and, if directed by a person entitled to those costs or fees, may retain the deposition until those costs or fees are paid.

Criminal Cases

§ 2945.50. Deposition in criminal cases.

At any time after an issue of fact is joined upon an indictment, information, or an affidavit, the prosecution or the defendant may apply in writing to the court in which such indictment, information, or affidavit is pending for a commission to take the depositions of any witness. The court or a judge thereof may grant such commission and make an order stating in what manner and for what length of time notice shall be given to the prosecution or to the defendant, before such witness shall be examined.

§ 2945.54. Conduct of examination.

The examination of witnesses by deposition in criminal cases shall be taken and certified, and the return thereof to the court made as for taking depositions under sections 2319.05 to 2319.31, inclusive, of the Revised Code. The commissioners appointed under section 2945.50 of the Revised Code to take depositions shall receive such compensation as the

court directs, to be paid out of the county treasury and taxed as part of the costs in the case.

[OHIO R. CIV. P.]

RULE 28. Persons before whom depositions may be taken.

(A) Depositions within state. Depositions may be taken in this state before: a person authorized to administer any oath by the laws of this state, a person appointed by the court in which the action is pending, or a person agreed upon by written stipulation of all the parties.

(B) Depositions outside state. Depositions may be taken outside this state before: a person authorized to administer oaths in the place where the deposition is taken, a person appointed by the court in which the action is pending, a person agreed upon by written stipulation of all the parties, or, in any foreign country, by any consular officer of the United States within his consular district.

(C) Disqualification for interest. Unless the parties agree otherwise as provided in Rule 29 depositions shall not be taken before a person who is a relative, employee or attorney of any of the parties, or is a relative or employee of such attorney, or is financially interested in the action.

LEGAL HOLIDAYS

[OHIO REV. CODE ANN.]

§ 1.14. First day excluded and last day included in computing time; exceptions; legal holiday defined.

The time within which an act is required by law to be done shall be computed by excluding the first and including the last day; except that when the last day falls on Sunday or a legal holiday, then the act may be done on the next succeeding day which is not Sunday or a legal holiday.

When a public office in which an act, required by law, is to be performed is closed to the public for the entire day which constitutes the last day for doing such act or before its usual closing time on such day, then such act may be performed on the next succeeding day which is not a Sunday or a legal holiday as defined in this section.

"Legal holiday" as used in this section means the following days:

(A) The first day of January, known as New Year's day;

(B) The third Monday in January, known as Martin Luther King day;

(C) The third Monday in February, known as Washington-Lincoln day;

(D) The day designated in the "Act of September

18, 1975," 89 Stat. 479, 5 U.S.C. 6103, as now or hereafter amended, for the commemoration of Memorial day;

(E) The fourth day of July, known as Independence day;

(F) The first Monday in September, known as Labor day;

(G) The second Monday in October, known as Columbus day;

(H) The eleventh day of November, known as Veterans' day;

(I) The fourth Thursday in November, known as Thanksgiving day;

(J) The twenty-fifth day of December, known as Christmas day;

(K) Any day appointed and recommended by the governor of this state or the president of the United States as a holiday.

If any day designated in this section as a legal holiday falls on Sunday, the next succeeding day is a legal holiday.

§ 5.20. Portion of election day a holiday.

The first Tuesday after the first Monday in November of each year, between the hours of twelve noon, eastern standard time, and five-thirty p.m., eastern standard time, is a legal holiday.

§ 5.21. Labor day; Columbus day; Veterans' day.

The first Monday in September of each year shall be known as "Labor day" and for all purposes shall be considered as the first day of the week.

The second Monday in October of each year shall be known as "Columbus day" and is a legal holiday.

The eleventh day of November of each year shall be known as "Veterans' day" and is a legal holiday. If said day falls on Sunday, the following Monday is the legal holiday.

OKLAHOMA

NOTARIES PUBLIC

[OKLA. STAT. ANN.]

Tit. 49, § 1. Appointment.

The Secretary of State shall appoint and commission in this state notaries public, who shall hold their office for four (4) years. An applicant for a notary commission shall be eighteen (18) years of age or older, a citizen of the United States, and a legal resident of the state. All notary commissions shall run in the name and by the authority of the State of Oklahoma, be signed by the Secretary of State and sealed with the Great Seal of the State of Oklahoma. Said commissions shall not be attested. Any person filing an application for a new notary commission shall pay Twenty-five Dollars ($25.00) to the Secretary of State with the application. Any person filing an application for a renewal of a notary commission shall pay Twenty Dollars ($20.00) to the Secretary of State with the application. These funds shall be deposited in the revolving fund created for the Secretary of State pursuant to the provisions of Section 276.1 of Title 62 of the Oklahoma Statutes.

Tit. 49, § 2. Oath, signature, bond and seal—fees.

A. Before entering upon the duties of his office

431

every notary public so appointed and commissioned shall file in the office of the court clerk, in his capacity as clerk of the district court, of the county in which such notary resides at the time he is commissioned, the commission issued to him, his oath of office, his official signature, an impression of his official seal, and a good and sufficient bond to the State of Oklahoma, in the sum of One Thousand Dollars ($1,000.00), with one or more sureties to be approved by the court clerk, conditioned for the faithful performance of the duties of his office.

B. Such commission, bond, and oath shall be recorded in the office of such court clerk, as clerk of the district court. The commission shall be returned to the notary. The bond and oath shall be transmitted by the court clerk to the Secretary of State to be filed and recorded in his office. The filing of such commission, bond, official signature, and impression of official seal in the office of the court clerk shall be deemed sufficient evidence to enable the court clerk to certify that the person so commissioned is a notary public, duly commissioned and acting as such, during the time such commission is in force. Upon the filing of his commission with the court clerk, every notary public shall pay to the court clerk the sum of Five Dollars ($5.00) to be held and accounted for by the court clerk as fees of his office.

C. The Secretary of State shall record and file the bond and oath of each notary of this state.

D. The court clerk shall charge a fee of Three Dollars ($3.00) for authenticating a notary commission.

Tit. 49, § 3. Blanks for bond and oath.

Blanks for bonds and oath of office shall be furnished with the commission by the Secretary of State.

Tit. 49, § 5. Official seal—types of seals—authentication of documents—penalties.

Every notary shall provide a notarial seal containing his name and county of residence. This seal may be either a metal seal which leaves an embossed impression or a rubber stamp used in conjunction with a stamp pad and ink. Each notary shall authenticate all his official acts, attestations and instruments with this seal; and he shall add to his official signature the date of expiration of his commission as such notary public. If a rubber stamp is used, this date may be a part of the stamp. If any notary public shall neglect or refuse to attach to his official signature the date of expiration of his commission he shall be deemed guilty of a misdemeanor, and upon conviction thereof shall be fined in any sum not exceeding Fifty Dollars ($50.00).

Tit. 49, § 6. Authority of notary.

Notaries public shall have authority within any county in this state to make the proof and acknowledgment of deeds and other instruments of writing to be proved or acknowledged; to administer oaths; to demand acceptance or payment of foreign or inland bills of exchange and promissory notes, and protest the same for nonacceptance or nonpayment, as the same may require, and to exercise such other powers and duties as by law of nations and commercial usage may be performed by notaries public. A notary may not notarize his own signature.

Tit. 49, § 7. Record of protests.

In cases of protests for banks, notaries shall keep a register thereof in a book provided for that purpose by the bank, and the notary shall not be required to deliver such register to the county clerk, but shall leave the same in the possession of such bank.

Tit. 49, § 8. Official record—certified copy.

Every notary shall keep a fair record of his official acts, and if required shall give a certified copy of any record in his office, upon the payment of the fees therefor.

Tit. 49, § 9. Vacancy.

If any notary die, resign, be disqualified or remove from the county, his record and official and public papers of his office, shall, within thirty days be delivered to the clerk of the county.

Tit. 49, § 10. Statute of limitations.

No suit shall be instituted against any such notary or his securities more than three (3) years after the cause of action accrues.

ADDITIONAL AUTHORITY

Tit. 6, § 904. Stockholder, director, officer or employee of bank as notary public—administration of oaths—protests.

It shall be lawful for any notary public who is a stockholder, director, officer or employee of a bank to take the acknowledgment of any party to any written instrument executed to or by such bank, or to administer an oath to any other stockholder, director, officer, employee or agent of such bank, or to protest for nonacceptance or nonpayment bills of exchange, drafts, checks, notes and other negotiable instruments which may be owned or held for collection by such bank; provided, it shall be unlawful for any notary public to take the acknowledgment of an instrument executed by or to a bank of which he is a stockholder, director, officer or employee, where such notary is a party to such instrument, either individually or as a representative of such bank, or to protest any negotiable instrument owned or held for collection by such bank where such notary is individually a party to such instrument.

Tit. 51, § 21. Oaths, officers authorized to administer.

The following officers are authorized to administer oaths:

* * *

5. Justices of the peace and notaries public within their respective counties.

* * *

FEES

Tit. 28, § 31. Fees of court clerks.

The clerk of the district court, or the clerk of any other court of record, shall charge and collect the following fees for services by them respectively rendered and none others, except as otherwise provided by law:

* * *

Certifying to any instrument (each) ...... $ .50

* * *

Tit. 28, § 47. Fees of notaries.

Each notary public shall charge and collect the following fees:

For protest and record of same .... $ .50
For each notice of protest .... .10
For each certificate and seal .... .25

Provided, that he may charge, receive and collect the fees provided in this article for the clerks of the district court for like service and none other.

OFFENSES

Tit. 21, § 1561. Wills, deeds and certain other instruments, forgery of.

Every person who, with intent to defraud, forges, counterfeits or falsely alters:

1st.   Any will or codicil of real or personal property, or any deed or other instrument being or purporting to be the act of another, by which any right or interest in real property is, or purports to be, transferred, conveyed or in any way changed or affected; or,

2nd.   Any certificate or endorsement of the acknowledgment by any person of any deed or other instrument which by law may be recorded or given in evidence, made or purporting to have been made by any officer duly authorized to make such certificate or endorsement; or,

3rd.   Any certificate of the proof of any deed, will, codicil or other instrument which by law may be recorded or given in evidence, made or purporting to have been made by any court or officer duly authorized to make such certificate,
is guilty of forgery in the first degree.

Tit. 21, § 1574. Making false certificate of acknowledgment.

If any officer authorized to take the acknowledgment or proof of any conveyance of real property, or of any other instrument which by law may be recorded, knowingly and falsely certifies that any such conveyance or instrument was acknowledged by any party thereto, or was proved by any subscribing witness, when in truth such conveyance or instrument was not acknowledged or proved as certified, he is guilty of forgery in the second degree.

Tit. 21, § 1621. Punishment for forgery.

Forgery is punishable by imprisonment in the penitentiary as follows:

1. Forgery in the first degree by imprisonment not less than seven (7) years nor more than twenty (20).

2. Forgery in the second degree not exceeding seven (7) years.

Tit. 51, § 24.1. Suspension or forfeiture of office or employment upon conviction of felony—vacancy—salary and benefits—governor notified in writing.

A. Any elected or appointed state or county officer or employee who, during the term for which he was elected or appointed, is, or has been, found guilty by a trial court of a felony in a state or federal court of competent jurisdiction shall be automatically suspended from said office or employment. The Governor shall appoint an interim successor to serve during the period of suspension of any county commissioner or any state officer other than a member of the State Legislature. A vacancy created by the suspension of a member of the State Legislature shall be filled as provided in Section 20 of Article V of the Oklahoma Constitution. A vacancy created by the suspension of a county officer other than a county commissioner shall be filled as provided by Section 10 of this title. In the event any elected or appointed state or county officer or employee who, during the term for which he was elected or appointed, pleads guilty or nolo contendere to a felony or any offense involving a violation of his official oath in a state or federal court of competent jurisdiction, he shall, immediately upon the entry of said plea, forfeit said office or employment. Any such officer or employee upon final conviction of, or pleading guilty or nolo contendere to, a felony in a state or federal court of competent jurisdiction shall vacate such office or employment and if such felony or other offense violates his oath of office shall forfeit all benefits of said office or employment, including, but not limited to, retirement benefits provided by law; provided however, that such forfeiture of retirement benefits shall not include such officer's or employee's contributions to the retirement system or retirement benefits that are vested on the effective date of this act. Any claims for payment of salary or wages, or any claims for payment of any other benefits, to any such officer or employee suspended from or forfeiting his office or employment shall be rejected by the proper authority. Such suspension or forfeiture shall continue until such time as said conviction or guilty plea is reversed by the highest appellate court to which said officer or employee may appeal. The attorney responsible for prosecuting such elected or appointed state or county officers or employees shall notify the retirement system in which such officer or employee is enrolled of the forfeiture of such officer's or employee's retirement benefits.

B. Within three (3) days of the conviction or plea of guilty or nolo contendere of a county commissioner, the district attorney of the county where such county commissioner served shall notify the Governor, in writing, of the suspension, the date of conviction or plea of guilty or nolo contendere resulting in suspension, and the felony committed.

C. Within three (3) days of the conviction or plea of guilty or nolo contendere of an elected or appointed state officer, the attorney responsible for prosecuting such state officer, shall notify the Governor in writing of the suspension, the date of conviction or plea of guilty or nolo contendere resulting in suspension, and the felony committed.

UNIFORM LAW ON NOTARIAL ACTS

Tit. 49, § 111. Short title.

Sections 1 through 11 [sections 111 et seq.] of this act shall be known and may be cited as the Uniform Law on Notarial Acts.

Tit. 49, § 112. Definitions.

As used in the Uniform Law on Notarial Acts:

1. "Notarial acts" means any act that a notary public of this state is authorized to perform, and includes taking an acknowledgment, administering an oath or affirmation, taking a verification upon oath or affirmation, witnessing or attesting a signature, certifying or attesting a copy, and noting a protest of a negotiable instrument.

2. "Acknowledgment" means a declaration by a person that the person has executed an instrument for the purposes stated therein and, if the instrument is executed in a representative capacity, that the person signed the instrument with proper authority and executed it as the act of the person or entity represented and identified therein.

3. "Verification upon oath or affirmation" means a declaration that a statement is true made by a person upon oath or affirmation.

4. "In a representative capacity" means:

a. for and on behalf of a corporation, partnership, trust, or other entity, as an authorized officer, agent, partner, trustee, or other representative;

b. as a public officer, personal representative, guardian, or other representative, in the capacity recited in the instrument;

c. as an attorney-in-fact for a principal; or

d. in any other capacity as an authorized representative of another.

5. "Notarial officer" means a notary public or any other person authorized to perform notarial acts in the place in which the act is performed.

Tit. 49, § 113. Taking acknowledgment or verification—witnessing or attesting signature—certifying or attesting copies—making or noting protest—evidence of true signature.

A. In taking an acknowledgment, the notarial officer must determine, either from personal knowledge or from satisfactory evidence, that the person appearing before the officer and making the acknowledgment is the person whose true signature is on the instrument.

B. In taking a verification upon oath or affirmation, the notarial officer must determine, either from a personal knowledge or from satisfactory evidence, that the person appearing before the officer and making the verification is the person whose true signature is on the statement verified.

C. In witnessing or attesting a signature the notarial officer must determine, either from personal knowledge or from satisfactory evidence, that the signature is that of the person appearing before the officer and named therein.

D. In certifying or attesting a copy of a document or other item, the notarial officer must determine that the proffered copy is a full, true, and accurate transcription or reproduction of that which was copied. In the case of official records, only the custodian of the official records may issue an official certified copy.

E. In making or noting a protest of a negotiable instrument the notarial officer must determine the matters set forth in Section 3-509 of the Uniform Commercial Code.

F. A notarial officer has satisfactory evidence that a person is the person whose true signature is on a document if that person is personally known to the notarial officer, is identified upon the oath or affirmation of a credible witness personally known to the notarial officer or is identified on the basis of identification documents.

Tit. 49, § 114. Person who may perform notarial acts—federal acts—genuineness of signature.

A. A notarial act may be performed within this state by the following persons:

1. a notary public of this state;

2. a judge, clerk, or deputy clerk of any court of this state;

3. all judge advocates, staff judge advocates, assistant judge advocates and all legal officers of the state military forces in performance of their official duties for military personnel and their dependents; or

4. any other person authorized to perform the specific act by the law of this state.

B. Notarial acts performed within this state under federal authority have the same effect as if performed by a notarial officer of this state.

C. The signature and title of a person performing a notarial act are prima facie evidence that the signature is genuine and that the person holds the designated title.

Tit. 49, § 115. Notarial acts performed in another state, commonwealth, territory, district, or possession of the United States.

A. A notarial act has the same effect pursuant to the laws of this state as if performed by a notarial officer of this state, if performed in another state, commonwealth, territory, district, or possession of the United States by any of the following persons:

1. a notary public of that jurisdiction;

2. a judge, clerk, or deputy clerk of a court of that jurisdiction;

3. all judge advocates, staff judge advocates, assistant judge advocates and all legal officers of the state military forces; or

4. any other person authorized by the law of that jurisdiction to perform notarial acts.

B. Notarial acts performed in other jurisdictions of the United States under federal authority have

the same effect as if performed by a notarial officer of this state.

C. The signature and title of a person performing a notarial act are prima facie evidence that the signature is genuine and that the person holds the designated title.

D. The signature and indicated title of an officer listed in this section conclusively establish the authority of a holder of that title to perform a notarial act.

Tit. 49, § 116. Notarial acts performed by certain federal officers.

A. A notarial act has the same effect pursuant to the laws of this state as if performed by a notarial officer of this state if performed anywhere by any of the following persons under authority granted by the law of the United States:

1. a judge, clerk, or deputy clerk of a court;

2. a commissioned officer on active duty in a military service of the United States;

3. an officer of the foreign service or consular officer of the United States; or

4. any other person authorized by federal law to perform notarial acts.

B. The signature and title of a person performing a notarial act are prima facie evidence that the signature is genuine and that the person holds the designated title.

C. The signature and indicated title of an officer listed in this section conclusively establish the authority of a holder of that title to perform a notarial act.

Tit. 49, § 117. Notarial acts performed by officer of foreign nation or multinational or international organization.

A. A notarial act has the same effect pursuant to the laws of this state as if performed by a notarial officer of this state if performed within the jurisdiction of and under authority of a foreign nation or its constituent units or a multinational or international organization by any of the following persons:

1. a notary public or notary;

2. a judge, clerk, or deputy clerk of a court of record; or

3. any other person authorized by the law of that jurisdiction to perform notarial acts.

B. An "Apostille" in the form prescribed by the Hague Convention of October 5, 1961, conclusively establishes that the signature of the notarial officer is genuine and that the officer holds the indicated office.

C. A certificate by a foreign service or consular officer of the United States stationed in the nation under the jurisdiction of which the notarial act was performed, or a certificate by a foreign service or consular officer of that nation stationed in the United States, conclusively establishes any matter relating to the authenticity or validity of the notarial act set forth in the certificate.

D. An official stamp or seal of the person performing the notarial act is prima facie evidence that the signature is genuine and that the person holds the indicated title.

E. An official stamp or seal of an officer listed in this section is prima facie evidence that a person with the indicated title has authority to perform notarial acts.

F. If the title of office and indication of authority to perform notarial acts appears either in a digest of foreign law or in a list customarily used as a source for that information, the authority of an officer with that title to perform notarial acts is conclusively established.

Tit. 49, § 118. Certification of notarial act.

A. A notarial act must be evidenced by a certificate signed and dated by a notarial officer. The certificate shall include identification of the jurisdiction in which the notarial act is performed and the title of the office of the notarial officer and may include the official stamp or seal of office. If the officer is a notary public, the certificate must also indicate the date of expiration, if any, of the commission of office, but omission of that information may subsequently be corrected. If the officer is a commissioned officer on active duty in the military service of the United States, it must also include the rank of the officer.

B. A certificate of a notarial act is sufficient if it meets the requirements of subsection A of this section and it:

1. is in the short form set forth in Section 9 of this act;

2. is in a form otherwise prescribed by the law of this state;

3. is in a form prescribed by the laws or regulations applicable in the place in which the notarial act was performed; or

4. sets forth the actions of the notarial officer and those are sufficient to meet the requirements of the designated notarial act.

C. By executing a certificate of a notarial act, the notarial officer certifies that the officer has made the determinations required by Section 3 of this act.

Tit. 49, § 119. Short form certificates of notarial acts.

The following short form certificates of notarial acts are sufficient for the purposes indicated, if

completed with the information required by subsection A of Section 8 of this act:

1. For an acknowledgment in an individual capacity:

State of

County of

This instrument was acknowledged before me on (date) by (name(s) of person(s)).

_____
(Signature of notarial officer)

(Seal, if any)

_____
Title (and Rank)
(My commission expires:)

2. For an acknowledgment in a representative capacity:

State of

County of

This instrument was acknowledged before me on (date) by (name(s) of person(s)) as (type of authority, e.g., officer, trustee, etc.) of (name of party on behalf of whom instrument was executed).

_____
(Signature of notarial officer)

(Seal, if any)

_____
Title (and Rank)
(My commission expires:)

3. For a verification upon oath or affirmation:

State of

County of

Signed and sworn to (or affirmed) before me on (date) by (name(s) of person(s) making statement).

_____
(Signature of notarial officer)

(Seal, if any)

_____
Title (and Rank)
(My commission expires:)

4. For witnessing or attesting a signature:

State of

County of

Signed or attested before me on (date) by (name(s) of person(s)).

_____
(Signature of notarial officer)

(Seal, if any)

_____
Title (and Rank)
(My commission expires:)

5. For attestation of a copy of a document:

State of

County of

I certify that this is a true and correct copy of a document in the possession of

Dated

_____
(Signature of notarial officer)

(Seal, if any)

———————————
Title (and Rank)
(My commission expires:)

Tit. 49, § 120. Construction and application of act.

A notarial act performed prior to November 1, 1985, is not affected by the provisions of the Uniform Law on Notarial Acts. The Uniform Law on Notarial Acts provides an additional method of proving notarial acts. Nothing in the Uniform Law on Notarial Acts diminishes or invalidates the recognition accorded to notarial acts by other laws or regulations of this state.

Tit. 49, § 121. Interpretation of act.

The Uniform Law of Notarial Acts shall be so interpreted as to make uniform the laws of those states which enact it.

ACKNOWLEDGMENTS

Tit. 16, § 33. Form of acknowledgment.

An acknowledgment by individuals of any instrument affecting real estate must be substantially in the following form, to wit:
State of Oklahoma,
              ss.
——————————— County.

Before me, ———————— in and for said county and State, on this ———————— day of ———————— 19___, personally appeared ———————— and ———————— to me known to be the identical person—who executed the within and foregoing instrument, and acknowledged to me that ———————— executed the same as ———————— free and voluntary act and deed for the uses and purposes therein set forth.

Tit. 16, § 34. Execution by mark.

When real estate is conveyed or encumbered by an instrument in writing by a person who cannot write his name, he shall execute the same by his mark, and his name shall be written near such mark by one of two persons who saw such mark made, who shall write their names on such instrument as witnesses. In case such instrument is acknowledged, then the officer taking the acknowledgment shall, in addition to the other necessary recitals in the acknowledgment, state that the grantor executed the instrument, by inserting in the ordinary form of acknowledgment by individuals

after the words "foregoing instrument" the words "by his mark, in my presence and in the presence of ———————— and ———————— as witnesses."

Tit. 16, § 35. Acknowledgment to be under seal—before whom taken.

Every acknowledgment must be under seal of the officer taking the same; and when taken in this State, it may be taken before any Notary Public, County Clerk, Clerk of the District Court, Clerk of the County Court, or County Judge; and when taken elsewhere in the United States, or United States possessions, or Canada (including Newfoundland), it may be taken before any Notary Public, Clerk of a Court of Record, or Commissioner of Deeds duly appointed by the Governor of the State for the County, State or Territory where the same is taken; and when taken in any other foreign country, it may be taken before any Court of Record or Clerk of such Court, or before any Consul of the United States, provided, that acknowledgments relating to military business of the State may be taken before an officer in charge of any summary Court-Martial * * * a certified copy of whose appointment is placed of record in the office of the Secretary of State by the Adjutant General.

Tit. 16, § 37b. Foreign execution and acknowledgments validated—exceptions.

All deeds, mortgages, releases, oil and gas leases, powers of attorney and other instruments of writing for the conveyance or incumbrance of any lands, tenements or hereditaments situated within this state, now of record or hereafter recorded which are executed and acknowledged or proved in any state, territory, District of Columbia or foreign country, in conformity with the law of such state, territory, District of Columbia or foreign country, or in conformity with the Federal Statutes, shall be as valid as to execution and acknowledgment thereof, only, as if executed and acknowledged within this state in conformity with the provisions of the laws of this state. Provided this act shall not validate any deed, mortgage, releases, oil and gas leases, powers of attorney, and other instruments of writing for the conveyance of any lands, tenements, or hereditaments the validity of which is in litigation upon the effective date of this act. Provided this act shall not validate any execution or acknowledgment fraudulently obtained.

Tit. 16, § 95. Acknowledgment by corporation—form.

Every deed or other instrument affecting real estate, executed by a corporation, must be acknowledged by the officer or person subscribing the name of the corporation thereto, which acknowledgment must be substantially in the following form, to wit: State of Oklahoma,

ss.

_____ County.

Before me, a _____ in and for said county and State, on this _____ day of _____ 19__, personally appeared _____, to me known to be the identical person who subscribed the name of the maker thereof to the foregoing instrument as its (attorney-in-fact, president, vice-president, or mayor, as the case may be) and acknowledged to me that he executed the same as his free and voluntary act and deed, and as the free and voluntary act and deed of such corporation, for the uses and purposes therein set forth.

Tit. 16, ch. 6., Appx. Title Examination Standards.

§ 6.2. Omissions and inconsistencies in instruments and acknowledgments. Omission of the date of execution from a conveyance or other instrument affecting the title does not, in itself, impair marketability. Even if the date of execution is of peculiar significance, an undated instrument will be presumed to have been timely executed if the dates of acknowledgment and recordation, and other circumstances of record, support that presumption.

An acknowledgment taken by a notary public in another state which does not show the expiration of the notary's commission is not invalid for that reason.

Inconsistencies in recitals or indication of dates, as between dates of execution, attestation, acknowledgment, or recordation, do not, in themselves, impair marketability. Absent a peculiar significance of one of the dates, a proper sequence of formalities will be presumed notwithstanding such inconsistencies.

* * *

Tit. 18, § 438.28. Acknowledgment of instruments.

No person who is authorized to take acknowledgments under the laws of this state shall be disqualified from taking acknowledgments of instruments executed in favor of a cooperative or to which it is a party, by reason of being an officer, trustee, member, or shareholder of such cooperative.

Tit. 84, § 55. Formal requisites in execution—self-proved wills.

Every will, other than a nuncupative will, must be in writing; and every will, other than a holographic will and a nuncupative will, must be executed and attested as follows:

1. It must be subscribed at the end thereof by the testator himself, or some person, in his presence and by his discretion, must subscribe his name thereto.

2. The subscription must be made in the presence of the attesting witnesses, or be acknowledged by the testator to them, to have been made by him or by his authority.

3. The testator must, at the time of subscribing or acknowledging the same, declare to the attesting witnesses that the instrument is his will.

4. There must be two attesting witnesses, each of whom must sign his name as a witness at the end of the will at the testator's request and in his presence.

5. Every will, other than a holographic and a nuncupative will, and every codicil to such will or to a holographic will may, at the time of execution or at any subsequent date during the lifetimes of the testator and the witnesses, be made self-proved, and the testimony of the witnesses in the probate thereof may be made unnecessary by the acknowledgment thereof by the testator and the affidavits of the attesting witnesses, each made before an officer authorized to take acknowledgments to deeds of conveyance and to administer oaths under the laws of this state, such acknowledgments and affidavits being evidenced by the certificate, with official seal affixed, of such officer attached or annexed to such testamentary instrument in form and contents substantially as follows:

THE STATE OF OKLAHOMA
COUNTY OF _____

Before me, the undersigned authority, on this day personally appeared _____, _____, and _____, known to me to be the testator and the witnesses, respectively, whose names are subscribed to the annexed or foregoing instrument in their respective capacities, and, all of said persons being by me first duly sworn, said _____, testator, declared to me and to the said witnesses in my presence that said instrument is his last will and testament or a codicil to his last will and testament, and that he had willingly made and executed it as his free and voluntary act and deed for the purposes therein expressed; and the said witnesses, each on his oath stated to me, in the presence and hearing of the said testator, that the said testator had declared to them that said instrument is his last will and testament or codicil to his last will and testament, and that he executed same as such and wanted each of them to sign it as a witness; and upon their oaths each witness states further that they did sign the same as witnesses in the presence of the said testator and at his request and that said testator was at that time eighteen (18) years of age or over and was of sound mind.

_____
Testator

_____
Witness

_____
Witness

Subscribed and acknowledged before me by the said _____, testator, and subscribed and sworn before me by the said _____, and _____ witnesses, this _____ day of _____, A.D., _____.

(SEAL)

(SIGNED) _____

_____
(OFFICIAL CAPACITY OF OFFICER)

A self-proved testamentary instrument shall be admitted to probate without the testimony of any subscribing witness, unless contested, but otherwise it shall be treated no differently than a will or codicil not self-proved. Furthermore, a self-proved testamentary instrument may be revoked or amended by a codicil in exactly the same fashion as a will or codicil not self-proved and such a testamentary instrument may be contested as a will not self-proved.

DEPOSITIONS

Tit. 20, § 1502. Duties of board.

The Board shall have the following duties:

a. Conduct preliminary investigations to determine the qualifications of applicants seeking to attain the status of certified shorthand reporters;

b. Conduct at least once a year, at a place and time to be published by ample notice given to all interested parties, an examination of those persons who seek to attain the status of certified shorthand reporters. The Board may also give examinations for a certificate of proficiency and for a certificate of merit;

c. Recommend to the Supreme Court for official enrollment as certified court reporters those persons who, on their examination, have established the requisite proficiency in taking testimony and proceedings and preparing accurate transcripts thereof;

d. Conduct proceedings, on reasonable notice, the object of which is to recommend to the Supreme Court the suspension, cancellation, revocation or reinstatement of the enrollment of a certified or licensed court reporter or of the status of any acting court reporter, regular or temporary, on the following grounds:

1. conviction of a felony or misdemeanor involving moral turpitude;

2. misrepresentation in obtaining enrollment;

3. any violation of, or noncompliance with any rule or directive of the Supreme Court;

4. fraud, gross incompetence or neglect;

5. any other violation of duties; or

6. nonpayment of renewal dues.

In all hearings or investigations on revocation, cancellation or suspension of enrollment, each Board member shall be empowered to administer oaths and affirmations, subpoena witnesses and take evidence anywhere in the state, after giving reasonable notice to the party whose status is sought to be affected.

e. Adopt, with the approval of the Chief Justice, examination standards and rules governing enrollment, discipline, suspension, cancellation and revocation proceedings and any other matter within the Board's cognizance.

f. Keep a current roll of certified court reporters and a file on all disciplined court reporters, official or unofficial, regular or temporary.

Tit. 20, § 1503. Examination for enrollment as certified or licensed shorthand reporter.

a. Every applicant who seeks to be examined for enrollment as a certified shorthand reporter shall prove to the satisfaction of the Board that he is of legal age, meets the requisite standards of ethical fitness and has at least a high school education or its equivalent.

b. Every applicant for enrollment as a certified shorthand reporter shall be required, on examination, to demonstrate proficiency in reporting testimony and proceedings at a speed of not less than two hundred (200) words per minute in taking a question-and-answer-type dictation only, and no other type, and in preparing an accurate transcription thereof that is reasonably free from spelling errors. Any examination or test given shall be approved by the Supreme Court. The Board may not increase or decrease such minimum speed requirement, by rule or otherwise.

c. As used in paragraph b hereof, the phrase "proficiency in reporting testimony and proceedings" means proficiency in verbatim reporting by use of any generally recognized system of symbols or abbreviations written with pen or pencil, stenotype or similar machines, or such other method as may be from time to time approved by the Supreme Court.

Tit. 20, § 1504. Enrollment without examination.

The following persons shall be entitled to enrollment as licensed court reporters without examination:

a. Any noncertified court reporter who was engaged and serving on March 1, 1969, as an official court reporter for the district or superior court;

b. Any person deemed by the Board to hold an equivalent license from another state who is a resident of Oklahoma, provided his credentials are found to be in proper order; and

c. Any person who, prior to July 1, 1978, was an acting shorthand reporter under a certificate issued by the Chief Justice of the Oklahoma Supreme Court.

Tit. 20, § 1505. Licensees from other states.

A person holding a license from another state which is deemed by the Board to be equivalent to that of an Oklahoma certified shorthand reporter may be enrolled without examination as an Oklahoma certified shorthand reporter upon satisfying the Board that his credentials are in proper order and that he is a resident of Oklahoma.

Tit. 20, § 1506. Fees.

The Board shall charge the following fees:

a. Seventy-five Dollars ($75.00) for an examination fee for a bona fide resident of the state;

b. One Hundred Fifty Dollars ($150.00) for an examination fee for a nonresident of the state;

c. One Hundred Fifty Dollars ($150.00) for an application to enroll a certified shorthand reporter without an examination;

d. Seventy-five Dollars ($75.00) as a bi-annual renewal fee to be paid by all persons enrolled as certified or licensed shorthand reporters.

Tit. 20, § 1507. Deposit of fees—withdrawals.

All fees authorized to be charged shall be paid to the Clerk of the Supreme Court who shall deposit them in the State Judicial Fund. The Chief Justice shall be authorized to draw against this fund for such amounts as are lawfully claimed by the Board for its necessary supplies and expenses. When performing essential duties each Board member shall be entitled to his actual expenses and shall receive, in addition thereto, the sum of Fifty Dollars ($50.00) for each full day of service or a fraction thereof for less than a day's service. On the effective date of this act the Clerk of the Supreme Court shall transfer and deposit to the State Judicial Fund all monies which he presently holds in the Certified Reporters Fund under the provisions of Section 962 of Title 59 of the Oklahoma Statutes.

Tit. 20, § 1508. Metal seals—use of abbreviations—powers of certified reporters.

Every person enrolled as a certified shorthand reporter shall be entitled to use the abbreviation C.S.R. after his name and shall receive from the Board, without additional charge, a metal seal with his name and the words "Oklahoma Certified Shorthand Reporter". Every person enrolled as a licensed shorthand reporter shall be entitled to use the abbreviation L.S.R. after his name and shall receive from the Board, without additional charge, a metal seal with his name and the words "Oklahoma Licensed Shorthand Reporter". Acting court reporters shall not be allowed to use the seal. The determination of the format and construction of the seal shall rest with the Supreme Court of the State of Oklahoma. The Oklahoma Supreme Court shall determine the procedures to be used in the distribution of all shorthand reporter seals. Certified shorthand reporters shall be authorized to issue affidavits in respect to their regular duties, to subpoena witnesses for depositions, administer oaths and affirmations, and to take depositions or other sworn statements, with authority equal to that of a notary public. Licensed shorthand reporters shall have the same authority while employed as official court reporters.

LEGAL HOLIDAYS

Tit. 25, § 82.1. Designation and dates of holidays.

The designation and dates of holidays in Oklahoma shall be as follows: Each Sunday, New Year's Day on the 1st day of January, Martin Luther King, Jr.'s Birthday on the third Monday in January, Washington's Birthday on the third Monday in February, Memorial Day on the last Monday in May, Independence Day on the 4th day of July, Labor Day on the first Monday in September, Veterans' Day on the 11th day of November, Thanksgiving Day on the fourth Thursday in November, Christmas on the 25th day of December; and if any of such holidays other than Sunday at any time fall on Sunday, the succeeding Monday shall be a holiday in that year. Any act authorized, required, or permitted to be performed on a holiday as designated in this section may be performed on the next succeeding business day, and no liability or loss of rights of any kind shall result from such delay.

Tit. 25, § 82.2. Additional holidays—acts performable—optional closing by banks and offices.

The following additional days are designated as holidays:

Jefferson Day on the 13th day of April; Oklahoma Day on the 22nd day of April; Mother's Day on the second Sunday in May; Indian Day on the first Saturday after the full moon in September; Cherokee Strip Day on the 16th day of September; Will Rogers Day on the 4th day of November; Citizenship Recognition Day on such date as may be fixed by the Governor; Oklahoma Historical Day on the 10th day of October; Senior Citizens' Day the 9th day of June; Youth Day on the third Sunday in March each year; each day in which a state election is held throughout the State of Oklahoma; and such other days as may be designated by the President of the United States or the Governor of the State of Oklahoma. Notwithstanding the day designated for Veterans' Day by Section 82.1 of this title, any bank, savings and loan or association or credit union may observe the fourth Monday in October as Veterans' Day. Any act authorized, required or permitted to be performed on any holiday as designated in this section may and shall be performed on said day the same as on any business day; provided any state, national or federal reserve bank, building and loan association, credit union, state, federal, county or municipal office may close on any day designated in this section as a holiday, and, upon such bank, building and loan association, credit union, or public office being closed on such day, any act authorized, required or permitted to be performed at or by such bank, building and loan association, credit union, public office or public official may be performed on the next succeeding business day and no liability or loss of rights of any kind shall result from such delay.

OREGON

NOTARIES PUBLIC

[Or. Rev. Stat.]

§ **194.005.** Definitions for ORS 194.005 to 194.200.

As used in ORS 194.005 to 194.200:

(1) "Commercial paper" means such instruments as are within the scope of ORS chapter 73, including drafts, checks, certificates of deposit and notes.

(2) "Commission" means to empower to perform notarial acts and the written authority to perform those acts.

(3) "Good moral character" means character other than that which reflects moral turpitude and conduct which would cause a reasonable person to have substantial doubts about an individual's honesty, fairness and respect for the rights of others and for the laws of the state and the nation. To be relevant to deciding whether a person is of "good moral character," conduct of questionable good moral character must be rationally connected to the applicant's fitness to be a notary public.

(4) "Notarial act" and "notarization" have the meaning given those terms under ORS 194.505.

(5) "Notarial certificate" and "certificate" mean the part of, or attachment to, a notarized document for completion by the notary and bearing the notary's signature and official seal.

(6) "Notarial journal" means the journal described under ORS 194.152.

(7) "Notary public" and "notary" mean any person commissioned to perform notarial acts under ORS 194.005 to 194.200.

(8) "Official misconduct" means a notary's performance of or failure to perform any act prohibited or mandated respectively by ORS 194.005 to 194.200 or 194.505 to 194.595, or any rule adopted under ORS 194.005 to 194.200 or 194.505 to 194.595, or any other law governing notarization.

§ 194.010. Appointment of notary public; certificate of authorization; office may be nonlucrative; functions not official duties.

(1) Upon application as prescribed under ORS 194.014, the Secretary of State shall appoint and commission individual persons as notaries public.

(2) Upon appointment as a notary public, the Secretary of State shall send to the person appointed a notarial commission and a Certificate of Authorization with which the person appointed shall obtain an official seal.

(3) The notary public shall retain the commission during the term of appointment.

(4)(a) Only upon presentation by the notary public of the Certification of Authorization is a vendor authorized to provide the notary with the official seal described under ORS 194.031.

(b) A vendor of official seals shall make note of the receipt of a Certificate of Authorization by a signature of the vendor or an authorized representative of the vendor upon the Certificate of Authorization.

(c) Subject to the procedures set forth under ORS 194.980, any vendor of official seals who furnishes an official seal to any person in violation of paragraph (a) of this subsection may incur a civil penalty in an amount, established by rule of the Secretary of State, that is within the limits set forth under ORS 194.980 (2)(a). Once incurred, the penalty shall be treated in all respects as a civil penalty incurred under ORS 194.980.

(5) Each notary public may file with the Secretary of State a statement waiving the fees specified under ORS 194.164 (1); and in such case the office of notary public is considered nonlucrative.

(6) The functions of a notary public are not considered official duties under section 1, Article III of the Oregon Constitution.

§ 194.012. Term of office.

The term of office of a notary public is four years

commencing with the effective date specified in the notarial commission. A notary public may perform notarial acts during the term of the commission, or until the commission is revoked, but may not perform notarial acts during any period when the commission is suspended.

§ 194.014. Application for appointment and commission.

Every individual person, before entering upon the duties of a notary public, shall file with the Secretary of State a completed application for appointment and commission as a notary public. Application shall be made on a form prescribed by the Secretary of State and shall include an oath of office, the legal name and an official signature. Each applicant for appointment and commission as a notary public shall swear, under penalty of perjury, that the answers to all questions on the application are true and complete to the best of the applicant's knowledge, and that the applicant is qualified to be appointed and commissioned as a notary public. The application process shall be ordered or arranged so that applications may be readily submitted by mail.

§ 194.020. Fee for application.

(1) To defray costs incurred by the Secretary of State to process the application made under ORS 194.014, each applicant for appointment as a notary public shall pay in advance to the Secretary of State a nonrefundable application fee not to exceed $20.

(2) Any fee received by the Secretary of State under subsection (1) of this section shall be deposited in the State Treasury and credited to the Notary Public Limitation Account, and is in lieu of any fee charged under ORS 177.130.

§ 194.022. Qualifications; written examination.

Every person appointed and commissioned as a notary public shall:

(1) Be at the time of appointment 18 years of age or older.

(2) Be at the time of appointment a resident of this state, or be a resident of an adjacent state and be regularly employed or carry on a trade or business within this state.

(3) At the time of appointment, be able to read and write the English language.

(4) Be of good moral character.

(5) Not have had a notary commission revoked for official misconduct during the five-year period preceding the date of application.

(6) Not have been convicted of a felony, or of a

lesser offense incompatible with the duties of a notary public, during the 10-year period preceding the date of application.

(7) Have satisfactorily completed a written examination prescribed by the Secretary of State to determine the fitness of the person to exercise the functions of the office of notary public. The written examination shall be included as part of the application form and the examination shall allow questions to be answered on an open-book basis. Answers to the questions shall be discernible from a review of the application materials furnished to the applicant.

§ 194.024. Investigation of applicant; consent.

(1) To assist in determining the identity of an applicant for notary public, or if the applicant has been convicted of a felony or of a lesser offense incompatible with the duties of a notary public, upon consent of the person making application for appointment as notary public and upon request of the Secretary of State, the Department of State Police shall furnish to the Secretary of State any information that the department may have in its possession from its central bureau of criminal identification, including but not limited to manual or computerized information and any information to which the department may have access, including but not limited to the Law Enforcement Data System maintained by the Executive Department and referred to in ORS 181.710. For purposes of receiving the information described in this subsection, the Secretary of State is a "criminal justice agency" under ORS 181.010 to 181.560 and the rules adopted under ORS 181.555.

(2) A person making application for appointment as notary public shall be deemed, upon signing or with signature upon the application filed under ORS 194.014, to have given the consent necessary for purposes of subsection (1) of this section.

§ 194.031. Notarial seal; filing of sample imprint; replacement seal.

(1) The official seal of a notary public shall be a stamp made of rubber or some other substance capable of making a legible imprint on paper in black ink. The imprint must legibly reproduce under photographic methods.

(2) The Secretary of State shall adopt rules prescribing the size and form of the imprint of the official seal to promote uniformity, legibility and permanency.

(3) The attempt to notarize an instrument required to be notarized shall be of no effect unless it bears an imprint of the official seal of the notary who performed the notarization made in the manner required under subsections (1) and (2) of this section.

(4) Upon delivery of an official seal to a notary public, the notary public shall cause an imprint of the official seal to be filed in the office of the Secretary of State, together with any other information that is by rule required. The filing shall be done in the manner and within the time prescribed by rule.

(5) Any notary whose official seal is lost, misplaced, destroyed, broken, damaged or that is otherwise unworkable shall immediately mail or deliver written notice of that fact to the Secretary of State. The Secretary of State shall issue a Certificate of Authorization which the notary public may use to obtain a replacement seal.

(6) A seal embosser may be used as an adjunct to the official seal. The use of the seal embosser shall be in compliance with any rules adopted by the Secretary of State.

§ 194.040. Record of appointments and commissions; Secretary of State's power to certify status of notary.

(1) The Secretary of State shall keep a record of appointment and commission of each notary public. The Secretary of State may certify as to the term of office of such notary public and imprint upon all instruments requiring a notarial certificate.

(2) Full faith and credit shall be given to all protestations, attestations and other instruments of publication of all notaries public appointed under ORS 194.010.

§ 149.043. Scope of appointment and commission.

Each notary public appointed and commissioned by the Secretary of State may perform notarial acts anywhere within this state. A notary public so appointed and commissioned may not perform notarial acts in another state, but may notarize a document originating in another state if the notarization is performed in this state.

§ 194.045. County clerk's power to certify status of notary.

Upon verification from the Secretary of State that a notary public is in good standing, the county clerk may certify as to the term of office of a notary public for instruments requiring such certificates.

§ 194.047. Change of address.

Any person appointed and commissioned as a notary public whose residential or business address is changed shall, within 30 days after the change, mail or deliver a notice of address change to the Secretary of State. The notice shall include the old address and the new address.

§ 194.052. Change of name.

(1) A notary public with a change of name under ORS 33.410. to 33.440 or otherwise may continue to use the current commissioned name until the expiration date of the commission. If the notary, however, wishes to use the new name in performing a notarial act, the notary must apply for an amended commission by completing a Change of Name Form and submitting the required fee for amended commission, as adopted by rule. The Secretary of State shall send an amended notarial commission to the person appointed, together with a Certificate of Authorization with which the notary shall obtain a new seal, the new seal to be as described under ORS 194.031.

(2) If a notary public whose name is changed does not wish to change the commission to the new name, the notary public shall, in any case, within 30 days after the change is effective, mail or deliver a notice of name change to the Secretary of State. The notice shall include the old name and the new name.

§ 194.063. Application for new commission; resignation.

(1) No person may be automatically reappointed as a notary public.

(2) Prior to expiration of a commission, a notary public may apply for a new commission in the manner provided by ORS 194.005 to 194.200, and subject to the qualifications prescribed therein.

(3) A person shall resign a notarial commission by mailing or delivering a letter of resignation indicating the effective date of the resignation to the Secretary of State, if:

(a) The person no longer desires to be commissioned as a notary public;

(b) The person ceases to reside in Oregon, or if the person is a nonresident notary, ceases to be regularly employed or to carry on a trade or business within Oregon; or

(c) The person becomes unable to read or write.

§ 194.070. Protesting commercial paper.

Each notary public who protests any commercial paper shall take such actions as are required by ORS 73.5090.

§ 194.090. Record of protest; effect as evidence.

Each notary public shall cause a record to be kept of all protests of commercial paper made by the notary public under ORS 73.5090. Such record is competent evidence to prove notice of dishonor for purposes of ORS 73.5100.

§ 194.100. Powers of notary connected with corporation; limitations.

(1) A notary public who is a stockholder, director, officer or employee of a bank or trust company or other corporation may:

(a) Take the acknowledgment of any party to any written instrument executed to or by such corporation;

(b) Administer an oath to any other stockholder, director, officer, employee or agent of such corporation; and

(c) Protest commercial paper owned or held for collection by such corporation.

(2) A notary public shall not:

(a) Take the acknowledgment of an instrument executed by or to a bank or trust company or other corporation of which the notary is a stockholder, director, officer or employee, if the notary is a party to such instrument, either individually or as a representative of such corporation; or

(b) Protest any commercial paper owned or held for collection by such corporation, if the notary is individually a party to the instrument.

§ 194.130. Disposition of records on vacancy in office; penalty for failure to properly dispose of records or for destroying or altering records.

(1) Whenever the office of a notary public becomes vacant, the record referred to in ORS 194.090 kept by the notary public, together with all the papers relating to such record, shall be deposited in the office of the Secretary of State. Any notary public neglecting for the space of three months after resignation or removal from office to deposit such record and papers in the Secretary of State's office, or any executor or administrator of a deceased notary public neglecting for the space of three months after the acceptance of that trust to lodge in the Secretary of State's office such record and papers as come into the hands of the notary public, shall forfeit not more than $500.

(2) If any person knowingly destroys, defaces, materially alters or conceals any record or paper of a notary public, that person shall forfeit not more than $500, and shall be liable to an action for damages by the party injured.

§ 194.150. Recovery of forfeitures.

All forfeitures under ORS 194.130 shall be recovered in a civil action in any court having jurisdiction of the same in the county where the notary public resides or is employed or is carrying on business. One-half shall be paid to the person bringing the action and one-half shall be paid to the State Treasurer to be credited to the General Fund.

§ 194.152. Journal of notarial acts; rules; disclosure.

(1) Each notary public shall provide, keep, maintain and protect one or more chronological journals of notarial acts performed by the notary public except for administering an oath or affirmation or certifying or attesting a copy.

(2) The Secretary of State shall adopt rules prescribing the form of the notarial journal to promote uniformity and establish the retention or disposition of the notarial journal and other notarial records, and prescribe rules to provide for exceptions to the notarial journal.

(3) A notary public who is an employee may enter into an agreement with the employer pursuant to which agreement the notarial journal or journals of the notary, in compliance with rules adopted under subsection (2) of this section, are retained or disposed of by the employer upon termination of employment.

(4) A notarial journal in the possession of a notary public who is not a public official or employee is exempt from disclosure under ORS 192.410 to 192.505. A notarial journal in the possession of the Secretary of State, or in the possession of a notary public who is a public official or employee, is not exempt from disclosure under ORS 192.410 to 192.505 unless the Secretary of State or other custodian determines that the public interest in disclosure is outweighed by the interests of the parties in keeping the journal record of the notarial act confidential. A determination by the Secretary of State or other custodian under this subsection is subject to review under ORS 192.410 to 192.505.

(5) This section does not apply to the record of protests of commercial paper which shall be as provided in ORS 194.090.

§ 194.154. Disposition of seal and notarial journal upon resignation, revocation or expiration of commission.

(1)(a) A notary public whose notarial commission is resigned or revoked shall deliver the official seal to the Secretary of State within the time specified under subsection (2) of this section for disposition of the notarial journal and records.

(b) Upon normal expiration of a notarial commission, the notary public shall destroy the official seal as soon as is reasonably practicable.

(2) Except as provided under subsection (3) of this section, a notary public whose notarial commission is resigned, revoked or expired shall dispose of the notarial journal and records pursuant to rules adopted by the Secretary of State within 30 days after the effective date of the resignation, revocation or expiration, whichever occurs first.

(3) A former notary who intends to apply for a new commission need not dispose of the notarial journal and records within 30 days after commission expiration, but must do so within three months after expiration unless newly commissioned within that period.

§ 194.156. Disposition of seal and notarial journal upon death of notary.

If a notary dies during the term of commission, the notary's heirs or personal representative, as soon as reasonably practicable after death, shall:

(1) Deliver the official seal to the Secretary of State; and

(2) Notify the Secretary of State in writing of the date of death and of the manner in which the notarial journal and records have been disposed. Disposition, after death, of the notarial journal and records shall be as provided by rule.

§ 194.158. Prohibited acts.

(1) A notary public may not perform a notarial act if the notary is a signer of or named in the document that is to be notarized.

(2) A notary may not indorse or promote any product, service, contest or other offering if the notary's title or seal is used in the indorsement or promotional statement.

§ 194.162. Misrepresentation of notarial powers; notice of notarial powers and fees.

(1) A notary public may select notarial certificates pursuant to ORS 194.005 to 194.200 and 194.505 to 194.595.

(2) A notary may not make representations to have powers, qualifications, rights or privileges that the office of notary does not have including the power to counsel on immigration matters.

(3) A notary who is not licensed to practice law in this state and who advertises notarial services in a language other than English shall include in the advertisement, notice or signs, in the same language and in English, the following:

(a) A statement, prominently displayed: "I am

not licensed to practice law in the State of Oregon and I am not permitted to give legal advice on immigration or other legal matters or accept fees for legal advice."; and

(b) The fees for notarial acts specified under ORS 194.164.

(4) The notary shall post the notice required under subsection (3) of this section in a conspicuous place in the notary's place of business.

(5) A person may not use the term "notario publico" or any equivalent non-English term, in any business card, advertisement, notice, sign or in any other manner that misrepresents the authority of a notary public.

§ 194.164. Maximum fees for notarial acts; exception.

(1) The Secretary of State shall adopt by rule a schedule fixing the maximum fees that a notary public may charge for performing notarial acts. The schedule shall include, but not be limited to, maximum fees for the following notarial acts:

(a) Acknowledgments.

(b) Oaths or affirmations without a signature.

(c) Verifications upon oath or affirmation.

(d) Copy certifications.

(e) Protesting commercial paper, except that no fees shall be allowed for protesting a check because of the insolvency of the bank upon which the check was written.

(2) A notary public may charge an additional fee for traveling to perform a notarial act if:

(a) The notary explains to the person requesting the notarial act that the fee is in addition to the fee specified under subsection (1) of this section and is not required by law; and

(b) The person requesting the notarial act agrees in advance upon the amount of the additional fee.

(3) Notaries shall display an English-language schedule of fees for notarial acts, as specified under subsection (1) of this section.

§ 194.166. Ground for refusal to issue; revocation or suspension of commission.

The Secretary of State may refuse to appoint any person as notary public or may revoke or suspend the commission of any notary public upon any of the following grounds:

(1) Failure to meet or maintain the qualifications required under ORS 194.005 to 194.200 or refusal of the consent described under ORS 194.024.

(2) Substantial and material misstatement or omission of fact in the application submitted to the Secretary of State.

(3) Engaging in official misconduct.

(4) Conviction of a felony, or of a lesser offense

incompatible with the duties of a notary public.

(5) Revocation, suspension, restriction or denial of a professional license issued by a governmental entity, if the revocation, suspension, restriction or denial was for misconduct, dishonesty or any cause substantially relating to the duties or responsibilities of a notary public.

(6) When adjudged liable for damages in any suit grounded on fraud or misrepresentation or in any suit based upon a failure to discharge fully and faithfully the duties as notary public.

(7) The use of false or misleading advertising wherein the notary public has represented that the notary public has powers, qualifications, rights or privileges that the office of notary does not have, including the power to counsel on immigration matters.

(8) Engaging in the unauthorized practice of law.

(9) Charging more than the maximum fees adopted by the Secretary of State by rule under ORS 194.164.

(10) Failure to comply with ORS 194.162 (3) and (4).

(11) Commission of any act involving dishonesty, fraud or deceit with the intent to substantially benefit the notary public or another or substantially injure another.

(12) Failure to complete an acknowledgment at the time the notary's signature and official seal are affixed to the document.

(13) Execution of any certificate as a notary public containing a statement known to the notary public to be false.

(14) Using officially an official seal, seal embosser or other device making an imprint or impression that does not conform to ORS 194.031 or to the rules of the Secretary of State.

(15) Failure to give notice of change of address as required under ORS 194.047 or apply for, or give notice of, a change of name as required under ORS 194.052.

§ 194.168. Hearing on refusal to issue; suspension or revocation of commission.

(1) If the Secretary of State proposes to refuse to issue, or to suspend or revoke, a commission of a notary public, opportunity for hearing shall be accorded as provided in ORS 183.310 to 183.550 for a contested case. If the notary public does not request a hearing, revocation or suspension of the commission shall be effective 10 days after service of the Secretary of State's order.

(2) Judicial review of orders under subsection (1) of this section shall be as provided under ORS 183.310 to 183.550 for a contested case.

§ 194.200. Action for damages for violation of ORS 194.166; attorney fees and costs; employer's liability.

In addition to other remedies provided by law:

(1) A person injured by a violation of ORS 194.166 (7), (8), (10) or (11) may bring an individual action in an appropriate court to recover actual damages or $200, whichever is greater. The court or the jury, as the case may be, may award punitive damages and the court may provide such equitable relief as it deems necessary or proper. In addition to any other remedies awarded by the court, the prevailing party may be awarded attorney fees and costs and disbursements, at trial and on appeal.

(2) The Secretary of State or any private individual injured by a violation of ORS 194.166 (7), (8), (10) or (11) may bring a civil suit to enjoin the violation. In addition to any other remedies awarded by the court, the prevailing party may be awarded attorney fees and costs and disbursements, at trial and on appeal.

(3) An employer of a notary is liable to the notary for all damages recovered from the notary as a result of official misconduct that was coerced by threat of the employer, if the threat, such as that of demotion or dismissal, was made in reference to the particular notarization.

§ 194.330. Attorney general to investigate or prosecute violation; payment of expenses.

If, in the opinion of the Secretary of State, any alleged violation of ORS 194.005 to 194.200, 194.505 to 194.595 or 194.990 is not being investigated or prosecuted, the Secretary of State may direct the Attorney General to take full charge of the investigation or prosecution. If so directed, the Attorney General shall take full charge of the investigation or prosecution and the provisions of ORS 180.070, 180.080 and 180.090 shall apply. Notwithstanding ORS 180.070 (3), expenses associated with the Attorney General's investigation or prosecution shall be paid from the Notary Public Limitation Account established by ORS 194.700.

§ 194.335. Rules.

Subject to ORS 183.310 to 183.550, the Secretary of State may adopt rules to carry out the purposes of ORS 194.005 to 194.200 and 194.505 to 194.595.

Uniform Law on Notarial Acts

§ 194.505. Definitions for ORS 194.505 to 194.595.

As used in ORS 194.005 to 194.200 and 194.505 to 194.595, unless the context requires otherwise:

(1) A "notarial act" or "notarization" is any act that a notary public of this state is authorized to perform, and includes taking an acknowledgment, administering an oath or affirmation, taking a verification upon oath or affirmation, witnessing or attesting a signature, certifying or attesting a copy and noting a protest of a negotiable instrument.

(2) An "acknowledgment" is a statement by a person that the person has executed an instrument for the purposes stated therein and, if the instrument is executed in a representative capacity, that the person signed the instrument with proper authority and executed it as the act of the person or entity represented and identified therein.

(3) A "verification upon oath or affirmation" is a statement by a person who asserts it to be true and makes the assertion upon oath or affirmation.

(4) "in a representative capacity" means:

(a) For and on behalf of a corporation, partnership, trust or other entity, as an authorized officer, agent, partner, trustee or other representative;

(b) As a public officer, personal representative, guardian or other representative, in the capacity recited in the instrument;

(c) As an attorney-in-fact for a principal; or

(d) In any other capacity as an authorized representative of another.

(5) "Notarial officer" means a notary public or any other officer authorized to perform notarial acts.

(6) "Oath" and "affirmation" mean a notarial act or part thereof in which a notary certifies that a person made a vow in the presence of the notary on penalty of perjury.

(7) "Personally known" means familiarity with an individual resulting from interactions with that individual over a period of time sufficient to eliminate every reasonable doubt that the individual has the identity claimed.

(8) "Satisfactory evidence," as it pertains to identification on the basis of documents as described under ORS 194.515, means identification of an individual based on at least one current document issued by the federal or a state government with the individual's photograph, signature and physical description, or at least two documents issued by an institution, business entity or federal or state government with at least the individual's signature.

§ 194.515. Notarial acts.

(1) In taking an acknowledgment, the notarial officer must determine, either from personal knowledge or from satisfactory evidence, that the person appearing before the officer and making the acknowledgment is the person whose true signature is on the instrument.

(2) In taking a verification upon oath or affirmation, the notarial officer must determine, either from personal knowledge or from satisfactory evidence, that the person appearing before the officer and making the verification is the person whose true signature is on the statement verified.

(3) In witnessing or attesting a signature the notarial officer must determine, either from personal knowledge or from satisfactory evidence, that the signature is that of the person appearing before the officer and named therein.

(4) In certifying or attesting a copy of a document or other item, the notarial officer must determine that the proffered copy is a full, true and accurate transcription or reproduction of that which was copied.

(5) In making or noting a protest of a negotiable instrument a notarial officer must determine the matters set forth in ORS 73.5090.

(6) A notarial officer has satisfactory evidence that a person is the person whose true signature is on a document if that person (a) is personally known to the notarial officer, (b) is identified upon the oath or affirmation of a credible witness personally known to the notarial officer or (c) is identified on the basis of identification documents.

§ 194.525. Who may perform notarial acts; acts performed under federal authority.

(1) A notarial act may be performed within the state by the following persons:

(a) A notary public of this state; or

(b) A judge, clerk or deputy clerk of any court of this state.

(2) Notarial acts performed within this state under federal authority as provided in ORS 194.545 have the same effect as if performed by a notarial officer of this state.

(3) The signature and title of a person performing a notarial act are prima facie evidence that the signature is genuine and that the person holds the designated title.

§ 194.535. Notarial acts in other jurisdictions of the United States.

(1) A notarial act has the same effect under the law of this state as if performed by a notarial officer of this state, if performed in another state, commonwealth, territory, district or possession of the United States by any of the following persons:

(a) A notary public of that jurisdiction;

(b) A judge, clerk or deputy clerk of a court of that jurisdiction; or

(c) Any other person authorized by the law of that jurisdiction to perform notarial acts.

(2) Notarial acts performed in other jurisdictions of the United States under federal authority as provided in ORS 194.545 have the same effect as if performed by a notarial officer of this state.

(3) The signature and title of a person performing a notarial act are prima facie evidence that the signature is genuine and that the person holds the designated title.

(4) The signature and title of an officer listed in paragraph (a) or (b) of subsection (1) of this section conclusively establish the authority of a holder of that title to perform a notarial act.

§ 194.545. Notarial acts under federal authority.

(1) A notarial act has the same effect under the law of this state as if performed by a notarial officer of this state if performed anywhere by any of the following persons under authority granted by the law of the United States:

(a) A judge, clerk or deputy clerk of a court;

(b) A commissioned officer on active duty with the military services of the United States;

(c) An officer of the foreign service or consular officer of the United States; or

(d) Any other person authorized by federal law to perform notarial acts.

(2) The signature and title of a person performing a notarial act are prima facie evidence that the signature is genuine and that the person holds the designated title.

(3) The signature and title of an officer listed in paragraphs (a) to (c) of subsection (1) of this section, conclusively establish the authority of a holder of that title to perform a notarial act.

§ 194.555. Foreign notarial acts.

(1) A notarial act has the same effect under the law of this state as if performed by a notarial officer of this state if performed within the jurisdiction of and under authority of a foreign nation or its constituent units or a multinational or international organization by any of the following persons:

(a) A notary public or notary;

(b) A judge, clerk or deputy clerk of a court of record; or

(c) Any other person authorized by the law of that jurisdiction to perform notarial acts.

(2) An "Apostille" in the form prescribed by the Hague Convention of October 5, 1961, conclu-

sively establishes that the signature of the notarial officer is genuine and that the officer holds the designated office.

(3) A certificate by a foreign service or consular officer of the United States stationed in the nation under the jurisdiction of which the notarial act was performed, or a certificate by a foreign service or consular officer of that nation stationed in the United States, conclusively establishes any matter relating to the authenticity or validity of the notarial act set forth in the certificate.

(4) An official stamp or seal of the person performing the notarial act is prima facie evidence that the signature is genuine and that the person holds the designated title.

(5) An official stamp or seal of an officer listed in paragraph (a) or (b) of subsection (1) of this section is prima facie evidence that a person with that title has authority to perform notarial acts.

(6) If the title of office and indication of authority to perform notarial acts appears either in a digest of foreign law or in a list customarily used as a source for that information, it conclusively establishes the authority of an officer with that title to perform notarial acts.

§ **194.565.** Certificate of notarial acts.

(1) A notarial act must be evidenced by a certificate signed and dated by a notarial officer. The certificate must include identification of the jurisdiction in which the notarial act is performed and the title of the office the notarial officer holds and may include the official stamp or seal of office. If the officer is a notary public, the certificate must also indicate the date of expiration, if any, of the commission of office, but omission of that information may subsequently be corrected. If the officer is a commissioned officer on active duty with the military services of the United States, it must also include the officer's rank.

(2) A certificate of a notarial act is sufficient if it meets the requirements of subsection (1) of this section and it:

(a) Is in the short form set forth in ORS 194.575;

(b) Is in a form otherwise prescribed by the law of this state;

(c) Is in a form prescribed by the laws or regulations applicable in the place in which the notarial act was performed; or

(d) Sets forth the actions of the notarial officer and those are sufficient to meet the requirements of the designated notarial act.

(3) By executing a certificate of a notarial act, the notarial officer certifies that the officer has made the determinations required by ORS 194.515.

§ **194.575.** Short forms.

The following short form certificates of notarial acts are sufficient for the purposes indicated, if completed with the information required by ORS 194.565 (1):

(1) For an acknowledgment in an individual capacity:

State of _____

County of _____

This instrument was acknowledged before me on _____ (date) by _____. (name(s) of person(s))

_____
(Signature of notarial officer)
(Seal, if any)

_____
Title (and Rank)
My commission expires: _____

(2) For an acknowledgment in a representative capacity:

State of _____

County of _____

This instrument was acknowledged before me on _____ (date) by _____. (name(s) of person(s)) as _____ (type of authority, e.g., officer, trustee, etc.) of _____ (name of party on behalf of whom instrument was executed.)

_____
(Signature of notarial officer)
(Seal, if any)

_____
Title (and Rank)
My commission expires: _____

(3) For a verification upon oath or affirmation:

State of _____

County of _____

Signed and sworn to (or affirmed) before me on _____ (date) by _____. (name(s) of person(s) making statement)

_____
(Signature of notarial officer)
(Seal, if any)

_____
Title (and Rank)
My commission expires: _____

(4) For witnessing or attesting a signature:

State of _____

County of _____

Signed or attested before me, on _____ (date) by _____. (name(s) of person(s))

_____
(Signature of notarial officer)
(Seal, if any)

_____
Title (and Rank)
My commission expires: _____

(5) For attestation of a copy of a document:

State of _____

County of _____

I certify that this is a true and correct copy of a document in the possession of _____.

Dated: _____

_____

(Signature of notarial officer)

(Seal, if any)

_____

Title (and Rank)

My commission expires: _____

§ 194.585. Uniformity of application and construction.

ORS 194.505 to 194.575 shall be applied and construed to effectuate its general purpose to make uniform the law with respect to the subject of ORS 194.505 to 194.575 among states enacting it.

§ 194.595. Short title.

ORS 194.505 to 194.595 may be cited as the Uniform Law on Notarial Acts.

§ 194.700. Notary public limitation account.

(1) The Notary Public Limitation Account is established in the General Fund of the State Treasury. All moneys received by the Secretary of State under this chapter shall be paid into the State Treasury and credited to the account. Such moneys are continuously appropriated and shall be used only for the administration and enforcement of this chapter.

(2) In order to facilitate financing the necessary costs of performing the duties under this chapter, the Secretary of State may transfer to the Notary Public Limitation Account such amounts considered necessary, not to exceed $50,000, from biennial appropriations to the Secretary of State. The funds so transferred shall be retransferred from the Notary Public Limitation Account to the appropriation from which the original transfer was made prior to the last day of each biennium.

§ 194.980. Civil penalty; factors; notice; hearing.

(1) In addition to any other penalty provided by law, any notary public who is found to have performed an act of official misconduct may incur a civil penalty in the amount adopted under subsection (2) of this section, plus any costs of service or recording costs.

(2)(a) The Secretary of State shall by rule estab-

lish the amount of civil penalty that may be imposed for a particular act of official misconduct. A civil penalty shall not exceed $1,500 per act of official misconduct.

(b) In imposing a penalty authorized by this section, the Secretary of State may consider the following factors:

(A) The past history of the person incurring a penalty in taking all feasible steps or procedures necessary or appropriate to correct any official misconduct.

(B) Any prior acts of official misconduct.

(C) The gravity and magnitude of the official misconduct.

(D) Whether the official misconduct was repeated or continuous.

(E) Whether the cause of the official misconduct was an unavoidable accident, negligence or an intentional act.

(F) Any relevant rule of the Secretary of State.

(G) The notary's cooperativeness and efforts to correct the act of official misconduct.

(c) The penalty imposed under this section may be paid upon those terms and conditions as the Secretary of State determines to be proper and consistent with the public benefit. Upon request of the notary incurring the penalty, the Secretary of State shall consider evidence of the economic and financial condition of the notary in determining whether a penalty shall be paid.

(3) Imposition or payment of a civil penalty under this section shall not be a bar to any action or suit described in ORS 194.200, to a criminal proceeding or to a proceeding under ORS 194.168.

(4) A civil penalty shall not be imposed under this section until the notary public incurring the penalty has been given notice in writing from the Secretary of State specifying the violation. The notice is in addition to the notice required under paragraph (a) of subsection (5) of this section and shall be provided in the same manner as described under paragraph (a) of subsection (5) of this section.

(5)(a) After initial notice as provided in subsection (4) of this section, any civil penalty imposed under this section shall become due and payable when the notice of penalty is served upon the person incurring the penalty. The notice shall be served personally, or shall be served by depositing the notice with the United States Postal Service, addressed to the notary at the address on file in the office of the Secretary of State, sent by certified mail, return receipt requested or by other means that allows a signed receipt via the United States Postal Service. The notice shall include:

(A) A reference to the particular sections of the statute or rule involved;

(B) A statement of the matters asserted or charged;

(C) A statement of the amount of the penalty or penalties imposed;

(D) A statement of the notary's right to request a hearing; and

(E) A statement that if the penalty becomes a judgment and is not paid within the time required under subsection (6) of this section, the penalty and any costs of service and recording costs will be recorded by the county clerk in the County Clerk Lien Record maintained under ORS 205.130.

(b) The notary to whom the notice is addressed shall have 20 days from the date of service or mailing of the notice in which to make written application for a hearing before the Secretary of State, after which time the notice becomes a final order. In no case shall a hearing be held less than 45 days from the date of the personal service or mailing of the notice.

(c) All hearings shall be conducted pursuant to the applicable provisions of ORS 183.310 to 183.550. The Secretary of State may delegate to a hearings officer appointed by the Secretary of State, upon such conditions as deemed necessary, all or part of the authority to conduct hearings required under this section.

(6) Unless the amount of penalty imposed under this section is paid within 10 days after the order becomes final, the order shall constitute a judgment and may be recorded with the county clerk in any county of this state in the County Clerk Lien Record maintained under ORS 205.130. The clerk shall record the name of the person incurring the penalty and the amount of the penalty, together with service and recording costs, in the County Clerk Lien Record. Where the service has been made by certified mail or other means providing a receipt, the returned receipt shall be attached to and made a part of the order recorded. The penalty provided in the order, and added costs, so recorded become a lien upon the real property and shall bear interest, expire, be renewed and be enforced in the same manner as a judgment docketed pursuant to ORS 18.350.

(7) Notwithstanding ORS 180.070 (3), expenses incurred by the Secretary of State or Attorney General under subsections (1) to (6) of this section or under ORS 194.200 (2) shall be paid from the Notary Public Limitation Account established under ORS 194.700.

(8) All civil penalties and costs recovered under this section shall be paid into the Notary Public Limitation Account established under ORS 194.700.

§ 194.985. Official warning to cease official misconduct.

In lieu of a civil penalty imposed under ORS 194.980, the Secretary of State may deliver a written Official Warning to Cease Official Misconduct to any notary whose actions are judged by the Secretary of State to be official misconduct.

§ 194.990. Penalities.

(1) If punishment therefor is not otherwise provided for:

(a) A notary who knowingly and repeatedly performs or fails to perform any act prohibited or mandated respectively by ORS 194.005 to 194.200 or 194.505 to 194.595, or rules adopted thereunder, is guilty of a Class B misdemeanor.

(b) Any person not a notary public who knowingly acts as or otherwise impersonates a notary public is guilty of a Class B misdemeanor.

(c) Any person who knowingly obtains, conceals, defaces or destroys the official seal, journal or official records of a notary public is guilty of a Class B misdemeanor.

(d) Any person who knowingly solicits, coerces or in any way influences a notary public to commit official misconduct is guilty of a Class B misdemeanor.

(2) The remedies of subsection (1) of this section supplement other remedies provided by law.

(3) The clerk of the court in which a conviction under any provision of subsection (1) of this section is had shall forthwith transmit to the Secretary of State a duly certified copy of the judgment, which is sufficient grounds for revocation of the commission of the convicted notary public.

OFFENSES

§ 161.625. Fines for felonies.

* * *

(4) As used in this section, "gain" means the amount of money or the value of property derived from the commission of the felony, less the amount of money or the value of property returned to the victim of the crime or seized by or surrendered to lawful authority before the time sentence is imposed. "Value" shall be determined by the standards established in ORS 164.115.

(5) When the court imposes a fine for a felony the court shall make a finding as to the amount of the defendant's gain from the crime. If the record does not contain sufficient evidence to support a finding the court may conduct a hearing upon the issue.

* * *

§ 161.635. Fines for misdemeanors and violations.

(1) A sentence to pay a fine for a misdemeanor shall be a sentence to pay an amount, fixed by the court, not exceeding:

* * *

(b) $1,000 for a Class B misdemeanor.

* * *

(4) If a person has gained money or property through the commission of a misdemeanor or violation, then upon conviction thereof the court, instead of imposing the fine authorized for the offense under subsection (1), (2) or (3) of this section, may sentence the defendant to pay an amount fixed by the court, not exceeding double the amount of the defendant's gain from the commission of the offense. In that event ORS 161.625 (4) and (5) apply.

(5) This section shall not apply to corporations.

§ 161.645. Standards for imposing fines.

In determining whether to impose a fine and its amount, the court shall consider:

(1) The financial resources of the defendant and the burden that payment of a fine will impose, with due regard to the other obligations of the defendant; and

(2) The ability of the defendant to pay a fine on an installment basis or on other conditions to be fixed by the court.

ACKNOWLEDGMENTS

§ 93.410. Execution and acknowledgment of deeds.

Deeds executed within this state, of lands or any interest in lands therein, shall be signed by the grantors and may be acknowledged before any judge of the Supreme Court, circuit judge, county judge, justice of the peace or notary public within the state. No seal of the grantor, corporate or otherwise, shall be required on the deed.

§ 93.420. Execution of deed where personal representative, guardian or conservator is unable or refuses to act.

If any person is entitled to a deed from a personal representative, guardian or conservator who has died or resigned, has been discharged, disqualified or removed or refuses to execute it, the deed may be executed by the judge before whom the proceeding is pending or by the successor of the judge.

§ 93.440. Proof of execution by subscribing witness.

Proof of the execution of any conveyance may be made before any officer authorized to take acknowledgments of deeds, and shall be made by a subscribing witness thereto, who shall state the place of residence of the witness, and that the witness knew the person described in and who executed the conveyance. Such proof shall not be taken unless the officer is personally acquainted with the subscribing witness, or has satisfactory evidence that the witness is the same person who was a subscribing witness to the instrument.

§ 93.450. Proof where witnesses are dead or absent.

When any grantor is dead, out of this state, or refuses to acknowledge the deed, and all the subscribing witnesses to the deed are also dead or reside out of this state, it may be proved before the circuit court, or any judge thereof, by proving the handwriting of the grantor and of any subscribing witness thereto.

§ 93.460. Subpoena to compel witness to testify to execution of deed.

Upon the application of any grantee, or any person claiming under the grantee, verified by the oath of the applicant setting forth that the grantor is dead, out of the state, or refuses to acknowledge the deed, and that any witness to the conveyance residing in the county where the application is made refuses to appear and testify touching its execution and that the conveyance cannot be proven without the evidence of the witness, any officer authorized to take the acknowledgment or proof of conveyances may issue a subpoena requiring the witness to appear and testify before the officer touching the execution of the conveyance.

§ 93.470. Indorsement of certificate of proof.

Every officer who takes the proof of any conveyance shall indorse a certificate thereof, signed by the officer, on the conveyance. In the certificate the officer shall set forth those matters required by ORS 93.440 to 93.460 to be done, known or proved, together with the names of the witnesses examined before the officer, and their places of residence, and the substance of the evidence given by them.

§ 93.480. Deed acknowledged or proved as evidence; recordability.

Every conveyance acknowledged, proved or certified in the manner prescribed by law by any of the authorized officers may be read in evidence without further proof thereof and is entitled to be recorded in the county where the land is situated.

§ 93.530. Execution, acknowledgment and recordation of assignments of sheriffs' certificates of sale.

All assignments of sheriffs' certificates of sale of real property on execution or mortgage foreclosure shall be executed and acknowledged and recorded in the same manner as deeds of real property.

DEPOSITIONS

§ 44.320. Authority to take testimony and administer oath or affirmation.

Every court, judge, clerk of a court, justice of the peace, certified shorthand reporter or notary public is authorized to take testimony in any action or proceeding, as are other persons in particular cases authorized by statute or the Oregon Rules of Civil Procedure and is authorized to administer oaths and affirmations generally, and every such other person in the particular case authorized.

§ 45.010. Testimony taken in three modes.

The testimony of a witness is taken by three modes:
(1) Affidavit.
(2) Deposition.
(3) Oral examination.

§ 45.020. Affidavit defined.

An affidavit is a written declaration under oath, made without notice to the adverse party.

LEGAL HOLIDAYS

§ 187.010. Legal holidays; acts deferred to next business day; effect on labor agreements.

(1) The following days are legal holidays in this state:
(a) Each Sunday.
(b) New Year's Day on January 1.
(c) Martin Luther King, Jr.'s Birthday on the third Monday in January.
(d) Presidents Day, for the purpose of commemorating Presidents Washington and Lincoln, on the third Monday in February.
(e) Memorial Day on the last Monday in May.
(f) Independence Day on July 4.
(g) Labor Day on the first Monday in September.
(h) Veterans Day on November 11.
(i) Thanksgiving Day on the fourth Thursday in November.
(j) Christmas Day on December 25.
(2) Each time a holiday, other than Sunday, listed in subsection (1) of this section falls on Sunday, the succeeding Monday shall be a legal holiday. Each time a holiday listed in subsection (1) of this section falls on Saturday, the preceding Friday shall be a legal holiday.
(3) Any act authorized, required or permitted to be performed on a holiday as designated in this section may be performed on the next succeeding business day; and no liability or loss of rights of any kind shall result from such delay.
(4) In enumerating legal holidays in subsection (1) of this section, the Legislative Assembly does not intend to limit or otherwise affect public or private collective bargaining or collective bargaining agreements.

§ 187.020. Additional legal holidays.

In addition to those specified in ORS 187.010, the following days are legal holidays in this state:
(1) Every day appointed by the Governor as a holiday.
(2) Every day appointed by the President of the United States as a day of mourning, rejoicing or other special observance only when the Governor also appoints that day as a holiday.

PENNSYLVANIA

NOTARY PUBLIC LAW OF 1953

[PA. STAT. ANN.]

Tit. 57, § 147. Short title.

This act shall be known and may be cited as "The Notary Public Law".

Tit. 57, § 149. Eligibility.

Any citizen of Pennsylvania, being eighteen (18) years of age or over, of known character, integrity and ability, shall be eligible to the office of notary public, if he shall have resided within this Commonwealth for at least one (1) year immediately preceding the date of his appointment, and if he shall be a registered elector in the Commonwealth.

Tit. 57, § 150. Disqualification; exception.

The following persons shall be ineligible to hold the office of notary public:

(1) Any person holding any judicial office in this Commonwealth, except the office of justice of the peace, magistrate, or alderman.

(2) Every member of Congress, and any person, whether an officer, a subordinate officer, or agent, holding any office or appointment of profit or trust under the legislative, executive, or judiciary departments of the government of the United States, to which a salary, fees or perquisites are attached.

Tit. 57, § 151. Application to become a notary public.

Applications for appointment to the office of notary public shall be made to the Secretary of the Commonwealth, on forms prescribed and furnished by him, and shall be accompanied by a non-refundable filing fee of twenty-five dollars ($25), payable to the order of "State Treasurer," by money order, check, or draft. Each application shall bear the endorsement of the Senator of the district in which the applicant resides, or, in the case of a vacancy in that senatorial district, shall be endorsed by the Senator of an adjacent district.

Before issuing to any applicant a commission as notary public, the Secretary of the Commonwealth shall satisfy himself that the applicant is of good moral character, and is familiar with the duties and responsibilities of a notary public. Such qualifying requirements may be waived in the case of reappointment or appointments of persons making application within six (6) months after the expiration of a previous term as notary public, or appointments of person who were prevented from applying for reappointment or from applying for appointment, within the six (6) month extension period mentioned above, by reason of their induction or enlistment in the armed forces of the United States, if application is made within one (1) year after military discharge of the applicant, under conditions other than dishonorable.

Tit. 57, § 152. Application for reappointment.

Applications for reappointment to the office of notary public shall be filed at least one month prior to the expiration of the commission under which the notary is acting.

Tit. 57, § 153. Vacation of office; change of residence.

In event of any change of address within the Commonwealth, notice in writing shall be given the Secretary of the Commonwealth and the recorder of deeds of the county of original appointment by a notary public within five (5) days of such change. For the purpose of this section, "address" means office address. A notary public vacates his office by removing from the Commonwealth, and such removal shall constitute a resignation from the office of notary public as of the date of removal.

Tit. 57, § 154. Oath of office; bond; recording.

Every notary, on his appointment and before he enters upon the duties of the office of notary public, shall take and subscribe the constitutional oath of office, and shall give a surety bond, payable to the Commonwealth of Pennsylvania, in such amount as shall be fixed by the Secretary of the Commonwealth, which bond shall, after being recorded, be approved by and filed with the Secretary of the Commonwealth. Every such bond shall have as surety a duly authorized surety company or two sufficient individual sureties to be approved by the Secretary of the Commonwealth, conditioned for the faithful performance of the duties of the office of notary public and for the delivery of his register and all other public papers into the office of the recorder of deeds of the proper county in case of his death, resignation, disqualification, or removal. Such bond, as well as his commission and oath of office, shall be recorded in the office of the recorder of deeds of the county in which he maintains an office at the time of appointment or reappointment. The commission of any notary hereafter appointed who shall, for the space of thirty (30) days after the beginning of his term, neglect to give bond and cause the same and his commission and oath to be recorded, as above directed, shall be null and void.

Tit. 57, § 155. Registration of notary's signature; fee.

The official signature of each notary public shall be registered, in the "Notary Register" provided for such purpose in the prothonotary's office of the county wherein he maintains an office, within thirty (30) days after the appointment or reappointment, and in any county to which he may subsequently move his office, within ten (10) days thereafter. In counties of the second class, such signature shall also be registered in the clerk of courts' office within said period. The fee to be charged by the prothonotary for recording a notary's signature shall be fifty ($.50) cents.

Tit. 57, § 156. Change of name.

Whenever the name of any notary is changed by decree of court, or otherwise, such notary may continue to perform official acts, in the name in which he or she was commissioned, until the expiration of his or her term, but he or she shall, within thirty (30) days after entry of such decree, or after such name change, if not by decree of court, notify the Secretary of the Commonwealth and the recorder of deeds of the county in which he or she maintains an office of such change of name. The Secretary of the Commonwealth shall mark the public records relating to the notary accordingly and the recorder of deeds shall record the notification. Application for reappointment of such notary shall be made in the new name.

Tit. 57, § 158. Notarial seal.

(a) A notary public shall provide and keep an official seal which shall be used to authenticate all the acts, instruments and attestations of the notary. The seal shall be a rubber stamp and shall show clearly in the following order: the words "Notarial Seal"; the name and surname of the notary and the words "Notary Public"; the name of the political subdivision and county in which the notary maintains an office; and the date the notary's commission expires.

(b) The seal shall have a maximum height of one (1) inch and width of three and one-half (3 1/2)

inches, with a plain border. It shall be stamped in a prominent place on the official notarial act near the notary's signature in such a manner as to be capable of photographic reproduction.

(c) In addition to the official seal required in subsection (a), a notary public shall also use and keep an embosser upon which shall be engraved the words "Notary Public, Commonwealth of Pennsylvania," and the name and surname of the notary. All documents executed shall bear a legibly embossed impression.

Tit. 57, § 161. Register; copies of records.

(a) Every notary public shall keep an accurate register of all official acts by him done by virtue of his office, and shall, when thereunto required, give a certified copy of any record in his office to any person applying for same. Said register shall contain the date of the act, the character of the act, and the date and parties to the instrument, and the amount of fee collected for the service.

(b) The register and other public papers of such notary shall not in any case be liable to be seized, attached or taken in execution for debt or for any demand whatsoever.

Tit. 57, § 162. Power to administer oaths and affirmations.

Notaries shall have power to administer oaths and affirmations, according to law, in all matters belonging or incident to the exercise of their notarial office. Any person who shall be convicted of having wilfully and knowingly made or taken a false oath or affirmation before any notary in any matters within their official duties shall be guilty of perjury and shall be subject to the penalties in such case made and provided.

Tit. 57, § 163. Power to take acknowledgment of instruments of writing relating to commerce or navigation and to make declarations.

Notaries shall have the power to receive the proof of acknowledgment of all instruments of writing relating to commerce or navigation, such as bills of sale, bottomries, mortgages and hypothecations of ships or vessels, charter parties of affreightment, letters of attorney, and such other writings as have been usually proved or acknowledged before notaries within this Commonwealth, and also to make declarations and testify the truth thereof, under their seals of office, concerning all matters by them done in virtue of their respective offices.

Tit. 57, § 164. Power to take depositions, affidavits and acknowledgment of writings relative to lands.

Notaries shall have power to take depositions and affidavits, to take and receive the acknowledgment or proof of all deeds, conveyances, mortgages, or other instruments or writing touching or concerning any lands, tenements or hereditaments, situate, lying and being in any part of this State.

Tit. 57, § 165. Limitation on powers; fees.

(a) No director or officer in any bank, banking institution or trust company, holding at the same time the office of notary public, shall do or perform any act or duty as notary public for any bank, banking institution or trust company in which he is a director or officer. Any act or duty performed by any such notary public for any such bank, banking institution or trust company is hereby declared invalid.

(b) No clerk in any bank, banking institution or trust company, holding at the same time the office of notary public, shall be authorized to protest checks, notes, drafts, bill of exchange, or any commercial paper, for any bank, banking institution or trust company in which he is employed.

(c) The fees of any such notary for other services rendered shall be the property of such notary and in no case belong to or be received by the corporation of which he is a director or clerk.

(d) No justice of the peace, magistrate or alderman, holding at the same time the office of notary public, shall have jurisdiction in cases arising on papers or documents containing acts by him done in the office of notary public.

(e) No notary public may act as such in any transaction in which he is a party directly or pecuniarily interests.

Tit. 57, § 167. Fees of notaries public.

NOTARY PUBLIC FEE SCHEDULE
AS OF FEBRUARY 11, 1984

THE SECRETARY OF THE
COMMONWEALTH

REVISED NOTARY FEES

Executing affidavits	$2.00
Executing acknowledgments	2.00
in executing acknowledgments, each additional name	1.00
Executing certificates	2.00
Administering oaths	2.00
Taking depositions, per page	2.00
Making protests, per page	2.00

Tit. 57, § 168. Rejection of application; removal.

The Secretary of the Commonwealth may, for good cause, reject any application, or revoke the commission of any notary public, but such action shall be taken subject to the right of notice, hearing and adjudication, and the right of appeal therefrom, in accordance with the provisions of the Administrative Agency Law, approved the fourth day of June, one thousand nine hundred forty-five (Pamphlet Laws 1388, Section 1710.1 *et seq.* of Title 71, State Government), or any amendment or reenactment thereof, relating to adjudication procedure.

Tit. 57, § 168.1. Surrender of seal.

Should an application or renewal be rejected, or should a commission be revoked or recalled for any reason, the applicant or notary shall deliver the seal of office to the Department of State within ten (10) days after notice from the department.

Any person who violates the provisions of this section shall be guilty of a summary offense and upon conviction thereof shall be sentenced to pay a fine not exceeding three hundred dollars ($300) or to imprisonment not exceeding ninety (90) days, or both.

Tit. 57, § 169. Revocation of commission of notaries issuing checks without funds on deposit.

The Secretary of the Commonwealth shall, upon written complaint of any aggrieved applicant, revoke the commission of any notary public who issues to the order of any State agency a personal check without funds on deposit in payment of moneys due the agency that were received by him from applicants. Any action taken by the Secretary of the Commonwealth shall be subject to the right of notice, hearing and adjucation and the right of appeal therefrom in accordance with the provisions of the Administrative Agency Law of June four, one thousand nine hundred forty-five (Pamphlet Laws 1388, Section 1710.1 *et seq.* of Title 71, State Government).

ADDITIONAL AUTHORITY

[PA. CONS. STAT. ANN.]

Tit. 42, § 6105. Acts of notaries public.

(a) **General rule.**—The official acts, protests and attestations of all notaries public, certified under their respective hands and seals of office, including the dishonor of all bills and promissory notes, and of notice to the drawers, acceptors or endorsers thereof, may be received and read in evidence, as proof of the facts therein stated. Any litigant may be permitted to contradict by other evidence any such certificate.

(b) Foreign notaries.—The official acts and exemplifications of foreign notaries in accordance with the laws of their respective countries shall be prima facie evidence of the matters therein set forth, if they are authenticated as provided in section 5328 (relating to proof of official records). Any litigant may be permitted to contradict by other evidence any such acts, exemplifications or certificates.

Tit. 65, § 1. State and federal offices.

Every person who shall hold any office, or appointment of profit or trust, under the government of the United States, whether an officer, a subordinate officer or agent, who is or shall be employed under the legislative, executive or judiciary departments of the United States, and also every member of congress, is hereby declared to be incapable of holding or exercising, at the same time, the office or appointment of justice of the peace, notary public, mayor, recorder, burgess or alderman of any city, corporate town, resident physician of the lazaretto, constable, judge, inspector or clerk of election under this commonwealth: Provided, however, That the provisions hereof shall not apply to any person who shall enlist, enroll or be called or drafted into the active military or naval service of the United States or any branch or unit thereof during any war or emergency as hereinafter defined.

Tit. 65, § 1.1. War defined.

As used in this act the term "war" shall mean the period between the opening and ending of hostilities, and shall not include the period after the ending of hostilities, notwithstanding the fact that no treaty of peace has been negotiated or concluded, and the term "emergency" shall mean the period between a declaration that a state of emergency exists and a declaration that the state of emergency has been terminated.

Tit. 65, § 2. Offices so holden void.

The holding of any of the aforesaid offices or appointments under this state, is hereby declared to be incompatible with any office or appointment under the United States, and every such commission, office or appointment, so holden under the government of this state, contrary to the true intent

and meaning of this act, shall be and is hereby declared to be null and void.

Tit. 65, § 3. Penalty for exercising.

If any person, after the expiration of six months from the passing of this act, shall exercise any offices or appointments, the exercise of which is by this act declared to be incompatible, every person so offending shall, for every such offense, being thereof legally convicted in any court of record, forfeit and pay any sum not less than fifty nor more than five hundred dollars, at the discretion of the court, one moiety of the said forfeiture to be paid to the overseers, guardians or directors of the poor of the township, district, county or place where such offense shall have been committed, to be applied to the support of the poor, and the other moiety thereof to the prosecutor who shall sue for the same.

FEES

Tit. 16, § 11411. Counties of the second class; schedule.

The fees to be charged and collected by the recorder of deeds, in counties of the second class, shall be as follows:

* * *

For recording or exemplifying of commission for notary public, with bond and oath, the minimum fee shall be eleven dollars ($11.00); city or county officer, with bond and oath, the minimum fee shall be fourteen dollars ($14.00); justice of the peace or alderman, with bond and oath, the minimum fee shall be twelve dollars and fifty cents ($12.50); special police officer, the minimum fee shall be ten dollars ($10.00).

* * *

For affidavit and acknowledgment of bondsmen for notary public, justice of the peace, or alderman, one person, the minimum fee shall be one dollar and twenty-five cents ($1.25); two persons, the minimum fee shall be one dollar and seventy-five cents ($1.75).

* * *

Tit. 72, § 3191. Tax on commissions.

In lieu of the fees now receivable by the secretary of the commonwealth, for the use of the commonwealth, there shall be demanded by and paid to the recorder of deeds within the city of Philadelphia and of the respective counties, upon the several commissions hereafter named, at or before the delivery thereof, to the several officers commissioned, viz.: ***; on the commission of a *** notary public, *** ten dollars.

OFFENSES

Tit. 18, § 4101. Forgery.

(a) Offense defined.—A person is guilty of forgery if, with intent to defraud or injure anyone, or with knowledge that he is facilitating a fraud or injury to be perpetrated by anyone, the actor:

(1) alters any writing of another without his authority;

(2) makes, completes, executes, authenticates, issues or transfers any writing so that it purports to be the act of another who did not authorize that act, or to have been executed at a time or place or in a numbered sequence other than was in fact the case, or to be a copy of an original when no such original existed; or

(3) utters any writing which he knows to be forged in a manner specified in paragraphs (1) or (2) of this subsection.

(b) Definition.—As used in this section the word "writing" includes printing or any other method of recording information, money, coins, tokens, stamps, seals, credit cards, badges, trademarks, and other symbols of value, right, privilege, or identification.

(c) Grading.—Forgery is a felony of the second degree if the writing is or purports to be part of an issue of money, securities, postage or revenue stamps, or other instruments issued by the government, or part of an issue of stock, bonds or other instruments representing interests in or claims against any property or enterprise. Forgery is a felony of the third degree if the writing is or purports to be a will, deed, contract, release, commercial instrument, or other document evidencing, creating, transferring, altering, terminating, or otherwise affecting legal relations. Otherwise forgery is a misdemeanor of the first degree.

Tit. 18, § 4103. Fraudulent destruction, removal or concealment of recordable instruments.

A person commits a felony of the third degree if, with intent to deceive or injure anyone, he destroys, removes or conceals any will, deed mortgage, security instrument or other writing for which the law provides public recording.

SAFE DEPOSIT BOXES

Tit. 71, § 733-724. Property in safe deposit vault or held for safe-keeping.

The secretary* may, any time after taking possession of an institution as receiver, give written notice to anyone claiming or appearing on the books of such institution to be the owner, or to be entitled to the possession, of any personal property left with such institution as bailee for safe-keeping or depository for hire, and to anyone appearing on the books of the institution to be the lessee of any safe, vault, or safe deposit box, notifying such bailor or lessee respectively, to remove all such personal property within the period fixed by the notice, provided that such period shall in no case be less than sixty days after the date of the notice.

At the expiration of such period if the lessee of a safe, vault, or safe deposit box has not removed the contents thereof, the secretary may cause such safe, vault, or safe deposit box to be opened either in his presence or in the presence of the deputy receiver of the institution, and in the presence of a notary public not an officer or employee of the institution or of the department. The contents, if any, of such safe, vault, or safe deposit box shall then be sealed and marked by such notary with the name and address of the lessee in whose name such safe, vault, or safe deposit box appeared on the books of the institution and with a list and description of the property therein. The secretary shall take such action as he shall deem desirable to safeguard such property until it is delivered to the owner or it is otherwise disposed of in accordance with law.

The secretary shall follow the same procedure and have the same powers with regard to the property left with the institution as bailee for safe-keeping or depository for hire and not called for within the period specified by the notice.

The contract of bailment or lease, if any, shall be considered at an end upon the date designated by the secretary for the removal of the property therein. The amount of unearned rent or charges, if any, paid by the bailor or lessee, shall become a debt of the institution.

* "Secretary" is defined by Pa. Stat. Ann. tit. 71, § 733-2 as The Secretary of Banking of this Commonwealth or his duly authorized deputy or representative.

ACKNOWLEDGMENTS

Tit. 21, § 81. Form of certificate of acknowledgment.

The form of certificate of acknowledgment of individuals (single or married) of any deed may be in the following words:—

Commonwealth of Pennsylvania,

ss:

County of _____

On this _____ day of _____ A.D. 19___, before me, a _____ in and for _____, came the above named _____ and acknowledged the foregoing deed to be _____ act and deed, and desired the same to be recorded as such.

Witness my hand and _____ seal, the day and year aforesaid.

(Seal)

_____
_____
(Official character.)

My commission expires _____.

Tit. 21, § 82. Acknowledgments by married women.

Acknowledgments of any married woman of any deeds, mortgages or other instruments of writing, required by law to be acknowledged, shall be taken by any judge, justice of the peace, notary public, or other person authorized by law to take acknowledgments of deeds, et cetera, in same manner and form as though said married woman were feme-sole; said acknowledgment to have the same force and effect as if taken separate and apart from the husband of said married woman.

Tit. 21, § 185. Acknowledgments in territories of United States.

The provisions of the third section of the act of assembly of this commonwealth, approved December 14, 1854, authorizing acknowledgments, in certain cases, to be taken before any officer or magistrate of the state wherein such deeds, powers of attorney, or other instruments of writing, therein mentioned, are executed, be and are hereby extended so as to authorize such acknowledgments to be taken before any officer or magistrate of any territory of the United States, created and organized by act of Congress, authorized by the laws of such territory to take acknowledgments of such deeds, powers of attorney, or other instruments of writing; and all deeds, powers of attorney or other instruments of writing, which have been executed prior to the passage of this act, in any territory, created by act of Congress, and acknowledged before any officer or magistrate of such territory, authorized by the laws of such territory to take acknowledgments of deeds, powers of attorney, or other instruments of writing, shall be as valid, to all intents and purposes, as if such territory had been one of the states of this Union.

Tit. 21, § 186. May be taken in the District of Columbia.

The provisions of the third section of the act of assembly entitled "An act relating to the authentication of letters of attorney, protests of notaries public and assignments made out of the state, and to the acknowledgment of deeds," approved December 14, 1854, for taking and certifying acknowledgments of deeds and other instruments of writing, executed in any of the United States, are hereby extended to the District of Columbia, with like effect as if the said district had been therein specially mentioned and included; and all such acknowledgments heretofore taken and certified in the said district, in the manner provided in said section, are hereby validated and confirmed, and the deeds and other instruments so acknowledged, and the records thereof when recorded, shall be deemed as valid and effectual as if said district had been mentioned and included in the provisions of said section.

Tit. 21, § 187. Acknowledgments in Cuba, and the island possessions, valid.

All deeds, mortgages or other instruments of writing, heretofore made or which may hereafter be made by any person or corporation, concerning lands, tenements, hereditaments or property, or any estate or interest therein, lying or being within this commonwealth, heretofore acknowledged or proved, or which may hereafter be acknowledged or proved, in the manner directed and provided by the laws of this commonwealth, before any person holding the rank of major or any higher rank in the military service of the United States in Cuba, or in Puerto Rico, the Phillippine Islands, or other possessions of the United States, whether in the regular or volunteer service, or before any civil officer in the service of the United States in any of the said places hereinbefore referred to, shall be valid to all intents and purposes, and be in like manner entitled to be recorded as if the same had been duly acknowledged and proven before a notary public or other officer within this commonwealth having authority to take such proofs or acknowledgments according to the existing laws of this commonwealth.

Tit. 21, § 190. Proof of official character of person taking acknowledgment.

And provided further, That the proof of the official character of the person taking such acknowledgment shall be his official seal, if he have one; and if not, then a certificate under the seal of any officer, of the United States who has an official seal, in any of said places.

Tit. 21, § 222. Ambassadors, public ministers, etc.

All ambassadors, ministers plenipotentiary, charges d'affaires, or other persons exercising public ministerial functions, duly appointed by the United States of America, shall have full power and authority to take all acknowledgments and proofs of any deeds, conveyances, settlements, mortgages, agreements, powers of attorney, or other instruments under seal relating to real or personal estate, made or executed in any foreign country or state, by any person or persons, or by husband and wife, in the manner and according to the forms required by the laws of this commonwealth, and to administer all oaths or affirmations necessary or required for the purposes aforesaid; and that all acknowledgments and proofs heretofore made by any or either of the persons aforesaid, before any of the officers aforesaid, in the manner and according to the forms aforesaid, are hereby ratified and confirmed, and the same, and the records of the instruments aforesaid, if the said instruments have been heretofore recorded, are declared to be as valid and effectual as if the said acknowledgments, proofs and records had been respectively made, taken and recorded under the provisions hereof.

Tit. 21, § 223. Deputy consuls and commercial agents, etc., of United States.

All conveyances, mortgages or other instruments of writing, heretofore made, or which may hereafter be made by any person or corporation, concerning any lands, tenements, hereditaments or property, or any estate or interest therein, lying or being within this commonwealth, heretofore acknowledged or proved, or hereafter acknowledged or proved, in the manner directed and provided by the laws of this commonwealth, before any deputy consul, commercial agents, vice and deputy commercial agents, or consular agents of the United States, duly appointed for and exercising the functions of his office, in the place where such acknowledgment has been or may be taken, and certified under the public official seal of such deputy consul, commercial agents, vice and deputy commercial agents or consular agents, shall be valid to all intents and purposes, and be in like manner entitled to be recorded, as if the same had been duly acknowledged and proven before a notary public, or other officer, within this commonwealth, having authority to take such proofs or acknowledgments according to the existing laws of this commonwealth, and where any such instruments so acknowledged before such consular officers have

heretofore been admitted to record in the proper office in this commonwealth, the record thereof shall be as good and valid as if they had been recorded subsequent to the passage of this act: Provided, That this act shall not apply to any case in which an action is now pending or has been heretofore judicially decided.

Tit. 21, § 224. Acknowledgments taken before commissioners in chancery in foreign countries.

In all cases of the sale, conveyance, mortgage or other instrument of writing, heretofore made or which may be hereafter made by any person, or husband and wife, concerning any lands, tenements or hereditaments, or any estate or interest therein, lying or being within this commonwealth, and heretofore acknowledged or proved, or hereafter acknowledged or proved, before any commissioner in chancery in any foreign country, according to the forms now or hereafter required by the laws of this state relative to such acknowledgment or probate, duly certified under the seal of office of such commissioner in chancery, shall be valid to all intents and purposes, and be in like manner entitled to be recorded, as if the same had been duly acknowledged or proven according to the existing laws of this commonwealth: Provided, That no case heretofore decided judicially shall be affected by this act.

Tit. 21, § 225. Acknowledgments by married women out of the United States.

In all cases of the sale, conveyance, mortgage or transfer of the property of any married woman, or of any powers of attorney to make and execute such sale, conveyance, mortgage or transfer, made and executed out of the United States, the written consent of such married woman, as required by the act relating to the rights of married women, may be acknowledged before any minister, ambassador, charge d'affaires, consul or vice-consul of the United States; and such acknowledgment so made shall be equally valid as if made before a judge of a court of common pleas of this commonwealth.

Tit. 21, § 289. Records of legal instruments having defective acknowledgments.

The records of all legal instruments which, by law, are directed to be recorded or are entitled to be recorded, and which have been duly executed by the proper party or parties, and which have been acknowledged to and certified by a qualified officer without this State but in the United States, a territory or insular possession of the United States or the District of Columbia, notwithstanding the absence of any authentication, affirming the official character of such officer in conformity with the laws of this Commonwealth in force at the time such instrument was acknowledged, are hereby severally made as valid and effective in law as if each such instrument had been fully acknowledged, certified and authenticated. The record of each such instrument, or the original of such instrument itself, shall be admitted as evidence in all courts of this Commonwealth, and shall be as valid and conclusive evidence as if such instrument had been in all respects acknowledged and the acknowledgment certified and authenticated in accordance with the then existing law.

Uniform Acknowledgment Act

Tit. 21, § 291.1. Acknowledgment of instruments.

Any instrument may be acknowledged in the manner and form now provided by the laws of this State or as provided by this act.

Tit. 21, § 291.2. Acknowledgment within the state.

The acknowledgment of any instrument may be made in this State before—

(1) A judge of a court of record;

(2) A clerk, prothonotary or deputy prothonotary or deputy clerk of a court having a seal;

(3) A recorder of deeds or deputy recorder of deeds;

(4) A notary public;

(5) A district justice, magistrate or alderman.

Tit. 21, § 291.3. Acknowledgment within the United States.

The acknowledgments of any instrument may be made without the State, but within the United States, or a territory or insular possession of the United States, or the District of Columbia, and within the jurisdiction of the officer before—

(1) A clerk or deputy clerk of any federal court;

(2) A clerk, prothonotary or deputy prothonotary or deputy clerk of any court of record of any state or other jurisdiction;

(3) A notary public;

(4) A recorder of deeds.

Tit. 21, § 291.4. Acknowledgment without the United States.

The acknowledgment of any instrument may be made without the United States before—

(1) An ambassador, minister, charge d'affaires, counselor to or secretary of a legation, consul general, consul, vice-consul, commercial attache or consular agent of the United States accredited to the country where the acknowledgment is made;

(2) A notary public of the country where the acknowledgment is made;

(3) A judge or clerk of a court of the country where the acknowledgment is made.

Tit. 21, § 291.5. Requisites of acknowledgment.

The officer taking the acknowledgment shall know or have satisfactory evidence that the person making the acknowledgment is the person described in and who executed the instrument.

Tit. 21, § 291.6. Acknowledgment by a married woman.

An acknowledgment of a married woman may be made in the same form as though she were unmarried.

Tit. 21, § 291.7. Forms of certificates.

An officer taking the acknowledgment shall endorse thereon or attach thereto a certificate substantially in one of the following forms:

(1) By individuals—

State of ....

County of ....

On this, the .... day of ...., 19....., before me ...., the undersigned officer, personally appeared ...., known to me (or satisfactorily proven) to be the person whose name .... subscribed to the within instrument, and acknowledged that .... he .... executed the same for the purposes therein contained.

In witness whereof, I hereunto set my hand and official seal.

....

....

Title of Officer.

(2) By a corporation—

State of ....

County of ....

On this, the .... day of ...., 19....., before me ...., the undersigned officer, personally appeared ...., who acknowledged himself to be the .... of ...., a corporation, and that he as such ...., being authorized to do so, executed the foregoing instrument for the purposes therein contained, by signing the name of the corporation by himself as ....

In witness whereof, I hereunto set my hand and official seal.

....

....
Title of Officer.

Any deed, conveyance, mortgage or other instrument in writing, made and executed by a corporation, may be acknowledged by any officer of said corporation whose signature appears on such deed, conveyance, mortgage or other instrument in writing, in execution or in attestation of the execution thereof.

(3) By an attorney in fact—
State of ....
County of ....
On this, the .... day of ...., 19....., before me ...., the undersigned officer, personally appeared ...., known to me (or satisfactorily proven) to be the person whose name is subscribed as attorney in fact for ...., and acknowledged that he executed the same as the act of his principal for the purposes therein contained.

In witness whereof, I hereunto set my hand and official seal.

....

....
Title of Officer.

(4) By any public officer or deputy thereof or by any trustee, administrator, guardian or executor—
State of ....
County of ....
On this, the .... day of ...., 19....., before me ...., the undersigned officer, personally appeared .... of the State (County or City as the case may be) of .... known to me (or satisfactorily proven) to be the person described in the foregoing instrument, and acknowledged that he executed the same in the capacity therein stated and for the purposes therein contained.

In witness whereof, I hereunto set my hand and official seal.

....

....
Title of Officer.

Tit. 21, § 291.8. Execution of certificate.

The certificate of the acknowledging officer shall be completed by his signature, his official seal, if he has one, the title of his office, and, if he is a notary public, the date his commission expires.

Tit. 21, § 291.9. Authentication of acknowledgments.

(1) If the acknowledgment is taken within the State, or if taken without this State by an officer of this State, or is made without the United States by an officer of the United States, no authentication shall be necessary.

(2) If the acknowledgment is taken without this State, but in the United States, a territory or insular possession of the United States or the District of Columbia, no authentication shall be necessary if the official before whom the acknowledgment is taken affixes his official seal to the instrument so acknowledged otherwise the certificate shall be authenticated by a certificate as to the official character of such officer, executed, (1) if the acknowledgment is taken by a clerk or deputy clerk of a court, by the presiding judge of the court, or, (2) if the acknowledgment is taken by some other authorized officer, by the official having custody of the official record of the election, appointment or commission of the officer taking such acknowledgment.

(3) If the acknowledgment is made without the United States and by a notary public or a judge or clerk of a court of record of the country where the acknowledgment is made, the certificate shall be authenticated by a certificate under the great seal of state of the country; affixed by the custodian of such seal, or by a certificate of a diplomatic, consular or commercial officer of the United States accredited to that country, certifying as to the official character of such officer.

Tit. 21, § 291.10. Acknowledgments under laws of other states.

Acknowledgments under laws of other states. Notwithstanding any provision of this act contained, the acknowledgment of any instrument without this State in compliance with the manner and form prescribed by the laws of the place of its execution, if in a state, a territory or insular possession of the United States, or in the District of Columbia, verified by the official seal of the officer before whom it is acknowledged or authenticated, in the manner provided by section 9, subsection (2) hereof, shall have the same effect as an acknowledgment in the manner and form prescribed by the laws of the State for instruments executed within the State.

Tit. 21, § 291.10a. Acknowledgment by persons serving in or with the armed forces of the United States or their dependents within or without the United States.

In addition to the acknowledgment of instruments in the manner and form and as otherwise now or hereafter authorized by the laws of this State or by this act, persons serving in or with the armed forces of the United States or their dependents, wherever located, may acknowledge the same before any commissioned officer in active service of the armed forces of the United States with the rank of Second Lieutenant or higher in the Army, Air Force, or Marine Corps, or Ensign or higher in the Navy or Coast Guard. The instrument shall not be rendered invalid by the failure to state therein the place of execution or acknowledgment. No authentication of the officer's certificate of acknowledgment shall be required but the officer taking the acknowledgment shall endorse thereon or attach thereto a certificate substantially in the following form:

"On this the .... day of .... 19....., before me ...., the undersigned officer, personally appeared ...., (Serial No.) .... (if any) known to me (or satisfactorily proven) to be (serving in or with the armed forces of the United States) (a dependent of .... (Serial No.) .... (if any) a person serving in or with the armed forces of the United States) and to be the person whose name is subscribed to the within instrument and acknowledged that he executed the same for the purposes therein contained. And the undersigned does further certify that he is at the date of this certificate a commissioned officer of the rank stated below and is in the active service of the armed forces of the United States.

_____
Signature of the Officer

_____
Rank and Serial No. of Officer and Command to which attached."

Tit. 21, § 291.11. Acknowledgments not affected by this act.

No acknowledgment heretofore taken shall be affected by anything contained herein.

Tit. 21, § 291.12. Uniformity of interpretation.

This act shall be so interpreted as to make uniform the laws of those States which enact it.

Tit. 21, § 291.13. Name of act.

This act may be cited as the Uniform Acknowledgment Act.

DEPOSITIONS

[PA. R. CIV. P.]

RULE 4015. Persons before whom depositions may be taken.

(a) Within the United States or within a territory or insular possession subject to the dominion of the United States, depositions shall be taken before an officer authorized to administer oaths by the laws of the United States or of this Commonwealth or of the place where the examination is held, or before a person appointed by the court in which the action is pending. A person so appointed shall have power to administer oaths and take testimony.

(b) In a foreign country, depositions may be taken

(1) on notice before a person authorized to administer oaths in the place in which the examination is held, either by the law thereof or by the law of the United States, or

(2) before a person commissioned by the court in which the action is pending, and a person so commissioned shall have the power by virtue of his commission to administer any necessary oath and take testimony, or

(3) pursuant to a letter rogatory.

A commission or a letter rogatory shall be issued on application and notice and on terms that are just and appropriate. It is not requisite to the issuance of a commission or a letter rogatory that the taking of the deposition in any other manner is impracticable or inconvenient; and both a commission and a letter rogatory may be issued in proper cases. A notice or commission may designate the person before whom the deposition is to be taken either by name or descriptive title. A letter rogatory may be addressed "To the Appropriate Authority in (here name the country)." Evidence obtained in response to a letter rogatory need not be excluded merely for the reason that it is not a verbatim transcript or that the testimony was not taken under oath or for any similar departure from the requirements for depositions taken within the United States under these rules.

(c) No deposition shall be taken before a person who is a relative, employee or attorney of any of the parties, or who is a relative or employee of such attorney, or who is financially interested in the action.

COMMISSIONERS

[PA. STAT. ANN.]

Tit. 21, § 971. Appointment of commissioners of deeds in other states.

The governor of this commonwealth be and he is

hereby authorized to name, appoint and commission one or more commissioners in each, or such of the other states of the United States, or in the District of Columbia, as he may deem expedient; which commissioners shall continue in office during the pleasure of the governor; and shall have authority to take the acknowledgments and proof of the execution of any deed, mortgage or other conveyance of any lands, tenements or hereditaments lying or being in this state; any contract, letter of attorney or any other writing under seal, to be used or recorded in this state, and such acknowledgment or proof taken or made in the manner directed by the laws of this state, and certified by any one of the said commissioners before whom the same shall be taken or made under his seal, which certificate shall be endorsed on or annexed to said deed or instrument aforesaid, shall have the same force and effect, and be as good and available in law for all purposes as if the same had been made or taken before a judge of the supreme court of the United States.

Tit. 21, § 972. Power to administer oaths.

Every commissioner appointed by virtue of this act shall have full power and authority to administer an oath or affirmation to any person who shall be willing and desirous to make such oath or affirmation before him, and such affidavit or affirmation made before such commissioner shall and is hereby declared to be as good and effectual to all intents and purposes as if taken by any magistrate resident in this commonwealth, and competent to take the same.

Tit. 21, § 973. Oath of office.

Every commissioner appointed as aforesaid, before he shall proceed to perform any duty under and by virtue of this law, shall take and subscribe an oath or affirmation before a justice of the peace, in the city or county in which such commissioner shall reside, well and faithfully to execute and perform all the duties of such commissioner under and by virtue of the laws of Pennsylvania, which oath or affirmation shall be filed in the office of the secretary of this commonwealth.

Tit. 21, § 975. Commissions to continue in force for five years.

All commissions hereafter issued for the appointment of commissioners to take acknowledgment and proof of deeds and instruments under seal, depositions and other papers, under and by virtue of the act *** and its supplements, shall continue in force for five years from their date, and no longer,

and may be revoked at any time by the governor; and shall each be subject to a tax of five dollars, which shall be paid to the secretary of the commonwealth at the time of issuing the commission, and accounted for as provided by law in the case of other fees.

Tit. 21, § 976. Appointment in the territories.

The provisions of the several sections of [this] act *** be and they are hereby extended so as to authorize the governor of this commonwealth to appoint and commission in like manner and with like powers one or more commissioners in each of the territories of the United States.

Tit. 21, § 977. Fees of commissioners of deeds in other states.

The commissioners appointed or hereafter to be appointed by the governor of this commonwealth, under the authority of [this] act *** be hereby authorized to demand as their compensation for taking each acknowledgment the fee of one dollar, and no more.

Tit. 21, § 978. Commissioners in foreign countries.

The governor shall have power to appoint one or more commissioners in any foreign country, who shall continue in office during the pleasure of the governor, and shall have the authority to take the acknowledgment and proof of the execution of any deed or other conveyance or lease of any lands lying in this state, or of any contract, letters of attorney, or of any other writing, under seal or not, to be used and recorded in this state.

Tit. 21, § 979. Oath of office.

Every such commissioner, before performing any duty, or exercising any power in virtue of his appointment, shall take and subscribe an oath or affirmation before a judge or clerk of one of the courts of record of the state, kingdom, or country in which said commissioner shall reside, well and faithfully to execute and perform all the duties of such commissioner, under and by virtue of the laws of the state of Pennsylvania, which oath, and a description of his seal of office, together with his signature thereto, shall be filed in the office of the secretary of this state.

Tit. 21, § 980. Fees.

The fees for all such services shall be the same as

for similar services rendered by commissioners of this state in other states of the Union, the same being reckoned in the money of the United States.

LEGAL HOLIDAYS

Tit. 44, § 11. Holidays designated; bank holidays; presentation and paying of instruments.

The following days and half days, namely: the first day of January, commonly called New Year's Day, the third Monday of January, known as Dr. Martin Luther King, Jr. Day, the third Monday of February, known as Presidents' Day, Good Friday, the last Monday in May, known as Memorial Day, the fourteenth day of June, known as Flag Day, the fourth of July, called Independence Day, the first Monday of September, known as Labor Day, the second Monday in October, known as Columbus Day, the first Tuesday after the first Monday of November, Election Day, the eleventh day of November, known as Veterans' Day, the fourth Thursday in November, known as Thanksgiving Day, the twenty-fifth day of December, known as Christmas Day; and every Saturday, after twelve o'clock noon until twelve o'clock midnight, each of which Saturdays is hereby designated a half holiday; and any day appointed or recommended by the Governor of this State or the President of the United States as a day of thanksgiving or fasting and prayer, or other religious observance; and in the event of a financial crisis in the State or Nation, any day or days appointed by the Governor of this State or the President of the United States as a bank holiday; and in the event of public calamity in any part of the State through fire, flood, famine, violence, riot, insurrection, or enemy action, any day or days appointed by the Governor of this State as a bank holiday for banking institutions affected by such public calamity shall, for all purposes whatever as regards the presenting for payment or acceptance, and as regards the protesting and giving notice of the dishonor of bills of exchange, checks, drafts, and promissory notes, made after the passage of this act, be treated and considered as the first day of the week, commonly called Sunday, and as public holidays and half holidays; and all such bills, checks, drafts, and notes otherwise presentable for acceptance or payment, on any of the said days, shall be deemed to be payable and be presentable for acceptance or payment on the secular or business day next succeeding such holiday or half holiday; except checks, drafts, bills of exchange, and promissory notes, payable at sight or on demand, which would otherwise be payable on any half holiday Saturday, shall be deemed to be payable at or before twelve o'clock noon of such half holiday: Provided, however, That for the purpose of protesting or otherwise holding liable any party to any bill of exchange, check, draft, or promissory note, and which shall not have been paid before twelve o'clock noon of any Saturday designated a half holiday as aforesaid, a demand for acceptance or payment thereof shall not be made, and notice of protest or dishonor thereof shall not be given, until the next succeeding secular or business day: And provided further, That when any person, firm, corporation or company shall, on any Saturday designated a half holiday, receive for collection any check, bill of exchange, draft, or promissory note, such person, firm, corporation, or company shall not be deemed guilty of any neglect or omission of duty, nor incur any liability, in not presenting for payment or acceptance or collection such check, bill of exchange, draft or promissory note, on that day: And provided further, That, in construing this section, every Saturday designated a half holiday shall, until twelve o'clock noon, be deemed a secular or business day; and the days and half days aforesaid, so designated as holidays and half holidays, shall be considered as public holidays and half holidays for all purposes whatsoever as regards the transaction of business, except that any day or days appointed as a bank holiday shall be regarded as secular or business days for all other purposes than those mentioned in this act: And provided further, That nothing herein contained shall be construed to prevent or invalidate the entry, issuance, service, or execution of any writ, summons, confession or judgment, or other legal process whatever, on any of the holidays or half holidays herein designated as holidays; nor to prevent any banking institution from keeping its doors open or transacting its business, on any Saturday afternoon, if by a vote of its directors it shall elect to do so, unless such Saturday is appointed as a bank holiday under the provisions of this act: And provided further, That any banking institution may, by a vote of its directors, or in the case of a private bank by action of the private banker or bankers, notice of which shall have been posted in its banking house for not less than fifteen days before the taking effect thereof, observe any Saturday throughout the year as a full holiday with like effect hereunder as though such day had been designated as a full holiday by the provisions of this act, and may in the same manner, observe as a full holiday any Monday next following the first day of January, the fourth day of July or the twenty-fifth day of December whenever any of such holidays shall occur on a Saturday with like effect hereunder as though such day had been designated as a full holiday by the provisions of this act.

Tit. 44, § 15. Execution of legal process; banks may transact business; bank holidays; optional observance of Saturdays and certain Mondays by banks.

Nothing herein contained shall be construed to prevent or invalidate the entry, issuance, service, or execution of any writ, summons, confession of judgement, or other legal process whatever, on any of the holidays or half holidays herein designated as holidays; nor to prevent any banking institution from keeping its doors open or transacting its business, on any Saturday afternoon, if by a vote of its directors it shall elect to do so, unless such Saturday is appointed as a bank holiday under the provisions of this act: And provided further, That any banking institution may, by a vote of its directors, or in the case of a private bank by action of the private banker or bankers, notice of which shall have been posted in its banking house for not less than fifteen days before the taking effect thereof, observe any Saturday throughout the year as a full holiday with like effect hereunder as though such day had been designated as a full holiday by the provisions of this act, and may in the same manner, observe as a full holiday any Monday next following the first day of January, [the thirtieth day of May, the fourth day of July] or the twenty-fifth day of December whenever any of such holidays shall occur on a Saturday with like effect hereunder as though such day had been designated as a full holiday by the provisions of this act.

Tit. 44, § 16. When Monday a holiday; validity of acts on Saturday afternoon and certain holidays; option of banks as to keeping open.

(a) Whenever the first day of January, the twelfth day of February, the fourteenth day of June, the fourth day of July, the eleventh day of November or the twenty-fifth day of December, shall any of them occur on Sunday, the following day (Monday) shall be deemed and declared a public holiday. All bills of exchange, checks, drafts, or promissory notes, falling due on any of the Mondays observed as holidays, shall be due and payable on the next succeeding secular or business day; and all Mondays observed as holidays shall, for all purposes whatever as regards the presenting for payment or acceptance, and as regards the protesting and giving notice of the dishonor of bills of exchange, checks, drafts, and promissory notes, made after the passage of this act, be treated and considered as if the first day of the week, commonly called Sunday.

(b) Nothing in any law of this Commonwealth shall in any manner whatsoever affect the validity of, or render void or voidable, the payment, certification, or acceptance of a check or other negotiable instrument or any other transaction by a banking institution in this State because done or performed or transacted on any Saturday between twelve o'clock noon and midnight, provided such payment, certification, acceptance or other transaction would be valid if done or performed on or before twelve o'clock on Saturday.

(c) Nothing in any law of this Commonwealth shall in any manner whatsoever affect the validity of, or render void or voidable the payment, certification, or acceptance of, any bill of exchange, check, draft, promissory note, or other negotiable instrument, or any other transaction by a banking institution in this State, because done or performed or transacted on any of the following legal holidays: the twelfth day of February, the third Monday in February, Good Friday, the fourteenth day of June, the second Monday in October, or the first Tuesday after the first Monday of November, the eleventh day of November or whenever any of said days shall occur on Sunday, done or performed or transacted on the following day (Monday): Provided, Such payment, certification, acceptance, or other transaction would be valid if done or performed on a secular or business day: Provided further, however, That for the purpose of protesting or otherwise holding liable any party to any bill of exchange, check, draft, promissory note, or other negotiable instrument which shall not have been paid on any of said holidays, a demand for acceptance or payment thereof shall not be made, and notice of protest or dishonor thereof shall not be given, until the next succeeding secular or business day. Nothing herein shall be construed to require any banking institution to keep open for the transaction of business on any of said holidays, or to require any banking institution which elects to be open for business on all or any part of any of said holidays, to do or perform any act or transaction on such holiday; but all acts and transactions done or performed on any such holiday shall be at the option of such banking institution.

Tit. 44, § 21. Election days made legal half-holidays.

The third Tuesday of February of each year, and the first Tuesday after the first Monday of November of each year, be and the same are hereby designated as legal half-holidays from twelve o'clock noon until midnight of such days, and shall for all purposes whatsoever as regards the presenting for payment or acceptance, and as regards the protesting and giving notice of the dishonor of bills of exchange, checks, drafts and promissory notes, made after the passage of this act, be treated and considered as the first day of the week, commonly called Sunday, and as public holidays, and half-holidays, and all such bills, checks, drafts and notes otherwise presentable for acceptance or payment on any of the said days, shall be deemed to be payable and be presentable for acceptance or payment at or before twelve o'clock noon on such half-holidays.

PUERTO RICO

NOTARIES PUBLIC

Subchapter I. The Notary and His Functions

[P.R. LAWS ANN.]

Tit. 4, § 2001. Short title.

This act shall be known as the "Puerto Rico Notarial Act".

Tit. 4, § 2002. Notary—concept.

The notary is a legal professional who practices a public function, authorized to attest and authenticate pursuant to the laws the juridical businesses and other acts and extrajudicial events executed before him, without prejudice of what is provided in the special laws. His function is to receive and interpret the will of the parties giving it a legal format, draft the notarial documents and deeds for such purpose and confer authority to them. The notary's public faith is complete with regard to the facts carried out and corroborated by him in the exercise of his functions, and also with regard to the manner, place, date and time of the execution.

Tit. 4, § 2003. —Autonomy.

The notary shall be authorized to practice his office throughout the Commonwealth of Puerto Rico. In that function he shall enjoy full autonomy and independence. He shall exercise it with impartiality and will be under the administrative direction of the Supreme Court of Puerto Rico, through the Office of Notarial Inspection created by this chapter.

Tit. 4, § 2004. —Public office; incompatibility.

In addition to the legal impediments that might exist, the office of notary shall be incompatible with any public office when there is a prohibition of the notarial practice by the public body for which he carries out his functions. The public bodies shall notify the Office of Notarial Inspection of the prohibitions they establish.

Tit. 4, § 2005. —Prohibitions; ineffectiveness.

(a) No notary may authorize documents he is a party to, or which include provisions in his favor. Neither may he authorize them if any one of the executing parties is related to him within the fourth degree of consanguinity or the second degree of affinity, except when he appears in the document as a representative.

(b) The provisions in favor of relatives of the notary who authorized the public document in which they were made within the fourth degree of consanguinity or the second degree of affinity shall have no effect.

Tit. 4, § 2006. —Deeds; protocols; deposits.

The notary shall write original notarial deeds, issue copies and draw up protocols. He shall be the depositary of the documents, securities and sums that the parties wish to deposit with the notary to secure their contracts. Admission of these deposits is voluntary and the notary may impose conditions on the depositor which will be consigned in the receipt or collateral agreement issued by the notary.

Subchapter II. Requirements for the Notarial Practice.

Tit. 4, § 2011. Notarial practice—requirements.

Only those presently authorized to practice the notarial profession and those attorneys who in the future are admitted to practice the profession, who are members of the Puerto Rico Bar Association and are thereafter authorized to practice as notaries by the Supreme Court of Puerto Rico, shall practice the notarial profession in the Commonwealth of Puerto Rico.

Every notary shall pledge an oath of fidelity to the Constitution of the United States of America and the Constitution and Laws of the Commonwealth of Puerto Rico before beginning the practice of his office.

No person authorized to practice the profession of notary in Puerto Rico may practice it without having posted and keeping in effect a bond for a sum of not less than fifteen thousand (15,000) dollars to answer for the proper performance of the functions of his office and damages caused by his acts or omissions in the exercise of his duties. This bond's limits do not impair the rights of the Commonwealth of Puerto Rico nor of natural or juridical persons under section 5141 of Title 31 or under any other legal or jurisprudential provision. The notary's surety shall be a mortgage bond, or posted by an insurance company authorized to do business in Puerto Rico, or by the Puerto Rico Bar Association, which is hereby authorized to charge the amount it deems reasonable for posting that security as provided in the act.

The surety bond must be renewed annually and approved by the Supreme Court of Puerto Rico which will review its sufficiency with regard to the mortgages, which shall be registered in the corresponding property registry office before its final approval.

The bond shall have preferent liability for the sums that the notary fails to deposit with the Commonwealth of Puerto Rico on account of Internal Revenue, notarial and other legally required stamps, for biding of protocols and any other necessary expense incurred as indicated by the Director of Notarial Inspection in order to carry out the inspection of notaries and their approval. Once the expenses are established, he may proceed against the bond directly to pay the obligations.

If the claimant is adjudicated all or part of the bond in a judicial claim against the notary, he shall not continue to practice until he posts a new bond.

All sums collected by the Bar Association for the posting of this security shall be covered [*sic*] into a fund designated as a "SPECIAL FUND" on account of notarial bond premiums, which shall be administered as it is established by section 2141 of this title.

Once the surety bond is approved and the notary takes the oath of office, he must register his signature, sign, seal and flourish at the Department of State pursuant to the provisions of section 2012 of this title as well as in a Register kept for that purpose in the office of the Clerk of the Supreme Court of Puerto Rico. That Register shall also include his place of residence and location of the notarial office. The notary is bound to notify the same officer of any change in residence or notarial office within five (5) days after it occurs.

Tit. 4, § 2012. —Certificate; display.

The Secretary of State shall issue a certificate to the notary attesting to his name and residence as well as membership number and the date on which the Supreme Court authorized him to practice as a notary, the date on which he registered his signature, sign, flourish and seal as a notary at the Department of State, and the facsimile of his registered signature, sign, seal or flourish, all attested to by the Secretary of State. It shall be the obligation of the notary to display the certificate on one of the walls of his office.

Tit. 4, § 2013. —Temporary substitutions.

The notary may appoint another notary to substitute for him when he is absent from his office for any nonpermanent cause, for a maximum period of three (3) months, which may be extended, if just cause is shown, for three (3) additional months after due request to the Director of Inspection of Notaries.

The notary as well as his substitute shall notify the Office of Notarial Inspection of the substitution in the same document and under their signatures.

The notary shall not authorize original documents in the name of the substituted notary. He shall be responsible for the custody and conservation of the protocols of the notary he is substituting for and, as such, may issue certified copies.

Subchapter III. Duties of the Notary

Tit. 4, § 2021. Duties of the notary—stamps; exemptions.

It shall be duty of every notary to attach and cancel on each original deed he executes and on the certified copies thereof that are issued the proper Internal Revenue Stamps and a stamp in the amount of one dollar ($1) that shall be adopted and issued by the Bar Association of Puerto Rico. The product of such sales shall be covered [*sic*] into the Association's funds.

The deed or certified copies of it shall be voidable or ineffective if the corresponding stamps are not attached to it. However, any of the parties to the document may deliver the amount of said fees to the corresponding official without impairing the provisions of the fifth paragraph of section 2011 of this title.

The Bar Association of Puerto Rico shall be bound to designate at least one third (1/3) of the total income derived from the notarial stamp to community services programs, such as free legal aid to indigents and continuing legal education programs for attorneys and the notaries themselves. No later than the month of February, the Association shall be bound to file an annual report before the Supreme Court specifying the income for the previous year from that concept, its use and the remainder.

Notaries from the Puerto Rico Legal Services Corporation, San Juan Legal Services, and any other nonprofit entity or organization certified by the Secretary of Justice whose purposes and functions are similar to those of these corporations shall not be bound to attach and cancel the stamps mentioned in this section when they execute documents for indigent persons following the eligibility criteria established by these bodies, but this circumstance shall be included in the document.

Tit. 4, § 2022. —Informative return on segregation, merging or transfer of real estate.

In the execution of deeds of segregation, merger or transfer of dominion the transferor or person who segregates or merges will be bound to complement and deposit at the office of the authorizing notary the Informative Return on the Segregation, Merging or Transfer of Real Estate.

That return shall include the following information:

(1) Number, date of the deed and legal business transacted.

(2) Name of those appearing, specifying the nature of their appearance and Social Security Number.

(3) Property or Cadastre Number.

The property cadastre number shall be taken from the latest available tax notice or receipt issued by the Secretary of the Treasury.

It is hereby provided that the District Office of the Bureau of Taxes on Property, Estate and Gifts of the Treasury Department of Puerto Rico shall offer the official records number or code within seven (7) days of its request. If this is not possible, it shall issue a negative certificate stating the reasons for not being able to offer the number requested. This certificate shall be sent to the Secretary of the Treasury together with the informative return.

(4) The real property registry's data including folio, volume, farm number and town.

(5) Price of transaction.

(6) Type of structure, if applicable.

(7) Type of property, location and address.

The return must be signed by the seller or by the person who segregates or merges, who shall certify the veracity of the information given with his signature and responsibility.

The notaries shall be bound to send to the Department of the Treasury during the first ten (10) days of each month the returns corresponding to the deeds executed before them during the previous month.

Tit. 4, § 2023. —Monthly indices.

The notaries shall send a monthly index of their notarial activities no later than the tenth calendar day of the month following the month reported to the Office of the Director of Notarial Inspection of Puerto Rico that will state, with respect to the original deeds and affidavits authorized by them during the preceding month, the numbers in numerical order, the name of those appearing, date, the subject of the instrument or testimony and the name of the witnesses, if any appeared.

In said report the notary shall certify to having sent the returns to the Treasury Department as required pursuant to section 2022 of this title.

If the notary has not had any notarial activity during a particular month, he shall send a negative report for said month to the Inspector of Notaries.

Subchapter IV. About Public Documents

Tit. 4, § 2031. Public documents—classes.

The original deed is the one that the notary shall write regarding the contract or act submitted for his authorization signed by the grantors, by the attesting witnesses or those having knowledge of the facts of his case, signed, marked, sealed and flourished by the notary himself.

The public documents include public deeds and notarial certificates whether they are originals or certified copies.

Tit. 4, § 2032. —Drawing; contents.

Notaries shall write the public documents according to the will of the grantors and adapt them to the juridical formalities necessary to their effectiveness.

Whenever the grantors hand over to the notary drafts or certificates concerning the act or contract they have submitted for his authorization, he must state it without impairing his review and editing, with their consent, to the effect that the meaning of the statements of will and agreements comprised therein are clearly and specifically stated.

Tit. 4, § 2033. —Formal requirements; cognizance; legal warnings.

In addition to the juridical business that motivates its execution, its background and the facts witnessed and consigned by the notary in the explanatory part and provisions, the public deed shall include the following:

(a) Its corresponding protocol number written in letters at the beginning thereof.

(b) The classification of the act or contract with its legally-recognized name unless it does not have a special one.

(c) The notary's name, his residence, the location of his office, as well as the day, month and year and place of execution which shall be that in which the last of the grantors signs the document if there are no attesting witnesses.

(d) The name and surname or surnames, as the case may be, age or legal age, civil status, profession, and residence of the grantors, their Social Security Number, if they have one, name and circumstances of the witnesses, if any, according to their statements. In the event that any of the grantors is married and the appearance of the spouse is not necessary, the spouse's name and surname shall be stated, even though the spouse does not appear at the execution.

(e) The attestation to by the notary as to his personal cognizance of the grantors or, in its absence, of having verified their identity by the means established by this chapter, that, in his judgment, they have the necessary legal capacity to execute the act or contract concerned, and of having read the deed to them and the witnesses, in their case, or having allowed them the option to read it before signing it, or of a waiver of their right to do so.

(f) Of having orally made the pertinent legal warnings and reservations to the grantors during the act of execution. This notwithstanding, there shall be consigned in the document those warnings that, in the notary's judgment, must be expressly detailed due to their importance.

Tit. 4, § 2034. —Signatures; initials; flourish and seal.

The grantors and witnesses shall sign the deed and shall also affix the initials of their name and surname or surnames to the margin of each one of the pages of the document which shall be flourished and sealed by the notary.

Tit. 4, § 2035. —Identification of parties.

In the absence of personal cognizance by the notary, the following shall be supplemental means of identification:

(a) An assertion of a person who knows the grantor and is responsible for the identification and is known by the notary, and the notary is responsible for the witness' identity.

(b) The identification of one of the contracting parties by the other, provided that the notary certifies his cognizance of the latter.

(c) Identification by identity document with a photograph and signature issued by competent public authorities of the Commonwealth of Puerto Rico, the United States or a state of the Union, whose purpose is to identify the persons, or by a passport duly issued by a foreign authority.

Witnesses as to identity shall be responsible for the identification of the grantors, as shall the grantor who attests to the identity of other grantors not known by the notary, and the notary shall be responsible for the cognizance of such witnesses.

Tit. 4, § 2036. —Representation.

The notary shall record the intervention of the grantors by stating whether they do so in their own name or in behalf of another, except when the representation arises from the law, in which case the grantor's investiture shall be accredited, unless it is of general knowledge, in which case the notary may take cognizance of it and record it.

The representative shall sign the document with his own signature without it being necessary to first place the name of the person he represents or use the firm name or name of the entity he represents.

Tit. 4, § 2037. —Evidence of representation.

Every grantor who appears in representation of another person shall always validate his designation before the notary with authenticating documents, except when there is the expressed agreement of the grantors. The full effectiveness of the documents shall be subordinated to the presentation of documentary evidence of the alleged representation.

There shall also be recorded the nature of the intervention of those grantors who appear only to the effect of complementing the capacity or give their authorization or consent to the contract.

Public officials legally authorized to represent the Commonwealth of Puerto Rico, municipalities, instrumentalities or corporations shall not have to validate their powers before the notary.

Tit. 4, § 2038. —Attesting witnesses.

The intervention of attesting witnesses shall not be necessary in the execution of deeds, except when required by the authorizing notary or any of the parties, or when one of the grantors does not know how to or cannot read or sign. This provision does not apply to wills which shall be governed by what is established by applicable legislation.

Attesting witnesses shall be present at the act of reading, consenting, signing and execution of the public document. Likewise, they may be identifying witnesses who, in turn, may be attestors if they meet the applicable legal requirements.

Tit. 4, § 2039. —Executing party who does not know how to or cannot read or sign.

When any of the grantors does not know how to, or cannot read, the document in question shall be read out loud twice, once by the notary and another by the witness designated by the grantor, all of which shall be attested to by the notary.

When any of the grantors is deaf or blind who does not know how to read and sign, he must designate a witness who upon his request shall read or sign the public document for him or both. The notary shall record these circumstances.

Tit. 4, § 2040. —Witnesses; qualifications.

The witnesses, including those as to identity, shall be of legal age, competent and know how to read and write and sign. Employees of the executing notary, his relatives or those of the interested parties within the fourth degree of consanguinity or the second of affinity shall not be attesting witnesses.

Tit. 4, § 2041. —Sufficient witnesses.

One person shall suffice as attesting witness designated by the grantors, if they or the notary so require it. However, any of the two may oppose that certain persons act as such.

Tit. 4, § 2042. —Unity of action.

When the witnesses appear at the execution of the document there shall be unity of action, to which the notary shall attest in the writ.

Tit. 4, § 2043. —Executing party who does not know how to or cannot sign.

Whenever any of the grantors does not know how to, or cannot sign, the notary shall require that they affix their two (2) thumb prints. If they do not have thumbs, any other fingers, next to the witness' signature who signs at his or their request, and on the margin of the rest of the document's folios, all which the notary shall attest to in the deed. If the grantor or grantors have no fingers, the notary shall state the circumstances and two (2) attesting witnesses shall sign at their request.

Tit. 4, § 2044. —Attestation by notary.

It shall not be necessary for the notary to state that he attests to the stipulation included in each clause of the deed, nor of the legal condition or circumstances of the persons or cases to which it refers, it being sufficient that it be consigned once at the end of the document, which will certify its entire contents, so that such statement is understood to apply to all the words, stipulations, statements and conditions, real or personal, contained in the instrument in accordance with the law.

Tit. 4, § 2045. —Use of arabic numbers or abbreviations; blanks; possible means of drawing.

Numbers shall not be used to express dates and amounts, unless they are also consigned in letters, except those included in direct quotations. Neither may abbreviations be used, nor blank spaces left in the text, and the originals may be handwritten as long as indelible ink, printing or a typewriter with an indelible ribbon are used, or through other mechanical or electronic mechanisms that produce indelible and permanent documents.

Tit. 4, § 2046. —Execution.

Those persons who sign a public document for any reason shall do so by signing at the end and affixing the initials of their name and surname or surnames in the margin of all the folios, in the manner they usually do so, and the notary shall do so after them, flourishing, signing and sealing it.

If there are no witnesses, it shall not be necessary for those appearing to sign the documents together in the notary's presence, since he may personally receive their signatures at any time within the same calendar day of the execution.

Tit. 4, § 2047. —Correction of defects.

The defects suffered by inter vivos notarial documents may be corrected without damage to third parties by the parties thereto or by their heirs or assigns, by means of a public deed which sets forth the defect, its cause and the correcting statement.

If the notary fails to record any data or circumstance provided by this chapter, or if it concerns an error in the statement as to the facts witnessed by the notary which is his duty to consign, they may be corrected by the executing notary at his own expense, on his own initiative or by petition of any of the parties, through a notarial certificate that shows the error or defect, its cause and the statement that corrects it.

If it is impossible to make the correction in any of the ways indicated above, it may be obtained by any legally-admitted means of proof, through the corresponding judicial procedure before the Superior Court.

In any case, the notary shall indicate the fact of the correction in the margin of the original document under his signature and seal, and shall indicate the deed or notarial certificate in which they were made.

Tit. 4, § 2048. —Certificates.

The notaries, at the request of a party or on their own initiative and under their oath, signature, sign, flourish and notarial seal, shall extend and execute certificates which consign facts and circumstances witnessed by them or of which they have personal knowledge and that due to their nature do not constitute a contract or juridical business.

Tit. 4, § 2049. —Contents and formalities of certificates.

The notarial certificates shall include the corresponding deed number, the date in which they are executed, the declaratory part and the notary's signature. The enjoiner may sign the certificate if he so wishes, or if required by the notary.

Tit. 4, § 2050. —Clerical errors; correction.

Any additions, annotations, interlineations, erasures and cross-outs in the public deeds shall be held as valueless unless they are certified after the last line, with the express approval and signature of those who must sign the document.

However, the mistaken words may be placed within parentheses followed by the words "I say" [I mean] to make it clear that they should not be read.

The blank spaces remaining at the end of a line or when a paragraph begins on the next line shall not be considered as such; but in this case the blank shall be filled with a line or dash.

Tit. 4, § 2051. —Acceptance deeds.

A party to a juristic act may appear in a public deed and make an offer to be accepted by another party in a different document that may be executed before another notary on another date and place.

In this case the main deed that sets forth the offer shall also include the personal circumstances of the party who will later appear in the deed of assent, as they are informed by the party thereto, as well as the complete text of the juristic act, without leaving any detail to be added by the deed of assent. It shall also fix the term within which the deed of assent will be executed, its requirements and the causes for the revocation or lapse of the offers, if any.

In the deed of assent, besides complying with the requirements for public documents imposed by this chapter, there shall be a precise and exact statement of the offer, or there shall be attached a certified copy of the deed of offer to which the deed of assent makes reference, and a statement by the person appearing to the effect that he knows, understands and accepts the offer made in said document.

In the event that the notary who executes or officially records the deed of assent is not the notary who executed the original deed, he will send a certified copy of the deed to the latter, under his notarial certification, personally, or by certified mail with acknowledgement of receipt, and he shall also notify the offerer of the acceptance, by certified mail with acknowledgement of receipt. The notary shall record, through a marginal note or at the end of the original deed, the existence of the deed of assent, identifying it by number, date and name of the executing notary. Once this requirement is complied with, it shall be understood that the offerer has knowledge of the acceptance of his offer.

If the offer is accepted outside Puerto Rico, the notary who executes the deed that sets forth the offer shall comply with what is mandated herein upon receipt of the acceptance in an authentic and duly executed document, and shall also comply with the official recording requirement of section 2056 of this title.

The assent may also be executed by inclusion in the same deed that sets forth the offer, and any other information that facilitates the identification and location of the executing notary.

Tit. 4, § 2052. —Null and void.

Public instruments shall be null:

(1) That include any provision in favor of the notary who executes it.

(2) Where the witnesses are relatives of the interested parties in the degree prohibited by section 2040 of this title, the relatives or employees of the notary himself.

(3) In which the signatures of the parties and witnesses when they should, and the notary's signature, do not appear.

Tit. 4, § 2053. —Voidable.

Public instruments in which the notary fails to attest to his cognizance of the grantors or does not supplement this deficiency in the form established by section 2035 of this title shall be voidable.

Tit. 4, § 2054. —Wills and mortis causa conveyances.

That which is provided by sections 2031-2053 of this title with regard to the form of the instruments and their nullity shall not be applicable to wills and other mortis causa provisions governed by Title 31.

Tit. 4, § 2055. —Paper; margins; binding.

Public notarial documents shall be written on sheets of paper or folios thirteen (13) inches long by eight-and-a-half (8 1/2) inches wide and on the side by which they are to be bound, they shall have a blank margin of twenty (20) millimeters plus another on the left side of the deed of sixty (60) millimeters and on the right a strip or margin of three (3) millimeters. If the reverse side of the sheet is used, the margins on it shall completely coincide with those on the face of the document.

Tit. 4, § 2056. —Executed outside Puerto Rico; protocolization.

In order for it to be valid as a public instrument, every notarial document executed outside Puerto Rico must be previously protocolized, with the notary being bound to cancel the same fees as if it had been originally executed in Puerto Rico.

The protocolization of certifications of resolutions adopted by a Board of Directors of a banking entity, corporation or trust, issued outside Puerto Rico shall not be necessary; but they must be duly attested before a notary and the notary's signature authenticated.

Subchapter V. About Copies of
Public Instruments.

Tit. 4, § 2061. Copies—certified.

A certified copy is the literal, total or partial transcript of a document executed before a notary that is issued by him or the person officially in charge of his protocol, with a certificate regarding the truth of the contents, and the number of folios of the document as well as the signature, sign and flourish, and the seal and flourish of the attesting notary on every page.

Tit. 4, § 2062. —Partial.

At the request of a party the notary may issue partial copies of documents found in his protocol, stating under his responsibility that there is nothing which broadens, restricts, modifies or conditions the excerpt in what is issued.

Tit. 4, § 2063. —Notation of issuance.

When issuing a certified copy the notary shall consign in the main deed, by means of a signed annotation, the name of the person to whom it is issued, the date and the number corresponding to the copy according to those already issued. These data shall appear in the copies.

Tit. 4, § 2064. —Documents incorporated.

When another document has been incorporated to the main deed, every page of the copy issued must be sealed and flourished by the notary and the notary shall likewise certify that it is a true and exact copy of the original joined to the main deed.

Tit. 4, § 2065. —Persons entitled to.

In addition to the grantors, their representatives and assigns, any person who is entitled to some right as a result of the deed, whether directly or already acquired through different deed and in the judgment of the notary or notarial registrar, establish a legitimate interest in the document, excepting wills prior to the death of the testator shall have a right to obtain copies at any time.

Tit. 4, § 2066. —Refusal to issue.

Once a notary has refused to issue a copy one may appear formally or informally before the Director of the Office of Notarial Inspection, who, having heard said notary and the complainant, shall dictate what is in order. If the decision directs that a copy be issued, the notary shall record it on the copy's issuance annotation in the main deed and in its certification annotation. Such a resolution shall be drafted in a brief and concise manner and the notary shall be notified.

The notary's denial, confirmed by the Director of the Office of Inspection of Notarial Offices, may be appealed before the competent part of the Superior Court. Said part may order the issuance of the copy or confirm the denial after examining the arguments of the appellant and the resolution of the Director of the Office of Inspection of Notarial Offices. Such resolution may be revised by the Supreme Court through certiorari.

Tit. 4, § 2067. —Means of production.

The notary is hereby empowered to issue certified photographic copies, or copies reproduced by any other electronic means, of original deeds which once they are certified by the notary shall be deemed valid for all legal purposes.

Tit. 4, § 2068. —Simple.

Notaries may issue simple copies of main deeds upon request of the same persons with a right to request certified copies, but without a guaranteed transcription of the document. These copies shall not be signed, sealed or flourished, nor shall a marginal note of its certified copy be placed on the original deed.

The notary shall allow the contents of documents of his protocol to be read by those who, in his judgment, show a legitimate interest as provided in section 2065 of this title.

Subchapter VI. Notarial Deeds Protocol

Tit. 4, § 2071. Protocol—concept and characteristics.

The protocol is the orderly collection of original deeds and acts executed during a calendar year by the notary, as well as the documents included therein.

The protocol shall be secret and shall only be examined according to the provisions of this chapter or by judicial order issued pursuant to the provisions of this chapter.

Tit. 4, § 2072. —State property; responsibility for custody.

The protocols belong to the State. Notaries shall conserve them in accordance with the provisions of this chapter and shall be responsible for their integrity. If they are damaged or lost due to neglect, the notaries shall replace them at their own expense, and the Supreme Court shall also be able to impose the sanctions established in section 2102 of this title, at its discretion. If there is reason to suspect the commission of a crime, the competent authority shall be informed, so that the corresponding action is taken.

Tit. 4, § 2073. —Foliated pages.

All of the protocol's pages, including its attachments, shall be permanently foliated on the upper right hand side with the corresponding numerical order, written in figures. Each folio shall bear its corresponding number according to the pages of the document.

Tit. 4, § 2074. —Opening and closing formalities.

The first face of the first document of each document of each protocol shall be labeled in the following manner:

"Protocol of public documents corresponding to the year (X)."

On the last day of each natural year, each protocol shall be closed in the same manner with the notary attesting the following annotation at the end of the last page of the last deed officially recorded:

"Hereby concludes the protocol for the year (X) which contains (so many) public instruments and (so many) folios authorized by me, the undersigned notary, to which I attest."

These notes, at the opening as well as the protocol's closing, shall be signed, sealed, flourished and dated by the attesting notary.

Tit. 4, § 2075. —Additional volumes.

If a protocol has more than one volume for any year, each additional volume shall be opened with the following note:

"Hereby commences Volume (X) of my protocol of public deeds corresponding to the year (X)."

By the same token each additional volume that is not the last shall be also closed with the following note:

"Hereby concludes Volume (X) of my protocol of public deeds that contains (so many) instruments and (so many) folios."

Tit. 4, § 2076. —Binding.

The protocols for the previous year with corresponding indexes of their contents shall be bound by the second month of each year. They shall be indexed by order of instrument and shall include the complete name of the parties appearing, the name of the person represented if that is the case, and the date and place of execution, the juridical business transacted and the number of the folios it includes.

Notwithstanding the above, the notaries may insert other indexes in the protocol as may be convenient to their practice and use as such.

Tit. 4, § 2077. —Removal from office prohibited; exceptions.

The protocol shall not be removed from the office where it is kept in custody except by judicial decree or by authorization of the Office of Notarial Inspection.

Tit. 4, § 2078. —Fire protection.

When the notary's office is located in a wooden or mixed construction building, it shall be provided with fireproof steel or iron boxes in which the protocols shall be kept.

Tit. 4, § 2079. —Loss or destruction; reconstruction.

In the case a protocol is rendered useless or is lost in whole or in part, the notary shall report the fact to the Chief Justice of the Supreme Court, who shall direct the reconstruction of the proper record by summoning the parties. The indexes and books shall be checked and all necessary records data shall be examined in order to restore insofar as practicable, what has been destroyed or rendered useless. The record shall be approved by the Supreme Court upon a recommendation of the Director of the Protocol Inspection Office.

Subchapter VII. Testimony or Statements of Authenticity

Tit. 4, § 2091. Testimony or statement of authenticity—concept; restrictions; extent of notarial responsibility.

By request of an interested party, the notary may give a notarial certificate, in a deed that is not the original deed, as to the legality of the signatures appearing in it, provided it does not deal with acts included in subsections (1) through (6) of section 3453 of Title 31, that it is a translation or a true and exact copy of any deed that is not in his protocol, or of the identity or any object or thing, in general.

Only notaries may give testimony as to facts, acts or contracts of a merely personal interest without prejudice of the provisions of any of the laws in effect. The statements of authenticity may or may not be part of the oath.

Notaries shall not authenticate affidavits in cases included in section 2005 of this title.

The notary does not assume any responsibility for the contents of the private documents whose signatures he authenticates.

Tit. 4, § 2092. —Forms; signature.

The forms to be used in the affidavits shall be brief and simple and shall include the authenticity of the act, always with the notaries' statement that they personally know the signers or the attesting witness, or certifying to having supplemented his personal knowledge in the manner indicated in section 2035 of this title.

In the event that the interested parties do not know how to, or cannot read or sign, the same norms of the public deed shall be applicable.

Tit. 4, § 2093. —Numbering.

The affidavits shall be numbered successively and continuously and shall be headed by their corresponding number which will correlate to that of the inscription in the registry established below.

Tit. 4, § 2094. —Registry.

Notaries shall keep a registry of affidavits in concise notes, dated, numbered, sealed and undersigned by them attesting as to the name of the grantors and a brief statement of the authenticated act.

The registry of affidavits shall be kept in duly bound books of not more than five hundred (500) sheets with successively numbered pages.

Tit. 4, § 2095. —Null and void.

Any testimony not included in the index that does not have the executing notary's signature or has not been recorded in the registry of affidavits shall be null.

Subchapter VIII. Regulation and Inspection of Notaries

Tit. 4, § 2101. Regulations.

The Supreme Court may approve regulations for the execution of this chapter, for the regulation of the notarial practice and the admission thereto, and to complement the provisions of this chapter.

Tit. 4, § 2102. Inspection and examination—officer in charge.

The Chief Justice of the Supreme Court of Puerto Rico shall be in charge of the inspection of notarial offices and the examination of protocols. He shall appoint a Director of the Office of Notarial Inspection and of experienced notaries as inspectors, all of whom shall be covered by the provisions of sections 521-525 of this title, known as the "Personnel Act of the Judiciary Branch" and the rules and regulations adopted by virtue thereof. One of the Protocol Inspectors shall reside in the district of San Juan, and another in the district of Ponce. The others shall reside in the location designated by the

Chief Justice. The Supreme Court, after giving the notary an opportunity to be heard in his defense, may discipline him through a reprimand, a fine not to exceed five hundred (500) dollars or a temporary or permanent suspension from office in case of any violation of the provisions of this chapter or any other act related to the notarial practice, all subject to the provisions of section 2105 of this title. The Supreme Court as well as the Chief Justice may delegate on the Director of Notarial Inspection whatever functions related to the supervision of the notaries and the notarial practice that they deem convenient with the exception of the power to impose disciplinary sanctions.

Tit. 4, § 2103. —Disparity of criteria; solution.

If, during the course of inspection of the notarial protocol, any difference of criteria arises between the Protocols Inspector and the notary with regard to the form and manner he keeps his protocols and registry of affidavits, with respect to compliance with this chapter, the cancelling of fees, or any other act related to the certification of the documents or instruments, the Inspector shall state it in his report, briefly listing the facts and the grounds of the controversy. This report shall be submitted to the Superior Court Part, without payment of fees or taxes of any type, so that after hearing the Inspector and the notary it may resolve the controversy. The ensuing resolution may be reviewed by the Supreme Court through certiorari filed within thirty (30) days after being notified; all of which is subject to the provisions of section 2105 of this title.

Tit. 4, § 2104. Death, disability or resignation of notary; surrender of protocol.

In case of the death or the permanent mental or physical disability of a notary, or when he voluntarily or compulsorily ceases in the performance of his functions, or in the event that the surety company requests the termination of his bond, or when he accepts permanent appointment to any judicial or executive office which, under the laws of Puerto Rico, is incompatible with the free exercise of the legal or notarial profession, it shall be the duty of the notary, his heirs, successors, or assigns, to surrender within thirty (30) days, his protocols and registries of affidavits, duly bound to the Office of Notarial Inspection for their inspection.

If this surrender is not made voluntarily within said term, the Supreme Court of Puerto Rico may issue the corresponding order to such effects.

Once the protocols surrendered pursuant to this section have been examined and approved they shall be placed under the custody of the custodian of notarial protocols of the corresponding district.

Tit. 4, § 2105. Disciplinary corrections; due process.

No notary may be disciplined, separated or suspended from notarial practice except through a process that complies, in all its phases, with all the guarantees of due process of law procedurally as well as substantively.

Tit. 4, § 2106. Delivery of protocol to general custodian; examination; return to the notary.

Once the protocols and registries of affidavits have been examined for the reasons established by section 2104 of this title, they shall be delivered to the General Custodian for the corresponding district, thus complying with section 2111(d) of this title with regard to registries of affidavits of less than thirty (30) years. If the result of the examination is that there has been a failure to affix the corresponding Internal Revenue, notarial tax or Legal Assistance stamps, the Attorney General shall proceed to sue for reimbursement of the pending amounts, from the notary, his heirs, successors or assigns or guarantors, in behalf of the Commonwealth, the Bar Association and legal assistance, and shall inform the Chief Justice of the outcome of these actions.

When the notary ceases to be disabled or to hold the judicial or executive office to which he was appointed, the General Custodian of the district shall return his protocols to him if he should resume the practice of the notarial profession, and the notary so requests it.

Tit. 4, § 2107. Notarial districts; general custodian; operation.

The territory of the Commonwealth shall be divided into the following notarial districts comprising the demarcation corresponding to the Parts of the Superior Court with seats in San Juan, Arecibo, Aguadilla, Mayaguez, Ponce, Guayama, Humacao, Caguas, Bayamon, Aibonito, Utuado, Carolina. The respective General Custodian of notarial protocols shall reside in each of these seats. He shall be a notary appointed by the Chief Justice of the Supreme Court, except as provided below with respect to the notarial archives custodian for San Juan. The Chief Justice of the Supreme Court shall pass upon all matters concerning said notarial archives and the resignations and vacancies of the custodians of protocols and shall take such measures he deems proper in connection with the general archives. The Chief Justice may delegate on the Director of Notarial Inspection whatever relevant powers he deems convenient.

General district custodians and, in the case of the

San Juan Notarial District, the Director of Notarial Inspection may issue literal, full or partial, handwritten, typewritten, photographic or photostatic copies, or copies reproduced by any other electronic means designed to obtain an exact reproduction of an original, of the original deeds in his custody through payment of their costs of reproduction and the scheduled fees prescribed for issuing copies, and payment of the corresponding internal revenue stamps required by law. In the San Juan General Archives, the fees shall be paid by receipts issued by the Collector of Internal Revenue, in addition to the Internal Revenue stamps that shall be cancelled on the copies of the deeds.

The copies thus issued of any deed duly certified by the district general custodian, or by the Director of Notarial Inspection in the case of the San Juan Notarial District Archives shall be admissible in evidence.

Present incumbents as general custodians of notarial protocols shall continue to hold office as long as they observe good conduct, or until they resign or are removed for any reason.

The Director of Notarial Inspection shall be in charge of the functioning of the notarial archives of San Juan as custodian. All the operational expenses of the San Juan notarial archives and the expenses of supervising the other district notarial archives shall be included in the annual expense budget of the Supreme Court.

Tit. 4, § 2108. Notarial inspection office; personnel.

The officers of the present Notarial Inspection Office shall continue in their office with the same prerogatives as long as they observe good conduct, until they resign, or are removed for any just cause.

Subchapter IX. General Archives of Protocols

Tit. 4, § 2111. General archives of protocols—contents and functions.

(a) The transfer to the General Archives of Puerto Rico of the notarial protocols that are kept conserved in the Archives of Notarial Protocols of Puerto Rico, which on the effective date of this act have been in existence more than sixty (60) years, is hereby authorized. The future transfer to the General Archives of Puerto Rico of those protocols that as time goes by reach that limit of antiquity, is also hereby authorized.

(b) The General Archives of Puerto Rico shall be the custodian of the notarial protocols transferred to the General Archives of Puerto Rico pursuant to subsection (a) of this section. It shall be the duty of the General Archives to take the necessary measures to ensure the proper conservation of the protocols placed in its custody, always conserving them in their original form and order.

(c) The protocols referred to this section shall continue to be secret pursuant to the provisions of this chapter. With regard to bona fide historical investigators, the General Custodian of Puerto Rico shall establish, through regulations to such effect, the norms necessary to establish their condition and to authorize investigations.

(d) The notarial custodian for the District of San Juan is hereby empowered, with the exclusion of any other official, to issue copies of the deeds found in the protocols referred to in this section, pursuant to the provisions of this chapter, including the cases of protocols transferred to the General Archives of Puerto Rico or of those documents in his custody and of those under temporary custody of the Director of Notarial Inspection.

The Director of Notarial Inspection may allow the destruction of all those registries of affidavits whose last entry has been in existence for more than thirty (30) years, and are deposited in each Notarial District's Archives, subject to prior authorization by the official designated to administer and regulate the Program of Administration of Public Documents in the Judiciary Branch.

The Director of Notarial Inspection shall likewise authorize notaries to destroy any book of affidavits whose last affidavit is dated over thirty (30) years ago. This authorization shall be issued in writing. No registry may be destroyed unless it has been previously examined and approved by an inspector of protocols. Once the destruction of these registries has been authorized, the notary may conserve them in his possession if he wishes, but they shall not be received in any notarial archive, unless so directed by the Supreme Court.

Tit. 4, § 2112. —Notarial custodians.

Notarial Custodians may be disciplined for the same causes and in the same manner as notaries, without impairing the provisions of section 3001 et seq. of Title 33.

Subchapter X. Registry of Wills

Tit. 4, § 2121. Registry of wills—creation and functions.

A registry of wills attached to the Office of Notarial Inspection is hereby created. The functions and faculties of the registry shall be exercised by the Director of Notarial Inspection under the direct supervision of the Chief Justice of the Supreme Court.

Tit. 4, § 2122. —Regulation.

The Supreme Court is hereby empowered to establish, by regulations, everything concerning the operation and functioning of the registry of wills created by this chapter in a manner not incompatible with its provisions.

Tit. 4, § 2123. —Certified reports.

The notaries shall remit to the Director of Notarial Inspection by certified mail with acknowledgement of receipt, or file personally before him, a certification authorized by them bearing their signature and notarial seal, of each original deed granting, modifying, revoking or extending a will, or recording of a holographic or sealed will, stating in said certification the number of the deed or record, the date, place and hour it was executed and the name and surname of the testator and of the witnesses, as the case may be, with their personal circumstances as they appear in the document, and any other information required, within twenty-four (24) hours of its execution, not counting Saturdays and Sundays or legal holidays.

Tit. 4, § 2124. —Acknowledgment of certified report; certification thereof.

It shall be the duty of the Director of Notarial Inspection to acknowledge receipt of said certification and maintain a register with the name and surname or surnames of the testator and other circumstances which are part of said notarial certification.

These certifications shall be conserved in custody of said official who shall keep them in the order in which they were remitted. He is hereby authorized to certify with his signature and official seal whether the execution of the will sought has been annotated, by written petition of an interested party or his attorney, accompanied by Internal Revenue stamps in the amount of three dollars ($3).

He may also certify, by payment of the same fees, that in the written records in his office there is no evidence that the designated person has executed a will.

Tit. 4, § 2125. —Negative certification, prerequisite for declaration of heirship.

The Superior Court shall not admit or process any petition of declaration of heirship whatsoever that is not filed with a negative certification from the Office of Notarial Inspection issued pursuant to section 2124 of this title.

Tit. 4, § 2126. Registry of powers of attorney.

In the case of granting a power of attorney the notary shall comply with the provisions of the Power of Attorney Registration Act, sections 921-927 of this title, and the Regulations of the Supreme Court of Puerto Rico.

Subchapter XI. Notarial Fees

Tit. 4, § 2131. Notarial fees—tariff.

Notaries are hereby authorized to charge the following fees for their notarial services:

(a) The notary may charge up to the sum of one hundred dollars ($100) for executing notarial documents concerning valuables or where a thing or amount of a determinable value is involved, whose value not exceeds ten thousand dollars ($10,000.00).

(b) The notary shall earn fees equal to one percent (1%) of their value, for executing notarial documents concerning valuables or where a thing or amount of determinable value is involved whose value exceeds ten thousand dollars ($10,000.00), but does not exceed five hundred thousand dollars ($500,000.00).

(c) For executing notarial documents concerning valuable objects or where a thing or amount of a determinable value is involved whose value exceeds five hundred thousand dollars ($500,000.00), the notary shall earn fees equivalent to one percent (1%) up to that amount, plus one half percent (.5%) on the excess of that sum.

(d) For executing nonvaluable notarial documents, including sworn statements, authentication of signatures or affidavits, the fees shall be fixed by agreement between the parties and the notary.

(e) For the issuing certified copies of deeds the charges shall be based on the document's amount, excluding costs, expenses and disbursements, in the following manner:

from	$00.00	to	$ 10,000.00	$15.00
from	$ 10,001.00	to	$500,000.00	$25.00
from	$500,001.00	and over		$40.00.

Tit. 4, § 2132. —Extra tariff.

The fees fixed above for executing the documents shall not impair or limit the notary from charging fees he believes reasonable and prudent in accordance with Canon 24 of Professional Ethics for the fixing of fees, for his prior and preparatory efforts, including the subsequent ones, such as background and titles, studies, consultations, opinions, preparation of certificates and compensated powers of attorney in which the notary renders an additional service as a lawyer.

Subchapter XII. Administration of Bonds

Tit. 4, § 2141. Notarial bond; administration.

The Notarial Bond Special Fund shall be governed by the Governing Board of the Bar Association.

The Governing Board shall have the following obligations:

(1) To establish and maintain a reserve sufficient to answer any legitimate claim against the Special Fund as a result of the notarial bond secured by the Bar Association and to cover expenses needed to administrate, operate and protect the Special Fund.

(2) To take custody of and invest in a prudent manner the balance of the Special Fund once the reserve amount required by the preceding subsection is discounted. The amount corresponding to this balance and its accrued interest may be used or invested for the following purposes:

(a) To carry out studies to modernize the property registries and collaborate in achieving this objective.

(b) To establish and maintain a continuing education program for all of Puerto Rico's attorneys through courses, seminars, conferences or any other educational programs the Board deems appropriate.

(c) To establish and maintain the proper coordination with educational institutions to provide a continuing education program for all members of the legal profession and improve teaching in our country's Law Schools.

(d) To sponsor a scholarship program so that distinguished members of the profession, judges of the General Court of Justice, professors and distinguished graduates of the Law Schools, may attend advanced studies in order to improve the quality of legal education, the quality of the profession and the quality of justice.

(e) To provide all of the country's lawyers with auxiliary legal investigation services through access to data banks or other means that would enable adequate legal investigation for the proper practice of the profession.

(f) To carry out the pertinent studies to draft a voluntary insurance plan within a term of one (1) year, counted from the effective date of this act that would cover professional malpractice in the practice of law. The plan can be offered by the Bar Association or by an insurance company authorized to do business in Puerto Rico. Any voluntary insurance plan that the Governing Board intends to institute shall be organized as an autonomous entity with an independent accounting system and resources, and limited liability, which shall be submitted to the Insurance Commissioner for his approval.

(g) To carry out the pertinent studies, within a term of one (1) year counted from the effective date of this act, to draft an incremented bonding plan based on the amounts involved in the transactions in the deeds executed by the notaries.

(h) To establish any other program or service that is compatible with the previously mentioned objectives.

Neither the resources of the Special Fund created by this section nor the interest they accrue may be used for purposes other than the ones established above.

ADDITIONAL AUTHORITY

[P.R.R. Sup. Ct.]

§ 9. Notaries.

(a) Any person entitled to practice law in the Commonwealth courts may be permitted to act as a notary. He shall file in the office of the secretary of his Court a petition together with a bond in duplicate for $2,500 in favor of the Commonwealth of Puerto Rico. Once the Court accepts said bond and the petitioner is permitted to act as notary, he shall take oath before the secretary of this Court. The notary shall then register in the Department of State of Puerto Rico and in the office of the secretary of this Court his signature, mark, seal, and paraph and shall notify the Part of the Superior Court within his domicile, as well as the protocol inspectors, his residence address, the place of his notarial office, and the date on which he will open the latter. He shall forward to said Court on Monday of every week his indices of deeds and affidavits. The notaries shall likewise notify any change of residence or notarial office to the Secretary of the Supreme Court, the secretary of the corresponding Part of the Superior Court and to the protocol inspectors.

(b) When the bond is furnished by a surety company it shall be sent to the Insurance Commissioner of Puerto Rico, who shall certify as to its sufficiency. When a notary submits a mortgage security it must be accompanied by a certificate from the Secretary of the Treasury of Puerto Rico setting forth the assessed value of the mortgaged property, and a certificate from the corresponding register of property in connection with liens on said property.

(c) The notaries shall send by registered mail, receipt requested, to the secretary of this Court, within twenty-four hours after its execution, a certificate authorized by them under their notarial seal, of each matrix of a will executed or protocolized by them, stating in said certificate the number of the deed, the date of its execution, and the name of the testator or testatrix, as well as their personal description; and it shall be the duty of the secretary of the Supreme Court to acknowledge receipt of this certificate to the notary and to proceed immediately after receipt thereof to annotate it in the Register of Wills in order that the secretary may thereafter issue, after payment of the proper fees and on petition of an interested party or of his attorney, a certificate stating whether or not the execution of the will in question is annotated in said book; Provided, That no part of the Superior Court of Puerto Rico shall admit or take into consideration any petition for declaration of heirs if the petition is not accompanied by a certificate from the secretary of this Court, in which certificate he states under his signature and the seal of this Court, that it does not appear from the entries in the said Register that the person referred to has executed any will.

(d) It shall be the duty of every notary before whom a deed to constitute, modify, extend, substitute, renounce, revoke or protocolize a power of attorney is executed, to send to the secretary of this Court, by registered mail within seventy-two hours following the execution thereof, a notice certified under his seal, setting forth therein the name or names of the grantor or grantors and of the witnesses, and the date, number and nature of the deed, specifying the person to whom the power of attorney is granted, extended, modified, or revoked. In case of substitution of a power of attorney, the name of the person substituted and of the attorney-in-fact shall be stated in said notice, and in cases of renunciation of the power of attorney, the name of the constituent thereof shall be given. Where the protocolization of a power of attorney executed outside of Puerto Rico is sought, it shall be the duty of the notary to set forth also the date and place of the execution of the power protocolized, name of the attorney-in-fact and the constituent of the power, notary before whom the power protocolized was executed and the officer who attested to the signature of said notary. It shall be the duty of the secretary of this Court to acknowledge to the notaries receipt of said notice and to proceed immediately after receipt thereof to make the corresponding entry in the register prescribed by law.

FEES

[P.R. Laws Ann.]

Tit. 4, § 847. Notarial tariff.

Notaries shall receive for the execution of instruments made before them and for the copies thereof, the fees contained in the following tariff:

Notarial Tariff

Article 1. The execution of documents or deeds of arras, dowry, articles of marriage, wills, associations, dissolutions thereof, contracts of work, simple obligations, obligations guaranteed by mortgage or pledges, securities, mandates or trusts, powers of attorney, protest, protest of bills of exchange and promissory notes, donations, services, usufruct, use, dwelling, tenancy, antichresis, acquittance, cancellations, exchange, purchase and sales, cessions, deposits, promises, annuities, subrogations, acknowledgments, redemption of annuities, loans with or without mortgage, renouncement or substitution of powers of attorney, furnishing capital to estates, engagements, appointment of arbiters or friendly arbitrators, allotments, partitions, protocolizations, acceptance or repudiation of inheritance, recognitions of natural children, rescissions of contracts, retraction sales on reversion, receipts through a third party, subrogation of mortgages, leases, subleases, pledgings of property, judicial declarations, marital licenses, paternal counsel and consent emancipation and any other kind of recordable deed of objects not appraisable or involving objects or sums not exceeding one thousand dollars, shall pay for each folio one dollar.

Article 2. For the execution of the same deeds mentioned in the preceding article, that is, deeds of appraisable objects or deeds involving objects or sums, as the price thereof, exceeding one thousand dollars, the fee of one-half percent shall be charged.

Article 3. For authenticating each act of acknowledgment of signatures in private documents containing nothing recordable or inscribable in the registry of deeds, there shall be charged a fee of fifty cents.

Article 4. For making a copy of recorded deeds, appertaining to any year, or issued from others, or from any public or private document, fifty cents per folio shall be charged.

Article 5. For each notification or note of issuance of copies to the parties concerned, forty cents shall be charged.

Article 6. For searching documents in the registry of the notarial archives or record, thirty cents for each year shall be charged.

General Provisions

The imposing of fees for the searching of a document in the notarial offices of the Commonwealth shall not exceed double the amount of the fees collected for the making of a copy therefor: Provided, That such limitation shall not apply to the General Archive of Protocols for the searching of documents dated before the last thirty years.

Tit. 30, § 1770a. Exemption of United States Government from certain fees.

The United States of America and its agencies

and instrumentalities, including The Federal Land Bank of Baltimore, the Federal Intermediate Credit Bank of Baltimore, The Baltimore Bank of Cooperatives, The Federal Land Bank Association of San Juan and The Puerto Rico Production Credit Association, are hereby exempted from payment of all kinds of duties, taxes or fees prescribed by the laws of the Commonwealth of Puerto Rico for the authentication of documents before a notary or before any public officer and for the registration of documents and other operations in the registries of property.

OATHS, AFFIDAVITS AND AFFIRMATIONS

Tit. 4, § 881. Administration of oaths, affidavits, and affirmations—mode; perjury.

All oaths, affidavits and affirmations shall be administered in the mode most binding upon the conscience of the individual taking the same, and shall be taken subject to the pains and penalties of perjury.

Tit. 4, § 882. Officers authorized to administer, in Puerto Rico.

All oaths, affidavits or affirmations, necessary or convenient or required by law, may be administered within Puerto Rico, and a certificate of the fact given, by any judge of the Supreme Court, or by any judge of the Superior Court, or by any secretary of either of the above mentioned courts, or by any justice of the peace or District Court judge, or by any notary public, or by any Commissioner of the United States for the District of Puerto Rico; Provided, That the prosecuting attorney of the Supreme Court of Puerto Rico is likewise authorized by this law to administer oaths in such cases in which the law permits prosecuting attorneys of the Superior Court to administer them, whenever by special delegation or substitution of any such prosecuting attorney of the Superior Court he shall conduct any investigation specially intrusted by law to said prosecuting attorneys of the Superior Court.

Tit. 4, § 883. Writing and signature of affidavits.

All affidavits provided by sections 881-885 of this title shall be in writing and signed by the party making the same.

Tit. 4, § 884. Affidavits within and outside Puerto Rico.

Affidavits may be made before either of the fol-

lowing officers who are authorized to take such affidavits and give a certificate thereof:

1. If taken within Puerto Rico before the officers named in section 882 of this title.

2. If taken without Puerto Rico and within the United States before any clerk of a court of record having a seal, any notary public, or any commissioner of deeds, duly appointed under the laws of Puerto Rico, within some state or territory.

3. If without the United States, before any notary public, or any minister, commissioner, or charge d'affaires of the United States resident in, and accredited to, the country where the affidavit may be taken; or any consul general; vice consul general, consul, vice consul, commercial agent, vice commercial agent, deputy consul or consular agent of the United States in such country, or any commissioner of deeds, duly appointed under the laws of Puerto Rico, within such country.

Tit. 4, § 887. Registry of affidavits or declarations of authenticity—definition.

By affidavit or declaration of authenticity is meant the act and the document by means of which a notary or any other of the officers designated by sections 887-895 of this title certifies to, or witnesses the truth or recognition of a signature, an oath, or any other fact or contract affecting real or personal property not made in a public instrument.

Tit. 4, § 889. Form of affidavit or declaration; numbering.

The affidavit or declaration of authenticity shall be drawn in the following form. In the case of the recognition of the signature under oath:

"Sworn to and subscribed before me, by .... (name, age, trade or occupation and residence) personally known to me (or who has been identified to my satisfaction by the two witnesses, known to me, whose statement to that effect is also signed by them), this, the ...... day of ...... 19....."

In the case of the recognition of a signature not made under oath, the same form shall be used, except that the words "sworn to" shall be stricken out.

A concise and simple form shall be used for all other cases and which shall include the authenticity of the act, but in all cases the officer authorizing same shall set forth that he knows personally the interested party; or knows the witnesses identifying such party.

Affidavits or declarations of authenticity shall be numbered in successive and continuous numbers and each declaration shall contain at its head the number corresponding to it and which shall be correlative with that of the entry in the Registry, referred to hereinafter.

Tit. 4, § 890. Officers who may authorize affidavits and declarations.

All notaries, Supreme Court justices, judges of the Court of First Instance, municipal judges, prosecutors, justices of the peace, the Secretary of State, the heads of the departments and the municipal treasurers shall authorize affidavits or declarations; but only notaries may authorize such affidavits and declarations when they have reference to facts, acts or contracts of a purely private nature; Provided, however, That municipal treasurers shall be authorized only and exclusively to administer oaths in those cases where required under Act No. 26 of March 28, 1914, with reference to certificates for industrial and commercial license taxes; Provided, further, That in towns where there is no notary with an open office, the district judges and justices of the peace may take affidavits, in which this fact shall appear, on recognition of signatures on instruments of credit and contracts of a private nature, the amount of which does not exceed two thousand five hundred (2,500) dollars.

The foregoing provisions shall not be so construed as to leave without effect any law in force under which authority is granted to other public officials, not mentioned in sections 887-895 of this title, to take affidavits, oaths and affirmations, which authorizations shall remain in full force.

Tit. 4, § 894. Unrecorded affidavit or declaration void.

Any affidavit or declaration not recorded in the Registry, or not included in the corresponding indice shall be null.

Tit. 4, § 895. Exemption of certain declarations.

There shall not be deemed to be included in sections 887-895 of this title any declarations in judicial, or administrative proceedings, made before judges or officers of any capacity, in matters under their jurisdiction.

ACKNOWLEDGMENTS

"Federal Relations Act"

§ 54. Acknowledgment of deeds and instruments.

That deeds and other instruments affecting land situate in the District of Columbia, or any other territory or possession of the United States, may be acknowledged in Puerto Rico before any notary public appointed therein by proper authority, or any officer therein who has ex officio the powers of any notary public; Provided, That the certificate by such notary shall be accompanied by the certificate of the Executive Secretary of Puerto Rico to the effect that the notary taking such acknowledgment is in fact such notarial officer.

In Puerto Rico

48 U.S.C. § 742. Acknowledgment of deeds.

Deeds and other instruments affecting land situate in the District of Columbia, or any other territory or possession of the United States, may be acknowledged in Puerto Rico before any notary public appointed therein by proper authority, or any officer therein who has ex officio the powers of a notary public: Provided, that the certificate by such notary shall be accompanied by the certificate of the executive secretary of Puerto Rico to the effect that the notary taking such acknowledgment is in fact such notarial officer.

DEPOSITIONS

[P.R.R. Civ. P. (tit. 32, app. III)]

RULE 25. Persons before whom depositions may be taken.

25.1 Within Puerto Rico and the United States

Within Puerto Rico, within the United States, or within any territory or possession subject to the dominion or jurisdiction thereof, depositions shall be taken before an officer authorized to administer oaths by the laws of Puerto Rico or of the place where the examination is held, or before a person appointed by the court in which the action is pending. A person so appointed has power to administer oaths, take testimony, and preside over the taking of depositions. It is not necessary for the person administering the oath to remain at the place where the deposition is to be taken after the deponent has been sworn.

When a person through an affidavit certifies before the court that he lacks the means to meet the expense of taking a deposition, the court may order that the deposition be taken under such conditions as it deems appropriate.

25.2 In foreign countries

In a foreign country, depositions may be taken on notice, (1) before a person authorized to administer oaths in the place in which the examination is held, or (2) before a person or officer commissioned by the court for this purpose, or (3) pursuant to a letter rogatory. A commission or a letter rogatory

Puerto Rico ANDERSON'S MANUAL FOR NOTARIES PUBLIC

shall be issued only when necessary and convenient, on application and on such terms and with such directions as are just and appropriate. Officers may be designated in notices or commissions either by name or descriptive title and letters rogatory may be addressed "To the Appropriate Authority in (here the name of the country)." Evidence obtained in response to a letter rogatory need not be excluded merely for the reason that it is not a verbatim transcript or that the testimony was not taken under oath or for any similar departure from the requirements for depositions taken within Puerto Rico.

25.3 Disqualification for interest

No deposition shall be taken before a person who is a relative within the fourth degree of consanguinity or the second degree of affinity, or employee or attorney of any of the parties, or is a relative within the degrees mentioned or employee of such attorney, or is financially interested in the action.

RULE 27. Depositions upon oral examination.

* * *

27.8 Certification and notice of deposition.

(a) The person before whom the deposition is taken or, in his absence, the person recording the examination shall certify on the deposition that the witness was duly sworn and that the deposition is a true and exact transcript of the testimony given by the witness. He shall then securely seal the deposition in an envelope indorsed with the title of the action and marked "Deposition of (here insert name of witness)" and shall promptly deliver it to the party taking it, who shall in turn be obliged to notify all other parties that the deposition is in his possession. Furthermore, he shall be obliged to keep the deposition and produce it at the trial, unless it is not to be used in the trial, in accordance with Rule 27.6.

(b) Documents and things produced for inspection during the examination of the witness shall, upon request of a party, be marked for identification and annexed to the transcript of the deposition. Said documents and things may be inspected and copied by any party. The person producing the documents or things may substitute copies to be marked for identification, if he affords to all parties fair opportunity to verify that the copies are true and exact to the originals. Also, if the person producing the documents or things requests their return, each party will be given an opportunity to inspect and copy them, and they will be returned to the person producing them after being duly marked by the parties and the materials may then be used in the same manner as if annexed to the deposition.

(c) Upon payment of a prescribed fee therefor, the person before whom the deposition is taken or, in his absence, the person taking or recording the examination shall furnish a copy of the deposition to any party to the action or to the deponent.

LEGAL HOLIDAYS

[P.R. Laws Ann.]

Tit. 1, § 71. Holidays generally.

Holidays, within the meaning of sections 71-73 of this title, are every Sunday, the first day of January, the twenty-second day of February, the twenty-second day of March, Good Friday, the thirtieth day of May, the fourth day of July, the twenty-fifth day of July, the first Monday of September, to be known as Labor Day, the twenty-fifth day of December, every day on which an election is held throughout the island and every day appointed by the President of the United States, by the Governor of Puerto Rico or by the Legislative Assembly, for a public fast, thanksgiving, or holiday. When any such day falls upon a Sunday, the Monday following is a holiday.

Tit. 1, § 73. Day of performance falling upon holiday.

Whenever any act is appointed by law or contract to be performed upon a particular day, which day falls upon a holiday, such act may be performed upon the next business day with the same effect as if it had been performed upon the day appointed.

Tit. 1, § 74. January 6.

The sixth day of January of each year is hereby declared to be an official and legal holiday in the Commonwealth of Puerto Rico.

Tit. 1, § 75. January 11; birthday of Eugenio Maria de Hostos.

January 11, the date of the anniversary of the birth of the illustrious Puerto Rican educator, philosopher, sociologist, writer, and patriot, is hereby declared a legal holiday every year.

Tit. 1, § 76. Second Sunday of April; Antonio R. Barcelo Day.

The second Sunday of April of 1941, and of each

succeeding year is hereby declared a legal holiday, and such day shall be known as Antonio R. Barcelo Day.

Tit. 1, § 77. April 16; Jose de Diego Day.

The sixteenth day of the month of April of each year shall be known in Puerto Rico as "Jose de Diego Day," and is hereby declared to be a legal holiday.

Tit. 1, § 78. July 17; Luis Munoz Rivera Day.

The 17th day of July of each year shall be commemorated in Puerto Rico as "Munoz Rivera Day," the same being hereby declared a legal holiday.

Tit. 1, § 79. July 25; Day of the Constitution.

July 25 of each year is hereby declared a legal holiday designated as Day of the Constitution.

Tit. 1, § 80. July 27; birthday of Dr. Jose Celso Barbosa.

The twenty-seventh day of July of each year is hereby declared an official and legal holiday in Puerto Rico, and during such day all public offices of Puerto Rico, Commonwealth and Municipal, shall remain closed.

Tit. 1, § 81. First Monday of September; Santiago Iglesias Pantin Day.

In addition to the declaration of Congress setting apart the first Monday of September of each year as Labor Day, the first Monday of September of 1940, and of each subsequent year is hereby declared a holiday consecrated to the memory of the eminent citizen, Santiago Iglesias Pantin.

Tit. 1, § 82. October 12; Columbus Day.

The twelfth day of October of each year is hereby declared to be and shall be kept as a legal holiday in Puerto Rico under the name of "Columbus Day."

Tit. 1, § 83. November 19; discovery of Puerto Rico.

The nineteenth day of November is declared a holiday in Puerto Rico.

Tit. 1, § 84. Transference of holidays.

The holidays listed below shall be held every year during the day and month set immediately after the holiday.

1. Washington's Birthday; shall be held the third Monday of February.

2. Memorial Day; shall be held the last Monday of May.

3. Discovery Day; shall be held the 12th of October.

4. Veterans Day; shall be held on the 11th day of November.

RHODE ISLAND

NOTARIES PUBLIC

[R.I. GEN. LAWS ANN.]

§ 42-30-3. Appointment of notaries and justices.

The governor shall, in the month of June, 1971, and in every fifth year thereafter, appoint as many notaries public for the state, and as many justices of the peace for the several towns and cities, as he or she may deem expedient; and every notary public and justice of the peace, so appointed, shall hold office until the first day of July, in the fifth year after his or her appointment. The governor may also appoint, from time to time, such other notaries public and justices of the peace as he or she may deem expedient, who shall hold office until the expiration of the tenure of office of those appointed under the preceding provisions of this section, or otherwise, until the first day of July, A. D. 1971.

§ 42-30-4. Commission fee—certificate of engagement.

(a) Except as otherwise provided, each notary public and justice of the peace shall, at the time of receiving his or her commission, pay to the secretary of state or the officer delivering the same, the sum of forty dollars ($40.00) for the use of the state, and shall, at his or her request upon payment of the actual cost thereof, receive a wallet-size identification card, and every such officer shall, within thirty (30) days after the date of his or her commission, deliver to the secretary of state a certificate that he or she has been duly engaged thereon, signed by the person before whom the engagement shall have been taken. The term of engagement shall be biennial.

§ 42-30-5. Application for appointment.

(a) Any qualified elector or member of the bar of this state desiring to be appointed a notary public, or a justice of the peace, shall make written application to the governor over his or her own signature, and stating that he or she is a qualified elector or a member of the bar, who is an actual resident of the state of Rhode Island, as the case may be, qualification as an elector of the state at the time of making application to be certified to by a member of the board of canvassers and registration, in cities having such boards, or by the city or town clerk of the city or town in which the applicant claims a right to vote, and except for members of the bar of this state, the member of the board of canvassers and registration or the city or town clerk shall satisfy himself or herself that the applicant for appointment to the office of notary public or justice of the peace can speak, read and write the English language and has sufficient knowledge of the powers and duties pertaining to that office. Qualification as a member of the bar shall be a certified copy of his or her certificate of admission to the bar.

(b) Provided, however, that all duly qualified notaries public and justices of the peace, whose commissions expire on the thirtieth day of June, 1986, or on the thirtieth day of June in every fifth year thereafter shall be exempted from the provisions of this section.

§ 42-30-7. Powers of notaries and justices.

The officers mentioned in §§ 42-30-3 to 42-30-6, inclusive, shall possess all the powers which now are or hereafter may be conferred by law upon justices of the peace or notaries public.

§ 42-30-8. Powers of notaries.

Notaries public may, within this state, act, transact, do, and finish all matters and things relating to protests and protesting bills of exchange and promissory notes, and all other matters within their office required by law, take depositions as prescribed by law, and acknowledgments of deeds and other instruments.

§ 42-30-9. Lists of appointees—certificates of appointment.

It shall be the duty of the secretary of state to make a list of all notaries public and justices of the peace appointed by the governor and duly qualified, and send a copy thereof to each of the clerks of the supreme, superior and family courts and to the clerks of the district courts for the second, third, fourth, ninth, tenth, eleventh and twelfth judicial districts, to be kept in the files of those courts, and the clerks shall, upon application, issue certificates of office to the person entitled thereto, and shall receive a fee of one dollar ($1.00) for every certificate.

§ 42-30-10. Removal of notaries, justices, and commissioners.

Any notary public, justice of the peace or commissioner of deeds, appointed by the governor, may be removed for cause by the governor, in his or her discretion, within the term for which that officer shall have been appointed, after giving to that officer a copy of the charges against him or her and an opportunity to be heard in his or her defense; provided however, that any notary public, justice of the peace or commissioner of deeds who is convicted of a felony and incarcerated shall have his or her commission revoked. Said notary public, justice of the peace or commissioner of deeds shall not be eligible to apply for a new commission until his or her voting rights are restored pursuant to Article 2, Section 1 of the Rhode Island Constitution.

§ 42-30-11. Continuation of powers without reappointment.

Every justice of the peace and notary public appointed by the governor and not reappointed, may continue to officiate for a space of thirty (30) days after the first day of July in the year in which his or her commission expires.

§ 42-30-12. Continuation of powers without new engagement.

Every such officer who may be reappointed or continued in office, may continue to officiate for the same length of time without taking a new engagement.

§ 42-30-13. Fees of notaries.

The fees of notaries public shall be as follows:
(1) For noting a marine protest, one dollar ($1.00);
(2) For drawing and extending a marine protest and recording it, one dollar and fifty cents ($1.50);
(3) For taking affidavits, twenty-five cents (25¢);
(4) For travel, per mile, ten cents (10¢);
(5) For taking acknowledgment of any instrument and affixing his seal, one dollar ($1.00);
(6) For the protest of a bill of exchange, order or draft, for nonacceptance or nonpayment, or of a promissory note or check for nonpayment, if the amount thereof is five hundred dollars ($500) or more, one dollar ($1.00), if it is less that five hun-

dred dollars ($500), for recording the same, fifty cents (50¢);

(7) For noting the nonacceptance or nonpayment of a bill of exchange, order or draft, or the nonpayment of a promissory note or check, seventy-five cents (75¢); and

(8) For each notice of the nonacceptance or nonpayment of a bill, order, draft, check, or note, given to a party liable for the payment thereof, twenty-five cents (25¢);

provided, that the whole cost of protest, including necessary notices and the record, shall not exceed two dollars ($2.00), and the whole cost of noting, including notices, shall in no case exceed one dollar and twenty-five cents ($1.25).

§ 42-30-14. Public officers having notarial powers.

Every state senator, state representative, chief, deputy, and assistant clerk of any state court, and worker's compensation commission during the period for which he or she has been elected or appointed, shall have the power to act as a notary public as in this chapter provided. No office holder set forth in this section shall be required to pay the commission fee as provided in § 42-30-4.

ADDITIONAL AUTHORITY

§ 19-4-4. Protests not to be made by bank officers.

No protest of any note, draft or check shall be made by any notary public who is the president, cashier, director, or officer of any bank, savings bank, or trust company wherein such note, draft or check has been placed for collection or has been discounted.

§ 36-1-3. Issuance of commissions.

A commission shall issue to every person elected to office by the general assembly, to every justice of the peace elected by any town council, to the clerk and each deputy clerk of the Rhode Island district court, and to every person appointed to office by the governor.

§ 36-2-1. Officers with statewide power.

The following persons may administer oaths anywhere within the state: the governor, lieutenant governor, secretary of state, attorney-general, assistant attorneys-general, general treasurer, active and retired justices of the supreme, superior, family and district courts, each member of the general assembly after he has filed his signature with the

secretary of state, commissioners appointed by other states to take acknowledgments of deeds and depositions within this state, and notaries public.

FEES

§ 36-2-4. Fees for acknowledgments and engagements.

To all officers empowered to take acknowledgments of deeds and administer oaths of engagement to office, there shall be allowed:

For taking acknowledgment of one or more parties to any instrument at one time .... $ .50
For engaging every officer .... .25.

ACKNOWLEDGMENTS

§ 15-4-5. Acknowledgment of deeds and letters of attorney.

The deed of a married woman conveying her separate interest in any lands, tenements, or hereditaments shall be acknowledged by her in the same manner as if she were single and unmarried. If any deed affecting her right of life estate created by chapter 25 of title 33 in any estate of her husband during his life be executed by attorney of the wife, the letter of attorney shall be acknowledged in the same manner as if she were single and unmarried.

§ 34-12-1. Form of acknowledgment— foreign acknowledgments.

Acknowledgment of any instrument hereafter made need not be in any set form, but shall be made of all the parties executing the instrument and the certificate thereof shall express the ideas that the parties were each and all known to the magistrate taking the acknowledgment, and known by the magistrate to be the parties executing the instrument, and that they acknowledge the instrument to be their free act and deed; Provided, however, That in case of any instrument executed without this state or within the limits of the United States or of any dependency thereof, if the instrument is acknowledged or proved in the manner prescribed by the law of the state, District of Columbia, territory or such dependency, where executed, it shall be deemed to be legally executed, and acknowledged and shall have the same effect as if executed and acknowledged in the mode above prescribed, including an acknowledgment by less than all parties if made in a jurisdiction the laws of which permit acknowledgments in such manner; Provided, however, That instruments requiring acknowledgements by parties having opposing interests must be acknowledged by at least one (1) party of each interest.

§ 34-12-2. Officers authorized to take acknowledgments.

Acknowledgment of any instrument required by any statute of this state to be acknowledged shall be made:

(1) Within this state, before any state senator, any state representative, judge, justice of the peace, clerk or assistant clerk of the superior court, mayor, notary public, town clerk or recorder of deeds.

(2) Without this state and within the limits of United States or any dependency thereof, before any judge or justice of a court of record or other court, justice of the peace, mayor or notary public, of the state, District of Columbia, territory or such dependency, in which such acknowledgment is made, or before any commissioner appointed by the governor of this state, or before any officer authorized by law to take acknowledgments of deeds in the place in which the acknowledgment is made.

(3) Without the limits of the United States, before any of the following officers acting within his territorial jurisdiction or within that of the court of which he is an officer:

(A) An ambassador, envoy, minister, charge d'affaires, secretary of legation, consul-general, consul, vice-consul, consular agent, vice-consular agent, or any other diplomatic or consular agent or representative of the United States, appointed or accredited to, and residing within the country where the acknowledgment or proof is taken.

(B) A judge or other presiding officer of any court having a seal or the clerk or other certifying officer thereof.

(C) A mayor or other chief civil officer of any city or other political subdivision.

(D) A notary public.

(E) A person residing in, or going to, the country where the acknowledgment or proof is to be taken, and specially authorized for that purpose by a commission issued to him under the seal of the superior court.

(F) Any person authorized, by the laws of the country where the acknowledgment or proof is made, to take acknowledgments of conveyances of real estate or to administer oaths in proof of the execution thereof.

§ 34-12-3. Acknowledgments in good faith before person claiming to be authorized—penalty for misrepresentation.

Any acknowledgment made in good faith before a person claiming to be one of the foregoing officials authorized to take acknowledgments within the respective jurisdictions as above, shall be valid, although the official before whom the same is made was not duly qualified in such office; but every person who shall, within this state, wilfully take and certify to the taking of any such acknowledgment, without being lawfully qualified thereunto, shall be liable in a criminal proceeding to a fine not exceeding fifty dollars ($50.00), one-half (1/2) to the use of the complainant and the other half thereto to the use of this state.

§ 34-12-4. Instruments executed by diplomatic officials outside United States.

Every instrument requiring acknowledgment, executed without the limits of the United States, concerning lands lying within this state, in which instrument any ambassador, minister, charge d'affaires, consul general, vice-consul general, consul, vice-consul, consular agent, commercial agent, of the United States, or commissioner appointed by the governor of this state, shall be grantor, may be executed in the presence of two (2) witnesses; and when so executed, an official certificate under the hand and official seal of the grantor that such instrument is his act and deed shall be equivalent to an acknowledgment of such instrument in the manner required by law.

§ 34-12-5. Power of armed forces officers to take acknowledgments.

In addition to the acknowledgment of instruments and the performance of other notarial acts in the manner and form and as otherwise authorized by law, instruments may be acknowledged, documents attested, oaths and affirmations administered, depositions and affidavits executed, and other notarial acts performed, before or by any commissioned officer in active service of the armed forces of the United States with the rank of second lieutenant or higher in the army, air force, or marine corps, or with the rank of ensign or higher in the navy or coast guard, or with equivalent rank in any other component part of the armed forces of the United States, by any person without the limits of the United States, and to any person who is a member of the armed forces who is within or without the limits of the United States and their lawful dependents.

§ 34-12-6. Effect of acknowledgment before armed forces officer.

Such acknowledgment of instruments, attestation of documents, administration of oaths and affirmations, execution of depositions and affidavits, and performance of other notarial acts, heretofore or hereafter made or taken, are hereby declared legal, valid and binding, and instruments and documents so acknowledged, authenticated, or sworn to shall be admissible in evidence and eligible to record in this state under the same circumstances, and with the same force and effect as if such acknowledgment, attestation, oath, affirmation, deposition, affidavit, or other notarial act, had been made or taken within this state before or by a duly qualified officer or official as otherwise provided by law.

§ 34-12-7. Contents of certificate of armed forces officer.

In the taking of acknowledgments and the performing of other notarial acts requiring certification, a certificate endorsed upon or attached to the instrument or documents, which shows the date of the notarial act and which states, in substance that the person appearing before the officer acknowledged the instrument as his act or made or signed the instrument or document under oath, shall be sufficient for all intents and purposes. The instrument or document shall not be rendered invalid by the failure to state the place of execution or acknowledgment.

§ 34-12-8. Proof of authority of armed forces officer.

If the signature, rank, and branch of service or subdivision thereof, of any such commissioned officer appear upon such instrument or document or certificate, no further proof of authority of such officer so to act shall be required and such action by such commissioned officer shall be prima facie evidence that the person making such oath or acknowledgment is within the purview of §§ 34-12-5 — 34-12-7, inclusive.

§ 34-12-9. Validation of prior acknowledgments before foreign notary public.

Any acknowledgment taken or made prior to April 27, 1928, of or upon any instrument used in conveying, directly or indirectly, any interest in real estate in this state, including power of attorney, and any other instruments heretofore acknowledged prior to April 27, 1928, before any notary public in any foreign country or territory without the United States, which instrument appears of record to have been duly recorded in any of the records of land evidence in this state, and the acknowledgment therein appearing was taken before a notary public outside the United States, which notary public was duly commissioned in such foreign place where the acknowledgment was taken, to take such acknowledgment, and the ac-

knowledgment is accredited, approved or affirmed, or the commission of such foreign notary public is attested or certified by any ambassador, minister, charge d'affaires, consul general, vice-consul general, consul, vice consul, or consular agent of the United States, or any commissioned officer in active service of the armed forces of the United States with the rank of second lieutenant or higher in the army, air force, or marine corps, or with the rank of ensign or higher in the navy or coast guard, or with equivalent rank in any other component of the armed forces of the United States, duly establishing the fact that such notary public was at the time of taking the acknowledgment duly authorized by the law, rules or regulations of his particular country or territorial section thereof, in which the acknowledgment was taken, to duly administer oaths or take such acknowledgments, then the acknowledgment and conveyance in connection with which the same was taken shall, for the purpose of the acknowledgment and execution thereof, be deemed a valid acknowledgment, and shall have the same effect as if acknowledged before a notary public in this state.

DEPOSITIONS

§ 9-17-3. Subpoenas issued by *** officials.

Auditors, referees, masters in chancery, and commissioners may issue subpoenas to witness in all cases and matters pending before them, respectively; and justices of the peace and notaries public may issue subpoenas to witnesses in any case, civil or criminal, before any court, and in any matter before any body or person authorized by law to summon witnesses.

§ 9-18-1. Officials authorized to take depositions.

Any justice of the supreme or superior or family court, justice of the peace or notary public may take the deposition of any witness, to be used in the trial of any civil suit, action, petition or proceeding, in which he is not interested, nor counsel, nor the attorney of either party, and which shall then be commenced or pending in this state, or in any other state, or in the District of Columbia, or in any territory, government, or country.

§ 9-18-2. Notice to adverse party.

Previous to the taking of any deposition as aforesaid within this state, the official authorized to take the same shall, in all cases, cause the adverse party or his attorney of record to be notified in writing of the time and place appointed for taking such depositions, so that he may attend and put interrogatories to the deponent if he think fit; Provided, That if the person to be notified cannot be found and his residence be not known and he has no attorney of record, the moving party or his attorney may make affidavit of such facts before any justice of the superior court at any time, and thereupon the justice shall prescribe the method in which notice shall be given to such person.

§ 9-18-3. Address and time of service of notice.

The notification issued by the magistrate, officer, or commissioner who shall take such deposition shall be directed to any proper officer, or to any impartial or disinterested person, and shall be served a reasonable time, not less than twenty-four (24) hours, exclusive of Sundays and legal holidays, before the time of taking such deposition.

§ 9-18-4. Service and return of notice.

The officer or other person charged as aforesaid with the service of such notification shall serve the same by reading it to the party to be cited, if to be found; and if not to be found, by leaving a copy thereof at his usual place of abode; and shall, in his return, state the manner and time of such service; and whenever such service shall be made by any person other than a sworn officer, he shall verify the same, under oath, before some officer authorized to administer oaths.

§ 9-18-5. Manner of taking depositions outside state for use in state.

Depositions may be taken without this state to be used in the tribunals of this state, upon an order obtained on motion from the court in which the case is pending, and when ordered shall be taken either by the person and in the manner and with the formalities required by the law of the state, district, territory, or country in which the same shall be taken; or second, shall be taken, if taken in any other state, district, or territory of the United States, before a commissioner appointed by the governor of this state, or before a judge, chancellor, justice of the peace, notary public, or civil magistrate of such state, district, or territory, respectively, or, if taken out of the United States, before a resident official of the United States, or, if the deponent be in the military, air, or naval service of the United States, before a colonel, lieutenant-colonel, or major in the army or air force, or before any officer in the navy not below the grade and rank of lieutenant-commander. And in every such case under the second method, the party causing such depositions to be taken shall notify the adverse party, or his attorney of record, of the time and place appointed for taking the same; and such notification issued by the official before whom such deposition is to be taken shall be served, in the manner hereinbefore provided, such reasonable time before the taking of such deposition as will give the adverse party a full opportunity to be present in person or by attorney and put interrogatories to the deponent, if he think fit.

§ 9-18-6. Oath of deponent—reduction of deposition to writing.

Every person, before deposing, shall be sworn to testify the truth, the whole truth, and nothing but the truth, and after giving such deposition shall subscribe his name thereto, if taken in longhand in the presence of the official before whom the same was taken. Such deposition may be reduced to writing by such official or by any person, including the deponent, under his direction and in his presence, or may be reduced to writing stenographically either by such official or by some person in his presence and under his direction, sworn by such official to correctly take down in shorthand, the evidence as given; and in the latter case, a transcript thereof in longhand writing, typewriting, print, or other reproduction, sworn to by the person stenographically reporting the same and signed by the deponent, shall be received in evidence. The signature in the latter case shall be attested by the official taking the deposition or by some magistrate authorized to administer oaths whether in this state or elsewhere.

§ 9-18-7. Sealing and delivery to court.

The deposition, so taken, shall be retained by such magistrate, officer, or commissioner until he delivers the same with his own hand to the court for which it is taken, or shall, together with a certificate of its having been duly taken, be by said magistrate, officer, or commissioner, sealed up and directed to such court and delivered to the clerk thereof, and remain so sealed until opened by order of the court or of some justice thereof, or by the clerk with the consent of the parties; and any person may be compelled to appear and depose as aforesaid within this state, in the same manner as to appear and testify in court.

§ 9-18-8. Deposition as evidence—use of certified copy.

The deposition of any person taken pursuant to this chapter may be used as evidence in the trial of any judicial proceeding in any court, or town council, or before commissioners, masters in chancery, referees, or auditors, in which it shall have been taken to be used; and if the party who took the same shall neglect to produce or use it, the adverse party may use the original or a copy of such deposition, certified by the magistrate before whom it was taken.

§ 9-18-9. Court grant of commission to take deposition.

Any court may, on the motion of either party in any action, suit, or proceeding, civil or criminal, pending therein, in which a deposition may be used, or before any commissioners, referees, or auditors appointed by any such court or under a rule from it, grant a commission to take depositions according to law, whenever it may be necessary to prevent a failure or delay of justice, on such terms as such court, by general or special order, may direct; and the deposition, so taken, may be used in any state of the cause, on appeal or otherwise.

§ 9-18-11. Depositions for use in foreign tribunals.

Depositions may be taken in this state, to be used on the trial of any cause pending in a tribunal of any other state, district, territory, or country, before any person residing in this state, to whom a commission shall be directed and sent by such tribunal, with the formalities prescribed in such commission, or, if there are none prescribed, then according to the laws of the jurisdiction whence said commission issues.

§ 9-29-3. Deposition fees.

To all officers empowered to take depositions, there shall be allowed:

For every hour necessarily employed ...... $.40
For every page of 200 words .... .30
For every mile's travel to the place of caption .10

§ 43-3-11. Oaths and affirmations.

The word "oath" shall be construed to include affirmation; the word "sworn," affirmed; and the word "engaged," either sworn or affirmed.

[R.I. R. Civ. P.]

RULE 28. Persons before whom depositions may be taken.

(a) Within the State. Within the state depositions shall be taken before an officer authorized to administer oaths by the law of the state or before a person appointed by the court. A person so ap-

pointed has the power to administer oaths and take testimony.

(b) Outside the State. Within another state, or within a territory or insular possession subject to the dominion of the United States, or in a foreign country, depositions may be taken (1) on notice before a person authorized to administer oaths in the place in which the examination is held, either by the law thereof or by the law of the United States, or (2) before a person commissioned by the court, and a person so commissioned shall have the power by virtue of his commission to administer any necessary oath and take testimony, or (3) pursuant to a letter rogatory. A commission or a letter rogatory shall be issued on application and notice and on terms that are just and appropriate. It is not requisite to the issuance of a commission or a letter rogatory that the taking of the deposition in any other manner is impracticable or inconvenient; and both a commission and letter rogatory may be issued in proper cases. A notice or commission may designate the person before whom the deposition is to be taken either by name or descriptive title. A letter rogatory may be addressed "To the Appropriate Authority in (here name the state, territory, or country)." Evidence obtained in a foreign country in response to a letter rogatory need not be excluded merely for the reason that it is not a verbatim transcript or that the testimony was not taken under oath or for any similar departure from the requirements for depositions taken within the United States under these rules.

(c) Disqualification for Interest. No deposition shall be taken before a person who is a relative or employee or attorney or counsel of any of the parties, or is a relative or employee of such attorney or counsel, or is financially interested in the action.

COMMISSIONERS

[R.I. Gen. Laws Ann.]

§ 42-31-1. Appointment of commissioners.

The governor may appoint, in any foreign country and in any state of the United States and in any territory of the United States and in the District of Columbia, one or more commissioners, under the seal of the state, to continue in office for the period of five (5) years.

§ 42-31-2. Oath of office.

Before any commissioner shall perform any duty of his office, he shall take and subscribe an oath before some officer authorized to administer oaths in the state, country or territory, or District of Columbia, for which such commissioner is appointed, that he will faithfully discharge all the duties of his office; a certificate of which shall be filed in the office of the secretary of state of this state within six (6) months after the taking of the same.

§ 42-31-3. Powers of commissioners.

Such commissioners may administer oaths and take depositions and affidavits to be used in this state; and may also take the acknowledgment of any deed or other instrument to be used or recorded in this state.

§ 42-31-4. Effectiveness of acts of commissioners.

All oaths administered by such commissioners, and all affidavits and depositions taken by them, and all acknowledgments aforesaid certified by them, shall be as effectual in law, to all intents and purposes, as if certified by any judge, justice of the peace, or notary public, within this state.

HOLIDAYS

§ 25-1-1. General holidays enumerated.

The first day of January (as New Year's day), the third Monday of January (as Dr. Martin Luther King, Jr.'s birthday), the third Monday of February (as Washington's birthday), the fourth day of May (as Rhode Island Independence day), the last Monday of May (as Memorial day), the fourth day of July (as Independence day), the second Monday of August (as Victory day), the first Monday of September (as Labor day), the second Monday of October (as Columbus day), the eleventh day of November (as Veterans day), the twenty-fifth day of December (as Christmas day), and each of said days in every year, or when either of the said days falls on the first day of the week, then the day following it, the Tuesday next after the first Monday in November in each year in which a general election of state officers is held (as election day), the first day of every week (commonly called Sunday), and such other days as the governor or general assembly of this state or the president or the congress of the United States shall appoint as holidays for any purpose, days of thanksgiving, or days of solemn fast, shall be holidays.

§ 25-1-2. Thanksgiving day.

The governor shall annually appoint a day of public thanksgiving, and shall announce the same by proclamation to the people of the state.

§ 25-1-3. Saturday bank closing—filing of resolution.

Any bank, savings bank, trust company, safe deposit company, building-loan association, national banking association or federal savings and loan association doing business within the state of Rhode Island or any branch or office of any such institution may remain closed on any Saturday or Saturdays upon the adoption of a resolution to close by the board of directors or the board of trustees thereof and upon filing a copy of the same as hereinafter required. Any such resolution shall be deemed effective for the purposes of this section and § 25-1-4 only when a copy thereof certified by the proper officer of such institution is filed in the office of the director of business regulation of this state, and any such resolution shall remain in full force and effect until a copy of a later resolution, certified in like manner, terminating any such prior resolution, is filed in such office of the director of business regulation.

§ 25-1-4. Effect of Saturday closing on rights and obligations.

Any Saturday upon which any such bank, savings bank, trust company, safe deposit company, building-loan association, national banking association or federal savings and loan association, or any branch or office thereof, shall remain closed pursuant to the provisions of §§ 25-1-3 and 25-1-4 shall, with respect to such closed institution, branch or office thereof, be a holiday for the purpose of chapter 3 of title 6A. If any such bank, savings bank, trust company, safe deposit company, building-loan association, national banking association or federal savings and loan association, or any branch or office thereof, shall close on any Saturday pursuant to the provisions of § 25-1-3, any act which would otherwise be required to be performed on any such Saturday at or by such institution, or any branch or office thereof, if such institution, branch or office thereof were not so closed, shall be performed on the next succeeding business day, and any act which would otherwise be authorized or permitted to be performed on any such Saturday at or by such institution, or any branch or office thereof, if such institution, branch or office thereof were not so closed, may be so performed on the next succeeding business day. No liability or loss of rights of any kind shall result from the failure to perform any of such acts on any such Saturday.

§ 25-1-5. Saturday closing of public offices.

The several administrative offices of state, city

and town governments may remain closed on any Saturday or Saturdays by executive order of the governor in the case of state administrative government and by the adoption of a resolution upon the part of the city and/or town council in the case of a city or town. Any Saturday upon which the several administrative offices of state, city and town governments, or any branch, division or independent agency thereof, shall remain closed pursuant to the provisions of this section shall, with respect to such closed administrative office, branch, division or independent agency thereof, be a holiday for the purpose of chapter 3 of title 6A. If any state, city and/or town administrative offices, or any branch, division or independent agency thereof, shall close on any Saturday pursuant to the provisions of this section, any act which would otherwise be required to be performed on any such Saturday at or by such administrative office, or any branch, division or independent agency thereof, if such administrative office, branch, division or independent agency thereof were not so closed, shall be so performed on the next succeeding business day, and any act which would otherwise be authorized or permitted to be performed on any such Saturday at or by such administrative office, or any branch, division or independent agency thereof, if such administrative office, branch, division or independent agency thereof were not so closed, may be so performed on the next succeeding business day. No liability or loss of rights of any kind shall result from the failure to perform any of such acts on any such Saturday.

SOUTH CAROLINA

NOTARIES PUBLIC

[S.C. Code Ann.]

§ 26-1-10. Appointment and term.

The Governor may appoint from the qualified electors as many notaries public throughout the State as the public good shall require, to hold their offices for a term of ten years. A commission shall be issued to each notary public so appointed and the record of such appointment shall be filed in the office of the Secretary of State. All commissions issued or renewed after July 1, 1967 shall be for the specified term. All commissions issued prior to July 1, 1967, unless renewed for the term herein provided, shall expire and terminate on January 1, 1970 for any person whose last name begins with A through K and on January 1, 1971 for any person whose last name begins with L through Z.

§ 26-1-20. Endorsement of application.

Each county legislative delegation shall determine whether the endorsement of notaries public must be by (1) one-half of the members of the legislative delegation representing that county in which the applicant resides or, (2) endorsement by the Senator and Representative in whose district the applicant resides, without other endorsers. Each county legislative delegation shall notify the Secretary of State in writing if it chooses to utilize method (2) within the individual county. If the county legislative delegation chooses to utilize method (2), the applicant, Senator, and Representative shall indicate their respective districts on the application provided to the Secretary of State. If the office of Senator or Representative from that district is vacant at the time the application is submitted, the notary public may be appointed upon the endorsement of a majority of the legislative delegation representing the county in which the applicant resides.

§ 26-1-30. Fees.

The fee for the issuance or renewal of a commission is twenty-five dollars, collected by the Secretary of State as other fees.

§ 26-1-40. Oath.

Every notary public shall take the oath of office prescribed by the Constitution, certified copies of which shall be recorded in the office of the Secretary of State.

§ 26-1-50. Enrollment of commission.

Every notary public shall, within fifteen days after he has been commissioned, exhibit his commission to the clerk of the court of the county in which he resides and be enrolled by the clerk.

§ 26-1-60. Seal of office; notary shall indicate date of expiration of commission.

Each notary public shall have a seal of office, which shall be affixed to his instruments of publications and to his protestations. He shall indicate below his signature the date of expiration of his commission. But the absence of such seal or date prior to and after May 30, 1968 shall not render his acts invalid if his official title be affixed thereto.

§ 26-1-70. Effect of change of name by notary.

Any notary public whose name is legally changed during his term of office may apply to the Secretary of State in such manner as may be prescribed by him, and the Secretary of State may change the name of the notary upon proper application and upon payment of a fee of ten dollars. The term expires at the same time as the original term.

§ 26-1-80. Jurisdiction.

The jurisdiction of notaries public shall extend throughout the State.

§ 26-1-90. Powers generally.

A notary public may administer oaths, take depositions, affidavits, protests for nonpayment of bonds, notes, drafts and bills of exchange, acknowledgments and proof of deeds and other instruments required by law to be acknowledged and renunciations of dower and perform all other acts provided by law to be performed by notaries public.

§ 26-1-95. False certification by notary.

A notary public who, in his official capacity, falsely certifies to affirming, swearing, or acknowledging of a person or his signature to an instrument, affidavit, or writing is guilty of a misdemeanor and, upon conviction, must be fined not more than two hundred dollars or imprisoned not more than thirty days. A notary public convicted under the provisions of this section shall forfeit his commission and shall not be issued another commission. The court in which the notary public is convicted shall notify the Secretary of State within ten days after conviction.

§ 26-1-100. No jurisdiction in criminal cases.

A notary public shall exercise no power or jurisdiction in criminal cases.

§ 26-1-110. Effect of employment of notary as attorney.

Any attorney at law who is a notary public may exercise all his powers as a notary notwithstanding the fact that he may be interested as counsel or attorney at law in any matter with respect to which he may so exercise any such power and may probate in any court in this State in which he may be counsel.

§ 26-1-120. Effect of status of notary as stockholder, director, officer or employee of corporation.

A notary public who is a stockholder, director, officer or employee of a corporation may take renunciation of dower in any written instrument, take the acknowledgment or the oath of a subscribing witness of any party to a written instrument executed to or by such corporation, administer an oath to any stockholder, director, officer, employee or agent of such corporation or protest for nonacceptance or nonpayment bills of exchange, drafts, checks, notes and other negotiable instruments which may be owned or held for collection by such corporation. But when a notary public is individually a party to an instrument it shall be unlawful for him to take the acknowledgment or probate to such instrument executed by or to a corporation of which he is a stockholder, director, officer or employee or to protest any such negotiable instrument owned or held for collection by such corporation.

FEES

§ 8-21-140. Fees of notaries public.

The fees of notaries public shall be as follows:

(1) For taking a deposition and swearing witnesses, twenty-five cents per copy sheet;

(2) For a duplicate of a deposition, protest and certificate, ten cents per copy sheet of one hundred words;

(3) For each attendance upon any person for proving a matter or thing and certifying the same, fifty cents;

(4) For every notarial certificate, with seal, fifty cents;

(5) For administering an oath for an affidavit, twenty-five cents;

(6) For taking a renunciation of dower or inheritance, one dollar; and

(7) For every protest, fifty cents, together with the cost of postage for transmitting notice thereof.

SAFE-DEPOSIT BOXES

§ 34-19-70. Opening box when rental one year in default.

If the rental due on a safe-deposit box has not been paid for one year, the lessor may send a notice by registered mail to the last known address of the lessee stating that the safe-deposit box will be opened and its contents stored at the expense of the lessee unless payment of the rental is made within thirty days. If the rental is not paid within thirty days from the mailing of the notice, the box may be opened in the presence of an officer, manager or assistant manager of the lessor and of a notary public who is not a director, officer, employee or stockholder of the lessor. The contents shall be sealed in a package by the notary public who shall write on the outside the name of the lessee and the date of the opening. The notary public shall execute a certificate reciting the name of the lessee, the date of the opening of the box and a list of its contents. The certificate shall be included in the package and a copy of the certificate shall be sent by registered mail to the last known address of the lessee. The package shall then be placed in the general vaults of the lessor at a rental not exceeding the rental previously charged for the box.

ACKNOWLEDGMENTS

§ 30-5-30. Prerequisites to recording.

Except as otherwise provided by statute, before any deed or other instrument in writing can be recorded in this State:

(1) The execution of the deed or other instrument must be first proved by the affidavit of a subscribing witness to the instrument, taken before some officer within this State competent to administer an oath. If the affidavit is taken without the limits of this State, it may be taken before:

(a) a commissioner appointed by dedimus issued by the clerk of the court of common pleas of the county in which the instrument is to be recorded,

(b) a commissioner of deeds of this State,

(c) a clerk of a court of record who shall make certificate of the deed or other instrument under his official seal,

(d) a justice of the peace who shall append to the certificate his official seal,

(e) a notary public who shall affix to the deed or other instrument his official seal within the State of his appointment, which is a sufficient authentication of his signature, residence, and official character,

(f) before a minister, ambassador, consul general, consul, or vice-consul, or consular agent of the United States of America, or

(g) in the case of any officer or enlisted man of the United States Army, Air Force, Navy, Marine Corps, or Coast Guard on active duty outside the State or any civilian employee of any such organization on active duty outside the continental confines of the United States, any commissioned officer of the Army, Air Force, Navy, Marine Corps, or Coast Guard, if the probating officer states his rank, branch, and organization;

(2) The Uniform Recognition of Acknowledgments Act must be complied with; or

(3) The person executing it shall submit an affidavit subscribed to before a person authorized to perform notarial acts herein or by the Uniform Recognition of Acknowledgments Act that the signature on the deed or other instrument is his signature and that the instrument was executed for the uses and purposes stated in the instrument.

§ 33-49-40. Acknowledgments.

No person who is authorized to take acknowledgments under the laws of this State shall be disqualified from taking acknowledgments of instruments executed in favor of a cooperative or to which it is a party by reason of being an officer, director or member of such cooperative.

Uniform Recognition of Acknowledgments Act

§ 26-3-10. Citation of chapter.

This chapter may be cited as the Uniform Recognition of Acknowledgments Acts.

§ 26-3-20. "Notarial acts" defined; persons by whom notarial acts may be performed outside State.

For the purposes of this chapter, *"notarial acts"* means acts which the laws and regulations of this

State authorized notaries public of this State to perform, including the administering of oaths and affirmations, taking proof of execution and acknowledgments of instruments, and attesting documents. Notarial acts may be performed outside this State for use in this State with the same effect as if performed by a notary public of this State by the following persons authorized pursuant to the laws and regulations of other governments in addition to any other person authorized by the laws and regulations of this State:

(1) A notary public authorized to perform notarial acts in the place in which the act is performed;

(2) A judge, clerk or deputy clerk of any court of record in the place in which the notarial act is performed;

(3) An officer of the foreign service of the United States, a consular agent or any other person authorized by regulation of the United States Department of State to perform notarial acts in the place in which the act is performed;

(4) A commissioned officer is active service with the Armed Forces of the United States and any other person authorized by regulation of the Armed Forces to perform notarial acts if the notarial act is performed for one of the following or his dependents: a merchant seaman of the United States, a member of the Armed Forces of the United States, or any other person serving with or accompanying the Armed Forces of the United States, and, further, such commissioned officers and other authorized persons, in the manner and under the conditions prescribed by this chapter, also may perform notarial acts inside this State for use in this State with the same effect as if performed by a notary public of this State;

(5) Any other person authorized to perform notarial acts in the place in which the act is performed.

§ 26-3-30. Proof of authority.

(a) If the notarial act is performed by any of the persons described in items (1) to (4), inclusive, of § 26-3-20, other than a person authorized to perform notarial acts by the laws or regulations of a foreign country, the signature, rank or title and serial number, if any, of the person are sufficient proof of the authority of a holder of that rank or title to perform the act. Further proof of his authority is not required.

(b) If the notarial act is performed by a person authorized by the laws or regulations of a foreign country to perform the act, there is sufficient proof of the authority of that person to act if:

(1) Either a foreign service officer of the United States resident in the country in which the act is performed or a diplomatic or consular officer of the foreign country resident in the United States certifies that a person holding that office is authorized to perform the act;

(2) The official seal of the person performing the notarial act is affixed to the document; or

(3) The title and indication of authority to perform notarial acts of the person appear either in a digest of foreign law or in a list customarily used as a source of such information.

(c) If the notarial act is performed by a person other than one described in subsections (a) and (b), there is sufficient proof of the authority of that person to act if the clerk of a court of record in the place in which the notarial act is performed certifies to the official character of that person and to his authority to perform the notarial act.

(d) The signature and title of the person performing the act are prima facie evidence that he is a person with the designated title and that the signature is genuine.

§ 26-3-40. What persons taking acknowledgment shall certify.

The person taking an acknowledgment shall certify that:

(1) The person acknowledging appeared before him and acknowledged he executed the instrument; and

(2) The person acknowledging was known to the person taking the acknowledgment or that the person taking the acknowledgment had satisfactory evidence that the person acknowledging was the person described in and who executed the instrument.

§ 26-3-50. Form of certification.

The form of a certificate of acknowledgment used by a person whose authority is recognized under § 26-3-20 shall be accepted in this State if:

(1) The certificate is in a form prescribed by the laws or regulations of this State;

(2) The certificate is in a form prescribed by the laws or regulations applicable in the place in which the acknowledgment is taken; or

(3) The certificate contains the words "acknowledged before me," or their substantial equivalent.

§ 26-3-60. "Acknowledged before me" defined.

The words *acknowledged before me* mean:

(1) That the person acknowledging appeared before the person taking the acknowledgment;

(2) That he acknowledged he executed the instrument;

(3) That, in the case of:

(a) A natural person, he executed the instrument for the purposes therein stated;

(b) A corporation, the officer or agent acknowledged he held the position or title set forth in the instrument and certificate, he signed the instrument on behalf of the corporation by proper authority, and the instrument was the act of the corporation for the purposes therein stated;

(c) A partnership, the partner or agent acknowledged he signed the instrument on behalf of the partnership by proper authority and he executed the instrument as the act of the partnership for the purposes therein stated;

(d) A person acknowledging as principal by an attorney in fact, he executed the instrument by proper authority as the act of the principal for the purposes therein stated;

(e) A person acknowledging as a public officer, trustee, administrator, guardian or other representative, he signed the instrument by proper authority and he executed the instrument in the capacity and for the purposes therein stated; and

(4) That the person taking the acknowledgment either knew or had satisfactory evidence that the person acknowledging was the person named in the instrument or certificate.

§ 26-3-70. Statutory short forms of acknowledgment.

The forms of acknowledgment set forth in this section may be used and are sufficient for their respective purposes under any law of this State. The forms shall be known as "Statutory Short Forms of Acknowledgment" and may be referred to by that name. The authorization of the forms in this section does not preclude the use of other forms.

(1) For an individual acting in his own right:
State of _____
County of _____
The foregoing instrument was acknowledged before me this (date) by (name of person acknowledged).
(Signature of Person Taking Acknowledgment)
(Title or Rank)
(Serial Number, if any)
(2) For a corporation:
State of _____
County of _____
The foregoing instrument was acknowledged before me this (date) by (name of officer or agent, title of officer or agent) of (name of corporation acknowledging) a (state or place of incorporation) corporation, on behalf of the corporation.
(Signature of Person Taking Acknowledgment)
(Title or Rank)
(Serial Number, if any)
(3) For a partnership:
State of _____
County of _____
The foregoing instrument was acknowledged be-

fore me this (date) by (name of acknowledging partner or agent), partner (or agent) on behalf of (name of partnership), a partnership.
(Signature of Person Taking Acknowledgment)
(Title or Rank)
(Serial Number, if any)
(4) For an individual acting as principal by an attorney in fact:
State of _____
County of _____
The foregoing instrument was acknowledged before me this (date) by (name of attorney in fact) as attorney in fact on behalf of (name of principal).
(Signature of Person Taking Acknowledgment)
(Title or Rank)
(Serial Number, if any)
(5) By any public officer, trustee or personal representative:
State of _____
County of _____
The foregoing instrument was acknowledged before me this (date) by (name and title of position).
(Signature of Person Taking Acknowledgment)
(Title or Rank)
(Serial Number, if any)

§ 26-3-80. Application of chapter.

A notarial act performed prior to May, 8, 1972 is not affected by this chapter. This chapter provides an additional method of proving notarial acts. Nothing in this chapter diminishes or invalidates the recognition accorded to notarial acts by other laws or regulations of this State.

§ 26-3-90. Construction.

This chapter shall be so interpreted as to make uniform the laws of those states which enact it.

DEPOSITIONS

[S.C.R. Civ. P.]

RULE 28. Persons before whom depositions may be taken; deposition in out of state actions.

28(a). Within the United States. Within any state or within a territory or insular possession subject to the jurisdiction of the United States, depositions shall be taken before an officer authorized to administer oaths by the laws of the United States or of the place where the examination is held, or before a person appointed by the court in which the action is pending. A person so appointed has power to administer oaths and take testimony. The term officer as used in Rules 30, 31 and 32 includes a person appointed by the court or designated by the parties under Rule 29.

28(b). In foreign countries. In a foreign country, depositions may be taken (1) on notice before a person authorized to administer oaths in the place in which the examination is held, either by the law thereof or by the law of the United States, or (2) before a person commissioned by the court, and a person so commissioned shall have the power by virtue of his commission to administer any necessary oath and take testimony, or (3) pursuant to a letter rogatory. A commission or a letter rogatory shall be issued on application and notice and on terms that are just and appropriate. It is not requisite to the issuance of a commission or a letter rogatory that the taking of the deposition in any other manner is impracticable or inconvenient; and both a commission and a letter rogatory may be issued in proper cases. A notice or commission may designate the person before whom the deposition is to be taken either by name or descriptive title. A letter rogatory may be addressed "To the Appropriate Authority in (here name the country)." Evidence obtained in response to a letter rogatory need not be excluded merely for the reason that it is not a verbatim transcript or that the testimony was not taken under oath or for any similar departure from the requirements for depositions taken within the United States under these rules.

28(c). Disqualification for interest. No deposition shall be taken before a person who is a relative or employee or attorney or counsel of any of the parties, or is a relative or employee of such attorney or counsel, or is financially interested in the action.

28(d). Depositions in out-of-state actions.

(1) When the deposition of a witness in South Carolina is to be taken in this State for use in an out-of-state action or proceeding, the clerk of court shall issue a subpoena, including a subpoena duces tecum, compelling the attendance of such witness at that deposition, pursuant to this rule, upon receipt of the filing fee set by Administrative Rule, and upon receipt of (Amended effective May 1, 1986);

(a) a certified copy of any mandate, writ, or commission issued by a court of record in any other state, territory, district, or foreign jurisdiction directing that such deposition be taken; or

(b) a certified copy of a notice or written agreement filed in a court of record in any other state, territory, district, or foreign jurisdiction directing that such deposition be taken.

(2) Such witness may be compelled to attend a deposition only in the county where he resides, where he is employed, or where he transacts his business in person.

(3) Such witness or a party may obtain a protective order pursuant to Rule 26(c) upon application

to the court in the county from which the subpoena is issued.

(4) If such witness fails to obey the subpoena or refuses to answer any question propounded upon oral examination, the provisions of Rule 37(a) and (b) shall apply, and the party requesting the deposition shall make application for such order to the court of the county from which the subpoena was issued.

(5) Such witness is entitled to the same compensation as provided to a witness pursuant to Rule or statute.

(6) The clerk of court, shall, upon receipt of the above described filing fee, file all papers received by him pursuant to this Rule.

LEGAL HOLIDAYS

[S.C. CODE ANN.]

§ 53-5-10. Legal holidays enumerated.

National Thanksgiving days, all general election days and also the first day of January, the nineteenth day of January, the third Monday in February (George Washington's birthday), the tenth day of May, the third day of June, the fourth day of July, the first Monday in September, the eleventh day of November and the twenty-fifth and twenty-sixth days of December in each year shall be legal holidays.

§ 53-5-20. Christmas Eve may be declared holiday for state employees.

The Governor of South Carolina is empowered to declare Christmas Eve of each year a holiday for state government employees.

§ 53-5-30. Certain Mondays declared holidays; effect on presentment of bills, notes and checks.

Whenever any of the legal holidays mentioned in §53-5-10 shall fall upon Sunday the Monday next following shall be deemed a public holiday for all the purposes aforesaid. But in such case all bills of exchange, checks and promissory notes which would otherwise be presentable for acceptance or payment on any such Monday shall be deemed to be presentable for acceptance or payment on the secular or business day next succeeding the holiday.

§ 53-5-40. Additional holidays for banks and cash depositories.

In addition to the holidays enumerated in §§ 53-5-10 to 53-5-30 the Governor, at the request of the chairman of the State Board of Bank Control and the president of the South Carolina Bankers' Association, may declare any other day or days of the year legal holidays for banks and cash depositories.

§ 53-5-50. Additional holidays for savings and loan and building and loan associations in case of special events.

In addition to the holidays enumerated in §§ 53-5-10 to 53-5-30, the Government at the request of the President of the South Carolina Savings and Loan League and the Chairman of the State Board of Bank Control may, in case of special events, declare any other day or days of the year legal holidays for savings and loan and building and loan associations.

§ 53-5-60. All first Mondays in month shall be business days for certain purposes.

Notwithstanding the provisions of §§ 53-5-10 and 53-5-30, each first Monday in any month shall be a legal day for judicial or sheriff's sales or the transaction of any legal business.

§ 53-5-70. Banks and cash depositories may do business on any day except Sunday.

Any business transacted by any bank or case depository on any day of the year other than Sunday shall be legal.

§ 53-5-80. Time at which commercial paper or other security maturing on Sunday or legal holiday shall be collectible.

Any commercial paper or other security which shall mature and become payable and collectible on Sunday or on any legal holiday shall be deemed and taken and treated as maturing and becoming payable and collectible on the next day thereafter if such next day shall not be Sunday or a legal holiday, in which latter event it shall be deemed, taken and treated as due, maturing and collectible on the first day thereafter which is not a Sunday or a legal holiday.

§ 53-5-90. Banks, building and loan associations and other financial institutions may close one additional day a week.

Any commercial bank, building and loan association, savings and loan association or cash depository doing business in the State may, in addition to Sunday and such legal holidays as are now provided by statute, remain closed one day of each week as its board of directors may from time to time determine.

§ 53-5-100. Days of closing under § 53-5-90 constitute legal holidays.

Any day on which any institution referred to in § 53-5-90 shall remain closed as permitted therein shall, as to such institution, constitute a legal holiday and any act authorized, required or permitted to be performed at, by, or with respect to any such institution on a day when it is closed may be performed on the next business day and no liability or loss of any rights of any kind shall result from such delay.

SOUTH DAKOTA

NOTARIES PUBLIC

[S.D. CODIFIED LAWS ANN.]

§ **18-1-1.** Appointment by secretary of state—term of office—authority.

The secretary of state shall appoint one or more notaries public, who shall hold their office for eight years unless sooner removed by the secretary of state. Each notary may, anywhere in this state, administer oaths and perform all other duties required of him by law.

§ **18-1-2.** Oath and bond of notary.

Each notary public before entering on the duties of his office, shall take an oath as required by § 3-1-5, and shall give a bond to this state, to be approved by the attorney general with one or more sureties, in the penal sum of five hundred dollars, conditioned for the faithful discharge of the duties of his office.

§ **18-1-3.** Seal, oath and bond filed with secretary of state.

Every notary public before entering upon the duties of his office, shall provide an official seal and file impression of the same, together with his oath and bond, in the office of the secretary of state.

§ **18-1-3.1.** Requirements of notary public seal—commission expiration date required on notarized document.

Any notary public shall have a seal which shall be used for the purpose of acknowledging documents. The seal shall be a type approved by the secretary of state and shall contain at least the following:

(1) The notary's name;
(2) The words "South Dakota";
(3) The words "notary public"; and
(4) A border surrounding the imprint.

In addition, rubber stamp seals shall have the word "seal."

If a seal is used by a notary public, he shall write, or print by a device made for such printing, below the seal's imprint or print and if not provided by the form, the words "my commission expires" and shall provide a date therefor. Any such device shall be separate and apart from the seal. Any notary public using a seal with the commission expiration date included as part of the imprint, prior to the effective date of this section, may use such seal until his current commission expires.

§ **18-1-4.** Issuance of commission—posting—records maintained by secretary of state.

The secretary of state shall issue a commission to each notary public which shall be posted in a conspicuous place in the notary's office for public inspection. The secretary of state shall keep in his office a record of such appointments and the date of their expiration.

§ **18-1-7.** Notarial acts valid despite notary's agency for party to transaction.

A notary public who is personally interested directly or indirectly, or as a stockholder, officer, agent, attorney, or employee of any person or party to any transaction concerning which he is exercising any function of his office as such notary public, may make any certificates, take any acknowledgments, administer any oaths or do any other official acts as such notary public with the same legal force and effect as if he had no such interest except that he cannot do any of such things in connection with any instrument which shows upon its face that he is a principal party thereto.

§ **18-1-9.** Fee chargeable by notary.

Notaries public are entitled to charge and receive

a fee not to exceed two dollars for each instrument notarized.

§ 18-1-10. Faith and credit to notarial acts.

Full faith and credit shall be given to all the protestations, attestations, and other instruments of publication, of all notaries public now in office or hereafter to be appointed under the provisions of this chapter.

§ 18-1-11. Notarizing without appearance by parties as misdemeanor.

It is a Class 2 misdemeanor for any notary public to affix his official signature to documents when the parties have not appeared before him.

§ 18-1-12. Acting after expiration of term or disqualification as misdemeanor.

It is a Class 2 misdemeanor for any notary public to exercise the duties of his office after the expiration of his commission or when he is otherwise disqualified.

§ 18-1-13. Removal of notary from office for violation.

Any notary public who commits an act which is designated as a Class 2 misdemeanor in this chapter shall be removed from office by the secretary of state.

§ 18-1-14. Notice to notary of revocation of commission.

Should the commission of any notary public be revoked, the secretary of state shall immediately notify such person by mail.

ADDITIONAL AUTHORITY

§ 18-3-1. Officers authorized to administer oaths.

The following officers are authorized to administer oaths:

(1) Supreme Court judges, circuit judges, magistrates, notaries public, and the clerk and deputy clerk of the Supreme Court, within the state;

(2) Members of the Legislature, while acting as a member of any committee thereof, while examining persons before such committee;

(4) [sic] The clerk of courts, the county auditor, the county treasurer, the register of deeds, and the deputy of each, within the county;

(5) Mayors, city auditors, deputy city auditors, town and township clerks, within their respective cities, towns, and townships;

(6) Each sheriff and his deputies in cases where they are authorized by law to select commissioners or appraisers, or to impanel juries for the view or appraisement of property, or are directed as an official duty to have property appraised, or take the answer of garnishees;

(7) Other officers in cases specifically provided by law.

§ 18-3-5. Affirmation in lieu of oath.

Persons conscientiously opposed to swearing may affirm, and shall be subject to the penalties of perjury as in case of swearing.

FEES

§ 1-8-10. Fees of secretary of state enumerated—collection.

Except as otherwise provided the secretary of state shall charge the following fees for services performed in his office and shall collect the same in advance:

* * *

(5) For filing application, bond, and issuing commission of notary public, five dollars;

* * *

OFFENSES

§ 3-1-9. Falsely pretending to be public officer as misdemeanor.

Every person who shall falsely assume or pretend to be any public executive or administrative officer, or who shall knowingly take upon himself to act as such, or to require any person to act as such, or assist him in any matter pertaining to such office, is guilty of a Class 1 misdemeanor.

§ 22-11-8. Impersonation of officer causing injury or fraud as misdemeanor.

Any person who intentionally impersonates any public officer or employee, civil or military, or any fire fighter or any person having special authority by law to perform any act affecting the rights or interests of another, or assumes, without authority, any uniform or badge by which such officer, employee, fire fighter or person is usually distinguished, and in such assumed character does any act where another person is injured or defrauded, is guilty of a Class 2 misdemeanor.

§ 22-39-36. Forgery defined—felony.

Any person who, with intent to defraud, falsely makes, completes or alters a written instrument of any kind, or passes such an instrument is guilty of forgery. Forgery is a Class 5 felony.

ACKNOWLEDGMENTS

§ 18-4-1. Officers authorized to take proof or acknowledgment within state.

The proof or acknowledgment of an instrument may be made at any place within this state before a justice or the clerk of the Supreme Court or a notary public.

§ 18-4-2. Officers authorized to take proof or acknowledgment within circuit, county or city.

The proof or acknowledgment of an instrument may be made in this state within the judicial circuit, county, or city for which the officer was elected or appointed, before either:

(1) A judge of the circuit court;
(2) A clerk of the circuit court;
(3) A county auditor;
(4) A register of deeds;
(5) A mayor of a city;
(6) A magistrate; or
(7) A United States magistrate.

§ 18-4-3. Indian agents authorized to take acknowledgment or proof in Indian country—recording of certificate of appointment.

Indian agents or superintendents are authorized to take acknowledgments or proofs of deeds or other instruments in writing, in Indian country, and acknowledgments or proof so taken shall have the same force and effect as if taken before a notary public. To qualify for taking such acknowledgments or proofs, such Indian agent or superintendent shall file for record in the office of the register of deeds of the county in which he is stationed, or the county to which said county is attached for judicial purposes, a certificate signed by the secretary of the interior of the United States showing his appointment and authority as such Indian agent or superintendent.

§ 18-4-4. Officers authorized to take proof or acknowledgment within United States.

The proof or acknowledgment of an instrument may be made without the state, but within the United States, and within the jurisdiction of the officer, before either:

(1) A justice, judge, or clerk of any court of record of the United States;
(2) A justice, judge, or clerk of any court of record of any state or territory;
(3) A notary public;
(4) Any officer of the state or territory where the acknowledgment is made, authorized by its laws to take such proof or acknowledgment; or
(5) A commissioner appointed for the purpose by the Governor of this state.

§ 18-4-5. Officers authorized to take proof or acknowledgment in foreign countries.

The proof or acknowledgment of an instrument may be made without the United States, before either:

(1) An ambassador, a minister, commissioner, or charge d'affaires of the United States, resident and accredited in the country where the proof or acknowledgment is made;
(2) A consul, vice consul, or consular agent of the United States, resident in the country where the proof or acknowledgment is made;
(3) A judge, clerk, register, or commissioner of a court of record of the country where the proof or acknowledgment is made;
(4) A notary public of such country;
(5) An officer authorized by the laws of the country where the proof of acknowledgment is taken, to take proof or acknowledgment; or
(6) When any of the officers mentioned in this chapter are authorized to appoint a deputy, the acknowledgment or proof may be taken before such deputy.

All proofs or acknowledgments heretofore taken according to the provisions of this section are hereby declared to be sufficiently authenticated and to be entitled to record, and any such record hereafter made shall be notice of the contents of the instrument so recorded.

§ 18-4-6. Acknowledgment before commissioned officer of armed forces—place of execution need not be shown.

In addition to the acknowledgment of instruments in the manner and form and as otherwise authorized by the laws of South Dakota, any person serving in or with the armed forces of the United States may acknowledge the execution of an instrument, wherever located, before any commissioned officer in active service of the armed forces of the United States with the rank of second lieutenant or higher in the army, air force or marine corps, or ensign or higher in the navy or United States coast guard. The instrument shall not be rendered invalid by the failure to state therein the place of execution or acknowledgment.

§ 18-4-7. Authentication of military certificate not required—form of certificate attached.

No authentication of the officer's certificate of acknowledgment taken pursuant to § 18-4-6 shall be required but the officer taking the acknowledgment shall endorse thereon or attach thereto a certificate substantially in the following form:

On this the _____ day of _____, 19__, before me _____, the undersigned officer personally appeared _____, known to me (or satisfactorily proven) to be serving in or with the armed forces of the United States and to be the person whose name is subscribed to the within instrument and acknowledged that __ he __ executed the same for the purposes therein contained. And the undersigned does further certify that he is at the date of this certificate a commissioned officer of the rank stated below and is in the active service of the armed forces of the United States.

_____
Signature of officer.

_____
Rank of officer and command to which attached.

§ 18-4-10. Identity of person making acknowledgment to be known or proved to officer.

The acknowledgment of an instrument must not be taken unless the officer taking it knows or has satisfactory evidence on the oath or affirmation of a credible witness, that the person making such acknowledgment is the individual who is described in and who executed the instrument; or, if executed by a corporation, that the person making such acknowledgment is an officer of the corporation authorized to execute the instrument.

§ 18-4-11. Certificate of officer taking acknowledgment to be attached.

An officer taking the acknowledgment of an instrument must endorse thereon or attach thereto a certificate substantially in the forms prescribed in §§ 18-4-12 to 18-4-15, inclusive.

§ 18-4-12. Form of general certificate of acknowledgment.

The certificate of acknowledgment of an instrument unless it is otherwise in this chapter provided must be substantially in the following form:

Territory of _____ or State of _____
County of _____ ss

On this _____ day of _____, in the year _____, before me personally appeared _____, known to me (or proved to me on the oath of _____) to be the person who is described in, and who executed the within instrument and acknowledged to me that he (or they) executed the same.

§ 18-4-13. Form of certificate of corporate acknowledgment.

The certificate of acknowledgment of an instrument executed by a corporation must be substantially in the following form:

Territory of _____ or State of _____
County of _____ ss
On this _____ day of _____, in the year _____, before me personally appeared _____, known to me (or proved to me on the oath of _____) to be the _____ of the corporation that is described in and that executed the within instrument and acknowledged to me that such corporation executed the same.

§ 18-4-14. Form of certificate of acknowledgment by attorney.

The certificate of acknowledgment by an attorney in fact must be substantially in the following form:

Territory of _____ or State of _____
County of _____ ss
On this _____ day of _____, in the year _____, before me personally appeared _____, known to me (or proved to me on the oath of _____) to be the person who is described in and whose name is subscribed to the within instrument as the attorney in fact of _____, and acknowledged to me that he subscribed the name of _____ thereto as principal and his own name as attorney in fact.

§ 18-4-15. Form of certificate of acknowledgment by deputy sheriff.

The certificate of acknowledgment by any deputy sheriff of South Dakota must be substantially in the following form:
State of South Dakota,

ss

County of _____

On this _____ day of _____, in the year _____, before me personally appeared _____, known to me (or proved to me on the oath of _____) to be the person who is described in and whose name is subscribed to the within instrument as deputy sheriff of said county and acknowledged to me that he subscribed the name of _____ thereto as sheriff of said county and his own name as deputy sheriff.

§ 18-4-16. Fees chargeable for acknowledgments—violation as petty offense.

Officers authorized by law to take and certify acknowledgment of deeds and other instruments are entitled to charge and receive twenty-five cents each therefor, and for administering oaths and certifying the same, ten cents. A violation of this section is a petty offense.

§ 18-4-17. Means of proving instrument not acknowledged.

Proof of the execution of an instrument, when not acknowledged, may be made either:

(1) By the party executing it, or either of them;

(2) By a subscribing witness; or

(3) By other witnesses, in cases mentioned in §§ 18-4-19 and 18-4-20, relating to proof of handwriting.

§ 18-4-18. Proof of instrument by subscribing witness.

If proof of the execution of an instrument is made by a subscribing witness, such witness must be personally known to the officer taking the proof to be the person whose name is subscribed to the instrument as a witness or must be proved to be such by the oath of a credible witness. The subscribing witness must prove that the person whose name is subscribed to the instrument as a party is the person described in it and that such person executed it and that the witness subscribed his name thereto as a witness.

§ 18-4-19. Circumstances permitting proof of instrument by handwriting.

The execution of an instrument may be established by proof of the handwriting of the party and of a subscribing witness, if there is one, in the following cases:

(1) When the parties and all the subscribing witnesses are dead;

(2) When the parties and all the subscribing witnesses are non-residents of the state;

(3) When the place of their residence is unknown to the party desiring the proof and cannot be ascertained by the exercise of due diligence;

(4) When the subscribing witness conceals himself or cannot be found by the officer by the exercise of due diligence in attempting to serve the subpoena or attachment; or

(5) In case of the continued failure or refusal of the witness to testify for the space of one hour after his appearance.

§ 18-4-20. Facts to be established for proof by handwriting.

The evidence taken under § 18-4-19 must satisfactorily prove to the officer the following facts:

(1) The existence of one or more of the conditions mentioned therein;

(2) That the witness testifying knew the person whose name purports to be subscribed to the instrument as a party and is well acquainted with his signature and that it is genuine;

(3) That the witness testifying personally knew the person who subscribed the instrument as a witness and is well acquainted with his signature and that it is genuine; and

(4) The place of residence of the witness.

§ 18-4-21. Powers of officers authorized to take proof of instruments.

Officers authorized to take the proof of instruments are authorized in such proceedings:

(1) To administer oaths or affirmations;

(2) To employ and swear interpreters;

(3) To issue subpoenas and to punish for contempt as provided in title 19 in regard to the means of producing witnesses.

§ 18-4-22. Contents of certificate of officer taking proof of instrument.

An officer taking proof of the execution of an instrument must in his certificate endorsed thereon or attached thereto set forth all the matters required by law to be done or known by him or proved before him on the proceeding, together with the names of all the witnesses examined before him, their places of residence respectively, and the substance of their evidence.

§ 18-4-23. Authentication of certificates of acknowledgment or proof.

Officers taking and certifying acknowledgments or proof of instruments for record must authenticate their certificates by affixing thereto their signatures, followed by the names of their offices; also their seals of office, if by the laws of the state, territory, or country where the acknowledgment or proof is taken or by authority of which they are acting, they are required to have official seals. Judges and clerks of courts of record must authenticate their certificates as aforesaid by affixing thereto the seal of the proper court; and mayors of cities, by the seal thereof.

§ 18-4-24. Clerk's certificate to accompany proof or acknowledgment taken by magistrate.

The certificate of proof or acknowledgment, if made before a magistrate, when used in any county other than that in which he resides, must be accompanied by a certificate under the hand and seal of the clerk of courts of the county in which the magistrate resides, setting forth that such magistrate at the time of taking such proof or acknowledgment was authorized to take the same, and that the clerk is acquainted with his handwriting and believes that the signature to the original certificate is genuine.

§ 18-4-25. False certification of acknowledgment or proof as forgery.

If any officer authorized to take the acknowledgment or proof of any conveyance of real property or of any other instrument which by law may be recorded, knowingly and falsely certifies that any such conveyance or instrument was acknowledged by any party thereto or was proved by any subscribing witness, when in truth such conveyance or instrument was not acknowledged or proved as certified, he is guilty of forgery.

Uniform Acknowledgment Law

§ 18-5-1. Acknowledgment permitted under chapter or other law.

Any instrument may be acknowledged in the manner and form now provided by the laws of this state, or as provided by this chapter.

§ 18-5-2. Officers permitted to take acknowledgment within state.

The acknowledgment of any instrument may be made in this state before:
(1) A judge of the circuit court;
(2) A clerk or deputy clerk of the circuit court;
(3) A register of deeds;
(4) A notary public; or
(5) A magistrate.

§ 18-5-3. Officers permitted to take acknowledgment within United States.

The acknowledgment of any instrument may be made without the state but within the United States or a territory or insular possession of the United States or the District of Columbia or the Philippine Islands and within the jurisdiction of the officer, before:
(1) A clerk or deputy clerk of any federal court;
(2) A clerk or deputy clerk of any court of record of any state or other jurisdiction;
(3) A notary public;
(4) A commissioner of deeds.

§ 18-5-4. Officers permitted to take acknowledgment in foreign country.

The acknowledgment of any instrument may be made without the United States before:
(1) An ambassador, minister, charge d'affaires, counselor to or secretary of a legation, consul general, consul, vice consul, commercial attache, or consular agent of the United States accredited to the country where the acknowledgment is made.
(2) A notary public of the country where the acknowledgment is made.
(3) A judge or clerk of a court of record of the country where the acknowledgment is made.

§ 18-5-5. Identity of person making acknowledgment to be known or proved to officer.

The officer taking the acknowledgment shall know or have satisfactory evidence that the person making the acknowledgment is the person described in and who executed the instrument.

§ 18-5-6. Acknowledgment by married person.

An acknowledgment of a married person may be made in the same form as an unmarried person.

§ 18-5-7. Officer taking acknowledgment to endorse or attach certificate.

An officer taking the acknowledgment shall endorse thereon or attach thereto a certificate substantially in one of the forms in §§ 18-5-8 to 18-5-12, inclusive.

§ 18-5-8. Form of certificates of acknowledgment by individual.

The form for certificate of acknowledgment by individuals is as follows: State of _____ County of _____
On this the _____ day of _____,

19___, before me, _____, the undersigned officer, personally appeared _____, known to me or satisfactorily proven to be the person whose name _____ subscribed to the within instrument and acknowledged that ___ he ___ executed the same for the purposes therein contained.

In witness whereof I hereunto set my hand and official seal.

_____

Title of officer.

§ 18-5-9. Form of certificate of corporate acknowledgment.

The form for certificate of acknowledgment by a corporation is as follows: State of _____ County of _____

On this the _____ day of _____, 19___, before me, _____, the undersigned officer, personally appeared _____, who acknowledged himself to be the _____ of _____, a corporation, and that he as such _____ being authorized so to do, executed the foregoing instrument for the purposes therein contained, by signing the name of the corporation by himself as _____.

In witness whereof I hereunto set my hand and official seal.

_____

Title of officer.

§ 18-5-10. Form of certificate of acknowledgment by attorney.

The form for certificate of acknowledgment by an attorney in fact is as follows: State of _____ County of _____

On this the _____ day of _____, 19___, before me, _____, the undersigned officer, personally appeared _____, known to me or satisfactorily proven to be the person whose name is subscribed as attorney in fact for _____, and acknowledged that he executed the same as the act of his principal for the purposes therein contained.

In witness whereof I hereunto set my hand and official seal.

_____

Title of officer.

§ 18-5-11. Form of certificate of acknowledgment by public officer or fiduciary.

The form for certificate of acknowledgment by any public officer or deputy thereof, or by any trustee, administrator, guardian or executor is as follows: State of _____ County of _____

On this the _____ day of _____, 19___, before me, _____, the undersigned officer, personally appeared _____, of the state, county or city as the case may be of _____, known to me or satisfactorily proven to be the person described in the foregoing instrument, and acknowledged that he executed the same in the capacity therein stated and for the purposes therein contained.

In witness whereof I hereunto set my hand and official seal.

_____

Title of officer.

§ 18-5-12. Form of certificate of acknowledgment by partner.

The form for certificate of acknowledgment by a partner is as follows: State of _____ County of _____

On this the _____ day of _____, 19___, before me, _____, the undersigned officer, personally appeared _____, who acknowledged himself to be one of the partners of _____, a partnership, and that he, as such partner, being authorized so to do, executed the foregoing instrument for the purposes therein contained, by signing the name of the partnership by himself as partner.

In witness whereof I hereunto set my hand and official seal.

_____

Title of officer.

§ 18-5-13. Signature of certificate by office—endorsement and seal—effect of failure to endorse—facsimile on fidelity or surety bonds.

The certificate of the acknowledging officer shall be completed by his signature and immediately following his signature and immediately preceding his official description, he shall endorse thereon his name with a typewriter or print the same legibly with a stamp or with pen and ink, his official seal, if he has one, the title of his office, and if he is a notary public, the date his commission expires. Failure of an acknowledging officer to endorse his name on an instrument as required herein shall not render such instrument invalid, but a recording officer may refuse to accept such instrument for record until such endorsement is made.

Notwithstanding any provision in this chapter, a facsimile of the original signature and notarization may be used in lieu of an original signature when acknowledging a fidelity or surety bond in a form as required herein.

§ 18-5-14. Authentication not required.

If the acknowledgment is taken within this state or is made without the United States by an officer of the United States no authentication shall be necessary.

§ 18-5-15. Acknowledgment recognized if valid where executed.

Notwithstanding any provision in this chapter contained the acknowledgment of any instrument without this state in compliance with the manner and form prescribed by the laws of the place of its execution, if in a state, a territory or insular possession of the United States, or in the District of Columbia, or in the Philippine Islands, verified by the official seal of the officer before whom it is acknowledged, shall have the same effect as an acknowledgment in the manner and form prescribed by the laws of this state for instruments executed within this state.

§ 18-5-16. Prior acknowledgments not affected by chapter.

No acknowledgment taken prior to July 1, 1941 shall be affected by anything contained in this chapter.

§ 18-5-17. Uniformity of interpretation of chapter.

This chapter shall be so interpreted and construed as to made uniform the laws of those states which enact it.

§ 18-5-18. Citation of chapter.

This chapter may be cited as the Uniform Acknowledgment Act.

DEPOSITIONS

[S.D. R. Civ. P. (Circuit Courts)]

RULE 15-6-28. Persons before whom depositions may be taken.

15-6-28(a). Taking depositions within the United States. Within the United States or within a territory or insular possession subject to the jurisdiction of the United States, depositions shall be taken before an officer authorized to administer oaths by the laws of this state, the United States or of the place where the examination is held, or before a person appointed by the court in which the action is pending. A person so appointed has power to administer oaths and take testimony. The term officer as used in §§ 15-6-30, 15-6-31 and 15-6-32 includes a person appointed by the court or designated by the parties under § 15-6-29.

15-6-28(b). Taking depositions in foreign countries. In a foreign country, depositions may be taken

(1) on notice before a person authorized to administer oaths in the place in which the examination is held, either by the law thereof or by the law of the United States, or

(2) before a person commissioned by the court, and a person so commissioned shall have the power by virtue of his commission to administer any necessary oath and take testimony, or

(3) pursuant to a letter rogatory.

A commission or a letter rogatory shall be issued on application and notice and on terms that are just and appropriate. It is not requisite to the issuance of a commission or a letter rogatory that the taking of the deposition in any other manner is impracticable or inconvenient; and both a commission and a letter rogatory may be issued in proper cases. A notice or commission may designate the person before whom the deposition is to be taken either by name or descriptive title. A letter rogatory may be addressed "To the Appropriate Authority in (here name the country)." Evidence obtained in response to a letter rogatory need not be excluded merely for the reason that it is not a verbatim transcript or that the testimony was not taken under oath or for any similar departure from the requirements for depositions taken within the United States under this chapter.

15-6-28(c). Disqualification to take deposition for interest. No deposition shall be taken before a person who is a relative or employee or attorney or counsel of any of the parties, or is a relative or employee of such attorney or counsel, or is financially interested in the action.

[S.D. Codified Laws Ann.]

§ 19-3-1. Means of testimony enumerated.

The testimony of witnesses is taken in three modes:
(1) By affidavit;
(2) By deposition;
(3) By oral examination.

§ 19-3-2. Affidavit defined.

An affidavit is a written declaration under oath made without notice to the adverse party.

§ 19-3-3. Deposition defined.

A deposition is a written declaration under oath made upon a notice to the adverse party for the purpose of enabling him to attend and cross-examine; or upon written interrogatories.

§ 19-3-7. Interpreter for witness unable to communicate in English—compensation.

When a witness cannot communicate or understand the English language the court shall procure and appoint a disinterested interpreter or translator for him who shall be compensated for those services as the court shall certify to be reasonable and just, to be paid and collected as other costs.

COMMISSIONERS

[S.D. Codified Laws Ann.]

§ 18-2-1. Appointment by governor—tenure—authority to take acknowledgment and proof.

The Governor shall have power to appoint one or more commissioners in any state of the United States or any of the territories belonging to the United States, who shall continue in office during the pleasure of the Governor and shall have authority to take acknowledgment and proof of the execution of any deed or other conveyance, or lease of any lands lying in this state, and of any contract, letter of attorney, or any other writing under seal or not, to be used or recorded in this state.

§ 18-2-2. Official seal of commissioner—contents.

Each commissioner appointed pursuant to § 18-2-1 shall have an official seal on which shall be engraved the words "Commissioner of South Dakota," with his surname at length and at least the initials of his Christian name; also the name of the state or territory in which he has been commissioned to act, which seal must be so engraved as to made a clear impression.

§ 18-2-3. Oath of office—filing of oath and seal with secretary of state.

Every such commissioner, before performing any duty or exercising any power by virtue of his appointment, must take and subscribe an oath or affirmation before some judge or clerk of some court of record having a seal of the state or territory in which such commissioner shall reside, well and faithfully to execute and perform all the duties of such commissioner under and by virtue of the laws of the state of South Dakota, with a description

and impression of his seal of office to be filed in the office of the secretary of this state.

§ 18-2-4. Administration of oaths by commissioner—depositions—validity.

Every commissioner appointed as mentioned in § 18-2-1 shall have power to adminster any oath which may be lawfully required in this state to any person willing to take the same, and to take and duly certify all depositions to be used in any of the courts of this state in conformity to the laws thereof, either on interrogatories proposed under a commission from any court in this state or by consent of the parties, or on legal notice given to the opposite party; and all such acts shall be as valid as if done and certified to according to law by a proper officer in this state.

§ 18-2-5. Force and effect of acknowledgments and proofs taken.

All acknowledgments and proofs as provided in § 18-2-1, taken according to the laws of this state and certified to by such commissioner under his seal of office and annexed to or endorsed upon such instrument, shall have the same force and effect as if the same had been taken before any officer authorized to perform such acts in this state.

LEGAL HOLIDAYS

§ 1-5-1. Holidays enumerated.

The first day of every week, known as Sunday; the first day of January, commonly known as New Year's Day; the third Monday in February, the anniversary of the birthdays of Lincoln and Washington; the last Monday of May, commonly known as Memorial Day; the fourth day of July, commonly known as Independence Day; the first Monday in September, commonly known as Labor Day; the second Monday in October, commonly known as Pioneer's Day; the eleventh day of November, known as Veterans' Day; the fourth Thursday in November, commonly known as Thanksgiving Day; and the twenty-fifth day of December, commonly known as Christmas Day; and every day appointed by the President of the United States, or by the Governor of this state for a public fast, thanksgiving, or holiday shall be observed in this state as a legal holiday.

If the fourth day of July, the first day of January, the eleventh day of November or the twenty-fifth of December falls upon a Sunday, the Monday following is a legal holiday and shall be so observed; and if any such day falls upon a Saturday, the preceding Friday is a legal holiday and shall be so observed.

§ 1-5-1.1. Martin Luther King, Jr. Day established.

The third Monday in January, to be known as Martin Luther King, Jr. Day shall be observed in this state as a legal holiday. Martin Luther King, Jr. Day is dedicated to the remembrance of Dr. Martin Luther King, Jr. and to the observance and appreciation of the various ethnic minorities who have contributed so much to the state and nation.

§ 1-5-1.2. Native Americans' Day established.

The second Monday in October to be known as Native Americans' Day, shall be observed in this state as a legal holiday. Native Americans' Day is dedicated to the remembrance of the great Native American leaders who contributed so much to the history of our state.

§ 1-5-2. Business and official acts permitted on holidays.

Any public or private business may be transacted or legal process or notices of any kind may be served or published on any of said days or next succeeding days designated herein as holidays, excepting Sundays, provided, that for good cause, a judge in whose court an action has been or is about to be brought, may endorse upon any process or notice permission to serve the same on Sunday, and if so endorsed, service thereof on Sunday shall be valid.

TENNESSEE

NOTARIES PUBLIC

[TENN. CODE ANN.]

§ 8-16-101. Election—residence requirement.

(a) There shall be elected by the members of the county legislative body as many notaries public for their county as they may deem necessary. All notaries must be residents of the county, or have their principal place of business in the county, from which they were elected. If an individual has his principal place of business in any county in the state of Tennessee he shall be eligible for election as a notary in that county, although he may reside in a state other than Tennessee.

(b) Nothing contained within the provisions of § 5-5-102(c)(2), or any other law, shall be construed to prohibit a member of a county legislative body from also serving as a notary public, provided such member complies with the requirements established within this part.

§ 8-16-102. Commission.

All notaries shall be commissioned by the governor.

§ 8-16-103. Term of office.

The term of office of notaries public shall be four (4) years, such term to begin on the date of the issuance of their commissions by the governor.

§ 8-16-104. Surety bond.

(a) Every notary public, before entering upon the duties of his office, shall give bond executed by some surety company authorized to do business in Tennessee as surety, or with two (2) or more good sureties, to be approved by the county legislative body, in the penalty of five thousand dollars ($5,000), payable to the state of Tennessee, conditioned for the faithful discharge of his duties. The bond shall be filed in the office of the county clerk in the county where elected.

(b)(1) Provided that in counties of more than six hundred thousand (600,000) population according to the 1980 federal census or any subsequent federal census, the amount of the above bond shall be ten thousand dollars ($10,000). Provided, further, that such bond requirement shall only apply to notaries in such counties upon the issuance of their commissions for terms of office which begin after this subsection becomes effective upon being approved as provided in subdivision (b)(2).

(2) This subsection shall have no effect unless it is approved by a two-thirds (2/3) vote of the county legislative body of any county to which it may apply. Its approval or nonapproval shall be proclaimed by the presiding officer of the county legislative body and certified by him to the secretary of state.

§ 8-16-105. Oath of office.

He shall also take and subscribe, before the county clerk or his deputy, within his county, an oath to support the constitutions of this state and of the United States, and an oath that he will, without favor or partiality, honestly, faithfully, and diligently discharge the duties of notary public.

§ 8-16-106. Payment of fee—issuance of commission.

It shall be the duty of any person elected a notary public, who desires to qualify for such office, to pay to the county clerk of the county in which he resides or has his principal place of business and was elected, the fee required to be paid into the office of the secretary of state for the issuance of a commission to a notary public. Thereupon, it shall be the duty of the county clerk to certify his election to the secretary of state and forward to the latter the fee. It shall be the duty of the secretary of state, upon receipt of the certificate and fee, to forward such commission to the county clerk, when the same shall have been issued by the governor, and the county clerk shall promptly notify the person to whom such commission is issued that the same has been received in his office. The county clerk shall be entitled to a fee of seven dollars ($7.00), due with payment of the fee to the secretary of state, for the services performed according to this section.

§ 8-16-107. Delivery of commission—clerk's record.

The county clerk shall not deliver the commission until the person elected shall have taken the oath and executed the bond, as required. The county clerk shall make a record of the date of the issuance and the expiration of the commission, noting the same on the bond executed by the notary public and also in the minute entry showing his qualification as such notary public.

§ 8-16-108. Location of office.

Every notary public shall keep his office in the county in which he shall be appointed.

§ 8-16-109. Qualification in other counties.

A notary public elected and commissioned for any county in the state, upon filing in the office of the county clerk for any other county his autograph signature and a certificate of the county clerk of the county for which he was elected, commissioned and qualified, setting forth the fact of his election, commission and date thereof and of qualifications as such notary public and paying to the county clerk of the other county a fee of two dollars ($2.00), may exercise all the functions of his office in the county in which such autograph signature and certificate are filed, with the same effect as if same were executed in the county in which he resided and for which he was appointed.

§ 8-16-110. Certificate of clerk of other county.

The county clerk of a county in whose office any notary public residing in another county has so filed his autograph signature and such certificate shall, when so requested, subjoin to any certificate of proof or acknowledgment signed by such notary public a certificate under his hand and seal, stating that such notary public has filed a certificate of his election, commission and qualification, with his autograph signature, in the office of such clerk, and was at the time of taking such proof or acknowledgment duly authorized to take the same, and that he is well acquainted with the handwriting of such notary public and believes that the signature to such proof or acknowledgment is genuine, and thereupon the instrument so proved or acknowledged and certified shall be entitled to be read in evidence or to be recorded in any of the counties of this state in respect to which a certificate of the county clerk may be necessary for either purpose.

§ 8-16-111. Certificate of qualification in other county.

Whenever a notary public takes an affidavit, proof or acknowledgment in a county other than the county for which he was elected, commissioned and qualified, he shall add to his certificate, following his official signature and the date of expiration of his commission, a statement that he is qualified in such other county under the provisions of §§ 8-16-109 and 8-16-110.

§ 8-16-201. Qualification as notary at large.

Any notary public who has been duly elected by the county legislative body of any county and who has otherwise qualified may, upon application to the secretary of state, be issued a certificate authorizing him to exercise the functions of a notary public in all the counties in Tennessee. He shall pay in to the secretary of state a fee of two dollars ($2.00) for such certificate and his name shall be registered in a book kept in the office of the secretary of state for that purpose, and the fees so collected by the secretary of state shall go into the same fund and be used for the same purposes that other fees in connection with the qualification of notaries public are used.

§ 8-16-202. Powers of notary at large.

The qualifications, powers, duties, fees and liabilities of such notaries shall be the same as those prescribed by law for notaries public elected by the county legislative bodies, except that they are authorized to act in any county in the state instead of only in the county of their residence and election. This part is not intended in any manner to repeal or modify the law with reference to notaries public elected by the county legislative bodies, but to create another class of notaries public with power to act in any county in Tennessee.

§ 8-16-203. Bond of notary at large.

Before the secretary of state shall issue the certificate provided for in § 8-16-201, the applicant therefor shall give a bond executed by some surety company authorized to do business in Tennessee as surety, or with two (2) or more good sureties, in the penal sum of five thousand dollars ($5,000), payable to the state of Tennessee, conditioned for the faithful performance of the duties of a notary public, as provided for in § 8-16-202, and the secretary of state, upon the issuance of the certificate provided for in § 8-16-201, shall note the date of the issuance of the certificate, together with the expira-

tion date of the commission of the notary public on the face of the bond.

§ 8-16-204. Oath of notary at large.

The secretary of state, upon the issuance of the certificate provided for in § 8-16-201, shall be authorized and empowered to administer, to notaries public granted the powers and privileges covered by this part, the following oath: "I do solemnly swear or affirm that I will well and truly perform the duties of a notary public at large for the state of Tennessee, so help me God," which shall be taken and subscribed by such notaries public before entering upon the duties of their office before the secretary of state or any officer authorized to administer oaths.

§ 8-16-205. Title of notary at large.

Any notary public receiving the certificate, as provided in § 8-16-204, shall be known as a notary public at large for the state of Tennessee, and his official signature shall so indicate.

§ 8-16-206. Seal of notary at large—imprinting of seal.

(a) The secretary of state shall prescribe and design an official seal to be used by a notary public at large for the state of Tennessee.

(b) The official seal may be imprinted by either an impression notary seal or by a rubber or other type stamp.

§ 8-16-207. Term of notary at large.

The term of any notary public thus authorized to act in any county in the state shall be coextensive with his term of service as regular notary public for the county of his residence and election, but the special authorization to act in any county of the state may be revoked, at any time, upon proper cause shown, by the secretary of state.

§ 8-16-301. Procurement and surrender of seal—imprinting of seal.

(a) Every notary shall, at his own expense, procure a seal of office, which he shall surrender to the county legislative body when he resigns, or at the expiration of his term of office, and which his representatives, in case of his death, shall likewise surrender, to be cancelled, on pain of indictment as for a misdemeanor.

(b) The seal of office may be imprinted by either an impression notary seal or by a rubber or other type stamp.

§ 8-16-302. Powers of notary.

Notaries public shall have power to administer oaths, to take depositions, to qualify parties to bills in chancery, and to take affidavits, in all cases; and in all such cases the notary's seal shall be affixed and the notary shall sign such documents in ink by his own hand.

§ 8-16-303. Expiration of commission indicated on instruments.

(a) All notaries public within this state shall be and they are required to have written, stamped, or printed on every certificate of acknowledgment, officially attached and affixed to any instrument, the true date of the expiration of their several commissions, when the same is attached and affixed to the instrument; provided, however, that the failure so to do shall not render void or invalidate such certificate of acknowledgment, but shall subject such notary public to the penalty below prescribed.

(b) A violation of the provisions of this section is a misdemeanor, and any person so offending shall pay a fine of not less than twenty-five dollars ($25.00) nor more than one hundred dollars ($100) for each offense.

§ 8-16-304. Receipt of instruments in evidence.

The attestations, protestations, and other instruments of publication or acknowledgment, made by any notary public under his seal, shall be received in evidence.

§ 8-16-305. Notice of deposition of notary.

The deposition of a notary may be taken, whether a suit be pending or not, on ten (10) days' notice to the opposite party, if resident in the state and forty (40) days' notice out of it, to be read as evidence between the same parties in any suit then or afterward depending, should the notary die or remove out of the state before the trial.

§ 8-16-306. Recording fee.

A fee of one dollar ($1.00) and no more is allowed to a notary public for recording in a well-bound book, to be by him kept for the purpose, each of his attestations, protestations, and other instruments of publication.

§ 8-16-307. Protest fee.

The fee of the notary for the protestation of negotiable instruments shall be one dollar and fifty cents ($1.50) for each instrument protested, without regard to the number of parties on each instrument.

§ 8-16-308. Acting after expiration of commission.

It shall be unlawful for any person, who has been commissioned as a notary public, either as a result of his election or upon direct appointment by the governor, to take acknowledgments or otherwise act in an official capacity after the expiration of his commission. Any person violating this section shall be guilty of a misdemeanor and punishable by a fine of not less than one hundred dollars ($100) nor more than one thousand dollars ($1,000) for each offense.

§ 8-16-309. Depositions taken by notaries of other states.

Notaries public, duly and lawfully commissioned by the proper authorities of other states and empowered by the law of such state to take depositions, are authorized to take depositions to be used in the courts of this state, upon the same terms that are provided for the taking of depositions by other officials in such states. But the certificate of such notary public shall show the date of the commencement and expiration of the commission under which he may be acting.

FEES

§ 8-21-201. Secretary of state—specific fees authorized.

The secretary of state is entitled to demand and receive, as above, and shall charge for the following services the fees annexed, among others, to be collected and paid into the state treasury:

* * *

(2) For commission of each notary public . 3.00

(3) For commission of each commissioner of deeds 10.00

* * *

§ 8-21-1201. Notaries public.

Notaries public are entitled to demand and receive the following fees and compensation for services:

(1) For recording, in a well-bound book, to be kept by him for that purpose, each attestation, protestation, and other instrument of publication .... $ 1.00

(2) For the protestation of negotiable instru-

ments, for each instrument protested, without regard to the number of parties on each instrument
.... 1.50

(3) For every acknowledgment or probate of deed, or other instrument of writing, with seal attached, the same as county clerks.

(4) For acknowledgment of notes for advances on tobacco .... .25

(5) For each deposition taken 1.00

(6) For any other service legally performed by him, the same fees allowed other officers for like services.

OFFENSES

§ 39-16-401. Definitions for public misconduct offenses.

The following definitions apply in this part, unless the context otherwise requires:

(1) "Act" means a bodily movement, whether voluntary or involuntary, and includes speech;

(2) "Law" means the constitution or a statute of this state or of the United States, a written opinion of a court of record, a municipal ordinance, or a rule authorized by and lawfully adopted under a statute; and

(3) "Public servant" means a person elected, selected, appointed, employed, or otherwise designated as one (1) of the following even if the public servant has not yet qualified for office or assumed the duties:

(A) An officer, employee, or agent of government;

(B) A juror or grand juror;

(C) An arbitrator, referee, or other person who is authorized by law or private written agreement to hear or determine a cause or controversy;

(D) An attorney at law or notary public when participating in performing a governmental function;

(E) A candidate for nomination or election to public office; or

(F) A person who is performing a governmental function under claim of right although not legally qualified to do so.

§ 39-16-402. Official misconduct.

(a) A public servant commits an offense who, with intent to obtain a benefit or to harm another, intentionally or knowingly:

(1) Commits an act relating to the servant's office or employment that constitutes an unauthorized exercise of official power;

(2) Commits an act under color of office or employment that exceeds the servant's official power;

(3) Refrains from performing a duty that is imposed by law or that is clearly inherent in the nature of the public servant's office or employment;

(4) Violates a law relating to the public servant's office or employment; or

(5) Receives any benefit not otherwise authorized by law.

(b) For purposes of subdivision (a)(2), a public servant commits an act under color of office or employment who acts or purports to act in an official capacity or takes advantage of such actual or purported capacity.

(c) It is a defense to prosecution for this offense that the benefit involved was a trivial benefit incidental to personal, professional or business contact, and involved no substantial risk of undermining official impartiality.

(d) An offense under this section is a Class E felony.

(e) Charges for official misconduct may be brought only by indictment, presentment or criminal information; provided, that nothing herein shall deny a person from pursuing other criminal charges by affidavit of complaint.

§ 39-16-403. Official oppression.

(a) A public servant acting under color of office or employment commits an offense who:

(1) Intentionally subjects another to mistreatment or to arrest, detention, stop, frisk, halt, search, seizure, dispossession, assessment or lien when the public servant knows the conduct is unlawful; or

(2) Intentionally denies or impedes another in the exercise or enjoyment of any right, privilege, power or immunity, when the public servant knows the conduct is unlawful.

(b) For purposes of this section, a public servant acts under color of office or employment if the public servant acts, or purports to act, in an official capacity or takes advantage of such actual or purported capacity.

(c) An offense under this section is a Class E felony.

(d) Charges for official oppression may be brought only by indictment, presentment or criminal information; provided, that nothing herein shall deny a person from pursuing other criminal charges by affidavit of complaint.

§ 39-16-404. Misuse of official information.

(a) A public servant commits an offense who, by reason of information to which the public servant has access in the public servant's official capacity and which has not been made public, attains or aids another to attain a benefit.

(b) An offense under this section is a Class B misdemeanor.

§ 39-16-406. Suspension, removal and discharge from office.

(a) A public servant convicted under § 39-16-402, § 39-16-403 or § 39-16-404 shall be removed from office or discharged from the position.

(b) A public servant elected or appointed for a specified term shall be:

(1) Suspended without pay immediately upon conviction in the trial court through the final disposition of the case;

(2) Removed from office for the duration of the term during which the conviction occurred if the conviction becomes final; and

(3) Barred from holding any appointed or elected office for ten (10) years from the date the conviction becomes final.

(c) A public servant who serves at-will shall be discharged upon conviction in the trial court. Subsequent public service shall rest with the hiring or appointing authority, provided that such authority has been fully informed of the conviction.

ACKNOWLEDGMENTS

§ 65-29-127. Acknowledgments by officers, directors or members.

No person who is authorized to take acknowledgments under the laws of this state shall be disqualified from taking acknowledgments of instruments executed in favor of a cooperative or to which it is a party, by reason of being an officer, director, or member of such cooperative.

§ 66-22-101. Authentication.

To authenticate an instrument for registration, its execution shall be acknowledged by the maker, if the maker is the natural person executing the instrument, or if the maker is another natural person or is a corporation, partnership, or other entity which is not a natural person, by the natural person acting on behalf of the maker or a constituent of the maker, or proved by two (2) subscribing witnesses, at least.

§ 66-22-102. Persons authorized to take acknowledgments within state.

If the person executing the instrument resides or is within the state, the acknowledgment shall be made before the county clerk, or legally appointed deputy county clerk, or clerk and master of chancery court of some county in the state or before a notary public of some county in this state.

§ 66-22-103. Acknowledgments in other states or territories.

If the person executing the instrument resides or is beyond or without the limits of the state, but within the union or its territories or districts the acknowledgment may be made:

(1) Before any court of record, or before the clerk of any court of record; or, before a commissioner for Tennessee, appointed by the governor; or before a notary public authorized there to take proof or acknowledgments. If the acknowledgment be made before a court of record, a copy of the entry of the acknowledgment on the record shall be certified by the clerk, under his seal of office; and the judge, chief justice, or presiding magistrate of the court shall certify as to the official character of the clerk.

(2) Or, before any other officer of such state, territory or district, authorized by the laws there to take the proof and acknowledgment of deed. There shall in cases under this paragraph be subjoined or attached to the certificate of proof or acknowledgment, signed by such other officer, a certificate of the secretary of state of the state or territory in which such officer resides, under the seal of such state, territory, or a certificate of the clerk of a court of record of such state, territory, or district, in the county in which said officer resides or in which he took such proof or acknowledgment under the seal of such court, stating that such officer was, at the time of taking such proof or acknowledgment duly authorized to take acknowledgments and proof of deeds of lands in said state, territory, or district, and that said secretary of state, or clerk of court is well acquainted with the handwriting of such officer, and that he verily believes that the signature affixed to such certificate of proof or acknowledgment is genuine.

§ 66-22-104. Acknowledgments in foreign countries.

(a) If the person executing the instrument resides or is beyond the limits of the union and its territories, the acknowledgment may be made:

(1) Before a commissioner for Tennessee appointed in the country where the acknowledgment is made, having an official seal;

(2) Before a notary public of such country, having an official seal; and

(3) Before a consul, charge d'affaires, envoy, minister, or ambassador of the United States in the country to which he is accredited and where the acknowledgment is made.

(b) When the seal affixed contains the name or official style of such officer, any error, in stating or failing to state otherwise such name or official style of the officer, shall not render the certificate defective.

§ 66-22-105. Authentication of instruments by or to county clerk.

The probate or acknowledgment of any deed or other instrument, made by or to a clerk of any county, may be taken and made before the judge having probate jurisdiction in his county, clerk and master or notary public, and the authentication entered on record in the office of the county clerk as other instruments; provided, that the clerk collect and account for the state tax on all such instruments as though the acknowledgment had been taken before him.

§ 66-22-106. Postponement pending identification.

(a) If the clerk or deputy clerk does not know, is not personally acquainted with, or does not have satisfactory evidence that, a person wishing to make acknowledgment of the execution of an instrument, he shall file it, and note, on his record of the probate of deeds, the date of the presentation of the instrument, and the reason of the postponement of the acknowledgment; and then, within twenty (20) days, the party may produce witnesses before the clerk or deputy clerk, to prove the identity of the person so offering to acknowledge the same; and the deed, when acknowledged after such proof, shall take effect from the filing with the clerk.

(b) For purposes of this chapter, "know" or "personally acquainted with" means having an acquaintance, derived from association with the individual in relation to other people and based upon a chain of circumstances surrounding the individual, which establishes the individual's identity with at least reasonable certainty.

(c) For the purposes of this chapter "satisfactory evidence" means the absence of any information, evidence, or other circumstances which would lead a reasonable person to believe that the person making the acknowledgment is not the individual he or she claims to be and any one of the following:

(1) The oath or affirmation of a credible witness personally known to the officer that the person making the acknowledgment is personally known to the witness.

(2) Reasonable reliance on the presentation to the officer of any one of the following, if the document is current or has been issued within five (5) years:

(A) An identification card or driver's license issued by the Tennessee department of safety; or

(B) A passport issued by the department of state of the United States.

(3) Reasonable reliance on the presentation of any one of the following, if the document is current or has been issued within five (5) years and contains a photograph and description of the person named on it, is signed by the person, bears a serial or other identifying number, and, in the event that the document is a passport, has been stamped by the United States Immigration and Naturalization Service:

(A) A passport issued by a foreign government;

(B) A driver's license issued by a state other than Tennessee;

(C) An identification card issued by a state other than Tennessee; or

(D) An identification card issued by any branch of the armed forces of the United States.

(d) An officer who has taken an acknowledgment pursuant to this section shall be presumed to have operated in accordance with the provisions of this chapter.

(e) Any party who files an action for damages based on the failure of the officer to establish the proper identity of the person making the acknowledgment shall have the burden of proof in establishing the negligence or misconduct of the officer.

§ 66-22-107. Form of certificate of acknowledgment.

(a) If the acknowledgment be made before a county clerk or deputy, or clerk and master, or notary public, or before any of the officers out of the state who are commissioned or accredited to act at the place where the acknowledgment is taken, and having an official seal, viz: those named in §§ 66-22-103 and 66-22-104, and, also, any consular officer of the United States having an official seal, such officer shall write upon or annex to the instrument the following certificate, in which he shall set forth his official capacity:

State of Tennessee,
County of _____]

Personally appeared before me, (name of clerk or deputy) clerk (or deputy clerk) of this county, (bargainor's name), the within named bargainor, with whom I am personally acquainted (or proved to me on the basis of satisfactory evidence), and who acknowledged that he executed the within instrument for the purposes therein contained. Witness my hand, at office, this _____ day of _____, 19___.

(b) Or, in the alternative, the following certificate, in case of natural persons acting in their own right:

State of Tennessee,

County of _____]

On this _____ day of _____,
19___, before me personally appeared
_____, to me known to be the person
(or persons) described in and who executed the
foregoing instrument, and acknowledged that he
(or they) executed the same as his (or their) free act
and deed.

(c) Or, in case of natural persons acting by attorney:

State of Tennessee,
County of _____]

On this _____ day of _____,
19___, before me personally appeared
_____, to me known (or proved to me
on the basis of satisfactory evidence) to be the person who executed the foregoing instrument in behalf of _____ acknowledged that he executed the same as the free act and deed of
_____.

§ 66-22-108. Acknowledgment for record of corporate or partnership instrument.

(a) The authentication or acknowledgment for record of a deed or other instrument in writing executed by a corporation, whether it has a seal or not, shall be good and sufficient, when made in substantially the following form:

State of _____,
County of _____]

Before me, _____ of the state and county mentioned, personally appeared _____, with whom I am personally acquainted (or proved to me on the basis of satisfactory evidence), and who, upon oath, acknowledged himself to be president (or other officer authorized to execute the instrument) of the _____, the within named bargainor, a corporation, and that he as such _____, executed the foregoing instrument for the purpose therein contained, by signing the name of the corporation by himself as _____.

Witness of my hand and seal, at office in _____, this _____ day of _____.

Or, alternatively as follows:
State of _____,
County of _____.

On this _____ day of _____,
19___, before me appeared A. B., to me personally known (or proved to me on the basis of satisfactory evidence), who, being by me duly sworn (or affirmed) did say that he is the president (or other officer or agent of the corporation or association) of (describing the corporation or association), and that the seal affixed to the instrument is the corporate seal of the corporation (or association), and that the instrument was signed and sealed in behalf of the corporation (or association), by authority of its Board of Directors (or Trustees) and A. B. ac-

knowledged the instrument to be the free act and deed of the corporation (or association).

(In case the corporation or association has no corporate seal omit the words "the seal affixed to the instrument is the corporate seal of the corporation or association and that," and add at the end of the affidavit clause, the words "and that the corporation (or association) has no corporate seal"). (In all cases add signature and title of officer taking the acknowledgment .)

(b)(1) The authentication or acknowledgment for record of a deed or other instrument in writing executed by a partnership shall be good and sufficient when made in substantially the following form:

STATE OF _____
COUNTY OF _____

Before me, _____ of the state and county aforesaid, personally appeared _____, with whom I am personally acquainted (or proved to me on the basis of satisfactory evidence), and who, upon oath, acknowledged himself to be a partner of _____, the within named bargainor, a partnership, and that he as such partner, executed the foregoing instrument for the purpose therein contained, by signing the name of the partnership by himself as partner.

Witness my hand and seal, this _____ day of _____, _____.

(2) The signing of a certificate of acknowledgment for a partnership will not change any requirement of the partnership agreement itself.

§ 66-22-109. Acknowledgment of married woman.

The acknowledgment of a married woman, when required by law, may be taken in the same form as if she were sole and without any examination separate and apart from her husband.

§ 66-22-110. Acknowledgments under seal.

All acknowledgments shall be under the seal of office of the officer taking same.

§ 66-22-114. Certificate of acknowledgment form.

(a) If the acknowledgment be made before any of the officers who are authorized to take such acknowledgment under the provisions of this chapter or any consular officer of the United States having an official seal, such officer shall write upon or annex to the instrument a certificate of acknowledgment. The following form shall constitute a valid certificate of acknowledgment:

State of _____

County of _____

Personally appeared before me, (name of officer), (official capacity of officer), (name of the natural person executing the instrument), with whom I am personally acquainted, and who acknowledged that he executed the within instrument for the purposes therein contained (the following to be included only where the natural person is executing as agent), and who further acknowledged that he is the (identification of the agency position of the natural person executing the instrument, such as "attorney-in-fact" or "president" or "general partner") of the maker or a constituent of the maker and is authorized by the maker or by its constituent, the constituent being authorized by the maker, to execute this instrument on behalf of the maker.

Witness my hand, at office, this _____ day of _____, 19___.

(b) Any certificate clearly evidencing intent to authenticate, acknowledge or verify a document shall constitute a valid certificate of acknowledgment for purposes of this chapter and for any other purpose for which such certificate may be used under the law. It is the legislative intent that no specific form or wording be required in such certificate and that the ownership of property, or the determination of any other right or obligation, shall not be affected by the inclusion or omission of any specific words.

DEPOSITIONS

§ 24-9-101. Deponents exempt from subpoena to trial but subject to subpoena to deposition.

Deponents exempt from subpoena to trial but subject to subpoena to a deposition are:

(1) An officer of the United States;

(2) An officer of this state;

(3) An officer of any court or municipality within the state;

(4) The clerk of any court of record other than that in which the suit is pending;

(5) A member of the general assembly while in session, or clerk or officer thereof;

(6) A practicing physician, psychologist, chiropractor, dentist, or attorney; and

(7) A jailer or keeper of a public prison in any county other than that in which the suit is pending.

§ 24-9-102. General sessions cases.

(a) Discovery pursuant to Rules 26-37 of the Tennessee Rules of Civil Procedure, excluding physical and mental examinations under Rule 35 of such rules, may be taken in all civil cases pending in the courts of general sessions in the discretion of the court after motion showing both good cause and exceptional circumstances and pursuant to an order describing the extent and conditions of such discovery.

(b) Depositions of custodians of hospital and medical records may be taken in all cases pending before the judges of the courts of general sessions, under the same rules, regulations, and restrictions as in cases pending in the courts of record.

§ 24-9-103. Depositions for use in foreign courts.

(a) Whenever any mandate, writ, or commission is issued out of any court of record in any other state, territory, district, or foreign jurisdiction, or whenever upon notice or agreement it is required to take the testimony of a witness or witnesses in this state, witnesses may be compelled to appear and testify in the same manner and by the same process and proceeding as may be employed for the purpose of taking testimony in proceedings pending in this state.

(b) The person whose deposition is required under a foreign commission or is taken upon agreement is entitled to the same fees as a person who is summoned to give testimony in the circuit courts of this state.

[TENN. R. CIV. P.]

RULE 28. Persons before whom depositions may be taken.

28.01. Within the United States.—Within the United States or within a territory or insular possession subject to the dominion of the United States, depositions shall be taken before an officer authorized to administer oaths by the laws of the United States or of the place where the examination is held, or before a person appointed by the court in which the action is pending. A person so appointed has power to administer oaths and take testimony.

28.02. In foreign countries.—In a foreign country, depositions may be taken (1) on notice before a person authorized to administer oaths in the place in which the examination is held, either by the law thereof or by the law of the United States, or (2) before a person commissioned by the court, and a person so commissioned shall have the power by virtue of his commission to administer any necessary oath and take testimony, or (3) pursuant to a letter rogatory. A commission or a letter rogatory shall be issued on application and notice and on terms that are just and appropriate. It is not requisite to the issuance of a commission or a letter rogatory that the taking of the deposition in any other manner is impracticable or inconvenient; and both a commission and a letter rogatory may be issued in proper cases. A notice or commission may designate the person before whom the deposition is to be taken either by name or descriptive title. A letter rogatory may be addressed "To the Appropriate Authority in (here name the country)." Evidence obtained in response to a letter rogatory need not be excluded merely for the reason that it is not a verbatim transcript or that the testimony was not taken under oath or for any similar departure from the requirements for depositions taken within the United Sates under these rules.

28.03. Disqualification for interest.—Except as provided in Rule 29, no deposition shall be taken before a person who is a relative (within the sixth degree, computed by the civil law) or employee or attorney or counsel of any of the parties, or who is a relative (within the sixth degree, computed by the civil law) or employee of such attorney or counsel, or who is financially interested in the action.

LEGAL HOLIDAYS

[TENN. CODE ANN.]

§ 15-1-101. Legal holidays.

The first day of January; the third Monday in January, "Martin Luther King, Jr. Day"; the third Monday in February, known as "Washington Day"; the last Monday in May, known as "Memorial" or "Decoration Day"; the fourth of July; the first Monday in September, known as "Labor Day"; the second Monday in October, known as "Columbus Day"; the eleventh day of November, known as "Veterans' Day"; the fourth Thursday in November, known as "Thanksgiving Day"; the twenty-fifth day of December; and Good Friday; and when any one of these days shall fall on Sunday then the following Monday shall be substituted; and when any of these days shall fall on Saturday, then the preceding Friday shall be substituted; also, all days appointed by the governor or by the president of the United States, as days of fasting or thanksgiving, and all days set apart by law for holding county, state, or national elections, throughout this state, are made legal holidays, and the period from noon to midnight of each Saturday which is not a holiday is made a half-holiday, on which holidays and half-holidays all public offices of this state may be closed and business of every character, at the option of the parties in interest of the same, may be suspended.

§ 15-1-102. Friday holidays—optional suspension of Saturday business.

Whenever the first day of January, the fourth day

of July or the twenty-fifth day of December shall fall on Friday, then any corporation, firm or individual shall, on the succeeding Saturday, have the privilege and option to suspend business activities completely or partially and shall not incur any liability for failure to exercise on such a Saturday all of the lawful functions authorized by law; provided, however, that nothing herein shall be construed to compel any corporation, firm or individual to suspend lawful business functions on such a Saturday, as it shall be optional whether this right is exercised.

§ 15-1-103. Banks—optional Saturday business.

Nothing in any law shall in any manner affect the validity of, or render void or voidable, the payment, certification, or acceptance of a check or other negotiable instrument or any other transaction by a bank in this state, because done or performed on any legal holiday or on any Saturday between twelve o'clock (12:00) noon and midnight; provided, that such payment, certificate, acceptance, or other transaction would be valid if done or performed on any business day other than a legal holiday, or if done or performed before twelve o'clock (12:00) noon on such Saturday; provided, further, that nothing herein shall be construed to compel any bank, which by law or custom is entitled to close on a legal holiday, or is entitled to close at twelve o'clock (12:00) noon on any Saturday, to keep open for the transaction of business or to perform any of these acts or transactions on any legal holiday or on any Saturday after twelve o'clock (12:00) noon, except at its own option.

§ 15-1-104. Banks—optional suspension of Wednesday, Thursday, or Saturday morning business.

Every corporation, firm or individual doing a banking business in this state shall have the privilege and option to suspend business activities completely or partially on Wednesday, Thursday or Saturday mornings of each week and shall not incur any liability for failure then to exercise all of the lawful functions authorized by law; provided, however, that nothing herein shall be construed to compel any corporation, firm or individual doing a banking business in this state to suspend lawful functions on Wednesday, Thursday, or Saturday mornings of each week.

TEXAS

NOTARIES PUBLIC

[TEX. GOV'T CODE ANN. (Vernon 1986)]

§ 406.001. Appointments.

The secretary of state may appoint a notary public at any time.

§ 406.002. Term.

The term of a notary public expires four years after the date the notary public qualifies.

§ 406.003. Jurisdiction.

A notary public has statewide jurisdiction.

§ 406.004. Residence and age.

To be eligible for appointment as a notary public an individual must be a resident of this state and at least 18 years old.

§ 406.005. Application.

(a) To be appointed a notary public an individual must apply to the secretary of state on a form prescribed by the secretary of state. The application must satisfy the secretary of state that the applicant is qualified. The application must state that the applicant has never been convicted of a crime involving moral turpitude and must also state:

(1) the applicant's name to be used in acting as a notary public;

(2) the applicant's post office address;

(3) the applicant's county of residence;

(4) the applicant's business address;

(5) the county in which the applicant's business is located; and

(6) the applicant's social security number.

(b) The secretary of state shall act on an application at the earliest practicable time and notify the applicant whether an appointment has been made.

§ 406.006. Qualification; reapplication.

(a) On receiving notice of appointment, the applicant must, not later than the 30th day after the date of appointment, qualify as provided by this subchapter. If the applicant does not qualify within that period, the appointment is void.

(b) An individual qualifies by:

(1) taking the official oath and providing the bond required by Section 406.010; and

(2) paying the fees required by Section 406.007.

(c) An individual whose appointment becomes void under Subsection (a) must reapply to be appointed.

§ 406.007. Fees paid to secretary of state.

(a) The applicant must submit to the secretary of state:

(1) a fee of $10 for approving and filing the bond of the notary public; and

(2) a fee of $1 to be appropriated to and used by the secretary of state only for hiring an investigator and for preparing and distributing the materials required to be distributed under Section 406.008.

(b) The secretary of state shall charge for use of the state a fee of $10 for a notary public commission. The applicant must pay the fee in advance to the secretary of state.

§ 406.008. Commission; notary materials.

(a) Immediately after the qualification of a notary public, the secretary of state shall issue a commission to the notary public. The commission is effective as of the date of qualification.

(b) When the commission is issued, the secretary of state shall supply the notary public with:

(1) materials outlining the powers and duties of the office;

(2) a list of prohibited acts; and

(3) sample forms for an acknowledgment, jurat, and verification and for the administering of an oath, protest, and deposition.

(c) This section does not prevent a qualified notary public from performing the duties of office after qualifying and before receiving the commission.

§ 406.009. Rejection of appointment; suspension or revocation of commission.

(a) The secretary of state may, for good cause, reject an application or suspend or revoke the commission of a notary public.

(b) An action by the secretary of state under this section is subject to the rights of notice, hearing, adjudication, and appeal.

(c) An appeal under this section is to the district court of Travis County. The secretary of state has the burden of proof, and the trial is conducted de novo.

(d) In this section, "good cause" includes:

(1) a final conviction for a crime involving moral turpitude;

(2) a false statement knowingly made in an application;

(3) the failure to comply with Section 406.017;

(4) a final conviction for a violation of a law concerning the regulation of the conduct of notaries public in this or another state; and

(5) the imposition on the notary public of an administrative, criminal, or civil penalty for a violation of a law or rule prescribing the duties of a notary public.

§ 406.010. Bond; oath.

(a) An individual appointed a notary public shall, before entering the official duties of office, execute a bond in the amount of $2,500 with a solvent surety company authorized to do business in this state as a surety. The bond must be approved by the secretary of state, payable to the governor, and conditioned on the faithful performance of the duties of office.

(b) The individual shall take the official oath of office and subscribe the individual's name and social security number to the oath. The oath and the certificate of the official administering the oath must be endorsed on the notary bond.

(c) The notary bond shall be deposited in the office of the secretary of state, is not void on first recovery, and may be sued on the name of the injured party from time to time until the whole amount of the bond is recovered.

(d) The State Board of Insurance may approve rates for a four-year notary bond issued after January 1, 1980, equivalent to twice the rate set previously for two-year notary bonds.

§ 406.011. Expiring term.

(a) Not later than the 90th day before the date on which a qualified notary public's term expires, the secretary of state shall send the notary public an application for reappointment, a notary bond, and an oath of office.

(b) On receiving the properly executed application for reappointment, notary bond, oath of office, and statutory fees, the secretary of state shall issue a commission to the notary public for another term of office unless the notary public has been convicted of a felony or a crime involving moral turpitude during the term of office.

(c) A notary public who is not reappointed before the expiration date of the term the notary public is serving must apply for appointment in the manner provided by Section 406.005.

§ 406.012. Inspection of records.

All records concerning the appointment and qualification of the notary public shall be kept in the office of the secretary of state. The records are public information.

§ 406.013. Seal.

(a) A notary public shall provide a seal of office that clearly shows, when embossed, stamped, or printed on a document, the words "Notary Public, State of Texas" around a star of five points, the notary public's name, and the date the notary public's commission expires. The notary public shall authenticate all official acts with the seal of office.

(b) The seal may be a circular form not more than two inches in diameter or a rectangular form not more than one inch in width and 2-1/2 inches in length. The seal must have a serrated or milled edge border.

(c) The seal must be affixed by a seal press or stamp that embosses or prints a seal that legibly reproduces the required elements of the seal under

photographic methods. An indelible ink pad must be used for affixing by a stamp the impression of a seal on an instrument to authenticate the notary public's official act.

§ 406.014. Notary records.

(a) A notary public other than a court clerk notarizing instruments for the court shall keep in a book a record of:

(1) the date of each instrument notarized;

(2) the date of the notarization;

(3) the name of the signer, grantor, or maker;

(4) the signer's, grantor's, or maker's residence or alleged residence;

(5) whether the signer, grantor, or maker is personally known by the notary public, was identified by an identification card issued by a governmental agency or a passport issued by the United States, or was introduced to the notary public and, if introduced, the name and residence or alleged residence of the individual introducing the signer, grantor, or maker;

(6) if the instrument is proved by a witness, the residence of the witness, whether the witness is personally known by the notary public or was introduced to the notary public and, if introduced, the name and residence of the individual introducing the witness;

(7) the name and residence of the grantee;

(8) if land is conveyed or charged by the instrument, the name of the original grantee and the county where the land is located; and

(9) a brief description of the instrument.

(b) Entries in the notary's book are public information.

(c) A notary public shall, on payment of all fees, provide a certified copy of any record in the notary public's office to any person requesting the copy.

(d) A notary public who administers an oath pursuant to Article 45.01, Code of Criminal Procedure, is exempt from the requirement in Subsection (a) of recording that oath.

§ 406.015. Copies certified by county clerk.

(a) A copy of a record, declaration, protest, or other official act of a notary public may be certified by the county clerk with whom the instrument is deposited.

(b) A copy of an instrument certified by the county clerk under Subsection (a) has the same authority as if certified by the notary public by whom the record, declaration, protest, or other official act was originally made.

§ 406.016. Authority.

(a) A notary public has the same authority as the county clerk to:

(1) take acknowledgments or proofs of written instruments;

(2) protest instruments permitted by law to be protested;

(3) administer oaths;

(4) take depositions; and

(5) certify copies of documents not recordable in the public records.

(b) A notary public shall sign an instrument in Subsection (a) in the name under which the notary public is commissioned.

(c) A notary public may not issue an identification card.

(d) A notary public not licensed to practice law in this state may not give legal advice or accept fees for legal advice.

§ 406.017. Representation as attorney.

(a) A notary public who is not an attorney and who advertises the services of a notary public in a language other than English, whether by signs, pamphlets, stationery, or other written communication or by radio or television, shall post or otherwise include with the advertisement a notice that the notary public is not an attorney.

(b) The notice must be in English and in the language of the advertisement and in letters of a conspicuous size. If the advertisement is by radio or television, the statement may be modified, but must include substantially the same message. The notice must include the fees that a notary public may charge and the following statement:
"I AM NOT AN ATTORNEY LICENSED TO PRACTICE LAW IN TEXAS AND MAY NOT GIVE LEGAL ADVICE OR ACCEPT FEES FOR LEGAL ADVICE."

(c) Literal translation of the phrase "Notary Public" into Spanish is prohibited. In this subsection, "literal translation" means the translation of a word or phrase without regard to the true meaning of the word or phrase in the language that is being translated.

(d) Failure to comply with this section is, in addition to a violation of any other applicable law of this state, a deceptive trade practice actionable under Chapter 17, Business & Commerce Code.

§ 406.018. Removal from office.

(a) A notary public guilty of wilful neglect of duty or malfeasance in office may be removed from office in the manner provided by law.

(b) A notary public indicted for and convicted of a wilful neglect of duty or official misconduct shall be removed from office. The court shall include the order for removal as part of its judgment.

§ 406.019. Change of address.

A notary public shall notify the secretary of state of a change of the notary public's address not later than the 10th day after the date on which the change is made.

§ 406.020. Removal from state.

A notary public who removes his residence from this state vacates the office.

§ 406.021. Removal from precinct.

An ex officio notary public who moves permanently from the notary public's precinct vacates the office.

§ 406.022. Effect of vacancy.

If the office of a notary public becomes vacant due to resignation, removal, or death, the county clerk of the county in which the notary public resides shall obtain the record books and public papers belonging to the office of the notary public and deposit them in the county clerk's office.

§ 406.023. Administration and enforcement.

(a) The secretary of state shall adopt rules necessary for the administration and enforcement of this subchapter. The rules must be consistent with the provisions of this subchapter.

(b) The secretary of state may employ an investigator to aid in the enforcement of this subchapter.

(c) The secretary of state may provide for the appointment of county clerks as deputy custodians for the limited authentication of notary public records deposited in the clerks' offices.

§ 406.024. Fees charged by notary public.

(a) A notary public may charge the following fees:

(1) for protesting a bill or note for nonacceptance or nonpayment, register and seal, a fee of $3;

(2) for each notice of protest, a fee of 50 cents;

(3) for protesting in all other cases, a fee of 50 cents for each 100 words;

(4) for certificate and seal to a protest, a fee of $3;

(5) for taking the acknowledgment or proof of a deed or other instrument in writing, for registration, including certificate and seal, a fee of $5 for

the first signature and $1 for each additional signature;

(6) for administering an oath or affirmation with certificate and seal, a fee of $5;

(7) for a certificate under seal not otherwise provided for, a fee of $5;

(8) for a copy of a record or paper in the notary public's office, a fee of 50 cents for each page;

(9) for taking the deposition of a witness, 50 cents for each 100 words;

(10) for swearing a witness to a deposition, certificate, seal and other business connected with taking the deposition, a fee of $5; and

(11) for a notarial act not provided for, a fee of $5.

(b) A notary public may charge a fee only for an acknowledgment or official act under Subsection (a). The fee charged may not exceed the fee authorized by Subsection (a).

ADDITIONAL AUTHORITY

[TEX. CONST.]

Art. 4, § 26. Notaries public.

(a) The Secretary of State shall appoint a convenient number of Notaries Public for the state who shall perform such duties as now are or may be prescribed by law. The qualifications of Notaries Public shall be prescribed by law.

(b) The terms of office of Notaries Public shall be not less than two years nor more than four years as provided by law.

Art. 5, § 19. Justices of the peace; jurisdiction; appeals; ex officio notaries public; times and places of holding court.

Justice of the peace courts shall have original jurisdiction in criminal matters of misdemeanor cases punishable by fine only, exclusive jurisdiction in civil matters where the amount in controversy is two hundred dollars or less, and such other jurisdiction as may be provided by law. Justices of the peace shall be ex officio notaries public.

[TEX. GOV'T CODE ANN. (Vernon 1986)]

§ 27.002. Commission; notary.

Each justice of the peace shall be commissioned as justice of the peace of the applicable precinct and ex officio notary public of the county.

[TEX. REV. CIV. STAT. ANN.]

Art. 852a. Savings and Loan Act.

* * *

Acknowledgments by members and employees

Sec. 11.02. No public officer qualified to take acknowledgments or proofs of written instruments shall be disqualified from taking the acknowledgments or proofs of any instrument in writing in which [a savings and loan] association or Federal [savings and loan] association is interested by reason of his membership in or stockholding in or employment by such an institution so interested, and any such acknowledgments or proofs heretofore taken are hereby validated.

* * *

Art. 1528c. Telephone Cooperative Act.

Short title

Sec. 1. This Act may be cited as the "Telephone Cooperative Act."

Definitions

Sec. 2. In this Act, unless the context otherwise requires:

(1) "Corporation" means any corporation organized under this Act or which becomes subject to this Act in the manner hereinafter provided.

* * *

Directors, officers or members—notaries

Sec. 27. No person who is authorized to take acknowledgments under the laws of this State shall be disqualified from taking acknowledgments of instruments executed in favor of a corporation or to which it is a party, by reason of being an officer, director, or member of such corporation.

* * *

Art. 342-509a. Stockholders, officers and employees [of banks]—authority to take acknowledgments.

No Notary Public or other Public Officer qualified to take acknowledgments or proofs of written instruments shall be disqualified from taking the acknowledgment or proof of an instrument in writing in which a State bank, national bank or private bank is interested by reason of his ownership of stock in or employment by the State or national or private bank interested in such instrument, and any such acknowledgment heretofore taken is hereby validated.

OFFENSES

[TEX. PENAL CODE ANN. (Vernon 1974)]

§ 12.21. Class A misdemeanor.

An individual adjudged guilty of a Class A misdemeanor shall be punished by:

(1) a fine not to exceed $2,000;

(2) confinement in jail for a term not to exceed one year; or

(3) both such fine and imprisonment.

§ 12.33. Second-degree felony punishment.

An individual adjudged guilty of a felony of the second degree shall be punished by confinement in the Texas Department of Corrections for any term of not more than 20 years or less than 2 years.

(b) In addition to imprisonment, an individual adjudged guilty of a felony of the second degree may be punished by a fine not to exceed $10,000.

§ 12.34. Third-degree felony punishment.

(a) An individual adjudged guilty of a felony of the third degree shall be punished by:

(1) confinement in the institutional division of the Texas Department of Criminal Justice for any term of not more than 10 years or less than 2 years; or

(2) confinement in a community correctional facility for any term of not more than 1 year.

(b) In addition to imprisonment, an individual adjudged guilty of a felony of the third degree may be punished by a fine not to exceed $10,000.

§ 32.21. Forgery.

(a) For purposes of this section:

(1) "Forge" means:

(A) to alter, make, complete, execute, or authenticate any writing so that it purports:

(i) to be the act of another who did not authorize that act;

(ii) to have been executed at a time or place or in a numbered sequence other than was in fact the case; or

(iii) to be a copy of an original when no such original existed;

(B) to issue, transfer, register the transfer of, pass, publish, or otherwise utter a writing that is forged within the meaning of Paragraph (A) of this subdivision; or

(C) to possess a writing that is forged within the meaning of Paragraph (A) with intent to utter it in a manner specified in Paragraph (B) of this subdivision.

(2) "Writing" includes:

(A) printing or any other method of recording information;

(B) money, coins, tokens, stamps, seals, credit cards, badges, and trademarks; and

(C) symbols of value, right, privilege, or identification.

(b) A person commits an offense if he forges a writing with intent to defraud or harm another.

(c) Except as provided in Subsections (d) and (e) of this section an offense under this section is a Class A misdemeanor.

(d) An offense under this section is a felony of the third degree if the writing is or purports to be a will, codicil, deed, deed of trust, mortgage, security instrument, security agreement, credit card, check or similar sight order for payment of money, contract, release, or other commercial instrument.

(e) An offense under this section is a felony of the second degree if the writing is or purports to be part of an issue of money, securities, postage or revenue stamps, or other instruments issued by a state or national government or by a subdivision of either, or part of an issue of stock, bonds, or other instruments representing interests in or claims against another person.

§ 37.10 Tampering with governmental record.

(a) A person commits an offense if he:

(1) knowingly makes a false entry in, or false alteration of, a governmental record;

(2) makes, presents, or uses any record, documents, or thing with knowledge of its falsity and with intent that it be taken as a genuine governmental record; or

(3) intentionally destroys, conceals, removes, or otherwise impairs the verity, legibility, or availability of a governmental record.

(b) It is an exception to the application of Subsection (a)(3) of this section that the governmental record is destroyed pursuant to legal authorization. With regard to the destruction of a local government record, legal authorization includes compliance with the provisions of Subtitle C, Title 6, Local Government Code.

(c) An offense under this section is a Class A misdemeanor unless the actor's intent is to defraud or harm another, in which event the offense is a felony of the third degree.

"Governmental record" means anything: (A) belonging to, received by, or kept by government for information; or (B) required by law to be kept by others for information of government. TEX. PENAL CODE ANN. § 37.01(1).

SAFE DEPOSIT BOXES

[TEX. REV. CIV. STAT. ANN.]

Art. 342-906. Safe deposit boxes—access by joint lessees—opening—lien—sale of content.

Any state, national or private bank, savings and loan association, hotel, or other private safe deposit company, hereinafter referred to as bank, financial institution, or company may maintain safe deposit boxes and rent the same. In all such transactions the relationship of the bank, financial institution, or company and the renter shall, in the absence of a contract to the contrary, be that of lessor and lessee and landlord and tenant and the rights and liabilities of the bank, financial institution, or company shall be governed accordingly, and the lessee shall be deemed in law for all purposes to be in possession of the box and the content thereof. If a safe deposit box is held in the name of two (2) or more persons jointly, any one of such persons shall be entitled to access to such box and shall be permitted to remove the content thereof and the bank, financial institution, or company shall not be responsible for any damage arising by reason of such access or removal by one of said persons. The death of one holder of a jointly held safe deposit box does not affect the right of any other holder of the box to have access to and remove contents from the box. If the box rental is delinquent for six (6) months, the bank, financial institution, or company, after at least sixty (60) days' notice by certified return receipt mail addressed to the lessee at his last known address on the books of the bank, financial institution, or company, may, if the rent is not paid within the time specified in said notice, open the box in the presence of two (2) employees, at least one of whom is an officer or manager of the bank, financial institution, or company and a notary public. The bank, financial institution, or company must inventory the content of the box in detail pursuant to state treasury reporting instructions and place the content of the box in a sealed envelope or container bearing the name of the lessee. The bank, financial institution, or company shall then hold the content of the box subject to a lien for its rental, the cost of opening the box and the damages in connection therewith. If such rental, cost and damages are not paid within two (2) years from the date of opening of such box, the bank, financial institution, or company may sell any part or all of the content at public auction in like manner and upon like notice as is prescribed for the sale of real property under deed of trust pursuant to Section 51.002, Property Code. Any unauctioned contents of boxes and/or any excess proceeds from such sale shall be remitted to the state treasury pursuant to Chapters 72 through 75, Property Code.

ACKNOWLEDGMENTS

[Tex. Rev. Civ. Stat. Ann. (Vernon)]

Art. 3905. Fee for acknowledgment.

Officers authorized by law to take acknowledgment or proof of deeds or other instruments of writing shall receive the same fees for taking such acknowledgment or proof as are allowed notaries public for the same services.

[Tex. Civ. Prac. & Rem. Code Ann. (Vernon 1986)]

§ 121.001. Officers who may take acknowledgments or proofs.

(a) An acknowledgment or proof of a written instrument may be taken in this state by:
(1) a clerk of a district court;
(2) a judge or clerk of a county court; or
(3) a notary public.
(b) An acknowledgment or proof of a written instrument may be taken outside this state, but inside the United States or its territories, by:
(1) a clerk of court of record having a seal;
(2) a commissioner of deeds appointed under the laws of this state; or
(3) a notary public.
(c) An acknowledgment or proof of a written instrument may be taken outside the United States or its territories by:
(1) a minister, commissioner, or charge d'affaires of the United States who is a resident of and is accredited in the country where the acknowledgment or proof is taken;
(2) a consul-general, consul, vice-consul, commercial agent, vice-commercial agent, deputy consul, or consular agent of the United States who is a resident of the country where the acknowledgment or proof is taken; or
(3) a notary public or any other official authorized to administer oaths in the jurisdiction where the acknowledgment or proof is taken.
(d) A commissioned officer of the United States Armed Forces or of a United States Armed Forces Auxiliary may take an acknowledgment or proof of a written instrument of a member of the armed forces, a member of an armed forces auxiliary, or a member's spouse. If an acknowledgment or a proof is taken under this subsection, it is presumed, absent pleading and proof to the contrary, that the commissioned officer who signed was a commissioned officer on the date that the officer signed, and that the acknowledging person was a member of the authorized group of military personnel or spouses. The failure of the commissioned officer to attach an official seal to the certificate of acknowledgment or proof of an instrument does not invalidate the acknowledgment or proof.

§ 121.002. Corporate acknowledgments.

(a) An employee of a corporation is not disqualified because of his employment from taking an acknowledgment or proof of a written instrument in which the corporation has an interest.
(b) An officer who is a shareholder in a corpora-

tion is not disqualified from taking an acknowledgment or proof of an instrument in which the corporation has an interest unless:

(1) the corporation has 1,000 or fewer shareholders; and

(2) the officer owns more than one-tenth of one percent of the issued and outstanding stock.

§ 121.003. Authority of officers.

In a proceeding to prove a written instrument, an officer authorized by this chapter to take an acknowledgment or a proof of a written instrument is also authorized to:

(1) administer oaths;

(2) employ and swear interpreters; and

(3) issue subpoenas.

§ 121.004. Method of acknowledgment.

(a) To acknowledge a written instrument for recording, the grantor or person who executed the instrument must appear before an officer and must state that he executed the instrument for the purposes and consideration expressed in it.

(b) The officer shall:

(1) make a certificate of the acknowledgment;

(2) sign the certificate; and

(3) seal the certificate with the seal of office.

§ 121.005. Proof of identity of acknowledging person.

(a) An officer may not take the acknowledgment of a written instrument unless the officer knows or has satisfactory evidence on the oath of a credible witness that the acknowledging person is the person who executed the instrument and is described in it.

(b) Except in a short form certificate of acknowledgment authorized by Section 121.008, the officer must note in the certificate of acknowledgment that:

(1) he personally knows the acknowledging person; or

(2) evidence of a witness was used to identify the acknowledging person.

§ 121.006. Alteration of authorized forms; definition.

(a) An acknowledgment form provided by this chapter may be altered as circumstances require. The authorization of a form does not prevent the use of other forms. The marital status or other status of the acknowledging person may be shown after the person's name.

(b) In an acknowledgment form "acknowledged" means:

(1) in the case of a natural person, that the person personally appeared before the officer taking the acknowledgment and acknowledged executing the instrument for the purposes and consideration expressed in it;

(2) in the case of a person as principal by an attorney-in-fact for the principal, that the attorney-in-fact personally appeared before the officer taking the acknowledgment and that the attorney-in-fact acknowledged executing the instrument as the act of the principal for the purposes and consideration expressed in it;

(3) in the case of a partnership by a partner or partners acting for the partnership, that the partner or partners personally appeared before the officer taking the acknowledgment and acknowledged executing the instrument as the act of the partnership for the purposes and consideration expressed in it;

(4) in the case of a corporation by a corporate officer or agent, that the corporate officer or agent personally appeared before the officer taking the acknowledgment and that the corporate officer or agent acknowledged executing the instrument in the capacity stated, as the act of the corporation, for the purposes and consideration expressed in it; and

(5) in the case of a person acknowledging as a public officer, trustee, executor or administrator of an estate, guardian, or other representative, that the person personally appeared before the officer taking the acknowledgment and acknowledged executing the instrument by proper authority in the capacity stated and for the purposes and consideration expressed in it.

§ 121.007. Form for ordinary certificate of acknowledgment.

The form of an ordinary certificate of acknowledgment must be substantially as follows:

"The State of _____,

"County of _____,

"Before me _____ (here insert the name and character of the officer) on this day personally appeared _____, known to me (or proved to me on the oath of _____) to be the person whose name is subscribed to the foregoing instrument and acknowledged to me that he executed the same for the purposes and consideration therein expressed.

(Seal) "Given under my hand and seal of office this _____ day of _____, A.D., _____."

§ 121.008. Short forms for certificates of acknowledgment.

(a) The forms for certificates of acknowledgment provided by this section may be used as alternatives to other authorized forms. They may be referred to as "statutory forms of acknowledgment."

(b) Short forms for certificates of acknowledgment include:

(1) For a natural person acting in his own right:

State of Texas
County of _____

This instrument was acknowledged before me on (date) by (name or names of person or persons acknowledging).

(Signature of officer)
(Title of officer)
My commission expires: _____

(2) For a natural person as principal acting by attorney-in-fact:

State of Texas
County of _____

This instrument was acknowledged before me on (date) by (name of attorney-in-fact) as attorney-in-fact on behalf of (name of principal).

(Signature of officer)
(Title of officer)
My commission expires: _____

(3) For a partnership acting by one or more partners:

State of Texas
County of _____

This instrument was acknowledged before me on (date) by (name of acknowledging partner or partners), partner(s) on behalf of (name of partnership), a partnership.

(Signature of officer)
(Title of officer)
My commission expires: _____

(4) For a corporation:

State of Texas
County of _____

This instrument was acknowledged before me on (date) by (name of officer), (title of officer) of (name of corporation acknowledging), a (state of incorporation) corporation, on behalf of said corporation.

(Signature of officer)
(Title of officer)
My commission expires: _____

(5) For a public officer, trustee, executor, administrator, guardian, or other representative:

State of Texas
County of _____

This instrument was acknowledged before me on (date) by (name of representative), (title of representative) of (name of entity or person represented).

(Signature of officer)
(Title of officer)
My commission expires: _____

§ 121.009. Proof of acknowledgment by witness.

(a) To prove a written instrument for recording, at least one of the witnesses who signed the instrument must personally appear before an officer who is authorized by this chapter to take acknowledgments or proofs and must swear:

(1) either that he saw the grantor or person who executed the instrument sign it or that that person acknowledged in the presence of the witness that he executed the instrument for the purposes and consideration expressed in it; and

(2) that he signed the instrument at the request of the grantor or person who executed the instrument.

(b) The officer must make a certificate of the testimony of the witness and must sign and officially seal the certificate.

(c) The officer may take the testimony of a witness only if the officer personally knows or has satisfactory evidence on the oath of a credible witness that the individual testifying is the person who signed the instrument as a witness. If evidence is used to identify the witness who signed the instrument, the officer must note the use of the evidence in the certificate of acknowledgment.

§ 121.010. Form of certificate for proof by witness.

When the execution of a written instrument is proved by a witness, the certificate of the officer must be substantially as follows:

"The State of _____,
"County of _____.
"Before me, _____ (here insert the name and character of the officer), on this day personally appeared _____, known to me (or proved to me on the oath of _____), to be the person whose name is subscribed as a witness to the foregoing instrument of writing, and after being duly sworn by me stated on oath that he saw _____, the grantor or person who executed such instrument of writing acknowledged in his presence that he had executed the same for the purposes and consideration therein expressed), and that he had signed the same as a witness at the request of the grantor (or person who executed the same.)

(Seal) "Given under my hand and seal of office this _____ day of _____, A.D., _____."

§ 121.011. Proof of acknowledgment by handwriting.

(a) The execution of an instrument may be established for recording by proof of the handwriting of persons who signed the instrument only if:

(1) the grantor of the instrument and all of the witnesses are dead;

(2) the grantor and all of the witnesses are not residents of this state;

(3) the residences of the grantor and the witnesses are unknown to the person seeking to prove the instrument and cannot be ascertained;

(4) the witnesses have become legally incompetent to testify; or

(5) the grantor of the instrument refuses to acknowledge the execution of the instrument and all of the witnesses are dead, not residents of this state, or legally incompetent or their places of residence are unknown.

(b) If the grantor or person who executed the instrument signed his name to the instrument, its execution must be proved by evidence of the handwriting of that person and at least one witness who signed the instrument. If the grantor or person who executed the instrument signed the instrument by making his mark, its execution must be proved by the handwriting of at least two of the witnesses who signed the instrument.

(c) Evidence taken for proof of handwriting must give the residence of the testifying witness. A testifying witness must have known the person whose handwriting is being proved and must be well acquainted with the handwriting in question and recognize it as genuine.

(d) Evidence offered for proof of handwriting must be given in writing by the deposition or affidavit of two or more disinterested persons. The evidence must satisfactorily prove to the officer each of the requirements provided by this section. The officer taking the proof must certify the witnesses' testimony. The officer must sign, officially seal, and attach this certificate to the instrument with the depositions or affidavits of the witnesses.

§ 121.012. Record of acknowledgment.

(a) An officer authorized by law to take an acknowledgment or proof of a written instrument required or permitted by law to be recorded must enter in a well-bound book and officially sign a short statement of each acknowledgment or proof. The statement must contain the date that the acknowledgment or proof was taken, the date of the instrument, and the names of the grantor and grantee of the instrument.

(b) If the execution of the instrument is acknowledged by the grantor of the instrument, the statement must also contain:

(1) the grantor's known or alleged residence;

(2) whether the grantor is personally known to the officer; and

(3) if the grantor is unknown to the officer, the

name and residence of the person who introduced the grantor to the officer, if any.

(c) If the execution of the instrument is proved by a witness who signed the instrument, the statement must also contain:

(1) the name of the witness;

(2) the known or alleged residence of the witness;

(3) whether the witness is personally known to the officer; and

(4) if the witness is unknown to the officer, the name and known or alleged residence of the person who introduced the witness to the officer, if any.

(d) If land is charged or conveyed by the instrument, the statement must also contain:

(1) the name of the original grantee; and

(2) the name of the county in which the land is located.

(e) The statements of acknowledgment recorded by the officer are original public records, open for public inspection and examination at all reasonable times. The officer must deliver the book to his successor in office.

§ 121.013. Subpoena of witness; attachment.

(a) On the sworn application of a person interested in the proof of an instrument required or permitted by law to be recorded, stating that a witness to the instrument refuses to appear and testify regarding the execution of the instrument and that the instrument cannot be proven without the evidence of the witness, an officer authorized to take proofs of instruments shall issue a subpoena requiring the witness to appear before the officer and testify about the execution of the instrument.

(b) If the witness fails to obey the subpoena, the officer has the same powers to enforce the attendance and compel the answers of the witness as does a district judge. Attachment may not be issued, however, unless the witness receives or is tendered the same compensation that is made to witnesses in other cases. An officer may not require the witness to leave his county of residence, but if the witness is temporarily present in the county where the execution of the instrument is sought to be proven for registration, he may be required to appear.

§ 121.014. Action for damages.

A person injured by the failure, refusal, or neglect of an officer to comply with a provision of this chapter has a cause of action against the officer to recover damages resulting from the failure, refusal, or neglect of the officer.

DEPOSITIONS

[TEX. CIV. PRAC. & REM. CODE ANN. (Vernon 1986)]

§ **20.001.** Persons who may take a deposition.

(a) A deposition of a witness who is alleged to reside or to be in this state may be taken by:
(1) a clerk of a district court;
(2) a judge or clerk of a county court; or
(3) a notary public of this state.
(b) A deposition of a witness who is alleged to reside or to be outside this state, but inside the United States, may be taken in another state by:
(1) a clerk of a court of record having a seal;
(2) a commissioner of deeds appointed under the laws of this state; or
(3) any notary public.
(c) A deposition of a witness who is alleged to reside or to be outside the Untied States may be taken by:
(1) a minister, commissioner, or charge d'affairs of the United States who is a resident of and is accredited in the country where the deposition is taken;
(2) a consul general, vice-consul, commercial agent, vice-commercial agent, deputy consul, or consular agent of the United States who is a resident of the country where the deposition is taken; or
(3) any notary public.
(d) A deposition of a witness who is alleged to be a member of the United States Armed Forces or of a United States Armed Forces Auxiliary or who is alleged to be a civilian employed by or accompanying the armed forces or an auxiliary outside the United States may be taken by a commissioned officer in the United States Armed Forces or United States Armed Forces Auxiliary or by a commissioned officer in the United States Armed Forces Reserve or an auxiliary of it. If a deposition appears on its face to have been taken as provided by this subsection and the deposition or any part of it is offered in evidence, it is presumed, absent pleading and proof to the contrary, that the person taking the deposition as a commissioned officer was a commissioned officer on the date that the deposition was taken, and that the deponent was a member of the authorized group of military personnel or civilians.

§ **20.002.** Testimony required by foreign jurisdiction.

If a court of record in any other state or foreign jurisdiction issues a mandate, writ, or commission that requires a witness's testimony in this state, either to written questions or by oral deposition, the witness may be compelled to appear and testify in the same manner and by the same process used for taking testimony in a proceeding pending in this state.

[TEX. R. CIV. P.]

District and County Courts

Rule 188. Depositions in foreign jurisdictions.

1. Whenever the deposition, written or oral, of any person is to be taken in a sister state or a foreign country, or in any other jurisdiction, foreign or domestic, for use in this state, such deposition may be taken (1) on notice before a person authorized to administer oaths in the place in which the examination is held, either by the law thereof or by the law of the State of Texas, or (2) before a person commissioned by the court in which the action is pending, and such person shall have the power, by virtue of such person's commission, to administer any necessary oath and take testimony, or (3) pursuant to a letter rogatory or a letter of request, or (4) pursuant to the means and terms of any applicable treaty or convention.

A commission, a letter rogatory, or a letter of request shall be issued on application and notice and on terms that are just and appropriate. It is not requisite to the issuance of a commission, a letter rogatory or a letter of request that the taking of the deposition in any other manner is impracticable or inconvenient; and a commission, a letter rogatory or a letter of request may all be issued in proper cases.

2. Upon the granting of a commission to take the oral deposition of a person under paragraph 1 above, the clerk of the court in which the action is pending shall immediately issue a commission to take the deposition of the person named in the application at the time and place set out in the application for the commission. The commission issued by the clerk shall be styled: "The State of Texas." The commission shall be dated and attested as other process; and the commission shall be addressed to the several officers authorized to take depositions as set forth in Section 20.001, Civil Practice and Remedies Code. The commission shall authorize and require the officer or officers to whom the commission is addressed immediately to issue and cause to be served upon the person to be deposed a subpoena directing that person to appear before said officer or officers at the time and place named in the commission for the purpose of giving that person's deposition.

Upon the granting of a commission to take the deposition of a person on written questions under paragraph 1 above, the clerk of the court in which the action is pending shall, after the service of the notice of filing the interrogatories has been completed, issue a commission to take the deposition of the person named in the notice. Such commission shall be styled, addressed, dated and attested as provided for in the case of an oral deposition and shall authorize and require the officer or officers to whom the same is addressed to summon the person to be deposed before the officer or officers forthwith and to take that person's answers under oath to the direct and cross interrogatories, if any, a copy of which shall be attached to such commission, and to return without delay the commission, the interrogatories and the answers of the person thereto to the clerk of the proper court, giving his official title and post office address.

3. Upon the granting of a letter rogatory under paragraph 1 above, the clerk of the court in which the action is pending shall issue a letter rogatory to take the deposition of the person named in the application at the time and place set out in the application for the letter rogatory. The letter rogatory issued by the clerk shall be styled, dated and attested as provided for in the case of a commission. The letter rogatory shall be addressed: "To the Appropriate Authority in [here name the state, territory or country"]. The letter rogatory shall authorize and request the appropriate authority to summon the person to be deposed before the authority forthwith and to take that person's answers under oath to the oral or written questions which are addressed to that person; the letter rogatory shall also authorize and request that the appropriate authority cause the deposition of the person to be reduced to writing, annexing to the writing any items marked as exhibits and to cause the written deposition, with all exhibits, to be returned to the clerk of the proper court under cover duly sealed and addressed.

4. Upon the granting of a letter of request, or any other device pursuant to the means and terms of any other applicable treaty or convention, to take the deposition, written or oral, of any person under paragraph 1 above, the clerk of the court in which the action is pending shall issue a letter of request or other device to take the deposition of the person named in the application at the time and place set out in the application for the letter of request or other device. The letter of request or other device shall be styled in the form prescribed by the treaty or convention under which the deposition is to be taken, such form to be presented to the clerk by the party seeking the deposition. Any error in the form of the letter of request or other device shall be waived unless objection thereto is filed and served on or before the time fixed in the order granting the letter of request or other device.

5. Evidence obtained in response to a letter roga-

tory or a letter of request need not be excluded merely for the reason that it is not a verbatim transcript or that the testimony was not taken under oath or for any similar departure from the requirements of depositions taken within the State of Texas under these rules.

RULE 205. Witness sworn.

Every person so deposing shall be first cautioned and sworn to testify the truth, the whole truth and nothing but the truth.

RULE 206. Examination.

The witness shall be carefully examined, his testimony shall be reduced to writing or typewriting by the officer taking the deposition, or by some person under his personal supervision, or by the deponent himself in the officer's presence, and by no other person, and shall, after it has been reduced to writing or typewriting, be subscribed by the deponent.

RULE 207. Objections to testimony.

The officer taking such oral deposition shall not sustain objections to any of the testimony taken, nor exclude same; but any of the parties or attorneys engaged in taking the testimony may have any objections they may make recorded with the testimony and reserved for the action of the court in which the cause is pending, but the court shall not be confined to objections made at the taking of the testimony.

RULE 208. Depositions certified and returned.

Such depositions shall be certified and returned by the officer taking the same, and opened and used as is provided in case of depositions on written questions. The party taking a deposition shall give prompt notice of its filing to all other parties.

RULE 209. Submission to witness; changes; signing.

When the testimony is fully transcribed the deposition shall be submitted to the witness for examination and shall be read to or by him, unless such examination and reading are waived by the witness and by the parties; provided that when the witness is a party to the suit with an attorney of record the deposition officer shall notify such attorney of record in writing by registered mail that the deposition is ready for such examination and reading at the office of such deposition officer, and if the witness does not appear and examine, read and sign his deposition within twenty (20) days after the mailing of such notice the deposition shall be returned as provided herein for unsigned depositions.

Any changes in form or substance which the witness desires to make shall be entered upon the deposition by the officer with the statement of the reasons given by the witness for making them. The deposition is not signed by the witness, unless the parties by stipulation waive the signing or the witness is ill or cannot be found or refuses to sign. If the deposition is not signed by the witness, the officer shall sign it and state on the record the fact of the waiver or of the illness or absence of the witness or the fact of the refusal to sign together with the reason, if any, given, therefor; and the deposition may then be used as fully as though signed; unless on motion to suppress, made as provided in Rule 212, the Court holds that the reasons given for the refusal to sign require rejection of the deposition in whole or in part.

RULE 210. Depositions opened.

Depositions, after being filed, may be opened by the clerk or justice at the request of either party or his counsel; and the clerk or justice shall indorse on such depositions upon what day and at whose request they were opened, signing his name thereto, and they shall remain on file for the inspection of either party.

[Tex. Code Crim. Pro. Ann.]

Art. 39.03. Officers who may take the deposition.

Upon the filing of such an affidavit and application, the court shall appoint, order or designate one of the following persons before whom such deposition shall be taken:

1. A district judge.
2. A county judge.
3. A notary public.
4. A district clerk.
5. A county clerk.

Such order shall specifically name such person and the time when and place where such deposition shall be taken. Failure of a witness to respond thereto, shall be punishable by contempt by the court. Such deposition shall be oral or written, as the court shall direct.

Art. 39.04. Applicability of civil rules.

The rules prescribed in civil cases for issuance of commissions, subpoenaing witnesses, taking the depositions of witnesses and all other formalities governing depositions shall, as to the manner and form of taking and returning the same and other formalities to the taking of the same, govern in criminal actions, when not in conflict with this Code.

Art. 39.05. Objections.

The rules of procedure as to objections in depositions in civil actions shall govern in criminal actions when not in conflict with this Code.

Art. 39.07. Certificate.

Where depositions are taken under commission in criminal actions, the officer or officers taking the same shall certify that the person deposing is the identical person named in the commission; or, if they cannot certify to the identity of the witness, there shall be an affidavit of some person attached to the deposition proving the identity of such witness, and the officer or officers shall certify that the person making the affidavit is known to them.

Art. 39.08. Authenticating the deposition.

The official seal and signature of the officer taking the deposition shall be attached to the certificate authenticating the deposition.

Art. 39.09. Nonresident witnesses.

Depositions of a witness residing out of the State may be taken before a judge or before a commissioner of deeds and depositions for this State, who resides within the State where the deposition is to be taken, or before a notary public of the place where such deposition is to be taken, or before any commissioned officer of the armed services or before any diplomatic or consular officer. The deposition of a nonresident witness who may be temporarily within the State, may be taken under the same rules which apply to the taking of depositions of other witnesses in the State.

Art. 39.10. Return.

In all cases the return of depositions may be made as provided in civil actions.

COMMISSIONERS

[Tex. Gov't Code Ann. (Vernon 1986)]

§ 406.051. Appointment.

(a) The governor may biennially appoint and commission one or more individuals in other states, territories, or foreign countries or in the District of Columbia to serve as commissioner of deeds.

(b) An appointment may be made only on the recommendation of the executive authority of the state, territory, or foreign country or of the District of Columbia.

§ 406.052. Term.

The term of office of a commissioner of deeds is two years.

§ 406.053. Oath.

Before performing the duties of office, a commissioner of deeds shall take and subscribe an oath to well and faithfully perform the duties of office under the laws of this state. The oath shall be:

(1) taken before the clerk of a court of record in the city, county, or country in which the commissioner resides;

(2) certified to by the clerk under the clerk's hand and seal of office; and

(3) filed in the office of the secretary of state of this state.

§ 406.054. Seal.

A commissioner of deeds shall provide a seal with a star of five points in the center and the words "Commissioner of the State of Texas" engraved on the seal. The seal shall be used to certify all official acts of the commissioner of deeds. An instrument that does not have the impression of the seal, or an act of the commissioner of deeds that is not certified by the impression of the seal, is not valid in this state.

§ 406.055. Authority.

A commissioner of deeds has the same authority as a notary public to take acknowledgments and proofs of written instruments, to administer oaths, and to take depositions to be used or recorded in this state.

LEGAL HOLIDAYS

[TEX. REV. CIV. STAT. ANN.]

Art. 4591. Enumeration.

The first day of January, the 19th day of January, the third Monday in February, the second day of March, the 21st day of April, the last Monday in May, the 19th day of June, the fourth day of July, the 27th day of August, the first Monday in September, the second Monday in October, the 11th day of November, the fourth Thursday in November, and the 25th day of December, of each year, and every day on which an election is held throughout the state, are declared legal holidays, on which all the public offices of the state may be closed and shall be considered and treated as Sunday for all purposes regarding the presenting for the payment or acceptance and of protesting for and giving notice of the dishonor of bills of exchange, bank checks and promissory notes placed by the law upon the footing of bills of exchange. The nineteenth day of January shall be known as "Confederate Heroes Day" in honor of Jefferson Davis, Robert E. Lee and other Confederate heroes. The 19th day of June is designated "Emancipation Day in Texas" in honor of the emancipation of the slaves in Texas on June 19, 1865.

Art. 342-910a. Legal holidays for banks or trust companies—alternative legal holidays for banks or trust companies—discrimination prohibited.

Sec. 1. Legal Holidays For Banks Or Trust Companies. Notwithstanding any existing provisions of law relative to negotiable or nonnegotiable instruments or commercial paper, but subject to the provisions of Section 2 of this article, only the following enumerated days are declared to be legal holidays for banking purposes on which each bank or trust company in Texas shall remain closed: Saturdays, Sundays, January 1, the third Monday in January, the third Monday in February, the last Monday in May, July 4, the first Monday in September, the second Monday in October, the 11th day of November, the fourth Thursday in November, and December 25.

When the dates July 4, November 11, or December 25 fall on Saturday, then the Friday immediately preceding such Saturday shall also be a legal holiday for banking purposes on which each bank or trust company in Texas shall remain closed. When the dates January 1, July 4, November 11, or December 25 fall on Sunday, then the Monday next following such Sunday shall also be a legal holiday for banking purposes on which each bank or trust company in Texas shall remain closed.

All such legal holidays shall be neither business days nor banking days under the laws of this State or the United States, and any act authorized, required or permitted to be performed at or by any bank or trust company on such days may be performed on the next succeeding business day and no liability or loss of right of any kind shall result therefrom to any bank or trust company.

Sec. 2. Alternative Legal Holidays For Banks Or Trust Companies. Any bank or trust company may elect to designate days on which it may close for general banking purposes pursuant to the provisions of this section, instead of Section 1 of this article, provided that any bank or trust company which has elected to be governed by this section shall remain closed on the following enumerated days, which days are declared to be legal holidays for banking purposes: Sundays, January 1, the third Monday in January, the third Monday in February, the last Monday in May, July 4, the first Monday in September, the second Monday in October, the 11th day of November, the fourth Thursday in November, and December 25. When the dates July 4, November 11, or December 25 fall on Saturday, then the Friday immediately preceding such Saturday shall also be a legal holiday for all banking purposes on which each bank or trust company shall remain closed. When the dates January 1, July 4, November 11, or December 25 fall on Sunday, then the Monday next following each Sunday shall also be a mandatory legal holiday for banking purposes on which each bank or trust company shall remain closed. Except as herein provided, any bank or trust company doing business in this state may, at its option, elect to be governed by this section and close for general banking purposes either on Saturday or on any other weekday of any week in the year in addition to mandatory legal holidays, provided:

(a) such day is designated at least 15 days in advance by adoption of a resolution concurred in by a majority of the board of directors thereof (or, if an unincorporated bank or trust company, by its owner or a majority of its owners, if there be more than one owner); and

(b) notice of the day or days designated in such resolution is posted in a conspicuous place in such bank or trust company for at least 15 days in advance of the day or days designated; and

(c) a copy of such resolution certified by the president or cashier of such bank or trust company is filed with the Banking Department of Texas.

The filing of such copy of resolution as aforesaid with the Banking Department of Texas shall be deemed to be proof in all courts in this state that such bank or trust company has duly complied with the provisions of this section. Any such election to so close shall remain in effect until a subsequent resolution shall be adopted and notice thereof posted and a copy thereof filed in the manner above provided.

If any bank or trust company elects to close for general banking purposes on Saturday or any other weekday as herein provided, it may, at its option, remain open on such day for the purpose of performing limited banking services. Notice of election to perform limited banking services shall be contained in the resolution and notices, above provided, with respect to closing for general banking purposes. Limited banking services may include such of the ordinary and usual services provided by the bank as the board of directors may determine, except the following: making loans, renewing or extending loans, certifying checks, and issuing cashier's checks.

Such day upon which such bank or trust company may elect to close for general banking purposes shall with respect to such institution be treated as a legal holiday for all purposes and not a business day; provided that if such bank shall elect to perform limited banking services on such day, the same shall not be deemed a legal holiday for the performance of limited banking services. Any bank or trust company which elects to close for general banking purposes on Saturday or any other weekday but which elects to perform limited banking services shall not be subjected to any liability or loss of rights for performing limited banking services or refusing to perform any other banking services on such day.

UTAH

NOTARIES PUBLIC

[UTAH CODE ANN.]

§ 46-1-1. Short title.

This chapter is known as the "Notaries Public Reform Act."

§ 46-1-2. Definitions.

As used in this chapter:

(1) "Acknowledgment" means a notarial act in which a notary certifies that a signer, whose identity is personally known to the notary or proven on the basis of satisfactory evidence, has admitted, in the notary's presence, having signed a document voluntarily for its stated purpose.

(2) "Copy certification" means a notarial act in which a notary certifies that a photocopy is an accurate copy of a document that is neither a public record nor publicly recordable.

(3) "Jurat" means a notarial act in which a notary certifies that a signer, whose identity is personally known to the notary or proven on the basis of satisfactory evidence, has made, in the notary's presence, a voluntary signature and taken an oath or affirmation vouching for the truthfulness of the signed document.

(4) "Notarial certificate" and "certificate" mean the part of or attachment to a notarized document for completion by the notary and bearing the notary's signature and seal.

(5) "Oath" and "affirmation" mean a notarial act or part thereof in which a notary certifies that a person made a vow or affirmation in the presence of the notary on penalty of perjury.

(6) "Personal knowledge of identity" means familiarity with an individual resulting from interactions with that individual over a period of time sufficient to eliminate every reasonable doubt that the individual has the identity claimed.

§ 46-1-3. Qualifications—commissioning—term.

(1) Except as provided in this section, the director of the Division of Corporations and Commercial Code shall commission as a notary any qualified person who submits an application in accordance with this chapter.

(2) To be qualified for a notarial commission, a person shall:

(a) be 18 years of age or older;

(b) be a resident of this state 30 days immediately preceding the filing for a notarial commission;

(c) be able to read and write English; and

(d) submit an application to the Division of Corporations and Commercial Code.

(3) An application for a notarial commission may be denied based on:

(a) the applicant's conviction for a criminal offense involving moral turpitude;

(b) any revocation, suspension, or restriction of a notarial commission issued to the applicant by this or any other state; or

(c) the applicant's official misconduct while acting in the capacity of a notary public.

(4) Each notary public shall be commissioned for the term of four years, unless the commission is revoked under Section 46-1-16, or resigned.

§ 46-1-4. Bond.

(1) A notarial commission may not become effective until a constitutional oath of office and $5,000 bond has been filed with and approved by the Division of Corporations and Commercial Code. The bond shall be executed by a licensed surety for a term of four years commencing on the commission's effective date and terminating on its expiration date, with payment of bond funds to any person conditioned upon the notary's misconduct while acting in the scope of his commission.

(2) The bond required under Subsection (1) may be executed by the Office of Risk Management for notaries public employed by a state office or agency.

§ 46-1-5. Recommissioning.

An applicant for recommissioning as a notary shall submit a new application and comply with the provisions of this chapter.

§ 46-1-6. Application.

(1) Each application for a notarial commission shall be verified under oath and shall be made on a form provided by the Division of Corporations and Commercial Code.

(2) Each applicant shall pay to the division an application fee determined under Subsection 63-38-3(2).

§ 46-1-7. Powers.

Notaries public may exercise the following notarial powers within the state:

(1) acknowledgments;

(2) oaths, affirmations, and jurats; and

(3) copy certifications.

§ 46-1-8. Improper notarizations.

A notary public may not perform a notarial act if the notary:

(1) is a signer of or named in the document that is to be notarized; or

(2) will receive directly from a transaction connected with the notarial act any commission, fee, advantage, right, title, interest, cash, property, or other consideration exceeding in value the fees specified in Section 46-1-12.

§ 46-1-9. Impartiality.

A notary public may not influence a person to enter into or not to enter into a lawful transaction involving a notarial act by the notary. A notary public shall perform notarial acts in lawful transactions for any requesting person who tenders the appropriate fee specified in Section 46-1-12.

§ 46-1-10. False certificate.

A notary public may not execute a certificate containing a statement known by the notary to be false or perform any official action with intent to deceive or defraud.

§ 46-1-11. Testimonials prohibited.

A notary may not endorse or promote any product, service, contest, or other offering if the notary's title or seal is used in the endorsement or promotional statement.

§ 46-1-12. Fees.

The maximum fees that may be charged by a notary public for notarial acts are for:

(1) acknowledgements, $5 per signature;

(2) oaths or affirmations without a signature, $5 per person;

(3) jurats, $5 per signature; and

(4) certified copies, $5 per page certified.

§ 46-1-13. Official signature—official seal—seal impression.

(1) In completing a notarial act, a notary shall sign on the notarial certificate exactly and only the name indicated on the notary's commission.

(2) A notary public shall keep an official notarial seal that is the exclusive property of the notary public and that may not be used by any other person. Upon the resignation, revocation, or expiration of a notarial commission or death of a notary public, the seal shall be destroyed.

(3) A new seal shall be obtained for any new commission or recommission after July 1, 1990. The seal impression shall consist of the following:

Near the notary's official signature on a notarial certificate, the notary shall affix in ink a sharp, legible, and photographically reproducible impression of the notarial seal that includes:

(a) the notary public's name exactly as indicated on the commission;

(b) the words "notary public," "state of Utah," and "my commission expires (commission expiration date)";

(c) the address of the notary's business or residence;

(d) a facsimile of the great seal of the state of Utah; and

(e) a rectangular border no larger than one inch by two and one-half inches surrounding the required words and seal.

(4) Notwithstanding Subsection (3), a seal obtained for any existing notarial commission which complied with the statutory requirements for seals in effect at the time the commission was issued may continue to be used until the expiration of the original commission.

(5) An embossed seal impression that is not photographically reproducible may be used in addition to but not in lieu of the photographically reproducible seal required in this section.

(6) The notarial seal shall be affixed in a manner that does not obscure or render illegible any information or signatures contained in the document or in the notarial certificate.

§ 46-1-14. Commission required to obtain seal.

A vendor may not provide a notarial seal to a person claiming to be a notary, unless the person presents to the vendor for his inspection a copy of the person's notarial commission.

§ 46-1-15. Liability.

A notary public is liable to any person for all damage to that person proximately caused by the notary's misconduct in performing a notarization. A surety for a notary's bond is liable to any person for damages proximately caused to that person by the notary's misconduct in performing a notarization, but the surety's liability may not exceed the penalty of the bond or of any remaining bond funds that have not been expended to other claimants. Regardless of the number of claimants, a surety's total liability may not exceed the penalty of the bond.

§ 46-1-16. Revocation.

The Division of Corporations and Commercial Code may revoke a notarial commission on any ground for which an application for a notarial commission may be denied under Section 46-1-3.

§ 46-1-17. Notice not invalidated.

If a notarial act is performed contrary to or in violation of this chapter, that fact does not of itself invalidate notice to third parties of the contents of the document notarized.

§ 46-1-18. Notarial acts affecting real property.

Notarial acts affecting real property in this state shall also be performed in conformance with Title 57.

FEES

§ 21-4-1. Fees of notaries public.

Every notary public may collect for his own use the following fees:

(1) for protesting the nonpayment of a promissory note, or nonpayment or nonacceptance of a bill of exchange, draft, or check, $2;

(2) for drawing and serving each notice of nonpayment of a promissory note, or the nonpayment or nonacceptance of a bill of exchange, order, draft, or check, $2;

(3) for recording each protest, $1;

(4) for drawing an affidavit, deposition, or other paper, for which provision is not made in this section: (a) for first folio, $2; and (b) for each subsequent folio, $1;

(5) for taking an acknowledgment or proof of a deed or other instrument, to include the seal and writing of the certificate: (a) for the first signature, $2; and (b) for each additional signature, $1;

(6) for administering an oath or affirmation, $2; and

(7) for every certificate, to include writing it and the seal, $2.

ACKNOWLEDGMENTS

§ 57-2-10. Proof of execution—how made.

The proof of the execution of any conveyance whereby real estate is conveyed or may be affected shall be:

(1) By the testimony of a subscribing witness, if there is one; or,

(2) When all the subscribing witnesses are dead, or cannot be had, by evidence of the handwriting of the party, and of a subscribing witness, if there is one, given by a credible witness to each signature.

§ 57-2-11. Witness must be known or identified.

No proof by a subscribing witness shall be taken unless such witness shall be personally known to the officer taking the proof to be the person whose name is subscribed to the conveyance as a witness thereto, or shall be proved to be such by the oath or affirmation of a credible witness personally known to such officer.

§ 57-2-12. Certificate of proof by subscribing witness.

No certificate of such proof shall be made unless such subscribing witness shall prove that the person whose name is subscribed thereto as a party is the person described in, and who executed, the same; that such person executed the conveyance, and that such person subscribed his name thereto as a witness thereof at the request of the maker of such instrument.

§ 57-2-13. Form of certificate.

The certificate of such proof shall be substantially in the following form, to wit:

State of Utah, County of _____

On this _____ day of _____, 19___,

before me personally appeared _____, personally known to me (or satisfactorily proved to me by the oath of _____, a competent and credible witness for that purpose, by me duly sworn) to be the same person whose name is subscribed to the above instrument as a witness thereto, who, being by me duly sworn, deposed and said that he resides in _____, county of _____, and state of Utah; that he was present and saw _____, personally known to him to be the signer of the above instrument as a party thereto, sign and deliver the same, and heard him acknowledge that he executed the same, and that he, the deponent, thereupon signed his name as a subscribing witness thereto at the request of said _____.

§ 57-2-14. Proof of handwriting.

No proof by evidence of the handwriting of a party, or of the subscribing witness or witnesses, shall be taken unless the officer taking the same shall be satisfied that all the subscribing witnesses to such conveyance are dead, out of the jurisdiction, or cannot be had to prove the execution thereof.

§ 57-2-15. What evidence required for certificate of proof.

No certificate of any such proof shall be made unless a competent and credible witness shall state on oath or affirmation that he personally knew the person whose name is subscribed thereto as a party, well knows his signature, stating his means of knowledge, and believes the name of the party subscribed thereto as a party was subscribed by such person; nor unless a competent and credible witness shall in like manner state that he personally knew the person whose name is subscribed to such conveyance as a witness, well knows his signature, stating his means of knowledge, and believes the name subscribed thereto as a witness was thereto subscribed by such person.

§ 57-2-16. Subpoena to subscribing witness.

Upon the application of any grantee in any conveyance required by law to be recorded, or of any person claiming under such grantee, verified under the oath of the applicant, that any witness to such conveyance residing in the county where such application is made refuses to appear and testify touching the execution thereof, and that such conveyance cannot be proved without his evidence, any officer authorized to take the acknowledgment or proof of such conveyance may issue a subpoena requiring such witness to appear before such officer and testify touching the execution thereof.

§ 57-2-17. Disobedience of subpoenaed witness—contempt—proof aliunde.

Every person who, being served with a subpoena, shall without reasonable cause refuse or neglect to appear, or, appearing, shall refuse to answer upon oath touching the matters aforesaid, shall be liable to the party injured for such damages as may be sustained by him on account of such neglect or refusal, and may also be dealt with for contempt as provided by law; but no person shall be required to attend who resides out of the county in which the proof is to be taken, nor unless his reasonable expenses shall have first been tendered to him; provided, that if it shall appear to the satisfaction to the officer so authorized to take such acknowledgment that such subscribing witness purposely conceals himself, or keeps out of the way, so that he cannot be served with a subpoena or taken on attachment after the use of due diligence to that end, or in case of his continued failure or refusal to testify for the space of one hour after his appearance shall have been compelled by process, then said conveyance or other instrument may be proved and admitted to record in the same manner as if such subscribing witness thereto were dead.

Recognition of Acknowledgments Act

§ 57-2a-1. Short title.

This chapter is known as the "Recognition of Acknowledgments Act."

§ 57-2a-2. Definitions.

As used in this chapter:

(1) "Acknowledged before me" means:

(a) that the person acknowledging appeared before the person taking the acknowledgment;

(b) that he acknowledged he executed the document;

(c) that, in the case of:

(i) a natural person, he executed the document for the purposes stated in it;

(ii) a corporation, the officer or agent acknowledged he held the position or title set forth in the document or certificate, he signed the document on behalf of the corporation by proper authority, and the document was the act of the corporation for the purpose stated in it;

(iii) a partnership, the partner or agent acknowledged he signed the document on behalf of the partnership by proper authority, and he executed the document as the act of the partnership for the purposes stated in it;

(iv) a person acknowledging as principal by an attorney in fact, he executed the document by proper authority as the act of the principal for the purposes stated in it; or

(v) a person acknowledging as a public officer, trustee, administrator, guardian, or other representative, he signed the document by proper authority, and he executed the document in the capacity and for the purposes stated in it; and

(d) that the person taking the acknowledgment:

(i) either knew or had satisfactory evidence that the person acknowledging was the person named in the document or certificate; and

(ii) in the case of a person executing a document in a representative capacity, either had satisfactory evidence or received the sworn statement or affirmation of the person acknowledging that the person had the proper authority to execute the document.

(2) "Notarial act" means any act a notary public is authorized by state law to perform, including administering oaths and affirmations, taking acknowledgments of documents, and attesting documents.

§ 57-2a-3. Persons authorized to perform notarial acts.

(1) Notarial acts performed in this state shall be performed by:

(a) a judge or court clerk having a seal;

(b) a notary public; or

(c) a county clerk or county recorder.

(2) The following persons authorized under the laws and regulations of other governments may perform notarial acts outside this state for use in this state with the same effect as if performed by a notary public of this state:

(a) a notary public authorized to perform notarial acts in the place where the act is performed;

(b) a judge, clerk, or deputy clerk of any court of record in the place where the notarial act is performed;

(c) an officer of the foreign service of the United States, a consular agent, or any other person authorized by regulation of the United States Department of State to perform notarial acts in the place where the act is performed;

(d) a commissioned officer in active service with the Armed Forces of the United States any any other person authorized by regulation of the Armed Forces to perform notarial acts if the notarial act is performed for any of his dependents, a merchant seaman of the United States, a member of the Armed Forces of the United States, or any other person serving with or accompanying the Armed Forces of the United States; or

(e) any other person authorized to perform notarial acts in the place where the act is performed.

§ 57-2a-4. Proof of authority—prima facie evidence.

(1) Except as provided in Subsections (2) and (3), the signature, title or rank, branch of service, and serial number, if any, of any person described in Subsections 57-2a-3(1) through (5) [Subsections 57-2a-3(2)(a) through (2)(e)] are sufficient proof of his authority to perform a notarial act. Further proof of his authority is not required.

(2) Proof of the authority of a person to perform a notarial act under the laws or regulations of a foreign country is sufficient if:

(a) a foreign service officer of the United States resident in the country in which the act is performed or a diplomatic or consular officer of the foreign country resident in the United States certifies that a person holding that office is authorized to perform the act;

(b) the official seal of the person performing the notarial act is affixed to the document; or

(c) the title and indication of authority to perform notarial acts of the person appears either in a digest of foreign law or in a list customarily used as a source of such information.

(3) The signature and title or rank of the person performing the notarial act are prima facie evidence that he is a person with the designated title and that his signature is genuine.

§ 57-2a-5. Certificate.

A person taking an acknowledgment shall cause a certificate in a form acceptable under Section 57-2a-6 or 57-2a-7 to be endorsed on or attached to the document or other written instrument.

§ 57-2a-6. Form of certificate.

The form of a certificate of acknowledgment used by a person whose authority is recognized under Section 57-2a-3 shall be accepted if:

(1) The certificate is in a form prescribed by the laws or rules of this state;

(2) The certificate is in a form prescribed by the laws or regulations applicable in the place where the acknowledgment is taken; or

(3) The certificate contains the words "acknowledged before me," or their substantial equivalent.

§ 57-2a-7. Form of acknowledgment.

The form of acknowledgment set forth in this section, if properly completed, is sufficient under any law of this state. It is known as "Statutory Short Form of Acknowledgment." This section does not preclude the use of other forms.

State of _____]
                     ] ss.
County of _____]

The foregoing instrument was acknowledged before me this (date) by (person acknowledging, title or representative capacity, if any).

_____
(Signature of Person Taking Acknowledgment)

(Seal)   (Title)

My commission   Residing at:

expires:

_____   _____

The phrases "My commission expires" and "Residing at" may be omitted if this information is included in the notarial seal.

§ 57-3-1. Certificate of acknowledgment, proof of execution, jurat, or other certificate required—notarial acts affecting real property.

(1) A certificate of the acknowledgment of any document, or of the proof of the execution of any document, or a jurat as defined in Section 46-1-2, or other notarial certificate containing the words "subscribed and sworn" or their substantial equivalent, that is signed and certified by the officer taking the acknowledgment, proof, or jurat, as provided in this title, entitles the document and the certificate to be recorded in the office of the recorder of the county where the real property is located.

(2) Notarial acts affecting real property in this state shall also be performed in conformance with Chapter 1, Title 46.

§ 69-1-2. Transmitting written instruments by telegraph or telephone authorized—entitled to record—force and effect of copies—documents submitted to recorder—requirements.

Any power of attorney or other instrument in writing duly proved or acknowledged and certified so as to be entitled to record may, together with the certificate of its proof or acknowledgment, be sent by telegraph or telephone, and the telegraphic or telephonic copy shall prima facie have the same force and effect in all respects, and may be admitted to record and recorded in the same manner and with the same effect, as the original. Documents submitted to the county recorder for recording shall be original or certified copies from other offices of public record, as required by Title 57.

§ 69-1-4. Transmitting certified instruments—burden of proof.

Except as hereinbefore otherwise provided, any

instrument in writing, duly certified under his hand and official seal by a notary public, commissioner of deeds or clerk of a court of record to be genuine to the personal knowledge of such officer, may, together with such certificate, be sent by telegraph or telephone. The telegraphic or telephonic copy thereof shall, prima facie only, have the same force, effect and validity in all respects as the original, and the burden of proof shall be on the party denying the genuineness or due execution of the original.

§ 78-25-7. Certificate of acknowledgment as evidence of execution.

Every private writing, except last wills and testaments, may be acknowledged or proved, and certified in the manner provided for the acknowledgment or proof of conveyances of real property, and the certificate of such acknowledgment or proof is prima facie evidence of the execution of the writing in the same manner as if it were a conveyance of real property.

DEPOSITIONS

§ 78-24-16. Oaths—who may administer.

Every court, every judge, clerk and deputy clerk of any court, every justice, every notary public, and every officer or person authorized to take testimony in any action or proceeding, or to decide upon evidence, has power to administer oaths or affirmations.

§ 78-24-17. Form.

An oath or affirmation in an action or proceeding may be administered, the person who swears or affirms expressing his assent when addressed, in the following form:

You do solemnly swear (or affirm) that the evidence you shall give in this issue (or matter) pending between _____ and _____ shall be the truth, the whole truth and nothing but the truth, so help you God (or, under the pains and penalties of perjury).

§ 78-24-18. Affirmation or declaration instead of oath allowed.

Any person may at his option, instead of taking an oath, make his solemn affirmation or declaration, by assenting, when addressed in the following form:

"You do solemnly affirm (or declare) that," etc., as in the preceding section.

§ 78-24-19. May be varied to suit witness' belief.

Whenever the court before which a person is offered as a witness is satisfied that he has a peculiar mode of swearing, connected with or in addition to the usual form, which in his opinion is more solemn or obligatory, the court may in its discretion adopt that mode.

If a person who is sworn believes in any other than the Christian religion, he may be sworn according to the peculiar ceremonies of his religion, if there are any.

§ 78-26-5. Taking of affidavits in this state.

An affidavit to be used before any court, judge, or officer of this state may be taken before any judge, the clerk of any court, any justice court judge, or any notary public in this state.

§ 78-26-6. If in another state.

An affidavit taken in another state or territory of the United States, to be used in this state, may be taken before a commissioner appointed by the governor of this state to take affidavits and depositions in such other state or territory, or before any notary public in another state or territory, or before any judge or clerk of a court of record having a seal.

§ 78-26-7. If in a foreign country.

An affidavit taken in a foreign country, to be used in this state, may be taken before an ambassador, minister, consul, vice consul or consular agent of the United States, or before any judge of a court of record having a seal, in such foreign country.

§ 78-26-8. If before foreign court or judge, clerk of court to certify.

When an affidavit is taken before a judge or court in another state or territory, or in a foreign country, the genuineness of the signature of the judge, the existence of the court, and the fact that such judge is a member thereof, must be certified by the clerk of the court under the seal thereof.

[Utah R. Civ. P.]

RULE 28. Persons before whom depositions may be taken.

(a) **Within the United States.** Within the United States or within a territory or insular possession subject to the jurisdiction of the United States, depositions shall be taken before an officer authorized to administer oaths by the laws of the United Sates or of the place where the examination is held, or before a person appointed by the court in which the action is pending. A person so appointed has power to administer oaths and take testimony. The term "officer" as used in Rules 30, 31, and 32 includes a person appointed by the court or designated by the parties under Rule 29.

(b) **In foreign countries.** In a foreign country, depositions may be taken (1) on notice before a person authorized to administer oaths in the place in which the examination is held, either by the law thereof or by the law of the United States, or (2) before a person commissioned by the court, and a person so commissioned shall have the power by virtue of his commission to administer any necessary oath and take testimony, or (3) pursuant to a letter rogatory. A commission or a letter rogatory shall be issued on application and notice and on terms that are just and appropriate. It is not requisite to the issuance of a commission or a letter rogatory that the taking of the deposition in any other manner is impracticable or inconvenient; and both a commission and a letter rogatory may be issued in proper cases. A notice or commission may designate the person before whom the deposition is to be taken either by name or descriptive title. A letter rogatory may be addressed "To the Appropriate Authority in [here name of country]." Evidence obtained in response to a letter rogatory need not be excluded merely for the reason that it is not a verbatim transcript or that the testimony was not taken under oath or for any similar departure from the requirements for depositions taken within the United States under these rules.

(c) **Disqualification for interest.** No deposition shall be taken before a person who is a relative or employee or attorney or counsel of any of the parties, or is a relative or employee of such attorney or counsel, or is financially interested in the action.

COMMISSIONERS

[UTAH CODE ANN.]

§ 21-4-2. Fees of commissioners of deeds.

Every commissioner of deeds may collect for his own use the same fees as those provided for a notary public.

§ 46-2-1. Appointment—term—removal.

The governor may appoint and commission in each state and territory of the United States, except this state, and in any foreign country, one or more commissioners of deeds, to hold office for the term of four years from and after the date of their com-

missions, but the governor may remove from office any commissioner during the term for which he was appointed. The commission shall be filed and recorded with the Division of Corporations and Commercial Code.

§ 46-2-2. Powers.

Every commissioner of deeds has power within the state or country for which he was appointed:

(1) To administer and certify oaths.

(2) To take and certify depositions and affidavits.

(3) To take and certify the acknowledgment or proof of powers of attorney, mortgages, transfers, grants, deeds or other instruments for record.

(4) To provide and keep an official seal, upon which must be engraved his name, the words "Commissioner of Deeds for the State of Utah," and the name of the state or country for which he is commissioned.

(5) To authenticate with his official seal all of his official acts.

§ 46-2-3. Place of residence and date commission expires affixed to signature.

To all acknowledgments, oaths, affirmations and instruments of every kind taken and certified by a commissioner of deeds he shall affix to his signature his official title and his place of residence and the date on which his commission expires.

§ 46-2-4. Force and effect of official acts.

All oaths administered, depositions and affidavits taken, and all acknowledgments and proofs certified, by commissioners of deeds have the same force and effect, to all intents and purposes, as if done and certified in this state by any officer authorized by law to perform such acts.

§ 46-2-5. Official oath.

Before a commissioner of deeds can perform any of the duties of his office, he shall take and subscribe an oath that he will faithfully perform his duties, which oath shall be taken and subscribed before some judge or clerk of a court of record in the state, territory or foreign country in which the commissioner is to exercise his functions, and shall be certified under the hand of the person taking it and the seal of his court.

§ 46-2-6. Oaths and seals of commissioners to be filed.

The official oaths of commissioners of deeds and

impressions of their official seals must be filed with the Division of Archives within six months after they are taken and adopted.

§ 46-2-7. Fees.

The fees of commissioners of deeds are the same as those prescribed for notaries public.

§ 46-2-8. Copy of laws to accompany commission.

The Division of Corporations and Commercial Code must transmit with the commission to the appointee a certified copy of this chapter and of the laws prescribing the fees of notaries public.

§ 46-2-9. Commissioners of other states and countries residing here.

Commissioner [Commissioners] of deeds for other states or countries residing in this state shall file with the Division of Archives a certified copy of their commissions, together with a statement of their places of residence.

LEGAL HOLIDAYS

§ 63-13-2. Legal holidays—personal preference day—Governor authorized to declare additional days.

(1) (a) The following-named days are legal holidays in this state:

(i) every Sunday;

(ii) January 1, called New Year's Day;

(iii) the third Monday of January, observed as the anniversary of the birth of Dr. Martin Luther King, Jr., also known as Human Rights Day;

(iv) the third Monday of February, observed as the anniversary of the birth of George Washington and Abraham Lincoln, also known as Presidents' Day;

(v) the last Monday of May, called Memorial Day;

(vi) July 4, called Independence day;

(vii) July 24, called Pioneer Day;

(viii) the first Monday of September, called Labor Day;

(ix) the second Monday of October, called Columbus Day;

(x) November 11, called Veterans' Day;

(xi) the fourth Thursday of November, called Thanksgiving Day;

(xii) December 25, called Christmas; and

(xiii) all days which may be set apart by the President of the United States, or the governor of this state by proclamation as days of fast or thanksgiving.

(b) If any of the holidays under Subsection (1)(a), except the first mentioned, namely Sunday, falls on Sunday, then the following Monday shall be the holiday.

(c) If any of the holidays under Subsection (1)(a) falls on Saturday the preceding Friday shall be the holiday.

(d) Each employee may select one additional day, called Personal Preference Day, to be scheduled pursuant to rules adopted by the Department of Human Resource Management.

(2)(a) Whenever in his opinion extraordinary conditions exist justifying the action, the governor may:

(i) declare, by proclamation, legal holidays in addition to those holidays under Subsection (1); and

(ii) limit the holidays to certain classes of business and activities to be designated by him.

(b) A holiday may not extend for a longer period than 60 consecutive days.

(c) Any holiday may be renewed for one or more periods not exceeding 30 days each as the governor may consider necessary, and any holiday may, by like proclamation, be terminated before the expiration of the period for which it was declared.

VERMONT

NOTARIES PUBLIC

[Vt. Stat. Ann.]

Tit. 24, § 441. Appointment; jurisdiction; ex officio notaries; application.

(a) The judges of the superior court may appoint as many notaries public for the county as the public good requires, to hold office until ten days after the expiration of the term of office of such judges, whose jurisdiction shall extend throughout the state.

(b) The clerk of the supreme court, county clerks, district court clerks and town clerks and their assistants shall be ex officio notaries public.

(c) Every applicant for appointment and commission as a notary public shall complete an application to be filed with the clerk of the superior court stating that the applicant is a resident of the county and has reached the age of majority, giving his business or home address and providing a handwritten specimen of the applicant's official signature.

(d) An ex officio notary public shall cease to be a notary public when he vacates the office on which his status as a notary public depends.

Tit. 24, § 441a. Nonresident notary public.

A nonresident may be appointed as a notary public, provided the individual resides in a state adjoining this state and maintains, or is regularly employed in, a place of business in this state. Before a nonresident may be appointed as a notary public, the individual shall file with the judges of the superior court in the county where the individual's place of employment is located, an application setting forth the individual's residence and the place of employment in this state. A nonresident notary public shall notify the judges of the superior court, in writing, of any change of residence or of place of employment in this state.

Tit. 24, § 442. Oath; certificate of appointment recorded; form.

A person appointed as notary public shall cause the certificate of his appointment to be filed and recorded in the office of the county clerk where issued. Before entering upon the duties of his office he, as well as an ex officio notary, shall take the oath prescribed by the constitution, and shall duly subscribe the same with his correct signature, which oath thus subscribed shall be kept on file by the county clerk as part of the records of such county.

The certificate of appointment shall be substantially in the following form:

STATE OF VERMONT,
ss.
. . . . County

This is to certify that AB of . . . . in such county, was, on the . . . . day of . . . . , 19. . ., appointed by the judges of the county court for such county a notary public for the term ending on February 10, 19. . .

Judges of the
county court.

. . . .
. . . .

. . . .
And at . . . . in such county, on this . . .
. day of . . . ., 19. . . personally appeared AB
. . . . and took oath of office prescribed in
the constitution.
> Before me,
>   CD . . . .
>   (Designation of the officer
>   administering the oath).

Tit. 24, § 443. Preservation of oaths.

The county clerk at the end of each biennial period shall cause the oaths aforesaid to be bound
into book form, which book shall then constitute
the final record thereof and shall be duly attested
by the clerk as such.

Tit. 24, § 445. Powers.

Every notary public is empowered to take acknowledgments, administer oaths and affirmations, certify that a copy of a document is a true
copy of another document, and perform any other
act permitted by law.

Tit. 24, § 446. Liabilities.

A notary public shall be liable to the persons involved for all damages caused by the notary's official misconduct.

ADDITIONAL AUTHORITY

Tit. 12, § 5852. Oaths of office; by whom administered.

When other provision is not made by law, oaths
of office may be administered by any justice of the
supreme court, superior judge, justice of the peace,
judge of the district court, notary public or the presiding officer, secretary or clerk of either house of
the general assembly.

Tit. 12, § 5854. Oaths, administering by court clerks, justices, notaries, etc.; certification.

The clerk of the supreme court, county clerks,
justices of the peace, judges and registers of probate, judges and clerks of the district court, notaries public and masters appointed by a county
court under an order of referee may administer
oaths in all cases where an oath is required, unless
a different provision is expressly made by law; and
a notary public need not affix his official seal to a
certificate of an oath administered by him. County
clerks and clerks of the district court may certify

the oaths administered by them under the seal of
the court.

Tit. 24, § 183. Certificate of appointment of notary public or master in chancery.

Immediately after the appointment of a notary
public or master, the county clerk shall send to the
secretary of state a certificate of such appointment,
on blanks furnished by such secretary, containing
the name, signature, and legal residence of the appointee, and the term of office of each notary public. Such secretary shall cause such certificate to be
bound in suitable volumes and to be indexed. Upon
request, such secretary may certify the appointment, qualification and signature of such notary
public or master in chancery on tender of his legal
fees.

FEES

Tit. 32, § 1759. Notaries public.

Notaries public shall receive for each protest under seal and the notices, $2.00; for each certificate
under seal, $.50.

ACKNOWLEDGMENTS

Tit. 11, § 231. Acknowledgments by stockholder or officer.

A person legally qualified to take acknowledgments shall not be disqualified to take such acknowledgments to an instrument in which a corporation is a party, by reason of his being a
stockholder in or an officer or employee of such
corporation.

Tit. 27, § 341. Requirements generally; recording.

(a) Deeds and other conveyances of lands, or of
an estate or interest therein, shall be signed by the
party granting the same and signed by two or more
witnesses and acknowledged by the grantor before
a town clerk, notary public, master, county clerk
or judge or register of probate and recorded at
length in the clerk's office of the town in which
such lands lie. Such acknowledgment before a notary public shall be valid without his official seal
being affixed to his signature.

(b) A deed or other conveyance of land which
includes a reference to a survey prepared or revised
after July 1, 1988 may be recorded only if it is accompanied by the survey to which it refers, or cites

the volume and page in the land records showing where the survey has previously been recorded.

Tit. 27, § 379. Acknowledgment out of state.

If deeds and other conveyances, and powers of attorney for the conveyance of lands, the acknowledgment or proof of which is taken without the state, are certified agreeably to the laws of the state, province or kingdom in which such acknowledgment or proof is taken, they shall be as valid as though the same were taken before a proper officer or court in this state. The proof of the same may be taken, and the same acknowledged with like effect before a justice, magistrate or notary public within the United States or in a foreign country, before a commissioner appointed for that purpose by the governor of this state, or before a minister, charge d'affaires, consul or vice consul of the United States in a foreign country.

Tit. 30, § 3036. Acknowledgments, members [of electric cooperatives] authorized.

A person who is authorized to take acknowledgments under the laws of this state shall not be disqualified from taking acknowledgments of instruments executed in favor of [an electric cooperative] or to which it is a party, by reason of being an officer, trustee or member of such cooperative.

DEPOSITIONS

Tit. 12, § 5810. Oath to be administered to witnesses.

You solemnly swear that the evidence you shall give, relative to the cause now under consideration, shall be the whole truth and nothing but the truth. So help you God.

Tit. 12, § 5811. Oath to be administered to interpreter of testimony.

You solemnly swear that you will justly, truly and impartially interpret to AB the oath about to be administered to him, and the testimony he shall give relative to the cause now under consideration. So help you God.

Tit. 12, § 5851. Affirmation.

In the administration of an oath, the word "swear" may be omitted, and the word "affirm" substituted, when the person to whom the obligation is administered is religiously scrupulous of swearing, or taking an oath in the prescribed form;

and, in such case, the words "so help you God" may be omitted, and the words "under the pains and penalties of perjury" substituted; and a person so affirming shall be considered, for every legal purpose or privilege, qualification or liability, as having been duly sworn.

[Vt. R. Civ. P.]

RULE 28. Persons before whom depositions may be taken.

(a) **Within the State.** Within the state depositions shall be taken before a justice of the peace or notary public or a person appointed by the court. A person so appointed has power to administer oaths and take testimony. The term "officer" as used in Rules 30, 31 and 32 includes a person appointed by the court or designated by the parties under Rule 29.

(b) **Outside the State.** Within another state, or within a territory or insular possession subject to the dominion of the United States, or in a foreign country, depositions may be taken (1) on notice before a person authorized to administer oaths in the place in which the examination is held, either by the law thereof or by the law of the United States, or (2) before a person appointed or commissioned by the court, and such a person shall have the power by virtue of the appointment or commission to administer any necessary oath and take testimony, or (3) pursuant to a letter rogatory. A commission or a letter rogatory shall be issued on application and notice and on terms that are just and appropriate. It is not requisite to the issuance of a commission or a letter rogatory that the taking of the deposition in any other manner is impracticable or inconvenient; and both a commission and a letter rogatory may be issued in proper cases. A notice or commission may designate the person before whom the deposition is to be taken either by name or descriptive title. A letter rogatory may be addressed "To the Appropriate Authority in (here name the state, territory or country)." Evidence obtained in a foreign country in response to a letter rogatory need not be excluded merely for the reason that it is not a verbatim transcript or that the testimony was not taken under oath or for any similar departure from the requirements for depositions taken within the United States under these rules.

(c) **Disqualification for interest.** No deposition shall be taken before a person who is a relative or employee or attorney or counsel of any of the parties, or is a relative or employee of such attorney or counsel, or is financially interested in the action.

(d) **Depositions for use in foreign jurisdictions.** Whenever the deposition of any person is to be taken in this state pursuant to the laws of another state or of the United States or of another country for use in proceedings there, any Superior Judge may, upon petition to the superior court in the county where the deponent resides or is employed or transacts business in person, make an order directing issuance of a subpoena as provided in Rule 45, in aid of the taking of the deposition, and may make any order in accordance with Rule 30(d), 37(a) or 37(b)(1).

[Vt. R. Crim. P.]

RULE 15. Depositions.

*   *   *

(d) How taken.

(1) *General.* A deposition shall be taken and filed in the manner provided in civil actions except as otherwise provided in these rules, provided that (i) in no event shall a deposition be taken of a party defendant without his consent and (ii) the scope and manner of examination and cross-examination shall be such as would be allowed in the trial itself. The state shall make available to the defendant or his counsel for examination and use at the taking of the deposition any relevant written or recorded statement of the witness being deposed which is in the possession or control of the state and to which the defendant would be entitled at trial.

(2) *Manner of recording.* A deposition shall be recorded stenographically unless the notice of taking states that it is to be recorded by other than stenographic means. A deposition recorded stenographically shall be transcribed only if a party or witness so requests. If a deposition is to be recorded nonstenographically, the notice of taking shall specify the method of recording; the equipment to be used; and the name, address, and employer of the operator of the equipment.

(3) *Concurrent recording.* Any party or witness may at his own expense concurrently record a deposition by a method other than that being used by the party taking the deposition. All parties present and the witness shall be advised that the concurrent recording is being made. A person making a concurrent recording shall permit the parties and the witness to review the recording and shall furnish a duplicate to the witness or any party upon request and tender of the actual cost of the duplicate.

(4) *Additional conditions.* Upon motion of a party or upon its own motion the court may impose such additional conditions upon the taking of a deposition as are necessary to assure that testimony to be recorded by nonstenographic means will be accurate and trustworthy and to protect the interests of the parties and the witness.

(e) Use. Any deposition may be used by any party as substantive evidence in the case if the deponent is unavailable for trial, as defined in subdivision (g) of this rule, or the witness gives testimony at the trial or hearing inconsistent with his deposition. Any deposition may also be used for the purpose of contradicting or impeaching the testimony of the deponent as a witness. The court may allow a deposition based on a concurrent recording to be used at trial provided that the deposition meets all requirements of this rule. If only a part of a deposition is offered in evidence by a party, an adverse party may require him to offer all parts of it which are relevant to the part offered, and any party may offer other parts.

*   *   *

(f) Objections to admissibility. Objections to receiving in evidence any deposition or part thereof may be made as provided in civil actions.

*   *   *

(h) Commission to examine witness out of state. When an issue of fact is joined upon an information or indictment, on application of the defendant or prosecuting attorney the court may grant a commission to depose material witnesses residing out of the state as provided in this rule, and the prosecuting attorney may join in such commission and name material witnesses to be examined on the part of the state.

(i) Deposition by agreement not precluded. Nothing in this rule shall preclude the taking of a deposition, orally or upon written questions, or the use of a deposition, by agreement of the parties.

COMMISSIONERS

[Vt. Stat. Ann.]

Tit. 4, § 851. Appointment and powers of commissioners.

The governor may appoint commissioners in other states and in foreign countries, who shall hold office for five years unless sooner removed by him. They may take depositions, affidavits and testimony to be used in any proceedings in superior court [a county court held by the presiding judge alone, sitting without a jury], administer oaths and take the acknowledgment of deeds and other instruments to be used or recorded in this state, and their acts therein shall have the same force as though performed by a justice or master in chancery in this state.

Tit. 4, § 852. Oath and bond.

Before entering upon his duties, each commissioner shall take and subscribe an oath of office before a magistrate of his locality and execute a bond to this state with sureties to the satisfaction of the governor in the sum of $500.00, conditioned for the faithful performance of his duties. The bond shall be kept in the office of the secretary of state, and an action may be maintained against any or all signers thereof, in the name of the state, for the benefit of a person injured by the act or neglect of the commissioner.

LEGAL HOLIDAYS

Tit. 1, § 371. Legal holidays.

(a) The following shall be legal holidays:

New Year's Day, January 1;

Martin Luther King, Jr.'s Birthday, the third Monday in January;

Lincoln's Birthday, February 12;

Washington's Birthday, the third Monday in February;

Town meeting day, the first Tuesday in March;

Memorial Day, May 30;

Independence Day, July 4;

Bennington Battle Day, August 16;

Labor Day, the first Monday in September;

Columbus Day, the second Monday in October;

Veterans' Day, November 11;

Thanksgiving Day, the fourth Thursday in November;

Christmas Day, December 25.

(b) All state departments, agencies and offices shall observe any legal holiday which falls on a Saturday on the preceding Friday and any legal holiday which falls on a Sunday on the following Monday; however, all other conditions of employment related to legal holidays, including but not limited to decisions such as the closing or opening of state offices and compensation for work performed on such a day, shall be proper matters for collective bargaining pursuant to section 904 of Title 3.

(c) The provisions of this section shall not affect any collective bargaining agreement in existence on the effective date hereof.

VIRGIN ISLANDS

NOTARIES PUBLIC

[V.I. CODE ANN.]

Tit. 3, § 771. Appointment of notaries public by Lieutenant Governor.

(a) The Lieutenant Governor may appoint and commission not more than 600 notaries public for the Virgin Islands, exclusive of notaries public ex officio and members of the Virgin Islands Bar, who shall hold office for a period of four years. The Executive Secretary of the Legislature of the Virgin Islands shall be granted a commission by the Lieutenant Governor as a notary public ex officio. Each official court reporter and assistant court reporter to the Territorial Court of the Virgin Islands and the District Court of the Virgin Islands, each official reporter of the Legislature of the Virgin Islands, and the Registrar and Deputy Registrars of Vital Statistics of the Department of Health shall be granted commissions by the Lieutenant Governor as notaries public ex officio. Any person admitted to practice law in the Virgin Islands as a member of the Virgin Islands Bar shall upon application and a showing of his membership be issued a commission for a period of four years.

(b) The Lieutenant Governor may promulgate such rules and regulations as he deems necessary, pursuant to the provision of Title 3, chapter 35, Virgin Islands Code, for the proper administration and enforcement of this chapter.

Tit. 3, § 772. Qualifications.

Every person appointed as a notary public shall—

(1) be a citizen of the United States at least 21 years of age and a resident of the Virgin Islands for at least 5 years preceding his appointment; Provided, however, That notaries ex officio and members of the Virgin Islands Bar commissioned in accordance with the provisions of section 771 of this title shall not be required to comply with the five year residency requirement imposed by this section; and

(2) be a graduate of an accredited high school or have passed the high school equivalency test;

(3) continue to reside within the Virgin Islands during the term of his office; and

(4) shall not have been convicted of any crime either within or without the Virgin Islands.

Every applicant for a notary appointment shall be investigated by the Office of the Lieutenant Governor with respect to his character so that prior to the issuance of a commission the Lieutenant Governor is satisfied with the applicant's good character and integrity for the office.

Removal from the Virgin Islands shall vacate his office and be the equivalent of a resignation.

Tit. 3, § 773. Commission fees; bonds; issuance of commission.

(a) Each notary public shall pay to the Treasury of the Virgin Islands an initial fee of $100.00 for the commission and thereafter, on the 1st day of January of each year, an annual fee of $25.00. Upon failure to pay the annual fee, the Lieutenant Governor shall, after giving the notary public 30 calendar days notice of his intention to do so, cancel such appointment.

(b) Each notary public shall execute a bond in favor of the Government of the Virgin Islands, in the sum of $5,000, from any insurance/bonding company authorized to do business in the Virgin Islands, or submit two (2) resident sureties who are owners, within the Virgin Islands, of real property with the value of $10,000 over and above encumbrances thereon, which bonds must be approved by the Presiding Judge of the Territorial Court; provided that the Presiding Judge of the Territorial Court shall notify the Office of the Lieutenant Governor and the applicant of the approval of the bond.

(c) Each notary public, upon the approval of his bond and after having taken the official oath, shall transmit such bond and oath, duly signed by him, to the Office of the Lieutenant Governor, whereupon the Lieutenant Governor may issue a commission.

(d) A notary public may, at the expiration of his or her term of office, apply for a renewal of the commission by the filing of an application accompanied with a new bond and a renewal fee of $75.00, and such application shall, if all other qualifications are in order, be given priority over other applications, provided it is postmarked no later than 60 days after the term ends.

(e) A notary public who fails to timely apply for a renewal shall be notified and a determination made regarding his or her desire to apply for renewal of the commission.

(f) The Lieutenant Governor shall have the authority to promulgate and issue an application for incorporating therein the qualifications and conditions as set forth in this chapter.

(g) The Lieutenant Governor may cancel a commission if there is satisfactory proof that the notary public is no longer qualified in accordance with the provisions of this chapter. Any such decision must be made known to the notary public within ten days after the Lieutenant Governor's determination, and such notary public shall have the right to appear in person or in writing to appeal the decision. The decision of the Lieutenant Governor, after hearing and determination on the appeal, shall be final; provided, an aggrieved notary shall have the right to appeal the final decision of the Lieutenant Governor to the Territorial Court.

Tit. 3, § 774. Liability of notaries and sureties.

Each notary public and the sureties on his bond shall be liable for all the damages sustained by a party injured by the official misconduct or neglect of that notary public.

Tit. 3, § 775. Records to be kept; inspection by United States attorney; filing.

(a) Each notary public shall keep an official record in which a memorandum of all official acts shall be noted.

(b) The Lieutenant Governor may inspect the official record of any notary public at any time.

(c) Upon the expiration of the term of office, the notary public's official record and seal shall be filed in the Office of the Lieutenant Governor, in the judicial division of his or her residence, for a period of five years. The Lieutenant Governor shall make an impression of such seal and keep such impression with the records of the notary public.

(d) The records kept by the notary public shall include, among other information, the date of the document, the nature or name of the document, the consideration named in the document, if any, the parties making the oath and such other information as the Lieutenant Governor may, by regulation, deem necessary.

(e) A notary public shall not be eligible for a renewal of office unless there is presented with the application for renewal a receipt showing the deposit of official records and seal with the Lieutenant Governor.

Tit. 3, § 776. Notarial seal; signature.

(a) Each notary public shall keep an official impression seal bearing his name, date of expiration of commission, and judicial division.

(b) The notary public must affix his impression seal to each document and either write, print or stamp his or her name in a legible fashion on the document.

(c) A document is not properly notarized until both the seal has been impressed thereon and the name of the notary public has been affixed thereto.

Tit. 3, § 777. Powers; limitations.

(a) Notaries public may take acknowledgments

of deeds and other instruments, administer oaths and affirmations, and perform such other acts as may be authorized by law.

(b) No notary public shall certify, attest or take an oath or acknowledgment for or to an instrument to which he is an interested party.

(c) Each notary public shall administer the oath or inquire of each person executing a document as to the truth and authenticity of such document; and shall request identification of the person(s) requiring his or her notarial services. Failure to do so shall subject the notary public to an administrative fine of $100.00 or to revocation of his or her commission, or both, by and in the discretion of the Lieutenant Governor.

Tit. 3, § 778. Fees; retention by notary.

(a) Each notary public may charge and retain a fee not to exceed $5.00 for each document notarized or for each time his or her seal is affixed to a document.

(b) A fee of $5.00 shall be collected by the office of the Lieutenant Governor for providing certificates of authenticity for documents to be sent out of the Territory or when such certificates are otherwise required.

Special Notaries Public

Tit. 3, § 801. Appointment of government employees as notaries public.

In addition to the notaries public provided for in subchapter I of this chapter, the Lieutenant Governor may authorize and empower employees of the Government of the Virgin Islands or of the United States, not exceeding 40 in number, to take acknowledgments of deeds and administer oaths and affirmations, and such employees shall be appointed and commissioned as notaries public with terms of office at the pleasure of the Lieutenant Governor.

Tit. 3, § 802. Oath of office; records to be kept.

Notaries public appointed and commissioned under section 801 of this title shall take an official oath and keep an official record in which a memorandum of all official acts shall be noted.

Tit. 3, § 803. Commission fees; bonds.

Notaries public appointed and commissioned under section 801 [above], of this title shall not be required to pay license fees, nor to give bond.

Tit. 3, § 804. Notarial seal.

(a) Notaries public appointed and commissioned under section 801 of this title shall keep an official impression seal which shall be furnished by the respective department.

(b) Chief clerks of the United States District Court for the Virgin Islands and the Territorial Court of the Virgin Islands shall submit, at least once a year, to and for the information of the Office of the Lieutenant Governor, a list of all persons authorized as ex officio notaries public.

Tit. 3, § 805. Restriction on powers; exception.

(a) Except as otherwise provided in subsection (b) of this section, notaries public appointed and commissioned under section 801 of this title, shall not be permitted to take acknowledgments of deeds and administer oaths and affirmations except on matters of official business of the Government of the Virgin Islands or the Government of the United States, and no fees for such acknowledgments and oaths or affirmations shall be charged.

(b) Not to exceed four of the notaries public commissioned under subsection (a) of section 801 of this title for the Island of St. John, two for the area of Cruz Bay and two for the area of Coral Bay, shall be permitted, in addition to the powers granted in that section, to take acknowledgments of deeds, and administer oaths and affirmations in matters not connected with official business of the Government of the Virgin Islands, in which cases the regular fees for such acknowledgments, oaths and affirmations shall be charged and deposited in the General Fund of the Treasury.

FEES

Tit. 4, § 519. Fees of notaries public.

Subject to the provisions of section 778 of Title 3, the following fees shall be charged by notaries public:

(1) Protest on notes and bills of exchange, when the note is issued in an amount
  (A) Not over $500 .... $3.50
  (B) Over $500 and not over $1,500 ...... 4.50
  (C) Over $1,500 and not over $3,000 .... 5.50
  (D) Over $3,000 and not over $5,000 .... 6.50
  (E) Over $5,000 .... 7.50
(2) Other protests, etc. 2.50
(3) Receiving marine note of protest 3.50
(A) For copy of the proceedings, double the amount of ordinary fees for copies under section 882 of Title 3.

(4) Authorization of journals for American vessels 2.50

(5) Oaths, affirmations and acknowledgments, as provided in section 520 of this title.

Tit. 4, § 520. Fees for oaths, affirmations and acknowledgments.

The fee of any person who takes an oath, affirmation or acknowledgment shall be $1.00, except that—

(1) if such service is performed outside the office in the town limits, the fee shall be $1.50; and

(2) if such service is performed outside the office in the country districts, the fee shall be $2.00.

ACKNOWLEDGMENTS

Uniform Recognition of Acknowledgments Act

Tit. 28, § 81. Acknowledgments within the Virgin Islands.

The acknowledgment of any instrument may be made in the Virgin Islands before—

(1) a notary public authorized to perform notarial acts in the Virgin Islands; or

(2) a judge, clerk, or deputy clerk of any court of record in the Virgin Islands having a seal; or

(3) a commissioner or recorder of deeds.

Tit. 28, § 82. Recognition of notarial acts performed outside the Virgin Islands.

For the purposes of this chapter, "notarial acts" means acts which the laws of the Virgin Islands authorize notaries public of the Virgin Islands to perform, including the administering of oaths and affirmations, taking proof of execution and acknowledgments of instruments, and attesting documents. Notarial acts may be performed outside the Virgin Islands for use in the Virgin Islands with the same effect as if performed by a notary public of the Virgin Islands by the following persons authorized pursuant to the laws and regulations of other governments in addition to any other person authorized by the laws of the Virgin Islands.

(a) A notary public authorized to perform notarial acts in the place in which the notarial act is performed.

(b) A judge, clerk, or deputy clerk of any court of record in the place in which the notarial act is performed.

(c) An officer of the foreign service of the United States, a consular agent or any other person authorized by regulation of the United States Department of State to perform notarial acts in the place in which the act is performed.

(d) A commissioned officer in active service with the armed forces of the United States and any other person authorized by regulation of the armed forces to perform notarial acts if the notarial act is performed for one of the following or his dependents: A merchant seaman of the United States, a member of the armed forces of the United States or any other person serving with or accompanying the armed forces of the United States.

(e) Any other person authorized to perform notarial acts in the place in which the act is performed.

Tit. 28, § 83. Authentication of authority of officer.

(a) If the notarial act is performed by any of the persons described in subsections (a) to (d) of section 82 of this chapter other than a person authorized to perform notarial acts by the laws or regulations of a foreign country, the signature, rank or title and serial number, if any, of the person are sufficient proof of the authority of a holder of that rank or title to perform the act. Further proof of his authority is not required.

(b) If the notarial act is performed by a person authorized by the laws or regulations of a foreign country to perform the act, there is sufficient proof of the authority of that person to act if any of the following exist:

(1) Either a foreign service officer of the United States resident in the country in which the acts is performed or a diplomatic or consular officer of the foreign country resident in the United States certifies that a person holding that office is authorized to perform the act;

(2) The official seal of the person performing the notarial act is affixed to the document; or

(3) The title and indication of authority to perform notarial acts of the person appears either in a digest of foreign law or in a list customarily used as a source of such information.

(c) If the notarial act is performed by a person other than one described in subsections (a) and (b) there is sufficient proof of the authority of that person to act if the clerk of a court of record in the place in which the notarial act is performed certifies to the official character of that person and to his authority to perform the notarial act.

(d) The signature and title of the person performing the act are prima facie evidence that he is a person with the designated title and that the signature is genuine.

Tit. 28, § 84. Certificate of person taking acknowledgment.

The person taking an acknowledgment shall certify that the person acknowledging appeared before him and acknowledged he executed the instrument; and the person acknowledging was known to the person taking the acknowledgment or that the person taking the acknowledgment has satisfactory evidence that the person acknowledging was the person described in and who executed the instrument.

Tit. 28, § 85. Recognition of certificate of acknowledgment.

The form of a certificate of acknowledgment used by a person whose authority is recognized under section 82 of this chapter shall be accepted in the Virgin Islands if one of the following is true:

(a) The certificate is in a form prescribed by the laws or regulations of the Virgin Islands;

(b) The certificate is in a form prescribed by the laws applicable in the place in which the acknowledgment is taken; or

(c) The certificate contains the words "acknowledged before me", or their substantial equivalent.

Tit. 28, § 86. Certificate of acknowledgment.

The words "acknowledged before me" mean

(1) that the person acknowledging appeared before the person taking the acknowledgment; and

(2) that he acknowledged he executed the instrument; and

(3) that, in the case of:

(i) a natural person, he executed the instrument for the purposes therein stated;

(ii) a corporation, the officer or agent acknowledged he held the position or title set forth in the instrument and certificate, he signed the instrument on behalf of the corporation by proper authority, and the instrument was the act of the corporation for the purpose therein stated;

(iii) a partnership, the partner or agent acknowledged he signed the instrument on behalf of the partnership by proper authority and he executed the instrument as the act of the partnership for the purposes therein stated;

(iv) a person acknowledging as principal by an attorney in fact, he executed the instrument by proper authority as the act of the principal for the purposes therein stated.

(v) a person acknowledging as a public officer, trustee, administrator, guardian, or other representative, he signed the instrument by proper authority and he executed the instrument in the capacity and for the purposes therein stated; and

(4) that the person taking the acknowledgment either knew or had satisfactory evidence that the person acknowledging was the person named in the instrument of certificate.

Tit. 28, § 87. Short form of acknowledgment.

(a) The forms of acknowledgment set forth in this section may be used and are sufficient for their purposes under any law of the Virgin Islands. The forms shall be known as "statutory forms of acknowledgment" and may be referred to by that name. The authorization of the forms in this section does not preclude the use of other forms.

(b) For an individual acting in his own rights:
Territory of the Virgin Islands
Judicial Division of
The foregoing instrument was acknowledged before me this (date) by (name of person acknowledged).
(Signature of person taking acknowledgment)
(Title or rank)
(Serial number, if any).

(c) For a corporation:
Territory of the Virgin Islands
Judicial Division of
The foregoing instrument was acknowledged before me this (date) by (name of officer or agent, title of officer or agent) of (name of corporation acknowledging) a (state or place of incorporation) corporation, on behalf of the corporation.
(Signature of person taking acknowledgment)
(Title or rank)
(Serial number, if any).

(d) For a partnership:
Territory of the Virgin Islands
Judicial Division of
The foregoing instrument was acknowledged before me this (date) by (name of acknowledging partner or agent), partner (or agent) on behalf of (name of partnership), a partnership.
(Signature of person taking acknowledgment)
(Title or rank)
(Serial number, if any).

(e) For an individual acting as principal by an attorney in fact:
Territory of the Virgin Islands
Judicial Division of
The foregoing instrument was acknowledged before me this (date) by (name of attorney in fact) as attorney in fact on behalf of (name of principal).
(Signature of person taking acknowledgment)
(Title or rank)
(Serial number, if any).

(f) By any public officer, trustee or personal representative:
Territory of the Virgin Islands
Judicial Division of
The foregoing instrument was acknowledged before me this (date) by (name of person acknowledged).
(Signature of person taking acknowledgment)
(Title or rank)
(Serial number, if any).

Tit. 28, § 88. Acknowledgments not affected by this chapter.

A notarial act performed prior to October 20, 1981, is not affected by this chapter.

Tit. 28, § 89. Uniformity of interpretation.

This chapter shall be so interpreted as to make uniform the laws of those jurisdictions which enact it.

Tit. 28, § 90. Acknowledgments under laws of other states.

Notwithstanding any provision in this chapter contained the acknowledgment of any instrument without the Virgin Islands in compliance with the manner and form prescribed by the laws of the place of its execution, if in a State of the United States, verified by the official seal of the officer before whom it is acknowledged, and authenticated in the manner provided by paragraph (2) of section 89 of this title, shall have the same effect as an acknowledgment in the manner and form prescribed by the laws of the Virgin Islands for instruments executed within the Virgin Islands.

DEPOSITIONS

[V.I. CODE ANN. tit. 5, App. I, CIVIL RULES]

RULE 28. Persons before whom depositions may be taken.

(a) WITHIN THE UNITED STATES. Within the United States or within a territory or insular possession subject to the dominion of the United States, depositions shall be taken before an officer authorized to administer oaths by the laws of the United States or of the place where the examination is held, or before a person appointed by the court in which the action is pending. A person so appointed has power to administer oaths and take testimony.

(b) IN FOREIGN COUNTRIES. In a foreign country, depositions may be taken (1) on notice before a person authorized to administer oaths in the place in which the examination is held, either by the law thereof or by the law of the United States, or (2) before a person commissioned by the court, and a person so commissioned shall have the power by virtue of the commission to administer any necessary oath and take testimony, or (3) pursuant to a letter rogatory. A commission or a letter rogatory shall be issued on application and notice and on terms that are just and appropriate. It is not requisite to the issuance of a commission or a letter rogatory that the taking of the deposition in any other manner is impracticable or inconvenient; and both a commission and a letter rogatory may be issued in proper cases. A notice or commission may designate the person before whom the deposition is to be taken either by name or descriptive title. A letter rogatory may be addressed "To the Appropriate Authority in [here name the country]." Evidence obtained in response to a letter rogatory need not be excluded merely for the reason that it is not a verbatim transcript or that the testimony was not taken under oath or for any similar departure from the requirements for depositions taken within the United States under these rules.

(c) DISQUALIFICATION FOR INTEREST. No deposition shall be taken before a person who is a relative or employee or attorney or counsel of any of the parties, or is a relative or employee of such attorney or counsel, or is financially interested in the action.

LEGAL HOLIDAYS

[V.I. CODE ANN.]

Tit. 1, § 171. Legal holidays; serving liquor on Good Friday; performance of acts under law or contract.

(a) The following days are legal holidays in the Virgin Islands:

Every Sunday
January 1 (New Year's Day)
January 6 (Three King's Day)
Third Monday in January (Martin Luther King, Jr.'s Birthday)
Third Monday in February (Presidents Day)
March 31 (Transfer Day)
Holy Thursday
Good Friday
Easter Monday
Last Monday in May (Memorial Day)
Third Monday in June (Organic Act Day)
July 3 (V.I. Emancipation Day)—Danish West Indies Emancipation Day
July 4 (Independence Day)
The Fourth Monday in July (Supplication Day)
First Monday in September (Labor Day)
Second Monday in October (Columbus Day and Puerto Rico Friendship Day)
Third Monday in October (Local Thanksgiving Day)
November 1 (D. Hamilton Jackson Day)
November 11 (Veterans Day)
Fourth Thursday in November (Thanksgiving Day)
December 25 (Christmas Day)
December 26 (Christmas Second Day)

and such other days as the President or the Governor may by proclamation declare to be holidays.

Whenever any holiday (other than Sunday) falls upon a Sunday, the Monday following shall be a legal holiday.

(b) Distilled liquor and drinks prepared therewith shall not be served in public places of refreshments between the hours of 9:00 o'clock in the morning and 4:00 o'clock in the afternoon on Good Friday. Whoever violates this subsection shall be fined not more than $200 or imprisoned not more than one year, or both.

(c) Whenever any act is appointed by law or contract to be performed upon a particular day, which day falls upon a holiday, that act may be performed upon the next business day with the same effect as if it had been performed upon the day appointed.

Tit. 1, § 171a. Exemption of banks and trust companies from Thursday half-holidays; option; validity of non-regular banking-hour transactions.

The Thursday half-holidays provided by law shall not be applicable to banks and banking business, provided, however, that any bank, trust company or national banking association may, at its option, observe Thursday afternoons as half-holidays, effective July 3, 1958. Nothing in any law of the Virgin Islands shall in any manner whatsoever affect the validity of, or render void or voidable, the payment, certification, or acceptance of a check or other negotiable instrument or any other transaction by a bank or trust company in the Virgin Islands, because done or performed during any time other than regular banking hours.

Tit. 1, § 171b. Banks and trust companies may close one business day each week.

Any bank or trust company and any national banking association or any branch or branches of any of them transacting business in the Virgin Islands may close on any one business day or any part thereof of each week and shall have this right even though there shall fall in such week a legal holiday.

VIRGINIA

NOTARIES PUBLIC

[VA. CODE ANN.]

§ 47.1-1. Short title.

This title may be cited as the "Virginia Notary Act."

§ 47.1-2. Definitions.

As used in this title, unless the context demands a different meaning:

1. *"Notarial act"* shall mean any official act performed by a notary under § 47.1-12 or § 47.1-13 of this Code or as otherwise authorized by law.
2. *"Oath"* shall include *"affirmation."*
3. *"Official misconduct"* means any violation of this title by a notary, whether committed knowingly, willfully, recklessly or negligently.
4. *"Secretary"* means the Secretary of the Commonwealth.
5. *"State"* includes any state, territory, or possession of the United States.

§ 47.1-3. Power of appointment.

The Governor may appoint in and for the Commonwealth as many notaries as to him shall seem proper.

§ 47.1-4. Qualification for appointment.

Each person appointed and commissioned as a notary shall be (i) at least eighteen years of age; (ii) a citizen of the United States; and (iii) able to read and write the English language. No person who has ever been convicted of a felony under the laws of the United States or this Commonwealth, or the laws of any other state, shall qualify to be appointed and commissioned as a notary public unless such person has been pardoned for such felony or has had his rights restored. A nonresident of Virginia may be appointed only if he is regularly employed in this Commonwealth and if such appointment will be necessary or useful to him in such employment. A member of the armed services of the United States shall be eligible for appointment and commission as a notary notwithstanding the provisions of § 2.1-30.

§ 47.1-5. Application; references.

No person shall be appointed a notary public pursuant to this chapter until he submits an application to the Secretary of the Commonwealth, in a form prescribed by the appointing authority, which shall include the following:

1. The oath of the applicant, signed and sworn before some officer authorized by law to administer oaths, that the answers to all questions on the application are true and complete to the best of his knowledge and that he is qualified to be appointed and commissioned as a notary public.
2. Endorsements from two registered voters of this Commonwealth, stating that, to the best of the endorser's knowledge, the applicant is a person of sound moral character and is possessed of all the qualifications for appointment set forth in this chapter.
3. A statement signed by any judge, clerk or deputy clerk of any court of this Commonwealth, or by any attorney for the Commonwealth or assistant attorney for the Commonwealth, or by the Attorney General or any of his assistants, or by any member of the General Assembly, that such official has examined the application and recommends the applicant for appointment.
4. An application fee as set forth in § 14.1-103 of this Code.

§ 47.1-6., 47.1-7. Reserved.

§ 47.1-8. Commission to be issued, etc.

Upon receipt of a completed application, proper endorsements and the correct fee, the Secretary, if satisfied the applicant is qualified to be appointed and commissioned as a notary public, shall prepare a notary commission for the applicant and forward the commission to the clerk of the circuit court in which the applicant shall elect to qualify. The Secretary shall thereupon notify the applicant that the commission has been granted and where and how it may be secured.

§ 47.1-9. Oath of notary; duties of clerks.

Before receiving his commission, each person appointed a notary shall appear before the clerk of the circuit court to which his commission has been sent and make oath as follows:

"I, ... , solemnly swear (or affirm) under penalty of perjury, that I have carefully read the notary laws of this Commonwealth, and am familiar with their provisions; that I will uphold the Constitution of the United States and the Constitution and laws of the Commonwealth of Virginia; and that I will faithfully perform, to the best of my ability, the duties of the office of notary public."

Such oath shall be signed by the applicant and attested by the clerk. The clerk shall thereupon issue to the applicant his commission as notary public. Within fourteen days of such qualification, the clerk shall certify the fact of such qualification to the Secretary of the Commonwealth.

No person shall be permitted to qualify who does not appear before the clerk within sixty days of his appointment. The clerk of each circuit court shall, at least once each month, return to the Secretary all commissions which have not been claimed within such sixty-day period, and the Secretary shall forthwith cancel the same.

§ 47.1-10. Records of the secretary.

The Secretary of the Commonwealth shall keep a book stating the names of all notaries public and the dates of their appointment and qualification. The Secretary shall also retain a specimen of the signature of each notary commissioned pursuant to this chapter. The specimen may be retained in photographic form.

The Secretary shall also be required to retain the completed applications of persons seeking appointment as notary public for a period of three months after their receipt; provided, however, that he shall retain the applications of persons refused appointment for not less than four years.

§ 47.1-11. Handbook.

The Secretary shall prepare, from time to time, a handbook for notaries public which shall contain the provisions of this title and such other information as the Secretary shall deem useful. Copies of the handbook shall be made available to persons seeking appointment as notaries public and to other interested persons.

§ 47.1-12. Powers.

Each notary shall be empowered to (i) take acknowledgments, (ii) administer oaths, (iii) certify that a copy of any document, other than a document in the custody of a court, is a true copy thereof, (iv) certify affidavits or depositions of witnesses, and (v) perform such other acts as may be specifically permitted by law.

§ 47.1-13. Jurisdiction; powers outside the Commonwealth.

The powers of any notary commissioned pursuant to this chapter of this title may be exercised anywhere within the Commonwealth of Virginia.

Any notary commissioned pursuant to Chapter 2 (§ 47.1-3 et seq.) of this title may likewise perform notarial acts outside the Commonwealth, where such notarial acts are performed in connection with a deed or other writing to be admitted to record in the Commonwealth of Virginia.

§ 47.1-14. Duty of care.

A notary shall exercise reasonable care in the performance of his duties generally. He shall exercise a high degree of care in ascertaining the identity of any person whose identity is the subject of a notarial act.

§ 47.1-15. Reserved.

§ 47.1-16. Notarizations to show date of act, etc.

A. Every notarization shall include the date upon which the notarial act was performed, and the county or city and state in which it was performed.

B. Upon every writing which is the subject of a notarial act, the notary shall, after his certificate, state the date of the expiration of his commission in substantially the following form:

"My commission expires the . . . . day of . . . . . , ..."

§ 47.1-17. Change of name.

Any notary duly appointed in this Commonwealth, who shall legally change his name during his term of office as a notary shall, after such change of name, when performing any notarial act, have written or printed in or annexed to his certificate the words: "I was commissioned notary as . . . . , or the equivalent.

§ 47.1-18. Notice of change of address; etc.

A. Any notary public who changes the address of his residence shall forthwith notify the Secretary of the Commonwealth of the fact by mailing or delivering a written notice which shall contain his new address.

B. Any notary who is commissioned as a nonresident shall notify the Secretary of the Commonwealth of any change in his place of employment.

§ 47.1-19. Fees.

A. A notary may, for taking and certifying the acknowledgment of any writing, or administering and certifying an oath, or certifying affidavits and depositions of witnesses, or certifying that a copy of a document is a true copy thereof, charge a fee of two dollars.

B. For other services a notary shall have the same fees as the clerk of a circuit court for like services.

C. Any person appointed as a member of an electoral board, a general registrar, or an officer of election shall be prohibited from collecting any fee as a notary from the time of such appointment.

D. It shall be unlawful for any notary to charge more than the fee established herein for any notarial act; provided, however, that a notary may recover, with the agreement of the person to be charged, any actual and reasonable expense of traveling to a place where a notarial act is to be performed if it is not the usual place in which the notary performs his office.

§ 47.1-20. Fee agreements with employer.

A. It shall be lawful for any employer to require a notary in his employment to perform notarial acts in connection with such employment without charging the fee allowed by law for the performance of such acts.

B. It shall not be lawful for any employer to require a notary in his employment to surrender to such employer a fee, if charged, or any part thereof.

§ 47.1-20.1. Validation of certain acts.

Oaths of office administered by a notary public on or before July 1, 1982, are hereby deemed to be valid and actions of any public officer taking such oaths are hereby deemed valid.

§ 47.1-21. Term of office.

The term of office of a notary public shall be four years, except as shall be otherwise provided in this chapter. The term of a notary public shall expire in the fourth calendar year after issuance of his commission on the last day of the month in which the notary was born.

§ 47.1-22. Resignation; removal from Commonwealth; etc.

A. A notary may resign his office by mailing or delivering to the Secretary a letter of resignation.

B. Any notary who ceases to be a resident of the Commonwealth of Virginia shall, from that time, cease to be a notary; provided, however, that such notary may retain his commission with the written consent of the Secretary if he meets the qualifications for nonresident appointment under § 47.1-4.

C. Any nonresident notary who ceases to be employed in this Commonwealth shall forthwith cease to be a notary.

D. Every notary who wishes to resign from office, or who ceases to be a notary pursuant to subsections B or C of this section, shall forthwith mail or deliver his commission to the Secretary, who shall cancel the same.

§ 47.1-23. Grounds for removal from office.

The Secretary of the Commonwealth may remove from office any notary who:

1. Submits or has submitted an application for commission and appointment as a notary public which contains a substantial and material misstatement of fact;

2. Is convicted or has been convicted of any felony under the laws of the United States or this Commonwealth, or the laws of any other state, unless the notary has been pardoned for such offense or has had his rights restored;

3. Is found to have committed official misconduct by a proceeding as provided in Chapter 5 (§ 47.1-24 et seq.) of this title;

4. Fails to exercise the powers or perform the duties of a notary public in accordance with this title; provided that if a notary is adjudged liable in any court of this Commonwealth in any action grounded in fraud, misrepresentation, impersonation, or violation of the notary laws of the Commonwealth, such notary shall be presumed removable under this section;

5. Uses false or misleading advertising wherein he represents or implies by virtue of his title to notary public, that he has qualifications, powers, duties, rights, or privileges that he does not possess by law;

6. Is convicted of the unauthorized practice of law pursuant to § 54.1-3904 of this Code;

7. Ceases to be a citizen of the United States; or

8. Becomes incapable of reading or writing the English language.

§ 47.1-24. Removal of notary by administrative process; surrender of commission; penalty.

A. Whenever the Secretary shall have reason to believe that a notary has been guilty of official misconduct pursuant to this chapter, or is otherwise subject to removal from office, an evidentiary proceeding under the provisions of the Administrative Process Act (§ 9-6.14:1 et seq.) shall be held.

B. through D. [Repealed.]

E. If the Secretary determines that the notary is guilty of official misconduct or grounds exist for the removal of the notary and his case decision is not thereafter reversed or suspended by a court of law, the Secretary may issue an order removing the notary from office, suspending the notary from office for a period of time not to extend beyond the date of expiration of the notary's commission, or reprimanding the notary.

F. Upon being notified that an evidentiary proceeding has been initiated under this section, the notary who is the subject of such a proceeding shall forthwith cease to serve as a notary for a period of sixty days, or until his case has been decided, whichever period shall be shorter. If the Secretary finds that grounds for removal exist, such notary shall be further suspended from serving as a notary until the Secretary has made a final disposition of the case under subsection E of this section; however, no notarial act shall be deemed invalid solely by reason of having been performed by a notary who has been suspended pursuant to this subsection.

G. Any notary ordered removed from office under this section shall forthwith mail or deliver his commission to the Secretary, who shall cancel the same. Any notary ordered suspended under this section shall forthwith surrender his commission to the Secretary for the duration of such suspension.

H. [Repealed.]

I. Any notary failing to deliver his commission to the Secretary pursuant to an order of the Secretary under this section shall be guilty of a Class 3 misdemeanor.

§ 47.1-25. Disqualification from office.

Any notary removed from office under the provisions of § 47.1-24 shall be disqualified from holding the office of notary public in this Commonwealth for a period of twenty years, unless such disqualification is sooner removed by the Governor.

§ 47.1-26. Civil liability of notary.

A notary public shall be liable for all damages proximately caused by his official misconduct.

§ 47.1-27. Civil liability of employer of notary.

The employer of a notary public shall also be liable for all damages proximately caused by the official misconduct by such notary if:

1. The notary public was acting within the scope of his employment at the time such damages were caused; and

2. The employer had actual knowledge of, or reasonably should have known of, such notary's misconduct.

§ 47.1-28. Willful misconduct a misdemeanor.

A. Any notary who knowingly and willfully commits any official misconduct under Chapter 5 (§ 47.1-24 et seq.) of this title shall be guilty of a Class 3 misdemeanor.

B. Any employer of a notary who willfully induces such notary to commit official misconduct under Chapter 5 of this title shall be guilty of a Class 3 misdemeanor.

§ 47.1-29. Impersonation of notary a felony.

Any person who shall willfully act as, or otherwise impersonate, a notary public while not lawfully commissioned as a notary public or other official authorized to perform notarial acts, shall be guilty of a Class 6 felony.

§ 47.1-30. Conflicts of interest.

No notary shall perform any notarial act with respect to any document or writing to which the notary or his spouse shall be a party, or in which either of them shall have a direct beneficial interest.

Any notary who violates the provisions of this section shall be guilty of official misconduct.

A notarial act performed in violation of this section shall not automatically be void for such reason, but shall be voidable in the discretion of any court of competent jurisdiction upon the motion of any person injured thereby.

ADDITIONAL AUTHORITY

§ 1-13.14. Notary or notaries.

The word "notary" or "notaries" shall be construed as if followed by the word "public."

§ 49-1. Form of general oath required of officers.

Every person before entering upon the discharge of any function as an officer of this Commonwealth shall take and subscribe the following oath: "I do solemnly swear (or affirm) that I will support the Constitution of the United States, and the Constitution of the Commonwealth of Virginia, and that I will faithfully and impartially discharge all the duties incumbent upon me as . . . . . . according to the best of my ability, (so help me God)."

Any person reappointed to any office filled by gubernatorial appointment for a subsequent term to begin immediately upon expiration of an existing term shall not be required to renew the oath set out in this section; however, the original oath taken shall continue in effect with respect to the subsequent term.

§ 49-2. Form of oath for out-of-state commissioners.

Where a person residing in another state is appointed a commissioner by the Governor, he shall only be required to take and subscribe the following oath or affirmation:

"I, ..., swear (or affirm) that I will faithfully perform the duties of commissioner to the best of my ability. So help me God."

§ 49-3. Who may administer oaths to officers.

The oaths to be taken by a person elected a member of either house of the General Assembly shall be administered by the clerk or presiding officer of the houses, respectively, or a notary. Those to be taken by any judge of any court of record elected by the General Assembly shall be administered in a court of record, or by a judge of such court, or by any officer authorized by law to administer an oath. Those to be taken by any person elected or appointed an officer of either house of the General Assembly shall be administered by the person and in the manner prescribed by the rules of such house. The oaths to be taken by a person elected or appointed to any other office or post shall, except in cases in which it may be otherwise directed by law, be administered by the judge or clerk of a court of record, by a Commissioner or clerk of the State Corporation Commission or by the Secretary of the Commonwealth. A magistrate or person holding a comparable position in another state may administer the oaths to be taken by a commissioner or other person residing therein.

§ 49-4. Magistrates and other officers who may administer oaths and take affidavits.

Any oath or affidavit required by law, which is not of such nature that it must be made in court, may be administered by a magistrate, a notary, a commissioner in chancery, a commissioner appointed by the Governor, a judge or clerk or deputy clerk of a court, a commissioner or clerk or deputy clerk of the State Corporation Commission, or clerks of governing bodies of local governments. In case of a survey directed by a court in a cause therein pending, an oath or affidavit may be administered by or before the surveyor directed to execute the order of survey.

FEES

§ 14.1-98. Officer to state fees, etc., on affidavit, deposition or report.

A notary or other officer returning affidavits or depositions of witnesses and a commissioner returning a report shall state at the foot thereof the fees therefor, to whom charged and, if paid, by whom.

§ 14.1-103. Secretary of commonwealth.

The Secretary of the Commonwealth shall charge for services rendered in his office the following fees, to be paid by the person for whom the service is rendered at the time it is done:

* * *

For issuing a commission to a commissioner in another state . . . . $ 7.00
For issuing a commission to a notary for the Commonwealth at large, including seal tax $25.00

* * *

§ 14.1-112. Clerks of circuit courts; generally.

A clerk of a circuit court shall, for services performed by virtue of his office, charge the following fees:

* * *

(19) For qualifying notaries public, including the making out of the bond and any copies thereof, administering the necessary oaths, and entering the order, ten dollars.

* * *

SAFE DEPOSIT BOXES

§ 6.1-334. Opening box; marking contents.

Upon the expiration of sixty days from the date of mailing the notice required by § 6.1-331 and the failure within such period of time of the renter or lessee in whose name the safe or box stands on the books of the company, bank, trust company, or other corporation to pay the amount due for the rental thereof to the time of payment, together with legal interest thereon, the company, bank, trust company, or other corporation may, in the presence of a notary public not in its employ, and of its president or any vice president, assistant secretary, assistant treasurer, secretary, treasurer, cashier or assistant cashier, cause such safe or box to be opened, and the contents thereof, if any, to be removed, inventoried and sealed up by such notary public in a package, upon which the notary shall distinctly mark the name of the renter or lessee in whose name the safe or box stood on the books of the company, bank, trust company or other corporation, and the date of removal of the property.

§ 6.1-335. Disposition of contents.

When a package has been marked for identification by a notary public as required under the provisions of the proceeding section (§ 6.1-334), it shall, in the presence of any one of the above-named officers of the company, bank, trust company or other corporation, be placed by the notary public in one of the general safes or boxes of the company, at a rental not to exceed the original rental of the safe or box which was opened, and shall remain in such general safe or box for a period of not less than two years, unless sooner removed by such renter or lessee.

§ 6.1-336. Certificate of notary.

The notary public who shall have placed a package as required under the provisions of the preceding section (§ 6.1-335) shall thereupon file with the company a certificate, under seal, which shall fully set out the date of the opening of such safe or box, the name of the renter or lessee in whose name it stood and a list of the contents, if any. Such certificate shall be sworn to by such notary public and shall be prima facie evidence of the facts therein set forth in all proceedings at law and in equity wherein evidence of such facts would be competent. A copy of such certificate shall, within ten days thereafter, be mailed to the renter or lessee in whose name the safe or box so opened stood on the

books of the company, bank, trust company, or other corporation, at his last known post office address, in a securely closed, post-paid, registered letter, together with a notice that the contents will be kept, at the expense of such renter or lessee, in a general safe or box in the vaults of the company, bank, trust company, or other corporation, for a period of not less than two years, unless sooner removed by such renter or lessee.

§ 6.1-337. Subsequent right of lessee to contents.

At any time after the mailing of such notice as is required by the preceding section (§ 6.1-336) and before the expiration of two years, such renter or lessee may require the delivery of the contents of the safe or box as shown by the certificate, upon the payment of all rentals due at the time of opening the safe or box, the cost of opening the safe or box, the fees of the notary public for issuing his certificate thereon, and the payment of all charges accrued during the period the contents remained in the general safe or box of the company, bank, trust company, or other corporation, together with legal interest on such rentals, costs, fees, and charges.

ACKNOWLEDGMENTS

§ 55-113. Acknowledgment within the United States or its dependencies.

[The] court or clerk *** shall admit any such writing to record as to any person whose name is signed thereto, except acknowledgment of contracts for the sale of real property shall require the seller or grantor of such real property to acknowledge his signature as herein provided, except for contracts recorded after the death of the seller pursuant to § 64.1-148 of the Code of Virginia.

(1) Upon the certificate of such clerk or his deputy, a notary public, a commissioner in chancery, or a clerk of any court of record within the United States or in Puerto Rico, or any territory or other dependency or possession of the United States that such writing had been acknowledged before him by such person. Such certificate shall be written upon or annexed to such writing and shall be substantially to the following effect, to wit:

I, _____, clerk (or deputy clerk, or commissioner in chancery) of the _____ court, (or a notary public) for the county (or corporation) aforesaid, in the State (or territory, or district) of _____, do certify that E.F., or E.F. and G.H. and so forth, whose name (or names) is (or are) signed to the writing above (or hereto annexed) bearing date on the _____ day of _____, has (or have) acknowledged the same before me in my county (or corporation) aforesaid.

Given under my hand this _____ day of _____.

(2) Upon the certificate of acknowledgment of such person before any commissioner appointed by the Governor, within the United States, so written or annexed, substantially to the following effect, to wit:

State (or territory, or district) of _____ to wit:

I, _____, a commissioner appointed by the Governor of the State of Virginia, for said State (or territory or district) of _____, do certify that E.F. (or E.F. and G.H., and so forth) whose name (or names) is (or are) signed to the writing above (or hereto annexed) bearing date on the _____ day of _____ has (or have) acknowledged the same before me in my State (or territory or district) aforesaid.

Given under my hand this _____ day of _____.

(3) Or upon the certificate of such clerk or his deputy, a notary public, a commissioner in chancery, or a clerk of any court of record within the United States, or in Puerto Rico, or any territory or other possession or dependency of the United States, or of a commissioner appointed by the Governor, within the United States, that such writing was proved as to such person, before him, by two subscribing witnesses thereto. Such certificate shall be written upon or annexed to such writing and shall be substantially to the following effect, to wit:

State (or territory, or district) of _____; county (or corporation) of _____, to wit: I, _____, clerk (or deputy clerk, or a commissioner in chancery) of the _____ court, (or a notary public) for the county (or corporation) aforesaid, in the State (or territory or district) of _____ (or a commissioner appointed by the Governor of the State of Virginia for said State, or territory, or district of _____), do certify that the execution of the writing above (or hereto annexed) bearing date on the _____ day of _____, by A.B. (or A.B. and C.D., and so forth), whose name (or names) is (or are) signed thereto, was proved before me in my county (or corporation, or State) aforesaid, by the evidence on oath of E.F. and G.H., subscribing witnesses to said writing.

Given under my hand this _____ day of _____.

When authority is given in § 55-106 or in this section to the clerk of a court in or out of this State, but within the United States, such authority may be exercised by his duly qualified deputy.

§ 55-114. Acknowledgments outside of the United States and its dependencies.

Such court or clerk shall also admit any such writing to record as to any person whose name is signed thereto upon the certificate under the official seal of any ambassador, minister plenipotentiary, minister resident, charge d'affaires, consul-general, consul, vice-consul or commercial agent appointed by the government of the United States to any foreign country, or of the proper officer of any court of record of such country or of the mayor or other chief magistrate of any city, town or corporation therein, that such writing was acknowledged by such person or proved as to him by two witnesses before any person having such appointment or before such court, mayor or chief magistrate.

§ 55-114.1. Acknowledgments by persons subject to Uniform Code of Military Justice; validation of certain acknowledgments.

Such court or clerk shall also admit any such writing to record as to any person whose name is signed thereto and who at the time of such acknowledgment:

(1) Was a member of any of the armed forces of the United States, wherever they may have been, or

(2) Was employed by, or accompanying such armed forces outside the United States and outside the Canal Zone, Puerto Rico, Guam and the Virgin Islands, or

(3) Was subject to the Uniform Code of Military Justice of the United States outside of the United States, upon the certificate of any person authorized to take acknowledgments under § 936(a) of Title 10 of United States Code Annotated as that section existed on October thirty, nineteen hundred sixty-three.

Such certification shall be in substantially the same form as required by § 55-115 of this Code.

Any acknowledgment heretofore taken which is in substantial conformity with this section is hereby ratified, validated and confirmed.

§ 55-115. Acknowledgments taken before commissioned officers in military service.

Such court or clerk shall also admit any such writing to record as to any person whose name is signed thereto who at the time of such acknowledgment was in active service in the armed forces of the United States, or as to the consort of such person, upon the certificate of any commissioned officer of the army, navy, marine corps, coast guard, any state national guard that is federally recognized or other branch of the service of which such person is a member, that such writing had been acknowledged before him by such person. Such certificate shall be written upon or annexed to such writing and shall be substantially to the following effect:

In the army (or navy, etc.) of the United States.

I, _____, a commissioned officer of the army (or navy, marine corps, coast guard or other branch of service) of the United States with the rank of lieutenant (or ensign or other appropriate rank) whose home address is _____, do certify that E.F. (or E.F. and G.H., and so forth), whose name (or names) is (or are) signed to the writing above (or hereto annexed), bearing date on the _____ day of _____, _____, and who, or whose consort, is a private (corporal, seaman, captain or other grade or rank) in the army (or navy, etc.) of the United States, and whose home address is _____, has (or have) acknowledged the same before me.

Given under my hand this _____ day of _____.

Such acknowledgment may be taken at any place where the officer taking the acknowledgment and the person whose name is signed to the writing may be. Such commissioned officer may take the acknowledgment of any person in any branch of the armed forces of the United States, or the consort of such person.

Every acknowledgment executed prior to January one, nineteen hundred seventy-two, in substantial compliance with the provisions of this section is hereby validated, ratified and confirmed, notwithstanding any error or omission with respect to any address, grade or rank.

Uniform Recognition of Acknowledgments Act

§ 55-118.1. "Notarial acts" defined; who may perform notarial acts outside State for use in State.

For the purposes of this article, "notarial acts" means acts which the laws and regulations of this State authorize notaries public of this State to perform, including the administering of oaths and affirmations, taking proof of execution and acknowledgments of instruments, and attesting documents. Notarial acts may be performed outside this State for use in this State with the same effect as if performed by a notary public of this State by the following persons authorized pursuant to the laws and regulations of other governments in addition to any other person authorized by the laws and regulations of this State:

(1) A notary public authorized to perform notarial acts in the place in which the act is performed;

(2) A judge, clerk, or deputy clerk of any court of record in the place in which the notarial act is performed;

(3) An officer of the foreign service of the United States, a consular agent, or any other person authorized by regulation of the United States Department of State to perform notarial acts in the place in which the act is performed;

(4) A commissioned officer in active service with the armed forces of the United States and any other person authorized by regulation of the armed forces to perform notarial acts if the notarial act is performed for one of the following or his dependents: a merchant seaman of the United States, a member of the armed forces of the United States, or any other person serving with or accompanying the armed forces of the United States; or

(5) Any other person authorized to perform notarial acts in the place in which the act is performed.

§ 55-118.2. Proof of authority of person performing notarial act.

(a) If the notarial act is performed by any of the persons described in paragraphs (1) through (4) of § 55-118.1, other than a person authorized to perform notarial acts by the laws or regulations of a foreign country, the signature, rank, or title and serial number, if any, of the person are sufficient proof of the authority of a holder of that rank or title to perform the act. Further proof of his authority is not required.

(b) If the notarial act is performed by a person authorized by the laws or regulations of a foreign country to perform the act, there is sufficient proof of the authority of that person to act if:

(1) Either a foreign service officer of the United States resident in the country in which the act is performed or a diplomatic or consular officer of the foreign country resident in the United States certifies that a person holding that office is authorized to perform the act;

(2) The official seal of the person performing the notarial act is affixed to the document; or

(3) The title and indication of authority to perform notarial acts of the person appears either in a digest of foreign law or in a list customarily used as a source of such information.

(c) If the notarial act is performed by a person other than one described in subsections (a) and (b), there is sufficient proof of the authority of that person to act if the clerk of a court of record in the place in which the notarial act is performed certifies to the official character of that person and to his authority to perform the notarial act.

(d) The signature and title of the person performing the act are prima facie evidence that he is a person with the designated title and that the signature is genuine.

§ 55-118.3. What person taking acknowledgment shall certify.

The person taking an acknowledgment shall certify that:

(1) The person acknowledging appeared before him and acknowledged he executed the instrument; and

(2) The person acknowledging was known to the person taking the acknowledgment or that the person taking the acknowledgment had satisfactory evidence that the person acknowledging was the person described in and who executed the instrument.

§ 55-118.4. When form of certificate of acknowledgment accepted.

The form of a certificate of acknowledgment used by a person whose authority is recognized under § 55-118.1 shall be accepted in this State if:

(1) The certificate is in a form prescribed by the laws or regulations of this State;

(2) The certificate is in a form prescribed by the laws or regulations applicable in the place in which the acknowledgment is taken; or

(3) The certificate contains the words "acknowledged before me," or their substantial equivalent.

§ 55-118.5. Meaning of "acknowledged before me."

The words "acknowledged before me" mean

(1) That the person acknowledging appeared before the person taking the acknowledgment,

(2) That he acknowledged he executed the instrument,

(3) That, in the case of:

(i) A natural person, he executed the instrument for the purposes therein stated;

(ii) A corporation, the officer or agent acknowledged he held the position or title set forth in the instrument and certificate, he signed the instrument on behalf of the corporation by proper authority, and the instrument was the act of the corporation for the purpose therein stated;

(iii) A partnership, the partner or agent acknowledged he signed the instrument on behalf of the partnership by proper authority and he executed the instrument as the act of the partnership for the purposes therein stated;

(iv) A person acknowledging as principal by an attorney in fact, he executed the instrument by proper authority as the act of the principal for the purposes therein stated;

(v) A person acknowledging as a public officer, trustee, administrator, guardian, or other representative, he signed the instrument by proper authority and he executed the instrument in the capacity and for the purposes therein stated; and

(4) That the person taking the acknowledgment either knew or had satisfactory evidence that the person acknowledging was the person named in the instrument or certificate.

§ 55-118.6. Statutory short forms of acknowledgment.

The forms of acknowledgment set forth in this section may be used and are sufficient for their respective purposes under any law of this State. The forms shall be known as "Statutory Short Forms of Acknowledgment" and may be referred to by that name. The authorization of the forms in this section does not preclude the use of other forms.

(1) For an individual acting in his own right:

State of ....
County of ....

The foregoing instrument was acknowledged before me this (date) by (name of person acknowledged).

          (Signature of Person Taking Acknowledgment)
          (Title or Rank)
          (Serial Number, if any)

(2) For a corporation:

State of ....
County of ....

The foregoing instrument was acknowledged before me this (date) by (name of officer or agent, title of officer or agent) of (name of corporation acknowledging) a (state or place of incorporation) corporation, on behalf of the corporation.

          (Signature of Person Taking Acknowledgment)
          (Title or Rank)
          (Serial Number, if any)

(3) For a partnership:

State of ....
County of ....

The foregoing instrument was acknowledged before me this (date) by (name of acknowledging partner or agent), partner (or agent) on behalf of (name of partnership), a partnership.

          (Signature of Person Taking Acknowledgment)
          (Title or Rank)
          (Serial Number, if any)

(4) For an individual acting as principal by an attorney-in-fact:

State of ....
County of ....

The foregoing instrument was acknowledged before me this (date) by (name of attorney-in-fact) as attorney-in-fact on behalf of (name of principal).

          (Signature of Person Taking Acknowledgment)
          (Title or Rank)
          (Serial Number, if any)

(5) By any public officer, trustee, or personal representative:

State of ....
County of ....

The foregoing instrument was acknowledged

before me this (date) by (name and title of position).

> (Signature of Person Taking Acknowledgment)
> (Title or Rank)
> (Serial Number, if any)

§ 55-118.7. Application of article; article cumulative.

A notarial act performed prior to June 26, 1970, is not affected by this article. This article provides an additional method of proving notarial acts. Nothing in this article diminishes or invalidates the recognition accorded to notarial acts by other laws or regulations of this State.

§ 55-118.8. Uniform interpretation.

This article shall be so interpreted as to make uniform the laws of those states which enact it.

§ 55-118.9. Short title.

This article may be cited as the Uniform Recognition of Acknowledgments Act.

§ 55-119. Deeds of corporations; how to be executed and acknowledged.

All deeds made by corporations shall be signed in the name of the corporation by the president or acting president, or any vice-president, or by such other person as may be authorized thereunto by the board of directors of such corporation, and, if such deed is to be recorded, the person signing the name of the corporation shall acknowledge the same in the manner provided by § 55-120.

§ 55-120. Acknowledgments on behalf of corporations and others.

When any writing purports to have been signed in behalf or by authority of any person or corporation, or in any representative capacity whatsoever, the certificate of the acknowledgment by the person so signing the writing shall be sufficient for the purposes of this and §§ ***, 55-113, 55-114, and 55-115, and for the admission of such writing to record as to the person or corporation on whose behalf it is signed, or as to the representative character of the person so signing the same, as the case may be, without expressing that such acknowledgment was in behalf or by authority of such other person or corporation or was in a representative capacity. In the case of a writing signed in behalf or by authority of any person or corporation or in any representative capacity a certificate to the following effect shall be sufficient:

State (or territory or district) of _____, county (or corporation) of _____, to wit: I, _____, a _____ (here insert the official title of the person certifying the acknowledgment) in and for the State (or territory or district) and county (or corporation) aforesaid, do certify that _____ (here insert the name or names of the persons signing the writing on behalf of the person or corporation, or the name of the person signing the writing in a representative capacity), whose name (or names) is (or are) signed to the writing above, bearing date on the _____ day of _____, has (or have) acknowledged the same before me in my county (or corporation) aforesaid. Given under my hand this _____ day of _____.

§ 55-121. Corporate acknowledgment taken before officer or stockholder.

Any notary or other officer duly authorized to take acknowledgments may take the acknowledgment to any deed or other writing, executed by a company, or to a company or for the benefit of a company, although he may be a stockholder, an officer, or both, in such company; provided he is not otherwise interested in the property conveyed or disposed of by such deed or other writing; and nothing herein shall be construed to authorize any officer to take an acknowledgment to any deed or other writing executed by such company by and through him as an officer or stockholder thereof, or to him for the benefit of such company.

§ 55-122. Act of notaries public, etc., who have held certain other offices.

All certificates of acknowledgment to deeds and other writings, taken and certified by notaries public and commissioners in chancery, and all depositions taken, accounts and reports made, and decrees executed by any notary public, commissioner in chancery or commissioner of accounts, who, since January 1, 1989, may have held the office of county treasurer, sheriff, attorney for the Commonwealth, county clerk, commissioner of the revenue, superintendent of the poor, county surveyor or supervisor shall be held and the same are hereby declared valid and effective in all respects, if otherwise valid and effective according to the law then in force.

§ 55-123. Validation of acknowledgments when seal not affixed.

When a certificate of acknowledgment was made prior to January 1, 1989, to any instrument in writing required by this chapter to be acknowledged and the notary or other official whether of this or some other state taking same failed to affix his official seal to such certificate of acknowledgment when a seal was necessary, the certificate of acknowledgment shall be as valid for all purposes as if such seal had been affixed, and the deed shall be, and shall since such date have been, notice to all persons as effectually as if such seal had been affixed, provided that such acknowledgment was in other respects sufficient.

§ 55-125.1. Certain acknowledgments taken and certified before January 1, 1989.

All certificates of acknowledgments to deeds and other writings, taken and certified prior to January 1, 1989, by commissioners of deeds of states other than Virginia, appointed or commissioned by the governor of such state, and by notaries public appointed or commissioned by the Governor of Virginia, or appointed or commissioned under the laws of any state other than this Commonwealth, or any other officer authorized under this chapter to take and certify acknowledgments of deeds and other writings, which omit the citation of the date of the deed or certificate where it is clear from the content of the entire certificate and the instrument which has been acknowledged that the identity of the instrument or the certificate is the same, or if it can reasonably be inferred from the certificate of the person recording the instrument or other writing that the certificate refers to the same instrument, shall be held and the same hereby declared valid and effective in all respects, if otherwise valid according to the law then in force, or otherwise appear valid upon their face, and all such deeds and other writings which have been admitted to record in any clerk's office in the Commonwealth upon such certificates shall be held to be duly and regularly recorded if such recordation be otherwise valid according to the law then in force.

§ 55-127. Acknowledgments taken by officers after expiration of terms.

All certificates of acknowledgment to deeds and other writings taken and certified prior to January 1, 1989, by commissioners of deeds of states other than Virginia, appointed or commissioned by the governor of such state, and by notaries public appointed or commissioned by the Governor of Virginia, or appointed or commissioned under the laws of any state other than this Commonwealth, or any other officer authorized under this chapter to take and certify acknowledgments to deeds and other writings who took and certified such acknowledgments after their term of office had expired, shall be held and the same are hereby declared valid and effective in all respects, if otherwise valid according to the law then in force or appear to be valid upon their face; and all such

deeds and other writings which have been admitted to record in any clerk's office in the Commonwealth upon such certificates shall be held to be duly and regularly recorded if such recordation be otherwise valid according to the law then in force.

§ 55-129. Acknowledgments before foreign officials who failed to affix seals.

All certificates of acknowledgment to deeds and other writings made and certified prior to January 1, 1989, before officials in any foreign country authorized by law to take and certify such acknowledgments, to which such officials failed to affix their official seals, shall be held, and the same are hereby declared, valid and effective in all respects if otherwise valid according to the law then in force.

§ 55-130. Acknowledgments taken by notaries in foreign countries.

All certificates of acknowledgment to deeds and other writings taken and certified prior to January 1, 1989, by notaries public residing in foreign countries shall be held, and the same are hereby declared, valid and effective in all respects, if otherwise valid according to the law then in force.

§ 55-131. Acknowledgments taken by officer who was husband or wife of grantee.

Any certificate of acknowledgment to a deed or other writings taken prior to January 1, 1989, by a notary public or other officer duly authorized to take acknowledgments, who at the time of taking such acknowledgment was the husband or wife of the grantee in the deed or other instrument, shall be held, and the same is hereby declared, valid and effective in all respects, if otherwise valid according to the law then in force. All acknowledgments of conveyances to a fiduciary taken before an officer, who is the husband or wife of the same and who has no beneficial or monetary interest other than possible commissions or legal fees shall be conclusively presumed valid.

§ 55-132. Acknowledgment when notary certifies erroneously as to expiration of commission.

All certificates of acknowledgment to deeds and other writings taken and certified prior to January 1, 1989, by a notary public appointed or commissioned by the Governor, or appointed or commissioned under the laws of any state other than the Commonwealth of Virginia, who mistakenly or by error certified that his commission had expired at the time he made such certificate, when in fact his commission had not at that time expired, shall be held, and the same are hereby declared, valid and effective in all respects if otherwise valid according to the law of the Commonwealth then in force, and the date and life of the notary's commission may be proved aliunde his certificate in any proceeding in which the capacity or authority of such notary is or shall be questioned; and all such deeds and other writings which have been admitted to record in any clerk's office in the Commonwealth, upon such certificates, shall be held to be duly and regularly recorded if such recordation be otherwise valid according to the law then in force.

§ 55-134. Acknowledgments taken before notary whose commission has expired; later date; intervening vested rights saved.

All certificates of acknowledgment to deeds and other writings taken and certified prior to January 1, 1989, by notaries public appointed or commissioned by the Governor, who took and certified such acknowledgments after their term of office had expired, shall be held, and the same are hereby declared, valid and effective in all respects, if otherwise valid according to the law then in force, and all such deeds and other writings which have been admitted to record in any clerk's office in the Commonwealth upon such certificates shall be held to be duly and regularly recorded, if such recordation be otherwise valid according to the law then in force; however, nothing in this section shall be so construed as to affect any intervening vested rights.

§ 55-134.1. Acknowledgments taken before notary who was appointed but failed to qualify; vested rights saved.

All certificates of acknowledgment to deeds and other writings taken and certified prior to January 1, 1989, by a person who was appointed as a notary public by the Governor but who failed to qualify as provided by law shall be held, and the same are hereby declared valid and effective in all respects, if otherwise valid, and all such deeds and other writings which have been admitted to record in any clerk's office in the Commonwealth upon such certificates shall be held to be duly and regularly recorded, if such recordation be otherwise valid according to law; however, nothing in this section shall be so construed as to affect any intervening vested rights.

§ 55-134.2. Acknowledgments taken before a notary at large who failed to cite the jurisdiction in which the acknowledgment was taken; vested rights saved.

All certificates of acknowledgment to deeds and other writings taken and certified prior to January

1, 1989, by a person who was appointed a notary public for the Commonwealth at large by the Governor, but who failed to include in such certificates of acknowledgment the city or county in which the notarial act was performed, shall be held, and the same are hereby declared, valid and effective in all respects, if otherwise valid, and all such deeds and other writings which have been admitted to record in any clerk's office in the Commonwealth upon such certificates shall be held to be duly and regularly recorded, if such recordation be otherwise valid according to law; however, nothing in this section shall be so construed as to affect any intervening vested rights.

§ 64.1-87.1. How will may be made self-proved.

A will, at the time of its execution or at any subsequent date, may be made self-proved by the acknowledgment thereof by the testator and the affidavits of the attesting witnesses, each made before an officer authorized to administer oaths under the laws of this Commonwealth or the laws of the state where acknowledgment occurred or before an officer of the foreign service of the United States, a consular agent, or any other person authorized by regulation of the United States Department of State to perform notarial acts in the place in which the act is performed, and evidenced by the officer's certificate, attached or annexed to the will. The officer's certificate shall be substantially as follows in form and content:

STATE OF VIRGINIA
COUNTY/CITY OF . . . .
Before me, the undersigned authority, on this day personally appeared . . . . . ., ..., and . . . . . ., known to me to be the testator and the witnesses, respectively, whose names are signed to the attached or foregoing instrument and, all of these persons being by me first duly sworn, ..., the testator, declared to me and to the witnesses in my presence that said instrument is his last will and testament and that he had willingly signed or directed another to sign the same for him, and executed it in the presence of said witnesses as his free and voluntary act for the purposes therein expressed; that said witnesses stated before me that the foregoing will was executed and acknowledged by the testator as his last will and testament in the presence of said witnesses who, in his presence and at his request, and in the presence of each other, did subscribe their names thereto as attesting witnesses on the day of the date of said will, and that the testator, at the time of the execution of said will, was over the age of eighteen years and of sound and disposing mind and memory.

. . . .
Testator

. . . .
Witness

. . . .
Witness

Subscribed, sworn and acknowledged before me by . . . . ., the testator, and subscribed and sworn before me by . . . . ., and . . . . ., witnesses, this . . . . day of . . . . ., A.D., ...

SIGNED . . . .

. . . .

(OFFICIAL CAPACITY OF OFFICER)

The sworn statement of any such witnesses taken as herein provided, whether before, on or after July 1, 1986, shall be accepted by the court as if it had been taken ore tenus before such court, notwithstanding that (i) the officer did not attach or affix his official seal thereto or (ii) the acknowledgment was before an officer authorized to administer oaths under the laws of another state. Any codicil which is self-proved under the provisions of this section which also, by its terms, expressly confirms, ratifies and republishes a will except as altered by the codicil shall have the effect of self-proving the will whether or not the will was so executed originally.

§ 64.1-87.2. Same; alternate method.

A will, at the time of its execution or at any subsequent date, may be made self-proved by the acknowledgment thereof by the testator and the attesting witnesses, each made before an officer authorized to administer oaths under the laws of the Commonwealth, or the laws of the state where the acknowledgment occurred or before an officer of the foreign service of the United States, a consular agent, or any other person authorized by regulation of the United States Department of State to perform notarial acts in the place in which the act is performed, and evidenced by the officer's certificate, attached or annexed to the will. The officer's certificate shall be substantially as follows in the form and content:

STATE OF VIRGINIA

CITY/COUNTY OF . . . .

Before me, the undersigned authority, on this day personally appeared . . . ., ..., and . . . ., known to me to be the testator and the witnesses, respectively whose names are signed to the attached or foregoing instrument and, all of these persons being by me first duly sworn, ..., the testator, declared to me and to the witnesses in my presence that said instrument is his last will and testament and that he had willingly signed or directed another to sign the same for him, and executed it in the presence of said witnesses as his free and voluntary act for the purposes therein expressed, that said witnesses stated before me that the foregoing will was executed and acknowledged

by the testator as his last will and testament in the presence of said witnesses who in his presence and at his request and in the presence of each other did subscribe their names thereto as attesting witnesses on the day of the date of said will and that the testator, at the time of the execution of said will, was over the age of eighteen years and of sound and disposing mind and memory.

Sworn and acknowledged before me by . . . . . ., the testator, and . . . . and . . . ., witnesses, this day of . . . . A.D., ...

SIGNED . . . .

. . . .

(OFFICIAL CAPACITY OF OFFICER)

DEPOSITIONS

§ 8.01-407. How summons for witness issued, and to whom directed; prior permission of court to summon certain officials and judges; attendance before commissioner of other state.

A. A summons may be issued, directed as prescribed in § 8.01-292, commanding the officer to summon any person to attend on the day and at the place that such attendance is desired, to give evidence before a court, grand jury, arbitrators, magistrate, notary, or any commissioner or other person appointed by a court or acting under its process or authority in a judicial or quasi-judicial capacity. The summons may be issued, if the attendance be desired at a court or in a proceeding pending in a court, by the clerk thereof; if before a commissioner in chancery or other commissioner of a court, by the clerk of the court in which the matter is pending, or by such commissioner in chancery or other commissioner; if before a notary or other officer taking a deposition, by such notary or other officer at the instance of the attorney desiring the attendance of the person sought; if before a grand jury, by the attorney for the Commonwealth, or the clerk of the court, at the instance of the attorney for the Commonwealth; and in other cases, by the clerk of the circuit court of the county or city in which the attendance is desired. It shall express on whose behalf, and in what case or about what matter, the witness is to attend. Failure to respond to any such summons shall be punishable by the court in which the proceeding is pending as for contempt.

B. No subpoena shall, without permission of the court first obtained, issue for the attendance of the Governor, Lieutenant Governor, or Attorney General of this Commonwealth, or a judge of any court thereof; the President or Vice-President of the United States; any member of the President's Cabinet; any ambassador or consul; or any military officer on active duty holding the rank of admiral or general.

C. This section shall be deemed to authorize a summons to compel attendance of a citizen of the Commonwealth before commissioners or other persons appointed by authority of another state when the summons requires the attendance of such witness at a place not out of his county or city.

Uniform Foreign Depositions Act

§ 8.01-411. Compelling attendance of witnesses for taking depositions and production of documents to be used in foreign jurisdiction.

Whenever any mandate, writ or commission is issued out of any court of record in any other state, territory, district or foreign jurisdiction, or whenever upon notice or agreement it is required to take the testimony of a witness or witnesses or produce or inspect designated documents in this Commonwealth, witnesses may be compelled to appear and testify and to produce and permit inspection or copying of documents in the same manner and by the same process and proceeding as may be employed for the purpose of taking testimony or producing documents in proceedings pending in this Commonwealth.

§ 8.01-412. Uniformity of interpretation; reciprocal privileges.

This article shall be so interpreted and construed as to effectuate its general purposes to make uniform the law of those states which enact it. The privilege extended to persons in other states by § 8.01-411 shall only apply to those states which extended the same privilege to persons in this Commonwealth.

§ 8.01-412.1. Short title.

This article may be cited as the Uniform Foreign Depositions Act.

§ 49-5. Officer of another state or country may take affidavit; authentication.

An affidavit may also be made before any officer of any state or country authorized by its laws to administer an oath, and shall be deemed duly authenticated if it be subscribed by such officer and there be annexed to it a certificate of the clerk or any other officer of a court of record of such state or country, under an official seal, verifying the genuineness of the signature of the first mentioned officer and his authority to administer an oath, ex-

cept that when such affidavit is made before a notary public of such other state or country the same shall be deemed and taken to be duly authenticated if it be subscribed by such notary with his official seal attached without being certified to by any clerk or other officer of a court of record.

§ 49-7. Affidavits for corporations, partnerships, and other entities.

An affidavit filed for a corporation or other entity may be made by its president, vice-president, general manager, cashier, treasurer, a director or attorney without any special authorization therefor, or by any person authorized by a majority of its stockholders, directors, partners or members to make the same.

COMMISSIONERS

§ 47.1-31. Appointment; lists of commissioners to be published.

The Governor shall appoint out of this Commonwealth, and within the United States, or within Puerto Rico, or any other territory subject to the jurisdiction of the United States, or over which the United States exercises authority, so many commissioners for such states, countries, and districts as to him shall seem proper, who shall hold their office, at the pleasure of the Governor, for the term of two years, and he shall, within thirty days after the beginning of each regular session of the General Assembly, communicate to it the names and residence of the persons holding office under such appointment. Lists of such commissioners shall be published with the acts and resolutions of the General Assembly.

§ 47.1-32. Fee of Secretary of Commonwealth.

The Secretary of the Commonwealth shall be entitled in each case to receive from the person appointed commissioner as aforesaid a fee of twenty-five dollars for making out and transmitting his commission to him.

§ 47.1-33. Certificate of acknowledgment.

A certificate of acknowledgment before any commissioner appointed under this chapter shall be under the form prescribed by §§ 55-113 and 55-120, and shall have like effect for all purposes as a certificate of acknowledgment before and by a notary public.

LEGAL HOLIDAYS

§ 2.1-21. Legal holidays.

It is the policy of the Commonwealth to fix and set aside certain days in the calendar year as legal holidays for the people of Virginia to honor and commemorate such holidays so established. In each year, the following days are designated as legal holidays:

January 1—New Year's Day.

The third Monday in January—Lee-Jackson-King Day to honor Robert Edward Lee (1806-1870), Thomas Jonathan (Stonewall) Jackson (1824-1863), and Martin Luther King, Jr., (1929-1968), defenders of causes.

The third Monday in February—George Washington Day to honor George Washington (1732-1799), the first President of the United States of America.

The last Monday in May—Memorial Day to honor all persons who made the supreme sacrifice in giving their lives in defense of Virginia and the United States of America in the following wars and engagements and otherwise: Indian Uprising (1622), French and Indian Wars (1754-1763), Revolutionary War (1775-1783), War of 1812 (1812-1815), Mexican War (1846-1848), War Between the States (1861-1865), Spanish American War (1898), World War I (1917-1918), World War II (1941-1945), Korean War (1950-1953), and the Vietnam War (1965-1973). On this day all flags, national, state, and local, shall be flown at half staff or mast to honor and acknowledge respect for those who made the supreme sacrifice.

July 4—Independence Day to honor the signing of the Declaration of Independence.

The first Monday in September—Labor Day to honor all people who work for a livelihood in Virginia.

The second Monday in October—Columbus Day and Yorktown Victory Day to honor Christopher Columbus (1451-1506), a discoverer of the Americas, and the final victory at Yorktown on October 19, 1781 in the Revolutionary War.

November 11—Veterans Day to honor all persons who served in the Armed Forces of Virginia and the United States of America in the following wars and engagements and otherwise: Indian Uprising (1622), French and Indian Wars (1754-1763), Revolutionary War (1775-1783), War of 1812 (1812-1815), Mexican War (1846-1848), War Between the States (1861-1865), Spanish American War (1898), World War I (1917-1918), World War II (1941-1945), Korean War (1950-1953), and the Vietnam War (1965-1973).

The fourth Thursday in November and the Friday next following—Thanksgiving Day to honor and give thanks in each person's own manner for the blessings bestowed upon the people of Virginia and honoring the first Thanksgiving in 1619.

December 25—Christmas Day.

Whenever any of such days falls on Saturday, the Friday next preceding such day, or whenever any of such days falls on Sunday, the Monday next following such day, and any day so appointed by the Governor of this Commonwealth or the President of the United States, shall be a legal holiday as to the transaction of all business.

§ 2.1-22. Acts, business transactions, legal proceedings, etc., on holidays valid.

No contract made, instrument executed, or act done on any of the legal holidays named in § 2.1-21, or on any Saturday, whether before or after twelve o'clock, noon, shall be thereby rendered invalid, and nothing in such section shall be construed to prevent or invalidate the entry, issuance, service or execution of any writ, summons, confession, judgment, order or decree, or other legal process whatever, or the session of the proceedings of any court or judge on any of such legal holidays or Saturdays, either before or after twelve o'clock, noon, nor to prevent any bank, banker, banking corporation, firm or association from keeping their doors open and transacting any lawful business on any of such legal holidays or Saturdays.

§ 2.1-23. Saturday closing of banks.

It shall be lawful for any bank as defined in § 6.1-4, including national banking associations and federal reserve banks, to permit any one or more or all of its offices to remain closed on any one or more or all Saturdays, as the bank, by resolution of its board of directors, may from time to time determine. Any Saturday on which an office of a bank shall remain closed, as herein permitted, shall, as to such office, constitute a legal holiday, and any act authorized, required or permitted to be performed at, by or with respect to any such office on a Saturday on which the office is so closed, may be performed on the next succeeding business day and no liability or loss of rights of any kind shall result from such delay.

WASHINGTON

NOTARIES PUBLIC

[Wash. Rev. Code Ann.]

§ 42.44.010. Definitions.

Unless the context clearly requires otherwise, the definitions in this section apply throughout this chapter.

(1) "Director" means the director of licensing of the state of Washington or the director's designee.

(2) "Notarial act" and "notarization" mean: (a) Taking an acknowledgment; (b) administering an oath or affirmation; (c) taking a verification upon oath or affirmation; (d) witnessing or attesting a signature; (e) certifying or attesting a copy; (f) receiving a protest of a negotiable instrument; (g) certifying that an event has occurred or an act has been performed; and (h) any other act that a notary public of this state is authorized to perform.

(3) "Notary public" and "notary" mean any person appointed to perform notarial acts in this state.

(4) "Acknowledgment" means a statement by a person that the person has executed an instrument as the person's free and voluntary act for the uses and purposes stated therein and, if the instrument is executed in a representative capacity, a statement that the person signed the document with proper authority and executed it as the act of the person or entity represented and identified therein.

(5) "Verification upon oath or affirmation" means a statement by a person who asserts it to be true and makes the assertion upon oath or affirmation administered in accordance with chapter 5.28 RCW.

(6) "In a representative capacity" means:

(a) For and on behalf of a corporation, partnership, trust, or other entity, as an authorized officer, agent, partner, trustee, or other representative;

(b) As a public officer, personal representative, guardian, or other representative, in the capacity recited in the instrument;

(c) As an attorney in fact for a principal; or

(d) In any other capacity as an authorized representative of another.

(7) "Serious crime" means any felony or any lesser crime, a necessary element of which, as determined by the statutory or common law definition of such crime, involves interference with the administration of justice, false swearing, misrepresentation, fraud, the unauthorized practice of law, deceit, bribery, extortion, misappropriation, theft, or an attempt, a conspiracy, or the solicitation of another to commit a serious crime.

§ 42.44.020. Qualifications—application—bond.

(1) The director may, upon application, appoint to be a notary public in this state, any person who:

(a) Is at least eighteen years of age;

(b) Resides in Washington state, or resides in an adjoining state and is regularly employed in Washington state or carries on business in Washington state; and

(c) Can read and write English.

(2) Each application shall be accompanied by endorsements by at least three residents of this state of the age of eighteen or more, who are not relatives of the applicant, in the following form:

I, __(name of endorser)__, being a person eligible to vote in the state of Washington, believe the applicant for a notary public appointment, __(applicant's name)__, who is not related to me, to be a person of integrity and good moral character and capable of performing notarial acts.

_____

(Endorser's signature and address, with date of signing)

(3) Every application for appointment as a notary public shall be accompanied by a fee established by the director by rule.

(4) Every applicant for appointment as a notary public shall submit an application in a form prescribed by the director, and shall sign the following declaration in the presence of a notary public of this state:

Declaration of Applicant

I, __(name of applicant)__, solemnly swear or affirm under penalty of perjury that the personal information I have provided in this application is true, complete, and correct; that I carefully have read the materials provided with the application describing the duties of a notary public in and for the state of Washington; and, that I will perform, to the best of my ability, all notarial acts in accordance with the law.

_____

(Signature of applicant)

State of Washington

County of _____

On this day _____ appeared before me, signed this Declaration of Application, and swore (or affirmed) that (he/she) understood its contents and that its contents are truthful.

Dated: _____

_____

Signature of notary public

(Seal or stamp)

Residing at _____

(5) Every applicant shall submit to the director proof from a surety company that a ten thousand dollar surety bond, insuring the proper performance of notarial acts by the applicant, will be affective for a term commencing on the date the person is appointed, and expiring on the date the applicant's notary appointment expires. The surety for the bond shall be a company qualified to write surety bonds in this state.

§ 42.44.030. Appointment denied certain persons.

The director may deny appointment as a notary public to any person who:

(1) Has been convicted of a serious crime;

(2) Has had a notary appointment or other professional license revoked, suspended, or restricted in this or any other state;

(3) Has engaged in official misconduct as defined in section 17(1) of this act, [42.44.160(1)] whether or not criminal penalties resulted; or

(4) Has performed a notarial act or acts in a manner found by the director to constitute gross negligence, a course of negligent conduct, or reckless disregard of his or her responsibility as a notary public.

§ 42.44.040. Certificate of appointment.

The director shall deliver a certificate evidencing the appointment to each person appointed as a notary public. The certificate may be signed in facsimile by the governor, the secretary of state, and the director or the director's designee. The certificate shall bear a printed seal of the state of Washington.

§ 42.44.050. Seal or stamp.

Every person appointed as a notary public in this state shall procure a seal or stamp, on which shall be engraved or impressed the words "Notary Public" and "State of Washington," the date the appointment expires, the person's surname, and at least the initials of the person's first and middle names. The director shall prescribe by rule the size and form or forms of the seal or stamp. It is unlawful for any person intentionally to manufacture, give, sell, procure or possess a seal or stamp evidencing the current appointment of a person as a notary public until the director has delivered a certificate evidencing the appointment as provided for in RCW 42.44.040.

§ 42.44.060. Term.

A person appointed as a notary public by the director may perform notarial acts in this state for a term of four years, unless:

(1) The notarial appointment has been revoked under RCW 42.44.130 or 42.44.140; or

(2) The notarial appointment has been resigned.

§ 42.44.070. Reappointment without endorsements.

A person who has received an appointment as a notary public may be reappointed without the endorsements required in RCW 42.44.020(2) if the person submits a new application before the expiration date of the current appointment.

§ 42.44.080. Standards for notarial acts.

A notary public is authorized to perform notarial acts in this state. Notarial acts shall be performed in accordance with the following, as applicable:

(1) In taking an acknowledgment, a notary public must determine and certify, either from personal knowledge or from satisfactory evidence, that the person appearing before the notary public and making the acknowledgment is the person whose true signature is on the document.

(2) In taking an acknowledgment authorized by RCW 64.08.100 from a person physically unable to sign his or her name or make a mark, a notary public shall, in addition to other requirements for taking an acknowledgment, determine and certify from personal knowledge or satisfactory evidence that the person appearing before the notary public is physically unable to sign his or her name or make a mark and is otherwise competent. The notary public shall include in the acknowledgment a statement that the signature in the acknowledgment was obtained under the authority of RCW 64.08.100.

(3) In taking a verification upon oath or affirmation, a notary public must determine, either from personal knowledge or from satisfactory evidence, that the person appearing before the notary public and making the verification is the person whose true signature is on the statement verified.

(4) In witnessing or attesting a signature, a notary public must determine, either from personal knowledge or from satisfactory evidence, that the signature is that of the person appearing before the notary public and named in the document.

(5) In certifying or attesting a copy of a document or other item, a notary public must determine that the proffered copy is a full, true, and accurate transcription or reproduction of that which was copied.

(6) In making or noting a protest of a negotiable instrument, a notary public must determine the matters set forth in RCW 62A.3-509.

(7) In certifying that an event has occurred or an act has been performed, a notary public must determine the occurrence or performance either from personal knowledge or from satisfactory evidence based upon the oath or affirmation of a credible witness personally known to the notary public.

(8) A notary public has satisfactory evidence that a person is the person described in a document if that person: (a) Is personally known to the notary public; (b) is identified upon the oath or affirmation of a credible witness personally known to the notary public; or (c) is identified on the basis of identification documents.

(9) The signature and seal or stamp of a notary public are prima facie evidence that the signature of the notary is genuine and that the person is a notary public.

(10) A notary public is disqualified from performing a notarial act when the notary is a signer of the document which is to be notarized.

§ 42.44.090. Form of certificate—general—seal or stamp as exclusive property.

(1) A notarial act by a notary public must be evidenced by a certificate signed and dated by a notary public. The certificate must include the name of the jurisdiction in which the notarial act is performed and the title of the notary public or other notarial officer and shall be accompanied by an impression of the official seal or stamp. It shall not be necessary for a notary public in certifying an oath to be used in any of the courts in this state, to append an impression of the official seal or stamp. If the notarial officer is a notary public, the certificate shall also indicate the date of expiration of such notary public's appointment, but omission of that information may subsequently be corrected.

(2) A certificate of a notarial act is sufficient if it meets the requirements of subsection (1) of this section and it:

(a) Is in the short form set forth in RCW 42.44.100;

(b) Is in a form otherwise permitted or prescribed by the laws of this state;

(c) Is in a form prescribed by the laws or regulations applicable in the place in which the notarial act was performed; or

(d) Is in a form that sets forth the actions of the notary public and the described actions are sufficient to meet the requirements of the designated notarial act.

If any law of this state specifically requires a certificate in a form other than that set forth in RCW 42.44.100 in connection with a form of document or transaction, the certificate required by such law shall be used for such document or transaction.

(3) By executing a certificate of a notarial act, the notary public certifies that he or she has made the determinations required by RCW 42.44.080.

(4) A notary public's seal or stamp shall be the exclusive property of the notary public, shall not be used by any other person, and shall not be surrendered to an employer upon termination of employ-

ment, regardless of whether the employer paid for the seal or for the notary's bond or appointment fees.

§ 42.44.100. Short forms of certificate.

The following short forms of notarial certificates are sufficient for the purposes indicated, if completed with the information required by this section:

(1) For an acknowledgment in an individual capacity:

State of Washington

County of _____

I certify that I know or have satisfactory evidence that _____ (name of person) _____ is the person who appeared before me, and said person acknowledged that (he/she) signed this instrument and acknowledged it to be (his/her) free and voluntary act for the uses and purposes mentioned in the instrument.

Dated: _____

_____
(Signature)

(Seal or stamp)

_____
Title
My appointment expires _____

(2) For an acknowledgment in a representative capacity:

State of Washington

County of _____

I certify that I know or have satisfactory evidence that _____ (name of person) _____ is the person who appeared before me, and said person acknowledged that (he/she) signed this instrument, on oath stated that (he/she) was authorized to execute the instrument and acknowledged it as the _(type of authority, e.g., officer, trustee, etc.)_ of _(name of party on behalf of whom instrument was executed)_ to be the free and voluntary act of such party for the uses and purposes mentioned in the instrument.

Dated: _____

_____
(Signature)

(Seal or stamp)

_____
Title
My appointment expires _____

(3) For a verification upon oath or affirmation:

State of Washington

County of _____

Signed and sworn to (or affirmed) before me on _(date)_ by _(name of person making statement)_ .

_____
(Signature)

(Seal or stamp)

_____
Title
My appointment expires _____

(4) For witnessing or attesting a signature:

State of Washington

County of _____

Signed or attested before me on _____ by _____

_____
(Signature)

(Seal or stamp)

_____
Title
My appointment expires _____

(5) For attestation of a copy of a document:

State of Washington

County of _____

I certify that this is a true and correct copy of a document in the possession of _____ as of this date.

Dated: _____

_____
(Signature)

(Seal or stamp)

_____
Title
My appointment expires _____

(6) For certifying the occurrence of an event or the performance of an act:

State of Washington

County of _____

I certify that the event or act described in this document has occurred or been performed.

Dated: _____

_____
(Signature)

(Seal or stamp)

_____
Title
My appointment expires _____

§ 42.44.110. Illegible writing.

The illegibility of any wording, writing, or marking required under this chapter does not in and of itself affect the validity of a document or transaction.

§ 42.44.120. Fees.

(1) The director shall establish by rule the maximum fees that may be charged by notaries public for various notarial services.

(2) A notary public need not charge fees for notarial acts.

§ **42.44.130.** Notarial acts by officials of other jurisdictions.

(1) A notarial act has the same effect under the law of this state as if performed by a notary public of this state, if performed in another state, commonwealth, territory, district, or possession of the United States by any of the following persons:

(a) A notary public of that jurisdiction;

(b) A judge, clerk, or deputy clerk of a court of that jurisdiction; or

(c) Any other person authorized by the law of that jurisdiction to perform notarial acts.

Notarial acts performed in other jurisdictions of the United States under federal authority as provided in RCW 42.44.140 have the same effect as if performed by a notarial officer of this state.

(2) The signature and title of a person performing a notarial act are prima facie evidence that the signature is genuine and that the person holds the designated title.

(3) The signature and title of an officer listed in subsection (1)(a) and (b) of this section conclusively establish the authority of a holder of that title to perform a notarial act.

§ **42.44.140.** Notarial acts by federal authorities.

(1) A notarial act has the same effect under the law of this state as if performed by a notary public of this state if performed by any of the following persons under authority granted by the law of the United States:

(a) A judge, clerk, or deputy clerk of a court;

(b) A commissioned officer in active service with the military forces of the United States;

(c) An officer of the foreign service or consular agent of the United States; or

(d) Any other person authorized by federal law to perform notarial acts.

(2) The signature and title of a person performing a notarial act are prima facie evidence that the signature is genuine and that the person holds the designated title.

(3) The signature and title or rank of an officer listed in subsection (1)(a), (b), and (c) of this section conclusively establish the authority of a holder of that title to perform a notarial act.

§ **42.44.150.** Notarial acts by foreign authorities.

(1) A notarial act has the same effect under the law of this state as if performed by a notary public of this state if performed within the jurisdiction of and under authority of a foreign nation or its constituent units or a multinational or international or-

ganization by any of the following persons:

(a) A notary public or notary;

(b) A judge, clerk, or deputy clerk of a court of record; or

(c) Any other person authorized by the law of that jurisdiction to perform notarial acts.

(2) An "apostille" in the form prescribed by the Hague Convention of October 5, 1961, conclusively establishes that the signature of the notarial officer is genuine and that the officer holds the designated office.

(3) A certificate by a foreign service or consular officer of the United States stationed in the nation under the jurisdiction of which the notarial act was performed, or a certificate by a foreign service or consular officer of that nation stationed in the United States, is prima facie evidence of the authenticity or validity of the notarial act set forth in the certificate.

(4) A stamp or seal of the person performing the notarial act is prima facie evidence that the signature is genuine and that the person holds that designated title.

(5) A stamp or seal of an officer listed in subsection (1)(a) or (b) of this section is prima facie evidence that a person with that title has authority to perform notarial acts.

(6) If the title of officer and indication of authority to perform notarial acts appears either in a digest of foreign law or in a list customarily used as a source for that information, the authority of an officer with that title to perform notarial acts is conclusively established.

§ **42.44.160.** Official misconduct—penalty.

(1) A notary public commits official misconduct when he or she signs a certificate evidencing a notarial act, knowing that the contents of the certificate are false.

(2) A notary public who commits an act of official misconduct shall be guilty of a gross misdemeanor.

(3) Any person not appointed as a notary public who acts as or otherwise impersonates a notary public shall be guilty of a gross misdemeanor.

§ **42.44.170.** Revocation of appointment—resignation.

(1) The director may revoke the appointment of any notary public for any reason for which appointment may be denied under RCW 42.44.030.

(2) The director shall revoke the appointment of a notary public upon a judicial finding of incompetency of the notary public. If a notary public is found to be incompetent, his or her guardian or

conservator shall within thirty days of such finding mail or deliver to the director a letter of resignation on behalf of the notary public.

(3) A notary public may voluntarily resign by mailing or delivering to the director a letter of resignation.

§ 42.44.180. Evidence of authenticity of notarial seal and signature.

(1) The authenticity of the notarial seal and official signature of a notary public of this state may be evidenced by:

(a) A certificate of authority from the director or the secretary of state; or

(b) An apostille in the form prescribed by the Hague Convention Abolishing the Requirement of Legalization for Foreign Public Documents of October 5, 1961.

(2) An apostille as specified by the Hague Convention shall be attached to any document requiring authentication that is sent to a nation that has signed and ratified the Hague Convention Abolishing the Requirement of Legalization for Foreign Public Documents.

§ 42.44.190. Rules.

On or before January 1, 1986, the director shall adopt rules to carry out this Chapter. Such rules shall include but shall not be limited to rules concerning applications for appointment, application and renewal fees, fees chargeable for notarial services, the replacement of lost or stolen seals or stamps, changes of names or addresses of notaries, resignations of notaries, appeals of denials and revocations of appointments, and issuance of evidences of authenticity of notarial seals and signatures.

§ 42.44.200. Transfer of records.

Records relating to the appointment and commissioning of notaries public that are in the custody of county clerks of this state on the effective date of this act shall be transferred to the director of licensing on or before December 31, 1985. Such records may be archived by the director.

§ 42.44.900. Savings—1985 c 156.

Nothing in this act may be interpreted to revoke any notary public appointment or commission existing on January 1, 1986. This act does not terminate, or in any way modify, any liability, civil or criminal, which exists on January 1, 1986. A notarial act performed before January 1, 1986, is not affected by this act.

§ 42.44.901. Construction.

RCW 42.44.010, 42.44.080, 42.44.090, 42.44.100, 42.44.130, 42.44.140, and 42.44.150 shall be applied and construed to effectuate their general purpose to make the law uniform with respect to the subject of this chapter among states enacting such sections of this chapter.

§ 42.44.902. Severability—1985 c 156.

If any provision of this act or its application to any person or circumstance is held invalid, the remainder of the act or the application of the provision to other persons or circumstances is not affected.

§ 42.44.903. Effective date—1985 c 156.

Sections 1 through 19, 21, and 23 through 26 shall take effect on January 1, 1986.

OFFENSES

§ 9A.20.021. Maximum sentences for crimes committed July 1, 1984, and after.

* * *

(2) Gross Misdemeanor. Every person convicted of a gross misdemeanor defined in Title 9A RCW shall be punished by imprisonment in the county jail for a maximum term fixed by the court of not more than one year, or by a fine in an amount fixed by the court of not more than five thousand dollars, or by both such imprisonment and fine.

* * *

§ 9A.60.040. Criminal impersonation.

(1) A person is guilty of a criminal impersonation if he:

(a) Assumes a false identity and does an act in his assumed character with intent to defraud another or for any other unlawful purpose; or

(b) Pretends to be a representative of some person or organization or a public servant and does an act in his pretended capacity with intent to defraud another or for any other unlawful purpose.

(2) Criminal impersonation is a gross misdemeanor.

§ 9A.60.050. False certification.

(1) A person is guilty of false certification, if, being an officer authorized to take a proof or acknowledgment of an instrument which by law may be

recorded, he knowingly certifies falsely that the execution of such instrument was acknowledged by any party thereto or that the execution thereof was proved.

(2) False certification is a gross misdemeanor.

ACKNOWLEDGMENTS

§ 64.08.010. Who may take acknowledgments.

Acknowledgments of deeds, mortgages and other instruments in writing, required to be acknowledged may be taken in this state before a justice of the supreme court, or the clerk thereof, or the deputy of such clerk, before a judge of the court of appeals, or the clerk thereof, before a judge of the superior court, or qualified court commissioner thereof, or the clerk thereof, or the deputy of such clerk, or a county auditor, or the deputy of such auditor, or a qualified notary public, or a qualified United States commissioner appointed by any district court of the United States for this state, and all said instruments heretofore executed and acknowledged according to the provisions of this section are hereby declared legal and valid.

§ 64.08.020. Acknowledgments out of state—certificate.

Acknowledgments of deeds conveying or encumbering real estate situated in this state, or any interest therein, and other instruments in writing, required to be acknowledged, may be taken in any other state or territory of the United States, the District of Columbia, or in any possession of the United States, before any person authorized to take the acknowledgments of deeds by the laws of the state, territory, district or possession wherein the acknowledgment is taken, or before any commissioner appointed by the governor of this state, for the purpose, but unless such acknowlegment is taken before a commissioner so appointed by the governor, or before the clerk of a court of record of such state, territory, district or possession, or before a notary public or other officer having a seal of office, the instrument shall have attached thereto a certificate of the clerk of a court of record of the county, parish, or other political subdivision of such state, territory, district or possession wherein the acknowledgment was taken, under the seal of said court, certifying that the person who took the acknowledgment, and whose name is subscribed to the certificate thereof, was at the date thereof such officer as he represented to himself to be, authorized by law to take acknowledgments of deeds,

and that the clerk verily believes the signature of the person subscribed to the certificate of acknowledgment to be genuine.

§ 64.08.040. Foreign acknowledgments, who may take.

Acknowledgments of deeds conveying or encumbering real estate situated in this state, or any interest therein and other instruments in writing, required to be acknowledged, may be taken in any foreign country before any minister, plenipotentiary, secretary of legation, charge d'affaires, consul general, consul, vice consul, consular agent, or commercial agent appointed by the United States government, or before any notary public, or before the judge, clerk, or other proper officer of any court of said country, or before the mayor or other chief magistrate of any city, town or other municipal corporation therein.

§ 64.08.050. Certificate of acknowledgment—evidence.

The officer, or person, taking an acknowledgment as in this chapter provided, shall certify the same by a certificate written upon or annexed to the instrument acknowledged and signed by him or her and sealed with his or her official seal, if any, and reciting in substance that the person, or persons, known to him or her as, or determined by satisfactory evidence to be, the person, or persons, whose name, or names, are signed to the instrument as executing the same, acknowledged before him or her on the date stated in the certificate that he, she, or they, executed the same freely and voluntarily. Such certificate shall be prima facie evidence of the facts therein recited. The officer or person taking the acknowledgment has satisfactory evidence that a person is the person whose name is signed on the instrument if that person: (1) Is personally known to the officer or person taking the acknowledgment; (2) is identified upon the oath or affirmation of a credible witness personally known to the officer or person taking the acknowledgment; or (3) is identified on the basis of identification documents.

§ 64.08.060. Form of certificate for individual.

A certificate of acknowledgment for an individual, substantially in the following form or, after December 31, 1985, substantially in the form set forth in RCW 42.44.100(1), shall be sufficient for the purposes of this chapter and for any acknowledgment required to be taken in accordance with this chapter:

State of . . . .]
                 ]   ss.
County of . . . . . .]

On this day personally appeared before me (here insert the name of grantor or grantors) to me known to be the individual, or individuals described in and who executed the within and foregoing instrument, and acknowledged that he (she or they) signed the same as his (her or their) free and voluntary act and deed, for the uses and purposes therein mentioned. Given under my hand and official seal this . . . . . day of . . . ., 19. . . (Signature of officer and official seal)

If acknowledgment is taken before a notary public of this state the signature shall be followed by substantially the following: Notary Public in and for the state of Washington, residing at . . . ., (giving place of residence).

§ 64.08.070. Form of certificate for corporation.

A certificate of acknowledgment for a corporation, substantially in the following form or, after December 31, 1985, substantially in the form set forth in RCW 42.44.100(2), shall be sufficient for the purposes of this chapter and for any acknowledgment required to be taken in accordance with this chapter:

State of . . . .]
                  ]   ss.
County of . . . . . .]

On this . . . . . day of . . . ., 19. . ., before me personally appeared . . . ., to me known to be the (president, vice president, secretary, treasurer, or other authorized officer or agent, as the case may be) of the corporation that executed the within and foregoing instrument, and acknowledged said instrument to be the free and voluntary act and deed of said corporation, for the uses and purposes therein mentioned, and on oath stated that he was authorized to execute said instrument and that the seal affixed is the corporate seal of said corporation.

In Witness Whereof I have hereunto set my hand and affixed my official seal the day and year first above written. (Signature and title of officer with place of residence of notary public.)

§ 64.08.090. Authority of superintendents, business managers and officers of correctional institutions to take acknowledgments and administer oaths—procedure.

The superintendents, associate and assistant superintendents, business managers, records officers and camp superintendents of any correctional institution or facility operated by the state of Washington are hereby authorized and empowered to take acknowledgments on any instruments of writing, and certify the same in the manner required by law, and to administer all oaths required by law to be administered, all of the foregoing acts to have the same effect as if performed by a notary public: *Provided*, That such authority shall only extend to taking acknowledgments for and administering oaths to officers, employees and residents of such institutions and facilities. None of the individuals herein empowered to take acknowledgments and administer oaths shall demand or accept any fee or compensation whatsoever for administering or taking any oath, affirmation, or acknowledgment under the authority conferred by this section.

In certifying any oath or in signing any instrument officially, an individual empowered to do so under this section shall, in addition to his name, state in writing his place of residence, the date of his action and affix the seal of the institution where he is employed: *Provided*, That in certifying any oath to be used in any of the courts of this state, it shall not be necessary to append an impression of the official seal of the institution.

§ 73.20.010. Acknowledgments.

In addition to the acknowledgment of instruments and the performance of other notarial acts in the manner and form and as otherwise authorized by law, instruments may be acknowledged, documents attested, oaths and affirmations administered, depositions and affidavits executed, and other notarial acts performed, before or by any commissioned officer in active service of the armed forces of the United States with the rank of second lieutenant or higher in the army or marine corps, or with the rank of ensign or higher in the navy or coast guard, or with equivalent rank in any other component part of the armed forces of the United States, by any person who either

(1) is a member of the armed forces of the United States; or

(2) is serving as a merchant seaman outside the limits of the United States included within the fifty states and the District of Columbia; or

(3) is outside said limits by permission, assignment or direction of any department or official of the United States government, in connection with any activity pertaining to the prosecution of any war in which the United States is then engaged.

Such acknowledgment of instruments, attestation of documents, administration of oaths and affirmations, execution of depositions and affidavits, and performance of other notarial acts, heretofore or hereafter made or taken, are hereby declared legal, valid and binding, and instruments and documents so acknowledged, authenticated, or sworn to shall be admissible in evidence and eligible to record in this state under the same circumstances, and with the same force and effect as if such acknowledgment, attestation, oath, affirmation, deposition, affidavit, or other notarial act, had been made or taken within this state before or by a duly qualified officer or official as otherwise provided by law.

In the taking of acknowledgments and the performing of other notarial acts requiring certification, a certificate endorsed upon or attached to the instrument or documents, which shows the date of the notarial act and which states, in substance, that the person appearing before the officer acknowledged the instrument as his act or made or signed the instrument or document under oath, shall be sufficient for all intents and purposes. The instrument or document shall not be rendered invalid by the failure to state the place of execution or acknowledgment.

If the signature, rank, and branch of service or subdivision thereof, of any such commissioned officer appear upon such instrument or document or certificate, no further proof of the authority of such officer so to act shall be required and such action by such commissioned officer shall be prima facie evidence that the person making such oath or acknowledgment is within the purview of this section.

DEPOSITIONS

§ 2.24.010. Appointment of court commissioners—qualifications—term of office.

There may be appointed in each county or judicial district, by the judges of the superior court having jurisdiction therein, one or more court commissioners for said county or judicial district. Each such commissioner shall be a citizen of the United States and shall hold the office during the pleasure of the judges making the appointment.

§ 2.24.020. Oath.

Court commissioners appointed hereunder shall, before entering upon the duties of such office, take and subscribe an oath to support the Constitution of the United States, the Constitution of the state of Washington, and to perform the duties of such office fairly and impartially and to the best of his ability.

§ 2.24.040. Powers of commissioners—fees.

Such court commissioner shall have power, authority, and jurisdiction, concurrent with the superior court and the judge thereof, in the following particulars:

* * *

(10) To grant adjournments, administer oaths, preserve order, compel attendance of witnesses, and to punish for contempts in the refusal to obey or the neglect of his lawful orders made in any matter before him as fully as the judge of the superior court.

(11) To take acknowledgments and proofs of deeds, mortgages and all other instruments requiring acknowledgment under the laws of this state, and to take affidavits and depositions in all cases.

(12) To provide an official seal, upon which shall be engraved the words "Court Commissioner," and the name of the county for which he may be appointed, and to authenticate his official acts therewith in all cases where same is necessary.

(13) To charge and collect, for his own use, the same fees for the official performance of official acts mentioned in subsections (4) and (11) of this section as are provided by law for referees and notaries public.

§ 5.28.010. Who may administer.

That every court, judge, clerk of a court, or notary public, is authorized to take testimony in any action, suit or proceeding, and such other persons in particular cases as authorized by law. Every such court or officer is authorized to administer oaths and affirmations generally, and every such other person in such particular case as authorized.

§ 11.20.030. Commission to take testimony of witness.

If any witness be prevented by sickness from attending at the time any will is produced for probate, or reside out of the sate or more than thirty miles from the place where the will is to be proven, such court may issue a commission annexed to such will, and directed to any judge, notary public, or other person authorized to administer an oath, empowering him or her to take and certify the attestation of such witness.

[Wash. Super. Ct. Civ. R.]

RULE 28. Persons before whom depositions may be taken.

Within the state. Depositions within the state may be taken before the following officers:

(1) Court Commissioners.
(2) Superior Courts.
(3) Judicial Officers.
(4) Judges of Supreme and Superior Courts.
(5) Inferior Judicial Officers.
(6) Notaries Public.
(7) Special Commissions.
(a) **Within the United States.** Within the United

States or within a territory or insular possession subject to the dominion of the United States, depositions shall be taken before an officer authorized to administer oaths by the laws of the United States or of the place where the examination is held, or before a person appointed by the court in which the action is pending. A person so appointed has power to administer oaths and take testimony.

(b) In foreign countries. In a foreign country, depositions may be taken (1) on notice before a person authorized to administer oaths in the place in which the examination is held, either by the law thereof or by the law of the United States, or (2) before a person commissioned by the court, and a person so commissioned shall have the power by virtue of his commission to administer any necessary oath and take testimony, or (3) pursuant to a letter rogatory. A commission or a letter rogatory shall be issued on application and notice, and on terms that are just and appropriate. It is not requisite to the issuance of a commission or a letter rogatory that the taking of the deposition in any other manner is impracticable or inconvenient; and both a commission and a letter rogatory may be issued in proper cases. A notice or commission may designate the person before whom the deposition is to be taken either by name or descriptive title. A letter rogatory may be addressed "To the Appropriate Authority in [here name the country]." Evidence obtained in response to a letter rogatory need not be excluded merely for the reason that it is not a verbatim transcript or that the testimony was not taken under oath or for any similar departure from the requirements for depositions taken within the United States under these rules.

(c) Disqualification for interest. No deposition shall be taken before a person who is a relative or employee or attorney or counsel of any of the parties, or is a relative or employee of such attorney or counsel, or is financially interested in the action.

LEGAL HOLIDAYS
[WASH. REV. CODE ANN.]

§ 1.16.050. "Legal holidays".

The following are legal holidays: Sunday; the first day of January, commonly called New Year's Day; the third Monday of January, being celebrated as the anniversary of the birth of Martin Luther King, Jr.; the third Monday of February to be known as Presidents' Day and to be celebrated as the anniversary of the births of Abraham Lincoln and George Washington; the last Monday of May, commonly known as Memorial Day; the fourth day of July, being the anniversary of the Declaration of Independence; the first Monday in September, to be known as Labor Day; the eleventh day of November, to be known as Veterans' Day; the fourth Thursday in November, to be known as Thanksgiving Day; the day immediately following Thanksgiving Day; and the twenty-fifth day of December, commonly called Christmas Day.

Employees of the state and its political subdivisions, except employees of school districts and except those nonclassified employees of institutions of higher education who hold appointments or are employed under contracts to perform services for periods of less than twelve consecutive months, shall be entitled to one paid holiday per calendar year in addition to those specified in this section. Each employee of the state or its political subdivisions may select the day on which the employee desires to take the additional holiday provided for herein after consultation with the employer pursuant to guidelines to be promulgated by rule of the appropriate personnel authority, or in the case of local government by ordinance or resolution of the legislative authority.

If any of the above specified state legal holidays are also federal legal holidays but observed on different dates, only the state legal holidays shall be recognized as a paid legal holiday for employees of the state and its political subdivisions except that for port districts and the law enforcement and public transit employees of municipal corporations, either the federal or the state legal holiday, but in no case both, may be recognized as a paid legal holiday for employees.

Whenever any legal holiday, other than Sunday, falls upon a Sunday, the following Monday shall be the legal holiday.

Whenever any legal holiday falls upon a Saturday, the preceding Friday shall be the legal holiday.

Nothing in this section shall be construed to have the effect of adding or deleting the number of paid holidays provided for in an agreement between employees and employers of political subdivisions of the state or as established by ordinance or resolution of the local government legislative authority.

The legislature declares that the twelfth day of October shall be recognized as Columbus Day but shall not be considered a legal holiday for any purposes.

The legislature declares that the ninth day of April shall be recognized as former prisoner of war recognition day but shall not be considered a legal holiday for any purposes.

WEST VIRGINIA

NOTARIES PUBLIC

[W. Va. Code Ann.]

Article 1.
General Provisions.

§ 29C-1-101. Short title.

This chapter shall be known and may be cited as the "uniform notary act."

§ 29C-1-102. Purposes and rules of construction.

(a) This chapter shall be construed and applied to promote its underlying purposes and policies.

(b) The underlying purposes and policies of this chapter are:

(1) To simplify, clarify and modernize the law governing notaries public;

(2) To make uniform notary laws among the states enacting it; and

(3) To promote, serve and protect the public interest.

(c) In this chapter, unless the context otherwise requires:

(1) Words in the singular number include the plural, and words in the plural number include the singular;

(2) Words of the masculine gender include the feminine and the neuter; and

(3) Words of the neuter gender may refer to any gender when the sense so indicates.

§ 29C-1-103. Prospective effect of chapter; exceptions.

Except as otherwise provided herein, this chapter applies prospectively and shall be applicable to all notaries public whether commissioned before, on or after the effective date of this chapter [July 1, 1984]: Provided, That the following sections in article two of this chapter shall apply only to those notaries public commissioned on or after the effective date of this chapter: Subsections (a) and (b) of section one hundred one, sections two hundred one, two hundred two, two hundred three, two hundred four, two hundred six, two hundred seven and three hundred one, relating to the appointment and qualifications of notaries, and section one hundred two, relating to jurisdiction and terms of notaries public.

§ 29C-1-104. Construction against implicit repeal.

This chapter is intended to provide comprehensive and unified coverage of the subject matter. Therefore, no part of it shall be construed to be impliedly repealed or amended by subsequent legislation if that construction can be avoided.

§ 29C-1-105. Notary public and notarization defined.

(a) The terms "notary public" or "notary" are used interchangeably to mean any individual appointed and commissioned to perform notarial acts.

(b) "Notarization" means the performance of a notarial act.

§ 29C-1-106. Effective date.

This chapter shall take effect the first day of July, one thousand nine hundred eighty-four.

Article 2.
Appointment Provisions.

Part I. Office Provisions.

§ 29C-2-101. Appointment.

(a) Upon application under this chapter, the governor may appoint and commission persons as a notary public in this state.

(b) The governor may not appoint and commission as a notary public any person who submits an application containing substantial and material misstatement or omission of fact.

(c) The secretary of state shall administer the chapter and may issue rules and regulations, in accordance with the provisions of chapter twenty-nine-a, to make the chapter effective.

§ 29C-2-102. Jurisdiction and term.

Notaries may perform notarial acts in any part of this state for a term of ten years, unless sooner removed.

Part II. Qualifying.

§ 29C-2-201. Application.

Every applicant for appointment and commission as a notary public shall complete an application to be filed with the secretary of state stating:

(a) That he is a citizen of the United States, or if he is not a citizen of the United States, that he is a citizen or national of a country that permits American citizens to become notaries public therein;

(b) If he is a citizen of the United States, that he is a qualified elector of a state at the time of his application;

(c) That he is able to read and write English;

(d) The address of his business or residence in this state;

(e) His social security number, if he has one; and

(f) That during the past ten years his commission as a notary public has not been revoked.

§ 29C-2-202. Qualifying fee.

Every applicant for appointment and commission as a notary public shall pay to the secretary of state a fee of fifty dollars.

§ 29C-2-203. Applicant's endorsers.

Every applicant for appointment and commission as a notary public shall submit to the secretary of state endorsements from three qualified electors of this state, in the following form:

I, ... (name of endorser), a qualified elector of this state, believe to the best of my knowledge, the applicant is a person of good moral character and integrity and capable of performing notarial acts.

. . . .
(Endorser's signature and address)

§ 29C-2-204. Applicant's oath.

Every applicant for appointment and commission as a notary public shall take the following oath in the presence of a person qualified to administer an oath in this state:

I, ... (name of applicant), solemnly swear or affirm, under the penalty of perjury, that the answers to all questions in this application are true, complete and correct; that I have carefully read the notaries public law of this state; and, if appointed and commissioned as a notary public, I will perform faithfully, to the best of my ability, all notarial acts in accordance with the law.

. . . .
(Signature of applicant)

Subscribed and sworn or affirmed before me this . . . . day of . . . . . ., 19. . . . The undersigned notary public further certifies that . . . . (name of applicant), is known to me to be the applicant and elector who executed the within application for appointment and commission as a notary public and acknowledged to me that he or she executed the same for the purposes therein stated.

. . . .

(Official signature and official seal of notary)

§ 29C-2-205. Repealed.

§ 29C-2-206. Confidential application.

Information in the application for appointment, except for the applicant's name and address, is confidential and may not be disclosed by an official or employee having access to it to any person other than the applicant, his authorized representative, or an employee or officer of the federal government, the state government or a local agency, acting in his official capacity. Such information shall be used by the governor and secretary of state for the sole purpose of performing his duties under this article.

§ 29C-2-207. Specimen official signature.

Every applicant for appointment and commission as a notary public shall mail or deliver to the secretary of state a handwritten specimen of his official signature which contains his surname and at least the initial of his first name. The fee payable to the secretary of state for recording a specimen of the official signature is two dollars.

§ 29C-2-208. Application by persons holding existing commissions.

Persons holding notary commissions on the effective date of this chapter and having been appointed pursuant to former section two, article four, chapter twenty-nine of this code, shall continue upon their bonds as previously posted until the expiration of their respective notarial commissions.

Part III. Government Notaries.

§ 29C-2-301. State and local government employees.

(a) The governor may appoint and commission such number of state and local government employees as notaries public, to act for and in behalf of their respective state and local government offices, as he deems proper. An appointee commissioned as a notary public under this section may act only for and in behalf of the government office or offices in which he is employed.

(b) An appointee under this section shall meet the requirements for qualification and appointment prescribed in article two of this chapter ex-

cept that the head of the state or local government office where the applicant is employed may execute a certificate that the application is made for the purposes of the office and in the public interest and submit it to the governor together with the application for appointment as a notary public, in which case the fee for appointment specified in article two, section two hundred two, is waived.

(c) The costs of all notary supplies for a commissioned state or local government employee shall be paid from funds available to the office in which he is employed.

(d) All fees received for notarial services by a notary public appointed for and in behalf of a state or local government office shall be remitted by him to the state or local government office in which he is employed.

(e) A notary public who is an employee of a state or local government office in this state must comply with all provisions of this chapter.

Article 3.
Powers.

§ 29C-3-101. Powers.

Every notary public is empowered to:
(1) Take acknowledgments;
(2) Administer oaths and affirmations;
(3) Certify that a copy of a document is a true copy of another document; and
(4) Perform any other act permitted by law.

§ 29C-3-102. Limitations of powers.

(a) A notary public who has a disqualifying interest, as hereinafter defined, in a transaction may not legally perform any notarial act in connection with the transaction.

(b) For the purposes of this chapter, a notary public has a disqualifying interest in a transaction in connection with which notarial services are requested if he:

(1) May receive directly, and as a proximate result of the notarization, any advantage, right, title, interest, cash or property, exceeding in value the sum of any fee properly received in accordance with section three hundred one, article four of this chapter, or exceeding his regular compensation and benefits as an employee whose duties include performing notarial acts for and in behalf of his employer; or

(2) Is named, individually, as a party to the transaction.

Article 4.
Duties.

Part I. Seek and Signature.

§ 29C-4-101. Official signature.

At the time of notarization a notary public shall sign his official signature on every notarial certificate.

§ 29C-4-102. Rubber stamp seal.

Under or near his official signature on every notarial certificate, a notary public shall rubber stamp clearly and legibly, so that it is capable of photographic reproduction:

(a) The words "Official Seal";

(b) His name exactly as he writes his official signature;

(c) The words "Notary Public," "State of West Virginia" and "My Commission expires (commission expiration date)";

(d) The address of his business or residence in this state; and

(e) A serrated or milled edge border in a rectangular form not more than one inch in width by two and one-half inches in length surrounding the information.

No person holding a notary commission pursuant to former section two [§ 29-4-2; repealed], article four, chapter twenty-nine of the effective date on this chapter [July 1, 1984] may be required to obtain or use a rubber stamp seal prior to the expiration of that commission. However, such a notary who was appointed for one or more counties of the state may obtain and use the rubber stamp seal prior to the expiration of that commission if the name of the county in which the notarial act is performed is on the seal used for that act.

§ 29C-4-103. Seal embosser.

(a) Every notary public may provide, keep and use a seal embosser engraved to show the words "Notary Seal," his name, "Notary Public," and "State of West Virginia."

(b) The indentations made by the seal embosser shall not be applied on the notarial certificate or document to be notarized in a manner that will render illegible or incapable of photographic reproduction any of the printed marks or writing.

§ 29C-4-104. Illegibility.

The illegibility of any of the information required by sections one hundred one through one hundred three, article four, does not affect the validity of a transaction.

Part II. Record Changes.

§ 29C-4-201. Change of address.

Every notary public shall mail or deliver notice to the secretary of state within thirty days after he changes the address of his business or residence in this state. The fee payable to the secretary of state for recording notice of change of address is two dollars.

§ 29C-4-202. Change of notary's name.

Every notary public shall mail or deliver notice to the secretary of state within thirty days after he changes his name, including with the notification a specimen of his handwritten official signature which contains his surname and at least the initial of his first name. The fee payable to the secretary of state for recording notice of change of notary's name is two dollars.

§ 29C-4-203. Lost official seal.

Every notary public shall mail or deliver notice to the secretary of state within thirty days after he loses or misplaces his official seal. The fee payable to the secretary of state for recording notice of a lost seal is two dollars.

Part III. Fees.

§ 29C-4-301. Maximum fees.

The maximum fee in this state for notarization of each signature and the proper recordation thereof in the journal of notarial acts is two dollars for each signature notarized.

(a) The maximum fee in this state for certification of a facsimile of a document, retaining a facsimile in the notary's file, and the proper recordation thereof in the journal of notarial acts is two dollars for each eight and one-half by eleven inch page retained in the notary's file.

(b) The maximum fee in this state is two dollars for any other notarial act performed.

(c) A notary public who charges more than the maximum fees specified is guilty of official misconduct.

Part IV. Termination of Commission.

§ 29C-4-401. Death.

If a notary public dies during the term of his appointment, his heirs or personal representative, as soon as reasonably possible after the notary's death, shall send by certified mail or deliver to the secretary of state the deceased notary's papers and copies relating to his notarial acts. His heirs or personal representative shall destroy forthwith his official seal.

§ 29C-4-402. Resignation or removal.

If a notary public no longer desires to be a notary public or has ceased to have a business or residence address in this state, he shall send forthwith by certified mail or deliver to the secretary of state a letter of resignation and all papers and copies relating to his notarial acts. He shall destroy forthwith his official seal. His commission shall thereupon cease to be in effect.

§ 29C-4-403. Revocation of commission.

Immediately after receiving notice from the secretary of state that his commission has been revoked, the person whose commission is revoked shall forthwith send by certified mail or deliver to the secretary of state all papers and copies relating to his notarial acts. He shall destroy forthwith his official seal.

§ 29C-4-404. Failure to be reappointed.

A notary public who is not reappointed to act as a notary public within thirty days after the expiration of his commission shall send forthwith by certified mail or deliver to the secretary of state all papers and copies relating to his notarial acts. He shall destroy forthwith his official seal.

§ 29C-4-405. Reappointment.

(a) No person may be automatically reappointed as a notary public.

(b) Every notary public who is an applicant for reappointment as a notary public shall recomply with the provisions of article two of this chapter.

Article 5.
Forms and Procedures.

§ 29C-5-101. Acknowledgment forms.

(a) The forms of acknowledgment set forth in section six [§ 39-1A-6], article one-a, chapter thirty-nine of this code, and known as "statutory short forms of acknowledgment" may be used and are sufficient for their respective purposes under any law of this state, whether the acknowledgment was taken within or without this state.

(b) Certificates of acknowledgment for the following purposes may be substantially in the following respective form:

(1) By a United States citizen who is outside of the United States . . . . . (description or location of place where acknowledgment is taken).

On this . . . . day of . . . . ., in the year . . . . ., before me . . . . . (name and title of person acting as a notary and refer to law or authority granting power to act as a notary), personally appear . . . . . (name of citizen) known to me to be the person who executed the within . . . . . (type of document)

and acknowledged to me that . . . . . (he) executed the same for the purposes therein stated.

. . . .
(Official signature and official seal of person acting as a notary and refer to law or authority granting power to act as a notary)

(2) By an individual who cannot write his name, State of . . . . ., County of . . . .
On this . . . . . day of . . . . ., in the year . . . . ., before me . . . . . (name of notary), a notary public in and for said state, personally appeared . . . . (name of individual), known to me to be the person who, being unable to write his name, made his mark in my presence. I signed his name at his request and in his presence on the within . . . . . (type of document) and he acknowledged to me and the two witnesses who have signed and printed their names and addresses hereto, that he made his mark on the same for the purposes therein stated.

. . . .
(Official signature and official seal of notary)
. . . .
. . . .
(Signatures of two witnesses and their addresses)

§ 29C-5-102. Oath; procedure; form.

(a) If the oath to be administered by the notary public is in writing and the person who took the oath has signed his name thereto, the notary public shall write or print under the text of the oath the following:

"Subscribed and sworn before me this . . . . . day of . . . . . ., 19. . . ."

. . . .
(Official signature and official seal of notary)

(b) If the oath to be administered by the notary public is not in writing, the notary public shall address the affirmant substantially as follows:

"You do solemnly swear, under the penalty of perjury, that the testimony you shall give in the matter in issue, pending between . . . . and . . . ., shall be the truth, the whole truth, and nothing but the truth, so help you God?"

§ 29C-5-103. Executing witness form.

(a) "Executing witness" as used in this section means an individual who acts in the place of a notary.

(b) An executing witness may not be related by blood or marriage or have a disqualifying interest as defined in subsection (b), section one hundred two, article three of this chapter.

(c) The affidavit of executing witness for acknowledgment by an individual who does not appear before a notary shall be substantially in the following form:

I, ... (name of executing witness), do solemnly swear under the penalty of perjury, that . . . . . . (name of person who does not appear before a notary), personally known to me, has executed the within . . . . . (type of document) in my presence, and has acknowledged to me that . . . . . (he) executed the same for the purposes therein stated and requested that I sign my name on the within document as an executing witness.

. . . .
(Signature of executing witness)
Subscribed and sworn before me this . . . . . day
of . . . ., 19. . . .

. . . .
(Official signature and official seal of
notary)

§ 29C-5-104. Certified facsimiles of documents; procedure; form.

(a) A notary public may certify a facsimile of a document if he receives a signed written request stating that:

(1) A certified copy or facsimile of the document cannot be obtained from the office of any recorder of public documents or custodian of documents in this state; and

(2) The production of a facsimile, preparation of a copy or certification of a copy of the document does not violate any state or federal law.

(b) Every notary public shall retain a facsimile of each document he has certified as a facsimile of another document, together with other papers or copies relating to his notarial acts.

(c) The certification of a facsimile shall be substantially in the following form:

State of . . . ., County of . . . .
I, ... (name of notary), a notary public in and for said state, do certify that on . . . . . (date) I carefully compared the attached facsimile of . . . . . (type of document) and the facsimile I now hold in my possession. They are complete, full, true and exact facsimiles of the document they support [purport] to reproduce.

. . . .
(Official signature and official seal of
notary)

Article 6.
Liability, Fines and Imprisonment.

Part I. Liability

§ 29C-6-101. Liability of notary.

A notary public is liable to the persons involved for all damages proximately caused by the notary's official misconduct.

§ 29C-6-102. Liability of employer of notary.

The employer of a notary public is also liable to the persons involved for all damages proximately caused by the notary's official misconduct, if:

(a) The notary public was acting within the scope of his employment at the time he engaged in the official misconduct; and

(b) The employer consented to the notary public's official misconduct.

§ 29C-6-103. Proximate cause.

It is not essential to a recovery of damages that a notary's official misconduct be the only proximate cause of the damages.

Part II. Misconduct.

§ 29C-6-201. Official misconduct defined.

The term "official misconduct" means the wrongful exercise of a power or the wrongful performance of a duty. The term "wrongful" as used in the definition of official misconduct means unauthorized, unlawful, abusive, negligent, reckless or injurious.

§ 29C-6-202. Official misconduct.

(a) A notary public who knowingly and willfully commits any official misconduct is guilty of a misdemeanor, and, upon conviction, shall be fined not more than five thousand dollars or imprisoned in the county jail not more than one year or both fined and imprisoned.

(b) A notary public who recklessly or negligently commits any official misconduct is guilty of a misdemeanor, and, upon conviction, shall be fined not more than one thousand dollars.

§ 29C-6-203. Willful impersonation.

Any person who acts as, or otherwise willfully impersonates, a notary public while not lawfully appointed and commissioned to perform notarial acts is guilty of a misdemeanor, and, upon conviction, shall be fined not more than five thousand dollars or imprisoned in the county jail not more than one year, or both fined and imprisoned.

§ 29C-6-204. Wrongful possession.

Any person who unlawfully possesses a notary's

official seal or any papers or copies relating to notarial acts, is guilty of a misdemeanor, and, upon conviction, shall be fined not more than one thousand dollars.

Article 7.
Revocation of commission; action for Injunction; Unauthorized Practice of Law.

Part I. Revocation.

§ 29C-7-101. Revocation of commission.

The governor or secretary of state may revoke the commission of any notary public who during the current term of appointment:

(a) Submits an application for commission and appointment as a notary public which contains substantial and material misstatement or omission of fact;

(b) Is convicted of any felony or official misconduct under this chapter;

(c) Fails to exercise the powers or perform the duties of a notary public in accordance with this chapter;

(d) Is adjudged liable in any suit grounded in fraud, misrepresentation, impersonation or violation of the state regulatory laws of this state, if his liability is not solely by virtue of his agency or employment relationship with another who engaged in the act for which the suit was brought;

(e) Represents or implies from unauthorized use of his title of notary public that he has qualifications, powers, duties, rights or privileges that by law he does not possess;

(f) Allows or permits his name or his title of notary public to be used deceptively, fraudulently or in false or misleading advertising;

(g) Engages in the unauthorized practice of law;

(h) Ceases to be a citizen of the United States or a national of a country which permits American citizens to become notaries public therein;

(i) Ceases to be a qualified elector of a state;

(j) Ceases to have a business or residence address in this state; or

(k) Becomes incapable of reading and writing the English language.

A notary's commission may be revoked under the provisions of this chapter only if action is taken subject to the rights of a notary public to notice, hearing, adjudication and appeal.

Part II. Injunctions.

§ 29C-7-201. Action for injunction; unauthorized practice of law.

Upon his own information or upon complaint of any person, the attorney general, or his designee, may maintain an action for injunctive relief in circuit court against any notary public who renders, offers to render or holds himself out as rendering any service constituting the unauthorized practice of the law. Any organized bar association in this state may intervene in the action, at any stage of the proceeding, for good cause shown. The action may also be maintained by an organized bar association in this state or by the secretary of state.

§ 29C-7-202. Remedies additional to those now existing.

The remedies provided in article seven are in addition to, and not in substitution for, other available remedies.

Article 8.
Certificate of Authority.

§ 29C-8-101. Certificate of authority.

Upon the receipt of a written request, the notarized document and a fee of two dollars payable to the secretary of state, the office of the secretary of state shall provide a certificate of authority in substantially the following form:

I, ... (secretary of state of the state of West Virginia, which office is an office of record having a seal) certify that . . . . . . (notary's name), by whom the foregoing or annexed document was notarized, was, at the time of the notarization of the same, a notary public authorized by the laws of this state to act in this state and to notarize the within . . . . . . (type of document), and I further certify that the notary's signature on the document is genuine to the best of my knowledge, information and belief and that such notarization was executed in accordance with the laws of this state.

In testimony whereof, I have affixed my signature and the seal of the state of West Virginia, this . . . . . day of . . . . . . , 19. . . .

. . . .
(Certifying officer's signature, title, jurisdiction, address and the seal affixed near the signature)

Article 9.
Curative Provisions.

§ 29C-9-101. Uniform application of chapter; validation of good faith notarial acts; nonliability for good faith notarial acts.

This article is to prevent or redress problems which might be caused by notaries public who in good faith performed notarial acts in substantial compliance with the laws which were replaced by the uniform notary act, chapter twenty-nine-c of this code, during a forgiveness period which begins with the effective date of that act [July 1, 1984] and ends with the effective date of this section [April 10, 1985].

With respect to notarial acts performed in good faith and in substantial compliance with prior law during the forgiveness period:

(a) Instruments so notarized shall be conclusively presumed to have been validly notarized;

(b) Notaries public and all parties to such notarial acts shall be immune from civil and criminal liability for such acts or the consequences of such acts. The rebuttable presumption created by section nine, article seven, chapter fifty-five of this code, that any violation of a statute which proximately causes injury constitutes negligence, does not apply; and

(c) The retrospective application of this section applies to all litigation which has not been fully adjudicated, including cases pending on appeal. This section does not apply to notarial acts performed prior to or subsequent to the forgiveness period.

The purposes of this article are remedial and shall be construed liberally to accomplish the purposes set forth herein.

ADDITIONAL AUTHORITY

§ 6-2-10. Bonds of county officers.

Every commissioner of a county commission and every clerk of a circuit court shall give bond with good security, to be approved by the circuit court, or the judge thereof in vacation; and every sheriff, deputy sheriff, surveyor of lands, clerk of a county commission, assessor, county superintendent of schools, notary public and magistrate shall give bond with good security, to be approved, unless otherwise provided by law, by the county commission of the county in which such officer is to act. The penalty of the bond of each commissioner of a county commission shall be not less than twenty thousand dollars and not more than two hundred thousand dollars, the amount to be fixed by the circuit court of the county, or the judge thereof in vacation, by order entered of record on the proper order books of both the county and circuit courts; of the clerk of the circuit court, not less than ten thousand nor more than fifty thousand dollars; of the sheriff, not less than one hundred thousand dollars nor more than the aggregate amount of all state, county, district, school, municipal and other moneys which will probably come into his hands during any one year of his term of office; of the deputy sheriff, not less than thirty-five thousand nor more than one hundred thousand dollars; of the surveyor of lands, not less than one thousand nor more than three thousand dollars; of the clerk of the county commission, not less than ten thousand nor more than fifty thousand dollars; of the assessor, not less than two thousand nor more than

five thousand dollars; of the county superintendent of schools, not less than ten thousand nor more than fifty thousand dollars; of a notary public, not less than two hundred fifty nor more than one thousand dollars. Any public body required to pay the premiums on official bonds may provide a blanket bond policy for two or more such official bonds: Provided, That the bond herein required to be given by a notary public may be given before the clerk of the county commission, in the vacation of said commission, and approved by it at its next regular session.

* * *

§ 6-2-13. Copies to be sent to the state tax commissioner; penalty for failure to send.

A copy of the official bond of every *** notary public, shall be sent to the state tax commissioner by the officer in whose office the original is filed, within two months after the same is filed in his office. If the officer whose duty it is to send any such copy fails to do so within the time specified, he shall forfeit fifty dollars.

§ 29-4-1. Notaries in office on January 1, 1931.

The notaries in office on the date this code takes effect [January 1, 1931] shall continue therein until their respective terms of office shall expire, unless otherwise sooner removed in the manner prescribed by law.

§ 29-4-3. Power as to oaths, affidavits and depositions.

When any oath may lawfully be administered, or affidavit or deposition taken, within any county, it may be done by a notary thereof, unless otherwise expressly provided by law.

§ 29-4-4. Power to take acknowledgments and as conservator of peace.

A notary, under the regulations prescribed by law, may take, within his county, and the county or counties to which his commission has been extended, acknowledgments of deeds and other writings. He shall be a conservator of the peace within the county of his residence, and as such conservator shall exercise all the powers conferred by law upon justices of the peace [now magistrate].

§ 29-4-5. Necessity for seal.

The certificate of a notary of this state, in cases specified in the two preceding sections, may be under his signature, without his notarial seal being affixed thereto: Provided, that a notary public who affixes his seal to any instrument or other writings shall affix his seal for the county in which the acknowledgment is taken and the certificate is made.

§ 29-4-6. Powers as to protests and other matters.

Notaries shall have authority to demand acceptance of foreign and inland bills of exchange, including checks, and to demand payment thereof, and of negotiable promissory notes, and protest the same for nonacceptance or nonpayment, as the case may require; and perform such other duties as by the law of nations or commercial usage may be performed by notaries public.

§ 29-4-7. Powers of notaries connected with banks or other corporations.

It shall be lawful for any notary who is a stockholder, director, officer or employee of a banking institution, including national banking associations, or other corporation, to take the acknowledgment of any party to any written instrument executed to or by such corporation, or to administer an oath to any other stockholder, director, officer, employee or agent of such corporation, or to protest, for nonacceptance or nonpayment, bills of exchange, drafts, checks, notes and other negotiable instruments which may be owned or held for collection by such corporation: Provided, That it shall be unlawful for any notary public to take the acknowledgment of an instrument by or to a banking institution, including national banking association, or other corporation, of which he is a stockholder, director, officer, or employee, when such notary is a party to such instrument, either personally or as a representative of such corporation; or to protest any negotiable instrument owned or held for collection by such corporation, when such notary is personally a party to such instrument.

§ 29-4-8. Signature of notary to state date of expiration of commission.

The official signature of any notary shall state the date of expiration of his commission, but a misstatement of such date shall not invalidate any official act of such notary, if his commission be at the time thereof in force.

FEES

§ 59-1-2. Fees to be charged by secretary of state.

Except as may be otherwise provided in article

one [§ 31-1-1 et seq.], chapter thirty-one of this code, the secretary of state shall charge for services rendered in his office the following fees to be paid by the person to whom the service is rendered at the time it is done:

For each certificate of incorporation or copy thereof, including restatements of any such certificates issued on new agreements, and/or consolidations or all certificates of merger or consolidation or certificates authorizing a foreign corporation to do business within this state	$10.00
For each certified copy of certificate of incorporation, not to exceed ten pages	10.00
If such copy contains in excess of ten pages, for each additional page	.20
For filing and recording a trademark	5.00
For each certificate of change of name, of increase or decrease of authorized capital stock, of change of principal office, or of amendment to certificate of incorporation	5.00
For recording a power of attorney and certificate thereof	3.00
For any other certificate, whether required by law or made at the request of any person	5.00

The foregoing fees shall include the tax on the great seal or the less seal impressed on any such document, as well as the filing, recording and indexing of the same.

For endorsing and filing reports of corporations, and all other papers, which shall include the indexing of the same, for each report or paper filed	$1.00
For any search, not less than	1.00
For searches of more than one hour, for each hour or fraction thereof consumed in making such search	5.00

The cost of the search shall be in addition to the cost of any certificate issued pursuant thereto or based thereon.

For entering statement of satisfaction of conditional sale contract	1.00
For filing each financing, continuation or termination statement or other statement or writing permitted to be filed under chapter forty-six [§ 46-1-101 et seq.] of the code	3.00
For recording any paper for which no specific fee is prescribed	1.00
Or at the rate, for each one hundred words recorded, of	.20
For issuing commission to a notary public, or to a commissioner of deeds, which shall include the tax on the state seal thereon and other charges	5.00
For a testimonial	1.50
For a copy of any paper, if one sheet	1.00

For each sheet of copy after the first ...... .75
For issuing a commission to a commissioner
in any other state.................... 5.00
For any other work or service not herein enumerated, such fee as may be elsewhere prescribed.

§ 59-1-7. Fees to be charged by notaries public.

A notary public may charge the following fees:
When there is a protest by him, for the record thereof, making out instrument of protest under his official seal and notice of dishonor to one person besides the maker of a note or acceptor of a bill $1.00
For every additional notice .... .10
For taking and certifying the acknowledgment of any deed or writing .... .50
For administering and certifying an oath, unless it be the affidavit of a witness ...... .25
For taking and certifying affidavits or depositions of witnesses, at the rate, for each hour actually employed in taking the same, of .... .75
For other services, where no specific fee is prescribed the same fees as are allowed by law to the clerk of the circuit court for similar services.

OFFENSES

§ 61-4-1. Forgery of public record, certificate, return or attestation of court or officer; penalty.

If any person forge a public record, or a certificate, return or attestation of a clerk of a court, notary public, judge, justice, or any public officer, in relation to any matter wherein such certificate, return, or attestation may be received as legal proof, or utter or attempt to employ as true such forged record, certificate, return or attestation, knowing the same to be forged, he shall be guilty of a felony, and, upon conviction, shall be confined in the penitentiary not less than two nor more than ten years.

ACKNOWLEDGMENTS

§ 31-1-74. Corporate acknowledgments.

A corporation may acknowledge any instrument required by law to be acknowledged by its attorney appointed under seal, and such appointment may be embodied in the deed or instrument to be acknowledged, or be made by a separate instrument; or such deed or other instrument may be acknowledged by the president or any vice president of such corporation without such appointment.

§ 39-1-2. Conditions under which county clerk shall admit deeds, contracts, etc., to record.

The clerk of the county court of any county in which any deed, contract, power of attorney, or other writing is to be, or may be, recorded, shall admit the same to record in his office, as to any person whose name is signed thereto, when it shall have been acknowledged by him, or proved by two witnesses as to him, before such clerk of the county court.

* * *

§ 39-1-2a. Other requirements for admission to record of certain instruments.

In addition to the other requirements prescribed by law, no instrument by which the title to real estate or personal property, or any interest therein or lien thereon, is conveyed, created, encumbered, assigned or otherwise disposed of, shall be recorded or admitted to record, or filed by the county clerk unless the name of the person who, and governmental agency, if any, which, prepared such instrument appears at the conclusion of such instrument and such name is either printed, typewritten, stamped, or signed in a legible manner: Provided, that the recording or filing of any instrument in violation of the provisions of this section shall not invalidate or cloud the title passing by or under such instrument or affect the validity of such instrument in any respect whatever, and such recorded or filed instrument shall constitute notice with like effect as if such instrument fully complied with the provisions of this section. An instrument will be in compliance with this section if it contains a statement in the following form: "This instrument was prepared by (name)."

This section does not apply to any instrument executed prior to the effective date hereof [June 7, 1965]; to any decree, order, judgment or writ of any court; to any will or death certificate; to any financing, continuation or termination statement permitted to be filed under chapter forty-six [§ 46-1-101 et seq.] of this Code; or to any instrument executed or acknowledged outside of this State.

§ 39-1-3. Who may take acknowledgment.

Upon the request of any person interested therein, such clerk of the county court shall also admit any such writing to record, as to any person whose name is signed thereto, upon a certificate of his acknowledgment before the president of a county court, a justice of the peace, notary public, recorder, prothonotary or clerk of any court, within the United States, the Philippine Islands, Island of Puerto Rico, Territory of Alaska, Territory of Hawaii, or any other territory, possession or dependency of the United States, or a commissioner appointed within the same by the governor of this State, written or annexed to the same; or upon a certificate so written or annexed under the official seal of any ambassador, minister plenipotentiary, minister resident, charge d'affaires, consul general, consul, deputy consul, vice consul, consular agent, vice consular agent, commercial agent, or vice commercial agent, appointed by the government of the United States to any foreign country, or of the proper officer of any court of record of such country, or of the mayor or other chief magistrate of any city, town or corporation therein, that such writing was acknowledged by such person, or proved as to him by two witnesses, before any person having such appointment, or before such court, mayor, or chief magistrate.

§ 39-1-4. Form of certificate of acknowledgment.

The certificate of acknowledgment mentioned in the preceding section [§ 39-1-3] may be in form or effect as follows:

State (territory or district) of _____, county of _____, to-wit:

I, _____, a commissioner, appointed by the governor of the State of West Virginia, for the said State (or territory or district) of _____; or I, _____, a justice of the peace of the county aforesaid; or I, _____, recorder of said county; or I, _____, a notary public of said county; or I, _____, a prothonotary (or clerk) of the _____ court of said county; (or other officer or person authorized to take acknowledgments by section three of this article, as the case may be), do certify that _____, whose name (or names) is (or are) signed to the writing above (or hereto annexed) bearing the date on the _____ day of _____, 19___, has (or have) this day acknowledged the same before me, in my said _____.

Given under my hand this _____ day of _____, 19___.

§ 39-1-4a. Acknowledgment of persons in the military service of the United States of America.

Upon the request of any person interested therein, the clerk of the county court of any county in which any deed, contract, power of attorney, or other writing is to be, or may be, recorded, shall admit the same to record as to any person whose name is signed thereto who is in the military service of the United States (including the Women's Army Auxiliary Corps, Women's Appointed Volunteers for Emergency Service, Army Nurse Corps, "Spars," Women's Reserve, or similar women's auxiliary unit officially connected with the military

service of the United States) or who is the spouse of any one in the military service of the United States (including the aforesaid components and auxiliary units officially connected therewith), upon the certificate of acknowledgment of such person before any commissioned officer of any branch of the military service of the United States, or auxiliary unit officially connected with such military service. Such acknowledgment may be taken at any place either within or outside of the United States of America, or any territory, possession or dependency thereof. The certificate of such acknowledgment need not state the place where same is taken and shall require no seal to be affixed thereto. The officer certifying such acknowledgment must state his rank, branch of military service, and identification number; and such certificate of acknowledgment may be in form and effect as follows:

IN THE MILITARY SERVICE OF THE UNITED STATES:

I, _____, a commissioned officer in the military service of the United States, do certify that _____, who is a member of the military service of the United States (or of _____, an auxiliary to the military forces of the United States), and/or _____, husband (or wife) of _____, a member of the military service of the United States (or of _____, an auxiliary to the military forces of the United States), whose name(s) is (are) signed to the foregoing writing bearing date on the _____ day of _____, 19___, has (have) this day acknowledged the same before me; and I further certify that I am a _____ (state rank) in the _____ of the United States and my identification number is _____.

Given under my hand this _____ day of _____, 19___.

_____
(Signature of Officer)

_____
(Official Title)

§ 39-1-5. Acknowledgment by husband and wife.

When a husband and wife have signed a writing purporting to sell or convey real estate, the wife may acknowledge the same together with, or separately from her husband. Either the husband or the wife may sign and acknowledge such writing before the other has signed or acknowledged it. If both acknowledge such writing at the same time, the certificate of such acknowledgments may be in form or effect as follows:

State (territory or district) of _____ county of _____, to-wit:

I, _____, a commissioner appointed by the governor of the State of West Virginia for the said State of _____, (or territory or district of

_____); or I, _____, a justice of the peace of the said county of _____; or I, _____, a notary public of the said county of _____; or I, _____, prothonotary (or clerk) of the _____ court or county of _____; (or other officer or person authorized to take acknowledgments by section three of this article, as the case may be),* do certify _____ and _____, his wife whose names are signed to the writing above (or hereto annexed) bearing date the _____ day of _____, 19__, have this day acknowledged the same before me in my said _____.

Given under my hand this _____ day of _____, 19__.

If the husband or wife acknowledge a deed or other writing separately from the other, the certificate of acknowledgment after the star in the foregoing form shall be in form or effect as follows: do certify that _____, the wife of _____, (or the husband of _____, as the case may be), whose name is signed to the writing above (or hereto annexed) bearing date the _____ day of _____, 19__, has this day acknowledged the same before me in my said _____.

Given under my hand this _____ day of _____, 19__.

§ 39-1-7. False certificate of acknowledgment.

If any person shall in any case wilfully make any false certificate of acknowledgment, contrary to the true facts in the case, or shall certify the acknowledgment of any person whom he does not personally know to be the person whose name is signed to the writing acknowledged, he shall be guilty of a misdemeanor, and, upon conviction thereof, be fined not more than five hundred dollars, and imprisoned not more than sixty days, at the discretion of the court.

§ 39-1-8. Form of certificate of acknowledgment by attorney-in-fact.

When any writing has been executed by an attorney-in-fact, and an acknowledgment of the execution thereof is required or authorized for any purpose, the certificate of acknowledgment may be in form or effect as provided in section four [§ 39-1-4] of this article as far as the words "do certify," and thence as follows: do certify that _____, whose name is signed to the writing above (or hereto annexed) bearing date the _____ day of _____, 19__, as attorney-in-fact for _____, has this day acknowledged the same before me in my said _____.

Given under my hand this _____ day of _____, 19__.

§ 39-1-9. Acknowledgment by corporations.

The certificate of acknowledgment of a corporation may be in form or effect as prescribed in section four [§ 39-1-4] of this article as far as the words "do certify" and thence as follows: do certify that _____, who signed the writing above (or hereto annexed), bearing date the _____ day of _____, 19__, for _____ (name of corporation), has this day in my said county, before me, acknowledged the said writing to be the act and deed of said corporation.

Given under my hand this _____ day of _____, 19__.

§ 39-1-10. When certificate to be under official seal.

If any acknowledgment be before a notary without this State, he shall certify the same under his official seal.

Uniform Recognition of Acknowledgments Act

§ 39-1A-1. "Notarial acts" defined; who may perform notarial acts outside State for use in State.

For the purposes of this article, "notarial acts" means acts which the laws and regulations of this State authorized notaries public of this State to perform, including the administering of oaths and affirmations, taking proof of execution and acknowledgments of instruments, and attesting documents. Notarial acts may be performed outside this State for use in this State with the same effect as if performed by a notary public of this State by the following persons authorized pursuant to the laws and regulations of other governments in addition to any other person authorized by the laws and regulations of this State:

(1) A notary public authorized to perform notarial acts in the place in which the act is performed;

(2) A judge, clerk, or deputy clerk of any court of record in the place in which the notarial act is performed;

(3) An officer of the foreign service of the United States, a consular agent, or any other person authorized by regulation of the United States department of state to perform notarial acts in the place in which the act is performed;

(4) A commissioned officer in active service with the armed forces of the United States and any other person authorized by regulation of the armed forces to perform notarial acts if the notarial act is performed for one of the following or his dependents: A merchant seaman of the United States, a

member of the armed forces of the United States or any other person serving with or accompanying the armed forces of the United States; or

(5) Any other person authorized to perform notarial acts in the place in which the act is performed.

§ 39-1A-2. Proof of authority of person performing notarial act.

(a) If the notarial act is performed by any of the persons described in subdivisions one to four, inclusive, section one [§ 39-1A-1] of this article, other than a person authorized to perform notarial acts by the laws or regulations of a foreign country, the signature, rank or title and serial number, if any, of the person are sufficient proof of the authority of a holder of that rank or title to perform the act. Further proof of his authority is not required.

(b) If the notarial act is performed by a person authorized by the laws or regulations of a foreign country to perform the act, there is sufficient proof of the authority of that person to act if:

(1) Either a foreign service officer of the United States resident in the country in which the act is performed or a diplomatic or consular officer of the foreign country resident in the United States certifies that a person holding that office is authorized to perform the act; and

(2) The official seal of the person performing the notarial act is affixed to the document; or

(3) The title and indication of authority to perform notarial acts of the person appears either in a digest of foreign law or in a list customarily used as a source of such information.

(c) If the notarial act is performed by a person other than one described in subsections (a) and (b) of this section, there is sufficient proof of the authority of that person to act if the clerk of a court of record in the place in which the notarial act is performed certifies to the official character of that person and to his authority to perform the notarial act.

(d) The signature and title of the person performing the act are prima facie evidence that he is a person with the designated title and that the signature is genuine.

§ 39-1A-3. What person taking acknowledgment shall certify.

The person taking an acknowledgment shall certify that:

(1) The person acknowledging appeared before him and acknowledged he executed the instrument; and

(2) The person acknowledging was known to the person taking the acknowledgment or that the person taking the acknowledgment had satisfactory

evidence that the person acknowledging was the person described in and who executed the instrument.

§ 39-1A-4. When form of certificate of acknowledgment accepted.

The form of a certificate of acknowledgment used by a person whose authority is recognized under section one [§ 39-1A-1] of this article shall be accepted in this States if:

(1) The certificate is in a form prescribed by the laws or regulations of this State;

(2) The certificate is in a form prescribed by the laws or regulations applicable in the place in which the acknowledgment is taken; or

(3) The certificate contains the words "acknowledged before me," or their substantial equivalent.

§ 39-1A-5. Meaning of "acknowledged before me."

The words "acknowledged before me" mean:

(1) That the person acknowledging appeared before the person taking the acknowledgment;

(2) That he acknowledged he executed the instrument;

(3) That, in the case of:

(a) A natural person, he executed the instrument for the purposes therein stated;

(b) A corporation, the officer or agent acknowledged he held the position or title set forth in the instrument and certificate, he signed the instrument on behalf of the corporation by proper authority, and the instrument was the act of the corporation for the purpose therein stated;

(c) A partnership, the partner or agent acknowledged he signed the instrument on behalf of the partnership by proper authority and he executed the instrument as the act of the partnership for the purposes therein stated;

(d) A person acknowledging as principal by an attorney in fact, he executed the instrument by proper authority as the act of the principal for the purposes therein stated;

(e) A person acknowledging as a public officer, trustee, administrator, guardian or other representative, he signed the instrument by proper authority and he executed the instrument in the capacity and for the purposes therein stated; and

(4) That the person taking the acknowledgment either knew or had satisfactory evidence that the person acknowledging was the person named in the instrument or certificate.

§ 39-1A-6. Statutory short forms of acknowledgment.

The forms of acknowledgment set forth in this

section may be used and are sufficient for their respective purposes under any law of this State. The forms shall be known as "Statutory Short Forms of Acknowledgment" and may be referred to by that name. The authorization of the forms in this section does not preclude the use of other forms.

State of ....

County of ....

The foregoing instrument was acknowledged before me this .... by

(date)

....

(name of person acknowledged)

....

(Signature of Person Taking Acknowledgment)

....

(Title or Rank)

....

(Serial Number, if any)

(2) For a corporation:

State of ....

County of ....

The foregoing instrument was acknowledged before me this ....by

(date)

....

(name of officer or agent,
title of officer or agent)

of ....

(name of corporation acknowledging)

a .... corporation,

(state or place of incorporation)

on behalf of the corporation.

....

(Signature of Person Taking Acknowledgment)

....

(Title or Rank)

....

(Serial Number, if any)

(3) For a partnership:

State of ....

County of ....

The foregoing instrument was acknowledged before me this .... by

(date)

.... partner (or

(name of acknowledging
parter or agent)

agent) on behalf of ....

(name of partnership)

a partnership.

....

(Signature of Person Taking Acknowledgment)

....

(Title or Rank)

....

(Serial Number, if any)

(4) For an individual acting as principal by an attorney-in-fact:

State of ....

County of ....

The foregoing instrument was acknowledged before me this .... by

(date)

.... as attorney-in-fact on

(name of attorney-in-fact)

behalf of ....

(name of principal)

....

(Signature of Person Taking Acknowledgment)

....

(Title or Rank)

....

(Serial Number, if any)

(5) By any public officer, trustee or personal representative:

State of ....

County of ....

The foregoing instrument was acknowledged before me this .... by

(Date)

....

(Name and Title of Position)

....

(Signature of Person Taking Acknowledgment)

....

(Title or Rank)

....

(Serial Number, if any)

§ 39-1A-7. Application of article; article cumulative.

A notarial act performed prior to the effective date of this article [May 6, 1971] is not affected by this article. This article provides an additional method of proving notarial acts. Nothing in this article diminishes or invalidates the recognition accorded to notarial acts by article one [§ 39-1-1 et seq.] of this chapter or by other laws or regulations of this State.

§ 39-1A-8. Uniform interpretation.

This article shall be so interpreted as to make uniform the laws of those states which enact it.

§ 39-1A-9. Short title.

This article may be cited as the "Uniform Recognition of Acknowledgments Act."

DEPOSITIONS

§ 56-3-5. To whom process directed; return of process; return of summons for witness.

Process from any court, whether original, mesne or final, may be directed to the sheriff of any county. Any process shall be returnable, within ninety days after its date, except as provided in section six, article two [§ 56-2-6] of this chapter, to the court on any day of a term, or in the clerk's office to the first day of any rules, designated as the first or last Monday, as the case may be, in any month and year, except that a summons for a witness shall be returnable on whatever day his attendance is desired, and an order of attachment may be returnable to the next term of the court, although more than ninety days from the date of the order, and process awarded in court may be returnable as the court may direct.

§ 57-4-1. Taking and certification of depositions—generally.

In any pending case the deposition of a witness, whether a party to the suit or not, may, without commission, be taken in or out of this State by a justice, or notary public, or by a commissioner in chancery, or before any officer authorized to take depositions in the county or state where they may be taken. And such depositions may be taken in shorthand, or stenographic characters or notes, and shall be written out in full and transcribed into the English language by the stenographer taking the same, and certified by the officer before whom the depositions are taken; and if certified by such officer under his hand and if further certified by him that such stenographic characters and notes were correctly taken and accurately transcribed by him, or under his direction and supervision, and that the witnesses were duly sworn, such depositions may be received and read in evidence without proof of the signature to such certificate and without the signature of the witness to such depositions. And in case the stenographer taking such depositions is not the officer before whom the same are being taken, then such stenographer, before proceeding to take any of said depositions, shall be sworn to take correctly and accurately transcribe the same, and the certificate of the officer before whom the depositions are taken shall state that the stenographer was so sworn.

§ 57-5-1. Summons for witnesses.

A summons may be issued, directed as described in section five, [§ 56-3-5] article three, chapter fifty-six of this Code, commanding the officer to summon any person to attend on the day and at the place that such attendance is desired, to give evidence before a court, grand jury, arbitrators, umpire, justice, surveyor, notary public, or any commissioner appointed by a court. The summons may be issued, if the attendance be desired at a court, by the clerk thereof; if before a grand jury, by the prosecuting attorney or the clerk of the court, at

the instance of the prosecuting attorney; and in other cases, by any person before whom, or the clerk of the circuit court of a county in which, the attendance is desired; or, if attendance be desired before a justice, by such or any other justice. The summons shall express on whose behalf, and in what case, or about what matter, the witness is to attend. This section shall be deemed to authorize a summons to compel attendance before commissioners or other persons appointed by authority of another state, but only in case they be citizens of this State, and the summons requires the attendance of a witness at a place not out of his county.

§ 57-5-6. Commitment to jail of person attending but refusing to testify or produce writing.

If a person, after being served with such summons, shall attend and yet refuse to be sworn, or to give evidence, or to produce any writing or document required, he may by order of the court whose clerk issued said summons, or of the person before whom he was summoned to attend, be committed to jail, there to remain until he shall, in custody of the jailer, give such evidence or produce such writing or document.

§ 57-5-7. Interpreters required.

(a) In any court proceeding wherein a party or witness cannot readily understand or verbally communicate the English language because he is deaf or a deaf mute or because of any other hearing impairment, such person shall have the right to have a qualified interpreter to assist him at every stage of the proceeding. Such right shall also pertain in any proceeding before administrative boards, commissions or agencies of this State or any political subdivision or municipality thereof, and in coroners' inquests and grand jury proceedings.

(b) The director of the administrative office of the supreme court of appeals shall establish a program to facilitate the use of interpreters in courts of this State and in extrajudicial criminal proceedings as provided for in this section.

(1) The director shall prescribe, determine and certify the qualifications of persons who may serve as certified interpreters in courts of this State in proceedings involving the hearing impaired. Persons certified by the director shall be interpreters certified by the national registry of interpreters for the deaf, or the West Virginia registry of interpreters for the deaf or approved by the chief of services for the deaf and hearing impaired of West Virginia of the West Virginia division of vocational rehabilitation, or shall be such other persons deemed by the director to be qualified by education, training and experience. The director shall maintain a current master list of all interpreters

certified by the director and shall report annually on the frequency of requests for, and the use and effectiveness of, interpreters.

(2) Each circuit court shall maintain on file in the office of the clerk of the court a list of all persons who have been certified as oral or manual interpreters for the hearing impaired by the director of the administrative office of the supreme court of appeals in accordance with the certification program established pursuant to this section.

(3) In any criminal or juvenile proceeding, or other proceeding described in section five [§ 51-11-5; repealed], article eleven, chapter fifty-one of this Code, the judge of the circuit court in which such proceeding is pending, or, if such proceeding is in a magistrate court, then the judge of the circuit court to which such proceeding may be appealed or presented for judicial review, shall, with the assistance of the director of the administrative office of the supreme court of appeals, utilize the services of the most available certified interpreter, or when no certified interpreter is reasonably available, as determined by the judge, the services of an otherwise competent interpreter, if the judge determines on his own motion or on the motion of a party that such party or a witness who may present testimony in the proceeding suffers from a hearing impairment so as to inhibit such party's comprehension of the proceedings or communication with counsel or the presiding judicial officer, or so as to inhibit such witness' comprehension of questions and the presentation of such testimony. The utilization of an interpreter shall be appropriate at any stage of the proceeding, judicial or extrajudicial, at which a person would be entitled to representation by an attorney and a waiver of the right to counsel shall not constitute a waiver of the right to an interpreter as provided for by this section.

(c) Whenever a qualified interpreter is appointed pursuant to the provisions of subsection (b) of this section, the court shall, at the conclusion of the proceedings or interrogation, by order, fix the compensation of such interpreter. The compensation shall be not less than fifteen dollars per hour, nor more than fifty dollars per day, plus reimbursement for all reasonable and necessary expenses actually incurred in the performance of such duties, but expenses shall not be incurred in excess of the prevailing rate for state employees. In all such cases, the compensation shall be paid by the state auditor from the fund out of which appointed counsel are paid in felony cases. In proceedings before administrative boards, commissions and agencies, the compensation shall be fixed by such board, commission or agency and paid, within the limit of available funds, by such board, commission or agency.

(d) In any proceeding described in subdivision (3), subsection (b) of this section, if the circuit judge does not appoint an interpreter, an individual requiring the services of an interpreter may seek the assistance of the clerk of the circuit court or the director of the administrative office of the supreme court of appeals in obtaining the assistance of a certified interpreter.

(e) Whenever an interpreter is necessary in any court proceeding because a witness or party speaks only a foreign language or for any other reason, an interpreter may be sworn truly to interpret.

§ 57-5-8. Who may administer oath to witness.

Any person before whom a witness is to be examined may administer an oath to such witness.

§ 57-5-9. Administration of oaths or taking of affidavits; authentication of affidavit made in another state or country; oaths and affidavits of persons in military service.

Any judge of this State may administer any oath that is or may be lawful for any person to take, including oaths of office, and also may swear any person to an affidavit, and administer an oath to any person in any proceeding.

Any oath or affidavit required by law, which is not of such a nature that it must be made otherwise or elsewhere may, unless otherwise provided, be administered by, or made before, a county commissioner, notary public, or a commissioner appointed by the governor, or by the clerk of any court, or, in case of a survey directed by a court in a case therein pending, by or before the surveyor directed to execute said order of survey.

An affidavit may also be made before any officer of another state or country authorized by its laws to administer an oath, and shall be deemed duly authenticated if it be subscribed by such officer, with his official seal annexed, and if he have none, the genuineness of his signature, and his authority to administer an oath, shall be authenticated by some officer of the same state or country under his official seal.

Any oath or affidavit required of a person in the military service of the United States (including the Women's Army Corps, Women's Appointed Volunteers for Emergency Service, Army Nurse Corps, Spars, Women's Reserve, or similar women's auxiliary unit officially connected with such military service of the United States), may be administered by or made before any commissioned officer of any branch of the military service of the United States, or any auxiliary unit officially connected with such military service. Such oath may be taken or affidavit made at any place either within or outside the United States of America, or any territory, possession or dependency thereof. The jurat to such oath and certificate to such affidavit need not state the place where the same is taken and shall require no seal to be affixed thereto. The certificate of the officer before whom such oath is taken or affidavit is made must state his rank, branch of military service, and identification number, and such certificate may be substantially in form and effect as follows:

IN THE MILITARY SERVICE OF THE UNITED STATES:

I, _____, being duly sworn on oath (affirmation), do swear (affirm) that I am a member of the military service of the United States (or of _____, an auxiliary to the military forces of the United States); that ***, etc.

_____

Taken, subscribed and sworn to before me, _____, a commissioned officer in the _____ service of the United States, by _____, a member of the military service of the United States (or of _____, an auxiliary to the military forces of the United States), this the _____ day of _____, 19___.

_____ (Signature of officer)

_____   _____
(Rank)   (Identification Number)

Any oath or affidavit heretofore taken or made by any person in the military service in substantial compliance with this section shall be valid.

Divorce

§ 48-2-24. Maturing of actions for divorce, annulment and separate maintenance; hearing; testimony and depositions; reference of action to commissioner.

Actions for divorce, annulment and separate maintenance shall mature in the same manner as other actions provided for in the Rules of Civil Procedure of the State of West Virginia, and when ready for hearing under said rules shall be tried before the court, in chambers, and all witnesses shall appear and testify at the hearing the same as witnesses in other civil actions. Such actions may be heard, when matured, and a judgment order entered, at any time irrespective of whether or not there is a term of court in session. The law governing the taking and reading of depositions, as provided for in the Rules of Civil Procedure, shall apply to depositions in the hearing of a divorce case. The court may, instead of proceeding with the action under this section, refer the same to a commissioner, or with a special commissioner, of said court as provided for in section twenty-five [§ 48-2-25] of this article.

§ 48-2-25. Reference to commissioner; taking of depositions; oral testimony before court.

Instead of proceeding with the action under the provisions of section twenty-four [§ 48-2-24] of this article, the court may, in its discretion, refer it to one of the commissioners of such court, or to a special commissioner, who shall take and return the testimony in such action, with a report of all such facts as the commissioner may be able to obtain as to property rights of the parties, their income, their character, conduct, health, habits, their children, their respective places of residence from the time of their marriage up to the time of such report, and any other matter deemed necessary by the court, together with his recommendation concerning whether a divorce, annulment or affirmation, as the case may be, should be granted, and concerning any other matter on which the court may request his recommendation. All such facts so reported and the recommendation of the commissioner shall be considered by the court in passing on the merits of the case, whether the same be referred to in the pleadings or evidence, or not. Except as otherwise expressly provided herein, the procedure in respect to the reference of such a case to a commissioner shall be governed in all respects by the rules applicable to references to commissioners generally.

If testimony is to be taken in a county other than that in which the action is pending, or of witnesses residing out of the State of West Virginia, the same shall be taken before some person duly authorized to take depositions in the county or state where taken. If such depositions are taken out of the county in which the action is pending, or without the State, the same shall be, by the person taking the same, filed with or forwarded to the clerk of the court wherein such action is pending, and on receipt of such depositions such clerk shall lay the same before the commissioner to whom such action has been referred, who shall consider the same in connection with his report hereinbefore mentioned. The person before whom depositions are taken hereunder shall be personally present at the time and place of taking depositions, and no deposition shall be taken or read in the action unless it appears therefrom that such person was personally present during the taking of the same. It is hereby made the duty of the person before whom such depositions are taken, to see that all witnesses are so examined as to elicit all facts within their knowledge pertaining to the action. If any person before whom any such depositions are taken certified falsely as to his presence at the taking of such depositions, he shall be guilty of a misdemeanor, and, on conviction thereof, shall be fined not less than fifty nor more than five hundred dollars.

The court in which such action is pending may so refer the same as often as, in its judgment, justice requires, and may, if it so elect, summon anyone to appear before such court, and give evidence with reference thereto, and base its findings on such oral evidence solely. The commissioner shall be allowed for his services the same compensation as is allowed in other court actions, and all costs, including stenographer's fees, shall be taxed as in other court actions.

[W. Va. R. Civ. P.]

RULE 28. Persons before whom depositions may be taken.

(a) *Within the United States.*—Within the United States or within a territory or insular possession subject to the dominion of the United States, depositions shall be taken before an officer authorized to administer oaths by the laws of the United States or of this State or of the place where the examination is held, or before a person appointed by the court in which the action is pending. A person so appointed has power to administer oaths and take testimony. The term officer as used in Rules 30, 31, and 32 includes a person appointed by the court or designated by the parties under Rule 29.

(b) *In foreign countries.*—In a foreign country, depositions may be taken (1) on notice before a person authorized to administer oaths in the place in which the examination is held, either by the law thereof or by the law of the United States or of this State, or (2) before a person commissioned by the court, and a person so commissioned shall have the power by virtue of his commission to administer any necessary oath and take testimony, or (3) pursuant to a letter rogatory. A commission or a letter rogatory shall be issued on application and notice and on terms that are just and appropriate. It is not requisite to the issuance of a commission or a letter rogatory that the taking of the deposition in any other manner is impracticable or inconvenient; and both a commission and a letter rogatory may be issued in proper cases. A notice or commission may designate the person before whom the deposition is to be taken either by name or descriptive title. A letter rogatory may be addressed "To the Appropriate Authority in [here name the country]." Evidence obtained in response to a letter rogatory need not be excluded merely for the reason that it is not a verbatim transcript or that the testimony was not taken under oath or for any similar departure from the requirements for depositions taken within the State under these rules.

(c) *Disqualification for interest.*—No deposition shall be taken before a person who is a relative or employee or attorney or counsel of any of the parties, or is a relative or employee of such attorney or counsel, or is financially interested in the action.

(d) *Depositions for use in foreign jurisdictions.*—Whenever the deposition of any person is to be taken in this State pursuant to the laws of another state or of the United States or of another country for use in proceedings there, any court having general civil jurisdiction in the county wherein the deponent resides or is employed or transacts his business in person may, upon petition, make and order directing issuance of a subpoena as provided in Rule 45, in aid of the taking of the deposition.

COMMISSIONERS

[W. Va. Code Ann.]

§ 29-4-12. Commissioners out of State; qualifications; fee.

The governor, if he deems it proper, may appoint any persons residing within or without this state and within the United States, its territories or possessions as commissioners to acknowledge signatures performed in or out of State by persons residing in or out of the state of West Virginia, covering deeds, leases and other writings pertaining to West Virginia property for recordation in the state of West Virginia.

Such commissioners shall hold office for ten years, unless sooner removed by the governor. Any commissioner in office upon the effective date of this act [June 3, 1974] shall continue therein until his term expires or until sooner removed in the manner prescribed by law.

Before performing any duties as such, the commissioner shall enter into a bond in the penalty sum of one thousand dollars with corporate surety to be approved by the secretary of state and filed in his office.

A fee of one hundred dollars for such commission issued shall be paid to the secretary of state.

§ 29-4-13. Power of commissioner appointed under § 29-4-12 as to oaths, affidavits and depositions.

When any oath may lawfully be administered, or affidavit or deposition taken, within the state, territory or district for which any such commissioner is appointed, to be used in this state, it may be done by such commissioner.

§ 29-4-14. Power of such commissioner to take acknowledgments.

Such commissioners, under regulations prescribed by law, may take, within or any place out of the state of West Virginia, the acknowledgments of deeds and other writings to be admitted to record in the state of West Virginia, but each such acknowledgment shall reflect where the acknowledgment was taken, as, for example, the state and county, the territory, etc.

§ 29-4-15. Seal of such commissioner.

Every such commissioner shall provide an official seal, on which shall be inscribed his name and residence, and the words "commissioner for West Virginia." An impression of such seal, together with his signature, shall be forthwith transmitted to and filed in the office of the secretary of state.

§ 29-4-16. Authentication of such commissioner's certificate.

Every certificate of such commissioner shall be authenticated by his signature and official seal.

LEGAL HOLIDAYS

§ 2-2-1. Legal holidays; official acts or court proceedings.

The following days shall be regarded, treated and observed as legal holidays, viz: The first day of January, commonly called "New Year's Day"; the third Monday of January, commonly called "Martin Luther King's Birthday"; the twelfth day of February, commonly called "Lincoln's Birthday"; the third Monday of February, commonly called "Washington's Birthday"; the last Monday in May, commonly called "Memorial Day"; the twentieth day of June, commonly called "West Virginia Day"; the fourth day of July, commonly called "Independence Day"; the first Monday of September, commonly called "Labor Day"; the second Monday of October, commonly called "Columbus Day"; the eleventh day of November, hereafter referred to as "Veterans Day"; the fourth Thursday of November, commonly called "Thanksgiving Day"; the twenty-fifth day of December, commonly called "Christmas Day"; any national, state or other election day throughout the district or municipality wherein the election is held; and all days which may be appointed or recommended by the

governor of this state, or the president of the United States, as days of thanksgiving, or for the general cessation of business; and when any of these days or dates falls on a Sunday, then the succeeding Monday shall be regarded, treated and observed as the legal holiday.

When the return day of any summons or other court proceeding or any notice or time fixed for holding any court or doing any official act shall fall on any of these holidays, the next ensuing day which is not a Saturday, Sunday or legal holiday shall be taken as meant and intended: Provided, That nothing herein contained shall increase nor diminish the legal school holidays provided for in section two, article five, chapter eighteen-a of this code.

§ 2-2-2. When acts to be done fall on Saturday, Sunday or legal holiday; adjournments from day to day.

When a proceeding is directed to take place or any act to be done on any particular day of the month or within any period of time prescribed or allowed, including those provided by article two [§ 55-2-1 et seq.], chapter fifty-five of this Code, if that day or the last day falls on a Saturday, Sunday or legal holiday, the next day which is not a Saturday, Sunday or legal holiday shall be deemed to be the one intended, and when the day upon which a term of court is directed by law to commence, falls on a Saturday, Sunday or legal holiday, the following day which is not a Saturday, Sunday or legal holiday shall be deemed to be the day intended. When an adjournment is authorized from day to day, an adjournment from Friday to Monday will be legal.

§ 2-2-3. Computation of time.

The time or period prescribed or allowed within which an act is to be done shall be computed by excluding the first day and including the last; or if the last be a Saturday, Sunday or legal holiday, it shall also be excluded, and any such Saturday shall be a legal holiday solely for the purpose of Rule 6(a) of the Rules of Civil Procedure for Trial Courts of Record; but the provisions of this section shall not be deemed to change any rule of law applicable to bills of exchange or negotiable notes.

WISInline CONSIN

NOTARIES PUBLIC

[Wis. Stat. Ann.]

§ 137.01. Notaries.

(1) **Notaries public who are not attorneys.** (a) The governor shall appoint notaries public who shall be Wisconsin residents and at least 18 years of age. Applicants who are not attorneys shall file an application with the secretary of state and pay a $15 fee.

(b) The secretary of state shall satisfy himself or herself that the applicant has the equivalent of an 8th grade education, is familiar with the duties and responsibilities of a notary public and, subject to ss. 111.321, 111.322 and 111.335, does not have an arrest or conviction record.

(c) If an application is rejected the fee shall be returned.

(d) Qualified applicants shall be notified by the secretary of state to take and file the official oath and execute and file an official bond in the sum of $500, with surety to be approved by the clerk of the circuit court for his or her county, or, if executed by a surety company, approved by the secretary of state.

(e) The qualified applicant shall file his signature, post-office address and an impression of his official seal, or imprint of his official rubber stamp with the secretary of state.

(f) A certificate of appointment as a notary public for a term of 4 years stating the expiration date of the commission shall be issued to applicants who have fulfilled the requirements of this subsection.

(g) At least 30 days before the expiration of a commission the secretary of state shall mail notice of the expiration date to the holder of a commission.

(h) A notary shall be entitled to reappointment.

(2) **Notaries public who are attorneys.** (a) Any Wisconsin resident who is licensed to practice law in this state is entitled to a permanent commission as a notary public upon application to the secretary of state and payment of a $15 fee. The application shall include a certificate of good standing from the supreme court, the signature and post-office address of the applicant and an impression of the applicant's official seal, or imprint of the applicant's official rubber stamp.

(b) The secretary of state shall issue a certificate of appointment as a notary public to persons who qualify under the requirements of this subsection. Such certificate shall state that the notary commission is permanent.

(c) The supreme court shall file with the secretary of state notice of the surrender, suspension or revocation of the license to practice law of any attorney who holds a permanent commission as a notary public. Such notice shall be deemed a revocation of said commission.

(3) **Notarial seal or stamp.** (a) Every notary public shall provide an engraved official seal which makes a distinct and legible impression or official rubber stamp which makes a distinct and legible imprint on paper. The impression of the seal or the imprint of the rubber stamp shall state, "Notary Public," "State of Wisconsin" and the name of the notary. But any notarial seal in use on August 1, 1959, shall be considered in compliance.

(b) The impression of the notarial seal upon any instrument or writing or upon wafer, wax or other adhesive substance and affixed to any instrument or writing shall be deemed an affixation of the seal, and the imprint of the notarial rubber stamp upon any instrument or writing shall be deemed an affixation of the rubber stamp.

(4) **Attestation.** (a) Every official act of a notary public shall be attested by his written signature.

(b) All certificates of acknowledgments of deeds and other conveyances, or any written instrument required or authorized by law to be acknowledged

617

or sworn to before any notary public, within this state, shall be attested by a clear impression of the official seal or imprint of the rubber stamp of said officer, and in addition thereto shall be written or stamped either the day, month and year when the commission of said notary public will expire, or that such commission is permanent.

(c) The official certificate of any notary public, when attested and completed in the manner provided by this subsection, shall be presumptive evidence in all cases, and in all courts of the state, of the facts therein stated, in cases where by law a notary public is authorized to certify such facts.

(5) **Powers.** Notaries public have power to act throughout the state. Notaries public have power to demand acceptance of foreign and inland bills of exchange and payment thereof, and payment of promissory notes, and may protest the same for nonacceptance or nonpayment, may administer oaths, take depositions and acknowledgments of deeds, and perform such other duties as by the laws of nations, or according to commercial usage, may be exercised and performed by notaries public.

(6) **Authentication.** (a) The secretary of state may certify to the official qualifications of any notary public and to the genuineness of his signature and seal or rubber stamp.

(b) Whenever any notary public has filed in the office of the clerk of the circuit court of his county of residence his signature, an impression of his official seal or imprint of his official rubber stamp and a certificate of the secretary of state, such clerk may certify to the official qualifications of such notary public and the genuineness of his signature and seal or rubber stamp.

(c) Any certificate specified under this subsection shall be presumptive evidence of the facts therein stated.

(6m) **Change of residence.** A notary public shall not vacate his office by reason of his change of residence within the state. Written notice of any change of address shall be given to the secretary of state within 5 days of such change.

(7) **Official records to be filed.** When any notary public ceases to hold office he, or in case of his death his executor or administrator, shall deposit his official records and papers in the office of the clerk of the circuit court of the county of his residence. If any such notary or any executor or administrator, after such records and papers come to his hands, neglects for 3 months to deposit them he shall forfeit not less than $50 nor more than $500. If any person knowingly destroys, defaces or conceals any records or papers of any notary public he shall forfeit not less than $50 nor more than $500, and shall be liable to the party injured for all damages thereby sustained. The clerks of the circuit courts shall receive and safely keep all such papers and records in their office.

(8) **Misconduct.** If any notary public shall be guilty of any misconduct or neglect of duty in office he shall be liable to the party injured for all the damages thereby sustained.

(9) **Fees.** A notary public shall be allowed the following fees:

(a) For drawing and copy of protest of the nonpayment of a promissory note or bill of exchange, or of the nonacceptance of such bill, $1 in the cases where by law such protest is necessary, but in no other case.

(b) For drawing and copy of every other protest, 50 cents.

(c) For drawing, copying and serving every notice of nonpayment of a note or bill, or nonacceptance of a bill, 50 cents.

(d) For drawing any affidavit, or other paper or proceeding for which provision is not herein made, 50 cents for each folio, and for copying the same 12 cents per folio.

(e) For taking the acknowledgment of deeds, and for other services authorized by law, the same fees as are allowed to other officers for similar services, but the fee per document shall not exceed 50 cents.

ADDITIONAL AUTHORITY

§ **19.01.** Oaths and bonds.

(1) **Form of oath.** Every official oath required by article IV, section 28, of the constitution or by any statute shall be in writing, subscribed, sworn to, and except as provided otherwise by s. 757.02 and SCR 40.13, shall be in substantially the following form:

STATE OF WISCONSIN,

County of . . . .

I, the undersigned, who have been elected (or appointed) to the office of . . . ., but have not yet entered upon the duties thereof, swear (or affirm) that I will support the constitution of the United States and the constitution of the state of Wisconsin, and will faithfully discharge the duties of said office to the best of my ability. So help me God.

. . . .,

Subscribed and sworn to before me this . . . . day of . . . ., 19. . . .

. . . .(Signature). . . .,

(1m) **Form of oral oath.** If it is desired to administer the official oath orally in addition to the written oath prescribed above, it shall be in substantially the following form:

I, ..., swear (or affirm) that I will support the constitution of the United States and the constitution of the state of Wisconsin, and will faithfully and impartially discharge the duties of the office of . . . . to the best of my ability. So help me God.

(2) **Form of bond.** (a) Every official bond re-

quired of any public officer shall be in substantially the following form:

We, the undersigned, jointly and severally, undertake and agree that . . . ., who has been elected (or appointed) to the office of . . . ., will faithfully discharge the duties of his said office according to law, and will pay to the parties entitled to receive the same, such damages, not exceeding in the aggregate . . . . dollars, as may be suffered by them in consequence of his failure so to discharge such duties.

Dated . . . ., 19. .

. . . .(Principal). . . .,
. . . .(Surety). . . .,

(b) Any further or additional official bond lawfully required of any public officer shall be in the same form and it shall not affect or impair any official bond previously given by him for the same or any other official term. Where such bond is in excess of the sum of $25,000, the officer may give 2 or more bonds.

(2m) Effect of giving bond. Any bond purportedly given as an official bond by a public officer, of whom an official bond is required, shall be deemed to be an official bond and shall be deemed as to both principal and surety to contain all the conditions and provisions required in sub. (2), regardless of its form or wording, and any provisions restricting liability to less than that provided in sub. (2) shall be void.

(3) Official duties defined. The official duties referred to in subs. (1) and (2) include performance to the best of his or her ability by the officer taking the oath or giving the bond of every official act required, and the nonperformance of every act forbidden, by law to be performed by the officer; also, similar performance and nonperformance of every act required of or forbidden to the officer in any other office which he or she may lawfully hold or exercise by virtue of incumbency of the office named in the official oath or bond. The duties mentioned in any such oath or bond include the faithful performance by all persons appointed or employed by the officer either in his or her principal or subsidiary office, of their respective duties and trusts therein.

(4) Where filed. Official oaths and bonds shall be filed:

(a) In the office of the secretary of state: Of all members and officers of the legislature; of the governor, lieutenant governor and state superintendent; of the justices, reporter and clerk of the supreme court; of the judges of the court of appeals; of the judges and reporters of the circuit courts; of all notaries public; of every officer, except the secretary of state, state treasurer, *district attorney* and attorney general, whose compensation is paid in whole or in part out of the state treasury, including every member or appointee of a board or commis-

sion whose compensation is so paid; and of every deputy or assistant of an officer who files with the secretary of state;

(b) In the office of the governor: Of the secretary of state, state treasurer and attorney general;

(c) In the office of the clerk of the circuit court for any county: Of all court commissioners, of all family court commissioners, of all municipal judges, and of all other judges or judicial officers elected or appointed for that county, or whose jurisdiction is limited thereto;

(d) In the office of the county clerk of any county: Of all county officers elected or appointed in and for such county, other than those enumerated in par. (c), and of all officers whose compensation is paid out of the treasury of such county. The members of the governing board, and the superintendent and other officers of any joint county school, county hospital, county sanatorium, county asylum or other joint county institution shall file in the county in which the buildings of such institutions are located;

(dd) Bonds specified in pars. (c) and (d) and bonds of any county employe required by statute or county ordinance to be bonded shall be approved by the district attorney as to amount, form and execution before the bonds are accepted for filing. The clerk of the circuit court and the county clerk respectively shall notify in writing the county board or chairperson within 5 days after the entry upon the term of office of a judicial or county officer specified in pars. (c) and (d) or after a county employe required to be bonded has begun employment. The notice shall state whether or not the required bond has been furnished and shall be published with the proceedings of the county board.

(e) In the office of any town clerk: Of all officers elected or appointed in and for such town except the town clerk who shall file in the office of the town treasurer;

(f) In the office of any city clerk: Of all officers elected or appointed in and for such city except the city clerk who shall file in the office of the city treasurer;

(g) In the office of any village clerk: Of all officers elected or appointed in and for such village, except the village clerk who shall file in the office of the village treasurer;

(h) The official oath and bond of any officer of a school district or of an incorporated school board shall be filed with the clerk of such school district or the clerk of such incorporated school board.

(j) With the secretary of a vocational, technical and adult education district: Of all members of the district board of such district.

(5) Time of filing. Every public officer required to file an official oath or an official bond shall file the same before entering upon the duties of his office; and when both are required, both shall be filed at the same time.

(6) Continuance of obligation. Every such bond continues in force and is applicable to official conduct during the incumbency of the officer filing the same and until his successor is duly qualified and installed.

(7) Interpretation. This section shall not be construed as requiring any particular officer to furnish or file either an official oath or an official bond. It is applicable to such officers only as are elsewhere in these statutes or by the constitution or by special, private or local law required to furnish such an oath or bond. Provided, however, that whether otherwise required by law or not, an oath of office shall be filed by every member of any board or commission appointed by the governor, and by every administrative officer so appointed, also by every secretary and other chief executive officer appointed by such board or commission.

(8) Premium on bond allowed as expense. The state and any county, town, village, city or school district may pay the cost of any official bond furnished by an officer or employe thereof pursuant to law or any rules or regulations requiring the same if said officer or employe shall furnish a bond with a licensed surety company as surety, said cost not to exceed the current rate of premium per year. The cost of any such bond to the state shall be charged to the proper expense appropriation.

§ 220.18. Bank or corporation notaries; permitted acts.

It shall be lawful for any notary public who is a stockholder, director, officer or employe of a bank or other corporation to take the acknowledgment of any party to any written instrument executed to or by such corporation, or to administer an oath to any other stockholder, director, officer, employe or agent of such corporation, or to protest for nonacceptance or nonpayment bills of exchange, drafts, checks, notes and other negotiable instruments which may be owned or held for collection by such corporation, if such notary is not a party to such instrument, either individually or as a representative of such corporation.

FEES

§ 59.42. Clerk of court; fees; investment of funds.

(1) The clerk of the circuit court shall collect the fees prescribed in ss. 814.60 to 814.63. The clerk may refuse to accept any paper for filing or recording until the fee prescribed in subch. II of ch. 814 or any applicable statute is paid.

(2) Except as provided in sub. (3), the clerk may invest any funds paid into his or her office and which are being held for repayment. The investments shall be made in suitably protected accounts in the manner specified in s. 66.04(2) and all income that may accrue shall be paid into the county general fund.

(3) A judge may direct that sub. (2) does not apply to certain funds paid into the office. The judge's authority applies only to funds relating to cases before his or her court.

§ 887.02. Duty to administer official and election oaths; no fees.

(1) Every person thereto authorized by law shall administer and certify, on demand, any official oath and any oath required on any nomination paper, petition or other instrument used in the nomination or election of any candidate for public office, or in the submission of any question to a vote of the people.

(2) No fee shall be charged by any officer for administering or certifying any official oath, or any oath to any person relative to his right to be registered or to vote.

OFFENSES

§ 943.39. Fraudulent writings.

Whoever, with intent to injure or defraud, does any of the following is guilty of a Class D felony:

* * *

(2) By means of deceit obtains a signature to a writing which is the subject of forgery under s. 943.38(1); or

(3) Makes a false written statement with knowledge that it is false and with intent that it shall ultimately appear to have been signed under oath.

ACKNOWLEDGMENTS

§ 706.06. Authentication.

(1) Any instrument may be acknowledged, or its execution otherwise authenticated by its signators, as provided by the laws of this state; or as provided in this section or s. 706.07.

(2) Any public officer entitled by virtue of his office to administer oaths, and any member in good standing of the state bar of Wisconsin, may authenticate one or more of the signatures on an instrument relating to lands in this state, by indorsing the instrument "Acknowledged", "Authenticated" or "Signatures Guaranteed", or other words to similar effect, adding the date of authentication,

his own signature, and his official or professional title. Such indorsement, unless expressly limited, shall operate as an authentication of all signatures on the instrument; and shall constitute a certification that each authenticated signature is the genuine signature of the person represented; and, as to signatures made in a representative capacity, that the signer purported, and was believed, to be such representative.

(3) Affidavits shall be authenticated by a certificate of due execution of the instrument, executed by a person entitled to administer oaths.

(4) In addition to any criminal penalty or civil remedy otherwise provided by law, knowingly false authentication of an instrument shall subject the authenticator to liability in tort for compensatory and punitive damages caused thereby to any person.

Uniform Law on Notarial Acts

§ 706.07. Uniform law on notarial acts.

(1) **Definitions.** In this section:

(a) "Acknowledgment" means a declaration by a person that the person has executed an instrument for the purposes stated therein and, if the instrument is executed in a representative capacity, that the person signed the instrument with proper authority and executed it as the act of the person or entity represented and identified therein.

(b) "In a representative capacity" means:

1. For and on behalf of a corporation, partnership, trust, or other entity, as an authorized officer, agent, partner, trustee, or other representative;

2. As a public officer, personal representative, guardian, or other representative, in the capacity recited in the instrument;

3. As an attorney in fact for a principal; or

4. In any other capacity as an authorized representative of another.

(c) "Notarial act" means any act that a notary public of this state is authorized to perform, and includes taking the acknowledgment, administering an oath or affirmation, taking a verification upon oath or affirmation, witnessing or attesting a signature, certifying or attesting a copy, and noting a protest of a negotiable instrument.

(d) "Notarial officer" means a notary public or other officer authorized to perform notarial acts.

(e) "Verification upon oath or affirmation" means a declaration that a statement is true made by a person upon oath or affirmation.

(2) **Notarial acts.** (a) In taking an acknowledgment, the notarial officer must determine, either from personal knowledge or from satisfactory evidence, that the person appearing before the officer and making the acknowledgment is the person whose true signature is on the instrument.

(b) In taking a verification upon oath or affirma-

tion, the notarial officer must determine, either from personal knowledge or from satisfactory evidence, that the person appearing before the officer and making the verification is the person whose true signature is on the statement verified.

(c) In witnessing or attesting a signature, the notarial officer must determine, either from personal knowledge or from satisfactory evidence, that the signature is that of the person appearing before the officer and named therein.

(d) In certifying or attesting a copy of a document or other item, the notarial officer must determine that the proffered copy is a full, true, and accurate transcription or reproduction of that which was copied.

(e) In making or noting a protest of a negotiable instrument, the notarial officer must determine the matters set forth in s. 403.509.

(f) A notarial officer has satisfactory evidence that a person is the person whose true signature is on a document if that person:

1. Is personally known to the notarial officer;

2. Is identified upon the oath or affirmation of a credible witness personally known to the notarial officer; or

3. Is identified on the basis of identification documents.

(3) **Notarial acts in this state.** (a) A notarial act may be performed within this state by the following persons of this state:

1. A notary public;

2. A judge, clerk or deputy clerk of a court of record;

3. A court commissioner;

4. A register of deeds or deputy register of deeds;

5. A municipal judge; or

6. A county clerk or deputy county clerk.

(b) Notarial acts performed within this state under federal authority as provided in sub. (5) have the same effect as if performed by a notarial officer of this state.

(c) The signature and title of a person performing a notarial act are prima facie evidence that the signature is genuine and that the person holds the designated title.

(4) **Notarial acts in other jurisdictions of the United States.** (a) A notarial act has the same effect under the law of this state as if performed by a notarial officer of this sate, if performed in another state, commonwealth, territory, district, or possession of the United States by any of the following persons:

1. A notary public of that jurisdiction;

2. A judge, clerk, or deputy clerk of a court of that jurisdiction; or

3. Any other person authorized by the law of that jurisdiction to perform notarial acts.

(b) Notarial acts performed in other jurisdictions of the United States under federal authority as provided in sub. (5) have the same effect as if performed by a notarial officer of this state.

(c) The signature and title of a person performing a notarial act are prima facie evidence that the signature is genuine and that the person holds the designated title.

(d) The signature and indicated title of an officer listed in par. (a) 1 or 2 conclusively establish the authority of a holder of that title to perform a notarial act.

(5) **Notarial acts under federal authority.** (a) A notarial act has the same effect under the law of this state as if performed by a notarial officer of this state if performed anywhere by any of the following persons under authority granted by the law of the United States:

1. A judge, clerk, or deputy clerk of a court;

2. A commissioned officer on active duty in the military service of the United States;

3. An officer of the foreign service or consular officer of the United States; or

4. Any other person authorized by federal law to perform notarial acts.

(b) The signature and title of a person performing a notarial act are prima facie evidence that the signature is genuine and that the person holds the designated title.

(c) The signature and indicated title of an officer listed in par. (a) 1, 2 or 3 conclusively establish the authority of a holder of that title to perform a notarial act.

(6) **Foreign notarial acts.** (a) A notarial act has the same effect under the law of this state as if performed by a notarial officer of this state if performed within the jurisdiction of and under authority of a foreign nation or its constituent units or a multinational or international organization by any of the following persons:

1. A notary public or notary;

2. A judge, clerk, or deputy clerk of a court of record; or

3. Any other person authorized by the law of that jurisdiction to perform notarial acts.

(b) An "apostille" in the form prescribed by the Hague convention of October 5, 1961, conclusively establishes that the signature of the notarial officer is genuine and that the officer holds the indicated office.

(c) A certificate by a foreign service or consular officer of the United States stationed in the nation under the jurisdiction of which the notarial act was performed, or a certificate by a foreign service or consular officer of that nation stationed in the United States, conclusively establishes any matter relating to the authenticity or validity of the notarial act set forth in the certificate.

(d) An official stamp or seal of the person performing the notarial act is prima facie evidence that the signature is genuine and that the person holds the indicated title.

(e) An official stamp or seal of an officer listed in par. (a) 1 or 2 is prima facie evidence that a person with the indicated title has authority to perform notarial acts.

(f) If the title of office and indication of authority to perform notarial acts appears either in a digest of foreign law or in a list customarily used as a source for that information, the authority of an officer with that title to perform notarial acts is conclusively established.

(7) **Certificate of notarial acts.** (a) A notarial act must be evidenced by a certificate signed and dated by a notarial officer. The certificate must include identification of the jurisdiction in which the notarial act is performed and the title of the office of the notarial officer and may include the official stamp or seal of office. If the officer is a notary public, the certificate must also indicate the date of expiration, if any, of the commission of office, but omission of that information may subsequently be corrected. If the officer is a commissioned officer on active duty in the military service of the United States, it must also include the officer's rank.

(b) A certificate of a notarial act is sufficient if it meets the requirements of par. (a) and it:

1. Is in the short form set forth in sub. (8);

2. Is in a form otherwise prescribed by the law of this state;

3. Is in a form prescribed by the laws or regulations applicable in the place in which the notarial act was performed; or

4. Sets forth the actions of the notarial officer and those are sufficient to meet the requirements of the designated notarial act.

(c) By executing a certificate of a notarial act, the notarial officer certifies that the officer has made the determination required by sub. (2).

(8) **Short forms.** The following short form certificates of notarial acts are sufficient for the purposes indicated, if completed with the information required by sub. (7)(a):

(a) For an acknowledgment in an individual capacity:

State of . . . .

County of . . . .

This instrument was acknowledged before me on (date) by (name(s) of person(s)).

. . . .

(Signature of notarial officer)

(Seal, if any)

. . . .

Title (and Rank)

[My commission expires: . . . .]

(b) For an acknowledgment in a representative capacity:

State of . . . .

County of . . . .

This instrument was acknowledged before me on (date) by (name(s) of person(s)) as (type of authority, e.g., officer, trustee, etc.) of (name of party on behalf of whom instrument was executed).

....
(Signature of notarial officer)
(Seal, if any)

....
Title (and Rank)
[My commission expires: ....]

(c) For a verification upon oath or affirmation:
State of . . . .
County of . . . .

Signed and sworn to (or affirmed) before me on (date) by (name(s) of person(s) making statement).

....
(Signature of notarial officer)
(Seal, if any)

....
Title (and Rank)
[My commission expires: ....]

(d) For witnessing or attesting a signature:
State of . . . .
County of . . . .

Signed or attested before me on (date) by (name(s) of person(s)).

....
(Signature of notarial officer)
(Seal, if any)

....
Title (and Rank)
[My commission expires: ....]

(e) For attestation of a copy of a document:
State of . . . .
County of . . . .

I certify that this is a true and correct copy of a document in the possession of . . . .
Dated: . . . .

....
(Signature of notarial officer)
(Seal, if any)

....
Title (and Rank)
[My commission expires: ....]

(9) Notarial acts affected by this section. This section applies to notarial acts performed on or after November 1, 1984.

(10) Uniformity of application and construction. This section shall be applied and construed to effectuate its general purpose to make uniform the law with respect to the subject of this section among states enacting it.

(11) Short title. This section may be cited as the uniform law on notarial acts.

DEPOSITIONS

§ 804.03. Persons before whom depositions may be taken.

(1) Within the United States. Within the United States or within a territory or insular possession subject to the dominion of the United States, depositions shall be taken before an officer authorized to administer oaths by the laws of the United States or of this state or of the place where the examination is held, or before a person appointed by the court in which the action is pending. A person so appointed has power to administer oaths and take testimony.

(2) In foreign countries. In a foreign country, depositions may be taken (a) on notice before a person authorized to administer oaths in the place in which the examination is held, either by the law thereof or by the law of the United States, or (b) before a person commissioned by the court, and a person so commissioned shall have the power by virtue of the commission to administer any necessary oath and take testimony, or (c) pursuant to a letter rogatory. A commission or a letter rogatory shall be issued on motion and notice and on terms that are just and appropriate. It is not requisite to the issuance of a commission or a letter rogatory that the taking of the deposition in any other manner is impracticable or inconvenient; and both a commission and a letter rogatory may be issued in proper cases. A notice or commission may designate the person before whom the deposition is to be taken either by name or descriptive title. A letter rogatory may be addressed "To the Appropriate Authority in (here name the country)". Evidence obtained in response to a letter rogatory need not be excluded merely for the reason that it is not a verbatim transcript or that the testimony was not taken under oath or for any similar departure from the requirements for depositions taken within the United States under this chapter.

(3) Disqualification for interest. No deposition shall be taken before a person who is a relative or employe or attorney or counsel of any of the parties, or is a relative or employe of such attorney or counsel, or is financially interested in the action.

§ 887.01. Oaths, who may administer.

(1) Within the state. An oath or affidavit required or authorized by law, except oaths to jurors and witnesses on a trial and such other oaths as are required by law to be taken before particular officers, may be taken before any judge, court commissioner, resident U.S. commissioner who has complied with s. 706.07, clerk, deputy clerk or calendar clerk of a court of record, court reporter, notary public, town clerk, village clerk, city clerk, municipal judge, county clerk or the clerk's deputy within the territory in which the officer is authorized to act, school district clerk with respect to any oath required by the elections laws; and, when certified by the officer to have been taken before him or her, may be read and used in any court and before any officer, board or commission. Oaths may be administered by any person mentioned in s. 885.01(3) and (4) to any witness examined before him or her.

(2) Without the state. Any oath or affidavit required or authorized by law may be taken in any other state, territory or district of the United States before any judge or commissioner of a court of record, master in chancery, notary public, justice of the peace or other officer authorized by the laws thereof to administer oaths, and if the oath or affidavit is properly certified by any such officer to have been taken before the officer, and has attached thereto a certificate of the clerk of a court of record of the county or district within which the oath or affidavit was taken, under the seal of his or her office, that the person whose name is subscribed to the certificate of due execution of the instrument was, at the date thereof, the officer as is therein represented to be, was empowered by law as such officer to administer the oath or affidavit, and that he or she believes the name so subscribed is the signature of the officer, the oath or affidavit may be read or used in any court within this state and before any officer, board or commission authorized to use or consider the oath or affidavit. Whenever any such oath or affidavit is certified by any notary public or clerk of a court of record and an impression of his or her official seal is thereto affixed no further attestation shall be necessary.

(3) Officer in armed forces. In every instance where an officer in the armed forces is authorized by s. 706.07 (5) to take an acknowledgment, he may administer an oath.

§ **887.03.** Oath, how taken.

Any oath or affidavit required or authorized by law may be taken in any of the usual forms, and every person swearing, affirming or declaring in any such form shall be deemed to have been lawfully sworn.

§ **887.04.** Affirmations.

(1) Every person who shall declare that he has conscientious scruples against taking the oath, or swearing in the usual form, shall make his solemn declaration or affirmation, which may be in the following form: Do you solemnly, sincerely and truly declare and affirm that the testimony you shall give in [here indicate the action, proceeding or matter on trial or being inquired into] shall be the truth, the whole truth and nothing but the truth; and this you do under the pains and penalties of perjury.

(2) The assent to the affirmation by the person making it may be manifested by the uplifted hand.

§ **887.23.** Deposition relative to public institutions.

(1) Who may require. The department of health and social services, the state superintendent or the board of regents of the university of Wisconsin system may order the deposition of any witness to be taken concerning any institution under his, her or its government or superintendence, or concerning the conduct of any officer or agent thereof, or concerning any matter relating to the interests thereof. Upon presentation of a certified copy of such order to any municipal judge, notary public or court commissioner, the officer shall take the desired deposition in the manner provided for taking depositions to be used in actions. When any officer or agent of any institution is concerned and will be affected by the testimony, 2 days' written notice of the time and place of taking the deposition shall be given him or her. Any party interested may appear in person or by counsel and examine the witness touching the matters mentioned in the order. The deposition, duly certified, shall be delivered to the authority which ordered it.

§ **887.26.** Depositions without this state by commission.

* * *

(6) Duty of commissioner. (a) The commissioner first named shall fix the time and place for executing the commission and give the other commissioner one day's notice if residing in the same place, and when not, one day's notice in addition for every 30 miles of distance between the place of residence and the place fixed for executing the commission. If the notice be by mail double time shall be allowed; but notice may be waived in writing or by appearance at the execution of the commission. If there be 2 commissioners the commission shall be executed in the county where they reside, unless they agree upon another. The commissioner first named shall have charge of and return the deposition, which return shall be in the form and manner directed by the commission or as provided by s. 804.05(7). If either commissioner shall not attend at the time and place so fixed, the other may execute the commission with like effect as if both were present, but such commissioner must certify in the return that the other had due notice but failed to attend.

* * *

(7) Fees. The persons who take depositions and the witness shall be entitled to the fees allowed court commissioners under s. 814.68(1) and witnesses for similar service by the law of this state, or such as may be prescribed by the law of the state or country where taken.

* * *

§ **137.02.** Commissioners of deeds.

(1) The governor shall have power to appoint one or more commissioners in any of the United States, or of the territories belonging to the United States and in foreign countries, who shall hold his office for the term of four years unless sooner removed. Every such commissioner shall take the official oath before a judge or clerk of one of the courts of record of the state or territory or country in which he shall reside, and file the same, with an impression of his seal of office and a statement of his post-office address, in the office of the secretary of state, and shall at the same time pay into the treasury the sum of five dollars; and thereupon his commission shall issue.

(2) Such commissioner shall have authority to take the acknowledgment and proof of the execution of deeds, conveyances and leases of any lands lying in this state, or written instruments relating thereto, or of any contract or any other writing, sealed or unsealed, to be used or recorded in this state; to administer oaths required to be used in this state; to take and certify depositions to be used in the courts of this state, either under a commission, by consent of parties or on notice to the opposite party; and all such acts done pursuant to the laws of this state and certified under his hand and seal of office shall be as valid as if done by a proper officer of this state.

§ **895.20.** Legal holidays.

January 1, January 15, the 3rd Monday in February (which shall be the day of celebration for February 12 and 22), the last Monday in May (which shall be the day of celebration for May 30), July 4, the 1st Monday in September which shall be known as Labor day, the 2nd Monday in October, November 11, the 4th Thursday in November (which shall be the day of celebration for Thanksgiving), December 25, the day of holding the September primary election, and the day of holding the general election in November are legal holidays. On Good Friday the period from 11 a.m. to 3 p.m. shall uniformly be observed for the purpose of worship. In every 1st class city the day of holding any municipal election is a legal holiday, and in every such city the afternoon of each day upon which a primary election is held for the nomination of candidates for city offices is a half holiday and in counties having a population of 500,000 or more the county board may by ordinance provide that all county employes shall have a half holiday on the day of such primary election and a holiday on the day of such municipal election, and that employes whose duties require that they work on such days be given equivalent time off on other days. Whenever any of said days falls on Sunday, the succeeding Monday shall be the legal holiday.

WYOMING

NOTARIES PUBLIC

[WYO. STAT. ANN.]

§ 32-1-101. Qualifications; application; term.

(a) The secretary of state shall commission as a notary any qualified person who submits an application in a form prescribed by the secretary of state.

(b) To be qualified for a notarial commission a person shall:

(i) Be at least nineteen (19) years of age;

(ii) Be a resident of the state of Wyoming and the county from which making application;

(iii) Be able to read and write the English language; and

(iv) Submit an application certifying compliance with the requirements of this subsection, accompanied by a fee of thirty dollars ($30.00).

(c) A person commissioned as a notary by the secretary of state may perform notarial acts in any part of the state for a term of four (4) years.

(d) A person holding a notarial commission who changes residence to a different county shall procure a new notary commission for the new county of residence.

§ 32-1-102. Name changes.

(a) When a notary changes surnames, the notary may continue to use the notarial commission and seal issued to the notary provided:

(i) When a notary marries or changes surnames, the notary shall file a certified copy of the certificate of marriage or order of name change in the office of the county clerk of the county where the notary resides and send a certified copy of the marriage certificate or order of name change and a three dollar ($3.00) filing fee to the secretary of state. The surname of the notary's spouse or the notary's new surname may then be added after the notary's name as it appears on the notary's commission;

(ii) When a notary divorces and the notary's previous name is restored by the court, the notary shall file a certified copy of the divorce decree in the office of the county clerk of the county where the notary resides and send a certified copy of the notary's divorce decree and a three dollar ($3.00) filing fee to the secretary of state. The notary's restored surname may then be added after the notary's name as it appears on the notary's commission.

(b) Instead of adopting the surname of the notary's spouse, a notary may continue to use or be commissioned as a notary by the name by which the notary is generally known.

§ 32-1-103. Transmittal of notarial commission to county clerks.

The secretary of state shall transmit each notarial commission to the office of the county clerk of the county in which the applicant resides where the commission shall be recorded.

§ 32-1-104. Bond and oath; notary commission forfeited upon failure to obtain another bond.

(a) No notarial commission becomes effective until the applicant files with the county clerk within sixty (60) days after issuance of the commission an oath and bond in the amount of five hundred dollars ($500.00) conditioned on the faithful performance of the duties of the office. The applicant shall swear or affirm under oath to support the constitution of the United States and the constitution of Wyoming and to faithfully and impartially discharge and perform all the duties of a notary. The bond shall be executed by the applicant and two (2) sureties, to be approved by the county clerk, or by a surety company licensed in this state. Upon the filing of the oath and bond the county clerk shall transmit the notarial commission to the notary and the county clerk shall send a written notice of qualification to the secretary of state.

(b) Upon cancellation of a notarial bond by a surety as a result of claims paid by the surety to persons injured as a result of the bonded notary's negligence or misconduct, the secretary of state shall notify the notary by certified mail return receipt requested that the notary's commission shall be revoked unless within twenty (20) days after the notary receives the notice the notary files proof with the secretary of state that the notary has secured another bond in the full amount of five hundred dollars ($500.00).

§ 32-1-105. Powers and jurisdiction.

(a) Every notary may administer oaths and affirmations, take depositions, receive acknowledgments of deeds, mortgages and powers of attorney and other instruments in writing.

(b) A notary serves as an impartial witness to the signing of a document, establishes the identity of the person signing the document and attests that the signature on the document was made in his presence. If the person did not appear before the notary and sign the document in the notary's presence, the notary may acknowledge the person's signature when the person appears before the notary, presents proper identification, acknowledges the signature is that of the person and the document was voluntarily executed by the person.

§ 32-1-106. Official seal generally.

(a) Each notary public before entering upon the duties of his office, shall provide himself with an official seal with which he shall authenticate all his official acts, which seal shall clearly show, when embossed, stamped, impressed or affixed to a document, his name, the words "notary public," the name of the county wherein he resides, and the word "Wyoming," and the seal of a notary public shall not be levied upon or sold. If the notary public changes his county of residence to a different county than that shown on the seal, he shall have the seal altered to indicate such change.

(b) The seal of every notary public may be affixed by a seal press or stamp that will print or emboss a seal which legibly reproduces under the photographic methods the name of the notary, the words "notary public," the name of the county in which he resides and the word "Wyoming." The seal may be circular not over two (2) inches in diameter or may be a rectangular form of not more than three-fourths of an inch in width by two and one-half (2 1/2) inches in length, with a serrated or milled edged border, and shall contain the information required by this section.

§ 32-1-107. Notary's certificate as presumptive evidence.

In all the courts within this state the certificate of a notary public over his hand and official seal, shall be received as presumptive evidence of the facts contained in such certificate; provided, that any person interested as a party to a suit may contradict, by other evidence the certificate of a notary public.

§ 32-1-108. Action on notarial bond.

If any person shall be damaged or injured by the

unlawful act, negligence or misconduct of any notary public, the person damaged or injured may maintain a civil action on the bond of such notary public against such notary public, and his sureties; and the recovery in such action shall not be a bar to any future action for other cause, to the full amount of the bond.

§ 32-1-109. Notary acting after term expires.

Whoever, having been appointed a notary public, does or performs any act as a notary public, after the expiration of his term of office, knowing that such term of office has expired, shall be fined not more than five hundred dollars ($500.00) nor less than twenty-five dollars ($25.00).

§ 32-1-110. Failure of county clerk to perform duties by chapter.

If any register of deeds shall fail or neglect to fulfill and perform any act imposed on him by this chapter, such person shall be liable in the penal sum of two hundred dollars ($200.00) recovered and applied as provided in the preceding section.

§ 32-1-111. When justice may protest paper in lieu of notary.

When the holder of any instrument desires it to be protested, and no notary public can be found, it shall be lawful for any justice of the peace of the county wherein said instrument is required to be protested, to perform the services herein required to be performed by notaries public, and to be entitled to the same fees as are hereinafter provided for notaries public for similar services.

§ 32-1-112. Fees.

A notary is entitled to receive a fee of two dollars ($2.00) for each oath or affirmation administered or for each signature notarized.

§ 32-1-113. Notary's interest in bank, etc., not disqualifying.

It shall be lawful for any notary public who is a stockholder, director, officer or employee of a bank or other corporation to take the acknowledgment of any party to any written instrument executed to or by said corporation, or to administer an oath to any other stockholder, director, officer, employee or agent of such corporation, or to protest for non-acceptance, or nonpayment, bills of exchange, drafts, checks, notes, and other negotiable instruments which may be owned or held for collection by any such bank or other corporation.

FEES

[Wyo. Const.]

Art. 14, § 2. Fees.

The legislature shall provide by law the fees which may be demanded by justices of the peace and constables in precincts having less than fifteen hundred population, and of court commissioners, boards of arbitration and notaries public, which fees the said officer shall accept as their full compensation. * * *

OFFENSES

[Wyo. Stat. Ann.]

§ 6-3-407. Obtaining property by false pretenses; penalties.

(a) A person who knowingly obtains property from another person by false pretenses with intent to defraud the person is guilty of:

(i) A felony punishable by imprisonment for not more than ten (10) years, a fine of not more than ten thousand dollars ($10,000.00), or both, if the value of the property is five hundred dollars ($500.00) or more; or

(ii) Repealed by Laws 1984, ch. 44, § 3.

(iii) A misdemeanor punishable by imprisonment for not more than six (6) months, a fine of not more than seven hundred fifty dollars ($750.00), or both, if the value of the property is less than five hundred dollars ($500.00).

§ 6-3-604. Fraud against testamentary instruments and government records; penalties; "government record" defined.

(a) A person is guilty of a felony punishable by imprisonment for nor more than ten (10) years, a fine of not more than ten thousand dollars ($10,000.00), or both, if he fraudulently steals, alters, defaces, destroys or secretes:

(i) An executed will, codicil or other testamentary instrument; or

(ii) A part or all of a government record.

(b) As used in this section, "government record" means a record, record book, docket or journal which is authorized by law or belongs or pertains to, or is filed with, a court of record, a county court, a justice of the peace or any governmental office of officer.

§ 6-5-108. Issuing false certificate; penalties.

(a) A public servant commits a felony punishable by imprisonment for not more than ten (10) years, a fine of not more than ten thousand dollars ($10,000.00), or both, if he makes and issues an official certificate or other official written instrument which he is authorized to make and issue containing a statement which he knows to be false with intent to obtain a benefit or maliciously to cause harm to another.

(b) A public servant commits a misdemeanor punishable by imprisonment for not more than one (1) year, a fine of not more than one thousand dollars ($1,000.00), or both, if he makes and issues an official certificate or other official written instrument which he is authorized to make and issue containing a statement which he knows to be false.

§ 6-5-114. Notaries public; issuance of certificate without proper acknowledgment; penalties.

A notary public commits a misdemeanor punishable by imprisonment for not more than six (6) months, a fine of not more than seven hundred fifty dollars ($750.00), or both, if he signs and affixes his seal to a certificate of acknowledgment when the party executing the instrument has not first acknowledged the execution of the instrument before the notary public, if by law the instrument is required to be recorded or filed and cannot be filed without a certificate of acknowledgment signed and sealed by a notary public.

§ 6-5-301. Perjury in judicial, legislative or administrative proceedings; penalties.

(a) A person commits perjury if, while under a lawfully administered oath or affirmation, he knowingly testifies falsely or makes a false affidavit, certificate, declaration, deposition or statement, in a judicial, legislative or administrative proceeding in which an oath or affirmation may be required by law, touching a matter material to a point in question.

(b) Perjury is a felony punishable by imprisonment for not more than five (5) years, a fine of not more than five thousand dollars ($5,000.00), or both.

§ 6-5-303. False swearing in nonjudicial or nonadministrative proceeding; false claims or vouchers; penalties.

(a) A person commits a felony punishable by imprisonment for not more than two (2) years, a fine of not more than two thousand dollars ($2,000.00), or both, if, while under a lawfully administered oath or affirmation in a matter where an oath is authorized by law, he knowingly makes a false cer-

tificate, affidavit, acknowledgment, declaration or statement other than in a judicial or administrative proceeding.

(b) A person is guilty of a felony punishable by imprisonment for not more than two (2) years, a fine of not more than two thousand dollars ($2,000.00), or both, if he knowingly submits a false claim or voucher with intent to defraud.

OATHS

§ 1-2-102. Officers authorized to administer.

(a) The following officers are authorized to administer oaths:

* * *

(vii) Notaries public;

* * *

ACKNOWLEDGMENTS

§ 19-1-103. Acknowledgment of instrument by members of armed forces and their dependents before commissioned officer; form of certificate.

In addition to the acknowledgment of instruments in the manner and form otherwise authorized by law, persons serving with the armed forces of the United States or their dependents, wherever located, may acknowledge the instruments before any commissioned officer in active service of the armed forces of the United States with the rank of second lieutenant or higher in the army, air force or marine corps, or ensign or higher in the navy or coast guard. The instrument is not invalid for failure to state therein the place of execution or acknowledgment. No authentication of the officer's certificate of acknowledgment is required, but the officer taking the acknowledgment shall endorse thereon or attach thereto a certificate substantially in the following form:

On this . . . . day of . . ., 19. ., before me, ..., the undersigned officer, personally appeared . . . ., Serial No. (If any) . . . ., known to me (or satisfactorily proven) to be serving with the armed forces of the United States (A dependent of . . . ., Serial No. (If any) . . . ., a person serving with the armed forces of the United States) and to be the person whose name is subscribed to the within instrument and acknowledged that . . . . he . . . . executed the same for the purposes therein contained, and the undersigned does further certify that he is, at the date of this certificate, a commissioned officer of the rank stated below and is in the active service of the armed forces of the United States.

> . . . . (Signature of the officer)
> . . . . (Rank and Serial No. of officer)
> and command to which attached.

§ 34-1-113. Acknowledgment of conveyances; generally.

Execution of deeds, mortgages or other conveyances of lands, or any interest in lands, shall be acknowledged by the party or parties executing same, before any judge or clerk of a court of record, or before any United States magistrate appointed under and by authority of the laws of the United States, or any county clerk, justice of the peace, district court commissioner, notary public, or other officer authorized under the laws of the State of Wyoming to take such acknowledgments, and the officer taking such acknowledgment shall endorse thereon a certificate of the acknowledgment thereof, and the true date of making the same, under his hand and seal of office, if there be one.

§ 34-1-114. Same—notary, etc., to state date of expiration of term of office, etc.

Every notary public, justice of the peace, and commissioner of deeds for Wyoming, who takes an acknowledgment to any written instrument to be recorded in any public office in Wyoming shall add to his certificate the date when commission or term of office expires.

§ 34-1-115. Same—execution out of state.

Any deed, mortgage, conveyance, power of attorney or instrument in writing requiring an acknowledgment executed outside of this state, may be acknowledged before any officer authorized by law to take acknowledgments at the place where such acknowledgment is taken. Whenever the officer taking such acknowledgment has no seal the certificate of such officer shall have attached thereto the certificate of the clerk of the court of record, or a county clerk, of the same place, having a seal, certifying that the officer taking the acknowledgment is authorized to take the same and that he believes that the signature appended to the acknowledgment is genuine. Each instrument of writing as aforesaid executed and acknowledged as aforesaid shall be as valid and have the same force and effect as if executed in Wyoming according to the provisions of [§ 34-1-113].

§ 34-1-116. Effect of conveyance executed in another state.

Any deed, mortgage or conveyance executed in any other state, territory, district or country, which shall be executed according to the laws of this state, and acknowledged before a clerk of a court of record, county clerk, or a commissioner appointed as aforesaid, shall have the same effect as if executed and acknowledged within this state.

§ 34-1-117. Execution, etc., in foreign countries; powers of attorney.

If any deeds, mortgages or conveyances of lands, or of any interest in lands, be executed in any foreign country, government, kingdom or empire, such deed, mortgage, or conveyance of land may be executed according to the laws of this state, and may be acknowledged before a consul general, consul or vice-consul of the United States; and when so acknowledged the officer taking the acknowledgment shall certify the same over his hand and official seal or the seal of the consulate to which he is attached, if there be any such seal; and in case he has no official seal, and there be no seal of his consulate, that fact shall be stated in the certificate; and no other or further authentication shall be required to entitle such instrument to record in this state. This section shall also apply to powers of attorney executed in any such foreign country, government, kingdom or empire.

§ 34-1-118. Where conveyance, etc., to be recorded.

A certificate of the acknowledgment of any deed, mortgage or conveyance, or proof of the execution thereof, before a court of record or a justice of the peace, signed by the clerk of such court (or by the justice), before whom the same was taken, as provided in this act, and in the cases where the same is necessary, the certificate required by [§ 34-1-115], shall entitle such deed, mortgage or conveyance, certificate or certificates aforesaid, to be recorded in the office of the register of deeds [county clerk] in the county where the land lies.

Wyoming Acknowledgment Act

§ 34-2-114. Acknowledgment Act—citation of act.

This act [§§ 34-2-114 to 34-2-118] shall be known as the "Wyoming Acknowledgment Act."

§ 34-2-115. Same; form of acknowledgment.

A certificate of acknowledgment substantially in the following form shall be sufficient for all instruments conveying, mortgaging or otherwise disposing of or encumbering real estate, including homestead property, and shall be sufficient for all other instruments affecting title to real estate and all other instruments required by the laws of this state to be acknowledged:

State of _____

　　　　　　　　ss.

County of _____

The foregoing instrument was acknowledged before me by _____, _____, this _____ day of _____, 19__.

Witness my hand and official seal.

_____

Title of officer

My Commission Expires: _____

§ 34-2-116. Same—requirements for implied acknowledgment.

Every certificate of acknowledgment substantially in the form provided for in [§ 34-2-115] shall for all purposes be deemed to be a certification by the officer making the certificate that

(a) If the instrument to which the same is affixed was executed by natural persons acting in their own right, that such person or persons personally appeared before such officer, were known to him to be the person or persons described in and who executed such instrument, and that such person or persons acknowledged that the same was executed and acknowledged freely and voluntarily.

(b) If the instrument to which the certificate is affixed was executed by an attorney-in-fact for a natural person: that such attorney personally appeared before such officer, was known by such officer to be the party who executed such instrument on behalf of such natural person, and that such attorney acknowledged that such instrument was executed and acknowledged as the free and voluntary act of such natural person.

(c) If the instrument to which the certificate is affixed was executed by a corporation or a joint-stock association: that the president or other official who signed such instrument on behalf of such corporation or association appeared before and was personally known to the officer making the certificate, and was by him duly sworn and upon oath represented that he was the president or other officer or agent of such corporation or association, that the seal affixed to the instrument is the corporate seal of such corporation or association, that the instrument was signed and sealed on behalf of such corporation or association by the authority of the board of directors or trustees thereof, and that the officer who executed such instrument on behalf of the corporation or association acknowledged said instrument to be the free act and deed of the corporation or association. If such corporation or association has no corporate seal a recital to that effect shall be inserted at the end of the certificate by the officer making the same.

§ 34-2-117. Same—acknowledgment of real estate transactions prior to January 1, 1966.

[Omitted.]

§ 34-2-118. Same—out-of-state transactions.

Any instrument conveying, mortgaging, or otherwise disposing of or encumbering real estate, excluding, however, homestead property, and any other instrument affecting title to real estate, and any other instrument required by the laws of this state to be acknowledged, which, prior to or after the effective date of this act [§§ 34-2-114 to 34-2-118], shall have been acknowledged out of this state before an officer empowered to take acknowledgments by the laws of the state, territory, or foreign country where the certificate of acknowledgment was made, if the form of such certificate of acknowledgment be in substantial compliance with the laws of the state, territory, or foreign country where taken or with the requirements of the laws of this state, shall for all purposes be conclusively deemed and regarded to be properly acknowledged.

DEPOSITIONS

[WYO. R. CIV. P.]

RULE 28. Persons before whom depositions may be taken.

(a) *Within the United States.* Within the United States or within a territory or insular possession subject to the jurisdiction of the United States, depositions shall be taken before an officer authorized to administer oaths by the laws of this state or of the United States or of the place where the examination is held, or before a person appointed by the court in which the action is pending. A person so appointed has power to administer oaths and take testimony. The term "officer" as used in Rules 30, 31 and 32 includes a person appointed by the court or designated by the parties under Rule 29.

(b) *In Foreign Countries.* In a foreign country, depositions may be taken (1) on notice before a person authorized to administer oaths in the place in which the examination is held, either by the law thereof or by the law of the United States, or (2) before a person commissioned by the court, and a person so commissioned shall have the power by virtue of his commission to administer any necessary oath and take testimony, or (3) pursuant to a letter rogatory. A commission or a letter rogatory shall be issued on application and notice and on terms that are just and appropriate. It is not requisite to the issuance of a commission or a letter rogatory that the taking of the deposition in any other manner is impractical or inconvenient; and both a commission and a letter rogatory may be issued in proper cases. A notice or commission may designate the person before whom the deposition is to be taken either by name or descriptive title. A letter rogatory may be addressed "To the Appropriate Authority in (here name the country)." Evidence obtained in response to a letter rogatory need not be excluded merely for the reason that it is not a verbatim transcript or that the testimony was not taken under oath or for any similar departure from the requirements for depositions taken within the United States under these rules.

(c) *Disqualification for Interest.* No deposition shall be taken before a person who is a relative, employee, attorney or counsel of any of the parties, or is financially interested in the action.

[WYO. R. CRIM. P.]

RULE 17. Depositions.

(a) *When Taken.* If it appears that a prospective witness may be unable to attend or prevented from attending a trial or hearing, that his testimony is material and that it is necessary to take his deposition in order to prevent a failure of justice, the court at any time after the filing of an indictment or information may upon motion of any party and notice to the other parties order that his testimony be taken by deposition and that any designated books, papers or documents or tangible objects, not privileged, be produced at the same time and place. If a witness is committed for failure to give bail to appear to testify at a trial or hearing, the court on written motion of the witness and upon notice to the parties may direct his deposition be taken. After the deposition has been subscribed, the court may discharge the witness.

(b) *Notice of Taking.* The party at whose instance the deposition is to be taken shall give to every other party reasonable written notice of the time and place for taking the deposition. The notice shall state the name and address of each person to be examined. On motion of a party upon whom the notice is served, and for cause shown on notice

and hearing, the court may extend or shorten the time for taking the deposition.

(c) *Defendant's Counsel and Payment of Expenses.* [Omitted.]

(d) *How Taken.* A deposition shall be taken in the manner provided in civil actions. The court at the request of a defendant may direct that a deposition be taken on written interrogatories in the manner provided in civil actions.

(e) *Use.* [Omitted.]

(f) *Objections to Admissibility.* Objections to receiving in evidence the deposition or part thereof may be made as provided in civil actions.

LEGAL HOLIDAYS

[WYO. STAT. ANN.]

§ 8-4-101. Legal holidays; dismissal of schools.

(a) The following days are legal holidays in and for the state of Wyoming:

(i) New Year's Day, January 1;

(ii) Washington's and Lincoln's birthdays, to be observed on the third Monday in February;

(iii) Memorial Day, to be observed on the last Monday in May;

(iv) Independence Day, July 4;

(v) Labor Day, to be observed on the first Monday in September;

(vi) Repealed by Laws 1990, ch. 21, § 2.

(vii) Veterans Day, November 11;

(viii) Thanksgiving Day, to be observed on the fourth Thursday in November;

(ix) Christmas Day, December 25;

(x) Repealed by Laws 1983, ch. 180, § 1.

(xi) Upon declaration by the governor of this state, any date appointed or declared by the president of the United States as an occasion of national mourning, rejoicing or observance of national emergency;

(xii) Martin Luther King, Jr., Wyoming Equality Day, to be observed on the third Monday in January.

(b) If New Year's Day, Independence Day, Christmas Day or Veterans Day fall upon a Sunday, the Monday following is a legal holiday.

(c) On Washington's and Lincoln's birthdays, Veterans Day, Martin Luther King, Jr., Wyoming Equality Day and all days upon which general elections are held, the public schools of any district shall not be dismissed except by order of the board of trustees of the district, but proper exercises may be held in the schools on these days to emphasize their significance and importance.

UNITED STATES

NOTARIES PUBLIC

5 U.S.C. § 2903. Oath; authority to administer.

* * *

(c) An oath authorized or required under the laws of the United States may be administered by—

(1) the Vice President; or

(2) an individual authorized by local law to administer oaths in the State, District, or territory or possession of the United States where the oath is administered.

10 U.S.C. § 936. Art. 136. Authority to administer oaths and to act as notary.

(a) The following persons on active duty or performing inactive-duty training may administer oaths for the purposes of military administration, including military justice, and have the general powers of a notary public and of a consul of the United States, in the performance of all notarial acts to be executed by members of any of the armed forces, wherever they may be, by persons serving with, employed by, or accompanying the armed forces outside the United States and outside Puerto Rico, Guam, and the Virgin Islands, and by other persons subject to this chapter [10 U.S.C. §§ 801 et seq.] outside of the United States:

(1) All judge advocates.

(2) All summary courts-martial.

(3) All adjutants, assistant adjutants, acting adjutants, and personnel adjutants.

(4) All commanding officers of the Navy, Marine Corps, and Coast Guard.

(5) All staff judge advocates and legal officers, and acting or assistant staff judge advocates and legal officers.

(6) All other persons designated by regulations of the armed forces or by statute.

(b) The following persons on active duty or performing inactive-duty training may administer oaths necessary in the performance of their duties:

(1) The president, military judge, trial counsel, and assistant trial counsel for all general and special courts-martial.

(2) The president and the counsel for the court of any court of inquiry.

(3) All officers designated to take a deposition.

(4) All persons detailed to conduct an investigation.

(5) All recruiting officers.

(6) All other persons designated by regulations of the armed forces or by statute.

(c) No fee may be paid to or received by any person for the performance of any notarial act herein authorized.

(d) The signature without seal of any such person acting as notary, together with the title of his office, is prima facie evidence of his authority.

12 U.S.C. § 73. Oath.

Each director, when appointed or elected, shall take an oath that he will, so far as the duty devolves on him, diligently and honestly administer the affairs of such association, and will not knowingly violate or willingly permit to be violated any of the provisions of this title, and that he is the owner in good faith, and in his own right, of the number of shares of stock required by this title, subscribed by him, or standing in his name on the books of the association, and that the same is not hypothecated, or in any way pledged, as security for any loan or debt. The oath shall be taken before a notary public, properly authorized and commissioned by the State in which he resides, or before any other officer having an official seal and authorized by the State to administer oaths, except that the oath shall not be taken before any such notary public or other officer who is an officer of the director's bank. The oath, subscribed by the director making it, and certified by the notary public or other officer before whom it is taken, shall be immediately transmitted to the Comptroller of the Currency and shall be filed and preserved in his office for a period of ten years.

12 U.S.C. § 131. Protest of notes—Waiver.

Whenever any national banking association fails to redeem in the lawful money of the United States any of its circulating notes, upon demand of payment duly made during the usual hours of business, at the office of such association, [or at its designated place of redemption,]* the holder may cause the same to be protested, in one package, by a notary public, unless the president or cashier of the association whose notes are presented for payment, [or the president or cashier of the association at the place at which they are redeemable,]* offers to waive demand and notice of the protest, and, in pursuance of such officer, makes, signs, and delivers to the party making such demand an admission in writing, stating the time of the demand, the amount demanded, and the fact of the nonpayment thereof. The notary public, on making such protest, or upon receiving such admission, shall forthwith forward such admission or notice of protest to the Comptroller of the Currency, retaining a copy thereof. If, however, satisfactory proof is produced to the notary public that the payment of the notes demanded is restrained by order of any court of competent jurisdiction, he shall not protest the same. When the holder of any notes causes more than one note or package to be protested on the same day, he shall not receive pay for more than one protest.

Obsolete language since no designated place of redemption currently exists.

22 U.S.C. § 4215. Notarial acts, oaths, affirmations, affidavits, and depositions; fees.

Every consular officer of the United States is required, whenever application is made to him therefor, within the limits of his consulate, to administer to or take from any person any oath, affirmation, affidavit, or deposition, and to perform any other notarial act which any notary public is required or authorized by law to do within the United States; and for every such notarial act performed he shall charge in each instance the appropriate fee prescribed by the President under section 4219 of this title.

28 U.S.C. § 636. Jurisdiction, powers, and temporary assignment.

(a) Each United States magistrate serving under this chapter shall have within the territorial jurisdiction prescribed by his appointment—

(1) all powers and duties conferred or imposed upon United States commissioners by law or by the Rules of Criminal Procedure for the United States District Courts;

(2) the power to administer oaths and affirmations, issue orders pursuant to section 3142 of title 18 concerning release or detention of persons pending trial, and take acknowledgments, affidavits, and depositions;

*   *   *

OFFENSES

18 U.S.C. § 1016. Acknowledgment of appearance or oath.

Whoever, being an officer authorized to administer oaths or to take and certify acknowledgments, knowingly makes any false acknowledgment, certificate, or statement concerning the appearance before him or the taking of an oath or affirmation by any person with respect to any proposal, contract, bond, undertaking, or other matter submitted to, made with, or taken on behalf of the United States or any department or agency thereof, concerning which an oath or affirmation is required by law or lawful regulation, or with respect to the financial standing of any principal, surety, or other party to any such proposal, contract, bond, undertaking, or other instrument, shall be fined not more than $2,000 or imprisoned not more than two years, or both.

DEPOSITIONS

[FED. R. CIV. P.]

RULE 28. Persons before whom depositions may be taken.

(a) **Within the United States.** Within the United States or within a territory or insular possession subject to the jurisdiction of the United States, depositions shall be taken before an officer authorized to administer oaths by the laws of the United States or of the place where the examination is held, or before a person appointed by the court in which the action is pending. A person so appointed has power to administer oaths and take testimony. The term officer as used in Rules 30, 31 and 32 includes a person appointed by the court or designated by the parties under Rule 29.

(b) In Foreign Countries. In a foreign country, depositions may be taken (1) on notice before a person authorized to administer oaths in the place in which the examination is held, either by the law thereof or by the law of the United States, or (2) before a person commissioned by the court, and a person so commissioned shall have the power by virtue of the commission to administer any necessary oath and take testimony, or (3) pursuant to a letter rogatory. A commission or a letter rogatory shall be issued on application and notice and on terms that are just and appropriate. It is not requisite to the issuance of a commission or a letter rogatory that the taking of the deposition in any other manner is impracticable or inconvenient; and both a commission and a letter rogatory may be issued in proper cases. A notice or commission may designate the person before whom the deposition is to be taken either by name or descriptive title. A letter rogatory may be addressed "To the Appropriate Authority in [here name the country]." Evidence obtained in response to a letter rogatory need not be excluded merely for the reason that it is not a verbatim transcript or that the testimony was not taken under oath or for any similar departure from the requirements for depositions taken within the United States under these rules.

(c) Disqualification for Interest. No deposition shall be taken before a person who is a relative or employee or attorney or counsel of any of the parties, or is a relative or employee of such attorney or counsel, or is financially interested in the action.

RULE 29. Stipulations regarding discovery procedure.

Unless the court orders otherwise, the parties may by written stipulation (1) provide that depositions may be taken before any person, at any time or place, upon any notice, and in any manner and when so taken may be used like other depositions, and (2) modify the procedures provided by these rules for other methods of discovery, except that stipulations extending the time provided in Rules 33, 34, and 36 for responses to discovery may be made only with the approval of the court.

RULE 30. Depositions upon oral examination.

(a) When Depositions May Be Taken. After commencement of the action, any party may take the testimony of any person, including a party, by deposition upon oral examination. Leave of court, granted with or without notice, must be obtained only if the plaintiff seeks to take a deposition prior to the expiration of 30 days after service of the summons and complaint upon any defendant or service

made under Rule 4(e), except that leave is not required (1) if a defendant has served a notice of taking deposition or otherwise sought discovery, or (2) if special notice is given as provided in subdivision (b)(2) of this rule. The attendance of witnesses may be compelled by subpoena as provided in Rule 45. The deposition of a person confined in prison may be taken only by leave of court on such terms as the court prescribes.

(b) Notice of Examination: General Requirements; Special Notice; Non-stenographic Recording; Production of Documents and Things; Deposition of Organization; Deposition by Telephone.

(1) A party desiring to take the deposition of any person upon oral examination shall give reasonable notice in writing to every other party to the action. The notice shall state the time and place for taking the deposition and the name and address of each person to be examined, if known, and, if the name is not known, a general description sufficient to identify the person or the particular class or group to which the person belongs. If a subpoena duces tecum is to be served on the person to be examined, the designation of the materials to be produced as set forth in the subpoena shall be attached to or included in the notice.

(2) Leave of court is not required for the taking of a deposition by plaintiff if the notice (A) states that the person to be examined is about to go out of the district where the action is pending and more than 100 miles from the place of trial, or is about to go out of the United States, or is bound on a voyage to sea, and will be unavailable for examination unless the person's deposition is taken before expiration of the 30-day period, and (B) set forth facts to support the statement. The plaintiff's attorney shall sign the notice, and the attorney's signature constitutes a certification by the attorney that to the best of the attorney's knowledge, information, and belief the statement and supporting facts are true. The sanctions provided by Rule 11 are applicable to the certification.

If a party shows that when the party was served with notice under this subdivision (b)(2) the party was unable through the exercise of diligence to obtain counsel to represent the party at the taking of the deposition, the deposition may not be used against the party.

(3) The court may for cause shown enlarge or shorten the time for taking the deposition.

(4) The parties may stipulate in writing or the court may upon motion order that the testimony at a deposition be recorded by other than stenographic means. The stipulation or order shall designate the person before whom the deposition shall be taken, the manner of recording, preserving and filing the deposition, and may include other provisions to assure that the recorded testimony will be accurate and trustworthy. A party may arrange to

have a stenographic transcription made at the party's own expense. Any objections under subdivision (c), any changes made by the witness, the witness' signature identifying the deposition as the witness' own or the statement of the officer that is required if the witness does not sign, as provided in subdivision (e), and the certification of the officer required by subdivision (f) shall be set forth in a writing to accompany a deposition recorded by non-stenographic means.

(5) The notice to a party deponent may be accompanied by a request made in compliance with Rule 34 for the production of documents and tangible things at the taking of the deposition. The procedure of Rule 34 shall apply to the request.

(6) A party may in the party's notice and in subpoena name as the deponent a public or private corporation or a partnership or association or governmental agency and describe with reasonable particularity the matters on which examination is requested. In that event, the organization so named shall designate one or more officers, directors, or managing agents, or other persons who consent to testify on its behalf, and may set forth, for each person designated, the matters on which the person will testify. A subpoena shall advise a non-party organization of its duty to make such a designation. The persons so designated shall testify as to matters known or reasonably available to the organization. This subdivision (b)(6) does not preclude taking a deposition by any other procedure authorized in these rules.

(7) The parties may stipulate in writing or the court may upon motion order that a deposition be taken by telephone. For the purposes of this rule and Rules 28(a), 37(a)(1), 37(b)(1) and 45(d), a deposition taken by telephone is taken in the district and at the place where the deponent is to answer questions propounded to the deponent.

(c) **Examination and Cross-Examination; Record of Examination; Oath; Objections.** Examination and cross-examination of witnesses may proceed as permitted at the trial under the provisions of the Federal Rules of Evidence. The officer before whom the deposition is to be taken shall put the witness on oath and shall personally, or by someone acting under the officer's direction and in the officer's presence, record the testimony of the witness. The testimony shall be taken stenographically or recorded by any other means ordered in accordance with subdivision (b)(4) of this rule. If requested by one of the parties, the testimony shall be transcribed.

All objections made at the time of the examination to the qualifications of the officer taking the deposition, or to the manner of taking it, or to the evidence presented, or to the conduct of any party, and any other objection to the proceedings, shall be noted by the officer upon the deposition. Evidence objected to shall be taken subject to the objections. In lieu of participating in the oral examination, parties may serve written questions in a sealed envelope on the party taking the deposition and the party taking the deposition shall transmit them to the officer, who shall propound them to the witness and record the answers verbatim.

(d) **Motion to Terminate or Limit Examination.** At any time during the taking of the deposition, on motion of a party or of the deponent and upon a showing that the examination is being conducted in bad faith or in such manner as unreasonably to annoy, embarrass, or oppress the deponent or party, the court in which the action is pending or the court in the district where the deposition is being taken may order the officer conducting the examination to cease forthwith from taking the deposition, or may limit the scope and manner of the taking of the deposition as provided in Rule 26(c). If the order made terminates the examination, it shall be resumed thereafter only upon the order of the court in which the action is pending. Upon demand of the objecting party or deponent, the taking of the deposition shall be suspended for the time necessary to make a motion for an order. The provisions of Rule 37(a)(4) apply to the award of expenses incurred in relation to the motion.

(e) **Submission to Witness; Changes; Signing.** When the testimony is fully transcribed the deposition shall be submitted to the witness for examination and shall be read to or by the witness, unless such examination and reading are waived by the witness and by the parties. Any changes in form or substance which the witness desires to make shall be entered upon the deposition by the officer with a statement of the reasons given by the witness for making them. The deposition shall then be signed by the witness, unless the parties by stipulation waive the signing or the witness is ill or cannot be found or refuses to sign. If the deposition is not signed by the witness within 30 days of its submission to the witness, the officer shall sign it and state on the record the fact of the waiver or of the illness or absence of the witness or the fact of the refusal to sign together with the reason, if any, given therefor; and the deposition may then be used as fully as though signed unless on a motion to suppress under Rule 32(d)(4) the court holds that the reasons given for the refusal to sign require rejection of the deposition in whole or in part.

(f) **Certification and Filing by Officer; Exhibits; Copies; Notice of Filing.**

(1) The officer shall certify on the deposition that the witness was duly sworn by the officer and that the deposition is a true record of the testimony given by the witness. Unless otherwise ordered by the court, the officer shall then securely seal the deposition in an envelope indorsed with the title of the action and marked "Deposition of [here insert

name of witness]" and shall promptly file it with the court in which the action is pending or send it by registered or certified mail to the clerk thereof for filing.

Documents and things produced for inspection during the examination of the witness, shall, upon the request of a party, be marked for identification and annexed to the deposition and may be inspected and copied by any party, except that if the person producing the materials desires to retain them the person may (A) offer copies to be marked for identification and annexed to the deposition and to serve thereafter as originals if the person affords to all parties fair opportunity to verify the copies by comparison with the originals, or (B) offer the originals to be marked for identification, after giving to each party an opportunity to inspect and copy them, in which event the materials may then be used in the same manner as if annexed to the deposition. Any party may move for an order that the original be annexed to and returned with the deposition to the court, pending final disposition of the case.

(2) Upon payment of reasonable charges therefor, the officer shall furnish a copy of the deposition to any party or to the deponent.

(3) The party taking the deposition shall give prompt notice of its filing to all other parties.

(g) **Failure to Attend or to Serve Subpoena; Expenses.**

(1) If the party giving the notice of the taking of a deposition fails to attend and proceed therewith and another party attends in person or by attorney pursuant to the notice, the court may order the party giving the notice to pay to such other party the reasonable expenses incurred by that party and that party's attorney in attending, including reasonable attorney's fees.

(2) If the party giving the notice of the taking of a deposition of a witness fails to serve a subpoena upon the witness and the witness because of such failure does not attend, and if another party attends in person or by attorney because that party expects the deposition of that witness to be taken, the court may order the party giving the notice to pay to such other party the reasonable expenses incurred by that party and that party's attorney in attending, including reasonable attorney's fees.

[FED. R. CRIM. P.]

RULE 15. Depositions.

(a) WHEN TAKEN. Whenever due to exceptional circumstances of the case it is in the interest of justice that the testimony of a prospective witness of a party be taken and preserved for use at trial, the court may upon motion of such party and notice to the parties order that testimony of such witness be taken by deposition and that any designated book,

paper, document, record, recording, or other material not privileged, be produced at the same time and place. If a witness is detained pursuant to section 3144 of title 18, United States Code, the court on written motion of the witness and upon notice to the parties may direct that the witness' deposition be taken. After the deposition has been subscribed the court may discharge the witness.

(b) NOTICE OF TAKING. The party at whose instance a deposition is to be taken shall give to every party reasonable written notice of the time and place for taking the deposition. The notice shall state the name and address of each person to be examined. On motion of a party upon whom the notice is served, the court for cause shown may extend or shorten the time or change the place for taking the deposition. The officer having custody of a defendant shall be notified of the time and place set for the examination and shall, unless the defendant waives in writing the right to be present, produce the defendant at the examination and keep the defendant in the presence of the witness during the examination, unless, after being warned by the court that disruptive conduct will cause the defendant's removal from the place of the taking of the deposition, the defendant persists in conduct which is such as to justify exclusion from that place. A defendant not in custody shall have the right to be present at the examination upon request subject to such terms as may be fixed by the court, but a failure, absent good cause shown, to appear after notice and tender of expenses in accordance with subdivision (c) of this rule shall constitute a waiver of that right and of any objection to the taking and use of the deposition based upon that right.

(c) PAYMENT OF EXPENSES. Whenever a deposition is taken at the instance of the government, or whenever a deposition is taken at the instance of a defendant who is unable to bear the expenses of the taking of the deposition, the court may direct that the expense of travel and subsistence of the defendant and the defendant's attorney for attendance at the examination and the cost of the transcript of the deposition shall be paid by the government.

(d) HOW TAKEN. Subject to such additional conditions as the court shall provide, a deposition shall be taken and filed in the manner provided in civil actions except as otherwise provided in these rules, provided that (1) in no event shall a deposition be taken of a party defendant without that defendant's consent, and (2) the scope and manner of examination and cross-examination shall be such as would be allowed in the trial itself. The government shall make available to the defendant or the defendant's counsel for examination and use at the taking of the deposition any statement of the witness being deposed which is in the possession of the government and to which the defendant would be entitled at the trial.

(e) Use. At the trial or upon any hearing, a part or all of a deposition, so far as otherwise admissible under the rules of evidence, may be used as substantive evidence if the witness is unavailable, as unavailability is defined in Rule 804(a) of the Federal Rules of Evidence, or the witness gives testimony at the trial or hearing inconsistent with that witness' deposition. Any deposition may also be used by any party for the purpose of contradicting or impeaching the testimony of the deponent as a witness. If only a part of a deposition is offered in evidence by a party, an adverse party may require the offering of all of it which is relevant to the part offered and any party may offer other parts.

(f) Objections to Deposition Testimony. Objections to deposition testimony or evidence or parts thereof and the grounds for the objection shall be stated at the time of the taking of the deposition.

(g) Deposition by Agreement Not Precluded. Nothing in this rule shall preclude the taking of a deposition, orally or upon written questions, or the use of a deposition, by agreement of the parties with the consent of the court.

LEGAL HOLIDAYS

5 U.S.C. § 6103. Holidays.

(a) The following are legal public holidays:
New Year's Day, January 1.
Birthday of Martin Luther King, Jr., the third Monday in January.
Washington's Birthday, the third Monday in February.
Memorial Day, the last Monday in May.
Independence Day, July 4.
Labor Day, the first Monday in September.
Columbus Day, the second Monday in October.
Veterans Day, November 11.
Thanksgiving Day, the fourth Thursday in November.
Christmas Day, December 25.

(b) For the purpose of statutes relating to pay and leave of employees, with respect to a legal public holiday and any other day declared to be a holiday by Federal statute or Executive order, the following rules apply:

(1) Instead of a holiday that occurs on a Saturday, the Friday immediately before is a legal public holiday for—

(A) employees whose basic workweek is Monday through Friday; and

(B) the purpose of section 6309 of this title.

(2) Instead of a holiday that occurs on a regular weekly nonworkday of an employee whose basic workweek is other than Monday through Friday, except the regular weekly nonworkday administra-

tively scheduled for the employee instead of Sunday, the workday immediately before that regular weekly nonworkday is a legal public holiday for the employee.

This subsection, except subparagraph (B) of paragraph (1), does not apply to an employee whose basic workweek is Monday through Saturday.

(c) January 20 of each fourth year after 1965, Inauguration Day, is a legal public holiday for the purpose of statutes relating to pay and leave of employees as defined by section 2105 of this title and individuals employed by the government of the District of Columbia employed in the District of Columbia, Montgomery and Prince Georges Counties in Maryland, Arlington and Fairfax Counties in Virginia, and the cities of Alexandria and Falls Church in Virginia. When January 20 of any fourth year after 1965 falls on Sunday, the next succeeding day selected for the public observance of the inauguration of the President is a legal public holiday for the purpose of this subsection.

26 U.S.C. § 7503. Time for performance of acts where last day falls on Saturday, Sunday, or legal holiday.

When the last day prescribed under authority of the internal revenue laws for performing any act falls on Saturday, Sunday, or a legal holiday, the performance of such act shall be considered timely if it is performed on the next succeeding day which is not a Saturday, Sunday, or a legal holiday. For purposes of this section, the last day for the performance of any act shall be determined by including any authorized extension of time; the term "legal holiday" means a legal holiday in the District of Columbia; and in the case of any return, statement, or other document required to be filed, or any other act required under authority of the internal revenue laws to be performed, at any office of the Secretary, or at any other office of the United States or any agency thereof, located outside the District of Columbia but within an internal revenue district, the term "legal holiday" also means a Statewide legal holiday in the State where such office is located.

TERRITORIES AND POSSESSIONS

48 U.S.C. § 1421f-1. Acknowledgment of deeds.

Deeds and other instruments affecting land situate in the District of Columbia or any Territory of the United States may be acknowledged in the islands of Guam [and Samoa or in the Canal Zone] before any notary public or judge, appointed therein by proper authority, or by any officer therein who has ex officio the powers of a notary public: Provided, That the certificate by such notary in Guam [, Samoa, or the Canal Zone, as the case may be,] shall be accompanied by the certificate of the governor or acting governor of such place to the effect that the notary taking said acknowledgment was in fact the officer he purported to be; and any deeds or other instruments affecting lands so situate, so acknowledged since the first day of January, nineteen hundred and five, and accompanied by such certificate shall have the same effect as such deeds or other instruments hereafter so acknowledged and certified.

48 U.S.C. § 1663. Acknowledgment of deeds.

Deeds and other instruments affecting land situate in the District of Columbia or any Territory of the United States may be acknowledged in the islands of [Guam and] Samoa [or in the Canal Zone] before any notary public or judge, appointed therein by proper authority, or by any officer therein who has ex officio the powers of a notary public: Provided, That the certificate by such notary in [Guam,] Samoa [, or the Canal Zone, as the case may be,] shall be accompanied by the certificate of the governor or acting governor of such place to the effect that the notary taking said acknowledgment was in fact the officer he purported to be; and any deeds or other instruments affecting lands so situate, so acknowledged since the first day of January, nineteen hundred and five, and accompanied by such certificate shall have the same effect as such deeds or other instruments hereafter so acknowledged and certified.

APPENDIX A
Uniform Commercial Code —
Table of Jurisdictions and Citations

Jurisdiction	Local Citation		Originial Effective Date of UCC
	U.C.C. Article 3	U.C.C. Article 4	
Alabama	ALA. CODE §§ 7-3-101 to 7-3-85	ALA. CODE §§ 7-4-101 to 7-4-504	Jan. 1, 1967
Alaska	ALASKA STAT. §§ 45.03.101 to 45.03.805	ALASKA STAT. §§ 45.04.101 to 45.04.504	Jan. 1, 1963
Arizona	ARIZ. REV. STAT. ANN. §§ 44-2501 to 44-2579	ARIZ. REV. STAT. ANN. §§ 44-2601 to 44-2637	Jan. 1, 1968
Arkansas	ARK. STAT. ANN. §§ 4-3-101 to 4-3-805	ARK. STAT. ANN. §§ 4-4-101 to 4-4-504	Jan. 1, 1962
California	CAL. COM. CODE §§ 3101 to 3805	CAL. COM. CODE §§ 4101 to 4504	Jan. 1, 1965
Colorado	COLO. REV. STAT. ANN. §§ 4-3-101 to 4-3-805	COLO. REV. STAT. ANN. §§ 4-4-101 to 4-4-504	July 1, 1966
Connecticut	CONN. GEN. STAT. ANN. §§ 42a-3-101 to 42a-3-805	CONN. GEN. STAT. ANN. §§ 42a-4-101 to 42a-4-504	Oct. 1, 1961
Delaware	DEL. CODE. ANN. tit. 6, §§ 3-101 to 3-805	DEL. CODE. ANN. tit. 6, §§ 4-101 to 4-504	July 1, 1967
District of Columbia	D.C. CODE ANN. §§ 28:3-101 to 28:3-805	D.C. CODE ANN. §§ 28:4-101 to 28:4-504	Jan. 1, 1965

Jurisdiction	Local Citation		Originial Effective Date of UCC
	U.C.C. Article 3	U.C.C. Article 4	
Florida	FLA. STAT ANN. §§ 673:3-101 to 673:3-805	FLA STAT. ANN. §§ 674:4-101 to 674:4-504	Jan. 1, 1967
Georgia	GA. CODE ANN. §§ 11-3-101 to 11-3-805	GA. CODE ANN. §§ 11-4-101 to 11-4-504	Jan. 1, 1964
Hawaii	HAW. REV. STAT. §§ 490:3-101 to 490:3-805	HAW. REV. STAT. §§ 490:4-101 to 490:4-504	Jan. 1, 1967
Idaho	IDAHO CODE §§ 28-3-101 to 28-3-805	IDAHO CODE §§ 28-4-101 to 28-4-504	Jan. 1, 1968
Illinois	ILL. ANN. STAT. ch. 26, §§ 3-101 to 3-805	ILL. ANN. STAT. ch. 26, §§ 4-101 to 4-504	July 2, 1962
Indiana	IND. CODE ANN. §§ 26-1-3-101 to 26-1-3-805	IND. CODE ANN. §§ 26-1-4-101 to 26-1-4-504	July 1, 1964
Iowa	IOWA CODE ANN. §§ 554.3101 to 554.3805	IOWA CODE ANN. §§ 554.4101 to 554.4504	July 1, 1964
Kansas	KAN. STAT. ANN. §§ 84-3-101 to 84-3-805	KAN. STAT. ANN. §§ 84-4-101 to 84-4-504	Jan. 1, 1966
Kentucky	KY. REV. STAT. ANN. §§ 355.3-101 to 355.3-805	KY. REV. STAT. ANN. §§ 355.4-101 to 355.4-504	July 1, 1960
Louisiana	LA. REV. STAT. ANN. §§ 10:3-101 to 10:3-807	LA. REV. STAT. ANN. §§ 10:4-101 to 10:4-504	Jan. 1, 1975

Jurisdiction	Local Citation		Originial Effective Date of UCC
	U.C.C. Article 3	U.C.C. Article 4	
Maine	ME. REV. STAT. ANN. TIT. 11, §§ 3-101 to 3-805	ME. REV. STAT. ANN. TIT. 11, §§ 4-101 to 4-504	Dec. 31, 1964
Maryland	MD. COM. LAW. CODE ANN. §§ 3-101 to 3-805	MD. COM. LAW. CODE ANN. §§ 4-101 to 4-504	Feb. 1, 1964
Massachusetts	MASS. GEN. LAWS §§ 3-101 to 3-805	MASS. GEN. LAWS §§ 4-101 to 4-504	Oct. 1, 1958
Michigan	MICH. COMP. LAWS ANN. §§ 440.31-101 to 440.38-805	MICH. COMP. LAWS ANN. §§ 440.4-101 to 440.4-504	Jan. 1, 1964
Minnesota	MINN. STAT. ANN. §§ 336.3-101 to 336.3-805	MINN. STAT. ANN. §§ 336.4-101 to 336.4-504	July 1, 1966
Mississippi	MISS. CODE ANN. §§ 75-3-101 to 75-3-805	MISS. CODE ANN. §§ 75-4-101 to 75-4-504	Mar. 31, 1968
Missouri	MO. ANN. STAT. §§ 400.3-101 to 400.3-805	MO. ANN. STAT. §§ 400.4-101 to 400.4-504	July 1, 1965
Montana	MONT. CODE ANN. §§ 87A-3-101 to 87A-3-805	MONT. CODE ANN. §§ 87A-4-101 to 87A-4-504	Jan. 2, 1965
Nebraska	NEB. REV. STAT. §§ 3-101 to 3-805	NEB. REV. STAT. §§ 4-101 to 4-504	Sept. 2, 1965
Nevada	NEV. REV. STAT. §§ 104.3-101 to 104.3-805	NEV. REV. STAT. §§ 104.4-101 to 104.4-504	Mar. 1, 1967

Jurisdiction	Local Citation		Originial Effective Date of UCC
	U.C.C. Article 3	U.C.C. Article 4	
New Hampshire	N.H. REV. STAT. ANN. §§ 382-A:3-101 to 382-A:3-805	N.H. REV. STAT. ANN. §§ 382-A:4-101 to 382-A:4-504	July 1, 1961
New Jersey	N.J. STAT. ANN. §§ 12A:3-101 to 12A:3-805	N.J. STAT. ANN. §§ 12A:4-101 to 12A:4-504	Jan. 1, 1963
New Mexico	N.M. STAT. ANN. §§ 55-3-101 to 55-3-805	N.M. STAT. ANN. §§ 55-4-101 to 55-4-504	Jan. 1, 1962
New York	N.Y. U.C.C. LAW §§ 3-101 to 3-805	N.Y. U.C.C. LAW §§ 4-101 to 4-504	Sept. 27, 1964
North Carolina	N.C. GEN. STAT. §§ 25-3-101 to 25-3-805	N.C. GEN. STAT. §§ 25-4-101 to 25-4-504	July 1, 1967
North Dakota	N.D. CENT. CODE §§ 41-03-01 to 41-03-81	N.D. CENT. CODE §§ 41-04-01 to 41-04-38	July 1, 1966
Ohio	OHIO REV. CODE ANN. §§ 1303.01 to 1303.78	OHIO REV. CODE ANN. §§ 1304.01 to 1304.34	July 1, 1962
Oklahoma	OKLA. STAT. ANN. TIT. 12A, §§ 3-101 to 3-805	OKLA. STAT. ANN. TIT. 12A, §§ 4-101 to 4-504	Jan. 1, 1963
Oregon	OR. REV. STAT. §§ 73.1010 to 73.8050	OR. REV. STAT. §§ 74.1010 to 74.5040	Sept. 1, 1963
Pennsylvania	PA. STAT. ANN. tit. 13, §§ 3101 to 3805	PA. STAT. ANN. tit. 13, §§ 4101 to 4504	July 1, 1954

| Jurisdiction | Local Citation | | Originial Effective Date of UCC |
	U.C.C. Article 3	U.C.C. Article 4	
Puerto Rico	None; not enacted.	None; not enacted.	None
Rhode Island	R.I. GEN. LAWS ANN. §§ 6A-3-101 to 6A-3-805	R.I. GEN. LAWS ANN. §§ 6A-4-101 to 6A-4-504	Jan. 2, 1962
South Carolina	S.C. CODE ANN. §§ 36-3-101 to 36-3-805	S.C. CODE ANN. §§ 36-4-101 to 36-4-504	Jan. 1, 1968
South Dakota	S.D. CODIFIED LAWS ANN. §§ 57A-3-101 TO 57A-3-805	S.D. CODIFIED LAWS ANN. §§ 57A-4-101 TO 57A-4-504	July 1, 1967
Tennessee	TENN. CODE ANN. §§ 47-3-101 to 47-3-805	TENN. CODE ANN. §§ 47-4-101 to 47-4-504	July 1, 1964
Texas	TEX. BUS. & COM. CODE ANN. §§ 3-101 to 3-805	TEX. BUS. & COM. CODE ANN. §§ 4-101 to 4-504	July 1, 1966
Utah	UTAH CODE ANN. §§ 70A-3-101 to 70A-3-805	UTAH CODE ANN. §§ 70A-4-101 to 70A-4-504	Jan. 1, 1966
Vermont	VT. STAT. ANN. tit. 9A, §§ 3-101 to 3-805	VT. STAT. ANN. tit. 9A, §§ 4-101 to 4-504	Jan. 1, 1967
Virgin Islands	V.I. CODE ANN. tit. 11A, §§ 3-101 to 3-805	V.I. CODE ANN. tit. 11A, §§ 4-101 to 4-504	July 1, 1965
Virginia	VA. CODE ANN. §§ 8.3-101 to 8.3-805	VA. CODE ANN. §§ 8.4-101 to 8.4-504	Jan. 1, 1966

Jurisdiction	Local Citation		Originial Effective Date of UCC
	U.C.C. Article 3	U.C.C. Article 4	
Washington	WASH. REV. CODE ANN. §§ 62A.3-101 to 62A.3-805	WASH. REV. CODE ANN. §§ 62A.4-101 to 62A.4-504	July 1, 1967
West Virginia	W. VA. CODE ANN.. §§ 46-3-101 to 46-3-805	W. VA. CODE ANN. §§ 46-4-101 to 46-4-504	Jan. 1, 1964
Wisconsin	WIS. STAT. ANN. §§ 403.101 to 403.805	WIS. STAT. ANN. §§ 404.101 to 404.504	July 1, 1965
Wyoming	WYO. STAT. ANN. §§ 34-21-301 to 34-21-379	WYO. STAT. ANN. §§ 34-21-401 to 34-21-493	Jan. 2, 1962

APPENDIX B
Table of Holidays by Jurisdiction

Holiday	Alabama	Alaska	Arizona	Arkansas
Sunday	×	×	×	
New Year's Day (Jan. 1)	×	×	×	×
Robert E. Lee's Birthday (Jan. 19)				
Dr. Martin Luther King, Jr.'s Birthday (3rd Mon. in Jan.)	×	×	×	×
Lincoln's Birthday (Feb. 12)		×		
Washington's Birthday (Feb. 22)				
President's Day (3rd Mon. in Feb.)	×	×	×	×
Thomas Jefferson's Birthday (Apr. 13)	×			
Mardi Gras (Shrove Tuesday)	×			
Confederate Memorial Day (May 10)				
National Memorial Day (May 30)				
Memorial Day (Last Mon. in May)		×	×	×
Jefferson Davis' Birthday (June 3)				
Independence Day (July 4)	×	×	×	×
Labor Day (1st Mon. in Sept.)	×	×	×	×
Columbus Day (2nd Mon. in Oct.)	×		×	
Veterans' Day (Nov. 11)	×	×	×	×
Thanksgiving Day (4th Thurs. in Nov.)	×	×	×	×
Christmas Day (Dec. 25)	×	×	×	×
Monday, if Holiday falls on Sunday	×	×	×	

Other Legal Holidays and Remarks

- **Alabama:** Robert E. Lee's birthday, third Monday in January; Washington's birthday, third Monday in February; Confederate Memorial day, fourth Monday in April; Jefferson Davis' birthday, first Monday in June. (Ala. Code § 1-3-8)
- **Alaska:** Seward's day, last Monday in March; Alaska day observed October 18; Friday if holiday falls on Saturday. (Alaska Stat. § 44.12.010)
- **Arizona:** Lincoln Day, second Monday in February. (Ariz. Rev. Stat. Ann. § 1-301)
- **Arkansas:** Robert E. Lee's birthday, third Monday in January; Christmas Eve, December 24; Friday if holiday falls on Saturday. (Ark. Stat. Ann. § 1-5-101)

649

Other Legal Holidays and Remarks

Holiday	California	Colorado	Connecticut	Delaware	District of Columbia	Florida
	Admission day, September 9; Good Friday, 12 noon to 3 p.m.; Friday when Nov. 11 falls on Saturday; Saturday half holidays. (CAL. GOV'T CODE §§ 6700, 6701, 6702)	Saturday half holidays. (COLO. REV. STAT. ANN. §§ 24-11-101, 24-11-103)	Martin Luther King Day, first Monday on or after January fifteenth; Friday, if holiday falls on Saturday. (CONN. GEN. STAT. ANN. §1-4)	Good Friday; Saturdays; General Election day and in Sussex County, Return Day, second day after General Election after 12:00 noon; Lincoln's birthday, first Monday in February; Friday following Thanksgiving Day; Friday when holiday falls on Saturday. (DEL. CODE ANN. tit. 1, § 501)	Saturday after 12:00 noon; Next preceding day if holidays falls on Saturday; Presidential inauguration day every fourth year. See also provisions concerning financial institutions. (D.C. Code Ann. § 28-2701)	Martin Luther King, Jr.'s birthday, Jan. 15; Susan B. Anthony's birthday, Feb. 15; Good Friday; General election day; Confederate Memorial day, April 26. (FLA. STAT. ANN. § 683.01)
Monday, if Holiday falls on Sunday	✕	✕	✕	✕	✕	✕
Christmas Day (Dec. 25)	✕	✕	✕	✕	✕	✕
Thanksgiving Day (4th Thurs. in Nov.)	✕	✕	✕	✕	✕	✕
Veterans' Day (Nov. 11)	✕	✕	✕	✕	✕	✕
Columbus Day (2nd Mon. in Oct.)	✕	✕	✕	✕	✕	✕
Labor Day (1st Mon. in Sept.)	✕	✕	✕	✕	✕	✕
Independence Day (July 4)	✕	✕	✕	✕	✕	✕
Jefferson Davis' Birthday (June 3)						✕
Memorial Day (Last Mon. in May)	✕	✕	✕	✕	✕	✕
National Memorial Day (May 30)						
Confederate Memorial Day (May 10)						
Mardi Gras (Shrove Tuesday)						✕
Thomas Jefferson's Birthday (Apr. 13)						
President's Day (3rd Mon. in Feb.)	✕	✕	✕	✕	✕	✕
Washington's Birthday (Feb. 22)						
Lincoln's Birthday (Feb. 12)			✕			✕
Dr. Martin Luther King, Jr.'s Birthday (3rd Mon. in Jan.)	✕	✕		✕	✕	
Robert E. Lee's Birthday (Jan. 19)						✕
New Year's Day (Jan. 1)	✕	✕	✕	✕	✕	✕
Sunday	✕					✕

Jurisdiction	Notes / Citation
Georgia	(GA. CODE ANN. § 1-4-1)
Hawaii	Prince Jonah Kuhio Kalanianaole Day, March 26; Good Friday; King Kamehameha I Day, June 11; Admission Day, third Friday in August; Discoverer's Day, second Monday in October; general election days. Preceding Friday, if holiday falls on Saturday. (HAW. REV. STAT. §§ 8-1, 8-2)
Idaho	Preceding Friday, if holiday falls on Saturday. (IDAHO CODE § 73-108)
Illinois	Casimir Pulaski's birthday, first Monday in March; Good Friday; General election day for House of Representatives; Saturday after 12:00 noon; day selected by a bank. (ILL. ANN. STAT. ch 17, ¶ 2201)
Indiana	Good Friday; Friday, if holiday falls on Saturday; Election Day. (IND. CODE ANN. § 1-1-9-1)
Iowa	(IOWA CODE ANN. § 33.1)
Kansas	(KAN. STAT. ANN. § 35-107)
Kentucky	Franklin D. Roosevelt day, January 30. (KY. REV. STAT. ANN. ¶ 2.110)
Louisiana	Battle of New Orleans, January 8; Good Friday; Confederate Memorial Day, June 3; Huey P. Long Day, August 30; All Saints Day, November 1; Inauguration Day in Baton Rouge; in certain parishes Saturdays and Wednesdays. See also Mardi Gras (1:55 A(3)), second Friday of Holiday in Dixie (§ 1:55 A(5)). (LA. REV. STAT. ANN. 1:55)

Holiday checkmark grid (columns = jurisdictions; row headers appear on the facing page):

Jurisdiction																
Georgia		x	x	x	x	x		x					x		x	x
Hawaii	x	x	x		x	x		x						x		x
Idaho		x	x	x	x	x		x					x		x	x
Illinois		x	x	x	x	x			x				x		x	x
Indiana	x	x	x	x	x	x		x					x		x	x
Iowa		x	x		x	x	x	x					x		x	x
Kansas		x	x	x	x	x		x		x			x		x	x
Kentucky	x	x	x	x	x	x		x	x				x		x	x
Louisiana		x	x	x	x	x		x	x				x	x		x

Other Legal Holidays and Remarks	Maine — Patriot's day, third Monday in April. (ME. REV. STAT. ANN. tit. 4, § 1051)	Maryland — Dr. Martin Luther King, Jr.'s Birthday, January 15; Maryland day, March 25; Good Friday; Defenders' day, September 12. General election days throughout the state. (MD. ANN. CODE ART. 1, § 27; MD. FIN. INST. CODE ANN. §§ 5-701 to 5-708)	Massachusetts — Third Monday in April; In Suffolk County, March 17 and June 17. (MASS. ANN. LAWS ch.4, § 7)	Michigan — Saturday after 12 noon. (MICH. COMP. LAWS ANN. §§ 435.101, 435.102)	Minnesota — Friday if certain holidays fall on Saturday. (MINN. STAT. ANN. § 645.44)	Mississippi — Confederate Memorial day, last Monday in April. (MISS. CODE ANN. § 3-3-7)	Missouri — May 8. (MO. ANN. STAT. §§ 9.010, 9.020)	Montana — State general election day; Heritage Day, date determined by political subdivisions and governor. (MONT. CODE ANN. § 1-1-216)
Monday, if Holiday falls on Sunday	×		×	×	×	×	×	×
Christmas Day (Dec. 25)	×	×	×	×	×	×	×	×
Thanksgiving Day (4th Thurs. in Nov.)	×	×	×	×	×	×	×	×
Veterans' Day (Nov. 11)	×	×	×	×	×	×	×	×
Columbus Day (2nd Mon. in Oct.)	×	×	×	×			×	×
Labor Day (1st Mon. in Sept.)	×	×	×	×	×	×	×	×
Independence Day (July 4)	×	×	×	×	×	×	×	×
Jefferson Davis' Birthday (June 3)								
Memorial Day (Last Mon. in May)	×	×	×	×	×	×	×	×
National Memorial Day (May 30)								
Confederate Memorial Day (May 10)								
Mardi Gras (Shrove Tuesday)								
Thomas Jefferson's Birthday (Apr. 13)								
President's Day (3rd Mon. in Feb.)	×	×	×	×	×	×	×	×
Washington's Birthday (Feb. 22)								
Lincoln's Birthday (Feb. 12)		×		×			×	
Dr. Martin Luther King, Jr.'s Birthday (3rd Mon. in Jan.)	×		×	×	×	×	×	
Robert E. Lee's Birthday (Jan. 19)								
New Year's Day (Jan. 1)	×	×	×	×	×	×	×	×
Sunday	×							×

Jurisdiction	Provisions
Nebraska	Arbor day, April 22; Veterans' Day, November 11 and/or federal holiday therefor; day after Thanksgiving. See also special provisions concerning banks.(Neb. Rev. Stat. §§ 62-301, 62-301.01)
Nevada	500th Anniversary of arrival of Columbus, Oct. 12, 1992; Nevada day, Oct. 31; Family Day, Friday following fourth Thursday in November; Friday, if holiday falls on Saturday; certain days appointed by President or governor. (Nev. Rev. Stat. § 236.015)
New Hampshire	Fast Day, fourth Monday in April; biennial election day. See also Saturday provisions for banks. (N.H. Rev. Stat. Ann. §§ 288.1 to 288.3)
New Jersey	Good Friday; general election day; Saturday; Friday, if holiday falls on Saturday (N.J. Stat. Ann. §§ 36:1-1 to 36:1-4)
New Mexico	(N.M. Stat. Ann. §§ 12-5-2, 12-5-3)
New York	General election day; half-holiday, Saturday noon to midnight. (N.Y. Gen. Constr. Law. § 24)
North Carolina	Greek Independence Day, March 25; Good Friday; Anniversary of signing Halifax Resolves, April 12; anniversary of Mecklenburg Declaration of Independence, May 20; Yom Kippur; Tuesday after first Monday in November of general election. (N.C. Gen. Stat. §§ 103-4, 103-5)
North Dakota	Good Friday; Friday, if holiday falls on Saturday. (N.C. Cent. Code §§ 1-03-01 to 1-03-05)

Other Legal Holidays and Remarks	First Tuesday after first Monday in November between noon and 5:30 p.m.; Saturday afternoon. (OHIO REV. CODE ANN. §§ 1.14, 5.20, 5.21)	Optional holidays for banks and public offices. (OKLA. STAT. ANN. §§ 82.1, 82.2)	Friday, if holiday falls on Saturday. (OR. REV. STAT. §§ 187.010, 187.020)	Good Friday; Flag day, June 14; Election Day, first Tuesday after first Monday of November. Saturdays and election days are half holidays. (PA. STAT. ANN. tit. 44, §§ 11, 21)	March 22; Good Friday; Island wide election day; Jan. 6; Jan. 11, birthday of Eugenio Maria de Hostos; second Sunday in April, Antonio R. Barcelo day; April 16, Jose de Diego day; July 17, Munoz Rivera day; July 25, Day of the Constitution; July 27, Dr. Jose Celso Barbosa's birthday; Oct. 12, Columbus Day; Nov. 19, discovery of Puerto Rico; Labor day also consecrated to memory of Santiago Iglesisas Pantin. (P.R. LAWS ANN. tit. 1, §§ 71 to 84)
Monday, if Holiday falls on Sunday	✕	✕	✕	✕	✕
Christmas Day (Dec. 25)	✕	✕	✕	✕	✕
Thanksgiving Day (4th Thurs. in Nov.)	✕	✕	✕	✕	✕
Veterans' Day (Nov. 11)	✕	✕	✕	✕	✕
Columbus Day (2nd Mon. in Oct.)	✕			✕	
Labor Day (1st Mon. in Sept.)	✕	✕	✕	✕	✕
Independence Day (July 4)	✕	✕	✕	✕	✕
Jefferson Davis' Birthday (June 3)					
Memorial Day (Last Mon. in May)	✕	✕	✕	✕	✕
National Memorial Day (May 30)					
Confederate Memorial Day (May 10)					
Mardi Gras (Shrove Tuesday)					
Thomas Jefferson's Birthday (Apr. 13)		✕			
President's Day (3rd Mon. in Feb.)	✕	✕	✕	✕	✕
Washington's Birthday (Feb. 22)					
Lincoln's Birthday (Feb. 12)					
Dr. Martin Luther King, Jr.'s Birthday (3rd Mon. in Jan.)	✕	✕	✕	✕	
Robert E. Lee's Birthday (Jan. 19)					
New Year's Day (Jan. 1)	✕	✕	✕	✕	✕
Sunday		✕	✕		✕
	Ohio	Oklahoma	Oregon	Pennsylvania	Puerto Rico

Jurisdiction	1	2	3	4	5	6	7	8	9	10	11	12	13	14	15	Other holidays / provisions
Rhode Island	×	×	×		×	×					×		×		×	Rhode Island Independence day, May 4; Victory day, second Monday of August; State election day, Tuesday after first Monday in November. Saturday bank and public offices closing provisions. (R.I. GEN. LAWS ANN. §§ 25-1-1 to 25-1-5)
South Carolina	×	×	×		×	×				×	×				×	December 26; general election days. See also provisions for state employees and banks. (S.C. CODE ANN. §§ 53-5-10 to 53-5-100)
South Dakota	×	×	×		×	×	×			×	×		×		×	Pioneer's Day and Native Americans' Day, second Monday in October; preceding Friday, if holiday falls on Saturday. (S.D. CODIFIED LAWS §§ 1-5-1 to 1-5-2)
Tennessee	×	×	×	×	×	×					×		×	×	×	Good Friday, days of local or national elections; preceding Friday, if holiday falls on Saturday; half-holidays on Saturdays. (TENN. CODE ANN. § 15-1-101)
Texas		×	×	×	×	×	×				×		×		×	March 2; April 21; Emancipation Day, June 19; August 27; state wide election days. (TEX. REV. CIV. STAT. ANN. art. 4591)
Utah	×	×	×	×	×	×	×				×		×	×	×	Pioneer Day, July 24; preceding Friday, if holiday falls on Saturday. (UTAH CODE ANN. § 63-13-2)
Vermont	×	×	×	×	×	×		×			×		×	×	×	Town meeting day, first Tuesday in March; Bennington battle day, August 16; preceding Friday if holiday falls on Saturday. (VT. STAT. ANN. tit. 1, § 371)
Virgin Islands	×	×	×		×	×	×				×		×		×	Three Kings' day, Jan. 6; Transfer day, March 31; Holy Thursday; Good Friday; Easter Monday; Organic Act day, third Monday in June; Emancipation Day, July 3; Supplication day, fourth Monday in July; Columbus day and Puerto Rico Friendship day, second Monday in Oct.; Local Thanksgiving day, third Monday in Oct.; D. Hamilton Jackson Day, Nov. 1; Christmas second day, Dec. 26. (V.I. CODE ANN. tit. 1, § 171)

Other Legal Holidays and Remarks	Lee-Jackson-King day, third Monday In January; Friday following Thanksgiving Day; preceding Friday, if holiday falls on Saturday. Saturday closing of banks permitted. (VA. CODE ANN. §§ 2.1-21 to 2.1-23)	Friday following Thanksgiving Day; preceding Friday, if holiday falls on Saturday. (WASH. REV. CODE ANN. § 1.16.050)	West Virginia day, June 20; local and national election days. (W. VA. CODE ANN. § 2-2-1)	January 15; Sept. primary election day; Nov. general election day. See also provisions concerning Good Friday, municipal elections and half holidays. (WIS. STAT. ANN. § 895.20)	(WYO. STAT. § 8-4-101)	Preceding Friday, if holiday falls on Saturday; Inauguration day. (5 U.S.C. § 6103).
Monday, if Holiday falls on Sunday	×	×	×	×	×	
Christmas Day (Dec. 25)	×	×	×	×	×	×
Thanksgiving Day (4th Thurs. in Nov.)	×	×	×	×	×	×
Veterans' Day (Nov. 11)	×	×	×	×	×	×
Columbus Day (2nd Mon. in Oct.)	×		×	×		×
Labor Day (1st Mon. in Sept.)	×	×	×	×	×	×
Independence Day (July 4)	×	×	×	×	×	×
Jefferson Davis' Birthday (June 3)						
Memorial Day (Last Mon. in May)	×	×	×	×	×	×
National Memorial Day (May 30)						
Confederate Memorial Day (May 10)						
Mardi Gras (Shrove Tuesday)						
Thomas Jefferson's Birthday (Apr. 13)						
President's Day (3rd Mon. in Feb.)	×	×	×	×	×	×
Washington's Birthday (Feb. 22)						
Lincoln's Birthday (Feb. 12)	×		×			
Dr. Martin Luther King, Jr.'s Birthday (3rd Mon. in Jan.)	×	×	×		×	×
Robert E. Lee's Birthday (Jan. 19)						
New Year's Day (Jan. 1)	×	×	×	×	×	×
Sunday		×				
	Virginia	Washington	West Virginia	Wisconsin	Wyoming	United States

GLOSSARY

Selected from The Law Dictionary (6th edition) *revised by Wesley Gilmer, Jr. Copyright 1986 by Anderson Publishing Co., Cincinnati.*

A

acceptance, the receipt of a thing, offered by another, with the intention of retaining it. (2) Of an offer (*q.v.*), a manifestation of assent (*q.v.*) to the terms of an offer, made by the offeree in a manner invited or required by the offer. Restatement (Second) of Contracts § 50(1). (3) The agreeing to terms or proposals by which a bargain (*q.v.*) is concluded and the parties are bound. (4) An agreement by the person, on whom a draft or bill of exchange is drawn, to pay the same according to its terms, generally expressed by writing the word "accepted" across the face and signing his name under it. (5) A drawee's (*q.v.*) signed engagement to honor a draft as presented. It must be written on the draft, and may consist of his signature alone. It becomes operative when completed by delivery or notification. U.C.C. § 3-410(1). (6) Of goods, occurs when the buyer (a) after a reasonable opportunity to inspect the goods signifies to the seller that the goods are conforming or that he will take or retain them in spite of their nonconformity, (b) fails to make an effective rejection, but such acceptance does not occur until the buyer has had a reasonable opportunity to inspect them, or (c) does any act inconsistent with the seller's ownership, but if such act is wrongful as against the seller it is an acceptance only if ratified by him. U.C.C. § 2-606(1). (7) Concerning goods, acceptance of a part of any commercial unit is acceptance of the entire unit. U.C.C. § 2-606(2).

accommodation paper, a promissory note or bill of exchange which a party makes, indorses, or accepts without consideration, for the benefit of another who receives money on it and is to provide for its payment when due. The want of consideration is a valid defense to an action brought on such paper by the person accommodated, but is no defense to an action by a third person who is a bona fide holder for value.

acknowledgment, the act of going before a competent officer or court and declaring the execution of a deed or other instrument. The acknowledgment is certified by the officer, and his certificate is sometimes called the acknowledgment. Acknowledgment of deeds, mortgages, and instruments conveying an interest in real property is required by the laws of most of the states, to entitle them to be recorded and to dispense with other proof of their execution.

affidavit, a written statement of fact, signed and sworn to before a person having authority to administer an oath.

affirmation, a solemn declaration without oath. The privilege of affirming in judicial proceedings is now generally extended to all persons who object to taking an oath.

attorney at law, a person licensed by a court to practice the profession of law. Such a license authorizes him to appear in court, give legal advice, draft written instruments, and do many other things which constitute the practice of law (*q.v.*).

average, a contribution, or adjustment of loss, made by merchants when goods have been thrown overboard for the safety of a ship. It is either general, *i.e.*, where the loss having been incurred for the general benefit, the owners of the ship and all that have cargo on board contribute proportionately toward making good the loss; or particular, where the loss has been accidental, or not for the general benefit, and therefore there is no general contribution. An average bond is an instrument executed by the several persons liable to contribute, empowering an arbitrator to assess the amount of their contributions. (2) Petty average, a small duty paid to masters of ships over and above the freight; known also as primage and average. (3) Formerly a service which an English tenant owed to his lord by doing work with his work beasts.

B

bill, a written statement of one's claim or account against another. (2) An unconditional, written, and signed, order to pay a sum certain in money to someone, drawn by a person on a third party, *e.g.*, *a bill of exchange*, also called a draft. It it is drawn on a bank and payable on demand, it is a check. U.C.C. § 3-104. (3) The original draft of a law presented to a legislative body for enactment. It is a bill until passed, and then becomes an act, or statute. The term is applied to some special acts after their passage: *e.g.*, *bill of attainder, bill of indemnity,* etc. (4) A document evidencing the receipt of goods for shipment, *i.e.*, *a bill of lading,* issued by a person engaged in the business of transporting or forwarding goods. U.C.C. § 1-201. (5) The written statement of an offense charged against a person, which is presented to a grand jury. If satisfied by the evidence that the charge is probably true, it is endorsed, "a true bill," and called an indictment.

bill of discovery, an application to a court which asks for the discovery of facts resting within the knowledge of the person against whom the bill is filed, or of deeds, writings, or other things, in his custody or control, and material to enable the party filing the bill to prosecute or defend some action at law. Under modern rules of practice, this procedure is less formal and is usually called discovery (*q.v.*).

bill of exchange, see *bill* (2).

bottomry, or **bummaree,** a species of mortgage or hypothecation of a ship, by which the ship is pledged as security for the repayment of a sum of money. If the ship be totally lost, the lender loses his money; but if the ship arrives safely, he recovers his principal, together with the interest agreed upon, which is at a high rate corresponding to the risk. The contract may be called a bottomry bill or a bottomry bond.

C

certified copy, a paper which is verified to be a faithful replica of a document which is in the custody of the officer making the certification. It is signed by the officer and usually has an official seal affixed to it.

charter party, the written contract by which the owner of a ship or other vessel hires her out to another person for a particular period or voyage.

check or **cheque,** an unconditional order to pay a sum certain in money to order or to bearer, drawn on a bank and payable on demand, which is signed by the drawer. U.C.C. § 3-104.

citation, reference to a constitution, statute, precedent case, or other persuasive material used in legal writing. (2) A summons to appear in court. (3) A compliment or award.

citizen, flexible term descriptive of a person who has the freedom and privileges of a city, county, state, or nation. (2) A person who is a member of a body politic, owes allegiance to its government, and may claim the protection of its government.

Citizen of the United States, any person born in the United States, or born out of the United States, if his parents were citizens, or one of foreign birth and parentage who has become naturalized. All persons born or naturalized in the United States, and subject to the jurisdiction thereof, are citizens of the United States and of the State wherein they reside. U.S. Const. Amend. XIV, Sec. 1.

city or **municipal corporation,** a public corporation established as a subdivision of a state for local government purposes, with various powers of government vested in its own officials.

commercial law, that branch of the law which concerns the relationships of persons engaged in business or doing business.

commercial paper, negotiable instruments (*q.v.*), *e.g.*, checks and promissory notes.

commission, an authorization or order to do some act, *e.g.*, to take depositions or to hold an inquest of lunacy. (2) The evidence of an officer's appointment and authority to discharge the duties of his office. (3) A body of persons appointed with necessary powers to do certain things. (4) The act of perpetrating an offense. (5) The compensation of a person employed to sell goods, usually a percentage on the amount realized from the sale.

commissioner, a court officer who is authorized to perform certain judicial or administrative functions and report his actions to the court for ratification. (2)

The title given by law to the heads of bureaus in certain departments of the United States government and to state officials charged with special duties.

common law, an ambiguous term. (1) A system of jurisprudence founded on principles of justice which are determined by reasoning and administration consistent with the usage, customs, and institutions of the people and which are suitable to the genius of the people and their social, political, and economic condition. The rules deduced from this system continually change and expand with the progress of society. (2) That system of law which does not rest for its authority upon any express statutes, but derives its force and authority from universal consent and immemorial usage, and which is evidenced by the decisions of the courts of law, technically so called, in contradistinction to those of equity and the ecclesiastical courts.

conflict of laws, the variance between the laws of two states or countries relating to the subject matter of a suit brought in one of them, when the parties to the suit, or some of them, or the subject matter, belong to the other. See also, *lex loci.*

conveyance, the transfer of the title to property from one person to another. (2) The instrument for affecting such transfer. (3) Every assignment, lease, mortgage, or encumbrance. Uniform Partnership Act § 2.

corporation, an artificial person composed of individuals. It usually has a corporate name and perpetual duration. Sometimes its duration is a fixed term of years. It substitutes for the individuals who compose it. See also *city or municipal corporation* and *professional service corporation.*

county, a civil division of a state for judicial, administrative, and political purposes.

cross-examination, the questioning of a witness by the party opposed to the party which called the witness for direct examination. This usually occurs after the direct examination but on occasion may be otherwise allowed. The form of the questions on cross-examination is designed for the purpose of eliciting evidence from a hostile witness. (2) Cross-examination should be limited to the subject matter of the direct examination and matters affecting the credibility of the witness. The court may, in the exercise of discretion, permit inquiry into additional matters as if on direct examination. Fed. R. Evid. 611(b).

curtesy, the estate which a husband has in his wife's fee simple or fee tail estates, general or special, after her death. In many jurisdictions, the extent and nature of this right are modified and defined by various statutes. Under the common law, the husband had an estate for his life. Three things were necessary to this estate: A legal marriage, seisin of the wife, and birth of issue capable of inheriting, alive and during the mother's life.

custom of merchants, see *law merchant.*

D

de be'ne es'se, a technical phrase applied to a thing done provisionally and out of due course, *e.g.*, evidence taken in advance of a trial, where there is danger that it may be lost owing to the age, infirmity, or intended absence of the witness.

dedi'mus potesta'tem, *l.* (we have given the power), formerly a writ or commission empowering the persons to whom it is directed to do a certain act.

deed, a written instrument designed for the purpose of conveying real property from a present owner to a new owner. (2) Sometimes any written instrument.

dep'osition, a written record of oral testimony, in the form of questions and answers, made before a public officer for use in a lawsuit. Depositions are used for the purpose of discovery of information, or for the purpose of being read as evidence at a trial, or for both purposes.

discovery, a plain method by which the opposing parties to a lawsuit may obtain full and exact factual information concerning the entire area of their controversy, via pre-trial depositions, interrogatories, requests for admissions, inspection of books and documents, physical and mental examinations, and inspection of land or other property. The purpose of these pre-trial procedures is to disclose the genuine points of factual dispute and facilitate adequate preparation for trial. Either party may compel the other party to disclose the relevant facts that are in his possession, prior to the trial. Fed. R. Civ. P. 26-37.

dishonor, to refuse to accept or pay a draft or to pay a promissory note when duly presented. An instrument (*q.v.*) is dishonored when a necessary or optional presentment is duly made and due acceptance or payment is refused, or cannot be obtained within the prescribed time, or in case of bank collections, the instrument is seasonably returned by the midnight deadline; or presentment is excused and the instrument is not duly accepted or paid. U.C.C. § 3-507(1).

dower, the common law life estate which a widow has in one-third of all the lands of which her husband was seized in fee simple, or fee tail, at any time during coveture. Dower is modified and defined by various state statutes.

draft, a preliminary or rough copy of a legal document. (2) See *bill* (2).

drawee, a person to whom a bill or draft is directed, *e.g.*, the drawee of a check is the bank on which it is drawn. See also, *bill* (2).

drawer, the person who draws a bill or draft, *e.g.*, the drawer of a check is the person who signs it. See also, *bill* (2).

E

encumbrance, see *incumbrance*.

F

fair, a flexible term for just, impartial, evenhanded, candid, or reasonable. (2) An event attended by persons having goods and chattels to exhibit and sell, held at stated intervals, or on special occasions.

felony, a type of crime which is of a relatively serious nature; usually various offenses in various jurisdictions for which the maximum penalty can be death or imprisonment in the state penitentiary, regardless of such lesser penalty as may in fact be imposed. Occasionally defined by various state statutes. (2) Formerly, every offense at common law which caused a forfeiture of lands or goods, besides being punishable by death, imprisonment, or other severe penalty.

G

general warranty, a covenant or undertaking that a grantor and his heirs and personal representatives will forever warrant and defend real property for the grantee, his heirs, personal representatives, and assigns, against the claims and demands of all persons whatever. Cf. *special warranty.*

guarantor, a person who makes a guaranty. See also, *surety.*

guaranty, or **guarantee,** a promise (*q.v.*) to a person to be answerable for the payment of a debt, or the performance of a duty by another, in case he should fail to perform his engagement. It may be for a single act, or be a continuing guaranty, covering all transactions of like kind and to a like amount, until revoked by the guarantor. (2) A promise (*q.v.*) to be surety (*q.v.*) for the performance of a contractual obligation made to the obligee. It is binding if the promise is in writing, signed by the promisor, and recites a purported consideration, the promise is made binding by statute, or the promisor should reasonably expect the promise to induce action or forebearance of a substantial character on the part of the promisee or a third person and the promise does induce such action or forebearance. Restatement (Second) of Contracts § 88.

H

holiday, a flexible term for a day specially designated by some governmental authority as a day of exemption from labor, or from the performance of legal business. Legal holidays often recognized in the United States are Sundays, New Year's Day, birthday of Martin Luther King, Jr., Presidents' Holiday, Memorial Day, Independence Day (Fourth of July), Labor Day, Veterans' Day, a day of National Thanksgiving, and Christmas Day.

hypothecation, the deposit of stocks, bonds, or negotiable securities with another, to secure the repayment of a loan, with power to sell the same in case the debt is not paid, and to pay the loan out of the proceeds. (2) In an older and unusual sense, a species of pledge in which the pledgor retained possession of the thing pledged. Analogous to mortgage (*q.v.*) and security agreement (*q.v.*).

I

incumbrance, a claim, lien or liability attached to property, *e.g.*, a mortgage or a judgment.

indorsement, something written on an instrument in writing, and having relation to it. (2) Especially, the writing put on the back of a bill or promissory note and signed, by which the party signing, called the indorser, transfers the property in the bill or note to another, called the indorsee. Indorsement may, however, be blank, *i.e.*, not specifying the name of the indorsee, in which case it may be transferred from hand to hand without further indorsement, and is payable to bearer. Indorsement may also be made without recourse, and thereby, the indorser relieves himself from liability in case the bill or note is not paid. Accord, U.C.C. §§ 3-201 to 3-206. (3) An indorsement must be written by or on behalf of the holder (*q.v.*) and on the instrument or on a paper so firmly affixed thereto as to become a part thereof. U.C.C. § 3-202(2). Words of assignment, condition, waiver, guaranty, limitation, or disclaimer of liability, and the like, accompanying an indorsement do not affect its character as an indorsement. U.C.C. § 3-202(4).

international law, is either public or private. (1) The former regulates the conduct of independent nations toward each other. (2) The latter decides the tribunal before which, and the law by which, private rights shall be determined. See also, *conflict of laws*.

J

ju'rat, a certificate or memorandum of the time, place, and person before whom an affidavit is sworn.

jurisdiction, the authority of a court to hear and decide an action or lawsuit. (2) The geographical district over which the power of a court extends. (3) Subject-matter jurisdiction defines the court's authority to hear a given type of case. (4) Personal jurisdiction requires that the court personally summon the defendant within its geographical district, or that it summon the defendant under the authority of a long-arm statute (*q.v.*). This protects the individual interest that is implicated when a nonresident defendant is haled into a distant and possibly inconvenient court. (5) Jurisdiction is limited when the court has power to act only in certain specified cases; general or residual when it may act in all cases in which the parties are before it, except for those cases which are within the exclusive jurisdiction of another court; concurrent when the same cause may be entertained by one court or another; original when the court has power to try the case in the first instance; appellate when the court hears cases only on appeal, certiorari, or writ of error from another court; exclusive when no other court has power to hear and decide the same matter.

justice of the peace, in some jurisdictions, a minor judicial officer with specifically enumerated powers, *e.g.*, preventing breaches of the peace, and causing the arrest and commitment of persons violating the law. Under various state statutes, they may have limited jurisdiction to try certain cases.

K

law merchant or **custom of merchants,** the general body of commercial usages which have become an established part of the law of the United States and England, and which relate chiefly to the transactions of merchants, mariners, and those engaged in trade. Unless displaced by the particular provisions of the U.C.C., the principles of law and equity, including, among other things, the law merchant, shall supplement its provisions. U.C.C. § 1-103.

ex lo'ci, the law of the place where a contract is made, *i.e.*, lex loci contractus; or thing is done, *i.e.*, lex loci actus; tort is committed, *i.e.*, lex loci delicti; or where the thing, *i.e.*, real estate, is situated, *i.e.*, lex loci rei sitae. It is usually applied in suits relating to such contracts, transactions, torts, and real estate.

lien, a security device by which there is created a right (1) to retain that which is in a person's possession, belonging to another, until certain demands of the person in possession are satisfied; or (2) to charge property in another's possession with payment of a debt, *e.g.*, a vendor's lien (*q.v.*). It may be either (a) particular, arising out of some charge or claim connected with the identical thing; (b) general, in respect of all dealings of a similar nature between the parties; or (c) conventional, by express or implied agreement between the parties, *e.g.*, a mortgage; or (d) by operation of law, *e.g.*, a lien for taxes or an attorney's lien.

M

maker, a person who signs a promissory note, and by so doing engages to pay it according to its tenor.

misdemeanor, any crime or offense not amounting to a felony (*q.v.*).

mortgage, (môr gāg), (a dead pledge), a conveyance of real or personal property to a person called the mortgagee, to secure the payment of money by the mortgagor and to become void upon the performance of such act. At common law, such conveyances became absolute upon failure to perform the condition, but in equity, the mortgagor is permitted to redeem. The manner in which the equity of redemption may be barred is regulated by various state statutes. A legal mortgage is one created by the conveyance or assignment of the property to the mortgagee. An equitable mortgage is one in which the mortgagor does not actually convey the property, but does some act by which he manifests his intention to bind it as security. (2) Any conveyance, agreement, or arrangement in which property is used as security or collateral. Uniform Probate Code §§ 1-201 (25), 5-103 (11). Cf. *lien* and *security agreement.*

municipal corporation, see *city.*

N

negotiability, that quality of certain written instruments by which a transferor may convey to an innocent transferee a better title than he has himself. See also, *negotiable instrument* and *negotiation (1)*.

negotiable instrument, a writing which is signed by the maker or drawer, and contains an unconditional promise or order to pay a sum certain in money and no other promise, order, obligation or power given by the maker or drawer, except as authorized by law, which is payable on demand or at a definite time, and which is payable to order or bearer. U.C.C. § 3-104(1). See also, *negotiability* and *negotiation (1)*.

negotiate, to perform a negotiation (*q.v.*).

negotiation, the transfer of an instrument (*q.v.*) in such form that the transferee becomes a holder (*q.v.*). If the instrument is payable to order, it is negotiated by delivery with any necessary indorsement; if payable to bearer, it is negotiated by delivery. U.C.C. § 3-202(1). See also *negotiability* and *negotiable instrument*. (2) Preliminary communications between parties, which seek to determine whether the parties can make a mutually agreeable sale, purchase, bargain, or contract.

notary, or **notary public,** a minor public official whose duties, powers, and manner of appointment vary in the different states. Commonly authorized to administer oaths, to take affidavits, acknowledgments and depositions, and to protest notes and bills of exchange for nonpayment.

note, a promissory note (*q.v.*). (2) A memorandum. (3) To note a dishonored bill is for a notary public to initial it, giving the date and the reason assigned for its not being paid.

nuncu'pative will, an oral disposition of property intended to take effect upon death, made during a final illness in the presence of witnesses. It usually disposes of personal property only. Regulated by various state statutes, which may require that it be reduced to writing.

O

oath, various solemn affirmations, declarations or promises, made under a sense of responsibility to God, for the truth of what is stated or the faithful performance of what is undertaken. Under various statutes, different forms of affirmation or solemn declaration are allowed in lieu of oaths, where an oath is not binding on the conscience of the individual, or the witness has conscientious scruples against making oaths. Oaths are judicial, *i.e.*, made in the course of judicial proceedings, or extrajudicial, *i.e.*, voluntary or outside of judicial proceedings, evidentiary, *i.e.*, relating to past facts, or promissory, *i.e.*, relating to the future performance of acts or duties, *e.g.*, those of a judge, corporate director, or other official.

oath of office, various declarations of promises, made by persons who are about to enter upon the duties of a public office, concerning their performance of that office. An oath of office is required by federal and state constitutions, and by various statutes to be made by major and minor officials, *e.g.*, President of the United States, governor, judge, notary public, juror, executor, administrator, guardian, and court commissioner. The oath of office required of the President of the United States is prescribed by U.S. Const., Art. II, Sec. 1.

obligee, a person to whom an obligation (*q.v.*) is due.

obligor, a person who is bound to perform an obligation (*q.v.*).

o're te'nus, *l.*, by word of mouth.

P

parish, in Louisiana, a civil division, corresponding to the county in other states.

payee, a person to whom a promissory note, check, or bill of exchange is made payable.

payment, the satisfaction of a debt, or obligation to pay money. It may be made in money, or anything of value which is unconditionally accepted by the payee as a substitute therefor.

practice of law, any service rendered, which involves legal knowledge or legal advice, *e.g.*, representation, counsel, advocacy, or drafting of instruments, which is rendered in respect to the rights, duties, obligations, liabilities, or business affairs of someone requiring the services. Often defined by various rules of court, and occasionally by various state statutes. See also *attorney at law.*

professional service corporation, a corporation (*q.v.*) which is organized by individuals who are licensed to render a professional service, *e.g.*, attorneys, dentists, or physicians, for the purpose of rendering those professional services to the public via the corporate organization, and not as individual practitioners. Usually authorized and regulated, and often defined, by various state statutes.

promissory note, an unconditional promise in writing, made by one person to another, signed by the maker, engaging to pay on demand or at a definite time, a sum certain in money, to the order of such other, or to bearer. U.C.C. § 3-104(1), (2).

protest, a solemn declaration, usually of dissent. (2) An express reservation, whereby a person protects himself against the effects of any admission that might be implied from his act, *e.g.*, payment under protest. (3) In commercial paper transactions, a certificate of dishonor (*q.v.*), made under the hand and seal of a United States consul or vice consul or a notary public or other person authorized to certify dishonor by the law of the place where dishonor occurs. It may be made upon information satisfactory to such person. U.C.C. § 3-509(1).

(4) A document drawn by the master of a ship, and formally attested, stating the circumstances under which damage has happened to the ship or her cargo.

Q

qua'si, *l.*, as if; almost. Often used to indicate significant similarity or likeness to the word that follows, while denoting that the word that follows must be considered in a flexible sense.

quitclaim deed, a written instrument that transfers a party's rights or claims concerning particular property, whatever those rights or claims might be. It is usually used to voluntarily divest a party of his or her undetermined rights and claims, and to merge them into the title of an owner who desires to perfect his title to the property.

R

real property, real estate, or realty, all land and buildings, including estates and interests in land and buildings which are held for life, but not for years, or some greater estate therein. (2) Real property includes land and any interest or estate in land. Uniform Partnership Act § 2.

S

scroll, formerly, a mark made with a pen, intended to take the place of a seal (*q.v.*).

seal, an impression on wax, paper, or other substance capable of being impressed, made for the purpose of authenticating the document to which it is attached. (2) In the law of contract, a manifestation in tangible and conventional form of an intention that a document be sealed. It may take the form of a piece of wax, a wafer, or other substance affixed to the document, or an impression made on the document. By statute or decision in most states in which the seal retains significance, a seal may take the form of a written or printed seal, word, scrawl, or other sign. Restatement (Second) of Contracts § 96. (3) The metal die or other device with which the impression is made. Cf. *scroll.*

security agreement, an agreement (*q.v.*) which creates or provides for a security interest (*q.v.*). U.C.C. § 9-105(1)(h).

security interest, an interest (*q.v.*) in personal property of fixtures which secures payment or performance of an obligation. The term also includes any interest of a buyer of accounts, chattel paper, or contract rights. U.C.C. § 1-201(37).

special warranty, a covenant or undertaking that a grantor and his heirs and personal representatives will forever warrant and defend real property for the grantee, his heirs, personal representatives, and assigns, against the claims and demands of the grantor and all persons claiming by, through, or under him. Cf. *general warranty.*

statute, a law enacted by the legislative body of a nation or a state for prospective application. It may be (a) declaratory, *i.e.*, one which does not alter the existing law, as opposed to remedial or amending; (b) enabling, *i.e.*, removing restrictions, as opposed to disabling. Statutes may also be either public or private, the latter including those which have a special application to particular persons or places. (2) Includes the Constitution and a local law or ordinance of a political subdivision of the state. Model Penal Code § 1.13(1).

subpoena (*sŭb pēnà*), a court order or writ commanding attendance in a court under a penalty for the failure to do so. A subpoena ad testificandum is personally served upon a witness to compel him to attend a trial or deposition and give evidence. (2) A subpoena duces tecum is personally served upon a person who has in his possession a book, instrument, or tangible item, the production of which in evidence is desired, commanding him to bring it with him and produce it at the trial or deposition. Cf. *citation* and *summons*.

summons, a court order or writ, commanding the sheriff to notify a party named therein to appear in court on or before a specified date, and defend the complaint in an action commenced against him. It should also notify the party that, in case of his failure to do so, judgment by default will be rendered against him for the relief demanded in the complaint.

surety, a person who makes himself responsible for the fulfillment of another's obligation, in case the latter, who is called the principal, fails himself to fulfill it. It includes a guarantor, U.C.C. § 1-201(40). See also, *guarantor* and *guaranty*.

INDEX

(References are to page numbers,